U.S. Master™

Compensation

Tax Guide

Fifth Edition

Includes Special Alert on KETRA and Proposed Regulations to Section 409A

Dennis R. Lassila, Ph.D., CPA
Bob G. Kilpatrick, Ph.D., CPA

CCH INCORPORATED
Chicago

A WoltersKluwer Company

This publication is designed to provide accurate and authoritative information in regard to the subject matter covered. It is sold with the understanding that the publisher is not engaged in rendering legal, accounting, or other professional service, and that the authors are not offering such advice in this publication. If legal advice or other expert assistance is required, the services of a competent professional person should be sought.

ISBN: 0-8080-9006-2

©2006, CCH INCORPORATED

4025 W. Peterson Ave.
Chicago, IL 60646-6085
1 800 248 3248
http://tax.cchgroup.com

Special Alert

As the 2006 edition of the *U.S. Master Compensation Tax Guide* goes to press, Congress has just passed the Katrina Emergency Tax Relief Act (KETRA) of 2005 (H.R. 3768), which President Bush signed into law on September 23, 2005. Relevant portions of the Act are summarized below. Also included is the Preamble to the Proposed Regulations regarding the application of section 409A to nonqualified deferred compensation plans.

KETRA gives Hurricane Katrina victims—individuals and businesses—temporary tax breaks scored by the Joint Committee on Taxation at over $6 billion.

The special relief provisions in the Katrina Emergency Tax Relief Act of 2005 are specific only to Hurricane Katrina victims. Victims of other disasters, past or future, are not covered by the new law and cannot rely on it.

HELP FOR INDIVIDUALS

The *Katrina Emergency Tax Relief Act of 2005* contains tax breaks not only for victims of the disaster but also for individuals and businesses helping in the recovery.

2005 Legislation Update

CHECKLIST OF MAJOR BENEFITS

The Katrina Emergency Tax Relief Act of 2005 includes provisions that include:

- Suspension of personal casualty loss AGI and dollar floors;
- Penalty waivers/income averaging for IRA/retirement plan withdrawals;
- Expanded qualified plan loan limits;
- Exemptions for housing displaced individuals;
- Higher standard mileage rate for vehicle use by volunteers;
- 2004 income to compute 2005 earned income/child tax credits;
- No discharge of indebtedness income;
- Extended replacement period for gain nonrecognition;
- Suspension of limits on charitable deductions;

- Expanded food/book donation deduction;
- Work Opportunity Credit to cover displaced workers;
- New Employee Retention Credit for small business;
- Relaxed mortgage revenue bond rules in the Hurricane Katrina disaster area on or after August 25, 2005, and that are attributable to Hurricane Katrina are not subject to these restrictions.

SCOPE OF KATRINA RELIEF

The "Hurricane Katrina disaster area" *is the area declared by the President to be a major disaster area before September 14 in connection with Hurricane Katrina. A "Core Disaster area" is that part of the generally declared disaster area determined by the President to warrant individual or individual and public assistance from the federal government.*

Benefits applied to the *general Hurricane Katrina disaster area* include:

- Retirement plan distributions/loans;
- Cancellation of nonbusiness debt (if economic loss);
- Replacement period for nonrecognition of gain;
- Earned income credit (only if displaced from principal residence);
- Exemption for housing a displaced individual;
- Suspension of personal casualty loss limitations;
- Exclusion for housing a displaced individual;
- Employee retention credit for businesses.

Benefits limited to *Core disaster areas* include:

- Work Opportunity Tax Credit;
- Employee Retention Credit for businesses;
- Cancellation of nonbusiness debt;
- Mortgage revenue bonds;
- Earned income credit qualification.

Benefits if *attributable to or in connection with* Hurricane Katrina:

- Suspension of charitable contribution limitations;
- Filing and payment deadlines extended;
- Exclusion from income of mileage reimbursements to charitable volunteers.

Early distributions from IRAs and pensions

Early distributions from IRAs, 401(k) plans, and other retirement savings vehicles are usually discouraged and taxpayers risk penalties for making early distributions unless there are special circumstances. The new law relaxes the tough restrictions for qualified Hurricane Katrina distributions.

Penalty-free withdrawals. Victims may withdraw up to $100,000 from an IRA, 401(k) plan, or similar savings plan without penalty for distributions made on or after August 25, 2005, and before January 1, 2007. Qualifying victims must have had their principal home in the Katrina disaster area on August 28, 2005, and must have sustained an economic loss. (The $100,000 limit is applied for each taxpayer and not to each retirement account.)

Extended rollover period. Taxpayers who are able to repay the distributions have three years to put the funds back and generally qualify for rollover treatment. Otherwise, they will be taxed on their distributions. Additionally, taxpayers who withdrew funds from an IRA after February 28, 2005, and before August 29, 2005, for a first-time home purchase but who could not complete that purchase, because of Hurricane Katrina, may put the funds back in their IRAs without penalty, if done by February 28, 2006.

Three-year income averaging. Taxpayers who cannot avoid income tax on their penalty-free withdrawals are allowed to spread that income evenly over three years (unless they elect out of this special treatment).

IMPACT: *Qualified Hurricane Katrina distributions are not subject to the 20 percent withholding normally required of distributions other than trustee-to-trustee rollovers. There also is no requirement on the size of the economic loss sustained by a qualifying taxpayer or on the necessity that any withdrawal be used to address an economic loss.*

Planning tip. *Victims who expect to be unemployed for awhile might want to defer withdrawals until 2006 and then elect not to 3-year income average, thereby putting all of their distribution income into the year when their gross income is otherwise low.*

The new law also increases the amount Hurricane Katrina victims can borrow from their pension plans. Instead of a maximum of $50,000, they can borrow up to $100,000. This provision is effective for loans made on or after September 23, 2005, and before January 1, 2007.

IMPACT: *Hurricane Katrina victims need to carefully weigh the pros and cons of taking early distributions and loans from IRAs and other savings plans. Taxpayers who are far from retirement may want to*

3

preserve their savings for when they retire and, in the meantime, seek a personal loan from a bank or possibly borrow from family members or friends.

Any qualified loan outstanding on or after August 25, 2005, with any required payment due date falling between August 25 and December 31, 2006, will have that required due date delayed for one year. Subsequent repayment schedules will be adjusted accordingly for the five-year and level-payment requirements.

IMPACT: *The IRS has separately made some changes to the hardship distribution and loan rules for 401(k) plans and similar plans. Plans can make loans or distributions based on the employee's authorization, without waiting for the normal documentation required to justify the distribution. The plan can make the loan or distribution even if its terms do not authorize the payment. Plan participants in another part of the country can take a loan or hardship distribution to help family members living in the disaster area.*

TIME LINE FOR KATRINA ACT BENEFITS

2005 deadlines:
- Qualified contributions   paid through 12/31/05
- Contributions of food/book inventory   after 8/28/05-12/31/05
- Employment retension credit for displaced employees   hired on or before 12/31/05

2006 deadlines:
- Housing displaced individuals   60 day period, through 2006
- Charitable use standard mileage rate   ending 12/31/06
- Vehicle expense reimbursement for charitable volunteers   ending 12/31/06
- Home purchase recontributions for distributions   after 2/28/05 and before 8/29/05
- Qualified distributions from retirement savings   before 1/1/07 Plan loans before 1/1/07
- Nonbusiness debt forgiveness   before 1/1/07

2007 deadlines:
- Work opportunity tax credit within core disaster areas hired to work in core disaster area   on or before 8/28/07

IRS Announces Relief for Those Affected By Hurricane Rita in Texas and Louisiana

On September 26, the Internal Revenue Service announced that it is extending deadlines for filing returns, paying taxes, and performing other time-sensitive acts for taxpayers affected by Hurricane Rita.

The Service said in a news release (IR-2005-110) that, generally, it is extending the deadline to February 28, 2006, the date set by Congress in the Katrina Emergency Tax Relief Act (H.R. 3768) signed September 23 by President Bush for taxpayers affected by Hurricane Katrina.

The extension does not apply to information returns in the W-2, 1098, 1099, or 5498 series, Forms 1042-S or 8027, or employment and excise tax deposits, IRS said, adding that existing procedures allow it to waive or abate for reasonable cause penalties for late filing or payment of these items.

Affected Areas Named

IRS said that nine Texas counties—Chambers, Galveston, Hardin, Jasper, Jefferson, Liberty, Newton, Orange, and Tyler—and five Louisiana parishes—Beauregard, Cameron, Calcasieu, Jefferson Davis, and Vermilion—have already been declared presidential disaster areas and residents will get automatic tax extensions.

PROPOSED REGULATIONS TO SECTION 409A

DEPARTMENT OF THE TREASURY
Internal Revenue Service
26 CFR Part 1
[REG-158080-04]
RIN 1545-BE79

Application of Section 409A to Nonqualified Deferred Compensation Plans

AGENCY: Internal Revenue Service (IRS), Treasury.

ACTION: Notice of proposed rulemaking and notice of public hearing.

. . . .

SUMMARY: This document contains proposed regulations regarding the application of section 409A to nonqualified deferred compensation plans. The regulations affect service providers receiving amounts of deferred compensation, and the service recipients for whom the service providers provide services. This document also provides a notice of public hearing on these proposed regulations.

DATES: Written or electronic comments must be received by January 3, 2006. Outlines of topics to be discussed at the public hearing scheduled for January 25, 2006, must be received by January 4, 2006.

ADDRESSES: Send submissions to: CC:PA:LPD:PR (REG-158080-04), room 5203, Internal Revenue Service, PO Box 7604, Ben Franklin Station, Washington, DC 20044. Submissions may be hand-delivered Monday through Friday between the hours of 8 a.m. and 4 p.m. to CC:PA:LPD:PR (REG-158080-04), Courier's Desk, Internal Revenue Service, 1111 Constitution Avenue, NW., Washington, DC or sent electronically, via the IRS Internet site at http://www.irs.gov/regs or via the Federal Rulemaking Portal at http://www.regulations.gov (IRS REG-158080-04). The public hearing will be held in the Auditorium, Internal Revenue Building, 1111 Constitution Avenue, NW., Washington, DC.

FOR FURTHER INFORMATION CONTACT: Concerning the proposed regulations, Stephen Tackney, at (202) 927-9639; concerning submissions of comments, the hearing, and/or to be placed on the building access list to attend the hearing, Richard A. Hurst at (202) 622-7116 (not toll-free numbers).

SUPPLEMENTARY INFORMATION:

Background

Section 409A was added to the Internal Revenue Code (Code) by section 885 of the American Jobs Creation Act of 2004, Public Law 108-357 (118 Stat. 1418). Section 409A generally provides that unless certain requirements are met, amounts deferred under a nonqualified deferred compensation plan for all taxable years are currently includible in gross income to the extent not subject to a substantial risk of forfeiture and not previously included in gross income. Section 409A also includes rules applicable to certain trusts or similar arrangements associated with nonqualified deferred compensation, where such arrangements are located outside of the United States or are restricted to the provision of benefits in connection with a decline in the financial health of the sponsor.

On December 20, 2004, the IRS issued Notice 2005-1 (2005-2 I.R.B. 274 (published as modified on January 6, 2005)), setting forth initial guidance with respect to the application of section 409A, and supplying transition guidance in accordance with the terms of the statute. Notice 2005-1 requested comments on all aspects of the application of Section 409A, including certain specified topics. Numerous comments were submitted and all were considered by the Treasury Department and the IRS in formulating these regulations. In general, these regulations incorporate the guidance provided in Notice 2005-1 and provide substantial additional guidance. For a discussion of the continued applicability of Notice 2005-1, see the Effect on Other Documents section of this preamble.

Explanation of Provisions

I. Definition of Nonqualified Deferred Compensation Plan

A. In General

Section 409A applies to amounts deferred under a nonqualified deferred compensation plan. For this purpose a nonqualified deferred compensation plan means any plan that provides for the deferral of compensation, with specified exceptions such as qualified retirement plans, tax-deferred annuities, simplified employee pensions, SIMPLEs and section 501(c)(18) trusts. In addition, section 409A does not apply to certain welfare benefit plans, including bona fide vacation leave, sick leave, compensatory time, disability pay, and death benefit plans. In certain instances, these regulations cross reference the regulations under section 3121(v)(2), which provide a special timing rule under the Federal Insurance Contributions Act (FICA) for nonqualified deferred compensation, as defined in section 3121(v)(2) and the regulations thereunder. However, unless explicitly cross-referenced in these regulations, the regulations under section 3121(v)(2) do not apply for purposes of section 409A and under no circumstances do these proposed regulations affect the application of section 3121(v)(2).

B. Section 457 Plans

Section 409A does not apply to eligible deferred compensation plans under section 457(b). However, section 409A applies to nonqualified deferred compensation plans to which section 457(f) applies, separately and in addition to the requirements applicable to such plans under section 457(f). Section 409A(c) provides that nothing in section 409A prevents the inclusion of amounts in gross income under any other provision of the Code. Section 409A(c) further provides that any amount included in gross income under section 409A will not be required to be included in gross income under any other Code provision later than the time provided in section 409A. Accordingly, if in a taxable year an amount subject to section 409A (but not required to be included in income under section 409A) is required to be included in gross income under section 457(f), that amount must be included in gross income under section 457(f) for that taxable year. Correspondingly, if in a taxable year an amount that would otherwise be required to be included in gross income under section 457(f) has been included previously in gross income under section 409A, that amount will not be required to be included in gross income under section 457(f) for that taxable year.

These proposed regulations are intended solely as guidance with respect to the application of section 409A to such arrangements, and should not be relied upon with respect to the application of section 457(f). Thus, State and local government and tax exempt entities may not rely upon the definition of a deferral of compensation under Sec. 1.409A-1(b) of these proposed regulations in applying section 457(f). For example, for purposes of section 457(f), a deferral of compensation includes a stock option and an arrangement in which an employee or independent contractor of a state or local government or tax-exempt entity earns the right to future payments for services, even if those amounts are paid immediately upon vesting and would qualify for the exclusion from the definition of deferred compensation under Sec. 1.409A-1(b)(5) of these proposed regulations. However, until further guidance is issued, State and local government and tax-exempt entities may rely on the definitions of bona fide vacation leave, sick leave, compensatory time, disability pay, and death benefit plans for purposes of section 457(f) as applicable for purposes of applying section 409A and Sec. 1.409A-1(a)(4) of these proposed regulations to nonqualified deferred compensation plans under section 457(f).

C. Arrangements With Independent Contractors

Consistent with Notice 2005-1, Q&A-8, these regulations exclude from coverage under section 409A certain arrangements between service providers and service recipients. Under these regulations, amounts deferred in a taxable year with respect to a service provider using an accrual method of accounting for that year are not subject to section 409A. In addition, section 409A generally does not apply to amounts deferred pursuant to an arrangement between a service recipient and an unrelated independent contractor (other than a director of a corporation), if during the independent contractor's taxable year in which the amount is deferred, the independent contractor is providing significant services to each of two or more service recipients that are unrelated, both to each other and to the independent contractor. In response to comments, these regulations clarify that the determination is made based upon the independent contractor's taxable year in which the amount is deferred.

Commentators also requested clarification of the circumstances in which services to each service recipient will be deemed to be significant, as required for the exclusion. Determining whether services provided to a service recipient are significant generally will involve an examination of all relevant facts and circumstances. However, two clarifications have been provided. First, the analysis applies separately to each trade or business in which the service provider is engaged. For example, a taxpayer providing computer programming services for one service recipient will not meet the exception if, as a separate trade or business, the taxpayer paints houses for another unrelated service recipient. To provide certainty to many independent contractors engaged in an active trade or business with multiple service recipients, a safe harbor has been provided under which an independent contractor with multiple unrelated service recipients, to whom the independent contractor also is not related, will be treated as providing significant services to more than one of those service recipients, if not more than 70 percent of the total revenue generated by the trade or business in the particular taxable year is derived from any particular service recipient (or group of related service recipients).

Commentators also requested clarification with respect to the application of section 409A to directors. As provided in these regulations, an individual will not be excluded from coverage under section 409A merely because the individual provides services as a director to two or more unrelated service recipients. However, the provisions of section 409A apply separately to arrangements between the service provider director and each service recipient. Accordingly, the inclusion of income due to a failure to meet the requirements of section 409A with respect to an arrangement to serve as a director of one service recipient will not cause an inclusion of income with respect to arrangements to serve as a director of an unrelated service recipient. In addition, the continuation of services as a director with one service recipient will not cause the termination of services as a director with an unrelated service recipient to fail to constitute a separation from service for purposes of section 409A, if the termination would otherwise qualify as a separation from service.

Commentators also requested clarification with respect to the application of the rule to directors who are also employees of the service recipient. In general, the provisions of section 409A will apply separately to the arrangements between the service recipient and the service provider for services as a director and the arrangements between the service recipient and the service provider for services as an employee. However, the distinction is not intended to permit employee directors to limit the aggregation of arrangements in which the individual participates as an employee by labeling such arrangements as arrangements for services as a director. Accordingly, an arrangement with an employee director will be treated as an arrangement for services as a director only to the extent that another non-employee director defers compensation under the same, or a substantially similar, arrangement on similar terms. Moreover, the separate application of

9

section 409A to arrangements for services as a director and arrangements for services as an employee does not extend to a service provider's services for the service recipient as an independent contractor in addition to the service provider's services as a director of the service recipient. Under those circumstances, both arrangements are treated as services provided as an independent contractor.

Commentators also requested clarification of the application of the exclusion to independent contractors who provide services to only one service recipient, when that service recipient itself has multiple clients. Specifically a commentator requested that the rule be applied on a look through basis, so that the independent contractor will be deemed to be providing services for multiple service recipients. The Treasury Department and the IRS do not believe that such a rule is appropriate. Where multiple persons have come together and formed an entity that is itself a service recipient of the independent contractor, the independent contractor is performing services for the single entity service recipient.

The Treasury Department and the IRS believe that where the service recipient is purchasing an independent contractor's management services, amounts deferred with respect to the independent contractor's performance of services should not be excluded from coverage under section 409A. Among the many objectives underlying the enactment of section 409A is to limit the ability of a service provider to retain the benefits of the deferral of compensation while having excessive control over the timing of the ultimate payment. Where the independent contractor is managing the service recipient, there is a significant potential for the independent contractor to have such influence or control over compensation matters so that categorical exclusion from coverage under section 409A is not appropriate. Accordingly, the regulations provide that compensation arrangements between an independent contractor and a service recipient that involve the provision of management services are not excluded from coverage under section 409A, and in such cases, the service recipient is not treated as unrelated for purposes of determining whether arrangements with other service recipients are excluded from coverage under section 409A under the general rule addressing independent contractors providing services to multiple unrelated service recipients. For this purpose, management services include services involving actual or de facto direction or control of the financial or operational aspects of the client's trade or business, or investment advisory services that are integral to the trade or business of a service recipient whose primary trade or business involves the management of investments in entities other than the entities comprising the service recipient, such as a hedge fund or real estate investment trust.

II. Definition of Nonqualified Deferred Compensation

A. In General

Consistent with Notice 2005-1, Q&A-4, these regulations provide that a plan provides for the deferral of compensation only if, under the terms of the plan and the relevant facts and circumstances, the service provider has a legally binding right during a taxable year to compensation that has not been actually or constructively received and included in gross income, and that, pursuant to the terms of the plan, is payable to (or on behalf of) the service provider in a later year. A legally binding right to compensation may exist even where the right is subject to conditions, including conditions that constitute a substantial risk of forfeiture. For example, an employee that in Year 1 is promised a bonus equal to a set percentage of employer profits, to be paid out in Year 3 if the employee has remained in employment through Year 3, has a legally binding right to the payment of the compensation, subject to the conditions being met. The right thus may be subject to a substantial risk of forfeiture, and accordingly be nonvested; however, the promise constitutes a legally binding right subject to a condition.

In contrast, a service provider does not have a legally binding right to compensation if that compensation may be unilaterally reduced or eliminated by the service recipient or other person after the services creating the right to the compensation have been performed. Notice 2005-1, Q&A-4 provides that, if the facts and circumstances indicate that the discretion to reduce or eliminate the compensation is available or exercisable only upon a condition that is unlikely to occur, or the discretion to reduce or eliminate the compensation is unlikely to be exercised, a service provider will be considered to have a legally binding right to the compensation. Commentators criticized the provision as being difficult to apply, because the standard is too vague, requiring a subjective judgment as to whether the discretion is likely to be exercised. The intent of this provision was to eliminate the possibility of taxpayers avoiding the application of section 409A through the use of plan provisions providing negative discretion, where such provisions are not meaningful. In response to the comments, these regulations adopt a standard under which the negative discretion will be recognized unless it lacks substantive significance, or is available or exercisable only upon a condition. Thus, where a promise of compensation may be reduced or eliminated at the unfettered discretion of the service recipient, that promise generally will not result in a legally binding right to compensation. However, where the negative discretion lacks substantive significance, or the discretion is available or exercisable only upon a condition, the discretion will be ignored and the service provider will be treated as having a legally binding right. In addition, where the service provider has control over, or is related to, the person granted the discretion to reduce or eliminate the compensation, or has control over all or any portion of such person's compensation or benefits, the discretion also will be ignored and the service provider will be treated as having a legally binding right to the compensation.

B. Short-Term Deferrals

Notice 2005-1, Q&A-4(c), set forth an exception from coverage under section 409A under which certain arrangements, referred to as short-term deferrals, would not be treated as resulting in the deferral of compensation. Specifically, Notice 2005-1, Q&A-4 provided that until further guidance a deferral of compensation would not occur if, absent an election to otherwise defer the payment to a later period, at all times the terms of the plan require payment by, and an amount is actually or constructively received by the service provider by, the later of (i) the date that is 2½ months from the end of the service provider's first taxable year in which the amount is no longer subject to a substantial risk of forfeiture, or (ii) the date that is 2½ months from the end of the service recipient's year in which the amount is no longer subject to a substantial risk of forfeiture. For these purposes, an amount that is never subject to a substantial risk of forfeiture is considered to be no longer subject to a substantial risk of forfeiture on the date the service provider first has a legally binding right to the amount. Under this rule, many multi-year bonus arrangements that require payments promptly after the amount vests would not be subject to section 409A.

The exception from coverage under section 409A for short-term deferrals set forth in Notice 2005-1, Q&A-4, has been incorporated into these proposed regulations. Commentators questioned whether a written provision in the arrangement requiring the payment to be made by the relevant deadline is necessary, or whether the customary practice of the service recipient is sufficient. These regulations do not require that the arrangement provide in writing that the payment must be made by the relevant deadline. Accordingly, where an arrangement does not otherwise defer compensation, an amount will qualify as a short-term deferral, and not be subject to section 409A, if the amount is actually paid out by the appropriate deadline. However, where an arrangement does not provide in writing that a payment must be paid by a specified date on or before the relevant deadline, and the payment is not made by the appropriate deadline (except due to unforeseeable administrative or solvency issues, as discussed below), the payment will result in automatic violation of section 409A due to the failure to specify the payment date or a permissible payment event. In addition, the rules permitting the service recipient limited discretion to delay payments of amounts subject to section 409A (for example, where the service recipient reasonably anticipates that payment of the amount would not be deductible due to application of section 162(m), or where the service recipient reasonably anticipates that payment of the amount would violate a loan covenant or similar contractual provision) would not be available, because the arrangement would not have specified a payment date subject to the delay. In contrast, where an arrangement provides in writing that a payment must be made by a specified date on or before the relevant deadline, and the payment is not made by the appropriate deadline so that section 409A becomes applicable, the rules contained in these regulations generally permitting the payment to be made in the same calendar year as the fixed payment date become applicable. In addition, the rules permitting a plan to provide for a delay in the payment in certain circumstances and the relief applicable to disputed payments and refusals to pay would also be available. Accordingly, it will often be appropriate to include a date or year for payment even when it is intended that the payment will be made within the short-term deferral period.

The short-term deferral rule does not provide a method to avoid application of section 409A if the legally binding right creates a right to deferred compensation from the outset. For example, if a legally binding right to payment in Year 10 arises in Year 1, but the right is subject to a substantial risk of forfeiture through Year 3, paying the amount at the end of Year 3 would not result in the payment failing to be subject to section 409A, but rather generally would be an impermissible acceleration of the payment from the originally established right to payment in year 10.

Commentators also questioned whether the 2½ month deadline for payment could be extended where the payment was not administratively practicable, or where the payment was made late due to error. These regulations provide that a payment made after the 2½ month deadline may continue to be treated as meeting the requirements of the exception from the definition of a deferral of compensation if the taxpayer establishes that it was impracticable, either administratively or economically, to avoid the deferral of the receipt by a service provider of the payment beyond the applicable 2½ month period and that, as of the time the legally binding right to the amount arose, such impracticability was unforeseeable, and the payment is made as soon as practicable. Some commentators had asked for a rule permitting delays due to unintentional error to satisfy the standard for the exclusion. However, the exception is based upon the longstanding position set forth in Sec. 1.404(b)-1T, Q&A-2(b) regarding the timing of the deduction with respect to a payment under a nonqualified deferred compensation plan. Similar to the deduction rule, the exclusion from coverage under section 409A treats a payment made within the appropriate 2½ month period as made within such a short period following the date the substantial risk of forfeiture lapses that it may be treated as paid when earned (and not deferred to a subsequent period). Also similar to the rule governing the timing of deductions, the exclusion from coverage under section 409A permits only limited exceptions to the requirement that the amount actually be paid by the relevant deadline. Pending further study, the Treasury Department and the IRS believe that providing further flexibility with respect to meeting the deadline would create the potential for abuse and enforcement difficulty.

C. Stock Options and Stock Appreciation Rights

In General

The legislative history states that section 409A does not cover grants of stock options where the exercise price can never be less than the fair market value of the underlying stock at the date of grant (a non-discounted option). See H.R. Conf. Rept. No. 108-755, at 735 (2004). Thus an option with an exercise price that is or may be below the fair market value of the underlying stock at the date of grant (a discounted option) is subject to the requirements of section 409A. Consistent with the legislative history and with Notice 2005-1, Q&A-4, these regulations provide that a non-discounted stock option, that has no other feature for the deferral of compensation, generally is not covered by section 409A. However, a stock option granted with an exercise price below the fair market value of the underlying shares of stock on the date of grant generally would be subject to section 409A except to the extent the terms of the option only permit exercise of the option during the short-term deferral period.

Commentators stressed that in many respects, a stock appreciation right can be the economic equivalent of a stock option, especially a stock option that allows the holder to exercise in a manner other than by the payment of cash (a cashless exercise feature). Accordingly, Notice 2005-1, Q&A-4 exempted from coverage certain non-discounted stock appreciation rights that most closely resembled stock options—stock appreciation rights settled in stock. The Treasury Department and the IRS were concerned that the manipulation of the purported stock valuation for purposes of determining whether the stock appreciation right was issued at a discount or settled at a premium could lead to a stock appreciation right being used to circumvent section 409A. Accordingly, the exception was limited to stock appreciation rights issued with respect to stock traded on an established securities market.

Commentators criticized the distinction between public corporations and non-public corporations, asserting that this distinction is not meaningful and unfairly discriminated against the latter corporations and placed such corporations at a severe competitive disadvantage. In addition, commentators questioned whether the distinction between stock-settled and cash-settled stock appreciation rights was relevant, where the amount of income generated would be identical.

In response to the comments, these regulations treat stock appreciation rights similarly to stock options, regardless of whether the stock appreciation right is settled in cash and regardless of whether the stock appreciation right is based upon service recipient stock that is not readily tradable on an established securities market. The Treasury Department and the IRS remain concerned that manipulation of stock valuations, and manipulation of the characteristics of the underlying stock, may lead to abuses with respect to stock options and stock appreciation rights (collectively referred to as stock rights). To that end, these regulations contain more detailed provisions with respect to the identification of service recipient stock that may be subject to, or used to determine the amount payable under, stock rights excluded from the application of section 409A, and the valuation of such service recipient stock, discussed below.

2. Definition of Service Recipient Stock

The legislative history of section 409A states that the exception from coverage under section 409A for certain nonstatutory stock options was intended to cover options granted on service recipient stock. H.R. Conf. Rept. No. 108-755, at 735 (2004). Section 409A(d)(6) provides that, for purposes of determining the identity of the service recipient under section 409A, aggregation rules similar to the rules in section 414(b) and (c) apply. Taxpayers requested that the definition of service recipient be expanded for purposes of the exception for stock rights to cover entities that would not otherwise be treated as part of the service recipient applying the rules under section 414(b) and (c). The Treasury Department and the IRS agree that the exclusion for nonstatutory stock rights was not meant to apply so narrowly. Accordingly, for purposes of the provisions excluding certain stock rights on service recipient stock, the stock right, or the plan or arrangement under which the stock right is granted, may provide that section 414(b) and (c) be applied by modifying the language and using "50 percent" instead of "80 percent" where appropriate, such that stock rights granted to employees of entities in which the issuing corporation owns a 50 percent interest generally will not be subject to section 409A.

Commentators also requested that the threshold be dropped below 50 percent to cover joint ventures and other similar arrangements, where the participating corporation does not have a majority interest. These regulations provide for such a lower threshold, allowing for the stock right, or the plan or arrangement under which the stock right is granted, to provide for the modification of the language and use of "20 percent" instead of "80 percent" in applying section 414(b) and (c), where the use of such stock with respect to stock rights is due to legitimate business criteria. For example, the use of such stock with respect to stock rights issued to employees of a joint venture that were former employees of a corporation with at least a 20 percent interest in the joint venture generally would be due to legitimate business criteria, and accordingly would be treated as service recipient stock for purposes of determining whether the stock right was subject to section 409A. A designation by a service recipient to use either the 50 percent or the 20 percent threshold must be applied consistently to all compensatory stock rights, and any designation of a different permissible ownership threshold percentage may not be made effective until 12 months after the adoption of such change.

The increased ability to issue stock rights with respect to a related corporation for whom the service provider does not directly perform services could increase the potential for service recipients to exploit the exclusion for certain stock rights by establishing a corporation within the group of related corporations, the purpose of which is to serve as an investment vehicle for nonqualified deferred compensation. Accordingly, these regulations provide that other than with respect to service providers who are primarily engaged in providing services directly to such corporation, the term service recipient for purposes of the definition of service recipient stock does not include a corporation whose primary purpose is to serve as an investment vehicle with respect to the corporation's interest in entities other than the service recipient (including entities aggregated with the corporation under the definition of service recipient incorporating section 414(b) and (c)).

Commentators also questioned whether the exception for certain stock rights could apply where a service recipient provides a stock right with respect to preferred stock or a separate class of common stock. The Treasury Department and the IRS believe this exception was intended to cover stock rights with respect to service recipient stock the fair market value of which meaningfully relates to the potential future appreciation in the enterprise value of the corporation. The use of a separate class of common stock created for the purpose of compensating service providers, or the use of preferred stock with substantial characteristics of debt, could create an arrangement that more closely resembles traditional nonqualified deferred compensation arrangements rather than an interest in appreciation of the value of the service recipient. An exception that excluded these arrangements from coverage under section 409A would undermine the effectiveness of the statute to govern nonqualified deferred compensation arrangements, contrary to the legislative intent. Accordingly, these regulations clarify that service recipient stock includes only common stock, and only the class of common stock that as of the date of grant has the highest aggregate value of any class of common stock of the corporation outstanding, or a class of common stock substantially similar to such class of stock (ignoring differences in voting rights). In addition, service recipient stock does not include any stock that provides a preference as to dividends or liquidation rights.

With respect to the foreign aspects of such arrangements, commentators requested clarification that service provider stock may include American Depositary Receipts (ADRs). These regulations clarify that stock of the service recipient may include ADRs, provided that the stock to which the ADRs relate would otherwise qualify as service recipient stock.

Commentators also requested that certain equity appreciation rights issued by mutual companies, intended to mimic stock appreciation rights, be excluded from coverage under section 409A. These regulations expand the exclusion for stock appreciation rights to include equity appreciation rights with respect to mutual company units. A mutual company unit is defined as a specified percentage of the fair market value of the mutual company. For this purpose, a mutual company may value itself under the same provisions applicable to the valuation of stock of a corporation that is not readily tradable on an established securities market. The Treasury Department and the IRS request comments as to the practicability of this provision, and whether such a provision should be expanded to cover equity appreciation rights issued by other entities that do not have outstanding shares of stock.

3. Valuation

Notice 2005-1, Q&A-4(d)(ii) provides that for purposes of determining whether the requirements for exclusion of a nonstatutory stock option have been met, any reasonable valuation method may be used. Commentators expressed concern that the standard was too vague, given the potential consequences of a failure to comply with the requirements of section 409A.

These regulations provide that with respect to service recipient stock that is readily tradable on an established securities market, a valuation of such stock may be based on the last sale before or the first sale after the grant, or the closing price on the trading day before or the trading day of the grant, or any other reasonable basis using actual transactions in such stock as reported by such market and consistently applied. Commentators pointed out that certain service recipients, generally corporations in certain foreign jurisdictions, would not be able to meet this requirement because the service recipient is subject to foreign laws requiring pricing based on an average over a period of time. To allow compliance with these requirements, these regulations further provide that service recipients (including U.S. service recipients) may set the exercise price based on an average of the price of the stock over a specified period provided such period occurs within the 30 days before and 30 days after the grant date, and provided further that the terms of the grant are irrevocably established before the beginning of the measurement period used to determine the exercise price.

Commentators asked for clarification of the definition of stock that is readily tradable on an established securities market. Specifically, commentators requested clarification of the scope of an established securities market, and whether that term includes over-the-counter markets and foreign markets. The regulations adopt the definition of an established securities market set forth in Sec. 1.897-1(m). Under that definition, over-the-counter markets generally are treated as established securities markets, as well as many foreign markets. However, the stock must also be readily tradable within such markets to qualify as stock readily tradable on an established securities market.

With respect to corporations whose stock is not readily tradable on an established securities market, these regulations provide that fair market value may be determined through the reasonable application of a reasonable valuation method. The regulations contain a description of the factors that will be taken into account in determining whether a given valuation method is reasonable. In addition, in an effort to provide more certainty, certain presumptions with respect to the reasonableness of a valuation method have been set forth. Provided one such method is applied reasonably and used consistently, the valuation determined by applying such method will be presumed to equal the fair market value of the stock, and such presumption will be rebuttable only by a showing that the valuation is grossly unreasonable. A method will be treated as used consistently where the same method is used for all equity-based compensation granted to service providers by the service recipient, including for purposes of determining the amount due upon exercise or repurchase where the stock acquired is subject to an obligation of the service recipient to repurchase, or a put or call right providing for the potential repurchase by the service recipient, as applicable.

Commentators specifically requested clarification as to whether a valuation method based upon an appraisal will be treated as reasonable, and if so with respect to what period. These regulations provide that the use of an appraisal will be presumed reasonable if the appraisal satisfies the requirements of the Code with respect to the valuation of stock held in an employee stock ownership plan. If those requirements are satisfied, the valuation will be presumed reasonable for a one-year period commencing on the date as of which the appraisal values the stock.

Commentators also specifically requested clarification of whether a valuation method based on a nonlapse restriction addressed in Sec. 1.83-5(a) will be treated as reasonable. Under Sec. 1.83-5(a), in the case of property subject to a nonlapse restriction (as defined in Sec. 1.83-3(h)), the price determined under the formula price is considered to be the fair market value of the property unless established to the contrary by the Commissioner, and the burden of proof is on the Commissioner with respect to such value. If stock in a corporation is subject to a nonlapse restriction that requires the transferee to sell such stock only at a formula price based on book value, a reasonable multiple of earnings or a reasonable combination thereof, the price so determined ordinarily is regarded as determinative of the fair market value of such property for purposes of section 83.

The Treasury Department and the IRS do not believe that this standard, in and of itself, is appropriate with respect to the application of section 409A. The Treasury Department and the IRS are not confident that a formula price determined pursuant to a nonlapse restriction will, in every case, adequately approximate the value of the underlying stock. The Treasury Department and the IRS are also concerned that such formula valuations, in the absence of other criteria, may be subject to manipulation or to the provision of predictable results that are inconsistent with a true equity appreciation right. Further, the Treasury Department and the IRS do not believe that the burden of proof with respect to valuation should be shifted to the Commissioner in all cases where such formulas have been utilized. Accordingly, the use of a valuation method based on a nonlapse restriction that meets the requirements of Sec. 1.83-5(a) does not by itself result in a presumption of reasonableness. However, where the method is used consistently for both compensatory and noncompensatory purposes in all transactions in which the service recipient is either the purchaser or seller of such stock, such that the nonlapse restriction formula acts as a substitute for the value of the underlying stock, the formula will qualify for the presumption that the valuation method is reasonable for purposes of section 409A. In addition, depending on the facts and circumstances of the individual case, the use of a nonlapse restriction to determine value may be reasonable, taking into account other relevant valuation criteria.

Commentators also expressed concern about the valuation of illiquid stock of certain start-up corporations. These commentators argued that the value of such stock is often highly speculative, rendering appraisals of limited value. Commentators also noted that such stock often is not subject to put rights or call rights that could be viewed as a nonlapse restriction. Given the illiquidity and speculative value, commentators argued that the risk that taxpayers would use rights on such shares as a device to pay deferred compensation is low. In response, these regulations propose additional conditions under which the valuation of illiquid stock in a start-up corporation will be presumed to be reasonable. A valuation of an illiquid stock of a start-up corporation will be presumed reasonable if the valuation is made reasonably and in good faith and evidenced by a written report that takes into account the relevant factors prescribed for valuations generally under these regulations. For this purpose, illiquid stock of a start-up corporation refers to service recipient stock of a service recipient that is in the first 10 years of the active conduct of a trade or business and has no class of equity securities that are traded on an established securities market, where such stock is not subject to any put or call right or obligation of the service recipient or other person to purchase such stock (other than a right of first refusal upon an offer to purchase by a third party that is unrelated to the service recipient or service provider), provided that this rule does not apply to the valuation of any stock if the service recipient or service provider reasonably may anticipate, as of the time the valuation is applied, that the service recipient will undergo a change in control event or participate in a public offering of securities within the 12 months following the event to which the valuation is applied (for example, the grant date of an award). A valuation will not be treated as made reasonably and in good faith unless the valuation is performed by a person or persons with significant knowledge and experience or training in performing similar valuations.

As stated in the preamble to Notice 2005-1, the Treasury Department and the IRS are concerned about the treatment of stock rights where the service recipient is obligated to repurchase the stock acquired pursuant to the stock right, or the service provider retains a put or call right with respect to the stock. Where the service provider retains such a right, the ability to receive a purchase price that differs from the fair market value of the stock could be used to circumvent the application of section 409A. Accordingly, these regulations generally require that where someone is obligated to purchase the stock received upon the exercise of a stock right, or the stock is subject to a put or call right, the purchase price must also be set at fair market value, the determination of which is also subject to the consistency requirements for the methods used in determining fair market value.

4. Modification

Commentators asked under what conditions a modification, extension, or renewal of a stock right will be treated as a new grant. The treatment as a new grant is relevant because although the original grant may have been excluded from coverage under section 409A, if the new grant has an exercise price that is less than the fair market value of the underlying stock on the date of the new grant, the new grant would not qualify for the exclusion from coverage under section 409A. Accordingly, the regulations set forth rules governing the types of modifications, extensions or renewals that will result in treatment as a new grant. The regulations provide that the term modification means any change in the terms of the stock right that may provide the holder of the right with a direct or indirect reduction in the exercise price of the stock right, or an additional deferral feature, or an extension or renewal of the stock right, regardless of whether the holder in fact benefits from the change in terms. Under this definition, neither the addition of a provision permitting the transfer of the stock right nor a provision permitting the service provider to exchange the stock right for a cash amount equal to the amount that would be available if the stock right were exercised would be modifications of the stock right. In addition, these regulations explicitly provide that both a change in the terms of a stock right to allow for payment of the exercise price through the use of pre-owned stock, and a change in the terms of a stock right to facilitate the payment of employment taxes or required withholding taxes resulting from the exercise of the right, are not treated as modifications of the stock right for purposes of section 409A.

Generally, a change to the exercise price of the stock right (other than in connection with certain assumptions or substitutions of a stock right in connection with a corporate transaction or certain adjustments resulting from a stock split, stock dividend or similar change in capitalization) is treated as a modification, resulting in a new grant that may be excluded from section 409A if it satisfies the requirements in these regulations as of the new grant date. However, depending upon the facts and circumstances, a series of repricings of the exercise price may indicate that the original right had a floating or adjustable exercise price and did not meet the requirements of the exclusion at the time of the original grant.

Generally, an extension granting the holder an additional period within which to exercise the stock right beyond the time originally prescribed will be treated as evidencing an additional deferral feature meaning that the stock right was subject to section 409A from the date of grant. Commentators stated that it is not uncommon upon a termination of employment to extend the exercise period for some brief period of time to allow the terminated employee a chance to exercise the stock right. In response, these regulations provide that it is not an extension of a stock right if the exercise period is extended to a date no later than the later of the fifteenth day of the third month following the date, or December 31 of the calendar year in which, the right would otherwise have expired if the stock right had not been extended, based on the terms of the stock right at the original grant date. The regulations further provide that it is not an extension of a stock right if at the time the stock right would otherwise expire, the stock right is subject to a restriction prohibiting the exercise of the stock right because such exercise would violate applicable securities laws and the expiration date of the stock right is extended to a date no later than 30 days after the restrictions on exercise are no longer required to avoid a violation of applicable securities laws.

These regulations also provide that if the requirements of Sec. 1.424-1 (providing rules under which an eligible corporation may, by reason of a corporate transaction, substitute a new statutory option for an outstanding statutory option or assume an old option without such substitution or assumption being considered a modification of the old option) would be met if the right were a statutory option, the substitution of a new right pursuant to a corporate transaction for an outstanding right or the assumption of an outstanding right will not be treated as the grant of a new right or a change in the form of payment for purposes of section 409A. Section 1.424-1 applies several requirements. Among them is the requirement under Sec. 1.424-1(a)(5)(ii) that the excess of the aggregate fair market value of the shares subject to the new option over the exercise price immediately after the substitution must not exceed the excess of the fair market value of the shares subject to the old option over the exercise price immediately before the substitution. In addition, Sec. 1.424-1(a)(5)(iii) requires that on a share by share comparison, the ratio of the exercise price to the fair market value of the shares subject to the option immediately after the substitution not be more favorable than the ratio of the exercise price to the fair market value of the shares subject to the old option immediately before the substitution.

Commentators expressed concern that the use of the regulations contained in Sec. 1.424-1, and specifically the ratio test prescribed in Sec. 1.424-1(a)(5)(iii), would prove difficult to apply in circumstances where, to reduce dilution, the acquiring corporation wished to issue a smaller number of shares than the shares underlying the old option, but also wished to retain the entire aggregate difference between the fair market value of the shares and the exercise price that had been available to the service provider before the substitution. In response, Notice 2005-1, Q&A-4 and these regulations provide that the requirement of Sec. 1.424-1(a)(5)(iii) will be deemed to be satisfied if the ratio of the exercise price to the fair market value of the shares subject to the right immediately after the substitution or assumption is not greater than the ratio of the exercise price to the fair market value of the shares subject to the right immediately before the substitution or assumption. For example, if an employee had an option to purchase 25 shares for $2 per share, and immediately prior to a substitution by reason of a corporate transaction the fair market value of a share was $5, then the aggregate spread amount would be $75 (25 shares multiplied by ($5 − $2) = $75). The ratio of the exercise price to the fair market value would be $2/$5 = .40. As a part of the transaction, new employer wishes to substitute for the option an option to purchase 5 shares of new employer, when the shares have a fair market value of $20 per share. To maintain the aggregate spread of $75, the new grant has an exercise price of $5 (5 shares multiplied by ($20 − $5) = $75). The ratio of the exercise price to the fair market value immediately after the substitution is $5/$20 = .25, which is not greater than the ratio immediately before the substitution. Provided that the other requirements of Sec. 1.424-1 were met, this substitution would not be considered a modification of the original stock option for purposes of section 409A.

One commentator asked for more flexible rules concerning adjustments to and substitutions of options following a spinoff or similar transaction because short-term trading activity in the period immediately following such a transaction frequently does not accurately reflect the relative long-term fair market values of the stock of the distributing and distributed corporations. To address this problem, the regulations provide that such adjustments or substitutions may be made based on market quotations as of a predetermined date not more than 60 days after the transaction, or based on an average of such market prices over a period of not more than 30 days ending not later than 60 days after the transaction.

These provisions addressing substitutions and assumptions of rights apply to stock appreciation rights, as well as stock options. However, the guidance provided in these regulations with respect to the assumption of stock appreciation right liabilities should not be interpreted as guidance with respect to issues raised under any other provision of the Code or common law tax doctrine.

D. Restricted Property

Consistent with Notice 2005-1, Q&A-4(e), these regulations provide that if a service provider receives property from, or pursuant to, a plan maintained by a service recipient, there is no deferral of compensation merely because the value of the property is not includible in income in the year of receipt by reason of the property being nontransferable and subject to a substantial risk of forfeiture, or is includible in income solely due to a valid election under section 83(b). However, a plan under which a service provider obtains a legally binding right to receive property (whether or not the property is restricted property) in a future year may provide for the deferral of compensation and, accordingly, may constitute a nonqualified deferred compensation plan.

Commentators asked for clarification with respect to how this provision applies to a promise to transfer restricted property in a subsequent tax year. Specifically, commentators questioned how section 409A would apply to a bonus program offering a choice between a payment in cash and a payment in substantially nonvested property. Because the promise grants the service recipient a legally binding right to receive property in a future year, this promise generally could not constitute property for section 83 purposes under Sec. 1.83-3(e), and could constitute deferred compensation for purposes of section 409A. However, the regulations provide that the vesting of substantially nonvested property subject to section 83 may be treated as a payment for purposes section 409A, including for purposes of applying the short-term deferral rule. Accordingly, where the promise to transfer the substantially nonvested property and the right to retain the substantially nonvested property after the transfer are both subject to a substantial risk of forfeiture (as defined for purposes of section 409A), the arrangement generally would constitute a short-term deferral because the payment would occur simultaneously with the vesting of the right to the property. For example, where an employee participates in a two-year bonus program such that, if the employee continues in employment for two years, the employee is entitled to either the immediate payment of a $10,000 cash bonus or the grant of restricted stock with a $15,000 fair market value subject to a vesting requirement of three additional years of service, the arrangement generally would constitute a short-term deferral because under either alternative the payment would be received within the short-term deferral period.

E. Arrangements Between Partnerships and Partners

The statute and legislative history to section 409A do not specifically address arrangements between partnerships and partners providing services to a partnership, and do not explicitly exclude such arrangements from the application of section 409A. The application of section 409A to such arrangements raises a number of issues, relating both to the scope of the arrangements subject to section 409A, and the coordination of the provisions of subchapter K and section 409A with respect to those arrangements that are subject to section 409A. The Treasury Department and the IRS continue to analyze the issues raised in this area, and accordingly these regulations do not address arrangements between partnerships and partners. Notice 2005-1, Q&A-7 provides interim guidance regarding the application of section 409A to arrangements between partnerships and partners. Until further guidance is issued, taxpayers may continue to rely on Notice 2005-1, Q&A-7.

Commentators have asked whether section 409A applies to guaranteed payments for services described in section 707(c). Until further guidance is issued, section 409A will apply to guaranteed payments described in section 707(c) (and rights to receive such guaranteed payments in the future), only in cases where the guaranteed payment is for services and the partner providing services does not include the payment in income by the 15th day of the third month following the end of the taxable year of the partner in which the partner obtained a legally binding right to the guaranteed payment or, if later, the taxable year in which the right to the guaranteed payment is first no longer subject to a substantial risk of forfeiture.

Treasury Department and the IRS continue to request comments with respect to the application of section 409A to arrangements between partnerships and partners.

F. Foreign Arrangements

The regulations provide guidance with respect to the application of section 409A to various foreign arrangements. As an initial matter, the regulations provide that an arrangement does not provide for a deferral of compensation subject to section 409A where the compensation subject to the arrangement would not have been includible in gross income for Federal tax purposes if it had been paid to the service provider at the time that the legally binding right to the compensation first arose or, if later, the first time that the legally binding right was no longer subject to a substantial risk of forfeiture, if the service provider was a nonresident alien at such time. Accordingly, if, for example, a foreign citizen works outside the United States and then retires to the United States, the compensation deferred and vested while working in the foreign country generally will not be subject to section 409A.

With respect to U.S. citizens or resident aliens working abroad, the regulations provide that an arrangement does not provide for a deferral of compensation subject to section 409A where the compensation subject to the arrangement would have constituted foreign earned income (within the meaning of section 911) paid to a qualified individual (as defined in section 911(d)(1)) and the amount of the compensation is less than or equal to the difference between the maximum section 911 exclusion amount and the amount actually excludible from gross income under section 911 for the taxable year for the individual. This hypothetical exclusion is applied at the time that the legally binding right to the compensation first exists or, if later, the time that the legally binding right is no longer subject to a substantial risk of forfeiture. Under section 911, a U.S. citizen or resident alien who resides in a foreign jurisdiction generally may exclude up to $80,000 of foreign earned income (to be adjusted for inflation after 2007). For example, an individual with $70,000 of foreign earned income excluded under section 911 in 2006 could also defer up to $10,000 of additional compensation that would not be subject to section 409A, if the additional compensation would qualify as foreign earned income if paid to the individual in 2006. This exception to coverage under section 409A is intended to be applied on an annual basis, so that individuals will not be entitled to carry over any unused portion of the exclusion under section 911 to a future year. This exception also is not intended to modify the rules under section 911 or the regulations thereunder.

Similarly, these regulations also address deferrals of compensation income that would be excluded from gross income for Federal income tax purposes under section 893 (generally covering compensation paid to foreign workers of a foreign government or international organization working in the United States), section 872 (generally covering certain compensation earned by nonresident alien individuals), section 931 (generally covering certain compensation earned by bona fide residents of Guam, American Samoa, or the Northern Mariana Islands) and section 933 (generally covering certain compensation earned by bona fide residents of Puerto Rico). The regulations provide that an arrangement does not provide for a deferral of compensation subject to section 409A where the compensation subject to the arrangement would have been excluded from gross income for Federal tax purposes under any of these sections, if the compensation had been paid to the service provider at the time that the legally binding right to the compensation first arose or, if later, the time that the legally binding right was no longer subject to a substantial risk of forfeiture.

The Treasury Department and the IRS understand that nonresident aliens may work for very limited periods in the United States. Many deferrals of the compensation earned by nonresident aliens for services rendered in the United States will not be covered by section 409A, because under an applicable treaty the amount of compensation deferred would not be includible in gross income for Federal tax purposes if paid at the time the legally binding right to the compensation deferred was no longer subject to a substantial risk of forfeiture. However, certain compensation earned in the United States by a nonresident alien might be includible in gross income under such circumstances, where there is no applicable treaty or where the treaty does not provide an exclusion. Where a nonresident alien defers such compensation earned in the United States under a foreign nonqualified deferred compensation plan—for example because the service in the United States is credited under the plan—the application of section

409A to the deferrals of the compensation subject to Federal income tax could be exceedingly burdensome in light of the relatively small amounts attributable to the service in the United States. Accordingly, these regulations adopt a de minimis exception, under which section 409A will not apply to an amount of compensation deferred under a foreign nonqualified deferred compensation plan for a given calendar year where the individual service provider is a nonresident alien for that calendar year and the amount deferred does not exceed $10,000.

Commentators requested clarification of the application of section 409A to participation by U.S. citizens and resident aliens in foreign plans. In this context, it should be noted that under these regulations, transfers that are taxable under section 402(b) of the Code generally are not subject to section 409A. See Sec. 1.409A-1(b)(6) of these regulations and Notice 2005-1, Q&A-4. Such transfers may consist of contributions to an employees' trust, where the trust does not qualify under section 501(a). Many foreign plans that hold contributions in a trust will constitute funded plans. To the extent that a contribution to the trust is subject to inclusion in income for Federal tax purposes under section 402(b), such a contribution will not be subject to section 409A.

These regulations also provide that section 409A does not override treaty provisions that govern the U.S. Federal taxation of participation in particular foreign plans. Where a treaty provides that amounts contributed to a foreign plan by or on behalf of a service provider are not subject to U.S. Federal income tax, section 409A will not cause such amounts to be subject to inclusion in gross income.

Some commentators requested that any participation in a foreign plan be exempted from section 409A, or that only deferrals of U.S. source compensation income be subject to section 409A. However, with respect to U.S. citizens working abroad, and with respect to resident aliens in the United States, compensation income generally is subject to U.S. Federal income tax absent an applicable treaty provision. Accordingly, the provisions of section 409A generally are applicable to this type of deferred compensation. In addition, the Treasury Department and the IRS are concerned that providing a broad exception for foreign plans or foreign source income would create opportunities for U.S. citizens and resident aliens to avoid application of section 409A through participation in a foreign plan, or through reallocations of deferrals among U.S. source and foreign source income.

The regulations provide, however, that with respect to non-U.S. citizens who are not lawful permanent residents of the United States, amounts deferred under certain broad-based foreign retirement plans are not subject to section 409A. This exception is intended to allow a worker who is not a green card holder to continue to participate in a broad-based foreign retirement plan that does not comply with section 409A without incurring adverse tax consequences due solely to the worker earning some income in the United States that is in some manner credited under the plan.

Commentators expressed concerns as to U.S. citizens and lawful permanent residents working abroad, and their ability to participate in broad-based plans of foreign employers. Generally, these workers' incomes are subject to Federal income tax, including section 409A. However, when U.S. citizens and lawful permanent residents work abroad for employers who sponsor broad-based foreign retirement plans providing relatively low levels of retirement benefits and such plans are nonelective, the worker's ability to control the timing of the income is limited. In such cases, the concerns with respect to the potential manipulation of the timing of compensation income addressed by section 409A are also limited, and do not outweigh the administrative burdens that would arise if a foreign employer's failure to amend these plans to be consistent with the provisions of section 409A would result in substantial adverse tax consequences to U.S. citizens and lawful permanent residents working abroad who are covered by such plans. Accordingly, an exception for foreign broad-based retirement plans also applies with respect to U.S. citizens and lawful permanent residents, but only with respect to nonelective deferrals of foreign earned income and only to the extent that the amount deferred in a given year does not exceed the amount of contributions or benefits that may be provided by a qualified plan under section 415 (calculated by treating the foreign source income as compensation for purposes of section 415).

Commentators also requested that certain types of payments, referred to as expatriate allowances, be exempted from coverage under section 409A. These payments were defined broadly to include many types of payments to U.S. citizens working abroad, intended to put the service providers in substantially the same economic position as the service providers would have been in had the services been provided in the United States. One very common arrangement involves payments intended to compensate the service provider for any differences in tax rates, often referred to as tax equalization plans. With respect to these plans, the Treasury Department and the IRS recognize that such payments often must be delayed because of the need to calculate foreign tax liabilities after the end of the year. In addition, where the amounts are limited to the amounts necessary to make up for difference in tax rates, the potential for abuse with respect to the timing of compensation income is not great, since the compensation will directly relate to taxes that the service provider has paid to a foreign jurisdiction. Accordingly, these regulations exempt tax equalization plans from coverage under section 409A provided that the payment is made no later than the end of the second calendar year beginning after the calendar year in which the individual's U.S. Federal income tax return is required to be filed (including extensions) for the year to which the tax equalization payment relates.

Other payments are not excluded from section 409A merely because they are denominated as expatriate allowances. The Treasury Department and the IRS believe that the rules provided in these regulations with respect to setting and meeting payment dates under a nonqualified deferred compensation plan will provide sufficient flexibility to permit arrangements involving expatriate allowances to satisfy the requirements of section 409A. For example, as discussed more fully below, these regulations generally provide that to meet the requirement that a payment be made upon a permissible payment event or a fixed date, the service recipient may make the payment by the later of the earliest date administratively practicable following, or December 31 of the calendar year in which occurs, the permissible payment event or fixed date. At the minimum, this should offer almost 12 months of flexibility with respect to a payment scheduled for January 1 of a calendar year. The Treasury Department and the IRS request comments, however, as to circumstances in which this flexibility will not be sufficient.

Commentators also requested a grace period during which arrangements with persons who have become resident aliens during a calendar year may be amended to comply with the requirements of section 409A. These regulations generally provide such relief. With respect to the initial year in which the service provider becomes a resident alien, the plan may be amended with respect to the service provider through the end of that year to comply with (or be excluded from coverage under) section 409A, including allowing the service provider the right to change the time and form of a payment. Provided that the election is made before the amount is paid or payable, initial deferral elections may also be made with respect to compensation related to services in that initial year, if the election is made by the end of the year or, if later, the 15th day of the third month after the service provider meets the requirements to be a resident alien. The relief generally does not extend further because a service recipient and service provider should reasonably anticipate the potential application of section 409A after the initial year in which the service provider attains the status of a resident alien. However, the Treasury Department and the IRS also recognize that there may be significant gaps between the years in which the service provider is treated as a resident alien. Accordingly, the grace period is available in a subsequent year, provided that the service provider has been a nonresident alien for at least five consecutive calendar years immediately preceding the year in which the service provider is again a resident alien.

Commentators also requested that amounts contributed or benefits paid under a foreign social security system that is the subject of a totalization agreement be exempted from coverage under section 409A. Totalization agreements refer to bilateral agreements between the United States and foreign jurisdictions intended to coordinate coverage under the Social Security system in the United States and similar systems of the foreign jurisdictions. These agreements are intended to minimize the potential for application of two different employment taxes, and correspondingly to coordinate the benefits under the two different social security systems. The Treasury Department and the IRS believe that section 409A was not intended to apply to benefits to which the service provider is entitled under the foreign jurisdiction social security system. Accordingly, these types of plans have been excluded from the definition of a nonqualified deferred compensation plan for purposes of section 409A. Similarly, for jurisdictions not covered by a totalization agreement, these regulations provide that amounts deferred under a government mandated social security system are not subject to section 409A.

G. Separation Pay Arrangements

1. In General

Many commentators requested clarification of the application of section 409A to plans or arrangements providing payments upon a termination of services, generally described as severance plans. Some commentators requested that all such arrangements be excluded from coverage under section 409A. However, section 409A(d)(1)(B) contains a list of welfare benefits that are specifically excluded from coverage under section 409A, including bona fide vacation leave, sick leave, compensatory time, disability pay and death benefit plans. Noticeably absent from this list is an exception for severance plans. This is particularly noteworthy because section 457(e)(11) contains the identical list of exclusions, with the one exception that the list of excluded plans under section 457(e)(11) includes severance pay plans, while the list of excluded plans under section 409A(d)(1)(B) does not. Therefore, it appears that Congress intended that severance payments could constitute deferred compensation under section 409A. To avoid confusion with other Code provisions, such as the specific exclusion from coverage under section 457(e)(11) for severance plans or the treatment of such arrangements under section 3121(v)(2), these regulations generally refer to such arrangements as separation pay arrangements.

With respect to payments available upon a voluntary termination of services, there is no substantive distinction between a plan labeled a severance plan or separation pay plan and a nonqualified deferred compensation plan that provides for payments upon a separation from service. If, as is often the case, the service recipient reserves the right to eliminate such arrangement at any time, the service provider may not have a legally binding right to the payment until payment actually occurs, or such other time as the service recipient's discretion to eliminate the right to the payments lapses. However, as provided in these regulations, where such negative discretion lacks substantive significance, or the person granted the discretion is controlled by, or related to, the service provider to whom the payment will be made, the service provider will be considered to have a legally binding right to the compensation.

Commentators requested that the exclusion from coverage under section 409A contained in Notice 2005-1, Q&A-19(d) for payments during the calendar year 2005 to non-key employees pursuant to severance plans that are classified as welfare plans, rather than pension plans, in accordance with the Department of Labor regulations, be made a permanent exclusion. This approach generally would be consistent with the regulations under section 3121(v)(2) of the Code. However, the Department of Labor regulations reflect different concerns with respect to separation pay arrangements from the concerns addressed in section 409A. The Department of Labor regulations focus on whether an arrangement sufficiently resembles a retirement plan to require funding of the obligations under such a plan, or rather is a welfare plan that would not require funding. In contrast, section 409A focuses on the manipulation of the timing of inclusion of compensation income. Accordingly, these regulations do not categorically exclude these arrangements from coverage under section 409A, although a modified version of this exception has been provided, as discussed below.

Some commentators requested that the Treasury Department and the IRS adopt an exclusion for all amounts payable upon an involuntary separation. This request is based upon the position under certain other Code provisions, and stated in certain court cases, that payments to which an individual becomes entitled upon an involuntary separation from service do not constitute nonqualified deferred compensation. See Kraft Foods North America v. U.S., 58 Fed. Cl. 507 (2003); Sec. 31.3121(v)(2)-1(b)(4)(iv). As discussed above, the statutory language and structure of section 409A strongly suggest that separation pay arrangements, including arrangements providing separation pay upon an involuntary separation, were meant to be covered by section 409A. Furthermore, the Treasury Department and the IRS believe that section 409A was not intended to be applied so narrowly. Section 409A addresses the manipulation of the timing of inclusion of compensation. Payments due to a separation from service, regardless of whether voluntary or involuntary, constitute a payment of compensation. Accordingly, the ability to manipulate the timing of the inclusion of income related to the receipt of those amounts is within the scope of section 409A.

Much of the discussion above relates to predetermined arrangements, where the right to the payment upon an involuntary termination of services arises as part of an arrangement covering multiple service providers, often covering a service provider from the time the service provider begins performing services. Where the separation pay arrangement involves an agreement negotiated with a specific service provider at the time of the involuntary separation from service, commentators asked how deferral elections could be provided that would meet the requirement that the election be made in the year before the year in which the services were performed. Commentators pointed out that even if the service provider does not already participate in any involuntary separation pay arrangement, the rule in section 409A(a)(4)(B) that allows an initial deferral election to be made within 30 days of initial eligibility under a plan applies only with respect to services performed after the election. To address these concerns, these regulations provide that where separation pay due to an involuntary termination has been the subject of bona fide, arm's length negotiations, the election as to the time and form of payment may be made on or before the date the service provider obtains a legally binding right to the payment.

The Treasury Department and the IRS recognize that separation pay arrangements providing for short-term payments upon an involuntary separation from service are common arrangements, and that compliance with the provisions of section 409A may be burdensome. In addition, the Treasury Department and the IRS recognize that where both the amount of the payments and the time over which such payments may be made are limited, these arrangements create fewer concerns with respect to manipulation of the timing of compensation income. Accordingly, these regulations generally exempt such arrangements where the entire amount of payments does not exceed two times the service provider's annual compensation or, if less, two times the limit on annual compensation that may be taken into account for qualified plan purposes under section 401(a)(17) ($210,000 for calendar year 2005), each for the calendar year before the year in which the service provider separates from service, and provided further that the arrangement requires that all payments be made by no later than the end of the second calendar year following the year in which the service provider terminates service. These limitations generally are consistent with the safe harbor under which severance plans may be treated as welfare plans under the applicable Department of Labor regulations, and should allow most of these arrangements to avoid coverage under section 409A.

The Treasury Department and the IRS further recognize that separation pay arrangements often occur in the context of a window program, where certain groups of service providers are identified as being subject to a separation from service, and the service recipient provides the identified service providers an incentive to voluntarily separate from service and obtain a benefit. Although technically these programs involve a voluntary separation from service, these regulations generally treat separations due to participation in a window arrangement the same as arrangements with respect to involuntary separations from service for purposes of the exceptions to coverage from section 409A.

These exclusions for separation pay are not intended to allow for rights to payments that would otherwise be deferred compensation subject to section 409A to avoid application of section 409A by being recharacterized as separation pay. Accordingly, the exclusions for separation pay do not apply to the extent the separation pay acts as a substitute for, or a replacement of, amounts that would otherwise be subject to section 409A. For example, a right to separation pay obtained in exchange for the relinquishment of a right to a payment of deferred compensation subject to section 409A will not be excluded from coverage under section 409A, but rather will be treated as a payment of the original amount of deferred compensation.

2. Treatment as a Separate Plan

Commentators have stated that arrangements involving payments due to an involuntary separation often operate separately from more traditional types of nonqualified deferred compensation plans. In addition, especially in the case of agreements covering an individual, the involuntary separation pay agreement may involve many different types of payments that are of a much smaller magnitude than amounts deferred under other types of nonqualified deferred compensation plans. Commentators expressed concerns that inadvertent violations of section 409A with respect to these unique arrangements could lead to much larger amounts being included in income and subject to the additional tax under section 409A due to the aggregation of such involuntary separation pay arrangements with other arrangements under the definition of a plan. The Treasury Department and the IRS have concluded that a nonqualified deferred compensation plan providing separation pay due to an involuntary separation from service, or participation in a window program, should be treated as a separate type of plan from account balance plans, nonaccount balance plans, and other types of plans (generally equity-based compensation arrangements) in which the service provider may participate that do not provide separation pay due to an involuntary separation from service, or participation in a window program.

3. Application of the Short-Term Deferral Rule to Separation Pay Arrangements

Many commentators asked for a clarification with respect to the application of the short-term deferral rule to separation pay arrangements. The right to a payment that will only be paid upon an involuntary termination of services generally would be viewed as a nonvested right. Accordingly, an involuntary separation pay arrangement may be structured to meet the requirements of the short-term deferral exception. Some commentators also requested that arrangements involving rights to payments upon termination of services for good reason be treated as a right subject to a substantial risk of forfeiture. These arrangements are common, especially following a transaction resulting in a change in control of the service recipient. The Treasury Department and the IRS are not confident that amounts payable upon a voluntary separation from service, and amounts payable only upon a termination of services for good reason, always may be adequately distinguished. Furthermore, even if the types of good reasons sufficient to constitute a substantial risk of forfeiture could be elucidated, the application of such a rule would involve intensive factual determinations, leaving taxpayers uncertain in their planning and creating a significant potential for abuse. Accordingly, the regulations do not treat the right to a payment upon a separation from service for good reason categorically as a right subject to a substantial risk of forfeiture. However, the Treasury Department and the IRS request comments as to what further guidance may be useful with respect to arrangements containing these types of provisions.

4. Reimbursement Arrangements

Many commentators requested clarification with respect to the application of section 409A to reimbursement agreements, involving the service recipient reimbursing expenses of the terminated service provider. Because the promise to reimburse the former service provider is not contingent on the provision of any substantial services for the service provider, the right to the payment generally would not be treated as subject to a substantial risk of forfeiture. Accordingly, if the period in which expenses incurred will be reimbursed extends beyond the year in which the legally binding right arises, the right to the amount generally would constitute deferred compensation. The

Treasury Department and the IRS recognize that reimbursement arrangements following a termination of services are common, and that requiring the service recipient to designate an amount at the time of the termination conflicts with the service recipient's desire to pay only amounts that the former service provider has actually incurred as an expense. However, a categorical exclusion for reimbursement arrangements is not tenable, because such an exclusion would allow for a limitless amount of deferred compensation to be paid without regard to the rules of section 409A, where such compensation took the form of the reimbursement of personal expenses (for example, reimbursements of home mortgage payments). These regulations provide that certain reimbursement arrangements related to a termination of services are not covered by section 409A, to the extent that the reimbursement arrangement covers only expenses incurred and reimbursed before the end of the second calendar year following the calendar year in which the termination occurs. The types of reimbursement arrangements excluded include reimbursements that are otherwise excludible from gross income, reimbursements for expenses that the service provider can deduct under section 162 or section 167, as business expenses incurred in connection with the performance of services (ignoring any applicable limitation based on adjusted gross income), outplacement expenses, moving expenses, medical expenses, as well as any other types of payments that do not exceed $5,000 in the aggregate during any given taxable year.

For purposes of this provision, reimbursement arrangements include the provision of in-kind benefits, or direct payments by the service recipient to the person providing the goods or services to the terminated service provider, if the provision of such in-kind benefits or direct payments would be treated as reimbursement arrangements if the service provider had paid for such in-kind benefits or such goods or services and received reimbursement from the service recipient.

H. Split-Dollar Life Insurance Arrangements

Commentators suggested that split-dollar life insurance arrangements should be excluded from the requirements of section 409A. However, the Treasury Department and the IRS believe that in applying the general definition of deferred compensation to split-dollar life insurance arrangements, the requirements of section 409A may apply to certain types of such arrangements (as described in Sec. 1.61-22). Split-dollar life insurance arrangements that provide only death benefits (as defined in these proposed regulations) to or for the benefit of the service provider may be excluded from coverage under section 409A under the exception from the definition of a nonqualified deferred compensation plan provided in these proposed regulations for death benefit plans. Also, split-dollar life insurance arrangements treated as loan arrangements under Sec. 1.7872-15 generally will not give rise to deferrals of compensation within the meaning of section 409A, provided that there is no agreement under which the service recipient will forgive the related indebtedness and no obligation on the part of the service recipient to continue to make premium payments without charging the service provider a market interest rate on the funds advanced. However, policies structured under the endorsement method, where the service recipient is the owner of the policy but where the service provider obtains a legally binding right to compensation includible in income in a taxable year after the year in which a substantial risk of forfeiture (if any) lapses, may provide for a deferral of compensation. Just as a promise to transfer property in a future year may provide for a deferral of compensation (even though the transfer itself is subject to section 83), an endorsement method split-dollar life insurance arrangement that grants the service provider a legally binding right to a future transfer of interests in a policy owned by the service recipient may provide for a deferral of compensation subject to section 409A. For example, where a service recipient enters into an endorsement method split-dollar life insurance arrangement with respect to a service provider, and irrevocably promises to pay premiums in future years, the arrangement may provide for a deferral of compensation within the meaning of section 409A.

Commentators raised concerns about the impact of changes to a split-dollar life insurance arrangement to comply with section 409A, where the split-dollar life insurance arrangement was entered into on or before September 17, 2003, and is not otherwise subject to the regulations set forth in Sec. 1.61-22 (a grandfathered split-dollar life insurance arrangement). Pursuant to Sec. 1.61-22(j)(2), if a grandfathered split-dollar life insurance arrangement is materially modified after September 17, 2003, the arrangement is treated as a new arrangement entered into on the date of the modification. Commentators expressed concern that modifications necessary to comply with section 409A may cause the split-dollar life insurance arrangement to be treated as materially modified for purposes of Sec. 1.61-22(j)(2). Comments are requested as to the scope of changes that may be necessary to comply with, or avoid application of, section 409A, and under what conditions those changes should not be treated as material modifications for purposes of Sec. 1.61-22(j)(2).

III. Definition of Plan

A. Plan Aggregation Rules

These regulations generally retain the plan aggregation rules set forth in Notice 2005-1, Q&A-9. Under the notice, all amounts deferred under an account balance plan are treated as deferred under a single plan, all amounts deferred under a nonaccount balance are treated as deferred under a single plan, and all amounts deferred under any other type of plan (generally equity-based compensation) are treated as deferred under a single plan. As discussed above, these regulations expand this rule so that all amounts deferred under certain separation pay arrangements are treated as a single plan. The purposes behind these aggregation rules are two-fold. First, because the provisions of section 409A are applied on an individual participant basis, rather than disqualifying the arrangement as to all participants, plan aggregation rules are necessary to implement the compliance incentives intended under the provision. Without such rules, multitudes of separate arrangements could be established for a single participant. Should the participant want access to an amount of cash, the participant would amend one or more of these separate arrangements and receive payments. The participant would argue that only those separate arrangements under which the amounts were paid failed to meet the requirements of section 409A and were subject to the income inclusion and additional tax, although in fact amounts were also available under the additional separate arrangements. Under that analysis, section 409A essentially would act as a 20 percent penalty required to receive a payment, similar to the haircut provisions that were intended to be prohibited by section 409A. The Treasury Department and the IRS do not believe that Congress intended that the consequences of section 409A could be limited in such a manner. However, the Treasury Department and the IRS also believe that complex plan aggregation rules, especially rules reliant on the particular facts and circumstances underlying each arrangement, would lead to unwarranted complexities and burdens with respect to service recipient planning and IRS enforcement. Accordingly, these regulations adopt rules intended to be simple and relatively easy to administer that retain the integrity of the compliance incentives inherent in the statute.

Commentators asked whether an isolated violation of a term of an arrangement with respect to one participant will be treated as a violation of the same arrangement term with respect to other participants covered by the same arrangement. First, the terms of the arrangement with respect to each participant must be determined, based upon the rights the individual participant has under the plan. Generally, these rights will be determined based upon the written provisions applicable under a particular arrangement, as evidenced by a plan document, agreement, or some combination of documents that specify the terms of the contract under which the compensation is to be paid. However, where the terms of a plan or arrangement comply with section 409A, but the service recipient does not follow such terms, an individual participant's actual rights under the arrangement may be unclear. Where a violation of a provision is not an isolated incident, or involves a number of participants or an identifiable subgroup of participants under the arrangement, the violation may result in a finding that even with respect to a participant who did not directly benefit from the violation, the actual terms of the arrangement differ from the written terms of the arrangement. For example, if a plan document provides for installment payments upon a separation from service, but participants in the arrangement repeatedly are offered the opportunity to receive a lump sum payment, the facts and circumstances may indicate that the arrangement provides for an election of a lump sum payment for all participants.

An analogous analytical framework applies where the service recipient offers different benefits to separate participants in the same plan or arrangement. Under the terms of the overall arrangement, the service provider may grant many different types of rights, including some rights that would not be subject to the requirements of section 409A and some rights that would be subject to those requirements. With respect to the application of section 409A, a plan or arrangement is analyzed as consisting of the rights and benefits that have actually been granted to a particular service provider. For example, with respect to an equity-based omnibus plan that permits the grant of discounted stock options that would be subject to the requirements of section 409A, as well as other types of stock options which would be excluded from coverage under section 409A, only those service providers actually granted the discounted stock options will be treated as having deferred an amount of compensation subject to section 409A, and then only with respect to the stock options subject to section 409A.

B. Written Plan Requirement

Although the statute does not explicitly state that a plan or arrangement must be in writing, the statute requires that a plan contain certain provisions in order to comply with section 409A. For example, section 409A(a)(2)(A) requires that a plan provide that compensation deferred under the plan may not be distributed earlier than certain specific events. Section 409A(a)(4)(B) requires that a plan provide certain restrictions with respect to initial deferral elections. Section 409A(a)(4)(C) requires that, if a plan permits under a subsequent election a delay in a payment or a change in the form of payment, the plan must require certain limits on the scope of such a delay or change. The clear implication of these provisions of section 409A is that the plan or arrangement must be set forth in writing and these regulations incorporate that requirement.

IV. Definition of Substantial Risk of Forfeiture

The scope of the definition of a substantial risk of forfeiture is central to the application of section 409A. In addition to the timing of the potential inclusion of income under section 409A, the existence of a substantial risk of forfeiture may also determine whether an amount is subject to section 409A or whether it qualifies for the exclusion under the short-term deferral rule. These regulations generally adopt the same definition as provided in Notice 2005-1, Q&A-10. This definition reflects the concerns of the Treasury Department and the IRS that the use of plan terms that purport to prescribe a substantial risk of forfeiture but, in fact, do not put the right to the payment at a substantial risk, may be used to circumvent the application of section 409A in a manner inconsistent with the legislative intent. The definition of a substantial risk of forfeiture in these regulations contains certain restrictions. Certain amendments of an arrangement to extend a substantial risk of forfeiture will not be recognized. The ability to periodically extend, or roll, the risk of forfeiture is sufficiently suspect to question whether the parties ever intended that the right be subject to any true substantial risk, or rather whether the period is being extended through periods in which the service recipient can be reasonably assured that the forfeiture condition will not occur. Similarly, the risk that a right will be forfeited due to the violation of a noncompete agreement can be illusory, such as where the service provider has no intent to compete or to provide such services. In addition, a rational service provider normally would not agree to subject amounts that have already been earned, such as salary payments, to a condition that creates a real possibility of forfeiture, unless the service provider is offered a material inducement to do so, such as an additional amount of compensation. Accordingly, these provisions will not be treated as creating a substantial risk of forfeiture for purposes of section 409A.

V. Initial Deferral Election Rules

A. In General

Section 409A(a)(4)(B)(i) provides that in general, a plan must provide that compensation for services performed during a taxable year may be deferred at the participant's election only if the election to defer such compensation is made not later than the close of the preceding taxable year or at such other time as provided in regulations. The legislative history indicates that the taxable year to which the statute refers is the service provider's taxable year, as it indicates that the Secretary may issue guidance "providing coordination rules, as appropriate, regarding the timing of elections in the case when the fiscal year of the employer and the taxable year of the individual are different."

H.R. Conf. Rep. No. 108-755, at 732 (2004). Accordingly, these regulations provide as a general rule that a service provider must make a deferral election in his or her taxable year before the year in which the services are performed. As discussed below, certain coordination rules for fiscal year employers have been provided.

An election to defer an amount includes an election both as to the time and form of the payment. An election is treated as made as of the date the election becomes irrevocable. Changes may be made to an initial deferral election, provided that the election becomes irrevocable (except to the extent the plan permits a subsequent deferral election consistent with these regulations) no later than the last date that such an election may be made. Commentators had questioned whether an evergreen deferral election, or a deferral election as to future compensation that remains in place unless the service provider changes the election, would be effective for purposes of section 409A. Such an election satisfies the initial deferral election requirements only if the election becomes irrevocable with respect to future compensation no later than the last permissible date an affirmative initial deferral election could have been made with respect to such compensation. For example, with respect to a salary deferral program under which an employee makes an initial deferral election to defer 10 percent of the salary earned during the subsequent calendar year, a plan may provide that the deferral election remains effective unless and until changed by the employee, provided that with respect to salary earned during any future taxable year, the election to defer 10 percent of such salary becomes irrevocable no later than the December 31 of the preceding calendar year.

B. Nonelective Arrangements

Some commentators asked whether the initial deferral election rules apply to nonelective arrangements. The requirement that the election be made in the year before the services are performed is not applicable where the participant is not provided any election with respect to the amount deferred, or the time and form of the payment. However, as stated in the legislative history, "[t]he time and form of distribution must be specified at the time of initial deferral." H.R. Conf. Rep. No. 108-755, at 732 (2004). In addition, the application of the subsequent deferral rules becomes problematic if the original time and form of deferred payment established by the service recipient is not viewed as an initial deferral election. Therefore, in order to avoid application of the initial deferral rules, a plan may not provide a service provider or service recipient with ongoing discretion as to the time and form of payment, but rather must set the time and form of payment no later than the time the service provider obtains a legally binding right to the compensation.

C. Performance-Based Compensation

Section 409A(a)(4)(B)(iii) provides that in the case of any performance-based compensation based on services performed over a period of at least 12 months, a participant's initial deferral election may be made no later than six months before the end of the period. The legislative history indicates that the performance-based compensation should be required to meet certain requirements similar to those under section 162(m), but not all requirements under that section. H.R. Conf. Rep. No. 108-755, at 732 (2004). An example in the legislative history, adopted in these regulations, is that the requirement of a determination by the compensation committee of the board of directors is not required.

Notice 2005-1 did not provide a definition of performance-based compensation. Rather, Notice 2005-1, Q&A-22 provided a definition of bonus compensation that, until further guidance was issued, could be used for purposes of applying the exception to the general rule regarding initial deferral elections.

Under these regulations, performance-based compensation is defined as compensation the payment of which or the amount of which is contingent on the satisfaction of preestablished organizational or individual performance criteria. Performance-based compensation does not include any amount or portion of any amount that will be paid either regardless of performance, or based upon a level of performance that is substantially certain to be met at the time the criteria are established.

Performance-based compensation generally may include payments based upon subjective performance criteria, provided that the subjective performance criteria relate to the performance of the participant service provider, a group of service providers that includes the participant service provider, or a business unit for which the participant service provider provides services (which may include the entire organization), and the determination that the subjective performance criteria have been met is not made by the service provider or a member of the service provider's family, or a person the service provider supervises or over whose compensation the service provider has any control.

Commentators requested that, similar to the provision contained in Sec. 1.162-27(e)(2) governing the requirements for establishing performance criteria for purposes of applying the deduction limitation under section 162(m), service recipients be allowed to establish performance criteria within 90 days of the commencement of a performance period of 12 months or more, rather than having to establish such criteria before the commencement of the period. These regulations adopt a similar provision with respect to the establishment of performance criteria for purposes of the exception under the deferral election rules, permitting the criteria to be established up to 90 days after the commencement of the period of service to which the criteria relates, provided that the outcome is not substantially certain at the time the criteria are established.

The legislative history indicates that to constitute performance-based compensation, the amount must be (1) variable and contingent on the satisfaction of preestablished organizational or individual performance criteria and (2) not readily ascertainable at the time of the election. H.R. Conf. Rep. No. 108-755, at 732 (2004). These regulations clarify that where the right to receive a specified amount is itself not substantially certain, the amount is not readily ascertainable as the amount paid could either be the specified amount or zero. Accordingly, these regulations provide that at the time of the initial deferral election, either the amount must not be readily ascertainable, or the right to the amount must not be substantially certain. So, for example, the right to a $10,000 bonus that otherwise qualifies as performance-based compensation could be deferred by an employee up to six months before the end of the performance period, provided that at the time of the deferral election the employee is not substantially certain to meet the criteria and receive the $10,000 payment.

Under the definition of bonus compensation provided in Notice 2005-1, Q&A-22, bonus compensation does not include any amount or portion of any amount that is based solely on the value of, or appreciation in value of, the service recipient or the stock of the service recipient. Commentators criticized this limitation as inconsistent with the provisions of Sec. 1.162-27 governing application of the deduction limitation under section 162(m), and the legislative history to section 409A indicating that the definition of performance-based compensation for purposes of section 409A would be similar to that provided under section 162(m) and the regulations thereunder. These proposed regulations eliminate this limitation, so that performance-based compensation may be based solely upon an increase in the value of the service recipient, or the stock of the service recipient, after the date of grant or award. However, if an amount of compensation the service provider will receive pursuant to a grant or award is not based solely on an increase in the value of the stock after the grant or award (for example, in the case of restricted stock units or a stock right granted with an exercise price that is less than the fair market value of the stock as of the date of grant), and that other amount would not otherwise qualify as performance-based compensation, none of the compensation attributable to the grant or award is performance-based compensation.

Nonetheless, an award of equity-based compensation may constitute performance-based compensation if entitlement to the compensation is subject to a condition that would cause a non-equity-based award to qualify as performance-based compensation, such as a performance-based vesting condition.

The Treasury Department and the IRS are concerned that the inclusion of such amounts in the definition of performance-based compensation could lead to a conclusion that an election to defer amounts payable under a stock right will necessarily comply with section 409A if the initial deferral election is made at least 6 months before the date of exercise. However, under these proposed regulations, a stock right with a deferral feature is subject to section 409A from the date of grant. To comply with section 409A, the arrangement would be required to specify a permissible payment time and a form of payment. The requirement would not be met if, at some point during the term of the stock right, the stock right becomes immediately exercisable and the holder may decide whether and when to exercise the stock right. In addition, where a deferral feature is added to an existing stock right the stock right generally would violate section 409A because the stock right would have a deferral feature and would not have specified a permissible payment time or event.

D. First Year of Eligibility

Section 409A and these proposed regulations contain an exception to the general rule regarding initial deferral elections, under which a service provider newly eligible for participation in a plan may make a deferral election within the first 30 days of participation in the plan, provided that the election may only apply to compensation with respect to services performed after the election. These regulations further provide that for compensation that is earned based upon a specified performance period (for example, an annual bonus), where a deferral election is made in the first year of eligibility but after the beginning of the service period, the election is deemed to apply to compensation paid for service performed subsequent to the election if the election applies to the portion of the compensation that is no greater than the total amount of compensation for the performance period multiplied by the ratio of the number of days remaining in the performance period after the election over the total number of days in the performance period.

Commentators had requested that the plan aggregation rules not apply in determining whether a service provider is newly eligible for participation in a plan. The concern is that a mid-year promotion, or management reorganization or other corporate event may make the service provider eligible for an arrangement that is of the same type as an arrangement in which the service provider already participates. For example, an employee participating in a salary deferral account-balance plan may become eligible for a bonus and a bonus deferral arrangement that would also be an account-balance plan.

The Treasury Department and the IRS believe that the plan aggregation rules are necessary in this context. Without such a rule, service providers may attempt to take advantage of the new eligibility exception by establishing serial arrangements. For example, an employer may argue that a 2007 salary deferral program is a new program, and not a continuation of the 2006 salary deferral program. Commentators argue that standards should be provided comparing the terms of the two plans to distinguish new arrangements from those that are merely continuations of existing arrangements. However, such rules would by necessity be complicated and burdensome, generally relying on the facts and circumstances of the individual arrangements and resulting in administrative burden and uncertainties. Accordingly, these regulations retain the plan aggregation rules.

However, as discussed below, certain other initial deferral election rules have been provided that address many of the situations in which service recipients desire to grant service providers the opportunity to make initial deferral elections due to eligibility in new programs. For example, the rule governing initial deferral elections with respect to certain forfeitable rights discussed below allows initial deferral elections upon eligibility for many bonus programs and ad hoc equity-based compensation grants. The Treasury Department and the IRS request comments as to whether these rules adequately address the concerns raised with respect to the definition of plan for purposes of applying the initial eligibility exception.

E. Initial Deferral Election With Respect to Short-Term Deferrals

As discussed above, an amount that is paid by the 15th day of the third month following the end of the first taxable year in which the payment is no longer subject to a substantial risk of forfeiture generally will not constitute a deferral of compensation. Commentators asked how the deferral election rules apply to an election to defer such an amount. Generally, once the service provider has begun performing the services required to vest, no election to defer could be made that would meet the timing requirements for initial deferral elections. Commentators suggested that the rules governing subsequent changes to the time and form of payment could be applied to elections to defer these amounts. The regulations provide that for purposes of an election to defer amounts that would not otherwise be subject to section 409A due to the short-term deferral rule, the date the substantial risk of forfeiture lapses is treated as the original time of payment established by an initial deferral election, and the form in which the payment would be made absent a deferral election is treated as the original form of payment established by an initial deferral election. Accordingly, the service provider may elect to defer the payment beyond the time at which the payment originally was scheduled to be made, in accordance with the rules governing subsequent changes in the time and form of payment. In general, this means that the service provider must make the election at least 12 months before the right to the payment vests, and must defer the payment for a period of not less than 5 years from the date the right to the payment could vest. Thus, no payment could be made within 5 years of the date the right to the payment vests (including upon a separation from service), except for instances of a change in control of the corporation, death, disability or an unforeseeable emergency. This would also mean that if the right to the payment actually vests within 12 months of the election, and the election is given effect so that the payment is not made within the short-term deferral period, the deferral of the payment would violate the requirements of section 409A.

For example, an employee may be entitled to the immediate payment of a bonus upon the occurrence of an initial public offering, where such a condition qualifies as a substantial risk of forfeiture so that the arrangement would constitute a short-term deferral. At some point after obtaining the right to the payment but before the initial public offering, the employee elects to defer any potential bonus payment to a date 5 years from the date of the initial public offering. To comply with the initial deferral election rules, that deferral election must not be given effect for 12 months. Accordingly, if the initial public offering occurred within 12 months of the deferral election, the payment must be made at the time of the initial public offering in accordance with the short-term deferral rules. If the payment is not made at such time, but rather is made, for example, 5 years from the date of the initial public offering, the payment would be deemed deferred pursuant to an invalid initial deferral election effective before the required lapse of 12 months and the arrangement would violate section 409A.

F. Initial Deferral Election With Respect to Certain Forfeitable Rights

Commentators asked how the initial deferral election rules would apply with respect to grants of nonqualified deferred compensation that occur in the middle of a taxable year, especially where such grants were unforeseeable by the service provider. Under these circumstances, an initial deferral election could not be made by the service provider during the taxable year before the year in which the award was granted, unless the service recipient had the foresight to request such an election in the prior year. The Treasury Department and the IRS do not believe that a categorical exclusion from the initial deferral election rules is appropriate, because such a rule would encourage the characterization of all grants of nonqualified deferred compensation as occurring in the middle of the year and in large part render ineffective the initial deferral election rules set forth in section 409A. However, these regulations provide that where a grant of nonqualified deferred compensation is subject to a forfeiture condition requiring the continued performance of services for a period of at least 12 months, the initial deferral election may be made no later than 30 days after the date of grant, provided that the election is made at least 12 months in advance of the end of the service period. Under these circumstances, the election still must be made in all cases at least 12 months before the service provider has fully earned the amount of compensation, analogous to the general requirement that the election be made no later than the end of the year before the services are performed. The Treasury Department and the IRS believe that such a rule will provide a reasonable accommodation to service recipients granting certain ad hoc awards, such as restricted stock units, that often are subject to a requirement that the service provider continue to perform services for at least 12 months.

G. Initial Deferral Election With Respect to Fiscal Year Compensation

The legislative history to section 409A indicates that the Treasury Department and the IRS are to provide guidance coordinating the initial deferral election rules with respect to compensation paid by service recipients with fiscal years other than the calendar year. H.R. Conf. Rep. No. 108-755, at 732 (2004). These regulations provide such a rule, generally permitting an initial election to defer fiscal year compensation on or before the end of the fiscal year immediately preceding the first fiscal year in which any services are performed for which the compensation is paid. For these purposes, fiscal year compensation does not encompass all compensation paid by a fiscal year service recipient. Where the compensation is not specifically based upon the service recipient's fiscal year as the measurement period, the timing requirements applicable to an initial deferral election are unchanged. Accordingly, the rule applies to compensation based on service periods that are coextensive with one or more of the service recipient's consecutive fiscal years, where no amount of such compensation is payable during the service period. For example, a bonus based upon a service period of two consecutive fiscal years payable after the completion of the second fiscal year would be fiscal year compensation. In contrast, periodic salary payments or bonuses based on service periods other than the service recipient's fiscal year would not be fiscal year compensation, and the deferral of such amounts would be subject to the general rule.

H. Deferral Elections With Respect to Commissions

Commentators requested clarification with respect to the application of section 409A to commissions. These regulations address commissions earned by a service provider where a substantial portion of the services provided by the service provider consists of the direct sale of a product or service to a customer, each payment of compensation by the service recipient to the service provider consists of a portion of the purchase price for the product or service (for example, 10 percent of the purchase price), or an amount calculated solely by reference to the volume of sales (for example, $100 per item sold), and each compensation payment is contingent upon the service recipient receiving payment from an unrelated customer for the product or services. In that case, the service provider is treated as having performed the services to which the commission compensation relates during the service provider's taxable year in which the unrelated customer renders payment for such goods or services. Accordingly, under the general initial deferral election rule an individual service provider could make an initial deferral election with respect to such compensation through December 31 of the calendar year preceding the year in which the customer renders the payment from which the commission is derived.

VI. Time and Form of Payment

A. In General

The regulations incorporate the statutory requirement that payments be made at a fixed date or under a fixed schedule, or upon any of five events: a separation from service, death, disability, change in the ownership or effective control of a corporation (to the extent provided by the Secretary), or unforeseeable emergency. As requested by commentators, these regulations provide guidance on what it means for a payment to be made upon one of these events. Where the time of payment is based upon the occurrence of a specified event (such as one of the five events listed above or upon the lapse of a substantial risk of forfeiture as discussed below), the plan must designate an objectively determinable date or year following the event upon which the payment is to be made. For example, the plan may designate the payment date as 30 days following a separation from service, or the first calendar year following a service provider's death. The Treasury Department and the IRS recognize that it may not be administratively feasible to make a payment upon the exact date or year designated. Furthermore, the Treasury Department and the IRS recognize that certain minimal delays that do not meaningfully affect the timing of the inclusion of income should not result in a violation of the requirements of section 409A. Accordingly, a payment will be treated as made

47

upon the designated date if the payment is made by the later of the first date it is administratively feasible to make such payment on or after the designated date, or the end of the calendar year containing the designated date (or the end of the calendar year if only a year is designated). This relaxation of the timing rules for administrative necessity is not intended to provide a method for the service provider to further defer the payment. Accordingly, any inability to make the payment that is caused by an action or inaction of the service provider, or any person related to, or under the control of, the service provider, will not be treated as causing the making of the payment to be administratively infeasible.

Once an event upon which a payment is to be made has occurred, the designated date generally is treated as the fixed date on which, or the fixed schedule under which, the payment is to be made (but not for purposes of the application of section 409A(a)(2)(B) generally requiring a six month delay in any payment upon a separation from service to a key employee of a corporation whose stock is traded on an established securities market). Accordingly, the recipient may change the time and form of payment after the event has occurred, provided that the change would otherwise be timely and permissible under these regulations. For example, a plan provides for payment of a lump sum on the third anniversary following a separation from service. A service provider has a separation from service on July 1, 2010. The July 1, 2013, payment date is now treated as the fixed date upon which the payment is to be made. Accordingly, the service provider generally could elect to defer the time and form of payment provided that the election were made on or before June 30, 2012, and deferred the payment to at least July 1, 2018. For a discussion of the application of the subsequent deferral rules when only a calendar year of payment is specified, see section VI.B of this preamble.

B. Specified Time or Fixed Schedule of Payments

Generally a plan will be deemed to provide for a specified time or fixed schedule of payments where, at the time of the deferral, the specific date upon which the payment or payments will be made may be objectively determined. As requested by commentators, these regulations permit plans to specify simply the calendar year or years in which the payments are scheduled to be made, without specifying the particular date within such year on which the payment will be made. Although this provision would be consistent with the flexibility allowed with respect to meeting the specified time or fixed schedule of payments requirement, the provision must be coordinated with the subsequent deferral rules. Section 409A(a)(4)(C)(iii) requires that if a plan permits under a subsequent election a delay in a payment or a change in the form of payment with respect to a payment payable at a specified time or a fixed schedule, the plan must require that the election be made not less than 12 months prior to the date of the first scheduled payment. Application of such a provision requires a specific date for the first scheduled payment. For a plan that does not designate a specific date, but rather only the year in which the payment is to be made, the first scheduled payment is deemed to be scheduled to be paid as of January 1 of such year for this purpose.

Commentators asked whether a specified time or fixed schedule of payments could be determined based upon the date the service provider vests in the amount of deferred compensation, where the vesting is based upon the occurrence of an event. These regulations provide that a plan provides for payment at a specified time or fixed schedule of payments if the plan provides at the time of the deferral that the payment will be made at a date or dates that are objectively determinable based upon the date of the lapsing of a substantial risk of forfeiture, disregarding any acceleration of the vesting other than due to death or disability. So, for example, a plan that provides at the time the service provider obtains a legally binding right to the payment that the payment will be made in three installment payments, payable each December 31 following an initial public offering, where the condition that an initial public offering occur before the service provider is entitled to a payment constitutes a substantial risk of forfeiture, would satisfy the requirement that the plan provide for payments at a specified time or pursuant to a fixed schedule.

C. Separation From Service

Section 409A(a)(2)(A)(i) provides that a plan may permit a payment to be made upon a separation from service as determined by the Secretary (except a payment to a specified employee, in which case the payment must be made subject to a six-month delay, discussed more fully below). These regulations provide guidance as to the circumstances under which service providers, including employees and independent contractors, will be treated as separating from service for purposes of section 409A. These rules are intended solely as guidance with respect to section 409A(a)(2)(A)(i), and should not be relied upon with respect to any other Code provisions, such as provisions with respect to distributions under qualified plans and provisions related to the service recipients' employment tax and information reporting obligations.

1. Employees

These regulations provide that an employee experiences a separation from service if the employee dies, retires, or otherwise has a termination of employment with the employer. However, the employment relationship is treated as continuing intact while the individual is on military leave, sick leave, or other bona fide leave of absence (such as temporary employment by the Government) if the period of such leave does not exceed six months, or if longer, so long as the individual's right to reemployment with the service recipient is provided either by statute or by contract. If the period of leave exceeds six months and the individual's right to reemployment is not provided either by statute or by contract, the employment relationship is deemed to terminate on the first date immediately following such six-month period.

Whether the employee has experienced a termination of employment is determined based on the facts and circumstances. The Treasury Department and the IRS do not intend for this standard to allow for the extension of deferrals through the use of consulting agreements or other devices under which the service provider technically agrees to perform services as demanded, but for which there is no intent that the service provider perform any significant services. Accordingly, the regulations provide an anti-abuse rule stating that where an employee either actually or purportedly continues in the capacity as an employee, such as through the execution of an employment agreement under which the service provider agrees to be available to perform services if requested, but the facts and circumstances indicate that the employer and the service provider did not intend for the service provider to provide more than insignificant services for the employer, an employee will be treated as having a termination of employment and a separation from service. For these purposes, an employer and employee will be deemed to have intended for the employee to provide more than insignificant services if the employee provides services at an annual rate equal to at least 20 percent of the services rendered and the annual remuneration for such services is equal to at least 20 percent of the average remuneration earned during the immediately preceding three full calendar years of employment (or, if the employee was employed for less than three years, such lesser period).

In addition, the Treasury Department and the IRS do not intend for this standard to be circumvented to create a separation from service where the service provider continues to perform significant services for the service recipient. For these purposes, the regulations provide that where an employee continues to provide services to a previous employer in a capacity other than as an employee, a separation from service will be treated as not having occurred if the former employee provides services at an annual rate that is 50 percent or more of the services rendered, on average, during the final three full calendar years of employment (or, if less, such lesser period) and the annual remuneration for such services is 50 percent or more of the average annual remuneration earned during the immediately preceding three full calendar years of employment (or if less, such lesser period).

Commentators asked whether the previous positions of the Treasury Department and the IRS with respect to a separation from service for purposes of section 401(k), generally referred to as the same desk rule, would apply in these circumstances. Under that rule, in certain situations where the identity of the employee's employer changed, such as with respect to a sale of substantially all of the assets of the original employer to a new employer who hired the employee, the employee would not be treated as having a separation from service where the duties and responsibilities of the employee had not materially changed. These regulations do not incorporate this standard.

Commentators had requested the ability to elect whether to apply the same desk rule in the case of a corporate transaction, such as a sale of substantially all of the assets of the original employer. The Treasury Department and the IRS do not believe that such a rule would be consistent with the provisions of section 409A, which generally restrict such control over the time and form of payment.

2. Independent Contractors

The definition of a separation from service of an independent contractor in these proposed regulations generally is derived from the definition of severance from employment provided in Sec. 1.457-6(b)(2). Comments are requested with respect to any changes that may be necessary to address issues arising under section 409A.

3. Delay for Key Employees

Section 409A(a)(2)(B)(i) provides that payments upon a separation from service to a key employee of a corporation whose stock is publicly traded on an established securities market must be delayed at least six months following the separation from service. For these purposes, a key employee is defined in accordance with section 416(i), disregarding section 416(i)(5). Commentators asked for guidance on when a determination as to whether an individual is a key employee must be made. Section 416 relies upon plan year concepts, which generally are not relevant to the application of section 409A. In addition, the Treasury Department and the IRS wish to establish rules that minimize the administrative burden, while implementing the legislative intent. Accordingly, the regulations provide that the identification of key employees is based upon the 12-month period ending on an identification date chosen by the service recipient. Persons who meet the requirements of section 416(i)(1)(A)(i), (ii) or (iii) during that 12-month period are considered key employees for the 12-month period commencing on the first day of the 4th month following the end of the 12-month period. For example, if an employer chose December 31 as an identification date, any key employees identified during the calendar year ending December 31 would be treated as specified employees for the 12-month period commencing the following April 1. In this manner, service recipients generally may know in advance whether the person to whom a payment is scheduled to be made will be subject to the provision. In addition, service recipients may choose an identification date other than December 31, provided that the date must be used consistently and provided that any change in the identification date may not be effective for a period of at least 12 months.

Some commentators had requested that certain types of payments, generally life annuities or longer-term installment payments, be excepted from the six-month delay requirement. The statutory language does not contemplate such an exception. Where an executive is aware that the source of funds to pay for his nonqualified deferred compensation are at significant risk, the executive may separate from service to obtain initial annuity or installment payments while such funds exist. Commentators argue that annuity payments or long-term installment payments generally would be less significant in amount. However, the Treasury Department and the IRS are not inclined to establish arbitrary limits, where such amounts may actually be quite significant due to the overall amount of the entire benefit, the number of installment payments, or the age of the participant, especially where the statutory language does not contemplate the creation of such an exception. Rather, the Treasury Department and the IRS believe that the provisions with respect to separation pay should provide service recipients the ability to provide reasonably significant amounts of benefits to terminating executives, that may respond to many of the concerns underlying the request to relax the six-month delay requirement.

To meet the six-month delay requirement, a plan may provide that any payment pursuant to a separation of service due within the six-month period is delayed until the end of the six-month period, or that each scheduled payment that becomes payable pursuant to a separation from service is delayed six months, or a combination thereof. For example, a nonqualified deferred compensation plan of a corporation whose stock is publicly traded on an established securities market may provide that a participant is entitled to 60 monthly installment payments upon separation from service, payable commencing the first day of the first month following the date of separation from service. To comply with the requirement of a six-month delay for payments to key employees, the plan may provide that in the case of an affected participant, the aggregate amount of the first seven months of installments is paid at the beginning of the seventh month following the date of separation from service, or may provide that the commencement date of the 60 months of installment payments is the first day of the seventh month following the date of separation from service, or may provide for a combination of these provisions. A plan may be amended to specify or change the manner in which the delay will be implemented, provided that the amendment may not be effective for at least 12 months. Because the delay requirement applies only to certain public corporations, a corporation or other entity not covered by the requirement may have failed to include a provision in its plans at the time the corporation is contemplating becoming a public corporation. These regulations provide that where the stock of the service recipient is not publicly traded on an established securities market, a plan may be amended to specify or change the manner in which the delay will be implemented, effective immediately upon adoption of the amendment. A plan may provide a service provider an election as to the manner in which the six-month delay is to be implemented, provided that such election is subject to otherwise applicable deferral election rules.

D. Death or Disability

As provided in section 409A(a)(2)(A)(ii) and (iii), these regulations state that the death or disability of the service provider are permissible payment events. The regulations incorporate the definition of disability provided in section 409A(a)(2)(C). These regulations clarify that a plan that provides for a payment upon a disability need not provide for a payment upon all disabilities identified in section 409A(a)(2)(C), as long as any disability upon which a payment would be made is contained within the definition provided in section 409A(a)(2)(C). In addition, these regulations provide that a service recipient may rely upon a determination of the Social Security Administration with respect to the existence of a disability.

E. Change in Ownership or Effective Control of the Corporation

The provisions defining a change in ownership or effective control of a corporation remain substantially unchanged from Notice 2005-1, Q&As-11 through 14. These provisions are based largely upon the discussion in the legislative history, indicating that the guidance should provide a similar, but more restrictive, definition of a change in the ownership or effective control of a corporation as compared to the definition used for purposes of the golden parachute provisions of section 280G. H.R. Conf. Rep. No. 108-755, at 730 (2004). Accordingly, the provisions largely mirror the regulations under section 280G, though the percentage changes in ownership necessary to qualify as permissible payment events have increased. However, unlike the golden parachute provisions, a change in control event may occur that does not relate to the entire group of affiliated corporations. Rather, the relevant analysis for purposes of section 409A generally is whether the corporation for whom the service provider performed services at the time of the event, the corporation or corporations liable for the payment at the time of the event, or a corporate majority shareholder of one of these corporations, experienced a change in control event.

Commentators asked whether the provisions relating to the change in ownership or effective control of a corporation will be extended to non-corporate entities. Specifically, some commentators asked whether change in control provisions could be applied in the case of a partnership or other pass-through entity. Neither the statute nor the legislative history refers to a permissible distribution upon a change in ownership or effective control of any type of entity other than a corporation.

However, the Treasury Department and the IRS plan to issue regulations under section 409A(a)(3) that will allow an acceleration of payments upon a change in the ownership of a partnership or in the ownership of a substantial portion of the assets of the partnership. Until further guidance is issued, the section 409A rules regarding permissible distributions upon a change in the ownership of a corporation (as described in proposed Sec. 1.409A-3(g)(5)(iv)) or a change in the ownership of a substantial portion of the assets of a corporation (as described in proposed Sec. 1.409A-3(g)(5)(vi)) may be applied by analogy to changes in the ownership of a partnership and changes in the ownership of a substantial portion of the assets of a partnership. For purposes of this paragraph, any references in proposed Sec. 1.409A-3(g)(5) to corporations, shareholders, and stock shall be treated as referring also to partnerships, partners, and partnership interests, respectively, and any reference to "majority shareholder" as applied by analogy to the owner of a partnership shall be treated as referring to a partner that (a) owns more than 50 percent of the capital and profits interests of such partnership, and (b) alone or together with others is vested with the continuing exclusive authority to make the management decisions necessary to conduct the business for which the partnership was formed. The Treasury Department and the IRS request comments with respect to the application of a change in control provision to partnerships and other non-corporate entities, as well as suggestions with respect to the formulation of which types of events should qualify and would be analogous to the corporate events described in the regulations.

Commentators also raised questions regarding the application of section 409A to earn-out provisions where an acquirer contracts to make an immediate payment at the closing of the transaction with additional amounts payable at a later date, subject to the satisfaction of specified conditions. In such situations, the later payments could create delays in payments of compensation calculated by reference to the value of target corporation shares. These regulations address this situation by providing that compensation payable pursuant to the purchase by the service recipient of service recipient stock or a stock right held by a service provider, or payment of amounts of deferred compensation calculated by reference to the value of service recipient stock, may be treated as paid at a specified time or pursuant to a fixed schedule in conformity with the requirements of section 409A if paid on the same schedule and under the same terms and conditions as payments to shareholders generally pursuant to a change in the ownership of a corporation that qualifies as a change in control event or as payments to the service recipient pursuant to a change in the ownership of a substantial portion of a corporation's assets that qualifies as a change in control event, and any amounts paid pursuant to such a schedule and such terms and conditions will not be treated as violating the initial or subsequent deferral election rules, to the extent that such amounts are paid not later than five years after the change in control event.

F. Unforeseeable Emergency

The regulations contain provisions defining the types of circumstances that constitute an unforeseeable emergency, and the amounts that may be paid due to the unforeseeable emergency. Generally these provisions are derived directly from section 409A(a)(2)(B)(ii). Commentators requested that in the case of an unforeseeable emergency, a service provider be permitted to cancel future deferrals. This issue is discussed in this preamble at paragraph VII.D.

G. Multiple Payment Events

The regulations permit a plan to provide that payments may be made upon the earlier of, or the later of, two or more specified permissible payment events or times. In addition, the regulations provide that a different form of payment may be elected for each potential payment event. For example, a plan may provide that a service provider will receive an installment payment upon separation from service or, if earlier, a lump sum payment upon death. The application of the rules governing changes in time and form of payment and the anti-acceleration rules to amounts subject to multiple payment events, is discussed below.

H. Delay in Payment by the Service Recipient

Commentators noted that for certain compelling reasons, a service recipient may be unwilling or unable to make a payment of an amount due under a nonqualified deferred compensation plan. These regulations generally provide that in the case of payments the deduction for which would be limited or eliminated by the application of section 162(m), payments that would violate securities laws, or payments that would violate loan covenants or other contractual terms to which the service recipient is a party, where such a violation would result in material harm to the service recipient, the plan may provide that the payment will be delayed. In addition, plans may be amended to add such provisions, but such an amendment cannot be effective for a period of at least 12 months. However, if a plan is amended to remove such a provision with respect to amounts deferred previously, the amendment will constitute an acceleration of the payment. In the case of amounts for which the deduction would be limited or reduced by the application of section 162(m), these regulations require that the payment be deferred either to a date in the first year in which the service recipient reasonably anticipates that a payment of such amount would not result in a limitation of a deduction with respect to the payment of such amount under section 162(m) or the year in which the service provider separates from service. In the case of amounts that would violate loan covenants or similar contracts, or would result in a violation of Federal securities laws or other applicable laws, the arrangement must provide that the payment will be made in the first calendar year in which the service recipient reasonably anticipates that the payment would not violate the loan contractual terms, the violation would not result in material harm to the service recipient, or the payment would not result in a violation of Federal securities law or other applicable laws. These regulations also provide that the Commissioner may prescribe through guidance published in the Internal Revenue Bulletin other circumstances in which a plan may provide for the delay of a payment of a deferred amount. The Treasury Department and the IRS specifically request comments as to what other circumstances may be appropriate to include in such guidance.

I. Disputed Payments and Refusals To Pay

In addition to situations in which a plan may delay payment due to certain business circumstances, commentators expressed concern about the possibility that a service recipient will refuse to pay deferred compensation when the payment is due, and whether such refusal to pay would result in taxation of the service provider under section 409A. Generally these situations will arise where either the obligation to make the payment, or the amount of the payment, is subject to dispute. But this situation may also arise where the service recipient simply refuses to pay. In either situation, these proposed regulations generally provide that the payment will be deemed to be made upon the date scheduled under the terms of the arrangement, provided that the service provider is acting in good faith and makes reasonable, good faith efforts to collect the amount. Factors relevant in determining whether a service provider is acting in good faith and making reasonable, good faith efforts to collect the amount include both the amount of the payment, or portion of a payment, in dispute, as well as the size of the disputed portion in relation to the entire payment. Although a payment may be delayed under this provision without violating section 409A because the service recipient refuses to make the payment, the payment may not be made subject to a subsequent deferral election because the payment was delayed. Rather, the payment must be made by the later of the end of the calendar year in which, or the 15th day of the third month following the date that, the service recipient and the service provider enter into a legally binding settlement of such dispute, the service recipient concedes that the full amount is payable, or the service recipient is required to make such payment pursuant to a final and nonappealable judgment or other binding decision. This paragraph is not intended to serve as a means of deferring payments without application of section 409A, by feigning a dispute or surreptitiously requesting that the service recipient refuse to pay the amount at the due date. Where the service provider is not acting in good faith, for example creating a dispute with no or tenuous basis, or where the service provider is not making reasonable, good faith efforts to collect the amount, the failure to receive the payment at the date originally scheduled may result in a violation of the permissible payment requirements. Among the factors to be considered is the practice of the service recipient with respect to payments of nonqualified deferred compensation. In addition, these regulations provide that the service provider is treated as having requested that a payment not be made, rather than the service recipient having refused to make such payment, where the decision that the service recipient will not make the payment is made by the service provider, or any person or group of persons under the supervision of the service provider at the time the decision is made.

VII. Anti-Acceleration Provision

A. In General

Under section 409A(a)(3), a payment of deferred compensation may not be accelerated except as provided in regulations by the Secretary. Certain permissible payment accelerations were listed in Notice 2005-1, Q&A-15, including payments necessary to comply with a domestic relations order, payments necessary to comply with certain conflict of interest rules, payments intended to pay employment taxes, and certain de minimis payments related to the participant's termination of his or her interest in the plan. All the permissible payment accelerations contained in Notice 2005-1, Q&A-15, are included in these regulations.

B. Payments Upon Income Inclusion Under Section 409A

These regulations provide that a plan may permit the acceleration of the time or schedule of a payment to a service provider to pay the amount the service provider includes in income as a result of the plan failing to meet the requirements of section 409A. For this purpose, a service provider will be deemed to have included the amount in income if the amount is timely reported on a Form W-2 "Wage and Tax Statement" or Form 1099-MISC "Miscellaneous Income", as appropriate.

C. Plan Terminations

Some commentators requested that service recipients be allowed to retain the right to accelerate payments upon a termination of the arrangement, where the termination is at the discretion of the service recipient. A general ability of a service recipient to make such payments raises the potential for abuse, especially with respect to arrangements with individual service providers. Where a service provider retains sufficient influence to obtain a termination of the arrangement, the service recipient's discretion to terminate the plan in substance would mean that amounts deferred were available to the service provider upon demand. Such a condition would be inconsistent with the provisions of and legislative intent behind section 409A.

Some commentators requested that service recipients be permitted to terminate arrangements where the arrangements are broad-based, covering a significant number of service providers. Due to concerns about administrability and equity, the regulations do not adopt the suggestion.

Some commentators also suggested that service recipients be permitted to terminate arrangements due to bona fide business reasons. However, the Treasury Department and the IRS are not confident that such a standard could be applied on a consistent and coherent basis, leaving service recipients unable to plan with confidence and creating the potential for abuse. The Treasury Department and the IRS are considering further guidance establishing criteria or circumstances under which a plan could be terminated. For that purpose, these regulations provide authority to the Commissioner to establish such criteria or circumstances in generally applicable guidance published in the Internal Revenue Bulletin.

These proposed regulations provide three circumstances under which a plan may be terminated at the discretion of the service recipient in accordance with the terms of the plan. The first addresses a service recipient that wants to cease providing a certain category of nonqualified deferred compensation, such as account balance plans, entirely. A plan may be terminated provided that all arrangements of the same type (account balance plans, nonaccount balance plans, separation pay plans or other arrangements) are terminated with respect to all participants, no payments other than those otherwise payable under the terms of the plan absent a termination of the plan are made within 12 months of the termination of the arrangement, all payments are made within 24 months of the termination of the arrangement, and the service recipient does not adopt a new arrangement that would be aggregated with any terminated arrangement under the plan aggregation rules at any time for a period of five years following the date of termination of the arrangement.

The remaining two exceptions relate to events that are both objectively determinable to have occurred—and so may be determined consistently—and are of such independent significance that they are unlikely to be related to any attempt to accelerate payments under a nonqualified deferred compensation plan in a manner inconsistent with the intent of the statute. These regulations provide that during the 12 months following a change in control of a corporation, the service recipient may elect to terminate a plan and make payments to the participants. In addition, a plan may provide that the plan terminates upon a corporate dissolution taxed under section 331, or with the approval of a bankruptcy court pursuant to 11 U.S.C. Sec. 503(b)(1)(A), provided that the amounts deferred under the plan are included in the participants' gross incomes by the latest of (i) the calendar year in which the plan termination occurs, (ii) the calendar year in which the amount is no longer subject to a substantial risk of forfeiture, or (iii) the first calendar year in which the payment is administratively practicable.

D. Terminations of Deferral Elections Following an Unforeseeable Emergency or a Hardship Distribution

Commentators noted that although section 409A provides that a service provider may receive a payment upon an unforeseeable emergency, there is no provision explicitly permitting or requiring the service provider to halt all elective deferrals to receive such a payment. In addition, commentators noted that to receive a hardship distribution under a qualified plan with a qualified cash or deferred arrangement under section 401(k), a participant generally would be required pursuant to the regulations under section 401(k) to halt any elective deferrals of compensation into a nonqualified deferred compensation plan. In response, these regulations provide that a plan may provide that a deferral election terminates if a service provider obtains a payment upon an unforeseeable emergency. Similarly, these regulations provide that a plan may provide that a deferral election is terminated if required for a service provider to obtain a hardship distribution under a qualified plan with a qualified cash or deferred arrangement under section 401(k). In each case, the deferral election must be terminated, and not merely suspended. A deferral election under the arrangement made after a termination of a deferral election due to a hardship distribution or an unforeseeable emergency will be treated as an initial deferral election.

E. Distributions To Avoid a Nonallocation Year Under Section 409(p)

Commentators noted that in the case of an S corporation sponsoring an employee stock ownership plan, under certain conditions distributions from a nonqualified deferred compensation plan may be necessary to avoid a nonallocation year (within the meaning of section 409(p)(3)). These regulations provide rules under which such distributions may be made to avoid such a nonallocation year.

VIII. Subsequent Changes in the Time and Form of Payment

A. In General

Section 409A(a)(4)(C) and these regulations provide that, in the case of a plan that permits a service provider to make a subsequent election to delay a payment or to change the form of a payment (provided that any such payment is the subject of an initial deferral election), the following conditions must be met:

(1) The plan must require that such election not take effect until at least 12 months after the date on which the election is made,

(2) In the case of an election related to a payment other than a payment on account of death, disability or the occurrence of an unforeseeable emergency, the plan requires that the first payment with respect to which such election is made be deferred for a period of not less than 5 years from the date such payment would otherwise have been made (the 5-year rule), and

(3) The plan requires that any election related to a payment at a specified time or pursuant to a fixed schedule may not be made less than 12 months prior to the date of the first scheduled payment.

B. Definition of Payment

Commentators requested clarification whether the individual amounts paid in a defined stream of payments, such as installment payments, are treated as separate payments or as one payment. This affects the application of the rules governing subsequent deferral elections, particularly the 5-year rule.

These proposed regulations provide generally that each separately identified amount to which a service provider is entitled to payment under a plan on a determinable date is a separate payment. Accordingly, if an amount is separately identified as a payment, either because the right arises under a separate arrangement or because the arrangement identifies the amount as a separate payment, the amount will not be aggregated with other amounts for purposes of the rules relating to subsequent changes in the time and form of payment and the anti-acceleration rule. For example, an arrangement may provide that 50 percent of the benefit is paid as a lump sum at separation from service, and that the remainder of the benefit is paid as a lump sum at age 60, which would identify each amount as a separate payment. However, once a payment has been identified separately, the payment may only be aggregated with another payment if the aggregation would otherwise comply with the rules relating to subsequent changes in the time and form of payment and the anti-acceleration rule.

The Treasury Department and the IRS recognize that most taxpayers view the ability to elect installment payments as a choice of a single form of payment. Accordingly, the entitlement to a series of installment payments under a particular arrangement generally is treated as a single payment for purposes of the subsequent deferral rules. However, taxpayers could also view each individual payment in the series of payments as a separate payment. Accordingly, these regulations provide that an arrangement may specify that a series of installment payments is to be treated as a series of separate payments.

An installment payment must be treated consistently both with respect to the rules governing subsequent changes in the time and form of payment, and with respect to the anti-acceleration rules. For example, if a 5-year installment payment is treated as a single payment and is scheduled to commence on July 1, 2010, then consistent with the 5-year rule a service provider generally could change the time and form of the payment to a lump sum payment on July 1, 2015, provided the other conditions related to a change in the time and form of payment were met. In contrast, if a 5-year installment payment is designated as five separate payments scheduled for the years 2010 through 2014, then the service provider could not change the time and form of the payment to a lump sum payment to be made on July 1, 2015 because the separate payments scheduled for the years 2011 through 2014 would not have been deferred at least 5 years. Rather, the service provider generally could change the time and form of payment to a lump sum payment only if the payment were scheduled to occur no earlier than 2019 (5 years after the last of the originally scheduled payments).

One exception to this rule is a life annuity, the entitlement to which is treated as a single payment. The Treasury Department and the IRS believe that taxpayers generally view an entitlement to a life annuity as a single form of payment, rather than a series of separate payments. In addition, treating a life annuity as a series of payments would lead to difficulty in applying the rules governing subsequent changes in the time and form of payment, because the aggregate amount of the payments and the duration of the payments are unknown, as their continuation depends on the continued life of the service provider or other individual. For example, if a single life annuity were treated as a series of separate payments, an election to change a form of payment to a lump sum payment could be made only if the lump sum payment were deferred to a date no earlier than five years after the death of the participant.

C. Application to Multiple Payment Events

As discussed above, a plan may provide that a payment will be made upon the earlier of, or the later of, multiple specified permissible payment events. In addition, a plan may provide for a different form of payment depending upon the payment event. For example, a plan may provide that a service provider is entitled to an annuity at age 65 or, if earlier, a lump sum payment upon separation from service.

The question then arises as to how the provisions governing changes in the time and form of payment and the anti-acceleration provision apply where there are multiple potential payment events, and possibly multiple forms of payment as well. The regulations provide that these provisions are to apply to each payment event separately. In the example above, these provisions would apply separately to the entitlement to the installment payment at age 65, and the entitlement to the lump sum payment at separation from service. Accordingly, the service provider generally would be able to delay the annuity payment date subject to the rules governing changes in the time and form of payment, while retaining a separate right to receive a lump sum payment at separation from service if that occurred at an earlier date. In other words, the 5-year rule would apply to the annuity payment date (delaying payment from age 65 to at least age 70) but not to the unchanged lump sum payment available upon separation from service before age 70.

Similarly, a plan may provide that an intervening event that is a permissible payment event under section 409A may override an existing payment schedule already in payment status. For example, a plan could provide that a participant would receive six installment payments commencing at separation from service, but also provide that if the participant died after the payments commenced, all remaining benefits would be paid in a lump sum.

An additional question arises where a new payment event, or a fixed time or fixed schedule of payments, is added to the plan. Generally, the addition of the payment event or date will be subject to the rules governing changes in the time and form of payment and the anti-acceleration rules. Accordingly, no fixed time of payment could be added that did not defer the payment at least five years from the date the fixed time was added. In addition, no payment due to any other added permissible event could be made within five years of the addition of the event. For example, a service provider entitled to a payment only on January 1, 2050, could not make a subsequent deferral election to be paid on the later of January 1, 2050, or separation from service, but could make a subsequent deferral election to be paid at the later of separation from service or January 1, 2055.

IX. Application of Rules to Nonqualified Deferred Compensation Plans Linked to Qualified Plans

A. In General

Commentators raised many issues concerning the application of section 409A to nonqualified deferred compensation plans linked to qualified plans. These linked plans exist in a variety of formats, and are referred to under various labels such as excess plans, wrap plans, and supplemental employee retirement plans (SERPs). Typically the purpose of such plans is to replace the benefits that would have been provided under the qualified plan absent the application of certain limits contained in the Code (for example, section 415, section 401(a)(17) or section 402(g)). Often the amounts deferred under the nonqualified deferred compensation plan are established through an offset formula, where the amount deferred equals an amount determined under a formula, offset by any benefits credited under the qualified plan. Because of the close relationship between the qualified plan and the nonqualified deferred compensation plan, sponsor and participant actions under the qualified plan may affect the calculation or payment of the amounts deferred under the nonqualified deferred compensation plan. Commentators asked for guidance regarding the circumstances under which an action (or failure to act) under the qualified plan may be treated as violating section 409A, to the extent the action (or failure to act) also affects the amounts deferred under the nonqualified deferred compensation plan.

These proposed regulations generally adopt rules under which nonqualified deferred compensation plans linked to qualified plans may continue to operate, though certain changes may be required. The intent of these rules generally is to permit the qualified plan to be established, amended and operated under the rules governing qualified plans, without causing the linked nonqualified deferred compensation plan to violate the rules of section 409A. However, the relief provided under certain rules to accommodate the linked plan structure is not intended to relax the rules generally with respect to all of the amounts deferred under the nonqualified deferred compensation plan, simply because a limited portion of the amounts deferred may be affected by actions under the qualified plan. Accordingly, in certain circumstances the relief provided relates solely to amounts deferred under the nonqualified deferred compensation plan that do not exceed the applicable limit on the qualified plan benefit for the taxable year.

B. Actions That Do Not Constitute Deferral Elections or Accelerations

Where amounts deferred under a nonqualified deferred compensation plan are linked to the benefits under a qualified plan, certain participant actions taken with respect to the benefit accrued under the qualified plan may affect the amounts deferred under the nonqualified deferred compensation plan. Where the amounts deferred under the nonqualified deferred compensation plan increase, the issue is whether the action taken with respect to the benefit accrued under the qualified plan constitutes a deferral election. Where the amounts deferred under the nonqualified deferred compensation plan decrease, the issue is whether the action taken with respect to the benefit accrued under the qualified plan constitutes an impermissible acceleration of a payment under the nonqualified deferred compensation plan.

With respect to the benefits provided under the qualified plan, these regulations provide generally that neither the amendment of the qualified plan to increase or decrease such benefits under the qualified plan nor the cessation of future accruals under the qualified plan is treated as a deferral election or an acceleration of a payment under the nonqualified deferred compensation plan. Similarly, the addition, removal, increase or reduction of a subsidized benefit or ancillary benefit under the qualified plan, or a participant election with respect to a subsidized benefit or ancillary benefit under the qualified plan, will not constitute either a deferral election or an acceleration of a payment under the nonqualified deferred compensation, even where such action results in an increase or decrease in amounts deferred under the nonqualified deferred compensation plan.

Additional relief is provided with respect to nonqualified deferred compensation plans linked to defined contribution plans that include a 401(k) or similar cash or deferred arrangement. Specifically, the regulations provide that a service provider's action or inaction under a qualified plan that is subject to section 402(g), including an adjustment to a deferral election under such qualified plan, will not be treated as either a deferral election or an acceleration of a payment under the linked nonqualified deferred compensation plan, provided that for any given calendar year, the service provider's actions or inactions under the qualified plan do not result in an increase in the amounts deferred under all nonqualified deferred compensation plans in which the service provider participates in excess of the limit with respect to elective deferrals under section 402(g) in effect for the year in which such actions or inactions occur. The Treasury Department and the IRS intend for this provision to address common arrangements whereby the amounts deferred under the nonqualified deferred compensation plan are linked to amounts deferred under a 401(k) arrangement (often referred to as 401(k) wrap plans), but only to the extent the amount of affected deferrals under the nonqualified deferred compensation plan does not exceed the maximum amount that ever could have been electively deferred under the qualified plan.

Similar relief is provided with respect to plans involving matching contributions. The regulations provide that a service provider's action or inaction under a qualified plan with respect to elective deferrals or after-tax contributions by the service provider to the qualified plan that affects the amounts that are credited under a nonqualified deferred compensation arrangement as matching amounts or other amounts contingent on service provider elective deferrals or after-tax contributions will not be treated as either a deferral election or an acceleration of payment, provided that such matching or contingent amounts, as applicable, are either forfeited or never credited under the nonqualified deferred compensation arrangement in the absence of such service provider's elective deferral or after-tax contribution, and provided the service provider's actions or inactions under the qualified plan do not result in an increase or decrease in the amounts deferred under all nonqualified deferred compensation plans in which the service provider participates in excess of the limit with respect to elective deferrals under section 402(g) in effect for the year in which such actions or inactions occur. Although the section 402(g) limit applies to elective deferrals, rather than matching contributions, the Treasury Department and the IRS believe that matching contributions in excess of 100 percent of the elective deferrals of pre-tax contributions or after-tax contributions will be rare.

X. Statutory Effective Dates

A. Effective Dates—Earned and Vested Amounts

Consistent with Notice 2005-1, Q&A-16, these regulations provide that an amount is considered deferred before January 1, 2005, and thus is not subject to section 409A, if the service provider had a legally binding right to be paid the amount and the right to the amount was earned and vested as of December 31, 2004. For these purposes, a right to an amount is earned and vested only if the amount is not subject to either a substantial risk of forfeiture or a requirement to perform further services. Some commentators questioned the application of section 409A to contractual arrangements entered into before the enactment of the statute. However, the statutory effective date is tied to the date the amount is deferred and the legislative history states that for these purposes, "an amount is considered deferred before January 1, 2005, if the amount is earned and vested before such date." H.R. Conf. Rep. No. 108-755, at 737 (2004). Accordingly, these regulations are consistent with the legislative intent that deferred amounts that were not earned, or were not vested, as of December 31, 2004, are subject to the provisions of section 409A.

Clarification has been provided with respect to when a stock right or similar right to compensation will be treated as earned and vested. The issue arises because often a stock right terminates upon a separation from service. Taxpayers questioned whether this meant that the right had not been earned and vested, because future services would be required to retain the right. These regulations clarify that a stock right or similar right will be treated as earned and vested by December 31, 2004, if on or before such date the right was either immediately exercisable for a payment of cash or substantially vested property, or was not forfeitable. Accordingly, stock options that on or before December 31, 2004, were immediately exercisable for substantially vested stock generally would not be subject to section 409A. In contrast, a nonstatutory stock option that was immediately exercisable on or before December 31, 2004, but only for substantially nonvested stock, generally would be subject to section 409A.

B. Effective Dates—Calculation of Grandfathered Amount

For account balance plans and plans that are neither account balance plans nor nonaccount balance plans (generally equity-based compensation), these regulations generally retain the method of calculating the grandfathered amount set forth in Notice 2005-1, Q&A 16. Accordingly, for account balance plans the grandfathered amount generally will equal the vested account balance as of December 31, 2004, plus any earnings with respect to such amounts. For equity-based compensation, the grandfathered amount generally will equal the payment that would be available if the right were exercised on December 31, 2004, and any earnings with respect to such amount. For this purpose, the earnings generally would include the increase in the payment available due to appreciation in the underlying stock.

Commentators argued that the definition of the grandfathered amount contained in Notice 2005-1, Q&A 16 with respect to nonaccount balance plans was not sufficiently flexible to account for subsequent increases in benefits unrelated to any further performance of services or increases in compensation after December 31, 2004. For example, a participant's benefit may increase if the participant becomes eligible for a subsidized benefit at a specified age that the participant reaches after December 31, 2004. In response, these proposed regulations provide that for nonaccount balance plans, the grandfathered amount specifically equals the present value as of December 31, 2004, of the amount to which the service provider would be entitled under the plan if the service provider voluntarily terminated services without cause on December 31, 2004, and received a payment of the benefits with the maximum value available from the plan on the earliest possible date allowed under the plan to receive a payment of benefits following the termination of services. Notwithstanding the foregoing, for any subsequent calendar year, the grandfathered amount may increase to equal the present value of the benefit the service provider actually becomes entitled to, determined under the terms of the plan (including applicable limits under the Code), as in effect on October 3, 2004, without regard to any further services rendered by the service provider after December 31, 2004, or any other events affecting the amount of, or the entitlement to, benefits (other than the participant's survival or a participant election under the terms of the plan with respect to the time or form of an available benefit).

Because separation pay plans with respect to involuntary terminations and window programs are now treated as separate plans, these regulations provide a rule for calculating the grandfathered amount under such plans. For these purposes, the principles used to calculate the grandfathered amounts under a nonaccount balance plan and an account balance plan are to be applied by analogy, depending upon the structure of the separation pay plan.

C. Material Modifications

Commentators have pointed out that a grandfathered plan may become subject to section 409A upon any material modification, even if such modification occurs many years after 2004. Given the substantial amounts of compensation that are deferred under grandfathered plans, as well as the potential for these amounts to grow through accumulated grandfathered earnings, the consequences of such a modification could be significant. Commentators expressed concern that as long as these plans exist, there will be the potential for a change to the plan to mistakenly cause the plan to become subject to section 409A. In response, these regulations include a provision stating that to the extent a modification is rescinded before the earlier of the date any additional right granted under the modification is exercised or the end of the calendar year in which the modification was made, the modification will not be treated as a material modification of the plan. For example, if a subsequent deferral feature is added that would allow participants to extend the time and form of payment of a grandfathered deferred amount, and if the right is removed before the earlier of the time the participant exercises the right or the end of the calendar year, then the modification will not be treated as a material modification of the plan. However, this provision is not intended to cover material modifications that are made with the knowledge that the modification will subject the amounts to section 409A, but are then rescinded.

Consistent with Notice 2005-1, Q&A-18(a), these regulations also provide that it is not a material modification to change a notional investment measure to, or to add, an investment measure that qualifies as a predetermined actual investment within the meaning of Sec. 31.3121(v)(2)-1(d)(2) of this chapter. Commentators requested similar flexibility with respect to investment measures reflecting reasonable rates of interest. These regulations provide such flexibility, generally adopting a modified version of the rules contained in Sec. 31.3121(v)(2)-1(d)(2) of this chapter. Under these regulations, it is not a material modification to change a notional investment measure to, or to add, an investment measure that qualifies as a predetermined actual investment within the meaning of Sec. 31.3121(v)(2)-1(d)(2) of this chapter or, for any given taxable year, reflects a reasonable rate of interest. For this purpose, if with respect to an amount deferred for a period, a plan provides for a fixed rate of interest to be credited, and the rate is to be reset under the plan at a specified future date that is not later than the end of the fifth calendar year that begins after the beginning of the period, the rate is reasonable at the beginning of the period, and the rate is not changed before the reset date, then the rate will be treated as reasonable in all future periods before the reset date. These proposed regulations also contain other clarifications of the application of the material modification rule.

XI. Transition Relief

A. In General

Until the effective date of these regulations, Notice 2005-1 generally remains in effect. Notice 2005-1, Q&As-18 through 23 provided transition relief that was limited to the 2005 calendar year. Commentators generally reacted favorably to the scope of the transition rules. The Treasury Department and the IRS intended for the transition rules to be generous during the calendar year 2005, both to enable taxpayers to familiarize themselves with the new provisions, and also to provide a period during which the Treasury Department and the IRS could develop regulations and taxpayers generally could be confident that either their plans were not in violation of section 409A, or could be corrected to avoid additional tax under the statute.

Because final regulations are not yet in place, the IRS and the Treasury Department are hereby extending through 2006 certain aspects of the transition relief provided for 2005 by Notice 2005-1. In addition, in response to questions, certain provisions of Notice 2005-1 are clarified below. However, because taxpayers will have had, by the end of 2005, over a year to implement the statute, certain other transition relief is not being extended through 2006.

B. Amendment and Operation of Plans Adopted on or Before December 31, 2006

Pursuant to Notice 2005-1, Q&A-19, a plan adopted on or before December 31, 2005, will not be treated as violating section 409A(a)(2), (3) or (4) only if the plan is operated in good faith compliance with the provisions of section 409A and Notice 2005-1 during the calendar year 2005, and the plan is amended on or before December 31, 2005, to conform to the provisions of section 409A with respect to amounts subject to section 409A. To allow time to finalize these regulations, and for practitioners to implement the final regulations, the deadline by which plan documents must be amended to comply with the provisions of section 409A and the regulations is hereby extended to December 31, 2006. Accordingly, in order to be treated as complying with section 409A(a)(2), (3) or (4), a plan adopted before December 31, 2006, must be amended on or before December 31, 2006, either to conform to the provisions of section 409A with respect to amounts subject to section 409A, or to provide a compensation arrangement that does not provide for a deferral of compensation for purposes of section 409A.

The good faith compliance period provided under Q&A-19 of Notice 2005-1 is also hereby extended through December 31, 2006. Accordingly, a plan adopted on or before December 31, 2006, will be treated as complying with section 409A(a)(2), (3) or (4) only if the plan is operated through December 31, 2006, in good faith compliance with the provisions of section 409A and Notice 2005-1. If any other guidance of general applicability under section 409A is published in the Internal Revenue Bulletin with an effective date prior to January 1, 2007, the plan must also comply with such published guidance as of its effective date. To the extent an issue is not addressed in Notice 2005-1 or such other published guidance, the plan must follow a good faith, reasonable interpretation of section 409A, and, to the extent not inconsistent therewith, the plan's terms.

These regulations are not proposed to become effective prior to January 1, 2007, and, accordingly, a plan is not required to comply with either these proposed regulations or the final regulations prior to January 1, 2007. However, compliance with either these proposed regulations or the final regulations will be good faith compliance with the statute. In general, these proposed regulations expand upon, and should be read consistently with, the provisions of Notice 2005-1. However, to the extent that a provision of either these proposed regulations or the final regulations is inconsistent with a provision of Notice 2005-1, the plan may comply with the provision of the proposed or final regulations in lieu of the corresponding provision of Notice 2005-1.

A plan will not be operating in good faith compliance if the plan sponsor exercises discretion under the terms of the plan, or a service provider exercises discretion with respect to that service provider's benefits, in a manner that causes the plan to fail to meet the requirements of section 409A. For example, if an employer retains the discretion under the terms of the plan to delay or extend payments under the plan and exercises such discretion, the plan will not be considered to be operated in good faith compliance with section 409A with regard to any plan participant. However, an exercise of a right under the terms of the plan by a service provider solely with respect to that service provider's benefits under the plan, in a manner that causes the plan to fail to meet the requirements of section 409A, will not be considered to result in the plan failing to be operated in good faith compliance with respect to other participants. For example, the request for and receipt of an immediate payment permitted under the terms of the plan if the participant forfeits 20 percent of the participant's benefits (a haircut) will be considered a failure of the plan to meet the requirements of section 409A with respect to that service provider, but not with respect to all other service providers under the plan.

C. Change in Payment Elections or Conditions on or Before December 31, 2006

Notice 2005-1, Q&A-19(c) provided generally that with respect to amounts subject to section 409A, a plan could be amended to provide for new payment elections without violating the subsequent deferral and anti-acceleration rules, provided that the plan was amended and the participant made the election on or before December 31, 2005. The period during which a plan may be amended and a service provider may be permitted to change payment elections, without resulting in an impermissible subsequent deferral or acceleration, is hereby extended through December 31, 2006, except that a service provider cannot in 2006 change payment elections with respect to payments that the service provider would otherwise receive in 2006, or to cause payments to be made in 2006. Other provisions of the Internal Revenue Code and common law doctrines continue to apply to any such election.

Accordingly, with respect to amounts subject to section 409A and amounts that would be treated as a short-term deferral within the meaning of Sec. 1.409A-1(b)(4), a plan may provide, or be amended to provide, for new payment elections on or before December 31, 2006, with respect to both the time and form of payment of such amounts and the election will not be treated as a change in the form and timing of a payment under section 409A(a)(4) or an acceleration of a payment under section 409A(a)(3), provided that the plan is so amended and the service provider makes any applicable election on or before December 31, 2006, and provided that the amendment and election applies only to amounts that would not otherwise be payable in 2006 and does not cause an amount to be paid in 2006 that would not otherwise be payable in such year. Similarly, an outstanding stock right that provides for a deferral of compensation subject to section 409A may be amended to provide for fixed payment terms consistent with section 409A, or to permit holders of such rights to elect fixed payment terms consistent with section 409A, and such amendment or election will not be treated as a change in the time and form of a payment under section 409A(a)(4) or an acceleration of a payment under section 409A(a)(3), provided that the option or right is so amended and any elections are made, on or before December 31, 2006.

D. Payments Based Upon an Election Under a Qualified Plan for Periods Ending on or Before December 31, 2006

For calendar year 2005, Notice 2005-1 Q&A-23 provides relief for nonqualified deferred compensation plans where the time and form of payment is controlled by the time and form of payment elected by the service provider under a qualified plan. Commentators indicated that this is a common arrangement with respect to nonqualified deferred compensation plans providing benefits calculated in relation to benefits accrued under a defined benefit qualified plan. Generally, the provisions with respect to the election of a time and form of a payment with respect to a qualified plan benefit would not comply with the requirements of section 409A were the plan subject to section 409A. Accordingly, election provisions under a nonqualified plan that mirrored or depended upon an election under a qualified plan generally would not comply with section 409A. The Treasury Department and the IRS were concerned that service providers, service recipients and plan administrators would not have sufficient time to solicit, retain and process new elections from service providers to comply with section 409A in 2005. Accordingly, relief was provided in Notice 2005-1, Q&A-23, under which an election under a nonqualified deferred compensation plan that was controlled by an election under a qualified plan could continue in effect during the calendar year 2005.

Commentators requested that this relief be a permanent provision in the regulations. Although the Treasury Department and the IRS understand that such a provision would make the coordination of benefits under a qualified plan and benefits under a nonqualified deferred compensation plan calculated by reference to the qualified plan benefits easier to administer, the provisions of section 409A are not as flexible with respect to the timing of such elections as the qualified plan provisions. Given that the benefits under a nonqualified deferred compensation plan often dwarf the benefits provided under a qualified plan, the Treasury Department and the IRS do not believe that the importation of the more flexible qualified plan rules would be consistent with the legislative intent behind the enactment of section 409A. Accordingly, the transition relief has not been made permanent. However, because other transition relief granting a participant the ability to change a time and form of payment through the end of the calendar year 2006 would, in many instances, allow a participant to elect the same time and form of payment that had been elected under the qualified plan, the relief is hereby extended through the calendar year 2006.

Accordingly, for periods ending on or before December 31, 2006, an election as to the timing and form of a payment under a nonqualified deferred compensation plan that is controlled by a payment election made by the service provider or beneficiary of the service provider under a qualified plan will not violate section 409A, provided that the determination of the timing and form of the payment is made in accordance with the terms of the nonqualified deferred compensation plan as of October 3, 2004, that govern payments. For this purpose, a qualified plan means a retirement plan qualified under section 401(a). For example, where a nonqualified deferred compensation plan provides as of October 3, 2004, that the time and form of payment to a service provider or beneficiary will be the same time and form of payment elected by the service provider or beneficiary under a related qualified plan, it will not be a violation of section 409A for the plan administrator to make or commence payments under the nonqualified deferred compensation plan on or after January 1, 2005, and on or before December 31, 2006, pursuant to the payment election under the related qualified plan. Notwithstanding the foregoing, other provisions of the Internal Revenue Code and common law tax doctrines continue to apply to any election as to the timing and form of a payment under a nonqualified deferred compensation plan.

E. Initial Deferral Elections

Notice 2005-1, Q&A-21 provides relief with respect to initial deferral elections, generally permitting initial deferral elections with respect to deferrals relating all or in part to services performed on or before December 31, 2005, to be made on or before March 15, 2005. No extension is provided with respect to this relief with respect to initial elections to defer compensation. The Treasury Department and the IRS believe that sufficient guidance has been provided so that timely elections may be solicited and received from plan participants. In combination with the extension of flexibility with respect to amending the time and form of payments, the Treasury Department and the IRS believe that participants should be sufficiently informed to make a decision with respect to deferral elections.

F. Cancellation of Deferrals and Termination of Participation in a Plan

Notice 2005-1, Q&A-20 provides a limited time during which a plan adopted before December 31, 2005, may provide a participant a right to terminate participation in the plan, or cancel an outstanding deferral election with regard to amounts subject to section 409A. Generally to qualify for this relief, if a plan amendment is necessary to permit the participant to terminate participation or cancel a deferral election, the plan amendment must be enacted and effective on or before December 31, 2005, and whether or not the plan is amended, the amount subject to the termination or cancellation must be includible in income of the participant in the calendar year 2005 or, if later, in the taxable year in which the amounts are earned and vested.

The period during which a service provider may cancel a deferral election or terminate participation in the plan is not extended. This relief was intended as a temporary period during which service providers could decide whether to continue to participate in an arrangement subject to section 409A. The Treasury Department and the IRS believe that the statute and existing guidance provide sufficient information for service providers to determine by December 31, 2005, whether to continue to participate in a particular arrangement, and that the further extension of this relief, and the relaxation of constructive receipt rules it entails, is not appropriate.

A termination or cancellation pursuant to Notice 2005-1, Q&A-20 is treated as effective as of January 1, 2005, for purposes of section

409A, and may apply in whole or in part to one or more plans in which a service provider participates and to one or more outstanding deferral elections the service provider has made with regard to amounts subject to section 409A. The exercise of a stock option, stock appreciation right or similar equity appreciation right that provides for a deferral of compensation, on or before December 31, 2005, will be treated as a cancellation of a deferral.

G. Terminations of Grandfathered Plans

Notice 2005-1, Q&A-18(c) provides that amending an arrangement on or before December 31, 2005, to terminate the arrangement and distribute the amounts of deferred compensation thereunder will not be treated as a material modification, provided that all amounts deferred under the plan are included in income in the taxable year in which the termination occurs. For the same reasons discussed above with respect to the period during which plans may allow participants to terminate participation in a plan, the relief provided in Notice 2005-1, Q&A-18(c) is not extended.

To qualify for the relief provided in Notice 2005-1, Q&A-18(c), the amendment to the plan must result in the termination of the arrangement and the distribution of all amounts deferred under the arrangement in the taxable year of such termination. An amendment to a plan to provide a participant a right to elect whether to terminate participation in the plan or to continue to defer amounts under the plan would not be covered by Q&A-18(c), and therefore would constitute a material modification of the plan. Accordingly, amounts that were not distributed pursuant to such an election and continued to be deferred under the plan would be subject to section 409A.

H. Substitutions of Non-discounted Stock Options and Stock Appreciation Rights for Discounted Stock Options and Stock Appreciation Rights

Notice 2005-1, Q&A-18(d) provides that it will not be a material modification to replace a stock option or stock appreciation right otherwise providing for a deferral of compensation under section 409A with a stock option or stock appreciation right that would not have constituted a deferral of compensation under section 409A if it had been granted upon the original date of grant of the replaced stock option or stock appreciation right, provided that the cancellation and reissuance occurs on or before December 31, 2005. The period during which the cancellation and reissuance may occur is extended until December 31, 2006, but only to the extent such cancellation and reissuance does not result in the cancellation of a deferral in exchange for cash or vested property in

2006. For example, a discounted option generally may be replaced through December 31, 2006 with an option that would not have provided for a deferral of compensation, although the exercise of such a discounted option in 2006 before the cancellation and replacement generally would result in a violation of section 409A.

Commentators pointed out that this relief could be interpreted as failing to cover discounted stock options or stock appreciation rights that were not earned and vested before January 1, 2005. Where replacement stock options or stock appreciation rights that would not constitute deferred compensation subject to section 409A are issued in accordance with the conditions set forth in Notice 2005-1, Q&A 18(d) and this preamble, such replacement stock options or stock appreciation rights will be treated for purposes of section 409A as if granted on the grant date of the original stock option or stock appreciation right. For example, provided that the conditions of Notice 2005-1, Q&A-18(d) and this preamble are met, a discounted stock option granted in 2003 that was not earned and vested before January 1, 2005, may be replaced with a stock option with an exercise price that would not have been discounted as of the original 2003 grant date, and the substituted stock option will be treated for purposes of section 409A as granted on the original 2003 grant date. Accordingly, if the substituted stock option would not have been subject to section 409A had it been granted on the original 2003 grant date, the substituted stock option will not be subject to section 409A.

Commentators noted that some service recipients may wish to compensate the service provider for the lost discount. Commentators proposed three methods to provide such compensation. First, the service recipient may wish to pay the amount of the discount in 2005 in cash. As a cancellation of a deferral of compensation on or before December 31, 2005 pursuant to Notice 2005-1, Q&A-20(a), this payment would not be subject to section 409A. Note that as a payment due to the cancellation of a deferral, such a payment could not be made in 2006 as this relief has not been extended beyond December 31, 2005. Where the stock option remains nonvested during the year of the option substitution, the service recipient may wish to make the compensation for the lost discount also subject to a vesting requirement. In that case, commentators also proposed granting restricted stock with a fair market value equal to the lost discount, subject to a vesting schedule parallel to the vesting schedule of the substituted option. As a transfer of property subject to section 83 that becomes substantially vested after the year of substitution, this grant would not be subject to section 409A. Finally, commentators proposed establishing a separate plan, promising a payment of the lost discount (plus earnings) subject to a vesting schedule parallel to the vesting schedule of the substituted option. Provided the right to the payment becomes substantially vested in a future year and otherwise meets the requirement of the short-term deferral exception in these regulations, the right to this payment would not constitute deferred compensation subject to section 409A. Alternatively, such an arrangement could itself provide for deferral of compensation beyond the year of substantial vesting and be subject to the requirements of section 409A, but if such requirements are met, would not affect the exclusion of the amended stock option or stock appreciation right from the treatment as a deferral of compensation subject to section 409A.

XII. Calculation and Timing of Income Inclusion Amounts

To more rapidly issue guidance necessary to allow service recipients to comply with section 409A, the Treasury Department and the IRS have not included in these regulations guidance with respect to the calculation of the amounts of deferrals, or of the amounts of income inclusion upon the violation of the provisions of section 409A and these regulations, or the timing of the inclusion of income and related withholding obligations. The Treasury Department and the IRS anticipate that these topics will be addressed in subsequent guidance. The Treasury Department and the IRS request comments with respect to the calculation and timing of the income inclusion under section 409A, and specifically request comments in two areas.

First, section 409A generally requires that for any taxable year in which an amount is deferred under a plan that fails to meet certain requirements, all amounts deferred must be included in income. This provision generally treats earnings (whether actual or notional) as amounts deferred subject to the inclusion provision. Service providers may experience negative earnings in a calendar year, such that the amounts to which a service provider has a right in a particular year are less than the amounts to which a service provider had a right in a previous year, even where no actual payments have been made. The Treasury Department and the IRS request comments with respect to whether and how such negative earnings may be accounted for in determining the amount of deferrals and the amount of income inclusion for a given taxable year, particularly where continuing violations of section 409A extend to successive tax years.

Second, the Treasury Department and the IRS understand that a method of calculation of current deferrals and of amounts to be included in income is needed for service recipients to meet their reporting and withholding obligations. Comments are requested as to what transitional relief may be appropriate depending upon when such future guidance is released. For interim guidance regarding the information reporting and wage withholding requirements applicable to deferrals of compensation within the meaning of section 409A, see

Notice 2005-1, Q&A-24 through Q&A-38. Until further guidance is provided, taxpayers may rely on Notice 2005-1 regarding information reporting and wage withholding obligations.

XIII. Funding Arrangements

Section 409A(b)(1) provides certain tax consequences for the funding of deferrals of compensation in offshore trusts (or other arrangements determined by the Secretary) or pursuant to a change in the financial health of the employer. The consequences of such funding are generally consistent with a violation of section 409A with respect to funded amounts. The Treasury Department and the IRS intend to address these provisions in future guidance. Commentators have requested guidance with respect to when assets will be treated as set aside, especially with respect to service recipients that are, or include, foreign corporations. Comments are requested as to what types of arrangements, other than actual trusts, should be treated similarly to trusts. In addition, these proposed regulations provide guidance with respect to the types of arrangements that constitute deferred compensation subject to section 409A. Because the funding rules of section 409A(b) apply only to amounts set aside to fund deferred compensation subject to section 409A, many issues raised by commentators with respect to foreign arrangements and funding may be addressed or limited through the definition of deferred compensation contained in these proposed regulations.

Proposed Effective Date

These regulations are proposed to be generally applicable for taxable years beginning on or after January 1, 2007. As discussed, taxpayers may rely on these proposed regulations until the effective date of the final regulations.

Effect on Other Documents

These proposed regulations do not affect the applicability of other guidance issued with respect to section 409A, including Notice 2005-1 (2005-2 I.R.B. 274 (published as modified on January 6, 2005)). However, upon the effective date of the final regulations, the Treasury Department and the IRS anticipate that Notice 2005-1 and certain other published guidance will become obsolete for periods after the effective date of the final regulations.

Special Analyses

It has been determined that this notice of proposed rulemaking is not a significant regulatory action as defined in Executive Order 12866.

Therefore, a regulatory assessment is not required. It has also been determined that section 553(b) of the Administrative Procedure Act (5 U.S.C. chapter 5) does not apply to these regulations, and because the regulation does not impose a collection of information on small entities, the Regulatory Flexibility Act (5 U.S.C. chapter 6) does not apply. Pursuant to section 7805(f) of the Code, this notice of proposed rule-making will be submitted to the Chief Counsel for Advocacy of the Small Business Administration for comment on its impact on small business.

Comments and Public Hearing

Before these proposed regulations are adopted as final regulations, consideration will be given to any written (a signed original and eight (8) copies) or electronic comments that are submitted timely to the IRS. The IRS and Treasury Department request comments on the clarity of the proposed rules and how they can be made easier to understand. All comments will be available for public inspection and copying.

A public hearing has been scheduled for January 25, 2006, beginning at 10 a.m. in the Auditorium of the Internal Revenue Building, 1111 Constitution Avenue, NW., Washington, DC. Due to building security procedures, visitors must enter at the Constitution Avenue entrance. In addition, all visitors must present photo identification to enter the building. Because of access restrictions, visitors will not be admitted beyond the immediate entrance area more than 30 minutes before the hearing starts. For information about having your name placed on the building access list to attend the hearing, see the FOR FURTHER INFORMATION CONTACT section of this preamble.

The rules of 26 CFR 601.601(a)(3) apply to the hearing. Persons who wish to present oral comments at the hearing must submit written or electronic comments and an outline of the topics to be discussed and the time to be devoted to each topic (a signed original and eight (8) copies) by January 4, 2006. A period of 10 minutes will be allotted to each person for making comments. An agenda showing the scheduling of the speakers will be prepared after the deadline for receiving outlines has passed. Copies of the agenda will be available free of charge at the hearing.

Drafting Information

The principal author of these regulations is Stephen Tackney of the Office of Division Counsel/Associate Chief Counsel (Tax Exempt and Government Entities). However, other personnel from the IRS and the Treasury Department participated in their development.

Preface

The field of taxation of employee and executive compensation is complex, dynamic, and ever-changing. Since 1980, there have been changes to the law affecting fringe benefits, qualified plans, and other types of compensation almost every year. The American Jobs Creation Act of 2004 (AJCA) (P.L. 108-357) made the most significant change to the taxation of nonqualified deferred compensation plans in over fifty years. The Medicare Prescription Drug Improvement and Modernization Act of 2003 (P.L. 108-173) enacted Health Savings Accounts, heralded as one of the most significant developments in the area of health care plans in many years. In addition, the Jobs Growth and Tax Relief Reconciliation Act of 2003 (JGTRRA) (P.L. 108-27) and the Economic Growth and Tax Relief Reconciliation Act of 2001 (EGTRRA) (P.L. 107-16) contain significant changes that affect the taxation of qualified retirement plans and other forms of executive and employee compensation.

The years 2003 through 2005 have been no exception to that trend of change. As mentioned above, the AJCA made significant changes to the taxation of nonqualified deferred compensation plans through the enactment of new Code Sec. 409A. These changes, which are generally applicable for compensation deferred after 2004, include requirements that must be met in order for employees to defer the taxation of nonqualified plan benefits and onerous tax consequences if those requirements are not met. While the provisions of new Code Sec. 409A directly affect many of the nonqualified plans covered in chapters 14 and 15, those provisions have an impact on compensation planning overall and, thus, affect other types of compensation discussed throughout the book. Other provisions of the AJCA impact other forms of compensation including rules concerning the amount that can be deducted by employers as a result of providing air transportation to executives and other employees. The Medicare Prescription Drug Improvement and Modernization Act of 2003 enacted the new Health Savings Account (HSA) provisions which became effective in 2004. The new rules permit employers to make tax-free contributions on behalf of employees who participate in high-deductible health plans and meet other specified requirements to HSAs, from which the employees can later make tax-free withdrawals to pay for eligible medical expenses. The Working Families Tax Relief Act of 2004 (P.L. 108-311) (1) changed the definition of the term "qualified dependent" which has an impact on many fringe benefit plans and other types of employee compensation and (2) extended the Archer MSA provisions by allowing taxpayers to establish new MSA accounts through the end of 2005. The Military Family Tax Relief Act of 2003 (P.L. 108-121) made a number of changes affecting the compensation of individuals in the military including the enactment of a new fringe benefit related to military base closures and realignments. The Pension Funding Equity Act of 2004 (P.L. 108-218) includes special relief provisions for underfunded pension plans for the 2004 and 2005 plan years increasing the interest rate used in computing pension liabilities, as well as other special relief for certain plans of employers in the airline and steel industries. JGTRRA made a number of changes including (1) the reduction in the top rate applicable to the receipt of qualified dividends by individuals in 2003 and later years to 15 percent (5 percent for individuals with marginal rates of 15 percent and lower), that has made it less desirable to pay current compensation as opposed to dividends to shareholder-employees of closely-held C corporations, (2) the reduction in the top rate applicable to the long-term capital gains received by individuals for sales and exchanges of stock and other capital assets after May 5, 2003, which will likely enhance the desirability of equity forms of deferred compensation, and (3) the acceleration in the reduction of individual marginal income tax rates from the schedule mandated by EGTRRA to the year 2003, which could affect planning for nonqualified deferred compensation and other forms of compensation.

From 2003 through 2005, there were also numerous and significant changes and additions to IRS regulations and administrative rulings concerning compensation taxation. For example, during this period, the following were issued: (1) final regulations pertaining to cash or deferred arrangements under Code Secs. 401(k) and 401(m); (2) proposed regulations pertaining to Roth Code Sec. 401(k) plans; (3) proposed regulations concerning the Code Sec. 415 limits and benefits and contributions for qualified plans (the first changes to such regulations in over 20 years); (4) final regulations pertaining to split-dollar life insurance plans under Code Secs. 61 and 7872; (5) final regulations governing group health plan portability, access and renewability under Code Secs. 9801, 9803, and 9831; (6) proposed regulations governing Code Sec. 403(b) tax-sheltered annuity plans (the first changes to such regulations in

over 40 years); and (7) IRS rulings, notices and other pronouncements concerning such issues as the first guidance relating to the
new Code Sec. 409A nonqualified deferred compensation rules
under Notice 2005-1, the new 2½ month grace period rules for
Health Flexible Savings Arrangements under Notice 2005-42, and
other issues such as the blended annual rate under low-interest
compensation-related loans and updated provisions concerning
employee expense reimbursement arrangements.

The continuing legislative, administrative, and judicial activity
in the compensation taxation field has increased the breadth and
complexity of the field, as well as the need for awareness of the legal
aspects and practical considerations. Likewise, the need for current
and comprehensive guidance with respect to compensation tax rules
has increased.

Accordingly, this book provides up-to-date coverage of the
federal tax laws concerning executive and employee compensation.
The American Jobs Creation Act of 2004 and other recent tax laws
plus pertinent regulations, administrative rulings, and case law
through the end of August 2005 are incorporated throughout. In
addition, this book fills a void left by other works on executive and
employee compensation (i.e., such works primarily cover qualified
plans and deferred compensation) by covering all the common forms
of compensation that are provided to executives and other
employees, including salary, bonuses, and other current compensation; employee fringe benefits (e.g., health and accident plans and
cafeteria plans); qualified deferred compensation (e.g., pension
plans and profit-sharing plans); and nonqualified deferred compensation (e.g., rabbi trusts and restricted stock plans).

This book is written in a guidebook style emphasizing the
fundamental tax consequences and related practical considerations
of the most common forms of executive and employee compensation.
Thus, the book is particularly useful to CPAs, attorneys, corporate
tax managers, qualified plan administrators, CFPs, CLUs, and
others needing a basic, working understanding of federal compensation tax rules in their practice and work. Yet, the coverage of
topics is sufficiently comprehensive that the book may be used as a
primary text or reference book for graduate-level compensation or
employee benefits tax classes and similar courses in law schools and
other continuing professional education programs.

Dennis R. Lassila
Bob G. Kilpatrick

August 2005

About the Authors

Dennis R. Lassila, Ph.D., CPA, is the Shelton Taxation Professor in the Professional Program of the Department of Accounting at Texas A&M University, College Station, Texas. There he teaches classes in executive compensation and estate and gift taxation; income taxation of trusts, estates, and partnerships; and introduction to the taxation of businesses, investments, and individuals. Dr. Lassila's extensive publications focusing on these and other tax areas have appeared in many nationally recognized accounting and taxation journals. He also coauthored (with Dr. Bob G. Kilpatrick) *Employment Taxes and Benefits,* a continuing professional education course book of the American Institute of Certified Public Accountants.

Bob G. Kilpatrick, Ph.D., CPA, is a Professor of Taxation and Accounting and Accounting Area Coordinator at Northern Arizona University in Flagstaff. He has held previous teaching positions at Texas A&M University (Graduate Tax Program), Oklahoma State University, and the University of Southern Mississippi. Dr. Kilpatrick has written numerous articles on compensation and tax issues for a large number of national journals, including several publications coauthored with Dr. Dennis R. Lassila.

Acknowledgments

The authors wish to thank students in the Compensation Tax and Estate Planning classes taught at Texas A&M University since the 1994 publication of The CCH Compensation Tax Guide and its successor, The CCH U.S. Master Compensation Tax Guide for helpful comments and suggestions that aided in the preparation of this book. Also, special thanks go to the University for its assistance in the preparation of draft chapters of the book.

Table of Contents

Detailed Table of Contents

Chapter 3:   Employee Fringe Benefits, in General

Chapter 6:   Requirements for Qualified Plans

Chapter 8: Employer Deduction and Funding Rules

Chapter 1

Overview

¶ 101   General Types of Compensation

The total compensation package for an executive or other employee generally consists of a mixture of current compensation (in the form of current salary and bonuses), fringe benefits, and deferred compensation. While current compensation still constitutes the largest element of most employees' compensation packages, other forms of compensation have become increasingly popular. For example, several recent studies have found that employee benefits account for approximately 40 percent of total payroll costs.

Generally speaking, most forms of compensation currently paid to or provided to or on behalf of employees can be classified into the following four basic compensation types:

(1) *Current Compensation*—compensation directly paid to the employee in the current year in cash or property and which is currently includible in the employee's gross income, is subject to payroll taxes, and is currently deductible by the employer (if reasonable in amount).

(2) *Employee Fringe Benefits*—supplemental compensation that is provided to or on behalf of employees on a current basis in forms such as life insurance coverage and health and accident insurance

coverage and which is typically partially or totally excludable from income to the employee, is not subject to payroll taxes, and is currently deductible (at cost) by the employer.

(3) *Qualified Deferred Compensation*—compensation plans under which the employer (and, in some cases, the employee) make contributions such that the employee and/or his spouse or beneficiaries will receive benefits in the future, typically at or after retirement, death, or separation from service. Under qualified deferred compensation plans: (a) the employer contributions are currently deductible but are not taxable to the employee; (b) the net earnings on the contributions to the plan are not subject to tax; (c) the benefits are only taxable when actually received; and (d) neither the employer contributions nor benefits paid are subject to payroll taxes. Special qualification requirements must be satisfied.

(4) *Nonqualified Deferred Compensation*—compensation which is deferred from the current year and which is payable in cash or property in some future year and which is typically includible in income by the employee, deductible by the employer, and subject to payroll taxes in the year actually paid. The special qualification requirements for qualified plans do not have to be satisfied.

Business organizations must continually assess their compensation and benefit packages to ensure that the most beneficial (from both the employee's and employer's perspective) compensation packages are provided to their employees. The need on the part of management and their outside advisors for a comprehensive, up-to-date, practical guide to the federal income tax treatment of the various forms of compensation was the stimulus for this book. The chapters that follow will review the common forms of compensation, the tax consequences of each type (from both the employer and employee perspective), and the special rules that pertain to each form. First, however, the four basic compensation classifications are summarized below.

¶ 102   Current Compensation

Current compensation is compensation which is generally paid in the current year to the employee in cash or in the form of property. Current compensation is usually fully taxable as ordinary income to the recipient, is currently deductible by the employer, and is subject to payroll taxes (Social Security (or FICA) taxes and Federal Unemployment Taxes (FUTA)).

Common Forms of Current Compensation. The typical types of current compensation provided to employees that are covered in this book include the following:

(1) wages and salaries;

(2) bonuses;

(3) vacation pay;

(4) commissions;

(5) tips and gratuities;

(6) drawing accounts;

(7) gifts;

(8) prizes and awards;

(9) reimbursement of employee expenses;

(10) employer payment of employee payroll taxes;

(11) standby pay;

(12) back pay and employment discrimination awards;

(13) dismissal and severance pay;

(14) unemployment and supplemental unemployment benefits;

(15) strike benefits;

(16) compensation paid in property and services; and

(17) bargain sales of employer property to employees.

The tax consequences of each of these forms of current compensation are covered in Chapter 2.

Reasonable Compensation Issue. Under Code Sec.162(a)(1), compensation paid to employees is not deductible unless it is reasonable in amount. Thus, the reasonableness of compensation is an important issue in determining the employer's deductibility of current compensation and other forms of compensation.

Typically, the question of whether compensation paid is reasonable in amount arises in the case of small, closely held corporations where the shareholders are also employees and executives of the corporation. Since compensation paid is deductible by the corporation but dividends paid to shareholders are not deductible, there has been a natural tendency for such corporations to pay more compensation and less dividends to shareholder-employees. It is too early to tell how much impact the reduction in the top tax rate applicable to qualified dividends received in 2003 and later years to 15 percent (5 percent for taxpayers with marginal tax rates of 15 percent or less) will have on this issue. However, it would seem that there would be less incentive to maximize compensation payments and minimize dividend payments to shareholder-employees of C corporations (particularly closely-held C corporations) in some cases. In general, whether compensation paid is reasonable in amount is determined by considering all of the facts and circumstances of each case. However, in general, a number of factors have been set forth by the courts for use in determining whether compensation paid is reasonable in amount. The factors include the background and qualifications of the employee, the nature and extent of the employee's duties, the amount of sales and net income of the employer in current and past years, and others.

$1 Million Deduction Limitation. In publicly traded corporations, a different limitation must be taken into account in structuring compensation packages for top executives. Under Code Sec. 162(m), the deduction for compensation paid to the CEO and the next four highest paid top executives is limited to $1 million each. The million dollar limitation is subject to certain exceptions including compensation paid in the form of commissions and certain incentive-based compensation as well as certain stock option compensation. In addition, the $1 million dollar limit can be partially circumvented and/or avoided through the provision of non-qualified deferred compensation (which is subject to the limit when it is includible in the recipient's gross income). Employer contributions to qualified deferred compensation plans and employer-provided fringe benefits which are excludable from the executive's gross income are not counted in determining the amount of compensation subject to the $1 million limitation.

¶ 103 Employee Fringe Benefits

Employee fringe benefits are supplemental compensation provided to or on the behalf of employees and/or their dependents on a current basis. It is typically provided in forms other than direct cash payments, such as meals and lodging for the convenience of the employer and life and health and accident insurance coverage for employees and family members. Employee fringe benefits are generally partially or totally excludable by the employee, are not subject to FICA and FUTA taxes, and are deductible (at cost) by the employer in the current year. Further, fringe benefits provided by the employer are beneficial to employees because employees can receive a much greater benefit per dollar of cost if the employer furnishes the fringe benefit than if the employees paid for the benefit on their own. However, many fringe benefits must be provided on a nondiscriminatory basis (that is, the benefits must be provided to rank-and-file employees as well as to the executives and shareholder-employees). This increases the cost of furnishing the benefits.

Common Forms of Employee Fringe Benefits. The following are employee fringe benefits that are commonly provided to employees and are covered in this book:

(1) group term life insurance coverage;

(2) split-dollar life insurance;

(3) employee death benefits;

(4) medical, accident, and disability benefits (including Archer MSAs and long-term care plans);

(5) health and accident insurance coverage;

(6) health savings accounts;

(7) meals and lodging furnished to employees for the convenience of the employer;

(8) group educational assistance plans;

(9) group dependent care programs;

(10) qualified adoption assistance plans;

(11) no-additional-cost services;

(12) qualified employee discounts;

(13) working condition fringe benefits;

(14) de minimis fringe benefits;

(15) qualified transportation fringes;

(16) qualified moving expense reimbursements;

(17) qualified retirement planning services;

(18) qualified military base realignment and closure fringes;

(19) qualified tuition reductions;

(20) interest-free and below-market-rate interest loans;

(21) employee use of company cars and airplanes; and

(22) golden parachute payments.

In addition, some fringe benefits such as group life insurance coverage and health and accident benefits can be made available to employees through cafeteria plans that allow employees to choose between receiving cash or certain specified fringe benefits. An employer may also provide certain fringe benefits through a voluntary employee benefit association. Fringe benefits, in general, are covered in Chapter 3. Cafeteria plans and voluntary employee benefit associations are covered in Chapter 4.

¶ 104 Qualified Deferred Compensation

One purpose of qualified deferred compensation plans is to provide tax-deferred income to an employee that is payable upon his retirement, at which time the employee's effective tax rate may be lower. Thus, the employee would receive a higher after-tax income than if he saved for retirement from current taxable compensation that is taxed at unfavorable rates. The tax law encourages such plans by providing tax benefits in the form of (1) a current deduction to the employer for contributions to the plan; (2) the tax-free accumulation of earnings on trust assets maintained under the plan; and (3) the deferral of income recognition by the employee until the actual payment of the benefits. However, in order to receive these benefits, qualified deferred compensation plans (i.e., pension, profit-sharing, stock bonus, and annuity plans) must meet the requirements under Code Sec. 401(a). In general, these provisions relate to minimum levels of employee coverage by the plan, vesting requirements, and nondiscrimination requirements.

Common Forms of Qualified Deferred Compensation. The following types of qualified plans are covered in this book:

(1) pension plans;

(2) profit-sharing plans;

(3) age-weighted profit-sharing plans;

(4) new comparability plans;

(5) stock bonus plans;

(6) money purchase pension plans;

(7) cash balance plans;

(8) target benefit pension plans;

(9) tax-sheltered annuity plans (403(b) plans);

(10) Keogh plans;

(11) cash or deferred arrangements (CODAs) or 401(k) plans;

(12) employee stock ownership plans (ESOPs);

(13) simplified employee pension plans (SEPs);

(14) savings incentive match plans for employees (SIMPLE);

(15) traditional individual retirement accounts (IRAs);

(16) Roth IRAs; and

(17) Deemed IRAs.

The requirements with respect to qualifying one of the above plans are quite extensive and complicated. Chapter 5 provides an introduction to qualified plans and describes the general characteristics of each plan. Chapter 6 describes the numerous requirements that a plan must meet in order to attain qualified status. Chapter 7 covers the qualification requirements for special types of qualified plans. Chapters 8 and 9 discuss the employer deductions for contributions and employee taxation upon distribution, respectively. Chapter 10 reviews the special rules regarding IRAs, simplified employee pension plans, and savings incentive match plans for employees (SEPs and SIMPLE plans). Chapter 11 presents an overview of the tax aspects of ESOPs. Chapter 12 discusses the duties and responsibilities imposed on the plan fiduciaries. Finally, Chapter 13 describes the basic reporting requirements for qualified plans.

¶105 Nonqualified Deferred Compensation

Nonqualified deferred compensation plans consist of plans that have failed to meet the Code Sec. 401(a) requirements, either by design or by accident. Nonqualified plans do not enjoy the tax advantages regarding deductions, earnings, and income recognition that qualified plans enjoy. For example, the employee is taxed when the right to the benefit becomes nonforfeitable (i.e., when the employee vests in the benefit). Thus, an employee may have to currently recognize income, despite the fact that the benefit is not payable until his retirement. In addition, the employer's deduction is allowed in the same year in which the employee recognizes income, as opposed to the year in which the contribution was made. Finally, if the plan is funded by employer contributions, the earnings are taxable to the trust. However, nonqualified plans have the significant advantage of flexibility. That is, nonqualified plans do not have to meet any minimum participation requirements or vesting standards. In addition, a nonqualified plan can discriminate with respect to contributions in favor of highly compensated employees.

Finally, the provisions of new Code Sec. 409A, which was enacted as part of the American Jobs Creation Act of 2004, will affect a large portion of nonqualified deferred compensation plans generally with respect to amounts deferred under such plans on or after January 1, 2005. Unless the requirements of the new section are met for amounts deferred under plans subject to the section, all amounts deferred under the plan after December 31, 2004 will be includible in gross income and will be subject to interest and a 20 percent additional tax.

Common Forms of Nonqualified Deferred Compensation. Nonqualified deferred compensation plans can take on a number of different forms. Some of the more common forms that are discussed in this book are:

(1) unfunded, unsecured plans;

(2) funded, unsecured plans (e.g., rabbi trusts, reserve funds);

(3) funded, secured plans (e.g., secular trusts);

(4) restricted property and stock plans;

(5) nonqualified stock options;

(6) incentive stock options;

(7) stock appreciation rights;

(8) performance share arrangements; and

(9) Code Sec. 457 deferred compensation plans.

Chapters 14 and 15 cover these nonqualified deferred compensation plans. In Chapter 14, the provisions of new Code Sec. 409A and general tax doctrines, such as the doctrine of constructive receipt and the economic benefit doctrine, are discussed because that section and such doctrines affect the income tax consequences of a large portion of nonqualified plans. In addition, Chapter 14 discusses the tax provisions Regarding property exchanged for services under Code Sec. 83. Chapter 15 provides a description of the most common forms of equity-oriented deferred compensation arrangements, along with the tax consequences of each and a review of typical financing techniques and the impact of new Code Sec. 409A on certain of those equity arrangements.

¶ 106   Coverage of the American Jobs Creation Act of 2004, the Jobs Growth and Tax Relief Reconciliation Act of 2003, the Economic Growth and Tax Relief Reconciliation Act of 2001, and Other Recent Tax Laws

The American Jobs Creation Act of 2004 (AJCA), which was signed into law on October 22, 2004, the Jobs Growth and Tax Relief Reconciliation Act of 2003 (JGTRRA), which was signed into law on May 28, 2003, and the Economic Growth and Tax Relief Reconciliation Act of 2001 (EGTRRA), which was signed into law on June 7, 2001, have a profound effect on the taxation of executive and employee compensation, and the applicable provisions of these Acts and other recently enacted tax laws such as the Job Creation and Worker Assistance Act of 2002 and the Working Families Tax Relief Act of 2004 are fully reflected in this book.

One interesting feature that is a prominent characteristic of both EGTRRA and JGTRRA are the sunset provisions contained in those Acts. Section 901 of EGTRRA provides that all provisions of and amendments made by EGTRRA will not apply to taxable, plan, or limitation years beginning after December 31, 2010. Thus, if the sunset provision were to stay in effect, the tax law (including qualified plan and elective deferral limits and other provisions affecting executive and employee compensation) would revert to the law in effect in 2001, as if EGTRRA did not exist. JGTRRA, as well, contains sunset provisions. For example, the JGTRRA provisions that (1) lower the top tax rate on qualified dividends received beginning in 2003 to 15 percent (5 percent for taxpayers with a marginal tax rate of 15 percent or less) and (2) lower the top tax rate on long-term capital gain income to 15 percent (5 percent for taxpayers with a marginal tax rate of 15 percent or less) for sales and exchanges of capital assets after May 5, 2003 both will not apply to taxable years beginning after December 31, 2008. Further, the provisions of JGTRRA that modify some of the changes instituted by EGTRRA, such as the acceleration of the reduction in individual marginal tax rates (JGTRRA moved up to 2003, the tax rate reductions that were slated to take effect in 2006 under EGTRRA), are subject to EGTRRA's Section 901 sunset provision described above. Congress will eventually need to pass legislation to eliminate or modify these sunset provisions before their scheduled expiration to eliminate or postpone this possibility. The potential impacts of the EGTRRA and JGTRRA sunset provisions are not covered in this text since what Congress will do in the next several years concerning the issue is a matter of speculation, and the IRS has not yet issued much definitive guidance on the issue. In its one reference to the provision so far, the IRS in Revenue Ruling 2001-51 has indicated that the sunset provisions of EGTRRA should not be taken into account for purposes of applying Code Secs. 412 and 404(j) (covered in Chapter 8) for years beginning on or before December 31, 2010. The IRS does not say what should be done after that. Does that mean that the sunset provision should be ignored for a while? That is difficult to say. Certainly for current compensation and fringe benefit planning, the sunset provisions of EGTRRA and JGTRRA should generally not be a concern for the next few years. But, for qualified and nonqualified deferred compensation, by 2007, the sunset provisions, if they are still in effect, will need to be taken into account in some fashion.

It should be noted that the provision of JGTRRA which, beginning in 2003, reduces the top tax rate on qualified dividends paid to individual taxpayers to 15 percent (5 percent for individuals with a marginal rate of 15 percent or less) could have a profound effect on compensation planning overall. As noted in the introduction to the topic of reasonable compensation earlier in this chapter, it can be expected that the special treatment of dividends will remove some of the incentive to pay compensation as opposed to dividends to shareholder-employees of corporations (especially closely-held C corporations and S corporations). Prior to the enactment of JGTRRA, in many cases there was a double taxation on dividend payments made by C corporations because dividends were taxed at regular tax rates to the recipient and are not deductible by the paying corporation, whereas, while taxable current compensation payments are also taxable at regular rates, compensation is deductible by the paying corporation. The reduction in the top tax rate on dividends substantially mitigates the double taxation disadvantage associated with dividend payments. Further, dividend payments are not subject to payroll taxes whereas most current compensation payments are. These factors can combine to make compensation payments less desirable relative to the payment of dividends, particularly when there is a possibility that the IRS may challenge the deductibility of some or all of the compensation payments. Certainly dividend payments won't replace all compensation paid to shareholder-employees in most cases for a variety of reasons including that certain fringe benefits and all retirement benefits depend on the provision of current compensation to the recipients. However, compensation planners need to take the new dividend taxation rules into account when designing executive compensation packages, particularly in the case of small, closely-held C and S corporations.

Finally, it should be noted that Code Sec. 409A, which was enacted as part of AJCA, is the most important development in the taxation of nonqualified deferred compensation in over 50 years. The provisions of this new section are primarily covered in Chapter 14. Provisions of the section which affect equity-oriented nonqualified deferred compensation are covered in Chapter 15. A large portion of existing nonqualified deferred compensation arrangements will have to be reviewed and, in many instances, altered or replaced to comply with the provisions of Code Sec. 409A which generally apply to amounts deferred after 2004 under plans subject to the new section. The consequences of failure to comply with the section are simply too great to ignore. If the provisions of the section are not met, all amounts deferred under the subject plans for employees or other service providers with respect to whom the section's requirements are violated, and all amounts deferred (generally after 2004) under the nonqualified plan covering them will be includible in gross income and subject to interest and a 20 percent additional tax. That is a consequence to be avoided if possible. Other parts of AJCA which affect compensation planning and compliance are also covered where applicable.

Chapter 2

Current Compensation

¶ 201 Introduction

Current compensation is the wages, salaries, bonuses, and other forms of remuneration that are paid or are directly provided to employees in the year in which they perform services for the employer. It is typically the largest segment of the total compensation package provided to rank-and-file employees and executives alike. Current compensation is the largest segment because most employees rely on it to satisfy their current consumption expenditure requirements. This chapter covers the more important types of current compensation that are paid to executives and other employees, when compensation must be reported by the employee, the rules governing the employer's deduction for current compensation, including the important issue of reasonableness of compensation, and when compensation is deductible.

¶ 202 Types of Current Compensation

Code Sec. 61(a)(1) specifies that compensation, in general, is includible in the gross income of the recipient. Taxable wages for income tax withholding purposes includes "all remuneration for services performed by an employee for his employer including the cash value of benefits paid in any medium other than cash."[1] Therefore, wages, salaries, bonuses, certain fringe benefits, commissions on sales or on insurance premiums, and preretirement leave benefits are taxable and

---

[1] Reg. § 31.3401(a)-1.

subject to payroll taxes. The more common forms of current compensation are covered in more detail in the following paragraphs.

.01 Wages and Salaries

In general, the term "wages" is defined as current compensation paid to employees on the basis of a certain rate per hour, such as $7 per hour. It is typically paid to rank-and-file employees. Salaries represent amounts paid over a period of time, sometimes regardless of the actual amount of time spent by the employee (up to a limit, of course). Salaries are typically paid to executives and professional and managerial employees. However, whether compensation is called wages or salary, it is subject to tax and income tax withholding as well as to FICA and FUTA taxes.

.02 Overtime Pay

In some cases, employees who work more than the normal hours during a particular day or other pay period will receive remuneration at a higher than normal rate, such as one and one-half times the normal rate. Overtime pay is treated the same as any other wages and salaries; that is, it is taxable when received.

.03 Bonuses

Bonuses are payments made to employees in addition to their regular salary as a reward for services performed. They are generally based on such factors as profitability, productivity, length of service, and others. For example, an executive may be given a Christmas bonus for outstanding performance during the year. Whatever the case, bonuses, as additional compensation, are includible in gross income of the employee.[2] They are also subject to income tax withholding and FICA and FUTA taxes. The IRS has recently publicly held that bonuses paid for signing an employment contract are subject to income tax withholding and FICA and FUTA taxes.[3] This ruling has particular impact on signing bonuses paid to baseball players and individuals employed in other sports. The ruling will be applied to any signing bonus, signing fee, or similar amount paid to an employee with respect to contracts entered into after January 12, 2005. In addition, bonus payments made to employees as a result of the ratification of a collective bargaining agreement between a union and the employer are subject to withholding, FICA taxes and FUTA taxes.[4]

---

[2] Reg. § 1.61-2(a)(1).
[3] Rev. Rul. 2004-109, 2004-50 IRB 958.   [4] *Id.*

.04 Vacation Pay

Employers frequently provide some of their employees with vacation time and, in some cases, pay them some compensation for that time. Such vacation pay directly received by the employee is taxable like other salaries and wages, whether the employee takes the vacation or works during the vacation period.

Vacation allowances that are paid to an employee from a vacation fund are taxable to the employee as compensation to the extent that they are based on services rendered.[5] Vacation allowances that are funded by a trust pursuant to a collective bargaining agreement, under which the employee vacation benefits are fixed and determinable from the time the employer makes contributions to the trust, are taxable to the employees when the contributions are made.[6]

.05 Commissions Received

Certain employees, such as salespersons, are paid commissions in lieu of, or in addition to, regular salaries and wages. Commissions are compensation based on the number or dollar value of units sold or serviced. As such, commissions paid are taxable as ordinary income under Code Sec. 61(a). Commissions received by real estate agents as a result of the sale of real estate are taxable even if they relate to real estate purchased by the agent. For example, in *K.W. Daehler,*[7] the Fifth Circuit Court of Appeals held that a real estate commission received by an agent as a result of the purchase of property (listed by another broker) for his own account was taxable compensation because the commission payment was made by his employer for services identical to services that would have been rendered if someone else had bought the property.

Similarly, commissions that a stockbroker earns on the purchase and sale of securities for his/her own account and for trading stock options for his/her own account are considered to be taxable compensation.[8]

.06 Tips and Gratuities

Tips, gratuities, and other rewards received by employees from customers for special services are taxable to the employees.[9] However, a waiter/waitress may deduct the portion of tips turned over to his/her assistants.[10] For example, a waitress is permitted to reduce

---

[5] Rev. Rul. 57-316, 1957-2 CB 626.
[6] Rev. Rul. 67-351, 1967-2 CB 86. *See also* IRS Letter Ruling 9110064, 12-13-90, CCH IRS Letter Rulings Reports.
[7] CA-5, 60-2 USTC ¶ 9565, 281 F2d 823, rev'g, 31 TC 722, Dec. 23,401 (1959).

[8] *L.J. Kobernat,* 31 TCM 593, Dec. 31,429(M), TC Memo. 1972-132; *E. Kelly,* 72 TCM 1389, Dec. 51,673(M), TC Memo. 1996-529.
[9] Reg. § 1.61-2(a)(1).
[10] *N.D. Cesanelli,* 8 TC 776, Dec. 15,705 (1947).

the amount of her reported tip income by amounts that are passed on to other employees, such as busboys, bartenders, cooks, and other waitresses.[11] Tips include amounts received directly from customers and amounts paid to the employee by the employer on behalf of the customers.

Employers must withhold both income tax and FICA taxes and pay FICA taxes on cash tips of $20 or more if the employee makes a written report of the tips to the employer.[12] In addition, such tips are subject to FUTA taxes.[13] Although noncash tips are includible in gross income, they are not subject to payroll taxes. The Supreme Court has held that the IRS may estimate the amount of tips earned in a restaurant for FICA tax purposes where the actual amount of tips reported by employees is less than tip amounts shown on other sources of tip information such as customers' credit card receipts.[14]

An employee must report cash tips to his/her employer if the tips equal or exceed $20 in a calendar month from work for a single employer. Tips received from one job do not have to be aggregated with tips from another job for reporting purposes.[15] For example, if Wilson earned tips of $16 in June from the Blake Cafe and $13 during the same month from the Alice Cafe, the tips would not have to be reported. However, Wilson would be subject to income tax on those tips.

In the case of large food and beverage establishments (that is, ones with more than ten employees), a portion of the gross receipts of the establishment may have to be allocated to tipped employees.[16] This rule does not apply to fast-food restaurants where tipping is not customary.

Food and beverage establishments are permitted to take a tax credit for FICA taxes paid with respect to tips reported that are in excess of the amount treated as wages for purposes of satisfying the minimum wage provisions of the Fair Labor Standards Act.[17] The credit is available for taxes paid after 1993, regardless of when the services for which the tips were received were performed. In addition, the credit is available whether or not the employer reported the tips on which the employer FICA taxes were paid pursuant to Code Sec. 6053(a).[18] After 1996, the credit also applies to tips received from customers relating to the delivery or serving of food or

---

[11] *K.A. Brown,* 72 TCM 59. Dec. 51,437(M), TC Memo. 1996-310.

[12] Code Secs. 3102(c) and 3402(k).

[13] Code Sec. 3306.

[14] *Fior D'Italia, Inc.,* SCt, 2002-1 USTC ¶ 50,459, 536 US 238, 122 SCt 2117, rev'g, CA-9, 2001-1 USTC ¶ 50,261, 242 F3d 844.

[15] IRS Pub. 505, at 13.

[16] See Code Sec. 6053.

[17] Code Sec. 45B.

[18] Code Sec. 45B(b)(1)(A), as amended by P.L. 104-188, Sec. 1112(a)(1) (Aug. 20, 1996).

beverages, whether or not the food or beverages will be consumed on the premises of the food and beverage establishment.[19]

.07 Drawing Accounts—Advances and Employee Loans

Advances against future commissions or other compensation are taxable when received if the employment agreement indicates that the advances are compensation for services to be performed in the future. However, advances that are actually loans (i.e., the advances must be repaid to the employer and are not compensation for future services) are not taxable. For example, advances provided to sales-persons against future salary and commissions for which the employees must perform services, but which the employees are not legally bound to repay, are taxable to them when received and are subject to withholding and FICA and FUTA taxes.[20] In addition, an advance commission paid to an insurance salesperson was held to be taxable and subject to employment taxes where there was no obligation to repay the advance in the event of a policy lapse.[21] However, if the employee signs a written acknowledgment of indebtedness and the advance is treated in the employer's accounting records as an "account due," it is an excludable loan.[22] For example, advances received by a corporate president and controlling stockholder over several years were held to be excludable because they were treated as loans when they were made (rather than as compensation or dividends).[23] Also, cash advances paid by a corporation to its president and major shareholder were held not to be taxable compensation where the amounts were credited against amounts that were previously loaned by the president to the corporation.[24] Finally, commissions paid in advance to an insurance company were held to be loans where the taxpayer was personally liable to repay the advances to the company.[25]

.08 Gifts

In general, gifts made to employees by employers are taxable and are subject to income tax withholding and FICA and FUTA taxes.[26] However, gifts of nominal value are excludable as de minimis fringe benefits (see the discussion of de minimis fringe benefits

---

[19] Code Sec. 45B(b)2, as amended by P.L. 104-188, 104th Cong., 2d Sess., Sec. 1112(b) (Aug. 20, 1996).

[20] Rev. Rul. 68-239, 1968-1 CB 414.

[21] *D.E. Warden,* 55 TCM 632, Dec. 44,711(M), TC Memo. 1988-165. *See also* IRS Letter Ruling 9519002, 2-3-95, CCH IRS LETTER RULINGS REPORTS and *M.D. Morgan,* 73 TCM 2313, Dec. 51,940(M), TC Memo. 1997-132.

[22] Rev. Rul. 68-337, 1968-1 CB 417.

[23] *I. Bartel,* 54 TC 25, Dec. 29,909 (1970).

[24] *G.K. Hagestad,* 66 TCM 87, Dec. 49,142(M), TC Memo. 1993-300.

[25] See, e.g., *J.J. Gales,* 77 TCM 1316, Dec. 53,231(M), TC Memo. 1999-27, *acq in result,* IRB 1999-40, 437, as corrected by Ann. 2000-102, 2000-2 CB 605. *See also* Technical Advice Memorandum 2000040004.

[26] Code Secs. 102(c), 3121(a), 3306(b), and 3401(a).

in Chapter 3). For example, a gift of a Christmas turkey to employees is excludable as a de minimis fringe benefit.

.09 Prizes and Awards

Prizes and awards received by employees are generally treated as taxable compensation whether paid in cash or not. For instance, cash awards made to employees for their suggestions concerning the efficiency of the employer's operations are taxable compensation subject to withholding and FICA and FUTA taxes.[27] Further, cash prizes awarded to salespersons are taxable compensation whether paid to the salesperson or his spouse.[28] And, incentive payments made by an automobile manufacturing company to a salesperson employed by an authorized dealership were treated as taxable compensation subject to income taxes and employment taxes because the incentive payments were considered to be an integral part of the compensation structure of the dealer.[29]

However, certain awards made to employees for safety achievement and/or length of service are excludable under Code Sec. 74(c). Code Sec. 74(c)(1) provides that the amount of an employee achievement award (that is, for safety or length of service) is excludable if the cost of the award does not exceed the amount that the employer can deduct under Code Sec. 274(j). In general, Code Sec. 274 permits a deduction of up to $400 of tangible personal property (not including cash, negotiable certificates, stocks, bonds, and services) per recipient under a nonqualified plan and up to $1,600 per recipient under a qualified plan as defined in Code Sec. 274(j)(3). Amounts received by employees in excess of the employer's deductible amount constitute gross income.

> **Example:** Ron was awarded a gold watch worth $1,750 under his employer's qualified plan for making awards for safety achievement. The first $1,600 of value to Ron is excludable because awards for safety achievement under a qualified plan of up to that amount are deductible by the employer and excludable by the employee. The excess $150 amount is taxable to the employee and not deductible by the employer.

.10 Reimbursement of Employee Business Expenses

Employee business expenses such as transportation incurred in pursuit of the employer's business and meals and lodging incurred away from home on an overnight basis are deductible by the

---

[27] Rev. Rul. 70-471, 1970-2 CB 199.
[28] Rev. Rul. 68-216, 1968-1 CB 413.

[29] Technical Advice Memorandum 9525003, 3-13-95, CCH IRS LETTER RULINGS REPORTS.

employee under Code Sec. 162. However, how such expenses are deductible depends upon (a) whether they are reimbursed and (b) whether such expenses are reimbursed under a "reimbursement or other expense allowance arrangement" as defined in the Code and regulations.

Unreimbursed Employee Expenses. Unreimbursed employee expenses (or the portion of such expenses not reimbursed) are only deductible from adjusted gross income (AGI) as miscellaneous itemized deductions. Further, unreimbursed meal and entertainment expenses are only 50 percent (80 percent before 1994) deductible under Code Sec. 274(n). After 1997, the percentage limitation on unreimbursed meal and entertainment expenses is being increased for employees subject to Department of Defense hours of service rules (e.g., airline pilots and crew, interstate truckers and bus drivers, and certain railroad employees).[30] In 2004 and 2005, the percentage for those employees was 70 percent, and for 2006 and 2007, the percentage will be 75 percent (eventually the percentage will increase to 80 percent by 2008). Wherever the 50 percent limit is discussed in the following paragraphs covering employee business expenses, the larger percentages will apply after 1997 with respect to employees subject to Department of Defense hours of service rules. Finally, the sum of unreimbursed employee expenses and other miscellaneous itemized deductions (such as Code Sec. 212 nonbusiness expenses) are deductible only to the extent that their sum exceeds two percent of the employee's AGI under Code Sec. 67.

Reimbursed Employee Expenses. The income tax and payroll tax treatment of reimbursed employee expenses depends upon whether the employee expenses are reimbursed under an "accountable" reimbursement plan or a "nonaccountable" plan. Reimbursements received under an accountable plan are excludable from the employee's gross income and are not subject to payroll taxes.[31] However, employees cannot exclude amounts paid as travel advances or reimbursements when such payments are combined with compensation payments unless there is specific identification of the travel advances or reimbursements at the time the amounts are paid.[32] The reimbursed expenses are not reported on the employee's tax return and the 50-percent limit on meals and entertainment expenses does not apply to the reimbursed expenses on the employee's tax return. The employer is permitted to deduct

---

[30] Code Sec. 274(n)(3), as added by P.L. 105-34. 105th Cong., 2d Sess., Sec. 969(a) (Aug. 5. 1997).
[31] Reg. § 1.62-2(c)(4), Reg. § 31.3121(a)-3, Reg.

§ 31.3306(b)-2, and Reg. § 31.3401(a)-4.
[32] See, e.g., Boyd Bros. Transportation Co., 27 Fed Cl 509, aff'd, 60 F3d 843 (Fed Cir., 1995).

the reimbursement amounts subject to the 50-percent limit on the reimbursements for meals and entertainment expenses.[33]

If an employee's expenses are not fully reimbursed under the employer's accountable plan, the unreimbursed portion of the expenses is deductible from AGI as a miscellaneous itemized deduction, subject to the two percent of AGI limitation under Code Sec. 67 (the unreimbursed portion of the meals and entertainment is only 50-percent deductible.[34])

Under Reg. § 1.62-2, an accountable plan is an expense reimbursement plan that meets the following requirements:

(1) *Business Connection*[35]—An arrangement is treated as having a business connection if it provides advances, allowances, or reimbursements for business expenses that are allowable as deductions by the employee and are paid or incurred by the employee in connection with the performance of services for the employer. However, Reg. § 1.62-2(h)(1) provides a limited exception to this rule. Under the exception, employer reimbursements of club dues and the cost of travel of a spouse or other companion accompanying the taxpayer on a business trip are not taxable if all other requirements for an accountable plan are met, even though these expenses are not deductible business expenses. The payment may be made by the employer or by a third party for whom the employee performs a service on behalf of the employer. If both wages and the reimbursement amount are combined in a single payment, the reimbursement must be identified either by making a separate payment or by specifically identifying the amount of the reimbursement. If an employer or other payor arranges to pay an amount to an employee regardless of whether the employee incurs or is reasonably expected to incur deductible business expenses, the arrangement does not meet the business connection requirement and is not an accountable plan.[36] However, the IRS has publicly held that where drivers of a courier service were paid on a tag-rate basis and were provided a mileage allowance which was a percentage of the tag rate, the mileage allowance met the business connection requirement.[37] As an example of applying the business connection requirement, the IRS has held that employer reimbursements for (1) meals and lodging expenses incurred by employees at temporary worksites (a site where the employee's work is expected to last one year or less) and (2) transportation to and from the employee's residence

---

[33] Code Sec. 274(c)(3) and (n).

[34] IRS Pub. 463 at 12 and IRS Form 2106.

[35] Reg. § 1.62-2(d)(1).

[36] *See,* e.g., *Trans Box Systems,* 225 F3d 664 (CA-9, 2000) and *World Labor Support of Mississippi, Inc.,* DC Miss., 2001-2 USTC ¶ 50,463.

[37] Rev. Rul. 2004-1, IRB 2004-4, 325.

and the temporary worksite are excludable.[38] The business connection requirement is met in these cases because the expenses would be deductible if paid or incurred by the employee and are employment-related. The U.S. Tax Court has held that an employer's payment of legal fees incurred by a former employee with respect to a wrongful termination suit brought by the former employee against the employer was not a reimbursement under an accountable plan.[39] The reimbursement did not meet the business connection requirement because the legal fees were not paid by an employee in pursuit of his employer's business. The legal fees were incurred after the employee's employment relationship with the employer ended, and thus, did not meet the requirement.

(2) *Substantiation*[40]—An arrangement must require each expense to be substantiated to the payor of the reimbursement in accordance with the provisions of Code Sec. 274(d) or Reg. § 1.162-17, whichever applies. Thus, for employee entertainment, transportation, and travel expenses, information sufficient to substantiate the amount, time, place or use, and business purpose of the expense must be submitted to the payor. Revenue Procedure 97-45[41] provides optional substantiation rules for use by employees of a federal government agency for reimbursed expenses. Under the optional rules, an employee may make an adequate accounting by submitting an account book, diary, or similar record without having to submit documentary evidence. The employer in such a case must maintain a written policy specifying certain requirements that are set forth in that revenue procedure. In response to the increasing use of ticketless travel on airlines, the IRS has privately ruled that an electronic itinerary is sufficient to meet the substantiation requirement where employees of a large corporation used ticketless travel in conducting business trips for the corporation.[42] In another instance, the IRS publicly held that the employer's reimbursement plan, which provided for electronic substantiation of employee business expenses that were incurred by employees and paid through use of an employee business credit card, met the substantiation requirements where the electronic substantiation provided all of the necessary information normally required for adequate substantiation.[43] Note that the amount of certain expenses is deemed to be substantiated if a per diem allowance or fixed allowance is provided within IRS prescribed amounts (see the discussion on per diem and fixed rate allowances below).

---

[38] Rev. Rul. 93-86, 1993-2 CB 71; Rev. Rul. 99-7, 1999-1 CB 361; and Chief Counsel Advice 200018052, 3-10-2000, Chief Counsel Advice 200002055, and Chief Counsel Advice 200026025, 5-31-2000, CCH IRS LETTER RULINGS REPORTS.

[39] *F. Biehl*, 118 TC 467, Dec. 54,760 (2002).

[40] Reg. § 1.62-2(e).

[41] 1997-2 CB 499.

[42] IRS Letter Ruling 9805007, 10-24-97, CCH IRS LETTER RULINGS REPORTS. *See also* IRS Letter Ruling 200304002, 8-6-2002, CCH IRS LETTER RULINGS REPORTS.

[43] Rev. Rul. 2003-106, 2003-2 CB 936. *See also* IRS Letter Ruling 200433010.

(3) *Returning Amounts in Excess of Substantiated Expenses*[44]—In general, a reimbursement plan must require an employee to return reimbursement amounts in excess of substantiated expenses to the payor within a reasonable period of time. For this purpose, Reg. § 1.62-2(g) states that what is considered to be a reasonable period of time generally depends upon the facts and circumstances. However, two safe-harbor provisions are provided, the fixed-date method (i.e., an excess reimbursement must be returned within 120 days of payment) and the periodic statement method (i.e., excess amounts must be returned within 120 days of receipt of a quarterly statement). In a recent case, the Tax Court found that the "returning amounts in excess of substantiated expenses" requirement was not met in an instance where (1) the taxpayer did not provide evidence that he was required to return amounts received that exceeded substantiated expenses, and (2) the annual reimbursement amount exceeded the taxpayer-employee's expenses.[45] Note that special rules (described below) apply in the case of expenses reimbursed on a per diem or fixed rate basis.

A recent Tax Court case provides an example of how payments made for travel expenses were excludable as payments under an accountable plan.[46] In that case, an individual, who was president of an accounting firm in Minneapolis, moved to Nashville to become an airline pilot for American Airlines. Two years later, the individual regularly traveled to Minneapolis to help the accounting firm represent itself in a criminal tax investigation concerning the firm's tax return preparation activities. The Tax Court found that the business connection requirement was met because the payments made were for travel expenses away from the individual's Nashville home and that the payments were directly related to his trade or business as the accounting firm's employee. The Tax Court also found that the payments, that were made on a per diem basis—see the discussion below—were adequately substantiated because (1) it was reasonable for the accounting firm to estimate that the federal per diem rate for Minneapolis would not exceed the individual's anticipated expenses, and (2) the other elements of substantiation were met by the furnishing of a handwritten log of the individual's activities and testimony from the individual's partner and an independent contractor associated with the firm. An example of payments held to be paid under a nonaccountable plan can be found in Rev. Rul. 2002-35.[47] In that ruling, the IRS found that amounts paid to workers that were engaged in pipeline construction and repair to

---

[44] Reg. § 1.62-2(f)(1).

[45] *Steven J. Namyst, et ux.,* TC Memo 2004-63.

[46] *N.M. Romer,* 76 TCM 8, Dec. 52,772(M), TC Memo. 1998-238.

[47] 2002-1 CB 1067.

reimburse the workers for the provision of their own tools, supplies, and equipment for use on the job were not paid under an accountable plan. The IRS found that none of the three accountable plan requirements were met.

If an arrangement does not satisfy one or more of the three accountable plan requirements, it is a "nonaccountable plan," and reimbursements made under such a plan (1) are includible in the employee's gross income, (2) must be reported to the IRS, and (3) are subject to payroll taxes.[48] In such a case, the expenses attributable to the reimbursements included in gross income of the employee are deductible by the employee from AGI as a miscellaneous itemized deduction (subject to the two percent of AGI floor under Code Sec. 67 and the 50 percent limitation on meal and entertainment expenses under Code Sec. 274(n) as long as the employee can substantiate the full amount of the expenses in accordance with the provisions of Code Sec. 274(d) and Reg. § 1.162-17.[49] However, a special rule applies where an employee fails to return, within a reasonable time period, reimbursements in excess of substantiated expenses. In that case, only the amounts paid in excess of the substantiated expenses are treated as paid under a nonaccountable plan.[50]

> **Example:** Norton is reimbursed for employee business expenses under an arrangement that permits him to keep any reimbursements that exceed his substantiated expenses. During 2006, he incurred $1,800 of substantiated expenses, but received $2,100 of reimbursement. In that case, $300 ($2,100 − $1,800) is considered as provided through a nonaccountable plan and is includible in Norton's gross income. The other $1,800 of reimbursement is considered to be provided through an accountable plan and is, therefore, excludable by Norton and need not be reported to the IRS.

Deemed Substantiation of Employee Travel Expenses. The return of excess reimbursement rule does not apply to employee travel expenses (meals, lodging, and incidentals) where: (1) the amount of the reimbursed expense is considered substantiated because the reimbursement is in the form of a per diem or fixed rate allowance that meets IRS guidelines; (2) the reimbursement or allowance is reasonably calculated not to exceed the amount of the employee's expenses or anticipated expenses; and (3) the employee is required to return to the payor, within a reasonable time, any portion of the reimbursement

---

[48] Reg. §§ 1.62-2(c)(3)(i) and (c)(5), Reg. § 31.3121(a)-2, Reg. § 31.3306(b)-2, and Reg. § 31.3401(a)-2.

[49] Reg. § 1.62-2(c)(5).

[50] Reg. § 1.62-2(c)(3)(ii).

or allowance that relates to days or miles of travel that are not for business purposes or are not substantiated. Under this exception, an employee need not be required to return the excess of the reimbursement or allowance in excess of substantiated expenses actually incurred. As long as the other elements of substantiation are provided to the payor, the reimbursement will be treated as made under an accountable plan. Only reimbursement amounts in excess of the allowable per diem or fixed rate will be taxable to the employee.[51]

The per diem or fixed rate allowance exception applies with respect to employee travel expenses if the reimbursement for meals, lodging, and incidentals does not exceed the allowable federal per diem rates specified in Rev. Proc. 2005-10[52] and subsequent revenue procedures in future years. Rev. Proc. 2005-10 is effective for per diem allowances that are paid both (a) to an employee on or after January 1, 2005, and (b) with respect to lodging, meals, and incidental expenses or with respect to meals and incidental expenses paid or incurred for travel away from home on or after January 1, 2005. However, taxpayers may apply Rev. Proc. 2004-60[53] (the immediate predecessor of Rev. Proc. 2005-10) for such items on or after January 1, 2005, and before March 1, 2005. Rev. Proc. 2004-60 was in effect from October 1 through December 31, 2004. Finally, the IRS recently issued Rev. Proc. 2005-67[53.1] which is effective for per diem allowances or expenses paid after September 30, 2005 for travel after that date. Previous revenue procedures beginning with the year 2000 were effective from October 1 of the year of issue until September 30 of the following year and contained transition rules for each affected calendar year.

Under Rev. Proc. 2005-10 and 2005-67, a per diem allowance is a payment pursuant to a reimbursement or other expense allowance arrangement that meets the requirements of Reg. § 1.62-2(c) (covered above) and that:

(1) is paid on account of employee business expenses for lodging, meals, and/or incidental expenses for travel away from home related to services performed for the employer;

(2) is reasonably calculated not to exceed the amount of the expenses or the anticipated expenses; and

(3) is paid at the applicable federal per diem rate, a flat rate or stated schedule, or in accordance with any other IRS-specified rate or schedule.

The applicable federal per diem rate is the sum of the federal lodging expense rate and the federal meal and incidental expense for

---

[51] Reg. § 1.62-2(f)(2).
[52] IRB 2005-3, 341.

[53] Rev. Proc. 2004-60, IRB 2004-42 682.
[53.1] IRB 2005-42, 1.

the locality of travel (rate varies by locality).[54] For purposes of these rules, the term "incidental expenses" has the same meaning as given to the term in the Federal Travel Regulations.[55] Thus, the term includes fees and tips paid to porters, baggage carriers, bellhops, hotel maids, stewards and stewardesses and other workers on ships, waiters and waitresses, and hotel servants in foreign countries. However, the term does not include expenses for laundry, cleaning and pressing of clothes, lodging taxes, and the costs of telegrams and telephone calls. For employees that use the federal per diem rates, a special transition rule applies for the first two months during 2005, under which the provisions of Rev. Proc. 2004-60 could be used with respect to per diem allowances rather than the provisions of Rev. Proc. 2005-10. A special transition rule applied to the year 2004 under which, for the last three months of that year, the employer could, on a consistent basis, use the rates in effect for the first nine months of the year or the ones in effect beginning October 1, 2003. If a payor reimburses only meal and incidental expenses at a per diem rate, the payor can use the federal meals and incidental expense per diem rate if: (1) the payor provides lodging to the employee in-kind; (2) the payor pays for the cost of lodging directly; or (3) the payor believes that the employee will not incur lodging costs. A similar transition rule applies to the year 2005 under Rev. Proc. 2005-67.

In the case of employees in the transportation industry, the employer can elect to use a specified meals and incidental-only rate of $41 per day (for October 1, 2004, through September 30, 2005) for travel within the continental United States and $46 per day (for October 1, 2004, through September 30, 2005) for travel outside of the continental United States, in lieu of the rates for the specific localities. The rates applicable after September 30, 2005 are $.52 and $.58, respectively under Rev. Proc. 2005-67. If elected, the special rates must be used consistently with respect to a particular employee during the calendar year. For this purpose, a special transition rule applied during the year 2004, under which an employer that used the special per diem rates for a particular employee during the first nine months of the year was obligated to use those rates for the remainder of the year. A change could not be made until January 1, 2005, with respect to that particular employee. A similar transition rule applies for the year 2005 under Rev. Proc. 2005-67.

In lieu of using the specified federal per diem rate with respect to an employee's travel within the continental United States, an

---

[54] The currently applicable federal per diem rates can be found, e.g., in the 2005 CCH STANDARD FEDERAL TAX REPORTER at ¶ 14,417.421.   [55] 41 CFR Part 300-3.1 (2004).

employer or other payor can use the "high-low" method. Under that method, an employer or other payor can use one specified per diem rate for any "high-cost locality" (e.g., New York City) and a lower specified rate for other localities within the continental United States. In such a case, the federal meals and incidental expense rate one specified dollar amount for high-cost localities and a lower fixed amount for others. Under Rev. Proc. 2005-10, the high-low rates applicable beginning January 1, 2005 were $204 for high-cost localities and $125 for other localities (as specified in that Revenue Procedure—the federal meals and incidental rate was $46 for high-cost localities and $36 for others). However, for January and February of 2005, employees could elect to use the high-low rates (and the indicated high and low rate locality designations) contained in Rev. Proc. 2004-60, rather than the rates (and locality designations) contained in Rev. Proc. 2005-10. The rates in Rev. Proc. 2004-60, which were effective from October 1 through December 31, 2004, were $199 for high-cost localities and $127 for low-cost localities (the federal meals and incidental expenses rate was $46 for high-cost localities and $36 for others). Finally, under Rev. Proc. 2005-67, the high-low rates applicable after September 30, 2005 are $226 for high-cost localities and $141 for other localities (the meals and incidental expense rate is $58 for a high-cost locality and $45 for others). If the high-low method is chosen for a particular employee, the method must be consistently used for that employee during the calendar year. With respect to the consistency rule, a special transition rule applies during the year 2004. Under that transition rule, an employer that used the high-low method with respect to a particular employee during the first nine months of 2004 has to use that method with respect to that employee during the last three months of 2004. A change may be made only on January 1, 2005. In addition, an employer that used the high-low method during the first nine months of 2004 has the option for the last three months of using the high-low rates in effect for the first nine months of 2004 or those listed in Rev. Proc. 2004-60 that took effect on October 1, 2004. A similar transition rule applies for the year 2005 under Rev. Proc. 2005-67.

Under the per diem substantiation method or the "high-low" method, the amount of travel expenses deemed substantiated is equal to the lesser of (1) the per diem allowance or (2) the amount computed at the applicable federal per diem rate or the applicable high-low rate, if the alternative method is used. Thus, as noted above, if the other substantiation requirements are met, the employee is not taxed if the reimbursement does not exceed the applicable federal rate. This is true even if the reimbursement exceeds the actual amount of the travel expenses and the employee is permitted to keep the excess. Only the reimbursement amounts in excess of the applicable federal per diem rate (or high-low rate, if used) are taxable. If the employer reimburses at a rate lower than the applicable federal rate, the difference between the applicable rate and what is reimbursed is deductible by the employee as a miscellaneous itemized deduction, subject to the two percent of AGI limit and 50-percent limit on meals and entertainment.

> **Example:** Charles, an employee of the Willis Corporation, spent five days on business travel in Rochester, Minnesota. He was reimbursed for meals and lodging at a rate of $100 per day for each of the five days. Assume that the federal per diem rate for meals and lodging is $86. Assuming that the other elements of substantiation have been supplied, Charles will have gross income of $14 per day ($100 − $86). If Charles had been reimbursed at a rate of only $50 per day, the excess of the per diem rate of $86 over the $50 reimbursement per day could be deducted as a miscellaneous itemized deduction on Charles' tax return.

The deemed substantiation rules of Rev. Proc. 2005-10 do not apply to reimbursement of travel expenses made to employees who are related to the employer or other payor under Code Sec. 267(b). For this purpose, an employee who directly or indirectly owns more than 10 percent of the employer or payor is considered to be a related party. Thus, more-than-10 percent owner-employees must provide actual substantiation of the amount of reimbursed travel expenses.

Deemed Substantiation of Employee Automobile Expenses. Rules similar to those provided above for the deemed substantiation of the amount of travel expenses reimbursed apply to employer reimbursements of employee automobile expenses on the basis of a rate per mile or under the fixed or variable rate (FAVR) method, as provided in Rev. Proc. 2004-64[56] and subsequent revenue procedures in future years.

Under Rev. Proc. 2004-64, if a mileage allowance is provided to an employee for the business usage of the employee's automobile, the amount deemed substantiated will equal the lesser of (1) the amount paid under the mileage allowance or (2) the applicable standard IRS mileage rate (generally 40.5 cents per mile for business miles driven during 2005 (37.5 cents per mile during 2004)). Finally, in IR 2005-99, the IRS increased the rate for the last four months of 2005 to 48.5 cents per mile. Thus the 40.5 cents per mile rate is applicable during the first eight months of 2005. Only amounts paid

---

[56] IRB 2004-49, 898.

in excess of the IRS rate will be taxable unless such amounts are actually substantiated. If the reimbursement is at a rate lower than the IRS rate, the employee may deduct the difference as a miscellaneous itemized deduction.

If the employer uses the per mile reimbursement method, parking fees and tolls attributable to the use of the automobile may be separately reimbursed, and the reimbursements are not taxable if the amounts are actually substantiated and the other elements of substantiation are provided. Interest may also be separately reimbursed, but such reimbursements are fully taxable since automobile interest is not deductible.

There are no rules indicating that the deemed substantiation rules concerning employee automobile expenses do not apply to employees that are related to the employer or other payor of the reimbursements. Thus, the deemed substantiation rules with respect to automobile expenses can be used for all of the employees of the employer.

Under the FAVR method for deemed substantiation, a periodic fixed payment is made to cover projected fixed costs (e.g., depreciation) of driving a "standard" automobile in the employee's work area. Also, a periodic variable cost payment is made to cover projected operating costs (such as gasoline and repairs). The FAVR allowance does not cover parking fees, tolls, interest, and taxes.

Under the FAVR method, the automobile expenses that are deemed substantiated equal the total FAVR allowance paid minus the sum of the following:

(1) the portion of a periodic variable payment that relates to miles in excess of the business-related miles substantiated by the employee, which the employee does not return within a reasonable time period;

(2) the portion of a periodic fixed payment that relates to a period during which the employee was not covered by a FAVR allowance, which the employee does not return within a reasonable time period; and

(3) the optional high-mileage payments (i.e., payments covering additional depreciation for a standard automobile attributable to business miles driven and substantiated by an employee for a calendar year in excess of the projected annual business mileage for the year).

> **Comment:** The FAVR deemed substantiation method is generally not favorable for potential users. The rules governing the calculations and definitions of terms under the approach are extremely complex, and numerous recordkeeping requirements

are associated with the use of the method. In addition, restrictions on the use of the method prevent its use for certain officers and shareholder-employees. In summary, the method is not advisable for most situations.

Optional Expense Substantiation Rule for Pipeline Builders. The IRS has provided a new optional expense substantiation rule that may be used by employers hiring rig welders and heavy equipment mechanics and that require, as a condition of employment, these employees to provide a welding rig or mechanics rig to be used in performing services in the construction, repair, or maintenance of transportation mainline pipeline.[57] Under the optional rules, expenses of up to $8 per hour for welding rigs and mechanics rigs will be deemed substantiated if an eligible employer either provides fuel or separately reimburses fuel expenses for such rigs assuming all of the other accountable plan requirements are met as specified by the IRS. Reimbursements of expenses of up to $13 per hour will be deemed substantiated if an employer does not provide or separately reimburse fuel used by the rigs. The deemed substantiation rules only apply with respect to (1) welding rigs that are 3/4 ton or heavier trucks that are equipped with a welding machine and other necessary equipment and (2) mechanics rigs that are heavy trucks equipped with a permanently installed mechanics bed and other necessary equipment used to repair and maintain heavy machinery at the job site. The optional rules are available to be elected as of September 9, 2002.[58]

Planning Pointer: Employees are frequently better off if their business expenses are reimbursed by their employer even if the employer pays them less compensation as a result. The reason is that if expenses are reimbursed under an accountable reimbursement plan where the reimbursements equal the substantiated expenses, the reimbursement is not includible in the employee's gross income, and no reporting of the reimbursement of expenses to the IRS is required. If the substantiated expenses are not fully reimbursed, the reimbursement amount is not taxable (and not subject to FICA and FUTA taxes), and the reimbursed portion of the expenses is not deductible by the employee. On the other hand, unreimbursed expenses may be partially deductible or not deductible at all because of the 50 percent limit on unreimbursed meals and entertainment expenses and the Code Sec. 67 two percent of AGI floor limitation. They are not deductible at all if the taxpayer does not take itemized deductions. For example, assume that Jack, who had AGI of $80,000 in 2000, incurred $1,500 of deductible meals and entertainment expenses and $1,200 of other deductible

---

[57] Rev. Proc. 2002-41, 2002-1 CB 1098.   [58] Notice 2002-55, 2002-1 CB481.

employee business expenses. If Jack's employer did not reimburse him for these expenses, he would be permitted to take a deduction from AGI of $350, assuming that he itemizes his deductions, computed as follows:

Deductible meals and entertainment ($1,500 × .5)	$ 750
Other deductible business expenses.	1,200
	$1,950
Minus .02 of $80,000 AGI	1,600
Total Deductible Amount	$ 350

On the other hand, if the employer reimbursed Jack for these expenses, none of the $2,700 would be includible in income, nor would the expenses be reported on Jack's tax return. It would be a wash for Jack.

Treatment of Reimbursed Uniform and Job Interview Expenses. Employer allowances for employee uniforms fall within the reimbursed expense rules if the uniforms are (1) specifically required as a condition of employment and (2) not acceptable or adaptable for general or continued usage. Uniforms worn by police officers, firefighters, nurses, and bus drivers are considered to meet the tests.[59] However, work clothing worn by painters is not considered a "uniform" even if required by the painters' union.[60]

Reimbursements received by a job applicant from a prospective employer for attending an employment interview are subject to the same general rules as employee business expenses, covered above. The reimbursements may cover round-trip transportation and meals and lodging.[61]

.11   Reimbursement of Employee Moving Expenses

Employer reimbursements of employee-incurred moving expenses are excludable from the employee's gross income as qualified moving expense reimbursements incurred after 1993 to the extent that the reimbursements apply to expenses that are deductible under Code Sec. 217.[62] Reimbursements in excess of the amount deductible under Code Sec. 217 are taxable to the employee under Code Sec. 82. In order for qualified moving expense reimbursements to be excludable, the employer's moving expense reimbursement plan must meet the same general requirements that apply to accountable plans for the reimbursement of employee business expenses covered above.[63]

---

[59] Rev. Rul. 70-474, 1970-2 CB 34.

[60] Rev. Rul. 57-143, 1957-1 CB 89.

[61] Rev. Rul. 63-77, 1963-1 CB 177.

[62] Code Sec. 132(g), as added by Sec. 13,213(d)(2), P.L. 103-66, 103rd Cong., 1st Sess. (Aug. 10, 1993).

[63] H.R. Rep. No. 213, 103rd Cong., 1st Sess. (1993).

Under this rule, the employer's moving expense reimbursement plan must meet the following requirements:

(1) Under the moving expense reimbursement plan, advances, allowances, or reimbursements must be provided only for deductible moving expenses incurred by the employee;

(2) The plan must require the employee to substantiate the expenses to the payor, unless the expenses are of a type for which substantiation is not required; and

(3) Advancements or reimbursements in excess of substantiated expenses covered under the plan must be required to be returned to the payor.

The reimbursements of employee moving expenses are not subject to withholding and FICA and FUTA taxes if it is reasonable to believe that the moving expenses are deductible under Code Sec. 217.[64] If the reimbursement exceeds the amount which is deductible under Code Sec. 217, the excess is subject to payroll taxes.[65]

Because meal expenses incurred as part of a move after 1993 are not deductible as moving expenses, employer reimbursements for such meals will be subject to withholding, FICA, and FUTA taxes.[66]

.12 Employer Payment of Employee Personal Debts and Expenses

In general, employer payments of the personal debts of employees and the reimbursement of personal expenses of the employee (such as commuting fares and travel expenses incurred while not away from home) are includible in the employee's gross income.

> **Example:** Construction Company XYZ provides free company transportation between its headquarters and job sites. Company XYZ also reimburses those employees who use their own vehicles for the same travel by paying them a flat per diem allowance. The allowance is considered to be additional compensation subject to income taxes.[67]

.13 Employer Payment of Employee Payroll Taxes

If an employer pays some or all of the employee's state or federal income taxes on the employee's salary or other compensation, such payments are taxable as additional compensation to the employee.[68]

---

[64] Code Secs. 3121(a)(11), 3306(b)(9), and 3401(a)(15).

[65] *See,* e.g., Reg. § 31.3121(a)(11)-1(b).

[66] Code Sec. 274(n)(2)(E) and Code Sec. 217(b)(1), as amended by Sec. 13,213(a)(1), P.L. 103-66, 103rd Cong., 1st Sess. (Aug. 10, 1993).

[67] Rev. Rul. 74-445, 1974-2 CB 325.

[68] *Old Colony Trust Co.,* SCt, 1 USTC ¶ 408, 279 US 716, 49 SCt 499 (1929).

The employer's payment of an employee's FICA taxes is also additional compensation to the employee if the employer has agreed to pay the employee's share of FICA taxes.[69]

The tax effect of the employer's payment of the employee's income taxes or FICA taxes is referred to as "pyramiding" because the amount of the employee's compensation is increased by such taxes, which, in turn, increases the taxable amount of the compensation, and so on. The formula to determine the amount of total compensation when the employer pays the employee's FICA taxes is shown below in cases where the employee's stated compensation is less than an amount equal to the wage limit for the OASDI portion of the FICA tax multiplied by .9235 (1 minus the FICA tax rate of .0765). The applicable amount for 2005 is $83,115 (the 2005 wage limit of $90,000 times .9235):[70]

$$\text{Total Compensation} = \frac{\text{Amount of Original Compensation}}{(1 - \text{Employee's FICA tax rate})}$$

Example: Bill's employer agrees to pay him $200 per week and also agrees to pay Bill's FICA taxes without deducting them from the $200. Bill's total compensation would be $216.57, computed as follows:

$$\text{Total Compensation} = \frac{\$200}{(1 - .0765)} = \frac{\$200}{.9235} = \$216.57$$

Once the employee's stated compensation equals or exceeds an amount equal to the OASDI wage limit multiplied by .9235 ($83,115 in 2005) the employer will only have to withhold and pay the Medicare portion of the FICA tax (at a rate of 1.45%) because the employee's compensation (including the employee's share of the OASDI taxes paid by the employer) will have already hit the OASDI wage limit—$90,000 in 2005. If, after that, the employer continues to pay the Medicare portion of the FICA tax (1.45 percent), only the 1.45 percent Medicare tax will be taken into account in the denominator of the above fraction.

Example: Ray's employer pays his FICA taxes on his monthly salary without deducting the taxes from Ray's pay. For October 2005, Ray earned a salary of $10,000. Prior to October, he had already earned $105,000. Since Ray's salary already exceeds $83,115 (the 2005 OASDI limit multiplied by .9235), only the Medicare tax portion of the FICA tax was paid

---

[69] Rev. Rul. 86-14, 1986-1 CB 304.   [70] IRS Pub. 15-A at 20 and 66 FR 54047-54052.

by the employer, and Ray would have total compensation of $10,147.13 for October, determined as follows:

$$\text{Total Compensation} = \frac{\$10,000\}}{(1-.0145)} = \frac{\$10,000}{.9855} = \$10,147.13$$

If it is necessary to determine the employee's total taxable compensation for the year for OASDI and Medicare tax purposes in a case where the employer pays the employee's share of the FICA tax (both OASDI and Medicare taxes), the way in which each total taxable amount is determined depends upon whether the employee's stated compensation equals or exceeds the OASDI limit multiplied by .9235. If the employee's stated pay is less than the OASDI limit multiplied by .9235, merely use the first formula presented above, i.e., divide the stated compensation by .9235 to yield total compensation for both OASDI and Medicare tax purposes. If the stated pay equals or exceeds the OASDI wage limit multiplied by .9235, the total compensation for OASDI tax purposes will be the OASDI wage base amount ($90,000 in 2005), while the total compensation for Medicare tax purposes will equal the following:[71]

$$\begin{array}{l}\text{Total Compensation} \\ \text{for Medicare Tax} \\ \text{Purposes}\end{array} = \begin{array}{l}\text{The OASDI Wage Limit for the Year +} \\ [(\text{Stated Compensation} - \text{the OASDI} \\ \text{Wage Limit} \times .9235)) \,/\, .9855]\end{array}$$

Example: Assume Mark's stated pay for 2005 is $105,000, and his employer paid Mark's OASDI and Medicare taxes. Mark's total 2005 compensation for OASDI tax purposes is $90,000 and is $112,207 for Medicare tax purposes ($90,000 + [($105,000 − $83,115) / .9855]).

.14 Standby Pay

Payments that are made to an employee after he/she attains the age of 62 and with the expectation that the employee will subsequently render services are called standby payments. Such payments are considered to be taxable compensation and are not exempt from payroll taxes.[72]

.15 Back Pay and Employment Discrimination Awards

Payments made by an employer to an employee who has been reinstated and granted back pay for time lost under a National Labor Relations Board order are taxable compensation subject to withholding and FICA and FUTA taxes.[73] Further, a court-ordered

---

[71] *See* Reg. §§ 1.62-2(d), (e), and (f).
[72] Code Secs. 61(a) and 3121(a).

[73] Rev. Rul. 57-55, 1957-1 CB 304, as amp'd by Rev. Rul. 75-64, 1975-1 CB 16.

back-pay award is taxable in the year paid.[74] For example, the District Court has held in two instances that the noninterest portion of payments made by the San Francisco Giants and Philadelphia Phillies to players and former players were considered to be taxable compensation since they represented amounts the players would have received if the ball clubs had not colluded to interfere with the rights of free agents.[75] Such awards are taxable using the tax rates in effect in the year in which the taxpayer receives the back-pay award. In addition, the United States Supreme Court has recently held that back-pay awards are subject to FICA taxes using the rates and wage limitation amounts that are in effect in the year in which the award is received.[76] Payments by an employer to compensate an employee for unpaid minimum wages and unpaid overtime under the Wage/Hour Law or the Walsh/Healy Act are also taxable.[77] But court-awarded legal fees and interest paid to employees under the Wage/Hour Law or under the Walsh/Healy Act are excludable.[78]

The tax treatment accorded to employment discrimination awards (i.e., for employment discrimination on account of race, color, religion, gender, national origin, or other similar classifications under Title VII of the Civil Rights Act, on account of age, or on account of disability under the Americans with Disabilities Act) has been the subject of much litigation and attention by the IRS and others in recent years. The current tax treatment of employment discrimination awards is based on Code Sec. 104(a)(2), as amended by the Small Business Job Protection Act of 1996[79] and the IRS interpretation of this amendment contained in Rev. Rul. 96-65.[80] Under revised Code Sec. 104(a)(2), only damages received on account of physical injury or physical sickness are excludable. Further, punitive damages are not excludable. According to the Conference Committee Report on the 1996 Act, emotional distress (including physical symptoms such as insomnia, headaches and stomach disorders) is not considered a physical injury or physical sickness.[81] Thus, there is no exclusion for damages (other than medical expenses, as noted below) received based on a claim of employment discrimination of any kind which is based on emotional

---

[74] Rev. Rul. 78-336, 1978-2 CB 225.

[75] *San Francisco Baseball Associates, L.P., aka San Francisco Giants,* DC Calif., 2000-1 USTC ¶ 50,358, and *The Phillies,* DC Pa., 2001-2 USTC ¶ 50,478.

[76] *Cleveland Indians Baseball Co.,* SCt, 2001-1 USTC ¶ 50,341, 532 US 200, 121 SCt 1433. rev'g, CA-6, 2000-1 USTC ¶ 50,469. The District Court has followed this holding in *The Phillies,* DC Pa., 2001-2 USTC ¶ 50,478. The decisions are in accord with the IRS ruling in Rev. Rul. 89-35, 1989-1 CB 280, but are contrary to some earlier

court decisions. *See also St. Louis Cardinals LP,* DC Mo., 2001-2 USTC ¶ 50,542 and IRS Letter Ruling 200214001, 10-19-2001, CCH IRS Letter Rulings Reports.

[77] Rev. Rul. 72-268, 1972-1 CB 313.

[78] Rev. Ruls. 72-268, 1972-1 CB 313 and 80-364, 1980-2 CB 294.

[79] Code Sec. 104(a)(2) as amended by Small Business Job Protection Act of 1996 (P.L. 104-188).

[80] Rev. Rul. 96-65, 1996-2 CB 6.

[81] Conference Committee Report to P.L. 104-188, Act Sec. 1605.

¶ 202.15

distress. However, the exclusion from gross income will continue to apply to (1) damages received based on a claim for emotional distress that is attributable to physical sickness or physical injury and (2) damages paid on account of medical care attributable to emotional distress. The provisions of revised Code Sec. 104(a)(2) apply to damage amounts received after August 20, 1996. However, the revised Section does not apply to damage amounts received under a written binding agreement, court decree, or mediation award in effect (or issued on or before) September 13, 1995.[82]

In Rev. Rul. 96-65, the IRS interpreted revised Code Sec. 104(a)(2) to specifically hold that (1) back pay received in satisfaction of a claim for denial of a promotion due to disparate treatment employment discrimination under Title VII of the Civil Rights Act is fully taxable because it is completely independent of damages on account of physical injury or physical sickness and (2) amounts received for emotional distress in satisfaction of such a claim are not excludable except to the extent they are paid for medical care attributable to emotional distress.[83] In a recent Technical Advice Memorandum, the IRS indicated that a taxpayer could exclude the portion of damages for emotional distress up to the amounts the taxpayer paid for medical care attributable to her emotional distress to the extent she was not permitted to take an income tax deduction for such expenses.[84] The IRS has given some indication as to what is considered to be physical injuries and physical sickness for purposes of applying revised Code Sec. 104(a)(2). The IRS has privately held that damages that are attributable to personal injury that does not result in observable physical manifestations such as bruises, cuts and scratches are not excludable under Code Sec. 104(a)(2).[85] The IRS did not refer to damages received on account of age discrimination under the Age Discrimination in Employment Act (ADEA) because the Supreme Court in *Schleier*[86] had ruled in 1995 that such damages are not excludable (owing to the fact that damages under the ADEA are not for tort-like actions and are not based on personal injury). A few recent cases apply to damage payments, taking into account revised Code Sec. 104(a)(2). Such cases are generally in accord with the requirement that the exclusion is permitted only on account of damages with respect to physical injuries and physical sickness. For example, in *Emerson*,[87] the Tax Court ruled that payment made to a taxpayer who stopped working for a company on account of intentional infliction of emotional distress was not excludable because the payment was not made on account of

---

[82] Code Sec. 104(a)(2), as amended by the Small Job Protection Act of 1996 (P.L. 104-188).

[83] Rev. Rul. 96-65, 1996-2 CB 6.

[84] Technical Advice Memorandum 200244004, 6-19-2002, CCH IRS LETTER RULINGS REPORTS.

[85] IRS Letter Ruling 200041022, 7-17-2000, CCH IRS LETTER RULINGS REPORTS.

[86] SCt, 95-1 USTC ¶ 50,309, 515 US 323, 115 SCt 2159.

[87] TC Memo 2003-82.

personal physical injuries or physical sickness. In *Oyelola*,[88] the Tax Court ruled that the taxpayer who received damages on account of racial discrimination was not entitled to exclude the amounts received because the taxpayer could not show that the recovery was received on account of physical injuries or physical sickness. The Court noted that the second requirement of the *Schleier* case (damages must be on account of personal injury to be excludable) means that the damages are payable with respect to personal injuries or physical sickness after the effective date of revised Code Sec. 104(a)(2).

> **Comment:** Presumably, revised Code Sec. 104(a)(2) also applies to damage awards under the Americans with Disabilities Act to the extent such awards are for back pay or for emotional distress and not for physical injury or physical sickness or medical expenses associated with emotional distress.

The tax treatment of employment discrimination awards under former Code Sec. 104(a)(2) (awards that do meet the effective date of revised Code Sec. 104(a)(2)) is also partially addressed in Rev. Rul. 96-65. The ruling states that back pay received in satisfaction of a claim for denial of a promotion due to disparate treatment employment discrimination under Title VII is taxable because it is completely independent of personal injuries or personal sickness. However, damages received for emotional distress in satisfaction of such a claim are excludable under former Code Sec. 104(a)(2) because they are received on account of personal injury or sickness. Presumably, the same analysis would apply to damages received under the Americans with Disabilities Act. As noted above, under the Supreme Court ruling in *Schleier*, age discrimination damages under the ADEA are taxable.

As noted above, Rev. Rul. 96-65 only partially addresses the treatment of employment discrimination awards under former Code Sec. 104(a)(2). That is because the ruling will not apply adversely to employment discrimination awards received (1) on or before June 14, 1995 (the date of the *Schleier* ruling) or (2) pursuant to a written binding agreement, court decree, or mediation award in effect on (or issued on or before) June 14, 1995. Earlier case law and revenue rulings, however, continue to provide guidance for certain awards that do not meet the effective date of Rev. Rul. 96-65. Thus, damage awards under Title VII of the Civil Rights Act, prior to its amendment on November 21, 1991, are taxable based on *T.A. Burke*[89] Supreme Court case ruling in 1992. For an example of a case involving damages received under the pre-1991 Title VII of the Civil Rights Act of 1964 and holding that the damages were wages on

---

[88] TC Summary Opinion 2004-28.
[89] SCt. 92-1 USTC ¶ 50,254, 504 US 229, 112 SCt 1867.

the basis of the *Burke* ruling, see *N.J. Hukkanen-Campbell*.[90] In addition, age discrimination awards are taxable under the *Schleier* decision covered above. Damage awards for disparate treatment discrimination under the amended Title VII and under the Americans with Disabilities Act that do not meet the effective date of Rev. Rul. 96-65 are still excludable under the provisions of Rev. Rul. 93-88,[91] which was obsoleted by Rev. Rul. 96-65. The treatment of other employment-related damage awards that do not meet the effective date of Rev. Rul. 96-65 is uncertain. Unless IRS guidance is released concerning such awards and in absence of a Supreme Court ruling, the treatment may be determined on a case-by-case basis and may be based on applicable state law. In one recent case concerning an employee who was discharged from employment in 1993, the District Court held that the portion of the settlement received by the employee from the employer that was attributable to nonphysical injuries as a result of the discharge was excludable.[92] The exclusion was permitted because state law in this case provided for remedies for injuries produced by a wrongful discharge.

As for punitive damages under former Code Sec. 104(a), such amounts were not excludable with respect to suits filed after July 10, 1989, except to the extent such damages relate to physical injury or sickness (courts differed as to the exclusion of punitive damages pertaining to physical injury or sickness). Thus, most employment-related punitive damages paid on account of suits entered into after that date are taxable.

.16 Dismissal and Severance Pay

Dismissal payments that an employer makes to an employee when that employee has been discharged are taxable regardless of whether the employer is legally bound to make the payments.[93] This rule also applies to lump-sum payments to employees who quit their jobs. For example, dismissal payments made to former employees by a company that had terminated its business operations were taxable to the employee.[94] In addition, a lump-sum payment received by a railroad employee in recognition of his agreement to relinquish certain rights with respect to his employment was considered to be taxable compensation.[95] In a recently released Legal Memorandum,

---

[90] CA-10, 2002-1 USTC ¶50,351. 274 F3d 1312, aff'g, 79 TCM 2122, Dec 53,909(M), TC Memo. 2000-180. Cert. denied, 4-13-2002.

[91] Rev. Rul. 93-88, 1993-2 CB 61.

[92] *D. Greer*, DC Ky., 98-2 USTC ¶50,821. The District Court's decision has been reversed by the Sixth Circuit Court of Appeals which disagreed with the District Court's holding that most of the settlement was based on nonphysical injuries that the taxpayer

suffered from being discharged from employment by the company. The Sixth Circuit remanded the case back to the District Court for a redetermmination of how the settlement should be divided between taxable and nontaxable portions. *See Greer*, CA-6, 2000-1 USTC ¶50,300, 207 F3d 322.

[93] Code Secs. 61 and 3401.

[94] Rev. Rul. 71-408, 1971-2 CB 340

[95] Rev. Rul. 75-44, 1975-1 CB 15.

the IRS has reviewed rulings in several recent cases that have held severance payments to be taxable and subject to payroll taxes and has affirmed its position that severance payments and dismissal pay is generally taxable. Further, the IRS has held that severance payments, in absence of a formal written plan, are not to be considered deferred compensation for FICA tax purposes under Code Sec. 3121(v) (covered in Chapter 14).[96] Back payments of severance pay are subject to FICA taxes using the rate in effect (and presumably the wage limitation in effect) in the year in which the payments are received.[97] Finally, in a recently issued revenue ruling, the IRS has held that if an employment contract is cancelled before the ending date of the contract as agreed upon, a payment that is made in the place of the remaining period of employment is subject to income tax withholding and FICA and FUTA taxes.[98] This ruling applies to payments made to employees and former employees on or after January 12, 2005.

.17 Unemployment Benefits and Supplemental Unemployment Benefits

Unemployment benefits paid to an employee from a state unemployment fund are fully includible in the employee's gross income under Code Sec. 85. (Such benefits were only partially includible before 1987.)

Supplemental unemployment benefits (SUB) plans pay private unemployment benefits to employees who have been laid off to supplement state unemployment benefit payments. The purpose of such plans is to provide jobless persons with a larger portion of their normal compensation than can be obtained just through state unemployment benefits.

Under trust fund SUB plans (such as the one in the auto industry), the employer establishes a trust fund and makes contributions into the fund for all covered employees. Laid-off employees who are eligible to receive state unemployment benefits are paid weekly cash benefits from the plan to supplement the state benefits. While the employer contributions made into the trust fund SUB plans are not taxable to the covered employees, the benefits paid to terminated employees under the plan are taxable to those employees in the year they receive the payments from an employer-

---

[96] Chief Counsel Advice 200033043, 6-13-2000. As examples of recent cases in this area, *see A. Pipitone,* CA-7, 99-1 USTC ¶ 50,600, 180 F3d 859, *J.H. Metelski,* 79 TCM 1705, Dec. 53,807(M), TC Memo. 2000-95, and *K.H. Donnel,* FedC1, 2001-2 USTC ¶ 50,664.

[97] *See, e.g.. D.A. Mazur,* DC N.Y., 97-2 USTC ¶ 50,981 and *G.A. Hemelt,* CA-4, 97-2 USTC ¶ 50,596, 122 F3d 204. *See also Cleveland Indians Baseball Co.,* SCt, 2001-1 USTC ¶ 50,341, 532 US 200, 121 SCt 1433, rev'g, CA-6, 2000-1 USTC ¶ 50,469.

[98] Rev. Rul. 2004-110, IRB 2004-50, 960.

financed plan.[99] If the employees also make contributions to the plan, the benefits are taxable only to the extent that they exceed the employee's contributions.[100] Trust fund SUB benefits are not subject to FICA and FUTA taxes according to a recent decision of the Court of Federal Claims.[101] The Court of Federal Claims held that the legislative history of Code Sec. 3402(o)(2)(A), which holds that Trust Fund SUB payments are not wages for income tax withholding purposes because they are nonwage payments, applies for all tax purposes. Therefore, such payments may not be treated as if they are wages for FICA (and FUTA) tax purposes. The Court's holding is in conflict with the IRS which has stated that lump-sum SUB benefits are subject to FICA and FUTA taxes because such benefits are not considered to be linked to state unemployment compensation benefits.[102]

Under the "Individual Income Security Account" plan, the employer must set up and make a cents-per-hour contribution into a separate account for each participating employee. Withdrawals may be made when the employee is laid off, becomes disabled, terminates employment, or dies. Employer contributions into "Individual Income Security Account" plans are taxable and subject to FICA and FUTA taxes in the year the contributions are made since the right to the benefits vests with each account holder regardless of whether or not the individual subsequently becomes unemployed.[103]

.18 Strike Benefits

Strike and lockout benefits paid by a union to striking or locked-out employees are generally taxable to the recipients. However, strike and lockout benefits are not taxable if the facts of the case show that the payments were meant to be a gift to the recipient. In *A. Kaiser*,[104] the Supreme Court upheld a jury finding that strike benefits in the form of food vouchers and rent payments provided for a nonunion worker, who was without work and income because of the union strike, constituted excludable gifts. Of particular importance was the fact that the worker was not required to picket or join the union in order to obtain the benefits. The *Kaiser* ruling was based on the specific facts of the case and did not state that strike benefits are nontaxable gifts as a matter of law.

In cases subsequent to *Kaiser*, courts have generally ruled that strike benefits are taxable. For example, in *W.A. Brown*,[105] the Tax

---

[99] Rev. Rul. 77-347, 1977-2 CB 362.
[100] Reg. § 1.501(c)(17)-3(a)(1).
[101] *CSX Corporation, Inc.*, FedCl, 2002-1 USTC ¶ 50,337.
[102] *See* Rev. Rul. 90-72, 1990-2 CB 211.
[103] Rev. Rul. 57-37, 1957-1 CB 18.

[104] SCt, 60-2 USTC ¶ 9517, 363 US 299, 80 SCt 1204.
[105] 47 TC 399, Dec. 28,311 (1967), aff'd, *per curiam*, CA-6, 68-2 USTC ¶ 9497, 398 F2d 832. Cert. denied, 393 US 1065. *See also R.A. Osborne, et al.*, 69 TCM 1895. Dec. 50,480(M), TC Memo. 1995-71.

Court held that strike benefits received by airline pilots were taxable where the payment of the benefits was not based on need, but rather was conditioned on their agreement not to fly for the airline on strike. The IRS has also ruled that strike benefits are generally taxable.[106] However, strike benefits are generally not subject to FICA and FUTA taxes.[107]

.19 Compensation Paid in Forms Other Than Money

If an employee receives property or services as compensation, rather than cash, the fair market value of the property or services is gross income to the employee. If a price has been stated for the property or services that are being rendered, that price is generally presumed to be the fair market value of the compensation received, in the absence of evidence showing a different value.[108] If the employee is required to pay a certain amount for the property or services received, the amount of the compensation is the fair market value of the property minus the amount payable by the employee.[109] The taxable amount must be reported in the year in which the property is received unless the employee's rights to the property are subject to a substantial risk of forfeiture and/or his rights of transferability of the property are substantially limited.[110] See Chapter 14 for a discussion of transfers of stock and property that are subject to a substantial risk of forfeiture.

One of the most common forms of compensation paid in property is employer stock. In general, the fair market value of stock received as compensation (minus whatever the employee has to pay for it) must be included in the employee's gross income.[111] Stock compensation is discussed extensively in Chapters 14 and 15.

If compensation is received in notes or other proof of indebtedness of the employer, the fair market value of this indebtedness at the time of the transfer is taxable.[112] Noninterest bearing notes that are expected to be collected at their face value upon maturity must be reported at their discounted value computed at the prevailing rate. The amount of the discount must be reported when it is collected. If the notes are payable in installments, a proportionate part of the discount is taxable at the time each installment is paid.[113]

If an employee is provided with services as compensation from the employer, the fair market value of such services is generally includible in gross income under Code Sec. 61. For example, an employer may pay a financial planner to provide personal financial

---

[106] *See,* e.g., Rev. Rul. 68-424, 1968-2 CB 419.
[107] *Id.*
[108] Code Sec. 83; Reg. § 1.61-2(d)(1).
[109] Code Sec. 83(a).
[110] *Id.*
[111] Code Sec. 83.
[112] Reg. § 1.61-2(d)(4).
[113] *Id.*

¶ 202.19

planning advice to its employees. Employer payments for personal financial planning and other financial-related services provided to employee are taxable to the employees.[114] However, after December 31, 2001, qualified retirement planning services provided to employees will be excludable as a miscellaneous fringe benefit under Code Sec. 132.[115] See Chapter 3 for a discussion of this excludable fringe benefit.

In recent years, employees have earned large amounts of frequent flier miles under various airline frequent flier mile programs (which, among other awards, offer free or discounted travel for accumulations of various air mileage levels) for business-related travel paid for or reimbursed by their employer. The issue is whether the value of such frequent flier miles is taxable as additional compensation. In a recent Announcement, the IRS stated that it will generally not pursue the issue. However, awards that are converted to cash and compensation paid in the form of travel will be taxable.[116] The Ninth Circuit Court of Appeals has held that frequent flier miles that are provided by an employer and which are converted into cash are taxable.[117]

In a recent private letter ruling, the IRS held that receipts of aid by needy employees through a company's charitable payroll plan were not taxable.[118] The amounts contributed to the plan are eligible for the charitable contribution deduction under Code Sec. 170. Under the plan, the company set up a tax-exempt Code Sec. 501(c)(3) charitable organization to receive voluntary contributions by means of payroll deductions from the company's managerial employees and any other employees that wished to participate. The principal activity of the charitable organization was to make grants and loans to the company's (and subsidiary company's) employees and their dependents on the basis of demonstrated need.

.20 Bargain Sales of Property

If an employer sells some of its property or stock to an employee at a price below market value, the employee must pay tax on the difference between the fair market value and his or her cost (i.e., the bargain element) in the year when the property is received unless his or her rights to the property are subject to a substantial risk of forfeiture.[119] (See Chapter 14 for a discussion of what constitutes a substantial risk of forfeiture.) This rule applies unless the discount

[114] Rev. Rul. 73-13, 1973-1 CB 42.

[115] Code Secs. 132(a)(7) and (m) as amended by P.L. 107-16, 107th Cong., 1st Sess., Sec. 665 (June 7, 2001).

[116] Announcement 2002-18, 2002-1 CB 621.

[117] *P.J. Charley*, CA-9, 96-2 USTC ¶50,399, 91 F3d 72.

[118] IRS Letter Ruling 200307084, 11-14-2002, CCH IRS LETTER RULINGS REPORTS.

[119] Code Sec. 83(a).

received by the employee can be considered a qualified employee discount under Code Sec. 132 (see Chapter 3 for a discussion of qualified employee discounts). For example, if the employee of an auto dealership buys a new car from the dealership at the dealership's cost, the difference between the fair market value of the car and the cost amount may be excludable from the employee's gross income, if the employee's discount percentage is not deeper than the company's gross profit percentage.

¶ 203   When Compensation Is Reported

Although current compensation is ordinarily taxable to the employee when it is received, the year in which compensation is reported may depend upon the accounting method of the taxpayer. Thus, compensation will normally be reported when it is received or accrued, depending upon whether the employee uses the cash or the accrual-basis method. In addition, certain problems may arise where compensation received or accrued in one taxable year must be returned to the employer in another year.

.01   Reporting by Cash-Basis Employees

Most employees use the cash-basis method of accounting for tax purposes. Therefore, most current compensation paid to employees is taxable to them in the year in which they receive it, subject to the doctrine of constructive receipt. Tips that are included in a written statement furnished to an employer by an employee are deemed received in the year the written report is furnished (see the discussion of when such reports are required to be reported earlier in this chapter).[120]

If the employer makes a periodic payment of compensation (e.g., bi-weekly or monthly), the first payroll period in January may overlap two taxable years of the employee. Nevertheless, the employee is taxable on the full amount of compensation in the year in which it is received. However, any payments of accrued compensation made to the employee before the end of the year are taxable in that year.[121]

Compensation paid by check must be reported in the year in which the check is received even if the check is not cashed or deposited until the following year.[122] But, a compensation check which is automatically deposited or mailed to the employee's bank for deposit on December 31 is taxable to the employee for the taxable year ending that December 31 because the amount of the check is considered to be constructively received as discussed below.

---

[120] Code Sec. 451(c).
[121] Rev. Rul. 75-478, 1975-2 CB 28.

[122] *See,* e.g., *U.A. Lavery,* CA-7, 46-2 USTC ¶ 9406, 158 F2d 859.

Constructive Receipt of Compensation. Compensation must be reported by cash-basis employees when it is constructively received even though not actually received. Under Reg. § 1.451-2, compensation is considered to be constructively received when it is made unqualifiably available to the taxpayer. Thus, if a compensation check is available to an employee in late December but is not actually picked up by the employee until January of the next year because the employee is on vacation, the check is considered to be income in the earlier year under the constructive receipt doctrine. Similarly, where an employer requests payment be made to him in January when the check is unqualifiably available to him in December, the amount of the check is taxable to him in the earlier year.

The doctrine of constructive receipt does not apply, however, if the employee's control of the receipt of the compensation is subject to substantial limitations and restrictions.[123] Thus, where an executive accrues a bonus from a corporation with the stipulation that the bonus will not be paid until the following year, the executive will not be considered to have constructively received the amount in the year it is accrued. The IRS has also ruled that where an employee and his employer enter into a binding agreement whereby the employer agrees not to pay or give a bonus or specified other compensation until a year following the year in which the related services are performed, the amount is not considered to be constructively received for the year the services are performed and is normally taxed in the year it is received.[124] Such an agreement is referred to as a nonqualified deferred compensation plan and is further discussed in Chapter 14. It should be noted, however, that generally for amounts deferred under nonqualified deferred compensation plans after December 31, 2004, new Code Sec. 409A imposes strict requirements that must be met in order to insure the deferral of income recognition.[125] These requirements are covered in Chapter 14. Finally, it should be noted that the IRS has privately held that the right of an employee to make an election to receive cash in lieu of vacation time in the year before the vacation is earned does not result in the constructive receipt of income.[126]

However, if an executive or other employee owns a controlling interest in a corporation, the constructive receipt doctrine applies if the corporation is liable for the salary or other compensation obligation and has the ability to pay the compensation. For instance, a controlling stockholder-employee and his wife constructively

---

[123] Reg. § 1.451-2.

[124] Rev. Rul. 60-31, 1960-1 CB 174. *See also* Rev. Procs. 71-21, 1971-1 CB 698 and 1992-65, 1992-2 CB 428.

[125] Code Sec. 409A, as added by P.L. 108-357, 108th Cong., 2d Sess., Sec. 885(a) (Oct. 22, 2004).

[126] IRS Letter Ruling 200130015, 4-26-2001, CCH IRS Letter Rulings Reports.

received salaries that were approved by the board of directors because the employee, as president, could authorize the payment of the compensation and the corporation had sufficient funds to make the payment.[127]

.02 Accrual-Basis Employees

If an employee is on the accrual-basis method, compensation income must be recognized by the employee in the year in which all the events have occurred which fix the right to receive that income as long as the amount of the income can be determined with reasonable accuracy.[128] Reg. § 1.451-1(a) indicates that in the case of compensation for services, no determination can be made as to the right to the compensation until the services have been performed. Thus, an accrual-basis employee is taxable on compensation when the services are completed, and the employer is liable for the compensation.

If an accrual-basis taxpayer receives compensation payments in advance, that is, before the services are performed, the advance compensation is ordinarily taxable when received. However, for taxable years ending on or after May 6, 2004, an accrual basis taxpayer may defer recognition of an advance payment under the provisions of Rev. Proc. 2004-34.[129] Under that revenue procedure, in the year of receipt, an advance payment only has to be included in gross income to the extent that the taxpayer includes the payment in his/her financial statements if that taxpayer elects to use the deferral method (if no financial statements are maintained, to the extent the payment is earned in the taxable year of the payment). The remainder of the advance payment is then to be recognized in the following year. Prior to the effective date of Rev. Proc. 2004-34, advance payments could be deferred based on the extent of the services performed, but only under contracts that called for completion of the related services by the end of the taxable year following the year in which the advance payment was received.[130]

.03 Impact of Compensation Adjustments

If part of the amount of compensation received by an employee is repaid during the year it is received, only the amount that is retained by the employee is taxable in that year.[131] However, if part of an employee's current compensation is not repaid to the employer until a later taxable year, the full amount of the compensation received is taxable to the employee in the current year if

---

[127] *E.J. Benes*, CA-6, 66-1 USTC ¶ 9205, 355 F2d 929.

[128] Reg. § 1.446-1(c)(1).

[129] Rev. Proc. 2004-34, IRB 2004-22, 991.

[130] Rev. Proc. 71-21, 1971-2 CB 549.

[131] *See, e.g., W.J. Smucker*, CA-6, 48-2 USTC ¶ 9396, 170 F2d 147

received under a claim of right. Ordinarily, income is considered to be received under a claim of right if the taxpayer claims the income rightfully belongs to him or her and his or her use of the income is not restricted even if: (1) his or her right to retain the income is disputed at the time of receipt, or later, and (2) there may be an obligation to repay the income in a later year.[132] For example, bonuses and commissions that were improperly computed and had to be repaid in a later year were taxable to the employees in the year of receipt under the claim of right doctrine.[133] Note that in situations where the taxpayer repays an amount previously included in income under the claim-of-right doctrine, the taxpayer is normally entitled to a deduction in the year of the repayment. However, if the amount repaid exceeds $3,000, Code Sec. 1341 allows taxes in the year of repayment to be reduced by the lesser of (a) or (b), where:

(a) = the repaid amount × the marginal tax rate for the year in which income was incorrectly reported; and

(b) = the repaid amount × the marginal tax rate for the year in which repayment occurs.

¶ 204 Employer's Deduction for Compensation

The employer may deduct compensation paid or incurred for personal services rendered to that employer in the carrying on of his trade or business.[134] If the compensation paid is partly for business purposes and partly for nonbusiness purposes, only the portion pertaining to business purposes is deductible. Under Reg. § 1.162-7(a), compensation is deductible only if:

(1) the payment is, in fact, compensation;

(2) the payment is made for services actually rendered by the employee; and

(3) the compensation payment is reasonable in amount.

All three conditions must be satisfied for compensation to be deductible. The following Sections cover these conditions in detail. In addition, the timing of compensation deductions will be explored.

.01 Deductible Compensation

As noted above, compensation is not deductible by an employer unless the payments made are, in fact, compensation payments

---

[132] *North American Oil Consolidated v. Burnet,* SCt, 3 USTC ¶943, 286 US 417, 53 SCt 613 (1932).

[133] *E.R. Lewis,* SCt, 51-1 USTC ¶9211, 340 US 590, 71 SCt 522.

[134] Code Sec. 162(a)(1).

made for services actually rendered to or for the employer and the payments are reasonable in amount.[135] The reasonableness criterion is separately covered below. This Section covers the first two requirements and related considerations.

Compensation Element. Under Reg. § 1.162-7(b)(1), a payment is deductible as compensation only if the payment is made for employee services and is not in substance a dividend or part of the purchase price of assets.

If "compensation" payments are actually payments for property, they cannot be deducted and, instead, must be capitalized. This may occur, for example, where a partnership sells all of its assets to a corporation and the partners become employees of the corporation. In such a case, some of the compensation paid to the former partners may constitute payment for the transfer of their business, and that portion is not deductible.[136] As another example, compensation for services rendered in organizing or starting a new company should be capitalized.[137]

An ostensible salary paid by a corporation may actually be a dividend payment. This may occur in the case of a corporation which has only a few shareholders, some or all of whom are compensated as employees. If in such a case, the payments are in excess of payments that would be paid for similar services, and the excessive payments correspond or bear a close relationship to the stockholdings of those shareholder-employees, some or all of the amounts paid will be treated as dividend payments. Such payments would not be deductible.[138] This point will be covered further in the discussion of reasonable compensation below.

Payments for Services Rendered. In general, compensation must be paid or incurred for personal services actually rendered in order to be deductible. Therefore, payments for services to be rendered in the future are not deductible.[139] Prepaid compensation is only deductible in the year the services are actually rendered.

Payments of compensation are deductible only if a bona fide employer-employee relationship exists. Thus, for example, reasonable compensation paid by a father to his minor child, who was found to be a bona fide employee rendering services to his father's business, was deductible.[140]

Compensation paid by corporations to their officers or employees for services rendered to related corporations is not deductible unless

---

[135] Reg. § 1.162-7(a).
[136] *See* Reg. § 1.162-7(b)(1).
[137] *Guarantee Bond and Mortgage Co.,* CA-6, 1930 CCH ¶ 9660, 44 F2d 297.

[138] Reg. § 1.162-7(b)(1).
[139] *See,* e.g., Code Sec. 461(h).
[140] Rev. Rul. 72-23, 1972-1 CB 43.

¶ 204.01

the payor corporation shows that it receives a direct benefit as a result of the services. Thus, a corporation cannot deduct payments to its officers for services performed for its subsidiaries to the extent that the services do not directly benefit the payor corporation.[141] However, compensation paid by a parent corporation to employees for services performed for a foreign subsidiary was deductible by the parent because the services were performed for the parent's benefit.[142]

If the services performed by employees benefit more than one corporation, the employing corporation may not deduct all of the compensation it pays to such employees. Some of the compensation may have to be allocated to each corporation that benefits from the services.

Form of the Compensation. Compensation need not be paid only in cash or by check. If the conditions for deductibility (listed above) are satisfied, compensation is deductible regardless of the form of payment (e.g., employer stock) or how the payments are referred to (e.g., bonuses, fees, commissions, etc.). Thus, most current compensation paid or provided to employees is deductible by the employer if the conditions of Code Sec. 162 are met. For example, the payment of household expenses of an employee for services rendered was held to be deductible compensation.[143] That is also true of most fringe benefits as indicated in Chapter 4. However, nonqualified deferred compensation is not covered by Code Sec. 162, and its deductibility depends upon the provisions of Code Sec. 404. Nonqualified deferred compensation is ordinarily deductible in the year it is taxable as ordinary income to the employee.

.02 Reasonable Compensation

The most prominent criterion underlying the deductibility of current and other forms of compensation is the requirement that the employer's payment of compensation must be "reasonable in amount." What is considered reasonable in amount will depend upon the facts and circumstances of each individual situation. Generally, but not always, the question of reasonableness arises in situations where compensation is paid to owner-employees of closely held corporations because of the actual or potential lack of arm's-length dealings in such situations. The IRS will scrutinize carefully any large payment of compensation to an officer of a corporation who is also a controlling shareholder, particularly in the cases where the corporation has a history of paying little or no dividends.

---

[141] *Great Island Holding Corp.*, 5 TC 150, Dec. 14,582 (1945).

[142] *Young & Rubicam, Inc.*, ClsCt, 69-1 USTC ¶ 9404, 410 F2d 1233, 187 ClsCt 635.

[143] *W.A. Montpetit*, 45 TCM 304, Dec. 39,561(M), TC Memo. 1982-715.

Historically, the reason for this close scrutiny is that C corporations have tended to favor making compensation payments, rather than dividends to shareholder-employees because, while both compensation and dividends have been fully taxable at regular rates to the recipients under Code Sec. 61, the compensation is deductible by the corporation, but the dividends are not. The payment of compensation, rather than dividends could maximize the overall wealth of the shareholders, since the compensation payments reduce the taxable income of the corporation, avoiding the double tax associated with dividend payments. The enactment of the special 15 percent tax rate for individual taxpayers (5 percent for taxpayers with marginal tax rates of 15 percent or less) on qualified dividend payments made by corporations in 2003 and later years under the Jobs Growth and Tax Relief Reconciliation Act of 2003 (JGTRRA) will lessen the disadvantage of dividend payments by dramatically reducing the impact of the double taxation of corporate income.[144] It is too early to tell how much impact this provision will have on the structure of payments made by C corporations (particularly closely-held C corporations) to their shareholder-employees. However, there should be somewhat less incentive for such corporations to make relatively large compensation payments and comparatively little or no dividend payments to their shareholder-employees while the special rates remain in effect. The enactment of the new special tax rates on dividends could also affect how unreasonable compensation payments are treated, as discussed below.

Reasonableness Factors. The Code does not specify any factors that can be used to determine the reasonableness of compensation. The regulations do not do much better. Under Reg. § 1.162-7(b)(3), reasonable compensation is "such amount as would ordinarily be paid for like services by like enterprises in like circumstances." Because of the lack of specific language in the regulations, the courts have developed most of the guidelines for determining whether compensation is reasonable in amount. However, the regulations do indicate that the circumstances existing at the date when the contract for services was made, not those existing at the date when the contract is questioned by the IRS, should be evaluated in determining the reasonableness of compensation.[145] Thus, contingent compensation (i.e., compensation, the amount of which is dependent upon the occurrence or nonoccurrence of certain events or the attainment of certain goals such as sales amounts) paid pursuant to an arm's-length agreement made prior to performance of

---

[144] Code Sec. 1(h)(11), as added by P.L. 108-27, 108th Cong., 1st Sess., Sec. 302(a) (May 28, 2003). The special rates on dividends are scheduled to be in effect for the years 2003 through 2008 under Sec. 303 of P.L. 108-27.

[145] Reg. § 1.162-7(b)(2).

the services will usually be considered reasonable.[146] However, contingent compensation payable to controlling shareholders who are also officers of a corporation may not be totally deductible particularly in cases where the corporation pays them little or no dividends. In such cases, some of the contingent compensation may actually be dividend payments.[147]

The courts have considered a variety of factors in deciding reasonable compensation cases. The importance of any particular factor or group of factors, however, can vary from case to case. In the final analysis, each case must be decided on the basis of its own facts.[148] Therefore, prior litigation can be best used to indicate the potential strength of various factors in particular types of factual situations.

One of the most widely quoted statements of the guidelines that courts have employed in deciding the issue of reasonableness of compensation appears in *Mayson Mfg. Co.*[149] The following factors are taken from the case:

(1) the employee's qualifications;

(2) the nature, extent, and scope of the employee's work;

(3) the size of the business;

(4) the complexities of the business;

(5) a comparison of salaries paid with the gross income and net income;

(6) the prevailing economic conditions;

(7) a comparison of salaries with distributions to stockholders;

(8) the prevailing rates of compensation for comparable positions in

(9) comparable concerns; and

(10) a presumption that salaries approved by a corporation's board of directors are reasonable and proper.

More recently, the Tax Court indicated that the reasonableness factors could be consolidated into the following five categories for the purpose of determining reasonableness of compensation (no one factor will be determinative in any particular case):[150]

(1) The employee's qualifications and role in the company, including factors such as the employee's position, hours worked, duties performed, and his/her overall contribution to the success of the company;

---

[146] Reg. § 1.162-7(b).

[147] *See,* e.g., *Hampton Corp.,* 23 TCM 899, Dec. 26,820(M), TC Memo. 1964-150, aff'd, CA-9, 65-2 USTC ¶ 9611.

[148] *See,* e.g., *Miller Mfg. Co., Inc.,* CA-4, 45-1 USTC ¶ 9293, 149 F2d 421.

[149] CA-6, 49-2 USTC ¶ 9467, 178 F2d 115.

[150] *See,* e.g., *Automotive Investment Development, Inc.,* 66 TCM 57, Dec. 49,140(M), TC Memo. 1993-298; and *Mortex Mfg. Co.,* 67 TCM 2412, Dec. 49,725(M), TC Memo. 1994-110.

(2) The character and condition of the company, including factors such as the size of the company, the complexity of its business, and the general economic conditions;

(3) A comparison of the employee's compensation with the compensation paid by similar companies for comparable services;

(4) The salary policy of the company for all its employees and the particular employee's salary history with the company; and

(5) The likelihood that a hypothetical, independent investor would be willing to compensate the employee at the levels paid by the company, taking into account dividends paid and capital growth.

The Ninth Circuit Court of Appeals in *Elliots, Inc.*[151] had earlier used a similar grouping of five factors. The court indicated that it is appropriate to evaluate the compensation payments from the perspective of a hypothetical independent investor under a factor category which it called "conflict of interest"—the primary issue in this category is whether some relationship exists between the employer company and its employee which might permit the company to disguise nondeductible distributions of income as deductible salary expenditures. As evidence that the five factors are still considered important in evaluating reasonable compensation cases, the Tax Court, in a 2004 case, used the five factors (because the case was appealable to the Ninth Circuit Court of Appeals) in determining that compensation paid to the 100 percent owner of the taxpayer-corporation was reasonable in amount.[152] It should be noted that the Seventh Circuit Court of Appeals has declined to use the multi-factor approach and has, instead, placed emphasis on the independent investor test (5th category above—see the discussion of the test below).[153] On the other hand, the Tenth Circuit Court of Appeals will continue to apply the multi-factor approach and not use the independent investor test.[154] The Fifth Circuit Court of Appeals continues to apply the ten factors listed above from the *Mayson Manufacturing* case (actually nine because that court combines the size and complexity of the business into one factor) in evaluating reasonable compensation cases.[155] It did say, however, that these include all of the factors listed in the five-factor grouping in the *Elliots* case stated above.

---

[151] CA-9, 83-2 USTC ¶ 9610, 716 F2d 1241, rev'g and rem'g, 40 TCM 802, Dec. 37,110(M). TC Memo. 1980-282. *See also Labelgraphics, Inc.*, CA-9, 2000-2 USTC ¶ 50,648, 221 F3d 1091, aff'g, 76 TCM 518, Dec. 52,889(M), TC Memo. 1998-343 and *Metro Leasing and Development Corp., et al*, 119 TC 8, Dec. 54,344(M), TC Memo. 2001-119.

[152] *Beiner, Inc.*, TC Memo 2004-219.

[153] *Exacto Spring Corp.*, CA-7, 99-2 USTC ¶ 50,964, 196 F3d 833, rev'g, 75 TCM 2522, Dec.

52,750(M). TC Memo. 1998-220 (*William J. Heitz*).

[154] *See Eberl's Claim Service, Inc.*, CA-10, 2001-1 USTC ¶ 50,396, 249 F3d 994, aff'g, 77 TCM 2336, Dec. 53,434(M). TC Memo. 1999-211.

[155] *See, e.g., Owensby and Kritikos, Inc.*, 819 F2d 1315 (CA-5, 1989); *Brewer Quality Homes*, CA-5, 94 AFTR2d 2004-7001, aff'g, TC Memo 2003-200; and *PK Ventures, Inc. and Subsidiaries*, TC Memo 2005-56.

Some of these factors from the *Mayson Manufacturing* case and the Tax Court grouping and others are discussed in the following paragraphs.

The qualification of the employee for the job is an important consideration in a majority of reasonable compensation cases. An employee with special training or experience can generally be paid a larger amount of compensation than an employee lacking such qualifications. For example, the Tax Court ruled that compensation paid to the president of eight corporations which operated retail gasoline stations and related businesses was reasonable, in large part because the president brought particular expertise, special knowledge of the petroleum industry, and experience in dealing with petroleum suppliers to the job.[156] In a more recent case, the Tax Court also held that compensation paid to an owner-employee who owned 60 percent of his company was reasonable on the basis of the employee's qualifications.[157] In that case, the Tax Court found the owner-employee, who is an engineer, possessed extensive technical expertise that few other individuals have and thus, was indispensable to the success of the company. Even a part-time employee with outstanding qualifications can be considered more valuable than a full-time employee without such special abilities.[158]

The nature, extent, and scope of the employee's work can also be an important factor. The more time an executive devotes to a company's business, the greater the amount of compensation that will be considered reasonable. For example, in *R. Clymer, Jr.,*[159] the Tax Court held that some of the compensation paid to Clymer, the sole stockholder and chief executive officer of Danison, was reasonable in amount, largely because Clymer worked long hours and controlled virtually every aspect of the firm's operations; he even opened the mail and signed most of the company's checks. Similarly, in *Hendricks Furniture, Inc.,*[160] the Tax Court carefully considered the owner-manager Hendricks's contributions to the employer's business in deciding that compensation paid to him was reasonable in amount. The Court stated that "we have before us a successful enterprise that is the progeny of Hendricks. He is the architect, enterprise general manager, and administrator of the business, and his ideas, efforts, and know-how have nursed it from its infancy." In another case, the Tax Court ruled that a relatively high amount of compensation paid to a director and chief executive officer

---

[156] *Bruce Oil Company,* 47 TCM 1728, Dec. 41,184(M), TC Memo. 1984-230.

[157] *W.J. Heitz.* TC Memo. 1998-220, 75 TCM 2522, Dec. 52.750(M).

[158] *Griswold Rubber Co., Inc.,* 24 TCM 184, Dec. 27,252(M), TC Memo. 1965-33.

[159] 47 TCM 1576, Dec. 41,152(M). TC Memo. 1984-203.

[160] 55 TCM 497, Dec. 44,666(M), TC Memo. 1988-133. *See also Law Offices of Richard Ashare, P.C.,* 78 TCM 348, Dec. 53,516(M), TC Memo. 1999-282.

of a corporation was reasonable in part because the corporation's growth and profitability were directly related to the executive's skills and to the services he provided.[161] For an example of a case where the courts have disallowed the deduction of compensation payments because the recipients did not play important roles in the corporation, see *Haffner's Service Stations*.[162] In that case, the First Circuit Court of Appeals upheld a Tax Court ruling that substantial bonuses that had been paid to two elderly shareholder-officers of a closely-held corporation were not deductible because the individuals had not made substantial contributions to the success of the corporation in the past and were not expected to in the future. If the employee divides his efforts between two or more businesses, the amount of work performed for each separate business is important in determining whether the compensation is reasonable.[163]

The size and complexity of the business is important. Key employees in large and complex businesses can often command greater compensation than their counterparts in smaller, less complex operations.[164] However, if the employee's influence over the business decreases as the business expands, the amount of compensation that will be considered reasonable will be less.[165] Thus, if an employee receives a substantial increase in salary without a corresponding increase in assigned duties or responsibilities, there is a presumption that some of the increased compensation is not reasonable.[166]

As noted earlier, the regulations indicate that reasonable compensation is the amount that is ordinarily paid for "like services" by "like enterprises" in "like circumstances."[167] Therefore, the amount of compensation received by individuals employed in similar positions in comparable businesses is an important factor in evaluating the reasonableness of compensation paid to an employee. If employees in substantially similar circumstances are paid less than the employee in question, it is likely that some of the compensation paid to that employee will be deemed unreasonable. For example, in *J.H. Rutter*,[168] compensation paid to shareholder-officers of Rutter Rex Corporation, a company in the garment industry, was found to be unreasonable where the top officers of similar companies were

---

[161] *Universal Mfg. Co, Inc., et al.,* 68 TCM 305, Dec. 50,014(M), TC Memo. 1994-367. *See also Max Burton Enterprises,* 74 TCM 652, Dec. 52,254(M), TC Memo. 1997-421.

[162] CA-1, 2003-1 USTC ¶ 50,333, 326 F3d 1. Aff'g 83 TCM 1211, Dec 54,644(M). TC Memo. 2002-38 (2002).

[163] *Henry Miller Spring and Mfg. Co.,* 34 TCM 1400. Dec. 33,485(M), TC Memo. 1975-323.

[164] *See,* e.g., *Idaho Livestock Auction, Inc.,* DC Ida., 60-2 USTC ¶ 9597, 187 FSupp 875.

[165] *Saia Electric, Inc.,* 33 TCM 1357, Dec. 32,846(M), TC Memo. 1974-290, aff'd, CA-5 (unpublished opinion 7-16-76).

[166] *Turkey Creek, Inc.,* 54 TCM 326, Dec. 44,151(M), TC Memo. 1987-429.

[167] Reg. § 1.167-7(b)(3).

[168] 52 TCM 326, Dec. 43,316(M), TC Memo. 1986-407, *aff'd,* CA-5, 88-2 USTC ¶ 9500.

¶ 204.02

generally paid less compensation on the average, based on a study by a compensation expert who testified before the court. Higher compensation than that paid to similarly situated employees in comparable firms would be justifiable only in cases where the employee possesses special qualifications and capabilities above those typically encountered in the particular line of work. It should be noted that the comparison of compensation paid in another company to that of the employee is relevant only if it shows that the other company is substantially similar to that of the employee's employer and that the positions being compared at the two companies are substantially similar. The comparison must be based on the duties performed by the employee rather than on the basis of the title of the position.[169]

The amount of a particular employee's compensation compared to the amount paid to other employees of the same business can be an important factor. If an employee's compensation is considerably larger than amounts paid to other employees of the business, that employee must perform services or possess qualifications which justify the additional compensation.[170] This factor can best be established by proving that similar amounts would have been paid by the corporation to a non owner-employee performing the same services.[171]

The comparability of compensation paid to the employee in the current year to that paid in previous years may also be considered by the courts. For example, in *R.J. Armstrong and Co., Inc.,*[172] the court held that the compensation of the corporation's officers was reasonable in amount in part because the compensation was based on the same percentage of gross sales that had been used to figure the officer's compensation during the previous eight years. An employee's current level of compensation may also be justified by showing that the employee was undercompensated in prior years.[173] For instance, in *United Title Insurance Company,*[174] the Tax Court held that at least some of the compensation paid to a majority stockholder-employee was reasonable because it was for services performed by the employee in previous years. The taxpayer was successful in proving that, as a new business, it could not afford to pay the employee much in its early years. It therefore paid the employee extra compensation in later, more profitable years to make up for the earlier underpayments. The Tax Court made a

---

[169] *Tricon Metals and Services, Inc.,* 74 TCM 287, Dec. 52,191(M), TC Memo. 1997-360.

[170] *See, e.g., Drexel Park Pharmacy, Inc.,* 39 TCM 788, Dec. 36,701(M), TC Memo. 1979-518

[171] *Affiliated Enterprises, Inc.,* CA-10, 41-2 USTC ¶ 9735, 123 F2d 665 (1941).

[172] 12 TCM 94, Dec. 19,452(M), TC Memo. 1953-38.

[173] *Old Colony Insurance Service, Inc.,* 41 TCM 1258, Dec. 37,827(M), TC Memo. 1981-177.

[174] 55 TCM 34, Dec. 44,552(M). TC Memo. 1988-38.

similar finding more recently in *Devine Brothers, Inc.*[175] In that case, the Tax Court determined that the taxpayer had been undercompensated in earlier years in order that his employer would meet bonding requirements. The taxpayer's compensation in the year at issue was reasonable because it was intended to compensate the taxpayer for his undercompensation in the prior years.

As noted above, the Tax Court has taken into account the likelihood that a hypothetical, independent investor would be willing to compensate the employee at the levels paid by the company, taking account of dividends paid and capital growth. For example, in *Donald Palmer Company, Inc.*[176] the Tax Court found that the compensation paid an officer-shareholder in the company resulted in negative retained earnings and a negative return on shareholder equity. Thus, the court could not conclude that an independent investor would sustain the amount of compensation paid. This factor contributed to the finding that the compensation paid was not reasonable in amount. In *Universal Manufacturing Co., Inc., et al.,*[177] the Tax Court in evaluating this factor determined that an independent investor would approve the amount of compensation paid to the chief executive and director of the company because the company earned an 18.7 percent return on equity. Recently, the Second Circuit Court of Appeals vacated and remanded a Tax Court decision (that had found some of the compensation paid to an employee to be reasonable) on the basis that the Tax Court should have assessed the entire company's situation from the viewpoint of an independent investor.[178] That is, given the company's dividend payments and return on equity, would that investor approve the compensation paid to the employee? According to the court, the "independent investor test" is not a separate autonomous factor; rather, it provides a lens through which the entire analysis should be viewed. On remand, the Tax Court found only the same amount of compensation to be reasonable as it did in its initial 1995 ruling holding that an independent investor would not have sustained the amount of compensation allowed to Lynn, the shareholder-employee, by the corporation.[179] In addition, the Ninth Circuit Court of Appeals also gave great weight to the independent investor test in a recent case in which it overturned a Tax Court decision.[180] That court stated that the test is "the most productive

---

[175] 85 TCM 768, Dec. 55,018(M), TC Memo. 2003-15.

[176] 69 TCM 1869, Dec. 50,474(M), TC Memo. 1995-65. *See also Brewer Quality Mobile Homes Inc.,* 86 TCM 29, Dec. 55,219(M), TC Memo. 2003-200.

[177] 68 TCM 305, Dec. 50,014(M), TC Memo 1994-367.

[178] *Dexsil Corp.,* CA-2, 98-1 USTC ¶ 50,471, 147 F3d 96, vac'g and rem'g, 69 TCM 2267, Dec. 50,552(M), TC Memo. 1995-135.

[179] *Dexsil Corp.,* 77 TCM 1973. Dec. 53,372(M), TC Memo. 1999-155. *See also Wagner Construction, Inc.,* 81 TCM 1869, Dec. 54,390(M), TC Memo. 2001-160.

[180] *Leonard Pipeline Contractors, Ltd.,* CA-9, 98-1 USTC ¶ 50,356, 142 F3d 1133. rev'g and rem'g. 72 TCM 83, Dec. 51,443(M), TC Memo. 1996-316. *See also Beiner, Inc.,* TC Memo 2004-219.

way to approach reasonable compensation cases in closely-held corporations." As indicated in an earlier paragraph, the Seventh Circuit Court of Appeals in *Exacto Spring Corporation*[181] has also endorsed the independent investor test which it said should be emphasized instead of a multi-factor test. The court stated that the multi-factor analysis used by the Tax Court in this case leaves "much to be desired being, like many other multi-factor tests, redundant, incomplete and unclear." In *Menard, Inc.,*[182] the Tax Court (in a case appealable to the Seventh Circuit Court of Appeals) recently applied the independent investor test in stating that the rate of return on investment raised a presumption of reasonableness as to the amount of compensation paid to John R. Menard, the president, CEO and 89 percent shareholder of the company. The court, however, found that this presumption was rebutted by the fact that John Menard's compensation significantly exceeded that of compensation paid to CEOs of comparable companies such as Lowe's. This holding was upheld by the Tax Court in an early 2005 reported decision when it denied Menard's motion for reconsideration of the case. In summary, it appears that the independent investor test is attaining greater importance in reasonable compensation cases as the new century begins.

Finally, the recently enacted burden of proof shifting rules enacted as part of the IRS Restructuring and Reform Act of 1998[183] could have an impact on some situations where the IRS is questioning the reasonableness of compensation paid to employees. Under these rules, the burden of proof will be shifted to the IRS in a civil court action if the taxpayer introduces credible evidence with respect to a factual issue (in reasonable compensation cases, credible evidence could presumably include objective, verifiable evidence relating to the compensation payments and why they are reasonable in amount). However, the burden of proof cannot be shifted in cases involving corporations, trusts, and partnerships which have a net worth in excess of $7 million.[184] Thus, only small or relatively unprofitable businesses will not be able to shift the burden of proof in reasonable compensation and other cases. Further, even if an employer business meets the net worth test, it must also meet two other standards. First, the taxpayer must comply with the various substantiation and record-keeping requirements of the Internal Revenue Code and Treasury Regulations.[185] Second, the taxpayer must cooperate with reasonable requests by the IRS for witnesses, information, documents, meetings, and interviews.[186] Because of

---

[181] *Exacto Spring Corp.,* CA-7, 99-2 USTC ¶ 50,964. 196 F3d 833, rev'g, 75 TCM 2522, Dec. 52,750(M), TC Memo. 1998-220 (*William J. Heitz*).
[182] TC Memo 2004-207 and TC Memo 2005-3.

[183] Code Sec. 7491, as added by P.L. 105–206, 105th Cong., 2d Sess. (July 22, 1998).
[184] Code Sec. 7491(a)(2)(C).
[185] Code Sec. 7491(a)(2)(A).
[186] Code Sec. 7491(a)(2)(B).

these requirements, and because (a) the IRS is likely to be more intrusive at the administrative and trial level to meet its potential burden of proof and (b) the taxpayer has to exhaust all administrative remedies before being able to attempt to shift the burden of proof, many taxpayers may want to steer clear of attempting to shift the burden of proof to the IRS in reasonable compensation cases.

The Corporation's Dividend Payments.   As noted at the beginning of this Section, the IRS has scrutinized large amounts of compensation paid to shareholder-employees when the corporation has been paying little or no dividends. This is particularly true where compensation is partly or totally paid in proportion to the ownership interests of the shareholder-employees.[187] As a result of the Court of Claims decision in *C. McCandless Tile Service,*[188] the IRS for many years tried to impose the "automatic dividend rule." In *McCandless Tile,* the court ruled that when no dividends are paid, some of the compensation paid to shareholder-employees must be characterized as a dividend even if it is reasonable in amount. Fortunately for taxpayers, the IRS lost time after time in later decisions when it tried to impose this guideline. The Ninth Circuit Court of Appeals in *Elliots, Inc.*[189] rejected the application of the automatic dividend rule, and the court will not presume an element of disguised dividend from the bare fact that a profitable corporation does not pay dividends. The Court gave three reasons for this rejection: (1) there is no statute that requires profitable corporations to pay dividends; (2) the automatic dividend rule is based on the faulty premise that shareholders of a profitable corporation will demand dividends; and (3) it may well be in the best interests of the corporations to retain and reinvest its earnings. Finally, in Rev. Rul. 79-8,[190] the IRS abandoned the automatic dividend rule. Nevertheless, it will continue to construe the amount of dividends paid to shareholders who are also receiving compensation in assessing the reasonableness of the compensation. To prevail against the negative impact of little or no dividend payments, the taxpayer will need to prove that legitimate reasons dictated the small or non-existent dividends. For example, in *W.C. Neils,*[191] the court ruled that although no dividends were paid during the company's first ten years of operation, there was a sufficient reason for this lack of payment. The company showed that it had engaged in numerous developments that required large amounts of capital.

---

[187] *See.* e.g., *RTS Investment Corp.,* 53 TCM 171, Dec. 43,717(M), TC Memo. 1987–98.

[188] CtCls, 70-1 USTC ¶ 9284, 422 F2d 1336, 191 CtCls 108.

[189] CA-9, 83-2 USTC ¶ 9610, 716 F2d 1241, rev'g and rem'g, 40 TCM 802, Dec. 37,110(M), TC Memo. 1980-282.

[190] 1979-1 CB 92.

[191] 43 TCM 982, Dec. 38,909(M). TC Memo. 1982-173.

¶ 204.02

Certain recent cases, however, tend to show an increased emphasis on the lack of dividend payments by corporations paying compensation to owner-employees. Despite its earlier rejection of the automatic dividend rule (noted in the above paragraph), the Ninth Circuit Court of Appeals concentrated on the lack of dividend payments in upholding a Tax Court ruling disallowing the deduction of all compensation paid to shareholder-employees in *O.S.C. Associates, Inc.*[192] While the Ninth Circuit did not embrace the automatic dividend rule in this case or attempt to adopt some other quantitative analysis, it agreed with the Tax Court that compensatory intent underlying payments to shareholders cannot be inferred merely because the total amounts paid represent reasonable compensation. The Ninth Circuit noted that if there is evidence that the payments contain disguised dividends, the corporation must separately satisfy both the reasonableness and the compensatory intent prongs of the test for deductibility of compensation. The Ninth Circuit went on to agree with the Tax Court that there was no compensatory intent behind the payments (for a number of reasons including that no dividends had been paid and that an extremely high percentage of net income had been paid to the shareholder-officers) and, thus, the payments were not deductible.

Finally, it should be noted that the enactment of the special 15 percent tax rate for individual taxpayers (5 percent for taxpayers with marginal rates of 15 percent or lower) on qualified dividend payments made by corporations beginning in 2003 under JGTRRA[193] could have an impact on how aggressively the IRS may pursue the reasonable compensation issue when little or no dividends are paid. If unreasonable compensation payments were treated as dividend payments eligible for the 15 percent or lower tax rate, the IRS would not gain as much revenue as in the past by successfully disallowing the corporate deduction of payments that would otherwise be taxed to the recipients at a rate as high as 35 percent (not counting payroll taxes).

Application of the Reasonableness Test. The general rule is that all compensation is subject to the reasonableness test. Thus, salaries, bonuses, commissions, and other forms of current compensation are subject to the test. Deferred compensation will also be reviewed by the IRS for reasonableness. The reasonableness of qualified deferred compensation is determined in the year the employer makes contributions to the trust or other funding vehicle rather than when distributions are received by the employee.[194]

---

[192] CA-9, 99-2 USTC ¶50,765, 187 F3d 1116, aff'g, 73 TCM 3231, Dec. 52,127(M), TC Memo, 1997-300. Cert. denied, 120 SCt 1831.

[193] Code Sec 1(h)(11). as added by P.L. 108-27, 108th Cong., 1st Sess., Sec 302(a) (May 28, 2003).

The special rates on qualified dividends will be in effect from 2003 through 2008 under Sec. 303 of P.L. 108-27.

[194] Reg. § 1.404(a)-1(b).

The reasonableness of nonqualified deferred compensation will be determined for the year the compensation is paid because the employer cannot deduct such compensation until the year in which it is taxable to the employee.[195] The new rules under Code Sec. 409A[196] that generally apply for amounts deferred under nonqualified plans after 2004 (see Chapter 14 for a coverage of those rules) will have an impact on this rule in cases where the deferred amounts are taxable in a year earlier than when paid pursuant to Code Sec. 409A.

Fringe benefits such as health and accident plans (Code Sec.104–106) and group-term life insurance plans (Code Sec. 79) must be reasonable in amount to be deductible.[197] However, there are few cases where the reasonableness of fringe benefits has been questioned. In *Ernest, Holdeman and Collet, Inc.,*[198] the Tax Court refused to consider health insurance premiums paid on behalf of officers of the corporation as unreasonable, even though it found that salaries paid to the same individuals were not totally reasonable in amount. However, in *Sanders and Sons, Inc.,*[199] the Tax Court stated that employer payments of medical expenses under a medical plan had to be reasonable in amount in order to be deductible. In addition, in *W.C. Neils*[200] the Tax Court held that the collective amount of compensation paid or provided to an employee, including bonuses and pension plan contributions, must be taken into account under the facts and circumstances in determining whether the compensation is reasonable in amount.

Impact of Compensation Being Found Unreasonable. Where it is ruled that part or all of the compensation paid to an employee is not reasonable in amount, the amount has been typically treated as a dividend distribution where a shareholder-employee is involved.[201] Thus, the unreasonable amount has been fully includible by the employee and not deductible by the corporation. The result has been a double tax that should be avoided. Perhaps the one bit of silver lining in this cloud is that the amount of compensation that is recharacterized as a dividend payment will not be subject to FICA and FUTA taxes, thereby reducing payroll taxes.

The enactment of the special 15 percent tax rate (5 percent for taxpayers with marginal rates of 15 percent or lower) on the receipt of qualified dividends by individual shareholders beginning in 2003

---

[195] *See* Temp. Reg. §§ 1.404(a)-1T and 1.404(b)-1T. *See also Nelson Brothers, Inc.,* 64 TCM 1594, Dec. 48,708(M), TC Memo. 1992-726.

[196] Code Sec. 409A, as added by P.L. 108-357, 108th Cong., 2d Sess., Sec. 885(a) (Oct. 22, 2004).

[197] Reg. § 1.162-10.

[198] 19 TCM 42, Dec. 24,030(M). TC Memo. 1960-10, aff'd, CA-7, 61-1 USTC ¶ 9398, 290 F2d 3.

[199] 26 TCM 671, Dec. 28,536(M). TC Memo. 1967-146.

[200] 43 TCM 982, Dec. 38,909(M). TC Memo. 1982-173.

[201] Reg. § 1.162-8.

¶ 204.02

under JGTRRA[202] could have an impact on the tax treatment of compensation found to be unreasonable in amount. Will unreasonable compensation be treated as qualified dividend payments subject to the special rates? The answer may hinge on whether the unreasonable compensation can be classified as dividend payments made out of earnings and profits. Unfortunately, the Committee Reports on the special rates do not provide any guidance concerning this issue.[203] As of the publication date of this book, the IRS had not issued any guidance concerning this issue.

Repayment of Disallowed Compensation. The double taxation of corporate income that results when compensation is declared unreasonable in amount can sometimes be avoided if the unreasonable portion of the compensation is paid back to the employer.

To protect against the possible double tax, the employee can contract with the employer to pay back the portion of any compensation that is determined to be unreasonable. But it should be noted that such a repayment arrangement could cause a court to find that the corporation's payments for compensation were unreasonable. In essence, such an agreement may raise a red flag to the IRS and the courts. For example, in *C. Schneider & Co., Inc.,*[204] a closely held corporation entered into an agreement that required the shareholder-officers to pay back any compensation received if the amounts were later declared by a court to be unreasonable. The court stated that the agreement indicated that the taxpayers believed that the payments would not be reasonable for tax purposes and thus did not permit a deduction for the full amount of bonuses paid.

¶ 205 $1 Million Limitation on Executive Compensation Deduction

After 1993, Code Sec. 162(m), as enacted by the Revenue Reconciliation Act of 1993, denies a deduction for compensation paid in excess of $1 million to certain top executives of publicly held U.S. corporations.[205]

.01 Publicly Held Corporations

Only executive compensation paid by publicly held corporations is subject to the $1 million limitation. Under Code Sec. 162(m)(2), a

---

[202] Code Sec. 1(h)(11), as added by P.L. 108-27, 108th Cong., 1st Sess., Sec. 302(a) (May 28, 2003). The special rates apply to qualified dividends received in the years 2003 through 2008 under Sec. 303 of P.L. 108-27.

[203] H.R. Conf. Rep. No 108-126, 108th Cong., 1st Sess (May 28, 2003).

[204] CA-8, 74-2 USTC ¶ 9563, 500 F2d 148, cert. denied, 420 US 908. *See also Menard, Inc.,* TC Memo 2004-207 and 2005-3.

[205] Code Sec. 162(m), as added by Sec. 13,211(a), P.L. 103-66, 103rd Cong., 1st Sess. (Aug. 10, 1993).

publicly held corporation is any corporation that issues common equity securities that must be registered under Section 12 of the Securities Exchange Act of 1934. This generally includes corporations whose securities are listed on a national securities exchange or who have $5 million or more of assets and 500 or more holders of such securities. A corporation is not considered publicly held if the registration of its securities is voluntary.[206]

Under Reg. § 1.162-27(c)(1), whether a corporation is a publicly held corporation is to be determined on the basis of the facts on the last day of its taxable year. Under this rule, if a corporation reports income on a calendar-year basis, the corporation is subject to Code Sec. 162(m) only if its common equity Securities are required to be registered under the Securities Exchange Act on December 31 of that year. Thus, a corporation that "goes private" during a given year is not subject to Code Sec. 162(m) for that year. Additionally, Code Sec. 162(m) will not apply to compensation plans or arrangements that are in existence when a corporation becomes a publicly held corporation if those plans or arrangements are adequately disclosed as part of the public offering.

Reg. § 1.162-27(c)(1) states that a publicly held corporation includes an affiliated group of corporations as defined in Code Sec. 1504. If a covered employee is paid compensation in a given year by more than one member of an affiliated group, compensation paid by each member of the group is aggregated. Any amount not allowed as a deduction by Code Sec. 162(m) must then be prorated among the payor corporations in proportion to the amount of compensation paid to the covered employee by each of the paying corporations.

For this purpose, an affiliated group does not include any subsidiary that is itself a publicly held corporation. Such a publicly held subsidiary and its subsidiaries are separately subject to the $1 million deduction limitation. However, under a special transition rule specified in Reg. § 1.162-27(j)(2), separate publicly held subsidiaries were not to be subject to the $1 million deduction limitation on their own until the first regularly scheduled meeting of the shareholders of the publicly held subsidiary that occurred more than 12 months after December 2, 1994. In addition, the $1 million deduction limitation does not apply to compensation paid to covered employees of a subsidiary that becomes a separate publicly held corporation pursuant to a plan or agreement that existed before December 2, 1994, provided that the treatment of that compensation as performance based is in accordance with a reasonable, good faith interpretation of the rules governing the $1 million deduction limitation.

---

[206] H.R. Rep. No. 103–213. 103rd Cong., 1st Sess. (1993), at p.93.

¶ 205.01

.02 Covered Executive Employees

Under Code Sec. 162(m)(3), executive employees whose pay is subject to the new limit are (1) the chief executive officer of the corporation (or an employee who acts in that capacity) as of the close of the year and (2) those employees whose total compensation must be reported to the corporation's shareholders because they are among the four highest compensated officers for the taxable year (other than the chief executive officer). If such disclosure is required with respect to fewer than four executives (other than the chief executive) under the rules of the Securities and Exchange Commission (SEC), only those for whom disclosure is required are covered employees.[207]

Reg. § 1.162-27(c)(2) further indicates that an individual is a "covered employee" if the individual's compensation is reported on the "summary compensation table" under the SEC's executive compensation disclosure rules. In addition, an individual must be employed as an executive officer on the last day of the taxable year before he or she can be considered a covered employee.

The IRS has privately held that corporate officers of a target corporation that was merged into an acquiring corporation were not covered employees of the target for the merger year where (1) the officers resigned before the last day of the tax year with no intent to resume their duties and (2) the target corporation was not required to file a summary compensation table with the SEC.[208]

.03 Covered Compensation

Only covered compensation (referred to as "applicable employee remuneration" in the statute) paid to the covered executives is subject to the limit. Under Code Sec. 162(m)(4), covered compensation includes all cash and noncash benefits paid for services performed as an employee of the corporation other than:

(1) compensation payable on a commission basis;

(2) compensation payable solely on the attainment of one or more performance goals if certain outside director and shareholder approval requirements are met;

(3) payments to or from a qualified retirement plan (including salary reduction contributions);

---

[207] *Supra* note 201, pp. 93 and 94.
[208] IRS Letter Ruling 200039028, 6-29-2000, CCH IRS LETTER RULINGS REPORTS. *See also* IRS Letter Ruling 200152003, 9-14-2001, IRS Letter Ruling 200216001, 10-17-2001, and IRS Letter Ruling 200219016, 2-5-2002, CCH IRS LETTER RULINGS REPORTS.

(4) amounts excludable from an executive's gross income (such as employer health and accident insurance plan contributions); and

(5) any compensation payable under a written binding contract which was in effect on February 17, 1993.

The $1 million threshold is reduced by excess golden parachute payments that are not deductible under Code Sec. 280G (discussed in Chapter 3).

An example of the determination of what constitutes covered compensation (applicable employee remuneration) in a specific fact situation is provided in Letter Ruling 9745002. In that ruling, the IRS held that payments made to a former CEO who retired from the employer corporation and, later returned as CEO within the same year were not applicable employer remuneration. The distributions received from the corporation's pension plan were excluded from the definition as payments made under a qualified plan. In addition, consulting fees paid to the retired CEO were not included in the definition because they were not for services performed as an employee. Finally, the IRS also held that director's fees paid to the CEO were not considered to be applicable employee remuneration because the CEO did not perform those services as an employee of the corporation.

The deduction limitation applies when the deduction is otherwise allowed to the employer. For example, in the case of nonqualified stock options (discussed in Chapter 15), the deduction is normally taken in the year the option is exercised rather than the earlier year of the grant. In the case of such compensation, the deduction limitation would apply in the exercise year if the employee is still covered by the $1 million limitation rules.[209]

.04 Commissions Paid

In order to qualify for the commissions-paid exception, the commission must be payable solely on account of income generated directly by the individual job performance of the executive receiving the compensation (e.g., compensation paid as a percentage of sales dollars generated by the executive).[210] Under Reg. § 1.162-27(d), compensation does not fail to be attributable directly to the job performance of the executive merely because support services, such as secretarial and research services, are utilized in generating the income. However, if compensation is paid because of broader performance standards, such as income produced by a business unit of the

---

[209] *Supra* note 201, p.94; Reg. § 1.162-27(c)(3)(i).   [210] *Supra* note 201, pp. 94 and 95.

¶ 205.04

corporation, the compensation does not qualify for the commissions-paid exception.

.05 Other Performance-Based Compensation

Under Code Sec. 162(m)(4)(C), covered compensation (applicable employee remuneration) does not include other compensation payable solely on account of the attainment of one or more performance goals if:

(1) the performance goals are established by a compensation committee of the board of directors which includes only two or more outside directors (as defined below);

(2) the material terms of the compensation, including performance goals, are disclosed to shareholders and approved by a separate majority vote before payment; and

(3) the compensation committee certifies that the performance goals and other material terms were satisfied before payment.

Performance-based compensation (other than stock options and other stock appreciation rights) is considered paid solely for the attainment of performance goals if it is paid pursuant to a preestablished objective performance standard by which a third party with knowledge of the performance results could calculate the amount paid. Specific performance standards include increases in stock price, market share, sales, and earnings per share.[211] However, Reg. § 1.162-27(e)(2)(i) indicates that a performance goal need not be based upon an increase or positive result under a business criterion and could include, for example, maintaining the status quo or limiting economic losses. A performance goal does not include the mere continued employment of the covered employee. Thus, a vesting provision based only on continued employment would not constitute a performance goal.

Under Reg. § 1.162-27(e)(2)(i), a performance goal is considered preestablished if it is established in writing by the compensation committee not later than 90 days after the commencement of the period of service to which the performance goal relates, provided that the outcome is substantially uncertain at the time the compensation committee actually establishes the goal. However, in no event will a performance goal be considered preestablished if it is established after 25 percent of the period of service (as scheduled at the time the goal is established) has elapsed. Thus, if a bonus is to be paid on the basis of an increase in sales during 2004, this performance goal would have to be established before the end of March of 2004.

---

[211] *Supra* note 201, p. 95; Reg. § 1.162-27(e)(2)(ii).

Under Reg. § 1.62-27(e)(2)(ii), the terms of the performance goal must, in general, be fixed and objective, and the amount of the compensation must be nondiscretionary. However, Reg. § 1.62-27(e)(2)(iii) indicates that a performance goal is not discretionary merely because the compensation committee reduces or eliminates the compensation that was due upon attainment of the goal. The exercise of negative discretion with respect to one employee cannot result in an increase in the amount payable to another. For example, in the case of a bonus pool, the sum of the individual percentages in the pool cannot exceed 100 percent. However, under a special transition rule contained in Reg. § 1.162-27(j)(2)(iv), the 100 percent limit on bonus pools did not apply to compensation paid before January 1, 2001, based on performance in any performance period that began before December 20, 1995. If compensation is payable upon or after the attainment of a performance goal, and a change is made to accelerate the payment of the compensation to an earlier date after the attainment of the goal, the change will be treated as an increase in the amount of the compensation, unless the amount of compensation paid is discounted to reasonably reflect the time value of money.

Under Reg. §§ 1.162-27(e)(2)(iv) and (v), the determination of whether compensation to be paid meets the performance goal exception is to be made on a grant-by-grant basis. For example, whether compensation attributable to a stock option grant meets the performance goal requirements is determined on the basis of the particular grant made and without regard to the terms of any other option grant, or other grant of compensation, to the same or another employee. Further, compensation will not meet the performance goal exception if the facts and circumstances indicate the employee would receive all or part of the compensation even if the performance goal is not attained.

Outside Director. For purposes of the performance-based compensation rules, the compensation committee requirement is met if the outside director members are not (1) current employees of the corporation, (2) former employees still receiving compensation for past services, (3) officers of the corporation, and (4) recipients of current compensation for any other reason than serving as directors.[212]

Under Reg. § 1.162-27(e)(3)(ii), for purposes of determining whether an individual is receiving additional compensation other than director's fees, direct and indirect payments for goods and

---

[212] *Supra* note 201, p.96; Reg. § 1.162-27(e)(3)(i). *See* IRS Letter Ruling 200423012 for an example of a situation where a former executive of a corporation qualified as an outside director who could help set the performance-based compensation goals of the corporation.

services must be considered. Compensation is considered to be received, directly or indirectly, by a director in each of the following circumstances:

(1) if compensation is paid to the director personally or to an entity in which the director has a beneficial ownership interest of greater than 50 percent;

(2) if compensation, other than de minimis compensation (covered below) was paid by the publicly held corporation in its preceding taxable year to an entity in which the director has a beneficial ownership interest of at least five percent but not more than 50 percent;

(3) if compensation, other than de minimis compensation, was paid by the publicly held corporation in its preceding taxable year to an entity by which the director is employed or self-employed other than as a director.

In general, compensation received by a director for other purposes is considered de minimis if the payments did not exceed the lesser of (a) $60,000 or (b) five percent of the gross revenue of the entity for its taxable year ending with or within the preceding taxable year of the corporation. For an example of the application of the de minimis compensation exception, see Letter Ruling 9731006.

Shareholder Approval. In the case of performance-based compensation other than stock options, the shareholder-approval requirement is met if the shareholders approve the specific terms of the compensation plan as well as the class of executives to which it applies. For stock option plans, the shareholders must approve the specific terms of the plan, the class of executives to which it applies, the option price or price-setting formula, and the maximum number of shares that can be awarded under the plan to any executive. Once the option plan has been approved, no further approval is required unless the plan is later materially changed.[213]

Disclosure to the shareholders should be specific. Reg. § 1.162-27(e)(4) indicates that the disclosure must include (1) a description of the broad class of employees (such as salaried employees or executive officers) who are eligible to receive compensation under a performance goal; (2) a general description of the terms of the goal; and (3) either the formula for computing the compensation or the maximum dollar amount that will be paid if the performance goal is satisfied. However, the specific targets under a performance goal need not be disclosed to shareholders. Thus, for example, if a performance goal were based on an increase in net profits of five

---

[213] *Supra* note 201, p. 97.

percent, the disclosure to shareholders would be required to state only that the performance goal is based on net profits. In addition, no disclosure is required of confidential commercial or business information. For this purpose, information is confidential if, under the facts and circumstances, disclosure of the information would adversely affect the publicly held corporation.

Reg. § 1.162-27(e)(4)(vi) states that once the material terms of a performance goal are disclosed to and approved by the shareholders, no additional disclosure or approval is required unless the compensation committee changes the material terms of the performance goal. For this purpose, the IRS ruled in Letter Ruling 9613006 that a proposed change to a compensation plan made in response to a modification of SEC rules is not a material change that must be approved by the employer corporation's shareholders. The material terms of a performance goal are considered approved by the shareholders if, in a separate vote, a majority of the votes cast on the issue are cast in favor of approval. Further, the IRS has held that in a case where (1) the performance goals of a performance-based compensation plan were approved by the shareholders of a corporation that was later merged into another corporation and (2) by operation of state law, the acquiring corporation assumed all rights, powers and obligations under the acquired corporation's compensation plans, the shareholders of the acquiring corporation did not have to approve the performance goals under the plan. In effect, the shareholder approval in the acquired corporation survived the merger and was held to constitute shareholder approval in the newly merged corporation. In addition, the IRS held that the eligibility criteria of the plan were not deemed to be modified as a result of the merger, and thus, no additional shareholder approval was required with respect to payments made under the plan to employees of the acquiring corporation's subsidiaries which were subsidiaries of the acquiring corporation prior to the merger.[214]

.06 Stock Option and Other Stock Appreciation Rights

Stock options and similar rights generally qualify for the performance-based compensation exception if the compensation committee and shareholder approval requirements are met. Specifically, Reg. § 1.162-27(e)(2)(vi) indicates that a stock option or stock appreciation right will satisfy the preestablished performance goal requirement where (1) the grant or award is made by the compensation committee; (2) the plan includes a per-employee limitation on

---

[214] IRS Letter Ruling 9801043, 10-2-97, CCH IRS LETTER RULINGS REPORTS. *See also* IRS Letter Ruling 200104022, 10-25-2000, CCH IRS LETTER RULINGS REPORTS, for a similar factual situation and ruling.

the number of shares for which options or stock appreciation rights may be granted during a specified period; and (3) the exercise price of the option or base amount of the stock appreciation right is no less than the fair market value of the stock on the date of the grant or award. The certification of the performance goal requirement need not be met because the amount of compensation depends exclusively on future stock prices. In the case of stock options, the directors may retain discretion as to the exact number to be granted to an executive if the maximum number that can be granted has been predetermined. The IRS has recently issued several private rulings in which it held that nonqualified stock options qualified as performance-based compensation not subject to the $1 million deduction limitation.[215] For example, the IRS held that compensation attributable to the exercise of stock options that were granted to an executive of the business when the business was formed qualifies as performance-based compensation. The IRS found that (1) the amount of the compensation was dependent solely upon the increase in the value of the stock after it was granted, (2) the number of shares were specifically stated, and (3) the shareholder approval and adequate disclosure requirements were satisfied.[216]

If the stock options are granted at prices below market value at the time of the grant or the employee is protected through a price-reducing feature, they are not treated as performance-based pay. In addition, restricted stock compensation (as covered in Chapter 14) does not qualify as performance-based compensation since the employee may receive the compensation regardless of the future stock price unless the grant or vesting of the stock is based on a performance goal and otherwise meets the performance-based compensation requirements.[217]

.07 Privately Held Company

Reg. § 1.162-27(f) covers rules concerning privately held companies that become publicly held during the year. If a corporation was not publicly held for the entire taxable year, the Code Sec. 162(m) deduction limit does not apply to any compensation plan or agreement that existed during the period in which the corporation was not publicly held to the extent that the prospectus accompanying the initial public offering disclosed information concerning such plans or agreements in accordance with established securities laws. For

---

[215] *See* IRS Letter Ruling 9942012, IRS Letter Ruling 200016024, 1-19-2000, IRS Letter Ruling 200027047, 5-10-2000, IRS Letter Ruling 200051018, 9-18-2000, and IRS Letter Ruling 200104020, 10-24-2000, CCH IRS Letter Rulings Reports. *See also* Chief Counsel Advice 200133014, 5-16-2001, CCH IRS Letter Rulings Reports.

[216] IRS Letter Ruling 200016024, 1-19-2000, CCH IRS Letter Rulings Reports.

[217] *Supra* note 201, p. 96.

example, the IRS has privately held that options issued by a wholly owned subsidiary limited liability company (LLC) of a foreign company will not be subject to the $1 million deduction limitation after the LLC becomes a publicly held C corporation.[218] The parent is not subject to the proxy compensation and disclosure requirements of the SEC and is not subject to Code Sec. 162(m). Because the parent is not subject to Code Sec. 162(m), the IRS held that the LLC is entitled to the transitional relief of Reg. § 1.162-27(f). However, this exemption does not apply to the extent that a plan is materially modified as defined in Reg. § 1.162-27(h)(1). In addition, the IRS has privately held that where a stock incentive plan was fully in effect at the time of an initial public offering of a corporation, and the terms of the arrangement were fully disclosed in the prospectus, the amounts under the plan were not subject to the Code Sec. 162(m) limitation.[219]

.08 Binding Contract Exception

Compensation established in written binding contracts effective on February 17, 1993, are excepted from the $1 million deduction limitation if the contracts are not materially modified after that date and before payment of the compensation. Under Reg. § 1.162-27(h)(1), state law is determinative as to whether a contract is binding. If a contract is materially modified, the contract is not subject to the grandfather rule. A material modification includes any change in the contract that provides an increase in compensation. As an example, the IRS recently privately ruled that amendments made to a company plan after February 17, 1993 were not material modifications because the amendments were found not to increase the compensation of the covered employees.[220] For purposes of determining whether a material modification has been made, the terms of new contracts or supplemental contracts may be taken into account. A contract that may be terminated or canceled at will by the corporation or that is renewable as of a specific date or event is treated as a new contract and thus is no longer grandfathered as of the first date on which it could be terminated, canceled, or renewed. The covered employee must have had the right to participate in the plan as of February 17, 1993. The mere existence of the plan then is not sufficient by itself to qualify under the binding contract exception.[221]

In addition to the grandfather rule, Reg. § 1.162-27(h)(2) and (3) provide two transition rules. The first is a transition rule for outside

---

[218] IRS Letter Ruling 200127006, 3-28-2001, CCH IRS Letter Rulings Reports. *See also* IRS Letter Ruling 200021050, 2-29-2000, CCH IRS Letter Rulings Reports.

[219] IRS Letter Ruling 200449012.
[220] IRS Letter Ruling 200229016, 4-11-2002, CCH IRS Letter Rulings Reports.
[221] *Supra* note 201, pp. 97 and 98.

directors under which a director who is a disinterested director was treated as satisfying the outside director requirements until the first meeting of shareholders at which directors are to be elected that occurs on or after January 1, 1996. Under the second transition rule, a plan that meets both the disinterested director and shareholder approval requirements of Rule 16b-3 under the Securities Exchange Act as of December 20, 1993 will be treated as having met the outside director and shareholder approval requirements until the earlier of (1) the termination or material modification of the plan or (2) the date of the first shareholder meeting that occurs after December 31, 1996.

> **Comment:** The scope of the $1 million limitation rules is quite limited. Privately-held companies are not subject to any specific dollar limitation. They only need be concerned with the reasonableness of compensation requirements covered earlier. Those companies subject to the $1 million rules could avoid the limit by setting the salary component of compensation at no more than $1 million and deferring payment of some or all of the rest of the compensation and/or paying it in the form of performance-based compensation. Alternatively, such companies could maintain their present compensation structure and not take a deduction for amounts paid over $1 million. It also should be noted that the IRS in 2004 initiated, on a pilot basis, an examination of executive compensation at 24 major U.S. corporations. This initiative included a focus on the Section 162(m) $1 million deduction limitation to make certain that the limitation and exceptions are being properly applied. In view of the IRS concern on this issue, care should be taken especially with respect to the exceptions and to which compensation is subject to the limitation.

¶ 206   Time for Deducting Compensation

The year in which compensation is deductible depends upon whether the employer is using the cash method or the accrual method of accounting. The accrual method has acquired more importance beginning in 1987 due to Sec. 801 of the Tax Reform Act of 1986 (TRA '86). Under Code Sec. 448, most C corporations, partnerships that have one or more C corporations as partners, tax shelters, and certain trusts must use the accrual method after 1986. Only farming and timber businesses, qualified personal service corporations, and entities with gross receipts of not more than $5 million are exempted from this rule.[222]

---

[222] Code Sec. 448(b).

.01   Deductions Under the Cash Basis

Although use of the cash basis has been substantially restricted for taxable years after 1986, many smaller companies, including S corporations, will still be able to use it. Hence, it is important to know when a cash basis business can deduct compensation. Under Reg. § 1.461-1(a), cash basis employers generally are permitted to deduct compensation in the year in which the compensation is paid or provided. Note that there is no counterpart to the constructive receipt rule that applies to income recognition when considering deductibility of compensation. Thus, compensation that is taxable to employees in one year under the constructive receipt doctrine is not deductible by the employer until the year in which it is actually paid.[223]

Prepaid compensation is not entirely deductible by a cash- or accrual-basis taxpayer when paid. Instead, the deduction is only allowed over the period in which the services are actually rendered.[224]

A cash-basis employee is permitted to deduct state and local income taxes that are withheld from the employee's compensation in the taxable year in which the taxes are withheld. But employment taxes that must be paid by the employer, such as the employer's FICA taxes and federal and state unemployment taxes, are deductible only in the year they are actually paid to the government.[225]

.02   Deductions Under the Accrual Basis

Under Reg. § 1.461-1(a)(2), accrual-basis employers are generally permitted to deduct current compensation as it accrues. Compensation is considered to be accrued when (1) all events have occurred which determine the fact of the liability, (2) the amount thereof can be determined with reasonable accuracy, and (3) economic performance has occurred with respect to the liability. This is the "all events test." Thus, accrued compensation amounts cannot be deducted until the year in which the employee performs the related services. Reserves for compensation representing amounts payable for services to be performed in future years are not deductible.

> **Example:** On January 2, 2006, the Casey Corporation entered into a three-year employment contract with Mr. Blake under which Blake is to be paid $150,000 per year for three years. Although Casey credits the entire $450,000 ($150,000 × 3) to its reserve for compensation account, only $150,000 will be

---

[223] *Vander Poel, Francis and Co., Inc.*, 8 TC 407, Dec. 15,628 (1947).
[224] Code Sec. 461(h).

[225] Rev. Rul. 80-164, 1980-1 CB 134; and *J.W. Tippin, et ux.*, 104 TC 518, Dec. 50,615 (1995).

¶ 206.01

deductible in 2006, the amount attributable to Casey's 2006 services.

Under the "all events test," the amount of the liability must be deducted in the year the liability is fixed and not in a later year when the amount is paid.[226] Further, the accrual of reasonable compensation must be made even if funds are not available with which to pay the compensation.[227] In summary, if all the events that determine the fact of an employer's liability have occurred, an accrual basis employer is entitled to deduct the entire liability for the compensation even if all or part of the compensation is not payable until a later year. However, special rules apply to payments made by accrual-basis taxpayers to certain cash-basis taxpayers (see below) and to the deduction of deferred compensation (see Chapter 14).

The IRS has ruled that an accrual basis taxpayer may deduct, in the current year, otherwise deductible FICA and FUTA taxes imposed on year-end wages that are properly accrued at the end of the current year but are not paid until the next year, provided that the requirements of the recurring item exception to the economic performance test (see Reg. § 1.461-5) are met.[228] Previously, the IRS held that FICA and FUTA taxes could not be deducted by an accrual basis taxpayer until paid.[229] The IRS changed its position due to losses in several court cases concerning the matter.[230]

Compensation Payable to Related Persons. Under Code Sec. 267(a)(2), an accrual-basis employer cannot deduct compensation that is to be paid to employees that are considered to be related parties until the compensation is actually paid to the employees. For this purpose, Code Sec. 267(b) specifies that an individual and a corporation whose stock is more than 50 percent owned by that individual (both directly and indirectly) are considered to be related parties. Thus, controlling shareholder-employees are considered to be related to the employer corporation. No deduction is permitted for accruals of compensation for controlling shareholder-employees until the payments are actually made.

Accrual of Contingent Compensation. Generally, only actual liabilities for which economic performance has occurred can be accrued. Thus, a contingent liability cannot be accrued until it becomes fixed and economic performance occurs. Under this rule, most forms of contingent compensation cannot be accrued. For

---

[226] Reg. § 1.461-1(a)(2).

[227] *Woodward Construction Co. v. Clark*, CA-10. 50-1 USTC ¶ 9133, 179 F2d 176.

[228] Rev. Rul. 96-51, 1996-2 CB 36.

[229] Rev. Rul. 74-40, 1974-1 CB 116, revoked by Rev. Rul. 96-51.

[230] *See*, e.g., *Eastman Kodak Co.*, CtCls, 76-1 USTC ¶ 9363, 534 F2d 252, 209 CtCls 365. Acq., 1996-2 CB 1.

example, bonuses credited to employees during one taxable year were not deductible by the employer in that year since a portion of the bonus was forfeitable by a terminated employee until the middle of the next year and, thus, the liability for the bonus was not fixed at the end of the year.[231]

Accrual of Uncertain Amounts.   Compensation may be accrued even if the amount to be paid is not exactly known, as long as the amount of the compensation liability is determinable with reasonable accuracy. The fact that the exact amount of the liability which has been incurred cannot be determined will not prevent the accrual of the portion that can be determined with reasonable accuracy.[232]

> **Example:** Randy performed services for Martin Company during 2006 and claims that he is owed $10,000. The Martin Company admits owing $5,000 to Randy, but contests the remainder. Martin Company may accrue only $5,000 as an expense for the year in which the services were performed. See below for a discussion of when contested compensation may be deducted.

Contested Compensation.   In general, the employer cannot deduct any portion of compensation payable to an employee that the employer contests. The deduction can be taken in the year in which the contest is settled.[233] However, if contested compensation is actually paid under protest, the amount is deductible in the year of payment if:

(1) the employer contests the amount of the compensation liability;

(2) the employer paid money in satisfaction of the asserted liability;

(3) the contest exists after the transfer; and

(4) a deduction would be allowed for the tax year in which the payment is made if the liability had not been contested.[234]

After the contest is settled, the employer will have to report as income, under Code Sec. 111, the excess of the contested amount deducted in the previous year (or current year) over the amount payable under the court's ruling or other contest agreement. If the settlement calls for an additional amount to be paid by the employer, that amount should be deductible.

Avoidance of Deferred Compensation Rules.   Year-end bonuses and other forms of compensation that are accrued within

---

[231] *Bennett Paper Corp.*, CA-8, 83-1 USTC ¶ 9208, 699 F2d 450 (1983).

[232] Reg. § 1.461-1(a)(2).

[233] *Dixie Pine Products Co.*, SCt, 44-1 USTC ¶ 9127, 320 US 516, 64 SCt 364.

[234] Code Sec. 461(f).

one taxable year, but not paid within that year must be paid shortly after the end of that taxable year to avoid being treated as compensation deferred under nonqualified plans. Since deductions are not permitted for compensation deferred under nonqualified plans until the year in which the amounts are paid (see Chapter 14), and since Code Sec. 404(b)(2)(A) states that any plan that defers compensation for employees and their spouses or dependents is a deferred benefit or deferred compensation plan, care must be taken to avoid deferred compensation treatment in the case of short-term accruals. In general, if a bonus or other short-term deferred amount is paid within two-and-one-half months after the close of the taxable year in which the related services were rendered, it is not considered payment under a deferred compensation plan or deferred benefit plan.[235] The two-and-one-half month rule is now of further importance due to the enactment of Code Sec. 409A which is generally applicable to nonqualified deferred compensation deferred after December 31, 2004 and is covered in Chapter 14.[236] The conference committee report on Section 409A indicates that the rules of Section 409A are not intended to apply to annual bonuses or other compensation amounts paid within two-and-one-half months after the close of the taxable year in which the relevant services required for payment have been performed.[237]

It should be noted that the amount of the compensation must "actually" be received by the employee by no later than two-and-one-half months following the close of the taxable year of the accrual in order to be treated as paid by the employer. Congress recently enacted Code Sec. 404(a)(11)[238] to specifically provide that compensation is not treated as having been paid to the employee unless it is actually received by the employee. This rule, which is effective for taxable years ending after July 22, 1998, was enacted to overrule the result in *Schmidt Baking Co., Inc.*[239] which allowed an accrual basis employer to deduct accrued vacation and severance pay in 1991 because the employer purchased a letter of credit for the employees (who were to receive the vacation and severance pay) on March 13, 1992, within two-and-one-half months after the end of 1991. The Tax Court reasoned that the purchase of the letter of credit, and the resulting income inclusion, constituted payment of the vacation and severance pay within two-and-one-half months after the close of the year, such that the vacation pay and severance pay were not deferred compensation. Now, Code Sec. 404(a)(11) requires actual receipt of

---

[235] Temp. Reg. § 1.404(b)-1T.

[236] Code Sec. 409A, as enacted by P.L. 108-357, 108th Cong., 2d Sess., Sec. 885(a) (Oct. 22, 2004).

[237] H.R. Conf. Rep. No. 108-755, 108th Cong., 2d Sess. (Oct. 22, 2004).

[238] Code Sec. 404(a)(11) as enacted by P.L. No 105-206, Sec. 7001(a) (July 22, 1998).

[239] 107 TC 271, Dec. 51,650 (1996).

the compensation to avoid classification of deferred compensation. The Conference Committee Report on the 1998 Act indicates letters of credit and similar arrangements such as the furnishing of a note or letter or other evidence of indebtedness, whether or not guaranteed by any other instrument or by a third party is not considered to be "actual" receipt. Further, actual receipt does not include a promise of the employer to provide property in the future, amounts transferred as loan, refundable deposit, or contingent payment, or amounts set aside in trust for employees.[240] Thus, actual receipt means that the employee must generally receive cash or a check.

Accrual of Vacation Pay. Accruals for vacation pay will generally be treated like other short-term accruals described above. That is, the deduction for vacation pay is generally limited to: (1) the amount that is paid to employees during the current taxable year, and (2) the amount that is vested with employees at the end of the current taxable year and paid to the employees within two-and-one-half months after the end of the year.[241] Amounts accrued during a particular year that are not paid within that two-and-one-half-month period are only deductible when they are actually paid. For this purpose, the amounts are not considered paid unless and until they are actually received by the employee under Code Sec. 404(a)(11), as discussed in the paragraph above.

---

[240] HR Rep. No. 105-599, 105th Cong., 2d Sess. (1998), p. 345.

[241] Omnibus Budget Reconciliation Act of 1987, Sec. 10201, repealing Code Sec. 463.

Chapter 3

Employee Fringe Benefits, in General

¶ 301 Introduction

Employee fringe benefits are a broad form of compensation which are generally provided by the employer to executives and other employees on a current basis as a supplement to current salary and bonus payments. There are many separate types of benefits that are included in this classification such as group-term life insurance, meals and lodging furnished by the employer, employer health and accident insurance, and others. While some types of the fringe benefits are partially or totally taxable to the recipient and subject to FICA and FUTA taxes, others are totally tax-free. In general, the employer can receive a current deduction for the cost of fringe benefit payments and contributions. In the case of some fringe benefits such as group-term life insurance provided by the employer, the employee may be required to pay a portion of the benefits desired. In such a case, the plan is a contributory plan. Nevertheless, the fringe benefit may be valuable to the employee since the employer can typically provide the employee with benefits such as life insurance coverage for a much lower cost than the employee would have to pay if he obtained the benefits on his own.

Today, fringe benefits are an important component of employee compensation packages in businesses ranging in size from the small to the very large. This chapter examines the more important types of fringe benefits that may be offered to employees and includes coverage of interest-free or below-market rate interest loans made to employees and golden parachute compensation. Cafeteria plans, i.e., employer plans which offer employees a choice among one or more fringe benefits and cash compensation, Health Reimbursement Arrangements

(HRAs), and welfare benefit plans are presented in Chapter 4. Finally, this chapter reflects provisions of recent tax acts, including the American Jobs Creation Act of 2004 (AJCA), the Working Families Tax Relief Act of 2004, the Medicare Prescription Drug, Improvement and Modernization Act of 2003 (which enacted the new Health Savings Account provisions covered in this chapter) and the Economic Growth and Tax Relief Reconciliation Act of 2001 (EGTRRA).

¶ 302 Statutory Fringe Benefits

Fringe benefits received as compensation in return for services performed are includible in the gross income of an employee or other service performer, unless the benefits are specifically excludable under one or more provisions of the Code.[1] In general, the amount includible by the employee is the fair market value of the fringe benefit, minus (1) the amount, if any, paid for the benefit and (2) the amount, if any, that is specifically excluded from gross income under a provision of the Code.[2] However, special rules apply to the valuation and reporting of certain benefits such as the employee's use of an employer-owned automobile or airplane.[3] The employer may deduct only the cost of providing the fringe benefit to the employee, not the value of the benefit that the employee may have to include in gross income.[4] Thus, if an employer allows an employee to use a company car, the employer cannot deduct the amount that the employee includes in income. Rather, the employer can only deduct the depreciation, insurance, and other expenses pertaining to the car. However, where the deductibility of a fringe benefit provided is affected by the provisions of Code Secs. 274(a) and (e) (pertaining to limitations on the deductibility of meals, entertainment, amusement, or recreation-related goods, services or facilities expenses), Congress in AJCA 2004 has changed the law to specifically limit the amount of the employer's deduction to the amount the employee is required to include in gross income.[5] This new rule applies with respect to such items provided by the employer to "specified individuals" (i.e., officers, directors, or 10 percent or more owners of the employer).[6] This new rule is applicable with respect to expenses incurred after October 22, 2004.[7] The IRS has issued Notice 2005-45[8] to provide interim guidance in applying the new rule with respect to use of company aircraft for entertainment-related purposes.

---

[1] Code Sec. 61(a)(1)

[2] Reg. § 1.61-21(b).

[3] See Reg. § 1.61-21(b)-(g).

[4] Reg. § 1.162-25T.

[5] Code Sec. 274(e)(2), as amended by P.L. 108-357, 108th Cong., 2d Sess., Sec. 907(a) (Oct. 22, 2004).

[6] Code Sec. 274(e)(2)(B), as amended by P.L. 108-357, 108th Cong., 2d Sess., Sec. 907(a) (Oct. 22, 2004).

[7] P.L. 108-357, 108th Cong., 2d Sess., Sec. 907(a) (Oct. 22, 2004).

[8] IRB 2005-24, 1228.

The IRS guidance is applicable to expenses incurred after June 30, 2005. As an example of the new rule applying to specified individuals, suppose that it was determined that $26X dollars were includible as compensation by a specified individual for personal use of an employer's airplane under the special valuation rules of Reg. § 1.61-21(g) (covered later in this chapter). In that situation, the employer would only be permitted to deduct $26X dollars where its claimed actual cost is more than that amount (e.g., $340X dollars). Expenses incurred on or before October 22, 2004 and expenses incurred with respect to employees who are not specified individuals are not subject to that limitation under rulings of the Tax Court and the Eighth Circuit Court of Appeals to which the IRS has acquiesced.[9] The employer's deduction under these rulings is not limited to the amount that the employees include in gross income. The IRS has acquiesced to the Eighth Circuit's ruling in indicating that if the employees provided the flights include the full value of the flights, the employer can deduct its full (higher) cost of providing the flights.[10] Thus, in the example given earlier, under the rulings and the IRS acquiescence that is applicable to employees who are not specified individuals both on or before and after October 22, 2004, and to specified individuals before that date, the amount deductible to the employer would not be limited to the $26X dollars included by the employee, and instead could be as high as the cost of providing the flight. Note that the requirements for deductibility of compensation, in general, that were discussed in Chapter 2 apply to fringe benefits as well. Therefore, fringe benefits must be provided for services performed and must be reasonable in amount.

The more common types of statutory fringe benefits and their tax treatment are covered in the following paragraphs. Specific rules apply to each separate benefit in determining the tax consequences, such as how much is includible and excludable by the recipient employee.

Reporting Requirements for Fringe Benefit Plans Several of the fringe benefits covered in the following paragraphs were subjected to reporting requirements under Code Sec. 6039D. Notice 90-24[11] indefinitely suspended the reporting requirements for Group-term life insurance plans under Code Sec. 79 (¶ 302.01), Accident and Health Plans under Code Secs. 105 and 106 (¶ 302.04), and Dependent Care Assistance Programs under Code Sec. 129

---

[9] *Sutherland Lumber-Southwest. Inc.*, CA-8, 2001-2 USTC ¶ 50,503, 255 F3d 495. Aff'g 114 TC 197. *National Bancorp of Alaska, Inc.*, 82 TCM 369, Dec. 54,436(M), TC Memo. 2001-202 and *Midland Financial Co.*, 82 TCM 371. Dec. 54,437(M), TC Memo. 2001-203.
[10] Acq. IRB 2002-6.
[11] 1990-1 CB 335.

(¶ 302.08). More recently, the IRS, in IR-2003-89, indicated it has terminated the Code Sec. 6039D reporting requirements for all of the types of fringe benefit plans that had been subject to those reporting requirements. In 2002, the IRS had issued Notice 2002-24[12] in which it had indicated that it had indefinitely suspended the Code Sec. 6039D reporting requirements for the remaining three types of fringe benefits for which the reporting requirements had not been suspended by Notice 90-24: Cafeteria Plans under Code Sec. 125 (covered in chapter 4), Educational Assistance Plans under Code Sec. 127 (¶ 302.07), and Adoption Assistance Plans under Code Sec. 137 (¶ 302.09).

.01 Group-Term Life Insurance

Group-term life insurance coverage for employees is one of the most common fringe benefits provided to employees. The employer or the employer and employee, in the case of contributory plans, pay premiums to provide death benefits to specified beneficiaries of the employee. No cash surrender value is built up in the case of group-term life insurance plans. Because the premium rates are group rates, the employee can be provided with coverage at a much lesser cost than he would have to pay on his own for comparable coverage.

In addition to the regular term insurance coverage, some plans provide supplemental life insurance (often paid for by the employee), accidental death and dismemberment insurance (which will pay various benefit amounts for certain serious injuries such as loss of a hand and for accidental death), survivor income benefit insurance (the beneficiaries receive installment payments over a period of years or for life rather than a lump-sum payment following the death of the insured employee), and dependent life insurance (an amount of coverage of a flat amount such as $1,000 or $2,000, or equal to some percentage of the insured's coverage). In recent years, some group policies have also been permitting the payment of accelerated death benefits to certain policy-holders who are terminally ill. The taxation of such benefits is discussed in the section below covering the taxation of life insurance benefits. But, first consider the taxation of employer-paid premiums on group-term life insurance policies.

Taxation of Employees. Employer-paid premiums on life insurance policies on the life of the employees, where the benefits are payable to beneficiaries designated by the employee, are ordinarily includible in the employees' gross income.[13] However, the premium

---

[12] 2002-1 CB 785.

[13] Reg. § 1.61-2(d).

¶ 302.01

cost of employer-provided group-term life insurance is taxable to an employee only to the extent that cost exceeds the sum of (a) the cost of the first $50,000 of coverage and (b) the amount (if any) of premiums paid by the employee.[14] If the coverage is more than $50,000, the employee is taxed on the cost of the excess coverage, computed in accordance with the employee's age from a table in Reg. § 1.79-3(d).[15] The table which provides a hypothetical cost per month per $1,000 of coverage for particular age groups is as follows:

Age at End of Tax Year	Cost per Month per $1,000
Under 25	5 cents
25 to 29	6 cents
30 to 34	8 cents
35 to 39	9 cents
40 to 44	10 cents
45 to 49	15 cents
50 to 54	23 cents
55 to 59	43 cents
60 to 64	66 cents
65 to 69	$1.27
70 and above	$2.06

The amount includible in the employee's income is determined by dividing the difference between the amount of the coverage provided and $50,000 by 1,000 and multiplying the result by the hypothetical rate per month from the regulations. This result is then multiplied by 12 to obtain the includible amount. The includible amount must be reduced by any premiums paid by the employee toward the cost of the policy.[16]

Example (1): Suppose that Martin, age 47, is provided with group-term life insurance coverage of $60,000 during 2006 by his employer. Under Reg. § 1.79-3(d), Martin's gross income on account of the employer's premium payments is $18.00, or $10,000 ($60,000 minus $50,000) divided by 1,000 multiplied by 15 cents times 12. If Martin had paid any amount of the premiums, that amount could have been subtracted from the $18.00 taxable amount. Thus, if Martin paid $10.00 in premiums, only $8.00 would have been taxable.

The $50,000 limit on tax-free coverage applies to all group-term life insurance policies provided to an employee by all of his employers.[17] Thus, if two or more employers provide group-term life

---

[14] Code Sec. 79(a).
[15] Code Sec. 79(c).

[16] Reg. § 1.79-3(e).
[17] Code Sec. 79(a).

insurance coverage to an employee, the employee must figure how much to include in income for the cost of all coverage that is more than $50,000.[18]

> **Example (2):** Baker, age 53, works for both the Weiss Company and the Hunter Company. In the year 2006, the Weiss Company provided Baker with $35,000 of group-term life insurance coverage, and the Hunter Company provided him with $45,000 of coverage. Baker paid a total of $56 for the coverage from both companies. Baker's gross income on account of this coverage would be $26.80, or $30,000 ($80,000 minus $50,000) divided by 1,000 multiplied by the hypothetical rate of 23 cents times 12 minus the $56 paid by Baker.

Under Code Sec. 79(b), the $50,000 limit on tax-free coverage does not apply if:

(1) the coverage is provided to the employee after he or she has retired for disability;

(2) the employer is the beneficiary of the policy for the entire period the insurance is in force during the tax year; or

(3) the only beneficiary of the amount over $50,000 is a charitable organization as defined in Code Sec. 170(c).[19]

Thus, in such cases, the employer-paid premiums are not taxable to the employee.

Prior to the enactment of the Tax Reform Act of 1984 (TRA '84), the $50,000 limit did not apply to retired employees. However, under Code Sec. 223(a)(2) of TRA '84, the $50,000 limit was generally extended to retired employees after 1983. See Sec. 223(a)(2) of TRA '84 for special transitional rules applicable to employees who retired on or before January 1, 1984.

Generally, the cost (as determined under the Code Sec. 79 regulations) of group-term life insurance on the life of the children or spouse of the employee paid by the employer is includible in the employee's gross income. However, employer-paid premiums for up to $2,000 payable on the death of a spouse or dependent of an employee are excludable as de minimis fringe benefits (see the discussion of de minimis fringe benefits later in this chapter).[20] For this purpose, the IRS has privately ruled that the de minimis fringe

---

[18] IRS Pub. No. 525, at 5.

[19] Code Sec. 79(b).

[20] Notice 89-110, 1989-2 CB 447. *See* Technical Advice Memorandum 200502040 for an example of this treatment for coverage provided by an employer under a group dependent universal life insurance program that was provided along with a group universal life insurance program provided to the employer's employees.

¶ 302.01

exclusion does not apply with respect to domestic partners of the employee and their dependents where the domestic partners and dependents are not considered qualified dependents of the taxpayer under Code Sec. 152.[21]

Group-term life insurance coverage provided by the employer through a qualified retirement plan, such as a qualified pension plan or annuity plan, is fully taxable to the covered employees. The $50,000 limit does not apply to such insurance. In the case of qualified pension or profit sharing plans, this rule applies if the proceeds of the contract are payable to a participant or beneficiary.[22]

Form, Coverage, and Nondiscrimination Rules. Group-term life insurance plans must satisfy certain formal requirements specified in the regulations as well as nondiscrimination rules specified in Code Sec. 79(d). The requirements specified in the regulations are described below. The nondiscrimination rules that apply to group-term life insurance plans are summarized below.

Formal Requirements. Life insurance protection provided by the employer is considered to be group-term life insurance for purposes of Code Sec. 79 only if it meets the following conditions:

(1) it provides a general death benefit that is excludable from gross income under Code Sec. 101(a);

(2) it is provided to a group of employees (defined below);

(3) it is provided under a policy carried directly or indirectly by the employer (defined below); and

(4) the amount of the coverage provided to each employee is based on a formula that precludes individual selection. The formula must be based on factors such as age, years of service, compensation, or position.[23]

Group of Employees. Generally, life insurance qualifies as group-term life insurance only if, at some time during the calendar year, it is provided to at least 10 full-time employees who are members of the group of employees.[24] However, this rule does not apply if the following conditions are met:

(1) the insurance is provided to all of the employer's full-time employees or, if evidence of insurability affects eligibility, to all full-time employees who provide satisfactory evidence of insurability to the insurer;

---

[21] IRS Letter Ruling 9717018, 1-22-97, CCH IRS Letter Rulings Reports.
[22] Code Secs. 79(b)(3) and 72(m)(3)(A).
[23] Reg. § 1.79-1(a).
[24] Reg. § 1.79-1(c)(1).

¶ **302.01**

(2) the insurance coverage is determined on the basis of a uniform percentage of employee compensation or on the basis of the insurer's coverage brackets. The amount computed under either method may be reduced for employees who do not provide evidence of insurability satisfactory to the insurer. In general, no bracket may be more than 2½ times larger than the next lower bracket, and the lowest bracket must be at least 10 percent of the highest bracket; and

(3) evidence of insurability is limited to a medical questionnaire completed by the employee that does not require a physical exam.[25]

Fewer than 10 employees may also be covered if the plan covers employees of two or more unrelated employers and participation is limited to and mandatory for all employees who belong to a particular group, such as a union.[26]

For purposes of the above rules, an "employee" is:

(1) a person who performs services for the employer and who is considered a common-law employee under Reg. § 31.3401(c)-1;

(2) a full-time life insurance salesperson as defined in Code Sec. 7701(a)(20); or

(3) a person who provides services as an independent contractor for his former employer is considered an employee only with respect to insurance provided on account of the person's prior services as an employee.[27]

A "group of employees" is all employees of the employer, or less than all if membership in the group is determined solely on the basis of age, marital status, or factors related to employment (such as membership in a union, some of whose members are employees of the employer).[28]

Nondiscrimination Rules. Under the nondiscrimination rules applicable to group-term life insurance plans, key employees are not eligible for the Code Sec. 79(a) $50,000 of coverage exclusion if the plan is discriminatory as to coverage or benefits. For this purpose, key employees are defined the same as for "top heavy" qualified deferred compensation plans under Code Sec. 416(i).[29] Under Code Sec. 79(d)(1), the key employees are taxable on the greater of (1) the hypothetical cost using the rates specified in Reg. § 1.79-3(d) or (2) the actual premiums paid by the employer if the plan is discriminatory.

---

[25] Reg. § 1.79-1(c)(2).
[26] Reg. § 1.79-1(c)(3).
[27] Reg. § 1.79-0(b).

[28] Id.

[29] Code Sec. 79(d)(6).

A group-term life insurance plan does not discriminate as to eligibility for coverage if: (1) at least 70 percent of all employees benefit; (2) at least 85 percent of all participants are not key employees; or (3) participants form a classification that the IRS considers not to be discriminatory.[30] A group-term plan that is part of a cafeteria plan that meets the Code Sec. 125 eligibility requirements is not discriminatory. For these purposes, employees can be excluded from participation if they: (1) have not completed three years of service, (2) are part-time or seasonal, (3) are nonresident aliens with no U.S.-source income, or (4) are covered by a collective bargaining agreement (i.e., union workers). Under Code Sec. 79(d)(4), benefits are not discriminatory if neither the type nor the amount of benefits discriminate in favor of key employees. For example, a plan is not discriminatory merely because the insurance provided to each participant bears a uniform relationship to compensation.[31]

Group-Term and Group-Permanent Insurance. Premiums paid by an employer for group-permanent insurance on the life of an employee are taxable to the employee if the employee's right to permanent insurance or equivalent benefits (paid-up or cash surrender value) is nonforfeitable upon the termination of employment.[32] However, group-term insurance coverage may be combined with group-permanent insurance coverage in one policy. If an employer provides such a combined policy which meets requirements specified in the regulations, an employee is taxable on the excess of: (1) the cost of the permanent benefits, plus (2) the cost of the term insurance coverage over $50,000, minus (3) the amount paid by the employee. The amount of the premium paid by the employer that is attributable to the permanent coverage is determined according to a formula specified in the regulations.[33]

Life insurance that includes permanent benefits is not group-term life insurance unless the following conditions are met:

(1) the policy or the employer must specify in writing the portion of each employee's death benefit that is considered group-term insurance; and

(2) the portion of each employee's death benefit that is designated as group-term insurance must not be less than the difference between the total death benefit provided under the policy and the employee's deemed death benefit at the end of the policy year.[34]

---

[30] Code Sec. 79(d)(3).
[31] Code Sec. 79(d)(5).
[32] Reg. § 1.79-1(d).

[33] Reg. § 1.79-1(b) and (d).

[34] Reg. § 1.79-1(b).

¶ **302.01**

Employer's Deduction. Under Code Sec. 162, premiums paid by the employer for either group-term or group-permanent insurance on the life of an employee are generally deductible if the employer is not a beneficiary and retains no incidents of ownership under the policy. It does not matter whether the employee-participants are eligible to exclude some or all of the cost of the coverage under Code Sec. 79.

In cases where the employer provides funding for life insurance coverage for employees after retirement through so-called retired lives reserve arrangements, special rules govern the amount deductible by the employer. These rules are covered in the discussion of welfare benefit plans in the next chapter.

Tax Treatment of Insurance Proceeds. Under Code Sec. 101(a), the proceeds of a group-term policy or a group-permanent policy are generally not taxed to the beneficiary if paid by reason of the death of the insured. If the proceeds are paid in installments, only the portion of the installments that represents interest is taxable.[35] For this purpose, what would have been received as a lump sum is prorated over the number of payments to be received.

> **Example:** Nellie is the beneficiary of a $100,000 life insurance policy on her father. Under a policy option, she elects to receive $11,500 per year for ten years rather than the $100,000 lump sum. Each year Nellie will be taxable on $1,500 ($11,500 – ($100,000 / 10)).

As noted above, a large number of group life insurance policies provide for the payment of accelerated death payments to terminally ill individuals to help them pay medical and other illness-related expenses. In response, the IRS issued Prop. Reg. § 1.101-8 allowing recipients to exclude "qualified accelerated death benefits." Effective for payments after 1996, Code Sec. 101(g), as enacted by the Health Insurance Portability and Accountability Act of 1996, provides for the exclusion of certain accelerated death benefit payments.[36] Payments before 1997 are excludable under the proposed regulations.

Under Code Sec. 101(g)(1), accelerated death benefit payments received under a life insurance contract on the life of an insured who is terminally ill or who is chronically ill are excludable from gross income. For this purpose, a terminally ill individual is an individual

---

[35] Code Sec. 101(d).

[36] Code Sec. 101(g), as added by P.L. 104-191, 104th Cong., 2d Sess., Sec. 331 (Aug. 21, 1996).

¶ 302.01

who has been certified by a physician as having an illness or physical condition which can reasonably be expected to result in death in no more than 24 months after the date of the certification.[37] A chronically ill individual is defined in the same way as for purposes of the recently enacted long-term care insurance rules of Code Sec. 7702B covered below under the discussion of Medical, Accident, and Disability Benefits. In brief, a person is considered chronically ill if he has been certified within the preceding 12-month period by a licensed health care practitioner as (1) not being able to perform at least two activities of daily living for a period of at least 90 days because of a loss of functional capacity, (2) having a similar level of disability under IRS regulations, or (3) requiring substantial supervision to protect the individual from threats to health and safety due to severe cognitive impairment (e.g., Alzheimer's disease).

However, the term "chronically ill" does not include terminally ill individuals.[38] Accelerated payments made to chronically ill individuals are excludable if the payments are for actual qualified long-term care costs (as defined in Code Sec. 7702B(c)) of the individual that are not reimbursed by insurance and the terms of the contract under which the payments are made meet the requirements of Code Sec. 7702B(b)(1)(B).[39] For purposes of the latter requirement, the contract must not pay or reimburse expenses that are reimbursable under Medicare, except when Medicare is a secondary payor, or when the contract makes payments on a per diem or periodic basis. In addition, the contract must meet certain consumer protection provisions under Code Sec. 101(g)(3)(B). Finally, payments made on a per diem or other periodic basis can be excluded only to the extent they do not exceed the equivalent of the dollar cap for per diem long-term care insurance contracts (which is $240 per day, $87,600 for 2005, adjusted for inflation after 2005).[40]

> **Example:** Morton, a chronically ill individual, received accelerated life insurance proceeds of $10,000 in 2005. His qualified long-term care expenses were $14,000, of which $8,000 were reimbursed by insurance. He can only exclude the $6,000 of unreimbursed expenses ($14,000 – $8,000). Therefore, $4,000 is includible income ($10,000 – $6,000). However, if he were to receive a flat per diem of $198 per day in 2005, instead of the reimbursement, the entire amount would be excludable, since the per diem is under the $240 (in 2005) per day cap amount.

---

[37] Code Sec. 101(g)(4)(A).

[38] Code Sec. 101(g)(4)(B).

[39] Code Sec. 101(g)(3)(A).

[40] Code Sec. 101(g)(3)(A); Code Sec. 7702B(d); Rev. Proc. 2004-71, IRB 2004-50, 970.

While accelerated payments made to chronically ill individuals are limited as noted above, accelerated death benefit payments are fully excludable.[41] They are not limited like payments made to chronically ill individuals.

If any portion of the accelerated death benefit payable to a terminally ill or chronically ill individual is sold or assigned to a licensed viatical settlement provider, the amount received by the individual is excludable.[42] A viatical settlement provider is any person who is regularly engaged in the business of purchasing, or taking assignments of, life insurance contracts on the life of the insured and is either licensed in the state in which the insured resides, or satisfies other requirements (specified under Code Sec. 101(g)(1)(B)) in the event the applicable state does not require licensing.

Finally, the exclusion under Code Sec. 101(g) does not apply to any amounts paid to any taxpayer other than the person insured if that taxpayer has an insurable interest on the life of the insured by reason of the insured being a director, officer, or employee of the taxpayer or because the insured has a financial interest in a trade or business carried on by the taxpayer.[43]

FICA and FUTA Taxation. The amount which is taxed to employees, on account of the employer payment of group-term life insurance premiums, is also subject to FICA taxes.[44] Thus, the rules covered above concerning the taxability of employer-paid group-term life insurance premiums apply in determining the amount of such payments subject to FICA taxes.

On the other hand, employer-paid group life insurance premiums (whether for term or permanent coverage) are not subject to FUTA taxes. The exclusion is permitted as long as the employer payments are made to or on the behalf of employees "... under a plan or system which makes provisions for employees generally ... or for a class or classes of his employees."[45]

Note that life insurance proceeds received by beneficiaries on account of the deaths of covered employees are not subject to FICA and FUTA taxes.[46]

.02 Split-Dollar Insurance

Due to the nondiscrimination and other requirements associated with group-term life insurance plans, employers desiring to provide life insurance coverage for certain key employees only,

---

[41] Rev. Rul. 2002-82, 2002-2 CB 978.
[42] Code Sec. 101(g)(2)(A).
[43] Code Sec. 101(g)(5).
[44] Code Sec. 3121(a)(2)(C).
[45] Reg. § 31.3306(b)(2)-1.
[46] Code Secs. 3121(a)(2)(C) and 3306(b)(2)(C).

such as executives and shareholder-employees, may desire to use other types of life insurance arrangements. One alternative is for the employer to pay premiums on group-permanent insurance as noted above. Another popular method is split-dollar life insurance. Under the classic type of split-dollar life insurance plan, the employer pays part of each premium equal to the increase in the cash surrender value of the policy each year. The employee pays the rest of the premium. The classic type of split-dollar life insurance plan has had two contractual forms: (1) the endorsement method, under which the employer is formally designated as the owner of the contract, and the employer endorses the contract to specify the portion of the proceeds payable to the employee's beneficiary, and (2) the collateral assignment method, under which the employee is formally designated as the owner of the contract, the employer's premium payments are characterized as loans from the employer to the employee, and the employer's interest in the proceeds of the contract is designated as collateral security for its loans.[47]

When the employee dies, the employer is paid an amount equal to the cash surrender value of the policy. The beneficiary named by the employee will receive the rest of the proceeds. The amount paid to the employer will be taxable, but the amount received by the beneficiary should be at least partially excludable under Code Sec. 101(a).

Due to the emergence of the equity split-dollar plans and variations of such plans, the IRS has recently felt it necessary to issue new guidance that would cover such plans. Under the formerly applicable guidance, which was meant to cover the classic type of plan, the employee was to be taxed on the net premium cost of current insurance (i.e., the value of the insurance protection) minus the amount of the premium the employee paid, if any.[48] The net premium cost was to be determined using the P.S. 58 table provided by the IRS in Rev. Rul. 55-747.[49] In 2001, the IRS issued Notice 2001-10[50] to bridge the gap and provide interim guidance concerning equity split-dollar arrangements. Due to the receipt of a significant amount of negative commentary concerning Notice 2001-10, the IRS revoked that Notice by issuing Notice 2002-8[51] which provided revised interim guidance concerning split-dollar plans. Finally, in September of 2003, the IRS issued comprehensive final regulations that provide treatment of split-dollar plans.[52] The final regulations apply to

---

[47] See e.g., T.D. 9092, 68 FR 54336 (Sept. 17, 2003).

[48] Former Reg. § 1.61-2(d)(2)(ii)(a).

[49] Rev. Rul. 66-110, 1966-1 CB 12.

[50] 2001-1 CB 459.

[51] 2002-1 CB 398.

[52] See T.D. 9092, 68 FR 54336 (Sept. 17, 2003).

any split-dollar life insurance arrangement entered into after September 17, 2003. In addition, the final regulations apply to any split-dollar life insurance arrangement entered into on or before September 17, 2003 if the arrangement is materially modified after that date.[53] However, certain plans described in Section IV of Notice 2002-8[54] will not be treated as materially modified if the change in the arrangement is made solely to comply with that Section of the Notice. In addition, the final regulations provide a nonexclusive list of changes that will not result in a material modification for purposes of the effective date. For instance, a change solely in the mode of premium payment or a change solely in the interest rate payable on a policy loan under the life insurance contract will not be treated as a material modification.[55] In the case of split-dollar arrangements entered into on or before September 17, 2003, taxpayers may continue to rely on previously issued revenue rulings, such as 66-110,[56] to the extent described in Notice 2002-8, but only if the arrangement is not materially modified after September 17, 2003.[57] The discussion below generally covers the rules concerning split-dollar life insurance arrangements between employer and employee under the final regulations. The treatment of other split-dollar arrangements (e.g., gift arrangements) is beyond the scope of this book. For coverage of rules concerning split-dollar arrangements issued on or before September 17, 2003 and that are not covered under the final regulations, see Notice 2002-8 and the revenue rulings cited therein.

The IRS Final Regulations. As mentioned above, the IRS in September of 2003 issued final regulations (Reg. §§ 1.61-22 and 1.7872-15, along with modifications to certain other regulations). The final regulations generally define a split-dollar life insurance arrangement as any arrangement between an owner of a life insurance contract and a non-owner of the contract under which either party to the arrangement pays all or part of the premiums, and one of the parties paying the premiums is entitled to recover (either conditionally or unconditionally) all or any portion of those premiums and that recovery is to be made from, or is secured by, the proceeds of the contract. The definition does not cover the purchase of an insurance contract in which the only parties to the arrangement are the policy owner and the life insurance company acting only in its capacity as issuer of the contract.[58] Under the final regulations, the tax treatment of split-dollar arrangements is based on the nature of arrangement and not how the parties would or

---

[53] T.D. 9092, 68 FR 54336 (Sept. 17, 2003) and Reg. § 1.61-22(j).

[54] 2002-1 CB 398.

[55] Reg. § 1.61-22(j)(2).

[56] 1996-1 CB 12.

[57] Rev. Rul. 2003-105, IRB 2003-40, 696.

[58] T.D. 9092, 68 FR 54336 (Sept. 17, 2003).

would like to characterize the arrangement. In general, the regulations provide two mechanisms for determining the tax consequences of such arrangements, including equity split-dollar arrangements. Thus, the consequences of the arrangement depends upon who is considered to be the owner of the policy (the employer or the employee, in the case of compensation-oriented arrangements).[59]

The first mechanism is the economic benefit approach provided by Reg. § 1.61-22. The economic benefit approach must be used when the policy owner, such as the employer, is considered to be providing certain benefits to an employee who is a non-owner (owners and non-owners are technically defined in Reg. § 1.61-22(c))—in general, the person named as the policy owner of the life insurance contract is the owner of that contract. Special rules apply where more than one person is named as policy owner).[60] The rules apply to endorsement arrangements which are equity split arrangements where the employer owns the policy and endorses certain rights to the employee. They also apply to non-equity split arrangements because in those, the employer also owns the policy. In the case of equity-split arrangements, Reg. § 1.61-22(d)(1) provides that the non-owner employee (and the owner employer for payroll tax purposes) must take into account the full value of all economic benefits from the policy, as described in the regulations, minus any consideration paid directly or indirectly by the non-owner for those economic benefits. Such net amount will be considered gross income to the employee and will be subject to payroll taxes. Under Reg. § 1.61-22(d)(2), the value of economic benefits provided to the non-owner (e.g., an employee) is to be equal to the sum of:

(1) The cost of current life insurance protection provided to the non-owner (This equals the amount of the current life insurance protection provided to the non-owner multiplied by the life insurance premium factor designated or permitted in guidance published in the Internal Revenue Bulletin);

(2) The amount of policy cash value to which the non-owner has current access to the extent such amount was not actually taken into account for a prior taxable year (for this purpose a non-owner is considered to have current access to that portion of the policy cash value that is directly or indirectly accessible by the non-owner, inaccessible to the owner, or inaccessible to the owner's general creditors); and

(3) The value of any economic benefits not described in (1) and (2) above to the extent not actually taken into account for a prior taxable year.

---

[59] *Id.*

[60] *See* Reg. § 1.61-22(c)(1)(i) and (ii).

Further, Reg. § 1.61-22(e) provides rules concerning the required income recognition by the owner employer and non-owner employee with respect to receipts of policy dividends and certain policy loans. In the case of a non-equity split-dollar arrangement, the regulations provide that the non-owner (the employee) receives current life insurance protection, subject to an anti-abuse rule, equal to the death benefit amount determined on the last day of the non-owner's taxable year (unless the parties agree to use the policy anniversary date) minus amounts payable to the employer-owner.[61] The cost of such insurance is to be determined from guidance to be published by the IRS and is to be reduced by the amount, if any paid by the non-owner employee. Finally, Reg. §§ 1.61-22(f) and (g) provide rules concerning the transfer (i.e., a policy rollout) by the owner employer to the non-owner employee which can cause the recognition of income to the parties.

The second approach mandated by the final regulations applies to collateral assignment equity-split arrangements where the employee is the owner and employer is the non-owner. In such case the non-owner is treated as a lender who advances funds to finance the split-dollar plan owned by the employee who is treated as the borrower. The employee owns the policy which is assigned as collateral to secure the employer's right to receive repayment of the premiums paid by the employer. If a split-dollar loan is not a below-market rate loan, the loan is generally governed by the rules that apply to debt instruments (including the rules for original issue discount under Sections 1271 through 1275).[62] Reg. § 1.7872-15 applies in cases where the split-dollar loan does not provide for adequate interest. In general, the taxation of the benefits under such loan arrangements depends upon whether the loan is a demand loan or a term loan (see the discussion of below-market rate loans in ¶ 303.01). Under Reg. § 1.7872-15(e)(3), the determination of income recognized in the case of a demand loan is made at the end of each year for which the loan is outstanding. The determination of income with respect to term loans is determined in the year in which the loan originates using the rules under Reg. § 1.7872-15(e)(4). Special exceptions are provided for term loan treatment. In the case of split-dollar term loans that are payable upon the death of an individual or which are conditioned upon the future performance of substantial services of an individual, the demand loan rules will be used to determine the timing of the income recognition.[63]

---

[61] T.D. 9092, 68 FR 54336 (Sept. 17, 2003).
[62] Reg. § 1.7872-15(a).

[63] T.D. 9092, 68 FR 54336 (Sept. 17, 2003).

Planning Note: Due to the enactment of the Corporate and Auditing Accountability, Responsibility and Transparency Act of 2002, better known as the Sarbanes-Oxley Act of 2002, split-dollar arrangements which are loans may be outlawed within publicly-traded companies under a provision of the Act which prohibits a public company from lending money to executives and directors of the company.[64] It is not clear whether this provision will apply to the payment of premiums on split-dollar life insurance policies by companies. The final split-dollar life insurance regulations issued in 2003 do not address this issue.[65]

.03 Medical, Accident, and Disability Benefits

One of the most common forms of fringe benefits provided to executives and other employees by employers is medical, accident, and disability coverage and/or benefits. These fringe benefits can take many forms. For example, the employer (and the employee, if the plan is contributory) may pay premiums to an insurance company for a policy that will reimburse the employee for medical expenses incurred as a result of an illness. The plan may require that certain deductibles must be met before benefits are paid, may provide for PPO and/or HMO coverage, may limit benefits for certain types of medical expenses, and so on. The employer may also provide disability coverage (either short- or long-term) on a contributory or noncontributory basis under which wage continuation payments may be made to disabled employees. In addition, the employer may provide the employee with accidental death and dismemberment insurance under which payments may be made on account of certain accidental injuries such as a loss of a foot or for accidental death. Or, the employer may make payments directly to employees or beneficiaries to reimburse them for medical expenses incurred, wage continuation, or for accidental death or dismemberment. As a result of tax legislation enacted in 1996 and revised in 2000, 2002 and 2004, Archer Medical Savings Accounts (Archer MSAs) in conjunction with high deductible health insurance policies have become available to reimburse medical expenses of employees of small employers and their qualified dependents. Medicare+ Choice MSAs, which are special Medical Savings Accounts available to persons eligible for Medicare after 1998 under Code Sec. 138, are not covered in this book because contributions can only be made to such plans by the Secretary for Health and Human Services or

---

[64] P.L. 107-204, 107th Cong., 2d Sess., Sec. 402(k)(1) (July, 2002), 116 Stat. 745 (2002).

[65] T.D. 9092, 68 FR 54336 (Sept. 17, 2003).

trustees of other Medicare+ Choice MSAs (in a trustee-to-trustee transfer). In addition, longterm care insurance policies, which reimburse certain long-term care expenses incurred by chronically-ill individuals are being provided by an increasing number of employers. The employer's payment of premiums on such policies is excludable if certain conditions are met, and, in certain cases, benefits received by employees or their beneficiaries under an insurance plan or directly from the employer may be tax free. In any event, the employer can usually provide medical, accident, and disability benefits for a far smaller cost than employees would have to pay on their own even under contributory plans.

In late 2003, as part of the Medicare Prescription Drug, Improvement, and Modernization Act of 2003, Congress enacted health savings accounts (HSAs) which allow participants, including employees, who participate in high deductible health plans to invest funds on a pre-tax basis in accounts to pay their qualified medical expenses and those of their spouses and dependents. Since these rules, which took effect in 2004, are much more widely applicable and important than those of Archer MSAs, mentioned above, they are separately discussed in the next section of this chapter (302.04).

Employer-Paid Health and Accident Insurance Premiums. Under Code Sec. 106(a), medical insurance premiums, including premiums for supplementary medical insurance (Medicare), paid on behalf of an employee, his/her spouse, and dependents by his or her employer (or former employer if the employee is retired) are excludable.[66] An example of the allowance of this exclusion is shown in a recent letter ruling issued by the IRS.[67] In the letter ruling, a company set up a plan under which the employer would make contributions measured by the value of a retiring employee's accumulated sick leave to pay for one of the two following supplemental benefits prior to an employee's retirement: (1) additional medical coverage that will commence after the lapse of

---

[66] Reg. § 1.106-1 and Rev. Rul. 67-369, 1967-2 CB 71. In Notice 2004-79, IRB 2004-49, 898, the IRS announced that Reg. § 1.106-1 would be amended effective for taxable years beginning after December 31, 2004, to reflect the same definition for the term dependent as given in Code Sec. 105(b), as amended by the Working Families Tax Relief Act of 2004. Under that change, a dependent will be defined as in Code Section 152 without regard to subsections (b)(1), (b)(2), and (d)(1)(B) thereof.

[67] IRS Letter Ruling 200222019, 2-27-02, CCH IRS LETTER RULINGS REPORTS. *See also* IRS Letter Ruling 200520014 for an additional example where the IRS held that contributions made by an employer and used exclusively to pay for accident and health coverage of retired employees and their spouses and dependents were excludable under Code Sec. 106.

the employer-provided retiree health insurance until the retiree's converted sick leave is exhausted or (2) contributions to a qualified deferred compensation plan that would begin on the date of retirement. The IRS held that the amounts contributed to provide the additional medical coverage were excludable under Code Sec. 106(a) as employer-paid medical insurance premiums for employees (retirees are considered employees for this purpose). The IRS has privately ruled that unmarried domestic partners of an employee are not treated as spouses, and the value of the health coverage with respect to the unmarried domestic partner is not excludable. In cases, where local governmental health plans recognize unmarried domestic partnerships, the IRS has stated that the exclusion from gross income for employer-paid premiums only applies if the domestic partner can be considered as a qualified dependent of the employee.[68] In addition, the value of health and accident insurance coverage provided under a VEBA (Voluntary Employee Benefits Association—see the coverage of VEBAs in Chapter 4) for unmarried domestic partners of a covered employee is not excludable.[69]

No exclusion is allowed for amounts an employer pays, without a plan, directly to an employee.[70] Further, no exclusion is permitted with respect to amounts paid by an employer to reimburse employees for health and accident insurance premiums that the employees paid on a salary-reduction basis (such as through a cafeteria plan as covered in chapter 4).[71] In addition, medical insurance premiums paid by partnerships and S corporations on behalf of partners and two percent or greater shareholders are not excludable and, instead, are recognized as guaranteed payments income or compensation.[72]

For purposes of the exclusion for employer-paid health and accident insurance premiums, a qualified long-term insurance contract, as defined under Code Sec. 7702B, is considered to be a health and accident insurance contract, and employer-paid premiums for such coverage are excludable for post-1996 tax years.[73] See the discussion below concerning long-term care insurance.

Archer MSA Premiums. Amounts contributed by eligible small employers to Archer Medical Savings Accounts (MSAs) of eligible employees are excludable by such employees as employer

---

[68] IRS Letter Ruling 9603011, 10-18-95, CCH IRS LETTER RULINGS REPORTS IRS Letter Ruling 9717018, 1-22-97. CCH IRS LETTER RULINGS REPORTS and IRS Letter Ruling 9850011, 9-10-98, CCH IRS LETTER RULINGS REPORTS.

[69] IRS Letter Ruling 200108010, 11-17-00, CCH IRS LETTER RULINGS REPORTS.

[70] *Supra* note 67.

[71] Rev. Rul. 2002-3, 2002-1 CB 316. *See also* Rev. Rul. 2002-80, 2002-2CB 925

[72] Rev. Rul. 91-26, 1991-1 CB 184.

[73] Code Sec. 7702B(a)(3), as added by P.L. 104-191, 104th Cong., 2d Sess., Sec. 321(a) (Aug. 21, 1996).

health and accident plan contributions. The maximum amount excludable is an amount not in excess of the applicable limitation under Code Sec. 220(b) for the year.[74] In addition, no amount is includible in gross income solely because an employee may choose between employer contributions to an Archer MSA and contributions to another health plan of the employer. The amount excludable from gross income is also not subject to FICA and FUTA taxes under Code Secs. 3121(a) and 3306(b)(17). However, Archer MSA contributions that are made through a salary reduction agreement under a cafeteria plan (as defined in Chapter 4) are not excludable.[75]

Briefly, an Archer MSA is a tax-exempt trust or custodial account which is created or organized in the United States to pay qualified medical expenses of eligible individual account holders in conjunction with a high-deductible health plan.[76] Qualified medical expenses are amounts paid by the Archer MSA account holder for medical expenses of the account holder, his/her spouse, and qualified dependents and which are not reimbursed by insurance or otherwise.[77] Coverage for employees under Archer MSAs can only be provided by small employers (generally defined as employers that had 50 or fewer employees during the previous two years).[78]

The Working Families Tax Relief Act of 2004 extended the applicability of the Archer MSA rules through the earlier of (1) the end of the year 2005 or (2) when the aggregate number of participants reaches the 750,000 cut-off limit, if that limit was reached before the end of 2004.[79] Since that limit was not reached, new contributions may be made to Archer MSAs and new accounts may be created until December 31, 2005.[80] After that, no new Archer MSA accounts may be established. However, contributions may continue to be made by or on behalf (including employer contributions) of participants in accounts in existence on December 31, 2005.

The maximum amount permitted to be contributed to an Archer MSA for a year is (1) for high deductible individual coverage, 65 percent of the deductible; and (2) for high-deductible family coverage, 75 percent of the deductible. The same maximum amount

---

[74] Code Sec. 106(b)(1), as added by P.L. 104-191, 104th Cong., 2d Sess., Sec. 301(c)(1) (Aug. 21, 1996), and amended by P.L. 106-554, 106th Cong. 2d Sess., Sec. 202(a)(2) (Dec. 21, 2000).

[75] Code Secs. 106(b)(2) and 125(f) and Notice 96-53, 1996-2 CB 219, Q&A 16.

[76] Notice 96-53, 1996-2 CB 219.

[77] Code Sec. 220(d)(2)(A), as added by P.L. 104-191, 104th Cong., 2d Sess., Sec. 301(a) (Aug. 21. 1996).

[78] Code Secs. 220(i)(4) and (c)(4). Conference Committee Report to P.L. 104-191.

[79] Code Sec. 220(i), as amended by P.L. 108-311, 108th Cong., 2d Sess., Sec. 220(j) (Oct. 4, 2004).

[80] Announcement 2005-12, IRB 2005-7, 555.

applies whether the employee or the employer make the plan contributions. However, if an employer makes a contribution to an Archer MSA for a given year, the account holder of that Archer MSA may not contribute to any Archer MSA for that same year.[81]

> **Example:** Assume that an individual has self-only coverage under a high deductible health plan with an annual deductible of $1,800. The annual contribution limit is 65 percent of $1,800 ($1,170), and the monthly contribution limit is $97.50 ($1,170/ 12). Thus, if the individual's employer contributed more than that, the excess would be gross income. Further, assume that the individual is eligible for only the first eight months of the year. In that case, the contribution limit for the year is $780 ($97.50 × 8).

An employee or other potential Archer MSA participant is an eligible individual if he/she is covered under a high deductible health plan and does not have other health coverage except for accidents, disability, dental care, vision care, long-term care, insurance for a specified disease or illness, and certain other forms of specific insurance.[82] A high deductible health plan is a health plan that: (1) has an annual deductible of at least $1,750, and not more than $2,650, for an individual (self-only coverage); or (2) has an annual deductible of at least $3,500, and not more than $5,250, for family coverage (coverage for more than one individual). In addition, annual out-of-pocket costs cannot exceed $3,500 for individual coverage and $6,450 for family coverage. The foregoing amounts are inflation-adjusted amounts applicable to the year 2005.[83] The amounts will be adjusted for inflation after 2005. Out-of-pocket expenses include deductibles, co-payments, and other amounts the participant must pay for covered benefits, but do not include premiums.[84] A family health plan will not be considered a high deductible plan under the MSA rules unless the annual deductible amount must be met before benefits are payable under the plan regardless of which member or members of the family incur the medical expenses.[85] Thus, if a plan which provides family coverage contains an individual deductible amount that is smaller than the lowest acceptable family deductible amount ($3,500 in 2005), the plan will not be considered a high deductible health plan.

---

[81] Notice 96-53, 1996-2 CB 219, Q&As 12 and 13.

[82] Code Sec. 220(c)(1)(B).

[83] Rev. Proc. 2004-71, IRB 2004-50, 970.

[84] Code Sec. 220(c)(2) and Notice 96-53, 1996-2 CB 219, Q&A 4.

[85] Rev. Rul. 97-20, 1997-1 CB 77.

Employers or other eligible individuals can establish an Archer MSA with a qualified MSA trustee or custodian (e.g., a bank or insurance company) in a manner similar to the way IRA accounts (discussed in Chapter 10) are established. No IRS permission is required. Because the aggregate participation in MSAs is limited, as noted above, the IRS will inform the public by a specified cut-off date (e.g., September 1 and October 1 for small employers) that MSAs can no longer be established. If the IRS makes such an announcement, no new MSAs can be established after that date.[86]

Note that Archer MSAs are meant to be portable. Thus, if a participating employee later changes employers or leaves the work force, the Archer MSA does not stay behind with the former employer, but stays with the individual employee. If that individual after leaving the employment, pays his own premiums, he/she may deduct them, subject to the limits noted earlier.[87]

Employers that maintain Archer MSAs are required to make available comparable contributions on behalf of all employees with comparable coverage during the year. Contributions are considered comparable if they are either the same amount or the same percentage of the deductible under the high deductible plan. If an employer fails to make comparable contributions, the employer is subject to an excise tax equal to 35 percent of the aggregate amount contributed by the employer to MSAs for the tax years of employees ending with or within that calendar year.

However, the IRS may waive part or all of the excise tax if the failure is due to reasonable cause and not willful neglect, and the payment would be excessive relative to the failure.[88]

Finally, it should be noted that self-employed individuals (or their spouses) can establish Archer MSAs subject to the same general rules and limits as discussed above. The contributions made by the self-employed individual or spouse are deductible for AGI within the limits discussed above.[89]

Premiums for Long-Term Care Insurance. Beginning in 1997, employer-paid premiums for employee coverage under a qualified longterm care insurance contract is excludable because it is

---

[86] Notice 96-53, 1996-2 CB 219, Q&As 26 and 27.

[87] *Id.,* Q&A 2.

[88] Code Secs. 4980E(a), (b), and (d), as added by P.L. 104-191, 104th Cong., 2d Sess., Sec. 301(c)(4) (Aug. 21, 1996).

[89] Notice 96-53, 1996-2 CB 219, Q&A 15.

considered coverage under an accident or health plan. However, employer-provided coverage for qualified long-term care services under a flexible spending arrangement (defined similar to flexible spending arrangements discussed under cafeteria plans in Chapter 4) is not excludable.[90]

A qualified long-term care insurance contract is an insurance contract that only provides coverage for specified long-term care services and meets the following requirements:[91]

(1) The contract must be renewable;

(2) The contract cannot provide a cash-surrender value or other money that can be paid, assigned, or pledged as collateral for a loan;

(3) Refunds and contract dividends may be used only to reduce future premiums or increase future benefits;

(4) The contract meets specified consumer protection provisions (for specific guidance concerning the consumer protection provisions, see Reg. § 1.7702B-1); and

(5) In general, the contract does not reimburse or pay expenses that can be paid by Medicare. Note that a contract will not fail to be a long-term care contract merely because payments under it can be made on a per diem or other periodic basis without regard to the expenses incurred during the period to which the payments relate. Further, the coordination with benefits under the contract with those provided under Medicare or cases where Medicare is only a secondary provider is not prohibited.[92]

In general, the requirements for determining what constitutes a qualified long-term care insurance contract apply to contracts issued after December 31, 1996.[93] However, under a special transition rule, any contract issued before January 1, 1997, which met the long-term care insurance requirements of the State at the time the contract was issued, will be treated as a qualified long-term care insurance contract. See Reg. § 1.7702B-2 for coverage of this rule and a determination of (1) which changes in a pre-1997 contract will be considered as the issuance of a new contract and (2) the treatment of the exchange of a pre-1997 contract for another contract (the new contract will be treated as issued after 1996).

---

[90] Code Secs. 7702B(a)(3) and 106(c) as added by P.L. 104-191, 104th Cong., 2d Sess., Secs. 321(a) and 321(c)(2) (Aug. 21, 1996).

[91] Code Sec. 7702B(b)(1).

[92] Code Sec. 7702B(b)(2).

[93] P.L. 104-191, 105th Cong., 1st Sess., Sec. 321(f) (Aug. 21, 1996).

Qualified long-term care services are necessary diagnostic, preventative, therapeutic, curing, treating, mitigating, rehabilitative services and maintenance or personal care services which are required by a chronically ill individual and are provided under a plan of care that is prescribed by a licensed health care practitioner as defined in Code Sec. 7702B(c)(4).[94]

A chronically ill individual is defined as any individual who has been certified by a licensed health practitioner as:[95]

(1) being unable to perform, without substantial assistance from another individual, at least two out of six activities of daily living (ADL's) listed in Code Sec. 7702B(c)(2)(b) for a period of at least 90 days due to a loss of functional capacity (the ADL Trigger);

(2) having a level of disability similar to the level of disability described in the ADL trigger to be stated in regulations to be issued by the IRS (the Similar Level Trigger); or

(3) requiring substantial supervision to protect the individual from threats to health and safety due to severe cognitive impairment (e.g., someone having alzheimers disease) (the Cognitive Impairment Trigger).

The six ADLs are eating, toileting, transferring, bathing, dressing, and continence.[96] A contract will not be treated as a qualified longterm care insurance contract unless the determination of whether an individual is a chronically ill individual, described under the ADL Trigger above, takes into account at least five of these factors.[97] Maintenance and personal care services means any care the primary purpose of which is the provision of needed assistance with any of the disabilities as a result of which the individual is a chronically ill individual.[98]

For purposes of the ADL Trigger, taxpayers may rely on any or all of the following safe harbor definitions:[99]

(1) Substantial assistance means hands-on assistance and standby assistance;

(2) Hand-on assistance means the presence of another person within arms reach of the individual that is necessary to prevent, by physical intervention, injury to that individual;

(3) Standby assistance is the presence of another person within arm's reach of the individual that is necessary to prevent, by physical intervention, injury to that individual while he/she is

---

[94] Code Sec. 7702B(c)(1).
[95] Notice 97-31, 1997-1 CB 417.
[96] *Id.*
[97] Code Sec. 7702B(c)(2) as modified by P.L.

105-34, 105th Cong., 2d Sess., Sec. 1602(b) (Aug. 5, 1997).
[98] Code Sec. 7702B(c)(3).
[99] Notice 97-31, 1997-1 CB 417.

¶ 302.03

performing the ADL (e.g., to prevent the individual from falling while getting into or out of a bathtub).

For purposes of the Cognitive Impairment Trigger, taxpayers may rely on one or both of the following safe harbor definitions:[100]

(1) Severe cognitive impairment is a loss or deterioration in intellectual capacity that is:

   (a) comparable to and includes Alzheimer's disease and similar forms of irreversible dementia and

   (b) measured by clinical evidence and standardized tests that reliably measure the individual's short-term or long-term memory, orientation as to people, places, or time, and deductive or abstract reasoning.

   (c) Substantial supervision means continual supervision (which may include cueing by verbal prompting, gestures, or other demonstrations) by another person that is necessary to protect the severely cognitively impaired individual from threats to his/her health (e.g., wandering away from a residence).

Disability (Wage Continuation) Payments. Disability or wage continuation payments made directly by the employer to an employee under a sick leave or other arrangement are fully includible in gross income under Code Sec. 105(a). In addition, wage continuation benefits received by an employee from an insurance plan or other plan are includible to the extent that the premiums for the coverage under the plan are paid by the employer. Thus, wage continuation or disability benefits are excludable only to the extent that the employee pays for the coverage.[101] For example, if an employee paid one-third of the premiums for wage continuation coverage, then one-third of any disability benefits received would be excludable. Finally, note that the IRS has recently publicly held that where an employer's disability benefits plan provides that employees can elect to treat employer-paid plan premiums as being provided on their behalf on an after-tax basis rather than on a pre-tax basis, employees that make such an election are treated as if they had made the employer contributions.[102] Thus, if the employer made 100 percent of the premium payments to a disability payment plan, and the employee elected to treat those contributions as provided on an after-tax basis, any benefits the employee receives under the plan would be totally tax-free.

---

[100] *Id.* at [12].
[101] Temp. Reg. § 32.1(d).
[102] Rev. Rul. 2004-55, IRB 2004-26, 1081.

The IRS has privately held that long-term disability benefits paid to employees under a policy for which the employees paid premiums on an after-tax basis were totally excludable. However, such benefits paid to employees who elected to exclude premiums paid by the employer for the plan year in which the employee becomes disabled are not excludable because the benefits were attributable to employer-paid contributions.[103]

Payment for Injuries. Under Code Sec. 104(a)(1), amounts received under workers' compensation laws by employees on account of personal injuries and sickness that are job-related are excludable from gross income. Further, an employee can exclude any amounts that he receives through health and accident insurance for personal injuries and sickness to the extent the benefits are attributable to the employee's contributions. For example, the IRS held that a portion of disability benefits received by firefighters under a state workmen's compensation act on account of service-related injuries or sickness and not determined by the employee's age, length of service, or prior contributions is excludable under Code Sec. 104(a) as worker's compensation payments.[104]

Under Code Sec. 105(c), benefits received under health and accident plans are excludable even when the benefits are paid by the employer or are attributable to employer contributions to a plan if the benefits are: (1) payments for permanent loss (or permanent loss of use) of a bodily member or function, permanent disfigurement of the employee, his spouse or a dependent (as defined in Code Sec. 152, determined without regard to subsections (b)(1), (b)(2), and (d)(1)(B) thereof, for taxable years beginning after December 31, 2004—as determined under Code Sec. 152 for taxable years beginning before January 1, 2005), and (2) computed without regard to any period of absence from work.[105]

> **Example:** Randy recently lost an arm while working at his employer's plant. He was paid $5,000 under an accidental death and dismemberment policy that was paid for by his employer. The $5,000 payment is excludable under Code Sec. 105(c).

Benefits that are excludable under Code Sec. 105(c) are not considered reimbursements for medical care and therefore do not have to be offset against the taxpayer's medical expenses for purposes of calculating the taxpayer's medical expense deduction.[106]

---

[103] IRS Letter Ruling 200305005, 9-27-02, CCH IRS LETTER RULINGS REPORTS.
[104] IRS Letter Ruling 200212009, 12-13-01, CCH IRS LETTER RULINGS REPORTS.

[105] Code Sec. 105(c), as amended by P.L. 108-311, 108th Cong., 2d Sess., Sec. 207(9) (Oct. 4, 2004).
[106] Code Sec. 105(f).

¶ 302.03

Medical Expense Reimbursements Directly and Through Insurance. Under Code Sec. 105(b), an employee can exclude amounts paid, directly or indirectly, to the employee to reimburse him for expenses incurred by him for the medical care (as defined in Code Sec. 213(d)) of the employee, his spouse, and his qualifying dependents (as defined in Code Sec. 152, determined without regard to subsections (b)(1), (b)(2), and (d)(1)(B) thereof, for taxable years beginning after December 31, 2004—as determined under Code Sec. 152 for taxable years beginning before January 1, 2005), except to the extent that the amounts are attributable to medical expense deductions taken in a prior year.[107] The exclusion under Code Sec. 105(b) applies to either amounts which the employer reimburses directly (under a noninsured plan) or through an insured plan for which the employer pays premiums. The employee can also exclude any benefits received under an accident and health insurance policy to the extent the benefits are attributable to the employee's own contributions.[108] The exclusion, however, does not apply to amounts provided by an employer to employees without regard to particular medical expenses to the employees incur. Thus, for example, where an employer provided advance reimbursement to employees for uninsured medical expenses (medical expenses not paid under the employer provided health insurance policy) and did not always require repayment of amounts advanced in excess of actual uninsured medical expenses of the employees, the IRS held that none of the advance payments were excludable under Code Sec. 105(b). Similarly, where an employer made loans to employees on account of possible uninsured medical expenses and treated the loans as repaid to the extent employees submitted evidence of actual uninsured medical expenses, no amounts were excludable under Code Sec. 105(b) because the amount advanced to the employees were not required to be repaid to the extent they exceed the employee uninsured medical expenses and, thus, were not loans.[109] Finally, in another ruling, the IRS held that amounts reimbursed under a self-insured employer medical plan were not excludable where the reimbursements pertained to medical expenses incurred by employees prior to the adoption of the medical plan.[110]

Medical expense reimbursements received in the same year as the expenses are incurred are excludable under Code Sec. 105(b). However, such reimbursements must be subtracted from the applicable medical expenses in determining the taxpayer's medical

---

[107] Code Sec. 105(b), as amended by P.L. 108-311, 108th Cong., 2d Sess., Sec. 207(9) (Oct. 4, 2004).

[108] Code Sec. 104(a)(3).

[109] Rev. Rul. 2002-80, 2002-2 CB 925.

[110] Rev. Rul. 2002-58, 2002-2 CB 541.

expense deduction under Code Sec. 213. However, if the reimbursements apply to medical expenses incurred in a prior taxable year, the reimbursements are includible in gross income to the extent that the earlier expense resulted in a Code Sec. 213 medical expense deduction.

> **Example:** Jenkins is covered under an employer-provided health and accident plan. During 2006, he incurred $1,500 of medical and dental expenses covered by the plan. He was reimbursed $1,300 as a result of the expenses in 2006. The reimbursement is excludable under Code Sec. 105(b). However, he must reduce his expenses that are eligible for the amount of the medical expense deduction by the amount of the reimbursement. If the expenses had been incurred in 2005 instead and had resulted in a $400 medical expense deduction for 2005, Jenkins would have had to report $400 as gross income in 2006 on account of the reimbursement.

Reimbursements Received Under Archer MSAs and Qualified Long-term Care Insurance Plans. For tax years beginning after 1996, distributions received by participants from Archer Medical Savings Accounts (Archer MSAs) are excludable from gross income of the recipient to the extent that the amounts are used to pay for medical expenses of the participant, his/her spouse, and dependents and are not reimbursed by insurance.[111] For this purpose medical expenses are those which are defined under Code Sec. 213 (i.e., the rules pertaining to the itemized deduction for medical expenses), but do not include expenses for insurance, other than long-term care insurance, premiums for "COBRA" -type health care continuation coverage, or premiums for heath care coverage while a participant is receiving unemployment insurance.[112]

However, distributions received to cover medical expenses will be includible in gross income if, for the month in which the expense was incurred, the individual for whom the expense was incurred was not covered by a high deductible health plan (defined in the discussion of contributions to Archer MSAs earlier) or had coverage that makes the individual ineligible for an Archer MSA. If included in gross income, distributions are generally subject to an additional 15-percent tax. But, if distributions that are included in gross income are made after the account holder turns age 65, becomes disabled, or dies, the additional 15-percent tax does not apply.[113]

---

[111] Code Sec. 220(f)(1), as added by P.L. 104-191, 104th Cong., 2d Sess., Sec. 301(a) (Aug. 21, 1996).

[112] Notice 96-53, 1996-2 CB 219, Q&A 22.
[113] *Id.*, Q&A 21.

Contributions which are not used to pay for qualified medical expenses can be returned to the participant free of tax on or before the due date of the participant's tax return for the year of the contribution.[114]

Amounts (other than policyholder dividends or premium refunds) that are received under a qualified long-term care insurance contract are generally excludable from gross income as amounts received for personal injuries and sickness and are treated as reimbursement for expenses actually incurred for medical care.[115] However, payments that are received under a per diem or periodic payment contract (paying amounts regardless of the amount of incurred expenses) are excludable only to the extent of the per diem limitation. The per diem limitation is the greater of (1) the equivalent of $175 per day or $63,875 per year (as adjusted for inflation after 1997—the inflation-adjusted amount for 2005 is $240 per day or $87,600 per year) or (2) the actual costs incurred for qualified long-term care services during the period reduced by the total reimbursements received by anyone on account of the longterm care services for the chronically ill individual.[116]

Coverage and Nondiscrimination Rules. Specific coverage and nondiscrimination rules under Code Sec. 105(h) apply to noninsured health and accident plans. For this purpose, a noninsured plan is a plan under which reimbursements were made directly to employees by the employer rather than under an insurance policy. The Code Sec. 105(h) rules do not apply to insured medical plans. Although insured plans are not subject to any specified nondiscrimination rules, employer contributions to insured MSA plans must be made on a comparable basis as discussed above under contributions to MSAs.

Under Code Sec. 105(h), special rules limit and, in some cases, deny the Code Sec. 105(b) exclusion to highly compensated employees for reimbursements made to them under a discriminatory noninsured plan. For this purpose, highly compensated employees include individuals who are:

(1) among the five highest paid officers;

(2) shareholders owning directly or indirectly more than 10 percent of the value of the employer's stock; or

(3) among the highest paid 25 percent of all employees.[117]

---

[114] Code Sec. 220(f)(3) as added by P.L. 104-191, 104th Cong., 2d Sess., Sec. 301(a) (Aug. 21, 1996).

[115] Code Sec. 7702B(a)(2).

[116] Code Secs. 7702B(d)(2) and (4); Rev. Proc. 2004-71, IRB 2004-50, 970.

[117] Code Sec. 105(h)(5).

Code Sec. 105(h) contains an eligibility test and a benefits test that must be satisfied in order for the highly compensated employees to fully exclude their medical expense reimbursements. Under the eligibility test, the plan must either (1) benefit (a) at least 70 percent of all employees, or (b) at least 80 percent of those eligible to benefit if at least 70 percent of all employees are eligible to benefit; or (2) benefit employees who qualify under a classification that does not discriminate in favor of highly compensated employees and their families.[118] For purposes of this test, employees can be excluded from consideration if they (1) have not completed three consecutive years of service before the start of the plan year, (2) have not reached age 25 before the start of the plan year, (3) are part-time or seasonal workers, (4) are covered by a collective bargaining plan, or (5) are nonresident aliens.[119]

> **Example:** Reymart Company employs 130 individuals. Thirty of these individuals have not reached the age of 25 or completed three years of service. Under the company's self-insured plan, all employees who work for some other employer cannot participate in the plan. Twenty-one employees are not eligible for this reason and 14 others choose not to participate. The plan fails the first eligibility test because only 65 employees actually participate, whereas 70 (70% times the 100 that cannot be excluded from consideration in the test) would have to participate to meet this test. However, the plan meets the second percentage test because 79 employees (which is more than 70 percent of 100) are eligible to participate (only the 21 moonlighters cannot participate), and of these 79 employees, 65 actually participate, which is more than the 64 minimum number required (80% of the 79 who are eligible) to meet the second percentage test. Thus, the plan meets the eligibility for coverage test of Code Sec. 105(h)(3).

Under the benefits test, the plan is not permitted to provide greater benefits for highly compensated employees, including non-participants, than for other employees.[120] However, a plan is not considered discriminatory just because more claims for benefits are made by highly compensated employees.[121]

If a plan is found to be discriminatory for a particular year, all or part of the reimbursements made to highly compensated employees are taxable to them. If the plan provides a benefit to a highly compensated employee that is not provided to all other participants,

---

[118] Code Sec. 105(h)(3).
[119] Reg. § 1.105-11(b)(2).

[120] Code Sec. 105(h)(4).
[121] Reg. § 1.105-11(c)(3).

the entire reimbursement paid to highly compensated employees is taxable.[122] If the plan does not meet the eligibility test, the payments made to highly compensated employees are taxable to them in proportion to the total amount of payments under the plan that are provided to highly compensated employees, unless the benefits are not provided to nonhighly compensated employees. However, under Code Sec. 3401(a)(20), the amounts taxable to the highly compensated employees are not subject to income tax withholding. Further, the nondiscrimination rules do not apply for FICA and FUTA tax purposes as discussed later in this chapter.

The Employer's Deduction. Employers may ordinarily deduct the amount of premiums they pay for employee health and accident insurance coverage as well as payments and reimbursements that they make directly to employees and their families under disability, health, and accident plans. In addition, employers are permitted to deduct amounts contributed on behalf of participating employees under Archer MSA Accounts and the amount of premiums paid on behalf of participating employees under qualified long-term care insurance plans.

Self-Employed Person's Deduction. A self-employed person can deduct 100 percent of the cost of medical insurance coverage for himself, his spouse and dependents for AGI in 2003 and later years.[123] Eligible long-term care insurance premiums under Code Sec. 7702B are considered as costs of medical insurance coverage for purposes of the deduction.[124] The amount deductible for AGI cannot be taken as an itemized medical expense deduction under Code Sec. 213 and cannot exceed the taxpayer's earned income from the trade or business with respect to which the plan providing the medical coverage is established.[125] In addition, the deduction is not permitted with respect to a taxpayer for any calendar month for which the taxpayer is eligible to participate in any subsidized health plan maintained by any employer of the taxpayer or his/her spouse.[126] This rule is applied separately to plans which include coverage for qualified long-term care services or are qualified long-term care insurance contracts and other types of insured plans. For example, the fact that the taxpayer is eligible to participate in his spouses' employer-provided health plan without long-term care coverage does not affect the deductibility of premiums paid by the taxpayer for coverage under a qualified long-term care insurance contract.[127]

---

[122] Code Sec. 105(h)(7)(A).
[123] Code Sec. 162(1)(1)(B), as amended by P.L. 105-277, 105th Cong., 2d Sess., Sec. 2002(a) (Oct. 21, 1998).
[124] Code Sec. 162(1)(2)(C).
[125] Code Sec. 162(1)(2) and (3).
[126] Code Sec. 162(1)(3).
[127] Code Sec. 162(1)(2)(B). as amended by P.L. 105-34, 105th Cong., 1st Sess., Sec. 1602(c) (Aug. 5, 1997).

Finally, the deduction is not permitted in determining the individual's self-employment income for purposes of the self-employment tax.[128]

Continuation Coverage Requirements of Group Health Plans. The Consolidated Omnibus Budget Reconciliation Act of 1985 (COBRA) added Code Secs. 162(k) and 106(b) to the Internal Revenue Code to require employer-sponsored group health plans to provide qualified beneficiaries, who so elected, continuing health care coverage for specified minimum periods. If a plan failed to provide required coverage to one or more qualified beneficiaries, (1) the employer-sponsor was not permitted to deduct the group health plan premiums it paid, and (2) the highly compensated employees of that employer were not entitled to exclude the employer-paid premiums on their behalf.[129] These rules applied to plan years beginning after June 30, 1986 and before January 1, 1989. Section 3011 of the 1988 TAMRA repealed Code Secs. 106(b) and 162(k) effective for plan years beginning after December 31, 1988 and enacted Code Sec. 4980B effective for plan years beginning after December 31, 1988. Code Sec. 4980B contains generally the same health care continuation rules found in former Code Sec. 162(k), but replaces the loss of deduction rule of that former section with an excise tax that will apply if the continuation rules are not met. On February 3, 1999, the IRS issued an extensive set of final regulations to explain and interpret the COBRA rules. These final regulations will be effective for qualifying events (defined below) occurring in plan years beginning on or after January 1, 2000.[130] On January 9, 2001, the IRS issued additional final regulations, which adopted, with certain changes, proposed regulations issued on February 3, 1999, and made a few changes to the 1999 final regulations.[131] The 2001 final regulations generally apply with respect to qualifying events occurring on or after January 1, 2002. Prior to that time, presumably reasonable compliance with the 1999 proposed regulations and the provisions of the 1999 final regulations that were changed in 2001 constituted a good faith compliance with reasonable interpretations of the statute. Reference is made to the final regulations, as modified in 2001, in the following paragraphs, as appropriate.

General Rule and Applicability of Excise Tax. Under Code Sec. 4980B(f)(1), a group health care plan must offer each "qualified beneficiary" who would otherwise lose coverage under the plan as a result of a "qualifying event" an opportunity to elect, within the

---

[128] Code Sec. 162(1)(4).
[129] Former Code Secs. 162(k) and 106(b).

[130] Reg. § 54.4980B-1, Q&A 2.
[131] T.D. 8928, 1/9/01.

applicable election period, continuation coverage under the plan and after August 10, 1993, must not reduce the coverage of costs of pediatric vaccines (as defined under section 262 of the Public Health Service Act) below the coverage provided by the plan as of May 1, 1993.[132] For these purposes, a group health plan is a plan maintained by an employer or employee organization to provide health care to individuals (such as employees and former employees) who have an employment-related connection to the employer or employee organization or to their families. Health care (which generally has the same meaning as medical care under Code Sec. 213) is provided under a plan whether provided directly or through insurance, reimbursement, or otherwise, and whether or not, in general, provided through an on-site facility, through a cafeteria plan (discussed in Chapter 4) or other flexible benefit arrangement such as a Health Flexible Spending Arrangement (Health FSA) (also discussed in Chapter 4).[133] However, COBRA coverage is not required with respect to a Health FSA if (1) the Health FSA is not subject to the Health Insurance Portability and Accountability Act (HIPAA) under Code Secs. 9831 and 9832 (discussed below) because the benefits provided under the Health FSA are excepted benefits and (2) in the plan year in which the qualifying event of a qualified beneficiary occurs, the maximum amount that the Health FSA could require to be paid for a full plan year of COBRA coverage equals or exceeds the maximumbenefit available under the Health FSA for the year.[134] Further, a Health FSA need not make COBRA coverage available to a qualified beneficiary if, as of the date of the qualifying event, the maximum benefit available under the Health FSA for the remainder of the plan year is not more than the maximum amount that the plan could require as payment for the remainder of that year to maintain coverage under that Health FSA.[135] Plans under which substantially all of the coverage is for qualified long-term care services (covered under Code Sec. 7702B discussed earlier) and Archer Medical Savings Account plans (covered under Code Sec. 220 discussed earlier) are not group health plans for purposes of the COBRA rules.[136] COBRA continuation coverage cannot be conditioned upon the employee's reimbursement of the employer for premiums the employer paid to maintain coverage under a group health plan during the time an employee is on leave under the Family and Medical Leave Act of 1993 (FMLA).[137]

---

[132] Code Sec. 4980B(f)(1), as amended by Sec. 13,422, P.L. 103-66, 103rd Cong., 1st Sess. (Aug. 10, 1993).

[133] Reg. § 54.4980B-2, Q&A 1(a) and (b).

[134] Reg. § 54.4980B-2, Q&A 8(c).

[135] Reg. § 54.4980B-2, Q&A 8 (f)(iv).

[136] Reg. § 54.4980B-2, Q&A 1(e) and (f).

[137] Reg. § 54.4980B-10, Q&A 5.

The health care continuation rules do not apply with respect to any qualified beneficiary if the qualifying event with respect to the beneficiary occurred during the calendar year immediately following a calendar year during which the employer or all employers (in the case of a multiemployer plan) are considered to be a small employer(s), that is, the employer(s) normally employed fewer than 20 employees during that previous calendar year.[138] For this purpose, an employer is considered to have normally employed fewer than 20 employees during a particular calendar year if it had fewer than 20 employees on at least 50 percent of its typical business days during the year. In determining the fewer than 20 threshold, only common law employees are taken into account, and each part-time employee counts as a fraction of an employee (based on the number of hours he/she works compared to the number required for full-time status).[139] Finally, in determining whether an employer is a small employer, that employer may count the number of its employees on a daily basis or a pay period basis (the method chosen must be consistently used for all employees within a particular year for which the determination is made).[140] It should be noted that although a small-employer plan is generally excepted from the COBRA rules, a plan that is not a small-employer plan for a period remains subject to COBRA for qualifying events that occurred during that period, even if it subsequently becomes a small-employer plan.[141] In addition, an employer that was formerly eligible for the fewer than 20 employee exception must begin to offer COBRA coverage once the number of employees it has exceeds the 20 employee threshold number, following the acquisition of the stock or assets of another employer. The IRS has recently issued Rev. Rul. 2003-70[142] to indicate when COBRA must be offered in such situations. The revenue ruling deals with two situations. In the first situation, a company that offers a group health plan and normally employed fewer than 20 employees during the previous calendar year, acquired the stock of another company, such that after the transfer, the two companies were considered to be part of a single employer. Further, that new single employer normally employed at least 20 employees during the previous calendar year. In that case, the IRS held that the new single employer becomes subject to the COBRA requirements as of the date of the stock transfer. In the second situation, a company that offers a group health plan and normally employed fewer than 20 employees during the previous calendar year, acquired substantially all of the assets of another company and continued the business operations

---

[138] Code Sec. 4980B(d)(1).
[139] Reg. § 54.4980B-2, Q&A 5 (a)-(c).
[140] Reg. § 54.4980B-2, Q&A 5 (e).

[141] Reg. § 54.4980B-2, Q&A 5 (g).

[142] IRB 2003-2 CB 3.

associated with those assets without interruption or substantial change. Together the first company and the acquired business normally employed at least 20 employees during the previous calendar year. In that case, the IRS held that the buying company would continue to be excepted from the COBRA rules with respect to its health plan until, with the normal application of the rules for determining whether a plan is a small employer plan, the January 1 following a year in which the buyer normally employed at least 20 employees. If, however, the buyer is considered to be a successor employer to the seller of the assets under the rules of Reg. § 54.4980B-9, the group health plan of the buyer will have the obligation to make COBRA coverage available to qualified beneficiaries of the seller, even though the buyer is otherwise excepted from COBRA. Other plans which are not subject to the COBRA rules are church plans and plans maintained by the federal government and the government of any State or political subdivision thereof, or by any agency or instrumentality of any of the foregoing (in the case of government plans, other sets of rules require continuation coverage).[143] The specific rules are described below.

If there is a failure to meet the continuation coverage requirements with respect to a qualified beneficiary, an excise tax of $100 for each day in the noncompliance period is imposed on the person or institution that is liable for the tax.[144] However, the excise tax cannot exceed $200 per day if the same failure relates to more than one qualified beneficiary (i.e., the failure affects a family).[145]

The noncompliance period is the period of time beginning on the date the failure to provide continuation coverage first occurs and ends on the earlier of (1) the date the failure is corrected or (2) the date that is six months after the last date on which the employer could have been required to provide continuing coverage to the qualified beneficiary (without considering the payment of premiums).[146] However, the noncompliance period will not start on the date the failure first occurred if the failure is inadvertent. Further, the excise tax does not apply if:

(1) with respect to a failure, it is established to the satisfaction of the IRS that none of the responsible persons knew or would have known, exercising reasonable diligence, that the failure existed; or

(2) the failure was due to reasonable cause and not to willful neglect, and the failure is corrected within 30 days after the

---

[143] Reg. § 54.4980B-2, Q&A 4(b).
[144] Code Sec. 4980B(b)(1).
[145] Code Sec. 4980B(c)(3).
[146] Code Sec. 4980B(b)(2).

day on which the responsible person knew or would have known, exercising reasonable diligence that the failure existed.[147]

However, the two rules above do not apply if the special audit rule of Code Sec. 4980B(b)(3) applies. Under the special audit rule, if one or more failures with respect to a qualified beneficiary (1) are not corrected before the date a notice of examination is sent to the employer, and (2) occur or continue to occur during the audit period, the amount of the excise tax cannot be less than the lesser of $2,500 or the excise tax that would otherwise apply. If the failures are more than de minimis, the minimum excise tax is the lesser of $15,000 or the excise tax that would otherwise apply.

The maximum excise tax liability for unintentional failures is the lesser of (1) 10 percent of the total amount paid or incurred by the employer or predecessor employer (or, for multiemployer plans, by the trust maintaining the plan) during the preceding taxable year for the employer's group health plans or (2) $500,000.[148] There is no dollar limit in the case of intentional failures. In the case of persons providing benefits, such as insurance companies, the maximum excise tax during a taxable year with respect to all plans cannot exceed $2 million for unintentional failures.

Under Code Sec. 4980B(g)(4), a failure to satisfy the health care continuation rules is to be treated as corrected if (1) the continuation rules are retroactively satisfied to the extent possible and (2) the qualified beneficiary is placed in a financial position which is as good as the beneficiary would have been in had the failure not occurred.

The excise tax can be imposed upon (1) the employer in the case of a single employer plan, (2) the plan, in the case of a multi-employer plan, and (3) persons (such as insurance companies) legally responsible for administering or providing benefits under the plan and that were responsible for the failure to satisfy the health care continuation rules.[149] In addition, another person may be liable for the excise tax if that person fails to comply with a written request of the employer (or qualified beneficiary or plan administrator) to make available to qualified beneficiaries the same benefits that the person provides to similarly situated active employees.[150]

Continuing Health Care Rules of Code Sec. 4980B(f). As noted above, the Code Sec. 4980B excise tax does not apply if the group health plan offers each "qualified beneficiary" who would otherwise lose plan coverage as a result of a "qualifying event" an

---

[147] Code Sec. 4980B(c)(1) and (2).
[148] Code Sec. 4980B(c)(4).
[149] Code Sec. 4980B(e)(1).

[150] Code Sec. 4980B(c)(2). *See also* Reg. § 54.4980B-2, Q&A 10(b).

opportunity to elect continuation coverage within the applicable election period.

Code Sec. 4980B(g)(1) defines a "qualified beneficiary" to include any covered employee's spouse or dependent child who was listed as a beneficiary under the plan on the day before the qualifying event. After 1996, the term "qualified beneficiary" also includes children born to, or placed for adoption with, the covered employee during the period of continuation coverage.[151] A covered employee is considered to be a qualified beneficiary only (1) in the event that the employee's employment is terminated (other than for gross misconduct), (2) in the event of a reduction in the employee's hours, and (3) in the event of the bankruptcy of the employer.[152] A covered employee is an individual who "is (or was) provided group health coverage under a group health plan" by virtue of performance of service by the individual for one or more persons maintaining the plan (including service as an independent contractor).[153] For a qualifying event that is the bankruptcy of the employer, any covered employee who retired on or before the date of any substantial elimination of group health coverage is also a qualified beneficiary as is any spouse, surviving spouse, or dependent child of such covered employee, if on the day before the bankruptcy qualifying event, such individual is a beneficiary under the plan.[154] If an individual is denied coverage under a group health plan in violation of applicable law (including the Health Insurance Portability and Accountability Act) and experiences an event that would be a qualifying event if the coverage had not been wrongfully denied, the individual is considered a qualified beneficiary.[155] An individual is not a qualified beneficiary if, on the day before the qualifying event, the individual is covered under the group health plan solely because of another individual's election of COBRA continuation coverage.[156] Finally, an individual ceases to be a qualified beneficiary if he/she does not elect COBRA continuation coverage by the end of the election period (discussed below) or once the plan's obligation to provide COBRA continuation coverage ends.[157]

A qualifying event that will enable a qualified beneficiary to elect continued coverage (that would otherwise be lost because of the event) is one of the following under Code Sec. 4980B(f)(3):

(1) the death of the covered employee;

---

[151] Code Sec. 4980B(g)(1)(A), as amended by P.L. 104-191. 104th Cong., 2d Sess., Sec. 421(c)(3), (d) (Aug. 21, 1996).

[152] Reg. § 54.4980B-3 Q&A 1(d).

[153] Code Sec. 4980B(f)(7). as amended by P.L. 101-239. Sec. 7862(c).

[154] Reg. § 54,4980B-3, Q&A 1(a)(2).

[155] Id., Q&A 1(a)(3).

[156] Id., Q&A 1(c).

[157] Id., Q&A 1(f).

(2) the termination of employment (except when due to gross misconduct as indicated in Reg. §54.4980B-4, Q&A 2),[158] or a reduction of hours of the covered employee's employment;

(3) the divorce or legal separation of the covered employee from his spouse;

(4) the covered employee's entitlement to Medicare benefits;

(5) a child of the covered employee ceasing to be a dependent; and

(6) a bankruptcy proceeding commencing on or after July 1, 1986, with respect to the employer from whose employment the covered employee retired at any time.

To lose coverage means to cease to be covered under the same terms and conditions as in effect immediately before the event. A loss of coverage also includes an increase in an employee premium or contribution resulting from one of the events listed above.[159] The loss of coverage need not be concurrent with the event; it is enough that the loss of coverage occur at any time before the end of the maximum coverage period (that is the length of time the continuation coverage must be made available as discussed below).[160] If coverage of a qualified beneficiary is eliminated in anticipation of a qualifying event, such as an employee's eliminating the coverage of the employee's spouse in anticipation of a divorce or legal separation, the elimination is disregarded in determining whether the qualifying event causes a loss of coverage.[161] Thus, where an employee eliminated the coverage of his spouse in anticipation of their divorce, the divorce was considered to be the qualifying event.[162] In the case of a bankruptcy proceeding, loss of coverage includes a substantial elimination of coverage with respect to a qualified beneficiary or his or her surviving spouse within one year before or after the date of commencement of the proceeding.[163]

If a qualifying event (such as separation from service or a reduction in hours) occurs less than 18 months after the date the covered employee becomes entitled to Medicare benefits, the period of coverage for qualified beneficiaries, other than the covered employee, will not terminate before the close of the 36-month period

---

[158] Note that the final regulations do not define what constitutes gross misconduct. However, recent court rulings provide some indication. For example, in *Bryant v. Food Lion Inc.,* 2001 U.S. App. LEXIS 7913, 26 EBC 1009 (CA-4, 2001), the Fourth Circuit Court of Appeals held that the firing of employees because of flagrant and repeated violations of the employer's rules of conduct constituted termination for gross misconduct. *See also Mc Knight v. School District of Philadelphia,* 105 F Supp 2nd 438 (E.D., PA, 2000), where the District Court held that the firing of a teacher because the teacher was charged with criminal sexual conduct against a former student was a termination for gross misconduct.

[159] Reg. §54,4980B-4, Q&A 1(c).

[160] *Id.*

[161] *Id.*

[162] Rev. Rul. 2002-88, 2002-2 CB 995.

[163] Code Sec. 4980B(f)(3).

beginning on the date the covered employee becomes entitled to the Medicare benefits.[164]

The taking of leave under the Family and Medical Leave Act of 1993 (FMLA) does not constitute a qualifying event under the COBRA rules unless:

(1) an employee (or the spouse or dependent child of the employee) is covered on the day before the first day of FMLA leave under a group health plan of the employee's employer;

(2) the employee does not return to employment with the employer at the end of the FMLA leave; and

(3) the employee (or the spouse or a dependent child of the employee) would, in absence of the COBRA continuation coverage, lose coverage under the group health plan before the end of the maximum coverage period.[165]

However, the satisfaction of the above conditions is not a qualifying event if the employer eliminates, on or before the last day of the employee's FMLA leave, coverage under a group health plan for the class of employees (while continuing to employ them) to which the employee would have belonged had he/she not taken the FMLA leave. If a qualifying event is deemed to occur under the above conditions, it is deemed to occur on the last day of the FMLA leave.[166] The fulfillment of the above conditions is a qualifying event even if the employee fails to pay the employee portion of premiums for plan coverage during the FMLA leave or declines coverage under a group health plan during the leave.[167]

If a qualified beneficiary makes an election to continue coverage, that beneficiary is entitled to the same coverage "as of the time the coverage is being provided," as the coverage that is provided to similarly situated non-COBRA beneficiaries for whom a qualifying event has not occurred.[168] If coverage under the plan is modified for any group of similarly situated non-COBRA beneficiaries, the coverage must also be modified in the same manner for all individuals who are qualified beneficiaries under the plan.[169] If the continuation coverage offered differs in any way from the coverage made available to similarly situated non-COBRA beneficiaries, the coverage offered does not constitute COBRA continuation coverage, and the group health plan is not in compliance with the COBRA rules, unless other coverage that does constitute COBRA continuation coverage is also offered.[170] A qualified beneficiary must be given credit for the

---

[164] Code Sec. 4980(B)(i)(V), as added by P.L. 101-239. sec. 7862(c).

[165] Reg. § 54.4980B-10, Q&A 1(a)

[166] *Id.*, Q&A 2.

[167] *Id.*, Q&A 3.

[168] Code Sec. 4980B(f)(2)(A).

[169] *Id.*

[170] Reg. § 54.4980B-5, Q&A 1(a).

amount earned toward any plan deductible before the qualifying event. The same rule applies to plan limits and co-payments. If a deductible is computed separately for each individual receiving coverage under the plan, each individual's remaining deductible amount (if any) on the date COBRA continuation coverage begins is equal to that individual's remaining deductible amount immediately before that date. If a deductible is computed on a family basis, the remaining deductible for the family on the date that COBRA continuation coverage begins depends on the members of the family electing the COBRA continuation coverage. In computing the family deductible that remains on the date COBRA continuation coverage begins, only the expenses of those family members receiving COBRA continuation coverage need be taken into account. If the qualifying event results in there being more than one family unit (for example, because of a divorce), the family deductible may be computed separately for each resulting family unit based on the members in each unit. These rules apply regardless of whether the plan provides that the family deductible is an alternative to individual deductibles or an additional requirement.[171]

In general, qualified beneficiaries need not be given an opportunity to change the plan coverage that he/she was receiving immediately before the qualifying event. This is true regardless of whether the coverage received by the qualified beneficiary ceases to be of value to the qualified beneficiary, such as in the case of a qualified beneficiary covered under a region-specific health maintenance organization (HMO) who leaves the HMO's service region. However, there are two exceptions to this rule. First, if a qualified beneficiary participates in a region-specific benefit package (such as an HMO or an on-site clinic) that will not service his/her health needs in the area to which he/she is relocating, the qualified beneficiary must be given an opportunity to elect alternative coverage that the employer or employee organization makes available to active employees. If the employer or employee organization makes group health plan coverage available to similarly situated non-COBRA beneficiaries that can be extended in the area to which the qualified beneficiary is relocating, then that coverage is the alternative coverage that must be made available to the relocating qualified beneficiary. If the employer or employee organization does not make group health plan coverage available to similarly situated non-COBRA beneficiaries that can be extended in the area to which the qualified beneficiary is relocating but makes the coverage available to other employees that can be extended in that area, then

---

[171] Reg. § 54.4980B-5, Q&As 2 and 3.

the coverage made available to those other employees must be made available to the relocating qualified beneficiary. However, the employer or employee organization is not required to make any other coverage available to the relocating qualified beneficiary if the only coverage the employer or employee organization makes available to active employees is not available in the area to which the qualified beneficiary relocates (because all such coverage is region-specific and does not service individuals in that area). Under the second exception, if an employer or employee organization makes an open enrollment period available to similarly situated active employees with respect to whom a qualified event has not occurred, the same open enrollment rights must be made available to each qualified beneficiary receiving COBRA continuation coverage. An open enrollment period means a period during which an active employee covered under a plan can choose to be covered under another group health plan or under another benefit package within the same plan, or to add or eliminate coverage of family members.[172]

The continuation coverage must last (that is the maximum coverage period must be) at least 18 months (the period extends to 29 months for persons becoming disabled (for social security benefit purposes) at any time during the first 60 days of COBRA continuation coverage if they have notified the employer of the disability) if the qualifying event is the employee's termination or reduction in hours of employment; otherwise, the coverage must last at least 36 months after the qualifying event. If a qualifying event that gives rise to an 18-month coverage period is followed by a second qualifying event (e.g., death of a covered employee or a divorce) within that 18-month period, coverage must be provided for up to 36 months from the first qualifying event.[173] In the case of a qualifying bankruptcy proceeding of the employer, coverage terminates at the date of death of the covered employee or qualified beneficiary, or in the case of the surviving spouse or dependent children of the covered employee, 36 months after the covered employee's death.[174]

The maximum coverage period will not be extended if alternative health coverage (for example, coverage as a result of state or local law, the Uniformed Services Employment and Reemployment Rights Act of 1994, industry practice, a collective bargaining agreement, severance agreement, or plan procedure) is provided to a qualified beneficiary after a qualified event without regard to COBRA continuation coverage. However, if the alternative coverage does not satisfy all the requirements for COBRA continuation

---

[172] Reg. § 54.4980B-5, Q&A 4.
[173] Code Sec. 4980(f)(2)(B)(i).

[174] Code Sec. 4980B(f)(2)(B)(i)(III).

coverage, or if the amount that the group health plan requires to be paid for the alternative coverage is greater than the amount required to be paid by similarly situated non-COBRA beneficiaries for the continuation coverage, the plan covering the qualified beneficiary immediately before the qualifying event must offer the qualified beneficiary receiving the alternative coverage the opportunity to elect COBRA continuation coverage. If an individual rejects COBRA continuation coverage in favor of alternative coverage, then, at the expiration of the alternative coverage period, the individual need not be offered a COBRA election. However, if the individual receiving alternative coverage is a covered employee and the spouse or a dependent child of the individual would lose that alternative coverage as a result of a qualifying event (such as the death of the covered employee), the spouse or dependent child must be given an opportunity to elect to continue that alternative coverage, with a maximum coverage period of 36 months measured from the date of that qualifying event.[175] If an employee takes an FMLA leave, the maximum coverage period will usually run from the last day of the FMLA leave.[176] However, if the employee notifies the employer, before the end of the FMLA period that he will not be returning to work, the maximum coverage period is measured from the day the employee notifies the employer.[177]

> **Example:** Employee Davidson is covered under the group health plan of Flexco on January 31, 2006. David takes FMLA leave beginning February 1, 2006. Davidson's last day of the leave is 12 weeks later, on April 25, 2006, and Davidson does not return to work with Flexco at the end of the FMLA leave. If Davidson does not elect COBRA continuation coverage, he will lose coverage under the group health plan of Flexco on April 26, 2006. Davidson experiences a qualifying event on April 25, 2006, and the maximum period (generally 18 months as covered above) is measured from that date.

Under Code Sec. 4980B(f)(2)(B), coverage may terminate before the end of the required coverage period for any of the following reasons:

(1) The employer terminates every group health plan for its employees.

(2) The qualified beneficiary fails to make a required premium payment (a 30-day (45 days for the first payment) grace period is allowed).

---

[175] Reg. § 54.4980B-7, Q&A 7.
[176] Reg. § 54.4980B-10, Q&A 2.
[177] *Id.*

(3) The qualified beneficiary first becomes covered under another group health plan (as an employee or otherwise) which does not contain any exclusion or limitation with respect to any preexisting condition of the beneficiary (other than such an exclusion or limitation which does not apply to or is satisfied by the beneficiary) by reason of the group health care plan portability, access, and renewability requirements of the Health Insurance Portability and Accountability Act of 1996 (see the discussion below concerning these requirements), the Employee Retirement Income Security Act or the Public Service Act.[178] The final regulations indicate that the employer may cut-off the right to COBRA continuation coverage based upon other group health coverage only if the qualified beneficiary first becomes covered under the other group health plan coverage after the date of the COBRA election (the same rule applies to becoming entitled to Medicare benefits described in (4) below).[179] Thus, coverage under a plan that took effect before the COBRA election date will not preclude the qualified beneficiary's ability to elect COBRA continuation coverage.

(4) The qualified beneficiary becomes entitled to Medicare benefits (for this purpose, the final regulations indicate that entitlement to Medicare benefits means being enrolled in Medicare and does not mean merely being eligible to enroll).[180]

(5) The qualified beneficiary who is entitled to extended coverage due to disability is no longer disabled.

In addition, a plan may discontinue providing COBRA continuation coverage to a qualified beneficiary for cause on the same basis that the plan could terminate coverage of a similarly situated non-COBRA beneficiary (except in the case of nontimely premium payments made within the allowable grace period). For example, if a plan terminates the coverage of similarly situated active employees for the submission of a fraudulent claim, then the COBRA continuation coverage of a qualified beneficiary can also be terminated for the submission of a fraudulent claim.[181]

The continuation coverage cannot be conditioned upon or otherwise discriminate on the basis of lack of insurability.[182] In addition, the plan during the 180 days before the expiration of the continuation period must provide a qualified beneficiary with a conversion option if such an option is otherwise available under the plan. But, this 180-day period evidently does not apply if the coverage ends earlier because of one of the reasons listed above.[183]

---

[178] Code Sec. 4980B(f)(2)(b)(iv)(I), as amended by P.L. 104-191, 104th Cong., 2d Sess., Sec. 421(c)(1)(B) (Aug. 21, 1996).

[179] Reg. § 54.4980B-7, Q&A 2.

[180] *Id.,* Q&A 3.

[181] *Id.,* Q&A 1(b).

[182] Code Sec. 4980B(f)(2)(D).

[183] Code Sec. 4980B(f)(2)(E).

A qualified beneficiary may be required to pay a premium for the continuation coverage. In general, the premium for any period of coverage may not exceed 102 percent (150 percent for any months after the 18th month of continuation coverage for certain disabled individuals) of the cost to the plan for coverage of similarly situated non-COBRA beneficiaries who have not reached a qualifying event.[184] A plan is not permitted to require the payment of an amount that exceeds 102 percent of the applicable premium for any period of COBRA continuation coverage to which a qualified beneficiary is entitled to without regard to the disability extension. Thus, if a qualified beneficiary entitled to a disability extension experiences a second qualifying event within the original 18 month maximum coverage period, then the plan is not permitted to require the payment of an amount that exceeds 102 percent of the applicable premium for any period of COBRA extension coverage.[185] The premium may, at the election of the payor, be paid in monthly installments. If an election is made after the qualifying event, the plan must permit payment for continuation coverage for the period preceding the election to be made within 45 days after the election is made.[186] A plan may not require the payment of any premium before the day that is 45 days after the day of the original election for continuation coverage.[187] The final regulations do not specify who must make the required payments. Thus, payments can be made on behalf of qualified beneficiaries by third parties such as a hospital or a new employer.[188] For self-insured plans, the premium must equal a reasonable estimate of the cost of providing coverage for similarly situated beneficiaries on an actuarial basis and take into account factors to be prescribed by the IRS (the final regulations do not address this issue). The plan may use a formula to set the premium by adjusting the previous year's cost (for similarly situated beneficiaries) for the change in the GNP implicit price deflator for a designated 12-month period.[189]

A series of notifications related to continuation coverage are required. First, when plan coverage commences or at the effective date of the continuation coverage rules, whichever is later, the plan must provide written notice to the employee and his/her beneficiaries of their rights to the continuation coverage.[190] This notice may be provided in a summary plan description, but it may not be provided by posting in a generally available location.[191] Note that

---

[184] Code Sec. 4980B(f)(2)(C).
[185] Reg. § 54.4980B-8, Q&A 1(b).
[186] Code Sec. 4980B(f)(2)(C).
[187] Code Sec. 4980B(f)(2)(C), as amended by P.L. 101-239, Sec. 7862(c).
[188] T.D. 8812, 2/3/99.
[189] Code Sec. 4980B(f)(4)(B).
[190] Code Sec. 4980B(f)(6)(A).
[191] H.R. Rep. No. 99-453, 99th Cong., 1st Sess. (1985), at 566-67.

¶ 302.03

employee benefit plans must provide this notice or risk sanctions under the Employee Retirement Income Security Act of 1974 (ERISA).

The second notice must be filed at about the time of the qualifying event. The employer of an employee under a plan must notify the plan administrator of the following qualifying events within 30 days after they occur:

(1) the death of the covered employee;

(2) the termination (except for gross misconduct) or reduction of hours of the covered employee's employment;

(3) the entitlement of the covered employee to Medicare benefits; and

(4) a bankruptcy proceeding with respect to the employer.[192]

The covered employee or qualified beneficiary must notify the plan administrator within 60 days of the divorce or legal separation of the covered employee from the spouse or the cessation of a child being a dependent.[193]

In addition, each qualified beneficiary, who is determined, under the Social Security Act, to have been disabled at any time during the first 60 days of continuation coverage is responsible for notifying the plan administrator of that determination within 60 days of the determination and for notifying the plan administrator within 30 days of the date of any final determination that the beneficiary is no longer disabled.[194]

Finally, under Code Sec. 4980B(f)(6)(D), the plan administrator must, within 14 days after it receives a notice, notify each qualified beneficiary of his/her right to elect continuation coverage. Notice provided to an employee's spouse is deemed to be notice provided to any other qualified beneficiaries in the family.

The Department of Labor, which has responsibility for issuing regulations concerning the COBRA continuation notice and disclosure requirements, covered in the above paragraphs, issued final regulations in May of 2004 addressing the notice requirements.[195] The regulations provide details as to the procedures governing, the content, and the timing of such notices. The regulations took effect on the first day of the first plan year beginning on or after November 26, 2004.

---

[192] Code Sec. 4980B(f)(6)(B).
[193] Code Sec. 4980B(f)(6)(C).
[194] Code Sec. 4980B(f)(6)(C), as amended by P.L. 104-191, 104th Cong., 2d Sess., Sec. 421(c)(2) (Aug. 21, 1996).
[195] Labor Reg. §§ 2590.606-1, 2590.606-2, 2590.606-3 and 2590.606-4, 69 FR 30084 (May 26, 2004).

A qualified beneficiary may elect continuation coverage during a specified election period under Code Sec. 4980B(f)(5). The election period must last for at least 60 days, beginning no later than the date that the coverage would have terminated on account of the qualifying event. If there is a choice among types of coverage under the plan, each qualified beneficiary is entitled to make a separate selection among the types of coverage. If an election is made within the 60-day period, coverage under an indemnity or reimbursement type of health plan must be provided from the date that such coverage would otherwise have been lost. As an alternative, the plan can permit retroactive reinstatement of a participant. Claims incurred by a qualified beneficiary during the election period do not have to be paid before the election is made.[196] In the case of a group health plan that provides health services (such as an HMO or a walk-in clinic), the plan can require with respect to a qualified beneficiary who has not elected and paid for COBRA continuation coverage that the qualified beneficiary choose between (1) electing and paying for the coverage; or (2) paying the reasonable and customary charge for the plan's services, but only if a qualified beneficiary who chooses to pay for the services will be reimbursed for that payment within 30 days after the election of COBRA continuation coverage (and, if applicable, the payment of any balance due for the coverage). In the alternative, the plan can provide continued coverage and treat the qualified beneficiary's use of the facility as a constructive election. In such a case, the qualified beneficiary is obligated to pay any applicable charge for the coverage, but only if the qualified beneficiary is informed that use of the facility will be considered a constructive election before using the facility.[197] If the qualifying beneficiary waives continuing coverage during the 60-day election period, the waiver may be revoked at any time before the end of the election period. However, coverage does not have to be retroactively provided in that case.[198] Finally, it should be noted that each qualified beneficiary must be offered the opportunity to make an independent election to receive COBRA continuation coverage. If the plan allows similarly situated active employees with respect to whom a qualifying event has not occurred to choose among several options during an open enrollment period (for example, to switch to another group health plan), then each qualified beneficiary must also be offered an independent election to choose during an open enrollment period among the options made available to similarly situated active employees with respect to whom a qualifying event has not occurred.[199]

---

[196] Reg. § 54.4980B-6, Q&A 3(b).
[197] Reg. § 54.4980B-6, Q&A 3(c).

[198] Reg. § 54.4980B-6, Q&A 4.
[199] Reg. § 54.4980B-6, Q&A 6.

¶ 302.03

A group health plan will be in compliance with the health care continuation rules if the plan provides for extension of the required periods (described above) such that (1) the period of extended coverage begins with the date of the coverage loss and (2) the applicable notice period begins with the date of the coverage loss.[200]

The final regulations issued in 2001 provide special rules concerning the application of the COBRA continuation rules in the cases of business reorganizations and employer withdrawals from multiemployer plans. See Reg. § 54.4980B-9 for details.

In summary, employers and other responsible persons should be careful to make certain that the required continuation coverage is available and that the required notices and other requirements of Code Sec. 4980B are taken care of. The rules have undoubtedly introduced more uncertainty and complexity into the maintenance of group health plans for employees. The rules also make it more costly for employers to provide health and accident coverage to its employees.

Excise Tax Applicable to Contributions to Nonconforming Group Health Plans. Under Code Sec. 5000(a), any employer or organization of employees, including self-employed individuals (after August 10, 1993), that contributes to a noncomforming group health plan must pay a tax equal to 25 percent of that employer's (or organization's) expenses incurred during the calendar year for each group health plan to which the employer or organization of employees contributes.[201] A nonconforming group health plan is a group health plan or large group health plan that (1) fails to provide the same benefits under the plan under the same conditions to any employee or employee's spouse age 65 or older as any employee or spouse of an employee under age 65 and/or (2) takes into account in furnishing an item or service to an individual 65 or older who is covered by the plan due to being currently employed (or the employment of his/her spouse), that the individual is entitled to Medicare hospital benefits.[202]

For purposes of these rules, a group health plan means a plan (including a self-insured plan) of, or contributed to, by an employer (including the self-employed) or employee organization to provide health care to employees, former employees, the employer, others associated with the employer in a business relationship or their families. A large group health plan is a plan of, or contributed to,

---

[200] Code Sec. 4980B(f)(8), as added by P.L. 101-239, Sec. 7891(d).

[201] Code Sec. 5000(a), as amended by Sec.

13,561(e)(2)(A)(i), P.L. 103-66, 103rd Cong., 1st Sess. (Aug. 10, 1993).

[202] 42 U.S.C.A. Sec. 1395y(b)(1)(A).

by an employer or employee organization (including a self-insured plan) that covers individuals as described above under a group health plan and that covers employees of at least one employer that normally employed at least 100 employees on a typical business day during the previous year. For purposes of the large group health plan definition, (1) all employers treated as a single employer under Code Sec. 52(a) or (b) will be treated as a single employer; (2) all employees of the members of an affiliated service group (as defined in Code Sec. 414(m) will be treated as a single employer; and (3) leased employees will be treated as employees of the person for whom they perform the service.[203]

The excise tax does not apply to federal or other government entities nor to small employers (those with fewer than 20 employees for each working day in each of 20 or more calendar weeks in the current or preceding year).[204] In addition, the excise tax with respect to actions related to an employee's age does not apply if an individual with end-stage renal disease is entitled to the special Medicare benefits for end-stage renal disease.[205]

An excise tax equal to 25 percent of group health plan expenses also applies where an employer's group health plan discriminates against beneficiaries having end-stage renal disease at any time during the year and where an employer's large group health plan (as defined above) discriminates against disabled individuals at any time during the year.[206]

Excise Tax For Failure to Comply with Group Health Plan Requirements. An excise tax is imposed on account of any failure of a group health plan to meet the recently enacted group health plan requirements specified in Code Secs. 9801 through 9803, 9811, and 9812. The requirements specified in Code Secs. 9801 through 9803 are the group health plan portability, access, and renewability requirements. Code Sec. 9811 contains rules concerning length of maternity stay requirements, and Code Sec. 9812 contains mental health parity requirements. The tax is imposed at the rate of $100 per day for each day in the noncompliance period on account of each individual to whom the failure relates.[207] Under Code Sec. 4980D(b)(2), the noncompliance period is the period starting on the date the failure first occurs and terminating on the date the failure is corrected. But, if there are one or more failures which

---

[203] Code Sec. 5000(b), as amended by Sec. 13,561(d)(2) and (e)(2)(A)(iv), P.L. 103-66, 103rd Cong., 1st Sess. (Aug. 10, 1993).
[204] Code Sec. 5000(d) and 42 U.S.C.A. Sec. 1395y(b)(1)(A).

[205] 42 U.S.C.A. Sec. 1395y(b)(1)(A).
[206] 42 U.S.C.A. Sec. 1395y(b)(1)(A) and (b)(1)(B).
[207] Code Sec. 4980D(b)(1).

are not corrected before an examination notice of income tax liability is sent to the employer, the excise tax will be at least $2,500.[208] Further, under Code Sec. 4980D(3)(B), the minimum excise tax is $15,000 where the failure in such circumstances is more than de minimis. These minimum tax provisions do not apply to church plans.[209] Code Sec. 4980D(e) indicates that the tax is generally imposed upon the employer, or in the case of a multiemployer plan, the plan.

The excise tax does not apply to any failure during any period for which it is established to the satisfaction of the IRS that the person otherwise liable for the tax did not know, and exercising due diligence would not have known, that the failure existed. In addition, Code Sec. 4980D(c)(2) indicates that the excise tax will not be imposed if:

(1) The failure is due to reasonable cause and not to willful neglect;

(2) For plans other than church plans, the failure is corrected during the 30-day period beginning on the first date the person otherwise liable for the tax knew, or exercising reasonable diligence, would have known, the failure existed; and

(3) For church plans, the failure is corrected before the end of the correction period.

Under Code Sec. 4980D(c)(3), for failures that are due to reasonable cause and not to willful neglect, an overall maximum equal to the lesser of (a) $500,000 or (b) 10 percent of the of the aggregate amount paid or incurred by the employer for a single employer plan (10 percent of the amount paid or incurred by a plan trust for a multiple employer plan). The IRS may waive part or all of the tax for a failure due to reasonable cause and not willful neglect to the extent the payment of the tax would be excessive relative to the failure involved.[210] Finally, Code Sec. 4980D(d) provides that the excise tax will not be imposed on any small employer that provides group health insurance through an insurer on account of any failure (other than failure relating to the maternity stay requirements of Code Sec. 9811) that is due solely to health insurance coverage offered by that insurer. A small employer, for this purpose, is one who employed on average at least two but not more than 50 employees on business days during the preceding calendar year and who employed at least two employees on the first day of the plan year.

The excise tax and the portability, access, and renewability rules do not apply to plan years beginning before July 1, 1997. The IRS

---

[208] Code Sec. 4980D(b)(3)(A).
[209] Code Sec. 4980D(b)(3)(C).

[210] Code Sec. 4980D(c)(4).

was required to issue regulations by April of 1997 and did so by issuing temporary and final regulations concerning those rules in TD 8716 (April 7, 1997). More recently, in December of 2004, the IRS issued final regulations under Code Secs. 9801, 9831, and 9833 (this latter section indicates the effective date of the new regulations). These final regulations are effective for plan years beginning on or after July 1, 2005.[211] For plan years beginning before July 1, 2005, the previously issued temporary regulations continue to be effective.[212] Previously, the IRS had issued final regulations in early 2001 under Code Sec. 9802 concerning the prohibition of discrimination against participants and beneficiaries based on a health factor (these final regulations are not as extensive as the 1997 temporary regulations).[213] In any event, the IRS will be permitted to take enforcement action with respect to the rules covered in these final regulations. Under the original legislation, no enforcement action could begin before the later of (a) January 1, 1998 or (b) the date final regulations are issued if the plan has sought to be in good faith compliance with the statutory requirements.[214] The final regulations (especially the ones issued in late 2004) contain detailed voluminous coverage and explanation of the rules, and general coverage of these regulations is beyond the scope of this book. Taxpayers should consult the regulations for details, particularly concerning the portability rules.

The length of maternity stay mandates and the mental health parity requirements are effective for group health plans for plan years beginning on or after January 1, 1998. The mental health parity provisions will not apply to benefits for services furnished on or after (a) on or after January 1, 2004, and before October 4, 2004, and (b) after December 31, 2005. The provisions of this section were also previously not applicable on or after September 30, 2001, and before January 10, 2002.[215] Temporary regulations were issued under the length of maternity stay mandates in late 1998 and under the mental health parity requirements in late 1997. See those regulations for more details concerning the rules.

The final and temporary regulations issued under the group health plan requirements indicated above do not apply to any group health plan for any plan year if, on the first day of the plan year, the plan has fewer than two participants who are current employees.[216] In addition, certain benefits, as indicated in Reg.

---

[211] Reg. § 54.9833-1 and T.D. 9166, 69 FR. 78720 (Dec. 30, 2004).

[212] T.D. 9166, 69 FR. 78720 (Dec. 30, 2004).

[213] *See* Reg. § 1.9802-1 and T.D. 8931, Jan. 5, 2001, amended March 8, 2001.

[214] P.L. 104-191, 104th Cong., 2d Sess., Secs. 301(c) and 401(e) (Aug. 21, 1996).

[215] Code Sec. 9812(f), as amended by P.L. 108-311, 108th Cong., 2d, Sess. Sec. 302(a) (Oct. 4, 2004).

[216] Reg. § 54.9831-1(b).

¶ 302.03

§ 54.9831-1(c), are not subject to the requirements of the final and temporary regulations. The benefits excepted in all circumstances include coverage only for accident, disability income coverage, liability insurance, worker's compensation or similar coverage, automobile medical payment insurance, credit-only insurance, and coverage for on-site medical clinics. Certain limited-scope benefits, such as dental benefits, vision benefits, and long-term care benefits, are excepted if they are provided under a separate policy, certificate or contract of insurance, or are otherwise not an integral part of a group health plan. Finally, benefits provided under a health flexible spending arrangement (as defined under Code Sec. 106(c)(2)) are excepted under specified circumstances.

Portability Rules. Under the portability rules of Code Sec. 9801, limitations are placed on coverage exclusions on account of preexisting conditions to make it easier for employees who change jobs to obtain full health care coverage from their new employer's plan. Under the Code Sec. 9801 final regulations, a *preexisting condition exclusion* means a limitation or exclusion of benefits relating to a condition based on the fact that the condition was present before the effective date of coverage under a group health plan or group health insurance coverage, whether or not any medical advice, diagnosis, care, or treatment was recommended or received before that day. A preexisting condition exclusion includes any exclusion applicable to an individual as a result of information relating to an individual's health status before the individual's effective date of coverage under a group health plan or group health insurance coverage, such as a condition identified as a result of a pre-enrollment questionnaire or physical examination given to the individual, or review of medical records relating to the pre-enrollment period.[217] Specifically, Code Sec. 9801(a) states that a group health plan may exclude coverage for preexisting conditions only for the first 12 months after enrollment of a new employee (18 months in the case of late enrollees). The 12 (or 18) month period must be reduced by the months of certain prior health care coverage (as discussed below). The preexisting condition exclusion can only relate to a condition (whether physical or mental) regardless of its cause, for which medical advice, diagnosis, care, or treatment was recommended or received within the 6-month period ending on the enrollment date. Under Code Sec. 9801(b)(1)(B), genetic information is not to be treated as a condition unless medical advice, diagnosis, care, or treatment was rendered with respect to a related condition within the 6-month period. Newborns of the employee may not be excluded from coverage under the new employer's

---

[217] Reg. § . 54.98701-3(a)(i).

plan if they were covered under another group health plan within 30 days of birth, and adoptees may not be excluded if they were covered within 30 days of adoption. Further, pregnancy may not be excluded.[218] See Reg. § 54.9801-3(b) for further details concerning the issues of genetic information, newborns, and pregnancy. The final regulations indicate that a group health plan that imposes a preexisting condition exclusion must provide a written general notice of such exclusion to participants under the plan and cannot impose a preexisting condition exclusion with respect to a participant or a dependent of the participant until such a notice is provided.[219]

Under Code Sec. 9801(c), an employee is credited with prior creditable coverage toward the 12 or 18 month exclusion period covered above. Creditable coverage includes coverage under a number of different specified arrangements including group health care plans, individual health care plans, HMOs, Medicare, and certain federal and state government plans. Reg. § 54.9801-4(a)(1) provides further specifics as to what can constitute creditable coverage, and Reg. § 54.9801-4(a)(2) indicates that creditable coverage does not include coverage of solely excepted benefits as described under Reg. § 54.9831-1 (see the discussion above of benefits that are not subject to the group health plan rules). However, prior coverage will not be counted, if there has been an intervening break in coverage of 63 days or more, not counting any waiting periods for the new coverage. Thus, if there has been a break of 63 days or more, only coverage after the break can be counted. For this purpose, Reg. § 54.9801-4(b)(2)(iv) states that days in a waiting period and days in an affiliation period are not taken into account in determining whether a significant break in coverage has occurred. In addition, for an individual who elects COBRA continuation coverage during the second election period provided under the Trade Act of 2002, the days between the date the individual lost group health plan coverage and the first day of the second COBRA election period are not taken into account in determining whether a significant break in coverage has occurred. Further, Code Sec. 9801(d)(4) provides that required coverage of newborns and adoptees under the new employer's plan will not apply if there has been a 63-day or more intervening break in coverage (this exception does not apply to pregnancy). Under Code Sec. 9801(c)(3), employers may count coverage under prior plans by not taking into account specific benefits provided by the prior plan or may elect to measure prior coverage by classes or categories of benefits that will be established in IRS regulations.

---

[218] Code Sec. 9801(d)(1)-(3).   [219] Reg. § 54.9801-3(c).

The final regulations issued in December of 2004 provide methods for counting creditable coverage, including the standard method in which the amount of creditable coverage is determined without regard to the specific benefits included in the coverage, or an alternative method which may be used for counting coverage for certain specific categories of benefits, including mental health, substance abuse treatment, prescription drugs, dental care, and vision care.[220]

The periods of creditable coverage with respect to an employee can be established through the presentation of certifications of that coverage or in any other manner the IRS specifies in regulations. Reg. § 54.9801-5 provides specific rules concerning certificates of prior coverage. An employee's previous health plan is required to provide the certification of the employee's prior coverage at the time the coverage ceases or at the request of the employee at any time within the next two years. In general, the certification is a written certification of the period of creditable coverage of the employee under the plan and coverage, if any, under the continuation coverage provision, and the waiting period, if any imposed on the employee for any coverage under the plan. An employer that credits prior coverage by classes or categories of benefits must secure such information from the prior plan and pay a reasonable fee to that plan, if requested.[221] No period before July 1, 1996 could be taken into account in determining creditable coverage unless the employee seeking to have that period taken into account followed procedures to be indicated by the IRS. No certification was required to be provided before June 1, 1997. In the case of an event occurring between June 30, 1996 and October 1, 1996, a certification was not required to be provided unless it is requested in writing.[222]

As noted above, employees who enroll late into a new employer's plan can face up to an 18-month exclusion period on account of preexisting conditions. However, under Code Sec. 9801(f), this rule does not apply if the employee declined coverage because he/she had other coverage under COBRA or another health plan (for the employee or a family member) and the other coverage is lost because (1) the other coverage was COBRA continuation coverage and the coverage was exhausted or (2) the other coverage was not under the continuation coverage rules and was terminated as a result of a loss of eligibility for coverage (e.g., due to death, divorce, termination of employment, etc.) or employer contributions towards such coverage were terminated. In such a case, the employee has to enroll within

---

[220] *See* Reg. § 54.9801-4(b) and (c).
[221] Code Sec. 4980D(e)(2).

[222] P.L. 104-191, 104th Cong., 2d Sess., Sec. 401(c)(2) (Aug. 21, 1996).

30 days of the date the other coverage is lost. A special 30-day period additionally applies for enrollment of new dependents the employee has because of marriage, birth, adoption, or placement for adoption.[223] See Reg. § 54.980-1-6 for detailed rules concerning the foregoing issues.

Prohibition Against Discrimination Based on Health Status. Under Code Sec. 9802(a)(1), a group health plan may not establish rules for eligibility (including continued eligibility) of any individual to enroll in the plan based on any of the following factors concerning the individual or a dependent of the individual: (1) health status, (2) medical condition (including both physical and mental illnesses), (3) claims experience, (4) receipt of health care, (5) medical history, (6) genetic information, (7) evidence of insurability (including conditions arising from acts of domestic violence, and (8) disability. However, Code Sec. 9802(a)(2) provides that these rules shall not be construed to (1) require a group health plan to provide particular benefits other than those provided under the terms of that plan or (2) prevent the plan from establishing limitations or restrictions on the amount, level, extent, or nature of the benefits or coverage for similarly situated individuals enrolled in the plan or coverage.

A group health plan may not require any individual (as a condition of enrollment or continued enrollment under the plan) to pay a premium or contribution which is greater than that premium or contribution for a similarly situated individual enrolled in the plan on the basis of any factor described in the previous paragraph concerning the individual or to an individual enrolled under the plan as a dependent of the individual. However, this rule is not to be construed to (1) restrict the amount that an employer may be charged for coverage under a group health plan or (2) prevent a group health plan from establishing premium discounts or rebates or modifying otherwise applicable co-payments or deductibles in return for adherence to programs of health promotion or disease prevention.[224] Thus, the regulations provide that a group health plan with a cost-sharing mechanism (such as a deductible, copayment, or coinsurance) that requires a higher payment from an individual, based on a health factor of that individual or a dependent of that individual, than for a similarly situated individual under the plan (and thus does not apply uniformly to all similarly situated individuals) does not violate the uniform premium rule if the payment differential is based on whether an individual has complied with the requirements

---

[223] Code Sec. 9801(f)(2)(B).   [224] Code Sec. 9802(b).

of a bona fide wellness program.[225] Further, a plan may establish a premium or contribution differential based on whether an individual has complied with the requirements of a bona fide wellness program.[226] Governmental plans, plans with fewer than two participants, and the benefits that are excepted from the preexisting condition rules covered above are excepted from these nondiscrimination rules.[227]

Guaranteed Renewability in Multiemployer Plans and Certain Multiemployer Welfare Arrangements. Under Code Sec. 9803(a), a group health plan which is a multiemployer plan or a multiple employer welfare arrangement may not deny an employer continued access to the same or different coverage under that plan, other than (1) for failure to pay contributions, (2) for fraud or other intentional misrepresentation of material fact by the employer, (3) for failure to comply with material plan provisions, (4) because the plan is ceasing to offer any coverage in a geographic area, (5) for a plan that offers benefits through a network plan, because no covered employee lives or works in the service area of the network plan and the plan uniformly applies this rule without regard to claims experience of employers or the health status of the employees and their dependents, or (6) for failure to meet the terms of an applicable collective bargaining agreement, to renew a collective bargaining or other agreement requiring or authorizing contributions to the plan, or to employ employees covered by that agreement. Code Sec. 9832(d)(4) provides that a network plan is health coverage or a health insurer under which the financing and delivery of medical care are provided in whole or in part through a defined set of providers that are under contract with the issuer. Governmental plans and plans that have less than two participants and the benefits which are excepted from the preexisting condition rules covered above are also not subject to these guaranteed renewability rules.[228]

Length of Maternity Stay Mandate. The Taxpayer Relief Act of 1997 incorporated into the Code provisions of the Newborns' and Mothers Protection Act of 1996 (P.L. 104-204). Under Code Sec. 9811(a)(1)(A), a group health plan may not restrict benefits for any hospital length of stay in connection with childbirth for the mother or newborn child following a normal delivery, to less than 48 hours. The minimum required stay is 96 hours following a caesarean

---

[225] Reg. § 54.9802-1(b)(2)(ii).
[226] Reg. § 54.9802-1(c)(3).
[227] *See* Code Secs. 9831(a)-(c) and 9832(c). Note that Code Secs. 9804, 9805, and 9806 were redes-

ignated as Code Secs. 9831 through 9833 by P.L. 105-34, 105th Cong., 1st Sess., Sec. 1531(a)(2) (Aug. 5, 1997).
[228] *Id.*

section. Further, a provider cannot be required to obtain authorization from the plan or the issuer for prescribing any length of stay required in Section 9811(a)(1)(A).[229] An attending health care provider, in consultation with the mother can approve a discharge earlier than the required 48 hours or 96 hours, as the case may be.[230]

Under Code Sec. 9811(b), a group health plan may not (1) deny to the mother or her newborn child eligibility or continued eligibility to enroll or renew plan coverage, solely for the purpose of avoiding the requirements of Section 9811(a)(1)(A); (2) provide monetary incentives or rebates to mothers to reduce the required minimum stays; (3) provide incentives or disincentives to health care providers to reduce the required minimum stays; or (4) restrict benefits for any portion of a period within a hospital length of stay required under the minimum stay rules in a manner that is less favorable than the benefits provided for any preceding portion of the stay. However, Code Sec. 9811(c) indicates that the minimum stay rules (1) are not to be construed as requiring mothers to give birth in hospitals or stay in a hospital following giving birth; (2) do not apply to group health plans that do not provide benefits for hospital stays connected with births; (3) are not to be construed as preventing a group health plan from imposing deductibles, coinsurance, or other cost sharing in relation to benefits for hospital lengths of stay in connection with childbirth except that such cost sharing for any portion of a period within the required minimum length of stay may not be greater than the cost sharing for any preceding portion of the stay. In addition, the minimum stay rules are not to be construed to prevent a group health plan from negotiating the level and type of reimbursement with a care provider in a manner that is consistent with the minimum stay rules.[231] Finally, the minimum length of stay rules do not apply in states where State law regulates such coverage in ways specified in Code Sec. 9811(e) (generally speaking, regulations that are consistent with or more stringent than the Section 9811 rules).

Mental Health Parity Requirements. The Taxpayer Relief Act of 1997 incorporated into the Code, provisions of the Mental Health Parity Act of 1996 (P.L. No. 104-204). Under Code Sec. 9812(a)(1), a group health plan that provides both medical and surgical benefits and mental health benefits may not impose an aggregate lifetime limit on mental health benefits if it does not impose such a limit on

---

[229] Code Sec. 9811(a)(1)(B), as enacted by P.L. 105-34, 105th Cong., 1st Sess., Sec. 1531(a)(4) (Aug. 5, 1997).

[230] Code Sec. 9811(a)(2).

[231] Code Sec. 9811(d).

the medical and surgical benefits. If an aggregate limit applies to medical and surgical benefits, the plan must either (a) apply that limit both to the medical and surgical benefits to which it would otherwise apply and to mental health benefits and not distinguish in the application of such limit between the two or (b) not include any aggregate lifetime benefit on mental health benefits that is less than that for medical and surgical benefits. In the case of a plan that contains no or different aggregate lifetime limits on different categories of medical and surgical benefits, the IRS is to establish rules under which the aggregate limit for mental health benefits should not be less than a weighted average of the aggregate lifetime for the various categories of medical and surgical benefits.[232] Similar rules apply in the case of annual benefit limits that apply to health plans which essentially require no worse than a parity in the annual limit that applies to medical and surgical benefits and the one applying to mental health benefits.[233]

The mental health parity rules are not to be construed as (1) requiring a group health plan to provide any mental health benefits or (2) affecting the terms and conditions (e.g., cost sharing limits on numbers of visits and days of coverage) relating to the amount, duration, or scope of mental health benefits provided under a plan except for the provisions concerning the parity of aggregate lifetime and annual limits for mental health benefits.[234] In addition, where a group health plan offers a participant or beneficiary two or more benefit package options under the plan, the mental health parity requirements will apply to each option separately.[235] Finally, Code Sec. 9812(c) indicates that the mental health parity rules will not apply (1) to any group health plan for a plan year of a small employer (as defined in Code Sec. 4980D(d)(2)—an employer generally with 50 or less employees on business days during the preceding calendar year) and (2) if the application of the rules results in an increase in the cost under the plan of at least one percent.

FICA and FUTA Taxation of Disability, Health, and Accident Benefits. Employer-paid premiums for disability, health, and accident insurance are excludable when the insurance premiums are paid on behalf of all employees or for a "class" or "classes" of employees.[236] There is no requirement that prohibits discrimination in favor of highly compensated individuals such as

---

[232] Code Sec. 9812(a)(1)(C), as enacted by P.L., 105-34, 105th Cong., 1st Sess., Sec. 1531(a)(4) (Aug. 5, 1997).

[233] Code Sec. 9812(a)(2).

[234] Code Sec. 9812(b).

[235] Code Sec. 9812(d).

[236] Reg. §§ 31.3121(a)(2)-1 and 31.3306(b)(2)-1.

officers and shareholder-employees. In addition, employer contributions to Archer MSAs and qualified long-term care insurance contracts are excludable for FICA and FUTA purposes.[237]

Under Code Secs. 3121(a)(2)(B) and 3306(b)(2)(B), any payments made to or on behalf of employees or their dependents on account of medical or hospitalization expenses attributable to sickness or disability under an employer plan or system, which provides for the employees generally or for a class or classes of employees, are excludable for FICA and FUTA tax purposes. The exclusion is permitted whether the plan is insured or noninsured. There is no requirement in the Code or regulations that the plan be nondiscriminatory in coverage. In addition, both distributions received from medical savings accounts to pay for qualified medical expenses and payments under long-term care insurance contracts are fully excludable for FICA and FUTA purposes under those code sections. On the other hand, if payments for medical-related expenses are made in a case where the employer maintains no plan or system and are made during the first six months the employee is off work, the payments are subject to FICA and FUTA taxes. The payments are excludable only if they are made after the expiration of six calendar months following the last calendar month in which the employee worked for the employer.[238]

In general, sickness and disability payments (i.e., sick pay or wage continuation payments) made directly to an employee or his dependents from the employer or under an employer plan during the first six months the employee is off work are subject to FICA and FUTA taxes. Under Code Secs. 3121(a)(4) and 3306(b)(4), sick pay received by an employee or his dependents is only excludable for FICA and FUTA tax purposes when received after the expiration of six calendar months following the last calendar month in which the employee worked for the employer. Note that this is in contrast to the fact that sick pay received from the employer or under an employer plan is subject to income taxes.

However, all sick pay received under a workers' compensation law is totally excludable for FICA and FUTA tax purposes under Code Secs. 3121(a)(2)(A) and 3306(b)(2)(A). In that regard, the IRS has recently issued proposed regulations which state that sick pay payments made under a statute in the nature of a workers' compensation act will be treated as having been made under a worker's compensation act and, thus, will be fully excludable for FICA tax

---

[237] *See,* e.g., Code Sec. 3306(c)(17) and Code Sec. 7702B(a)(1).

[238] Code Secs. 3121(a)(4) and 3306(b)(4).

¶ 302.03

purposes (presumably the same rule would apply for FUTA tax purposes).[239] The IRS provides an example in which a local government employee is injured while performing work-related activities. The employee is not covered by the state workers' compensation law, but is covered by a local government ordinance that requires the local government to pay the employee's full salary when the employee is out of work as a result of an injury incurred while performing services for the local government. The ordinance does not limit or otherwise affect the local government's liability to the employee for the work-related injury. The local ordinance is not a workers' compensation law, but it is in the nature of a workers' compensation act. Therefore, the salary the employee receives while out of work as a result of the work-related injury is not subject to FICA taxes.[240] In addition, the portion of any sick pay that is attributable to the employee's own contributions is excludable for FICA and FUTA tax purposes. Thus, if an employee paid for 65 percent of the cost of a policy providing for sick pay, 65 percent of the sick pay received under the plan would be excludable. Finally, the IRS has recently publicly held that where an employer's disability benefits plan provides that employees can elect to treat employer-paid plan premiums as being provided on their behalf on an after-tax basis rather than on a pre-tax basis, employees that make such an election are treated as if they had made the employer contributions.[241] Thus, if the employer made 100 percent of the premium payments to a disability payment plan, and the employee elected to treat those contributions as provided on an after-tax basis, any benefits the employee receives under the plan would be totally excludable for FICA and FUTA tax purposes.

> **Example:** Roy Moore was injured on the job during July 2006. He was off work for 5 months. His employer, which maintains no plan or system for the payment of medical and disability benefits, paid Moore $1,800 in sick pay and reimbursed him for $2,000 of medical expenses he incurred as a result of the accident. In addition, Moore received $1,600 in workers' compensation payments. The $1,800 in sick pay received from the employer as well as the medical expense reimbursements are subject to FICA and FUTA taxes since they were paid within the first six months that Moore was off work. The workers' compensation payments are excludable.

---

[239] Prop. Reg. § 31.3121(a)(2)-1(d)(3).
[240] Prop. Reg. § 31.3121(a)(2)-1(e).

[241] Rev. Rul. 2004-55, IRB 2004-26, 1081.

.04   Health Savings Accounts (HSAs)

In late 2003, Congress enacted the Health Savings Account (HSA) provisions as part of the Medicare Prescription Drug, Improvement, and Modernization Act of 2003.[242] In many respects, HSAs are similar to Archer MSAs (which were covered in ¶ 302.03), that is, contributions are made by or on behalf of the HSA account holders. Then, the holder can use the contributed amounts and any earnings thereon to pay qualified medical expenses or for other purposes. To the extent the amounts withdrawn are used to pay qualified medical expenses, they are totally excludable. However, HSAs are much more useful than Archer MSAs in that they are much more universally applicable. That is, their use is not limited to self-employed individuals and employees of small employers (those with 50 or fewer employees). Any individual who is covered by a high-deductible health plan and is otherwise eligible can contribute to (or have contributions made on his/her behalf) to HSAs. Further, the contribution limits are much more liberal for HSAs than for Archer MSAs. Finally, there is no time limit or numerical limit on when and the number of HSAs that can be set up. In summary, HSAs combine the best attributes of traditional IRAs and Roth IRAs discussed in Chapter 10. Contributions made to HSAs (within the limits) are in pre-tax dollars like deductible contributions made to traditional IRAs. Distributions from HSAs used to pay qualified medical expenses are totally excludable like qualified distributions from Roth IRAs. The discussion will generally focus on HSAs made available by employers to their employees. However, much of the discussion is also applicable to HSAs held by self-employed individuals.

General Rules and Contribution Limits. Beginning in 2004, amounts contributed by an employer with respect to an employee (who is an eligible individual) to a Health Savings Account (HSA) are excludable as employer health plan contributions. The exclusion is permitted to the extent that the amounts (reduced by contributions, if any, made by or on behalf of the eligible individual to an Archer MSA) do not exceed the applicable limitation under Code Sec. 223(b) for the year.[243] The excludable employer contributions are not subject to income tax withholding, FICA taxes, and

---

[242] Code Sec. 223, as added by P.L. 108-173, 108th Cong., 1st Sess., Sec. 1201(a) and (k) (Dec. 8, 2003).
[243] Code Sec. 106(d), as added by P.L. 108-173, 108th Cong., 1st Sess., Sec. 1201(d)(1) and (k)

(Dec. 8, 2003) and Sec. 223(b), as added by P.L. 108-173, 108th Cong., 2d Sess., Sec. 1201(a) and (k) (Dec. 8, 2003).

FUTA taxes.[244] HSA contributions may also be made on an excludable basis through a cafeteria plan (see the coverage of cafeteria plans in Chapter 4).[245] An HSA is a tax-exempt trust or custodial account which is created or organized in the United States exclusively for the purpose of paying the qualified medical expenses of the employee or other account beneficiary who, for the months for which contributions are made to the HSA, is covered by a high-deductible health plan.[246] Contributions to HSAs can only be made by or on behalf of eligible individuals. An eligible individual is anyone who, for a particular month, is (1) covered by a high-deductible health plan (HDHP); and (2) not also covered by a plan (a) that is not an HDHP and (b) which provides coverage for any benefit that is covered under the HDHP, other than certain permitted or limited purpose plans covered below.[247] Note that the Conference Committee and the IRS have adopted a more stringent definition than the statute by indicating that an eligible individual must (1) be covered by an HDHP and (2) not be covered by another health plan that is not an HDHP, other than certain permitted insurance or limited purpose plans.[248] Thus, the IRS has publicly held that an individual, who is covered by an HDHP and also has coverage under the HDHP or another plan for prescription drugs not subject to as high a deductible as is required under HDHPs, is not an eligible individual.[249] In addition, the IRS has publicly ruled that an employee is not eligible to participate in an HSA if the employee is covered by an HDHP and a Flexible Spending Account (FSA) (for coverage of FSAs, see ¶ 402.04) or a Health Reimbursement Arrangement (HRA) (for coverage of HRAs, see ¶ 403) which reimburses the employee for medical expenses which are not covered under the HDHP because of the HDHP deductible and co-pay arrangements.[250] However, under a limited exception, the IRS does permit coverage under (1) limited purpose FSAs or HRAs (those that provide coverage similar to "permitted insurance"); (2) post-deductible FSAs or HRAs that cover medical expenses only after the HDHP deductible is met; (3) suspended HRAs, where the employee

---

[244] Code Sec. 3401(a)(22), as amended by P.L. 108-173, Sec. 1201(d)(2)(C) and (k), 108th Cong., 1st Sess. (Dec. 8, 2003) and Sec. 3306(b)(18), as amended by P.L. 108-173, Sec. 1201(d)(1)(B), 108th Cong., 1st Sess. (Dec. 8, 2003); Notice 2004-2, Q&A 19, IRB 2004-2, 269.

[245] Code Sec. 125(d)(2)(D), as amended by P.L. 108-173, Sec. 1201(i) and (k); Notice 2004-2, Q&A 33, IRB 2004-2, 269.

[246] Code Sec. 223(d); Notice 2004-2, Q&A 1, IRB 2004-2, 269.

[247] Code Sec. 223(c)(1).

[248] See H.R. Conf. Rep. No. 391, 108th Cong., 1st Sess. (2003) 841; Notice 2004-2, Q&A 2, IRB 2004-2, 269.

[249] Rev. Rul. 2004-38, IRB 2004-15, 717. Note that the IRS has provided transition relief from the application of this ruling for 2004 and 2005. See Rev. Proc. 2004-22, IRB 2004-15, 727. Thus, for 2004 and 2005, an individual is an eligible individual for HSA purposes when he/she is covered by an HDHP and has coverage for prescription drugs not subject to the general HDHP deductible.

[250] See Rev. Rul. 2004-45, IRB 2004-22, 971.

who is covered by an HDHP elects to forgo reimbursements under the HRA; and (4) HRAs that only provide coverage to retired employees.[251] In the exception cases where an individual can be covered both by an HSA and a Health FSA, Notice 2004-50[252] indicates that the following three requirements that apply to Health FSAs (as discussed in ¶402.04) do not apply to HSAs: (1) the prohibition against a benefit that defers compensation by permitting employees to carry over unused elective contributions from one plan year to another (note that, more recently, the IRS has provided a two-and-one-half-month grace rule (see ¶402.02) that modifies that FSA requirement and that where FSAs adopt the grace rule, they may not be usable in conjunction with an HSA even under the rules of Notice 2004-50); (2) the requirement that the maximum amount of reimbursement be available at all times during the coverage period; and (3) the mandatory 12-month period of coverage. Finally, an individual (1) cannot be entitled to Medicare benefits (i.e., the individual must not be age 65 or more and otherwise eligible for Medicare); and (2) may not be claimed as a dependent on the tax return of another person.[253]

An HDHP is a health plan that meets specified requirements concerning deductibles and out-of-pocket expenses. For 2005, a health plan that only covers the HSA account holder is an HDHP only if the plan has an annual deductible of at least $1,000 and a maximum annual out-of-pocket cost (exclusive of plan premiums) of $5,115 (both amounts will be adjusted for inflation after 2005). For family coverage, the 2005 deductible must be at least $2,050, and the maximum annual out-of-pocket cost cannot exceed $10,250 (amounts adjusted for inflation after 2005).[254] Under family plans, no amounts can be payable from the plan with respect to any covered family member until the $2,050 deductible is met in total.[255] A health plan will not fail to be an HDHP solely because the plan has a smaller or no deductible for preventive care.[256] The IRS has issued Notice 2004-23,[257] which provides guidance as to what constitutes preventive care for purposes of the definition of HDHPs. Preventive care includes, but is not limited to, the following:

(1) Periodic health evaluations, including tests and diagnostic procedures ordered in connection with routine examinations, such as annual physicals;

---

[251] *Id.*
[252] IRB 2004-33, 196.
[253] Code Sec. 223(c).
[254] Rev. Proc. 2004-71, IRB 2004-50, 970.

[255] Notice 2004-2, Q&A 3, IRB 2004-2, 269.
[256] Code Sec. 223(c)(2)(D); Notice 2004-2, Q&A 3, IRB 2004-2, 269.
[257] IRB 2004-15, 725.

(2) Routine prenatal and well-child care;

(3) Child and adult immunizations;

(4) Tobacco cessation programs;

(5) Obesity weight-loss programs; and

(6) Specified screening services.

A listing of safe harbor screening services can be found in the appendix of the Notice.

Individuals are eligible to participate in HSAs even if they are covered by certain permitted insurance plans (limited purpose plans) in addition to an HDHP. Permitted insurance plans are plans under which substantially all of the coverage relates to (1) liabilities resulting under worker's compensation laws; (2) tort liabilities; (3) liabilities related to use or ownership of property (e.g., automobile liability insurance); (4) insurance for a specified disease or illness (e.g., cancer insurance); and (5) insurance that pays a fixed amount per daily (or other period) of hospitalization.[258] Further, an individual can have coverage through insurance or otherwise for accidents, disability, dental care, vision care, and long-term care. But note that if a plan that is intended to be an HDHP is one in which substantially all of the plan coverage is through permitted insurance or coverage described in the previous sentence, the plan is not an HDHP.[259]

Contributions to HSAs generally cannot exceed the sum of the applicable monthly limitations for months during the applicable year that the employee is an eligible individual. The monthly dollar contribution limitation for calendar year 2005 is one-twelfth of the lesser of (1) the annual deductible under the plan or (2) (a) $2,620 (for self-only coverage), or (b) $5,250 (for family coverage). The dollar maximums will be adjusted for inflation after 2005.[260] For purposes of applying the HSA monthly limitations, all HSA contributions made by or on behalf of an eligible individual (including by the individual's employer) are taken into account. Further, the annual limit is to be reduced by any Archer MSA contributions made by or on behalf of the eligible individual.[261]

Example: Roy, age 47, began to be covered by an HSA on July 1, 2005. He is not also covered by any other HSA or an Archer MSA. He is covered by a family coverage HDHP with a

---

[258] Code Sec. 223(c)(3); Notice 2004-2, Q&A 7, IRB 2004-2, 269.

[259] Notice 2004-2, Q&A 7, IRB 2004-2, 269.

[260] Code Sec. 223(b)(2) and (g); Notice 2004-2, Q&A 12, IRB 2004-2, 269; Rev. Proc. 2004-71, IRB 2004-50, 970.

[261] Notice 2004-2, Q&A 12, IRB 2004-2, 269.

¶ 302.04

$2,200 yearly deductible. Assume that his employer contributes $100 per month to the HSA on John's behalf. John could contribute up to $83.33 per month to that HSA. The monthly limit in this case is $183.33 total (the lesser of one-twelfth of (a) the $2,200 plan deductible, or (b) $2,650).

Code Sec. 223(b)(5) provides special rules for determining the contribution limit in the case of married individuals. In general, if either spouse has family coverage, both spouses are treated as having only such family coverage. Also, if each spouse has family coverage under different health plans, both spouses are treated as having family coverage under the plan with the lowest deductible. However, if a spouse has HDHP family coverage and the other spouse has non-HDHP self-only coverage, the spouse with the HDHP family coverage is an eligible individual and may contribute to an HSA up to the amount of the annual contribution limit. Because the other spouse is covered by a non-HDHP and is therefore not an eligible individual, the other spouse may not contribute to an HSA, notwithstanding the special rule in Code Sec. 223(b)(5) treating both spouses as having family coverage.[262] Recently, the IRS has issued Rev. Rul. 2005-25[263] to clarify the treatment of contributions of married persons to HSAs. In its holdings in that revenue ruling, the IRS states that (1) an individual who otherwise qualifies as an eligible individual does not fail to be an eligible individual merely because the individual's spouse has non-HDHP family coverage, if the spouse's non-HDHP does not cover the individual. Accordingly, that individual may contribute to an HSA; and (2) the maximum amount under Code Sec. 223(b) that an eligible individual may contribute to an HSA is based on whether the individual has self-only or family HDHP coverage.

Eligible individuals (and their spouses covered under an HDHP) between the ages of 55 and 65 can make (or have made on their behalf) an additional monthly contribution of one-twelfth of $600 (or $50.00 per month) in 2005 over and above the limits discussed above. This "catch-up amount" will increase in $100 increments annually, until it reaches $1,000 per year in calendar year 2009. Once an individual reaches age 65, contributions can no longer be made to the individual's HSA.[264]

Taxation of Amounts Withdrawn from HSAs. Qualified distributions received by participants from health savings accounts (HSAs) are totally excludable and are not subject to payroll taxes.

---

[262] Notice 2004-50, Q&A 33, IRB 2004-33, 196.
[263] IRB 2005-18, 1.

[264] Code Sec. 223(b)(3); Notice 2004-2, Q&A 14, IRB 2004-2, 269.

¶ **302.04**

"Qualified" distributions from HSA are distributions that are used exclusively to pay qualified medical expenses of the account beneficiary (the participant), his/her spouse, and dependents. Further, such amounts may be withdrawn in any year, even after the account holder is not an eligible individual for HSA purposes (see the definition of eligible individuals above). Eligible individuals may use debit, credit, or stored value cards to receive distributions from an HSA for qualified medical expenses as an alternative to receiving distributions by check. Withdrawals used to pay qualified medical expenses will not be treated as expenses paid for medical care for purposes of the Code Sec. 213 medical expense deduction.[265]

On the other hand, any amounts withdrawn from an HSA that are not used to pay such qualified medical expenses are taxable and subject to an additional 10 percent penalty tax except for distributions received after the account holder's death, disability or becoming age 65.[266]

> **Example:** Joy, age 59, a participant in an HSA, withdrew $5,000 from the HSA in 2006. Of that amount, $3,900 was used to pay qualified medical expenses. As a result, $1,100 of the withdrawal is subject to income taxes and the 10 percent penalty tax ($5,000 − $3,900). The other $3,900 is not taxable and cannot be considered part of her medical expense deduction.

Qualified medical expenses are expenses paid by the account holder, his/her spouse, and dependents for medical care incurred after the HSA is established and not compensated by insurance and which are described in Code Sec. 213(d), as extended by Rev. Rul. 2003-102.[267] Health insurance premiums are generally not considered qualified medical expenses. However, the payments of premiums for the following types of coverage are considered to be qualified medical expenses: (1) qualified long-term care insurance; (2) COBRA health care continuation coverage; (3) health insurance coverage an individual receives while the individual is receiving unemployment compensation; and (4) for individuals over the age of 65, premiums for (a) Medicare Part A or B, (b) Medicare HMO, and (c) the employee's share of premiums for employer-sponsored health insurance or employer-sponsored retiree health insurance. Premiums for Medigap policies are not qualified medical expenses.[268]

---

[265] Code Sec. 223(f)(2) and (4); Notice 2004-2, Q&A 25, IRB 2004-2, 269.

[266] Code Sec. 223(d)(2); Notice 2004-2, Q&A 27, 2004-2 IRB 269.

[267] 2003-2 CB, 559. Therefore, qualified medical expenses will not only include prescribed medi-

cine and drugs but will also include certain over-the-counter items specified in the ruling, including aspirin, cold medicines, and antacids.

[268] Code Sec. 223(d)(2); Notice 2004-2, Q&A 27, 2004-2 IRB, 269.

Example: Denton, age 67, has an HSA account and, in 2008, he withdrew $4,000 to pay $2,800 in uninsured doctor's bills, $500 of premiums for Medicare Part B coverage and $700 for premiums for a Medigap policy. As a result, $700 of the withdrawal is taxable since the last expenditure is not for qualified medical expenses.

.05   Meals and Lodging Furnished for the Convenience of the Employer

Meals and lodging can be a very valuable fringe benefit for executives and other employees in cases where their value can be excluded from gross income. And, unlike all of the other tax-free fringe benefits covered in this chapter, meals and lodging can, in some cases, be provided exclusively to shareholder-employees and officers where the circumstances warrant such provision. This can be of particular benefit in the case of small, closely held corporations where the shareholders are also the major employees of the corporation. The provision of meals and lodging to shareholder-employees in appropriate circumstances can result in a tax-free benefit to the shareholder-employees and a deductible business expense to the corporation (reducing corporate taxable income). For example, meals and lodging furnished to shareholder-employees of a ranching business have been held to be excludable. There are no specific nondiscrimination rules that have to be satisfied. But, it should be noted that the exclusion for owner-employees is only applicable in C corporations. Two percent or greater owners of S corporations, partners of partnerships and sole proprietors are not considered to be employees for purposes of obtaining the exclusion.[269] Further, the meals and lodging must be provided with respect to the work of the individuals involved as employees of the business. For example, in instances where the owners and sole employees of family farming businesses set up their farms as C corporations, then conveyed all of the farm property, including the family residence, to the corporation, and then leased the farms from the corporations, the meals and lodging exclusion was not permitted for the food and lodging that was provided to those owner-employees. The Tax Court held that the taxpayers performed their work as tenants rather than as employees of the corporation, and thus were not permitted the Code Sec. 119 exclusion.[270]

---

[269] *See* FSA 200031003; Reg. § 1.707-1(c).

[270] *See* e.g., *Ricky Schmidt*, TC Memo 2003-325; *Ronald D. Weeldreyer*, TC Memo 2003-324.

General Rules. Under Code Sec. 119(a), the gross income of an employee does not include the value of meals and lodging furnished to him, his spouse, or any of his dependents by or on behalf of his employer for the convenience of the employer, but only if:

(1) in the case of meals, the meals are furnished on the business premises of the employer; or

(2) in the case of lodging, the employee is required to accept the lodging on the business premises of his employer as a condition of his employment.

Thus, meals and lodging are excludable only if they are furnished for the convenience of the employer on the business premises of that employer. Further, in the case of lodging only, the value of the lodging must be accepted as a condition of employment. Obviously, an understanding of the terms "for the convenience of the employer," "the employer's business premises," and "accepted as a condition of employment" is critical to determining whether meals and lodging are excludable in particular cases. Each of the terms will be covered in detail below.

In general, only meals and lodging furnished to employees "in kind" are excludable. Reg. § 1.119-1(e) states that to be excludable, meals and lodging must be furnished directly to the employee. Thus, cash allowances or employer reimbursements for meals and lodging purchased by employees are not excludable. This rule was upheld in the 1977 Supreme Court case *Kowalski,*[271] in which the Court held that cash allowances for meals furnished to a highway patrolman were taxable to him. In another case, the Tax Court recently ruled that reimbursements provided to employees for groceries purchased by the employees were not excludable because the reimbursements did not constitute meals furnished in kind.[272] However, supper money or other sporadic meal reimbursements are excludable.[273] The Supreme Court in *Kowalski* indicated that it was not ruling on the tax status of supper money. So, apparently, supper money is still excludable. As an additional example of the in-kind requirement, in two recently issued Technical Advice Memoranda, the IRS has held that housing allowances (in one instance paid by a private school to its head mistress and in the other instance paid by a hospital to residents) were not excludable because the value of lodging is only excludable if provided in-kind.[274]

---

[271] SCt, 77-2 USTC ¶ 9748, 434 US 77, 98 SCt 315.
[272] *Bernardus A.P. Dobbe,* 80 TCM 577, Dec. 49,096(M), TC Memo. 2000-30. Aff'd, CA-9 (unpublished opinion), 2005-1 USTC ¶ 50,377.
[273] O.D. 514, 2 CB 90 (1920).

[274] See Technical Advice Memorandum 9801023, 9-30-97, CCH IRS LETTER RULINGS REPORTS and Technical Advice Memorandum 9824001, 2-11-98, CCH IRS LETTER RULINGS REPORTS.

In cases where employees are charged a fixed and unvarying amount for meals and/or lodging furnished for the employer's convenience on the business premises, the amount charged can be excluded from the employee's gross income under Code Sec. 119(b)(3). However, the exclusion is permitted only if the employee is required to make the payment whether he or she accepts or rejects the meals (or lodging). The exclusion is permitted whether the employee pays the fixed charge out of his stated compensation or directly. The exclusion is not permitted where the employee is charged a varying amount or can decline to take some of the meals.[275]

Special rules apply in the case of lodging furnished to employees that live in a "camp" in certain foreign countries and to qualified campus lodging furnished to faculty. These provisions are covered below.

For the Convenience of the Employer. Meals and lodging must be furnished for the convenience of the employer in order to be excludable. Under Reg. § 1.119-1(a)(2), meals furnished by the employer will be regarded as furnished for the convenience of the employer if the meals are furnished for a "substantial noncompensatory business reason." Basically, that means that the employer must have a good business reason for providing the meals other than giving the employees more pay.[276] All of the surrounding facts and circumstances must be evaluated in determining whether meals are furnished for a substantial noncompensatory business reason. In determining the reason why an employer furnishes meals, a mere statement that the meals are not intended as pay is not sufficient to establish that the meals are furnished for the employer's convenience. In general, meals furnished before or after hours of the employee are not for the employer's convenience (except in the case of restaurant and food service employees, see below). Meals furnished on nonworking days are not excludable as a general rule. However, if meals are furnished to the employee in lodging on the employer's premises that the employee is required to accept as a condition of employment, the value of meals furnished at any time is excludable.[277]

Reg. § 1.119-1(a)(2)(ii) indicates a number of specific instances in which the meals are considered to be furnished for a substantial noncompensatory business reason and, thus, for the employer's convenience. For example, meals furnished during working hours

---

[275] Reg. § 1.119-1(a)(3)(ii).
[276] Reg. § 1.119-1(a)(2)(i).
[277] *Id.*

so that the employee will be available for emergency calls during the meal period can qualify (e.g., in the case of hospital employees). Meals are also furnished for the employer's convenience if the meals are furnished during working hours because the nature of the employer's business restricts the employee to a short meal period (such as 30 or 40 minutes) and the employee cannot be expected to eat elsewhere in such a short time. For example, meals may qualify if there are insufficient eating facilities near the place of employment, or if the peak workload period occurs during the normal lunch hour.[278] Meals furnished to restaurant employees and other food service employees for each meal period they work will be excludable if the meal is served during the working hours or immediately before or after the employee's working hours. In its recent decision in *Boyd Gaming Corporation*,[279] the Ninth Circuit Court of Appeals noted that meals furnished to food service employees sometime during the working day should be excludable. Meals furnished to employees whose duties require their presence at a remote facility that is far away from alternative dining facilities will also meet the test.

The "convenience of the employer" test for lodging is basically the same as for meals. That is, the employer must have a valid business reason for furnishing the lodging other than as additional pay.[280]

> **Example:** John, a construction worker, is employed at a remote job site in Alaska. Due to the inaccessibility of facilities and prevailing weather conditions, John and other employees working at the job cannot get food and lodging. Thus, the employer has to furnish meals and lodging to John at the camp site in order to carry on the construction project. John is required to pay $40 per week for the meals and lodging. Neither the weekly charge of $40 nor the value of the meals and lodging is taxable to John.

Note that the courts have stated that there is little distinction between the "convenience of the employer" test and the "condition of employment" test (discussed below) in the case of lodging.[281]

Finally, under a recently enacted safe harbor provision, all meals that are furnished to employees on the business premises of the employer will be regarded as furnished for the convenience of

---

278 IRS Pub. No. 15B, at 13.
279 CA-9, 99-1 USTC ¶ 50,530, 177 F3d 1096. Rev'g 74 TCM 759, Dec. 52,280(M). TC Memo. 1997-445. Acq. 1999-2 CB xvi.

280 *See* IRS Pub. No. 15B, at 13.
281 *United States Junior Chamber of Commerce*, CtCls, 64-2 USTC ¶ 9637, 334 F2d 660, 167 CtCls 392.

the employer if, without regard to the safe harbor rule, more than one-half of the meals that are furnished on such premises to the employer's employees are considered to be furnished for the convenience of the employer (as determined under the guidelines discussed in the above paragraphs).[282] This provision is intended to apply both in years before, during, and after the date of enactment of the IRS Restructuring and Reform Act of 1998.[283]

> **Example:** Ronco serves meals to 160 employees on its business premises, and 94 of those employees are furnished the meals for the convenience of the employer. Thus, under the new safe harbor rule, all of the meals furnished to the 160 employees will be excludable as being furnished for the convenience of the employer. Such meals will also be fully deductible by the employer.

Business Premises of the Employer. The value of meals and lodging furnished to an employee are excludable only if furnished on the employer's business premises. Unfortunately, the term "business premises" has been the source of considerable IRS-taxpayer litigation. This may be due to the rather vague definition provided for the term in the regulations and IRS publications. Under Reg. § 1.119-1(c)(1), the business premises of the employer is "the place of employment of the employee."

In *Dole*,[284] the Tax Court held that the term "business premises" should mean either the living quarters that constitute an integral part of the employer's business property or premises on which the company conducts some of its business activities. The court did not allow the Code Sec. 119 exclusion because it found that the housing that was furnished to the employee was located some distance away from the employer's premises and that no business was carried on at the furnished lodging.

However, the fact that lodging is located close to the place where the employee performs services will not necessarily satisfy the requirement. In *Anderson*,[285] the Sixth Circuit Court of Appeals held that the employer's business premises is the location where either the employee performs a significant portion of his duties or the premises where the employer conducts a significant portion of his business. The court ruled that lodging located only two blocks from

---

[282] Code Sec. 119(b)(4), as added by P.L. 105-206, 105th Cong., 2d Sess., Sec 5002(a) (July 22, 1998).

[283] H.R. 2676, 105th Cong., 2d Sess., (1998), p. 161.

[284] 43 TC 697, Dec. 27,253 (1965). Aff'd, *per curiam,* CA-1, 65-2 USTC ¶9688, 351 F2d 308 (1965).

[285] CA-6, 67-1 USTC ¶9136, 371 F2d 59, *rev'g* 42 TC 410, Dec. 26,806.

¶ 302.05

where the employee worked did not constitute business premises because no duties were performed at the home. Further, in Letter Ruling 8938014, the IRS ruled that garden apartments provided by a hospital to certain medical personnel and located across the street from the hospital did not meet the business premises test because the hospital failed to show that any significant portion of the employees' duties was performed there or that the hospital conducted any significant business there. The IRS used similar reasoning in another private ruling in which they held that an apartment building located near the campus of a private school was not on the business premises of the school because the apartment was not an integral part of the school's business property.[286] On the other hand, even if a residence is provided at a location that is not the regular office or work site, the Code Sec. 119 exclusion may be allowed if the employee performs substantial services for the employer at that location. Thus, in *Adams,*[287] a residence furnished to the employee was considered on the employer's business premises because the employee, a chief executive officer, often performed substantial services at the residence that benefited the employer, including entertaining members of the business community. Finally, it should be noted that if the employee is furnished lodging on the employer's physical business premises, it is not necessary for the employee to perform services within the lodging to obtain the Code Sec. 119 exclusion. For example, in Rev. Rul. 90-64,[288] the business premises test was met where a residence was furnished to a principal representative of the United States stationed in a foreign country without cost because the U.S. government owned or rented the building in which the residence was located.

Condition of Employment. Lodging must also be accepted as a condition of employment in order to be excludable. Reg. § 1.119-1(b) indicates that "condition of employment" means that an employee must be required to accept the lodging in order to enable him or her to properly perform the duties of his or her employment. Lodging will be regarded as furnished to enable the employee to properly perform the duties of his or her employment, when, for example, the lodging is furnished because the employee must be available for duty at all times or because the employee could not perform the services required of him or her unless he or she was furnished the lodging. Thus, if the employee has the option of accepting or rejecting the lodging, no exclusion will be allowed. But,

---

[286] IRS Letter Ruling 9801023, 9-30-97, CCH IRS LETTER RULINGS REPORTS. *See also* AOD 1992-001 (Jan. 21, 1992) and IRS Letter Ruling 9824001, 2-11-98, CCH IRS LETTER RULINGS REPORTS.

[287] CtCls. 78-2 USTC ¶ 9752, 585 F2d 1060 (1978).

[288] 1990-2 CB 35.

there has to be something more than a stated requirement of the employer that the lodging must be accepted as a condition of employment. The lodging must be necessary in order for the employee to properly do his job or the employee must be on call at all times. For example, the IRS held that rent-free lodging provided by a prep school to a nurse and to dorm parents was excludable because they were on duty during the evenings and the weekends to respond to emergencies and performed substantial services at their residences. Further, they were required to live on the school property. Thus, the condition of employment test was met.[289]

Although the taxpayer must demonstrate some business necessity in order to satisfy the condition of employment test, it is not necessary to show that the employee's duties would be impossible to perform without the provision of the lodging.[290] The test may be satisfied if the employer-furnished lodging provides important benefits or advantages to the employer or otherwise facilitates job performance.[291]

Exclusion Only Available to Employees and Their Dependents. It is clear that shareholder-employees of closely held corporations can, in appropriate circumstances, take advantage of the Code Sec. 119 exclusion. However, owners of unincorporated businesses generally have not been entitled to the Code Sec. 119 exclusion. Sole proprietors and partners are not regarded as employees for purposes of Code Sec. 119. Although at least one court has held that a partner may, under appropriate circumstances, take advantage of Code Sec. 119,[292] the IRS and most courts have held that only common-law employees (sole proprietors and partners are not common-law employees) are eligible for the Code Sec. 119 exclusion.[293]

Lodging Furnished in Foreign Camps. Under Code Sec. 119(c), a camp located in a foreign country is part of the business premises of the employer. A camp is defined as lodging which is:

(1) provided by or on behalf of the employer for the employer's convenience because the place at which the employee renders services is in a remote area where satisfactory housing is not available to the employee on the open market within a reasonable commuting distance of that place;

---

[289] Technical Advice Memorandum 9602001, 9-15-95, CCH IRS Letter Rulings Reports.

[290] *Caratan*, CA-9, 71-1 USTC ¶ 9353, 442 F2d 606 (1971).

[291] *See*, e.g., *United States Junior Chamber of Commerce, supra* note 111.

[292] *See*, e.g., *Armstrong*, CA-5, 68-1 USTC ¶ 9355, 394 F2d 661 (1968).

[293] *See*, e.g., *Wilson*, ClsCt, 67-1 USTC ¶ 9378, 376 F2d 280 (1967). *See also* FSA 200031003 and Reg. § 1.707-1(c).

¶ 302.05

(2) located, as near as practicable, in the vicinity of the place at which the employee renders services; and

(3) furnished in a common area or enclave which is not available to the general public for lodging or accommodations and which normally accommodates ten or more employees.[294]

The regulations provide many technical definitions as to what constitutes satisfactory housing, the availability of housing, reasonable commuting distance, and a common area or enclave.[295] Note that this special rule only applies for purposes of the business premises test. The convenience of employer test and the condition of employment test (covered above) must also be satisfied.

Exclusion for Certain Faculty Housing. Under Code Sec. 119(d), the value of qualified campus lodging furnished to an employee of an educational institution during the taxable year is not taxable to the employee. However, the exclusion does not apply if the rent is inadequate. Specifically, the employee (faculty member) must include in income the excess of the lesser of (1) five percent of the appraised value of the qualified campus lodging, or (2) the average of the rentals paid by individuals (other than employees or students of the educational institution) for comparable lodging furnished by the educational institution, over the rent paid by the employee for the qualified campus lodging.[296]

> **Example:** A faculty member pays $200 per month for lodging. Other employees pay $400 for similar lodging. The appraised value of the lodging is $55,000. Five percent of this amount is $2,750. The faculty member would have to report $350 of gross income for the year ($2,750 − (12 × $200)).

The appraised value of the qualified campus lodging is to be determined as of the close of the calendar year in which the taxable year begins. If the rental period is not greater than one year, the appraised value may be determined at any time during the calendar year in which the rental period begins.[297] Also, the appraisal must be made by a qualified appraiser. The appraisal may not be made by the educational institution, or any of its officers, trustees, or employees. A new appraisal need not be obtained each year, but the appraisal must be reviewed annually in accordance with IRS regulations that have yet to be issued.[298]

---

[294] Reg. § 1.119-1(d).

[295] *See* Reg. § 1.119-1(d)(2) and (5). *See Roy L. Abeyta,* TC Summary Opinion 2005-44, as an example of where a taxpayer on an overseas assignment was not permitted to exclude the value of a home in a suburban neighborhood as lodging furnished by his employer because while the first two requirements were met, the third was not. Thus, the lodging was not furnished in a foreign camp as required for the exclusion.

[296] Code Sec. 119(d)(2).

[297] *Id.*

[298] 1986 Act Conference Committee Report, at 545.

Qualified campus lodging is lodging to which the normal Code Sec. 119 exclusion does not apply, which is (1) located on, or in the proximity of, a campus of the educational institution, and (2) furnished to the employee, his or her spouse and any of his or her dependents by, or on behalf of, the educational institution for use as a residence.[299] Under Code Sec. 119(d)(4), an educational institution is an organization that normally maintains a regular faculty and normally has a regularly enrolled body of students in attendance at the place where its educational activities are regularly carried on or an academic health center. An academic health center is an organization the principal purpose of which is the provision of medical or hospital care, medical education, or medical research, which receives payments under section 1886 of the Social Security Act, and which has as one of its principal purposes, the providing and teaching of basic and clinical medical science and research by the entity's own faculty.

FICA and FUTA Taxation of Meals and Lodging. Employer-provided meals and lodging that are excludable from an employee's gross income under Code Sec. 119 are also excludable for FICA and FUTA tax purposes.[300]

.06 Educational Assistance Plans

Generally, employees are not taxable on the value of educational benefits provided by employers if the benefits are furnished under a qualifying group educational assistance program of the employer.[301] Under Code Sec. 127(a)(2), the maximum amount that can be excluded per year per individual is $5,250. Educational benefits that are excludable under Code Sec. 127 are also excludable for FICA and FUTA tax purposes.[302] Since 1997, the Section 127 exclusion has only been available for the costs of education at the undergraduate level. However, with respect to classes that begin after December 31, 2001, the Economic Growth and Tax Relief Reconciliation Act of 2001 (EGTRRA) has extended the applicability of that exclusion to education at the graduate level.[303] Employer payments or reimbursements are deductible under Code Sec. 162.

Under Code Sec. 127(b), an educational assistance program is a separate written plan under which the employer provides employees with educational assistance (as defined below). The program does not have to be funded or approved in advance by the IRS.[304]

---

[299] Code Sec. 119(d)(3).
[300] Code Secs. 3121(a)(19) and 3306(b)(14).
[301] Code Sec. 127(a)(1).
[302] Code Secs. 3121(a)(18) and 3306(b)(13).

[303] Code Sec. 127(c), as amended by P.L. 107-16, 107th Cong., 1st Sess., Sec. 411(b) (June 7, 2001).
[304] Code Sec. 127(b)(5).

An educational assistance program must not provide employees with a choice between educational assistance and taxable compensation.[305]

Nondiscrimination Rules. A qualified educational assistance plan must satisfy specified coverage, eligibility, and concentration rules. The plan must benefit employees who qualify under a classification in a way that does not discriminate in favor of highly compensated employees (as defined in Code Sec. 414(q)).[306] For this purpose, Code Sec. 127(b)(2) indicates that employees not included in the educational assistance program but who are included in a unit of employees covered by an agreement which the IRS deems to be a good faith collective bargaining agreement between representatives of the employees and the employer do not have to be taken into account.

Educational assistance plans must also satisfy the concentration test of Code Sec. 127(b)(3). Under that test, not more than five percent of the amounts paid or incurred by the employer for educational assistance during the year may be provided to shareholders or owners of the business each of whom (on any day of the year) owns directly or indirectly more than five percent of the business.

Meaning of Educational Assistance. Excludable educational assistance includes the payment or provision of tuition, fees, and similar expenses, as well as the cost of books, supplies, and equipment paid for or provided by the employer.[307] However, excludable educational assistance does not include: (1) the cost of tools or supplies that may be retained by the employee after completion of the educational course, (2) meals, lodging, or transportation provided by the employer, and (3) courses that involve sports, games, or hobbies unless those courses are directly related to the taxpayer's business or are required as part of a degree program.[308] Sports, games, or hobbies for purposes of Code Sec. 127 do not include education that instructs employees how to maintain and improve health as long as the education does not involve the use of athletic facilities or equipment and is not recreational in use. Excludable educational assistance did not include any payment for, or the provision of benefits for, any graduate level course of a kind normally taken by an individual pursuing a program leading to a law, business, medical or other advanced academic or professional degree for taxable years beginning before January 1, 2002.[309] However, note that benefits for

---

[305] Code Sec. 127(b)(4).

[306] Code Sec. 127(b)(2).

[307] Code Sec. 127(c)(1).

[308] Reg. § 1.127-2(c)(3).

[309] Code Sec. 127(c)(1), as amended by P.L. 107-16, 107th Cong., 1st Sess., Sec. 441(b) (June 7, 2001).

graduate level courses beginning before January 1, 2002, and educational assistance benefits that exceeded the $5,250 limitation under Code Sec. 127(a)(2) (covered above) may have been excludable as a working condition fringe benefit under Code Sec. 132(j)(8) (see the discussion of working condition fringe benefits later in this chapter).

Education paid or provided for under a qualified program may be furnished directly by the employer or through a third party, such as an educational institution. Education is not limited to courses that are job related or part of a degree program.[310]

Under Code Sec. 117(d)(4), tuition reductions granted by a college or university to graduate students who are engaged in teaching or research activities for their college or university are not taxable to the student. However, Code Sec. 117(c) provides that this exclusion does not apply to that portion of any amount received which represents payment for teaching, research, or other services by the student required as a condition for receiving the qualified tuition reduction.

Deductions or Credits. Any amount excluded under Code Sec. 127 cannot be taken as a deduction or credit by an employee under some other Code Section.[311] However, any educational expenses that are not eligible for the Code Sec. 127 exclusion are treated under the normal rules of Code Secs. 117, 162, and 212 and Code Sec. 132(j)(8), as indicated above. Thus, in cases where an employer reimburses selected employees for educational expenses that the employees can deduct under Reg. § 1.162-5, the employee would not have to report the reimbursement (and would not take a deduction) if an adequate accounting is made to the employer (see Chapter 2).

Repeal of the Sunset of the Code Sec. 127 Exclusion. Under prior law, the Code Sec. 127 rules were set to expire for expenses with respect to courses beginning after December 31, 2001. However, EGTRRA has made the exclusion permanent.[312]

.07   Group Dependent Care Programs

Dependent care programs are an important fringe benefit in the 1990s. As the proportion of families with two working parents grows, the demand for such programs is increasing.

---

[310] Reg. §§ 1.127-1(a) and 1.127-2(c)(4).
[311] Reg. § 1.127-1(b).
[312] Code Sec. 127(d), as amended by P.L. 106-170, 106th Cong., 1st Sess. (1999) and as stricken and redesignated by P.L. 107-16, 107th Cong., 1st Sess., Sec. 411(a) (June 7, 2001).

Under Code Sec. 129(a)(1), employees can exclude amounts paid or incurred by the employer for dependent care assistance provided to such employees under qualified dependent care assistance programs. The amount that may be excluded with respect to dependent care services provided during a taxable year is limited to $5,000 ($2,500 for a married person filing a separate return).[313] Further, the value of dependent care assistance in excess of the exclusion limit must be included in gross income in the taxable year in which the dependent care services are provided (even if payment for those services is made in another year).[314]

> **Example:** Mason, a calendar-year taxpayer, incurred and paid $6,000 for dependent care services in 2005 and $5,000 in 2006. During 2005, Mason's employer maintained a qualified dependent care assistance program. Under the program, the employer reimbursed Mason for $2,000 of the 2005 expenses in 2005 and the remaining $4,000 in 2006. The employer reimbursed $3,000 of the 2006 expenses in 2006 and $2,000 in 2007. Under Code Sec. 129(a)(2)(B), Mason must recognize $1,000 of gross income in 2005 since the total amount of reimbursements for child care incurred in 2005 exceeded the exclusion limit by $1,000, but nothing in 2006 since the total amount of reimbursements for child care incurred in 2006 equaled the exclusion limit in 2006. The timing of the employer's reimbursements does not affect the result.

Dependent care assistance that is excludable under Code Sec. 129 is not subject to FICA and FUTA taxes.[315] The employer's payments or reimbursements are deductible under Code Sec. 162.

Earned Income Limitation. The amount excludable under Code Sec. 129 cannot exceed: (1) the earned income of an unmarried employee; or (2) in the case of an employee who is married, the lesser of (a) the employee's earned income, or (b) the earned income of the employee's spouse.[316] However, earned income may be imputed (under the same rules that apply for purposes of the dependent care credit under Code Sec. 21(d)(2)) for spouses who are physically or mentally incapable of caring for themselves or who are full-time students.

Payments to Related Individuals. No exclusion is permitted to the extent employer dependent care assistance payments are

---

[313] Code Sec. 129(a)(2)(A).
[314] Code Sec. 129(a)(2)(B).

[315] Code Secs. 3121(a)(18) and 3306(b)(13).
[316] Code Sec. 129(b)(1).

made (1) to an individual who qualifies as a dependent (within the meaning of Code Sec. 151(c)) of the employee or his or her spouse, or (2) to a child (within the meaning of code Sec.152(f)(1) for taxable years beginning after December 31, 2004—within the meaning of Code Sec. 152(c)(3) for taxable years beginning before January 1, 2005) of the employee under age 19 as of the close of the taxable year.[317]

Dependent Care Assistance Programs. Under Code Sec. 129(d)(1), a qualified dependent care assistance program is a separate written plan of an employer for the exclusive benefit of his employees, under which the employer provides employees with dependent care assistance. The program need not be funded to qualify.[318] A dependent care plan must furnish to an employee, on or before January 31 of the next year, a written statement showing amounts paid or expenses incurred by the employer in providing dependent care assistance to that employee during the year.[319] Finally, note that if a plan would qualify as a dependent care assistance program but for a failure to meet the requirements of Code Sec. 129(d) (e.g., the nondiscrimination rules), the plan will nevertheless be treated as a dependent care assistance program for nonhighly compensated employees (i.e., the nonhighly compensated employees would still be entitled to the Code Sec. 129 exclusion).[320]

Nondiscrimination Rules. Qualified dependent care plans must satisfy certain coverage, eligibility, concentration, and benefits tests. Under Code Sec. 129(d)(2), the contributions and benefits provided under the plan cannot discriminate in favor of highly compensated individuals (as defined under Code Sec. 414(q)) or their dependents. Further, the program must benefit employees under a classification set up by the employer which is found by the IRS not to discriminate in favor of highly compensated employees.[321]

In addition, the employer's dependent care plan must satisfy the concentration test specified in Code Sec. 129(d)(4). Under that test, not more than 25 percent of the amounts paid or incurred by the employer for dependent care assistance may be provided for the class of individuals who are shareholders or owners (or their spouses and dependents) each of whom (on any day of the year) owns directly or indirectly more than five percent of the stock or of the capital or profits interest in the employer. Finally, a special benefits test under Code Sec. 129(d)(8) must be satisfied. Under that rule, the average benefits provided to employees who are not highly compensated under all plans of the employer must be at least 55 percent of

---

[317] Code Sec. 129(c), as amended by P.L. 108-311, 108th Cong., 2d Sess., Sec. 207(12) (Oct. 4, 2004).
[318] Code Sec. 129(d)(5).
[319] Code Sec. 129(d)(6).
[320] Code Sec. 129(d)(1).
[321] Code Sec. 129(d)(3).

the average benefits provided to highly compensated employees. For purposes of that rule, any benefits provided through a salary reduction agreement to employees with compensation of less than $25,000 can be disregarded.

For purposes of the eligibility test of Code Sec. 129(d)(3) and the benefits test of Code Sec. 129(d)(4) described above, the following employees can be excluded from consideration:[322]

(1) employees who have not attained the age of 21 and completed one year of service (as defined under Code Sec. 410(a)(3) for pension plan purposes; see Chapter 6); and

(2) employees not included in a dependent care assistance program who are included in a unit of employees covered by an agreement that the IRS finds to be a bona fide collective bargaining agreement between representatives of the employees and the employer.

Note that the line of business rules (described in Chapter 6) are applicable for purposes of determining compliance with the dependent care assistance program nondiscrimination rules covered above.[323]

Definition of Terms and Special Rules. Earned income is defined in the same way as it is for purposes of the earned income credit, but the term does not include amounts paid or incurred by an employer for dependent care assistance.[324]

The term "employee" includes individuals who are self-employed.[325] A sole proprietor will be treated as his or her own employer and a partnership is treated as the employer of its partners.[326] Thus, dependent care assistance, unlike most other fringe benefits, is available on a tax-free basis to the self-employed, partners in partnerships and S corporation shareholder-employees.

In the case of an on-site facility maintained by an employer, the amount of dependent care assistance provided to an employee and excludable under Code Sec. 129 is to be based on (1) the utilization of the facility by a dependent of the employee and (2) the value of the services provided with respect to the dependent.[327]

No deduction or credit shall be permitted to employees with respect to amounts that are excludable under Code Sec. 129.[328]

No exclusion is permitted for dependent care assistance with respect to an employee unless the name, address, and taxpayer

---

[322] Code Sec. 129(d)(9).
[323] Code Sec. 414(r)(1), as amended by P.L. 101-140, Sec. 204(b)(2).
[324] Code Sec. 129(e)(1).

[325] Code Sec. 129(e)(3).
[326] Code Sec. 129(e)(4).
[327] Code Sec. 129(e)(8).
[328] Code Sec. 129(e)(7).

identification number of the person or organization performing the services are included on the employee's return.[329] However, this rule does not apply if it is shown that the employee exercised due diligence in attempting to provide the required information.

.08   Qualified Adoption Assistance Programs

Under Code Sec. 137(a), gross income of an employee does not include amounts paid or expenses incurred by the employee's employer for qualified adoption expenses in connection with the adoption of a child by the employee where the amounts are furnished under an adoption assistance program.[330] The exclusion applies to tax years beginning after 1996 (prior to amendment by EGTRRA, the provision was set to become inapplicable as of January 1, 2002).[331] In addition, EGTRRA made increases in the amounts that can be excluded under Code Sec. 137. The maximum amount excludable for all taxable years on account of the adoption of a child by an employee cannot exceed $10,000 ($5,000 in the case of taxable years beginning before January 1, 2002).[332] For adoptions involving a child with special needs, the maximum exclusion amount is also $10,000 ($6,000 for taxable years beginning before January 1, 2002).[333] For an adoption of a child with special needs which becomes final during a particular taxable year, the qualified adoption expenses connected with that adoption for that year can be increased by amount equal to the excess, if any, of $10,000 over the actual aggregate qualified adoption expenses pertaining to that adoption during that taxable year and all prior taxable years.[334] This provision is applicable for taxable years beginning after December 31, 2002.[335] These maximum exclusion amounts will be adjusted upward on account of inflation for taxable years beginning after December 31, 2002.[336] The inflation adjusted figure for taxable years beginning in 2005 is $10,360.[337]

The exclusion is a per-child limit. In addition, the Code Sec. 137(a) excludable amount for any taxable year is phased out ratably for employees with AGI (not taking into account the foreign earned income exclusion and with certain other adjustments specified in

---

[329] Code Sec. 129(e)(9).

[330] Code Sec. 137 as added by P.L. 104-188, 104th Cong., 2d Sess., Sec. 1807(b) (Aug. 20, 1996).

[331] Code Sec. 137(f), as amended by P.L. 107-16, 107th Cong., 1st Sess., Sec. 202(e)(2) (June 7, 2001).

[332] Code Secs. 137(a) and (b), as amended by P.L. 107-16, 107th Cong., 1st Sess., Sec. 202(a)(2) (June 7, 2001).

[333] Code Sec. 137(a)(2), as amended by P.L. 107-16, 107th Cong., 1st Sess., Sec. 202(a)(2) (June 7, 2001).

[334] Code Sec. 137(a)(2), as amended by P.L. 107-47, 107th Cong., 2d Sess., Sec 411(c)(2)(A) (March 9, 2002).

[335] Id.

[336] Code Sec. 137(f), as amended by P.L. 107-16, 107th Cong., 1st Sess., Sec. 202(e)(2) (June 7, 2001).

[337] Rev. Proc. 2004-71, IRB 2004-50, 970.

Code Sec. 137(b)(3)) of from $150,000 to $190,000 ($75,000 to $115,000 for taxable years beginning before January 1, 2002).[338] These dollar figures are to be adjusted upward for inflation for taxable years beginning after December 31, 2002.[339] The inflation-adjusted range applicable for taxable years beginning in 2005 is $159,450 to $199,450.[340] Thus, the amount excludable cannot exceed $10,160 and is reduced by an amount equal to the amount incurred or paid by the employer multiplied by a fraction, the numerator of which is the taxpayer's modified AGI in excess of $159,450 in 2005 and the denominator of which is $40,000. This phaseout calculation applies without regard to the $10,360 (in 2005) maximum dollar limit. Thus, before doing the phaseout, the taxpayer must first take into account the lesser of the actual allowable costs or the $10,360 (in 2005) limit.

> **Example:** In 2005, Charles adopted a child and, under an adoption assistance program, his employer paid $8,000 of qualified adoption expenses in connection with that adoption. If Charles had AGI of $137,500, all $8,000 of the employer's payments would be excludable. If Charles had AGI of $179,450, the exclusion would be reduced to $4,000 [$8,000 − ($8,000× ($179,450 − $159,450 / $40,000))]. Thus, $4,000 ($8,000 − $4,000) would be includible in his gross income.

Under Code Sec. 137(c), an adoption assistance program is a separate written program of an employer for the exclusive benefit of that employer's employees under which the employer provides the employees with adoption assistance. Further, the program must meet requirements similar to the nondiscrimination and eligibility rules, the concentration test, and the plan notification rules that apply under Code Sec. 127(b) for educational assistance plans discussed earlier.

Qualified adoption expenses include reasonable and necessary adoption fees, court costs, attorney's fees, and other expenses which are (1) directly related to, and the principal purpose of which is for, the legal adoption of a qualified child by the employee, (2) not incurred in the violation of State or Federal law or in carrying out any surrogate parenting arrangement, and (3) not incurred in connection with the adoption of a child of the employee's spouse. An eligible child is any individual who is less than 18 years old, who is

---

[338] Code Sec. 137(b)(2), as amended by P.L. 107-16, 107th Cong., 1st Sess., Sec. 202(b)(2)(B) (June 7, 2001).

[339] Code Sec. 137(f), as amended by P.L. 107-16, 107th Cong., 1st Sess., Sec. 202(e)(2) (June 7, 2001).

[340] Rev. Proc. 2004-71, IRB 2004-50, 970.

physically or mentally incapable of caring for himself/herself, or who his a child with special needs. A child with special needs is a child where (1) a State has determined that the child cannot or should not be returned to the home of his/her parents, (2) a special factor or condition makes it reasonable to conclude that the child cannot be placed with adoptive parents unless assistance is provided, and (3) the child is a citizen or resident of the United States. Special factors or conditions creating special needs could include the child's ethnic background, age, membership in a minority or sibling group, medical condition, or physical, mental, or emotional handicap.[341]

Certain other special rules also apply for allowance of the exclusion including that (1) in the case of foreign adoptions, no exclusion is allowed until the adoption becomes final (in that case, adoption expenses incurred before that event can be taken into account—for this purpose, Notice 2003-15[342] has announced a proposed revenue procedure which indicates the circumstances under which foreign adoptions are deemed to be final), (2) married couples must file joint returns to get the exclusion, and (3) the name, age, and taxpayer identification number of the child must be placed on the employee's return.[343]

Notice 97-9 provides information concerning how the provisions for the adoption assistance program exclusion relate to the adoption credit provisions of Code Sec. 23.[344] An individual may claim a credit and an exclusion in connection with the adoption of an eligible child. However, the individual may not claim both a credit and an exclusion for the same expense.

> **Example:** Assume that in 2005, an unmarried individual pays $11,500 in qualified adoption expenses to an adoption agency for the final adoption of a child who is not a child with special needs. In that same year, the individual's employer, under an adoption assistance program meeting the Code Sec. 137 requirements, pays an additional $5,000 of other qualified adoption expenses pertaining to the child. Assuming the individual has AGI of $114,000, the individual may claim a credit of $10,360 (in 2005) (the limit under Code Sec. 23) for the first expenses and may exclude $5,000 of the second expense because the exclusion and credit are not for the same expenses.

An individual may not claim a credit under Code Sec. 23 for any expense that is reimbursed by the individual's employer, whether or

---

[341] Code Secs. 137(d) and 23(d) as added by P.L. 104-188 and Notice 97-9, 1997-1 CB 365, II. B.

[342] Notice 2003-15, 2003-1 CB 540.

[343] Code Secs. 137(e), 23(e) as added by P.L. 104-188, and 23(f) as added by P.L. 104-188 and Notice 97-9, 1997-1 CB 365, II. H. and IV.

[344] Notice 97-9, 1997-1 CB 365.

¶ 302.08

not the reimbursement is under an adoption assistance program qualifying under Code Sec. 137.

The adoption assistance exclusion is not applicable for FICA and FUTA purposes. Hence, adoption assistance provided to employees is subject to FICA and FUTA taxes.[345]

.09   Code Sec. 132 Fringe Benefits and Qualified Tuition Reductions

TRA '84 codified the tax treatment of a number of miscellaneous fringe benefits that were previously treated (in some cases in an uncertain fashion) by administrative and judicial law. For many years, Congress had enacted rules prohibiting the IRS from issuing regulations concerning the tax treatment of miscellaneous fringe benefits pending a congressional study on the matter. Finally, in 1984, Congress decided to provide statutory rules to end the uncertainty of the treatment of these items. Congress enacted Code Secs. 132 and 117(d) to provide statutory treatment of miscellaneous fringe benefits. The following types of fringe benefits are (under appropriate circumstances) excludable from gross income:

(1) no-additional-cost services;

(2) qualified employee discounts;

(3) working condition fringes;

(4) de minimis fringe benefits;

(5) qualified transportation fringes;

(6) qualified moving expense reimbursements;

(7) qualified retirement planning services;

(8) qualified military base realignment and closure fringe; and

(9) qualified tuition reductions.

Further, if the above miscellaneous fringe benefits are excludable for income tax purposes, they are also excludable for FICA and FUTA tax purposes.[346] The employer will ordinarily be permitted to take a deduction for its cost of providing the fringe benefits rather than for the value of such benefits to the employee.[347] The above miscellaneous fringe benefits are discussed in the following paragraphs.

---

[345] Notice 97-9, 1997-1 CB 365.
[346] Code Secs. 3121(a)(20) and 3306(b)(16).

[347] Temp. Reg. § 1.162-25T.

.10 No-Additional-Cost Services

A no-additional-cost service is any service provided to an employee for use by the employee if (1) the service is offered for sale to nonemployee customers in the ordinary course of the line of business of the employer in which the employee is performing services, and (2) the employer incurs no substantial additional cost (including foregone revenue) in providing the service to the employee (determined without regard to the amount paid by the employee for the service).[348] Examples of no-additional-cost services include excess airline, bus, or train tickets, unused hotel rooms, or telephone services provided free or at a reduced price to employees working in those lines of business.[349] Services that are not eligible for treatment as no-additional-cost services are non-excess capacity services, such as the use of a stock brokerage firm or a mutual fund to purchase stock or an interest in a mutual fund.[350] The no-additional cost service exclusion does not apply to cash received by employees in lieu of employee services. Thus, airline attendants were not permitted to exclude the amount of cash awarded by a court that was allocable to travel passes they did not receive.[351] A number of definitions and special rules apply in the case of no-additional-cost services. These are discussed below.

Employee. The term "employee" is broadly defined under Code Sec. 132(h) and includes the following:

(1) any individual who is currently employed by the employer in the line of business;

(2) any individual who was formerly employed by the employer in the line of business and who separated from service because of retirement or disability;

(3) a surviving spouse of an individual who died while still employed or who at the time of his or her death was a "former employee" in the line of business; and

(4) any partner who performs services for the partnership.[352]

Also included are the employee's spouse and children (within the meaning of Code Sec. 152(f)(1) for tax years beginning after December 31, 2004—within the meaning of Code Sec. 152(c)(3) for tax years beginning before January 1, 2005) of the employee (1) who are qualified dependents of the employee, or (2) both of whose parents are deceased and who have not attained age 25.[353] Further,

---

[348] Code Sec. 132(b)(1).
[349] Reg. § 1.132-2(a)(2).
[350] *Id.*
[351] *A.H. McKean,* 33 FedCl 535, 95-2 USTC ¶ 50,382 (1995).

[352] Reg. § 1.132-1(b)(2).

[353] Code Sec. 132(h)(2), as amended by P.L. 108-311, 108th Cong., 2d Sess., Sec. 207(13) (Oct. 4, 2004).

parents of airline employees and of employees who retired or went on disability are considered to be employees if the flights are provided as no-additional-cost services.[354]

Line of Business. A no-additional-cost service provided to an employee must be for services that are offered for sale to customers in the ordinary course of the same line of business in which the employee receiving the service performs substantial services.[355] Note that the exclusion does not apply to services sold primarily to employees. An employee who performs services in more than one line of business may exclude no-additional-cost services only in the lines of business in which he or she performs substantial services.[356] If an employee performs substantial services that benefit more than one line of business of the employer, the employee is treated as performing substantial services in all such lines of business.[357]

> **Example (1):** Baker Co. operates three lines of business—a chain of hotels, general retail merchandise stores, and a chain of grocery stores. Bob Adams manages one of the retail merchandising stores. Bob cannot exclude hotel services he receives because he only performs substantial services in the general retail merchandise store line of business.

> **Example (2):** Assume the same facts as in Example (1). Jackie Peters is an accountant with Baker Co. and performs accounting work for all three lines of business. She is considered to perform substantial services for all three lines of business and, thus, can exclude no-additional-cost services from the hotel line of business.

If the employee's employer has a minor line of business that is significantly related to a major line of business, only employees of the minor line who perform services that directly benefit both the major and the minor line are considered employees of both the major and minor lines.[358] A minor line of business is significantly interrelated with a major line of business when the activity of the minor line is directly related to, but is a minor part of, the major line of business (such as laundry services provided at a hospital).

Under IRS regulations, an employer's line of business is determined by reference to the Enterprise Standard Industrial Classification Manual (ESIC Manual) prepared by the Statistical Policy Division of the U.S. Office of Management and Budget.

---

[354] Code Sec. 132(h)(3).
[355] Reg. § 1.132-4(a)(1).
[356] Reg. § 1.132-4(a)(1)(iii).

[357] Reg. § 1.132-4(a)(1)(iv).
[358] *Id.*

An employer is generally considered to have more than one line of business if the employer offers for sale products or services in more than one two-digit classification referred to in the ESIC manual.[359] Examples of two-digit classifications are general retail merchandise stores; hotels and other lodging places; auto repair, services, and garages; and food stores.[360] Under these rules, a sporting goods store and an auto repair shop would be considered two different lines of business, but a general merchandise or department store is considered one line of business. Further, if an employer's retail operations are located on the same premises and are in separate lines of business, but would be considered to be one line of business if the merchandise for sale in the lines of business were offered for sale at a department store, the operations are treated as one line of business. For example, if, on the same premises, an employer sells women's clothing and jewelry and if they were sold together in a department store, they would be considered one line of business, the two different operations are considered one line of business. However, the IRS has privately ruled that an employer's optical stores and clothing stores located within one mall were two separate lines of business. The IRS reasoned that those two lines of business would not have been treated as a single line of business had the operations of both lines been conducted in a department store.[361]

Special Rules for Certain Airline Affiliates. If an employee is employed by a qualified airline affiliate and is directly engaged in providing airline-related services, he or she is not taxable on the value of air transportation provided by the airline. A qualified airline affiliate is any corporation affiliated with an airline, predominantly engaged in providing airline-related services such as: catering, baggage handling, ticketing and reservations, flight planning and weather analysis, and restaurants and gift shops located at an airport.[362]

Special Rules Applying to All Cargo Operations. Under Code Sec. 132(j)(7), the transportation of cargo by air and the transportation of passengers by air are treated as the same service. As a result, employees performing services in the air cargo division of an airline can receive free air passenger travel from the airline without any tax consequences as a no-additional-cost service.

Aggregation of Lines of Business. If an employer has more than one line of business, such lines of business will be treated as one

---

[359] Reg. § 1.132-4(a)(2)(i).

[360] Reg. § 1.132-4(a)(2)(ii).

[361] IRS Letter Ruling 9328016, 4-16-93, CCH IRS LETTER RULINGS REPORTS.

[362] Code Sec. 132(j)(6); Reg. § 1.132-4(d)(3).

line of business if one or more of the following aggregation rules apply:

(1) If it is uncommon in the industry of the employer for any of the separate lines of business of the employer to be operated without the others, the separate lines of business are treated as one line of business.

(2) If it is common for a substantial number of employees (other than employees who work at the headquarters or main office of the employer) to perform substantial services for more than one line of business of the employer (making determination of which employees perform substantial services for particular divisions difficult), the separate lines of business may be aggregated.

(3) If separate retail lines of business would be aggregated if they were part of a department store, they may be aggregated.[363]

Conglomerates that made a special election by March 31, 1986, can continue to furnish certain multiline fringes to all employees of all lines of business existing before 1985. However, multiline fringes that exceed one percent of the employer's payroll are subject to a 30-percent excise tax.[364]

Reciprocal Agreements. Under Code Sec. 132(i), employees can exclude no-additional-cost services provided by another unrelated employer in the same line of business if:

(1) the service provided to the employees of both employers is the same type of service provided to the customers of the employers, both in the line of business in which the employees perform substantial services and the line of business in which the service is provided to customers; and

(2) neither employer incurs substantial additional cost (including foregone revenue) in providing the service to the employees of the other employer.[365]

Each employee can exclude the services as if they were provided by his own employer. For example, the exclusion is available if two unrelated airlines provide free standby flights to each other's employees. However, employees of a hotel cannot exclude free standby flights provided by an unrelated airline company.

No Substantial Additional Cost to the Employer. The exclusion for a no-additional-cost service applies only if the employer does not incur substantial additional cost in providing the service to the employee. The term "cost" includes foregone revenue because the service is provided to an employee rather than a customer.[366]

---

[363] Reg. § 1.132-4(a)(3).
[364] Reg. §§ 1.132-4(g) and 54.4977-1T.

[365] Reg. § 1.132-2(b).
[366] Reg. § 1.132-2(a)(5).

Whether the employer incurs substantial additional cost must be determined without regard to what the employee pays for the service. Thus, any reimbursement by an employee for the cost of providing the service does not affect the determination of whether the employer incurs substantial additional cost.[367]

The employer must include the cost of labor incurred in providing services to an employee. If a substantial amount of time is spent by the employer or other employees in providing the service, the employer is considered to have incurred a substantial additional cost, whether or not nonlabor costs are incurred. The same result occurs whether or not the time spent by the employer or other employees would have been idle or if the services were provided outside of normal business hours.[368]

The employer incurs no substantial additional cost if the services provided to an employee are merely incidental to the primary service being provided by the employer.[369]

Example: Airline employees traveling on a space-available basis are provided in-flight services by flight attendants and in-flight meals. The services and meals are not considered substantial in relation to the air transportation provided. The value of the flight is excludable.

Nondiscrimination Rules. Under Code Sec. 132(j)(1), the exclusion for no-additional-cost services and qualified employee discounts (discussed below) is available for highly compensated employees (as defined under Code Sec. 414(q)) only if the fringe benefit is available on substantially identical terms to each member of a group of employees which is defined under a reasonable classification set up by the employer which does not discriminate in favor of the highly compensated employees. If no-additional-cost services and/or qualified employee discounts are provided in a manner that discriminates in favor of highly compensated employees, only the nonhighly compensated employees will be permitted to exclude the benefits.[370] However, a finding that one fringe benefit program (e.g., no-additional-cost services) is discriminatory will not, by itself, cause another fringe benefit program of the same employer to be treated as discriminatory, unless the programs are related.[371]

---

[367] *Id.*
[368] Reg. § 1.132-2(a)(5)(ii).
[369] *Id.*

[370] Reg. § 1.132-8(a)(1).

[371] Reg. § 1.132-8(a)(2).

.11 Qualified Employee Discounts

In general, a "qualified employee discount" is a discount allowed to employees and their families that does not exceed 20 percent of the price of qualified services offered to customers of the employer or the gross profit percentage of qualified property offered for sale to customers of the employer.[372] To be excludable, the discounts must apply to qualified property and/or services that are offered for sale to customers in the ordinary course of the line of business of the employer in which the employee performs services.

> **Comment:** Qualified property does not include personal investment property such as stock, gold coins, bonds, or real property (such as residential real estate or mineral leases), whether or not the purchase is made for investment.[373] Thus, no exclusion is allowable for discounts on such items.

For purposes of the qualified employee discount exclusion, the terms "employee" and "line of business" have the same general meaning as in the case of no-additional-cost services (described above). In addition, the same nondiscrimination rules apply. However, the term "customer" includes employee customers for purposes of the qualified employee discount exclusion, whereas the term "customer" does not include employees for no-additional-cost services and any other Code Sec. 132 fringe benefits.[374] Note that this rule reduces the excludable qualified employee discount amount since the price at which merchandise and services are sold to employees affects the overall normal price of the merchandise on which the allowable discounts are computed.

Merchandise Discounts. The amount excludable for discounts permitted to employees on qualified property cannot exceed the gross profit percentage (for the representative period) of the price at which the property is being offered for sale to customers in the ordinary course of business in the line of business in which the employee normally works. An employer's gross profit percentage for a representative period is the employer's gross profit (gross receipts minus the cost of goods sold) divided by its aggregate sales price (gross receipts).[375] The representative period is ordinarily the taxable year of the employer immediately preceding the taxable year in which the discount is available.

> **Example:** If gross receipts for the qualified property offered at a discount to employees are $2 million and the cost of goods sold is $1,400,000, the gross profit percentage is 30% (($2,000,000 − 1,400,000) ÷ $2,000,000). Thus, if the employee

---

[372] Code Sec. 132(c).
[373] Reg. § 1.132-3(a)(2).
[374] Code Sec. 132(k).
[375] Reg. § 1.132-3(c).

discount does not exceed 30% of the normal selling price, the discount is excludable. If the discount is more than 30%, (e.g., 45%) the excess discount is subject to taxation.

In general, an employer must determine the gross profit percentage on the basis of all property offered to customers (including employees) in each separate line of business. However, an employer can select a classification of merchandise that is narrower than the applicable line of business. Such a classification must be reasonable. For example, a retail department store may compute a gross profit percentage for the department store as a whole, or may compute different gross profit percentages for different departments or types of merchandise.[376] In any event, the percentage must be based on the employer's experience during a representative period, such as the previous year.[377] Therefore, the IRS ruled that the classification of a company's products into four different categories (i.e., (a) general merchandise, (b) footwear and men's and women's apparel and accessories, (c) children's and infant's clothing, and (d) sports equipment) was a reasonable classification of property for purposes of calculating gross profit percentages.[378]

Discount on Services. In the case of services, the discount cannot exceed 20 percent of the price at which the service is offered to customers in the normal course of the line of business in which the employee works.[379] If the discount exceeds 20 percent, the excess is subject to income taxes.

Leased Sections of Department Stores. If a department store leases floor space to another employer (e.g., a cosmetics firm), and the employees of the other employer engage in over-the-counter sales of merchandise which appear to the public to be made by department store employees, special rules under Code Sec. 132(j)(2) apply. For purposes of the qualified employee discount exclusion, the leased section is treated as part of the line of business of the employer operating the department store, and the employees of the leased section are treated as employees of the department store as well as employees of their own employer.[380] Thus, employees of the leasing employer are permitted the qualified employee discount exclusion for purchases they make in the department store. In addition, employees of the department store can exclude discounts on merchandise they purchase from the leased section.[381]

Special Grandfather Rule for Certain Retail Stores. The line of business requirement has been relaxed for an affiliated group that

---

[376] Reg. § 1.132-3(c)(2).
[377] Code Sec. 132(c)(1)(B).
[378] IRS Letter Ruling 8936041, 6-12-89, CCH IRS LETTER RULINGS REPORTS.

[379] Code Sec. 132(c)(1)(B).
[380] Reg. § 1.132-3(d).
[381] Id.

operates retail department stores under a grandfather rule. The rule applies if (1) on October 5, 1983, 85 percent of the employees of one member were entitled to discounts at department stores of another member, and (2) more than 50 percent of the group's current year are attributable to the operation of retail department stores. Under the rule, the first affiliate is treated as engaged in the same line of business as the second affiliate. Therefore, employees of the first affiliate may exclude qualified employee discounts received at the retail department stores of the second affiliate. However, employees of the second affiliate may not exclude discounts they receive from stores of the first affiliate.[382]

.12 Working Condition Fringes

Under Code Sec. 132(d), the fair market value of any property or services provided to an employee is excluded from gross income to the extent the costs of such property or services would be deductible by the employee under Code Sec. 162 or 167, as an employee business expense, if the employee paid for the property or services. The provision of such property or services is excludable as a working condition fringe benefit.

Employee. For purposes of the working condition fringe exclusion, the term "employee" means (1) an individual currently employed, (2) any partner who performs services for a partnership, (3) any director of the employer, or (4) any independent contractor who performs services for the employer.[383] Thus, the IRS has privately held that financial counseling services provided by a firm to survivors of its deceased employees and to family members of eligible employees who have been diagnosed with a terminal illness are not excludable as working condition fringe benefits because the recipients are not employees of the firm.[384] Independent contractors cannot exclude the use of consumer goods provided under a product testing program (discussed below) and a director cannot exclude the use of consumer goods provided under a product testing program.[385]

General Conditions to Be Satisfied. As noted above, the property or services provided as a working condition fringe must be deductible under Code Sec. 162 (as an ordinary and necessary business expense) or 167 (depreciation by the employee if the employee paid for the item). The value of property or services provided to an employee cannot be excluded as a working condition fringe benefit unless the applicable substantiation requirements of either Code Sec. 274(d) or Code Sec. 162 (whichever applies) and the regulations thereunder are

---

[382] Reg. § 1.132-4(b)(1).

[383] Reg. § 1.132-1(b)(2).

[384] IRS Letter Ruling 199929043, 4-22-99, CCH IRS LETTER RULINGS REPORTS.

[385] Reg. § 1.132-1(b)(2).

satisfied.[386] As an application of the rules mentioned in this paragraph, the Eleventh Circuit Court of Appeals reversed a ruling of the U.S. District Court in *Tounsend Industries,*[387] by holding that the cost of a company fishing trip provided to employees of the company was an excludable working condition fringe benefit because the expenses would have been deductible as an employee business expense under Code Sec. 162 if paid directly by the employees. The Court of Appeals determined on the basis of testimony from the company employees and officials that the fishing trip was associated with the active conduct of the employer's business. Thus, the expenses of the trip would have been deductible if the employees had paid for those expenses.

No nondiscrimination rules apply with respect to working condition fringes. In addition, the rules of Code Sec. 280F for listed property do not apply in determining the amount of working condition fringes.[388] However, a service or property offered by an employer in connection with a flexible spending account is not excludable as a working condition fringe.[389] For this purpose, a flexible spending account is an agreement entered into between an employer and an employee that makes available to the employee over a time period a certain level of unspecified noncash benefits with a predetermined cash value. In addition, a cash payment made by an employer to an employee will not qualify as a working condition fringe unless the employer requires the employee to:[390]

(1) use the payment for expenses in connection with a specific or prearranged activity or undertaking for which a deduction is allowable under Code Sec. 162 or 167;

(2) verify that the payment is actually used for such expenses; and

(3) return to the employer any part of the payment not so used.

The third requirement does not apply in the case of a plan under which only substantiated business expenses are reimbursed. For example, the IRS has privately held that reimbursements that could not exceed properly substantiated business expenses of the employer's employees were excludable as working condition fringe benefits.[391]

Further, if the value of the property or service would be allowable as a deduction with respect to a trade or business of the employee other than the employee's trade or business of being an employee of the employer, it is not considered to be a working

---

[386] Reg. § 1.132-5(c).
[387] CA-11 2003-2 USTC ¶ 50,666, rev'g, and rem'g, DC-Iowa, 2002-2 USTC, ¶ 50,518.
[388] Reg. § 1.132-5(j).

[389] Reg. § 1.132-5(a)(1)(i).
[390] Reg. § 1.132-5(a)(1)(v).
[391] IRS Letter Ruling 9822044, 3-2-98, CCH IRS LETTER RULINGS REPORTS.

¶ 302.12

condition fringe.[392] Finally, a physical examination program that is provided by an employer cannot be considered a working condition fringe benefit. This is true even if the value of the program might be deductible by the employee as a medical expense and without regard to whether the employer makes the program mandatory for some or all of its employees.[393]

The Code Sec. 67 two percent of AGI limitation does not apply in determining the amount of a property or service that would be deductible if paid for by the employee, and, therefore, that limitation does not affect the amount excludable as a working condition fringe.[394]

Examples of Working Condition Fringes. A prime example of a working condition fringe is an employee's use of a company car or airplane for valid business purposes. However, the use of company vehicles and airplanes for personal purposes is not excludable. Further, employer-provided transportation must meet all of the requirements for excludability as a working condition fringe benefit in order to be excludable. Thus, the IRS ruled that the cost of round-trip commercial airline tickets furnished to an employee to take the employee from his residence in one state to a job cite in a remote area of another state was not excludable because the cost would not have been deductible had the employee paid for the tickets under the circumstances.[395] In addition, the U.S. Court of Federal Claims has held, in summary judgment, that per diem payments made by an airline to crew members on "turnaround flights" were not excludable as working condition fringe benefits because there was no requirement that expenses incurred by those employees be adequately substantiated to the employer.[396]

> **Example (1):** An employer provides an employee with a car for the entire year. Assume that the value of the use of the car is $4,000. If the employee drove the car 8,000 miles for the employer's business purposes and 2,000 miles for personal use, the working condition fringe amount that is excludable would be $3,200 (8,000 / 10,000 or 80% × $4,000). The other $800 would not be excludable.

If more than one automobile is provided to an employee, the amount excludable as a working condition fringe must be determined on a vehicle-by-vehicle basis.[397]

---

[392] Reg. § 1.132-5(a)(2).
[393] Reg. § 1.132-5(a)(l)(iv).
[394] Reg. § 1.132-(a)(1)(vi).
[395] IRS Letter Ruling 9641003, 6-21-96, CCH IRS LETTER RULINGS REPORTS.

[396] *American Airlines, Inc.,* FedCl, 98-1 USTC ¶ 50,323, Aff'd on other issue and rem'd on other issue, 2000-1 USTC ¶ 50,236.

[397] Reg. § 1.132-5(b)(2).

> **Example (2):** Assume that automobile Y is available to employee Sanders for 3 days in January and for 5 days in March, and automobile Z is available to Sanders for a week in July. Assume further that the Daily Lease Value (see the discussion of automobile lease value later in this chapter) of the cars is $50 each. For the eight days of availability in January and March, Sanders uses car Y 90% for business purposes, and during July he uses car Z 60% for business purposes. The value of the working condition fringes are determined separately for each automobile. Therefore, the working condition fringe exclusion for car Y is $360 ($400 × .90), and it is $210 ($350 × .60) for car Z. The remaining amounts for the cars are taxable.

If an employer vehicle is used by more than one employee, the miles accumulated on the vehicle by all of the employees driving it are taken into account in determining the amount of working condition fringe benefit with respect to a particular employee's use of the vehicle. If, however, substantially all of the use of the employer's vehicle by other employees is limited to a certain period, such as the last two months of a calendar year, the miles driven by the other employees would not be taken into account in determining the value of the taxpayer-employee's working condition fringe benefit exclusion.[398]

In the case of vehicles used in connection with the business of farming and also used partly for personal purposes, the working condition fringe exclusion is the value of the availability of the vehicle multiplied by 75 percent.[399]

In lieu of excluding the value of a working condition fringe benefit with respect to an automobile, an employer that uses the lease valuation rule of Reg. § 1.61-21 (covered later in this chapter) may include in an employee's gross income the entire annual lease value of the automobile. In that case, the employee can take a miscellaneous itemized deduction on his/her tax return for the business-related use of the automobile. The total inclusion method cannot be used with respect to any other automobile valuation method covering the vehicle.[400]

> **Comment:** Use of the total inclusion approach is not generally advisable since it may result in required income tax withholding and additional payroll taxes on account of the amount included. In addition, the employee may not be able to deduct the

---

[398] Reg. § 1.132-5(b)(1)(i).
[399] Reg. § 1.132-5(g)(1).

[400] Reg. § 1.132-5(b)(1)(iv).

entire value of the business-related use of the automobile because of the Code Sec. 67 two percent of AGI limitation. The employee would not get any deduction for such use if he/she takes the standard deduction.

If an employee is provided with the services of a chauffeur, the amount excludable as a working condition fringe is the amount that would be allowable as a deduction under Code Sec. 162 or 167 if the employee paid for the chauffeur services, and the working condition fringe with respect to a chauffeur is determined separately from the amount of the working condition fringe with respect to the vehicle. An employee may exclude from gross income the excess of the value of the chauffeur services over the value of the chauffeur services for personal purposes (such as commuting), as determined under the taxable fringe benefit valuation rules of Reg. § 1.61-21 (covered later in this chapter).[401]

> **Example (3):** Assume that an employer makes available to an employee an automobile and a chauffeur. Assume further that the value of the chauffeur services determined in accordance with the fringe benefit valuation rules of Reg. § 1.61-21 is $30,000 and that the chauffeur spends 30 percent of each day driving the employee for personal purposes. Only $21,000 ($30,000 − .30 × $30,000) is excludable as a working condition fringe.

Other examples of working condition fringes include payment of bar association dues by a law firm, the subscription cost of business-related periodicals, and the value of fringes provided for an employee's safety, where necessary, including a bodyguard, a car and driver, or a car designed for security.[402] In order to obtain the exclusion for employer-provided transportation for security concerns, there must be a demonstration of bona fide business-oriented security concern. In general, a bona fide business-oriented security concern exists only if the facts and circumstances establish a specific basis for concern regarding the safety of the employee (e.g., a threat of death or kidnapping or serious bodily harm). In addition, the employee's employer must establish that an overall security program has been provided with respect to the employee involved.[403] An example of an employer-provided service that is not considered to be a working condition fringe benefit is employer-provided tax preparation for employees.[404] The IRS found that the employer did not

---

[401] Reg. § 1.132-5(b)(3).
[402] Reg. § 1.132-5(m).
[403] Reg. § 1.132-5(m)(2).

[404] Field Service Advice 200137039, 6-19-01, CCH IRS Letter Rulings Reports.

derive a substantial business benefit from provision of the service, and the underlying expense would not have been deductible under Code Sec. 162 if paid for by the employees.

Auto Salespeople. The fair market value of "qualified automobile demonstration use" by a full-time auto salesperson is excludable as a working condition fringe.[405] But, it should be noted that the exclusion is only permitted if the general requirements applicable to the excludability of working condition fringe benefits, in general, are met. Thus, the IRS has privately ruled that the value of dealer provided demonstration automobiles provided to sales personnel was not excludable as a working condition fringe benefit because the employer did not require employees to provide substantiation or records concerning their use of the vehicles and that the vehicles were provided to both sales and non-sales personnel for both business and non-business purposes.[406] The term "qualified automobile demonstration use" means any use of a demonstration automobile by a full-time automobile salesperson in the sales area in which the automobile sales office is located if:

(1) the use is provided primarily for the purpose of helping the salesman sell cars; and

(2) there are substantial restrictions on the personal use of the automobile by the salesperson.[407]

A full-time automobile salesperson is any individual who:

(1) is employed by an automobile dealer;

(2) customarily spends at least half of a normal business day on the sales floor selling automobiles to customers of the dealer;

(3) is employed on a full-time basis (not less than 1,000 hours per year);

(4) derives at least 25 percent of his/her gross income from the dealer as a result of selling automobiles; and

(5) directly engages in substantial promotion and negotiation of sales to customers.[408]

The sales area is the geographic area surrounding the automobile dealer's sales office from which the office regularly derives customers. However, with respect to a particular full-time salesperson, the sales area may be treated as the larger of the area within a 75-mile radius of the dealer's office or the one-way commuting distance (in miles) of the particular salesperson.[409]

---

[405] Code Sec. 132(j)(3)(A).
[406] IRS Letter Ruling 9801002, 9-3-97, CCH IRS LETTER RULINGS REPORTS.
[407] Reg. § 1.132-5(o).
[408] Reg. § 1.132-5(o)(2).
[409] Reg. § 1.132-5(o)(5).

¶ 302.12

A demonstration auto is one that is currently in the inventory of the dealer and is available for test drives by customers during the normal business hours of the employee.[410]

The salesperson's use of the automobile is considered to be substantially restricted if:

(1) use of the car by others is prohibited;

(2) use for personal vacation trips is prohibited;

(3) the storage of personal possessions in the auto is not allowed; and

(4) the total use by mileage of the automobile by the salesperson outside working hours is limited.[411]

The IRS issued Rev. Proc. 2001-56[412] in late 2001 to provide simplified methods that can be used by auto dealerships to value the use of demonstration automobiles provided to their employees. In all, four different valuation methods are presented ranging from a full-exclusion method to a full inclusion general valuation approach. For the full exclusion approach to be applicable, the overall requirements specified on the previous page based on the final regulations must generally be met. But, certain leeway is provided. For example, the personal use of a demonstration automobile will be considered limited if the vehicle is driven not more than 10 miles per day for personal purposes in addition to commuting usage. A partial exclusion approach is applicable where the overall requirements are met but the employee fails to meet the 10 miles per day personal usage guideline.

Product Testing. The value of the use of consumer goods manufactured for sale to nonemployee customers and provided to employees for product testing and evaluation outside the employer's office is excluded as a working condition fringe if the following conditions are satisfied:[413]

(1) consumer testing and evaluation of the product is an ordinary and necessary business expense of the employer;

(2) business reasons necessitate that the testing and evaluation be performed off the employer's business premises;

(3) the product is furnished to the employee for purposes of testing and evaluation;

(4) the product is made available to the employee for no longer than necessary to test and evaluate its performance;

(5) the product must be returned to the employer after completion of the testing and evaluation;

---

[410] Reg. § 1.132-5(o)(3).
[411] Reg. § 1.132-5(o)(4).
[412] 2001-2 CB 590.
[413] Reg. § 1.132-5(n)(1).

(6) the employer imposes limitations on the employee's use of the product which significantly reduce the value of any personal benefit to the employee; and

(7) the employee is required to submit detailed reports on the testing and evaluation.

The sixth requirement is met, for example, if (1) the employer places limitations on the employee's ability to select among different models or varieties of the consumer product that is furnished for testing and evaluation purposes, (2) the employer's policy requires the employee, in appropriate cases, to purchase or lease at his own expense the same type of product being tested (so that personal use by the employee's family will be limited), and (3) the employer requires that members of the employee's family generally cannot use the item. In addition, personal use of such consumer products, which otherwise does not qualify for exclusion under the above rules, is excludable to the extent that the employee pays or reimburses the employer for such personal use.[414]

If products are furnished under a testing and evaluation program only to highly compensated employees, the products may not be considered a working condition fringe unless the employer can show a business reason for only providing the products to such employees (e.g., automobiles furnished by an automobile manufacturing company to its design engineers and supervisory mechanics for testing and evaluation).[415] For example, the IRS privately ruled that the value of products provided under one firm's product testing program was not excludable where almost 93 percent of the participants were the firm's highest paid employees, or they made salaries sufficient to qualify them for bonuses, and because there were insufficient limitations on the personal use of the products by the employees' families.[416]

Employer-Provided Educational Assistance. Under Code Sec. 132(j)(8), amounts paid or expenses incurred by the employer for education or training provided to the employee that are not excludable under Code Sec. 127 (e.g., because the amounts paid exceed the Code Sec. 127 exclusion limit of $5,250) are excludable if the amounts or expenses meet the requirements (covered above) for exclusion as a working condition fringe benefit.[417] Thus, for example, the educational assistance costs would have to be deductible by the employee under Code Sec. 162 if the employee paid

---

[414] Reg. § 1.132-5(n)(2).
[415] Reg. § 1.132-5(n)(3).
[416] IRS Letter Ruling 9401002, 9-24-93. CCH IRS LETTER RULINGS REPORTS.

[417] Code Sec. 132(j)(8), as amended and redesignated by Secs. 13,101(b) and 13,213(d)(2), P.L. 103-66, 103rd Cong., 1st Sess. (Aug. 10, 1993).

directly for the education. However, the IRS has privately ruled in Field Advice that tuition reductions which are not excludable under Code Sec. 117(d) cannot be excluded as working condition fringe benefits under Code Sec. 132.[418] There is no statutory provision comparable to Code Sec. 132(j)(8) allowing for such treatment.

Working Condition Fringe Exclusion for Volunteer Workers. A bona fide volunteer (including an officer or director) who performs services for an exempt organization or for a government employer is entitled to the working condition fringe benefit exclusion with respect to working condition fringe benefits furnished to him/ her.[419] An individual is considered to be a bona fide volunteer for this purpose only if the total value of the fringe benefits received by him/her is substantially less than the value of the volunteer services that the individual provides to the exempt organization or government employer.[420]

Job Placement Assistance. Under Rev. Rul. 92-69,[421] job placement assistance provided by a worker's employer can be excluded as a working condition fringe benefit if the employer obtains a "substantial business benefit" from providing the job placement assistance to the workers. A substantial business benefit is obtained by the employer if the job placement assistance is established to promote a positive corporate image, maintain employee morale, avoid wrongful termination suits, foster a positive work atmosphere, and/or help attract quality employees. It is not necessary to provide the same type of job placement assistance to every terminated employee, and such assistance does not have to be provided to certain terminated employees who the employer believes do not need such assistance. The exclusion, however, is not available if an employee can elect to receive cash or other taxable benefits in place of the job placement assistance.

Employer Payment of Club Dues and Spouse Travel Allowances. The IRS has issued final regulations under which (1) the payment by an employer of club dues to provide membership in a club to an employee can be excludable as a working condition fringe benefit and (2) the provision of travel allowances for the spouse or other companion of an employee on a business trip for the employer is excludable as a working condition fringe benefit.[422] However, the exclusions for these benefits are not allowed if the employer treats them as deductible compensation payments.

---

[418] Field Service Advice 200231016, 3-12-02. CCH IRS Letter Rulings Reports.
[419] Reg. § 1.132-5(r)(1).
[420] Reg. § 1.132-5(r)(3).
[421] 1992-2 CB 51.
[422] Reg. §§ 1.132-5(s) and (t).

.13   De Minimis Fringe Benefits

Under Code Sec. 132(e)(1), the value of any property that (after taking into account the frequency with which similar fringes are provided by the employer) has such a small value that accounting for it would be "unreasonable or administratively impractical" is considered to be excludable as a de minimis fringe benefit. For example, the U.S. Court of Federal Claims has held that the value of American Express vouchers provided to employees of an airline were not excludable as de minimis fringe benefits because the airline did not prove that it would have been administratively impractical to account for the vouchers.[423] The fringes that qualify for exclusion as de minimis fringe benefits are ones that otherwise would be includible in gross income. The IRS has recently issued Field Service Advice in which it analyzes in detail the general requirements for the exclusion of employer-provided benefits as de minimis fringe benefits.[424] For example, the IRS indicates that the method of accounting chosen by an employer with respect to a particular employee benefit is not determinative in deciding whether it is administratively impractical to account for the value of a benefit. Further, the less frequent an item is furnished, the more likely it can be classified as a de minimis fringe benefit. It is up to the employer to provide an accounting system that will adequately show the frequency with which items are furnished to employees. Finally, the lower the value of an item which is furnished to employees, the more likely the item can be excluded as a de minimis fringe benefit.

Excludable de minimis fringe benefits include (1) the occasional typing of a letter by a company secretary, (2) occasional personal use of employer copying machines, (3) infrequent use of the employer's automobile, and (4) certain holiday gifts or property with a low market value, such as a holiday turkey given to employees.[425] In addition, the electronic filing of an employee's individual income tax return by the employer and the provision of income tax preparation services by VITA (Volunteer Income Tax Assistance) volunteers at the employer's headquarters, but not payments by an employer to an income tax preparer for services provided in preparing an employee's income tax return, are considered de minimis fringe benefits.[426] The IRS repeated that position in an Information Letter it released in 2004.[427] However, the IRS did state that employers may offer electronic filing services that are limited to the electronic

---

[423] *American Airlines, Inc.,* FedCl, 98-1 USTC ¶ 50,323. Aff'd on other issue and rem'd on other issue, 2000-1 USTC ¶ 50,236.

[424] Field Service Advice 200219005, 12-31-01, CCH IRS LETTER RULINGS REPORTS.

[425] Reg. § 1.132-6(e).

[426] IRS Letter Ruling 9442003. 7-11-94, CCH IRS LETTER RULINGS REPORTS.

[427] IRS Information Letter 2004-0035 (Jan. 22, 2004).

¶ 302.13

transmittal of employee tax returns as an excludable de minimis fringe benefit. In a 2004 letter ruling, the IRS held that the provision of a holiday gift coupon with a value of $35 and redeemable at several local grocery stores to each of its employees is not an excludable de minimis fringe benefit.[428] The IRS held that the gift coupons were indistinguishable from cash equivalent fringe benefits, such as gift certificates, and as such were not administratively impractical to account for.

When determining whether the value of an item or service is de minimis, the frequency with which similar fringes are provided by the employer to his/her employees must be taken into account. For example, the IRS has privately ruled that meal allowances provided to employees of a utility company were not excludable as de minimis fringe benefits where the employees were entitled to the meal allowances on a routine basis, rather than an occasional basis.[429] Generally, this frequency is determined by reference to how often the employer provides the fringe to each employee. However, where it would be administratively difficult to determine frequency with respect to individual employees, the determination may be made by reference to how frequently the fringe is provided to all employees.[430]

Eating Facilities. The operation by the employer of any eating facility for employees is excludable as a de minimis fringe if the facility is located on or near the business premises of the employer and the revenue derived from the facility normally equals or exceeds the direct operating costs of the facility.[431] For this purpose, in taxable years beginning after 1997, an employee entitled under Code Sec. 119 (Meals and Lodging Furnished for the Convenience of the Employer discussed earlier in this chapter) to exclude the value of a meal provided at the eating facility will be treated as having paid an amount for that meal equal to the direct operating costs of the facility attributable to that meal.[432] In addition, if more than one half of employees to whom meals are provided by an employer on the employer's business premises are provided for the convenience of the employer, then all of the meals furnished by the employer on its business premises to employees will be regarded as furnished for the convenience of the employer.[433] Thus, as long as

---

[428] Technical Advice Memorandum 200437030.
[429] IRS Letter Ruling 9148001, 2-15-91, CCH IRS LETTER RULINGS REPORTS.
[430] Reg. § 1.132-6(b)(2).
[431] Code Sec. 132(e)(2).
[432] Code Sec. 132(e)(2), as amended by P.L. 105-35. 105th Cong., 1st Sess., Sec. 970(a) (Aug. 5, 1997). This new rule brings Code Sec. 132(e)(2) in line with Reg. § 1-32-7(a)(2) and the Tax Court ruling in *Boyd Gaming Corporation,* 106 TC 343 (1996). In that case, the Tax Court held

that meals provided by a casino in an eating facility, free-of-charge were excludable de minimis fringe benefits and were deductible by the employer. The Court agreed with the employer that it had reasonably determined that the meals were excludable under Code Sec. 119 and that the employer did not have to meet the revenue versus expense test normally required.
[433] Code Sec. 119(b)(4), as added by P.L. 105-206. 105th Cong., 2d Sess., Sec. 5002(a) (July 22, 1998).

over one half of the meals furnished in an eating facility are provided for the convenience of the employer, all employees provided meals in the facility will be treated as having paid an amount for that meal equal to the direct operating costs of the facility attributable to those meals. The exclusion is not available, however, to highly compensated employees (as defined in Code Sec. 414(q)) unless the facility is made available on substantially the same terms to each member of a group of employees defined under a reasonable classification set up by the employer that does not discriminate in favor of the highly compensated employees.

An employer-operated eating facility for purposes of the exclusion is a facility that meets all of the following conditions:

(1) the facility is owned or leased by the employer;

(2) the facility is operated by the employer;

(3) the facility is located on or near the business premises of the employer; and

(4) the meals furnished at the facility are provided during or immediately before or after the employees' working hours.[434]

.14   Athletic Facilities

Under Code Sec. 132(j)(4), the value of any on-premises athletic facility provided by an employer to its employees is not taxable to the employees. The term "on-premises athletic facility" is any gym or athletic facility:

(1) that is located on the premises of the employer;

(2) that is operated by the employer; and

(3) substantially all the use of which is by employees of the employer, their spouses, and their dependent children.[435]

No nondiscrimination rules have to be satisfied.

The athletic facility need not be located on the business premises of the employer. However, the facility must be located on premises owned and operated by the employer and cannot be a facility for residential use, such as a resort.[436] An athletic facility is considered to be located on the employer's premises if the facility is located on the premises of a voluntary employees' beneficiary association funded by the employer.[437] An employer is deemed to be operating a facility if the employer operates the facility through its own employees, or if the employer contracts out to another (such as

---

[434] Reg. § 1.132-7(a)(2).
[435] Code Sec. 132(a)(5)(B).

[436] Reg. § 1.132-1(e)(2).
[437] Id.

an independent contractor) to operate it.[438] If an athletic facility is operated by a voluntary employees' beneficiary association funded by the employer, the employer is considered to operate the facility.[439] Qualifying facilities include gyms, swimming pools, tennis courts, golf courses, and running and bicycle paths.

The athletic facilities exclusion does not apply to any membership in an athletic facility (including health clubs or country clubs) unless the facility is owned or leased and operated by the employer and used substantially by the employer's employees.[440]

.15   Qualified Transportation Fringes

Under Code Sec. 132(f)(1), the following fringe benefits are excludable as qualified transportation fringes:

(1) transportation of the employee in a commuter highway vehicle between the employee's residence and place of employment;

(2) any transit pass provided to an employee; and

(3) qualified employee parking.

The maximum amount excludable with respect to the first two qualified transportation fringes provided alone or for both combined is $100 per month in 2002 (adjusted for inflation after 2002) and $175 per month in 2002 for qualified employee parking (after 2002, the amount is to be adjusted upward for inflation—the inflation adjusted figures for 2005, are $105 and $200, respectively).[441] Cash reimbursements made to employees for qualified transportation expenses can also be excluded. However, a reimbursement for a purchased transit pass is excludable only if a voucher or similar item which may be exchanged only for a transit pass is not readily available for direct distribution to employees by the employer.[442] For taxable years beginning after 1997, qualified transportation fringes are excludable even if they are provided in lieu of compensation that would be includible in the gross income of the recipient employee.[443] Prior to 1998, the exclusion was not available for qualified transportation fringe benefits that were made available in lieu of, as opposed to in addition to, taxable compensation.[444] That rule applied even if state and local law required employers to offer the choice of receiving a qualified transportation fringe or a larger amount of taxable compensation.[445]

---

[438] Reg. § 1.132-1(e)(4).

[439] Id.

[440] Reg. § 1.132-1(e)(3).

[441] Code Secs. 132(f)(2) and (6), as amended by P.L. 105–178, 105th Cong., 2d Sess., Sec. 9010(c), (June 9, 1998), effective for tax years beginning after 2001. See also Rev. Proc. 2004-71, IRB 2004-50, 970.

[442] Code Sec. 132(f)(3).

[443] Code Sec. 132(f)(4), as amended by P.L. 105-178, 105th Cong., 2d Sess., Sec. 9010(a)(1) (June 9, 1998).

[444] Former Code Sec. 132(f)(4).

[445] Notice 94-3, 1994-1 CB 327, Q&A 4.

For purposes of the exclusion rules, a commuter highway vehicle is a highway vehicle (1) that can seat at least six adults and (2) at least 80 percent of the mileage of which can be reasonably expected to be for commuting purposes and trips during which the number of employees transported are at least one-half of the adult seating capacity of the vehicle, exclusive of the driver.[446]

A transit pass is any pass, token, farecard, or similar item that entitles an individual to free or reduced-fare transportation if the transportation is provided (1) on mass transit facilities or (2) by anyone in the business of transporting individuals for compensation as long as the transportation is provided in a commuter highway vehicle (as defined above).[447]

Qualified employee parking is parking provided to an employee on or near the business premises of the employer or on or near a location from which the employee commutes to work in a commuter highway vehicle (as defined above).[448] The IRS has privately held that employer-provided parking and reimbursements made for employee parking at nontemporary work locations is excludable to the extent that the statutory limitation (noted above) is not exceeded.[449] As noted above, cash reimbursements made to employees for qualified transportation fringes, including qualified parking, can be excluded as qualified transportation fringes. However, no exclusion is permitted where the employee receives double benefits (i.e., double-dipping). In that respect, the IRS has publicly ruled that where (1) a company implemented a payroll arrangement under which the amount of its employees' cash compensation is reduced in return for company-provided parking, and (2) the company makes "reimbursement" payments to the employees with respect to the parking expenses in amounts that cause employees' net after-tax pay from the company to be the same amount as it would have been if there were no compensation reduction for the parking, the reimbursement was not excludable as a qualified transportation fringe.[450] Because the reimbursement payments were not reimbursement of expenses incurred by the employee for parking, it was not reasonable for the employer to believe at the time the reimbursements were made that the employee would be able to exclude the payments under Code Sec. 132(a)(5). The IRS also noted that its ruling applies to arrangements with respect to benefits other than parking where (1) the employee's salary (and gross income) is reduced in return for a non-taxable benefit, and (2) the employer reimburses the employee for some or all of the cost of the non-taxable benefit and excludes the

---

[446] Code Sec. 132(f)(5)(B).
[447] Code Sec. 132(f)(5)(A).
[448] Code Sec. 132(f)(5)(C).

[449] IRS Legal Memorandum 200105007.
[450] Rev. Rul. 2004-98, IRB 2004-42, 664. *See also* Information Letters 2004-0201 and 2005-0059.

reimbursement from the employee's salary (and gross income), even though that cost was paid by the employer and not the employee.

The IRS issued final regulations in 2001[451] to address some specific issues concerning the provision and excludability of transportation fringes. The regulations indicate that an employer may simultaneously provide more than one of three benefits (described above) at the same time. The regulations also indicate that if an employee pays an employer for a qualified transportation fringe, the amount that is taxable to the employee equals the value of the benefit minus the sum of (1) the amount paid by the employee plus (2) the amount excludable under Code Sec. 132 or another Code Section. If both commuter highway vehicle transportation and transit passes are provided, the $105 limit (in 2005) applies in total, not to each separately. If less than the limit is provided to an employee during one month, the unused amount cannot be carried over to a subsequent month.

Before 1993, employer-provided parking was excludable without limit as a working condition fringe benefit, and transit passes provided to employees at a discount of no more than $21 per month were excludable as a de minimis fringe benefit.[452]

.16 Qualified Moving Expense Reimbursement

After 1993, qualified moving expense reimbursements by the employer are excludable as a fringe benefit under Code Sec. 132(g).[453] A qualified moving expense reimbursement is considered to be any amount received (directly or indirectly) by an individual from an employer as a payment for (or a reimbursement of) moving expenses of the individual that would be deductible under Code Sec. 217 if paid for by the individual. However, no exclusion is permitted with respect to payments for (or reimbursements of) any expenses actually deducted by the individual in a prior taxable year. For further coverage concerning this topic, see the discussion of reimbursements of employee moving expenses in Chapter 2.

.17 Qualified Retirement Planning Services

A new fringe benefit has been made available as a result of the enactment of EGTRRA. In taxable years beginning after December 31, 2001, the value of qualified retirement planning services provided to employees will be excludable.[454] Under new Code Sec. 132(m),

---

[451] Reg. § 1.132-9.

[452] Former Code Sec. 132(h)(4) and Reg. § 1.132-6(d)(4).

[453] Code Sec. 132(g), as added by Sec. 13,213, P.L. 103-66, 103rd Cong., 1st Sess. (Aug. 10, 1993).

[454] Code Sec. 132(a)(7), as added by P.L. 107-16, 107th Cong., 1st Sess., Sec. 665(a) (June 7, 2001).

qualified retirement planning services are defined as any retirement planning advice or information that is provided to an employee and his/her spouse by an employer maintaining a qualified employer plan. However, the exclusion is not available to highly compensated employees unless the retirement planning services are available on substantially the same terms to each member of the group of employees normally provided education and information regarding the employer's qualified retirement plan.[455]

For purposes of the qualified retirement planning services exclusion rules, qualified employer plans are defined as a plan, contract, pension or account that is described in Code Sec. 219(g)(5).[456] These are the typical qualified plans offered by employers and discussed in Chapter 5, including Code Sec. 401(k) plans, SIMPLE plans, defined benefit pension plans, and others. Qualified retirement planning services are retirement planning advice and information. The exclusion is not limited to information concerning the qualified plan, and therefore, for example, applies to advice and information about retirement income planning for an employee and his/her spouse and how the employer's plan fits into the employee's overall retirement income plan. However, the exclusion does not apply to services that may be related to retirement planning, such as tax preparation, accounting, legal, or brokerage services.[457]

.18 Qualified Military Base Realignment and Closure Fringe

As enacted by the Military Family Tax Relief Act of 2003,[458] the amount of a qualified military base realignment and closure fringe as defined in new Code Sec 132(n) is excludable from gross income. The term "qualified military base realignment and closure fringe" means one or more payments under the authority of Section 1013 of the Demonstration Cities and Metropolitan Development Act of 1966 (42 U.S.C. Sec. 3374, as in effect on the date of enactment of Sec. 132(n)—November 11, 2003) to offset the adverse effects on housing values that result from the realignment or closure of a military base.[459] The exclusion applies to payments made under the Department of Defense Homeowners Assistance Program (HAP) as authorized under the 1966 Act. Those payments reimburse military homeowners for losses that result from the sale of their

---

[455] Code Sec. 132(m)(2), as added by P.L. 107-16, 107th Cong., 1st Sess., Sec. 665(b) (June 7, 2001).

[456] Code Sec. 132(m)(3), as added by P.L. 107-16, 107th Cong., 1st Sess., Sec. 665(b) (June 7, 2001).

[457] HR Conf. Rep. No. 107-84, 107th Cong., 1st Sess. (June 7, 2001).

[458] P.L. 108-121, 108th Cong., 1st Sess. (Nov. 11, 2003).

[459] Code Sec. 132(n)(1), as added by P.L. 108-121, 108th Cong., 1st Sess., Sec 103(a) (Nov. 11, 2003).

homes following the closure of a base or a reduction in the operations of a base.

The amount excludable as a qualified military base realignment and closure fringe for any particular property will not include payments related to that property to the extent they exceed the maximum amount described in clause (1) of subsection (c) of the 1966 Act (as in effect on November 11, 2003).[460] Thus, the amount received under HAP, under the 1966 Act, is an amount not in excess of the difference between (1) 95 percent of the fair market value of the property as determined by the Department of Defense before the public announcement of the intention to close all or part of the military base or installation, and (2) the fair market value of the property at the time of the sale.

.19 Qualified Tuition Reduction Plans

A qualified tuition reduction is not taxable to the recipient under Code Sec. 117(d). The term "qualified tuition reduction" means the amount of any tuition reduction provided to an employee of an educational institution for education at that institution below the graduate level.[461] For example, employees of a college would not be taxed if they were permitted to take one undergraduate class at no cost.

However, a special rule under Code Sec. 117(d)(4) applies to graduate students who are teaching or are research assistants at the educational institution where they are enrolled. They are entitled to exclude the value of tuition reductions they receive on account of their teaching and research activities. This exclusion does not apply to amounts received which represent payment for teaching, research, or other services by the students required as a condition for receiving the qualified tuition reduction.[462]

For purposes of Code Sec. 117(d), the term "employee" has the same meaning (under Code Sec. 132(h)) as it does for no-additional-cost services (described above). Thus, the term includes the employee's family and certain former employees and their families.

The exclusion is not permitted to highly compensated employees (as defined under Code Sec. 414(q)) unless the tuition reduction plan is available on substantially identical terms to each member of a group of employees defined under a reasonable classification set up by the employer that is not discriminatory in favor of the highly compensated employees.[463]

---

[460] Code Sec. 132(n)(2), as added by P.L. 108-121, 108th Cong., 1st Sess., Sec. 103(a) (Nov. 11, 2003).
[461] Code Sec. 117(d)(2).

[462] Code Sec. 117(c).

[463] Code Sec. 117(d)(3).

The IRS has privately ruled in Field Advice that tuition reductions which are not excludable under Code Sec. 117(d) cannot be excluded as working condition fringe benefits under Code Sec. 132.[464]

¶303 Other Fringe Benefits

The remainder of this chapter covers certain other fringe benefits that may be provided to employees. Some of the following benefits are excludable in some circumstances and others are fully taxable. The benefits covered are:

(1) interest-free and below-market-rate-interest, compensation-related loans;

(2) employee use of company cars and airplanes; and

(3) golden parachute payments.

.01 Interest-Free and Below-Market-Rate-Interest, Compensation-Related Loans

Under Code Sec. 7872, if an employer loans an employee more than $10,000 at less than the applicable federal rate (AFR), the employer is deemed to have paid additional compensation to the employee equal to the foregone interest (the interest that would have been collected by the employer if the employer had charged a rate of interest equal to the AFR minus the amount of interest actually collected by the employer). Further, this rule applies to any employer-employee loan, regardless of amount, if one of the principal purposes of the loan is the avoidance of federal tax.[465] The amount that is treated as additional compensation is taxable to the employee and is deductible by the employer as compensation paid under Code Sec. 162. That amount is also treated as a payment of imputed interest by the employee (which is not deductible by the employee unless the interest could be classified as investment interest) that is includible in the gross income of the employer. This additional compensation to the employee is subject to FICA and FUTA taxes.[466] The provisions of Code Sec. 7872 apply to term loans made after June 6, 1984, and to demand loans outstanding after that date and not repaid before September 18, 1984.

Compensation-Related Loans. A compensation-related loan is a below-market rate loan that is made in connection with the performance of services, directly or indirectly, between:

(1) an employer and an employee;

---

[464] Field Service Advice 200231016, 3-12-02, CCH IRS LETTER RULINGS REPORTS.

[465] Code Sec. 7872(c)(3)(B).
[466] Prop. Reg. § 1.7872-11(d).

(2) an independent contractor and a person for whom the independent contractor provides services; and

(3) a partnership and a partner if the loan is made in consideration for services performed by the partner acting other than in his capacity as a member of the partnership.[467]

The term "in connection with the performance of services" has the same meaning as the term has for purposes of Code Sec. 83 (which covers deferred compensation in the form of restricted property plans under which the payment of the deferred compensation is subject to a substantial risk of forfeiture). Except in the case of loans made by a corporation to shareholder-employees (as discussed below), a loan which is made in part in exchange for services and in part for other reasons is treated as a compensation-related loan only if more than 25 percent of the amount loaned is attributable to the performance of services of the recipient. If 25 percent or less of a loan is made with respect to the performance of services by the employee, none of the loan amount is treated as a compensation-related loan (some or all the loan may still be subject to Code Sec. 7872 on some other basis, however).[468]

An arrangement will be treated as a compensation-related loan only if, in substance, there is a debtor-creditor relationship between the employee and the employer at the time the loan is made.[469] For example, if an employer makes a payment to an unrelated third-party lender to buy down a mortgage loan for an employee, and considering all the facts and circumstances, the transaction is, in substance, a loan by a third-party lender to the employee and a payment by the employer to secure the benefit for the employee, the employer's payment to the lender will be treated as compensation to the employee. To that extent, the below-market interest rules do not apply. However, if the transaction is actually a loan by the employer made with the aid of services provided by the third-party lender acting as an agent for the employer, there is, in fact, a compensation-related loan subject to the rules of Code Sec. 7872.[470]

In addition, if an employee receives payment from a customer for services rendered on behalf of an employer and is permitted to retain the money for a period of time without paying interest at a rate at least equal to the AFR, there is generally a compensation-related loan.[471] For example, if an investment banker is permitted by an issuing company to retain the proceeds of a public offering of

---

[467] Prop. Reg. § 1.7872-4(c)(1).
[468] Prop. Reg. § 1.7821-4(c)(2).
[469] H.R. Rep. No. 861, 98th Cong., 2d Sess. (1984), at 1018.

[470] Prop. Reg. § 1.7872-4(c)(3).
[471] H.R. Rep. No. 861, 98th Cong., 2d Sess. (1984), at 1018.

stock without paying interest, there is a below-market loan from the issuer to the banker. To the extent the benefit is in lieu of a fee for services, the loan is considered to be compensation-related.

When a below-market rate loan is made to a shareholder-employee, that loan could be a compensation-related loan or a corporation-shareholder loan which could give rise to dividend income. Fortunately, the final regulations under Code Sec. 7872 provide some guidelines that can be used in classifying loans made to shareholder-employees. The final regulations indicate that a loan to a shareholder-employee will be considered to be a corporation-shareholder loan if:

(1) in the case of a publicly held corporation, the shareholder-employee owns directly and indirectly more than 0.5 percent of the total voting power of all classes of stock entitled to vote, or more than 0.5 percent of the total value of shares of all other classes of stock, or 0.5 percent of the value of shares of all classes of stock (including voting stock) of the corporation; or

(2) in the case of a nonpublicly traded corporation, the shareholder-employee owns directly or indirectly more than five percent of the total voting power of all classes of stock entitled to vote, or more than five percent of the total number of shares of all other classes of stock, or five percent of the total value of shares of all classes of stock (including voting stock) of the corporation.

Such a loan is presumed to be a corporation-shareholder loan unless there is clear and convincing evidence that the loan is made solely in connection with the performance of services.[472]

> **Example:** Michaels, a 60 percent shareholder and chairman of the board of the Michaels Corporation, was provided with a $275,000 below-market interest rate loan from the corporation in June 2006. There was no clear evidence to indicate that the loan was made in connection with Michaels's services. The loan is thus considered to be a corporation-shareholder loan. In that case, the foregone interest is considered to be a dividend which is not deductible by the corporation and not subject to FICA and FUTA taxes.

Computation of Foregone Interest. In the case of a demand compensation-related loan, the amount of the foregone interest which is taxable as compensation to the employee is the excess of:

(1) the amount of interest that would have been payable in that year if the interest had accrued at the AFR over

---

[472] Prop. Reg. § 1.7872-4(d)(2).

(2) any interest payable on the loan that is properly allocable to that year.[473]

The AFR to be used in the calculation is determined according to rules contained in Prop. Reg. § 1.7872-13. For example, if a fixed-principal below-market compensation-related loan remains outstanding for an entire year, the AFR is the "blended annual rate" for the year as announced by the IRS. The blended annual rate for 2005 was 3.11 percent.[474]

In the case of a term compensation-related loan, the amount of foregone interest that is taxable as compensation to the employee and deductible by the employer (and subject to FICA and FUTA taxes) is the amount of the loan minus the present value of all payments which are required to be made under the terms of the loan. That present value is determined using the AFR that applies to the loan (based on the length of the term of the loan).[475] In addition, the amount which is deemed to be paid by the employee to the employer (the imputed interest) must be determined using the original issue discount (OID) rules.[476] However, a compensation-related term loan will be treated as a demand loan for purposes of determining the compensation and imputed interest consequences if the benefit derived by the employee from the interest arrangement is (1) nontransferable, and (2) conditioned upon the future performance of substantial services by the employee. For example, a benefit is treated as nontransferable and conditioned on future performance of substantial services if, on the termination, for any reason, of the employee's employment, the interest rate is increased so that the rate for the remaining term of the loan equals or exceeds the AFR.[477] Under this provision, the cumbersome OID rules can be avoided.

Exemptions from Imputed Interest Treatment. There are four exceptions to the general rule that foregone interest must be recognized as income. These exceptions are (1) for loans made available to the general public at the same below market rate, (2) loans without significant tax effect on either the employer or employee, (3) the $10,000 de minimis exception, and (4) the exception for employee relocation loans.

Under Temp. Reg. § 1.7872-5T(b)(1), no income recognition is required with respect to loans made to employees that are also made to the general public at the same or lower below-market rate (e.g., insurance policy loans).

---

[473] Prop. Reg. § 1.7872-6(c).
[474] Rev. Rul. 2005-38, IRB 2005-27, 6.
[475] Code Sec. 7872(b)(1) and (f).

[476] Code Sec. 7872(b)(2).
[477] Code Sec. 7872(f)(5); H.R. Rep. No. 861, 98th Cong., 2d Sess, (1984).

Under the second exception, no imputed interest will be recognized with respect to loans that have no significant tax effect on either the employer or employee because of offsetting income and deductions, a de minimis amount of income relative to the cost of compliance, or significant nontax reasons for structuring the loan with a below-market interest rate.[478]

Under Code Sec. 7872(c)(3), a de minimis exception is provided for compensation-related loans. Under this exception, the rules of Code Sec. 7872 do not apply to any day on which the aggregate outstanding amount of loans between the employer and employee is $10,000 or less. The de minimis exception does not apply, however, if the principal purpose of the interest arrangement is the avoidance of any federal tax.

For purposes of the de minimis exception, all loans between an employer and a particular employee must be combined.[479] Further, deemed transfers from the employer to the employee-borrower are treated as occurring on the later of the dates on which the loans are made or the first date on which the loans are subject to Code Sec. 7872.

> **Example:** If there are no other outstanding loans between an employer and an employee, and the employer makes a $9,000 compensation-related term loan to an employee on April 1, and a $2,000 compensation-related term loan to the same employee on May 3, the parties are treated as if the employer made an $11,000 compensation-related loan to the employee on May 3. Further, once Code Sec. 7872 applies to a term loan, Code Sec. 7872 continues to apply to the loan regardless of whether the $10,000 limitation applies at some later date.[480]

The foregone interest on employee relocation loans is exempted from Code Sec. 7872 treatment. In the case of a compensation-related loan to an employee, where the loan is secured by a mortgage on the employee's new principal residence (as defined under Code Sec. 217) of the employee, acquired in connection with the transfer of that employee to a new principal place of work (that meets the requirements in Code Sec. 217(c)), the loan will be exempt from Code Sec. 7872 if the following conditions are satisfied:

(1) the loan is a demand loan or a term loan under which the benefits of the interest arrangements are not transferable by the employee and are conditioned on the future performance of substantial services by the employee;

---

[478] Temp. Reg. § 1.7872-5T(c)(3).
[479] Prop. Reg. § 1.7872-9(b).

[480] H.R. Rep. No. 861, 98th Cong., 2d Sess. (1984).

(2) the employee certifies to the employer that he reasonably expects to be entitled to and will itemize deductions for each year the loan is outstanding; and

(3) the loan agreement requires that the loan proceeds be used only to purchase the new principal residence of the employee.[481]

If a compensation-related loan is not secured by a mortgage but is used to purchase a new principal residence of the employee acquired in connection with the transfer of that employee to a new principal place of work, the loan will be exempt from the below-market interest rules if the following conditions are satisfied:

(1) the three conditions stated above for employee relocation loans are met;

(2) the loan agreement provides that the loan is repayable within 15 days after the date of the sale of the employee's immediately preceding former residence;

(3) the aggregate principal amount of such loans does not exceed the employee's equity (and the equity of his/her spouse) in the employee's immediately preceding former residence; and

(4) the employee's immediately preceding former principal residence is not converted to business or investment use.[482]

Such a loan is called a "bridge loan."

.02 Employee Use of Employer Automobiles or Other Vehicles

A common fringe benefit provided to employees is the use of a company automobile or other vehicle. As noted earlier in this chapter, the use of a company-owned car for business purposes is not taxable under Code Sec. 132(d) as a working condition fringe benefit. However, the personal use of an employer's vehicle is taxable to the employee unless that use is de minimis.

Ordinarily, the amount taxable to the employee equals (1) the fair market value of the availability of the automobile or other vehicle or the amount a third party would have to pay to rent or lease a comparable vehicle on comparable terms, multiplied by (2) the personal use percentage.[483] The fair market value of the use of the vehicle cannot be computed on the basis of a cents-per-mile rate times the number of miles the employee actually drives the vehicle during the period unless the employee can prove that such a vehicle could have been leased on a cents-per-mile basis.[484] See the example of valuation of personal usage of an employer-provided automobile in the discussion of working condition fringe

---

[481] Temp. Reg. § 1.7872-5T(c).
[482] Temp. Reg. § 1.7872-5T(c)(1)(ii).

[483] Reg. § 1.61-21(b)(2).
[484] Reg. § 1.61-21(b)(4).

benefits above. For purposes of the vehicle-use valuation rules, a vehicle is any motorized vehicle, including an automobile, that is manufactured primarily for use on public streets, roads, and highways. An automobile is any four-wheeled vehicle manufactured primarily for use on public streets, roads, and highways.[485]

The following discussion covers rules concerning determination of the value of an employee's use of employer automobiles and other vehicles primarily contained in Reg. § 1.61-21.

Optional Valuation Methods. Instead of using the general rule for valuing the employee's use of an employer automobile or other vehicle, an employer can elect to use one of the following special valuation rules:

(1) the vehicle cents-per-mile valuation rule;

(2) the automobile lease valuation rule (applicable only for valuing automobiles); or

(3) the commuting valuation rule (if applicable).[486]

In addition, a special valuation rule pertains to the commuting use of employer-provided transportation for security reasons under Reg. § 1.61-21(k).

Use of any of the above special valuation rules is optional. An employer does not have to use the same special valuation rule for all vehicles provided to all employees. For example, an employer may use the lease valuation rule for automobiles provided to some employees and the cents-per-mile rule for vehicles provided to other employees.[487] However, once an employer chooses to use the lease valuation rule or the cents-per-mile rule for a particular vehicle, that method must continue to be used for subsequent years on that vehicle except for years in which the commuting valuation rule applies.[488] The same valuation rule must also be used by each employee who shares the use of a vehicle. The value determined using the applicable rule must be allocated among the employees based on the relevant facts and circumstances.[489]

Neither the employer nor the employee may use the special valuation rules unless one of the following four conditions is met:

(1) The employer treats the value of the benefit as wages for reporting purposes within the time for filing the tax returns for the particular taxable year;

---

[485] Reg. § 1.61-21(d)(1)(ii) and (e)(2).
[486] Reg. § 1.61-21(c).
[487] Reg. § 1.61-21(c)(2)(iii).

[488] *See,* e.g., Reg. § 1.61-21(d)(7).

[489] Reg. § 1.61-21(c)(2)(iii)(B).

(2) The employee includes the value of the benefit in gross income within the time for filing the returns for the taxable year (including extensions) in which the benefit is provided;

(3) The employee is not a control employee as defined in Reg. § 1.61-21(f)(5) or (6) (see the discussion concerning control employees later in this chapter); or

(4) The employer demonstrates a good-faith effort to treat the benefit correctly for reporting purposes.[490]

The special valuation rules may be used for income tax, employment tax, and reporting purposes. As noted above, the employer may use any of the special valuation rules if one of the requirements noted above is met. An employee may use a special valuation rule, only if (1) the employer uses that rule or (2) the employer does not report the use of the vehicle as wages and one of the last three requirements noted above is met.[491] The latter instance provides a circumstance under which the employee may use a different special valuation rule than the employer. Alternatively, the employee may use the general fair market value rule even if the employer uses a special valuation rule. If a special valuation rule is used, it must be used for all income tax, employment tax, and reporting purposes. If an employer properly uses a special valuation rule and the employee uses the same rule, the employee must include in gross income the amount determined by the employer under the special rule minus the sum of:

(1) Any amount reimbursed by the employee to the employer; and

(2) Any amount excludable under another section of the Code.

If some of the benefit is excludable as a Code Sec. 132 working condition fringe benefit which is determined under the general rule or a special valuation rule, the employee must include in gross income the amount determined by the employer less any amount reimbursed by the employee to the employer.[492] Finally, if an employee properly chooses to use a special valuation rule, the employee must continue to use that method in subsequent years except for years in which the commuting-only rule applies.[493]

The special valuation rules are individually described in the following paragraphs.

Vehicle "Cents-Per-Mile" Optional Valuation. The optional cents-per-mile rule is probably the simplest method to use in valuing the availability of a company automobile or other vehicle.

---

[490] Reg. § 1.61-21(c)(3)(ii).
[491] Reg. § 1.61-21(c)(2)(ii).
[492] Reg. § 1.61-21(c)(2)(ii).
[493] See, e.g., Reg. § 1.61-21(d)(7)(iv).

Under this rule, the value of the employee's personal use of a company automobile is the number of miles the automobile is driven for personal purposes multiplied by the IRS standard mileage rate.[494] For 2005, the standard mileage rate is 40.5 cents per mile (for the first eight months) and 48.5 cents per mile (for the last four months) for all business miles that the employer's vehicle was driven during 2005.[495]

The cents-per-mile rate includes the fair market value of maintenance and insurance for the vehicle. For miles driven in the United States, its territories, Canada, and Mexico, the cents-per-mile rate includes the fair market value of fuel provided by the employer. If the employer does not provide fuel for the automobile, the rate may be reduced by no more than 5.5 cents or the amount specified in any applicable revenue ruling or revenue procedure.[496] The value of any other services, such as those of a chauffeur (see the discussion on the valuation of chauffeur services later in this chapter) is not reflected in the mileage rate and must be valued separately.[497]

The cents-per-mile rule may only be used to value the miles driven by the employee for personal purposes. The term "personal miles" means all miles driven by the employee except for miles driven by the employee in connection with the employer's trade or business.[498]

> **Example:** An employer bought a car for $9,000 and allows employee Benson to use the car for business and personal purposes. During 2005, the employer and Benson have chosen to use the cents-per-mile method of valuing Benson's personal usage. During the first eight months of 2005, Benson drove the car 8,500 miles for business use and 3,500 miles for personal use. During the last four months, the mileage figures were 3,200 and 2,800, respectively. As a result, Benson's 2005 gross income from the personal use of the car is $2,775.50 (3,500 miles times $.405 plus 2,800 miles times $.485).

The cents-per-mile method can be used for a calendar year only if the fair market value of the automobile does not exceed the sum of the maximum recovery deductions available under Code Sec. 280F(a)(2) for a five-year period for an automobile first placed into service during that calendar year (as adjusted for inflation under Code Sec. 280F(d)(7)).[499] The limitation on value of a vehicle placed

---

[494] Reg. § 1.61-21(e)(1).
[495] Rev. Proc. 2004-64, IRB 2004-49, 898 and IR 2005-99.
[496] Reg. § 1.61-21(e)(3)(ii).

[497] Reg. § 1.61-21(e)(3)(iii).
[498] Reg. § 1.61-21(e)(4).
[499] Reg. § 1.61-21(e)(1)(iii).

¶ 303.02

into service before January 1, 1989, was to be at least $12,800. With respect to a vehicle placed into service in or after 1989, the limitation on value is $12,800 (as adjusted for inflation under Code Sec. 280F(d)(7)).[500] For automobiles placed into service in 2005, the limitation on value was approximately $14,800; it was also $14,800 in 2004.[501] If an employee contributes an amount toward the purchase price of a vehicle in return for a percentage ownership interest in the vehicle, the fair market value of the vehicle (to be compared against the fair market value limitation) is reduced by the lesser of:

(1) the amount contributed; or

(2) an amount equal to the employee's percentage ownership interest multiplied by the unreduced fair market value of the vehicle.[502]

In the case of a vehicle leased by the employer, if an employee contributes an amount toward the cost of the lease in return for a percentage interest in the lease, the fair market value of the vehicle (to be compared against the fair market value limitation) is reduced by an amount equal to the market value multiplied by the lesser of the following percentages:

(1) the employee's percentage interest in the lease; or

(2) a fraction, the numerator of which is the amount contributed and the denominator of which is the entire lease cost.[503]

In addition, the cents-per-mile valuation rule can be used for a vehicle only if:

(1) the employer reasonably expects that the vehicle will be regularly used in the employer's business throughout the calendar year (or such shorter period as the vehicle may be owned or leased by the employer); or

(2) the vehicle is actually driven at least 10,000 miles in the particular year and use of the vehicle during the year is primarily by employees. If the employer does not own or lease the vehicle for the entire year, the 10,000-mile threshold is to be reduced proportionately.[504]

The consistency rules described earlier must also be satisfied. Thus, under Reg. § 1.61-21(e)(5), employers must adopt the cents-per-mile method for a vehicle by the later of the period that begins on January 1, 1989, or the first period in which the vehicle is used by any employee of the employer for personal use. If the commuting only

---

[500] Id.
[501] Rev. Procs. 2005-48, IRB 2005-32, 271 and 2004-20, IRB 2004-13, 642.
[502] Reg. § 1.61-21(e)(1)(iii).
[503] Id.
[504] Reg. § 1.61-21(e)(1).

method was adopted when the vehicle was first used by an employee for personal purposes, the employer may use the cents-per-mile method in the first period the commuting method is not used.[505] Once the employer has adopted the cents-per-mile method for a particular vehicle, the method must be used for subsequent periods except periods when the vehicle fails to qualify for use of the cents-per-mile method (in which case another method may be used) or when the commuting-only method is applicable.[506]

An employee can generally use the cents-per-mile rule only if the rule is adopted by the employer for the first applicable period (as covered above). The employee must then continue to use the method as long as the employer does for the vehicle (except that the commuting rule may be used when applicable).[507] If the employee does not adopt the cents-per-mile method when the employer adopts it, the employee must use the general valuation method, unless the employee qualifies for using another special method under Reg. § 1.61-21(c)(2)(ii) as discussed previously.

Optional Lease Valuation Rule. Under the optional lease valuation rule, the personal use of an employer-provided automobile (or other vehicle) is valued using the annual lease value (ALV) of the car.[508] The ALV of an automobile provided to an employee for the entire calendar year can be found in a table in Reg. § 1.61-21(d)(2)(iii), which is reproduced below. The values in the table are based on a four-year term. The ALV includes the fair market value of maintenance and insurance for the automobile. The ALV does not include the fair market value of fuel provided or reimbursed. Fuel may be valued separately at 5.5 cents per mile.[509] Fuel that is reimbursed or charged to the employer may be valued at its actual cost. proposed regulations indicate that the 5.5 cents-per-mile rate applied for the years 1989 through 1992 and that rates for subsequent years are to be set forth in revenue procedures concerning the optional standard mileage rates used in computing deductible costs of operating a passenger automobile for business purposes. No rates different than 5.5 cents have been specified for 1993 or later years at the time of this writing.[510] Finally, the fair market value of any service other than maintenance and insurance (such as the services of a chauffeur) must be added to the ALV.[511]

---

[505] Reg. § 1.61-21(e)(5)(iii).
[506] Id.
[507] Reg. § 1.61-21(e)(5)(iv).
[508] Reg. § 1.61-21(d).

[509] Reg. § 1.61-21(d)(3)(ii).
[510] Prop. Reg. § 1.61-21(d)(3)(ii)(B). *See also* IRS Pub No 15-B, p. 20.
[511] Reg. § 1.61-21(d)(3)(iii).

¶ 303.02

Annual Lease Value Table

Automobile Fair Market Value	Annual Lease Value
$0—999	$ 600
1,000—1,999	850
2,000—2,999	1,100
3,000—3,999	1,350
4,000—4,999	1,600
5,000—5,999	1,850
6,000—6,999	2,100
7,000—7,999	2,350
8,000—8,999	2,600
9,000—9,999	2,850
10,000—10,999	3,100
11,000—11,999	3,350
12,000—12,999	3,600
13,000—13,999	3,850
14,000—14,999	4,100
15,000—15,999	4,350
16,000—16,999	4,600
17,000—17,999	4,850
18,000—18,999	5,100
19,000—19,999	5,350
20,000—20,999	5,600
21,000—21,999	5,850
22,000—22,999	6,100
23,000—23,999	6,350
24,000—24,999	6,600
25,000—25,999	6,850
26,000—27,999	7,250
28,000—29,999	7,750
30,000—31,999	8,250
32,000—33,999	8,750
34,000—35,999	9,250
36,000—37,999	9,750
38,000—39,999	10,250
40,000—41,999	10,750
42,000—43,999	11,250
44,000—45,999	11,750
46,000—47,999	12,250
48,000—49,999	12,750
50,000—51,999	13,250
52,000—53,999	13,750
54,000—55,999	14,250
56,000—57,999	14,750
58,000—59,999	15,250

For automobiles having a fair market value in excess of $59,999, the annual lease value is equal to 25% of the automobile's fair market value plus $500.

The ALV of a particular automobile is figured as follows:

(1) Determine the fair market value of the automobile (as discussed below) as of the first date on which the automobile is made available to an employee for personal use.

(2) Using the ALV table, pick the ALV that corresponds to the dollar range of fair market value in which the value of the automobile falls.[512] The ALV used by the employer must be used by the employee unless the employee uses the general valuation rule.

As noted above, the ALV is for a four-year term and, thus, the ALV figured for the first year will remain the same for the period that begins with the first date the employer uses the ALV rule and ends on December 31 of the fourth calendar year following that date. The ALV for each subsequent four-year period is figured by (1) determining the fair market value of the automobile on January 1 of the first year of each subsequent four-year period and (2) selecting the appropriate ALV figure.[513]

> **Example (1):** The fair market value of an automobile is $9,000 on January 1, 2003, when the auto is first provided by the Dixon Company for use by its employee, Blake. The car is made available to Blake for the entire year and is used partly for personal purposes by Blake. The ALV from the lease table is $2,850. That value would be used for the years 2003-2006 by the employer and Blake, if he elects to use an optional method. The auto would be re-valued on January 1, 2007, and a new ALV would be used for the succeeding four years.

> Once the ALV is determined, the amount taxable to the employee is determined by multiplying the personal use percentage times the ALV.

> **Example (2):** Assume the same facts as given in the example above. If Blake used the car 30 percent of the time for personal purposes during 2003, he would include $855 ($2,850 × 30%) in gross income.

If an employee contributes an amount toward the purchase price of an automobile in return for a percentage ownership interest in the automobile, the ALV (or the daily lease value, discussed below) is determined by reducing the fair market value by the lesser of:

(1) the amount contributed; or

---

[512] IRS Pub. No. 15-B at 19.   [513] Reg. § 1.61-21(d)(2)(iv).

¶ 303.02

(2) an amount equal to the employee's percentage ownership interest multiplied by the unreduced fair market value of the automobile.[514]

In the case of an automobile leased by the employer, if an employee contributes an amount toward the cost of the lease in return for a percentage interest in the lease, then the ALV (or daily lease value, if applicable) is determined by reducing the market value of the automobile by the unreduced market value of the automobile multiplied by the lesser of:

(1) the employee's percentage interest in the lease; or

(2) a fraction, the numerator of which is the amount contributed and the denominator of which is the entire lease cost.[515]

Fair Market Value. For purposes of determining the ALV of an automobile using the IRS table, the fair market value (FMV) of an automobile is the amount (including all amounts attributable to the purchase of an automobile such as sales tax and title fees in addition to the purchase price) that a person would have to pay a third party to purchase the particular automobile.[516] However, under Reg. § 1.61-21(d)(5), the following safe-harbor values may be used as the FMV of the automobile (as applicable):

(1) for an automobile that is owned by the employer, the employer's cost of purchasing the automobile (including sales tax, title fees, and other expenses attributable to purchase), as long as the purchase was made at arm's length. This safe-harbor rule, however, does not apply to an automobile manufactured by the employer; or

(2) for an automobile that is leased by the employer, either the manufacturer's suggested retail price of the automobile less eight percent (including sales tax, title, and other purchase-related expenses), or the retail value of the automobile as reported by a nationally recognized pricing source that regularly reports applicable new or used automobile retail values.

In addition to the above-specified safe-harbor values, IRS Notice 89-110[517] indicates that employers who lease a vehicle will be permitted to use the manufacturer's invoice price (including options) plus four percent as an estimate of fair market value. The safe harbor rule is not available with respect to vehicles that are owned by the employer. Thus, a distributor of vehicles manufactured by its subsidiary could not use the safe harbor rule in applying the lease valuation rule, because the distributor owned rather than leased the vehicles.[518]

---

[514] Reg. § 1.61-21(d)(2)(ii).
[515] *Id.*
[516] Reg. § 1.61-21(d)(5)(i).

[517] 1989-2 CB 447.
[518] IRS Letter Ruling 9816007, 12-31-97, CCH IRS Letter Rulings Reports.

¶ **303.02**

The FMV of the special equipment that is added to or carried in the automobile does not have to be included in the automobile's FMV if the presence of such equipment is necessitated by, and attributable to, the employer's business needs. However, the value of special equipment that is used in a separate trade or business of the employee or is susceptible to the employee's personal use must be included in the FMV of the automobile.[519]

If an employer transfers an automobile from one employee to another employee, the employer may recalculate the FMV of the automobile as of January 1 of the year of the transfer. However, the FMV cannot be recalculated at that time if the primary purpose of the transfer is to reduce federal taxes.[520]

Fleet Average Valuation Rule. An employer with a fleet of 20 or more cars may use a fleet-average value for purposes of calculating the ALV of the automobiles in the fleet. The average value of all cars in the fleet is the fleet average value. Once determined, the ALV for the fleet of automobiles will remain in effect until the end of the following calendar year. The ALV for each subsequent two-year period is calculated by determining the fleet average value as of the first January 1 of that period. The fleet valuation rule may not be used for any automobile with a market value in excess of $16,500 (as adjusted for inflation in accordance with the provision of Code Sec. 280F(d)(7). Based on the formula for calculating the inflation adjusted figures, the 2004 dollar limitation is $19,700 (it was $20,200 in 2003). In addition, the special rule may only be used for automobiles that the employer reasonably expects will regularly be used in the employer's trade or business. This special valuation does not have to be consistently used.[521]

Prorated Annual Lease Value. If an employer-provided vehicle is available for continuous periods of 30 days or more but less than a full year, the value of the use of the automobile is the prorated annual lease value. The prorated annual lease value equals the applicable ALV multiplied by a fraction, using the number of days of availability as the numerator and 365 as the denominator. A prorated annual lease value may not be used when the primary reason the automobile is unavailable to an employee during a calendar year is the reduction of federal taxes.[522]

Daily Lease Value. If an employer-provided automobile is available for continuous periods of less than 30 days, the automobile's value is the daily lease value. The daily lease value equals the ALV multiplied by a fraction, the numerator of which is four times the number of days

---

[519] Reg. § 1.61-21(d)(5)(iv).
[520] Reg. § 1.61-21(d)(2)(v).

[521] Reg. § 1.61-21(d)(5)(v).
[522] Reg. § 1.61-21(d)(4).

¶ 303.02

of availability and the denominator is 365. However, the employer may apply a prorated annual lease value instead by treating the automobile as if it had been available for 30 days if that would produce a better result.[523]

> **Comment:** Ordinarily, the election to use the prorated annual lease value instead of the daily lease value is advantageous if the automobile is actually available more than 7½ days at a time (e.g., a seven-day availability is valued at 28/365 of the ALV).

Consistency Requirements. An employer may adopt the ALV rule only if the rule is adopted to take effect the first day of the first period the automobile is available to any employee for personal use (or the first period for which the commuting-only method cannot be used). Once the method is adopted, it must continue to be used in succeeding periods except when the commuting-only method can be used.[524]

If the employer adopts the ALV method, the employee must generally begin using the ALV method for the first period it is adopted by the employer and continued for later periods (except periods for which the commuting-only method can be used).[525] If the employee does not adopt the ALV method, the employee must use the general valuation method unless the employee qualifies for using another special method under Reg. § 1.61-21(c)(2)(ii) as discussed previously.

Optional Commuting-Only Valuation Rule. If an employee is required for bona fide noncompensatory business reasons to commute in an employer-provided vehicle that is not otherwise available for the employee's personal use, a flat $1.50 one-way rate (a $3.00 round trip amount) can be used to value the use of the automobile.[526] The $1.50 value includes the value of any goods or services directly related to the vehicle (e.g., fuel). If more than one employee uses the same vehicle for purposes of commuting, the amount taxable to each employee is the $1.50 per one-way commute. Note that this rule, when applicable, can be used no matter what distance the employee has to commute. However, this rule does not apply to passengers in a chauffeur-driven vehicle.

To qualify for the commuting method of valuation, all of the following conditions must be satisfied:

(1) the vehicle is owned or leased by the employer and is provided to one or more employees for use in connection with the employer's trade or business;

---

[523] *Id.*
[524] Reg. § 1.61-21(d)(7)(i).

[525] Reg. § 1.61-21(d)(7)(iii).
[526] Reg. § 1.61-21(f)(1) and (3).

(2) for bona fide noncompensatory reasons, the employer requires the employee to commute to and/or from work in the vehicle;

(3) the employer has a written policy under which neither the employee nor any individual whose use would be taxable to the employee may not use the vehicle for personal purposes other than for commuting or de minimis personal use (such as a lunch stop between business meetings);

(4) the employee does not use the vehicle for any personal purpose other than commuting and de minimis personal use; and

(5) the employee required to use the vehicle for commuting is not a control employee as defined in the regulations (control employees are discussed in the section of this chapter describing the valuation of employee transportation on employer-owned airplanes).[527]

The commuting rule can be used for any year in which it is applicable to a particular vehicle of the employer even if the employer has previously chosen to use the cents-per-mile method or the ALV method.

Special Valuation of Employer-Provided Transportation Due to Unsafe Conditions. A special value of $1.50 per one-way trip may be used to determine the amount included in gross income relating to transportation furnished solely because of unsafe conditions to employees who would otherwise walk or use public transportation. In order for the special rule to apply, the following conditions, specified by the IRS in Reg. § 1.61-21(k), must be met:

(1) the transportation is provided solely because of unsafe conditions to an employee who would ordinarily walk or use public transportation to commute to and from work;

(2) the employer has established a written policy that the transportation is not provided for the employee's personal purposes other than for commuting due to unsafe conditions, and the employer's practice corresponds with the policy;

(3) the transportation is not used for other purposes by the employee; and

(4) the employee receiving the transportation is a "qualified employee."[528]

Unsafe conditions exist if a reasonable person would consider it unsafe to walk to or from home, or to walk or use public transportation at the time of day that he/she has to commute.[529]

---

[527] Reg. § 1.61-21(f)(2).
[528] Reg. § 1.61-21(k)(1).

[529] Reg. § 1.61-21(k)(5).

The special valuation rules apply on a trip-by-trip basis. Thus, if the requirements are not met for any particular trip (e.g., because the employee uses the trip for some other purpose), the amount includible in the employee's gross income is the fair market value of the transportation for that particular trip.[530]

Qualified employees are those who do not receive compensation in excess of $50,000 and who are paid on an hourly basis. Further, the employee must not be claimed to be exempt from the minimum wage and maximum hour provisions of the Fair Labor Standards Act.[531]

Valuation of Chauffeur Services. Under Reg. § 1.61-21(b)(5), chauffeur services that are provided to the employee must be valued separately from the employer-provided vehicle. In general, the value of a chauffeur's services is the amount that an individual would have to pay in an arm's-length transaction to obtain the same or comparable services in the same geographic area for the period in which the services are provided. That value includes the amount of time the chauffeur is on call to provide services to the employee, regardless of the amount of time he actually drives the employee. Finally, the value also includes all other aspects of the chauffeur, such as special qualifications of the chauffeur or the employee's ability to choose a particular chauffeur.

Alternatively, under Reg. § 1.61-21(b)(5)(i)(B), the value of a chauffeur's services may be based on the chauffeur's annual compensation plus the fair market value of any nontaxable lodging that the chauffeur receives during the year. For this purpose, a chauffeur's compensation is reduced proportionately to reflect the amount of time during which the chauffeur performs substantial services for the employer other than as a chauffeur and is not on call as a chauffeur.[532]

.03 Plane Flights Provided to Employees

Generally, the fair market value of plane flights taken for personal use by the employee and/or members of his family is taxable to the employee unless the value of the plane flights is excludable as a noaddy-additional-cost service or a working condition fringe benefit under Code Sec. 132(b) and (d), respectively.[533] However, there are special valuation rules that can be used to determine the value of commercial and noncommercial (or company) aircraft flights. If chosen, the special rules must be used for all flights provided by the employer

---

[530] Reg. § 1.61-21(k)(4).
[531] Reg. § 1.61-21(k)(6).

[532] Reg. § 1.61-21(b)(5)(ii).
[533] Reg. § 1.61-21(b)(6).

during a particular taxable year.[534] Despite this general rule, the IRS has privately ruled that an employer may use the special valuation rules to determine the value of personal flights provided to employees on employer-provided aircraft even if one or more employees intend to use the general valuation rules in valuing their flights.[535]

If the special valuation rules are not used, the fair market value of a plane flight provided to an employee depends upon whether the employer furnishes the pilot of the plane. If the employee takes a flight on an employer-provided piloted aircraft, and that employee's flight is primarily personal, the value of the flight equals the amount that an individual would have to pay in an arm's-length transaction to charter the same or comparable piloted aircraft for that period for the same or a comparable flight. That value is allocated among the employees taking the flight if more than one is on the flight unless one or more of them control the flight (i.e., determine where and when the flight goes). In that case, the value is allocated among the employees who control the flight.[536]

However, if an employee takes a flight on an employer-provided aircraft for which the employer does not furnish a pilot, the value of that flight equals the amount that an individual would have to pay in an arm's-length transaction to lease the same or comparable aircraft on the same or comparable terms for the same period in the geographic area in which the aircraft is used. If more than one employee is benefited, the value of the flight is allocated among them.[537]

Special Rule for Commercial Flights. Free or discounted flights provided to airline employees, their spouses, dependent children, and parents, which are subject to space-available standby-basis restrictions, are ordinarily excludable as a no-additional-cost fringe benefit under Code Sec. 132(b) (covered earlier in this chapter). However, a free or discounted commercial airline flight provided to other guests of the employee does not qualify for the exclusion and is ordinarily taxed to the employee. Under a special rule set forth in Reg. § 1.61-21(h), the value of a space-available flight on a commercial aircraft is 25 percent of the airline's highest unrestricted coach fare in effect for the particular flight taken. A space-available flight is a flight on a commercial aircraft for which the airline incurs no substantial additional cost (including forgone revenue) to any amount paid for the flight. The flight must be subject to the same

---

[534] Reg. § 1.61-21(g)(14) and (h)(5).
[535] IRS Letter Ruling 9840015, 6-29-98, CCH IRS LETTER RULINGS REPORTS.

[536] Reg. § 1.61-21(b)(6)(ii).

[537] Reg. § 1.61-21(b)(7)(ii).

¶ 303.03

restrictions customarily associated with flying on an employee "standby" or "space-available" basis. Flights to customers must be offered on a per-seat basis. Thus, the rule cannot be used with respect to flights for the transportation of cargo.

If the airline does not offer, in the ordinary course of business, air transportation to customers on a per-seat basis, the commercial flight valuation rule cannot be used. In that case, the flight may be valued under the noncommercial flight valuation rule discussed below.[538]

Optional Rule for Valuing Flights on Noncommercial Aircraft. Reg. § 1.61-21(g) sets forth a special, optional rule for valuing United States or international flights on employer-provided aircraft (including helicopters) by employees, their families, and guests. The value of the flight for each employee (or his guest) passenger is expressed as a percentage of the Standard Industry Fare Level (SIFL) rates. The SIFL is a per-mile formula rate which is calculated and revised on a semiannual basis by the Department of Transportation.[539]

Under Reg. § 1.61-21(g)(5), the value of an employee's flight equals (1) the "base aircraft valuation formula" (SIFL mileage rate formula for the particular flight) multiplied by (2) the "aircraft multiple" (the percentage applicable to the employee taken from the IRS table in Reg. § 1.61-21(g)(7); the exact percentage depends upon the takeoff weight of the aircraft and whether the employee is a "control" or a "noncontrol" employee as indicated in the schedule below), plus (3) the SIFL terminal charge. The value of a flight during the first six months of a calendar year is determined using the SIFL formula (and terminal charge) in effect on December 31 of the preceding year, and the value of a flight during the last six months of a calendar year is determined using the SIFL formula (and terminal charge) in effect on June 30 of the same year.[540] For flights taken from January 1, 2005, through June 30, 2005, the terminal charge was $35.59 and the SIFL mileage rates were $.1942 per mile for the first 500 miles traveled, $.1423 per mile for miles between 500 and 1,500 and $.1514 per mile for any miles traveled in excess of 1,500.[541] See CCH STANDARD FEDERAL TAX REPORTS ¶ 694.04 for terminal charges and SIFL rates applicable to other periods.

---

[538] Reg. § 1.61-21(h)(3).
[539] Reg. § 1.61-21(g)(5).

[540] *Id.*
[541] Rev. Rul. 2005-14, IRB 2005-14, 749.

Aircraft Multiples

Maximum Certified Takeoff Weight of the Aircraft	Aircraft Multiple for a Control Employee	Aircraft Multiple for a Noncontrol Employee
6,000 lbs. or less	62.5 percent	15.6 percent
6,001—10,000 lbs.	125 percent	23.4 percent
10,001—25,000 lbs.	300 percent	31.3 percent
25,001 lbs. or more	400 percent	31.3 percent

Example (1): Charlie Smith, who is not a control employee, received a one-way company flight for personal purposes. The flight distance was 800 miles and the flight took place on June 14, 2005. The company's aircraft weighed 12,000 pounds, so the aircraft multiple is 31.3 percent. The value of the flight is [.313 × ($.1942 × 500 + $.1423 × 300) + $35.59], or $79.34.

Except for the rules concerning intermediate stops, the length of an employee's flight is the distance (in statute miles) from the place where the employee boards the aircraft to the place where he or she gets off.[542]

The value of a noncommercial flight under the special rule is determined separately for each flight. Thus, a round-trip consists of two flights.

Example (2): Wilson takes a personal trip on an employer-provided aircraft from New York City to Denver, Denver to Los Angeles, and Los Angeles to New York. He has taken three flights and must value each flight separately.

The value of a flight must be determined on a passenger-by-passenger basis. For example, if someone accompanies the employee and the flight taken by the other person would be taxable to the employee, the employee would have to include the value of both flights.[543]

If an intermediate stop must be made due to weather conditions, an emergency, the need to refuel or obtain other services for the aircraft, or for the employer's business purposes unrelated to the employee whose flight is being valued, the distance between the place at which the trip originates and the place at which the intermediate stop occurs is not a separate flight.[544]

Seating Capacity Rule. If 50 percent or more of the regular passenger seating capacity of an employer-provided aircraft is occupied by individuals who are flying for the employer's business

---

[542] Reg. § 1.61-21(g)(3).
[543] Id.
[544] Id.

purposes and whose flights are thus excludable as a working condition fringe benefit (discussed earlier in this chapter), the value of a flight on that aircraft to an employee who is not flying primarily for the employer's business purposes or whose flight is not excludable as a working condition fringe benefit is considered to be zero. Thus, all employees on the flight can exclude the value of the flight. Note that this rule applies only to employees and partners of the employer providing the aircraft and does not include independent contractors and directors.

The 50-percent seating rule does not apply to individuals who are not actual employees but who are treated as employees under the fringe benefit exclusion rules of Code Sec. 132(h) (former employees and spouses and dependents of the employees). If a flight taken by such an individual is not excludable as a working condition fringe benefit (as defined under Code Sec. 132) the individual is taxed on the value of the flight as a non-control employee.[545] The seating capacity rule must be met both at the time the individual whose flight is being valued boards the aircraft and at the time he or she gets off. Otherwise, the individual is taxed on the value of the flight.[546]

Combination Business and Pleasure Trips. If an employee combines, in one trip, personal and business flights on an employer-provided aircraft and the trip is primarily business, the amount includible in income equals the value of all the flights comprising the trip minus the value of flights that would have been taken had there been no personal flights but only business flights. If the trip is primarily personal, the employee is taxable on the value of personal flights that would have been taken had there been no business flights but only personal flights.[547]

> **Example:** Employee Wilson flies on a primarily personal trip—from San Francisco to Los Angeles on business, then to Palm Springs for personal reasons and then back to Los Angeles. His income includes the values of the flight from San Francisco to Palm Springs and from Palm Springs to San Francisco. If the trip were primarily for business (e.g., San Francisco to Palm Springs on business, then to Los Angeles for personal reasons and then back to San Francisco), Wilson would include in income only the value of all flights minus the value of the business-only flights (San Francisco to Palm Springs and Palm Springs to San Francisco).

---

[545] Reg. § 1.61-21(g)(12).
[546] *Id.*

[547] Reg. § 1.61-21(g)(4).

Control Employees. A "control" employee of a nongovernmental employer includes the following employees and their spouses and other family members (as defined under Code Sec. 267(c)(4)):[548]

(1) board-elected or shareholder-appointed, confirmed, or elected officers limited to the lesser of (a) one percent of all employees or (b) ten employees;

(2) individuals whose compensation equals or exceeds the compensation of the top one percent most highly paid employees of the employer, limited to a maximum of 50 employees;

(3) five percent or more owners of the employer; and

(4) directors of the employer.

Note that for purposes of determining who is a control employee under the first two categories, individuals who earn less than $85,000 (applicable in 2005) of compensation (as adjusted for inflation after 2005) are not to be treated as control employees.[549] Further, in determining who is a one-percent or five-percent owner, the Code Sec. 318 attribution rules apply. Finally, instead of applying the control employee definition given above, an employer can elect to treat employees who are highly compensated employees pursuant to Code Sec. 414(q) (see the discussion of highly compensated employees in Chapter 6) as control employees.[550]

In the case of a governmental employer, a control employee is any:[551]

(1) elected official; or

(2) employee whose compensation equals or exceeds the compensation paid to a Federal Investment employee holding a position at Executive Level V, determined under Chapter 11 of title 2, United States Code, as adjusted by Sec. 5318 of title 5, United States Code.

The term "government" includes any federal, state, or local government unit, and any agency or instrumentality thereof. Instead of applying the definition of control employee given above, a governmental employer may elect to treat highly compensated employees as defined in Code Sec. 414(q) as control employees.[552]

The amount includible with respect to a flight provided to a control employee is much higher than in the case of a noncontrol

---

[548] Reg. § 1.61-21(g)(8).

[549] Reg. §§ 1.61-21(g)(8)(ii)(B) and (g)(10) and Code Sec. 414(q)(1) as amended by P.L. 104-188, 104th Cong., 2d Sess., Sec. 1431 (Aug. 20, 1996); IR 2004-127 (Oct 20, 2004).

[550] Reg. § 1.61-21(g)(8)(ii)(A).

[551] Reg. § 1.61-21(g)(9).

[552] *Id.*

employee since the aircraft multiple for the control employees is significantly higher than for noncontrol employees.

Example: The Blake Company general manager, his wife, and two children took a 500-mile trip in the Blake Company's plane, which has a takeoff weight of 15,000 pounds. The trip was taken on June 23, 2005. The general manager's gross income from the flight is $1,200.69 [(4 × 300% × $.1942 × 500 miles) + $35.49]. For a noncontrol employee, the amount includible would have been only $156.95 [(4 × 31.3% × $.1942 × 500 miles) + $35.49].

.04 Golden Parachute Payments

In recent years corporate takeover activity has been very common, and executives and other key employees have increasingly been negotiating contracts that require their employer to make large cash and/or property payments to them in the event of a successful corporate takeover. These payments, known as golden parachute payments, are used as a defense against takeover activity because an acquiring corporation may be reluctant to complete a takeover if the takeover could obligate the acquiring corporation to make large payments to certain key employees of the acquired corporation. Alternatively, the payments could reduce resistance to a takeover by certain key employees who would receive large payments after a takeover is completed.

Because Congress became concerned that the payment of large amounts of money to certain executives and other key employees during corporate takeover battles was not always in the best interests of the acquired corporation or its shareholders, Code Secs. 280G and 4999 were enacted as part of the Tax Reform Act of 1984 to discourage such payments. Under Code Sec. 280G(a), excess golden parachute payments made to "disqualified individuals" are not deductible. Further, under Code Sec. 4999, the recipients of excess golden parachute payments are subject to a nondeductible 20 percent excise tax on the excess and the employer must deduct and withhold the excise tax from payments made to an employee. Excess parachute payments are also fully taxable to the recipient and are subject to FICA and FUTA taxes. With respect to taxable years beginning after December 31, 1993, the Code Sec. 162(m) $1 million deduction limitation on an executive's compensation is reduced by the amount of that executive's excess parachute payments under Code Sec. 280G (see the discussion of the $1 million executive compensation deduction limit in Chapter 2).[553] Finally, on August 4, 2003, the IRS issued final regulations concerning golden parachute payments. The final regulations apply to any payments that are contingent on a change in ownership or control if the change in ownership and control occurs on or after January 1, 2004.[554] Previously, the IRS issued two sets of final regulations (Prop. Reg. § 1.280G-1) to apply to golden parachute payments. The first set of final regulations was issued in 1989, and taxpayers are permitted to rely on the 1989 final regulations with respect to changes in ownership or control that occur before January 1, 2004.[555] Alternatively, taxpayers can rely on the second set of final regulations that were issued in 2002 until the effective date of the final regulations noted above.[556] Taxpayers are permitted to rely on the 2002 final regulations, including for purposes of amended returns with respect to the following: (1) That a shareholder who owns stock with a fair market value of $1 million is not a disqualified individual and (2) that the base amount includes the amount of compensation included in gross income under Code Sec. 83(b).[557] The final regulations are referred to in the following paragraphs as appropriate. For coverage of the 1989 and 2002 final regulations, see those regulations, as referenced below.

Disqualified Individuals. For purposes of the golden parachute rules, a disqualified individual is any individual who is an employee or independent contractor of the corporation and is, with respect to the corporation, a shareholder, officer or highly compensated individual.

Under the final regulations, "shareholder" is defined as an individual who owns stock of a corporation with a fair market value that exceeds one percent of the fair market value of the outstanding shares of all classes of stock of the corporation.[558]

An "officer" is defined under both sets of final regulations as an administrative executive who is in regular and continued service; however, no more than 50 employees (or, if less, the greater of three employees or ten percent of the employees, rounded up to the next whole integer) can be officers.[559]

A "highly compensated individual" is defined under the newer golden parachute final regulations as an individual who is, or would

---

[553] Code Sec. 162(m)(4)(F), as amended by Sec. 13,211(a), P.L. 103-66, 103rd Cong., 1st Sess. (August 10, 1993).

[554] Reg. § 1.280G-1, TD 9083, 68 FR 45745 (August 4, 2003).

[555] TD 9083, 68 FR 45745 (August 4, 2003). Prop. Reg. § 280G-1, PS-217-84 (May 5, 1989).

[556] TD 9083, 68 FR 45745 (August 4, 2003). Prop. Reg. § 1.280G-1, REG-209114-20 (February 20, 2002).

[557] TD 9083, 68 FR 45745 (August 4, 2003).

[558] Reg. § 1.280G-1, Q&A 17.

[559] Reg. § 1.280G-1, Q&A 18.

be if the individual were an employee, a member of the group which consists of the lesser of (a) the highest paid one percent of the employees of the corporation (rounded up to nearest integer), or (b) the highest paid 250 employees of the corporation, when ranked on the basis of compensation (as determined under Reg. § 1.280G-1, Q&A 21) earned during the disqualified individual's determination period (as determined under Reg. § 1.280G-1, Q&A 20). However, no individual whose annualized compensation is less than the amount described in Code Sec. 414(q)(1)(B)(i) (see the discussion of highly compensated individuals in chapter 6—for 2003 the threshold figure is $90,000 as announced in IR 2002-111 (Oct 18, 2002)).[560]

Personal service corporations are treated as individuals for purposes of these provisions.[561]

Definition of Parachute Payments. Under Code Sec. 280G(b)(2), parachute payments are payments in the nature of compensation to or for the benefit of a disqualified individual if:

(1) the payment is contingent on a change in the ownership or effective control of the corporation or in the ownership of a substantial portion of the assets of the corporation; and

(2) the aggregate present value of the payments in the nature of compensation to the individual which are contingent on the change equals or exceeds an amount equal to three times the individual's base amount.

For this purpose, payments in the nature of compensation include all payments—in whatever form—if they arise out of an employment relationship and are associated with the performance of services. Thus, the term includes (but is not limited to) wages and salary, bonuses, severance pay, fringe benefits, and pension benefits and other deferred compensation (including interest thereon).[562] On the other hand, the IRS has privately held that payments made under a covenant not to compete are not parachute payments.[563] The IRS indicated that a reasonable value attributable to the refraining from performing services pursuant to a noncompetition clause could be considered a payment for services. Finally, note that the District Court has held that payments can be considered parachute payments regardless of whether the payments are made by the target (acquired) corporation or the acquiring corporation.[564]

---

[560] Reg. § 1.280G-1, Q&A 19.

[561] Code Sec. 280G(c).

[562] Reg. § 1.280G-1, Q&A 11.

[563] IRS Letter Ruling 200110025, 12-8-00, CCH IRS LETTER RULINGS REPORTS.

[564] *H.S. Hemingway*, DC-Utah, 99-2 USTC ¶ 50,667

A payment in the nature of compensation under the final regulations is generally considered made (and is subject to the excise tax on excess parachute payments) in the taxable year in which it is includable in the gross income of the disqualified individual or, in the case of excludable fringe benefits and other excludable items, in the taxable year in which the benefits are received.[565] Transfers of property are treated as payments for purposes of what is considered to be payments in the nature of compensation.[566] A transfer of property is considered a payment made (or to be made) in the taxable year in which the property transferred is includable in the gross income of the disqualified individual under Code Sec. 83 and the regulations thereunder (see the discussion in chapters 14 and 15 concerning Code Sec. 83 and restricted property compensation plans).[567] Since the Code Sec. 83(b) election (as discussed in chapters 14 and 15) will not apply for golden parachute payment purposes, ordinarily the amount of the payment is equal to the fair market value of the property at the time the property becomes substantially vested minus the amount, if any, paid for the property.[568] In the case of nonqualified stock options and incentive stock options (see the discussion of stock options in chapter 15), an option is treated as transferred no later than the time at which the option becomes substantially vested. Therefore, in general, the vesting of incentive stock options and nonqualified stock options is considered a payment in the nature of compensation.[569] The IRS has issued Rev. Proc. 2003-68[570] to provide guidance concerning how to value stock options for purposes of the golden parachute rules.

An "excess parachute payment" equals the excess of a parachute payment over the base amount (defined below) allocated to it.[571] The term "parachute payment" does not include payments to a disqualified individual with respect to a small business corporation (defined similarly to S corporations) or a corporation whose stock was not readily traceable on an established securities market, or otherwise if the shareholder approval requirements are met.[572] In addition, payments made under qualified deferred compensation plans, such as pension and profit-sharing plans, Code Sec. 403(a) annuity plans and simplified employee pension plans, are not considered to be parachute payments.[573] For purposes of the golden parachute rules, all members of the same affiliated group (as defined in Code Sec. 1504) are treated as a single corporation under Code Sec. 280G(d)(5).

---

[565] Reg. § 1.280G-1, Q&A 11(b)
[566] Reg. § 1.280G-1, Q&A 12(a).
[567] Reg. § 1.280G-1, Q&A 12(a) and (b).
[568] *Id.*
[569] Prop. Reg. § 1.280G-1, Q&A 13

[570] 2003-2 CB 398.
[571] Code Sec. 280G(b)(1).
[572] Code Sec. 280G(b)(5).
[573] Code Sec. 280G(b)(6).

¶ 303.04

Payments Contingent on Change in Ownership or Control. A payment is not subject to the golden parachute rules unless it is contingent on a change in the ownership or effective control of a corporation or in the ownership of its assets.[574] In general, a payment is treated as contingent on a change in ownership or control if the payment would not in fact have been made to the disqualified individual had no change in ownership or control occurred. A payment is also generally treated as contingent on a change in ownership or control if (a) the payment is contingent on an event that is closely associated with a change in ownership or control, (b) a change in ownership or control actually occurs, and (c) the event is materially related to the change in ownership or control.[575] Thus, the IRS privately held that a merger of two corporations did not result in a change of ownership and effective control of the target company where, after the merger, shareholders of the acquired company do not act in a concerted way to control the management and policies of the acquiring company.[576] A payment is deemed to be contingent on a change in ownership or control if such change determines the time when the payment is to be made, such as the onset of a tender offer, a substantial increase in the corporation's market price before the change, or a five percent acquisition of the corporation's stock.[577] A payment may be a parachute payment even if the employment or similar relationship of the disqualified individual involved is not voluntarily or involuntarily terminated.[578]

Any payment pursuant to (1) an agreement entered into within one year of a takeover or (2) an amendment made within such a one-year period of a previous agreement is presumed to be contingent on the change unless otherwise proven.[579] Under Code Sec. 280G(b) (2)(B), a payment in the nature of compensation to or for the benefit of a disqualified individual, which is made pursuant to an agreement which violates any securities laws or regulations, is also considered a parachute payment. The burden of proof is on the IRS to establish that such payments are made under an agreement that would violate any securities laws or regulations. Finally, property that becomes substantially vested (as defined in Reg. § 1.83-3(b) as discussed in Chapter 14) as a result of a change in ownership or control is treated as a payment contingent on a change in ownership or control.[580]

---

[574] Code Sec. 280G(b)(2)(A).

[575] Reg. § 1.280G-1, Q&A 22. *See* IRS Letter Ruling 9847011, 8-19-98, CCH IRS Letter Rulings Reports for an application of this rule. *See also Richard Cline*, 94-2 ustc ¶ 50, 468 (4th Cir., 1994).

[576] IRS Letter Ruling 200108008, 11-15-00, CCH IRS Letter Rulings Reports.

[577] Reg. § 1.280G-1, Q&A 22.

[578] *Id.*

[579] Code Sec. 280G(b)(2)(C).

[580] Reg. § 1.280G-1. Q&A 22.

The final regulations provide specifics in Q&As 27 through 29 as to the circumstances under which a change in ownership or control is considered to occur. Under these regulations, more than one person will not be considered to be acting as a group merely because they happen to purchase or own stock of the same corporation at the same time, or due to the same public offering. Rev. Proc. 2004-87[581] provides guidance for determining whether a change in ownership or control occurs when creditors acquire the stock of a company in a bankruptcy reorganization.

The IRS has recently publicly ruled that the nonvested shares of restricted stock that are taxable in the current year because the employee or other service provider has made the Code Sec. 83(b) election (as discussed in Chapter 14) are to be treated as outstanding shares of stock in the corporation for determining whether (1) the employing corporation has had a change of ownership or control, and (2) a shareholder is a disqualified individual (as discussed earlier in this section) for purposes of Code Sec. 280G.[582]

Determination of Excess Parachute Payments. Payments which are contingent on a change in ownership or control of the payor corporation are not "parachute payments" under the golden parachute rules unless their aggregate present value equals or exceeds three times the recipient's "base amount." Under Code Sec. 280G(b)(3), the base amount is the individual's annualized includible compensation for the base period. The term "annualized includible compensation for the base period" is the average annual compensation that (1) was payable by the corporation being taken over, and (2) was taxable to the disqualified individual for the taxable years in the base period.[583] The base period is the most recent five taxable years ending before the date on which the takeover occurs or, if less, the portion of that period of time during which the disqualified individual performed personal services for the corporation taken over.[584] If the disqualified individual did not perform services for the corporation prior to the individual's tax year in which the change of ownership or control occurred, the individual's base period compensation is the annualized compensation includible in gross income for that portion, prior to such change, of the individual's taxable year in which the change occurred.[585]

The amount treated as a parachute payment can be reduced by (1) the portion of the payment that the taxpayer establishes is reasonable compensation for personal services to be rendered on or

---

[581] IRB 2004-32, 154.
[582] Rev. Rul. 2005-39, IRB 2005-27, 998.
[583] Code Sec. 280G(d)(1).

[584] Code Sec. 280G(d)(2).

[585] Reg. § 1.280G-1, Q&A 36.

after the date of the takeover and (2) the portion of the payment which the taxpayer proves is reasonable compensation for services actually rendered by the taxpayer before the change in ownership or control occurs.[586]

If there is only one payment to the disqualified individual, the entire base amount is allocated to it. If there is more than one parachute payment payable to an individual, the portion of the base amount to be allocated to any parachute payment is an amount which bears the same ratio to the base amount as the present value of the parachute payment bears to the present value of all parachute payments payable to the individual.[587] The present value of a parachute payment is determined at the time of the event that causes the parachute payment(s) to be made. The present value of a parachute payment is determined by using a discount rate equal to 120 percent of the AFR (determined under Code Sec. 1274(d)), compounded semiannually.[588]

> **Example (1):** Warren Wallace was a director of the Axis Corporation, which was taken over by the Daniels Corporation. Under an agreement, Axis Corporation paid Warren $500,000 on the date of the takeover. Warren's base amount is $120,000. The $500,000 payment to Warren was an excess parachute payment since it exceeded the $360,000 base amount ($120,000 times three). The excess payment of $380,000 ($500,000 minus $120,000) is not deductible by the corporation, and Warren must pay an excise tax of $76,000 ($380,000 times 20 percent).

> **Example (2):** Assume that Wilma Mertz, also a director of Axis Corporation, was to receive a parachute payment to be paid over five years with a present value of $1,000,000. Assume that her base amount was $250,000. The payment is an excess parachute payment since the present value exceeds $750,000 (three times her base amount of $250,000). Assuming that Wilma receives a $200,000 payment in the first year, the amount that is not deductible is $150,000, determined as follows:
> (1) ratio of present payment to present aggregate value of all payments is 20 percent ($200,000/$1,000,000);
> (2) portion of base amount allocable to the first payment is $50,000 ($250,000 × 20 percent);
> (3) the excess payment is $150,000 ($200,000 − $50,000).

---

[586] Code Sec. 280G(b)(4).
[587] Code Sec. 280G(b)(3)(B).
[588] Code Sec. 280G(d)(4).

Wilma must also pay an excise tax of $30,000 for the first year. To determine the amount of the excess and excise tax on payments in future years, the value of the payment and the present value of the total payments will have to be determined under Code Sec. 1274.

Chapter 4

Employee Fringe Benefit Plans

¶401   Introduction

Chapter 3 covered the taxation of the more common forms of fringe benefits payable to executives and other employees. In recent years, employers have established plans in which employees can choose between receiving certain types of excludable fringe benefits or receiving taxable cash compensation. These flexible benefit plans—called cafeteria plans—are specifically covered by Code Sec. 125. In addition, the IRS, in 2002, issued public guidance concerning Health Reimbursement Arrangements (HRA's), under which the employer makes contributions, and the amounts contributed under the plan can be used to reimburse employees for medical expenses that the employees and their dependents incur. Finally, employers have set up formal plans under which employer contributions are made to a plan which provides covered employees with medical benefits, life insurance benefits, and/or certain other types of fringe benefits. These plans are called welfare benefit plans, of which the most important is voluntary employee benefit associations (VEBAs). VEBAs must satisfy certain statutory requirements, and after 1985, the deductions for employer contributions to welfare benefit plans are subject to strict limitations. This chapter covers cafeteria plans, health reimbursement arrangements, and welfare benefit plans.

¶402   Cafeteria Plans

Cafeteria plans are employer-maintained plans that permit participating employees to choose between one or more qualified benefits (certain fringe benefits as specified in Code Sec. 125) and taxable cash.

Under Code Sec. 125, excludable benefits are not subject to the doctrine of constructive receipt merely because the employee has the right to choose particular benefits. As a general rule, employer contributions to cafeteria plans are only includible to the extent that the participants actually choose to receive taxable cash available under the plan. However, highly compensated participants and/or key employee participants may be taxable on some or all of the benefits that they receive under a cafeteria plan if the plan is discriminatory.

.01 Cafeteria Plan Defined

A cafeteria plan is a separate written plan maintained by an employer for the benefit of its employees under which all participants are employees and which permits participating employees to choose between two or more benefits consisting of taxable cash compensation and qualified benefits (as defined in Code Sec. 125(f)).[1] Benefits received under a cafeteria plan are not taxed solely because employee participants may choose among the benefits of the plan.[2] Further, benefits provided under a cafeteria plan are not subject to FICA and FUTA taxes solely because employee participants may choose among benefits provided by the plan.[3] The tax treatment of benefits provided by cafeteria plans is generally based on the provisions of the Code that pertain to the specific benefits. The IRS publicly ruled in 2002 that contributions made by employees under a cafeteria plan salary reduction arrangement to pay for health insurance coverage are not includable in gross income (and subject to FICA and FUTA taxes) solely because the plan provides for automatic enrollment for employee-only coverage.[4] The facts of the situation indicated that employees are provided with written notice that they can elect to receive cash instead of the coverage or additionally obtain family coverage. On the other hand, qualified retirement plan distributions that cafeteria plan participants chose to be used to pay health insurance premiums of the participants under the cafeteria plan were held to be taxable.[5] The IRS held that there is no provision under Code Sec. 402 (which governs the taxability of retirement plans as discussed in chapter 9) which permits the exclusion of qualified retirement plan benefits that are used to pay health insurance premiums under a cafeteria plan.

Written Document Requirement. Under Prop. Reg. § 1.125-1 (Q&A-3), a written document for the cafeteria plan must be maintained and must contain at least the following information:

(1) a specific description of each benefit available under the plan, including the period(s) during which the benefits are provided;

---

[1] Code Sec. 125(d)(1).
[2] Code Sec. 125(a).
[3] Code Secs. 3121(a)(5) and 3306(b)(5).

[4] Rev. Rul. 2002-27, 2002-1 CB 925.
[5] Rev. Rul. 2003-62, 2003-1 CB 1034.

¶ 402.01

(2) the plan's eligibility rules governing participation;

(3) the procedures governing participant's elections under the plan;

(4) the manner in which employer contributions may be made under the plan, such as by means of a salary reduction agreement or by nonelective employer contributions to the plan;

(5) the maximum amount of employer contributions available to any plan participant; and

(6) the plan year on which the cafeteria plan operates.

The written plan document must also specify the maximum amount of elective contributions (salary reduction contributions) available to any participant under the plan either by stating the maximum dollar amount or maximum percentage of compensation that may be contributed or by stating the method for determining such maximum.[6]

The written document need not be self-contained. That is, the plan document may include by reference benefits established under other separate written plans, such as coverage under a dependent care assistance program, without describing in full the benefits available under the separate plans.[7]

Eligible Participants. A cafeteria plan can only have employee participants.[8] Although the term "employees" is not defined in Code Sec. 125, Prop. Reg. § 1.125-1, Q&A-4, states that the term "employees" includes present and former employees of the employer. Leased employees, as defined in Code Sec. 414(n)(2), can also be covered by an employer receiving their services, since they are treated as employees of that employer.[9] Further, all employees who are treated as employed by a single employer under Code Sec. 414(b), (c), or (m) (controlled groups of corporations, partnerships and proprietorships under common control, and affiliated service groups) are treated as employed by a single employer for purposes of Code Sec. 125. However, self-employed individuals (as described in Code Sec. 401(c)) are not employees for purposes of Code Sec. 125 and cannot participate in a cafeteria plan (see, however, the discussion concerning full-time life insurance salespersons below). In addition, even though former employees can participate in cafeteria plans, a cafeteria plan may not be established predominantly for the benefit of former employees of the employer.

Although spouses and other beneficiaries of employee-participants may not participate in a cafeteria plan, a cafeteria plan may provide benefits to such spouses and other beneficiaries.

Example: An employee's spouse may not be given the opportunity to purchase or select medical insurance or other benefits

---

[6] Prop. Reg. § 1.125-2, Q&A 3.
[7] Prop. Reg. § 1.125-1, Q&A 3.
[8] Code Sec. 125(d)(1).
[9] Code Sec. 414(n)(1).

offered by a cafeteria plan, but such spouse may benefit from the employee's selection of medical insurance protection under the plan. Such insurance could be used to pay medical bills of the spouse.

An employee-participant's spouse will not be treated as actively participating in a cafeteria plan just because the spouse has the right, upon the death of that employee, to select among various settlement options available with respect to a death benefit selected by the employee under the cafeteria plan or to elect among permissible distribution options with respect to the deceased employee's benefits under a cash or deferred arrangement that is part of the plan.[10]

Under Code Sec. 7701(a)(20), full-time life insurance salespersons are also eligible to participate in cafeteria plans with respect to benefits that the salespersons are permitted to exclude from income (benefits under Code Secs. 79, 101(b) 104, 105, and 106).

.02 Permitted Benefits Under Code Sec. 125

Under Code Sec. 125(d)(1), cafeteria plan participants may select between two or more benefits consisting of taxable cash compensation and qualified benefits (as defined in Code Sec. 125(f)). The permitted benefits under a cafeteria plan may be provided pursuant to a salary reduction agreement with the employer.[11] That is, employees can elect to receive less taxable compensation and have the employer contribute like amounts with respect to qualified benefits under the cafeteria plan. Such amounts are treated as employer contributions, and are not treated as constructively received by the employee-participants.

> **Example:** Employer-paid medical insurance premiums are a qualified benefit (see the discussion on qualified benefits below). Suppose that Wilson, a participant in his employer's cafeteria plan, has to pay $100 per month (the employer pays $125) for group medical insurance coverage available through the employer. Under the cafeteria plan, the employee, through a salary reduction arrangement, can elect to receive $100 per month less of taxable compensation and have the employer pay that $100 for the medical insurance coverage. Under the proposed regulations, each $100 payment is treated as an employer contribution to the plan and is excludable by the employee. Those amounts are also not subject to FICA and FUTA taxes.

Qualified Benefits. Under Code Sec. 125(f), qualified benefits are fringe benefits that are excludable under specific sections of the Code other than fringe benefits excludable under Code Secs. 106(b), 117, 127,

---

[10] Prop. Reg. § 1.125-1, Q&A 4.   [11] Prop. Reg. § 1.125-1, Q&A 6.

and 132 and any product which is advertised, marketed, or offered as long-term care insurance. Qualified benefits also include:

(1) any group-term life insurance which is includible in gross income only because it exceeds the $50,000 limitation under Code Sec. 79; and

(2) other benefits permitted under IRS regulations (note, that the exclusion for group legal service benefits expired on July 1, 1992, so beginning on that date, such benefits are not a nontaxable fringe benefit). In accordance with its regulatory authority on the matter of qualified benefits, the IRS has stated that group-term life insurance on the lives of the employee's spouse or children is a qualified benefit when that amount is included in income (this would be the case when the face value exceeds $2,000; see the discussion in Chapter 3 under group-term life insurance).[12] In addition, Notice 97-9 provides that an adoption assistance program that meets the requirements of Code Sec. 137 constitutes a qualified benefit that may be offered through a cafeteria plan.[13] Employer contributions to Archer MSA accounts under Code Sec. 106(b) do not constitute a qualified benefit and cannot be provided through a cafeteria plan. However, high deductible health plans that are used in conjunction Archer MSAs (see the discussion in Chapter 3) can be provided through a cafeteria plan.[14]

Thus, the following fringe benefits constitute qualified benefits:

(1) coverage under group-term life insurance plans (Code Sec. 79);

(2) coverage under accident or health plans including coverage under high deductible health plans but not including Archer MSA accounts (Code Secs. 105 and 106);

(3) coverage under a dependent care assistance program (Code Sec. 129);

(4) coverage under an employer-maintained adoption assistance program (Code Sec. 137); and[15]

(5) beginning in 2004, coverage under a health savings account (HSA) under Code Sec. 223 (see ¶ 302.04).[16]

In addition, Prop. Reg. § 1.125-2, Q&A-4(a), provides that accident or health coverage, group-term life insurance coverage, and benefits under a dependent care assistance program do not fail to be qualified benefits merely because they are includible in gross income under the applicable nondiscrimination rules. However, in

---

[12] Temp. Reg. § 1.125-2T.
[13] Notice 97-9, 1997-1 CB 365, II E.
[14] Notice 96-53, 1996-2 CB 219, Q&A 8.
[15] *Id.*, Notice 97-9, 1997-1 CB 365, II. E., and Notice 96-53, 1996-2 CB 219, Q&A 8.

[16] Code Sec. 125(d)(2)(D), as amended by P.L. 108-173, 108th Cong., 1st Sess., Sec. 1201 (Dec. 8, 2003).

a case where an employer reimbursed employees for the amount of health insurance premiums that the employees paid under a salary reduction agreement as part of a cafeteria plan, the reimbursements were not qualified benefits.[17] The reimbursements constituted gross income and are subject to FICA and FUTA taxes. A cafeteria plan may offer employee-participants the opportunity to purchase, with after-tax contributions, coverage under the above listed plans. Finally, a cafeteria plan may permit employees to elect to receive either additional or fewer paid vacation days than otherwise provided by the employer, on a nonelective basis. However, such election cannot be provided in a way that results in the deferral of compensation. In determining whether the opportunity to defer compensation exists, nonelective vacation days are deemed to be used before elective days. An employee may be granted the opportunity to receive cash in exchange for unused elective vacation days as long as the cash is received on or before the last day of the plan year and the last day of the employee's taxable year to which the elective contributions used to purchase the unused vacation days relate.[18]

The following fringe benefits cannot be provided by a cafeteria plan:

(1) medical savings accounts under Code Sec. 106(b);

(2) scholarships and fellowships under Code Sec. 117;

(3) meals and lodging under Code Sec. 119;

(4) vanpooling under Code Sec. 124;

(5) educational assistance under Code Sec. 127;

(6) miscellaneous fringe benefits excludable under Code Sec. 132; and

(7) long-term care insurance under Code Sec. 7702B.[19]

Currently Taxable Benefits Treated as Cash. The cafeteria plan rules state that participants should be permitted to choose between qualified benefits and cash. Under Prop. Reg. § 1.125-2, Q&A-4(c), a benefit is treated as cash if the benefit does not defer the receipt of compensation and an employee who receives the benefit purchases it with after-tax employee contributions, or is treated, for all tax purposes, as receiving, at the time the benefit is received, cash compensation equal to full value of the benefit and then purchasing the benefit with after-tax employee contributions. For example, long-term disability coverage is treated as cash if the cafeteria plan permits an employee to purchase the coverage under the

---

[17] Rev. Rul. 2002-3, 2002-1 CB 316.
[18] Prop. Reg. § 1.125-2, Q&A 5(c).

[19] Temp. Reg. § 1.125-2T(a), Code Sec. 125(f), and Notice 97-9, 1997-1 CB 365, II. E.

plan with after-tax employee contributions, or provides that the employee receiving such coverage is treated as having cash compensation equal to the value of the coverage and then as having purchased the coverage with after-tax employee contributions.

Deferred Compensation. In general, deferred compensation cannot be a qualified benefit.[20] As an example, the IRS privately held that a state plan for funding retiree health coverage would not qualify as a cafeteria plan because the plan provided for deferred compensation by permitting payment of benefits beyond the year in which the employee retired. The plan also failed to qualify because it would permit unused amounts to be paid to a retiree's beneficiaries.[21] However, in the case of profit-sharing or stock bonus plans or rural electric cooperative plans that include Code Sec. 401(k) cash or deferred payment arrangements (see Chapters 5 and 7 for a description of these plans), under which an employee can elect to have pre-tax contributions made to the plan pursuant to a salary reduction agreement, the amounts so contributed are treated as qualified benefits.[22]

Similarly, a cafeteria plan may permit employees to make after-tax contributions subject to Code Sec. 401(m) under a qualified plan. In addition, a cafeteria plan will not be treated as including a benefit that is deferred compensation merely because, under the qualified plan, employer matching contributions (as defined in Code Sec. 401(m)(4)(A)) are made with respect to such elective or after-tax employee contributions.[23] Finally, reasonable premium rebates or policy dividends paid with respect to cafeteria plan benefits do not constitute prohibited deferred compensation if they are paid before the end of the 12-month period immediately following the plan year to which the rebates and dividends relate.[24]

Employees of educational institutions can elect to have their employer pay contributions for post-retirement life insurance under a cafeteria plan if (1) all contributions for that insurance must be made before retirement, and (2) the life insurance does not have a cash surrender value.[25]

In summary, unless one of the exceptions noted above is applicable, the proposed regulations have prohibited cafeteria plans from offering benefits that defer the receipt of compensation. For example, a plan that permits employees to carry over unused elective contributions or plan benefits from one plan year to another operates to defer compensation and, under the existing proposed regulations,

---

[20] Code Sec. 125(c)(2).
[21] IRS Legal Memorandum 200015021.
[22] Code Sec. 125(c)(2).

[23] Prop. Reg. § 1.125-2. Q&A 5(b).
[24] *Id.*
[25] Code Sec. 125(d)(2)(C).

could not qualify as a cafeteria plan. Thus, under the existing proposed regulations, a plan that enables participants to use contributions for one plan year to purchase a benefit that will be provided in a subsequent plan year would not qualify as a cafeteria plan. Under this rule, commonly referred to as the "use-it-or-lose-it" rule, unused cafeteria plan contributions or benefits remaining at the end of the plan year are forfeited. This rule has had particular relevance for flexible spending arrangements, covered below. Recently, the IRS issued Notice 2005-42,[26] in which it has modified that rule to permit a two-and-one-half-month grace period following a particular plan year. During that grace period, expenses for qualified benefits incurred may be paid or reimbursed from benefits or contributions remaining unused at the end of the immediately preceding plan year. The qualified benefit that is paid or reimbursed in the grace period must be the same as would have qualified for payment or reimbursement from contributions during that immediately preceding plan year. Thus, unused contributions relating to medical expenses at the end of one plan year can only be used to pay or reimburse medical expenses during the grace period, not some other type of expenses, such as dependent care costs. Any contributions from the previous plan year that remain unused by the end of the two-and-one-half-month grace period cannot be carried forward after the grace period. The IRS will amend the proposed regulations to reflect the new grace period provisions.

Flexible Spending Arrangements. Under a flexible spending arrangement (FSA), participating employees elect to have pretax compensation dollars contributed by their employer to the plan (also referred to as a tax-saver plan) frequently pursuant, to a salary reduction plan. Then, the participants can have the plan reimburse them for medical expenses, dependent care expenses, and other eligible expenses incurred during the plan year from the contributions made on their behalf by the employer to the plan during that plan year. The amounts contributed by the employer to the FSA and the amounts reimbursed by the FSA are not taxable to the participant as long as specific requirements in the proposed regulations are satisfied. The IRS has recently issued a revenue ruling concerning employee participants in an FSA of one company which sells all of its assets to another company, and the selling company's employees afterward become employees of the buying company, which agrees to cover those employees under its own FSA. Such employees may continue to exclude (1) the salary reduction contributions they make to the buying company's FSA and (2) medical reimbursements they

---

[26] IRB 2005-23, 1204.

¶ 402.02

receive under that FSA at the same level of coverage that they had under the selling company's plan.[27] In another recent ruling, the IRS analyzed circumstances where electronic reimbursements for medical expenses made under an FSA through the use of debit or credit cards of participants can be excluded.[28] The IRS indicated that when procedures were in place sufficient to allow for only the reimbursement of eligible medical expenses of the FSA participants, reimbursements made through debit or credit cards were permissible under the FSA and were not taxable to the recipients. Under a typical plan that uses debit or credit cards, a participant will present the debit or credit card to a merchant, drug store, or other vendor for payment for eligible expenses (expenses normally allowed to be reimbursed under health FSAs). If electronic documentation is sufficient in a case where the card is used, the plan administrator will reduce the participant's account balance by the amount of the expense. If further documentation is needed, the administrator will send notification to the participant. The participant then will have a specified period of time (e.g., 45 days) to provide the additional documentation. If such documentation is not timely provided, the expense will not be allowed, and the participant's card may be deactivated.

For plan years beginning after December 31, 1989, Prop. Reg. § 1.125-2, Q&A-7, provides a specific definition for FSAs and extensive and specific requirements that must be met by FSAs (many of the requirements are for health FSAs). Under Prop. Reg. § 1.125-2, Q&A-7(c), an FSA is a benefit program that provides employees with reimbursement of specified incurred expenses (subject to reimbursement maximums and other reasonable conditions) and under which the maximum amount of reimbursement does not substantially exceed the total premiums paid (including both employee- and employer-paid portions). Under this rule, the maximum amount of the reimbursement cannot exceed 500 percent of the total premium for the participant's coverage.

Health plans that are FSAs must qualify as health and accident plans (as defined in Code Secs. 105 and 106, discussed in Chapter 3). Thus, in general, while the health coverage under the FSA need not be insured, health FSAs must exhibit the risk-shifting and risk-distribution characteristics of insurance. Similarly, reimbursements under health FSAs must be paid specifically to reimburse the participant for medical expenses incurred previously during the period of coverage. Further, a health FSA cannot operate in a manner that enables participants to receive coverage only for periods for which

---

[27] Rev. Rul. 2002-32, 2002-1 CB 1069.   [28] Rev. Rul. 2003-43, 2003-1 CB 935.

the participants expect to incur medical expenses if such periods are less than one year.[29]

A health FSA must also satisfy a number of specific requirements as follows:

(1) *Uniform coverage throughout the coverage period.*[30] The maximum amount of reimbursement under the plan must be available at all times during the period of coverage, regardless of the amount of premiums that have been paid. Reimbursement will be considered available at all times if it is paid monthly or when the total amount of the claims submitted is at least a specified, reasonable minimum amount.

(2) *Twelve-month period of coverage.*[31] There must be a 12-month period of coverage, except in the case of a short plan year. Changes of plan elections are not permitted during the 12-month period except in cases where a change of election is permitted under the general cafeteria plan rules (elections and revocation of election rules are covered below).

(3) *Prohibited reimbursement.*[32] Under the proposed regulations, a health FSA can only reimburse medical expenses as defined in Code Sec. 213. A health FSA may not reimburse the costs of coverage under another health plan or other types of expense. A 2003 revenue ruling issued by the IRS has expanded the types of medicines and drugs that may be reimbursed under a health FSA.[33] Prior to the revenue ruling, only prescription drugs and insulin were permitted to be reimbursed. After the issuance of the ruling, certain over-the-counter drugs, such as antacids, allergy and cold medicines, and pain relievers (such as aspirin and ibuprofen) may be reimbursed under a health FSA. However, dietary supplements, such as vitamins, that are merely beneficial to a participant's overall health may not be reimbursed under a health FSA.

(4) *Claims substantiation.*[34] Plan participants must provide a written, independent third-party statement as proof that the expense was incurred, the amount of the expense, and that the expense has not otherwise been reimbursed. Note that as discussed above, in certain circumstances, electronic substantiation through the participant's use of a debit or credit card provided by the health FSA administrator will be now be acceptable. A health FSA cannot make advance reimbursements of future or projected expenses.

(5) *Claims incurred.*[35] Under the proposed regulations issued in 1989, claims for reimbursement must be for expenses incurred

---

[29] Prop. Reg. § 1.125-2, Q&A 7(a).
[30] Prop. Reg. § 1.125-2, Q&A 7(b)(2).
[31] Prop. Reg. § 1.125-2, Q&A 7(b)(3).
[32] Prop. Reg. § 1.125-2, Q&A 7(b)(4).

[33] Rev. Rul. 2003-102, 2003-2 CB 559.
[34] Prop. Reg. § 1.125-2, Q&A 7(b)(5).
[35] Prop. Reg. § 1.125-2, Q&A 7(b)(6).

during the applicable plan year, and thus cannot be for a later year even if billing for the medical services is not made until the next year. Thus, under this rule, participants could not carry over unused FSA contributions at the end of one plan year to be used to reimburse medical expenses incurred in the following plan year. However, as discussed in the section above concerning deferred compensation, the IRS has issued Notice 2005-42,[36] under which a cafeteria plan may now incorporate a two-and-one-half-month grace period into its health FSA plan. Under this grace period rule, FSA participants in plans which permit the grace period may use unused FSA plan contributions at the end of one plan year to pay medical expenses incurred during the first two-and-half months of the immediate following plan year. It should be noted that an FSA that incorporates the grace period rule and that is used in conjunction with an HSA (see the discussion of HSAs in ¶ 302.04) may jeopardize the qualified status of the HSA. The IRS is expected to issue guidance concerning this issue.

(6) *FSA experience gains.*[37] If a health FSA has an experience gain for a coverage year, the excess of the premiums paid and income (if any) of the FSA over the FSA's total claims reimbursements and administrative costs for the year may be used to reduce premium payments for the following year or may be returned to the participants.

In the case of dependent care assistance FSAs, rules similar to those applicable to health FSAs apply for plan years beginning after 1989.[38] The new two-and-one-half-month grace period rule described above under health FSAs also applies.

> **Example:** Charles Edwards is an employee of Clark Company, which maintains an FSA. Under a salary reduction agreement, Charles contributed $100 per month to the FSA plan for the plan year of September 1, 2005 through August 31, 2006. He can receive reimbursements under the plan for eligible medical expenses incurred by him and his spouse and dependents during the plan year. Although he can make a claim for medical expenses incurred any time during the plan year, the maximum amount of claims he can make is limited to the total of his twelve monthly plan contributions, or $1,200. If he fails to make claims of totaling $1,200 for the year, and during the first two and one-half months of the following plan year, the unused contributions cannot be returned to him. However, if the plan has an experience gain, he can receive his allocable share during the next year.

---

[36] IRB 2005-23, 1204.
[37] Prop. Reg. § 1.125-2, Q&A 7(b)(7).

[38] Prop. Reg. § 1.125-2, Q&A 7(b)(8).

Under the proposed regulations and Notice 2005-42, Clark Company's plan is a qualified health FSA, and none of the plan contributions or reimbursements are taxable to Charles.

.03   Family and Medical Leave Act (FMLA) and Cafeteria Plans

Recently published Reg. § 1.125-3 covers the impact of provisions of the Family Medical and Leave Act (FMLA) on cafeteria plan operations. In brief, the FMLA (P.L. 103-3 (1993)) requires employers to make available unpaid leaves of absence to employees for certain health-related and maternity reasons of the employee or immediate family members and imposes certain requirements on employers concerning coverage under group health care plans for employees taking FMLA leave. Reg. § 1.125-3 applies when an employee who participates in a cafeteria plan takes leave under the FMLA. The final regulations are applicable for cafeteria plan years beginning on or after January 1, 2002.[39] For earlier years, compliance with Prop. Reg. § 1.125-3, issued in 1995, should be acceptable. Important provisions in the final regulations are covered in the following paragraphs.

Under Reg. § 1.125-3, Q&A-2, an employer can require an employee who chooses to continue group health plan coverage while on an FMLA leave to be responsible for the share of group health premiums that would be allocable to the employee if the employee were working, and, for this purpose, treats amounts paid pursuant to a pre-tax salary reduction agreement as amounts allocable to the employee. The employer must continue to contribute the share of the cost that the employer contributed prior to the time the FMLA leave started. The employer may offer certain premium payment options (covered below) to an employee that continues coverage during the FMLA leave and may, in addition, on a nondiscriminatory basis, waive the obligation of the employee to pay his/her premiums.[40]

An employer must either allow an employee on unpaid FMLA leave to revoke coverage or continue coverage but allow the employee to discontinue payment of his/her share of the premium for group health plan coverage (including a health FSA) under a cafeteria plan for the period of the FMLA leave. An employer need not require an employee to revoke coverage if the employer pays the employee's share of premiums. Under such circumstances, as noted below, the employer may recover the employee's share of the premiums when the employee returns to work. If the employee on unpaid FMLA leave revokes coverage or has coverage terminated due to lack of

---

[39] Reg. § 1.125-3, Q&A 8.   [40] Reg. § 1.125-3, Q&A 3.

¶ 402.03

premium payments during the leave, that employee must be permitted to be reinstated in the group health plan coverage (including a health FSA) upon his/her return to work. Such an employee must, to the extent required by the FMLA, be reinstated on the same terms as prior to taking FMLA leave (including family or dependent coverage), subject to any changes in benefit levels that may have taken place during the period of FMLA leave. If the employee does not elect to be reinstated in the group health plan upon return from FMLA leave, the employer may nevertheless require the employee to resume participation if the employer also requires employees who return from unpaid non-FMLA leave to resume participation upon return from the leave. Finally, employee-participants, while on FMLA leave, must have the right to revoke or change elections under Reg. § 1.125-4 (discussed below—e.g., because of changes in status or cost or coverage changes as provided in Reg. § 1.125-4) under the same terms and conditions as are available to plan participants who are not on FMLA leave.[41]

An employer is not required under the FMLA to maintain other types of cafeteria plan benefits (e.g., non-health benefits such as adoption assistance) during an employee's FMLA leave. The entitlement of an employee to other benefits while on FMLA leave is determined under established policies of the employer for the provision of such benefits during other types of leave.[42] Further, an employee's revocation and/or changes of elections with respect to other cafeteria plan benefits are subject to the same rules that apply to employees who are not on FMLA leaves (see the discussion below). However, in certain cases, an employer may continue other cafeteria plan coverage while an employee is on an FMLA leave in order that the employer can meet its responsibility to provide equivalent benefits to the employee when the employee returns to work.

If an employer continues those other benefits while the employee is on FMLA leave, the employer can recoup the costs it incurred in paying the employee's share of the cost of the other benefits while the employee was on leave. Finally, an employee whose coverage has been terminated during the employee's FMLA leave must be permitted to be reinstated when the employee returns to work.[43]

Under Reg. § 1.125-3 Q&A 3(a), three payment options can be offered on a nondiscriminatory basis under a cafeteria plan to an employee who will be continuing his/her group health plan coverage (including a health FSA) while on unpaid FMLA leave: (1) the prepay option, (2) the pay-as-you go option, or (3) the catch-up option.

---

[41] Reg. § 1.125-3, Q&A 1; T.D. 8966, 10/17/01.   [43] Id.
[42] Reg. § 1.125-3, Q&A 7.

The final regulations detail how payments are to be made under each of these options. In all instances the employee's payments can be made on a pre-tax basis.

In general, a participant in a health FSA who takes FMLA leave is subject to the same rules discussed earlier regarding other employees who take FMLA leave. That is, they may (1) continue coverage under the FSA while on the leave or (2) revoke an existing health FSA under the cafeteria plan for the rest of the coverage period. In addition, an employee whose health FSA coverage has been terminated during the leave must be allowed to reinstate the coverage after he/she returns to work on the same terms as those prior to the beginning of the FMLA leave. In addition, a plan may require an employee to be reinstated in health coverage upon return from a period of unpaid FMLA leave, provided that employees who return from a period of unpaid leave not covered by the FMLA are also required to resume participation upon return to work.[44]

The maximum amount of coverage (minus reimbursements already made) must be available at all times during the FMLA leave provided that the employee continues coverage (or if the employer continues the coverage of an employee who fails to make the required premium payments) during the leave period. If an employee's coverage under the health FSA terminates while the employee is on FMLA leave, the employee is not entitled to receive reimbursements for claims incurred during the period when the coverage is terminated. If an employee subsequently elects or the employer requires the employee to be reinstated in the health FSA upon return from FMLA leave for the remainder of the plan year, the employee may not retroactively elect health FSA coverage for claims incurred during the period when the coverage was terminated. Upon reinstatement into a health FSA upon return from FMLA leave, the employee has the right under FMLA to (1) resume coverage at the level in effect before the FMLA leave and make up the unpaid premium payments, or (2) resume coverage at a level that is reduced and resume premium payments at the level in effect before the FMLA leave. If an employee chooses to resume health FSA coverage at a level that is reduced, the coverage is prorated for the period during the FMLA leave for which no premiums were paid. In both cases, the coverage level is reduced by prior reimbursements. Finally, FMLA requires that an employee on FMLA leave have the right to revoke or change elections (because of events described in Reg. § 1.125-4, discussed below) under the same terms and conditions that apply to plan participants who are not on FMLA leave.[45]

---

[44] Reg. § 1.125-3, Q&A 6(a).   [45] Reg. § 1.125-3, Q&A 6(b).

¶ 402.03

.04 Tax Rules and Consequences

Under the general rule of Code Sec. 125(a), amounts received or provided to employees under cafeteria plans are not taxable merely because the employees have the right to choose among the benefits of the plan. Thus, except in the case of discriminatory plans (discussed below), Code Sec. 125 does not specify the tax treatment of benefits received under a cafeteria plan. Rather, other individual Code sections which specifically govern the tax consequences of particular benefits apply in the case where such benefits are provided under a cafeteria plan. Further, benefits receivable under a cafeteria plan are not subject to FICA and FUTA taxes just because the employee has a choice of which benefits to receive.[46]

Cafeteria Plan Election Rules. A plan does not qualify as a cafeteria plan unless the plan requires participants to make elections among the benefits offered under the plan. The elections provided for under the cafeteria plan must be prospective only. Retroactive elections (e.g., elections applying to a previous year) are not permitted. Where a retroactive election is provided during a particular year under a cafeteria plan, the cafeteria plan is disqualified for that particular year.[47] For example, reimbursements that were made to employees for medical care and dependent care assistance benefits under a cafeteria plan were taxable to the recipients because the plan allowed retroactive payment for expenses before the plan was in effect.[48] In general, an election will not be deemed to have been made if a participant can revoke the election, even if the revocation is only for the remainder of the plan year.[49] However, the IRS has issued final regulations in 2000 and modifications to those final regulations in early 2001 (including an adoption, with certain changes, of proposed regulations issued in 2000) that indicate some limited circumstances under which a participant may revoke an existing election and make a new one (consistent with the reasons for making the change) for the remaining portion of the period of coverage.[50] One purpose of the new regulations is to conform these rules with the rules under the Health Insurance Portability and Accountability Act of 1996, discussed earlier. The final regulations (Reg. § 1.125-4), as modified in 2001, cover all qualified benefits (as defined above) and the circumstances under which election changes can be made with respect to those benefits. The final regulations generally apply to cafeteria plan years that begin on or after January 1, 2001.[51] However, the change in status

---

[46] Code Secs. 3121(a)(5) and 3306(b)(5).
[47] Prop. Reg. § 1.125-1, Q&A 8.
[48] *American Family Mutual Insurance Co.*, DC-Wis., 93-1 USTC ¶ 50,025.

[49] Reg. § 1.125-4(a).
[50] *See* Reg. § 1.125-4.
[51] Reg. § 1.125-4(j)(1).

rules found in Reg. § 1.125-4(c) applies to qualified benefits, other than accident and health plans and group-term life insurance (to which the January 1, 2001 date applies), in cafeteria plan years beginning on or after January 1, 2002. That same delayed effective date also applies to (1) Reg. § 1.125-4(d)(1)(ii)(B) (concerning a spouse, former spouse, or other individual obtaining accident of health plan coverage for an employee's child on account of a judgment, decree, or other order), (2) Reg. § 1.125-4(f) (describing election changes that are due to plan cost or coverage changes), and (3) Reg. § 1.125-4(i)(9) (which defines similar plan coverage).[52] For these provisions, taxpayers had the option, until January 1, 2002, of relying on either the final regulations, the proposed regulations issued in 2000 (Prop. Reg. § 1.125-4) or the plan cost or coverage change rules that were contained in Prop. Reg. § 1.125-2, Q&A 6 (issued in 1989).[53]

First, Reg. § 1.125-4(b) provides that a cafeteria plan may permit an employee to revoke an election for accident or health coverage during a period of coverage and to make a new election that corresponds with the special enrollment rights provided under Code Sec. 9801(f) (under the Health Insurance Portability and Accountability Act of 1996) for persons who lose other health and accident coverage. This rule applies regardless of whether or not the change in election is permitted under the changes in status rules of Reg. § 1.125-4(c).

The final regulations contain rules under which a change in status constitutes a circumstance under which an election can be revoked and a new election can be made during the same coverage period. Under the regulations, the revocation and new election must generally be consistent with the change in status. Under Reg. § 1.125-4(c)(2), the following events are considered to be a change in status:

(1) Events that change an employee's legal marital status (e.g., marriage, divorce, death of a spouse);

(2) Events that change an employee's number of qualified dependents (e.g., birth or death of a dependent);

(3) A termination or commencement of employment by the employee, spouse, or dependent;

(4) A reduction or increase in hours of employment by the employee, spouse, or dependent, including a switch between part-time and full-time;

(5) An event that causes an employee's dependent to satisfy the requirements for coverage due to attainment of an age, student status, and or similar circumstances;

---

[52] Reg. § 1.125-4(j)(2).   [53] T.D.8921, 1/10/01, 66 FR 1837.

(6) A change in the place of residence or work of the employee, spouse, or dependent; and

(7) The commencement or termination of adoption proceedings under a qualified adoption assistance plan that is provided through a cafeteria plan.

Under Reg. § 1.125-4(c)(3), a revocation of coverage and a new election for the remaining portion of a period is consistent with a change in status with respect to accident or health coverage if (1) the change in status (a) results in the employee, spouse, or dependent gaining or losing eligibility for accident or health coverage under either the cafeteria plan or an accident or health plan of spouse's or dependent's employer, or (b) is due to an increase or decrease in the number of an employee's dependents or family members that may benefit from being covered under the plan; and (2) the election change corresponds with that gain or loss of coverage. Similar rules apply generally in the case of group-term life insurance coverage.[54] An election change satisfies the consistency requirements for other qualified benefits if the election change is due to and corresponds with a change in status that has an effect on eligibility for coverage under an employer's cafeteria plan. Under Reg. § 1.125-4(c)(3)(ii), an election change also satisfies the consistency requirements if the change is due to and corresponds with a change in status that affects expenses with respect to dependent care assistance (covered by Code Sec. 129) or expenses for adoption assistance (including qualified adoption expenses covered in Code Sec. 137(d)). Notwithstanding these consistency requirements, if the employee, spouse, or dependent becomes eligible for continuation coverage under the employer's group health plan as provided under the COBRA continuation rules (discussed in Chapter 3) or any similar State law, the employee may elect to increase payments under the employer's cafeteria plan to pay for the continuation coverage.[55] In addition, a cafeteria plan may permit a change in election that results from a judgment, decree, or order resulting from a divorce, legal separation, annulment, or change in legal custody that requires accident or health coverage for a child of an employee or permit the employee to make an election to cancel coverage for the child if the order requires the former spouse to provide coverage, and such coverage is actually provided.[56] If an employee, spouse, or dependent, who is enrolled in an accident or health plan, becomes eligible for Medicare or Medicaid coverage, a cafeteria plan may permit the employee to make an election change to cancel coverage of that employee, spouse, or dependent under the accident or health plan.[57]

---

[54] Reg. § 1.125-4(c)(3)(i).
[55] Reg. § 1.125-4(c)(3)(i).

[56] Reg. § 1.125-4(d).
[57] Reg. § 1.125-4(e).

¶ **402.04**

The final regulations also contain provisions concerning cafeteria plan cost and coverage related election changes under which (the cost and coverage change rules do not apply to Health FSAs covered above):

(1) *Cost Changes.*[58] If the cost of a qualified benefit plan increases (or decreases) during a period of coverage and, under the terms of the plan, employees have to make a corresponding change in their payments, the cafeteria plan may, on a reasonable and consistent basis, automatically make a prospective increase (or decrease) in affected employees' elective contributions for the plan.

If the cost charged to an employee for a benefit package option (a qualified benefit under Code Sec. 125(f) that is offered under a cafeteria plan, or an option for coverage under an underlying accident or health plan such as an HMO option) significantly increases or significantly decreases during a period of coverage, the cafeteria plan may permit the employee to make a corresponding change in election under the cafeteria plan. Changes that may be made include commencing participation in the cafeteria plan for the option with a decrease in cost, or, in the case of an increase in cost, revoking an election for that coverage and, in lieu thereof, either receiving on a prospective basis coverage under another benefit package option providing similar coverage or dropping coverage if no other benefit package option providing similar coverage is available. For example, if the cost of an indemnity option under an accident or health plan significantly increases during a period of coverage, employees who are covered by the indemnity option may make a corresponding prospective increase in their payments or may instead elect to revoke their election for the indemnity option and, in lieu of that, elect coverage under another benefit package option including an HMO option (or drop coverage under the accident or health plan if no other benefit package option is offered).

(2) *Coverage Changes.*[59] If an employee (or an employee's spouse or dependent) experiences a significant curtailment of coverage (that is not a total loss of coverage) under a plan during a period of coverage (for example, there is a significant increase in the deductible, the copay, or the out-of-pocket cost sharing limit under an accident or health plan), the cafeteria plan may permit any employee who had been participating in the plan and receiving that coverage to revoke his/her election for that coverage and, in lieu thereof, to elect to receive on a prospective basis, coverage under another benefit package that provides similar coverage. Coverage under a plan is significantly curtailed only if

---

[58] Reg. § 1.125-4(f)(2).   [59] Reg. § 1.125-4(f)(3)-(5).

¶ 402.04

there is an overall reduction in coverage provided under the plan so as to constitute reduced coverage, in general. Therefore, in most cases, the loss of one particular physician in a network is not considered a significant curtailment.

If an employee (or the employee's spouse or dependent) has a significant curtailment that is a loss of coverage, the plan may permit that employee to revoke his/her election under the cafeteria plan and, in lieu thereof, to elect either to (1) receive, on a prospective basis, coverage under another benefit package option that provides similar coverage or (2) drop coverage if no similar benefit package option is available. For purposes of these rules, a loss of coverage means a complete loss of coverage under the benefit package option or other coverage option (including, e.g., an HMO ceasing to be available in the area where the individual resides). Also, the cafeteria plan may, at its option, treat the following as a loss of coverage: (1) a substantial decrease in medical care providers under the plan option; (2) a reduction in the benefits of a specific type of medical condition or treatment with respect to which the employee or the employee's spouse or dependent is currently in a course of treatment; or (3) any other similar fundamental loss of coverage.

If a plan adds a new benefit package option or other coverage option, or if coverage under an existing benefit package option or other coverage option is significantly improved during a period of coverage, the cafeteria plan may permit eligible employees (whether or not they have previously made an election under the cafeteria plan or have previously elected the benefit package option) to revoke their election under the cafeteria plan and, in lieu thereof, to make an election on a prospective basis for coverage under the new or improved benefit package.

A cafeteria plan may permit an employee to make a prospective election change that is on account of and corresponds with a change made under another employer plan (including a plan of the same employer or of another employer) if (1) the other cafeteria plan or qualified benefits plan permits participants to make an election change that would be permitted under Reg. § 1.125-4(b)(g), with the exception of this provision or (2) the cafeteria plan permits participants to make an election for a period of coverage that is different from the period of coverage under the other cafeteria plan or qualified benefits plan.

A cafeteria plan may permit an employee to make an election on a prospective basis to add coverage under a cafeteria plan for the employee, spouse, or dependent if the employee, spouse, or dependent loses coverage under any group health coverage sponsored by (1) a governmental or education institution including, e.g., a state health benefits risk pool and (2) a foreign government group health plan.

¶ **402.04**

The final regulations contain provisions concerning elective contributions under a qualified cash or deferred arrangement.[60] Under the regulations, a cafeteria plan may permit a participant who has elected to make contributions under a qualified cash or deferred arrangement (within the meaning of Code Sec. 401(k)) or who has elected to make after-tax employee contributions subject to Code Sec. 401(m) to modify or revoke the election in accordance with the provisions of Code Secs. 401(k) and 401(m) and the regulations, thereunder.

The final regulations indicate special requirements relating to the Family and Medical Leave Act (FMLA). Under these requirements, an employee taking leave under the FMLA may revoke an existing election of accident or health plan coverage and make such other election for the remaining portion of the period of coverage as may be provided for under the FMLA.[61] These requirements are consistent with those indicated in Reg. § 1.125-3 which is covered earlier in this chapter.

Finally, the final regulations do not contain a provision indicating the impact of a cessation of required contributions under the cafeteria plan by a covered employee. However, Prop. Reg. § 1.125-2 Q&A 6(b) covers that issue. Under that proposed regulation, a cafeteria plan may provide that a benefit will terminate if the employee fails to make the required premium payment. However, such an employee-participant may not make a new election for the same coverage period.

Nondiscrimination Rules. Cafeteria plans must satisfy, under Code Sec. 125(b), (1) an eligibility test, (2) a contributions and benefits test, and (3) a concentration test.

Under Code Sec. 125(b)(1)(A), a cafeteria plan cannot discriminate in favor of highly compensated employees as to eligibility to participate. Code Sec. 125 (g)(3) provided that a cafeteria plan does not discriminate in favor of highly compensated employees with respect to eligibility to participate if:

(1) the plan covers employees in sufficient number to satisfy the IRS (on a facts and circumstance basis) that the plan does not discriminate in favor of highly compensated employees;

(2) no employee is required to complete more than three years of employment as a condition of participation (the employment requirement applies to all employees); and

(3) any employee, who meets the employment requirement (number (2) above) and who is otherwise entitled to participate in the plan, commences participation no later than the first day of the first

---

[60] Reg. § 1.125-4(h). [61] Reg. § 1.125-4(g).

plan year beginning after the date the employment requirement is satisfied (assuming that employee is still employed).

Under Code Sec. 125(b)(1)(B), cafeteria plans also cannot discriminate in favor of highly compensated employees with respect to contributions and benefits. For that purpose, Code Sec. 125(c) states that a cafeteria plan does not discriminate in favor of highly compensated employees if the provision of qualified benefits and total benefits or employer contributions allocable to qualified benefits does not discriminate in favor of highly compensated employees. Except in the case of health benefits and collectively bargained plans, a cafeteria plan is not discriminatory if the plan gives each participant an equal opportunity to select qualified benefits and if the actual selection of qualified benefits is not discriminatory (i.e., highly compensated employees did not disproportionately select nontaxable benefits while nonhighly compensated employees selected taxable benefits).[62] A cafeteria plan automatically meets the eligibility and benefits tests if it is maintained under an agreement found by the IRS to be a collective bargaining agreement between employee representatives and one or more employers.[63] A cafeteria plan does not discriminate in favor of highly compensated employees as to contributions and benefits in the case of health and accident benefits if (1) contributions for each participant are at least (a) 100 percent of the cost of the health benefit coverage under the plan of similarly situated highly compensated employees, or (b) 75 percent of the cost of the most expensive health benefit coverage elected by a similarly situated highly compensated participant, and (2) contributions and benefits under the plan in excess of the limits described in (1) bear a uniform relationship to the participant's compensation.[64]

For purposes of the preceding two nondiscrimination rules, highly compensated employees include the following employees:

(1) officers;

(2) stockholders owning more than five percent of the voting power or value of all classes of stock of the employer;

(3) the highly compensated; and

(4) spouses or dependents (as defined in Code Sec. 152, determined without regard to subsections (b)(1), (b)(2), and (d)(1)(B) thereof) of the above classes.[65]

---

[62] Prop. Reg. § 1.125-1, Q&A 19.
[63] Code Sec. 125(g)(1).
[64] Code Sec. 125(g)(2).
[65] Code Sec. 125(e), as amended by P.L. 108-311, 108th Cong., 2d Sess., Sec. 207(11) (Oct. 4, 2004), effective for taxable years beginning after December 31, 2004. For taxable years prior to January 1, 2005, dependents were as defined in Code Sec. 152. The third category, "the highly compensated" is not specifically defined, and the Committee Reports do not indicate if the term has the same meaning as it is given in the context of qualified plans as covered in Chapter 6.

The third nondiscrimination test (a concentration test) specifies that in the case of key employees (within the meaning of Code Sec. 416(i)(1) in connection with the qualified plan top-heavy rules; see Chapter 7), the qualified benefits provided to key employees cannot exceed 25 percent of the aggregate of qualified benefits provided to all employees under the plan.[66]

Consequences of Failure to Meet the Nondiscrimination Tests. Under Prop. Reg. § 1.125-1, Q&A-10, if a cafeteria plan does not meet the eligibility, benefits and contributions, and/or concentration tests, the highly compensated participants in the plan (key employees in the case of failure of the concentration test) are to be taxed on the combination of taxable benefits with the greatest aggregate value that could have been selected for the plan year.

> **Example:** Kent is a highly compensated individual and participates in his employer's cafeteria plan. During 2006, he has the opportunity to select total benefits of $4,000, consisting of cash of up to $2,500 and qualified benefits costing from $1,500 to $4,000. He chooses to receive $1,500 of cash and qualified benefits costing $2,500. Assuming that the plan fails to satisfy the eligibility test for 2006, Kent will have to include $2,500 in gross income, the greatest amount of taxable benefits that he could have received under the plan. Of that $2,500, $1,500 is allocated to the cash he received, and the other $1,000 is allocated pro rata among the qualified benefits he actually selected.[67]

.05   Cafeteria Plan Reporting Requirements

Code Sec. 6039D imposes specified reporting requirements relating to cafeteria plans and certain other fringe benefit plans. In 2002, the IRS issued Notice 2002-64[68] under which it indicated that it was suspending the reporting requirements until it evaluated whether reporting the information is appropriate. Immediately prior to the issuance of that notice, the IRS was only enforcing reporting requirements for cafeteria plans, Code Sec. 127 Educational Assistance Plans, and Code Sec. 137 Adoption Assistance Plans. Finally, the IRS in IR-2003-89 indicated it has terminated the reporting requirements for these three types of plans. It should be noted that the 2002 suspension and the 2003 termination of reporting requirements do not affect reporting requirements under ERISA.

---

[66] Code Sec. 125(b)(2).
[67] Prop. Reg. § 1.125-1, Q&A 11.

[68] 2002-1 CB 785.

Under Code Sec. 6039D(b), each employer maintaining a cafeteria plan must maintain records as may be necessary to determine whether the requirements for the applicable exclusions under the plan are being met.

¶ 403 Health Reimbursement Arrangements

A recent development in employer health plan coverage provided to employees has been the emergence of defined contribution type health plans. Such plans are similar to defined contribution retirement plans discussed in chapter 5 since employers make a set amount of contributions to the plans to cover medical and other health related expenses of employees and their dependents. If the contributed amounts are insufficient to reimburse employees for all of their expenses, the employees have to pay the rest of the costs. Until recently, there was no formal guidance from the IRS concerning the tax treatment afforded such arrangements. In 2002, the IRS broke its silence by issuing Notice 2002-45[69] and Rev. Rul. 2002-41[70] to provide guidance concerning defined contribution health plans which are specifically called health reimbursement arrangements (HRAs). The following paragraphs cover HRAs and the IRS guidance. The analysis is based upon the guidance supplied in Notice 2002-45, except where otherwise noted.

.01 Health Reimbursement Arrangements (HRAs), in General

An HRA is an employer-provided arrangement that:

(1) Is paid for solely by the employer and is not provided through a salary reduction arrangement nor under a cafeteria plan;

(2) Reimburses a covered employee for medical care expenses (as defined in Code Sec. 213) that are incurred by the employee and the employee's spouse and dependents (as defined in Code Sec. 152); and

(3) Provides reimbursements up to a specified maximum dollar amount for a coverage period and any unused portion of the maximum dollar amount that is left at the end of a coverage period can be carried forward to increase the maximum reimbursement that is available in subsequent coverage periods.

To the extent that an HRA is an employer-provided health and accident plan, the provided coverage and reimbursements provided to employees under the plan for medical expenses of the employees and their spouses and dependents are generally excludable from gross income under Code Secs. 105 and 106. In a more recent ruling,

---

[69] 2002-2 CB 93.   [70] 2002-2 CB 76.

the IRS analyzed circumstances where electronic reimbursements for medical expenses made under an HRA through the use of debit or credit cards of participants can be excluded.[71] The IRS indicated that when procedures were in place sufficient to allow for only the reimbursement of eligible medical expenses of the HRA participants, reimbursements made through debit or credit cards were permissible under the HRA and were not taxable to the recipients.

.02 Benefits Provided Under an HRA

To qualify for the exclusions allowed under Code Sees. 105 and 106, an HRA may only provide benefits that reimburse expenses for medical care as defined in Code Sec. 213(d) or for insurance covering medical care expenses as defined under Code Sec. 213(d)(1)(D). Each medical care expense that is submitted for reimbursement must be substantiated (presumably through medical care provider itemized receipts). However, an HRA may not reimburse a medical care expense that is attributable to a deduction allowed under Code Sec. 213 for any prior year (this rule would not apply for persons who took the standard deduction). Further if an HRA is also considered to be a flexible spending arrangement as defined in Code Sec. 106(b) (note that is not same type of arrangement and should be distinguished from FSAs that are provided under cafeteria plans discussed in paragraph 401 above), qualified long-term care services as defined under Code Sec. 7702B(c) may not be reimbursed under the HRA.

Reimbursements provided under an HRA will not be excludable under Code Sec. 105(b) if a covered employee or any other person has the right to receive cash of any other taxable or non-taxable benefit under the HRA other than the reimbursement of medical care expenses. If an employee or any other person has this kind of right under the arrangement for the current or any future year, all distributions to all persons made from the arrangement in the current tax year are taxable, even amounts that are paid to reimburse medical care expenses. For example, if an arrangement pays a death benefit without regard to medical care expenses, no amounts paid under the arrangement to any of the participants will be excludable. The IRS will consider arrangements that are formally outside the HRA to determine whether benefits provided under an HRA qualify for exclusion. For example, if in the year that an employee retires, he/she received a bonus that is related to that employee's maximum reimbursement remaining in an HRA, no exclusion will be permitted. Similarly, if an employer provides severance pay only to employees who have reimbursement amounts remaining in an

---

[71] Rev. Rul. 2003-43, 2003-1 CB 937.

HRA at the time of termination of employment, no amounts paid under the HRA will be excludable under Code Sec. 105(b) as reimbursements for medical care.

In early 2005, the IRS issued Revenue Ruling 2005-24,[72] in which it provides additional guidance concerning the benefits that can be provided under an HRA. In the ruling, the IRS analyzed four hypothetical situations and assessed whether the medical reimbursements in each situation were excludable. In the first situation, an employer sponsors a reimbursement plan (the Plan) that reimburses an employee solely for medical care expenses (as defined in Code Sec. 213(d)) that are substantiated. The Plan reimburses the medical care expenses of both current and former employees (including retired employees), their spouses and dependents (as defined in Code Sec. 152, determined without regard to subsections (b)(1), (b)(2), and (d)(1)(B)). The Plan also reimburses the medical care expenses of the surviving spouse and dependents of a deceased employee. No other person may receive reimbursements from the Plan. Upon the death of the deceased employee's surviving spouse and last dependent, or upon the death of the employee if there is no surviving spouse or dependents, any unused reimbursement amount is forfeited. The Plan is paid for solely by the employer and is not provided pursuant to a salary-reduction election or otherwise under a Code Sec. 125 cafeteria plan. The Plan provides reimbursements up to an annual maximum dollar amount for the coverage period, which is the plan year. The Plan reimburses medical care expenses only to the extent that the employee or the employee's spouse or dependents have not been reimbursed for the expense from any other plan.

Under the Plan, a portion of each employee's reimbursement amount available at the end of each plan year is forfeited if not used to reimburse medical expenses. The remaining unused reimbursement amount is carried forward for use in subsequent plan years. Neither the employee nor any other person has the right, currently or for any future year, to receive cash or any taxable or nontaxable benefit other than the reimbursement of medical care expenses incurred by the employee and his or her spouse and dependents.

When an employee retires, the employer automatically and on a mandatory basis (as determined under the Plan) contributes an amount to the reimbursement plan equal to the value of all or a portion of the retired employee's accumulated unused vacation and sick leave. Under no circumstances may the retired employee or the

---

[72] IRB 2005-16, 892.

retired employee's spouse or dependents receive any of the designated amount in cash or other benefits. The Plan satisfies the nondiscrimination requirements of Code Sec. 105(h) for a self-insured medical expense reimbursement plan.

The facts in the second situation are the same as the first, except the Plan provides that the employee will receive a cash payment equal to all or a portion of the unused reimbursement amount available to that employee at the end of the plan year or upon termination of employment, if earlier. The employer treats the cash payment as taxable compensation to the employee.

The facts in the third situation are the same as the first, except the Plan provides that upon the death of an employee, all or a portion of the unused reimbursement amount is paid in cash to a beneficiary or beneficiaries designated by the employee, and if no beneficiary is designated, to the deceased employee's estate.

Finally, the facts in the fourth situation are the same as in the first, except that the employer has an "option plan" which purports to be separate and apart from the reimbursement plan. Under the option plan, an employee elects, prior to the beginning of the plan year, to participate in the option plan. If an employee elects to participate in the option plan, any unused reimbursement amount available at the end of the plan year is "forfeited." However, the option plan provides that the employee may elect to transfer all or a portion of the forfeited amount to one of several retirement plans or to receive the amount as a cash payment. If an employee does not elect to participate in the option plan, any reimbursement amount unused at the end of the plan year is carried forward for use in future plan years.

Based on an analysis of Notice 2002-45 and other applicable authorities, the IRS held that the reimbursement plan described in the first situation is an HRA that meets the requirements for tax-favored treatment under Code Secs. 105(b) and 106. The Plan is an employer-provided accident or health plan under Code Sec. 106 and payments are limited solely to reimbursements of substantiated medical care expenses incurred by current and former employees and their spouses and dependents. No person has the right, currently or in the future, to receive cash or any other taxable or nontaxable benefit under the Plan other than the reimbursement of medical care expenses as required by Code Sec. 105(b).

On the other hand, the reimbursement plans described in the last three situations do not meet the requirements for tax-favored treatment. The Plan in the second situation provides for a cash payment equal to all or a portion of the unused reimbursement amount available at the end of the plan year or upon termination of employment, if earlier. The Plan in the third situation provides for a death benefit upon the death of the employee of all or a portion of the unused reimbursement amount without regard to medical care expenses. The Plan in the fourth situation permits conversion of unused reimbursement amounts to cash or other benefits regardless of whether or not medical expenses have been incurred. Although the option plan in the fourth situation purports to be formally outside the reimbursement arrangement, the option plan and the reimbursement arrangement constitute one plan. Therefore, since the Plans in the last three situations pay amounts "irrespective" of whether medical care expenses have been incurred, no amount paid under the Plans to any person is excludable from gross income under Code Sec. 105(b).

.03 Coverage Under an HRA

Medical care expense reimbursements under an HRA are excludable under Code Sec. 105(b) to the extent that the reimbursements are provided with respect to medical expenses deductible under Code Sec 213 to the following individuals: (1) current and former employees (including retired employees), their spouses and dependents (as defined in Code Sec. 152 as modified by the last sentence in Code Sec. 105(b)) and (2) the spouses and dependents of deceased employees. Self-employed individuals as defined in Code Sec. 401(c) are not considered employees for this purpose, and, thus, cannot be eligible participants in HRAs.

An HRA may continue to reimburse former employees or retired employees for medical care expenses after they terminate employment or retire (even if the employee does not elect COBRA continuation coverage—see the discussion of COBRA continuation coverage in ¶ 302.04). For example, an HRA may provide reimbursement to a former employee for medical expenses up to the remaining amount in that employee's HRA account when that employee retires or terminates employment. Rev. Rul. 2002-41 provides an example of a plan allowing for the use of carried over amounts under an HRA by terminated employees and retirees and indicates that reimbursements of medical expenses from those carried over amounts are excludable. An HRA may also provide that the maximum reimbursement amount remaining at retirement may be reduced for any administrative costs of continuing such coverage. An HRA may provide additional employer contributions following an employee's retirement or termination of employment (this is true even if the employee does not elect COBRA continuation coverage).

.04 HRAs and Cafeteria Plans

Employer contributions to an HRA may not come from or be attributable to salary reduction contributions or otherwise provided under a cafeteria plan (see cafeteria plans as covered in ¶401). A plan funded using salary reduction contributions is subject to the cafeteria plan rules. However, an HRA will not be treated as having been paid for by salary reduction amounts merely because it is provided in conjunction with a cafeteria plan (i.e., the HRA and cafeteria plan are separate plans). Additionally, if an employer offers employees a choice between employer-provided non-taxable benefits (e.g., coverage under an HRA and coverage under a health maintenance organization (HMO)), with no cash or other taxable benefits available, that choice is not considered a cafeteria plan election.

If an employer provides an HRA only in conjunction with another health and accident plan and that other plan is provided on a salary reduction basis under a cafeteria plan, then all of the facts and circumstances have to be considered in ascertaining whether the salary reduction election is attributable to the HRA. Assuming that the terms of the salary reduction agreement indicate that the reduction is to be used only to provide the other health coverage and not to pay for coverage under the HRA, the fact that an employee can participate in the HRA only if he/she elects the other coverage will not necessarily result in the salary reduction being attributed to the HRA. In such cases, if the salary reduction election for a coverage period to fund the specified health and accident plan offered in conjunction with the HRA exceeds the actual cost of the specified health and accident plan for that coverage period, the salary reduction is attributable to the HRA. For this purpose, the actual cost of the other coverage can be pegged to the cost of the COBRA coverage for the period.

For the sole of purpose of determining whether a salary reduction election exceeds the cost of coverage during any coverage period, the actual cost of the specified accident or health plan coverage for the coverage period may be determined using the rules for determining the COBRA continuation coverage applicable premium under Code Sec. 4980B(f)(4). For example, assume that an employer offers an HRA and an employee who participates in that HRA also has to participate in corresponding employee-only or family coverage offered in a high-deductible health and accident plan. If the COBRA applicable premium for the high-deductible health and accident coverage would be $1,800 for the employee-only coverage and $4,500 for family coverage if that coverage were offered separately from the HRA, then the annual maximum allowable salary reduction election in this case is the $1,800 or $4,500 depending on the level of coverage in order for the salary reduction to be treated as not attributable to the HRA.

In an addition, an arrangement will not be treated as an HRA if that arrangement interacts with a cafeteria plan in a way that permits employees to use salary reduction amounts to indirectly fund the HRA. Therefore, if (1) an employee participating in a reimbursement arrangement has a choice among two or more specified health and accident plans to be used in conjunction with the reimbursement arrangement (or a choice among various maximum reimbursement amounts credited for a coverage period) and (2) there is a correlation between (a) the maximum amount available under the HRA for the coverage period (disregarding any amounts carried over from previous periods) and (b) the amount of salary reduction election for the specified health and accident plan, then the salary reduction is attributed to the reimbursement arrangement. This rule applies even if the amount of salary reduction election is equal to or less than the actual cost of the other health and accident coverage.

Example: An employer offers a reimbursement arrangement plus other specified health and accident plan coverage that costs $4,500 for family coverage. The employee is given a choice to reduce his/her salary by $2,500 or $3,500 to pay for this coverage. An employee who elects family coverage and the $2,500 salary reduction receives a $1,000 maximum reimbursement amount under the reimbursement arrangement for the coverage period, whereas an employee who elects family coverage and the $3,500 salary reduction receives a $2,000 maximum reimbursement amount. Although the maximum allowable salary reduction is not exceeded, a portion of the salary reduction is attributed to the reimbursement arrangement because the increase in salary reduction is related to a larger maximum reimbursement amount in the reimbursement arrangement for the coverage period. Therefore, the described reimbursement arrangement is not an HRA and is subject to the Code Sec. 125 cafeteria plan rules.

Finally, the IRS indicates that a reimbursement arrangement will not qualify as an HRA if the amount credited to the reimbursement arrangement is directly or indirectly tied to amounts forfeited under a Code Sec. 125 health flexible spending arrangement (FSA— see the discussion of FSAs at ¶ 402.02). For purposes of making this determination, such considerations as the manner in which salary reduction is implemented for other health and accident plans offered by the employer will be taken into account.

.05 HRAs and Flexible Spending Arrangements (FSAs)

HRAs are closely related to health flexible spending arrangements (FSAs) that were covered in ¶402.02 in the discussion of cafeteria plans. Recall that FSAs permit employees to direct that specified amounts be withheld from their salary on a pre-tax basis to be used to pay medical expenses that are not otherwise reimbursed and that are incurred during the FSA coverage period. Because HRAs are paid solely through employer contributions and not pursuant to salary reduction amounts, the IRS indicates that the following restrictions on health FSAs under the Code Sec. 125 proposed regulations do not apply to HRAs:

(1) The prohibition against being able to carry over unused salary reduction FSA contributions (in situations where the amount of medical expenses submitted for reimbursement is less than the contributions made to the FSA) from one coverage period to the next—unused HRA contributions can be carried over as indicated in an example presented by the IRS in Rev. Rul. 2002-41;

(2) The requirement that the maximum amount of reimbursement must be available throughout the coverage period—the maximum reimbursement for a coverage period (not including amounts carried over from previous coverage periods) does not have to be available throughout the coverage period;

(3) The mandatory twelve-month period of coverage—HRAs may specify a coverage period that is shorter than 12 months; and

(4) The general limitation that expenses reimbursed must be incurred during the period of coverage—under an HRA, claims incurred during one coverage period may be reimbursed in another coverage period provided that the employee requesting the reimbursement was covered under the HRA when the claim was incurred.

Additionally, the maximum reimbursement amount credited under an HRA in the future (not including amounts carried forward from previous coverage periods) may be increased or decreased. But, with respect to such increases, employers should take into account the provisions of Reg. § 1.105-11(c)(3)(ii) regarding operational discrimination in favor of highly compensated individuals under self-insured health plans (see the discussion of those nondiscrimination rules in ¶302.04) because such increases with respect to highly compensated employees may violate the nondiscrimination rules.

A medical care expense may not be reimbursed from a Code Sec. 125 health FSA if the expense has been reimbursed or can be reimbursed under any other health or accident plan including an HRA. If coverage is provided to an employee under both an HRA and a health FSA for the same medical care expenses, the IRS requires that amounts under the FSA must be exhausted before reimbursements may be made from the FSA. However, an FSA may reimburse an expense that is not covered by the HRA. In no case may an employee be reimbursed for the same medical care expense by both an HRA and a health FSA.

Finally, the IRS does provide a reasonable planning opportunity for employers that want to offer both an HRA and health FSA for their employees taking into account the rules discussed in the previous paragraph. The IRS indicates that prior to the beginning of a health FSA plan coverage year, the employer could indicate in the HRA plan documents that HRA reimbursements could only be used for medical care expenses of an employee that exceed the amount available for reimbursements under the FSA.

.06 Other Rules Affecting HRAs

The IRS indicates that HRAs are subject to a number of other rules that apply to health and accident plans. These rules include:

(1) The Code Sec. 105(h) nondiscrimination rules applicable to self-insured medical reimbursement plans as applied under Reg. § 1.105-11-to the extent an HRA is a self-insured medical reimbursement plan, the nondiscrimination rules of Code Sec. 105(h) apply;

(2) The COBRA continuation coverage rules of Code Sec. 4980B—an HRA is a group health plan generally subject to the COBRA continuation requirements (as discussed in ¶ 302.04). Thus, an HRA complies with the COBRA requirements by providing for the continuation of the maximum reimbursement amount for an individual at the time of the COBRA qualifying event and by increasing the maximum amount at the same time and by the same increment that it is increased for similarly situated non-COBRA beneficiaries (and by decreasing it for claims reimbursed). However, an HRA may provide for continued reimbursements after the COBRA qualifying event regardless of whether a qualified beneficiary elects continuation coverage.

(3) The deduction limitations under Code Secs. 419 and 419A (for employer contributions to welfare benefit funds to the extent an HRA is part of such a plan—see ¶ 404.05 below) and under Code Sec. 404 (for amounts paid or accrued under plans providing for deferred amounts that are not provided through a welfare benefit fund);

(4) The application of the nondiscrimination requirements under the Health Insurance Portability and Accountability Act of

1996—Code Secs. 9801–9803, 9811, and 9812 as discussed in ¶302.04—including the extent to which underwritten individual health insurance policies purchased and reimbursed by an HRA are treated as health insurance coverage offered under a group health plan; and

(5) The requirements for welfare benefit plans under the Employee Retirement Income Security Act of 1974 (ERISA).

See ¶302.04 for a discussion of the relationship of HRAs, health FSAs and Health Savings Accounts (HSAs).

¶404   Voluntary Employee Benefit Associations (VEBAs) and Welfare Benefit Plans

Another vehicle through which an employer can provide executives and other employees with life insurance, health and accident benefits, and other fringe benefits is the welfare benefit plan, of which the most common form is the VEBA. Under a VEBA or other welfare benefit plan, the employer makes contributions to the plan which, in turn, pays benefits to employee-participants according to the terms of the plan. This section of the chapter covers VEBAs, including the statutory and regulatory requirements that VEBAs must satisfy, the nondiscrimination standards that must be satisfied, and the rules governing taxation of employees under the plans. In addition, the rules governing the deductions for employer contributions to VEBAs and other welfare benefit plans are discussed.

.01   Definition of a VEBA

A VEBA is a tax-exempt organization which provides for the payment of life, sick, accident, or similar benefits to the members of the VEBA and/or their dependents.[73] Under a VEBA, no part of the net earnings can inure (other than through the payment of permitted benefits) to the benefit of any private shareholder or individual. To achieve tax-exempt status, a VEBA must satisfy a number of specific requirements.

.02   Statutory and Regulatory Requirements for VEBAs

In general, a VEBA must satisfy the following four basic requirements:

(1) the organization is an association of employees;

(2) the membership in the association is voluntary;

(3) the organization provides for the payment of life, sick, accident, or other benefits to its members and/or their dependents or

---

[73] Code Sec. 501(c)(9).

beneficiaries, and substantially all of its operations are to provide such benefits; and

(4) no part of the net earnings of the association can inure (other than through the payment of permitted benefits) to the benefit of any private shareholder or individual.[74]

In considering the basic requirements above, questions can arise concerning the meaning of specific terms such as the meaning of the term "membership," the meaning of the term "voluntary," and the meaning of other key terms. These issues are covered below.

Meaning of Membership. The membership of a VEBA must consist of individuals (1) who are entitled to participate because they are employees and (2) whose eligibility for membership is defined by objective standards that constitute a "common employment-related bond" between the individuals.[75] The regulations provide that membership is typically defined according to the following objective standards:

(1) a common employer or affiliated employers;

(2) coverage under one or more collective bargaining agreements (with respect to benefits provided by reason of such agreements);

(3) membership in a labor union or in one or more locals of a national or international labor union; or

(4) one or more employers engaged in the same line of business in the same geographic locale.[76]

> **Example:** Membership in a VEBA that is open to all employees of a particular employer would satisfy the guidelines. Or, membership might be open to employees at specific locations and who are entitled to benefits because of one or more collective bargaining agreements.

With respect to the geographic locale requirement (number 4 above), it should be noted that the Seventh Circuit Court of Appeals has ruled that the geographic requirement unreasonably narrows the scope of the exemption granted to VEBAs and is thus invalid.[77] While the IRS has not withdrawn this requirement in its final regulations, it has issued proposed regulations creating a three-state safe harbor for determining if an area is a single geographic

---

[74] Reg. § 1.501(c)(9)-1.
[75] Reg. § 1.501(c)(9)-2(a).
[76] Reg. § 1.501(c)(9)-2(a)(1).

[77] *Water Quality Association Employees' Benefit Corp.*, CA-7, 86-2 USTC ¶ 9527, 795 F2d 1303.

area.[78] An area is a single geographic locale if it does not exceed the boundaries of three contiguous states. Under this rule, three states are contiguous if each one shares a land or river border with at least one of the others. Alaska and Hawaii are considered to be contiguous with each other and with Washington, Oregon, and California.[79]

The IRS also has the authority to recognize some other specified area as a single geographic locale if: (1) it would not be economically feasible to cover employees of employers engaged in that line of business in that area under two or more separate VEBAs, each extending over fewer states, and (2) employment characteristics in that line of business, population characteristics, or other regional factors support the particular states included. This requirement is met if the states are contiguous.[80]

The regulations also permit a VEBA to include a limited number of persons who are not employees if those persons share an employee-related common bond with the employee-members.[81] Further, the regulations limit the number of nonemployees that can be members of a VEBA by requiring that 90 percent of the total membership of the VEBA on one day of each quarter of the VEBA's taxable year must consist of employees.

> **Example:** Persons who are eligible for membership in a VEBA can include employees of the VEBA, employees of a union whose members are included in a VEBA, and the proprietor of a business whose employees are members of a VEBA.

Meaning of Voluntary. Membership in a VEBA must be voluntary. The regulations state that membership is voluntary if an affirmative act is required on the part of an employee to become a member.[82] However, a VEBA will be considered voluntary although membership is required of all employees if the employees do not incur a detriment (for example, through deductions from pay) as a result of membership in the VEBA. In addition, an employer is not deemed to be the victim of imposed involuntary membership if membership is required as the result of a collective bargaining agreement or as an incident of membership in a labor organization.

Meaning of Employees. The regulations define the term "employee" for purposes of the VEBA rules in a broader sense

---

[78] Notice of Proposed Rulemaking, EE-23-92 (Aug. 6.1992).

[79] Prop. Reg. § 1.501(c)(9)-2(d)(1).

[80] Prop. Reg. § 1.501(c)(9)-2(d)(2).

[81] Reg. § 1.501(c)(9)-2(a)(1).

[82] Reg. § 1.501(c)(9)-2(c)(2).

than the common-law definition. Under Reg. § 1.501(c)(9)-2(b), the term "employee" includes the following:

(1) an individual who is considered an employee for employment tax purposes or for purposes of a collective bargaining agreement;

(2) an individual who became entitled to membership in the VEBA by reason of being or having been an employee. Thus an individual will continue to qualify as an employee even though the individual is on a leave of absence, works temporarily for another employer or as an independent contractor, or has been terminated because of retirement, disability, or layoff; and

(3) the surviving spouse and dependents of an employee.

Comment: The broad definition of the term "employee" in the regulations gives VEBAs considerable leeway to provide benefits to all persons who have any reasonable employment-related common bond. Therefore, disputes between the IRS and VEBAs concerning this matter should be rare.

A VEBA can maintain its tax-exempt status even if some of its members are not employees provided that the nonemployee members maintain an employment-related bond with the employee members. Under a safe-harbor rule in the regulations, a VEBA can include nonemployees if at least 90 percent of its members are employees on one day of each quarter of the tax year of the VEBA.[83] For example, outside directors of a corporation can belong to a VEBA under this rule. The IRS has indicated that the 90 percent rule of the regulations is more than a safe-harbor rule because it is the only meaningful standard concerning the membership of nonemployees.[84]

Control Requirement. A VEBA cannot be controlled by an employer. The regulations state that a VEBA must be controlled by (1) its membership, (2) an independent trustee or trustees, such as a bank, or (3) trustees or other fiduciaries at least some of whom are designated by, or on behalf of, the membership.[85] For these purposes, a VEBA will be considered controlled by independent trustees if it is an "employee welfare benefit plan," as defined in Sec. 3(1) of ERISA and, thus, subject to the reporting and disclosure requirements and fiduciary responsibility rules of ERISA.

Similarly, a plan will be considered to be controlled by its membership when the membership, either directly or through its representatives, designates a person or persons to serve as chief

---

[83] Reg § 1.501(c)(9)-2(a)(1).
[84] GCM 39835, Dec. 11, 1990

[85] Reg. § 1.501(c)(9)-2(c)(3).

operating officer, administrator or trustee of the VEBA.[86] In addition, the control requirement is met if the VEBA is controlled by one or more trustees designated under a collective bargaining agreement.

> **Example:** Pursuant to a collective bargaining agreement, a VEBA is established to provide health benefits for employees of the employer. Under the collective bargaining agreement, two persons, Smith and Jones, were designated to serve as trustees. The control requirement is met.

An example of a VEBA that did not meet the control requirement is the case of a plan controlled by trustees who were appointed by a self-perpetuating board of directors, instead of a board designated by the plan members.[87] In addition, a plan that limited the trustee to a custodial role whereby benefit payments were required to be authorized by the employer failed to meet the control requirement.[88]

Definition of Association. According to Reg. § 1.501(c)(9)-2, a VEBA is an entity that has an existence independent of the member-employees and their employer. A VEBA may take the form of a nonprofit corporation or tax-exempt trust, as noted above.

Permissible Recipients of Benefits. The permissible benefits from a VEBA must only be paid or provided to the members of the VEBA and their dependents or their designated beneficiaries.[89] For this purpose, the term "dependent" means the following:

(1) the member's spouse;

(2) any child of the member or the member's spouse who is either a minor or a student (within the meaning of Code Sec. 151(e)(4));

(3) any other minor child residing with the member; and

(4) any other individual who a VEBA, relying on information furnished to it by a member, in good faith, believes is a person described in Code Sec. 152(a) (i.e., a relative).

Permissible Benefits. In general, a VEBA is permitted to provide life, sick, accident, or other similar benefits in the form of cash or noncash benefits.[90] For example, sick and accident benefits

---

[86] *Id.*

[87] *American Assn. of Christian Schools VEBA Welfare Trust,* CA-11, 88-2 USTC ¶9452, 850 F2d 1510. Aff'g DC-Ala., 87-1 USTC ¶9328, 663 F Supp 275.

[88] *Lima Surgical Associates, Inc. VEBA Plan Trust,* CtCls, 91-2 USTC ¶50,473, 944 F2d 885, 20 CtCls 674.

[89] Reg. § 1.501(c)(9)-3(a).

[90] *Id.*

¶ 404.02

can be furnished by providing clinical care services by visiting nurses and transportation furnished for medical care.[91]

A VEBA must operate primarily to provide permissible benefits.[92] A VEBA will not be qualified if it systematically and knowingly provides nonpermissible benefits of more than a de minimis amount.

The term "life benefit" means a benefit, including a burial benefit or wreath, payable by reason of the death of a member or dependent.[93] A life benefit may be provided directly by the VEBA or through insurance. In general, only term insurance protection can be provided. However, the benefit may also include a right to convert to individual coverage on termination of eligibility for coverage through the association, or a permanent benefit pursuant to the Code Sec. 79 regulations. In addition, a life benefit includes the benefit provided under any life insurance contract purchased directly from an employee-funded VEBA by a member or provided by the association to a member.[94] A benefit payable on account of death can be settled in either lump-sum or annuity form. A VEBA can provide whole-life coverage that does not meet the conditions for group-term life insurance if the policies are owned by the VEBA and are funded by level premiums over the expected lives or working lives of the employees, and the cash reserves accrue to the VEBA.[95] Finally, the IRS has privately ruled that self-funded paid-up life insurance constitutes a qualified benefit even if the state insurance authority does not consider paid-up life insurance to be life insurance. The paid-up life insurance is a qualified benefit because the payment of the benefit under the plan only comes due upon the unanticipated death of a member.[96]

"Sick and accident benefits" are amounts furnished to or on behalf of a member or member's dependents in the event of illness or personal injury to a member or dependent.[97] Similarly, amounts paid to a member in lieu of income during a period in which the member is unable to work due to sickness or injury and benefits designed to safeguard or improve the health of members and their dependents are "sick and accident benefits." The benefits can be paid directly to members or their dependents or through the payment of premiums or fees to an insurance company, medical clinic, or similar entity. The IRS has privately held that health benefits paid to nondependent domestic partners of plan participants, while ordinarily a nonpermissible benefit, would not affect the VEBA's

---

[91] Reg. § 1.501(c)(9)-3(c).
[92] Reg. § 1.501(c)(9)-3(a).
[93] Reg. § 1.501(c)(9)-3(b).
[94] Id.

[95] GCM 39440, Nov. 7, 1985.
[96] IRS Letter Ruling 199930040, 4-7-99, CCH IRS LETTER RULINGS REPORTS.
[97] Reg. § 1.501(c)(9)-3(c).

tax-exempt status where the total amount of benefits paid to such nondependent domestic partners did not exceed three percent of the total benefits paid by the plan and were, thus, considered to be de minimis.[98] Similarly, the IRS gave the same ruling in a situation where the cost of providing health coverage to nondependent domestic partners ranged from about two percent to between 2.88 percent and 3.31 percent of the VEBA's total benefit expenditures.[99] In addition, the IRS has held that home health care and long-term care benefits provided under a VEBA constitute qualified benefits since both constitute medical benefits under Code Sec. 213(d)(1).[100]

Under Reg. § 1.501(c)(9)-3(d), "other benefits" include only benefits that are similar to life, sick, or accident benefits. For this purpose, a benefit is similar if: (1) it is intended to safeguard or improve the health of a member or a member's dependents, or (2) it protects against a contingency that interrupts or impairs a member's earning power. Examples of "other benefits" include the following:

(1) paying vacation benefits;

(2) providing vacation facilities;

(3) reimbursing vacation expenses;

(4) subsidizing recreational activities, such as athletic leagues;

(5) providing child-care facilities for preschool and school-age dependents;

(6) providing job readjustment allowances;

(7) providing income maintenance payments in the event of economic dislocation;

(8) providing temporary living expense loans and grants at times of disaster (such as fires and floods);

(9) paying supplemental unemployment compensation benefits defined in Code Sec. 501(c)(17)(D);

(10) paying severance benefits under a severance pay plan within the meaning of 29 C.F.R. § 2510.3-2(b); and

(11) providing educational or training benefits or courses, such as apprentice training programs.[101]

Severance pay benefits under a severance pay plan that meet specified conditions can be considered other benefits.[102] Among

---

[98] IRS Letter Ruling 9850011, 9-10-98, CCH IRS LETTER RULINGS REPORTS.

[99] IRS Letter Ruling 200108010, 11-17-00, CCH IRS LETTER RULINGS REPORTS.

[100] IRS Letter Ruling 200028007, 4-10-00, CCH IRS LETTER RULINGS REPORTS.

[101] Reg. § 1.501(c)(9)-3(e).

[102] GCM 39879, Jan. 6, 1986.

the conditions that severance pay plans must meet are that the payments must not be directly or indirectly contingent, upon an employee's retirement and the payments must not exceed twice an employee's most recent annual compensation. For example, the Court of Appeals for the Federal Circuit held that a plan which provided severance benefits to participants whose employment was terminated for any reason except death was providing nonqualifying benefits.[103] The court held that the severance payments were contingent directly or indirectly upon the employee's retirement, and hence, did not qualify as "other benefits." The court concluded that the subject plan pays retirement benefits which are nonqualifying benefits as noted below.

Recently, the IRS privately held that social, cultural, and recreational benefits provided by a VEBA to retired members constituted permissable benefits because the benefits and related activities provided by the VEBA are similar to the "other benefits" listed above.[104] The IRS indicated that the benefits were intended to safeguard or improve the health of the retired members. Among the benefits and activities that were held to be permissable included arts and crafts classes, exercise classes, bowling, and bingo, with canned goods distributed as prizes.

Nonqualifying Benefits. Under Reg. § 1.501(c)(9)-3(f), nonqualifying benefits include the following:

(1) paying commuting expenses (such as bridge tolls or train fares);

(2) providing accident or homeowner's insurance benefits for damage to property;

(3) providing malpractice insurance;[105]

(4) providing loans to members except in times of distress;

(5) providing savings facilities to members;

(6) paying any benefit similar to a pension or annuity at the time of voluntary or mandatory retirement; and

(7) paying any benefit similar to that provided by a stock bonus or profit-sharing plan.

A benefit will be considered similar to that provided under a pension, annuity, stock bonus, or profit-sharing benefit if it provides for deferred compensation that becomes payable by reason of the

---

[103] *Lima Surgical Associates, Inc.*, CA-FC, 91-2 USTC ¶50,473, 944 F2d 885. Aff'g 90-1 USTC ¶50,329, 20 ClsCt 674.

[104] IRS Letter Ruling 9802038, 10-14-97, CCH IRS LETTER RULINGS REPORTS.

[105] *See* e.g., *Anesthesia Service Medical Group Inc.*, 85 TC 1031. Dec. 42,556 (1985), in which the Tax Court held to be valid the part of Reg. § 1.501(c)(9)-3(f) holding that the provision of malpractice insurance is a nonqualifying benefit.

¶404.02

passage of time, rather than as the result of an unanticipated event.[106]

> **Example:** Annuity benefits payable upon and after retirement are not qualifying benefits. However, supplemental unemployment benefits that become payable on account of an unanticipated layoff are permissible benefits because they are payable by reason of an unanticipated event, and not on account of the passage of time.

Inurement Prohibited. No part of the net earnings of a VEBA can inure to the benefit of any private shareholder or individual other than through the payment of permissible benefits.[107] Prohibited inurement is to be determined with reference to all of the facts and circumstances of a particular case. The regulation states that the following transactions generally will constitute prohibited inurement:

(1) the disposition of property to, or the performance of services for, a person for less than the greater of fair market value or cost to the VEBA, other than as a life, sick, accident, or other permissible benefit;

(2) the payment of unreasonable compensation to the trustees or employees of the VEBA; or

(3) the purchase of insurance or services for amounts in excess of their fair market value from a company in which one or more of the VEBA's trustees, officers, or fiduciaries have an interest.

Prohibited inurement may also be considered to occur if it appears from the facts and circumstances that the employer is operating the VEBA for the employer's own advantage or for the primary benefit of the owner or owners of the employer.[108] However, even though a high percentage of benefits under a plan may be paid to the owners of the employer, the plan may be a tax-exempt VEBA where the funding of the plan is actuarially sound, the assets are prudently invested, the benefits that were provided were commensurate with the compensation and ages of the plan's members, the funds in the plan would not revert to the employer, and the plan generated sufficient income to pay for the benefits under the plan.[109] The IRS has recently privately held that the transfer of assets

---

[106] Reg. § 1.501(c)(9)-3(f). *See also Canton Police Benevolent Assn. of Canton, Ohio*, CA-6, 88-1 USTC ¶ 9285, 844 F2d 1231. Aff'g DC-Ohio, 87-1 USTC ¶ 9209 and *Bricklayers Benefit Plans of Delaware Valley Inc.*, 81 TC 735, Dec. 40,543 (1983).

[107] Reg. § 1.501(c)(9)-4.

[108] *Sunrise Construction Co.. Inc.*, 52 TCM 1358, Dec. 43,625(M), TC Memo. 1987-21. Aff'd CA-9 (unpublished opinion 11/21/88).

[109] *W.L. Moser*, Dec. 45,583(M), 56 TCM 1604, TC Memo. 1989-142. Aff'd on other issue, CA-8, 90-2 USTC ¶ 50,498.

¶ 404.02

between two VEBAs within an employing company would not constitute prohibited inurement.[110] The assets of the first VEBA were made available to provide benefits on a nondiscriminatory manner to employees of the company covered by the second VEBA, after the employing company sold an operating division to another company, and all of the employees of that division (who were covered by the first VEBA) went to work for that other company. The transfer of assets did not constitute prohibited inurement since the assets of the first VEBA were not being returned to the employing company, but instead were being expended by the second VEBA for employee welfare benefits.

The regulations state that the rebate of excess insurance premiums, based on the mortality or morbidity experience of the insurer to which premiums were paid, to the person whose contributions were applied to such premiums, does not constitute prohibited inurement.[111] In addition, a VEBA may make administrative adjustments strictly incidental to the provision of benefits to its members.

Recordkeeping. Under Reg. § 1.501(c)(9)-5, every VEBA must maintain records indicating the amount contributed by each member and contributing employer, and the amount and type of benefits paid by the VEBA to or on behalf of each member. In addition, a VEBA must maintain records concerning any unrelated business taxable income and must comply with the provisions concerning information returns on account of payments pursuant to Code Sec. 6041.

.03 Nondiscrimination Rules

The Tax Reform Act of 1984 (TRA '84) established statutory coverage and benefits nondiscrimination standards for VEBAs and qualified group legal service organizations (GLSOs). Essentially, these nondiscrimination rules are similar to those applicable to other employee benefits, such as those for medical reimbursement plans under Code Sec. 105(h). A VEBA or GLSO will not be exempt from tax under Code Sec. 501(a) unless the plan meets the Code Sec. 505(b) nondiscrimination requirements.[112] However, this rule does not apply to an organization that is part of a plan maintained pursuant to a good-faith collective bargaining agreement.[113]

---

[110] IRS Letter Ruling 200122047, 6-4-01. CCH IRS LETTER RULINGS REPORTS and IRS Letter Ruling 200122051, 6-4-01, CCH IRS LETTER RULINGS REPORTS. *See also* IRS Letter Ruling 200225041, 3-25-02, CCH IRS LETTER RULINGS REPORTS and IRS Letter Ruling 200301030, 9-30-02, CCH IRS LETTER RULINGS REPORTS.

[111] Reg. § 1.501(c)(9)-4(c).
[112] Code Sec. 505 (a).
[113] Code Sec. 505(a)(2). *See* IRS Letter Ruling 9640024, 7-9-96, CCH IRS LETTER RULINGS REPORTS for an example of a situation where the IRS held a VEBA was exempt from the nondiscrimination rules because the collective bargaining agreement exception was met.

Code Sec. 505(b)(1) provides that the coverage of a VEBA or GLSO must be nondiscriminatory and benefits must be provided on a nondiscriminatory basis. A VEBA or GLSO is nondiscriminatory only if (1) each class of benefits is made available to a classification of employees set forth in the plan and is found by the IRS to not favor the highly compensated, and (2) each class of benefits is not provided in a manner that discriminates in favor of highly compensated employees. However, a life insurance, disability, severance pay, or supplemental unemployment compensation benefit will not fail to meet the nondiscrimination tests merely because the benefits available bear a uniform relationship to the total compensation, or the basic or regular rate of compensation, of employees covered by the plan.[114] In addition, a VEBA plan is considered discriminatory if the annual compensation taken into account under the plan for any year exceeds $200,000, as adjusted for inflation after 2002 (the 2005 inflation adjusted amount is $210,000).[115] The compensation dollar limit does not apply, however, if, under the VEBA administration rule, a plan must meet the Code Sec. 79 group-term life insurance nondiscrimination rules (as discussed in Chapter 3).

In testing whether a plan is discriminatory, certain employees may be excluded from consideration. Under Code Sec. 505(b)(2), employees who (1) have not attained the age of 21, (2) have not completed three years of service with the employer, (3) work less than half-time, (4) are included in a collective bargaining unit (if the benefits involved have been the subject of good-faith bargaining), or (5) are nonresident aliens, may be excluded.

Highly compensated individuals are defined in the same manner as under Code Sec. 414(q), which provides the definition of highly compensated employees for qualified deferred compensation purposes (see Chapter 6).[116]

If any benefit provided by a VEBA or GLSO is covered by nondiscrimination provisions specifically under some other Code section, those specific provisions take precedence over the requirements of Code Sec. 505(b)(1). However, the nondiscrimination provisions of Code Sec. 505 will be met in such cases only if the specific nondiscrimination requirements for the benefit are satisfied.[117]

---

[114] Code Sec. 505(b)(1).
[115] Code Sec. 505(b)(7), as amended by P.L. 107-16, 107th Cong., 1st Sess., Sec. 611(c)(1) (June 7, 2001). IR 2004-127, 10/20/2004.

[116] Code Sec. 505(b).

[117] Code Sec. 505(b)(3).

¶ 404.03

Finally, Code Sec. 505(b)(4) provides that, in testing a VEBA or GLSO for discrimination, employers may elect to treat two or more plans as one plan.

.04 Taxation of Benefits Received Under VEBAs

There are no specific statutory rules, other than those under the nondiscrimination rules described above, that cover the taxation of benefits received by employees and their dependents under VEBAs. Instead, the taxation of each particular benefit received is based on the taxation rules applicable to that benefit under the Code. For example, reimbursements received by an employee from a VEBA on account of medical expenses incurred by the employee would be excludable under Code Sec. 105(b). Also, the IRS has privately held that scholarships provided by a VEBA were not excludable from gross income based on the fact that the requirements for exclusion under Code Sec. 117 were not met.[118] In another ruling, the IRS held that while the value of health coverage provided under a VEBA to domestic partners of covered employees constituted qualified benefits, the value of such coverage was includible in the employee's gross income since it is not excludable under Code Sec. 106.[119]

.05 Deduction for Employer Contributions to Welfare Benefit Plans

If employer contributions to a welfare benefit plan qualify as ordinary and necessary business expenses, they are deductible under Code Sec. 419 in the year paid to the extent the contributions do not exceed the "qualified cost" of the welfare benefit fund for the fund's taxable year that relates to the employer's taxable year.[120] This limitation applies to employer contributions made after 1985. (Note that prior to 1986, there was virtually no limit on the deduction for contributions made to welfare benefit plans.)[121]

"Qualified cost" is the sum of the "qualified direct cost" of the plan plus any allowable addition to "qualified asset account" minus the welfare benefit fund's "after-tax income."[122] Carryovers of excess contributions are permitted.[123]

Welfare Benefit Fund Defined. Under Code Sec. 419(e)(1), a "welfare benefit fund" is any "fund" which is part of an employer's plan and through which the employer provides "welfare benefits" to employees or their beneficiaries.

---

[118] IRS Letter Ruling 200043007, 7-22-00, CCH IRS LETTER RULINGS REPORTS.
[119] IRS Letter Ruling 200108010, 11-17-00, CCH IRS LETTER RULINGS REPORTS.

[120] Temp. Reg. § 1.419-IT Q&A 4.
[121] TRA '84, Sec. 511(e).
[122] Code Sec. 419(c).
[123] Code Sec. 419(d).

Welfare benefits do not include the following:

(1) benefits paid under deferred compensation plans (to which Code Sec. 404 or 404A applies); and

(2) transfers of restricted property covered under Code Sec. 83.[124]

In general, allowable welfare benefits include sickness, accident, hospitalization, medical expense, some life insurance, severance pay, and unemployment benefits.

Under Code Sec. 419(e)(3), a "fund" includes the following:

(1) a tax-exempt social club, a VEBA, a supplemental unemployment benefits compensation trust, or a GLSO;

(2) any trust, corporation, or other organization not exempt from tax; and

(3) as provided in regulation, any account held for any employer by any person.

However, the term "fund" does not include (1) amounts held by an insurance contract on the life of an officer, employee, or person financially interested in the employer's trade or business if the employer is the direct or indirect beneficiary of the policy, or (2) amounts held under certain "qualified nonguaranteed insurance contracts."[125]

According to Code Sec. 419(c)(3), the "qualified direct cost" with respect to any taxable year is the aggregate amount which would have been allowable as a deduction to the employer if the benefits under the plan had been directly provided by the employer and the employer had used the cash method of accounting. Thus, a deduction is allowed for benefits paid out by the fund. On that basis, the IRS has ruled that an employer may not deduct vacation pay in the year it was accrued by a welfare benefit plan where the accrued amounts were not paid until the next year.[126]

In addition, qualified direct cost includes properly allocable administrative costs and insurance premiums.[127]

> **Example (1):** Under a non-insured medical reimbursement plan, the qualified direct cost would not only include the actual medical expense reimbursements made by the plan, but also a properly allocable share of the administrative costs.

If depreciable property is owned by the fund, the employer can take a deduction for the amount of depreciation that would have

---

[124] Code Sec. 419(e)(2).
[125] Code Sec. 419(e)(4).

[126] FSA 200009010.
[127] Temp. Reg. § 1.419-1T, Q&A 6.

¶ 404.05

been allowed if the employer had directly owned the property. With respect to child-care facilities, the cost of the facility is deductible using the straight-line amortization method over 60 months.[128]

Note that the rules which limit the amount of deductible business expenses also apply in the case of determining qualified direct cost. Thus, contributions by the employer that are used by the fund to buy land and other assets whose cost must be capitalized are not deductible because they are capital expenditures under Code Sec. 263.[129]

In determining whether a benefit is provided during the taxable year for purposes of determining the qualified cost, a benefit is provided if it would be includible in the gross income of the employee without regard to a particular provision of the Code that may exclude it.[130]

> **Example (2):** If an employer contributes to a welfare fund that pays premiums for a medical insurance policy for participating employees, the amount deductible is the amount of the premiums paid without regard to the exclusion rule of Code Sec.106.

Reduction in Qualified Cost by After-Tax Income. Employer contributions to a welfare benefit fund must be reduced by the after-tax income of the fund during the year in determining the qualified cost for that year.[131] Under Code Sec. 419(c)(4), the after-tax income of a welfare benefit fund is its gross income reduced by (1) the deductions that are directly connected with the production of that gross income for the year, and (2) the income tax (if any) imposed on the fund for the year.

Carryovers of Excess Contributions. Employer contributions in excess of the amount deductible under Code Sec. 419 can be carried over to later taxable years. The carryover is permitted for amounts contributed that would otherwise be deductible.[132] Amounts that are carried over must be reduced by any nondeducted contribution that reverts to the benefit of the employer.[133]

Qualified Asset Account. The qualified cost of a welfare benefit fund includes a permitted addition to the plan's qualified assets account (QAA). Under Code Sec. 419A(a), the QAA is any account consisting of assets of the plan that are set aside to provide for the payment of disability, medical or supplemental unemployment

---

[128] Code Sec. 419(c)(3)(C).
[129] Temp. Reg. § 1.419-1T, Q&A 6.
[130] Code Sec. 419(c)(3)(B).

[131] Code Sec. 419(c)(2).
[132] Code Sec. 419(d).
[133] Code Sec. 4976(b)(3).

benefits (SUB), severance pay benefits, or life insurance benefits. Thus, a deduction is not permitted where an employer is found not to have set aside assets for the payment of such benefits. For example one court held that the failure to disclose the existence of trusts established for the payment of benefits and contributions to such trusts to employees, retirees, unions, or shareholders in addition to the failure to pay out any benefits indicated that the employer did not set aside assets for the payment of benefits.[134] Thus, the employer was not permitted a deduction for most of the plan contributions made in that case. Note that an "accounts receivable" entered on the books of a VEBA by a sponsoring accrual-basis employer is not considered an "asset set aside" to provide employee benefits because the entry is insufficient to create a funded reserve. The amount is not deductible because an unfunded obligation of an employer cannot be considered an addition to a reserve to provide for the payment of future benefits.[135]

The amount that can be added to a QAA for a particular year is limited under Code Sec. 419A(c). In general, the account limit for any QAA is the amount reasonably and actuarially necessary to fund: (1) claims incurred but unpaid (as of the close of the taxable year) for QAA benefits, and (2) administrative costs with respect to such claims.[136] Also, the account limit for any taxable year may include a reserve funded over the working lives of the covered employees and actuarially determined on a level and reasonable basis for:

(1) post-retirement medical benefits payable to covered employees; and

(2) post-retirement life insurance benefits to be provided to covered employees.[137]

Unless there is an actuarial certification of the account limits for any taxable year, the account limits cannot exceed the sum of specified safe-harbor limits (covered below) for the year.[138] Thus, an actuarial certification is necessary to permit deduction of amounts in excess of the safe-harbor amounts. But, note that meeting the safe-harbor amount only eliminates the need for obtaining an actuarial certification. Even if amounts set aside meet the safe-harbor limit, they nevertheless must be reasonable in amount under the facts and circumstances to be deductible. Meeting one of the safe

---

[134] *Parker-Hannifin Corp.*, CA-6, 98-1 USTC ¶ 50,278, partially rev'g 72 TCM 191, TC Memo. 1996-337.

[135] *National Presto Industries, Inc.*, 104 TC 559, Dec. 50,623 (1995).

[136] Code Sec. 419A(c)(1).

[137] Code Sec. 419A(c)(2). *See Wells Fargo and Co*, 120 TC 69 (2003), for a case involving the method for calculating the reserve for post-retirement life insurance benefits to be provided to covered employees.

[138] Code Sec. 419A(c)(5).

¶ 404.05

harbors does not automatically entitle the employer to a deduction.[139] Conversely, even amounts significantly in excess of the actuarial limit may be deductible if it can be shown that they are reasonable and necessary. (For example, the IRS privately ruled that a VEBA reserve for medical claims equal to 49.76 percent of the prior year's medical claims was reasonable and necessary based on the facts of the case even though this amount was far in excess of the 35 percent safe-harbor limit (the safe-harbor limits are discussed below.)[140]

For purposes of the deduction limits, claims incurred but unpaid include claims incurred but unreported as well as claims reported but unpaid. A claim is incurred only when an event has occurred entitling an employee (or his or her beneficiary) to the benefit. For example, a claim is incurred under a noninsured medical benefit plan when a covered employee has received medical services and, thus, incurred a covered expense. A claim would not be incurred at the time a covered employee becomes ill unless he or she receives covered medical services. Insurance premiums, whenever payable, are not regarded as claims incurred but unpaid.[141]

Contributions to a fund will not be deductible to the extent they cause the total amount in the fund to exceed the applicable account limit. For this purpose, contributions made to a welfare benefit fund during the taxable year of the employer but after the end of the last related taxable year of the fund, and contributions accrued and deducted with respect to a fund during the taxable year of the employer or during any prior taxable year of the employer (but not actually paid to the fund on or before the end of a taxable year of the employer), are to be treated as an amount in the fund as of the end of the last taxable year of the fund that related to the taxable year of the employer. Contributions that are not deductible under this rule are in excess of the qualified cost of the fund for the taxable year of the fund that relates to the employer's taxable year and are treated as contributed to the fund on the first day of the employer's next taxable year.[142]

Addition for SUB/Severance Pay Benefits. The QAA limit for SUB and severance pay benefits is 75 percent of the average annual qualified direct costs for SUB and severance pay benefits for any two of the immediately preceding seven years (as selected

---

[139] *General Signal Corp.*, 103 TC 216, Dec. 50,058. Aff'd on other issue, CA-2, 98-1 USTC ¶ 50,357, 142 F3d 546.

[140] Technical Advice Memorandum 9446002, 7-12-94, CCH IRS LETTER RULINGS REPORTS.

[141] H.R. Rep. No. 98-861, 98th Cong., 2d Sess. (1984), at 1156 (hereafter referred to in this chapter as '84 Act Conference Report).

[142] Temp. Reg. § 1.419-1T, Q&A 5(b)(1).

by the welfare plan) plus the average administrative costs for such years allocable to the provision of those benefits.[143]

Limitation of Disability, SUB, and Severance Pay. Disability benefits payable to an individual will not be taken into account to the extent such benefits are paid at an annual rate in excess of the lower of (1) 75 percent of average annual compensation for his/her highest paid three years, or (2) the dollar limitation on annual defined benefit pension plan benefits ($170,000 in 2005—the amount will be adjusted for inflation after 2005). Further, any SUB or severance pay benefit payable to an individual cannot be taken into account to the extent it is payable at an annual rate in excess of 150 percent of the defined contribution plan limitation ($42,000 in 2005).[144] Finally, the amount of SUB or severance pay benefits that can be taken into account for any tax year is 75 percent of the average annual qualified direct costs for such benefits in any two of the immediately preceding seven tax years.[145] This amount also is the safe-harbor limit for such benefits as covered below.

The funding of claims for disability for an indefinite period of time is allowed only if the disabilities are determined to be long-term. Long-term disabilities are those that (1) a medical evaluation determines are expected to last for at least 12 months, and (2) have persisted for at least five months. For such disabilities, current deductions are permitted for contributions necessary to fund the expected future stream of benefit payments using actuarial assumptions that are reasonable, including assumptions as to morbidity, mortality, and fund earnings. Other disabilities that have persisted for at least two weeks are considered to be short-term, and no more than five months of benefit payments may be deemed to have been incurred for such disabilities.[146] However, under TRA '86, funding of up to 12 months is permitted with respect to disabilities expected to last more than five months but less than twelve.[147]

Reserves for Post-Retirement Medical and Life Insurance Benefits. The QAA limit may include a reserve for post-retirement medical benefits or post-retirement life insurance benefits to be provided to covered employees.[148] However, no reserve may be taken into account for post-retirement medical benefits or life insurance benefits to be provided to covered employees unless the plan meets the nondiscrimination requirements of Code Sec. 505(b)

---

[143] Code Sec. 419A(c)(3) and '84 Act Conference Report, at 1158.

[144] Code Sec. 419A(c)(4).

[145] Code Sec. 419A(c)(5)(B)(iii).

[146] '84 Act Conference Report, at 1156.

[147] *See* S. Rep. No. 99-313, 99th Cong., 2d Sess. 1006 (1986).

[148] Code Sec. 419A(c)(2).

¶ 404.05

with respect to the benefits. Plans maintained pursuant to a collective bargaining agreement are not subject to this rule.[149]

Life insurance benefits cannot be taken into account in determining the QAA limit to the extent that the aggregate amount of such benefits to be provided for a particular employee exceeds $50,000.[150] The $50,000 limit is applicable to the aggregate of all life insurance benefits under all funds maintained by the employer.

In a recent decision, the Tax Court ruled that a taxpayer's method used in computing its contribution to a VEBA trust for postretirement medical benefits did not result in a contribution in excess of the account limit permitted for the reserve under the Code.[151] The IRS had sought to disallow full funding of the postretirement benefits reserve in the year in which the reserve is created. The IRS asserted that the funding of a reserve over the working lives of the covered employees cannot start until the reserve is created. However, the Tax Court held that for employees who were retired when the reserve is created, the present value of the projected benefits for those individuals may be allocated to the year in which the reserve is created.

Post-Retirement Benefits for Key Employees. If post-retirement medical and life insurance benefits are to be provided to key employees, (1) a separate account must be maintained for each key employee for that purpose, and (2) medical and life insurance benefits can only be paid from that account.[152] Further, any amount attributable to medical benefits for key employees is to be treated as an annual addition to a defined contribution qualified retirement plan.[153] However, such amounts are not subject to the annual defined contribution dollar limit.

For purposes of the separate account rules, a key employee is defined in the same fashion as a key employee under the top-heavy pension plan rules (under Code Sec. 416(i)).

Safe-Harbor Limits. Unless there is an actuarial certification of the QAA limit for any taxable year, the QAA limit is not permitted to exceed the following safe-harbor limits:

(1) *short-term disability*—17.5 percent of qualified direct costs (other than insurance premiums) for the immediately preceding taxable year;

---

[149] Code Sec. 419A(e)(1).
[150] Code Sec. 419A(e)(2).
[151] *Wells Fargo and Company (F.K.A. Norwest Corporation)*, 120 TC 69 (2003).

[152] Code Sec. 419A(d)(1).
[153] Code Sec. 419A(d)(2).

(2) *medical benefits*—35 percent of qualified direct costs (other than insurance premiums) for the immediately preceding taxable year;

(3) *SUB or severance pay*—75 percent of the average annual qualified direct costs for any two of the immediately preceding seven taxable years plus allocable administrative costs for each period; and

(4) *long-term disability/life insurance benefits*—IRS regulations are to specify the appropriate safe-harbor limits—there is no safe-harbor limit at this time since no regulations have been issued. Thus, an actuarial certification is required with respect to any addition to the account limit for long-term disability claims that are incurred, but are unpaid.[154]

Note that the safe-harbor limits do not establish the amount of the deduction but merely provide a maximum dollar figure. Thus, despite the safe-harbor limits, no deduction is permitted for an amount in excess of the amount that is reasonably necessary to fund claims that are incurred, but unpaid.[155]

Account Limitations for Collectively Bargained Welfare Benefit Funds. No account limits apply in the case of any QAA under a separate welfare benefit fund under (1) a collective bargaining agreement, or (2) a VEBA if: (a) the VEBA covers at least 50 employees (determined without regard to the aggregation rules that treat all welfare benefit funds as one fund for certain purposes), and (b) no employee is entitled to a refund with respect to amounts in the fund, other than a refund based on the experience of the entire fund.[156] For purposes of these rules, a fund is not considered to be maintained under a collective bargaining agreement unless 50 percent or more of the employees eligible to receive benefits under the fund (90 percent with respect to funds formed after July 1, 1985) are covered by the agreement.[157] Thus, where the benefits provided through union VEBA sub-trusts were found to be the subject of arm's-length negotiations between employee representatives and the employers, and none of the represented employees are executives, officers, or owners of more than a de minimis amount of employer stock, the IRS concluded that the sub-trusts are maintained pursuant to a collective bargaining agreement. In that case, the sub-trusts did not have to meet the account limit requirements described above.[158] Finally, it should be noted that the IRS issued a

---

[154] Code Sec. 419A(c)(5)(B), IRS Letter Ruling 9818001, 6-13-97, CCH IRS LETTER RULINGS REPORTS.

[155] *General Signal Corp.*, 103 TC 216, Dec. 50,058 (1994). Aff'd on other issue, CA-2, 98-1 USTC ¶50,357, *Square D Co.*, 109 TC 200, Dec. 52,295 (1997).

[156] Code Sec. 419A(f)(5).

[157] Temp. Reg. § 1.419A-2T, Q&As 2 and 4.

[158] IRS Letter Ruling 200119064, 2-15-01, CCH IRS LETTER RULINGS REPORTS. *See also* IRS Letter Ruling 200137062, 6-18-01, CCH IRS LETTER RULINGS REPORTS in which the IRS held that the account limits did not have to be met with

notice in 2003 designed to curb deductions for employer contributions to welfare benefit funds that are set up as a result of sham labor negotiations designed to take advantage of the no account limit in the case of plans set up through a collectively bargained agreement.[159] The notice outlines several approaches the IRS can take to impose the normal account limits where the welfare benefit fund is found not to be a bona-fide separate welfare benefit fund set up under a collectively bargained agreement. The notice also indicates that arrangements of this general type are listed transactions that not only are not eligible for the collective bargaining contribution limitation of Code Sec. 419A(f)(5), but are also potentially subject to the penalties that are associated with abusive tax shelters.

Aggregation of Funds. For purposes of determining the limits applicable to the reserves for disability benefits, SUB and severance pay benefits, and post-retirement medical and life insurance benefits, all welfare benefit funds of a single employer are to be treated as one fund.[160] In addition, an employer may- elect to treat two or more welfare benefit funds as being one fund for other purposes. Finally, the commonly controlled corporation, commonly controlled trade or business, affiliated service group, and employee leasing rules of Code Sec. 414 apply to welfare benefit funds.[161]

Exception to Application of Deduction Limits for Ten-or-More Employer Plans. Under Code Sec. 419A(f)(6), the welfare benefit plan deduction limitations do not apply to a welfare benefit fund which is part of a ten-or-more employer plan. For this purpose, a ten-or-more employer plan is a plan:

(1) to which more than one employer contributes; and

(2) to which no employer contributes more than 10 percent of the total contributions contributed under the plan by all the participating employers.

However, the ten-or-more employer plan exemption does not apply to any plan which maintains experience-rating arrangements with respect to individual employers.[162] The IRS has recently issued final regulations to provide guidance for determining whether a welfare benefit fund is part of a 10 or more employer plan so as to be excepted from the limits of Code Sees. 419 and 419A.[163] The final regulations are generally effective for contributions paid or incurred in taxable years beginning on or after July 11, 2002.[164] In general, a

---

respect to a physician's welfare benefit plan since the IRS found that the plan was established under a collective bargaining agreement.

[159] Notice 2003-24, 2003-1 CB 853.
[160] Code Sec. 419A(h)(1).
[161] Code Sec. 419A(h)(2).
[162] Code Sec. 419A(f)(6)(A).

[163] Reg. § 1.419A(f)(6)-1, TD 9079, July 16, 2003.
[164] Reg. § 1.419A(f)(6)-1(g). For contributions made before this effective date, the IRS has indicated that it will apply formerly applicable law including Notice 95-34, 1995-1 CB 309 and relevant case law.

10 or more employer plan is a plan to which more than one employer contributes and to which no employer normally contributes more than 10 percent of the total contributions contributed under the plan by all employers. The plan must be maintained pursuant to a written document that (1) requires the plan administrator to maintain records sufficient for the IRS or any participating employer to readily verify the plan's compliance with Code Sec. 419A(f)(6) and (2) provides the IRS and each participating employer with the right to inspect and copy all such records. The requirements in the final regulations are substantially consistent with the contents of Notice 95-34,[165] in which the IRS identified certain types of arrangements which may be experience rated and thus do not satisfy the Code Sec. 419A(f)(6) requirements. For an example case of an arrangement using a separate accounting system that did not qualify for the 10 or more employer exception, see *Booth*.[166]

.06 Taxation of Unrelated Business Income of Nonexempt Welfare Benefit Fund

In the case of any welfare benefit fund that is not exempt from income tax either as a VEBA, SUB, GLSO, or other tax-exempt fund, the employer who maintains the fund must include in gross income an amount equal to the fund's "deemed unrelated income" for the fund's taxable year ending within the employer's taxable year.[167]

Deemed Unrelated Business Income. The deemed unrelated income of a nonexempt welfare benefit fund is the amount that would be treated as unrelated business taxable income if the fund were a VEBA, SUB, or GLSO.[168]

If any amount is included in the gross income of an employer for a taxable year as deemed unrelated income with respect to a welfare benefit fund, then: (1) the income tax imposed on that income is treated as a contribution paid by the employer to the fund on the last day of the taxable year, and (2) that tax shall be treated as a deduction in determining the fund's "after-tax" income.[169]

For purposes of determining unrelated business income, the employer may elect to treat two or more non-exempt welfare benefit funds as a single fund.[170]

---

[165] 1995-1 CB 309. *See also* Notice 2001-51, 2001-2 CB 190.
[166] 108 TC 524, Dec. 52,097.
[167] Code Sec. 419A(g)(1).
[168] Code Sec. 419A(g)(2).
[169] Code Sec. 419A(g)(3).
[170] Code Sec. 419A(h)(1).

.07 Excise Tax on Disqualified Benefits

Under Code Sec. 4976(a), a nondeductible excise tax of 100 percent is imposed on a welfare benefit fund that provides a disqualified benefit. Disqualified benefits include:

(1) any post-retirement medical or life insurance benefit provided with respect to a key employee if a separate account is required to be established for that employee and the payment is not from the account;

(2) any post-retirement medical or life insurance benefit provided to an individual in whose favor discrimination is prohibited unless the plan meets the nondiscrimination requirements of Code Sec. 505(b) with respect to the benefit, whether or not those requirements apply to such plans; and

(3) any portion of a welfare benefit fund reverting to the benefit of the employer.[171]

Benefits covered under the rule described in (1) above will not be disqualified even if they are not provided through a separate account if the cost of the benefit is paid by the employer in the tax year in which the benefit is provided and no separate account is maintained or required to be maintained for the key employee.[172]

A benefit covered under the rule described in (2) above will not be disqualified if it is the subject of good-faith bargaining under a recognized collective bargaining agreement.[173]

The rule in (3) above in which reversions to the benefit of the employer constitute disqualified benefits does not apply to a contribution which is not deductible for the taxable year or any prior year.[174]

Under Code Sec. 4976(b)(4), the rules described in (1) and (2) above will not apply to post-retirement benefits that are charged against an existing reserve for post-retirement medical or life insurance benefits or charged against the income of such reserve.

The IRS has recently issued a number of private letter rulings concerning situations where the 100-percent excise tax will not apply.[175] In one of the rulings, the IRS held that a transfer of

---

[171] Code Sec. 4976(b)(1).
[172] Temp. Reg. § 54.4976-1T, Q&A 2.
[173] Code Sec. 4976(b)(2).
[174] Code Sec. 4976(b)(3).
[175] IRS Letter Ruling 9814049, 7-7-98, CCH IRS LETTER RULINGS REPORTS. IRS Letter Ruling 9815057, 1-13-98, CCH IRS LETTER RULINGS REPORTS, IRS Letter Ruling 9815058, 1-13-98, CCH IRS LETTER RULINGS REPORTS, IRS Letter Ruling 199952094, 10-8-99, CCH IRS LETTER RULINGS REPORTS, IRS Letter Ruling 200003054, 10-27-99. CCH IRS LETTER RULINGS REPORTS, IRS Letter Ruling 200009051, 11-30-99, CCH IRS LETTER RULINGS REPORTS, IRS Letter Ruling 200023052. 3-10-00, CCH IRS LETTER RULINGS REPORTS, IRS Letter Ruling 200024054, 3-22-00, CCH IRS LETTER RULINGS REPORTS, IRS Letter Ruling 200111046, 12-15-00, CCH IRS LETTER RULINGS REPORTS, IRS Letter Ruling 200136028, 6-12-01, CCH IRS LETTER RULINGS REPORTS, IRS

retirement funding account's assets from a parent corporation to its subsidiary to provide for the payment of its employees' post-retirement life insurance benefits is exempt from the 100-percent excise tax. Positive rulings were given with respect to similar situations in the other rulings. Finally, in another ruling, the IRS privately held that a trust's payment of demutualization proceeds to a company (where the insurance company demutialized and became a stock insurance company) was not subject to the excise tax of Code Sec. 4976(b)(1)(C).[176]

Letter Ruling 200450040, and IRS Letter Ruling 200503027.

[176] IRS Letter Ruling 200219002, 9-28-01, CCH IRS LETTER RULINGS REPORTS.

¶ 404.07

Chapter 5

Introduction to Multiemployee Qualified Deferred Compensation Plans

¶501 Introduction

This chapter introduces multiemployee deferred compensation plans. Qualified deferred compensation plans are the most important form of compensation used to provide retirement and separation from service benefits to employees as a whole. Although the characteristics and tax requirements of various deferred compensation plans may be different, qualified deferred compensation overall has a number of specific unique characteristics. Within limits, the employer can deduct contributions it makes to qualified deferred compensation plans. Second, the amounts contributed to qualified plans are not taxable to the employees in the year of the contribution. Third, the net earnings on both employer and employee contributions are not subject to tax when earned. Finally, the participating employee or his beneficiary is taxed on benefits from a qualified deferred compensation plan only when the benefits are actually received, usually at or after retirement. Employer contributions to qualified plans are also excludable for FICA and FUTA tax purposes under Code Secs. 3121(a)(5) and 3306(b)(5). To attain these basic characteristics, qualified plans must satisfy a number of specific nondiscrimination and reporting standards. In addition, there are limits on the contributions that can be made to and/or benefits that can be paid under qualified plans.

After comparing qualified and nonqualified deferred compensation plans, this chapter presents a summary of the major forms of multiemployee qualified deferred compensation plans and a comparison of the most important of such plans. Chapter 6 then covers the major requirements for qualification of deferred compensation plans; Chapter 7 specifically covers certain special qualified plans such as Code Sec. 401(k) plans; and Chapters 8 and 9 cover the tax rules governing qualified plan contributions and the taxation of plan distributions respectively. The Economic Growth and Tax Relief Reconciliation Act of 2001 (EGTRRA) made numerous and significant changes that affect the rules and planning concerning qualified deferred compensation plans. Among the changes are substantial increases in the maximum amount of annual additions that can be made to defined contribution plans; elective deferral contributions that can be made into Code Sec. 401(k), Code Sec. 403(b) and other plans permitting elective deferral contributions; and the maximum amount of benefits that can be paid under defined benefit plans. These changes and others will be covered and evaluated in this chapter and in the following chapters on qualified plans. In addition, the decrease in marginal income tax rates that was enacted by EGTRRA and accelerated by the Jobs Growth and Tax Relief Reconciliation Act of 2003 (JGTRRA) should enhance the desirability of qualified plans, since benefits paid under or with respect to such plans may be subject to lower tax rates than those that applied in 2001 and 2002.

¶ 502 Types of Qualified Deferred Compensation Plans and General Characteristics

The following paragraphs cover the distinctions between qualified and nonqualified deferred compensation plans, the distinctions between defined contribution and defined benefit plans, and specific qualified plans, such as pension plans, profit-sharing plans, stock bonus plans, and others.

.01 Qualified v. Nonqualified Plans

A qualified deferred compensation plan is a plan that meets specified requirements in order to obtain special tax treatment. In general, qualified deferred compensation plans must satisfy the following requirements:

(1) minimum participation standards under Code Sec. 410;

(2) nondiscrimination standards (the plan cannot discriminate in favor of highly compensated employees) under Code Sec. 401(a)(4);

(3) minimum vesting standards under Code Sec. 411;

(4) minimum funding standards (for defined benefit plans and money purchase plans) under Code Sec. 412; and

(5) specified limits on benefits and contributions under Code Sec. 415.

In addition, reporting and disclosure requirements mandated by the Employee Retirement Income Security Act of 1974 (ERISA) have to be met.

There are four major tax advantages associated with qualified plans:

(1) The employer can deduct contributions it makes to the plan (within limits) in the current year even though the participants in the plan receive no benefits from the plan during the year.

(2) Generally, the net income on amounts contributed to the plan is exempt from taxation as long as the assets stay in the plan, and, thus, the amounts held in the qualified plan grow at a tax-free rate of return.

(3) Participants in the plan are taxed on benefits only when they actually receive distributions from the plan, usually at or after retirement. Further, in some cases distributions received in lumpsum form may be eligible for taxation at special rates using the long-term capital gain rules and/or ten-year forward averaging or eligible to be rolled over to an IRA or, qualified plan in order to defer taxation even longer.

(4) Employer contributions to and benefits payable under qualified plans are generally not subject to FICA and FUTA taxes.

Nonqualified plans, on the other hand, do not have the characteristics noted above. First of all, the participants can avoid being taxed until deferred compensation is actually paid under a nonqualified plan only if the doctrines of constructive receipt and economic benefit do not apply and, generally with respect to amounts deferred under nonqualified plans after December 31, 2004, the requirements of new Code Sec. 409A are met to permit the deferral of income recognition until the year in which the deferred compensation is paid (see Chapter 14). Secondly, the employer is permitted to take a deduction for amounts paid under a nonqualified plan only in the year in which the employee includes the amount in income according to Code Sec. 404. Third, the net income on amounts set aside to pay deferred compensation under a nonqualified plan is generally taxable (note that amounts set aside must remain subject to the claims of the general creditors of the employer in order to defer the recognition of income). If the nonqualified plan provides for the payment of property to the employee at some future time, the provisions of

Code Sec. 83 apply, and income will be recognized at the time the employee's rights to the property are no longer subject to a substantial risk of forfeiture. The employer can take a deduction in the year in which the employee includes the value of the property in his gross income. Finally, amounts payable under nonqualified plans are subject to FICA and FUTA taxes in the later of the year in which the related services are performed or the year in which the employee's rights to the deferred compensation are no longer subject to a substantial risk of forfeiture.[1]

As a result of comparing qualified and nonqualified plans, it can be concluded that an employee will be able to receive much larger benefits from a qualified plan than under a nonqualified plan, assuming the same amount of contributions are made by the employer.

> **Example:** Assume that Wilson's employer contributes 10 percent of his $50,000 compensation annually to a qualified plan that earns a 10 percent rate of return. Further assume that the $5,000 annual contributions begin when Wilson is age 40 and end when he is age 65. In that case, the accumulated balance in Wilson's retirement account would be $491,735.50. On the other hand, assume that the employer made a promise to pay Wilson at age 65 an amount equivalent to what $5,000 yearly in a nonqualified plan set aside per year would grow credited with after-tax interest. Assume also that the employer is able to earn 10 percent interest and is subject to a 30 percent marginal income tax rate, yielding an after-tax rate of return of 7 percent. On that basis, Wilson would receive only $316,245 (before tax) at age 65. Also note that Wilson may be able to use ten-year averaging and/or long-term capital gains treatment to tax the benefits from the qualified plan if received in lump-sum form (assuming that Wilson was at least 50 on January 1, 1986). Or, Wilson could elect to roll over (on a tax-free basis) part or all of the balance into a traditional IRA or another qualified retirement plan as discussed in Chapter 9. However, amounts received from the nonqualified plan would be taxed as ordinary income at regular rates no matter how they are received. Amounts received under nonqualified plans cannot be rolled over.

Disadvantages of Qualified Plans. There are three basic disadvantages of qualified plans as compared to nonqualified plans. First, under qualified plans, the employer typically must make substantial contributions on a nondiscriminatory basis on behalf of

---

[1] Code Secs. 3121(v)(2) and 3306(r)(2).

most of its employees, which increases the costs of providing similar benefits to highly compensated employees. There is no such requirement in the case of nonqualified plans. As few as one employee can be covered under a nonqualified plan. Secondly, even though EGTRRA made substantial increases, the maximum amounts of yearly additions that can be made to defined contribution qualified plans and the maximum benefits that can be paid under defined benefit qualified plans are still rather limited (the dollar limit on annual additions is $40,000 for plan limitation years beginning on or after January 1, 2002—the inflation adjusted amount for 2005 plan years is $42,000, whereas it was $35,000 for plan limitation years beginning on or after January 1, 2001, and the limit on benefits is $160,000 for plan limitation years ending after December 31, 2001— for plan years beginning after December 31, 2004, the amount is $170,000, whereas it was $140,000 for plan limitation years ending after December 31, 2000); in addition, only the first $200,000 (in 2002 (the amount for 2005 is $210,000), as increased by EGTRRA from $170,000 in 2001) of employee compensation can be used to determine how much can be contributed on behalf of an employee to a qualified plan, whereas there are no such limits under nonqualified plans. Finally, higher start-up and administration costs are incurred for qualified plans as compared with nonqualified plans.

.02 Defined Contribution v. Defined Benefit Plans, in General

Qualified plans can be broadly divided into two major categories, defined contribution and defined benefit plans. The fundamental difference between defined contribution and defined benefit plans (which will be described in more detail below) is that under defined benefit plans the employer has the risk and obligation to make sufficient contributions to the plan to insure that the benefits that the participant is entitled to receive under the plan at retirement will be paid. On the other hand, under a defined contribution plan, the employee-participants are not entitled to any particular level of benefits, and the amount of benefits that will be received is dependent upon the amount of contributions the employer and employee make to the plan and the plan earnings on those contributions. The employee, not the employer, bears the risk as to the amount of benefits that will be received under a defined contribution plan. Other differences between the two types of plans are that (1) typically, the benefits under defined contribution plans such as Section 401(k) Cash or Deferred Arrangement Plans are more portable (i.e., can be moved to other plans by those changing jobs) than defined benefit plans and (2) employees, in many cases, control how contributed funds are invested under defined contribution plans (e.g., employees can direct that such amounts can be invested in certain mutual funds), whereas under defined benefit plans the investment decisions are made by the qualified plan trustee.

These plan differences, other tax factors, and certain demographic factors including a shift in employment away from industries in which employers traditionally favored defined benefit plans (e.g., the steel industry) have led to a tremendous increase in the percentage of employers offering defined contribution plans and a decrease in those offering defined benefit plans. For example, a Government Accounting Office (GAO) study found that in 1993, 88 percent of private employers with single-employer-sponsored qualified plans sponsored only defined contribution plans, compared to 68 percent in 1984. Those sponsoring defined benefit plans only decreased from 24 percent to nine percent over the 1984 to 1993 period.[2] As further evidence of this trend, statistics reported by the Congressional Research Service show that in 1975 there were 103,646 defined benefit plans in the United States with 27.2 million participants compared to 207,748 defined contribution plans with 11.2 million participants. By 1996, the number of defined benefit plans had fallen to 63,657 with 23.3 million participants, whereas the number of defined contribution plans had risen to 632,566 with 44.6 million participants. Actually, the change for defined benefit plans is even more dramatic over the 1983 to 1996 period. From 1975 to 1983, the number of defined benefit plans increased from 103,646 to 172,642. After that, the number of defined benefit plans decreased sharply to the 63,657 figure. Much of that decrease coincided with the sharp increase in the number of Code Sec. 401(k) plans (a popular type of defined contribution plan) from 17,203 in 1984 to 230,808 in 1996.[3] More recently available reports showed that these trends have continued through the present time. By 2004, the number of private defined benefit pension plans had declined to around 26,000, covering just under 17 percent of the private-sector workforce. The number of defined contribution plans had increased to 840,300 (up from 673,626 in 1998 and 208,750 in 1975), and about 42 million workers participate in such plans.[4] Only very large employers continue to use defined benefit plans in a larger proportion than defined

---

[2] General Accounting Office, "Private Pensions Most Employers That Offer Pensions Use Defined Contribution Plans," GAO/GGD-97-1, October 3, 1996.

[3] Purcell, Patrick J., "Retirement Savings and Household Wealth in 1997: Analysis of Census Bureau Data," Congressional Research Service Report to Congress, April 5, 2001, Secs. 18-23.

[4] *See*, e.g., Weisman, Jonathon, "Death of the Pension," *Houston Chronicle*, Oct. 14, 2004, p. D2, citing data from the Employee Benefit Research Institute. *See also* Employee Benefit Research Institute, "Private Pension Plans, Participation, and Assets: Update," Facts From EBRI, January 2003.

contribution plans. Even as the number of defined benefit plans continues to decline, the financial condition of many of such plans is also deteriorating. In its 2004 Annual Report, the Pension Benefit Guaranty Corporation, which insures private defined benefit plan benefit payments for participants in single employer plans, reported a net loss of $14.7 billion in fiscal 2004, in part because of significant increases in the number of plan terminations and in the number of plan participants for which the corporations have taken responsibility for benefit payments.[5] Another development that has occurred in recent years is the conversion of traditional defined benefit pension plans into cash balance plans (discussed later in this chapter). Companies such as AT&T, Bell Atlantic, Cigna, Xerox, and other large corporations have converted their traditional defined benefit plans into cash balance plans. Evidence that these types of conversions are widespread is shown in the 1999 GAO survey of Fortune 1000 firms which indicated that about 19 percent of those firms sponsor cash balance plans covering an estimated 2.1 million participants; more than half of these plans were established after 1993.[6] A 2002 report published in *The New York Times* estimated that as many as one-third of the largest public companies have cash balance plans.[7] One motivation for making the conversions is that the conversions reduce (and, in some cases eliminate for one year or more) the amounts that the employers must contribute to their plans. The general impact of the conversion is a reduction in the amount that must be contributed on behalf of older workers. That is because contributions into cash balance plans are made more evenly over time (therefore benefiting younger workers), whereas the contributions tend to increase as a worker nears retirement under a traditional defined benefit plan. Thus, the benefits that older workers will receive under cash balance plans will likely be smaller than the amount they would have been entitled to under a traditional defined benefit plan. Several recent articles have covered this issue and indicate that some workers are beginning to fight such conversions on the basis that the conversions result in age discrimination against them.[8] In response to an IRS request in IR-1999-79 for comments from employees, employers, and their

---

[5] Pension Benefit Guaranty Corporation, 2004 Annual Report.

[6] General Accounting Office, "Cash Balance Plans, Implications For Retirement Income," GAO/GEHS-00-207, Oct. 3, 2000.

[7] Oppel, Richard A., "Administration Proposes Rules That Can Alter Pension Plans," *New York Times,* Dec. 10, 2002, p. C1.

[8] *See,* e.g., Schultz, Ellen, "Some Workers Facing Pension Hit," *Wall Street Journal,* Dec. 4.

1998. p. C1; Schultz, Ellen and Elizabeth McDonald, "Employers Win Big With a Pension Shift; Employees Often Lose," *Wall Street Journal,* Dec. 4, 1998, pp. A1 and A6; Schultz, Ellen. "Ins and Outs of 'Cash-Balance' Plan," *Wall Street Journal.* Dec. 4, 1998, p. C1; "The Down-Aging of Pension Plans," *Tax Notes,* Jan. 11, 1999, pp. 171-179; and Shepard, Lee A., "Polemics Versus Facts in the Cash Balance Plan Debate," *Tax Notes,* Oct. 9, 2000, pp. 178-181.

representatives concerning cash balance plans and conversions to cash balance plans, a substantial number of negative comments were received.[9] A number of court actions have been brought by disgruntled employees on account of such plan conversions. Three federal district court cases have addressed whether cash balance plans violate age discrimination rules. In *Eaton v. Onan*,[10] the court held that a cash balance plan did not violate the prohibition on reducing the rate of benefit accrual because of age. Under the plan, participants received pay credits for each year of service as well as front-loaded interest credits. The court examined how the rate of an employee's benefit accrual was determined and found that the statute does not require that the rate of benefit accrual be measured solely in terms of change in the value of an annuity payable at normal retirement age. The court found that requiring the rate of benefit accrual to be measured in such a way would produce a result inconsistent with the goal of the pension age discrimination provisions. The court found that in the case of a cash balance plan, the rate of benefit accrual should be defined as the change in the employee's cash balance account from one year to the next, thus determining that the cash balance plan was not age discriminatory. In the second case, a federal district court in *Cooper v. IBM Personal Pension Plan*[11] held that cash balance formulas are inherently age discriminatory because identical interest credits necessarily buy a smaller age annuity at normal retirement age for older workers than for younger workers due to the time value of money. The court interpreted "rate of benefit accrual" as referring to an employee's age 65 annual benefit (i.e., annuity payable at normal retirement age) and the rate at which the age 65 annual benefit accrues. The court held that the interest credits must be valued as an age 65 annuity, so that interest credits would always be more valuable to a younger employee as opposed to an older employee, thus violating the prohibition on reducing the rate of benefit accrual because of age. More recently, the U.S. District Court for the District of Maryland followed *Eaton v. Onan* and rejected the argument that cash balance plans are age discriminatory in *Tootle v. ARISC Inc.*[12] The court held that in examining the age discrimination issue, benefit accrual should be measured by examining the rate at which amounts are allocated and the changes in a participant's account balance over time. According to the court, the accrued benefit should be

---

[9] *See,* e.g., "Employees Continue to Bash Cash Balance Plan Conversions," *Tax Notes,* Feb. 7, 2000, p. 787; and "Controversy Over Cash Balance Plan Conversions Continues," *Tax Notes,* March 27, 2000, pp. 1856 and 1857.

[10] *See* 117 F Supp 2d 812 (SD, IND, 2000).

[11] 274 F Supp 2d 1010 (SD, ILL, 2003).

[12] DC, MD, June 10, 2004.

calculated under ERISA's provisions for defined contribution plans, rather than in terms of an age 65 annuity as required for defined benefit plans.

There has been some action by the IRS, but little congressional action concerning cash balance plans. In late 1999, the Clinton Administration announced a moratorium on the issuance of determination letters concerning cash balance plans while it studied related age discrimination questions.[13] Plan sponsors have to ask the IRS for technical advice, instead.[14] In late 2002, the IRS issued proposed regulations which indicate requirements that must be met by cash balance plans in order that they pass muster.[15] These proposed regulations have been subsequently withdrawn by the Bush Administration, which has proposed legislation in its fiscal year 2006 budget to address cash balance plans and conversions to cash balance plans.[16] The only congressional action on cash balance plans that has been enacted into law is in the form of a provision (covered in the discussion of cash balance plans below) enacted as part of EGTRRA under which notices must be provided to plan participants with respect to certain conversions of defined benefit plans into cash balance plans. Defined contribution plans, defined benefit plans, and cash balance plans are further discussed below.

Defined Contribution Plans. Under a defined contribution plan, amounts are contributed on behalf of each participant employee by the employer into a separate account maintained by the qualified plan fund holder. In some cases, the employee may also make or be required to make after-tax contributions to the plan (contributory plans), and amounts forfeited by other employees who terminate employment before their rights to benefits are 100 percent vested may be credited to the employee's account. In other cases, employee participants, may make pre-tax, salary reduction contributions to plans such as Section 401(k) Cash or Deferred Arrangement Plans (covered below and in Chapter 7) and employers may make matching contributions to such plans under Code Sec. 401(m). The employee pre-tax contributions are, however, considered to be employer contributions for purposes of determining the taxation of benefits paid under the plan. The employee's account is then credited with the net income on such contributions and forfeiture amounts. Finally, the employee will receive benefits

---

[13] *See* Shepard, Lee A., "A Square Peg in a Round Hole: Cash Balance Plans Ratified," Tax Notes, Dec. 16, 2002, pp. 1386-1389.

[14] *See* e.g., Rev. Proc. 2005-5, IRB 2005-1, 170.

[15] *See* REG-209500-86 and REG-164464-02, 67 FR 76123 (December 11, 2002).

[16] *See* Announcements 2003-22, 2003-1 CB 846 and 2004-57, IRB 2004-27, 15.

under the plan based upon the amounts contributed, the forfeitures credited, and the earnings on such amounts. Thus, the employee's benefits under the plan are entirely dependent upon the amounts contributed to the plan, forfeitures, and the net income on such amounts. There is no promise by the employer concerning the amount of benefits that will ultimately be paid, and there is no limit on the amounts that can be paid. Thus, it is possible that a participant in a defined contribution plan can receive much larger benefits than under a defined benefit plan because benefits are limited (see below) under a defined benefit plan.

However, the maximum amount that can be added (through employer and employee contributions and allocated forfeitures) to a defined contribution plan with respect to a particular employee is still quite limited even after increases enacted as part of EGTRRA. For plan limitation years beginning on or after January 1, 2002, the maximum amount that can be added to a participant's plan is the lesser of (a) 100 percent of the employee's compensation or (b) $40,000 (for plan limitation years beginning on or after January 1, 2001, the limit was the lesser of (a) 25 percent of compensation or (b) $35,000). The dollar maximum is $42,000 for plan limitation years beginning on or after January 1, 2005. EGTRRA also changed the definition of compensation for this purpose, and after 2001, elective deferrals under Code Sec. 401(k) and other plans will be included in the definition of compensation. Special limits apply if more than one defined contribution plan is maintained or if a defined contribution and defined benefit plan are maintained by the employer. Also, special limitations apply if the plan is integrated with Social Security. These are discussed in Chapter 6.

In summary, the employee rather than the employer is at risk in the case of defined contribution plans since his or her benefits under the plan are not predetermined and are based on circumstances that are, in most cases, largely beyond his/her control. For example, even though a large portion of defined contribution plan participants can direct how the plan contributions made on their behalf are to be invested, their control over the rate of return that can be earned on the investment varies according to the riskiness of the investments they make (those that invest contributions into growth stock funds might receive extraordinary high rates of return or might lose a large portion of their contributions invested). In addition, employee's account balances in defined contribution plans are not insured by the Pension Benefits Guaranty Corporation (PBGC) like defined benefit plans are (see Chapter 6 for a discussion of the PBGC). On the other hand, the employer incurs no such risk and operates in a rather certain environment in which its obligation is to contribute a determinable amount to the plan on behalf of participants.

Defined Benefit Plans. A defined benefit plan under Code Sec. 414(j) is a qualified plan that is required to pay a participant definitely determinable benefits beginning at some time in the future, usually at or after retirement. The "promised" benefits must be paid regardless of earnings or losses incurred on amounts contributed by the employer (and the employee, if the plan is contributory) to the qualified plan. As a consequence, it is necessary for the employer to make contributions that, on an actuarial basis, are sufficient to enable payment of the "promised benefits" to the participants. To enforce this requirement, Code Sec. 412 mandates that the employer make minimum contributions to a defined benefit plan as discussed in Chapter 6.

The maximum benefits that can be paid annually under a defined benefit plan are still quite limited despite increases made by EGTRRA. EGTRRA increased the dollar limit to $160,000 for plan limitation years ending after December 31, 2001 (adjusted for inflation after 2002 and up from $140,000 for plan limitation years ending after December 31, 2000). The dollar limit for plan years ending after December 31, 2004 (i.e., 2005 plan years) is $170,000. Specifically, the limitation is the lesser of the dollar limitation or 100 percent of the participant's average compensation in his or her three consecutive highest paid years under a defined benefit plan.[17] Further, this maximum is reduced actuarially in a method similar to that under which Social Security benefits are reduced for persons who retire at ages below age 62 (this age limit applies in 2002 and later years and was reduced from age 65 by EGTRRA—see Chapter 6 for further discussion). The manner in which defined benefit plan benefits are determined is summarized below in the discussion of pension plans.

Forfeitures do not increase the benefits of participants, but, instead reduce the employer's funding obligations.

In summary, the employer takes most of the risk in the case of defined benefit plans since it must make contributions sufficient to fund the promised benefits to employees. If the qualified plan fund holder experiences losses or below-normal earnings, the employer will have to make additional contributions to actuarially make up for that poor performance. Further, in the case of employees that begin employment with an employer only a few years before retirement

---

[17] Code Sec. 415(b), IR 2004-127 (Oct. 20, 2004). *See also* Rev. Rul. 2001-51, 2001-2 CB 427.

¶ **502.02**

and are promised retirement benefits, contributions will have to be substantial to fund the promised benefits. Employees, on the other hand, face less risk than under defined contribution plans because their plan benefits are "promised." Employee-participants may not get as large benefits as they could obtain from a defined contribution plan where invested funds earned extremely high rates of return, but they will not suffer, either, as would participants in a defined contribution plan who experience a negative rate of return on investments. Finally, most employers that maintain defined benefit plans are required to provide for plan termination insurance with the Pension Benefit Guaranty Corporation.

A general side-by-side comparison of defined benefit and defined contribution plans is presented following the discussion of specific qualified plans at the end of the chapter.

Phased Retirement Plans or Arrangements. A developing trend in recent years is that of phased retirement. That is, instead of the traditional situation under which an employee works full-time and then retires at or near retirement age (e.g., 65), more and more older employees in the range of ages 55-70 continue working for their employer for less than a full-time basis rather than retiring outright. This demographic condition raises questions as to the role of pension plans (primarily defined benefit pension plans) with respect to those employees.

In order to provide an answer as to how an employee who works less than full-time in a phased retirement scenario can be provided retirement benefits under a qualified plan, the IRS issued proposed regulations in November of 2004 concerning phased retirement arrangements.[18] The proposed regulations would amend Reg. § 1.401(a)-1(b) and add Reg. § 1.401(a)-3 in order to permit a pro rata share of an employee's accrued benefit to be paid under a bona fide phased retirement program and would apply to plan years beginning on or after the date the final regulations are published. The pro rata share is based on the extent to which the employee has reduced hours under the program. Under this pro rata approach, an employee maintains a dual status (i.e., partially retired and partially in service) during the phased retirement period. Under the proposed regulations, a plan would be permitted to pay a pro rata portion of the employee's benefits under a bona fide phased retirement program before attainment of normal retirement age. The proposed regulations define a bona fide phased retirement program as a

---

[18] REG-114726-04, 69 FR 65108 (Nov. 10, 2004).

written, employer-adopted program pursuant to which employees may reduce the number of hours they customarily work beginning on or after a retirement date specified under the program and receive phased retirement benefits. Payment of phased retirement benefits is permitted only if the program meets certain conditions, including that employee participation is voluntary and the employee and employer expect the employee to reduce, by 20 percent or more, the number of hours the employee works during the phased retirement period.

Consistent with the pro rata approach discussed above, the maximum amount that is permitted to be paid is limited to the portion of the employee's accrued benefit equal to the product of the employee's total accrued benefit on the date the employee commences phased retirement (or any earlier date selected by the plan for administrative ease) and the employee's reduction in work. The reduction in work is based on the employee's work schedule fraction, which is the ratio of the hours that the employee is reasonably expected to work during the phased retirement period to the hours that would be worked if the employee were full-time. Based in part on commentators' concerns regarding early retirement subsidies, the proposed regulations generally require that all early retirement benefits, retirement-type subsidies, and optional forms of benefit that would be available upon full retirement be available with respect to the phased retirement accrued benefit. However, the proposed regulations would not permit payment to be made in the form of a single-sum distribution (or other eligible rollover distribution) in order to prevent the premature distribution of retirement benefits. The phased retirement benefit is an optional form of benefit protected by Code Sec. 411(d)(6) and the election of a phased retirement benefit is subject to the provisions of Code Sec. 417, including the required explanation of the qualified joint and survivor annuity.

Cash Balance Plans. A special type of plan which combines some of the characteristics of a defined contribution plan and a defined benefit plan is the cash balance plan. A cash balance plan is a defined benefit plan that defines plan benefits for each employee participant by reference to a hypothetical account for the employee participant. An employee's hypothetical account balance is determined by reference to hypothetical allocations and interest adjustments that are analogous to actual allocations of contributions and plan earnings to an employee participant's account under a defined contribution plan.[19] The practical difference between the

---

[19] Reg. § 1.401(a)(4)-8(c)(3).

cash balance plan and many traditional defined benefit plans is the way in which required employer plan contributions are determined. Under a cash balance plan, for each working year a participant earns a rate of his/her compensation, called a "pay credit" which is a certain percentage (which may be the same for all age groups or may increase somewhat as an employee becomes older) of compensation credited to the participant's hypothetical account plus interest credits (hypothetical interest accruals) to that hypothetical account. By contrast, traditional defined benefit plans do not include an interest element and instead base the required accrual on the amount necessary to fund the promised benefit payments at retirement (which typically means that relatively high amounts must be accrued for older workers nearing retirement as compared to younger workers). Otherwise, a cash balance plan is a defined benefit plan and so must provide for the funding of promised benefits, provide for vesting, and meet other requirements associated with defined benefit plans. The nondiscrimination rules under Reg. § 1.401(a)(4) apply, and whether a cash balance plan meets those rules is decided by considering the equivalent amount of contributions under the plan or, if applicable, a safe-harbor test under Reg. § 1.401(a)(4)-8(c)(3). At retirement, the accumulated balance may be available as a lump sum or paid in annuity form (as noted in Chapter 6, a joint and survivor annuity must be available if the participant is married).

As indicated earlier, conversions of traditional defined benefit plans into cash balance plans can be disadvantageous to older workers. Conversions to cash balance plans can result in periods during which some workers do not earn additional pension benefits while other workers accrue benefits. This amounts to a freeze in future benefit accruals, and the concept is known as "wearaway," which tends to last longer for older workers.[20] Partly because of this phenomenon, Congress enacted a new notice requirement as part of EGTRRA under which disclosure is required when qualified plan amendments (such as a conversion of a defined benefit plan to a cash balance plan) could have the effect of reducing the rate of future benefit accruals of affected plan participants. Under Code Sec. 4980F, a notice must be provided to each participant in the plan whose future benefit accrual may reasonably be expected to be significantly reduced as a result of the plan amendment. An excise tax of $100 per day per each recipient and beneficiary can be imposed on the employer (or the plan if the plan is a multiemployer plan) for

---

[20] Government Accounting Office, "Private Pensions: Implications of Conversions to Cash Balance Plans," GAO/HEHS-00-185 (September 29, 2000).

¶ 502.02

failure to meet the notice requirements.[21] Further, as noted above, the IRS suspended issuing determination letters concerning cash balance plans, and noted that plan administrators have to seek technical advice instead.[22] In December of 2002, the IRS issued proposed regulations that provide age discrimination requirements for cash balance plans under Code Secs. 411(b)(1)(H), 411(b)(2) and 401(a)(4).[23] Broadly, the proposed regulations under Section 411 indicated how cash balance plans and conversions to such plans would be acceptable to the IRS with respect to the issue of age discrimination. The proposed regulations provide guidance on the requirements of Code Sec. 411(b)(1)(H), under which a defined benefit plan fails to be a qualified plan, if, under the plan, benefit accruals on behalf of a participant are ceased or the rate of benefit accrual on behalf of a participant is reduced because of the participant's attainment of any age. Similarly, the proposed regulations provide guidance under Code Sec. 411(b)(2) which applies a similar determination with respect to defined contribution plans.

At the same time the Section 411 proposed regulations were issued, the IRS issued proposed regulations under Section 401(a)(4). These proposed regulations provided that an "eligible cash basis plan" as defined in the proposed regulations under Section 411(b)(1)(H) may not demonstrate that the benefits under the plan do not discriminate in favor of highly compensated employees using the rules for defined benefit plans unless the plan complies with a modified version of the special Section 401(a)(4) regulations related to cross-testing by defined contribution plans and certain arrangements involving combinations of defined contribution and defined benefit plans. This restriction on the use of inconsistent testing methods between Sections 411(b)(1)(H) and 401(a)(4) was intended to ensure that plan sponsors could not avoid the "new comparability" rules applicable to a defined contribution plan and those combination arrangements through the use of a cash balance plan (which has a benefit accrual pattern similar to that of a defined contribution plan).[24]

In April of 2003, the IRS withdrew the December 2002 proposed regulations under Section 401(a)(4) due to significant negative comments by practitioners which raised serious concerns about the impact of the proposed regulations on cash balance conversions.[25]

---

[21] Code Sec. 4980F, as enacted by P.L. 107-16, 107th Cong., 1st Sess., Sec. 659(a)(1) (June 7, 2001).

[22] See Shepard, Lee A., "A Square Peg in a Round Hole: Cash Balance Plans Ratified," *Tax Notes,* Dec. 16, 2002, pp. 1386-1389.

[23] REG-209500-86 and REG-164464-02, 67 FR 76123 (December 11, 2002).

[24] Id.

[25] Announcement 2003-22, 2003-1 CB 846.

And, in Announcement 2004-57,[26] the IRS withdrew the Code Sec. 411 proposed regulations concerning cash balance plans. Rather than issuing replacement proposed regulations, the Bush Administration has included a legislative proposal in its Fiscal Year 2006 budget addressing cash balance plans and conversions to cash balance plans. The proposal would require companies converting to cash balance plans to protect current employees through a five-year "hold harmless" period and would prohibit any benefit wearaway. The proposals also would provide rules under which cash balance formulas would not be considered age-discriminatory and rules regarding interest crediting rates.[27]

As of the date of publication of this book, no further proposed regulations have been promulgated and the Administration's legislative proposals have not been enacted. As a result, the moratorium on the issuance of new determination letters on cash balance plan conversions remains in effect.

Previously, the IRS had issued Notice 96-8[28] which provided guidance on the application of Code Secs. 411(a) and 417(e) (the latter dealing with joint and survivor annuities) to deal with cash balance plan issues. Some of its provisions are similar to the withdrawn proposed regulations under Section 411 that were summarized in the above paragraphs. The validity of the provisions in Notice 96-8 were upheld in two recent court cases concerning cash balance plans.[29]

For further discussion of cash balance plan issues, see chapters 6 and 8.

.03 Noncontributory v. Contributory Plans

A noncontributory qualified plan is one under which only the employer makes contributions to the plan. The employee makes no contributions to the plan. Note that Section 401(k) Cash or Deferred Arrangement Plans (covered later in this chapter and in Chapter 7) and SIMPLE plans (covered in this chapter and Chapters 7 and 10) are considered to be noncontributory plans, since employee contributions made to such plans are in pre-tax dollars and are, therefore, considered to be employer contributions. Under these circumstances, all benefits received under the plan will be taxable to the recipient (see Chapter 9).

A contributory plan is one under which the employee-participants are required to or are permitted to make after-tax

---

[26] IRB 2004-27, 15.
[27] Announcement 2004-57, IRB 2004-27, 15.
[28] 1996-1 CB 359.

[29] See, e.g., *Lyons vs. Georgia Pacific.* CA-11, 221 F3d 1235 (2000) and *Edsen vs. Bank of Boston*, CA-2, 2000-2 USTC ¶ 50, 738, 229 F3d 154 (2000).

contributions to the plan. Before 1987, employees were permitted to make voluntary deductible contributions of up to $2,000 per year to qualified plans permitting such contributions. However, voluntary deductible contributions were repealed by the Tax Reform Act of 1986 (TRA '86). Note that employee contributions are counted along with employer contributions toward the maximum annual addition ($40,000 for plan limitation years beginning on or after January 1, 2002, adjusted for inflation after 2002 (the maximum for 2005 plan limitation years is $42,000) and up from $35,000 for plan limitation years beginning on or after January 1, 2001, as a result of the enactment of EGTRRA) permitted for defined contribution plans.[30]

There are certain advantages associated with contributory plans. The primary advantage is that the benefits payable under the plan can be higher if the employee is required to make contributions to the plan than if only the employer makes contributions. In addition, the employee contributions constitute a form of forced savings for participating employees. Finally, the employee contributions to a qualified plan provide one of the few tax-sheltered investments available for the participants.

However, there are a number of disadvantages associated with contributory plans. The primary disadvantage is that employee contributions are made in after-tax dollars, whereas employer contributions are not taxable to the participating employees. A second disadvantage is that employees may resent having amounts withheld to fund benefits that may be received in some distant future year. In addition, employees may desire a greater influence over the administration of a contributory plan. Finally, employee contributions are given priority in the case of distributions made pursuant to the termination of a qualified plan (see Chapter 6).

In addition to considering the advantages and disadvantages, employers, in deciding whether to make a plan contributory, should take into account: (1) how employee contributions will affect the cost of the plan, (2) whether employee contributions will conflict with any state law or labor agreement, and (3) registration requirements of the SEC. If the decision is made to make the plan contributory, then the employer must decide upon the amount of the employee contributions, taking into account the allowable maximums specified above and the amount of matching employer contributions, if any.

---

[30] Code Sec. 415(c)(2). *See also* Rev. Rul. 2001-51, 2001-2 CB 427 and IR-2004-127 (October 20, 2004).

.04   Qualified Pension Plans

A qualified pension plan is ordinarily a qualified plan under which the amount of retirement benefits to be paid to the participants is a determined amount, and the required amount of contributions to fund such benefits is actuarially computed. Thus, pension plans are ordinarily defined benefit plans.

Reg. § 1.401-1(b)(i) states:

> A pension plan within the meaning of Code Sec. 401(a) is a plan established and maintained by an employer primarily to provide systematically for the payment of definitely determinable benefits to his employees over a period of years, usually for life, after retirement. Retirement benefits generally are measured by, and based on, such factors as years of service and compensation received by employees. The determination of the amount of retirement benefits and the contributions to provide such benefits are not dependent upon profits. . . A plan designed to provide benefits for employees or their beneficiaries to be paid upon retirement or over a period of years after retirement will, for purposes of Code Sec. 401(a), be considered a pension plan if the employer contributions under the plan can be determined actuarially on the basis of definitely determinable benefits, or, as in the case of *money purchase pension plans,* such contributions are fixed without being geared to profits.

The above regulation also states that money purchase plans are pension plans (see the discussion below concerning money purchase plans). With the exception of money purchase plans which are defined contribution plans, pension plans are, as noted above, defined benefit plans. Note that the definition stated in the regulations may be changed in the near future to take account of phased retirement plans as discussed above in ¶ 502.02.

Methods of Determining Benefits Under Defined Benefit Pension Plans. Pension plans must ordinarily pay definitely determinable benefits to retirees. There are three common ways of determining benefits under a pension plan: (1) flat benefits, (2) flat percentage benefits, and (3) unit benefits. In addition, pension plans can provide for cost of living adjustments. Under the flat benefit method, the retirement benefit will be a set dollar amount, such as $1,000 per month, beginning at the normal retirement age. The amount of the benefit is not based on the amount of compensation paid to or the years of service contributed by the participant. Note that under this method, benefits would be the same for assembly line workers as for the president of the company.

Under the flat percentage benefit method, pension benefits equal a certain percentage of the compensation of the participant. In some cases, the benefit may equal a certain percentage of the participant's average annual career compensation.

Example (1): Wilson will retire in early 2006. During his career, his average yearly compensation was $70,000. His employer's pension plan pays annual benefits equal to 10 percent of average career compensation for life. Thus, Wilson would receive yearly benefits of $7,000 for life ($70,000 × 10%).

In other cases, the pension benefit may be equal to a certain percentage of the employee's average compensation paid in his three highest paid years or for some other period of time. The advantage of the flat percentage benefit approach is that it ties pension benefits to the individual's compensation which basically rewards employee performance. The disadvantage of the method is that large benefits may have to be paid to individuals hired only a few years prior to retirement. In such cases, the company has only a short time in which to fund the promised benefits.

Under the unit benefit method, the pension benefit equals either: (1) a specified dollar amount times the years of service of the participant, or (2) a certain percentage of compensation times the years of service of the participant.

Example (2): Walt's employer pays a pension equal to $50 per month for each year of credited service with the employer. Walt accumulated 28 years of service by the time he retired. Walt's pension would be $1,400 per month ($50 × 28).

Example (3): Ken's employer pays a pension amount equal to two percent multiplied by (1) a retiring employee's average compensation for that employee's last five years of service and (2) the number of years of service of the retiring employee. Suppose that Ken had average compensation of $60,000 in his last five years of service and that he worked 22 years for the employer. Ken's pension would equal $26,400 per year (.02 × $60,000 × 22).

A plan which pays a pension equal to a certain dollar amount per month for each year of credited service would seem best suited for companies whose work force is largely made up of individuals earning about the same amount of compensation. On the other hand, companies with large disparities in payroll may be better off paying a pension equal to a percentage of compensation times years of service.

Types of Funding Arrangements and Benefits. Under Code Sec. 401, a pension plan may be funded through the use of a trust, a custodian (which is usually a bank), an insurance company, or an investment company operating as a "face-amount certificate" company.

Benefits from a pension plan are generally paid in annuity form for the participant's life (in joint or survivor annuity form if the participant is married). However, benefits may also be paid in lump-sum form. Payments of pension benefits may begin at the time of the employee's death, disability, termination of employment, or at retirement.[31] Life insurance benefits may be provided, but health and accident benefits can only be provided for retirees and their dependents.[32] Pension and annuity plans can provide for the payment of benefits for sickness, accident, hospitalization and medical expenses for retired employees if the plan meets certain requirements. The benefits must be subordinate to the plan retirement benefits, and a separate account must be established to which the employer makes contributions to provide for such expenses.[33] In general, the aggregate amount of contributions for medical benefits when added to actual contributions for life insurance cannot exceed 25 percent of the total actual contributions to the plan (other than contributions in respect to past service costs). However, certain transfers of assets from fully funded pension plans can be made to pension plan medical accounts under Code Sec. 420 from January 1, 1991 to December 31, 2013.

Loans Made to Participants. Loans may be made by pension plans and other qualified plans to participants. However, participants must pay tax if some or all of the principal amount of the loan is treated as a distribution of plan benefits under Code Sec. 72. See Chapter 9 for a discussion of the tax consequences of loans from qualified plans to participants.

.05 Profit-Sharing Plans

A profit-sharing plan is a defined contribution qualified plan under which the employer makes contributions on behalf of participating employees under a definite predetermined formula that may, in part, be based upon profits. The benefits receivable by the

---

[31] Reg. § 1.401-1(b)(1)(i); Rev. Rul. 56-693, 1956-2 CB 282, and Rev. Rul. 69-277, 1969-1 CB 116.

[32] Code Sec. 401(h).
[33] Code Sec. 401(h).

participants (or beneficiaries) will depend upon the amounts contributed, any earnings on the contributed amounts, and forfeitures allocated to the participants.

Under Reg. § 1.401-1(b)(1)(ii), a profit-sharing plan is:

> a plan established and maintained by an employer to provide for the participation in his profits by his employees or their beneficiaries. The plan must provide a definite predetermined formula for allocating contributions made to the plan among the participants and for distributing the funds accumulated under the plan after a fixed number of years, the attainment of a stated age, or upon the prior occurrence of some event such as layoff, illness, disability, retirement, death or severance of employment. A formula for allocating the contributions among the participants is definite, if, for example, it provides for an allocation in proportion to the basic compensation of each participant. A plan . . . does not qualify under Code Sec. 401(a) if the contributions to the plan are made at such times or in such amounts that the plan in operation discriminates in favor of . . . highly compensated employees.

Profit-sharing plan contributions need not be made each year. All that is necessary is that contributions be recurring and substantial.[34] Further, it is not necessary that the employer have profits in order to make contributions into profit-sharing plans.[35] Thus, tax-exempt organizations can maintain profit-sharing plans. Note that this provision does not mean that employers cannot base contributions on profits. It means that profits may be ignored in computing contributions.

A special type of profit-sharing plan that has become popular in recent years is the age-weighted profit-sharing plan. An age-weighted plan makes use of the nondiscrimination rules contained in Reg. § 1.401(a)(4)-2 or § 1.401(a)(4)-8 (the Reg. § 1.401(a)(4) rules are covered in Chapter 6) to provide relatively greater percentage contributions on behalf of older workers as compared to younger workers, so as to accumulate retirement funds more quickly for the older workers. A newer variation of this type of plan is called the "new comparability plan." A new comparability plan is a cross-tested, age-and-salary-weighted defined contribution plan that has the objective of distributing benefits upward (to the more highly compensated workers and officers) while satisfying nondiscrimination rules on

---

[34] Reg. § 1.401-1(b)(2). [35] Code Sec. 401(a)(27).

the basis of benefits testing.[36] The IRS has recently released final regulations applicable to new comparability plans.[37] The final regulations describe when such plans will be permitted to satisfy the Code Sec. 401(a)(4) nondiscrimination requirements based on projected benefits. The new regulations are effective as of June 29, 2001.

Allocating Contributions to Participant Accounts. The regulation above states that a profit-sharing plan must contain a predetermined formula for allocating contributions to the plan among the accounts of the participating employees. Contributions typically are allocated: (1) in proportion to compensation, (2) on the basis of salary plus years of service, or (3) on the basis of salary weighted by years of service. These formulas and others must not result in discrimination in favor of highly compensated employees.

If contributions are allocated in proportion to compensation, the total amount contributed is credited to each participating employee based on that employee's compensation relative to total compensation of all participating employees. For example, if an employee's compensation equals one percent of the compensation of all participants, one percent of the employer's contribution would be allocated to his account. EGTRRA has increased the maximum amount of compensation for each employee that can be taken into account for purposes of determining contributions to $200,000 in 2002 (adjusted for inflation after 2002—the limit for 2005 is $210,000, while the limit in 2001 was $170,000).[38]

If contributions are allocated on the basis of salary plus years of service, an employee would receive a certain portion of the employer's total contribution based on the employee's salary with an additional credit based on his number of years of service.

Finally, if the allocations are based on salary weighted by years of service, the contribution would be a certain amount allocated for each $1,000 (or some other amount) of compensation multiplied by the number of years of service performed for the employer.

Benefits Under Profit-Sharing Plans. The payment of benefits from a profit-sharing plan can begin at any of the times specified for pension plans (i.e., death, disability, termination of employment, or at retirement), and, in addition, for reasons of hardship, or after a fixed number of years.[39] In fact, Rev. Rul.

---

[36] Shepard, Lee A., "New Comparability Plan Rules and Cross-Testing Generally," *Tax Notes,* Oct. 16, 2000, pp. 336-343.

[37] Reg. § 1.401(a)(4)-8(b), as amended by T.D. 8954, 6/28/01. *See also* Rev. Rul. 2001-30, 2001-2 CB 46.

[38] Code Sec. 401(a)(17), as amended by P.L. 107-16, 107th Cong., 1st Sess., Sec 611(c) (June 7, 2001). IR-2004-127 (October 20, 2004).

[39] Reg. § 1.401-1(b)(1)(ii); Rev. Rul. 71-295, 1971-2 CB 184, and Rev. Rul. 73-553, 1973-2 CB 130.

71-295[40] has held that payments from profit-sharing plans can be made in as few as two years after contributions have been made to the plan.

Benefits may be paid in annuity or lump-sum form. In addition, incidental benefits in the form of life insurance and health and accident benefits may be provided, within limits.[41]

Employer's Deduction for Contributions Made. Deductions for employer contributions to profit-sharing plans are generally governed by the provisions of Code Sec. 404. Under Code Sec. 404(a), the maximum amount that an employer can deduct with respect to contributions to profit-sharing plans is the greater of (1) 25 percent (in 2002, and later years, up from 15 percent in 2001 and earlier years as a result of EGTRRA) of the compensation of all participants in the plan for the taxable year ending with or within a plan year or (2) in the case of profit-sharing plans that are Code Sec. 401(k) plans, the amount of contribution necessary to meet the nondiscrimination tests described in Code Sec. 401(k)(11). For example, if an employer had a total payroll in 2006 of $1,500,000, but the participants in the employer's profit-sharing plan received compensation of just $900,000, the maximum amount the employer could deduct on account of his profit-sharing plan contributions would be $225,000 (25 percent of $900,000). If an amount in excess of the 25 percent limitation is contributed during a given year, the employee may carry forward the excess to the next year to be considered along with contributions made in the next year. Such contributions in the next year would be subject to the 25 percent limit. Further carryovers are permitted if the excess cannot be fully used in the next year.

> **Example:** Assume the same facts as in the example described in the above paragraph. If the employer contributed $260,000 to the profit-sharing plan, only $225,000 would be deductible and the $35,000 that is not deductible for the current year can be carried forward to the next year to be considered with contributions made in that next year in determining the amount deductible for the year.

.06 Stock Bonus Plans

Stock bonus plans are defined contribution qualified plans that are similar to profit-sharing plans. The major difference between

---

[40] 1971-2 CB 184.

[41] Reg. § 1.401-1(b)(1)(ii).

stock bonus plans and profit-sharing plans is that the benefits from a stock bonus plan are payable in the form of the employer's stock.

Reg. § 1.401-1(b)(1)(iii) defines a stock bonus plan as follows:

> A stock bonus plan is a plan established and maintained by an employer to provide benefits similar to those of a profit-sharing plan, except that . . . the benefits are distributable in the stock of the employer company. For the purpose of allocating and distributing the stock of the employer . . . such a plan is subject to the same requirements as a profit-sharing plan.

A special type of stock bonus plan, the employee stock ownership plan is briefly described below and is more thoroughly covered in Chapter 11 of this book.

Advantaged Treatment of Distributions from Stock Bonus Plans. A distribution of employer stock or securities is not treated like other qualified plan distributions. If employer stock is distributed as a lump sum, the employee is not taxed at the time of the distribution on the appreciation in value of the stock that has occurred since it was contributed to the qualified plan by the employer.[42] That unrealized appreciation on the stock will be taxed as a capital gain when the employee actually sells or exchanges the stock. But, if the stock is distributed to the employee in a nonlump-sum distribution, only the portion of the unrealized appreciation that is attributable to the portion of the stock that was paid for by the employee can be excluded. For further discussion on the matter, see Chapter 9.

.07 Money Purchase Pension Plans

A money purchase pension plan is a defined contribution qualified plan under which the employer must make definitely determinable contributions to the account of each participant in the plan each year.

Determination of Employer Contributions. Under a money purchase plan, the employer must make yearly contributions using a definitely determinable formula. Thus, contributions cannot be dependent on profits or some other criteria.[43] Further, contributions cannot be limited by action of the board of directors.[44]

Employer contributions under a money purchase plan are normally a specified percentage of a participant's compensation.

---

[42] Code Sec. 402(e)(4).
[43] Rev. Rul. 72-302, 1972-1 CB 111, and Rev. Rul 73-412, 1973-2 CB 125.
[44] Rev. Rul. 73-379, 1973-2 CB 124.

The percentage may, for example, equal 12 percent of the employee's annual compensation, or 12 percent of the first $100,000 of annual compensation and 15 percent of earnings in excess of that amount. But, of course, the amounts contributed cannot discriminate in favor of highly compensated employees, and only the first $200,000 in 2002 (adjusted for inflation after 2002—the 2005 maximum is $210,000—the dollar maximum was increased up from $170,000 in 2001 as a result of the enactment of EGTRRA) of compensation of each participant can be taken into account in determining employer contributions (see Chapter 6).

Determination of Benefits Payable Under Money Purchase Plans. In general, the benefits payable under a money purchase plan, like any other defined contribution plan, are based on the account balance of the employee at the time the benefit payments are to begin. This account balance equals the amount of employer contributions and forfeitures, if any, that are allocated to the employee's account, employee contributions, plus the net earnings received by the fund holder.

.08 Target Benefit Plans

A target benefit plan is a pension plan that is a hybrid of a defined benefit pension plan and a money purchase pension plan. Under a target benefit plan, a "target" defined benefit is established, and contributions are determined by actuarial assumptions to fund the target benefit.[45] But, after the initial contribution formula is established, no adjustments are made to that formula. In that respect, the plan is a defined contribution plan.

All of the other features of a target benefit plan are similar to those of money purchase pension plans.

.09 Cash or Deferred Arrangements (Code Sec. 401(k) Plans)

A qualified cash or deferred arrangement (CODA) (Code Sec. 401(k) plan) is an arrangement within a qualified profit-sharing, stock bonus, pre-ERISA money purchase, or rural electric cooperative plan, under which a participant can elect either to receive current cash compensation or have the employer contribute like amounts on a pretax basis to the qualified plan. The arrangement typically contains a salary reduction agreement under which employer contributions are made only if the participant elects to reduce his or her compensation or not to take a pay increase. The agreement may also give the participant the option to receive a

---

[45] *See* Reg § 1.401(a)(4)-8(b)(3).

portion of the total amount subject to election as cash compensation, and have the remainder contributed to the qualified plan fund holder.[46] A second means of setting up employee participation in Code Sec. 401(k) plans is by automatic enrollment. An automatic enrollment (or negative election) is a feature meant to encourage participation by employees in their employer's Code Sec. 401(k) plan (automatic enrollment is also being used with Code Sec. 403(b) plans covered in ¶502.13 and Code Sec. 457 plans covered in chapter 14). Under automatic enrollment, unless an eligible employee affirmatively elects to receive cash compensation, the employee's compensation is automatically reduced by a fixed percentage of the cash compensation, and that amount is contributed into the employer's Code Sec. 401(k) plan. Recently, the IRS issued a General Information Letter in which it stated that (1) the amount which is deducted from the employee's cash compensation and contributed to the plan can be any amount that is allowable under the plan up to the annual contribution limits under Code Sec. 402(g) (covered below); and (2) the plan can automatically increase the employee's contribution over time, such as after the employee receives an increase in compensation. The final Code Sec. 401(k) regulations also provide for automatic election provisions.[47]

Contributions to CODAs. Two types of contributions may be made to CODAs. Employers may make nonelective contributions which are basically treated the same way for tax purposes as employer contributions to other qualified plans (i.e., they are excludable to the participant). The other type of contributions is elective deferrals made under a salary reduction plan. They are also excludable for income tax purposes when contributed but are subject to FICA and FUTA taxes under Code Secs. 3121(v)(1) and 3306(r)(1). The employer may also make matching contributions equal to the amount of or a certain percentage of the employees' elective contributions.

Under Code Sec. 402(g), the maximum dollar amount of elective contributions under CODAs that can be excluded has been increased as a result of the enactment of EGTRRA to $11,000 in 2002 and has been increased by $1,000 per year up to $14,000 in 2005 (up from $10,500 in 2001). The limit will increase by an additional $1,000 to reach $15,000 in 2006 and will be adjusted upward on account of inflation after that.[48]

---

[46] Code Sec. 401(k)(2).

[47] IRS General Information Letter (April 7, 2004); Rev. Ruls. 98-30, 1998-1 CB 1273, and 2000-35, 2000-2 CB 138; Reg. § 1.401(k)-1(a)(3).

[48] Code Sec. 402(g)(1), as amended by P.L. 107-16, 107th Cong., 1st Sess., Sec. 611(d)(1)(June 7, 2001).

¶502.09

EGTRRA also includes a provision under which, beginning in the year 2002, certain plan participants may be permitted to make additional "catch-up" contributions to Code Sec. 401(k) plans and other plans which allow elective deferral contributions, such as Code Sec. 403(b) plans (covered in ¶502.13, below).[49] Recently issued Reg. § 1.414(v)-1 provides guidance on the new "catch-up" contribution provisions. Under Reg. § 1.414(v)-1, which is generally effective for taxable years beginning on or after January 1, 2004, plan participants who are "catch-up eligible participants" may make additional elective deferral (pre-tax) contributions. A catch-up eligible participant is any plan participant who is at least or will become age 50 before the end of the applicable calendar year. Catch-up contributions are defined as elective deferrals made by catch-up eligible participants in excess of any of the following limits and that do not exceed the statutory dollar limits for catch-up contributions:

(1) the statutory limit (which would be the Code Sec. 402(g) dollar limits listed above—e.g., $15,000 in 2006 or, if smaller, the participant's compensation for the year);

(2) an employer-provided limit which is not the statutory limit (e.g., a contribution that a catch-up eligible participant may make in excess of an employer plan limit such as 15 percent of an employee's compensation would be a catch-up contribution—thus, if an employee had compensation of $20,000 in 2006, any contribution permitted in excess of $3,000 (15% of $20,000) would be a catch-up contribution);

(3) the actual deferral percentage (ADP) limit that applies to Code Sec. 401(k) plans (see the discussion of the ADP limit in Chapter 7) and salary reduction simplified employee pension plans (discussed in Chapter 10).

The maximum amount of the catch-up contribution that can be made (the dollar limit) for Code Sec. 401(k) plans and other elective deferral plans other than SIMPLE plans started out at $1,000 in 2002 and has been increased by $1,000 per year after that up to $4,000 in 2005 and $5,000 in 2006. After 2006, the $5,000 additional contribution limit will be adjusted upward for inflation.

Based on the discussion in the two paragraphs above, the maximum elective deferral contributions that can be made by any Code

---

[49] Code Sec. 414(v), as added by P.L. 107-16, 107th Cong., 1st Sess., Sec. 631(a) (June 7, 2001).

Sec. 401(k) plan participants for the years 2001 through 2006 are as follows:

Year	Elective Deferral Limit	Additional Contribution Limit for Participants Age 50 or More	Total Elective Deferral Limit for Participants Age 50 or More
2001	$10,500	$0	$10,500
2002	11,000	1,000	12,000
2003	12,000	2,000	14,000
2004	13,000	3,000	16,000
2005	14,000	4,000	18,000
2006	15,000	5,000	20,000

Example: A 30-year-old participant could make elective deferrals of up to $15,000 in 2006 to a Code Sec. 401(k) plan. If that participant were at least age 50, the maximum elective deferral contribution will be $20,000.

The elective deferral (and additional catch-up elective deferral) limits apply to all of the employee's elective contributions under simplified employee pension plans and Code Sec. 403(b) tax-sheltered annuity plans. In addition, elective deferrals made by an employee under a Savings Incentive Match Plan for Employees (SIMPLE) are considered to be elective deferrals for purposes of the limitation.

Qualified Roth Contribution Programs. Effective for tax years beginning after 2005, participants in Code Sec. 401(k) plans will be permitted to make after-tax contributions in lieu of some or all of the elective deferral contributions they would have otherwise made to a qualified Roth contribution program, if the employer's plan then incorporates such a program.[50] Such contributions would be made to a separate designated Roth IRA account (see Chapter 10 for a discussion of Roth IRAs in general) for each participating employee. The elective deferral limits covered above will apply to the combined amount of elective deferral and after-tax contributions made by each participating employee. Employees may be better off making their Code Sec. 401(k) contributions to designated Roth IRA

---

[50] Code Sec. 402A, as added by P.L. 107-16, 107th Cong., 1st Sess., Sec 617(a) (June 7. 2001); and Code Sec. 402(g)(1), as amended by P.L. 107-16, 107th Cong., 1st Sess., Sec. 617(a) (June 7, 2001)—effective for taxable years beginning after December 31, 2005.

¶502.09

accounts instead of making elective deferral contributions, since (as noted in Chapter 10) there will no tax levied on withdrawals from such accounts (including earnings on plan contributions) if the withdrawals are considered qualified distributions (generally those taken on or after when the participant reaches age 59½). In late 2005, the IRS issued proposed regulations which explain the Roth IRA option for Code Sec. 401(k) plans.[51] For further discussion of qualified Roth contribution programs, see Chapter 7.

Special Requirements for CODAs. In addition to satisfying the normal pension plan qualification rules, a CODA must also satisfy the following requirements:

(1) The employee's right to accrued benefits attributable to the elective deferral must be nonforfeitable at all times.

(2) Amounts attributable to the elective deferrals may not be distributed to participants or their beneficiaries earlier than:

(a) severance from employment, death, or disability;

(b) termination of the plan without the establishment of a successor plan;

(c) the attainment of age 59½, in the case of a profit-sharing or stock bonus plan; or

(d) hardship of the employer in the case of profit-sharing or stock bonus plans.

Such plans must also satisfy special nondiscrimination rules relating to plan contributions and participation, unless the special safe-harbor rules of Code Sec. 401(k)(12) apply. In December of 2004, the IRS issued new comprehensive final regulations under Code Sec. 401(k) to incorporate statutory changes (including those in EGTRRA) and administrative developments since final regulations were last published in 1994.[52] For further discussion, see Chapter 7.

.10 Savings Incentive Match Plan for Employees (SIMPLE)

The Small Business Job Protection Act of 1996 established two new qualified deferred compensation plans effective for plan years beginning after 1996—SIMPLE Section 401(k) plans and SIMPLE IRA plans.[53] SIMPLE Section 401(k) plans are covered in detail

---

[51] *See* REG-152354-04 (Mar. 2, 2005), 70 FR 10062.
[52] *See* T.D. 9169 (Dec. 28, 2004), 69 FR 78143.

[53] *See*, e.g., Code Secs. 408(p) and 401(k)(11), as added by P.L. 104-188. 104th Cong., 2d Sess. (Aug. 20, 1996), Secs. 1421 and 1422.

in Chapter 7 and SIMPLE IRA plans are further discussed in Chapter 10. SIMPLE plans have been very popular. For example, in the first two months of 1997, Fidelity Investments reported setting up about 1,000 new SIMPLE plans, whereas it had anticipated that it would set up only about 40 such plans per month.[54] Some general characteristics of SIMPLE plans are noted below.

In general, a SIMPLE plan may be established only by an employer that had no more than 100 employees who received at least $5,000 of compensation during the preceding year.[55] In addition, the employer cannot maintain any other qualified deferred compensation plan that covers employees covered by a SIMPLE plan (i.e., none of the other qualified plans described in this chapter or other parts of this book).[56] Employees must be notified of the existence of the plan and permitted to elect to participate in the SIMPLE plan.

Employees that elect to participate in a SIMPLE plan will have their employer make elective pre-tax contributions, expressed as a percentage of compensation or as a specific dollar amount. EGTRRA increased the maximum allowable employee elective deferral contributions starting in 2002. In 2002, the maximum amount was $7,000 (up from $6,500 in 2001), and that amount has been increased by $1,000 each year after 2002 up to $10,000 in 2005. After 2005, the $10,000 limit will be adjusted upward for inflation.[57] In addition, eligible catch-up participants (those who are at least or will become age 50 during an applicable calendar year) can make additional "catch-up" elective deferral contributions to SIMPLE plans beginning in 2002. Recently issued Reg. § 1.414(v)-1 provides guidance concerning the definition of catch-up contributions and other issues (see the discussion of this regulation in ¶502.09 above). The additional contribution dollar limit started out at $500 in 2002 and has been increased by $500 each year since up to $2,000 in 2005 and $2,500 in 2006. After 2006, the then $2,500 limit will be adjusted upward for inflation.[58] Thus, the elective deferral limits for SIMPLE plans for the years 2001 through 2005 are as follows:

---

[54] Federal Bar Association Briefs, *Tax Notes,* March 10, 1997, p. 1260.

[55] Code Secs. 401(k)(11)(D)(i) and 408(p)(2)(C)(i).

[56] Code Secs. 401(k)(11)(C) and 408(P)(2)(D).

[57] Code Sec. 408(p)(2)(E), as amended by P.L. 107-16, 107th Cong., 1st Sess., Sec. 611(f) (June 7, 2001).

[58] Code Sec. 414(v)(2)(B)(ii), as added by P.L. 107-16, 107th Cong., 1st Sess., Sec. 631(a) (June 7. 2001)

Year	Elective Deferral Limit	Additional Elective Deferral for Participants Age 50 or More	Total Elective Deferral Limit for Participants Age 50 or More
2001	$6,500	$ 0	$6,500
2002	7,000	500	7,500
2003	8,000	1,000	9,000
2004	9,000	1,500	10,500
2005	10,000	2,000	12,000

Example: A 30-year-old participant in a SIMPLE plan could make elective deferral contributions of up to $10,000 to the plan in 2005. If, instead, the participant were at least age 50 in 2005, the maximum elective deferral contribution could be $12,000.

In general, the employer must match the amount each participating employee contributes up to three percent of the employee's compensation for the year. In lieu of making a matching contribution, an employer can make a nonelective contribution equal to two percent of compensation on behalf of each employee who is eligible to participate in the plan.[59] The amount of the pre-tax employee contributions and the employer contributions are excludable from the employee's gross income. However, the pre-tax employee contributions are subject to FICA and FUTA taxes.[60]

SIMPLE plans are exempt from the nondiscrimination rules that apply to other qualified deferred compensation plans under Code Sec. 401 (discussed in Chapter 6) and the top heavy plan rules covered in Chapter 7. However, all employees with at least $5,000 of compensation must be permitted to participate in a SIMPLE IRA plan; SIMPLE 401(k) plans may require one year of service and attainment of age 21 for eligibility; participating employees must be permitted to terminate participation in the plan at any time; all contributions made on behalf of participating employees must be completely vested when made; and participating employees in SIMPLE IRAs (SIMPLE 401(k)s subject to qualified plan distribution rules) must be permitted to make withdrawals from their plan at any time.[61] Amounts withdrawn and distributions received by employees from SIMPLE plans are fully taxable when received, and, in some cases, may be subject to additional penalty taxes, unless such amounts are rolled over into another SIMPLE plan or an IRA.

---

[59] Code Secs. 401(k)(11)(B)(ii) and 408(p)(2)(B).
[60] Notice 98-4, 1998-1 CB 269.

[61] *See* Code Secs. 401(k)(11)(A) and 408(p)(3) and (4) and Notice 98-4, 1998-1 CB 269.

.11 Employee Stock Ownership Plans

An employee stock ownership plan (ESOP) is a defined contribution plan which is a qualified stock bonus plan or a qualified stock bonus and a money purchase plan which is designed to invest primarily in qualifying employer securities.[62] An ESOP must satisfy the qualification requirements of Code Sec. 401 and the requirements of Code Sec. 409(e) and 409(h) (if the employer has registration-type securities).

The distinction between a stock bonus plan (described earlier) and an ESOP is important because ESOPs are not subject to certain prohibited transactions rules while stock bonus plans are. For example, an ESOP may borrow funds to buy the securities of the employer corporation. Otherwise, the tax treatment of ESOPs is largely the same as the tax treatment of stock bonus plans. Since ESOPs are more widely used than regular stock bonus plans, an entire chapter of this book—Chapter 11—covers, in detail, the tax treatment of ESOPs.

.12 Code Sec. 403(a) Annuity Plans

An annuity plan is a qualified plan under which retirement benefits are provided through the use of annuity or insurance contracts.[63] The basic statutory difference between a Code Sec. 403(a) annuity plan and a pension plan is that an annuity plan does not have to meet the requirements concerning the existence and terms of a trust that apply to a qualified pension plan. Thus, in general, the rules governing contributions made to and benefits payable under annuity plans are similar to those concerning pension plans.

A Code Sec. 403(a) annuity plan usually will pay retirement benefits under an annuity contract issued by an insurance company. However, it can also include a face amount certificate, as defined in Sec. 2(a)(15) of the Investment Company Act of 1940.[64] However, an annuity plan cannot include any contract or certificate issued after 1962 if the contract or certificate is transferable and is owned by a person other than the trustee of a Code Sec. 401(a) trust. A contract or certificate is nontransferable if the owner cannot sell, sign, discount, or pledge as collateral for a loan or as security for the performance of an obligation his interest in the contract to any person other than the issuer. However, the employee may designate a beneficiary to receive the proceeds of the annuity upon the employee's death or may elect to have annuity benefits paid in joint and survivor form.[65]

---

[62] Code Sec. 4975(e)(7).
[63] Reg. § 1.404(a)-3(a).

[64] Code Sec. 401(g).
[65] Reg. § 1.401-9(b)(3).

.13 Code Sec. 403(b) Annuity Plans

Contributions made by a tax-exempt Code Sec. 501(c)(3) religious, charitable, scientific, etc. organization, or a public school to a Code Sec. 403(b) annuity plan may be wholly or partly excludable to the employee (depending upon the amount of the contribution relative to the employee's exclusion allowance). Further, even if an employee's rights under the contract are nonforfeitable at the time of the contribution, the employee is not taxed until benefits are actually received under the plan. For taxable years beginning after December 31, 1995, participants in Code Sec. 403(b) tax-sheltered annuity plans may enter into more than one salary reduction agreement per year.[66] Prior to 1996, participants in those accounts were only permitted to enter into one salary reduction agreement per year. In November of 2004, the IRS issued comprehensive proposed regulations under Code Sec. 403(b) intended to replace final regulations last issued in 1964 to take account of legislative changes and administrative developments since then.[67] The proposed regulations, upon promulgation of final regulations, are generally intended to apply for taxable years beginning after December 31, 2005.[68] Reference will be made to the proposed regulations as appropriate in the following introduction to Code Sec. 403(b) plans.

Exclusion Allowance. In taxable years prior to January 1, 2002, a maximum exclusion allowance applied with respect to Code Sec. 403(b) plans.[69] The exclusion allowance has been repealed with respect to years beginning after December 31, 2001. Thus, after 2001, for defined contribution Code Sec. 403(b) plans, only the maximum contribution (addition to account) limit under Code Sec. 415(c) applies as the limit for how much can be excluded by the participant employee.

Maximum Benefit and Contribution Limitations. The Code Sec. 415 maximum benefit limitations apply to Code Sec. 403(b) plans. Thus, the maximum benefit cannot exceed $160,000 for plan limitation years ending after December 31, 2001 (adjusted for inflation after 2002—the limit is $170,000 for 2005 plan years, and the limit was increased from $140,000 in 2001 by EGTRRA).[70] If the Code Sec. 403(b) plan is treated as a defined

---

[66] Code Sec. 402(e)(3) as amended by P.L. 104-188, 104th Cong., 2d Sess., Sec 1450(a) (Aug. 20, 1996).

[67] REG-155608-2, Nov. 16, 2004, 69 FR 67075.

[68] Prop. Reg. § 1.403(b)-11(a).

[69] Code Sec. 403(b)(2), as stricken by P.L. 107-16, 107th Cong., 1st Sess., Sec. 632(a)(2) (June 7, 2001).

[70] Code Sec. 415(b)(1)(A), as amended by P.L. 107-16, 107th Cong., 1st Sess., Sec. 611(a)(1)(A) (June 7, 2001). *See also* Rev. Rul. 2001-51, 2001-2 CB 427, IR 2004-127 (October 20, 2004).

contribution plan, the maximum allowable account addition (including contributions) for plan limitation years beginning on or after January 1, 2002, is the lesser of (1) 100 percent of the employee's compensation or (2) $40,000 (adjusted for inflation after 2002—the 2005 plan year limit is $42,000).[71] As noted in the above paragraph, the Code Sec. 403(b)(2) exclusion allowance does not apply in years after 2001. For purposes of this calculation, compensation does not include contributions to a Code Sec. 403(b) plan.[72] If the contributions exceed the Code Sec. 415(c) limits, the plan will not be disqualified. Instead, the excess amount is reported as gross income.[73]

Special Exclusion Allowance and Contribution Rules. EGTRRA made significant changes to the special exclusion allowance and contribution rules under Code Sec. 403(b), effective for years beginning after December 31, 2001. Beginning in 2002, the only special provision remaining is under revised Code Sec. 415(c)(7).[74] Under that revised section, at the election of a participant who is an employee of a church or a convention or association of churches, including organizations described in Code Sec. 414(e)(3)(B)(ii), contributions and other additions to a Code Sec. 403(b) plan will not be treated as exceeding the Code Sec. 415(c)(1) limit (covered in the above paragraph) if that annual addition does not exceed $10,000. For this purpose, the total amount of additions for any participant for all years that may be considered under this exception shall not exceed $40,000. The rest of the special exclusion allowance and contribution limit rules were repealed by EGTRRA effective for years beginning after December 31, 2001.

Salary Reduction 403(b) Plans. Amounts that are contributed by employers on behalf of employees to a Code Sec. 403(b) plan under a salary reduction agreement are excludable to the employees within limits. Starting in 1996, an employee can enter into more than one salary reduction agreement per year.[75] This means that 403(b) participants can change their deferral percentage during a plan year if the plan allows.

In addition to the exclusion allowance (effective for years beginning before January 1, 2002) and the Code Sec. 415(c) limitations,

---

[71] Code Sec. 415(c)(1), as amended by P.L. 107-16, 107th Cong., 1st Sess., Sec. 611(b)(1) (June 7, 2001). *See also* Rev. Rul. 2001-51, 2001-2 CB 427; IR-2004-127 (October 20, 2004); Prop. Reg. § 1.403(b)-4(a).

[72] Code Sec. 415(c)(3); Reg. § 1.415-2(d)(3); Prop. Reg. § 1.403(b)-4(b).

[73] Prop. Reg. § 1.403(b)-4(f)(1).

[74] Code Sec. 415(c)(7), as amended by P.L. 107-16, 107th Cong., 1st Sess., Sec. 632(a)(3)(F) (June 7, 2001). Code Secs. 403(b)(2) and 415(c)(4), as stricken by P.L. 107-16, 107th Cong., 1st Sess., Secs. 632(a)(3)(E) and 632(a)(2) (June 7, 2001).

[75] Code Sec. 402(e)(3), as amended by P.L. 104-188, 105th Cong., 1st Sess., Sec. 1450(a) (Aug. 20, 1996).

there is a cap on the amount that an employee can exclude pursuant to a Code Sec. 403(b) salary reduction agreement. Thus, the limit in the case of elective deferral plans is for years beginning after 2001, the lesser of (1) the Code Sec. 415(c)(1) limitation (covered above) or (2) the elective deferral limit covered in this paragraph.[76]

The elective deferral limit is being increased after 2001 as a result of the enactment of EGTRRA. The applicable dollar limit was increased to $11,000 in 2002 and has been increased by $1,000 per year since then to $14,000 in 2005 and $15,000 in 2006 (the limit was $10,500 in 2001). After 2006, the then $15,000 limit will be adjusted for inflation.[77] Further, beginning in 2002, eligible catch-up participants (those who are at least or will become age 50 during an applicable calendar year) will be permitted to make additional "catch-up" contributions. Recently issued Reg. § 1.414(v)-1 provides guidance concerning the definition of catch-up contributions and other issues (see the discussion of that regulation in ¶502.09). The maximum additional contribution started out at $1,000 in 2002 and has been increased by $1,000 per year up to $4,000 in 2005 and $5,000 in 2006. After 2006, the then $15,000 limit will be adjusted upward on account of inflation.[78] Thus, the elective deferral limits for Code Sec. 403(b) plans for the years 2001 through 2006 are as follows:

Year	Elective Deferral Limit	Additional Elective Deferral Limit for Participants Age 50 or More	Total Elective Deferral Limit for Participants Age 50 or More
2001	$10,500	$ 0	$10,500
2002	11,000	1,000	12,000
2003	12,000	2,000	14,000
2004	13,000	3,000	16,000
2005	14,000	4,000	18,000
2006	15,000	5,000	20,000

Example: A 30-year-old participant in a Code Sec. 403(b) elective deferral plan can make elective deferral contributions in 2006 of up to $15,000 (assuming this amount is smaller than the Code Sec. 415(c)(1) limitation). If that participant were at least 50 in 2006, the maximum elective deferral contribution would be $20,000.

---

[76] Prop. Reg. Sec. 1.403(b)-4(b) and (c).
[77] Code Secs. 402(g)(1) and (4), as amended by P.L. 107-16, 107th Cong., 1st Sess., Secs. 611(d)(1) and (2) (June 7, 2001).

[78] Code Secs. 414(v)(2)(B) and (C), as added by P.L. 107-16, 107th Cong., 1st Sess., Sec. 631(a) (June 7, 2001). See also Prop. Reg. § 1.403(b)-4(c).

The limit on elective deferrals under Code Sec. 403(b) plans applies to all Code Sec. 403(b) plans, CODAs, and elective deferral simplified employee plans (SEPs) in which the employee participates. For years beginning before January 1, 2002, a Code Sec. 403(b) plan participant who also participated in a Code Sec. 457 deferred compensation plan (see the discussion of Code Sec. 457 plans in Chapter 14) was subject to a combined elective deferral limit that was equal to the limit applying to Code Sec. 457 plans (in 2001, that limit was $8,500).[79] This provision was repealed effective for years beginning after December 31, 2001.[80] Thus, after 2001, elective deferrals can be made into Code Sec. 403(b) plans up to the limits covered above and also into Code Sec. 457 plans up to the limit applying to those plans (covered in Chapter 14).[81] Effective for taxable years beginning after December 31, 1995, the elective deferral limit applies to the tax-sheltered annuity contract of each participant, rather than to the tax-sheltered annuity plan.[82] Therefore, excess deferrals made with respect to one participant in the plan do not affect the excludability of contributions by other plan participants. Note that employer contributions to a Code Sec. 403(b) annuity plan are not treated as elective deferrals if the contributions are made pursuant to a one-time irrevocable election made by the employee at the time of initial eligibility to participate in the agreement or is made pursuant to a similar arrangement involving a one-time irrevocable election specified in IRS regulations.[83]

Amounts of elective deferrals that exceed the maximum allowable exclusion for a particular year are taxable to the employee in that year and must be allocated among the Code Sec. 403(b) plans and other elective deferral plans in which the employee participates by March 1 of the next year. The plans must distribute such excess amounts along with the income allocable to them to the participant by the following April 15.[84] Such distribution will not be subject to the 10-percent premature distribution penalty tax described in Chapter 9. However, the excess deferrals must be taken into account in applying the special nondiscrimination tests.

Catch-up Election Under Salary Reduction Plans. Code Sec. 402(g)(7) provides an exception to the annual limit on elective deferrals under Code Sec. 403(b) plans. A qualified employee who has completed at least 15 years of service with an educational institution, hospital, home health service or agency, health or welfare

---

[79] *See* e.g., former Code Sec. 457(c)(2).

[80] See P.L. 107-16, 107th Cong., 1st Sess., Sec. 615(a) (June 7, 2001).

[81] *See*, e.g., IRS Pub. No. 571 at 7.

[82] Code Sec. 403(b)(1)(E), as amended by P.L. 104-188, 104th Cong. 2d Sess., Sec. 1450(c) (Aug. 20, 1996).

[83] Code Sec. 402(g)(3). *See also* IRS Pub. 571 at 3.

[84] Prop. Reg. § 1.403(b)-4(f)(2).

service agency, or certain churches can make additional elective deferrals. The maximum allowable additional contribution for a particular year is the least of the following:[85]

(1) $3,000;

(2) $15,000 minus additional elective deferrals made in prior years; or

(3) the excess of $5,000 multiplied by the number of years of service of the employee for the qualified organization over elective deferrals made by the employee with respect to that organization in prior years.

Example: Kellee, age 40, is employed at Crane University, and began her employment there on January 1, 1987. Thus, she had accumulated 19 years of service by the end of 2005. Her elective deferrals in prior years amounted to $78,000. On January 2, 2006, Kellee and her employer agreed to a salary reduction of $1,300 per month to be contributed to a tax-sheltered annuity. Kellee's total elective deferrals to the tax-sheltered annuity for 2006 equal $15,600, which is more than the $15,000 elective deferral limit for 2006. However, since Kellee is an employee of an educational institution with more than 15 years of service, she may increase her elective deferral limit by the lesser of:

(1) $3,000,

(2) $15,000,

(3) ($5,000 × 19) − $78,000 = $17,000.

Kellee's total elective deferral limit under the Code Sec. 402(g)(7) election is $18,000 ($15,000 + $3,000). Therefore, her elective deferrals do not exceed the elective deferral limit.

The proposed Code Sec. 403(b) regulations indicate how to determine the contribution limits for a Code Sec. 403(b) participant who is eligible for both an age 50 or greater additional elective deferral contribution and the special Code Sec. 403(b) catch-up contribution pursuant to Code Sec. 402(g)(7), as described above. The proposed regulations indicate that any catch-up amount contributed by such an employee is treated first as an amount contributed as a special Code Sec. 403(b) catch-up, to the extent a special Code Sec. 403(b) catch-up is permitted, and then as an amount contributed as an age 50 or greater catch-up (to the extent the catch-up amount exceeds the maximum special Code Sec. 403(b) catch-up).[86]

---

[85] Prop. Reg. § 1.403(b)-4(c)(3).   [86] Prop. Reg. § 1.403(b)-4(c)(3)(iv).

Example: Assume the same facts as in the previous example, except that Kellee is age 50 in 2006. According to the proposed regulations, Kellee could have contributed as much as $23,000 to the plan for 2006—(1) the $15,000 regular elective deferral limit, plus (2) the special Code Sec. 403(b) catch-up contribution of $3,000, plus (3) the additional $5,000 elective deferral contribution for those participants age 50 or more.[87]

Qualified Roth Code Sec. 403(b) Contributions. Effective for tax years beginning after 2005, participants in elective deferral Code Sec. 403(b) plans will be permitted to make after-tax contributions in lieu of part or all of the elective deferral contributions that they would have otherwise made to a qualified Roth contribution plan, if the employer's plan then incorporates such a program.[88] See the discussion of this rule concerning Code Sec. 401(k) plans in ¶502.10 and in Chapter 7.

Nondiscrimination Rules. The type of nondiscrimination rules that apply to a Code Sec. 403(b) plan depends upon whether the plan is a nonelective deferral or an elective deferral plan. When the proposed regulations issued in 2004 become final, Code Sec. 403(b) nonelective deferral plans will have to meet all of the following requirements (collectively referred to as nondiscrimination requirements) in the same manner as a qualified plan under Code Sec. 401(a): (1) Code Sec. 401(a)(4) (relating to nondiscrimination in contributions and benefits), taking Code Sec. 401(a)(5) into account; (2) Code Sec. 401(a)(17) (limiting the amount of compensation that can be taken into account—that limit is $210,000 in 2005); (3) Code Sec. 401(m) (relating to matching and after-tax contributions); and (4) Code Sec. 410(b) (relating to minimum coverage).[89] See Chapter 6 for a general discussion of these requirements. However, for nonelective deferral plans of state and local governments and political subdivisions thereof, only the Code Sec. 401(a)(17) compensation limitations apply.[90] Other governmental nonelective deferral plans will be deemed to satisfy the nondiscrimination rules until the first day of the first plan year beginning on or after the date the proposed regulations become final.[91] Until then, such plans must be operated in accordance with a reasonable good-faith interpretation of the

---

[87] Prop. Reg. § 1.403(b)-4(c)(4).

[88] Code Sec. 402A, as added by P.L. 107-16, 107th Cong., 1st Sess., Sec. 617(a) (June 7, 2001); Code Sec. 402(g)(1), as amended by P.L. 107-16, 107th Cong., 1st Sess., Sec. 617(a) (June 7, 2001), effective for taxable years beginning after December 31, 2005.

[89] Code Sec. 403(b)(12)(A)(i). Prop. Reg. § 1.403(b)-5(a)(1).

[90] Code Sec. 403(b)(12)(C), as added by P.L. 105-34, 105th Cong., 1st Sess., Sec. 1505(c) (Aug. 5, 1997); Prop. Reg. § 1.403(b)-5(a)(5).

[91] Notice 2003-6, 2003-1 CB 298 and Prop. Reg. § 1.403(b)-11(a).

¶502.13

statutory provisions. Alternatively, until then, other governmental nonelective deferral plans can satisfy the nondiscrimination rules if they meet one of three safe harbor tests first specified in Notice 89-23:[92] (1) the maximum disparity safe harbor; (2) the lesser disparity safe harbor; or (3) the no-disparity safe harbor. In general, these safe-harbor tests place limits on the allowable difference between the amounts that can be contributed for the highly and nonhighly compensated employees of the organizations and provide that specified minimum numbers or percentages of nonhighly compensated employees must benefit under the plan.[93]

The nondiscrimination rules do not apply to Code Sec. 403(b) plans maintained (i.e., contracts purchased by) a church.[94] For this purpose, the term "church" means a church as defined in Code Sec. 3121(w)(3)(A) and a qualified church-controlled organization defined in Code Sec. 3121(w)(3)(B).[95] In addition, retirement plans maintained by the YMCA Retirement Fund as of January 1, 2003 are treated as church plans.[96] Prop. Reg. § 1.403(b)-9, when finalized, will contain special rules for church-maintained Code Sec. 403(b) plans.

The nondiscrimination rules described above do not apply to elective deferral Code Sec. 403(b) plans.[97] Under Code Sec. 403(b)(12)(A)(ii), all employees of the eligible employer must be permitted to have Section 403(b) elective deferrals contributed on their behalf if any employee of the eligible employer may elect to have the organization make Code Sec. 403(b) elective deferrals. The employee's right to have Code Sec. 403(b) elective deferrals made on his or her behalf includes the right to Code Sec. 403(b) elective deferrals up to the lesser of (1) the applicable elective deferral dollar limitations (covered above), or (2) the applicable limits under the contract with the largest limitation, and applies to part-time employees as well as full-time employees.[98] Further, the plan must provide an employee with an effective opportunity to make (or change) a cash or deferred election (as defined in Reg. § 1.401(k)-1(a)(3)) at least once during each plan year. Whether an employee has an effective opportunity is determined based on all the relevant facts and circumstances, including notice of the availability of the election, the period of time during which an election may be made, and any other conditions on elections. An effective opportunity is not considered to exist if there are any other rights or benefits that are

---

[92] Prop. Reg. § 1.403(b)-5(d).

[93] 1989-1 CB 654, modified by Notice 90-73, 1990-2 CB 253, and 96-64, 1996-2 CB 229.

[94] *Id.*

[95] Prop. Reg. § 1.403(b)-2(a)(5).

[96] P.L. 108-476, 108th Cong., 2d Sess., Sec. 1(a)(1) (Dec. 21, 2004).

[97] Prop. Reg. § 1.403(b)-5(a)(2).

[98] Prop. Reg. § 1.403(b)-5(b)(1).

conditioned (directly or indirectly) upon a participant making or failing to make a cash or deferred election with respect to a contribution to a Code Sec. 403(b) contract.[99] If a Code Sec. 403(b) plan covers the employees of more than one Code Sec. 501(c)(3) organization, the universal availability requirement applies separately to each common law entity, i.e., to each Code Sec. 501(c)(3) organization. In the case of a Code Sec. 403(b) plan that covers the employees of more than one State entity, this requirement applies separately to each entity that is not part of a common payroll. An employer may condition the employee's right to have Code Sec. 403(b) elective deferrals made on his or her behalf on the employee electing a Section 403(b) elective deferral of more than $200 for a year.[100]

In applying the nondiscrimination rules with respect to Code Sec. 403(b) plans, nonresident aliens with no U.S. source income from the employer, employees who participate in an eligible deferred compensation arrangement, CODA, or another Code Sec. 403(b) plan that permits employees to make elective deferrals, employees who work less than 20 hours per week, and students whose pay is exempt from social security taxes under Code Sec. 3121(b)(10) may be excluded from consideration.

Permitted Distributions and Taxability of Distributions. Beginning in 1989, distributions of elective deferrals (and the earnings on such contributions) may not be made before the employee:

(1) reaches age 59½;

(2) has a severance from employment (prior to 2002, the wording was "has a separation from service")

(3) dies;

(4) becomes disabled; or

(5) experiences financial hardship.[101]

Distributions on account of financial hardship are limited to the amount of the elective deferrals (and not the earnings thereon). However, the Code Sec. 403(b)(11) rules only apply with respect to distributions that are attributable to assets other than assets held as of the close of the last year beginning before January 1, 1989.[102] Thus, distributions with respect to pre-1989 assets in the plan can be made at any time. Further, plans under which the employee makes a one-time election upon beginning participation in the plan are not

---

[99] Prop. Reg. § 1.403(b)-5(b)(2).
[100] Prop. Reg. § 1.403(b)-5(b)(3).
[101] Code Sec. 403(b)(11), as amended by P.L. 107-16, 107th Cong., 1st Sess., Sec. 646(a)(2)

(June 7, 2001). *See also* Prop. Reg. § 1.403(b)-6(d)(1)(i).

[102] Prop. Reg. § 1.403(b)-6(d)(1)(ii).

considered elective deferral plans. Thus, distributions from such plans and other Code Sec. 403(b) plans that do not contain salary reduction agreements can be made at any time.

Applicability of FICA and FUTA Taxes. Employer contributions to Code Sec. 403(b) plans are not subject to FICA and FUTA taxes.[103] However, employee contributions under elective deferral Code Sec. 403(b) plans are subject to FICA and FUTA taxes.[104] In addition, mandatory employee contributions (that is, contributions made under a one-time irrevocable employee election) to Code Sec. 403(b) plans, are, in the view of the IRS, subject to FICA and FUTA taxes.[105] For purposes of FICA and FUTA taxes, the IRS believes that that there is no distinction between elective deferral and non-elective deferral contributions such as there is for income tax purposes as described in earlier paragraphs.

.14 Keogh Plans

Self-employed individuals (i.e., sole proprietors and partners) and their employees may receive qualified retirement benefits under a Keogh (or H. R. 10) plan. As a result of the Tax Equity and Fiscal Responsibility Act of 1982 (TEFRA), Keogh plans are treated for tax purposes in basically the same fashion as other qualified plans. Thus, the same basic requirements for plan qualification and the same limitations on contributions and benefits apply in the case of Keogh plans. However, there are still a few important differences, and these are covered in detail in Chapter 7.

Annual additions to a defined contribution Keogh plan on behalf of owner-employees (sole proprietors and partners with more than 10 percent capital or profits interest in the partnership) may not exceed the lesser of (1) 100 percent of compensation or (2) $40,000 for plan limitation years beginning on or after January 1, 2002 (the $40,000 is adjusted for inflation after 2002—the 2005 dollar limit is still $40,000).[106] The annual addition limit for 2001 was the lesser of (1) 25 percent of compensation or (2) $35,000 in 2001.[107] However, the maximum deduction percentage for contributions on behalf of owner-employees to defined contribution plans remains at 25 percent. Thus, the maximum deduction for such contributions in 2005 is the lesser of (1) 25 percent of compensation or (2) $42,000 in 2005.[108] This means that the maximum possible deduction for such

---

[103] Code Secs. 3121(a)(5)(D) and 3306(b)(5)(D).
[104] Temp. Reg. § 3121(a)(5)-2(T).
[105] *Id.*
[106] Code Sec. 415(c)(1), as amended by P.L. 107-16, 107th Cong., 1st Sess., Secs. 611(b)(1) and 632(a)(1) (June 7, 2001). *See also* Rev. Rul.

2001-51, 2001-2 CB 427. IR-2002-111 (October 18, 2002).
[107] Former Code Sec. 415(c)(1)
[108] IRS Pub. 560, Retirement Plans for Small Business at 3. *See also* IR 2004-127 (Oct. 20, 2004).

contributions in 2002 and later years is smaller than the maximum possible account addition on behalf of owner-employees. For purposes of the maximum annual account addition and deduction rules, compensation is defined as earned income reduced by qualified plan contributions made on behalf of the owner-employee.[109] Thus, a self-employed person may deduct a maximum of only 20 percent of earned income. Further, note that earned income for this purpose must be reduced by the self-employed individual's self-employment tax deduction (one-half of self-employment taxes is deductible under Code Sec. 164(f)).

> **Example:** Carl is a 20 percent partner in the Wyatt Brothers Partnership. Assuming that his earned income from the partnership (before the Keogh plan contribution) was $130,000 after subtracting his self-employment tax deduction for 2005, his maximum allowable Keogh plan contribution deduction for 2005 is $26,000, calculated from the following formula: $C = .25 \times (\$130,000 - C)$, where C is the amount of the contribution. Notice that $26,000 is exactly 25 percent of $130,000 minus $26,000 or the earned income after subtraction of the contribution. In order to achieve the maximum contribution deduction of $42,000, Carl would have to have at least $210,000 (20% × $210,000) of earned income.

If a Keogh plan is a profit-sharing plan, the maximum deduction that can be made with respect to contributions made on behalf of an owner-employee is 25 percent (in 2002 and later years—in 2001 and earlier years, the percentage was 15 percent) of earned income minus the amount of the contribution.[110] Thus, only a maximum of 20 percent (13.04 percent in years before 2002) of earned income of a self-employed individual may be deducted on account of contributions made to a profit-sharing plan.

A Keogh plan can include a cash or deferred arrangement (Code Sec. 401(k) plan, summarized earlier in this chapter) under which participants can elect to have the employer contribute part of their before-tax compensation to the plan rather than receive the compensation in cash.[111] As a participant in the plan, the self-employed individual can contribute part of his/her before-tax net income from the business. This contribution (which is an elective deferral) is subject to the same $14,000 limit (in 2005 plus the additional

---

[109] Code Sec. 404(a)(8).
[110] Code Sec. 404(e)(3) as amended by P.L. 107-16, 107th Cong., 1st Sess., Sec. 616(a)(1) (June 7, 2001).

[111] IRS Pub. 560 at 13.

¶502.14

$4,000 elective deferral contribution that can be made by individuals who are or become age 50 during the calendar year) on elective deferrals discussed earlier. Further, since, beginning in 2002, the definition of compensation (for purposes of determining the maximum amount that can be deducted on account of contributions to defined contribution plans including Keogh plans) will include (rather than exclude) elective deferral contributions, an owner-employee making contributions to a Code Sec. 401(k) plan will be permitted to make up to $14,000 of elective deferral contributions in 2005 (plus another $4,000 if he/she is at least age 50), and *in addition,* make a deductible contribution equal to 20 percent of earned income, as covered above.[112] The total possible before-tax contributions will increase yearly as the maximum amount of elective deferral contributions increases, as discussed earlier in this chapter. Note that the total amount of deductible and elective deferral contributions cannot exceed the $42,000 (in 2005) annual contribution addition limitation. However, the additional elective deferral contributions for those 50 or older can be made over and above the annual addition dollar limit.

> **Example:** In 2005, Jack, a 52-year-old sole proprietor, has earned income (after the self employment deduction) of $100,000 and maintains a Code Sec. 401(k) Keogh plan. He can make a deductible contribution of $20,000 ($100,000 times the maximum percentage of 20%). Also, he can make an elective deferral contribution of $14,000 and an additional elective deferral contribution of $4,000 for a total of $38,000. However, if Jack had $200,000 of earned income (after the self employment tax deduction), the combined total of deductible and elective deferral contributions cannot exceed the annual addition limitation of $42,000. Thus, he would make $28,000 of deductible contributions and $14,000 of elective deferral contributions for a total of $42,000. He would also be able to make the additional elective deferral contribution of $4,000 raising the total to $46,000.

In general, a Keogh plan can include a Code Sec. 401(k) plan only if the Keogh is (1) a profit-sharing plan or (2) a money purchase pension plan in existence on June 27, 1974, that included a salary reduction arrangement on that date. If the plan permits, the self-employed individual(s) can make additional (matching) contributions for an employee on account of elective deferral contributions made by the employee. In addition, the self-employed individual(s) can also make matching contributions on behalf of themselves. After 1997, the matching contributions on behalf of the self-employed

---

[112] Code Sec. 404(a)(12), as added by P.L. 107-16, 107th Cong., 1st Sess., Sec. 616(b)(1) (June 7, 2001).

individuals will not be considered to be elective contributions subject to the elective deferral limit. Rather, such contributions will receive the same tax treatment as the matching contributions for other employees. Finally, the self-employed individuals can make nonelective contributions (other than matching contributions) on behalf of the participating employees without giving them the choice to take cash instead.

If the self-employed individual's plan contribution rate is less than the 25 percent maximum deduction percentage permitted for defined contribution plans (15 percent for profit-sharing plans in years beginning before 2002), IRS Pub. No. 560 provides a method for determining the allowable rate for the self-employed individual to use with respect to his/her own contribution. In general, that method provides that the self-employed individual's rate equals (1) the percentage contribution rate divided by (2) one plus the contribution rate. For example, if the contribution rate is 8.5 percent, the allowable contribution deduction rate for the self-employed individual is 7.83 percent (.085 ÷ 1.085).

SEP IRA Self-Employed Retirement Plan. In lieu of setting up a defined contribution Keogh plan, a self-employed individual can set up a Simplified Employee Contribution (SEP) IRA plan. The maximum allowable deductible contribution for 2005 would be the lesser of (1) 20 percent of earned income less the self-employment tax deduction, or (2) $42,000 (the same as for the Keogh plan without a Code § 401(k) plan addition).[113] The amount would be contributed directly into the self-employed individual's IRA account. Thus, the administration costs associated with the plan would be minimal (much less than for a normal defined contribution Keogh plan). See chapter 10 for a discussion of SEP IRA plans.

Defined Benefit Keogh Plan. Under a defined benefit Keogh plan, the benefit payable to an owner-employee or other employee is limited to the smaller of $160,000 (in 2002—as adjusted for inflation after 2002 (in 2005, the limit is $170,000); the dollar maximum in 2001 was $140,000), or 100 percent of the employee's average compensation for the highest three years of employment.[114] Again, compensation means earned income, reduced by deductible plan contributions as well as the self-employment tax deduction. It should be noted that, in some cases, a great deal more can be contributed by a self-employed individual to a defined benefit Keogh plan in a tax deductible or advantaged manner than to a defined contribution

---

[113] IRS Pub. 560, Retirement Plans for Small Business, at 5.

[114] Code Sec. 415(b)(1), as amended by P.L. 107-16, 107th Cong., 1st Sess., Sec. 611(a)(1) (June 7, 2001). IR-2002-111 (October 18, 2002).

¶ 502.14

Keogh plan, as discussed above. Note that the maximum amount that could be contributed by an individual over age 50 to a Keogh plan combined with a Code § 401(k) plan in 2005 is $46,000 (the $42,000 defined contribution plan limitation plus the additional $4,000 elective deferral contribution). On the other hand, a self-employed individual who has net income after the self-employment tax deduction of $150,000 and who wants to contribute as much as possible on a tax-advantaged basis to a defined benefit Keogh plan could contribute $150,000 to the plan for 2005.[115] Of course, this strategy is best applied to a case where the self-employed individual has no employees (i.e., it is a solo Keogh plan). In addition, the administration cost would be high because actuarial certification would be required for the contribution. However, if a Code § 412(i) plan is maintained by the self-employed individual, the actuarial certification would not have to be met because the plan is considered to be fully funded.[116]

Earned Income. Self-employed individuals are eligible for retirement plan coverage only if they have earned income. Earned income is earnings from self-employment as defined in Code Sec. 1402(a). Fundamentally, this is the net income of a sole proprietor or a partner's share of the net income from a partnership in which the individual's services are a material income-producing factor.[117]

Taxation of Keogh Plan Benefits. Benefits paid to employees and self-employed individuals or their beneficiaries from Keogh plans are subject to tax under Code Sec. 72 in the same way as other qualified plan benefits. Keogh plan benefits paid in lump-sum form may be eligible for special capital gains and/or ten-year forward averaging taxation under Code Sec. 402, as are pension plan benefits. For a discussion of other particular rules concerning Keogh plans, see Chapter 7.

¶ 503   Nonrefundable Credit for Qualified Plan and IRA Contributions

Code Sec. 25B, as enacted by EGTRRA, provides a nonrefundable tax credit for contributions made by eligible taxpayers to qualified plans and IRAs.[118] The new Code section is effective for taxable years beginning after December 31, 2001 and before January 1, 2007.[119] The maximum annual credit under Code Sec. 25B is $2,000.[120]

---

[115] See e.g., Opkyke, Jeff D., "Firms Offer Pension Plans for Self-Employed," *The Wall Street Journal*, Jan. 18, 2005, p. D3.
[116] See Code § 412(i).
[117] Code Sec. 401(c)(2).

[118] Code Sec. 25B, as added by P.L. 107-16, 107th Cong., 1st Sess., Sec. 618(a) (June 7, 2001).
[119] Code Sec. 25B(g).
[120] Code Sec. 25B(a).

The amount of the credit equals the applicable credit rate multiplied by the amount of eligible qualified plan and IRA contributions. The applicable credit rate depends upon the amount of adjusted gross income (AGI) of the taxpayer. Only joint returns with AGI of $50,000 or less, head of household returns of $37,500 or less, and single returns of $25,000 or less are eligible for the credit. The AGI limits applicable to single taxpayers apply to married persons that file separate returns. The credit rates are as follows:[121]

Joint Filers AGI	Heads of Households	All Other Filers	Credit Rate
$0–$30,000	$0–$22,500	$0–$15,000	50%
$30,000–$32,500	$22,500–$24,375	$15,000–$16,250	20%
$32,500–$50,000	$24,375–$37,500	$16,250–$25,000	10%
Over $50,000	Over $37,500	Over $25,000	0

The credit offsets alternative minimum tax liability as well as regular tax liability.[122] The credit is available to individuals who are 18 or over, other than individuals who are full-time students or claimed as a dependent on another taxpayer's return.[123]

The credit is available with respect to (1) elective contributions to Code Sec. 401(k) plans, Code Sec. 403(b) tax-sheltered annuity plans, Code Sec. 457 governmental deferred compensation plans, SIMPLE plans, and simplified employee pension plans; (2) contributions to a traditional IRA or Roth IRA (see the discussion concerning these plans in Chapter 10); and (3) voluntary after-tax contributions to a qualified retirement plan (such as a pension or profit-sharing plan).[124] The credit is in addition to any deduction or exclusion that otherwise applies with respect to the contribution.[125] Thus, the new Code Sec. 25B tax credit rules have no impact on the rules relating to qualified plans, in general. Further, the credit amount has no impact in determining the taxpayer's investment in the contract for purposes of determining the taxable amount of qualified plan distributions as discussed in Chapter 9.[126]

> **Example:** Fred and Marliss are both under age 50 and are married and file a joint income tax return. Their AGI is $28,100. Fred participates in a Code Sec. 401(k) plan and made elective deferral contributions of $3,000 to that plan in 2006. Marliss does not participate in a qualified plan, and the couple did not contribute anything into an IRA. Assuming neither receives any

---

[121] Code Sec. 25B(b).
[122] Code Sec. 25B(h).
[123] Code Sec. 25B(c).
[124] Code Sec. 25B(d)(1).

[125] S. Rep. No. 107-30, 107th Cong., 1st Sess. (June 7, 2001).

[126] Code Sec. 25B(f).

distributions from qualified plans, the Code Sec. 25B credit is $1,500 (50% of the $3,000 of Code Sec. 401(k) elective deferral contributions).

The amount of any contribution that is eligible for the credit must be reduced (for purposes of determining the credit) by taxable distributions received by the taxpayer and his/her spouse, if any, from any qualified plan arrangement described above or any other qualified plan during the taxable year for which the credit is claimed, the two taxable years prior to the year the credit is claimed, and during the period after the end of the taxable year and prior to the due date for filing the taxpayer's return for the year. In the case of a distribution from a Roth IRA, this rule applies to any such distributions, taxable or not taxable.[127] However, certain specified distributions listed under Code Sec. 25B(d)(2)(C) are not taken into account for purposes of determining the credit. For example, distributions related to qualified plan loans under Code Sec. 72(p), distributions of excess contributions to Code Sec. 401(k) plans, and distributions to which Code Sec. 408A(d)(3) applies (relating to rollovers from an IRA that is not a Roth IRA).

¶504 Summary Comparisons of Plan Types

.01   General Comparison of Defined Benefit and Defined Contribution Plans

The following chart summarizes the basic differences (advantages and disadvantages) of defined benefit and defined contribution plans.

Defined Benefit Plan	*Defined Contribution Plan*
Always a pension plan; includes any plan that is not a defined contribution plan.	Includes profit-sharing plans, money purchase and target benefit plans, stock bonus plans, and ESOPs.
(1) A determinable benefit, usually based on average compensation and years of service, is provided after retirement.	Provides for an individual account for each participant with benefits based solely on the amount contributed to the account and upon any income, expense, gains and losses, and any forfeitures of accounts of other participants which may be allocated to the account.

---

[127] Code Sec. 25B(d)(2).

(2) A determinable retirement benefit stipulated under a formula.

The ultimate benefit depends upon investment performance.

(3) Highest annual benefit payable may not exceed the lessor of: $170,000 (in 2005) or 100% of the participant's average earnings for the year in his three highest years of employment (with certain exceptions). The $170,000 (in 2005) is adjusted downward, actuarially, if the individual retires and starts receiving benefits before age 62.

Annual addition to each employee's account cannot exceed the lesser of: $40,000 (in 2002—as adjusted for inflation after 2002—in 2005, the dollar maximum is $42,000) or 100% of the employee's compensation for the year. The amount of the benefits payable is not subject to any limitation.

(4) It is possible to fund comparatively higher benefits over a shorter period of time; therefore, the plan is more favorable to employees who are older at the time of the adoption of the plan.

Over a longer period of time, higher benefits may be obtained; therefore, it is more favorable to younger employees.

(5) Employee forfeitures must reduce funding cost in pension plans and may not be applied to increase the benefits any employee would receive under the plan.

Forfeitures can be allocated to the accounts of the remaining participants.

(6) The amount of annual contributions is subject to minimum funding requirements which must be met to avoid penalties.

Except for money purchase pension and target benefit plans, defined plans are exempt from funding requirements.

(7) Can be subject to plan termination insurance (not applicable to plans maintained for owners and spouses or certain professionals (such as doctors) who have 25 or fewer employees.

Not subject.

(8) Defined benefit plans will generally require greater administrative and actuarial costs and greater reporting requirements.

¶ 504.01

(9) Defined benefit plans are more risky for the employer since poor actuarial experience will necessitate greater employer contributions to fund future benefits.

Defined contribution plans provide the employer with much more certainty since a specified amount of benefits are not set out. Contributions are set without regard to future benefit levels.

.02 Comparison of Pension, Money Purchase Pension, Profit-Sharing, and Stock Bonus Plans

The following is a side-by-side comparison of the four most important qualified deferred compensation plans: pension, money purchase pension, profit-sharing, and stock bonus plans.

Plan	Contributions	Distributions	Plan's Investments
Pension	Determined actuarially.	Made at death, retirement, disability, or termination of employment.	Any prudent investment; does not have to be employer's stock.
Money Purchase Pension	Made yearly to individual employee accounts, based on a percentage of compensation.	Same as for pension plans.	Same.
Profit-Sharing	Allocation to individual employee accounts, based on a percentage of compensation.	Made after a fixed number of years (at least two); certain age; event such as disability, severance, retirement, or hardship.	Same.
Stock Bonus	Same as profit-Sharing.	Same as profit-Sharing, but must be in employer stock.	Same.

Chapter 6

Requirements for Qualified Plans

¶601   Introduction

In 1974, the private pension area was massively overhauled with the passage of the Employee Retirement Income Security Act (ERISA). One of the results of ERISA was the division of jurisdiction over pensions between the Internal Revenue Service (IRS), the Department of Labor (DOL), and the Pension Benefit Guaranty Corporation (PBGC). The IRS has responsibility for all plans which are qualified under the Internal Revenue Code. Although the DOL has some responsibility in this area, it is primarily concerned with fiduciary responsibilities and prohibited transactions. The PBGC is a pseudo-government entity, similar to the SEC and FDIC, which insures the benefits of participants in pension plans.

In order to be "qualified," a plan must meet several requirements under Code Sec. 401(a). These rules are very complex and detailed. However, this is the cost that an employer must pay in order to reap the tax benefits of qualified plans. As a reminder, qualified plans have four major tax advantages over nonqualified plans:

(1) The employer is allowed to take a deduction for contributions made to the trust in the year of the contribution (within certain limits).

(2) The trust accumulates earnings on a tax-free basis. Thus, the earnings can accumulate to a much higher level.

(3) The employees are taxed only when they actually receive payments from the trust, rather than when they have a nonforfeitable right to the benefits (i.e., become vested). In addition, favorable tax treatment (IRA rollovers) is available upon those distributions.

(4) Employer contributions to, and benefits payable under, the plan are generally not subject to FICA and FUTA taxes.

The purpose of this chapter is to discuss the rules which must be met in order to obtain qualified plan status. As mentioned above, the general rules are set out in Code Sec. 401(a). More than 30 provisions are listed in Code Sec. 401(a), many of which lead into the more detailed provisions from Code Sec. 401 through Code Sec. 418E. The chart below serves as a guide to some of the more significant sections of the Code relating to qualified plans that are covered in this chapter.

Major Code Secs. Dealing with Qualified Plans

Code Sec.	Area of Coverage
401	Requirements for Qualification
402, 403, 72	Taxation of the Beneficiary
404	Employer's Deduction for Contributions
410	Participation Requirements
411	Vesting Requirements
412	Funding Requirements
413	Collectively Bargained & Multiemployer Plans
414	Definitions and Special Rules
415	Contribution and Benefit Limitations
416	Special Rules for Top-Heavy Plans
417	Survivor Annuity Requirements
418	Special Rules for Multiemployer Plans
501	Tax Exemption of the Trust
4971-5	Penalty Provisions
6057-8	Registration and Information Requirements

¶602 Obtaining Qualified Status

Many qualified plans follow a standard form (i.e., either a master or prototype plan), which is pre-approved by the IRS. These master and prototype plans are made available by plan providers, such as banks, insurance companies, mutual funds, and other organizations, for adoption by employers. Alternatively, an employer may establish an individually-designed plan to meet its specific needs.

As long as a plan meets all the requirements for qualification under Code Sec. 401(a), qualified status and the tax advantages resulting therefrom are automatic. Thus, obtaining advance IRS approval is not required. However, it certainly is advisable to do so. By obtaining a favorable IRS "determination letter," the employer is assured that the plan has no drafting errors which would violate the requirements necessary to obtain the qualified status. Thus, any defects can be corrected. In addition, the IRS will most likely indicate any part of the plan which it considers to be a potentially disqualifying feature.

It should be noted, however, that a favorable determination letter is not a complete guarantee that a plan is qualified. That is, the determination letter is based on the plan as it is written. If, in actual operation, the plan becomes discriminatory in favor of certain highly compensated employees, it can still become disqualified either on a prospective basis (the usual case) or on a retroactive basis.

A request for a determination letter is made on a Form 5300 for individually designed defined benefit plans and defined contribution plans. A request for a determination letter concerning a plan amendment may also be made on these forms or on a Form 6406.

Prior to filing a request for a determination letter, a notification to "interested parties" must be made. These "interested parties" generally include all employees eligible to participate in the plan and all other present employees who have the same place of business as any employee who is eligible to participate.[1] In general, this notice must contain the following information:[2]

(1) a brief description identifying the class(es) of eligible employees, the name of the plan, the name and identification of the plan administrator, and the name and identification number of the applicant;

(2) a statement as to the type of determination letter requested (initial, amendment, termination);

(3) the procedure under which any interested party may submit comments upon the request for the determination letter; and

(4) a description of the procedure whereby interested parties may obtain additional information.

¶603 General Requirements

There are three basic forms of qualified plans: pension plans, profit-sharing plans, and stock bonus plans. The general features of these, as well as some other "hybrid" plans, were discussed in

---

[1] Reg. § 1.7476-1

[2] Rev. Proc. 2005-6, IRB 2005-1, 200.

Chapter 5. The qualification requirements for all of these plans are identical, except that certain fundamental differences in the plans require variations in the application of some rules.

Prior to 1983, these types of qualified plans were available only to C corporations. S corporations and unincorporated entities (proprietorships and partnerships) were subject to much less favorable restrictions, especially regarding the level of benefits or contributions which could be provided under the plan. These plans, called Keogh or H.R. 10 plans, were essentially put on an equal footing with corporate plans by the Tax Equity and Fiscal Responsibility Act of 1982 (TEFRA). Thus, the rules which are discussed in this chapter apply to qualified plans under any form of entity. There are, however, some important differences which still remain between plans for self-employed individuals (Keogh plans) and corporate plans. These differences are discussed in detail in Chapter 7.

.01 The Plan

A qualified pension, profit-sharing, or stock bonus plan must be a definite written program and arrangement which is communicated to the employees and which is established and maintained by an employer.[3]

Communicated to Employees. A plan must actually be reduced to a formal written document and communicated to employees by the end of the employer's taxable year, in order to be qualified for such year. According to Rev. Rul. 72-509,[4] a plan did not qualify until the terms of the plan were communicated to employees, even though it was reduced to writing and approved by the employer in a prior year.

Under ERISA, a summary plan description must be furnished to participants within 120 days after the plan is established or, if later, 90 days after an employee becomes a participant.[5] The summary plan description must be written in such a manner that it will be understood by the average plan participant and must be sufficiently comprehensive in its description of the participant's rights and obligations under the plan.[6]

The description must include the following information:[7]

(1) the name and type (e.g., profit-sharing, defined benefit) of the plan, including the type of administration of the plan (e.g., insurer administration);

(2) the name, address, and employer identification number of the plan sponsor;

---

[3] Reg. § 1.401-1(a)(2)
[4] 1972-2 CB 221
[5] DOL Reg. § 2520.104b-2(a).

[6] DOL Reg. § 2520.102-2.

[7] DOL Reg. § 2520.102-3.

(3) the names and addresses of the plan administrator, trustees, and legal agent;

(4) the plan's requirements with respect to eligibility for participation and benefits;

(5) a statement describing any joint and survivor benefits provided under the plan;

(6) a statement clearly identifying circumstances which may result in disqualification, ineligibility and forfeiture of benefits;

(7) a description of plan provisions for determining vesting of benefits;

(8) a statement as to whether benefits under a pension plan are guaranteed by the PBGC;

(9) how the plan will be funded (e.g., by employer contributions only or partly by employee contributions), and the identity of the funding medium used to accumulate the assets through which benefits are provided (e.g., trust fund, insurance company); and

(10) the procedures for claiming benefits under the plan and the remedies available if claims are denied in part or in whole.

Established by the Employer. The plan must be established and maintained by the employer. Thus, a plan established by employees will not qualify, even if the employer makes contributions to the plan.[8] However, it is acceptable for a qualified plan to be entirely funded by employees, as long as the plan is not established by the unilateral action of the employees, since Code Sec. 401(a)(1) requires that contributions be made by the employer, employees, *or* both.[9]

No particular entity form (sole proprietor, partnership, corporation, association, etc.) is required. Code Sec. 401(c), however, provides a definition of "employer" for purposes of unincorporated entities. An individual who owns the entire interest in an unincorporated trade or business is treated as his own employer, whereas the partnership is treated as the employer of each partner. Thus, the partnership, and not the individual partners, must establish and maintain a qualified plan.

A single qualified plan may be maintained by more than one employer, whether or not the employers are under common control. However, as discussed later in this chapter, separate employers under common control are viewed as one employer for certain qualification requirements.

---

[8] *See Times Publishing Company,* CA-3, 50-2 USTC ¶ 9465, 184 F2d 376.

[9] Rev. Rul. 80-306, 1980-2 CB 131.

.02 The Trust

The assets of a qualified plan must be held in a valid trust created or organized in the United States.[10] As an alternative, a custodial account or an annuity contract issued by an insurance company or a custodial account held by a bank (for a plan which uses IRAs) may be used.[11] Under Code Sec. 401(f), these custodial accounts and annuity contracts will be treated as a qualified trust, and the person holding the assets of the account or contract will be treated as the trustee thereof.

Trust Requirements. A trust is a matter of state law. In order to be a valid trust, three requirements must be met:

(1) the trust must have a corpus (property);

(2) the trust must have a trustee; and

(3) the trust must have a beneficiary.

Both the plan and the trust must be *written* instruments. They may, however, be two separate instruments or one combined instrument.[12] Even though some states recognize oral trusts as valid, an oral agreement to create a plan is not sufficient for purposes of Code Sec. 401.[13]

In order to obtain a deduction for a year, the trust must be established prior to year end, although the actual contribution is not required until the due date of filing the employer tax return (including extensions).[14] Although this contradicts the requirement that a valid trust have a corpus, the IRS has held that if the trust is valid in all respects under local law except for the existence of corpus, and if the contribution is made within the above prescribed time limits, it will be deemed to have been in existence on the last day of the year.[15]

Domestic Trust. The trust generally must be created, organized, and maintained in the United States to attain a tax-exempt status under Code Sec. 501(a). However, a trust under a qualified Puerto Rican plan is treated as exempt under U.S. law at the election of its administrators.[16] In addition, an employee trust created in Canada which operates exclusively in the United States for the benefit of U.S. employees is treated as a domestic trust.[17] Regulations provide tests for determining whether a trust will be treated as a domestic trust for federal tax purposes.[18]

---

[10] DOL Reg. § 2550, 403a-1 and Code Sec. 401(a).

[11] ERISA Sec. 403(b).

[12] Reg. § 1.401-1(a)(2).

[13] Rev. Rul. 69-231, 1969-1 CB 118.

[14] Code Sec. 404(a)(6); Rev. Rul. 76-28, 1976-1 CB 106.

[15] Rev. Rul. 81-114, 1981-1 CB 207.

[16] Reg. § 1.401(a)-50.

[17] Rev. Rul. 70-242, 1970-1 CB 89.

[18] Reg. § 301.7701-7.

For purposes of deducting contributions made by an employer and postponing the recognition of taxable income by employees, the trust situs makes no difference, if it otherwise meets the qualification requirements.[19] However, the income earned by a foreign trust under a plan which meets the requirements would nevertheless be taxable to that trust, except for the Puerto Rican and Canadian trusts described in the preceding paragraphs.

.03 Permanency Requirement

The plan must be intended to be a permanent and continuing program. It must not be a temporary arrangement set up in high tax years as a tax savings scheme to benefit the employer. Although the employer may reserve the right to terminate the plan and discontinue further contributions, the abandonment of a plan for any reason other than business necessity can indicate that the plan was not a bona fide program from its inception.[20] Thus, if a plan is discontinued after only a short period of years, or soon after the pensions have been fully funded for individuals who are owners, the IRS may retroactively disqualify the plan.

The tax effects of such a retroactive disqualification can be very negative for the employer, the employees, and the trust. A retroactive disqualification would require a recomputation of taxable income for all three parties for all years which are still open for adjustment under Code Sec. 6501 (generally, three years) to account for the amounts involved as if the plan were nonqualified. The tax treatment of nonqualified plans is formally discussed in Chapters 14 and 15.

If the plan is retroactively disqualified, the employees must recognize taxable income in the year and to the extent which he has a nonforfeitable right to the employer contributions (i.e., becomes vested), even though he has no current claim to receive the funds. The employer is allowed a deduction for the amount and for the year in which the employee recognizes this income. Finally, the earnings of the trust are taxable to it. Thus, the negative impacts are that the employee must pay a tax on amounts on which he cannot withdraw until retirement, the employer is allowed a deduction only upon vesting rather than as contributions are made, and the earnings do not accumulate tax free.

As discussed in Chapter 5, a profit-sharing plan differs from pension plans in that it is not necessary that the employer contribute every year or that contributions be made in the same amount or in

---

[19] Code Secs. 404(a)(4) and 402(c).   [20] Reg. § 1.401-1(b)(2).

the same ratio each year. However, merely making a single or occasional contribution does not establish permanency. There must be recurring and substantial contributions for the employees. The IRS has ruled that a trust can retain its exempt status even though contributions under a qualified profit-sharing plan have been discontinued and the trust is retained solely to make distributions in accordance with the plan.[21] Such a plan, known as a frozen plan, must continue to meet all of the requirements (e.g., recordkeeping and filing requirements, providing survivor annuities)[22] in order to retain its qualified status, except those requiring additional benefit accruals.

Permanency has not been defined in an exact number of years for pension plans, either. The IRS hints in its *Employee Plans—Plan Termination Guidelines* that a plan which terminates within ten years after inception without a valid business reason may not satisfy the permanency requirement, although it appears that as few as five years may be the general rule applied in practice.[23]

.04   Exclusive Benefit of Employees or Beneficiaries

A qualified plan must be established and operated for the exclusive benefit of the employees or their beneficiaries. It cannot be designed as a subterfuge for the distribution of profits to shareholders (although shareholders and owner-employees may also be included under the plan). It must benefit the employees in general, although it need not provide benefits for all employees. Thus, the plan cannot discriminate in favor of certain highly compensated employees.[24] The plan cannot include as participants individuals who are not employees. Thus, for example, individuals such as corporate directors cannot participate in the plan, unless they have some employment relationship with the employer.[25]

Investment of Trust Assets. No specific limitations are provided in Code Sec. 401(a) with respect to investments that may be made by the trustees of a qualified trust.[26] To ensure that the plan is solely for the exclusive benefit of employees and not for the employer, Code Sec. 4975(c) lists six "prohibited transactions" which restrict the dealings between the plan and certain "disqualified persons." This list prohibits certain transactions such as the acquisition by the plan of employer securities and other property owned by the

---

[21] Rev. Rul. 69-157, 1969-1 CB 115.

[22] Rev. Rul. 89-87, 1989-2 CB 81.

[23] Internal Revenue Manual, ¶ 7.12.1.2.5.1. *See,* e.g., Rev. Rul. 83-83 (1983-1 CB 86), in which the IRS accepted a plan as permanent where contri-

butions were guaranteed only for the five-year period of a collective bargaining agreement.

[24] Reg. § 1.401-1(a)(3)(ii) and 1.401-1(b)(3).

[25] Rev. Rul. 69-493, 1969-2 CB 88.

[26] Reg. § 1.401-1(b)(5).

employer (with certain exceptions) and the lending of money by the plan to the employer. These prohibited transactions and other fiduciary standards of conduct are discussed in detail in Chapter 12.

Nondiversion of Trust Assets to Employer. The trust instrument must make it impossible, before the satisfaction of *all* liabilities to employees and beneficiaries, for assets to be used for, or diverted to, purposes other than for the exclusive benefit of employees or beneficiaries. This provision must be specifically written into the trust instrument.[27]

"All liabilities" is defined by Reg. § 1.401-2(b)(2) as including both fixed and contingent liabilities. For example, if there are some employees who have met all the requirements for a monthly pension and some who have not yet completed the required period of service, both types fall within the meaning of liabilities as it relates to this issue.

One exception to this nondiversion-reversion rule is that, if the plan so provides, a return of assets to the employer is allowed if:

(1) a good-faith mistake was made in determining the deductibility of a contribution;

(2) a good-faith mistake of fact (and not law) was made; or

(3) the contribution was made on the condition that the plan would qualify under Code Sec. 401(a).[28]

The reversion is the difference between the actual contribution and the amount which would have been contributed if no mistake had been made. No earnings on the mistaken contribution may be returned; however, any losses resulting from the investments of the contribution must be deducted in computing the allowable return. The reversion must not reduce any employee's account below the balance that would have prevailed had the mistake not occurred. The return must be made within one year of the mistaken contribution, denial of qualification, or disallowance of deduction.[29]

The only other time at which a reversion of assets to the employer may occur is at the termination of a defined benefit plan. Thus, after all liabilities have been paid off, any amount remaining may be returned to the employer. However, any such reversions are subject to a 20 (or even 50) percent nondeductible excise tax on the amount returned to the employer under Code Sec. 4980. Under only one circumstance (other than the above exceptions under ERISA Sec. 403(c)) can a defined contribution plan return any of its assets to the

---

[27] Reg. § 1.401-2.
[28] ERISA Sec. 403(c)(2).
[29] Rev. Rul. 91-4, 1991-1 CB 57.

employer. A defined contribution plan may provide for the reversion to the employer, upon termination of the plan, of amounts held in a suspense account which the plan has created in connection with excess contributions under Code Sec. 415(c).[30] Thus, upon termination, a profit-sharing, money purchase, or stock bonus plan must generally allocate any forfeitures to other participants.[31]

¶604   Assignment and Alienation Prohibited

Code Sec. 401(a)(13) requires qualified plans to provide that the participants' benefits under the plan may not be assigned, alienated or subject to attachment, garnishment, levy, execution or other equitable process. Thus, arrangements which provide for the payment to the employer of plan benefits which would otherwise be due to the participant and arrangements (direct or indirect) whereby a party acquires a right or interest enforceable against the plan in any part of a plan benefit payment which is due to the participant or his beneficiary are prohibited.[32] However, these rules do not preclude the enforcement of federal tax levies or the collection by the United States on a judgment resulting from an unpaid tax assessment,[33] although the IRS cannot force the plan to distribute a levy before the benefits become due under the plan terms (e.g., at retirement).[34]

Several exceptions to this rule exist in the Code and Regulations.

(1) A participant's benefits may be reduced to satisfy liabilities of the participant to the plan due to (a) the participant being convicted of committing a crime involving the plan, (b) a civil judgment (or consent order or decree) entered by a court in an action brought in connection with a violation of the fiduciary provisions of ERISA, or (c) a settlement agreement between the Secretary of Labor or the Pension Benefit Guaranty Corporation and the participant in connection with a violation of the fiduciary provisions of ERISA. The court order establishing the liability must require the participant's benefit in the plan be applied to satisfy the liability. If the participant is married, however, certain spousal consent rules (see *Forms of Distribution— QJSA and QPSA* section of this chapter) must be followed.[35]

(2) Any voluntary revocable assignment of an amount which does not exceed ten percent of any benefit payment may be made by a participant or beneficiary, as long as the purpose of the assignment is not to defray the costs of plan administration.[36]

(3) A loan by the plan to the participant or beneficiary that is secured by the participant's accrued benefit will not be considered an

---

[30] Reg § 1.401(a)-2(b).
[31] Rev. Rul. 71-149, 1971-1 CB 118.
[32] Reg. § 1.401(a)-13(c).
[33] Reg. § 1.401(a)-13(b)(2).

[34] IRS Chief Council Advice 200032004, 5-10-00, CCH IRS Letter Rulings Reports.
[35] Code Sec. 401(a)(13)(C).
[36] Reg. § 1.401(a)-13(d)(1).

assignment or alienation, if the loan is exempt from the prohibited transaction tax of Code Sec. 4975 because it meets the requirements under Code Sec. 4975(d)(1).[37] These loans are discussed in Chapter 12.

(4) The following arrangements are deemed not to be an assignment or alienation:

    (a) arrangements for the withholding of federal, state, or local taxes from plan benefits;

    (b) arrangements for the recovery by the plan of overpayments of benefits previously made to a participant;

    (c) arrangements for the transfer of benefit rights from the plan to another plan;

    (d) arrangements for the direct deposit of benefit payments to a bank, savings and loan association or credit union, provided that the arrangement does not constitute an assignment of benefits; and

    (e) arrangements whereby a participant directs the plan to pay any portion of a benefit to a third party if it is revocable at any time by the participant or beneficiary and the third party acknowledges in writing that he has no enforceable right to the benefit payments.[38]

(5) The assignment and alienation prohibition does not apply to the creation, assignment, or recognition of a right to any benefit payable pursuant to a "qualified domestic relations order" (QDRO).[39]

.01 Qualified Domestic Relations Orders (QDROs)

Code Sec. 401(a)(13)(B) was added to the Code in 1984 to clarify the treatment of certain domestic relations orders, as related to the assignment and alienation provisions. In general, a plan must prohibit the creation, assignment, or recognition of a right to benefits by a domestic relations order, unless it is a "qualified domestic relations order." That is, the enforcement of a QDRO against a plan is permitted.

Definitions. A "domestic relations order" means any judgment, decree, or order (including approval of a property settlement agreement) that relates to the provision of child support, alimony

---

[37] Reg. § 1.401(a)-13(d)(2).
[38] Reg. § 1.401(a)-13(c)(2) and (e).

[39] Code Sec. 401(a)(13)(B).

payments, or marital property rights to a spouse, former spouse, child, or other dependent of a participant and that is made pursuant to a state domestic relations law (including a community property law).[40]

To be a "qualified domestic relations order," a domestic relations order must create or recognize the existence of the right of an alternate payee (spouse, former spouse, child or other dependent) to receive all or a portion of the benefits payable with respect to a participant under the plan.[41] In addition, the order must clearly specify the following four items: (1) the name and last known mailing address (if any) of the participant and the name and mailing address of each alternate payee covered by the order, (2) the amount or percentage of the participant's benefits to be paid by the plan to each such alternate payee, or the manner in which such amount is to be determined; (3) the number of payments or period to which the order applies; and (4) each plan to which the order applies.[42] Finally, the order must not require the plan to (1) provide any form of benefit, or any option, not otherwise provided by the plan; (2) provide increased benefits (determined on the basis of actuarial value); or (3) pay to an alternate payee any benefits required to be paid to another alternate payee under a previous QDRO.[43]

The IRS has provided a discussion of issues that should be considered for a QDRO, intended to assist domestic relations attorneys, plan participants, their spouses and former spouses, and plan administrators in drafting and reviewing a QDRO. Included in the same notice is sample language that may be included in a QDRO.[44]

Payments to the Alternate Payee. A QDRO may require the payment of benefits to be made to an alternate payee prior to the participant's separation from service, provided the participant has attained the earliest retirement age. For this purpose, earliest retirement age means the earlier of (1) the earliest date benefits are payable under the plan, or (2) the later of the date the participant attains age 50 or the date on which the participant could obtain a distribution from the plan if the participant separated from service. The benefits are determined as if the participant had retired on the date on which the payment is to begin under the QDRO, taking into account only the present value of the benefits actually accrued and not taking into account the present value of any employer subsidy for early retirement. (The present value is determined using the interest rate specified in the plan or, if no rate is specified, five

---

[40] Code Sec. 414(p)(1)(B).
[41] Code Sec. 414(p)(1)(A).
[42] Code Sec. 414(p)(2).
[43] Code Sec. 414(p)(3).
[44] Notice 97-11, 1997-1 CB 379.

percent.) The payments may be required in any form in which the benefits may be paid under the plan to the participant, other than in the form of a qualified joint and survivor annuity (QJSA) with respect to the alternate payee and his or her spouse.[45]

As further explained in Chapter 9, if the alternate payee is the spouse or former spouse of the participant, the payee is treated as a distributee of benefits for tax purposes.[46] Any employee contributions are apportioned between the participant and the alternate payee.[47] If the alternate payee is other than a spouse or former spouse (e.g., a child), the payments are included in the participant's income, and all employee contributions made by the participant are recoverable under the general basis recovery rules of Code Sec. 72. These amounts are not subject to the ten percent penalty tax for early distributions from qualified plans and can be rolled over tax-free into an IRA.[48]

¶605 Participation Requirements

Generally, plans may impose a variety of requirements for participation in a plan, such as restricting coverage to only salaried employees, specific divisions, and employees who meet a minimum service period requirement.[49] Code Sec. 401(a)(3) requires that a plan meet the minimum participation standards of Code Sec. 410. Code Sec. 410 divides these participation standards into two general categories:

(1) age and service requirements (that is, the rights of an employer to exclude certain employees on account of age or years of service), and

(2) coverage requirements, which relate to the portion of the employer's total work force that must participate in the plan.

.01 Minimum Age and Service Requirements

Under tax law, a plan can exclude from coverage virtually any class of employees for any reason. However, if the reason includes age or service requirements, certain restrictions apply. A qualified plan cannot exclude any employee from participation on account of his age or years of service, except for the exclusion of employees who:

(1) are under age 21, or

(2) have less than one "year of service" (In general, this means 1,000 hours of work within a 12-month period. Note that this level of service could include potential part-time employees.)

---

[45] Code Sec. 414(p)(4).
[46] Code Sec. 402(e)(1)(A).
[47] Code Sec. 72(m)(10).

[48] Code Sec. 72(t)(2)(D).
[49] *See*, e.g., *Bauer v. Summit Bancorp*, CA-3, 325 F3d 155 (2003).

Thus, the only age and service restrictions that may be imposed are minimum requirements, i.e., employees may not be excluded because of age or service requirements if they are at least age 21 and have completed one year of service. A plan may not impose any maximum age limitations for participation in the plan.[50] Thus, an employee may not be excluded because he exceeds a certain age, such as age 65, if all other entry requirements are met. Employees may, however, be excluded from participation due to some other factor, such as a salaried-only plan.

Two exceptions to the general rule of minimum age and service requirements exist under Code Sec. 410(a)(1)(B):

(1) A plan that provides for 100 percent vesting after no more than two years of service may require a two-year period of service for eligibility to participate.

(2) Plans maintained by educational institutions which are tax exempt under Code Sec. 501(a) may require a minimum age of 26, but only if the plan provides for 100 percent vesting after no more than one year of service.

.02   Required Starting Date

An employee who has satisfied the minimum age and service requirements of a plan that requires attainment of age 21 and one year of service must actually begin participation (i.e., enter the plan) no later than the earlier of:

(1) the first day of the first plan year beginning after the employee satisfied the requirements; or

(2) six months after the employee satisfied the requirements.[51]

> **Example:** Ned was hired by the W Corporation on June 18, 2005. W Corporation's qualified profit-sharing plan requires a one-year service requirement for participation. Assuming that Ned has completed one "year of service" by June 17, 2006, the plan must admit Ned no later than December 17, 2006.

If the plan were to admit participants only once a year—for example, on the first day of each plan year—it would violate the starting date requirements. Thus, it would be necessary to admit participants on virtually every day of the year. Because of the record-keeping required to track participants for purposes of vesting and benefit accrual, however, this is usually considered to be

---

[50] Code Sec. 410(a)(2).   [51] Reg. § 1.410(a)-4(b).

cumbersome. Accordingly, many plans allow semi-annual entry dates, such as July 1 and January 1 for a calendar plan year. This makes it technically impossible to violate the starting date requirements, since participants are admitted on dates which are no more than six months apart. As an alternative, a plan could provide only one entry date, usually the first day of the plan year, but reduce any age and service requirements by six months; that is, participants must be admitted on the first day of the plan year after they attain age 20½ or have six months of service. Although both of these methods accelerate the admission date for participation, they do provide a "fail-safe" mechanism to prevent any violation of the qualification requirements and a potential disqualification.

.03 Years of Service Defined

A "year of service" for participation purposes is a 12-consecutive-month period (referred to as the computation period) during which the employee has at least 1,000 "hours of service."[52] Of course, a plan may be more liberal, i.e., it may credit an employee with a year of service for fewer hours of service during the computation period.

The counting of the 1,000 hours begins on the date of hire for an employee's initial eligibility computation period. After the initial computation, the plan may adopt a computation period which begins either on the employment date anniversary, or, if the plan provides, on the first day of each plan year. However, if the plan year is used, an employee who is credited with 1,000 hours of service in both the initial eligibility computation and the plan year which includes the first anniversary of the employment commencement date must receive credit for two years of service for participation purposes.

> **Example:** Nancy began work on June 18, 2005, and completed 1,000 hours of service by June 17, 2006, and also completed 1,000 hours of service from January 1 through December 31, 2006. If the plan elects to use a calendar year plan year as its computation period, Nancy must be credited with two years of service as of the end of 2006.

A plan may require more than 1,000 hours of service for a full year of participation for benefit accrual purposes under a defined benefit plan. However, such a plan must give pro rata credit to those participants who have at least 1,000 hours of service during the computation period.[53] For example, suppose a plan requires 2,000 hours of service for a full year of participation. An employee who has

---

[52] Code Sec. 410(a)(3).

[53] DOL Reg. § 2530.204-2(c).

completed 1,000 hours of service during the benefit accrual period will be credited with a half year of participation. This method is allowed only for defined benefit plans with certain types of formulas, such as a unit benefit plan. For example, a plan that provides a benefit of $25 per month (payable at age 65) for each year of participation could use this method to scale benefits for those employees who are less than full time but who nevertheless meet the 1,000-hour requirement. For vesting purposes, however, the employee must receive a full year of service for any vesting computation period in which the employee is credited with 1,000 hours of service, regardless of whether the employee is employed on the first day or the last day of the computation period.[54]

"Hours of service" include:

(1) hours for which the employee is paid, or entitled to payment, for the performance of duties;

(2) hours for which the employee is paid, or entitled to payment, during periods when no duties are performed, such as vacation, illness, disability, maternity or paternity leave (however, the plan does not have to credit the employee with more than 501 hours of service for this category); and

(3) hours for which back pay is awarded or agreed to by the employer (no double counting of hours which have already been credited is required, though).[55]

These hours of service may be actual hours worked or the equivalent of hours by reference to work-time, periods of employment, or earnings, as determined under DOL Reg. § 2530.200b-3(d), (e), and (f).

A special alternative for counting hours of service is the *elapsed-time* method. Under this method, instead of counting actual or equivalent hours, periods of service are determined by reference to the total period of time that elapses while the employee is employed, regardless of his number of hours of service.[56] In general, an employee is credited with one year of service for each anniversary of his employment commencement date, up to the date he terminates employment. Thus, record-keeping is greatly simplified. Depending on the nature of the employer's work force, there may be relatively little difference between the elapsed-time method and the actual counting of hours of service. Of course, the plan must state how the years of service are to be credited. This may be done by reference to the DOL rules.[57]

---

[54] DOL Reg. § 2520.200b-1(b).
[55] DOL Reg. § 2530.200b-2(a).

[56] Reg. § 1.410(a)-7.
[57] DOL Reg. § 2530b.200-2(f).

.04   Counting Years of Service

In general, years of service are cumulative. All years of service for the employer and members of the same controlled group are counted. If a plan is maintained by more than one employer (i.e., a multiple employer plan), service or work for all the employers in the plan is counted.[58] Also, if a successor employer continues the same plan, service with the predecessor employer must count.[59]

The manner in which service is credited for all purposes under a plan must not discriminate in favor of highly compensated employees. Any credit for service for a specific purpose will be deemed nondiscriminatory if each combination of service-crediting provisions applied for that purpose would be nondiscriminatory if it were another right or feature. The nondiscrimination regulations provide that the use of different service-crediting methods, such as counting hours of service for hourly paid employees and using the elapsed-time method for salaried employees, will be treated as nondiscriminatory if they are fundamentally equivalent.[60]

Breaks in Service. Exceptions to the general rule of counting *all* years of service are the "break in service" rules of Code Sees. 410(a)(5) and 411(a)(6)(C). A "break in service" is defined in Code Sec. 411(a)(6)(A) as a 12-month computation period in which an employee fails to receive credit for more than 500 hours of service. (Note, then, that less than 501 hours is considered a break in service, while more than 999 hours is considered a year of service. Thus, a computation period in which the total hours of service are between 501 and 999 constitutes neither a break in service nor a year of service.) For plans using the elapsed time method, a one-year break in service is any period of 12 consecutive months beginning on the date of the participant's separation from service, or any anniversary thereof, and ending on the next anniversary thereof, provided that the participant does not complete one hour of service in the 12-month period.[61]

These rules permit (but do not require) a plan to provide that certain consecutive breaks in service result in a loss of years of service that have been credited toward participation or vesting. Note, however, a break in service due to qualified military service cannot result in a loss of years of service for participation or vesting.[62] There are three break-in-service rules, each of which is discussed below.

---

[58] Code Sec. 413(c)(1).
[59] Code Sec. 414(a)(1).
[60] Reg. § 1.401(a)(4)-11(d)(2).

[61] Reg. § 1.411(a)-6(c)(2).
[62] Code Sec. 414(u)(8)(A).

¶ **605.04**

(1) *The two-year, 100 percent vesting rule:* A plan offering 100 percent vesting after two years may require the employee to complete two years of service without an intervening break in service (but not two *consecutive* years).[63]

Example (1): An employee completes the following service:

Year	Hours of Service
1	1,000
2	400
3	1,000
4	600
5	1,000
6	1,000

The employee completed one year of service with at least 1,000 hours in year 1, but failed to work for more than 500 hours in year 2. Upon receiving credit for more than 1,000 hours in year 3, he would have credit for only one year of service because of the break in service in year 2. If the employee is credited with 600 hours in year 4 (neither a year of service nor a break in service), and 1,000 hours in year 5, he would become 100% vested at the end of year 5, i.e., 2 years of service without an intervening break.

(2) *The one-year wait following a break-in-service rule:* If an employee incurs a one-year break in service, a plan may provide that none of the years of service before the break will be counted until the employee completes a year of service after the break in service. Thus, the employer is not required to consider service before the one-year break immediately upon an employee's return to work. After completing the year of service upon returning to work (measured from the date of reemployment), the employee must receive credit for the previous years, i.e., the employee participates retroactively.[64] This rule, known as the "look-back rule," is illustrated below.

Example (2): Maria completes a year of service in 2004 under a plan that uses the calendar year as the computation period. She then incurs a one-year break in service for the 12-month period that ends on December 31, 2005. In January 2006, she begins work again and completes a year of service for 2006. Prior to December 31, 2006, in computing her period of service as of any date occurring in 2006, her service prior to December 31,

---

[63] Code Sec. 410(a)(5)(B) and Temp. Reg. § 1.410(a)-8T(c)(2).

[64] Code Sec. 410(a)(5)(C) and Reg. § 1.410(a)-5(c)(3)

2005, is not required to be taken into account for participation purposes. Because she completed a year of service for the 12-month period ending December 31, 2006, however, her period of service is redetermined as of January 1, 2006. Thus, upon completion of a year of service for 2004, her periods of service will include service prior to December 31, 2005.

(3) *The rule of parity for nonvested participants:* If an employee incurs a one-year break in service, years of service before the break may be disregarded completely if:

(a) the employee had no vested rights to any benefits; and

(b) the number of consecutive one-year breaks in service equals or exceeds the *greater* of

   (i) five, or

   (ii) the total number of years of service earned before the break in service.[65]

Example (3): Karen had been credited with four years of service in the W Corporation pension plan as of December 31, 1998, but had no nonforfeitable rights in her accrued benefits according to the plan's vesting schedule. She incurred six consecutive one-year breaks in service from 1999 through 2004. In January 2005, she returned to work and completed a year of service for 2005. Assuming that the plan requires an employee to complete one year of service to become a participant, Karen will become a participant in the plan on January 1, 2006. Because Karen had incurred six consecutive one-year breaks in service and had no vested benefits, upon her readmission to the plan on January 1, 2006, she will have no accrued benefits, as they will have been forfeited. Had Karen incurred only four consecutive one-year breaks in service, she would have been subject to the "one-year break in service" rule discussed in the previous paragraph. That is, she would not have lost her previous credit for years of service upon the completion of a year of service after her return.

Maternity and Paternity Leaves. In determining whether a one-year break in service has occurred, special rules apply for certain maternity or paternity absences. If an absence from work is due to the employee's pregnancy, the birth of the employee's child,

---

[65] Code Sec. 410(a)(5)(D) and Reg. § 1.410(a)-5(c)(4).

adoption of a child by the employee, or the caring for such child for a period immediately following the birth or adoption, the plan must credit the employee for hours of service that would normally have been credited. (If the plan is unable to determine how many hours would have been credited, eight hours per day of absence is credited.) However, the plan is required to credit no more than 501 hours of service for a year. The effect of this provision is that the employee will not incur a break in service (nor is the employee necessarily given credit for a year of service) due to such absences. The plan is required to give this credit for only one year. Normally, that year is the one in which the absence begins. However, if the employee would not have incurred a one-year break in service despite the absence, service must be credited in the following year.[66]

.05 Comprehensive Example

W Corporation maintains a defined benefit pension plan. Employees are admitted to the plan on January 1 or July 1 upon the attainment of age 21 and the completion of one year of service. After the initial eligibility computation period, the plan uses the calendar year as the computation period for vesting and accrual (participation) purposes. The plan requires that 2,000 hours of service are needed for a full year of participation but that employees with at least 1,000 hours of service will receive pro rata credit. Employee B was hired on October 16, 1995 at age 30. He completed 2,000 hours of service for his initial eligibility computation period, which ended on October 15, 1996. His number of hours of service during each calendar year is shown in the following table.

Year	Hours of Service
1995	900
1996	2,000
1997	1,500
1998	900
1999	1,000
2000	2,000
2001	1,500
2002	1,500
2003	2,000
2004	400
2005	1,000
2006	1,500

B was first admitted to the plan on January 1, 1997, which is the first admission date after his completion of one year of service, October

---

[66] Code Sec. 410(a)(5)(E).

15, 1996. Thus, the starting date requirement is met, since B was admitted within six months of meeting the eligibility requirements.

Vesting. As of the end of 2006, B has 10 years of service for vesting purposes. This includes each year in which B has at least 1,000 hours of service, and begins with the date of hire. Note that since the plan uses the calendar year as the computation period after the initial eligibility computation period, the rules require that B receive credit for a year of service for his initial eligibility year and the computation year which includes the anniversary of his employment. Thus, at the end of 1996, B was credited with two years of service for vesting purposes.

Accrual (Participation). As of the end of 2006, B has six full years of participation for accrual purposes. Years of service for this purpose begin on January 1, 1997, when B was admitted to the plan. The calculation of the six years is as follows: 1997—$\frac{3}{4}$ year; 1998—no credit; 1999—$\frac{1}{2}$ year; 2000—1 year; 2001—$\frac{3}{4}$ year; 2002—$\frac{3}{4}$ year; 2003—1 year; 2004—no credit; 2005—$\frac{1}{2}$ year; and 2006—$\frac{3}{4}$ year. 1998 was neither a year of service nor a break in service. 2004 was a break in service, so B had to complete a year of service (1,000 hours) in 2005 in order to participate. Since he did this, B was admitted to the plan retroactively as of the beginning of 2005.

¶606 Coverage Requirements

The government has chosen to encourage savings by individuals by subsidizing the private pension system through tax savings. Because tax savings are more significant to individuals with higher incomes (and, thus, higher income taxes), the government has, in essence, provided more encouragement for savings by these people than it has for lower-income individuals. As mentioned in the preceding discussion, a plan can impose restrictions to entry into a plan on any basis other than age and service (such as a salaried-only plan). However, to ensure that lower-paid employees are also provided for, the tax law requires qualified plans to provide coverage for lower-paid employees.

.01 Minimum Coverage Tests

A plan must meet one of two alternative tests to comply with the minimum coverage requirements of Code Sec. 410(b): the ratio percentage test or the average benefits test. (Technically, the Code contains three tests. Regulations combine the ratio test and the percentage test into one test.) These minimum coverage requirements are generally applied to each plan, unless the employer elects to aggregate plans (discussed later in this chapter). A second set of tests under Code Sec. 401(a)(26) imposes a specific minimum number of employees that must be covered for defined benefit plan qualification.

The Ratio Percentage Test.[67] Regulations combine the percentage test and the ratio test found in the Code, since the computations would yield the same result. In order to meet this test, a plan's ratio percentage for the plan year must be at least 70 percent. This is met if the plan "benefits" a percentage of nonhighly compensated employees which is at least 70 percent of the percentage of highly compensated employees benefiting under the plan. The applicable percentages are determined by dividing the number of active employees benefiting under the plan in each category by the total number of active employees in such category.[68]

> **Example:** Assume that an employer has two highly compensated employees and 20 nonhighly compensated employees who may not be excluded under Code Sec. 410(b)(3) or (4). If the plan covers both of the highly compensated employees (100 percent), it must cover at least 14 of the nonhighly compensated employees (70 percent of 100 percent = 70 percent required coverage). If the plan covers only 1 of the highly compensated employees (50 percent), it must cover at least seven of the nonhighly compensated employees (70 percent of 50 percent = 35 percent required coverage).

Certain employees are excluded in computing the ratio percentage test under Code Sec. 410(b)(3) or (4). These include employees covered under a good-faith collective bargaining agreement, certain air pilots, nonresident aliens, and employees who do not meet the plan's minimum age or service requirements.

The Average Benefits Test.[69] A plan will meet the average benefits test if:

(1) the plan meets a nondiscriminatory classification test (using the Code Sec. 414(q) definition of highly compensated employees); and

(2) the average benefit percentage of nonhighly compensated employees, considered as a group, is at least 70 percent of the average benefit percentage of the highly compensated employees, considered as a group.

Classification Test. The classification test is met for a plan year if the classification system (established by the employer) is reasonable and established under objective business criteria that identify

---

[67] Code Sec. 410(b)(1).
[68] Reg. § 1.410(b)-9.

[69] Code Sec. 410(b)(2).

the employees who benefit under the plan. Reasonable classifications include, e.g., specified job categories, nature of compensation (salaried or hourly), geographic location, etc.

This classification must meet a safe- and unsafe-harbor range that compares the percentage of nonhighly compensated employees to the percentage of highly compensated employees benefiting under the plan.[70] This classification process requires three steps, discussed below.

The first step in the classification process is to determine the nonhighly compensated employee (NHCE) concentration percentage, which is computed by dividing the total NHCEs by the total number of all employees. (Both the numerator and denominator take into account the same employees excluded under the ratio percentage test.)

The second step in the process is to determine the safe-harbor percentage and the unsafe-harbor percentage for the plan. The safe-harbor percentage is 50 percent, reduced by three-quarters of a percentage point for each whole percentage point by which the nonhighly compensated employee concentration percentage exceeds 60 percent. The unsafe-harbor percentage is 40 percent, reduced by three-quarters of a percentage point for each whole percentage point by which the nonhighly compensated employee concentration percentage exceeds 60 percent, subject to a minimum unsafe-harbor percentage of 20 percent. The regulations provide a table for various levels of safe-and unsafe-harbor percentage points.[71]

> **Example (1):** Employer A has 200 employees after applying the allowable exclusions; 120 are nonhighly compensated employees and 80 are highly compensated employees. The nonhighly compensated employee concentration percentage is 60 percent (120 / 200). Employer A maintains a plan that benefits 72 highly compensated employees, so the highly compensated employee benefiting percentage is 90 percent (72 / 80). The safe-harbor percentage is 50 percent and the unsafe-harbor percentage is 40 percent.

Finally, the third step is a comparison of the plan's ratio percentage with the safe- and unsafe-harbor percentages. Three possibilities exist in this comparison: (1) if the plan's ratio percentage is at least equal to the safe harbor percentage, the plan satisfies the test; (2) if the plan's ratio percentage is less than the unsafe harbor percentage, the plan fails the test; and (3) if a plan's ratio percentage is between the safe and unsafe harbors, relevant facts

---

[70] Reg. § 410(b)-4(b) and (c).   [71] Reg. § 410(b)-4(c)(4)(iv).

and circumstances must be examined to determine whether the classification system is nondiscriminatory. These relevant facts and circumstances include the underlying business reason for the classification, the percentage of employees benefiting under the plan, whether or not the employees benefiting in each salary range are representative of the employer's work force, and the difference between the percentage of the two groups benefiting under the plan.[72]

Example (2): Refer to the facts in Example (1). The safe-harbor percentage is 50 percent and the unsafe-harbor percentage is 40 percent. If the plan benefits at least 45 percent (50% X 90%) of the nonhighly compensated employees, or 54 employees, the classification is below the safe harbor and thus is considered nondiscriminatory. If the plan benefits less than 36 percent (40% X 90%) of the nonhighly compensated employees, or 44 employees, the classification is below the unsafe harbor and thus is considered discriminatory. If the plan benefits from 44 to 53 nonhighly compensated employees, the IRS may determine that the classification is nondiscriminatory based on all the facts and circumstances.

Average Benefit Percentage. The second part of the average benefits test requires the plan's average benefit percentage of the NHCEs to equal at least 70 percent of the average benefit percentage of the HCEs. This test is computed as: (1) NHCEs' average benefit percentage, divided by (2) HCEs' average benefit percentage. To compute the average benefit percentage for each group, a benefit percentage is first calculated individually for each employee. It is equal to the employer-provided contribution or benefit (including elective deferrals and forfeitures) under *all* qualified plans of the employer, expressed as a percentage of the employee's total compensation (within the meaning of Code Sec. 414(s)).[73] (Since employer-provided contributions and benefits for all plans must be used, one must convert all plans into a comparable benefit percentage, i.e., based either on contributions or on benefits. See the discussion on plan comparability in ¶ 607.01 for details on how this is accomplished.) At the election of the employer, the benefit percentage for any plan year is computed on the basis of contributions or benefits for that plan year, or any consecutive plan year period (not greater than three years) which ends with that plan year. An election to use the consecutive plan year may not be revoked without the consent of

---

[72] Reg. § 410(b)-4(c)(3). [73] Code Sec. 410(b)(2)(C)(i).

the Secretary of the Treasury.[74] These benefit percentages are then averaged over the employees within each group (highly compensated or nonhighly compensated), whether or not a particular employee is a participant in any plan.[75]

As in the ratio percentage coverage test, the employer excludes employees under a collective bargaining agreement, employees in a qualified separate line of business (discussed later in this section), certain air pilots, and nonresident aliens. However, an employer may not exclude any employees because of age or service in applying the average benefits test, unless it elects to do so. If no election is made, those employees must be taken into account for purposes of the average benefit percentage test. However, if the employer makes this election, it must use the lowest age and service requirements of all qualified plans which are maintained by the employer.[76] For example, if an employer maintains two plans, where one plan requires age 19 and one year of service and the other requires age 21 but no minimum service, the employer could exclude only those employees who are under age 19, regardless of their service. It would appear to be advantageous to make this election, since those employees who do not meet the minimum age or service would probably be included in the nonhighly compensated group. By electing to not consider them, the resulting zero percent benefit would not have to be averaged in with the other employees.

Example: The qualified profit-sharing plan of Company X covers all salaried employees who have at least one year of service. Information concerning the employees of X is below:

Employee	Pay Status	Completed Years of Service	Compensation	Employer Contribution
A	Salaried	30	$100,000	$10,000
B	Salaried	25	100,000	10,000
C	Salaried	25	100,000	10,000
D	Salaried	0	100,000	-0-
E	Salaried	10	20,000	2,000
F	Salaried	5	20,000	2,000
G	Salaried	5	20,000	2,000
H	Salaried	0	20,000	-0-
I	Salaried	0	20,000	-0-
J	Hourly	4	20,000	-0-

---

[74] Code Sec. 410(b)(2)(C)(ii).
[75] Reg. § 1.410(b)-5(c).

[76] Code Sec. 410(b)(2)(D)(ii).

The average benefit percentage of the highly compensated employees group (which includes A, B, C, and D) is 7.5 percent ($30,000 total contributions divided by $400,000 total compensation). It equals 5.00 percent for the nonhighly compensated group of employees ($6,000 total contributions divided by $120,000 total compensation). Assuming the plan would pass the classification test, it still would not pass the average benefit test, since the average benefit percentage for the nonhighly compensated employees (whether or not in the plan) is not at least 70 percent of the average benefit percentage for the highly compensated employees, i.e., 5 percent < (70% × 7.5%).

However, if X elected to exclude those individuals who do not meet the minimum service requirement (one year, since this is the only plan of Company X), the average deferred percentage is 10 percent for the highly compensated employees ($30,000 total contributions divided by $300,000 total compensation, since employee D must be excluded for not meeting the one year requirement) and 7.5 percent for the nonhighly compensated employees ($6,000 total contributions divided by $80,000 total compensation, which excludes employees H and I for not meeting the one year requirement). Since the 7.5 percent average deferred percentage of the nonhighly compensated employees is at least 70 percent of the 10 percent average deferred percentage of the highly compensated employees, the plan would pass the average benefits test for the year.

Line of Business Exception. In general, the coverage requirements of Code Sec. 410(b) are applied to a controlled group as a whole, rather than to each individual employer within the group. That is, the employees of all trades or businesses in a controlled group are treated as being employed by a single employer. (See the section on related employers, below.) However, the coverage tests may be applied separately to each "line of business" of an employer, provided that the reasonable classification test can be satisfied on an employer-wide basis. Thus, the overall costs of providing a qualified plan can be significantly reduced by applying the separate lines of business rules since a smaller number of employees will have to be covered. An employer that chooses to apply the minimum coverage tests separately to its qualified separate lines of business must also apply the nondiscrimination rules separately to those same lines of business.[77]

The regulations provide a three-step process for determining whether an employer operates a qualified separate line of business.

---

[77] Reg. § 1.414(r)-8(c)(1).

First, the employer must define its lines of business (LOBs). The second step is to determine whether the lines of business are separate lines of business under the regulations (SLOBs). Finally, the separate lines of business must meet a three-pronged test to determine if they are qualified separate lines of business (QSLOBs). The regulations provide a flowchart of this complex process; a summary of the requirements for each step is presented below.[78]

The employer is given a great deal of discretion to identify its own lines of business. The only requirement is that the determination must be reasonable and consistent with its existing bona fide business operations. This first step requires the employer to identify all the property and services it provides to its customers for the testing year and to designate which portion of the property and services is provided by each of its lines of business. Alternatively, the employer may designate lines of business that provide the same property or services but that do so in different geographical areas or for different types of customers. One restriction in identifying lines of business is that any designation cannot result in separating employees of an "affiliated service group" (see discussion of related employers later in ¶606.05) from other employees of the employer.[79]

The second step requires that the employer-identified LOBs meet the four tests for separateness. First, the LOB must be a formal organizational unit (such as a corporation, division, or similar unit), and it must exist on each day of the testing year. Second, each LOB must have separate financial accountability, i.e., it must maintain books and records that provide separate revenue and expense information. Third, the LOB must have its own work force. This test is met if at least 90 percent of the employees who provide services to the specific LOB perform at least 75 percent of their services for that LOB. (In addition, the employer may treat an employee who provides at least 50%, but less than 75%, of his services to a LOB as a substantial service employee, provided it does so for all purposes under the SLOB rules. The employer can apply this rule separately for each employee.)[80] Finally, each LOB must have its own separate management. This test is met if at least 80 percent of the top-paid employees (those in the top 10 percent by compensation) who provide services to that LOB are not "substantial-service" employees with respect to any other LOB.[81] In computing this fraction, the numerator is the number of employees who meet both the top-paid and substantial service definitions, and the denominator is the total

---

[78] Reg. § 1.414(r)-0(c).
[79] Reg. § 1.414(r)-2.

[80] Reg. § 1.414(r)-11(b)(2).
[81] Reg. § 1.414(r)-11(b)(3).

number of top-paid employees providing any services to the particular LOB.[82]

The final step in the process is the three-pronged test to determine if the SLOBs are qualified under the regulations. First, each SLOB must have at least 50 employees on each day of the testing year who provide their services to the SLOB and do not provide services to any other SLOBs of the employer. Second, the employer must provide notice to the IRS that it is applying the SLOB rules by filing Form 5310-A (Notice of Plan Merger or Consolidation, Spinoff, or Transfer of Plan Assets or Liabilities; Notice of Qualified Separate Lines of Business) with the relevant key district director of the IRS, generally within ten-and-a-half months after the close of the testing year. (Rev. Proc. 93-40[83] contains the specific information required with the notice.) Third, the SLOB must meet either the statutory safe harbor or one of five other safe harbors provided in the regulations. The statutory safe harbor is satisfied if either: (1) the "highly compensated employee percentage ratio" is at least 50 percent, but not more than 200 percent. This is a straightforward computation where the numerator is the percent of employees of the SLOB who are highly compensated employees (HCEs), and the denominator is the percent of all employees of the employer who are HCEs;[84] or (2) at least 10 percent of all HCEs of the employer provide their services exclusively to the SLOB.[85] If the statutory safe harbor is not met, the regulations provide five additional safe-harbor tests:[86]

(1) *SLOBs in different industries.* A SLOB meets this test if it is in a different industry from every other SLOB of the employer. In Rev. Proc. 91-64,[87] the IRS has established twelve industry categories to use for this test.

(2) *SLOBs reported as industry segments.* This test is met if the employer is required to report, on its annual Form 10-K or Form 20-F filed with the Securities and Exchange Commission, a SLOB as an industry segment, as defined in Statement of Financial Accounting Standards No. 14 (Financial Reporting for Segments of a Business Enterprise).

(3) *Minimum and maximum benefits.* If a SLOB does not meet the 50 percent test under the statutory safe harbor, it will be deemed satisfied if at least 80 percent of all nonhighly compensated employees of the SLOB receive a minimum defined contribution allocation of 3 percent of compensation, a minimum defined benefit accrual of 0.75 percent of average compensation over

---

[82] Reg. § 1.414(r)-(3).
[83] 1993-2 CB 535.
[84] Code Sec. 414(r)(3); Reg. § 1.414(r)-5(b)(1).
[85] Reg. § 1.414(r)-5(b)(4).
[86] Reg. § 1.414(r)-5.
[87] 1991-2 CB 866.

a five-year period (payable in the form of a straight-life annuity beginning at age 65), or a combination of both that is the equivalent. (Alternatively, the 80 percent can be reduced to 60 percent if the average accrual and/or allocation rates are equal to the minimum levels.) If a SLOB does not meet the 200 percent test under the statutory safe harbor, it will be deemed satisfied if either: (a) none of the highly compensated employees of the SLOB receives a maximum defined contribution allocation of 10 percent of compensation, accrues a maximum benefit of 2.5 percent of compensation, or attains a combination of both that is the equivalent; or (b) the average allocation or accrual rate of all highly compensated employees is not larger than 80 percent of the maximum amount for any individual employee.

(4) *Mergers and acquisitions.* This safe harbor applies to employers that acquire a SLOB through certain mergers or acquisitions described in Code Sec. 410(b)(6)(C). To meet this safe harbor, the employer must designate the acquired business as a LOB, and the acquired LOB must meet the tests discussed earlier to become a SLOB. Finally, there cannot be any significant change in the work force of the acquired LOB, as detailed in the regulations.

(5) *Same average benefits.* If a SLOB does not meet the 50 percent test under the statutory safe harbor, it will still qualify if the actual benefit percentage (discussed in the minimum coverage tests) of nonhighly compensated employees in the SLOB is at least equal to the actual benefit percentage of all other nonhighly compensated employees. If a SLOB does not meet the 200 percent test under the statutory safe harbor, it will still qualify if the actual benefit percentage of the highly compensated employees in the SLOB is no greater than the actual benefit percentages of all highly compensated employees.

If the SLOB does not satisfy either the statutory safe harbor or any of the five safe harbors in the regulations, it may still qualify if the employer receives a determination letter from the IRS that the line of business may be treated as separate. The regulations provide some guidance as to the facts and circumstances that the IRS will take into account in determining whether to grant a favorable determination of the SLOB.[88]

The IRS has provided special simplified rules for demonstrating that an employer operates QSLOBs under Rev. Proc. 93-42.[89] Whether or not an employer uses the special single-day snapshot testing for demonstrating compliance with the minimum coverage requirements (discussed later in this section), it may apply

---

[88] Reg. § 1.414(r)-6   [89] 1993-2 CB 540.

the QSLOB rules on a snapshot basis on a three-year testing cycle. However, the special snapshot test does not apply to the requirement that a separate line of business have at least 50 employees.

Employees Benefiting Under the Plan. For purposes of applying the coverage tests, an active employee who receives an allocation of contributions or forfeitures (in a defined contribution plan) or a benefit accrual (in a defined benefit plan) for a plan year is deemed to benefit under the plan for that year.[90] In addition, employees who are eligible to make contributions either to a cash or deferred arrangement under Code Sec. 401(k) or to a plan to which matching employer contributions are made under Code Sec. 401(m) are deemed to benefit under the plan.[91]

Failure to Meet the Coverage Rules. If any requirement under Code Sec. 401(a) is not met, the plan and trust are disqualified with respect to all employees. However, if a plan fails to qualify solely because the coverage requirements under Code Sec. 410(b) are not met, the trust will be treated as exempt with respect to employees who are not highly compensated, and not exempt with respect to employees who are highly compensated.[92] Thus, all highly compensated employees are taxable on their *entire* vested accrued benefit (other than employee contributions) as of the close of the employer's taxable year which ends with or within the taxable year of the trust. (This is in contrast to the normal operating rules which result in taxation only on the vested portion of employer contributions made during the year.) If a plan fails to meet the coverage requirements for more than one taxable year, any portion of the vested accrued benefit which becomes taxable is included in income only once.[93]

Minimum Participation for Defined Benefit Plans. The second set of participation requirements was added to the Code to eliminate perceived discrimination in favor of highly compensated employees through the use of multiple defined benefit plans, each of which covers only a few employees. Plans which would not meet the participation tests on their own are allowed to designate another plan(s) and itself as one combined plan for purposes of the participation requirements. (See ¶ 606.04.) Because of possible selective use of actuarial assumptions, plans may give the appearance of being comparable (a requirement for combining) when, in fact, they are not. Code Sec. 401(a)(26) limits the ability of smaller employers to aggregate such plans by providing that a defined benefit plan will

---

[90] Reg. § 1.410(b)-3(a)(1).
[91] Code Sec. 410(b)(6)(E); Reg. § 1410(b)-3(a)(2)(i).
[92] Code Sec. 402(b)(4).
[93] Code Sec. 402(b)(4)(A).

¶ 606.01

not be qualified unless it benefits the lesser of:

(1) 50 employees; or

(2) the greater of: 40 percent of "all employees" (within the meaning discussed earlier in this section), or 2 employees (one employee if there is only one employee.)

Thus, each plan must have a minimum number of employees covered, without regard to any designation of another plan. Note, then, that a plan maintained by an employer who has only 2 employees must benefit both employees.

The minimum participation rule must be met on each day of the plan year. However, a plan is treated as satisfying the requirement if it does so on any single day during the plan year ("snapshot testing"), provided that day is reasonably representative of the employer's work force and the plan's coverage.[94] A plan that fails to meet the minimum participation requirements may be retroactively amended to include previously excluded employees or merged with another plan as late as ten-and-a-half months after the end of the plan year, effective for the first day of the plan year.[95] Any such retroactive amendments must satisfy the nondiscrimination requirements discussed later in this chapter.

Regulations provide that certain single plans will be considered as two or more plans for purposes of the minimum participation tests. An arrangement under a defined benefit plan that provides an employee with a greater interest in a portion of the plan assets in a way that has the effect of creating separate accounts is treated as comprising separate plans. If an employer is treated as operating qualified separate lines of business, the portions of the plan that benefit employees of each separate line of business are treated as separate plans.[96]

Certain plans are not subject to the minimum participation rules. A plan, other than a frozen defined benefit plan, satisfies Code Sec. 401(a)(26) if it is not top-heavy, does not benefit any current or former highly compensated employee, and is not aggregated with any other plan of the employer for purposes of satisfying the nondiscrimination rules of Code Sec. 401(a)(4) or the minimum benefit rule (other than the average benefits test) of Code Sec. 410(b).[97]

The determination of employees who benefit under the plan is performed in the same manner as under the coverage requirements.

---

[94] Reg. § 1.401(a)(26)-7(b).
[95] Reg. § 1.401(a)(26)-7(c).

[96] Reg. § 1.401(a)(26)-2(d)(1).
[97] Reg. § 1.401(a)(26)-2(b)(1).

Generally, this means that an employee benefits under a defined benefit plan only if he or she receives an increase in the dollar amount of benefit accrual for the plan year, unless the failure to receive a benefit accrual was due to the limitations on benefits.[98] Similarly, the determination of employees included and excluded in the test is the same as the coverage rules. Thus, all employees of a controlled group of employers are counted, and employees who are either statutorily excluded or in a separate line of business are excluded.

An employer who has designated QSLOBs for purposes of meeting the minimum coverage requirements is not required to apply the QSLOB designation for purposes of meeting the minimum participation rules, and vice versa.[99] If the employer elects QSLOBs for minimum participation purposes, each plan would be tested separately with regard to each QSLOB, and the employees in every other QSLOB would be treated as excludable employees.[100]

.02 Highly Compensated Employees Defined

"Highly compensated employees" is a term that is specifically defined in Code Sec. 414(q). The determination of highly compensated employees is based on all the entities that are required to be aggregated under the rules discussed in ¶ 606.05.

A highly compensated employee (HCE) is any employee who:[101]

(1) was a 5-percent owner, regardless of compensation, at any time during the current year or the preceding (or "look-back") year; or

(2) received compensation from the employer for the preceding (look-back) year in excess of $95,000 in 2005, and if the employer so elects, was in the top-paid 20 percent of employees for the preceding year.

For purposes of the 5-percent owner test, the constructive ownership rules of Code Sec. 318 apply (under which family, entity, and option ownership are attributed to the taxpayer.) Ownership is measured by either the value of the outstanding stock or combined voting power of all stock of the corporation. If the employer is not a corporation, ownership is measured by either capital or profits interest in the employer.[102] (Technically, 5-percent ownership is defined as ownership of *more than* 5 percent.[103])

---

[98] Reg. § 1.401(a)(26)-5(a).
[99] Reg. § 1.414(r)-1(c)(2)(i).
[100] Reg. § 1.414(r)-9(b).
[101] Code Sec. 414(q)(1).

[102] Temp. Reg. § 1.414(q)-1T, Q&A 8, Notice 97-45, § VIII(3), 1997-33 IRB 7.

[103] Code Sec. 416(i)(1)(B).

¶606.02

Example: Harry is a 100% shareholder in X Co. in 2006. Wilma, Harry's spouse, is also considered a 100% shareholder through the constructive ownership rules. Thus, Harry and Wilma are considered separate highly compensated employees.

For purposes of classifying HCEs, compensation generally means the same as that used for defined contribution plans. Thus, it includes compensation received from the employer (earned income for a self-employed individual), including deferrals under a cash or deferred arrangement (Code Sec. 401(k) plan), cafeteria plan (Code Sec. 125), tax sheltered annuity (Code Sec. 403(b)), government-deferred compensation plan (Code Sec. 457), qualified transportation fringe benefit plan (Code Sec. 132(f)(4)), and SIMPLE plan (Code Sec. 408(p)).[104] An employer may elect to treat the calendar year beginning with or within the preceding year as the look-back year for determining whether an employee is a highly compensated employee due to his compensation. A calendar year data election, once made, applies for all subsequent determination years unless changed by the employer. (Note, however, that this calendar year election does *not* apply to the 5-percent owner test.)

Note that not all employees who earned more than $95,000 in the preceding year need be classified as highly compensated employees. The employer may elect to rank all employees by compensation and identify those who were also in the top 20 percent of the total number of active employees of the employer for the year (thus, having the effect of reducing the number of employees included in the HCE group). If the employer makes this election, it applies for all subsequent determination years unless changed by the employer. Thus, some employees in that general range may be classified as nonhighly compensated. However, in determining the number of active employees, the following employees are excluded:

(a) employees with less than six months of service;

(b) employees who normally work less than 17½ hours per week

(c) employees who normally work not more than six months during any year;

(d) employees under age 21;

(e) employees covered by a collective bargaining agreement;

(f) nonresident aliens with no U.S. source of earned income.[105]

If a former employee was classified as a highly compensated employee when he separated from service or at any time after

---

[104] Code Sec. 414(q)(4) and 415(c)(3).   [105] Code Sec. 414 (q)(5).

attaining age 55, that employee is treated as a highly compensated employee.[106] An employee is deemed to have separated from service in any year in which his annual compensation is less than 50 percent of his average annual compensation for the three immediately preceding calendar years.[107]

classifying HCEs, compensation generally means the same as that used for defined contribution plans. Thus, it includes

(thus, having the effect of reducing the number of employees included in the HCE group).

.03 Meeting the Minimum Coverage Requirements

Plans must meet the minimum coverage requirements and minimum participation requirements (with respect to defined benefit plans) on each day of the plan year. However, most plans can use an optional test period in applying the ratio percentage test. The employer can apply the test to either at least one day in each quarter, or to the last day of the plan year. Under either option, the employer takes into account for the day selected only those employees who are employed on that day.[108] The IRS has issued guidelines that simplify the testing for coverage and minimum participation. If an employer maintaining a plan does not have precise data at a reasonable cost, then a substitute day may be used as long as there is a high likelihood that the plan would satisfy the nondiscrimination requirements using precise data. Employers may substantiate that a plan complies with the requirements on the basis of the employer's work force on a single day during the plan year (the snapshot day), provided that day is reasonably representative of the work force and coverage throughout the plan year. Further, such testing will not be required more than once every three years, provided there are no significant changes.[109]

.04 Designating Two or More Plans as a Single Plan

Code Sec. 410(b)(6)(B) permits an employer to designate two or more plans as constituting one plan for purposes of meeting the coverage requirements of Code Sec. 410(b). Thus, a plan, which by itself, does not have adequate coverage may be deemed to be adequate when considered as one of a group of plans. As noted above, each individual defined benefit plan so designated must still meet certain minimum participation requirements under Code Sec. 401(a)(26).

---

[106] Code Sec. 414 (q)(6).
[107] Temp. Reg. § 1.414(q)-1T, Q&A 5.

[108] Reg. § 1.410(b)-8(a).
[109] Rev. Proc. 93-42, 1993-2 CB 540.

¶ 606.03

One of the basic requirements for this combination is that the plans so designated be comparable as to contributions or benefits. Regulations under Code Sec. 401(a)(4) demonstrate how such comparability is attained. However, this involves an understanding of the discrimination requirements and Social Security integration rules. After these are covered in the next section of this chapter, the working rules of such a combination are discussed in ¶607.04.

.05 Related Employers

An employer could attempt to circumvent the coverage requirements of Code Sec. 410(b) by operating its business through multiple entities. For example, all of the highly compensated employees could work for one member of the group, and all of the lower-paid employees could work for another member. Thus, the entity employing the highly paid group could set up a plan to cover all its employees and the entity with the lower-paid group could have no plan. Because of the obvious undesirability of such a scheme from a congressional viewpoint, certain related employers are treated as a single employer for purposes of the coverage tests. That is, all employees of each entity in the group are used in computing the percentage or classification tests. The related employers which fall into this classification consist of trades or businesses under common control (both parent-subsidiary and brother-sister forms), affiliated service groups, and leased employee arrangements. Each of these is defined below.

Parent-Subsidiary Group Under Common Control (Code Sec. 414(b) and (c)). A parent-subsidiary group under common control consists of one or more chains of organizations conducting trades or businesses which are connected through the ownership of a controlling interest by a common parent. Controlling interest is defined as (1) in the case of a corporation, 80 percent ownership of the total combined voting power of all classes of stock entitled to vote, or at least 80 percent of the total value of shares of all classes of stock of the corporation; (2) in the case of a trust or estate, 80 percent ownership of the trust or estate; (3) in the case of a partnership, 80 percent ownership of the profits or capital interest; and (4) in the case of a proprietorship, 100 percent ownership of the business.[110] Examples of the parent-subsidiary group of controlled trades or businesses are provided in Reg. § 1.414(c)-2(e), Examples (1)-(3).

Brother-Sister Group Under Common Control (Code Sec. 414(b) and (c)). A brother-sister group of trades or businesses

---

[110] Reg. § 1.414(c)-2(b).

consists of two or more organizations in which: (1) the same five or fewer persons who are individuals, estates, or trusts, own, directly or indirectly, singly or combined, a controlling interest of each organization; and (2) taking into account the ownership of each such person only to the extent such ownership is identical with respect to each such organization, such persons are in effective control of each organization. "Effective control" is given the same meaning as "controlling interest" (above), except that only a 50 percent identical interest or ownership is required instead of the 80 percent identical interest or ownership.[111] However, 80 percent of the stock of each corporation must be owned by the same five or fewer persons. Examples of the brother-sister group of trades or businesses under common control are provided in Reg. § 1.414(c)-2(e), Examples (4) and (5).

Affiliated Service Groups (Code Sec. 414(m)). Code Sec. 414(m) was added to the Code in 1980 as the result of the *Kiddie* and *Garland* decisions.[112] In these cases, professional corporations formed a partnership to employ all of the common-law employees, leaving only the doctors under the qualified plans of each of the professional corporations. This arrangement did not constitute a parent-subsidiary group since there was no common parent, nor did it constitute a brother-sister group since the owners are corporations and not individuals, trusts, or estates.

An organization is a member of an affiliated group under any of the following arrangements:

(1) *A organization.* It is a service organization that is a shareholder or partner in another service organization and regularly performs services for it or is regularly associated with it in performing services for others. (Examples of A organizations are provided in Prop. Reg. § 1.414(m)-2(b)(3).)

(2) *B organization.* It is any other organization, if: (a) a significant portion of its business is performing services for another service organization, if such services are normally performed by employees, and (b) 10 percent or more of the organization is owned by officers, highly compensated employees, or owners of the organization for which services are being performed. (Examples of B organizations are provided in Prop. Reg. § 1.414(m)-2(c)(8).)

(3) *Organization performing management functions.* It is a group consisting of (a) an organization, the principal business of which is performing on a regular and continuing basis "management

---

[111] Reg. § 1.414(c)-2(c).

[112] *T. Kiddie, M.D., Inc.*, 69 TC 1055, Dec. 35,076 (1978), and *L.M. Garland, M.D., F.A.C.S., P.A.*, 73 TC 5, Dec. 36,376 (1979).

functions" for one organization (including related organizations) and (b) the organization (and related organizations) for which such functions are performed.

Leased Employees (Code Sec. 414(n)). "Leased employees" are treated as employees of an organization for purposes of the coverage requirements, unless the special safe-harbor provisions are met. A leased employee is an individual who performs services for another individual (the recipient), but who is not an employee of the service recipient. Rather, he is an employee of someone else who has an agreement with the recipient to provide the services (a leasing organization). If the individual has performed services for the recipient (or related persons) on a substantially full-time basis for a period of at least 12 months, and those services are under the primary direction or control of the recipient, then the individual will be treated as an employee of the recipient.

Factors that are relevant in determining whether an individual is under the primary direction or control of the service recipient include whether the individual is subject to the direct supervision of the recipient and whether the individual must perform services in the manner dictated by the recipient. Thus, clerical and similar support staff (e.g., secretaries and nurses in a doctor's office) generally would be considered to be subject to primary direction or control of the service recipient and would be considered leased employees, assuming the other requirements were met. This does not mean that the recipient organization is necessarily required to cover the leased employees; instead, the leased employees are treated as employees for purposes of testing the coverage tests of Code Sec. 410(b).

Code Sec. 414(n)(5) provides a safe-harbor exception. Leased employees will not be considered employees of the recipient if:

(1) leased employees do not comprise more than 20 percent of the recipient's nonhighly compensated work force; and

(2) the leasing organization provides a money purchase pension plan which:

    (a) covers 100 percent of its employees with annual compensation of at least $1,000,

    (b) provides immediate participation with full and immediate vesting, and

    (c) provides contributions of at least ten percent of compensation, including compensation earned for services rendered to recipient organizations (with no Social Security integration).

¶607   Nondiscrimination Requirements

The coverage requirements (see ¶606) ensure that minimum levels of participation by lower-paid employees in a qualified plan are met. Once those coverage requirements are met, however, employers must ensure that the plan does not discriminate against those lower-paid employees who are covered under the plan. Two main areas of concern under the nondiscrimination requirements are (1) the contributions or benefit provided under the plan are nondiscriminatory, and (2) the availability of benefits, rights, and other features of the plan are nondiscriminatory. These two sets of rules are coordinated, so that however a plan is defined for one purpose is also the definition used for the other, e.g., if an employer has designated two or more plans as constituting one plan for purposes of the meeting the coverage requirements (see ¶606.04), that same designation is used for testing nondiscrimination within the combined plan.

A plan must be written so that it will be nondiscriminatory as to benefits or contributions. It must also be nondiscriminatory in actual operation to be qualified. That is, while a plan may give the appearance, on paper, to be nondiscriminatory, it must be in fact nondiscriminatory in application. However, employees who are covered under a collective bargaining agreement and nonresident aliens who receive no U.S. source income are excluded in considering whether this requirement is met.[113]

Note that Code Sec. 401(a)(4) requires only that a plan not discriminate in relation to benefits or contributions, but not both. Generally, this requires defined benefit plans to demonstrate that they do not discriminate as to benefits, and defined contribution plans to show that they do not discriminate as to contributions.

A plan is not discriminatory merely because contributions or benefits bear a uniform relationship to total compensation.[114] That is, just because the highly compensated group members receive a larger absolute amount of contributions or benefits does not mean that discrimination exists. Rather, discrimination (with respect to benefits or contributions) is based strictly on the amount provided as a percentage of compensation. However, compensation must be defined in accordance with the uniform definition that applies for many purposes relating to qualified plans.

---

[113] Code Secs. 401(a)(4) and 410(b)(3)(A) and (C).   [114] Code Sec. 401(a)(5)(B); Reg. § 1.401(a)(5)-1(c).

Example: Karen and Jack are employees of L Company and earn salaries of $200,000 and $20,000, respectively. Under the L Company profit-sharing plan, Karen receives an allocation of $20,000, and Jack receives an allocation of $2,000. Despite the fact that Karen receives an employer allocation that is ten times the amount received by Jack, the plan allocation is nondiscriminatory, as each has received an employer allocation equal to 10 percent of their compensation.

Definitions of Compensation. Code Sec. 414(s) provides a uniform definition of compensation for purposes of the Code Sec. 401(a)(4) antidiscrimination rules. "Compensation" is defined to be the total compensation from the employer for the year. This would include compensation received from all members of a related group of employers.

The basic definition of compensation includes, but is not limited to, the following items if actually paid or made available to the employee during the year:[115] wages, salaries, and other amounts received in cash or otherwise for personal services actually rendered with the employer; amounts paid for injury or sickness, or under an accident or health plan to the extent includible in gross income; moving expenses paid or reimbursed by the employer to the extent not deductible by the employee; the value of nonqualified stock options to the extent includible in gross income for the year of the grant (see Chapter 15); and the amount includible in gross income on account of an election under Code Sec. 83(b).

The basic definition of compensation also includes elective contributions that are contributed by the employer that are not includible in gross income under a cafeteria plan, cash or deferred arrangement, SEP, SIMPLE, a plan of state or local government, qualified transportation fringe benefit plan, or tax-sheltered annuity program. However, an employer may elect to not treat these deferrals as compensation for this purpose.[116]

The following items are not included in the basic definition of compensation:[117]

(1) employer contributions to a deferred compensation plan, to the extent not includible in the employee's gross income for the year, without regard to dollar limits on contributions or benefits;

---

[115] Reg. § 1.415-2(d)(2).
[116] Code Sec. 415(c)(3)(D).
[117] Reg. § 1.415-2(d)(3).

(2) distributions from a deferred compensation plan, regardless of whether they are included in gross income;

(3) amounts realized from the exercise of a nonqualified stock option or when restricted stock or property becomes freely transferable or is no longer subject to a substantial risk of forfeiture;

(4) amounts realized from the disposition of stock acquired under qualified stock options; and

(5) other amounts receiving special tax benefits, such as premiums for group-term life insurance to the extent not includible in gross income.

Alternative Definitions. Alternative definitions of compensation are also allowed, but any such definition must be reasonable and meet the nondiscrimination requirements. An alternative definition is reasonable if it excludes on a consistent basis irregular or additional compensation, e.g., overtime pay and bonuses. Any alternative definition will meet the nondiscrimination requirement if the average percentage of total compensation included for the employer's highly compensated employees does not exceed the average percentage of total compensation included for the employer's nonhighly compensated employees by more than a de minimis amount.[118]

Self-Employed Individuals. For self-employed individuals, compensation is defined as their earned income, as defined in Code Sec. 401(c)(1). Thus, it is net earnings from self-employment determined with respect to a trade or business in which the individual's services are a material income-producing factor. Net earnings from self-employment are reduced for one-half of self-employment taxes and for contributions to a qualified plan. Any alternative definitions of compensation used for other employees must be translated to an equivalent amount based on the self-employed's earned income.

Compensation Limit. The maximum amount of an employee's compensation that may be taken into account is $210,000 (in 2005). The application of this rule may be demonstrated by the following example.

> **Example:** A money purchase plan covers two employees in 2005, Betty (who has compensation of $400,000) and Aaron (who has compensation of $30,000). Since the maximum amount that may be allocated to Betty's account in 2005 is $42,000, contribution rate of only 10.5 percent would be required without a compensation limit. However, under the 2005 limit on compensation

---

[118] Reg. § 1.414(s)-1(d).

of $210,000 which may be considered, a 20 percent contribution rate would be required to obtain the maximum $42,000 contribution to Betty's account ($210,000 X 20% = $42,000). Thus, Aaron would also receive a contribution of 20 percent of his compensation, assuming Betty wishes to provide the maximum contribution to her account.

Availability of Benefits, Rights, and Features. A plan is considered nondiscriminatory only if the benefits, rights, and features provided under the plan are made available to employees in the plan in a nondiscriminatory manner. These benefits, rights, and features must be currently available to a nondiscriminatory group of employees, and the group of employees to whom they are effectively available cannot substantially favor highly compensated employees.

The benefits, rights, and features to which this requirement applies are all optional forms of benefits, ancillary benefits, and other rights and features available to any employee under the plan. An optional form of benefit is a distribution alternative that is available under the plan with respect to retirement benefits, early retirement benefits, or retirement-type subsidies. Generally, distribution options result from differences in payment schedule, timing, commencement, medium of distribution, election rights, and similar options. Ancillary benefits include Social Security supplements, disability benefits, ancillary life and health insurance benefits, death benefits under a defined contribution plan, preretirement death benefits under a defined benefit plan, shut-down benefits, and other similar benefits. Examples of other rights and features include plan loan provisions, the right to direct investments, the right to a particular form of investment or type of employer securities, the right to make each rate of elective contributions, the right to make after-tax employee contributions to a defined benefit plan that are not allocated to separate accounts, the right to an allocation of each rate of matching contributions, and the right to make rollover transfers to and from the plan. Different optional forms of benefits, ancillary benefits, and other rights and features will exist under a plan if they are not available on substantially the same terms.[119]

Any optional form of benefit, ancillary benefit, or other right or feature must be currently available to a nondiscriminatory group of employees during the plan year. A group of employees is nondiscriminatory if it satisfies either the ratio percentage test or the

---

[119] Reg. § 1.401(a)(4)-4(e).

nondiscriminatory classification test under the minimum coverage requirements of Code Sec. 410(b). In addition, optional forms of benefits, ancillary benefits, or other rights or features must be effectively available to a group of employees that does not substantially favor highly compensated employees. This determination is made on the basis of all the facts and circumstances.[120]

> **Example:** Employer X maintains Plan A, a defined benefit plan that covers both of its highly compensated nonexcludable employees and nine of its 12 nonhighly compensated nonexcludable employees. Plan A provides for a normal retirement benefit payable as an annuity and based on a normal retirement age of 65, and an early retirement benefit payable upon termination in the form of an annuity to employees who terminate from service with the employer on or after age 55 with 30 or more years of service. Both HCEs of Employer X currently meet the age and service requirement, or will have 30 years of service by the time they reach age 55. All but two of the nine NHCEs of Employer X who are covered by Plan A were hired on or after age 35 and, thus, cannot qualify for the early retirement benefit. Even though the group of employees to whom the early retirement benefit is currently available satisfies the ratio percentage test, absent other facts, the group of employees to whom the early retirement benefit is effectively available substantially favors HCEs.[121]

Catch-Up Contributions. EGTRRA '01 provides a special catch-up provision for individuals who are at least age 50. Under this provision, qualifying individuals may make additional elective deferrals to a 401(k) plan (as well as a 403(b) plan, SEP, SIMPLE, or 457 government plans) above the normal limitations that apply. (See Chapter 7 for a discussion of this new provision.)

An employer is not required to provide for catch-up contributions in any of its plans. However, if any employer plan provides for catchup contributions, all other plans of the employer that provide elective deferrals must provide catch-up eligible participants with the same effective opportunity to make the same dollar amount of catch-up contributions. This universal availability requirement does not require plans that do not otherwise provide for elective deferrals to provide for catch-up contributions. However, for purposes of this universal availability requirement, all plans maintained by related employers (see

---

[120] Reg. § 1.401(a)(4)-4(b) and (c).   [121] Reg. § 1.401(a)(4)-4(c)(2), Example 1.

¶ 606.05) that do provide for elective deferrals are treated as a single plan if the related employers are treated as a single employer.[122]

.01   Testing Discrimination in Contributions and Benefits

Generally, defined contribution plans demonstrate nondiscrimination with respect to contributions, and defined benefit plans demonstrate nondiscrimination with respect to benefits. However, any plan may be tested for nondiscrimination on the basis of contributions or benefits without regard to whether it is a defined benefit or a defined contribution plan. Such testing is referred to in the regulations as cross-testing.

Defined Contributions Testing. Two safe-harbor tests are available for determining whether contributions under a plan are nondiscriminatory. If a plan cannot satisfy one of these two safe harbors, it must satisfy a general test for nondiscrimination.

Uniform Allocation Formula. A plan with a uniform allocation formula will satisfy the first safe harbor. Such a plan allocates all contributions and forfeitures under a formula that allocates the same percentage of plan year compensation, the same dollar amount, or the same dollar amount for each uniform unit of service (not to exceed one week) performed by the employee during the plan year. A plan that meets the Social Security integration rules in form does not fail to have a uniform formula because of the differences in employee's allocations attributable to uniform disparities permitted under the integration rules (discussed later in this chapter).[123]

Uniform Points Plan. A uniform points plan meets the second safe harbor. Under a uniform points plan, each employee's allocation for the plan year equals the product determined by multiplying all amounts allocated to all employees in the plan for the plan year by a fraction, the numerator of which is the employee's points for the plan year and the denominator of which is the sum of the points of all employees in the plan for the plan year. An employee's points equal the sum of the employee's points for age, service, and units of plan year compensation for the plan year. Each employee must receive the same number of points for age, service, and unit of compensation. Any combination of these three points methods may be used; however, the plan must grant points for either age or service. A unit of compensation is not required to be used, but if it is, it must be a single dollar amount not in excess of $200.

---

[122] Code Sec. 414(v)(4); Reg. § 1.414(v)-1(e).   [123] Reg. § 1.401(a)(4)-2(b)(2).

Once allocations are determined, the average of the allocation rates for highly compensated employees (HCEs) in the plan may not exceed the average of the allocation rates for the nonhighly compensated employees (NHCEs) in the plan.[124]

Example: Plan A has a single allocation formula that applies to all employees, under which each employee's allocation for the plan year equals the product of the total of all amounts taken into account for all employees for the plan year and a fraction, the numerator of which is the employee's points for the plan year and the denominator of which is the sum of the points of all employees for the plan year. Plan A grants each employee 10 points for each year of service and one point for each $100 of plan year compensation. For the plan year, the total allocations are $71,200, and the total points for all employees are 7,120. Each employee's allocation for the plan year is set forth in the table below.

Employee	Years of Service	Plan Year Compensation	Points	Amount of Allocation	Allocation Rate
H1	20	$150,000	1,700	$17,000	11.3%
H2	10	150,000	1,600	16,000	10.7%
H3	30	100,000	1,300	13,000	13.0%
H4	3	100,000	1,030	10,300	10.3%
N1	10	40,000	500	5,000	12.5%
N2	5	35,000	400	4,000	11.4%
N3	3	30,000	330	3,300	11.0%
N4	1	25,000	260	2,600	10.4%
Total			7,120	$71,200	

For the plan year, the average allocation rate for the HCEs (HI through H4) is 11.3 percent, and the average allocation rate for NHCEs (N1 through N4) is 11.3 percent. Because the average of the allocation rates for the HCEs does not exceed the average of the allocation rates for the NHCEs, Plan A satisfies the safe harbor for the plan year.

General Test. If neither of the above safe-harbor tests is met, contributions will be nondiscriminatory if they can satisfy the gen-

---

[124] Reg. § 1.401(a)(4)-2(b)(3).

eral test for contributions. This general test is met if each rate group under the plan satisfies the minimum coverage requirements of Code Sec. 410(b). A rate group exists for each highly compensated employee in the plan and consists of that highly compensated employee and all other employees in the plan who have an allocation rate greater than or equal to the highly compensated employee's allocation rate. Thus, an employee is in the rate group for each highly compensated employee in the plan who has an allocation rate less than or equal to that employee's allocation rate.

The allocation rate of an employee under this test is the sum of the allocations to the employee's account for the plan year, expressed either as a percentage of compensation or as a dollar amount. Amounts taken into consideration for this purpose include employer contributions and forfeitures but exclude income, expenses, gains, and losses attributable to the employees' account. An employer may group employees' allocation rates within a range of no more than five percent (not five percentage points) above and below a midpoint rate chosen by the employer. If allocation rates are determined as a percentage of compensation, such rates may be grouped within a range of no more than a quarter of a percentage point. However, grouping is allowed only if the allocation rates of highly compensated employees within the range are not significantly higher than the allocation rates of nonhighly compensated employees within the range.[125]

> **Example:** Employer Y has only seven employees, all of whom benefit under Plan D. The HCEs are H1 and H2, and the NHCEs are N1 through N5. For the plan year, H1 and N1 through N3 have allocation rates of 5.0 percent of plan year compensation. For the same plan year, H2, N4, and N5 have allocation rates of 7.5 percent of plan year compensation.
>
> There are two rate groups in Plan D. Rate group 1 consists of H1 and all those employees who have an allocation rate greater than or equal to H1's allocation rate (5.0 percent). Thus, rate group 1 consists of H1, H2, and N1 through N5. Rate group 2 consists of H2, and all those employees who have an allocation rate greater than or equal to H2's allocation rate (7.5 percent). Thus, rate group 2 consists of H2, N4, and N5. Rate group 1 satisfies the ratio percentage test, because the ratio percentage of the rate group is 100 percent—i.e., 100 percent (the percentage of all NHCEs who are in the rate group) divided by 100 percent

---

[125] Reg. § 1.401(a)(4)-2(c).

(the percentage of all NHCEs who are in the rate group). Rate group 2 also satisfies the ratio percentage test, because the ratio percentage of the rate group is 80 percent—i.e., 40 percent (the percentage of all NHCEs who are in the rate group) divided by 50 percent (the percentage of all HCEs who are in the rate group).

Defined Benefit Testing. Three safe harbors are available for determining whether benefits are nondiscriminatory. If a plan cannot satisfy one of these three safe harbors, it must pass the general test for nondiscrimination.

In order to use any of the safe harbors for benefits, a plan must satisfy the following uniformity requirements:

(1) The same benefit formula applies to all employees in the plan.

(2) Annual benefits provided to all employees are payable in the same form, commencing at the same uniform normal retirement age, and are the same percentage of average annual compensation (computed over at least a three-year period) or the same dollar amount for all employees in the plan who will have the same number of years of service at normal retirement age. The annual benefit must equal the employee's accrued benefit at normal retirement age and must be the normal retirement benefit under the plan.

(3) With respect to an employee with a given number of years of service at any age after normal retirement age, the annual benefit commencing at the employee's age is the same percentage of average annual compensation or the same dollar amount that would be payable commencing at normal retirement age to an employee who had the same number of years of service at normal retirement age.

(4) Each subsidized optional form of benefit is available to substantially all employees in the plan.

(5) The plan must not be a contributory plan (i.e., no employee contributions).

(6) Each employee benefit must be accrued over the same years of service that are taken into account in applying the benefit formula.[126]

Unit Credit Plans. The first safe harbor concerns unit credit plans. Such a plan will be nondiscriminatory if: (1) it satisfies the $133\frac{1}{3}$ rule on benefit accruals (discussed later in this chapter) under

---

[126] Reg. § 1.401(a)(4)-3(b)(1) and (2).

¶**607.01**

Code Sec. 411(b)(1)(B); and (2) each employee's accrued benefits under the plan as of any plan year are determined by applying the plan's benefit formula to the employee's years of service and average annual compensation, both determined as of that plan year.[127]

> **Example (1):** Plan A is a unit credit plan that provides an accrued benefit for each employee equal to the employee's average annual compensation times a percentage that depends on the employee's years of service determined as of that plan year. The percentage is 2 percent for each of the first 10 years of service, plus 1.5 percent for each of the next 10 years of service, plus 2 percent for all additional years of service. The accrual rate meets the $133\frac{1}{3}$ rule since the accrual rate after the second 10 years (2%) does not exceed $133\frac{1}{3}$% of the accrual rate in any prior year of service (i.e., 1.5% × $133\frac{1}{3}$% = 2%). Thus, Plan A would meet the safe-harbor provision.

Fractional Accrual Plans. The second safe harbor concerns fractional accrual plans, including flat benefit plans. Such a plan will be nondiscriminatory if: (1) it satisfies the fractional rule on benefit accruals (discussed later in this chapter) under Code Sec. 411(b)(1)(C); (2) an employee's accrued benefit under the plan as of any plan year before the employee reaches normal retirement age is determined by multiplying the employee's fractional accrual rule benefit by a fraction, the numerator of which is the employee's years of service determined as of the plan year, and the denominator of which is the employee's projected years of service as of normal retirement age; and (3) one of the following:

(a) No employee in the plan can accrue in any one year more than $133\frac{1}{3}$ percent of the benefit than any other employee in the plan can accrue (employees with more than 33 years of service at normal retirement age are not taken into account for this test);

(b) The normal retirement benefit under the plan is a flat benefit that requires a minimum of 25 years of service at normal retirement age for an employee to receive the unreduced flat benefit; or

(c) The plan meets the requirements of (b), above, other than the 25-year requirement, and the average normal accrual rate of nonhighly compensated employees as a group is at least 70 percent of the average normal accrual rate of highly compensated employees as a group.[128]

---

[127] Reg. § 1.401(a)(4)-3(b)(3).

[128] Reg. § 1.401(a)(4)-3(b)(4).

Example (2): Plan B provides a normal retirement benefit equal to 4 percent of average annual compensation times each year of service up to 10, and 1 percent of average annual compensation times each year of service in excess of 10 and not in excess of 30. Plan B further provides that an employee's accrued benefit as of any plan year equals the employee's fractional rule benefit multiplied by a fraction, the numerator of which is the employee's years of service as of the plan year and the denominator of which is the employee's projected years of service as of normal retirement age. The greatest benefit that an employee could accrue in any plan year is 4 percent of average annual compensation (the case for an employee with 10 or fewer years of projected service at normal retirement age). Among employees with 33 or fewer years of projected service at normal retirement age, the lowest benefit that an employee could accrue in a plan year is 1.82 percent of average annual compensation (the case for an employee with 33 years of projected service at normal retirement age). Plan B would fail to satisfy the safe harbor because the 4 percent accrual rate is more than $133\frac{1}{3}$ percent of the 1.82 percent accrual rate.

Insurance Contract Plans. The third safe harbor concerns insurance contract plans. To meet the safe harbor, the plan must be funded exclusively by the purchase of insurance contracts of the same series, under which an employee's accrued benefit on any applicable date is not less than the cash surrender value of his insurance contracts on that date. The scheduled premium payments under the contract must be level annual payments to normal retirement age and, for an employee who continues participation beyond normal retirement age, must be equal to the amount necessary to fund additional benefits that accrue under the plan's benefit formula. Any experience gains, dividends, forfeitures and similar items must be used solely to reduce future premiums. Finally, the benefit formula must satisfy the fractional accrual formula safe harbor if the stated normal retirement benefit under the formula accrued ratably over each employee's period of plan participation through normal retirement age.[129]

General Test. If a defined benefit plan cannot satisfy any of the three safe harbors, it must pass the general nondiscrimination test for benefits. Similar to the general test for contributions, this test is met if each rate group under the plan satisfies the minimum coverage requirements of Code Sec. 410(b). For defined benefit plan purposes, a rate group consists of each highly compensated employee

---

[129] Reg. § 1.401(a)(4)-3(b)(5).

and all other employees who have a normal accrual rate greater than or equal to the highly compensated employee's normal accrual rate and who also have a most valuable accrual rate greater than or equal to the highly compensated employee's most valuable accrual rate. However, a plan is deemed to satisfy the general test if it would do so by treating as not benefiting no more than five percent of the highly compensated employees in the plan and the IRS determines that, based on the relevant facts and circumstances, the plan does not discriminate with respect to benefits.

An employee's normal accrual rate for a plan year is the increase in his accrued benefit during the measurement period, divided by his years of service used in applying the benefit formula under the plan (referred to as testing service) during the measurement period, and expressed either as a dollar amount or as a percentage of his average annual compensation. An employee's most valuable accrual rate is computed in the same manner, but uses the employee's most valuable optional form of payment. The measurement period can be the current plan year, the current plan year and all prior plan years, or the current plan year and all prior and future years. As in the general test for contributions, an employer may group the accrual rates of employees. An employer may group accrual rates within a range of 5 percent of the midpoint rate for normal accrual rates and 15 percent of the midpoint rate for most valuable accrual rates. If accrual rates are determined as a percentage of average annual compensation, such rates may be grouped within one twentieth of a percentage point of the midpoint rate.[130]

Cross-Testing. Cross-testing provides an alternative method for a defined contribution or defined benefit plan to satisfy the requirement that a plan must be nondiscriminatory in amount. Cross-testing allows a defined contribution to be tested on a benefits basis (referred to as an equivalent accrual) under the general nondiscrimination test (rather than the safe harbor rules) for defined benefit plans. Similarly, a defined benefit plan may be tested on a contributions basis (referred to as an equivalent allocation) under the general nondiscrimination test for defined contribution plans.[131]

Converting benefits to equivalent contributions under a defined benefit plan. A defined benefit plan is nondiscriminatory with respect to equivalent allocations for a plan year if each rate group under the plan satisfies the minimum coverage requirements. A rate group exists under a plan for each highly compensated employee in the plan and consists of that highly compensated employee and all other employees in the plan who have an equivalent normal alloca-

---

[130] Reg. § 1.401(a)(4)-3(c).   [131] Reg. § 1.401(a)(4)-8(a).

tion rate greater than or equal to the highly compensated employee's equivalent normal allocation rate and who also have an equivalent most valuable allocation rate greater than or equal to the highly compensated employee's equivalent most valuable allocation rate.

An employee's equivalent normal and most valuable allocation rates for a plan year are the actuarial present value of the increase over the plan year in the benefit that would be taken into account in determining the employee's normal and most valuable accrual rates for the plan year, expressed either as a dollar amount or as a percentage of the employee's plan year compensation. The actuarial present value must be determined using a standard interest rate and a standard mortality table, assuming no mortality prior to the employee's testing age. Equivalent allocation rates must be determined in a consistent manner for all employees for the plan year.[132]

Converting contributions to equivalent benefits under a defined contribution plan. The most common types of plans that rely on cross-testing are age-weighted plans and new comparability plans. Both of these plans are usually designed as profit-sharing plans (in order to take advantage of contribution flexibility), but are tested for discrimination on the basis of benefits, rather than contributions.

A defined contribution plan is nondiscriminatory with respect to benefits for a plan year if the plan's equivalent accrual rates were substituted for each employee's allocation (contribution) rate and the plan either:[133]

(1) provides broadly available allocation rates;

(2) uses certain age-based allocation rates; or

(3) satisfies a minimum allocation gateway.

A plan provides broadly available allocation rates if each allocation rate under the plan is currently available to a nondiscriminatory group of employees. For example, if, within one plan, an employer provides different allocation rates for nondiscriminatory groups of employees at different locations or different profit centers, the plan would meet this requirement.[134]

Plans that use gradual age or service schedules, or provide allocation rates based on a uniform target benefit allocation also meet the conditions for cross-testing. A plan has a gradual age or service schedule if the formula for all employees under the plans provides for a single schedule of allocation rates (based on age,

---

[132] Reg. § 1.401(a)(4)-8(c).
[133] Reg. § 1.401(a)(4)-8(b)(1)(i).
[134] Reg. § 1.401(a)(4)-8(b)(1)(iii).

service, or the sum of age and service) and provides for allocation rates that increase smoothly at regular intervals. However, increases in rate allocations between intervals, or bands, (e.g., allocation rates for 6-10 years of service versus 0-5 years of service) are limited to the lesser of five percentage points or twice the prior allocation rate. Generally, the age and/or service intervals (bands) used in the allocation rate schedule must be the same length, except for the one associated with the highest age and/or service interval.[135]

If the plan does not meet the above conditions, it must satisfy a minimum allocation gateway. This gateway test requires that the allocation rate for each nonhighly compensated employee (NHCE) be at least the lesser of: (1) one-third of the allocation rate of the highly compensated employee (HCE) with the highest allocation rate; or (2) five percent of the NHCE's compensation (as defined under Code Sec. 415(c)(3)).[136]

An employee's equivalent accrual rate for a plan year is the annual benefit that is the result of normalizing the increase in the employee's account balance during the measurement period, divided by the number of years in which the employee benefited under the plan during the measurement period, and expressed either as a dollar amount or as a percentage of the employee's average annual compensation.

The increase in the account balance during the measurement period taken into account does not include income, expenses, gains, or losses allocated during the measurement period that are attributable to the account balance as of the beginning of the measurement period, but does include any additional amounts that would have been included in the increase in the account balance except for the fact that they were previously distributed. The account balances are normalized by treating them as single-sum benefits that are immediately and unconditionally payable to the employee. A standard interest rate, and a straight life annuity factor that is based on the same or a different standard interest rate and on a standard mortality table, must be used in normalizing these benefits.[137]

Cash balance plans. A cash balance plan is a defined benefit plan that defines benefits for each employee by reference to the employee's hypothetical account. That is, while a traditional defined benefit plan defines an employee's benefit as a series of monthly

---

[135] Reg. § 1.401(a)(4)-8(b)(1)(iv).
[136] Reg. § 1.401(a)(4)-8(b)(1)(vi).

[137] Reg. § 1.401(a)(4)-8(b)(2).

payments for life to begin at retirement, a cash balance plan instead defines the benefit in terms of a stated account balance. In a typical cash balance plan, an employee's hypothetical account is credited each year with hypothetical allocations (often referred to as pay credits) and hypothetical earnings (often referred to as interest credits), and are therefore, analogous to actual allocations of contributions and earnings to an employee's account under a defined contribution plan.

Cash balance plans are normally the result of an employer's amendment to a traditional defined benefit formula that converts it to a cash balance formula. For many employees (who are often the older employees), the benefit already accrued under the old defined benefit formula will exceed the amount determined under the new cash balance formula. Thus, those employees may not earn any additional benefits until the cash balance formula exceeds their benefits already accrued under the old formula for some period of time after the conversion. (This period of time is often referred to as the "wear away" period.)

Because of concern regarding potential age discrimination in the rate of benefit accrual during this wear away period, the IRS issued proposed regulations in December 2002 addressing testing for nondiscrimination for these types of plans. The proposed regulations would have required eligible cash balance plans to pass a modified version of the cross-testing regulations discussed earlier. However, because those proposed regulations would have made it difficult, if not impossible, for many plan sponsors converting traditional pension plans to cash balance plans to provide the required different types of transition relief to participants, the IRS withdrew the proposed regulations after only four months. In a subsequent announcement, the IRS has indicated its permanent withdrawal of the proposed regulations in order to give Congress the opportunity to consider legislation on cash balance and other hybrid plans.[138] Thus, plan sponsors considering conversions to cash balance plans should be aware of these issues.

New Comparability Plans. New comparability plans have built-in disparities between the allocation rates for HCEs and the allocation rates for NHCEs. In a typical new comparability plan, HCEs (typically older) receive high allocation rates, while NHCEs, regardless of their age or years of service, receive comparatively low

---

[138] Announcement 2004-57, IRB 2004-27, 15.

allocation rates. For example, HCEs in such a plan might receive allocations of 20 percent of compensation, while NHCEs receive allocations of three percent of compensation. These plans demonstrate compliance with the nondiscrimination rules by comparing the actuarially projected value of the employer contributions for the younger nonhighly compensated employees (NHCEs) with the actuarial projections of the larger contributions (as a percentage of compensation) for the older highly compensated employees (HCEs). As a result, these plans are generally able to provide higher rates of employer contributions to HCEs, while NHCEs are not allowed to earn the higher allocation rates as they work additional years for the employer or grow older. However, new comparability plans must meet the requirements discussed in the preceding section in order to continue using cross-testing.

Age-Weighted Plans. Age-weighted plans take into account participants' ages in addition to their compensation. Thus, allocations of contributions to older owners can be maximized, while allocations to younger employees are minimized. For example, consider the following small profit-sharing plan that covers one highly compensated, older employee (the owner) and four nonhighly compensated, younger employees. Contributions for the year are set at 10 percent of total compensation.

Name	Age	Compensation	Contribution
HC	50	$150,000	$15,000
A	40	40,000	4,000
B	35	40,000	4,000
C	30	40,000	4,000
D	30	30,000	3,000
Totals		300,000	30,000

Under an age-weighted plan, each participant's compensation is weighted by an age factor. A simple method of calculating age-weighted compensation is to discount each participant's compensation from the normal retirement age under the plan to his current age at an allowable interest rate (the standard rate, a rate between 7.5 percent and 8.5 percent, is typically used). Using a normal retirement age of 65 and a discount rate of 8.5 percent, the age-weighted compensation levels and contribution levels in the above example are:

Name	Age	Age-Weighted Compensation	Contribution
HC	50	$ 44,121	$23,298
A	40	5,204	2,748
B	35	3,461	1,827
C	30	2,302	1,215
D	30	1,726	911
Totals		$ 56,813	$30,000

Thus, the contributions are allocated proportionately, but based on the age-weighted compensation levels. In this illustration, the owner is allocated 78 percent of the total allocation under age-weighting, compared to 50 percent under the traditional profit-sharing allocation. While the uniform age-weighted formula in this plan is nondiscriminatory, the allocation rate for the highly compensated employee exceeds the average allocation rate for the nonhighly compensated employees by a considerable amount. Thus, the plan would not meet the nondiscrimination requirements by testing contributions. By converting the contributions to equivalent benefits the plan would meet the cross-testing provisions. Note, however, that this desirable result depends entirely on having the right employee population, i.e., an older highly compensated employee and younger nonhighly compensated employees.

Note that in allocating contributions under an age-weighted profit-sharing plan, it may be necessary to adjust participants' accounts to reflect all limits applicable to qualified plans. For example, if any participant's allocation exceeds the annual additions limitation (100 percent of compensation or $42,000), such excess must be reallocated to other employees in a nondiscriminatory manner. Additionally, since age-weighted profit-sharing plans are common for smaller employers, many will be subject to the top-heavy rules (discussed in Chapter 7). In the above illustration, the age-weighted allocation would cause the plan to be top heavy. While the minimum contribution of three percent of salary was met, the plan must comply with the remaining restrictions of top-heavy plans.

Target Benefit Plans. Target benefit plans are normally tested for nondiscrimination based on contributions, but can be tested in terms of their equivalent benefits. Unlike the cross-testing of defined contribution plans, target benefit plans can satisfy the safe-harbor tests for the fractional accrual type of defined benefit plans if the following are satisfied: each employee's stated benefit would satisfy the safe harbors for defined benefit plans if the plan were a defined benefit plan with the same benefit formula; employer contributions with respect to each employee are based exclusively on the employee's stated benefit, and computed under a special provision in the regulations; forfeitures under the plan are used exclusively to reduce employer contributions; and employee contributions are not used to fund the stated benefit.[139]

Permitted Disparity. The tests above can take into account the disparity permitted under the Social Security integration rules of Code Sec. 401(1). The disparity between contributions or benefits with respect to compensation subject to Social Security and contributions or benefits with respect to compensation not subject to Social Security can be done in two ways. The plan may take permitted disparity into account under its contribution or benefit formula in compliance with Code Sec. 401(1). Alternatively, this permitted disparity may be imputed in accordance with the regulations. That is, the plan formula does not actually integrate with Social Security, but would nevertheless meet the permitted disparity rules if it actually incorporated them.[140] The permitted disparity rules and Social Security integration are discussed later in this chapter.

.02 Contributory Plans

Plans may require employee contributions (on an after-tax basis) as a condition of participation in the plan or to receive additional employer contributions (i.e., matching contributions). These employer-matching contributions and employee contributions are tested separately from employer contributions in determining whether they are nondiscriminatory in amount.[141] Under Code Sec. 401(m), a plan will meet the antidiscrimination test for matching contributions and employee contributions for the plan year only if the "actual contribution percentage" (ACP) for eligible highly compensated employees (as defined under Code Sec. 414(q)) does not exceed the greater of:

(1) 125 percent of the ACP for all other eligible employees for the preceding plan year; or

(2) the lesser of:

  (a) 200 percent of the ACP for all other eligible employees for the preceding plan year, or

  (b) the ACP for all other eligible employees for the preceding plan year plus two percentage points.[142]

---

[139] Reg. § 1.401(a)(4)-8(b)(3).
[140] Reg. § 1.401(a)(4)-7.

[141] Reg. § 1.401(a)(4)-1(b)(2)(ii)(B).
[142] Code Sec. 401(m)(2)(A).

The ACP for a specified group of employees is the average of the actual contribution ratios (ACRs) of eligible employees in the group for that year. The ACR of an eligible employee is computed by dividing (a) by (b), where:

(a) is the sum of employee contributions, matching contributions, and qualified nonelective contributions (QNECs) paid under the plan for each employee, and

(b) is the employee's compensation (within the meaning of Code Sec. 414(s)).[143]

Thus, the working rules of Code Sec. 401(m) are quite similar to those applicable to cash or deferred arrangements under Code Sec. 401(k) in that two distinct groups of employees are identified —the group of highly compensated employees and the group of nonhighly compensated employees. The test is applied to employee contributions and matching contributions, rather than elective employee contributions, and is based on the groups as a whole, rather than non individual employees. Indeed, many of the tests under the Sec. 401(m) regulations are written by reference to those in Sec. 401(k).

The current year ACP for highly compensated employees is compared with the preceding year ACP for nonhighly compensated employees. In the first year of existence for a plan, the employer can treat the ACP of the nonhighly compensated employees as three percent, or alternatively, the employer can elect to use the first plan year's ACP for the nonhighly compensated employees.[144] An employer may also elect to use the current year ACP for nonhighly compensated employees instead of the prior year ACP for all plan years. While the IRS requires that the plan state which method (prior-year testing or current-year testing) it will use, a change from the prior-year testing method to the current-year testing method may be made at any time (although a change back to the prior-year testing method is subject to certain restrictions).[145]

Safe Harbors. Two safe-harbor methods of satisfying the ACP tests exist with respect to matching contributions. First, the ACP test will be deemed met for a plan year if the plan meets the contribution, exclusive plan, and immediate vesting requirements applicable to SIMPLE 401(k) plans (discussed in ¶ 704.10).[146]

---

[143] Code Sec. 401(m)(3); Reg. § 1.401(m)-2(a)(2) and (3).

[144] Code Sec. 401(m)(3); Reg. § 1.401(m)-2(c)(2).

[145] Notice 98-1, 1998-1 CB 327; Reg. § 1.401(m)-2(c)(1).

[146] Code Sec. 401(m)(10); Reg. § 1.401(m)-1(b)(1).

Second, a plan is treated as meeting the ACP test if:

(1) the plan satisfies the contribution and notice requirements applicable to SIMPLE 401(k) plans (discussed in ¶ 704.10); and

(2) the following limitations on matching contributions are met:

(a) employer-matching contributions with respect to employee contributions or elective deferrals do not exceed six percent;

(b) the rate of matching contributions does not increase as the rate of an employee's contributions or elective deferrals increases; and

(c) the matching contribution rate for any highly compensated employee is not greater than that for any nonhighly compensated employee.[147]

Definitions. A "matching contribution" is any employer contribution made to the plan on behalf of an employee on account of an employee contribution, any employer contribution made to the plan on behalf of an employee on account of an employee's elective deferral and any forfeiture allocated on the basis of employee contributions, matching contributions, or elective deferrals. An "elective deferral" means any employer contribution to the extent it is not includible in the employee's gross income under a cash or deferred arrangement as defined in Code Sec. 401(k). A "qualified nonelective contribution (QNEC)" is any employer contribution (other than a matching contribution) that the employee may not elect to have been paid in cash rather than have contributed to the plan and that meets the vesting and withdrawal restrictions of cash or deferred arrangements under Code Sec. 401(k).[148] (These are discussed in detail in ¶ 704.09.)

Example: S Company maintains a qualified profit-sharing plan which covers all five of its employees. Under the plan, S Company will contribute an amount equal to each employee's contribution. Assume Employees A and B both meet the definition of highly compensated employee, and that S Company elects to compute the ACP for its nonhighly compensated employees based on current year data. The information for the current year is below:

---

[147] Code Sec. 401(m)(11); Reg. § 1.401(m)-3(d).   [148] Code Sec. 401(m)(4); Reg. § 1.401(m)-5.

Employee	Total Compensation	Employee Contribution	Ratio of Employee and Employer Contribution to Compensation
A	$100,000	$4,000	$8,000/$100,000
B	80,000	2,800	$5,600/$80,000
C	30,000	1,500	$3,000/$30,000
D	20,000	500	$1,000/$20,000
E	10,000	100	$200/$10,000

The actual contribution percentage for the nonhighly compensated group (C, D, and E) is 5.67% [(10.00% + 5.00% + 2.00%)/3]. The contribution percentage for the highly compensated group (A and B) is 7.50% [(8.00% + 7.00%)/2].

To meet the ACP test, the ACP of the highly compensated employees (7.5%) must not exceed the greater of:

7.09%, computed as 125% of the ACP for nonhighly compensated employees (125% × 5.67%); or

7.67%, which is the lesser of: (a) 11.34%, computed as 200% of the ACP for the nonhighly compensated employees (200% × 5.67%); or (b) 7.67%, computed as the ACP for the nonhighly compensated employees plus two percentage points (5.67% + 2.0%).

The test is met, as 7.5% is less than 7.67%, and the plan is deemed nondiscriminatory with respect to this feature. Note that although employee A does exceed the limits on all tests, the plan is still nondiscriminatory, because the tests are based on the groups of highly compensated and nonhighly compensated employees, rather than on individual employees.

Employees Taken into Consideration. Any employee who is eligible to make an employee contribution (or elective contributions, if the employer takes them into account) or to receive a matching contribution under the plan being tested is considered to be an eligible employee for purposes of the antidiscrimination test. If an employee contribution is required as a condition of participation in the plan, any employee who would be a participant in the plan if he made such a contribution is also treated as an eligible employee on behalf of whom no employer contributions are made.[149]

---

[149] Code Sec. 401(m)(5); Reg. § 1.401(m)-5.

Multiple Plans. If two or more plans of an employer to which matching contributions, employee contributions, or elective deferrals are made are treated as one plan for purposes of meeting the coverage rules of Code Sec. 410(b), all of these plans are treated as one plan for purposes of this discrimination test. If a highly compensated employee participates in two or more plans of the employer to which such contributions are made, all such contributions are aggregated for purposes of applying this test.[150]

Distribution of Excess Aggregate Contributions. Because this is an annually determined test, a plan may meet the test one year and fail it the next. The plan can avoid disqualification if the excess aggregate contributions are distributed (or, if forfeitable, forfeited) before the end of the following plan year. However, a 10 percent excise tax under Code Sec. 4979 applies to the employer unless the excess contributions (and earnings) are distributed within two-and-one-half months after the plan year ends.

The amount of the corrective distribution which is attributable to the employee contribution is not taxable. All other amounts (including earnings and/or employer contributions) are taxable for the employee's tax year ending with or within the plan year for which the excess contributions were made, or if distributed more than two-and-one-half months after the plan year for which the excess contributions were made, in the taxable year of the employee in which distributed. The corrective distribution of excess contributions (and income) is not subject to the 10 percent early distribution tax of Code Sec. 72(t) and is not treated as a distribution for purposes of the 15 percent excise tax under Code Sec. 4980A on excess distributions.[151]

For purposes of this rule, "excess aggregate contributions," with respect to any plan year, is defined as the excess of:

(1) the aggregate amount of the matching contributions and employee contributions (and any qualified nonelective contribution or elective contribution taken into account in computing the contribution percentage) actually made on behalf of highly compensated employees for the plan year, over

(2) the maximum amount of the contributions allowed under the ACP test (discussed above).[152]

---

[150] Code Sec. 401(m)(2)(B); Reg. § 1.401(m)-2(a)(3)(ii).

[151] Reg. § 1.401(m)-5.
[152] Code Sec. 401(m)(6)(B).

Any excess aggregate contributions for any plan year are distributed to highly compensated employees in order of their dollar amount of contributions, rather than to the employees receiving the largest percentage-of-compensation matching contributions. (This distribution method is the same one used for distributing excess contributions under a CODA 401(k) plan. ¶ 704.09 presents an example of such a distribution). Forfeitures of excess aggregate contributions may not be allocated to participants whose contributions are reduced because of a distribution. The determination of the amount of excess aggregate contributions is made after determining any excess deferrals under a cash or deferred arrangement of Code Sec. 401(k) (those in excess of $14,000 for 2005), a simplified employee pension plan, and a tax-sheltered annuity under Code Sec. 403(b).[153]

Income Allocable to Excess Contributions. The income allocable to the excess contribution is equal to the sum of the income for the plan year in which the excess contribution was made, plus the income for the period between the end of the plan year and the date of distribution. A plan may use any reasonable method for computing the income allocable to excess aggregate contributions, provided that it is nondiscriminatory, used consistently for all participants, and is the method used for allocating income to participants' accounts. Alternatively, income attributable to excess contributions may be computed by multiplying income for the plan year by a fraction, the numerator of which is the excess contribution, and the denominator of which is the total account balance as of the beginning of the plan year plus additional contributions made during the plan year.[154]

A safe-harbor exists for allocating the income attributable to the period between the end of the plan year and the date of the corrective distribution, but not for the year of the excess contribution. Under this method, the allocable income for this period is equal to ten percent of the income allocable to excess contributions for the excess contribution year, multiplied by the number of calendar months that have elapsed since the end of the excess contribution year. A distribution occurring on or before the 15th day of the month is treated as made on the last day of the preceding month. A distribution occurring after the 15th day is treated as made on the first day of the next month.[155]

---

[153] Code Sec. 401(m)(6)(C) and (D).
[154] Reg. § 1.401(m)-2(b)(2)(iv)(B) and (C).

[155] Reg. § 1.401(m)-2(b)(2)(iv)(D).

¶ 607.02

.03 Social Security Integration

Every employer is, in effect, already providing a retirement plan for its employees through its contributions to the Social Security system. Because the OASDI part of Social Security is based on taxable wages only up to a specified level ($90,000 in 2005), it actually discriminates in favor of lower-paid employees. For example, consider the case of two employees, one of whom earns $90,000 and the other earns $180,000. The OASDI taxes paid by the employer and the benefit to be derived from their earnings are exactly the same for 2005. Since the contribution and the benefit are the same, but the total compensation of each employee is very different, the contribution or benefit as a percentage of compensation is twice as high for the $90,000 earner as it is for the $180,000 earner.

Social Security integration allows an employer to consider the total retirement benefits or contributions made on behalf of employees to both the Social Security system and the employer's private qualified plan in determining whether discrimination exists. Thus, because Social Security discriminates in favor of the nonhighly compensated employees, the employer's plan is allowed to make up this difference, i.e., the plan is allowed to discriminate in favor of the highly compensated employees if it properly integrates. Code Sec. 401(a)(5) provides the basis for Social Security integration by reference to Code Sec. 401(1)'s permitted disparity limitations.

Permitted Disparity. Social Security integration may be achieved in one of two basic ways. A plan can be an excess plan, in which an employee's contributions or benefits are increased based on his compensation in excess of a specified integration level. Alternatively, a plan can be an offset plan, in which an employee's benefit is reduced based on his compensation below a specified integration level. Integration in a defined contribution plan may only be in the form of an excess plan, whereas integration in a defined benefit or target benefit plan may be in either form.

Defined Contribution Plans. Integration is accomplished in a defined contribution plan by reference to employer contributions. Thus, the permitted disparity is based on the rates of contribution above and below the integration level. For this purpose, the following definitions are necessary:

(1) The "excess contribution percentage" is the percentage of compensation that is contributed with respect to that portion of each participant's compensation in excess of the integration level.

(2) The "base contribution percentage" is the percentage of compensation that is not in excess of the integration level.[156]

A defined contribution plan meets the disparity limit if the excess contribution percentage does not exceed the base contribution percentage by the lesser of:

(1) the base contribution percentage; or

(2) the greater of: (a) 5.7 percent; or (b) the portion of the OASDI that is attributable to old age insurance.[157]

The effect of this disparity limit is that all employees must receive some contribution. In order to achieve the maximum disparity allowed (5.7 percent), the employer must also contribute that level on compensation below the integration level.

The disparity provided under the plan must use the same base and excess contribution percentages for all employees in the plan. Similarly, the integration level used in a defined contribution plan must be a single dollar amount that is one of the following:

(a) the taxable wage base in effect at the beginning of the plan year ($90,000 in 2005);

(b) no greater than the larger of $10,000 or one-fifth of the taxable wage base in effect at the beginning of the plan year; or

(c) an amount between (a) and (b). If this amount is used, however, the 5.7 percent disparity limit is reduced to 4.3 percent if the integration level is not more than 80 percent of the taxable wage base (i.e., the level is less than $72,000 in 2005), or 5.4 percent if the integration is greater than 80 percent of the taxable wage base (i.e., the level is between $72,000 and $90,000 in 2005).[158]

Example: A profit-sharing plan provides for contributions on behalf of each employee equal to 4.3% of compensation up to the Social Security taxable wage base and 10% of compensation in excess of the wage base. This plan would not meet the disparity limits. The excess contribution percentage (10%) exceeds the base contribution percentage (4.3%) by 5.7%. This amount is larger than the limit of 4.3%, which is lesser of the base contribution percentage (4.3%) or 5.7%.

---

[156] Code Sec. 401(1)(2)(B).
[157] Code Sec. 401(1)(2)(A).

[158] Reg. § 1.401(1)-2(d).

¶ 607.03

Defined Benefit Excess Plans. Integration is accomplished in a defined benefit plan by reference to employer benefits. In order to be within the disparity limits under a defined benefit excess plan, any optional form of benefit, preretirement benefit, actuarial factor, or other benefit or feature which is provided for compensation in excess of the integration level must also be provided for compensation below the integration level.[159] In addition, benefits must be based on average annual compensation, which is defined as the greater of final average compensation (defined below) or the highest average annual compensation for any three consecutive years.[160] The "excess benefit percentage" under a defined benefit excess plan cannot exceed the "base benefit percentage" (both terms are defined in the same manner as excess and base contribution percentages, above) by the lesser of:

(1) 200 percent of the "base benefit percentage"; or

(2) with respect to any year of service, 3/4 percent, and with respect to total benefits, 3/4 percent times all years of service with the employer (not to exceed 35 years).[161]

The effects of these restrictions are similar to those under defined contribution plans in that plans must provide some benefits for compensation below the integration level. Note also that the maximum disparity between the rates above and below the integration level is 26 1/4 percent × 35 years maximum).

Example (1): A flat benefit plan has a benefit formula which provides a retirement benefit for any participant retiring at age 65 with at least 15 years of service equal to 20% of the participant's final average compensation not in excess of the applicable integration level. The plan provides for the accrual of benefits under the fractional rule (discussed in the vesting section of this section). In order to satisfy the disparity limits with respect to a participant retiring at age 65 with 20 years of participation, the plan may not provide a benefit in excess of 35% of compensation over the integration level. This is the lesser of (1) 40%, which is 200% of the base benefit level (20%), or (2) 35%, which is the base benefit level (20%) plus ¾ times 20 years of service. If the participant had 35 years of service, the plan would be precluded from providing a benefit with respect to final average compensation over the integration level in excess of 40%, which is the lesser of (1) 40% (200% of the base benefit level),

---

[159] Code Sec. 401(1)(3)(A)(i).
[160] Code Sec. 401(1)(5)(C).

[161] Code Sec. 401(1)(4)(A); Reg. § 1.401(1)-3(b)(2).

or (2) 46.25% (the base benefit level of 20% plus 3/4% X 35 years of service).

Example (2): A unit credit benefit plan provides a benefit at normal retirement age (65) of 1% of final average compensation up to covered compensation for each year of service, not to exceed 25 years, and 1.5% of compensation over covered compensation for each year of service up to the 25-year maximum. The plan meets the disparity limits because the excess benefit percentage, 1.5% (37.5% in total), does not exceed the lesser of (1) 2% (50% in total), which is 200% of the base benefit percentage, or (2) with respect to any year of service, $1\frac{3}{4}$%, which is the base benefit percentage of 1% plus 3/4% per year, and with respect to total benefits, 43.75%, which is the total base benefit percentage plus 3/4% times 25 years of service.

The disparity provided under a defined benefit excess plan must be uniform. That is, the plan must use the same base and excess benefit percentages for all employees with the same number of years of service.

Similarly, the integration level must be uniform and be one of the following amounts:

(1) covered compensation;

(2) a single dollar amount either specified in the plan or determined under a formula specified in the plan that does not exceed the greater of $10,000 or one-half of the covered compensation of an individual who attains Social Security retirement age in the calendar year in which the plan year begins;

(3) a uniform percentage greater than 100 percent of each participant's covered compensation, not exceeding the taxable wage base (final average compensation is the limit in a defined benefit offset plan); or

(4) a single dollar amount either specified in the plan or determined under a formula specified in the plan that is greater than the amount determined in (2), above, but does not exceed the taxable wage base (again, final average compensation is the limit in a defined benefit offset plan).[162]

Covered compensation is the average of the Social Security taxable wage bases in effect for each calendar year during the 35-year period ending with the last day of the calendar year in which the

---

[162] Reg. § 1.401(1)-3(d).

participant attains the social security retirement age. The IRS periodically provides tables which determine the covered compensation for employees who reach Social Security retirement age in a given year. Presented below is the Rounded Table from Rev. Rul. 2004-104[163] for covered compensation for plan years beginning in 2005.

Year of Birth	Covered Compensation
1937	$39,000
1938-1939	45,000
1940	48,000
1941	51,000
1942-1943	54,000
1944	57,000
1945	60,000
1946-1947	63,000
1948	66,000
1949-1950	69,000
1951-1952	72,000
1953-1954	75,000
1955	78,000
1956-1958	81,000
1959-1961	84,000
1962-1965	87,000
1966 and later	90,000

Defined Benefit Offset Plans. The maximum offset to a participant's accrued benefits derived from employer contributions is limited to the lesser of:

(1) one-half of the employee's gross benefit percentage, multiplied by a fraction, the numerator of which is the employee's average compensation (as defined earlier), and the denominator of which is the employee's final average compensation up to the offset level; or

(2) with respect to any year of service, 3/4 percent of the employee's final average compensation, and with respect to total benefits, $\frac{3}{4}$ percent times the total years of service taken into account under the plan (not to exceed 35 years).[164]

The gross benefit percentage, referred to above, is the rate at which employer-provided benefits are determined under an offset plan (before application of the offset) with respect to an employee's average compensation.

---

[163] IRB 2004-46, 837.

[164] Code Sec. 401(1)(4)(B); Reg. § 1.401(1)-3(b)(3).

The disparity provided under a defined benefit offset plan must be the same gross benefit percentage and the same offset percentage for all employees with the same number of years of service. Similarly, the integration level must be uniform. It is defined the same as for defined benefit excess plans, with the two exceptions noted earlier in numbers (3) and (4).

For purposes of calculating final average compensation, the plan must compute the participant's average annual compensation for the three-consecutive-year period ending with the current year or, if shorter, the participant's full period of service.[165]

.04 Combining Plans—Comparability

An employer may elect to have two or more plans treated as a single plan for purposes of meeting the ratio percentage and nondiscriminatory classification tests. However, any plans so aggregated must also be aggregated for purposes of the nondiscrimination tests.[166] That is, the combined plans must be comparable with respect to benefits or contributions, and not discriminate in favor of highly compensated employees when viewed as one plan.

In designating two plans as a single plan for purposes of meeting the coverage requirements, three combinations of the general forms of plans are possible: those involving only defined contribution plans; those involving only defined benefit plans; and those involving defined contribution and defined benefit plans. The discrimination that is most likely to occur in such a combination is from two sources: differences in vesting and differences in the rate of contributions or benefits. All plans must meet one of two vesting schedules: the 5-year cliff schedule or the 3-to-7-year graded schedule. These schedules are treated as equivalent in determining whether the manner in which employees vest in their accrued benefits under the aggregated plan is discriminatory.[167] Testing for nondiscrimination of contributions or benefits is satisfied by meeting one of the safe harbors or the general tests for defined contribution plans and defined benefit plans.

Combining Defined Contribution Plans and Defined Benefit Plans. If the aggregated plan consists of a defined contribution plan and a defined benefit plan, it must meet the cross-testing provisions (discussed in ¶ 607.01). The requirement

---

[165] Code Sec. 401(1)(5)(D).
[166] Code Sec. 410(b)(6)(B) and Reg. § 1.401(a)(4)-1(c)(4).
[167] Reg. § 1.401(a)(4)-11(c)(2).

that benefits, rights, and features be currently available to a non-discriminatory group of employees can be applied separately to the defined contribution and the defined benefit portions of an aggregated plan containing both types with respect to features other than single sum benefits, loans, ancillary benefits, or benefit commencement dates, including in-service withdrawals.[168]

A combined defined contribution plan and a defined benefit plan can demonstrate nondiscrimination on the basis of benefits if the combined plan (the DB/DC plan):[169]

(1) is primarily defined benefit in character;

(2) consists of broadly available separate plans; or

(3) satisfies a minimum gateway allocation.

A DB/DC plan is primarily defined benefit in character if, for more than 50 percent of the nonhighly compensated employees (NHCEs) in the plan, the normal accrual rate under the defined benefit plan for the NHCE exceeds the equivalent accrual rate for the NHCE attributable to contributions under the defined contribution plan. For example, a DB/DC plan is primarily defined benefit in character where the defined contribution plan covers only salaried employees, the defined benefit plan covers only hourly employees, and more than half of the NHCEs participating in the DB/DC plan are hourly employees participating only in the defined benefit plan.[170]

A DB/DC plan consists of broadly available separate plans if the defined contribution plan and the defined benefit plan, tested separately, would each satisfy the coverage tests of Code Sec. 410(b) and the nondiscrimination test, assuming satisfaction of the average benefit percentage test. This alternative is useful, for example, where an employer maintains a defined contribution plan that provides a uniform allocation rate for all covered employees at one business unit and a safe harbor defined benefit plan for all covered employees at another unit, and where the group of employees covered by each of those plans is a group that satisfies the nondiscriminatory classification test of Code Sec. 401(b). Because the employer provides broadly available separate plans, it may continue to aggregate the plans and test for nondiscrimination on the basis of benefits, as an alternative to using the qualified separate lines of business (SLOB) rules (discussed in ¶ 606.01) or meeting the average benefit percentage test.[171]

---

[168] Reg. § 1.401(a)(4)-9(b)(3).
[169] Reg. § 1.401(a)(4)-9(b)(2)(v).

[170] Reg. § 1.401(a)(4)-9(b)(2)(v)(B).
[171] Reg. § 1.401(a)(4)-9(b)(2)(v)(C).

DB/DC plans that cannot meet either of the above conditions must satisfy a minimum aggregate allocation gateway test. In order to apply this test, each employee's aggregate normal allocation rate is determined by adding the employee's allocation rate under the defined contribution plan to the employee's equivalent allocation rate under the defined benefit plan. The aggregate normal allocation rate for each NHCE must meet the following minimum allocation, based on the aggregate normal allocation rate of the highly compensated employee (HCE) with the highest aggregate normal allocation rate under the plan (HCE rate):[172]

HCE Rate	Minimum NHCE Rate
less than 15%	$\frac{1}{3}$ of the HCE rate
15–25%	5%
25–30%	6%
30–35%	7%
over 35%	7½%

(Note: The above table incorporates the rule under the regulations in which a NHCE rate of at least 7½% is deemed to satisfy the minimum aggregate allocation gateway.)

¶ 608 Vesting Requirements

Vesting refers to the percentage of accrued benefit to which an employee would be entitled if he left employment prior to attaining the normal retirement age under the plan. In other words, it represents that portion of the employee's benefit which is nonforfeitable. For example, if an employee separates from service from the employer at a time when he is 70 percent vested in his account balance of $1,000 in a defined contribution plan, he would be entitled to $700. The remaining $300 would be forfeited and either used to reduce the next year's contribution for the employer or allocated to the remaining participants' accounts. Had the plan been a defined benefit pension plan and his accrued balance were $1,000 per month for life beginning at age 65, upon leaving employment, the participant would likewise be entitled to a $700 per month annuity beginning at age 65. Thus, under a defined benefit plan, the vested benefit is not one which is determined for distribution at termination of employment. Rather, it is defined in terms of payments upon reaching normal retirement age. Thus, the employee would either wait until normal retirement age, or most likely, would receive the present value of the vested benefit upon termination.

---

[172] Reg. § 1.401(a)(4)-9(b)(2)(v)(D).

The above example demonstrates an important concept, that of accrued benefits. After all, it is the accrued benefit in which a participant vests. Under a defined contribution plan, a participant's accrued benefit is the participant's account balance. Under a defined benefit plan, however, a participant's accrued benefit is determined by the manner of accrual as specified by the plan. If a plan were to provide employees with immediate vesting in a defined benefit plan, but not accrue any benefits until after the employee had worked for a number of years, it would be meaningless to the employee if he terminated employment at an early age, since he might be 100 percent vested in nothing. Thus, in order to prevent employers from avoiding the intention of vesting by providing little benefits in the first few years of employment, and then substantially increasing the rate of accrual in later years (known as "backloading"), the Code also provides some minimum accrual rules in Code Sec. 411(b), the same section under which the vesting rules appear.

Code Sec. 401(a)(7) requires a plan to meet the rules under Code Sec. 411, regarding vesting standards. These vesting standards contain three general classes of vesting: (1) those relating to situations calling for full and immediate vesting; (2) those relating to the minimum vesting schedules of Code Sec. 411(a)(2); and (3) those relating to compliance with the Code Sec. 401(a)(4) nondiscrimination requirements.

.01 Situations Requiring Full and Immediate Vesting

Certain situations require full and immediate vesting. These relate to (1) the attainment of normal retirement age; (2) employee contributions; and (3) the complete or partial termination of, or discontinuance of contributions to, a plan.

Attainment of Normal Retirement Age. Under the general rule of Code Sec. 411(a), a participant's normal retirement benefit derived from employer contributions must be nonforfeitable upon the attainment of normal retirement age, regardless of where the employee happens to fall on the plan's vesting schedule at normal retirement age. The normal retirement benefit is generally the benefit payable at normal retirement age, unless an early retirement benefit is larger.[173]

Normal retirement age is the earlier of:[174]

(1) the age stated under the plan; or

---

[173] Code Sec. 411(a)(9). [174] Code Sec. 411(a)(8).

(2) the later of:

   (a) age 65; or

   (b) in the case of a plan participant who commences participation in the plan within five years before attaining the normal retirement age under the plan, the fifth anniversary of the time the plan participant commences participation in the plan.

If no normal retirement age is stated in the plan, then the normal retirement age is the earliest day beyond which benefits will not accrue due to additional age or service.[175]

Employee Contributions. Code Sec. 411(a)(1) requires that a participant must be fully vested at all times in the accrued benefit derived from the employee's own contributions to the plan. This requirement applies regardless of whether the employee contributions are voluntary or mandatory.

Defined contribution plans pose no problems in determining the accrued benefit derived from employee contributions, since the employee's "accrued benefit" is his account balance. Thus, if separate accounts are maintained for employee and employer contributions, the accrued benefit attributable to employee contributions is simply the balance of that account. If, on the other hand, separate accounts are not maintained, the accrued benefit from an employee's contributions is the total account balance multiplied by the ratio of employee contributions (less withdrawals) to the total contributions by the employer and the employee (less withdrawals).[176]

> **Example:** Employee Raymond terminates employment at a time when he was 40% vested (in employer-derived accrued benefits) in his employer's qualified profit-sharing plan. The total of his account balance on that date was $30,000. During his employment, Raymond had contributed $2,000 to the plan, and the employer had contributed $18,000. Raymond had made no withdrawals during his time of participation in the plan. Of the total contributions of $20,000 to the plan, $2,000 (10%) were employee contributions. Raymond is fully vested in $3,000 (10%) of the total accrued benefit, and 40% vested in the remaining $27,000 (90%), which represents the accrued benefit derived from employer contributions. Thus, his total accrued benefit is $13,800 ($3,000 + 40% of $27,000).

Determining the accrued benefit derived from voluntary employee contributions under a defined benefit plan which allows

---

[175] Reg. § 1.411(a)-7(b).   [176] Code Sec. 411(c)(2)(A).

them is equally easy. This is due to the fact that such plans are required to maintain a separate accounting for the portion of the accrued benefit derived from the employee's voluntary employee contributions. Such contributions are treated as if they were contributions to a defined contribution plan.[177]

In the case of a defined benefit plan which provides for mandatory employee contributions, determining the accrued benefit derived from employee contributions is relatively complex, since there is no separate accounting required under such a plan. Because of the complexity involved, only a general discussion will be provided; the exact manner in which the accrued benefit is determined is provided in proposed regulations.[178] The basic idea is to first determine the employee's "accumulated contributions," which is the total of the mandatory contributions made to the plan plus interest. This balance is then converted into an accrued benefit that is expressed as a single life annuity without ancillary benefits and commencing at normal retirement age. The proposed regulations provide appropriate interest rates and conversion factors for varying normal retirement ages, as well as for different forms of payments.

Termination, Partial Termination, and Complete Discontinuance of Contributions. Code Sec. 411(d)(3) requires that a qualified plan provide that accrued benefits, to the extent funded, become nonforfeitable for participants who are affected by a complete or partial termination of a plan, and in the case of a profit sharing or stock bonus plan, upon the complete discontinuance of contributions to the plan.

Determining whether a partial termination or a complete discontinuance of contributions has occurred are questions of fact, and are not always easy to determine. Reg. § 1.411(d)-2 provides guidelines for determining whether either has occurred. (¶ 612.03 discusses these guidelines.) The IRS has ruled that when a defined benefit plan temporarily freezes benefit accruals, a partial termination has occurred. Thus, all benefits accrued as of the date of the freeze were immediately vested, to the extent funded. Moreover, if benefit accruals are resumed under a different formula (or the plan is merged into a new plan), service during the freeze period must be included for vesting of benefits accrued after the resumption of the plan.[179]

---

[177] Code Sec. 411(b)(3) and (d)(5).
[178] Prop. Reg § 1.411(c)-1(c).

[179] Rev. Rul. 2003-65, 2003-25 IRB 1035.

.02   The Minimum Vesting Schedules of Code Sec. 411(a)(2)

All plans must satisfy at least one of two vesting schedules provided in Code Sec. 411(a)(2). It should be noted that these are *minimum* vesting schedules (which set the maximum number of years required to vest); a plan may use a more rapid, or liberal, vesting schedule. If a plan uses any schedule which is different from these two schedules, it will still qualify if it produces at least as high a vesting percentage as either statutory schedule for all years of service. Note, however, that a plan may not use a vesting schedule which meets the requirements of one statutory schedule only in some years, despite meeting another statutory schedule in other years, if it does not satisfy one schedule for all years.[180]

Five-Year Cliff Vesting. Under this schedule, participants who have completed five years of service with the employer must receive a 100 percent nonforfeitable claim to employer-derived benefits.[181] Thus, the schedule is as follows:

Completed Years of Service	Nonforfeitable Percentage
1-4	0%
5	100%

Three-to-Seven-Year Graded Vesting. Under this schedule, participants become vested at the rate of 20 percent per year, beginning with the third year of service.[182] The schedule is:

Completed Years of Service	Nonforfeitable Percentage
1-2	0%
3	20%
4	40%
5	60%
6	80%
7	100%

Top-Heavy Plans. A top-heavy plan is a plan in which more than 60 percent of the accrued benefits in the trust belong to so-called "key employees." Such plans are required to provide minimum contributions or benefits to all participants and to provide a more rapid vesting schedule. While the specific rules concerning top-heavy plans will be discussed in Chapter 7, the minimum vesting schedules applicable to such plans are provided here as well. A

---

[180] Reg. § 1.411(a)-3(a)(2); Temp. Reg. § 1.411(a)-3T(a)(2) and (f).

[181] Code Sec. 411(a)(2)(A).
[182] Code Sec. 411(a)(2)(B).

top-heavy plan must provide either:

(1) 100 percent vesting after three years of service; or

(2) 2-to-6-year graded vesting beginning with 20 percent after two years of service and 20 percent more for each year of service thereafter (100 percent after six years).[183]

Note that there is very little difference (only one year) between the three-to-seven-year graded schedule and the two-to-six-year graded schedule. Thus, it would probably be easier, from an administrative point of view, for a plan which may be potentially top heavy to simply adopt the two-to-six-year graded schedule.

Employer-Matching Contributions. Employer-matching contributions made to a plan are subject to faster vesting schedules. Employer-matching contributions are those made on account of an employee contribution or elective deferral to a defined contribution plan. (See ¶607.02 for discussion of matching contributions.) These schedules are the same as those imposed on top-heavy plans (discussed above), i.e., the matching contributions must provide either:[184]

(1) 100 percent vesting after three years of service; or

(2) 2-to-6-year graded vesting as follows:

Completed Years of Service	Nonforfeitable Percentage
1	0%
2	20%
3	40%
4	60%
5	80%
6	100%

(Note that these faster vesting schedules apply only to employer-matching contributions made after 2001. Matching contributions made before 2002 may remain under the previous vesting schedule in effect at the time of the contribution.)

Other Special Plans. Two other plans require special vesting provisions. Both of those plans are the result of the age and service exceptions for participation under Code Sec. 410(a)(1)(B). The first of these plans is a plan that requires two years of service as a condition of participation. Such a plan must provide full and immediate vesting no later than completion of two years of service.[185]

---

[183] Code Sec. 416(b).
[184] Code Sec. 411(a)(12).

[185] Code Sec. 410(a)(1)(B)(i).

The second type of plan is one maintained by certain educational institutions that requires, as a condition of participation, the attainment of age 26 (rather than age 21). Such plans must provide full and immediate vesting upon completion of one year of service.[186]

Changes in Vesting Schedules. If a qualified plan is amended with respect to its vesting schedule, two restrictions apply:

(1) the plan cannot reduce the vested rights to already accrued benefits; and

(2) each participant who has at least three years of service (as of the amendment date) must be given the right to elect to remain under the old vesting schedule.[187]

The period for electing to remain under the old vesting schedule must begin no later than the date the amendment was adopted and must end no earlier than 60 days after the latest of (1) the date the amendment was adopted, (2) the date the amendment becomes effective, or (3) the date the participant is issued written notice of the amendment by the employer or plan administrator.[188]

.03 Nondiscrimination in Vesting Requirements

Even if a plan adopts one of the two statutory vesting schedules, it may still discriminate in favor of highly compensated employees in practice. A plan that meets the minimum vesting standards will not be treated as discriminatory, unless there is a pattern of abuse under the plan (such as dismissal of lower-paid employees prior to vesting in their accrued benefits) tending to discriminate in favor of highly compensated employees. Likewise, if there has been, or there is reason to believe that there will be, an accrual of benefits or forfeitures tending to discriminate in favor of highly compensated employees, a plan will be discriminatory.[189]

The determination of whether a plan actually discriminates in favor of highly compensated employees is based on all the facts and circumstances. Under a safe harbor provided in the nondiscrimination regulations, the manner in which employees vest in their accrued benefits under a plan does not discriminate in favor of highly compensated employees if each combination of plan provisions that affect the vesting of any employee's accrued benefit would satisfy the nondiscriminatory availability requirements (see earlier discussion of the nondiscrimination rules) if that combination were another right or feature.[190] Two or more plans may be aggregated to

---

[186] Code Sec. 410(a)(1)(B)(ii).
[187] Code Sec. 411(a)(10).
[188] Reg. § 1.411(a)-8(b)(2).

[189] Code Sec. 411(d)(1).

[190] Reg. § 1.401(a)(4)-11(c)(3).

determine whether they are discriminatory. The 5-year cliff vesting schedule and the 3-to-7-year graded vesting schedule are treated as equivalent in determining whether the manner in which employees vest in their accrued benefits under the aggregated plan is discriminatory.[191]

.04 Service for Vesting Purposes

The general rules for counting years of service for vesting are similar to those for participation, which were covered earlier in the chapter. Thus, a year of service for vesting purposes is a 12-consecutive-month period during which an employee is credited with 1,000 hours of service.[192] Alternatively, if the plan employs the elapsed time method for counting hours of service, a year of service for vesting would be counted in a manner similar to that used in counting participation. However, three important differences between service for vesting and participation exist. First, all years of service after the attainment of age 18 (rather than age 21) must be counted. Years of service before age 18 may be disregarded. Second, contributory plans (those with mandatory employee contributions) may disregard any years of service in which an employee failed to make a contribution. Finally, years of service during which the employer did not maintain the plan or a predecessor plan may be disregarded.[193] (Note that service after a plan is terminated may be excluded for vesting purposes. However, this rule does not apply to a partial termination.[194] Thus, when a defined benefit plan was frozen for several years, and then resumed either under a different formula or merged into a new plan (resulting in a partial termination), service during the freeze period was included for vesting of benefits accrued upon the resumption of the plan.)[195]

Breaks in Service. The rules regarding breaks in service also apply to vesting. Thus, an employee failing to complete more than 500 hours of service in the computation period may lose credit for one or more years of service for vesting purposes in the following situations:

(1) If an employee incurs a one-year break in service, the plan may provide that all years of service before the break will not count toward vesting until the employee has completed a year of service after the break.[196]

Example: Plan X employs the 3-to-7-year graded vesting schedule. Roger, who had completed three years of service

---

[191] Reg. § 1.401(a)(4)-11(c)(2).
[192] Code Sec. 411(a)(5).
[193] Code Sec. 411(a)(4).

[194] Reg. § 1.411(a)-5(b)(3)(iii).
[195] Rev. Rul. 2003-65, 2003-25 IRB 1035.
[196] Code Sec. 411(a)(6)(B).

from 2002-2004 and was 20 percent vested at the end of 2004, incurs a one-year break in service in 2005. If Roger returns to work in 2006, Plan X is not required to apply this 20 percent vesting to any additional accrued benefits earned during 2006 until Roger has completed a year of service. If Roger completes a year of service in 2006, he will be credited with another 20 percent vesting for 2006 (according to the vesting schedule), and the original 20 percent vested level earned before the break in service will be combined with it to total 40 percent.

(2) A defined contribution plan (and certain insured defined benefit plans) may provide that following five consecutive one-year breaks in service, any years of service earned after the break are not taken into account for purposes of determining the vested percentage in the benefit accrued prior to the break. Thus, plans are safe to allocate forfeitures to remaining participants after any such five consecutive one-year breaks in service.[197]

Example (2): Profit-sharing Plan Y employs the 3-to-7-year graded vesting schedule. Tara had earned five years of service for vesting (and was 60 percent vested in her accrued benefit), but incurred five consecutive one-year breaks in service. Plan Y distributed 60 percent of Tara's accrued benefit to her and allocated the remaining 40 percent forfeited to other participants in the plan after Tara had incurred the breaks in service. Tara subsequently returned to work and earned two additional years of service. Thus, Tara has a total of seven years of service and will be 100 percent vested in all benefits accrued after the breaks in service, but will receive no additional vesting in her benefit accrued before the breaks.

(3) The rule of parity, which applies only to nonvested participants, requires a plan to count years of service earned before a break in service toward post-break vesting if the break period is less than five years or, if greater, the number of years of service earned before the break in service. Note that this rule is different from the preceding five-year rule, in that the rule of parity concerns whether pre-break service can increase vesting of post-break accrued benefits, whereas the five-year defined contribution plan rule concerns whether post-break service can increase vesting of pre-break accrued benefits.[198]

---

[197] Code Sec. 411(a)(6)(C).

[198] Code Sec. 411(a)(6)(D).

Example (3): Plan Z employs the five-year cliff vesting schedule. Corey had earned four years of service (and no vesting in his accrued benefit) prior to incurring six consecutive one-year breaks in service. If Corey subsequently returns to work, Plan Z may disregard his prior four years of service earned, since his break in service exceeded his pre-break years and was longer than five consecutive years. Had Corey returned after only four consecutive one-year break periods, Plan Z would have to count his four years earned prior to the break. Thus, upon the completion of one year of service after returning to work, Corey would be 100 percent vested in his benefit accrued after the break period.

An exception to the break in service rule applies to veterans who are reemployed under USERRA. Such individuals are treated as not having incurred a break in service with the employer by reason of the employee's period of qualified military service.[199]

.05 Forfeitures of Accrued and Vested Benefits

Generally, once a participant has a vested right in an accrued benefit, it is nonforfeitable under any circumstances. However, a plan can provide for forfeitures of vested rights attributable to employer contributions as long as the plan would still meet the minimum vesting schedules. Thus, a plan that vests participants 25 percent after one year and 100 percent after five years could provide for a forfeiture for any reason before year five, since the plan would meet the five-year vesting schedule. In addition, Code Sec. 411(a)(3) contains provisions under which certain forfeitures are permitted (but not required) under a plan. Those exceptions which relate to single employer plans are discussed below.

Forfeiture on Account of Death. A qualified retirement plan is required to provide retirement benefits, but not death benefits. Thus, a plan may provide that accrued benefits derived from employer contributions will be forfeited upon the death of the participant, unless the death requires the payment of a survivor annuity to the participant's spouse under the provisions of Code Sec. 401(a)(11). Moreover, a plan may also treat the accrued benefit from the employee's contribution as forfeitable if the participant's death occurs after the commencement of annuity or pension payments in a defined benefit form provided under the plan.[200]

Suspension of Benefits upon Reemployment of a Retiree. Benefit payments to a retired employee who returns to work for the

---

[199] Code Sec. 414(u)(8).

[200] Reg. § 1.411(a)-4(b)(1).

employer may be suspended during the reemployment period under Code Sec. 411(a)(3)(B). Generally, benefits may be suspended for each calendar month in which the participant is reemployed for 40 or more hours.[201]

Retroactive Plan Amendments. Ordinarily, no plan amendment may be adopted which would retroactively decrease accrued benefits. However, under Code Sec. 412(c)(8), a plan may be allowed to retroactively reduce accrued benefits within certain limits if the employer demonstrates to the IRS that such action is necessary due to a "substantial business hardship," as defined in Code Sec. 412(d)(2).[202] Any such amendment must be adopted within two-and-a-half months after the close of the plan year to which it applies. The amendment must not reduce the accrued benefit of any participant computed as to the beginning of the plan year to which the amendment applies.

The term "accrued benefits" is generally defined as the annual benefit commencing at normal retirement age. (See ¶ 608.06 for discussion.) However, it is also construed to mean different forms of benefits. Indeed, the Code provides that any plan amendment that eliminates an optional form of benefit with respect to benefits attributable to service before the amendment (e.g., a single sum distribution or early retirement benefit) is treated as reducing accrued benefits.[203] Thus, a plan amendment that reduces or eliminates early retirement benefits, retirement-type subsidies, or optional forms of benefit that are already accrued is not allowed. (Note that this provision does not prohibit amendments that reduce or eliminate optional forms of benefit that are not yet accrued on the amendment date.) Under regulations finalized in 2005, however, employers are allowed to eliminate some optional forms of benefit under limited circumstances. An optional form of benefit may be eliminated generally if: (1) the eliminated form is redundant with respect to a retained optional form of benefit; or (2) the amendment is not effective for benefits that begin in the next four years and certain core options are made available to participants.[204] If the retained optional form of benefit or each core option does not have the same annuity starting date or has a lower actuarial present value than the optional form being eliminated, the employer must also demonstrate that the eliminated form creates significant burdens and complexities for the plan, and that the elimination does not reduce the actuarial present value of any participant by more than

---

[201] DOL Reg. § 2530.203-3.

[202] Code Sec. 411(a)(3)(C).

[203] Code Sec. 411(d)(6)(B); Reg. § 1.411(d)-4, Q&A 1.

[204] Reg. § 1.411(d)-3(c) and (d).

a *de minimis* amount (defined as the greater of 2% of the present value of the retirement-type subsidy under the eliminated optional form prior to the amendment or 1% of the greater of the participant's compensation for the prior plan year or the participant's average compensation for his or her high three years.[205])

However, an amendment to a defined contribution plan may eliminate a form of distribution previously available, provided that (1) a single sum distribution that is otherwise identical to the optional form of benefit that is eliminated is available to the participant at the same time or times as the form of distribution eliminated by the amendment, and (2) the single sum distribution is based on the same or greater portion of the participant's accrued benefit as the form of distribution eliminated by the amendment.[206]

Withdrawal of Mandatory Employee Contributions. A plan may provide that if a participant who is less than 50 percent vested in employer contributions withdraws any of his mandatory employee contributions (or the earnings thereon) all or part of benefits attributable to employer contributions will be forfeited. However, the plan must restore the forfeited benefit upon the timely repayment of the amount withdrawn (plus interest at 120 percent of the mid-term applicable rate in a defined benefit plan) by the employee.[207] The plan may require that the repayment must be made: (1) in the case of a withdrawal on account of separation from service, before the earlier of five years after the resumption of employment by the participant or the last day of the first period of five consecutive breaks in service commencing after the withdrawal, or (2) in the case of any other withdrawal, five years from the date of withdrawal.[208]

Matching Contributions Forfeited by Reason of Excess Deferral or Contribution. A matching employer contribution (within the meaning of Code Sec. 401(m)) is not treated as a forfeiture if the plan requires such matching contribution to be forfeited if it relates to an employee contribution that is an excess contribution under Code Sec. 401(k)(8), an excess deferral under Code Sec. 402(g)(2)(A), or an excess aggregate contribution under Code Sec. 401(m)(6)(B).[209]

"Cash-Out" Rules. Another provision quite similar to those above are the "cash-out" rules contained in Code Sec. 411(a)(7)(B). These rules apply generally to distributions resulting from a parti-

---

[205] Reg. § 1.411(d)-3(e).
[206] Code Sec. 411(d)(6)(E); Reg. § 1.411(d)-4, Q&A 2(e), as amended by T.D. 9176, 2005-10 IRB 661.
[207] Code Secs. 401(a)(19) and 411(a)(3)(D).
[208] Code Sec. 411(a)(3)(D)(ii).
[209] Code Sec. 411(a)(3)(G); Reg. § 1.411(d)-4, Q&A 2(e), as amended by T.D. 9176, 2005-10 IRB 661.

cipant's termination of employment. Recall under the break-in-service rules that a participant's years of service after incurring five consecutive one-year breaks in service don't have to be counted for purposes of determining the vested percentage of his account balance before the break. Thus, the employer would know the amount of the potential forfeiture. However, because of the five-year requirement, the plan must keep the balance in an unallocated suspense account, or else the employer will remain contingently liable to restore the balance if the participant returns within the five-year period.

If the distribution qualifies as a "cash-out," however, the plan can immediately allocate the forfeiture to other participants' accounts or use the forfeiture to reduce the next year's employer contribution. The Code identifies two kinds of cash-outs: involuntary and voluntary.

Involuntary Cash-Outs. A distribution meets the definition of an involuntary cash-out if it meets the following requirements:[210]

(1) the distribution is the present value of the participant's entire vested benefit (in the case of a defined contribution plan, this means the participant's vested account balance; in the case of a defined benefit plan, the present value is determined using the mortality and interest assumptions provided under Reg. § 1.417(e)-1);

(2) the amount of the distribution which is attributable to the present value of employer-derived benefits does not exceed $5,000 (excluding any rollover contributions and related earnings);

(3) the distribution is made on account of termination of the employee's participation in the plan; and

(4) if the participant was not fully vested, the plan contains a "buyback" provision (discussed below).

In computing the $5,000 threshold, the plan may disregard rollovers (and related earnings) from participants who have transferred retirement benefits from a previous employer or an IRA.[211]

For any involuntary cash-out exceeding $1,000, the default method of distribution is a direct rollover to a designated IRA. However, a participant must be allowed to affirmatively elect to have the distribution transferred to a different IRA or another qualified plan, or to receive it directly. Note, however, that this provision does not become effective until the Department of Labor issues regulations to provide safe harbors under which the plan

---

[210] Code Secs. 411(a)(7)(B) and (C).   [211] Code Sec. 411(a)(11)(D).

administrator's designation of an institution and the investment of the funds for the designated IRA are deemed to satisfy the fiduciary responsibilities under ERISA Sec. 404(a).[212]

Voluntary Cash-Outs. A distribution meets the definition of a voluntary cash-out if it meets the following requirements:[213]

(1) the distribution is made on account of termination of the employee's participation in the plan;

(2) the employee consents to receive the cash-out distribution;

(3) the distribution equals the present value of the participant's accrued benefit under the plan; and

(4) the plan contains a buy-back provision.

An employee consent to the cash-out is valid only if the employer provides to the employee a description of the material features and an explanation of the relative values of the optional forms of benefit available, and informs the employee of his right to defer receipt of the distribution. The employee must be given the opportunity to consider the decisions for at least a 30-day period.

Buy-Back Provision. In either type of cash-out distribution, the plan must contain a "buy-back" provision so that, if a participant who received a cash-out which was less than the present value of his accrued benefit later resumes employment before a five-consecutive-year break in service has occurred, the participant can restore his nonvested benefit by repaying the amount of the previous cash-out distribution. (Otherwise, the plan may not disregard a participant's accrued benefit attributable to service for which he or she received the earlier distribution.[214]) In the case of a defined contribution plan, the participant must repay the amount he actually received. Under a defined benefit plan, however, the employee must repay the full amount of the distribution plus interest at the rate of 120 percent of the midterm applicable rate for the interim period.[215]

A plan may require that if the distribution was made on account of separation from service, the participant must repay the full amount of the distribution (as defined in the preceding paragraph) by the earlier of:

(1) five years after the first date on which the participant is subsequently reemployed; or

(2) the end of the first period of five consecutive one-year breaks in service beginning with the date of the cash-out distribution.

---

[212] Code Sec. 401(a)(31)(B).
[213] Code Secs. 411(a)(7)(B) and (C).

[214] Reg. § 1.411(a)-7(d)(6)(i).
[215] Code Sec. 411(a)(7)(C).

In the case of a withdrawal not on account of separation from service, the plan may require that the buy-back be made no later that five years after the date of the withdrawal.[216]

Example (1): Sue terminates her employment with Blue Company after five years when she was 60% vested in her $7,000 account balance in Blue's profit-sharing plan. The Blue plan may distribute the $4,200 vested balance to Sue without consulting her about whether she wants the cashout.

Example (2): Continuing with the facts in the above example, assume that Sue returns to work for Blue Company three years later. The Blue plan must allow Sue to restore her $2,800 nonvested benefit by repaying the previous $4,200 cash-out to the plan.

"Bad Boy" Clauses. Code Sec. 411(a)(3) is intended as an exclusive list for forfeitures of vested benefits. Thus, a plan may not have a "bad boy" clause providing for forfeitures of vested benefits for misconduct (e.g., dishonesty) or engaging in competition with the employer (a practice which was common prior to the passage of ERISA). However, it is possible to provide for switching to another vesting schedule which satisfies Code Sec. 411(a)(2). Thus, a plan which has 100 percent vesting after three years could include a provision for complete forfeiture of benefits for employees with less than five years of service for such actions by the employee. Alternatively, a plan could provide two vesting schedules, the longer of which applies to bad boys, as long as both schedules satisfy the same statutory vesting schedule and are not discriminatory.[217] Of course, any such provisions must satisfy the nondiscrimination requirements.

.06 Accrual of Benefits Under Defined Benefit Plans

A participant's accrued benefit under a defined contribution plan is simply the participant's account balance. Thus, there is no difficulty in determining the dollar amount of vested benefit; it is the account balance derived from employer contributions multiplied by the vested percentage, plus the total amount derived from employee contributions. Under a defined benefit plan, a participant's accrued benefit is determined by the plan's formula. The amount of a participant's accrued benefit under a defined benefit plan is the annual

---

[216] *Id.*

[217] Reg. § 1.411(a)-4(c) and Rev. Rul. 85-31, 1985-1 CB 153.

benefit, expressed as a single life annuity, beginning at normal retirement age, or the actuarial equivalent of such benefit.[218] If a participant leaves employment before normal retirement age, he would receive a smaller retirement benefit than if he stayed until normal retirement age, even though he is fully vested.

Code Sec. 411(b)(1) provides three alternative benefit accrual tests. These tests represent the minimum rate of accrual under a defined benefit plan. Their purpose is to prevent "backloading." That is, the formula cannot provide substantially, higher accruals after attainment of a specified age or years of service. For example, a plan formula cannot accrue benefits at the rate of one percent per year for the first 20 years of service and five percent per year thereafter. As in the case of vesting standards, a plan need meet only one of the three tests.

The Three-Percent Rule. Under the three-percent rule, a participant must accrue, for each year of participation (up to $33\frac{1}{3}$ years), at least three percent of the benefit which he would receive if he became a participant at the earliest possible age under the plan and stayed until normal retirement age or age 65 (whichever is earlier).[219]

The following examples, adapted from the regulations,[220] illustrate this rule.

Example (1): The defined benefit plan of M Company provides an annual benefit commencing at age 65 of $480 per year for each year of participation. There is no limit on the number of years of credited service. The plan requires an employee to have attained age 21 as a condition of participation. The normal retirement age under the plan is age 65. Mr. Adler, age 40, has completed 12 years of participation in the plan. If Mr. Adler had become a participant at the earliest possible entry age (21) and served continuously until normal retirement age (65), he would be entitled to an annual benefit of $21,120 ($480 × 44 years). Under the 3% rule, Mr. Adler must have an accrued benefit of at least $7,603 (.03 × $21,120 × 12) as of the close of the plan year. Under the M Company plan, Mr. Adler is entitled to an accrued benefit of only $5,760 (12 × $480) as of the close of the plan year. Thus, with respect to Mr. Adler, the accrual rate does not meet the 3% rule.

---

[218] Code Sec. 411(a)(7)(A)(i) and (c)(3).
[219] Code Sec. 411(b)(1)(A).

[220] Reg. § 1.411(b)-1.

Example (2): If, however, the M Company plan provides that only the first 30 years of participation are taken into account, the 3% rule would be met. That is, the maximum annual benefit which Mr. Adler could receive is $14,400 ($480 X 30 years). Under the 3% rule, he must have accrued at least $5,184 (.03 X $14,400 X 12) as of the close of the plan year. Since Mr. Adler's accrued benefit is $5,760 as of the close of the plan year, it would now meet the 3% rule.

Example (3): N Company's defined benefit plan provides an annual retirement distribution, commencing at age 65, of 50% of average compensation for the highest 3 consecutive years of compensation for an employee with 25 years of participation. Employees who separate from service prior to age 65 are entitled to 2% of average compensation for the highest 3 consecutive years of compensation, not to exceed 25 years. Normal retirement age under the plan is 65; the plan has no minimum age or service requirement for participation. Ms. Dowd, who became a participant in the N Company plan on January 1, 1996, is age 40 as of December 31, 2006. The normal retirement benefit to which Ms. Dowd would be entitled if she had commenced participation at the earliest possible entry age under the plan (age 0, since the plan has no minimum age requirement) and stayed until normal retirement age is 50% of average compensation for the highest 3 consecutive years of compensation. Under the 3% rule, Ms. Dowd must have accrued an annual benefit of at least 16.5 percent of her highest 3 consecutive years of compensation commencing at age 65 (.03 × 50% of average compensation for the highest 3 consecutive years of compensation × 11 years). Under the N Company plan, Ms. Dowd has accrued an annual benefit of 22 percent of average compensation for her highest 3 consecutive years of compensation commencing at age 65. Thus, with respect to Ms. Dowd, the benefit accrual rate satisfies the 3% rule.

The 133⅓ Percent Rule. Under this rule, the benefit accrual rate for any year cannot be more than 133⅓ percent of the accrual rate for any prior year (excluding accruals due to plan amendments).[221]

Example: A defined benefit plan provides for an annual benefit (commencing at age 65) of a percentage of a participant's average compensation for his final five years of participation,

---

[221] Code Sec. 411(b)(1)(B).

where the percentage is 1% for each of the first five years of participation; $1\frac{1}{3}$% for each of the next five years of participation; and $1\frac{7}{9}$% for each year thereafter. This rate of benefit accrual would not meet the $133\frac{1}{3}$% rule, because the accrual rate after the first 10 years of participation ($1\frac{7}{9}$%) exceeds $133\frac{1}{3}$% of the rate of accrual for the first five years of participation (1%).

The Fractional Rule. To meet this rule, the accrued benefit of a participant must be at least proportionate to the ratio of his actual years of participation to the total possible years of participation (assuming the participant stayed until normal retirement age) times his projected benefit at retirement age. Under this rule, if a participant's projected benefit is based on compensation, the participant is assumed to earn the same rate of compensation until retirement as he earns at the measurement date, but the assumption may take into account no more than the 10 years of service immediately preceding the determination.[222]

Thus, the accrued benefit under this rule must be at least equal to:

$$\text{Projected Annual Benefit at normal retirement age} \times \frac{\text{Actual Years of Participation}}{\text{Total Years of Participation if he remains until normal retirement age}}$$

Example: A defined benefit plan provides a normal retirement benefit of 1% per year of a participant's average compensation. The annual benefit for participants who separate from service prior to normal retirement age (65) is 1% of average compensation times the number of years of plan participation. Mr. Carr, age 55 in 2006, became a participant in the plan on January 1, 1996. His compensation history is as follows:

Year	Compensation
1996	$ 17,000
1997	18,000
1998	20,000
1999	20,000
2000	21,000
2001	22,000
2002	23,000
2003	25,000
2004	26,000
2005	29,000
2006	32,000
Total	$253,000

---

[222] Code Sec. 411(b)(1)(C).

To determine whether the plan meets the fractional rule as of December 31, 2006, the fractional rule benefit must be calculated. This is his average annual compensation, based on only the 10 years' compensation immediately prior to the determination date (1997-2006), which equals $23,600. Thus, his fractional rule benefit would be calculated as follows: $253,000 (from above) plus 10 more years (Mr. Carr is age 55, and the normal retirement age is 65) of the assumed $23,600 earnings, divided by 21 years of total possible participation equals a projected annual compensation of $23,286. Thus, the fractional rule benefit is $4,890 ($23,286 × 1% per year × 21 projected years). Under the fractional rule, Mr. Carr must have an accrued benefit of at least:

$$\$4,890 \times \frac{11 \text{ Actual Years of Participation}}{21 \text{ Total Possible Years of Participation}} = \$2,561$$

Mr. Carr's actual accrued benefit under the plan as of December 31, 2006, is $2,530, which is (1% × 11 years of participation × $23,000 average compensation for all years of participation (from 1996-2006)). Thus, because his actual accrued benefit is less than the minimum required benefit of $2,561, the plan does not meet the fractional rule test.

¶609 Limitations on Contributions and Benefits

Code Sec. 401(a)(16) requires a plan to comply with the Code Sec. 415 limitations for contributions and benefits. These limitations set the maximum amounts which the employer may provide to participants under the plan (but not necessarily deduct; employer deductions are determined under Code Sec. 404, which is covered in Chapter 8). A plan must include provisions to ensure that these limitations are never exceeded for any participant; otherwise, the entire plan will become disqualified for the year.

.01 General Rules

Before considering the actual limitations, some fundamental rules should be noted. As usual, all employees of a controlled group or affiliated service group are treated as if they were with a single employer.[223] Thus, these limits apply to all plans maintained by all members in the group, considered as if all the plans were a single plan, i.e., if an employee is covered by more than one plan, even

---

[223] Reg. § 1.415-2(d)(6); Prop. Reg. § 1.415(a)-1(e) and (f).

though maintained by another employer in the group, the limits apply to the total amounts provided under all such plans.

In addition, all defined benefit (or contribution) plans, without regard to whether the plans have been terminated, ever maintained by the employer or a member of the same controlled group are treated as one defined benefit (or contribution) plan.[224] Thus, an employer cannot establish a defined benefit plan which provides the maximum allowable benefit, fully fund it, terminate it, and then establish a new defined benefit with the same intentions. This rule requires that all such plans be combined to determine if the total benefit or contributions are within the limits.

Compensation Defined. The limitations imposed on both defined contribution and defined benefit plans are based on the participant's compensation. For purposes of the limitations under Code Sec. 415, the basic definition of compensation (as defined earlier in the nondiscrimination section) applies. It includes all remuneration received for personal services rendered for the employer, as well as employee elective deferrals to a CODA, cafeteria plan, SARSEP, Code Sec. 457 government plan, qualified transportation fringe benefit plan or a tax-sheltered annuity.[225]

For a self-employed individual, "compensation" is earned income, which is the total net earnings from self-employment from a trade or business in which personal services of the taxpayer are a material income-producing factor. Earned income is reduced by the deduction for one-half of self-employment taxes and by the amount of the deduction allowed for a contribution to a defined benefit or a defined contribution plan.[226] To illustrate, the limitation on deductions for defined contribution plans is 25 percent of the participant's compensation. If a self-employed individual has $100,000 of earned income (after the deduction for one-half of self-employment taxes), that limitation is applied after taking the deduction into account as follows:

$$\text{Deduction} = 25\% \times (100,000 - \text{Deduction})$$

$$\text{Deduction} = \$25,000 - .25\ (\text{Deduction})$$

$$\text{Deduction} = \$20,000$$

Thus, for the self-employed individual, the limitation on deductions for defined contribution plans is, in effect, 20 percent of earned income. See ¶ 702.02 for a detailed discussion.

---

[224] Code Sec. 415(f) and Reg. § 1.415-8(a); Prop. Reg. § 1.415(a)-1(e).

[225] Code Sec. 415(c)(3)(D); Prop. Reg. § 1.415(c)-2(a).
[226] Code Sec. 401(c)(2).

Limit on Compensation. The amount of annual compensation that may be taken into account under a qualified plan is $210,000 (in 2005).[227] This limit applies not only for determining the amount of benefits or contributions, but for all of the nondiscrimination rules as well.

The compensation limit has been subject to COLAs and other increases through legislation (most notably EGTRRA '01). Annual limits in prior years were: $150,000 for 1994-1996; $160,000 for 1997-1999; $170,000 for 2000-2001; $200,000 for 2002-2003; and $205,000 for 2004. This historical perspective is important, because in determining an employee's allocation or benefit accrual for the current plan year, the dollar limit in effect for the current year applies only to the compensation for that year. An employee's compensation for any prior plan year is subject to the applicable annual compensation limit in effect for that prior plan year. Thus, the limit applies separately to each year's compensation, rather than to the final average compensation.[228]

Example (1): Gina is a participant in the Green Company profit-sharing plan. The Green plan has a calendar plan year, and a contribution formula that provides for a contribution of 10 percent of compensation. Gina's compensation for each of the years 2003, 2004, and 2005 is $250,000. Gina's annual contributions under the plan formula are $20,000 for 2003 ($200,000 limit × 10%), $20,500 for 2004 ($205,000 limit × 10%), and $21,000 for 2004 ($210,000 limit × 10%).

Example (2): Rita is a participant in the Red Company defined benefit plan. The Red plan has a calendar plan year, and a benefit formula that provides for an annual benefit at normal retirement age equal to the product of: (years of service) × (1%) × (high 3-year average compensation). For this purpose, high 3-year average compensation is the average of the compensation over the 3 consecutive plan years for which the average is the highest, and compensation for each year is limited to the maximum annual compensation allowed under Code Sec. 401(a)(17). As of December 31, 2004, Rita has 10 years of service and compensation of $250,000 for each of the 3 years 2002, 2003, and 2004. Rita's high 3-year average compensation of $201,667 is determined as the average of annual compensation (as limited by Code Sec. 401(a)(17)) of $200,000 for 2002, $200,000 for 2003, and $205,000 for 2004. Rita's annual benefit under the plan

---

[227] Code Sec. 401(a)(17).   [228] Reg. § 1.401(a)(17)-1(b)(2).

¶609.01

formula as of December 31, 2004, is $20,167, calculated as (10) × (1%) × ($201,667).

In 2005, Rita has annual compensation of $250,000. Rita's high 3-year average compensation of $205,000 is determined as of December 31, 2005, as the average of annual compensation of $200,000 for 2003, $205,000 for 2004, and $210,000 for 2005. Rita's annual benefit as of December 31, 2005, would be $22,550, calculated as (11) × (1%) × ($205,000).

As mentioned above, EGTRRA '01 significantly increased the compensation limit from prior years, beginning in 2001. In addition to this increase, provisions under EGTRRA '01 also allow a plan that uses annual compensation for periods prior to the first plan year beginning on of after January 1, 2002, for determining accruals or allocations for a plan year beginning on or after January 1, 2002, to provide that the $200,000 compensation limit applies to annual compensation for those prior periods in determining accruals or allocations.[229] The IRS ruled that plans could be amended to also apply this increased compensation limit to all *former* employees (or all former employees who retain accrued benefits under the plan).[230]

.02   Code Sec. 415 Limitations

The total amount of benefits provided under defined benefit plans or contributions to defined contribution plans on behalf of any participant is subject to annual limitations. These limits are determined on the basis of a limitation year, which is generally the calendar year, unless the employer elects to use another 12-month period.

Several transition rules have been provided to protect plans (and participants) that had met requirements under prior law, but would not meet the limits imposed under subsequent acts. Thus, in the discussion below, several references are made to the limitations under old law, since plans which were in existence as of the enactment of new legislation would be affected.

.03   Defined Benefit Plans

A defined benefit plan may not provide "annual benefits" in excess of the lesser of:

(1) a dollar limit of $170,000 (in 2005); or

(2) 100 percent of the participant's average annual compensation for the three consecutive years in which his compensation was

---

[229] Committee Reports, EGTRRA Sec. 611.   [230] Rev. Rul. 2003-11, IRB 2003-3, 285.

the highest.[231] (The compensation limit does not apply to governmental plans; only the dollar limit applies.[232])

The $170,000 limit is subject to cost of living adjustments in multiples of $5,000. As a matter of historical perspective, the dollar limit placed on benefits has been the target of several changes. Prior to TEFRA, the limit was $75,000, adjusted for the cost of living. By 1982, these adjustments had increased the limit to $136,425. TEFRA reduced the limit to $90,000, but by 2001, COLAs had increased the limit to $140,000. EGTRRA '01 increased the limit to $160,000, beginning in 2002, after which subsequent COLAs are in multiples of $5,000.

Again, annual compensation (for purposes of computing the three highest consecutive years) is limited by the annual dollar amount in effect for each year. Proposed regulations would also restrict compensation used for this purpose to compensation earned in periods during which the employee was an active participant in the plan.[233]

If a defined benefit plan provides for postretirement cost of living adjustments, the limitation based on the average compensation is also subject to cost of living adjustments for participants who have separated from service.

"Annual Benefit" Defined. The "annual benefit" to which the above limitations apply means a benefit payable annually at age 62 in the form of a straight-life annuity, with no ancillary benefits, under a plan to which employees do not contribute and under which no rollover contributions are made by the employee. Employee contributions, whether mandatory or voluntary, are considered to be a separate defined contribution plan to which the limitations thereon apply.[234]

If the annual benefit under a plan is payable in any form other than a straight-life annuity, such as an annuity which includes a post-retirement death benefit and an annuity providing for a guaranteed number of payments, it must be actuarially adjusted to the equivalent of such a benefit.[235] No adjustment is required, however, if the benefit is payable in the form of a qualified joint and survivor annuity (as defined in Code Sec. 401(a)(11)). In addition, ancillary benefits which are not directly related to retirement income benefits, such as post-retirement medical benefits and pre-retirement

---

[231] Code Sec. 415(b)(1).
[232] Code Sec. 415(b)(11).
[233] Prop. Reg. § 1.415(b)-1(a)(5).

[234] Reg. § 1.415-3(d); Prop. Reg. § 1.415(b)-1(b).
[235] Reg. § 1.415-3(c)(1); Prop. Reg. § 1.415(b)-1(c).

death and disability benefits, do not require adjustment, i.e., they are disregarded in determining the amount of the annual benefit.[236] The steps and procedures for determining these actuarial adjustments are provided in Rev. Rul. 98-1[237] and in proposed regulations.[238]

Adjustments to the Dollar Limit. The $170,000 limit applies to benefit payments commencing between the ages of 62 and 65. In the event that benefit payments begin before a participant reaches age 62, the dollar limit must be actuarially reduced to the equivalent of a $170,000 annuity beginning at age 62. (However, no reduction is made in the case of early benefits paid from a government plan on account of a participant's death or disability.) Similarly, the dollar limit is increased for benefit payments which begin after a participant reaches age 65 to the equivalent of a $170,000 annuity beginning at age 65. The steps and procedures for determining these actuarial adjustments are provided in Rev. Rul. 98-1[239] (as are those for determining different forms of the annual benefit, discussed above), except that the defined benefit dollar limit is modified to reflect the increase provided under EGTRRA.[240]

The dollar limitation for benefits commencing prior to age 62 is reduced to the actuarial equivalent of the limitation for benefits commencing at age 62. This actuarial equivalence must be determined using the mortality table contained in Rev. Rul. 2001-62[241] and an interest rate which is not less than the greater of five percent (5.5% for plan years 2004 and 2005)[242] or the rate specified in the plan for determining actuarial equivalence for early retirement.[243] However, no reduction is made in the case of early benefits paid from a governmental plan on account of a participant's death or disability.[244]

Similarly, the dollar limitation for benefits commencing after the participant attains age 65 may be actuarially increased to the equivalent of a $160,000 annual benefit commencing at age 65.[245] Unlike reducing benefits for pre-age 62 retirees, the interest rate used in the calculation must not exceed the *lesser* of 5 percent or the rate specified in the plan.[246] Of course, the adjusted benefit cannot exceed the participant's compensation limitation.

Adjustments to the Compensation Limit. For participants who have separated from service with a vested benefit, a plan may

---

[236] Reg. § 1.415-3(c)(2); Prop. Reg. § 1.415(b)-1(c)(4).

[237] 1998-1 CB 249, modified by Rev. Rul. 2001-62, 2001-2 CB 632.

[238] Prop. Reg. § 1.415(b)-1(c)(5).

[239] 1998-1 CB 249, modified by Rev Rul.2001-62, 2001-2 CB 632.

[240] Rev. Rul. 2001-51, 2001-45 IRB 1, Q&A 3.

[241] 2001-2 CB 632.

[242] PFEA '04, Sec. 101 (P.L. 108-218).

[243] Code Sec. 415(b)(2)(E)(iii).

[244] Code Sec. 415(b)(2)(I).

[245] Code Sec. 415(b)(2)(D).

[246] Code Sec. 415(b)(2)(E)(iii).

provide cost-of-living adjustments. The compensation limitation (i.e., the high three consecutive years) may be adjusted annually to take into account cost-of-living increases after the separation occurs. The annual adjustment factor is a fraction, the numerator of which is the adjusted dollar limitation for the limitation year in which the compensation limitation is being adjusted and the denominator of which is the adjusted dollar limitation for the calendar quarter beginning July 1 of the calendar year preceding the calendar year in which such separation occurs.[247]

> **Example:** Jack's average compensation for his high 3 years is $50,000. In the year in which Jack separates from service, the dollar limitation was $160,000. Thus, the maximum benefit that may be provided for Jack is $50,000. For the 2005 plan year, the dollar limitation is $170,000. Thus, if the plan provides for post-retirement cost-of-living adjustments, Jack's maximum annual benefit could be increased to $53,125 ($50,000 × $170,000/ $160,000) for the 2005 plan year.

De Minimis Benefit. A defined benefit may provide an annual benefit of up to $10,000, regardless of the above limitations, provided that the participant has not at any time participated in a defined contribution plan maintained by the employer.[248] The amount is not adjusted for early or late retirements. This $10,000 limit applies to employer-derived benefits only. Employee contributions are not considered as separate defined contribution plans for purposes of this section.[249]

Reduction of Limits for Participation or Service of Less than Ten Years. If a participant has completed less than ten years of *participation* in the plan, the dollar limit of Code Sec. 415(b)(1)(A) is reduced. Specifically, the dollar limit is multiplied by a fraction, the numerator of which is the number of years (including fractional parts thereof) of participation in the plan, and the denominator of which is ten. However, this reduction is not made in the case of payments from a governmental plan or a multiemployer plan on account of a participant's death or disability.[250]

The compensation limitation of Code Sec. 415(b)(1)(B) and the special $10,000 de minimis benefit of Code Sec. 415(b)(4) are similarly reduced for participants with less than ten years of *service with the employer* (not participation in the plan). However, in no event

---

[247] Code Secs. 415(d)(1)(B), (3)(B), and (3)(C).
[248] Code Sec. 415(b)(4); Prop. Reg. § 1.415(b)-1(f)(1).
[249] Reg. § 1.415-3(f)(3); Prop. Reg. § 1.415(b)-1(f)(4).
[250] Code Sec. 415(b)(11); Prop. Reg. § 1.415(b)-1(g)(1) and (3).

will either adjustment reduce the amounts to less than one-tenth of the limitation.[251]

> **Example:** Kay begins employment with Daily Corporation at age 58 and becomes a participant in Daily's defined benefit plan one year later. When she retires in 2005 at age 65 and begins to receive benefits under the plan, the average of Kay's highest three years' compensation is $180,000. Because Kay has less than 10 years of service and participation (she has seven years of service with Daily and six years of participation in the plan), her maximum permissible annual benefit is the lesser of: (1) $102,000 ($170,000 limitation in 2005 × 6/10); or (2) $126,000 ($180,000 average compensation × 7/10).

Special Rules for Governmental and Tax-Exempt Plans. For participants in a plan maintained by a state or political subdivision thereof, who are credited with at least 15 years of service for benefit accrual as an employee in a police department, fire department, or emergency medical service, or as a member of the Armed Forces of the U.S., the dollar limit is not reduced for benefits commencing before age 62.[252]

For commercial airline pilots who are required to separate from service as a commercial airline pilot after age 60 but before age 62, the $170,000 limit is not reduced. However, if separation from service occurs before age 60, the $170,000 limit is reduced to the equivalent of a $170,000 annuity beginning at age 62.[253]

.04 Defined Contribution Plans

A defined contribution plan's "annual additions" to a participant's account for any limitation year may not exceed the lesser of:

(1) $42,000 (in 2005); or

(2) 100 percent of the participant's compensation.[254]

The $42,000 limit is subject to COLAs in increments of $1,000.

If any contribution is made by reason of an employee's reemployment rights resulting from qualified military service, the contribution is not subject to the limit on annual additions as applied for the limitation year in which the contribution is made, and the contribution is not taken into account in applying the limit to any other contributions made during that. limitation year. Instead, the

---

[251] Code Sec. 415(b)(5); Prop. Reg. § 1.415(b)-1(g)(2).

[252] Code Sec. 415(b)(2)(G) and (H).

[253] Code Sec. 415(b)(9).

[254] Code Sec. 415(c)(1); Prop. Reg. § 1.415(c)-1(a).

contribution is subject to the limit on annual additions as applied for the limitation year to which the contribution relates.[255]

"Annual Additions" Defined. Annual additions is defined as the sum, for any year, of:

(1) employer contributions;

(2) employee contributions; and

(3) forfeitures.[256]

For these purposes, employee contributions do not include: any rollover contributions or direct transfers from another qualified plan, repayments and restorations from cash-out buy-backs, contributions to a SEP that are excluded from gross income, repayments of loans, restorations of losses resulting from a breach of fiduciary duty, or the special catch-up contributions that may be made by participants age 50 or older.[257]

Excess Annual Additions. If excess annual additions are made to any participant's account as the result of forfeiture allocations (the usual case), a reasonable error in estimating a participant's annual compensation, or other limited facts and circumstances, the excess amounts will not be treated as such if they are handled in accordance with any one of the following provisions:[258]

(1) The excess in the participant's account must be reallocated to other participants' accounts. If all participants exceed the limits, the excess amounts may be held in a suspense account. Such amounts must be allocated to participants' accounts before any employer contributions and employee contributions may be made to the plan.

(2) The excess amounts can be used to reduce the employer contribution for the next limitation year.

(3) The excess amounts may be held in a suspense account and allocated to all participants in the next year, with a corresponding reduction in employer contributions for that year.

(4) Employee contributions may be returned to reduce the excess amount.

.05 Participation In Both a Defined Benefit Plan and a Defined Contribution Plan

If an employee participates or has participated in both a defined benefit and a defined contribution plan of the same employer, he can

---

[255] Code Sec. 414(u)(1).
[256] Code Sec. 415(c)(2).

[257] Code Sec. 415(c)(2) and 414(u)(1); Reg. § 1.415-6(b)(3); Prop. Reg. § 1.415(c)-1(b)(2)(ii).
[258] Reg. 1.415-6(b)(6).

receive a combined ultimate benefit greater than that which he would have received under a single plan. (Before 2000, a special overall limit applies to the benefits and contributions provided to such participants under Code Sec. 415(e). However, SBA '96 repealed this special limit for plan years beginning after 1999.[259]) Thus, employees can participate in both a defined benefit plan and defined contribution plan and be subject to only the regular benefit and contribution limits under Code Sec. 415.

¶610   Distribution Requirements

Code Sec. 401 contains three provisions which relate to distributions: those regarding the commencement of the payment of benefits; requirements concerning the minimum amounts and timing of distributions; and provisions which relate to the form of benefit payments. Each of these areas is discussed in this section of the chapter.

.01   Commencement of Distributions

Code Sec. 401(a)(14) requires that qualified plans provide that the payment of benefits to a participant must commence not later than 60 days after the close of the plan year in which the latest of the following events occurs:

(1) the participant attains the earlier of age 65 or the normal retirement age stated under the plan;

(2) the tenth anniversary of the year in which the participant commenced participation in the plan; or

(3) the participant terminates his service with the employer.

The regulations also provide that a plan may permit a participant to delay the commencement of his benefit payments to a date later than the above dates. The plan must require that the election be in writing and specify the date on which the payment of the benefits shall commence.[260] There are limits, however, on the extent to which such deferrals may be made. (See the discussion of Code Sec. 401(a)(9), below.)

Many pension plans provide for an early retirement option. In order to qualify for early retirement, participants must usually reach a certain age and have a certain number of years of service, for example, age 55 and 20 years of service. In such a plan, if a participant satisfies the service requirements for early retirement benefits, but separates from service prior to reaching the early

---

[259] SBA '96 § 1452. repealing Code Sec. 415(e).   [260] Reg. § 1.401(a)-14(b).

retirement age, the plan must provide that the participant will be eligible to receive the early retirement benefit (actuarially reduced from normal retirement age) only upon the attainment of the required age.[261]

Example: X Corporation's defined benefit pension plan provides that a normal retirement benefit will be payable to a participant upon attainment of age 65. The plan also provides that an actuarially reduced retirement benefit will be payable upon application to any participant who has completed 10 years of service with X Corporation and attained age 60. When she is 55 years of age and has completed 10 years of service with X Corporation, Alice leaves the service of X Corporation and does not return. The plan will not be qualified unless, upon attainment of age 60 and application for benefits, Alice is entitled to receive an actuarially reduced normal retirement benefit.[262]

.02 Required Minimum Distributions

Code Sec. 401(a)(9) contains provisions requiring the commencement and duration of benefit payments to a participant and to the participant beneficiary after the death of the participant. Failure to meet the minimum distributions required under this section can result in a 50 percent penalty assessment on the shortfall under Code Sec. 4974.

Distributions During Participant's Lifetime. A participant's entire interest must be distributed or commence to be distributed by the required beginning date, which is April 1 of the calendar year following the later of:

(1) the calendar year in which the participant attains age 70½; or

(2) the calendar year in which the participant retires.[263]

Note that this required beginning date is considered to be for a minimum distribution for the preceding calendar year. Minimum distributions for each subsequent calendar year must be made by December 31 of that year. Thus, the first minimum distribution and the second minimum distribution may occur in the same calendar year.

The delayed required beginning date for individuals who continue to work past age 70½ is not available to five-percent owners and IRA holders, i.e., such individuals must begin receiving distri-

---

[261] Code Sec. 401(a)(14).
[262] Reg. § 1.401(a)-14(c)(4).

[263] Code Sec. 401(a)(9)(A) and (C)(i); Reg. § 1.401(a)(9)-2, Q&A 2.

butions no later than April 1 of the calendar year following the year in which they reach age 70½.[264] However, a delayed beginning date beyond age 70½ for a 5-percent owner could be accomplished by a rollover into another plan in which the individual is not a 5-percent owner.[265] (Note that a rollover into an IRA would not delay the beginning date, since an IRA has the same required beginning date of age 70½.)

In the case of an employee who retires in a calendar year after the year in which he attains age 70½, the employees' accrued benefit must be actuarially increased for the period of time after age 70½ during which the employee was not receiving benefits. Thus, the employee's adjusted accrued benefit reflects the value of the benefit that he would have received if he had retired at age 70½ and had begun receiving benefits at that time.[266]

(Note: The actuarial adjustment rule and the rule requiring five percent owners to begin receiving distributions after attainment of age 70½ do not apply in the case of a governmental plan or church plan.)

The distributions must be made in accordance with one of the following manners:[267]

(1) in a lump-sum distribution;

(2) over the life of the participant or over the joint-life of the participant and a designated beneficiary (note that the beneficiary does not have to be the spouse of the participant); or

(3) over a fixed period of time which does not extend beyond the life expectancy of the participant or the joint life expectancy of the participant and a designated beneficiary.

The period over which required minimum distributions must be made (referred to as the "applicable distribution period") is determined using the Uniform Lifetime Table (found in Table A-2 of Reg. § 1.401(a)(9)-9), based on the participant's age as of his or her birthday in the relevant distribution calendar year. If the sole designated beneficiary is the participant's spouse, the applicable distribution period is the longer of the period determined using the Uniform Lifetime Table (based solely on the participant's age) or the joint life expectancy of the employee and spouse from the Joint and Last Survivor Table (found in Table A-3 of Reg. § 1.401(a)(9)-9), based on the participant's and spouse's ages as of their birthdays in the distribution calendar year.[268]

---

[264] Code Sec. 401(a)(9)(C)(ii).
[265] IRS Letter Ruling 200453015.
[266] Code Sec. 401(a)(9)(C)(iii).

[267] Code Sec. 401(a)(9)(A).

[268] Reg. § 1.404(a)(9)-5, Q&A 4.

Defined Contribution Plans. In an individual account plan, the benefit used to compute the minimum distribution in a distribution calendar year is the participant's account balance as of the last valuation date in the previous calendar year. This amount is adjusted for subsequent contributions, forfeitures, and distributions made in the calendar year after the valuation date.[269]

> **Example:** Logan, born October 12, 1935, retires on his 65th birthday in 2000. Logan attains age 70½ in 2006, and accordingly, his required beginning date for minimum distributions is April 1, 2007. As of December 31, 2005, the value of Logan's account is $379,500. No additional contributions or forfeitures were allocated to Logan's account during 2006. The applicable distribution period from the regulations Uniform Lifetime table for an individual age 71 is 26.5 years. Thus, the required minimum distribution for calendar year 2006 is $14,302 ($379,500/26.5). That amount is distributed to Logan on April 1, 2007.
>
> Assume that on December 31, 2006, the balance in Logan's account is $393,200. No contributions or forfeitures were allocated to Logan's account during 2007. In order to determine the amount to be used in calculating the minimum required distribution for 2007, the account balance of $393,200 is reduced by the $14,302 distribution made on April 1. Consequently, the benefit for purposes of determining the required minimum distribution for 2007 is $378,898 ($393,200—$14,302). The applicable distribution period for an individual age 72 is 25.6. Thus, the required minimum distribution that must be made by December 31, 2007 is $14,801 ($378,898/25.6).

Defined Benefit Plans. In a defined benefit plan, minimum distributions that commence on or after the participant's required beginning date must be paid in the form of periodic annuity payments for the participant's life (or the joint lives of the participant and beneficiary). Alternatively, the annuity payment may be made over a period certain that does not exceed the applicable distribution period for the participant (i.e., using the Uniform Lifetime Table), or, in the case of a sole spousal beneficiary, over a period certain that does not exceed their joint life expectancy (i.e., using the Joint and Last Survivor Table). The interval between payments for the annuity must be uniform over the entire distribution period and must not exceed one year.[270] In general, the periodic payments

---

[269] Reg. § 1.401(a)(9)-5, Q&A 3.   [270] Reg. § 1.401(a)(9)-6, Q&A 1.

must be nonincreasing. However, regulations permit increases for: adjustments to reflect cost-of-living increases; any increase in benefits pursuant to a plan amendment; a pop-up in payments in the event of the death of the beneficiary or the divorce of the employee and spouse; or return of employee contributions upon an employee's death.[271]

If the distributions are made in the form of a joint and survivor annuity where the beneficiary is not the employee's spouse, an additional requirement (referred to as the incidental benefit) must be met. The basic purpose of this requirement to is to ensure that distributions are primarily to provide retirement benefits to the employee. Accordingly, the survivor percentage may be limited, depending on the difference between the participant's and beneficiary's ages. A table provided in the regulations computes the maximum survivor percentages based on this age difference. The range in the table indicates that a joint-and-50%-survivor annuity is allowed under any age difference, but a joint-and-100%-survivor annuity is allowed only if the beneficiary is nor more than ten years younger than the participant.[272]

Distributions After Participant's Death. The commencement and duration of the distribution of a deceased participant's interest to a beneficiary depends on whether or not distributions to the participant had already begun prior to death and whether the beneficiary is the participant's spouse.

Employee's Death Before Distributions Commence. If a participant dies before his or her required beginning date (and, thus, before distributions are treated as having begun), distribution of the participant's entire interest must be made in accordance with one of the following methods:[273]

(1) the five-year rule;

(2) the life expectancy rule; or

(3) special rules where the designated beneficiary is the surviving spouse of the participant.

The five-year rule requires that the entire interest of the participant be distributed by the end of the calendar year that contains the fifth anniversary of the date of the participant's death. For example, if a participant dies on January 1, 2006, the entire interest must be distributed by the end of 2011 (and no distribution would be required in any year before that fifth year). Plans may adopt

---

[271] Reg. § 1.401(a)(9)-6, Q&A 14(a).
[272] Reg. § 1.401(a)(9)-6, Q&A 2(c).

[273] Reg. § 1.401(a)(9)-3, Q&A 1.

provisions that make the five-year rule the default distribution method, or that permit participants (or beneficiaries) to elect whether the five-year rule applies to distributions after the death of the participant.[274]

The life expectancy rule requires that distributions to a non-spouse designated beneficiary commence on or before the end of the calendar year immediately following the calendar year in which the participant died. The applicable distribution period is measured by the beneficiary's life expectancy, determined using the beneficiary's age as of the beneficiary's birthday in the calendar year immediately following the calendar year of the participant's death. In each subsequent calendar year, this initial applicable distribution period is reduced by one, rather than redetermined annually.[275]

If the sole designated beneficiary is the participant's surviving spouse, distributions must commence by the later of (1) the end of the calendar year immediately following the calendar year in which the participant died, or (2) the end of the calendar year in which the participant would have attained age 70 ½. The applicable distribution period is measured by the surviving spouse's life expectancy using the surviving spouse's birthday for each distribution calendar year after the calendar year of the participant's death up through the calendar year of the spouse's death.[276]

(Note that the applicable distribution periods for spouses and other beneficiaries use different tables than that used by the participant (i.e., either the Single Life Table in A-1 or the Joint and Last Survivor Table in A-3 of Reg. § 1.401(a)(9)-9.[277])

Employee's Death After Distributions Commence. If the participant dies after his or her minimum distribution period has begun, the remaining portion of the participant's interest must be distributed at least as rapidly as under the distribution method being used as of the date of death. The amount required to be distributed for. each distribution calendar year following the year of death depends on whether the distributions are from an individual account under a defined contribution plan or annuity payments under a defined benefit plan.[278]

The applicable distribution period for distributions to beneficiaries after the calendar year of the participant's death is: (1) if the participant has a designated beneficiary, the longer of the remaining

---

[274] Reg. § 1.401(a)(9)-3, Q&As 2 and 4.

[275] Reg. § 1.401(a)(9)-3, Q&A 3(a) and Reg. § 1.401(a)(9)-5, Q&A 5(c)(1).

[276] Reg. § 1.401(a)(9)-3, Q&A 3(b) and Reg. § 1.401(a)(9)-5, Q&A 5(c)(2).

[277] Reg. § 1.401(a)(9)-5, Q&A 6.

[278] Reg. § 1.401(a)(9)-2, Q&A 5.

life expectancy of the beneficiary or the remaining life expectancy of the participant; or (2) if the participant does not have a designated beneficiary, the remaining life expectancy of the participant. In subsequent calendar years for either situation, the initial distribution period is reduced by one of each calendar year that has elapsed after the calendar year of the participant's death.[279]

Any amount paid to a child shall be treated as if it had been paid to the surviving spouse if the amount will become payable to the surviving spouse upon the child's reaching majority age.[280]

.03 Forms of Distribution—Qualified Joint and Survivor Annuities and Qualified Preretirement Survivor Annuities

Most qualified plans must provide automatic survivor benefits: (1) in the case of a married participant who retires under the plan, in the form of a "qualified joint and survivor annuity," and (2) in the case of a married participant who dies before the annuity starting date and who has a surviving spouse, in the form of a "qualified preretirement survivor annuity."[281] Thus, the survivor annuity is the automatic form of benefit payment, unless a proper election to the contrary has been made by the participant or the participant's spouse.

The annuity starting date is the first day of the first period for which an amount is payable as an annuity. If the benefits are not payable as an annuity, the annuity starting date is the first day on which all events have occurred which entitle the participant to a benefit.[282]

This rule applies to all pension plans (defined benefit, money purchase, and target benefit). It also applies to profit-sharing and stock bonus plans unless:

(1) the plan *requires* that the participant's vested accrued benefit is payable *in full,* on the participant's death, to the surviving spouse (or, if there is no surviving spouse or the surviving spouse consents, to a designated beneficiary);

(2) the participant does not elect the payment of benefits in the form of a life annuity; and

(3) with respect to the participant, the plan is not a direct or indirect transferee from a plan that is subject to the annuity requirement.[283] (Note: According to the regulations, a rollover does not constitute a transfer that subjects the plan to the survivor annuity rules.)[284]

---

[279] Reg. § 1.401(a)(9)-5, Q&A 5(a).
[280] Code Sec. 401(a)(9)(F).
[281] Code Secs. 401(a)(11) and 417

[282] Code Sec. 417(f)(2).
[283] Code Sec. 401(a)(11)(B).
[284] Reg. § 1.401(a)-20, Q&A 5.

Definitions. A "qualified joint and survivor annuity" (QJSA) is defined as an annuity for the life of the participant, with a survivor annuity for the life of the spouse which is not less than 50 percent (and not greater than 100 percent) of the amount that is payable during the joint lives of the participant and the spouse. That is, each benefit payment to the surviving spouse must be at least 50 percent of the benefit payment made to the participant and the spouse while they were both alive. The annuity must be the actuarial equivalent of a single annuity for the life of the participant.[285] In the case of a participant who is not married, a qualified joint and survivor annuity means an annuity for the life of the participant.[286]

A "qualified preretirement survivor annuity" (QPSA) is an annuity for the life of the surviving spouse in which the payments to the surviving spouse are not less than the payments that would have been made under a qualified joint and survivor annuity. In the case of a participant who dies after attaining the earliest retirement age under the plan, the annuity payments are not less than the amount that would be payable if the participant had retired with an immediate qualified joint and survivor annuity on the day before the participant's death. In the case of a participant who dies on or before the earliest retirement age under the plan, the annuity payments are calculated as if the participant had:

(1) separated from service on the date of death;

(2) survived to the earliest retirement age under the plan;

(3) retired with an immediate qualified joint and survivor annuity at the earliest retirement age; and

(4) died on the day after the day on which the participant would have reached the earliest retirement age.[287]

For participants who separate from service, the benefits are calculated as of the day of separation, i.e., benefits do not continue to accrue after separation from service.

In the case of a defined contribution plan, a qualified preretirement survivor annuity is an annuity for the life of the surviving spouse that is actuarially equivalent to at least 50 percent of the participant's account balance as of the date of death.[288] The earliest date that payments to the surviving spouse must commence under a QPSA is the month in which the participant would have attained the earliest retirement age under the plan.[289]

---

[285] Code Sec. 417(b).
[286] Reg. § 1.401(a)-20, Q&A 25.
[287] Code Sec. 417(c)(1).

[288] Code Sec. 417(c)(2).

[289] Code Sec. 417(c)(1)(B).

Waivers of QJSA and QPSA. A plan must provide participants with an election, during the applicable "election period," to receive benefits in a form other than a QJSA and to waive the QPSA right. The plan must also permit the revocation of any such election during the applicable election period. The waiver election is not effective unless either: (1) the participant's spouse consents in writing to the election and is witnessed by a plan representative or a notary public; or (2) the plan representative can establish that consent cannot be obtained because there is no spouse, because the spouse cannot be located, or because of such other circumstances as regulations may prescribe. The consent waiver must either name a nonspouse beneficiary to receive any death benefits which become payable and the form of the death benefit, or acknowledge that the spouse relinquishes the right to name the beneficiary and/or specify the form of payment.[290]

The IRS has provided sample language that can be included in a form used for a spouse to consent to a participant's waiver of a QJSA or QPSA, or to a participant's choice of a non-spouse beneficiary in a defined contribution plan not subject to the QJSA and QPSA requirements. This language is designed to assist plan administrators in preparing spousal consent forms that meet the statutory requirements.[291]

The election to waive the QJSA form of benefit (and any revocation of the election) must be made within the 90-day period which ends on the annuity starting date. The election to waive the QPSA (and any revocations of the election) must be made during the period which begins on the first day of the plan year in which the participant attains age 35 and ends on the date of the participant's death.[292]

A plan loan to a participant is not treated as a distribution. However, the reduction of an account balance or accrued benefit to satisfy an unpaid plan loan is treated as a distribution which requires the consent of the participant and spouse at the time of the reduction, assuming the plan is subject to the QJSA and QPSA requirements. Thus, a plan must require the participant and spouse to consent to the loan and the possible reduction in the accrued benefit within the 90-day period before making the loan. If spousal consent is obtained at the time of making the loan to a married participant, spousal consent is not required at the time of any setoff of the loan against the accrued benefit resulting from nonpayment, even if the participant is married to a different spouse at the time of

---

[290] Code Sec. 417(a)(2).
[291] Notice 97-10, 1997-1 CB 370.

[292] Code Sec. 417(a)(6).

the setoff. Similarly, if an unmarried participant gives consent to the loan and possible reduction in the accrued benefit within the prescribed time period, the consent requirement will have been satisfied even if the participant is married at the time of the setoff. On the other hand, if the plan does not obtain consent of a current spouse at the time of a loan secured by some portion of the participant's accrued benefit, the plan will not be certain that it will be able to execute on the security by reducing the participant's accrued benefit without violating Code Sec. 417(e).[293]

Plan Notices. The plan must provide a written explanation of the joint and survivor annuity and preretirement survivor annuity to each participant. The written explanation must contain a general description of the eligibility conditions and other material features of the optional forms of benefit and sufficient additional information to explain the relative values of the optional forms of benefit available under the plan (e.g., the extent to which optional forms are subsidized relative to the normal form of benefit or the interest rates used to calculate the optional forms).[294] In addition, the explanation of the joint and survivor annuity must set out the following information:

(1) the terms and conditions of the QJSA and QPSA;

(2) the participant's right to make, and the effect of, an election to waive the QJSA and QPSA;

(3) the rights of the participant's spouse to consent to the election; and

(4) the right to revoke an election and the effect of such revocation.[295]

Generally, the written explanation of the terms and conditions of a QJSA must be provided no less than 30 days and no more than 90 days before the annuity starting date. However, a plan may permit a participant (with spousal consent, if applicable) to elect to waive the 30-day minimum waiting period between the notification and the annuity starting date, and reduce it to a seven-day period. In addition, a plan may provide the written explanation of the QJSA after the annuity starting date, if the distribution begins at least 30 days after the explanation is provided (subject to the same waiver of the 30-day minimum waiting period described in the preceding sentence).[296]

---

[293] Code Sec. 417(a)(4) and Reg § 1.401(a)-20, Q&A 24.

[294] Reg. § 1.401(a)-20, Q&A 36.

[295] Code Sec. 417(a)(3)(A) and Reg. § 1.417(a)-1(b)(3).

[296] Code Sec. 417(a)(7)(A); Reg. § 1.417(e)-1(b)(3).

In practical terms, the above rules mean that a married participant, with the consent of the spouse, can receive or rollover a lump sum payment eight days after the couple receives the QJSA notice (note also that the participant would also be required to waive the 30-day waiting period regarding rollover).

The plan must also provide a similar written explanation of the QPSA by the latest of (1) the period beginning on the first day of the plan year in which the participant attains age 32 and ending with the close of the plan year preceding the plan year in which the participant attains age 35; (2) a reasonable period after the individual becomes a participant; (3) a reasonable period ending after the plan ceases to fully subsidize the cost of the QPSA benefit; or (4) a reasonable period after the survivor annuity provisions apply to the participant. If a participant separates from service before attaining age 35, the explanation must be provided within a reasonable period (one year) after such separation.[297]

Exclusions from the QJSA and QPSA Requirements. A plan is not required to provide the notice of the right to waive the QJSA or QPSA if the plan fully subsidizes the cost of the benefits and does not allow a participant to waive the benefit or to select a nonspouse beneficiary. A plan fully subsidizes the costs of a benefit if the failure to waive the benefit by a participant would not result in a decrease in any plan benefits to the participant and would not result in increased contributions from the participant.[298]

A plan is not required to provide a QJSA or a QPSA to the spouse of a participant, if the participant and the spouse have been married for less than one year ending on the earlier of (1) the participant's annuity starting date or (2) the date of the participant's death. If a participant marries within one year before the annuity starting date, and if the participant and the participant's spouse have been married for at least one year as of the participant's death, the spouse will be treated as having been married throughout the required one-year period.[299]

If the present value of a participant's QJSA or QPSA is not more than $5,000, the plan may provide for a cash-out (i.e., distribute the benefit in a lump sum), even if no waiver was elected. However, such a cash-out is not allowed if the participant dies after the annuity starting date, unless the participant and the spouse (or surviving spouse if the participant has died) consent to the cash-out. A cash-

---

[297] Code Sec. 417(a)(3)(B); Reg. § 1.401(a)-20, Q&A 35(c).

[298] Code Sec. 417(a)(5) and Reg. § 1.401(a)-20, Q & A 37&38.
[299] Code Sec. 417(d).

out of a benefit which has a present value that exceeds $5,000 may be made only if the participant and the participant's spouse (or surviving spouse if the participant has died) consent in writing. The IRS has published mortality tables and interest rates to be used in determining the present values of plan benefits in these situations.[300]

Assignment of Plan Benefits for Fiduciary Breach. If a court order reduces a married participant's benefits on account of a breach of fiduciary duty (see *Assignment and Alienation Prohibited* section earlier in this chapter), one of the following three conditions must be satisfied:[301]

(1) Spousal consent must be obtained or the spouse must have waived his or her rights to a QJSA or a QPSA. If spousal consent cannot be obtained, this requirement may still be satisfied if the plan representative can establish that there is no spouse or the spouse cannot be located (or other circumstances to be specified in future regulations).

(2) The spouse is also required to pay an amount to the plan in the judgment, order decree or settlement in connection with a breach of fiduciary duty.

(3) In the judgment, order, decree, or settlement, the spouse is provided with a survivor annuity under a QJSA and under a QPSA, determined as if: (a) the participant terminated employment on the offset date, (b) there was no offset, (c) the plan allowed benefits to begin only on or after normal retirement age, (d) the plan provided only the minimum required QJSA, and (e) the amount of the QPSA is equal to the amount of the survivor annuity payable under the minimum-required QJSA. The minimum-required QJSA is a QJSA that is the actuarial equivalent of the participant's accrued benefit and under which the survivor annuity is 50 percent of the amount of the annuity that is payable during the joint lives of the participant and the spouse.

¶ 611 Top-Heavy Requirements

Most qualified plans must contain special provisions which will take effect if the plan becomes "top-heavy" for a given plan year.[302] In general, the plan must meet certain minimum vesting and accrual rules in such a year. The specific rules, found in Code Sec. 416, are discussed in depth in ¶ 703.

---

[300] Code Sec. 417(e). Reg. § 1.417(e)-1(d); Rev. Rul. 2001-62, 2001-52 IRB 632.

[301] Code Sec. 401(a)(13)(C) and (D).

[302] Code Sec. 401(a)(9)(B).

¶612 Plan Termination and Mergers

.01 Pension Benefit Guaranty Corporation

Title IV of ERISA established the Pension Benefit Guaranty Corporation (PBGC) to provide termination insurance for most defined benefit pension plans. All qualified plans are covered by the insurance rules, except for the following: defined contribution plans, plans maintained by professional service employers that do not have more than 25 participants covered under the plan, and governmental and church-maintained plans.

Under the program, sponsors of pension plans must pay an annual premium to the PBGC, currently a flat rate of $19 per participant, plus a variable premium of $9.00 for each $1,000 of unfunded vested benefits as of the end of the preceding plan year. From these premiums, the PBGC maintains a fund to guarantee certain benefits to participants of pension plans, in the event that the plan's assets are insufficient to pay its promised benefits.[303]

A plan administrator is required to notify the PBGC of certain "reportable events" which may adversely affect the plan within thirty days of their occurrence, one of which is the intent to terminate the plan. (Chapter 13 discusses these reporting requirements.) In the event of a voluntary termination by the plan sponsor, the PBGC determines whether the plan has sufficient assets to pay its guaranteed benefits when they become due. If so, the PBGC gives approval to the termination and is otherwise uninvolved. On the other hand, if the assets are insufficient to meet the benefits, and the employer request qualifies as a distress termination, the PBGC will step in as the plan trustee and administer the payment of benefits. As explained later, the sponsor remains liable to the PBGC for any shortfall, up to a statutory limitation.

The PBGC can also force the involuntary termination of a plan, although it does not often exercise this power. Nevertheless, the PBGC has the power to do so under ERISA Sec. 4042 for the following situations:

(1) the plan has not met the minimum funding requirements of Code Sec. 412

(2) the plan is unable to pay benefits when due;

(3) the plan has made a distribution of $10,000 or more to a substantial (ten percent) owner and immediately afterward has unfunded vested liabilities; or

---

[303] Instructions to PBGC Form 1.

(4) the possible long-run loss to the PBGC is expected to increase unreasonably if the plan is not terminated.

Guaranteed Benefits. The PBGC does not guarantee the payment of all benefits promised under a plan. Rather, it guarantees only those basic pension benefits (i.e., ancillary benefits, such as health care, are not guaranteed) which were vested at termination (but not those vested under Code Sec. 411(d)(3) because of termination), up to a maximum amount. The guaranteed benefit is one which is in the form of a straight life annuity commencing at age 65 and payable monthly. The maximum monthly benefit is limited to the lesser of (1) one-twelfth of the participant's average annual compensation from the employer during his highest five consecutive years; or (2) for 2005, $3,801.14 (adjusted annually).[304]

Certain benefits are not guaranteed or are subject to limitations. These include benefits under a plan or amendment which has been in effect for less than 60 months before the plan terminates; benefits which were increased from amendments made within 60 months before the plan terminates; benefits payable to a substantial (ten percent) owner; and benefits accrued after the date on which the IRS issues notice that the plan does not qualify under Code Sec. 401(a) or 404(a)(2).[305]

Asset Allocation upon Termination. Under ERISA Sec. 4044(a), benefits under a terminated pension plan must be allocated in the following order of priorities:

(1) voluntary employee contributions;

(2) mandatory employee contributions plus interest at 5 percent;

(3) benefits in payment status at least three years prior to plan termination, excluding any increases resulting from plan amendments within five years prior to termination, and benefits which would have been in payment status for at least three years if the employee had retired (e.g., at the early retirement age stated in the plan);

(4) all other benefits guaranteed by the PBGC;

(5) all other vested (as of the termination date) benefits; and

(6) all other benefits.

If any assets remain after all of the above liabilities have been satisfied, they may be returned to the employer (subject to an excise tax, discussed below) if the plan allows, or allocated to participants in a nondiscriminatory manner.

---

[304] ERISA Sec. 4022(b)   [305] *Id.*

¶ 612.01

Contingent Employer Liability. The employer will be liable to the PBGC for the amount of unfunded guaranteed benefits as of the termination date. If the liability exceeds 30 percent of the net worth of the employer (and members of the same controlled group), the PBGC provides commercially reasonable terms for the liability in excess of 30 percent of the employer's net worth.[306] In determining net worth, current value is to be used. In addition, any unusual or improper transfers to related parties will be added back.[307] If the employer refuses to pay the amount of its liability, the PBGC may attach a lien on the employer's property which has the same status as a federal tax lien.[308]

.02 Complete Terminations

Upon the formal termination of a qualified plan, Code Sec. 411(d)(3) requires that all participants become fully vested in their accrued benefits to the extent funded. As the above section indicated, the termination of a defined benefit pension plan is a very formal process. For defined contribution plans, however, the complete discontinuance of employer contributions will constitute a termination, despite the fact that the employer has not formally terminated the plan.

The difference between a complete discontinuance versus a mere "suspension" of contributions in a profit-sharing or stock bonus plan is not always clear. A complete discontinuance of contributions may occur although some amounts are contributed by the employer to the plan, if the amounts are not substantial enough to reflect the intent on the part of the employer to continue to maintain the plan. On the other hand, a suspension of contributions to the plan is a temporary cessation of contributions that may or may not ripen into a discontinuance. For example, the IRS ruled that where an employer did not contribute to a profit-sharing plan for five consecutive years because the corporation had no current or accumulated profits, but the plan required that contributions be resumed as soon as the employer had profits, there was not a complete discontinuance of contributions for purposes of the full vesting requirements of Code Sec. 411(d)(3).[309]

Potential Retroactive Disqualification. According to Reg. § 1.401-1(b)(1), a qualified plan is supposed to be a permanent program. Although the employer may reserve the right to terminate the plan and to discontinue contributions thereunder, if a plan is abandoned for any reason other than business necessity within a few

---

[306] ERISA Sec. 4062(b)(1)(A).
[307] ERISA Sec. 4062(c).

[308] ERISA Sec. 4068.
[309] Rev. Rul. 80-146, 1980-1 CB 90.

years after it has taken effect, it is presumed that the plan, from its inception, was not a bona fide program for the exclusive benefit of employees. As mentioned earlier in this chapter, termination of a pension plan within five years of adoption without a business reason may be the rule of thumb used by the IRS in determining whether the plan was intended to be permanent.

If it is determined that a plan was not intended to be a permanent program, the IRS will retroactively disqualify the plan. Thus, the plan would be treated as a nonqualified plan, losing its favorable tax treatment. As a review of the tax treatment of a nonqualified plan, the participant must recognize income when he has a nonforfeitable right (vests) in the benefits. The employer is entitled to a deduction only when the participants claim the income and then only if (according to Reg. § 1.83-6(a)(2)) withholding of income taxes is made; otherwise, no deduction is allowed. Thus, since the employer would not have withheld any taxes, it could lose all deductions. Finally, any income of the trust is taxable to it. However, if the plan becomes disqualified because of the failure to meet the minimum coverage requirements or the minimum participation requirements, highly compensated employees and nonhighly compensated employees are taxed differently under Code Sec. 402(b)(4). A highly compensated employee must include in income (for his year within which the trust's tax year ends) his entire vested accrued benefit, less any investment in the contract. If the sole reason for plan disqualification was due to the plan's failure to meet the minimum coverage or minimum participation requirements, nonhighly compensated employees report income only at the time of actual distribution from the trust.

A retroactive disqualification would require the participants, the employer, and the trust to recalculate taxable income for all years which are still open under the statute of limitations. Generally, this is three years, unless the understatement in gross income was more than 25 percent for the particular taxpayer.[310]

Restrictions on Distributions. A defined benefit plan is required to incorporate provisions restricting benefits to highly compensated employees and former highly compensated employees in order to meet the nondiscrimination requirements. This restriction also applies to benefit payments in the event of a plan termination. Specifically, the plan must restrict annual payments to highly compensated employees to an amount equal to a single life annuity that is the actuarial equivalent of the sum of the employee's

---

[310] Code Sec. 6501(a).

accrued benefit and the employee's other benefits (such as death benefits and loans) under the plan. These restrictions also apply to money purchase pension plans that have an accumulated funding deficiency or an unamortized funding waiver.[311]

These restrictions generally apply to all highly compensated employees and former highly compensated employees. However, the plan may limit the total number of employees whose benefits are restricted to a group of the 25 employees with the highest amounts of compensation.[312]

The restrictions do not apply, however, if:

(1) after payment of all benefits to the highly compensated employee, the value of the plan assets equals or exceeds 110 percent of the value of the current liabilities;

(2) the value of the benefits for the highly compensated employee is less than one percent of the value of the current liabilities before the distribution; or

(3) the value of the benefits for the highly compensated employee does not exceed $5,000.[313]

For these purposes, the value of plan assets and current liabilities may be determined under any reasonable and consistent method.

Reversions of Plan Assets. Recall that Code Sec. 401(a)(2) requires that, before the satisfaction of all liabilities (fixed and contingent), a plan's assets may not be used for any purpose other than for the exclusive benefit of employees and beneficiaries. Reg. § 1.401-2(b), however, allows an employer to reserve the right to recover at the termination of the trust, and only at such termination, any balance remaining in the trust which is due to erroneous actuarial computations during the previous life of the trust. Thus, any surplus arising from unanticipated excess earnings or a high level of forfeitures may revert to the employer after paying the benefits of participants, but only if the plan expressly permits such reversion.

Because reversion is limited to erroneous actuarial computations, reversions from defined contribution plans would not be permitted, since they do not use any actuarial assumptions. The only exception to this rule is in the event that unallocated forfeitures are still in a suspense account because of the Code Sec. 415 limitations, then the excess assets may revert to the employer when the plan is terminated.[314] Thus, with that one possible exception, rever-

---

[311] Reg. § 1.401(a)(4)-5(b)
[312] Reg. § 1.401(a)(4)-5(b)(3)(ii).

[313] Reg. § 1.401(a)(4)-5(b)(3)(iv).
[314] Rev. Rul. 71-149, 1971-1 CB 118.

sions are permitted only in the case of excess assets after the termination of a defined benefit pension plan.

In past years, a significant increase in terminations of pension plans with asset reversions to sponsoring employers occurred. Because Congress apparently felt that it is undesirable for employers to "tap" these pension funds, a 20 percent nondeductible excise tax on the amount of the reversion is imposed on the employer. The 20 percent excise tax is increased to 50 percent, unless the employer either (a) transfers 25 percent of the excess assets to a qualified replacement plan or (b) provides pro rata benefit increases to plan participants of the terminating plan equal to at least 20 percent of the excess assets.[315] However, the excise tax remains at 20 percent if the employer is in bankruptcy liquidation.[316]

A qualified replacement plan (typically, a defined contribution plan) is one which is established or maintained by the employer in which:

(1) at least 95 percent of the active participants in the terminated plan and who remain as employees following the termination are active participants in the replacement plan; and

(2) at least 25 percent of the amount that would otherwise revert to the employer is transferred to the replacement plan. However, this amount is reduced by an amount equal to the present value of the aggregate increases in accrued benefits under the terminated plan that were adopted within 60 days prior to the termination of the old plan, if such increases take effect immediately upon plan termination.

Any such amounts transferred are not includible in the gross income of the employer or allowed as a deduction, nor are they treated as an employer reversion.[317]

Rather than establish a qualified replacement plan to avoid the increase in the excise tax, the employer can provide pro rata increases in the accrued benefits of all qualified participants in the terminating pension plan. The aggregate present value of the increases must be at least 20 percent of the amount that the employer would otherwise receive as a reversion and must take effect immediately upon termination of the plan. However, total benefit increases for individuals who are not active participants are limited to 40 percent of 20 percent of the potential reversion amount.[318]

---

[315] Code Sec. 4980(d).
[316] Code Sec. 4980(d)(6).

[317] Code Sec. 4980(d)(2); *see also* Rev. Rul. 2003-85, 2003-32 IRB 291.
[318] Code Sec. 4980(d)(3).

While ERISA provides that an employer may not recover excess assets unless the plan permits a recovery, employers may amend the plan prior to termination to permit such a recovery. However, any provision or amendment that either provides for a reversion or increases the amount that may revert will not be effective before the end of the fifth calendar year following the date of adoption of the provision. In the case of a plan that has been in effect for less than five years, and the plan, from its inception, has a provision for reversion of residual assets, such a distribution is allowed.[319]

Excess assets from a terminated qualified pension plan may be transferred to a welfare benefit plan to pay retiree health benefits. For purposes of this provision (1) the qualified pension plan and welfare plan must be jointly administered pursuant to a collective bargaining agreement between the employer and one or more employee representatives; (2) the welfare benefit plan must provide retiree health benefits; and (3) the qualified pension plan must have assets in excess of its termination liability and the welfare plan must have assets that are less than the present value of projected benefits (determined at the time the pension plan is terminated). Any such assets transferred under this provision are includible in the employer's gross income and are subject to the 20 percent excise tax on reversions.[320]

.03 Partial Terminations

Code Sec. 411(d)(3) also requires immediate vesting for the "affected" employees upon the partial termination of a qualified plan. The Code does not define what constitutes a partial termination. Regulations state that whether a partial termination has occurred is determined on a facts-and-circumstances basis and describe three situations in which a partial termination may occur:[321]

(1) a plan amendment which has the effect of excluding from coverage a group of employees who were previously covered under the plan;

(2) a plan amendment which reduces or ceases future benefit accruals under a defined benefit plan if a potential reversion to the employer is created or increases; and

(3) a plan amendment that makes the plan provisions less liberal, such as a slowing down of the vesting schedule or a reduction in the rate of employer contributions if a potential reversion

---

[319] ERISA Sec. 4044(d).
[320] TRA '86 Sec. 1132, as amended by RRA '89 Sec. 7861(a).

[321] Reg. § 1.411(d)-2(b).

is created or increased or the potential for discrimination increases.

Several rulings and cases have been made by the IRS in determining the level of reduction in coverage that would constitute a partial termination.[322] While there is no definite number or percentage which makes a reduction significant enough to constitute a partial termination, it appears that somewhere around a 20 percent reduction in coverage may be the cutoff. In a recent ruling concerning this issue, the Seventh Circuit ruled that this 20 percent reduction level is a rebuttable presumption of partial termination; a reduction below 10 percent should be conclusively presumed not to be a partial termination; and a reduction above 40 percent should be conclusively presumed to be a partial termination. For reductions between 10 percent and 40 percent, the examination of the facts and circumstances surrounding the changes to the plan should focus solely on the tax motives and tax consequences involved in the reduction in plan coverage.[323]

The safest approach to take with respect to whether a partial termination has occurred pursuant to a plan amendment is to file for a determination letter with the IRS on Form 6406. (See Chapter 13 for an explanation of the determination letter process.)

.04   .04 Mergers and Consolidations

Code Secs. 401(a)(12) and 414(1) both provide that in the event of any merger or consolidation of qualified plans, or the transfer of assets or liabilities to another plan, each participant must be entitled to a benefit immediately after the merger, consolidation, or transfer which is equal to or greater than the benefit he would have been entitled to receive immediately before the merger or transfer.

If defined contribution plans are merged, Reg. § 1.414(1)-1(d) specifies that these requirements will be met if:

(1) the sum of the account balances in each plan equals the fair market value (determined as of the date of the merger) of the entire plan assets;

(2) the assets of each plan are combined to form the assets of the plan as merged; and

(3) immediately after the merger, each participant in the plan as merged has an account balance equal to the sum of the account

---

[322] *See* e.g., Rev. Rul. 72-439, 1972-2 CB 223; Rev. Rul. 72-510, 1972-2 CB 223; Rev. Rul. 73-284, 1973-2 CB 139; and Rev. Rul. 81-27, 1981-1 CB 228.

[323] *Matz v. Household International Tax Reduction Investment Plan*, (CA-7, 2004-2 USTC ¶ 50,403.

balances the participant had in the plans immediately prior to the merger.

If the plans are defined benefit plans, the satisfaction of the rule depends on whether both plans were fully funded. If the plan assets are at least equal to the present values of the accrued benefits (whether or not vested), the requirements of Code Sec. 414(1) will be satisfied merely by combining the assets and preserving each participant's accrued benefits. However, if an underfunded plan merges with a fully funded plan, i.e., if the total assets are less than the sum of the present values of all participants' accrued benefits (whether or not vested), Reg. § 1.414(1)-1(e) provides additional requirements. A special schedule of benefits must be developed, which provides for the payout of benefits as if the premerged plans were terminated and benefits distributed. Its purpose is to ensure that the plan participants in the more fully funded plan would receive benefits at least equivalent to those if their plan had terminated prior to the merger.

¶613 Amendments to Qualified Plans

An employer may decide to amend its qualified plan for just about any purpose it desires. However, as mentioned earlier in this chapter, certain restrictions apply to prevent amendments from reducing the vested accrued benefits of participants. (See ¶608.05 for discussion of these restrictions.) These amendments may be made either on a prospective or a retroactive basis. Of course, either type of amendment could cause the plan to become disqualified. Thus, it is advisable to request a determination letter from the IRS concerning a proposed amendment of a significant plan feature, such as the benefit formula. The procedures which need to be followed in applying for this determination letter are the same as those required to apply for an initial determination, discussed in the beginning of this chapter.

The timing of any plan amendment must not discriminate in favor of highly compensated employees or former highly compensated employees. Whether the timing of a plan amendment is discriminatory is based on the relevant facts and circumstances. These would include the relative number of highly compensated employees and nonhighly compensated employees affected by the amendment and the relative accrued benefits of both groups both before and after the amendment. For example, suppose a defined benefit plan that has covered highly and nonhighly compensated employees for most of its existence is amended to increase benefits at a time when the plan covers only highly compensated employees and then terminates. The timing of this plan amendment would have the effect of discriminating significantly in favor of highly compensated employees and would, therefore, cause the plan to lose its qualified status.[324]

A plan amendment that provides for past service credits is deemed not to discriminate significantly in favor of highly compensated employees if:

(1) the period for which credit is granted does not exceed the five years immediately preceding the year in which the amendment is first effective;

(2) past service credit is granted on a reasonably uniform basis to all employees;

(3) the credit is determined by applying the current plan formula to the years credited; and

(4) the period for which past service is granted is service with the employer or a previous employer.

However, this safe harbor is not available if a plan amendment granting past service credit is part of a pattern of amendments that discriminate in favor of highly compensated employees.[325]

.01 Retroactive Amendments

Retroactive amendments can also be made to correct defects in the plan which could cause its disqualification, as long as they are made within the time period prescribed in Code Sec. 401(b). Generally, this would require that the employee benefit rights be retroactively restored to the levels they would have been had the plan been in compliance with the qualification requirements from the date the plan defect arose.

The amendment must be made, however, within the "remedial amendment period" to be effective for a particular year. This remedial amendment period begins on the date on which the defect arose (plan establishment or amendment) and ends generally on the date on which the employer is required to file its income tax return (including extensions) for the taxable year in which the defect arose. However, if an application for a determination letter has been made, this period is automatically extended to 91 days after the issuance of the determination letter by the IRS.[326]

---

[324] Reg. § 1.401(a)(4)-5(a).
[325] Reg. § 1.401(a)(4)-5(a)(3).
[326] Reg. § 1.401(b)-1.

Chapter 7

Special Rules for Keogh, Top-Heavy, and 401(k) Plans

¶ 701   Introduction

The purpose of this chapter is to discuss the qualification requirements which are applicable to certain types of plans. Qualified plans for unincorporated businesses are usually referred to as Keogh, or H.R. 10, plans. As discussed in Chapter 6, the Tax Equity and Fiscal Responsibility Act of 1982 (TEFRA) generally eliminated the differences between corporate and noncorporate plans. However, there are still some distinctions between the two which require attention. The top-heavy rules apply to all qualified plans, but are only in effect under specific circumstances. Finally, 401(k) plans (also referred to as cash or deferred arrangements) are a specific form of qualified plan and must meet additional qualification requirements.

¶ 702   Keogh Plans

Prior to TEFRA, there were significant differences between corporate and noncorporate plans, all of which favored the corporate form of business. TEFRA eliminated most of the disparities in qualified plans between corporate and noncorporate entities. Thus, all of the requirements discussed in Chapter 6 apply to noncorporate (Keogh) plans, as well as corporate plans. Although many of the differences in the requirements for a Keogh plan were discussed in that chapter, they are reviewed in this section as well, in order to highlight the disparities which remain, all of which affect the self-employed individual only, rather than the employees under the plan.

Before reviewing these differences, however, it is important to be familiar with the terminology used in distinguishing the Keogh plans.

.01 Definitions

The following definitions and provisions relate specifically to plans established by an unincorporated trade or business, i.e., a sole proprietorship or a partnership. These definitions are all found in Code Sec. 401(c).

Self-Employed Individual. Recall from Chapter 6 that a qualified plan of an employer must be established for the exclusive benefit of its *employees* or their beneficiaries. Thus, without a special provision, a self-employed individual could not benefit under a qualified plan, since he is technically not a common-law employee. For qualified plan purposes, however, a self-employed individual is treated as an employee.

The term "self-employed individual" means, with respect to any taxable year, an individual who has "earned income" for the year. It also includes an individual who would meet the above definition, except for the fact that the trade or business operated at a loss, and an individual who has been a self-employed individual for any prior taxable year.[1] Thus, a self-employed individual includes sole proprietors and partners.

If a self-employed individual is engaged in more than one trade or business, each different trade or business will be considered a separate employer. Thus, only the earned income derived from the specific trade or business under which a plan is established may be taken into account.[2]

Earned Income. Many. of the provisions for qualified plans are based upon an employee's compensation. For example, the limitations on contributions and benefits under Code Sec. 415, the deduction limitations under Code Sec. 404 (discussed in Chapter 8), and the discrimination provisions under Code Sec. 401(a)(4) and (5) all refer to compensation. For the self-employed individual, there is no "compensation," but there is "earned income."

Earned income is defined as the net earnings from self-employment, as defined in Code Sec. 1402(a) for purposes of the self-employment tax. Thus, net earnings generally means the gross income derived by an individual from the trade or business, less any deductions allowed. It also includes a partner's distributive share of income or loss from a trade or business carried on by a partnership under Code Sec. 702(a)(9).

---

[1] Code Sec. 401(c)(1).

[2] Reg. § 1.401-10(b)(2).

¶ 702.01

However, the trade or business must be one in which personal services of the individual are a material income-producing factor. Thus, earned income would exclude certain types of passive income, such as dividends, interest, real estate rental income, capital gains, and a limited partner's distributive share of partnership income.[3] (Note, however, that any guaranteed payments made to a limited partner are treated as earned income, if the payments are for services to the partnership.)

Self-employed individuals who have elected out of the self-employment system based on religious grounds may treat their exempt self-employment income as compensation for purposes of establishing and contributing to a qualified plan.[4]

The pass-through income to a shareholder in an S corporation is not considered earned income. Since a shareholder who performs services to his/her corporation is considered an employee, only the actual wages paid to the shareholder-employee meets the definition of compensation.[5]

Earned income does not include the amount excludable from gross income resulting from a contribution to a qualified plan. That is, the earned income of a self-employed individual is reduced by the amount of the deduction allowed under Code Sec. 404 for a contribution to a qualified plan. Earned income is also reduced by the deduction allowed under Code Sec. 164(f) for one-half of self-employment taxes.[6]

Owner-Employee. An owner-employee includes an employee who owns a sole proprietorship or who owns more than ten percent of either the capital interest or the profits interest in a partnership.[7] Note that all owner-employees are also self-employed individuals. However, the reverse is not true, since a five percent partner would be considered a self-employed individual, but not an owner-employee.

Employer. While the term "employer" may seem obvious, it is important to identify who the employer is, because it is the employer who must establish and maintain the plan, and not the employee(s). An individual who owns a sole proprietorship is treated as his own employer, not the business itself. A partnership, and not the individual partners, is treated as the employer of each partner who is an employee within the definition of self-employed individuals.[8] Thus, an individual partner cannot establish a qualified plan with respect to his earned income from a partnership.

---

[3] Code Sec. 401(c)(2)(A)(i) and Reg. § 1.401-10(c)(1).
[4] Code Sec. 401(c)(2)(A).
[5] *Durando*, CA-9, 95-2 USTC ¶ 50,615, 70 F3d 548.

[6] Code Sec. 401(c)(2).
[7] Code Sec. 401(c)(3).
[8] Code Sec. 401(c)(4).

Contributions on Behalf of Owner-Employees. This term includes contributions made to a qualified plan by the employer for an owner-employee and by an owner-employee as an employee.[9]

Note, however, that matching contributions made to Sec. 401(k) plans or SIMPLE IRAs that are made on behalf of self-employed persons are not treated as employee elective contributions. Thus, the matching contributions are not subject to the annual dollar limits on elective contributions ($14,000 for 401(k) plans (in 2005) and $10,000 for SIMPLE IRA plans (in 2005)).[10]

.02 Differences Between Keogh and Corporate Plans

Despite the significant changes made by TEFRA in eliminating most of the differences between Keogh plans and corporate plans, there are several remaining differences which generally favor corporate plans over Keogh plans. The chief areas of disparity which still remain concern the contribution and deduction limitations, the taxation of distributions to owner-employees, and plan loans.

Contribution and Benefit Limitations. Contributions and benefits on behalf of an owner-employee are based on the earned income of the individual, as defined in Code Sec. 1402(a). Although this includes earned income from all trades or businesses, including a partner's distributive share of partnership income, Code Sec. 401(d)(3) restricts the amount of earned income to that which is derived from the trade or business with respect to which a plan is established.

> **Example (1):** Adam is a 60% owner in the AB Partnership. He also is the sole proprietor of C Company. AB Partnership and C Company are not considered as a single employer for qualified plan purposes. Thus, either AB Partnership or C Company may establish a plan under which Adam benefits, as long as the Code Sec. 410(b) coverage requirements are met. Assume Adam establishes a qualified plan with respect to C Company (the proprietorship). Adam may base plan contributions or benefits only on the income derived from C Company.

As discussed in Chapter 6 and in the definitions of this section, "earned income" is reduced by the deduction for one-half of self-employment taxes and by the deduction allowed for contributions to

---

[9] Code Sec. 401(c)(5).

[10] Code Sec. 402(g)(9) for Sec. 401(k) plans (effective 12/31/97), and Code Sec. 408(p)(8) for SIMPLE IRAs.

¶ 702.02

a plan on behalf of the self-employed individual. The annual benefit provided on behalf of a self-employed individual under a defined benefit Keogh plan is limited under Code Sec. 415(b) to the lesser of $170,000 (in 2005) or 100% of average earned income for the highest three consecutive years. Similarly, with respect to self-employed individuals, contributions to a defined contribution plan are limited under Code Sec. 415(c) to the lesser of $42,000 (in 2005) or 100 percent of earned income. Again, in computing earned income for both the benefit and contribution limitation, earned income is reduced by the deduction for one-half of self-employment taxes and by the Keogh deduction.

Deduction Limitations. As discussed in Chapter 8, the annual employer *deduction* allowed under Code Sec. 404(a) is subject to a different limitation from the maximum contribution and benefit provided on behalf of a self-employed individual under Code Sec. 415.

Deductions for contributions to a defined benefit Keogh plan are subject to the normal limitations for qualified defined benefit plans. The maximum deduction is equal to the greatest of the amount: (1) necessary to satisfy the minimum funding standard; (2) determined under the level cost method; or (3) determined under the normal cost method. These amounts are discussed in detail in § 803.01.

The maximum *deduction* allowed under Code Sec. 404(a) for contributions on behalf of a self-employed individual to a defined contribution plan is set at 25 percent of earned income, reduced by one-half of self-employment taxes and the Keogh deduction. Mathematically, this works out to a maximum contribution of 20 percent of the amount equal to earned income minus one-half the self-employment taxes, i.e.:

Maximum
Deduction=25%(Earned Income−50% Self-Employment Taxes−Deduction)

Maximum
Deduction=20%(Earned Income−50% Self-Employment Taxes)

Note that this reduction is to be computed regardless of the rate stated for other employees. That is, if the contribution rate is 10 percent of compensation, the contribution on behalf of the self-employed individual is reduced by the contribution, resulting in a contribution of 9.09 percent of earned income before the contribution [.10/(1 + .10)]. IRS Publication 560 contains a worksheet for computing the maximum deductible contribution on behalf of a self-employed individual for various plan contribution rates.[11]

---

[11] IRS Publication 560, Retirement Plans for Small Businesses (SEP, SIMPLE, & Keogh Plans), published annually.

Example: Ann is a sole proprietor of a business. She maintains a plan under which she contributes 10% of compensation. Ann's business earned a profit of $800,000 in 2005, after taking into account contributions made to the plan on behalf of her employees. Ann's self-employment taxes total $11,304 ($80,000 × .9235 × 15.3%). Thus, the deduction for one-half of self-employment taxes ($5,652) reduces her net earnings from self-employment taxes to $74,348. Ann's maximum contribution and deduction is $6,758 ($74,348 × 9.09%).

Additional Deduction Limits. Annual additions are defined for self-employed individuals as employer contributions and employee contributions. Self-employed individuals cannot participate in forfeiture allocations from other participants' accounts.[12]

Another difference between corporate and Keogh plans concerning deductions is the determination of a net operating loss (NOL). Under the provisions of Code Sec. 172(d)(4), a deduction for a contribution to a qualified Keogh plan on behalf of a self-employed individual is limited to income. That is, the deduction cannot create or increase an NOL.

Distributions. The definition of lump-sum distributions also differs for self-employed individuals. Generally, a distribution is treated as a lump-sum distribution only if it is made on account of the employee's death, attainment of age 59½, separation from service, or disability. However, separation from service as an event which triggers a lump-sum distribution is limited to employees who do not meet the definition of self-employed individuals at any time during their participation in the plan. On the other hand, disability as an event which triggers a lump-sum distribution is available only for self-employed individuals.[13] Thus, a common-law employee can receive a lump-sum distribution prior to age 59½ by separating from service. A self-employed individual, however, can qualify for a lump-sum distribution only on account of death, disability, or the attainment of age 59½.

Before 1987, long-term capital gain treatment was available on the pre-1974 portion of a lump-sum distribution. Although TRA '86 eliminated this treatment for all post-1986 distributions, it did grandfather individuals who were at least 50 years old as of the beginning of 1986. Thus, these individuals may elect to treat the pre-1974 portions of lump-sum distributions as long-term capital gains. Under old Code Sec. 402(a)(2) (which was eliminated by

---

[12] Reg. § 1.401-11(b)(3).   [13] Code Sec. 402(d)(4)(A).

TRA '86), in order for a self-employed individual to receive this capital gains treatment, he also must elect the ten-year averaging under Code Sec. 402(e)(4) for the remainder of his distribution. Any other employee may elect to treat the pre-1974 portion of a lump-sum distribution without regard to making the averaging election. Because TRA '86 allows the averaging election to be made only once in a lifetime, and only after the attainment of age 59½, a self-employed individual, unlike his corporate counterpart, has only one opportunity to receive capital gain treatment.

Plan Loans. A loan from a qualified plan to a plan participant is generally a "prohibited transaction" which is subject to an excise tax under Code Sec. 4975, unless the loan meets the requirements of Code Sec. 4975(d)(1). (See Chapter 12 for a discussion of prohibited transactions.) Moreover, owner-employees (sole proprietors, more-than-ten-percent partners, and more-than-five-percent S corporation owners) are generally considered to be disqualified persons for purposes of prohibited transactions. Under provisions added by EGTRRA '01, plan loans to such owner-employees are specifically allowed.[14]

¶703 Top-Heavy Plans

As discussed earlier, TEFRA generally eliminated the differences between qualified plans of corporations and self-employed individuals. However, in bringing about this parity, TEFRA introduced restrictions on all plans, whether corporate or self-employed, which benefit the employer's key employees. Under Code Sec. 401(a)(10)(B), all qualified plans, except for SIMPLE retirement plans and governmental plans, must include the restrictive top-heavy provisions contained in Code Sec. 416.

In general terms, a top-heavy plan is a plan under which more than 60 percent of the accumulated benefits or contributions are attributable to "key employees." For employers who maintain both a defined benefit and a defined contribution plan, an additional calculation for "super top-heavy" status must be made. A plan is super top heavy if more than 90 percent of the accumulated benefits in the plan are attributable to key employees. In the case of a defined contribution plan, these determinations are based on the total account balances of the employees under the plan. For a defined benefit plan, the determinations are based on the present value of the accrued

---

[14] Code Sec. 4975(f)(6)(B)(iii).

benefits under the plan's formula. In both cases, the accumulated benefits include those which are attributable to both employer and employee (whether mandatory or voluntary) contributions.

Certain plans are specifically excluded from the definition of a top-heavy plan. Sec. 401(k) plans that meet the safe harbor requirements for the ADP nondiscrimination test under Sec. 401(k)(12) and that meet the requirements for matching contributions under Sec. 401(m)(11) are specifically excluded from the definition of a top-heavy plan.[15] (Both of these requirements are discussed later in this chapter.) Revenue Ruling 2004-13 examines four specific plan scenarios in determining whether a 401(k) plan meets the safe harbor requirements.[16]

If a plan is determined to be top heavy for the plan year, it must satisfy one of two special (more accelerated) vesting schedules under Code Sec. 416(b) and provide a minimum level of employer-derived benefits or contributions to non-key employees (with no Social Security integration) under Code Sec. 416(c).

All qualified plans, other than SIMPLE retirement plans and governmental plans, must incorporate the provisions of Code Sec. 416 into the plan document. These provisions must include (1) the criteria for determining which employees are key employees, (2) in the case of a defined benefit plan, the actuarial assumptions and benefits considered to determine the present value of accrued benefits, (3) a description of how the top-heavy ratio is computed, (4) a description of what plans will be aggregated in testing whether the plan is top heavy, and (5) a definition of the determination date and the valuation date applicable to the determination date. In addition, the plan must specifically contain the provisions concerning vesting, minimum benefit, the compensation limitation, and the combined plan limitations referred to in the preceding paragraph.

Of course, a plan may concede top-heavy status by incorporating the restrictions under the plan terms, thereby alleviating the need to make annual top-heavy determinations. This would eliminate the possibility that the top-heavy rules would be violated for a particular plan year.

The top-heavy status is determined on an employer basis which incorporates the commonly controlled group and affiliated service group rules of Code Secs. 414(b), (c), and (m).[17] In applying the tests and rules of Code Sec. 416 to this group, however, one

---

[15] Code Sec. 416(g)(4)(H).
[16] 2004-7 IRB 485.

[17] Reg. § 1.416-1, Q&A T-1.

must identify the plans which are to be reviewed and the key employees under those plans. After these plans have been identified, the actual test is performed, and if it is determined that the plan or plans are top heavy for the year, the plans must meet the special vesting and benefit limitations. Accordingly, the remainder of this discussion is divided into the following sections: the top-heavy calculation, the plans to consider in making the calculation, the determination of key employees, and the requirements which must be met if a plan is top heavy.

.01 The Top-Heavy Calculation

The Determination Date. Whether a plan is top heavy for a particular year is determined as of the determination date for that plan year. That is, the determination date is the date on which the present values of accrued benefits for the employees are calculated under the plan. The determination date for a plan year is the last day of the preceding plan year. In the case of the first plan year, the determination date is the last day of the current plan year.[18]

When two or more plans constitute an "aggregation group" (discussed in the next section), the present values of all employees' accrued benefits are determined separately for each plan as of each plan's determination date. The plans are then aggregated by adding together the results for each plan as of the determination dates for the plans which fall within the same calendar year.

> **Example:** Suppose an employer maintains two plans, A and B. Plan A's plan year commences July 1 and ends June 30, and Plan B's plan year is the calendar year. For Plan A's plan year commencing July 1, 2006, the determination date is June 30, 2006. For Plan B's plan year in 2007, the determination date is December 31, 2006. If these two plans are aggregated under the rules described later, each of the plans will separately calculate the present value of the accrued benefits for all employees as of its own determination date. Since both of these determination dates are within the calendar year 2006, the present value of accrued benefits for all employees are added together to determine top heaviness. If the results show that the group is top heavy, Plan A will be top heavy for the plan year commencing July 1, 2006, and Plan B will be top heavy for the 2007 calendar year.

The above example demonstrates a potential problem area in determining the top-heavy status for aggregation groups of plans.

---

[18] Code Sec. 416(g)(4)(C).

Suppose, for example, that Plan A's plan year begins on February 1. Thus, its determination date for the 2006-2007 year would be January 31, 2006. However, it would not be until December 31, 2006 (at the earliest) that Plan A would be determined as top heavy for that year. If there is some time lag in calculating the accrued benefits under Plan B, it could result that Plan A's top-heavy determination would not be known until the year in question was already over. This situation would cause some uncertainty for determining the amount of vested benefits which are due to participants who terminate during the year, since their rates of benefit accrual and vesting may change as a result of a top-heavy determination.

General Calculation Rules. Before considering the calculations of accrued benefits for specific types of plans, some general rules applicable to all top-heavy determinations should be covered. The determination date discussed above serves not only as a date for valuing accrued benefits, but also as the date which sets the top-heavy test period. That is, the top-heavy calculation considers more than the status of employees and accrued benefits as of the determination date. Rather, the calculation involves a lookback test period.

One such calculation concerns distributions which have occurred during this lookback period. All distributions made within the plan year that includes the determination date are added to the account balances of all employees.[19] However, if an inservice distribution is made (one made for a reason other than separation from service, death, or disability, e.g., a loan), a five-year lookback period applies.[20] In the case of distributions made after the valuation date and prior to the determination date, such distributions are not added to the account balance since they are already included in the valuation amount. That is, the distributions are not double-counted.[21]

A second calculation which employs this lookback test period concerns the key employee status. Code Sec. 416(i) provides that a key employee is one who meets the definition of a key employee during the plan year containing the determination date. Note, however, that the status of an employee (i.e., key or non-key employee) for the plan year being tested is irrelevant. This is because the key employee determination is to be made for the year which contains the determination date, which is the year prior to the year under consideration. Thus, an employee who becomes a key employee during the plan year will not be considered as such until the following year.

---

[19] Code Sec. 416(g)3.
[20] Code Sec. 416(g)(3)(B).

[21] Reg. § 1.416-1, Q&A T-30.

¶ 703.01

Another important aspect of the calculation is the treatment of former key employees. A *former* key employee is defined as an employee who is currently classified as a non-key employee for the plan year, but who was classified as a key employee for any prior plan year. In calculating the accrued benefits of all employees, the accrued benefits of former key employees are excluded entirely.[22]

Example: Suppose a plan has the following employees for 2006:

Employee	Last Year Classified as a Key Employee	Status for 2006
A	2005	Key
B	2005	Key
C	2003	Former Key
D	Never	Non-Key
E	Never	Non-Key

The plan will be considered top heavy if the total present values of the accrued benefits of A and B exceeds 60 percent of the total present values of accrued benefits of A, B, D and E. That is, employee C is left out of the top-heavy calculation since he is a former key employee.

Similarly, if an individual has not performed services for the employer at any time during the year ending on the determination date, any accrued benefit for the individual is not taken into account.[23]

Accrued Benefits. A participant's accrued benefit includes his mandatory or voluntary employee contributions. Although "catch-up" contributions (additional contributions that may be made by individuals who are at least age 50—see ¶ 704.03 for discussion) are generally disregarded for most limit calculations, catchup contributions for *prior* plan years are taken into account for purposes of determining the top-heavy status. Thus, catch-up contributions for prior years are included in the account balances that are used in determining whether the plan is top-heavy.[24]

Certain plans provided for deductible employee contributions prior to 1987. (These plans were required to account for these contributions separately, because those contributions were treated as if they were in an IRA, rather than a qualified plan.) Regulations provide that such deductible employee contributions are not considered to be part of the accrued benefits.[25]

---

[22] Code Sec. 416(g)(4)(B).
[23] Code Sec. 416(g)(4)(E).
[24] Code Sec. 414(v)(1); Prop. Reg. § 1.414(v)-1(d)(iv).
[25] Reg. § 1.416-1, Q&A T-28.

Rollovers and plan-to-plan transfers may or may not be included in the calculation of accrued benefits, depending on whether they are related or unrelated. An unrelated rollover or transfer is one which is initiated by the employee where the plans involved are maintained by unrelated employers. In such a case, the original plan which made the distribution is required to add it back for one year, under the rules discussed previously, and the receiving plan does not include the amount in determining the accrued benefit of the employee. In the case of a related rollover or transfer (one which was either not initiated by the employee or which was made to a plan maintained by the same employer), the plan accepting the rollover or transfer counts the amount in the present value of accrued benefits, while the original plan which made the distribution ignores the amount.[26]

Defined Contribution Plan Calculations. A defined contribution plan is top heavy if, as of the determination date, the sum of the account balances for key employees exceeds 60 percent of the sum of the account balances for all employees. In determining the account balance for any individual, the value as of the most recent valuation date occurring within a 12-month period ending on the determination date is used, increased by any contribution actually made to the account after the valuation date and before the determination date. In the case of a money purchase pension plan, contributions which are due, but not yet made, to an individual's account on or before the determination date are added to the most recent value. In the first year of a plan, contributions made after the determination date that were allocated as of a date in that first year are also to be added.[27] (Again, note that the account balance includes employee contributions.)

> **Example:** Assume an employer maintains a profit-sharing plan (Plan X), which covers four employees. The plan year is the calendar year. The determination date for the plan year 2006 is December 31, 2005. As of that date, the following account balances were accrued under the plan:

Employee	Status	Account Balance December 31, 2005	Distributions Since January 1, 2005
A	Key	$50,000	$10,000
B	Non-Key	25,000	-0-
C	Non-Key	15,000	-0-
D	Non-Key	10,000	-0-

---

[26] Reg. § 1.416-1, Q&A T-32.   [27] Reg. § 1.416-1, Q&A T-24.

The plan would not be top heavy for the plan year 2006, since the account balances (plus distributions within the last year) for all the key employees do not exceed 60% of the account balances (plus distributions within the last year) for all employees, i.e., $60,000 < (60% \times $110,000).

Defined Benefit Plans Calculations. A defined benefit plan is top heavy if, as of the determination date, the total present value of the accrued benefits for the key employees exceeds 60 percent of that for all employees. In determining the present value of an accrued benefit, the most recent valuation date which is within a 12-month period ending on the determination date is used. The accrued benefit for a participant is computed as if the individual terminated service as of the valuation date. For this purpose, the valuation date must be the same valuation date for computing plan costs for minimum funding, regardless of whether a valuation is performed that year. In the first year of the plan, however, the accrued benefit is determined as if the individual terminated service either as of the determination date or as of the valuation date (but taking into account the estimated accrued benefit as of the determination date).[28]

No specific actuarial assumptions, other than reasonable assumptions, are prescribed by the IRS. In fact, the assumptions need not relate to the actual plan and investment experience. The present value of accrued benefits is to be based on the benefit which would be payable at normal retirement age, using a reasonable interest rate. (The IRS provides a safe-harbor rate of between five and six percent, but indicates that plans are not required to use a rate in this range.)[29] The method of benefit accrual must be the method which is used by all plans of the employer being tested. If no single method is used by all plans, the benefits must be treated as accruing ratably under the fractional rule of Code Sec. 411(b)(1)(C).[30]

Example: Assume an employer maintains defined benefit plan Y that uses the calendar year as its plan year and has a normal retirement age of 65. The determination date for the plan year 2006 is December 31, 2005. As of that date, the following information is available:

---

[28] Reg. § 1.416-1, Q&A T-25.
[29] Reg. § 1.416-1, Q&A T-26.

[30] Code Sec. 416(g)(4)(F).

Employee	Status	Projected Annual Benefit	Age at 12/31/05	Age at Entry	Fractional Rule Accrued Benefit	Present Value of Accrued Benefit
E	Key	$60,000	55	45	$30,000	$162,690
F	Non-Key	30,000	50	45	7,500	30,390
G	Non-Key	30,000	40	30	8,571	19,396
H	Non-Key	20,000	45	30	8,571	25,955
			Total			$238,431

Plan Y would be top heavy for the 2006 plan year because $162,690 (the total present values of accrued benefits for all key employees) is greater than 60% of $238,431 (the total present values of accrued benefits for all employees), i.e., ($162,690 / $238,431 = 68.2%).

.02   Plans to Consider

All qualified plans maintained by any entity within an employer group, except SIMPLE plans, must comply with the top-heavy rules. This includes not only those plans which are qualified under Code Sec. 401(a), but also SEPs and plans which qualify under Code Sec. 403(a). Certain plans will fall under an aggregation group status, in which case the top-heavy computation is applied to the group rather than separately to each plan. Aggregation may be required or permissive. The results of a required aggregation group classification are that, if the group is top heavy, then all plans under the group are top heavy, whether or not the plan considered alone would be top heavy. Such is not the case with a permissive aggregation group, though.

A special rule applies to 401(k) plans that meet the new safe harbor provision for exclusion from top-heavy status, but nevertheless belong to an aggregation group that is a top-heavy group. All contributions under such 401(k) plans may be taken into account in determining whether any other plan in the group meets the minimum contribution requirements.[31]

Required Aggregation Group. A required aggregation group includes each plan of the employer in which a key employee participates in the plan year ending on the determination date. In addition, each other plan of the employer which, during the same period, enables a plan covering key employees to meet the nondiscrimination rules of Code Sec. 401(a)(4) and the coverage rules of

---

[31] Code Sec. 416(g)(4)(H).

Code Sec. 410(b) is part of the required aggregation group. That is, if the plan covering key employees cannot meet the coverage requirements of Code Sec. 410(b) by itself, but can meet those requirements by designating another plan (with comparable benefits or contributions under the rules discussed in ¶607.01), both plans are part of a required aggregation group. Of course, the plan which was designated to support the key employee plan would typically be one in which mostly rank-and-file employees participated.

A required aggregation group will be top heavy if the total of: (1) the present values of the accrued benefits for key employees under all defined benefit plans, and (2) the account balances for key employees under all defined contribution plans exceed 60 percent of the totals of the same amounts for all employees in all plans in the required aggregation group. If the required aggregation group is top heavy, all plans in the group are top heavy. Thus, each plan (whether or not top heavy when considered separately) must meet the top-heavy rules for the plan year. On the other hand, if the required aggregation group is not top heavy, no plan in the group is top heavy. Thus, even if a plan, when considered separately, is top heavy, it would not convert to top-heavy status for the plan year if the group is not top heavy.

> **Example:** Assume that Plans X and Y in the last two examples were maintained by the same employer. Since each plan covers a key employee, the plans constitute a required aggregation group. Thus, the determination of top heavy status must be made on the group basis, as follows:

Employee	Status	Account Balance Under Defined Contribution Plan X on 12/31/05, Adjusted for Distributions	Present Value of Accrued Benefits Under Plan Y on 12/31/05
A	Key	$ 60,000	
B	Non-Key	25,000	
C	Non-Key	15,000	
D	Non-Key	10,000	
E	Key		$162,690
F	Non-Key		30,390
G	Non-Key		19,396
H	Non-Key		25,955
	Totals	$110,000	$238,431

The total present values of accrued benefits for all key employees in the group is $222,690, and the total present values of accrued benefits for all employees is $348,431. Because $222,690 exceeds 60% of $348,431 (it's 63.9%), the required aggregation group is top heavy. Thus, both Plan X and Plan Y must comply with the top-heavy provisions for 2006.

Permissive Aggregation Group. A permissive aggregation group consists of plans of an employer that are required to be aggregated, plus one or more other plans that are not part of a required aggregation group. As long as the plan which is not required to be aggregated can meet the comparability standards of Code Sec. 401(a)(4) and Code Sec. 410(b) (see ¶607.01 for discussion), the plan may be considered together with the required aggregation group. Keep in mind that this added plan was not one which had been designated as a single plan for purposes of meeting the coverage tests. Rather, it is considered together with these other plans only for the top-heavy determination.

If a permissive aggregation group is not top heavy, then no plan in the group is considered top heavy, regardless of its status when considered separately or in the required aggregation group. If the permissive aggregation group is top heavy, only those plans that are part of the required aggregation group are subject to the top-heavy rules for the plan year. Thus, it is only necessary to consider a permissive aggregation group if the required aggregation group has been determined top heavy.

Example: Suppose the same employer, as in the above example, also maintains money purchase Plan Z, which covers only nonkey employees. Assume Plans X, Y, and Z meet the comparability standards discussed in ¶607.01. As of December 31, 2005, Plan Z's determination date, the participant's account balances are as below.

Employee	Status	Account Balance December 31, 2005
I	Non-Key	$20,000
J	Non-Key	$20,000
K	Non-Key	15,000
L	Non-Key	10,000
	Total	$65,000

Plans X, Y, and Z now comprise a permissive aggregation group. The total present values of accrued benefits of all key employees in the plans is $222,630, which is 53.8% of the total present values of accrued benefits of $413,431 for all employees in the plans. Thus, the permissive aggregation group is not top heavy for 2006, which means that none of the plans must satisfy the top-heavy requirements for that year.

Terminated Plans. A terminated plan is treated like any other plan for purposes of the top-heavy rules. Thus, if the plan would have been part of a required aggregation group had it not terminated, it is still aggregated with other plans if it was maintained by the employer within the year ending on the determination date for the plan year in question. In addition, distributions which have taken place within the one-year period (five years for in-service distributions, such as loans) ending on the determination date must be added to the accrued benefit or account balance of an employee.[32]

.03   Key Employees

Under Code Sec. 416(i), a key employee is any employee (including a terminated employee) who, at any time during the preceding plan year, was:

(1) an officer of the employer having annual compensation from the employer for a plan year greater than $135,000 (in 2006) for the calendar year in which the plan year ends;

(2) a five-percent owner of the employer (regardless of the level of compensation); or

(3) a one-percent owner of the employer with compensation in excess of $150,000.

An individual may be considered a key employee in a plan year for more than one reason. For example, an individual may be both an officer and a five-percent owner. However, in testing whether a plan or group is top heavy, an individual's accrued benefit is counted only once.[33]

Officers. The first group of key employees are employees who are "officers" and who earn more than $135,000 (subject to COLAs). Officer status is determined on a facts and circumstances basis. Generally, an officer is an administrative executive who is in regular and continued service. Thus, an employee who merely has the title of an officer but not the authority of an officer will not be considered as such for the top-heavy test. Similarly, an employee who does not have the title of an officer but has the authority of an officer will be considered as an officer in the top-heavy test.[34]

---

[32] Code Sec. 416(g); Reg. § 1.416-1, Q&A T-4.
[33] Reg. § 1.416-1, Q&A T-12.
[34] Reg. § 1.416-1, Q&A T-13.

Officer classification is not restricted to corporations. Thus, noncorporate entities (sole proprietorships, partnerships, associations, trusts, etc.) may also have individuals who will be classified as officers.[35] However, a partner of a partnership will not be treated as an officer merely because he owns a capital or profits interest in the partnership, votes, and is authorized to act as an agent of the partnership. In the case of related employers under Code Secs. 414(b), (c), or (m), officer status is determined based upon responsibilities with respect to the employer for which the individual is directly employed, and not with respect to the controlled or affiliated group.[36]

No minimum number of officers must be taken into account. However, there is a maximum number of officers that will be considered key employees in the top-heavy determination. (This maximum number of officers which will be considered is based on the employer group, as aggregated under Code Sec. 414(b), (c), or (m), rather than for each individual employer.) The number of officers will not exceed 50, or if less, the greater of three officers or ten percent of the total employees. The number of employees to be used is the greatest number of employees (for all employers in the employer group) during the preceding plan year. Thus, the number of officers is limited to the following:

Maximum Number of Employees	Maximum Number of Officers
Under 30	3
31-500	10% of employees
Over 500	50

In the event that the maximum limit applies, two rules are provided in the regulations. First, if the greatest number of employees during the test period is between 30 and 500 (i.e., the 10 percent limit applies), and 10 percent of total employees is not a whole integer, then the maximum number of officers is to be rounded up to the next whole integer. Second, if any of these limits apply, the employees who are to be included as officers are those who had the largest annual plan-year compensation during the preceding plan year.[37]

Five-Percent Owners. The second category of key employees are employees who, at any time during the preceding plan year, owned more than five percent of the employer. Ownership, for this

---

[35] Reg. § 1.416-1, Q&A T-15.
[36] Reg. § 1.416-1, Q&A T-13.
[37] Reg. § 1.416-1, Q&A T-14.

¶ **703.03**

purpose, is based on the total value of outstanding stock or the total combined voting power of all stock of a corporation. With respect to a noncorporate employer, ownership is based on an individual's capital or profits interest in the employer. The other rules which apply under this category are identical to those under the top ten owners. That is, the attribution rules of Code Sec. 318 apply for ownership, and the five-percent ownership is based on each individual entity in an employer group.[38]

One-Percent Owners. The one-percent owner category of key employees has identical rules as the five-percent category. Thus, Code Sec. 318 attribution rules apply and, in the case of a corporation, ownership is based on the total value of outstanding stock or total voting power of all stock. In the case of a noncorporate entity, ownership is based on capital or profits interest, and the test is made at the individual employer level in the case of an employer group.[39]

The one-percent owner must also have an annual compensation in excess of $150,000 during the year of his ownership. This compensation is the total compensation derived from all employers within an employer group, and has the usual meaning of compensation, as defined in Code Sec. 414(q).

Beneficiaries of Key Employees. Under Code Sec. 416(i)(5), a beneficiary of a deceased key employee is deemed to be a key employee. (The same rule applies to non-key employees.) Thus, if the beneficiary is a key employee independently of his beneficiary status, both the present value of his own accrued benefits and the present value of his inherited accrued benefits will be considered as the accrued benefit of a key employee.

.04 Consequences of Top-Heavy Status

If a plan is determined to be top heavy for the plan year, it must meet the requirements in Code Secs. 416(b) regarding minimum vesting, 416(c) regarding minimum contributions or benefit accruals, and 416(d) regarding the maximum compensation which may be recognized for contribution or benefit accruals. If the employer maintains both a defined contribution plan and a defined benefit plan, it must also meet restrictions with regard to the limitations of Code Sec. 415(e).

Vesting Schedules. Code Sec. 416(b) provides special vesting schedules for years in which a plan becomes top heavy. A top-heavy plan must meet one of the two alternative vesting schedules below:

---

[38] Reg. § 1.416-1, Q&A T-17.   [39] Reg. § 1.416-1, Q&A T-16.

(1) three-year cliff vesting, i.e.,

Years of Service	Nonforfeitable Percentage
0-2	0%
3	100%

(2) two-to-six year graded vesting, i.e.,

Years of Service	Nonforfeitable Percentage
0-1	0%
2	20%
3	40%
4	60%
5	80%
6	100%

Years of service are to be counted in accordance with the vesting provisions of Code Sec. 411(a). Note that the top-heavy rules require that all years of service which must be counted under Code Sec. 411(a) are counted for the top heavy vesting schedules. That is, years of service in nontop-heavy years are also counted. Of course, years of service which may be disregarded under the break in service rules of Code Sec. 411(a)(4) also apply to the top-heavy schedules.[40]

The top-heavy vesting schedules apply to all accrued benefits, including those which were accrued in nontop-heavy years and in years before Code Sec. 416 was in effect. However, the accrued benefits of any employee who does not have at least one hour of service in a top-heavy year are not required to be subject to the top-heavy vesting schedule. In addition, any accrued benefits which have already been forfeited are not restored because a plan becomes top heavy.[41]

When a top-heavy plan ceases to be top heavy, the plan may revert to its original vesting schedule, e.g., the five-year cliff vesting schedule. However, such a change is subject to the rules discussed in Chapter 6, regarding changes in vesting schedules. That is, the nonforfeitable percentage of any employee's accrued benefit must not be reduced. In addition, any employee with at least three years of service must be allowed to elect to remain under the prior (i.e., the top-heavy) vesting schedule.[42] In switching to the nontop-heavy vesting schedule, an employee (absent an election to remain under the top-heavy vesting schedule) remains vested in his accrued benefit as of the date the plan becomes nontop heavy only, and no further vesting is required for additional accrued benefits.

---

[40] Code Sec. 416(b)(2).
[41] Reg. § 1.416-1, Q&A V-3.

[42] Reg. § 1.416-1, Q&A V-7 and Code Sec. 411(a)(10).

Example: Plan A uses the five-year cliff vesting schedule for nontop-heavy years and the two-to-six year graded vesting schedule for top-heavy years. If an employee is 40-percent vested under the top-heavy schedule (i.e., he has three years of service) in his accrued benefit of $10,000 on the date the plan ceases to be top heavy, he will remain 40 percent vested in that accrued benefit ($10,000) until he completes his fifth year of service.

Minimum Benefits-Top-Heavy Defined Benefit Plans. Each non-key employee who is a participant in a top-heavy defined benefit plan and who has at least 1,000 hours of service (or equivalent) in the computation period must have an accrued benefit of at least two percent of his average compensation for his highest paid five consecutive years, times his years of service, up to a maximum of ten years (20 percent maximum). This minimum accrued benefit is expressed as a single life annuity (with no ancillary benefits), commencing at normal retirement age. It must be from employer-derived contributions, with no Social Security integration.[43]

Certain non-key employees who are excluded from participation in the plan must also accrue the minimum benefit. These include employees: (1) who are excluded merely because their compensation is less than a stated amount (e.g., in a Social Security integrated plan); and (2) who fail to make a mandatory employee contribution.[44]

Years of service for the minimum benefit accrual are generally determined under the normal rules of Code Secs. 411(a)(4), (5), and (6). That is, an employee is credited with a year of service for a year in which he performs at least 1,000 hours of service. Note that years of service as they relate to vesting, rather than participation, are counted. Thus, for example, a plan which contains participation and/or age requirements before admission to the plan must count the years of service before an employee became a participant. In addition, a plan which contains mandatory employee contributions must count years in which an employee failed to make such a contribution, if the employee has completed at least 1,000 hours of service. However, a plan may disregard any year of service for minimum benefit accrual purposes if the plan was not top heavy for the plan year ending during such year of service. (Recall, however, that these years of service do count for top-heavy vesting purposes.)[45] Further, years of service do not include years during which the plan benefits no key or former key employee (i.e., frozen plan years).[46]

---

[43] Reg. § 1.416-1, Q&A M-2, -3 and -11.
[44] Reg. § 1.416-1, Q&A M-4.

[45] Reg. § 1.416-1, Q&A M-2(b) and -4.
[46] Code Sec. 416(c)(1)(C)(iii).

If a non-key employee has already accrued more than the minimum accrued benefit under Code Sec. 416(c)(1), no additional minimum accruals are required.[47]

> **Example:** Plan A provides a benefit accrual of one percent per year of service, times the employee's highest five years' average compensation. For 2006, Plan A is determined to be top heavy for the first time. Thus, the minimum benefit accrual for all non-key employees must be two percent (times one year), if they have completed at least 1,000 hours during 2006. Employee B, who has completed three years of service, would receive his regular benefit accrual of one percent for 2006, since he has already accrued a total of three percent of his average salary. On the other hand, employee C, who has completed only one year of service (2006), would receive a benefit accrual of two percent, since he would have accrued a total of only one percent of his average salary, which is less than the minimum.

The minimum benefit is based on an employee's average annual compensation for a period of consecutive years (not to exceed five years) during which the employee had the largest aggregate compensation. Thus, even though an employee may have accrued more than the maximum 20 percent of average compensation, an additional accrual will be required if his average compensation increases. In computing this average, compensation earned during the following years are disregarded: (1) plan years which began prior to 1984; (2) years beginning after the last top-heavy plan year; and (3) years in which the employee did not earn a year of service.[48]

Minimum Contributions-Top-Heavy Defined Contribution Plans. Each non-key employee a top-heavy defined contribution plan must receive a minimum allocation to his account of three percent of compensation for the top-heavy year. This allocation consists of employer-derived contributions, reallocated forfeitures, elective deferrals under a 401(k) plan, and employer matching contributions.[49] As in the case of a top-heavy defined benefit plan, this minimum contribution may not be integrated with Social Security.[50]

A special rule allows for a lower minimum contribution, if the total allocation (employer contribution, forfeitures, and 401(k) contribution) to key employees' accounts is less than three percent.[51] In

---

[47] Reg. § 1.416-1, Q&A M-2(e).
[48] Reg. § 1.416-1, Q&A M-2(c).
[49] Code Sec. 416(c)(2)(A).

[50] Code Sec. 416(c)(2) and Reg. § 1.416-1, Q&A M-7 and -11.
[51] Reg. § 1.416-1, Q&A M-7.

this case, the minimum contribution to the non-key employee's accounts does not have to exceed this rate. Thus, if an employer makes no contribution to a profit-sharing plan and there are no forfeiture allocations, no minimum contribution is required on behalf of the non-key employees. (This special rule does not apply to any defined contribution plan which is required to be included in an aggregation group if such plan enables a defined benefit plan required to be included in the group to meet the coverage or antidiscrimination requirements.) As in all qualified plans, no more than $210,000 (in 2005) of compensation is to be considered.[52]

> **Example:** Joe, a key employee with a $300,000 salary, wants to receive a profit sharing contribution of $5,000. However, because only $210,000 of his compensation may be considered, a $5,000 contribution made on his behalf equals a contribution of 2.38 percent ($5,000/$210,000). Consequently, a minimum contribution of only 2.38 percent must be made for all non-key employees.

Individuals who are at least age 50 may make special "catch-up" contributions. (See ¶ 704.30 for discussion.) Under proposed regulations, catch-up contributions with respect to the current year are not taken into account for purposes of the top-heavy minimum contribution rate. Thus, for example, if the only contributions made for a plan year by key employees are catch-up contributions, the applicable percentage under Code Sec. 416(c) is 0%, and no minimum top-heavy contribution is required for the year.[53]

All non-key employees who are participants in a top-heavy defined contribution plan who have not separated from service by the end of the plan year must receive the minimum contribution. This includes those who: (1) have become participants but who subsequently failed to complete 1,000 hours of service during the top-heavy year; (2) were excluded from the plan because of social security integration. No minimum contribution is required for non-key employees who are not participants, e.g., those excluded because of age or service requirements or because the class of employees in which they belong is completely excluded from coverage.[54]

If an employer maintains two top-heavy defined contribution plans, only one of the plans must provide the minimum contribution for each non-key employee who participates in both plans. However, the other plan must provide for the top-heavy vesting and must limit compensation in providing benefits.[55]

---

[52] Code Sec. 401(a)(17).
[53] Prop. Reg. § 1.414(v)-1(d)(2)(iv).

[54] Reg. § 1.416-1, Q&A M-10.
[55] Reg. § 1.416-1, Q&A M-8.

Two or More Plans. If a non-key employee participates in both a defined benefit plan and a defined contribution plan maintained by the same employer, Code Sec. 416(f) provides that the employer is not required to meet both the defined benefit minimum accrual and the defined contribution minimum contribution. The regulations provide four safe-harbor rules which a plan may use in determining which minimum must be provided to non-key employees who are covered under both defined benefit and defined contribution plans.

First, the employer may provide the two percent defined benefit accrual with no minimum defined contribution. Second, a floor off-set approach (see Rev. Rul. 76-259[56]) may be used whereby the two percent defined benefit minimum is provided, subject to an offset by the actuarial equivalent of the employee's defined contribution account balance. Third, in the case of employees covered under both plans, the employer may prove, using the comparability analysis of Reg. § 1.401(a)(4)-8 (see ¶ 607.01), that the plans are providing a benefit which is at least equivalent to the two percent defined benefit minimum. Finally, the employer may provide a five percent defined contribution minimum allocation to the non-key employees' accounts.[57]

An employer may not use a different method each year to meet the above requirements. The plan document must set forth the specific method to be used by the employer to meet the requirements. If an employer wishes to change the method, the plan document must be amended.[58]

¶ 704   Code Sec. 401(k) Plans

Probably the most popular type of qualified plan is the Code Sec. 401(k) plan, sometimes referred to as a cash or deferred arrangement or CODA. A 401(k) plan is an arrangement that is part of a qualified profit-sharing or stock bonus plan (or certain pre-ERISA money purchase plans) under which an eligible employee may elect to have the employer contribute up to $14,000 (in 2005) to a trust under the plan, or to have the amount paid to the employee in cash.[59]

Elective contributions under a qualified 401(k) plan generally are not included in the employee's gross income at the time the cash is available or at the time contributed to the plan. However, if the contributions are designated Roth contributions, the amount so elected is included in the employee's gross income. (Roth 401(k) plans are discussed in ¶ 704.11.)

---

[56] 1976-2 CB 111.
[57] Reg. § 1.416-1, Q&A M-12.
[58] Reg. § 1.316-1, Q&A M-15.
[59] Reg. § 1.401(k)-1(a)(2), (3).

A plan that allows an employee to make a one-time irrevocable election, upon the employee's first becoming eligible to participate in *any* qualified deferred compensation plan (as described in Code Sec. 219(g)(5)(D), whether or not terminated) of the employer to have a specified amount or percentage of compensation contributed by the employer for the duration of the employee's service is not considered a 401(k) plan. Thus, any such contributions would not fall under the 401(k) plan requirements or limitations.[60]

A 401(k) plan is either in the form of a bonus or a salary reduction arrangement. Under the bonus form of a 401(k) plan, an employee may elect to have the employer contribute to the trust all or any portion of some amount in excess of his normal compensation; any amounts not so elected may be paid to the employee. For example, a 401(k) plan may allow employees to elect to split five percent of their compensation, in any manner, between current cash or a contribution to the trust. Under the salary reduction form of a 401(k) plan, the employee elects to reduce his normal compensation, or elects to forgo an increase in his compensation, and have the amount instead contributed to the trust.

Any amount that an employee elects to have contributed to the trust is not subject to federal income tax for the period in which they were earned (assuming the plan meets the special qualification requirements).[61] These elective contributions are, however, subject to FICA and FUTA taxes for the period in which they were earned.[62]

Individual 401(k) Plans. In the past couple of years, many mutual fund and investment management companies have begun marketing what is being called a "new" type of 401(k) plan. Depending on the specific company offering the plan, these individual plans are sold under different trademarked names, such as Solo(k), Uni(k), Individual(k), etc. These plans are designed for self-employed individuals or business owners with no employees—hence the name.

Technically, there is no "new" plan under the Code. Instead, these plans are based on the change (that became effective under EGTRRA in 2002) including elective deferrals under a 401(k) plan in defining compensation for qualified plan purposes. (See ¶607 for discussion of compensation.) The effect of this change is to increase the total amount of contributions that can be made and deducted by the individual, since any elective deferral under a 401(k) plan is not counted in the employer's maximum deductible amount.

---

[60] Reg. § 1.401(k)-1(a)(3)(v).
[61] Code Sec. 402(a)(8).

[62] Code Secs. 3121(v)(1) and 3306(r).

.01 General Qualification Requirements

In order to receive special tax treatment, a 401(k) plan must first satisfy the general qualification requirements for profit-sharing and stock bonus plans under Code Sec. 401(a). In addition, a 401(k) plan must meet special provisions, which relate mainly to nondiscrimination, nonforfeitability, and distribution requirements.

A 401(k) plan must be a part of a qualified profit-sharing or stock bonus plan. (It may also be a part of a rural electric cooperative plan, a plan maintained by Indian tribal governments, a plan maintained by tax-exempt employers, or a pre-ERISA money purchase plan.) Both the 401(k) plan and the underlying plan must meet their respective qualification requirements. If the 401(k) plan meets the special rules, but the underlying plan does not qualify under Code Sec. 401(a), the entire arrangement is nonqualified. However, the underlying plan which contains the 401(k) plan can still be qualified as long as it meets the Code Sec. 401(a) requirements, even though the 401(k) plan fails to meet the separate requirements.[63] In such a case any contributions to the plan made at the election of the employee for the year are includible in the employee's gross income.[64] Of course, this could cause a qualification problem for the underlying plan, because of the restrictions on nondeductible employee contributions under Code Sec. 401(m), discussed in ¶ 607.02.

Self-Employed Individuals. A partnership or sole proprietorship may maintain a 401(k) plan, and individual partners or owners may make cash or deferred elections with respect to compensation attributable to services rendered to the entity. In the case of a partnership, any arrangement whereby an individual partner is permitted to directly or indirectly vary the amount of his contribution to a plan is deemed to be a 401(k) plan, and is thus subject to the qualification requirements for such a plan if the contributions are to be treated as elective contributions.

Under Code Sec. 402(g)(8), matching contributions made on behalf of a self-employed individual are not treated as elective contributions made pursuant to a cash or deferred election.[65]

.02 Annual Election

The plan must allow the employee to elect to have the employer contribution made to the trust or paid to him in cash. Any contributions made by the employer pursuant to a deferral election by an employee are not deemed to be made available (i.e., constructively

---

[63] Reg. § 1.401(k)-1(a)(5)(iv).
[64] Reg. § 1.402(a)-1(d).

[65] Prop. Reg. § 1.401(k)-1(a)(6)(ii).

received) merely because the employee had the election to receive the benefit in cash.[66]

The election is made on an annual basis, so an employee may elect different amounts or percentages each year. The election may be made at any time permitted by the plan with regard to amounts that are not currently available to the electing employee as of the date of the election.[67] However, prefunding of elective contributions and matching contributions is generally not allowed. Thus, the actual contribution must be made (1) after the deferral election is made, and (2) after the employee performs services related to the compensation.[68]

> **Example:** An employer maintains a profit-sharing plan under which each eligible employee has an election with respect to a bonus of 10% of his compensation payable on January 30 each year based on the prior year's profits. Deferred amounts are not treated as after-tax employee contributions. An election made prior to January 30 (the date on which the compensation is to be paid) to defer all or part of the bonus qualifies as a 401(k) election.

The IRS has ruled that this annual election does not have to be an affirmative action by the employee. Thus, for example, a plan may provide for an automatic salary reduction, as long as the employee is notified of his right to elect to receive cash both when hired and at later annual dates.[69]

Self-Employed Individuals. A partner's or sole proprietor's compensation is deemed currently available on the last day of the entity's tax year; therefore, any election must be made no later than the last day of that year.[70] Assuming a timely election, the restriction on prefunding does not prohibit self-employed individuals from deferring amounts during the year even though their earned income is not determined until year-end. For example, a partner could defer an amount paid to him or her throughout the year on account of services performed during the year, as long as those payments do not exceed a reasonable estimate of the partner's earned income for the tax year.[71]

---

[66] Code Sec. 402(e)(3).

[67] Reg. § 1.401(k)-1(a)(3).

[68] Prop. Reg. § 1.401(k)-1(a)(3)(iii)(B).

[69] Rev. Rul. 2000-8, 2000-1 CB 617; Prop. Reg. § 1.401(k)-1(a)(3)(ii).
[70] Reg. § 1.401(k)-1(a)(6)(ii)(B); Prop. Reg. § 1.401(k)-1(a)(6)(iii).
[71] Reg. § 1.401(k)-1(a)(6)(iv).

.03   Dollar Limitations on Amount Deferred

Elective deferrals may be limited in amount because of any one of the following three restrictions: the special nondiscrimination requirements, the defined contribution plan limitations of Code Sec. 415(c), or the $12,000 limitation for all elective deferrals under Code Sec. 402(g). The nondiscrimination requirements are discussed in a later section of this chapter; the remaining limitations are discussed below.

Code Sec. 415(c) Limitations. Recall from ¶ 609.04 that annual additions to a defined contribution plan are limited to the lesser of (1) 100 percent of compensation, or (2) $42,000 (in 2005). For purposes of these rules, elective deferrals under a qualified 401(k) plan (including designated Roth contributions—see ¶ 704.11) are considered to be employer contributions.[72]

Compensation, as defined in Code Sec. 414(s), includes any amounts deferred under a 401(k) plan. Elective deferrals under Code Secs. 125 (cafeteria plans), 402(h) (SEPs), 403(b) (tax-shelter annuity programs), 457 (deferred compensation plans of state or local governments), and 132(f)(4) (qualified transportation fringe benefit plans) are also included in defining compensation for purposes of Code Sec. 414(s). Consider the example below.

> **Example:** Plan X is a qualified 401(k) plan and is a part of a qualified profit-sharing plan. Under Plan X, employees may elect to reduce their salary by a certain percentage and have it instead paid to the trust. Employee A elects to defer $7,000 as a 401(k) plan contribution from his $25,000 salary. Information concerning Employee A is below:
>
> | | |
> |---|---:|
> | Compensation before reduction . . . . | $25,000 |
> | Employer contribution under the profit-sharing plan | 10,500 |
> | Amount elected as salary reduction by A . . . . | 7,000 |
> | Includible compensation ($25,000 − $7,000) . . . . | 18,000 |
>
> For purposes of the Code Sec. 415(c) percentage limitation, $17,500 (total annual additions) divided by $25,000 (total compensation) equals 70 percent.

Dollar Limit on Elective Deferrals. Any plan that provides for elective deferrals cannot be a qualified plan unless it provides that the total amount of elective deferrals for an individual during a calendar year under the plan and all other plans, contracts, and

---

[72] Reg.   § 1.401(k)-1(a)(4)(ii);   Prop.   Reg.
§ 1.401(k)-1(a)(4)(ii).

¶ 704.03

arrangements of the employer maintaining the plan may not exceed this limitation.[73] A maximum of $14,000 per employee for 2005 may be electively deferred under all plans in which the employee participates.[74] Under EGTRRA '01 scheduled annual increases, the dollar limit will increase to $15,000 in 2006, after which it will be subject to COLAs beginning in 2007.[75]

The annual dollar limit applies to all cash or deferred arrangements in which the employee participates, not just those of related employers (as Code Sec. 415 limits apply). In addition, elective deferrals under SEPs (Code Sec. 408(k)), tax-sheltered annuities (Code Sec. 402(b)), and certain union plans under Code Sec. 501(c)(18) count toward the annual dollar limit.[76]

> **Example:** If in 2005 Mr. A works for two unrelated employers and defers $7,000 in one plan and $8,000 in the other, only $14,000 may be deferred; the remaining $1,000 will be taxable in that year (absent any special catch-up provision).

The dollar limit applies only to elective deferrals; nondeductible employee contributions and employer contributions (matching or otherwise) are subject only to the normal provisions of Code Secs. 415 and 401(m).[77]

Special Catch-Up Provisions. The annual dollar limit on elective deferrals is increased for individuals who are at least age 50 by the end of the plan year and who are not allowed to make additional elective deferrals because of some restriction or limitation. These additional elective deferrals, referred to as catch-up contributions are determined by reference to statutory limits (the $14,000 limit on elective deferrals or the $42,000 limit on annual additions), employer-provided limits (e.g., a plan limits elective deferrals by highly compensated employees to 10 percent of compensation), and the ADP test (discussed in ¶ 704.09).[78]

If an elective deferral is treated as a catch-up contribution, it is not subject to otherwise applicable limits under the plan or taken into account in applying any of the dollar limitations imposed on employee or employer contributions or deductions.[79]

Catch-up contributions generally are elective deferrals made by a catch-up eligible participant that exceed an otherwise applicable limit and that are treated as catch-up contributions under the plan,

---

[73] Code Sec. 401(a)(30).
[74] Code Sec. 402(g)(1).
[75] Code Sec. 402(g)(1).
[76] Code Sec. 402(g)(3).

[77] Code Sec. 402(g)(9).
[78] Reg. § 1.414(v)-1(b)(1).
[79] Reg. § 1.414(v)-1(d)(1).

but only to the extent they do not exceed the maximum amount of catch-up contribution permitted for the taxable year. The maximum amount of annual catch-up contributions that may be made by a participant is the lesser of:[80]

(1) the participant's compensation for the year (as reduced by any other elective deferrals made by the participant for the year); or

(2) the applicable dollar amount. This applicable dollar amount is $4,000 for 2005, and is scheduled to increase to $5,000 in 2006. Beginning in 2007, the $5,000 amount is subject to COLAs.

> **Example:** Sue, age 52, is a participant in the Blue Co. 401(k) plan. Under the terms of the plan, the maximum deferral is 10% of compensation, up to the annual dollar limit. The plan also provides that a catch-up eligible participant is permitted to defer amounts in excess of 10 percent of compensation, up to the applicable dollar catch-up limit for the year. For the 2006 plan year, Sue's compensation is $60,000; therefore, the maximum elective deferral allowed under the plan is $6,000 (as this amount is less than the $15,000 limit for 2006). Under the catch-up provision, however, Sue may contribute up to $11,000 for the year ($6,000 under the normal limits of the plan, plus the $5,000 allowed under the catch-up provision for 2006).

The amount of elective deferrals in excess of an applicable limit is generally determined as of the end of a plan year by comparing the total elective deferrals for the plan year with the applicable limit for the plan year. (In the above example, since the Blue Co. 401(k) plan limits elective deferrals to 10 percent of compensation, then whether Sue has elective deferrals in excess of 10 percent of her compensation is determined at the end of the plan year.) However, for a limit that is determined on the basis of a year other than a plan year (such as the $15,000 calendar 2006 year limit on elective deferrals), the determination of whether elective deferrals are in excess of the applicable limit is made on the basis of the calendar year. This timing rule is most important for a plan with a plan year that is not the calendar year.[81]

> **Example:** The Blue Co. 401(k) plan uses an October 31 plan year-end. For the year ending on October 31, 2006, any employee's elective deferrals in excess of the employer-imposed 10% of compensation limit for the plan year would be treated as catch-up contributions as of the last day of the plan year (October 31,

---

[80] Code Sec. 414(v).   [81] Reg. §§ 1.414(v)-1(b)(2) and (c)(3).

2006), up to the catch-up contribution limit for 2006 ($5,000). Any employee's elective deferrals in excess of the $15,000 limit for the 2006 calendar year are treated as catch-up contributions at the time they are deferred, up to the $5,000 limit, after reduction by the elective deferrals treated as catch-up contributions as of October 31, 2006.

Excess Deferrals. Generally, if an individual defers more than the maximum amount under a single plan or under plans of the same employer, the plan or plans will be disqualified. On the other hand, if more than the annual maximum is deferred under two or more plans of unrelated employers, none of the plans is disqualified because of the excess; however, the individual must include the excess deferrals in income.[82] Any plan is allowed to distribute this excess (and any earnings thereon) by April 15 with no penalties to the employee or consequences to the qualified status of the plan (assuming, of course, the plan document so provides). This distribution does not require the consent of the participant's spouse, nor will it be treated as violating an outstanding qualified domestic relations order (QDRO). If the individual has deferrals in more than one plan for the year, he must allocate the amount of the excess deferrals among the plans in any manner and notify the administrator of the plans by March 1 of the following year of the allocated amounts.[83]

An excess deferral which is distributed by April 15 of the following year is not subject to income tax, since it was already included by the employee in the year of the deferral. That is, it is treated as if it had not been made to the plan. Any earnings distributed as a result of the excess deferral are taxable in the actual year of distribution. Neither of these amounts is subject to the ten-percent penalty tax on early withdrawals from qualified plans under Code Sec. 72(t).[84] Excess deferrals are treated as employer contributions, even if they are distributed. However, excess deferrals of a nonhighly compensated employee are not taken into account for purposes of the ADP test (discussed later in this chapter) to the extent that they are prohibited under Code Sec. 401(a)(30). Excess deferrals are treated as annual additions for purposes of annual limitation of Code Sec. 415(c), unless they are distributed under these rules.[85]

Code Sec. 402(g)(7) provides a double taxing of excess deferrals which are not distributed by the required April 15 deadline. Excess deferrals that are not distributed by April 15 are not treated as an

---

[82] Reg. § 1.402(g)-1(e)(3)(i).
[83] Code Sec. 402(g)(2)(A).
[84] Code Sec. 402(g)(2)(C).
[85] Reg. § 1.402(g)-1(e)(1)(ii).

employee investment in the contract. Thus, these undistributed excess deferrals are taxed not only in the year of the elective deferral but also upon distribution. Moreover, the amounts are subject to the ten-percent penalty tax on early withdrawals under Code Sec. 72(t) and subject to the distribution restrictions applicable to elective deferrals (discussed in ¶ 704.04).

A plan may use any reasonable method for computing the income allocable to excess deferrals, provided that it is nondiscriminatory and is used consistently.[86] Alternatively, a plan can determine income allocable to excess deferrals by multiplying the income for the tax year allocable to elective contributions by a fraction, the numerator of which is the excess deferrals by the employee for the tax year, and the denominator of which is the sum of the total account balance of the employee attributable to elective contributions as of the beginning of the tax year, plus the employee's elective contributions for the tax year.[87] These methods may also be used for computing income between the end of the tax year and the distribution date, as well as a safe harbor method contained in the regulations.[88]

If the entire amount of excess deferral and the income attributable to the excess is not distributed, the distribution is treated as made proportionately from the excess deferral and the income.[89]

> **Example:** Ted has excess deferrals of $1,000 for the year in his employer's 401(k) plan. The income attributable to excess deferrals is $100. The plan distributes $1,000 to Ted by April 15. Because the plan did not distribute the entire excess deferral and the income, $909 is treated as a distribution of excess deferrals, and $91 is treated as a distribution of earnings. With respect to amounts remaining in the account, $91 is treated as an elective deferral and is not included in Ted's investment in the contract. Because it was not distributed by the required date, the $91 is includible in gross income upon distribution as well as in the year of deferral.

.04 Distribution Restrictions

Employer and nonelective employee contributions to the underlying plan of a 401(k) plan are subject to the normal distribution restrictions discussed in Chapter 6. However, the distribution of amounts which are attributable to an employee's elective deferral

---

[86] Reg. § 1.402(g)-1(e)(5)(ii).
[87] Reg. § 1.402(g)-1(e)(5)(iii).

[88] Reg. § 1.402(g)-1(e)(5)(iv).
[89] Code Sec. 402(g)(2)(D); Reg. § 1.402(g)-1(e)(10).

is further restricted. Such amounts may not be distributable earlier than:[90]

(1) severance from employment, death, or disability;

(2) termination of the plan without establishment or maintenance of another defined contribution plan, other than an ESOP (however, this rule applies only if the employee receives a lump-sum distribution because of the termination);

(3) in the case of a profit-sharing or stock bonus underlying plan, the attainment of age 59½; or

(4) in the case of a profit-sharing or stock bonus underlying plan, upon the hardship of the employee.

The Code specifically prohibits employee deferred amounts from being distributable by reason of the completion of a stated period of participation or the lapse of a fixed number of years.[91]

Severance from Employment. A severance from employment occurs when an employee ceases to be an employee of the employer maintaining the plan. Conversely, a severance from employment does not occur if, in connection with a change of employment, the employee's new employer maintains the plan with respect to the employee. For example, if there is a transfer of the plan assets and liabilities attributable to an employee's benefits from the former employer plan to a plan of the new employer (other than a rollover or elective transfer), then that employee is not considered to have severed employment with the former employer. Thus, distribution of the employee's elective deferrals are not allowed under these circumstances.[92]

Hardship Withdrawals. Plans are not required to permit hardship distributions, but instead are allowed to provide them if the plan complies with the hardship distribution requirements. Hardship withdrawals are not eligible for rollover and are subject to the normal withholding rules that apply to such distributions and to the 10 percent penalty tax imposed on early distributions.

In defining what constitutes a hardship, the regulations offer general guidelines. In order to be on account of hardship, a distribution must be necessary on account of immediate and heavy financial needs of the employee and is necessary to satisfy those financial needs. Generally, for example, the need to pay the funeral expenses of a family member would constitute an immediate and heavy financial need. On the other hand, the purchase of a television

---

[90] Code Sec. 401(k)(2)(B)(i).
[91] Code Sec. 401(k)(2)(B)(ii).

[92] Reg. § 1.401(k)-1(d)(2).

or a boat would generally not meet this standard. A distribution will be deemed to be made on account of immediate and heavy financial need of the employee if the distribution is on account of: medical expenses; purchase of a principal residence for the employee; payment of tuition and room and board for the next 12 months for postsecondary education for the employee, his or her spouse, children, or dependents; payments to prevent the eviction of the employee from, or the foreclosure on the mortgage of, his principal residence; and expenses for repair of damage to the employee's principal residence resulting from a casualty loss.[93] Of course, this list is not all-inclusive.

The amount of a distribution which may be made on account of hardship is limited to that which is required to meet the immediate financial need created by the hardship and not reasonably available from other resources of the employee. Regulations include assets of the employee's spouse and minor children; and expenses for repair of damage to the employee's principal residence resulting from a casualty loss. (other than assets held under an UGMA) as available resources.[94] This amount may be "grossed up" to pay any federal, state, or local income taxes or penalties reasonably anticipated to result from the distribution.[95]

A distribution generally may be treated as necessary to satisfy a "financial need" if the employer reasonably relies upon the employee's representation that the need cannot be relieved through reimbursement or compensation by insurance; by reasonable liquidation of the employee's assets, to the extent such liquidation would not itself cause an immediate and heavy financial need; by cessation of elective contributions or employee contributions to the plan; or by other distributions or nontaxable loans from plans maintained by the employer (or by any other employer), or by borrowing from commercial sources on reasonable commercial terms.[96]

The dollar amount of these distributions is generally limited to the amount of the employee's elective deferrals, reduced by any previous distributions on account of hardship. Earnings on the elective deferrals are not available for hardship distribution. In addition, employer matching contributions and nonelective employee contributions which are taken into account for the special nondiscrimination tests (discussed below) may not be distributed on account of hardship.[97]

---

[93] Reg. § 1.401(k)-1(d)(3)(iii)(B).

[94] Reg. § 1.401(k)-1(d)(3)(iv)(B).

[95] Reg. § 1.401(k)-1(d)(3)(iv)(A).

[96] Reg. § 1.401(k)-1(d)(3)(iv)(C).

[97] 86 Conference Committee Report, at II-389; Reg. § 1.401(k)-1(d)(3)(ii).

A distribution will be deemed to be necessary to satisfy an "immediate and heavy financial need" of an employee if all of the following requirements are satisfied:

(1) the distribution is not in excess of the amount of the immediate and heavy financial need of the employee;

(2) the employee has obtained all distributions, other than hardship distributions, and all nontaxable loans currently available under all plans maintained by the employer; and

(3) the plan, and all other plans maintained by the employer, provide that the employee's elective contributions and employee contributions will be suspended for at least six months after receipt of the hardship distribution.

As expected for a qualified plan, the hardship provisions must meet certain nondiscrimination standards. The determination of the existence of financial hardship and the amount required to be distributed to meet the need created by the hardship must be made in accordance with "nondiscriminatory and objective" standards set forth in the plan. However, no specific guidelines are provided in the regulations.

.05 Vesting Requirements

The accrued benefit derived from amounts contributed to the plan pursuant to an employee's elective deferral must be fully vested at all times.[98] Thus, the provisions for forfeitures of vested benefits under Code Sec. 411(b)(3) (see the discussion in Chapter 6) cannot apply to the elective deferrals.[99]

Accrued benefits from employer contributions and nonelective employee contributions are subject to the regular vesting rules of Code Sec. 411, with three exceptions. First, for the employer contributions or nonelective employee contributions to be "qualified," i.e., taken into account for the special nondiscrimination requirements (discussed below), they must be immediately and fully vested.[100] Second, if the employer contributions or nonelective employee contributions are not separately accounted for (as discussed in the next section), they must also be immediately and fully vested.[101] Third, any employer matching contributions made after 2001 are subject to the faster vesting schedules (i.e., the 3-year cliff schedule or the 2-to-6 year graded schedule).[102] Chapter 6 discusses these vesting schedules.

---

[98] Code Sec. 401(k)(2)(C).
[99] Reg. § 1.401(k)-1(c).
[100] Reg. § 1.401(k)-1(c)(1).

[101] Reg. § 1.401(k)-1(e)(3)(ii).
[102] Code Sec. 411(a)(12).

.06 Separate Accounting Required

Unless the plan provides a separate accounting of elective employee contributions, the entire balance of the employee's account must be subject to the distribution rules and full and immediate vesting provisions which were discussed above. Thus, all amounts held under the plan, including the accrued benefits derived from employer contributions, and contributions made for years when the 401(k) plan was not qualified, are deemed to be elective employee contributions.[103]

This separate accounting must allocate investment gains and losses on a reasonable pro rata basis, with adjustments for withdrawals and contributions. The separate accounting will not be acceptable unless gains, losses, withdrawals, forfeitures and other credits or charges are separately allocated to the accrued benefits subject to the distribution and vesting requirements and other benefits on a reasonable and consistent basis.[104]

.07 Service Requirements

As discussed in Chapter 6, a qualified plan cannot require more than one year of service as a condition for participation, except that a plan which provides 100-percent vesting after no more than two years may require a two-year service period for participation. However, this two-year exception is not available for 401(k) plans; thus, no plan which contains a qualified 401(k) plan may require more than one year of service for participation.[105]

.08 Nondiscrimination Requirements—Coverage Tests

A 401(k) plan must not discriminate in favor of highly compensated employees with respect to coverage (i.e., Code Sec. 410(b)(1) and Code Sec. 401(a)(26)) and benefits or contributions (i.e., Code Sec. 401(a)(4)). Specifically, a 401(k) plan must satisfy Code Sec. 410(b) tests and the special "actual deferred percentage" (ADP) tests.[106]

Code Sec. 410(b) requires that a plan must satisfy one of the coverage tests. The Code Sec. 410(b) coverage tests include a percentage test, a ratio test, and an average benefits test. Because many 401(k) plans would not meet the actual participation requirements due to the lack of contributions by many of the rank-and-file employees, a special provision is made. In determining whether a

---

[103] Reg. § 1.401(k)-1(e)(3).
[104] Reg. § 1.401(k)-1(e)(3); Reg. § 1.401(k)-1(e)(3)(i).
[105] Code Sec. 401(k)(2)(D).
[106] Code Sec. 401(k)(3)(A).

401(k) plan meets the coverage tests of Code Sec. 410(b)(1), all *eligible* employees (rather than *covered* employees) under the arrangement are treated as benefiting under the plan.[107] Thus, the 70-percent test of Code Sec. 410(b)(1)(A) will be met if at least 70 percent of "all employees" are *eligible* to participate in the 401(k) plan.

For purposes of the coverage requirements, the underlying plan and the 401(k) arrangement are, in general, tested on an aggregate basis. If the employer plan contains separate 401(k) arrangements (e.g., different groups of employees are eligible for separate 401(k) plans), all such arrangements are treated as a single plan.[108] Employer plans that have been either aggregated or disaggregated for purposes of applying the coverage tests (see ¶ 606) are treated in the same manner for purposes of testing the 401(k) arrangement.[109]

.09   Nondiscrimination Requirements—Actual Deferred Percentage (ADP) Tests

The second set of nondiscrimination tests, which relate to nondiscrimination as to benefits or contributions under Code Sec. 401(a)(4), are the actual deferred percentage (ADP) tests in Code Sec. 401(k)(3)(A)(ii). These tests require a specific comparison of the elective deferrals, expressed as a percentage of compensation, by highly compensated and nonhighly compensated employees.

This comparison is based on prior year data in determining the ADP for nonhighly compensated employees, while current year data is used for highly compensated employees. (Thus, the highly compensated employees know in advance the overall limit on their combined deferrals.) However, employers may elect to use current year data for determining the ADP for both highly compensated and nonhighly compensated employees for any plan year. (Note, however, that a single testing method must apply with respect to all 401(k) arrangements under a plan,[110] and that changing back to the prior-year testing method is subject to certain restrictions.)[111]

The plan may elect to ignore all nonhighly compensated employees who are eligible to participate in the plan before they have completed one year of service and reached age 21. To make this election, however, the plan must separately satisfy the minimum

---

[107] Code Sec. 401(a)(26)(C); Reg. § 1.401(k)-1(b)(1).

[108] Reg. § 1.401(k)-1(b)(4)(ii).

[109] Reg. § 1.401(k)-1(b)(4)(iii)(A).

[110] Reg. § 1.401(k)-1(b)(4)(iii)(B).

[111] Notice 98-1, 1998-1 CB 327; Reg. § 1.401(k)-2(c).

coverage rules taking into account only those employees who have not met the minimum age and service requirements. Instead of applying two separate ADP tests, a plan may adopt a single ADP test that compares the ADP of the highly compensated employees with the ADP of the nonhighly compensated employees who are eligible to participate and who have met the minimum ages and service requirements.[112]

Computing the ADP. The calculation of the actual deferred percentage is required for (1) the group of highly compensated employees (as defined in Code Sec. 414(q)), and (2) the group of nonhighly compensated employees. The ADP for each group is computed as the simple average of the employee's deferred percentages. Thus, the first step is to compute, for each employee who is eligible to make elective deferrals under the plan, the actual deferred ratio (ADR) of: (1) the amount of elective contributions actually paid over to the trust on his behalf for the plan year, to (2) the employee's compensation for the plan year. (However, any special "catch-up" contributions, and earnings attributable thereto, under Code Sec. 414(v) are disregarded when determining ADP ratios for a plan year.) Next, the simple average of these ratios is computed for the group of highly compensated employees and for the group of non-highly compensated employees.[113]

The period used to determine compensation may be either the plan year or the calendar year ending within the plan year.[114] As discussed earlier, any elective deferrals are counted as compensation. However, Code Sec. 414(s)(2) allows an employer to elect *not* to include as compensation any amount which is contributed by the employer pursuant to an elective deferral and which is not includible in the gross income of an employee under a cafeteria plan, 401(k) plan, tax-sheltered annuity, or SEP. Of course, these definitions do not affect the taxability of such amounts.

Finally, Code Sec. 401(a)(17) limits the amount of compensation which may be taken into account under any plan to $210,000 (in 2005). Thus, if an employee who has compensation of $300,000 elects to defer $8,000 in 2005, his ratio is 3.81 percent ($8,000/$210,000), rather than 2.67 percent ($8,000/$300,000).

> **Example:** Assume an employer maintains a profit-sharing plan with a 401(k) plan that allows employees to defer up to 10 percent of their total compensation, up to a maximum contribution of $14,000 for the 2005 plan year. Information for employees

---

[112] Code Sec. 401(k)(3)(F); Reg. § 1.401(k)-2(a)(1)(iii).

[113] Code Sec. 401(k)(3)(B); Reg. § 1.401(k)-2(a)(2).

[114] Code Sec. 401(k)(3)(D); Reg. § 1.401(k)-6.

¶ 704.09

A and B, who comprise the entire nonhighly compensated group, is as follows:

Employee	Compensation	Deferred Amount	ADR
A	$20,000	$2,000	10%
B	10,000	-0-	0%

Thus, the ADP for the group is 5%, the average of 10% and 0%, and not 6.67%, which is the total deferred amount divided by the total compensation.

If two or more plans which include 401(k) plans are considered as one plan for purposes of meeting the requirements of Code Secs. 401(a)(4) and 410(b), the 401(k) plans included in those plans are treated as one arrangement for purposes of computing the ADP. (However, any such permissively-aggregated plans must use the same testing method, current-year or prior-year, to compute the ADP.) Additionally, if a highly compensated employee is a participant under two or more 401(k) plans of the employer, for purposes of calculating the deferral percentage with respect to that employee, all such 401(k) plans are treated as one 401(k) plan.[115]

In calculating the ADR as above, the employer contribution made on behalf of any employee includes the amount made pursuant to the employee's deferral election. In addition, employer contributions and qualified nonelective employee contributions will be included, if they meet the safe-harbor requirements described later.[116] The period used to determine compensation may be either the plan year or the calendar year ending within the plan year.[117]

The ADP Tests. Once the ADP for each of the two groups of employees has been calculated, a comparison for discrimination is made. The standard method for this comparison is based on the prior-year ADP for nonhighly compensated employees, while the current year ADP is used for highly compensated employees. That is, the maximum permitted ADP for the highly compensated employee group for a tax year is determined by reference to the ADP for nonhighly compensated employees for the preceding year. In the case of the first plan year, the ADP for the nonhighly compensated employees is 3 percent, or at the employer's election, the ADP of the nonhighly compensated employees for the first plan year.[118]

---

[115] Code Sec. 401(k)(3)(A); Reg. § 1.401(k)-2(a)(3)(ii).
[116] Code Sec. 401(k)(3)(D); Reg. § 1.401(k)-2(a)(3)(i).
[117] Reg. § 1.401(k)-6.
[118] Code Sec. 401(k)(3), Notice 98-1, 1998-1 CB 327; Reg. § 1.401(k)-2(c)(2).

Alternatively, an employer may elect to use the current year ADP for nonhighly compensated employees. The plan document must indicate which method, current-year testing or prior-year testing, it will use. Generally, if the current-year method is elected, it may be revoked only with IRS permission. However, permission is automatic if the change is due to plan aggregation or certain employer changes.

One of the following two tests must be met in order for the 401(k) plan to be qualified:[119]

(1) the ADP for the group of highly compensated employees cannot be more than the ADP of the other eligible employees multiplied by 1.25; or

(2) the ADP for the group of highly compensated employees cannot be more than 2 percentage points over the ADP of the other eligible employees *and* the ADP for the group of highly compensated employees cannot be more than the ADP of the other eligible employees multiplied by two.

Thus, the maximum spreads between the ADPs for the highly compensated employees and the nonhighly compensated employees are as follows:

Prior Year ADP for the *Nonhighly Compensated*	*Current Year Maximum ADP* *for the Highly Compensated*
0-2%	2 times that rate
2-8%	2 percentage points more
above 8%	1.25 times that rate

The regulations under Code Sec. 401(k) provide several examples of how these rules operate.

Example: Company X has three employees, A, B, and C. Company X sponsors a profit-sharing plan that includes a 401(k) plan. Under the plan, each eligible employee may elect to receive none, all, or any part of a bonus (equal to 10 percent of salary) in cash; Company X contributes the remainder to the plan. Employee A is a highly-compensated employee; employees B and C are nonhighly-compensated employees. The plan uses the prior year testing method and defines compensation to include elective contributions and bonuses paid during the plan year. For the plan year, A, B, and C make the following elections:

---

[119] Code Sec. 401(k)(3)(A)(ii).

Employee	Salary	Elected Contribution to Plan	Cash Election	Total Compensation
A	$120,000	$8,000	$4,000	$132,000
B	60,000	3,000	3,000	66,000
C	40,000	1,600	2,400	44,000

The ratios of employer contributions to the trust on behalf of each eligible employee to the employee's compensation for the plan year (calculated separately for each employee) are:

Employee	Ratio of Contribution to Total Compensation	ADR
A	8,000/132,000	6.06%
B	3,000/66,000	4.55%
C	1,600/44,000	3.64%

The ADP for the nonhighly compensated group is 4.10% (the average of 4.55% and 3.64%, rounded to the nearest 0.01%). Thus, in the following plan year, A's maximum deferral is 6.10% of his compensation (i.e., 2 percentage points more than the ADP of the nonhighly compensated employees).

"Fail-Safe" Provisions in Regulations. One of the chief hazards of a 401(k) plan is the uncertainty of passing the ADP tests. That is, a plan could be qualified in one year and not qualified in the next, simply because the nonhighly compensated employees elect to defer a smaller percentage of their compensation. Although most of this uncertainty has been removed with the change to using the prior year ADP of the nonhighly compensated employees in the discrimination test, it still exists for employers who elect to use current-year ADP ratios for the nonhighly compensated employee group. The regulations provide employers more control with a "fail-safe" measure, under which the employer provides qualified nonelective contributions (QNECs) and/or qualified matching contributions (QMACs), in addition to elective contributions.

For example, an employer could provide a nonelective contribution on behalf of all employees equal to five percent of salary and an elective contribution of two percent of salary. Thus, even if all of the nonhighly compensated employees elected to receive the two percent in cash and all of the highly compensated employees elected to have it contributed to the plan, the CODA would still meet the ADP tests, since by design, it could never fail the test. However, in order to combine the nonelective or matching contribution with the elective contribution for purposes of the ADP test, the nonelective or matching portion must comply with the distribution restrictions and full and immediate vesting provisions for elective deferrals.[120] In addition, the QNECs and QMACs must meet the general nondiscrimination requirements and must be allocated to the employees' accounts within the plan year.[121]

> **Example:** Assume that Plan A is a qualified profit-sharing plan that contains a 401(k) plan. Plan A elects to compute the ADP for nonhighly compensated employees based on current year data and provides that elective contributions are not included in compensation (as provided under Code Sec. 414(s)(2)). Employer contributions on behalf of its nine employees are as follows:

(1) a qualified nonelective contribution (QNEC) of 2% of each employee's compensation, where such amounts satisfy the distribution restrictions of Code Sec. 401(k)(2)(B) and the full and immediate vesting requirements of Code Sec. 401(k)(2)(C), and

(2) up to 2% of each employee's compensation which the employee may elect to receive as a direct cash payment or to have that amount contributed to the plan.

For the plan year, employees 1 thru 9 received compensation and deferred contributions as indicated below:

Employee	Wages	2% Non-Elective Contribution	2% Elective Contribution Deferred	Total Compensation (excluding elective deferrals)	ADR
1	$98,000	$2,000	$2,000	$100,000	2.00%
2	78,400	1,600	1,600	80,000	2.00%
3	58,800	1,200	1,200	60,000	2.00%
4	39,600	800	400	40,400	0.99%
5	27,700	600	300	30,300	0.99%
6	20,000	400	-0-	20,400	-0-
7	20,000	400	-0-	20,400	-0-
8	10,000	200	-0-	10,200	-0-
9	5,000	100	-0-	5,100	-0-

Assume that employees 1 and 2 are the only highly compensated employees. In this case, the 2% elective portion (considered alone) does not satisfy the ADP tests. The ADP for the highly compensated group is 2.00% (the average ADR for employees 1 and 2), and the ADP for the nonhighly compensated group is 0.57%. However, since

---

[120] Reg. § 1.401(k)-6.   [121] Reg. § 1.401(k)-2(a)(6)(i) and (ii).

the two percent QNEC meets the distribution and vesting require-ments, it may be considered in computing the ADP for the groups. The ADP for the highly compensated group, when the nonelective contributions are considered, is 4.00%, and for the nonhighly com-pensated group, the ADP is 2.54%. Although the plan does not meet the 1.25 ADP test, it does meet the second test, since 4.00% is less than 5.08% (2.54% × 2.0) and less than 4.54% (2.54% + 2.0%).

The regulations provide that QNECs and qualified matching contributions (QMACs) may be made with respect to *any or all* employees, as long as they meet the nondiscrimination rules or Code Sec. 401(a)(4). In order to prevent employers from targeting disproportionately large QNECs on behalf of the lowest paid employ-ees (and, thus, skewing the ADP at a low cost), QNECs for any nonhighly compensated employee are not taken into account to the extent that they exceed the product of that employee's compensation and the greater of 5 percent or twice the plan's representative con-tribution rate. The representative contribution rate is defined as the lowest contribution rate (i.e., the sum of QNECs and QMACs divided by the employee's compensation) among a group of nonhighly com-pensated employees that is half of all the eligible nonhighly compensated employees under the plan (or, if greater, the lowest contribution rate among all eligible nonhighly compensated employ-ees under the plan who are employed on the last day of the year).[122]

In order to be taken into account in the calculation of the ADP or ACP for a year under the prior-year testing method, a QNEC or QMAC must be allocated as of a date within the year and must actually be paid to the trust by the end of the testing year. Thus, for example, if the prior-year testing method is used for the 2006 testing year, QNECs that are allocated to the accounts of nonhighly compensated employees for the 2005 plan year (i.e., the prior year) must be contributed to the plan by the end of the 2006 plan year in order to be treated as elective contributions for purposes of the ADP test for the 2006 testing year.[123]

Note, however, that an employer is not required to include nonelective or matching contributions in the ADP tests. For exam-ple, suppose an employer maintains a 401(k) plan in which the employer matches the elective contributions. If the ADP, with re-spect to the elective deferrals only, is seven percent for the highly compensated employees and five percent for the nonhighly compen-sated employees, the plan would satisfy the tests. However, if the

---

[122] Reg. § 1.401(k)-2(a)(6)(iv).

[123] Notice 98-1, 1998-1 CB 327; Reg. § 1.401(k)-2(a)(6)(i).

matching employer contributions were considered, the ADP test would not be satisfied, i.e., the 14 percent and 10 percent rates would not meet the ADP tests.

Safe Harbor Provisions in Code. The Code also provides a safe harbor provision, under which the plan may automatically satisfy the nondiscrimination rules. The safe harbor requires an employer contribution that is either a matching contribution or a nonelective contribution. Similar to the fail-safe provision described in the preceding section, employer matching and nonelective contributions used to satisfy the safe harbor rules must be nonforfeitable and subject to the distribution restrictions that apply to employee elective deferrals.[124]

Under the matching contribution safe harbor, the employer matches each nonhighly compensated employee's elective contribution in an amount equal to:[125]

(1) 100% of the employee's elective contribution, up to 3% of the employee's compensation; and

(2) 50% of the employee's elective contribution on the next 2% of the employee's compensation.

The match rate for highly compensated employees cannot be greater than the match rate for nonhighly compensated employees at any level of compensation. As an alternative, the matching safe harbor is deemed met if the employer's match rate does not increase as an employee's elective contribution increases and the match amount at least equals the amount that would be made under the matching levels above.

Under the nonelective contribution safe harbor, the plan must require the employer to make a contribution, on behalf of each eligible nonhighly compensated employee, of an amount equal to at least three percent of the employee's compensation, without regard to any employee contribution.[126]

Normally, a plan that intends to satisfy the safe harbor requirements for a plan year must, prior to the beginning of the plan year, contain language to that effect and must specify which safe harbor will be used. Nevertheless, a plan may be amended, not later than 30 days before plan year-end, to use the safe harbor rules for that plan year.[127] (Thus, if it appears that the plan will probably not meet the ADP and ACP tests, an employer can adopt the safe harbor

---

[124] Code Sec. 401(k)(12)(E).
[125] Code Sec. 401(k)(12)(B); Reg. § 1.401(k)-3(b).
[126] Code Sec. 401(k)(12)(C); Reg. § 1.401(k)-3(b).
[127] Notice 2000-3, Q&A 1, 2000-1 CB 413; Reg. § 1.401(k)-3(f).

3% employer nonelective contribution for the year as late as December 1 of that year.) Conversely, a plan may also be amended during the plan year to not use the matching contribution safe harbor, but will instead meet the ADP and ACP tests.[128] (Of course, any matching contributions already contributed or earned before the effective date of the amendments cannot be changed.) In the event matching contributions will not be provided, the plan must allow employees to make changes to their elective contributions.

Under either safe harbor contribution provision, each eligible employee must be given written or electronic (if it is likely that all employees can access the notice and obtain a free hard copy) notice of their rights and obligations under the plan within a reasonable period of time before the plan year, or for the year in which an employee becomes eligible, within a reasonable period before the employee becomes eligible. IRS Notices 98-52 and 2000-3 provide the content and timing requirements for the employee notifications.[129] In the event of plan amendments during a plan year to either use the safe harbor contributions or to reduce or eliminate matching contributions, supplemental notices must be given to all eligible employees.

Excess Contributions. If the elective deferrals (including the QNECs and QMACs treated as elective deferrals) of the highly compensated employees exceed the level permitted by the ADP tests, the plan must distribute the excess contributions (and income) to the highly compensated employees by the end of the following plan year in order to maintain the qualified status of the plan.[130] This distribution is not subject to the ten percent tax on early distributions under Code Sec. 72(t), nor is it subject to spousal consent or in violation of any qualified domestic relations order.

However, a ten-percent excise tax may be imposed on the employer for allowing these excess contributions. This excise tax will not be imposed if the excess contributions (plus income) are distributed within two-and-one-half months after the end of the plan year in which the excess was contributed (March 15 for calendar plans).[131] Thus, if the distribution is made within the two-and-one-half-month period, the plan will still be qualified, and no excise tax will be imposed. The contributions, and the income earned thereon, will be taxed in the employee's taxable year in which the excess contributions were made.[132]

---

[128] Notice 2000-3, Q&A 6, 2000-1 CB 413; Reg. § 1.401(k)-3(g).
[129] 1998-2 CB 634, § V.C.; and 2000-1 CB 413.
[130] Code Sec. 401(k)(8).
[131] Code Sec. 4979.
[132] Code Sec. 4979(f).

On the other hand, if the distribution was made after the two-and-one-half-month period but before the end of the next plan year, the penalty tax will be imposed. The plan will still be qualified, since the distribution was made prior to the end of the following plan year. However, the employee will be taxed on the distribution (the excess contributions plus the income) in the year of the distribution, rather than in the year of the deferral.

Recharacterizing Excess Contributions. Instead of distributing the excess contributions, the plan may allow the employee to recharacterize the excess contribution, and the earnings thereon, as distributed to the employee and then contributed by the employee to the plan as an after-tax contribution.[133] As with distributions, the excess contribution must be recharacterized no later than two-and-one-half months after the close of the plan year. In addition, the presumed distribution is not subject to any other provisions such as the early distribution penalty, spousal consent, or qualified domestic relations order restrictions. However, since after-tax employee contributions must also meet a similar ADP test under Code Sec. 401(m), the underlying plan could be in danger of disqualification.

Excess Contributions Treated as Catch-Up Contributions. A 401(k) plan that satisfies the ADP test through correction under Code Sec. 401(k)(8)(C) (discussed below) must retain any elective deferrals that are treated as catch-up contributions because they exceed the ADP limit. The plan is not treated as failing to satisfy the requirements imposed on excess contributions merely because the catch-up contributions are not distributed or recharacterized as employee contributions.[134]

> **Example:** Dave, age 58, is a highly compensated employee who is eligible to make elective deferrals under the Sand Co. 401(k) plan. During 2006, Dave elects to defer $15,000. The ADP test is run for the 2006 plan year, and it is determined that the Sand plan must take corrective action in order to pass the ADP test. After determining the excess contributions allocable to the highly compensated employees (discussed below), the maximum deferrals which may be retained by any highly compensated employee in the Sand plan is $9,500. Accordingly, $5,500 of Dave's elective deferrals exceed the applicable limit under the plan. The Sand plan treats $5,000 of Dave's elective deferrals as catch-up contributions (the maximum catch-up

---

[133] Code Sec. 401(k)(8)(A)(ii); Reg. § 1.401(k)-2(b)(3).

[134] Reg. §§ 1.414(v)-1(d)(2)(111) and (h), Example 4.

deferral for 2006) and must retain that amount. However, the remaining $500 in excess of the 2006 limit can not be treated as catch-up contributions and must either be distributed to Dave or recharacterized, as discussed in the preceding paragraphs.

Determining Excess Contributions. To determine the amount of excess contributions (including earnings thereon) and the employees to whom the excess contributions are to be distributed or recharacterized, the elective deferrals of highly compensated employees are reduced in the order of their actual deferral amounts (in terms of dollars, not percentages), beginning with the highly compensated employee who has deferred the largest amount during the plan year. This leveling process is repeated until the 401(k) plan satisfies the ADP test. The excess contributions must be recharacterized or distributed to those highly compensated employees for whom a reduction is made in order to satisfy the special ADP nondiscrimination tests.[135] Any income attributable to the excess contribution is determined in the same manner as under Code Sec. 401(m). The calculation of the income attributable to such excess contributions was discussed in Chapter 6.

Example: Plan A is a profit-sharing plan that contains a 401(k) plan. The ADP of the nonhighly compensated employees for the preceding plan year is 3%. For the current plan year, Plan A's two highly compensated employees have the following elective contributions:

Employee	Compensation	Contribution Elective	ADR
A	$ 85,000	$8,500	10%
B	158,333	$9,500	6%

As a result, the ADP for the two highly compensated employees under the plan (A and B) is 8%. Under the ADP test, the ADP of the two highly compensated employees may not exceed 5% (i.e., 2 percentage points more than the prior-year ADP of the nonhighly compensated employees under the plan. Therefore, the excess contributions for the highly compensated employees are determined as follows:

Step 1: The elective contributions of employee A (the highly compensated employee with the highest ADR) are reduced by

---

[135] Code Sec. 401(k)(8)(B) and (C); Reg. § 1.401(k)-2(b)(2).

$3,400 to reduce A's ADR to 6% ($5,100/$85,000), which is the ADR of employee B. Because the ADP of the highly compensated employees still exceeds 5%, further reductions in elective contributions are necessary. Thus, the elective contributions of A and B are each reduced by 1% of compensation ($850 and $1,583, respectively).

Step 2: The total excess contributions for the highly compensated employees that must be distributed equal $5,833, the total reductions in elective contributions determined in step 1 ($3,400 + $850 + $1,583).

Step 3: The plan distributes $1,000 in excess elective contributions to employee B (the highly compensated employee with the highest dollar amount of elective contributions) in order to reduce B's dollar amount of elective contributions to $8,500, which is the dollar amount of A's elective contributions.

Step 4: Because the total amount distributed ($1,000) is less than the total excess contributions ($5,833), step 3 must be repeated. Because the dollar amount of remaining elective contributions for both A and B are equal, the remaining $4,833 of excess contributions is then distributed equally to A and B in the amount of $2,416.50 each.

Note in the above example, employee A must receive a total distribution of $2,416.50 of excess contributions plus allocated income, and employee B must receive a total distribution of $3,416.50 of excess contributions plus allocated income. This is true even though the ADR of employee A exceeded the ADR of employee B.[136]

.10 SIMPLE 401(k) Plans

Savings Incentive Match Plans for Employees (SIMPLE plans) may be either in the form of an IRA arrangement (discussed in Chapter 9) or adopted as part of a 401(k) plan (discussed below). As its name implies, a SIMPLE arrangement simplifies certain rules, the most significant of which concerns the nondiscrimination requirements (ADP tests) applicable to traditional CODAs. A SIMPLE 401(k) plan that allows only contributions required to satisfy the requirements of Section 401(k)(11), discussed below, is exempt from the top-heavy provisions.[137]

Qualification Requirements. SIMPLE 401(k) plans are available only to employers that: (1) employed 100 or fewer employees who earned $5,000 or more during the preceding year; and (2) do not maintain another qualified plan covering the employees who are

---

[136] Reg. § 1.401(k)-2(b)(C).   [137] Code Sec. 401(k)(11)(D)(ii).

eligible to participate in the SIMPLE 401(k) plan. An employer who establishes and maintains a SIMPLE plan for one or more years, and who fails to be eligible in a subsequent year (e.g., has more than 100 employees), may continue to maintain a SIMPLE plan for the two years following the last year that it met the eligibility requirements.[138]

The following special rules apply to SIMPLE 401(k) plans. First, the plan is not subject to the top-heavy rules.[139] Second, eligibility for participation applies to all employees who received at least $5,000 in compensation from the employer during any 2 preceding calendar years and who are reasonably expected to receive at least $5,000 in compensation during the calendar year (although union employees, air pilots, and nonresident aliens may be excluded).[140] Third, the plan does not have to satisfy the special ADP and ACP tests otherwise applicable to plans containing CODAs and matching contributions. Instead, those special tests are deemed met if:[141]

(1) each eligible employee may elect to make salary reduction contributions for a year of up to $10,000 (in 2005);

(2) the employer makes a matching contribution equal to the employee's salary reduction contribution, limited to three percent of the employee's compensation for the year, or alternatively, makes a nonelective contribution for all eligible employees equal to two percent of the employee's compensation for the year;

(3) no other contributions are made under the SIMPLE 401(k) arrangement, nor are any contributions or benefit accruals under any other qualified plan of the employer covering the employees eligible to participate in the SIMPLE 401(k); and

(4) all amounts contributed under the SIMPLE 401(k) provisions are nonforfeitable (i.e., fully vested) at all times.

(Note that if the employer elects to make nonelective contributions equal to 2 percent of compensation, it must notify its employees of the election within a reasonable period of time before the 60th day before the beginning of the year.)

The plan year of a plan containing the SIMPLE 401(k) provisions must be the calendar year. Thus, existing 401(k) plans must convert the plan to a calendar year in order to adopt the SIMPLE provisions. The IRS has issued a model amendment for incorporating the SIMPLE provisions in plans that contain a CODA or matching contribution arrangement.[142]

---

[138] Code Sec. 401(k)(11)(D)(i).
[139] Code Sec. 401(k)(11)(D)(ii).
[140] Code Sec. 408(p)(4).

[141] Code Sec. 401(k)(11)(A).

[142] Rev. Proc. 97-9, 1997-1 CB 624

Limit on Elective Deferrals. As discussed in the preceding section, employee elective deferrals are subject to an annual dollar limit. For 2005, the limit is $10,000, which is subject to COLAs beginning in 2006.[143]

The special catch-up provisions that apply to individuals who are at least age 50 by year-end also apply to SIMPLE 401(k) plans. However, the maximum amount of additional elective deferral under SIMPLE 401(k) plans is smaller than that allowed under regular 401(k) plans. The limit for 2005 is $2,000, which is scheduled under EGTRRA '01 provisions to increase to $2,500 for 2006. Beginning in 2007, the $2,500 amount is subject to COLAs.[144]

Annual Election and Termination Provisions. The plan must allow each eligible employee to make or modify an elective deferral during the 60-day period immediately preceding each January 1. For the year in which an employee becomes eligible to participate in the plan, the election period is a 60-day period that includes either the date the employee becomes eligible or the day before. The employer must notify each eligible employee of the employee's rights to make the election within a reasonable time period before the applicable election period.[145]

The plan must allow a participant in a SIMPLE 401(k) plan to terminate an elective deferral at any time during the year. If an employee terminates an elective deferral, the plan may refuse to allow the employee to resume participation until the beginning of the next calendar year.[146]

Comparison of SIMPLE 401(k) Arrangements with Traditional CODAs. Several factors should be considered in deciding whether to adopt a traditional 401(k) plan or a SIMPLE plan. Besides the obvious limited availability to only smaller employers, are the following.

Annual employer contributions are required under the SIMPLE plan, whether the employer matches employee deferrals (up to three percent of compensation) or makes the two percent nonelective contribution. Annual employer contributions are discretionary under a traditional 401(k) plan, except for years in which the plan is top heavy or years in which one of the safe harbor provisions is used to ensure the ADP test is met.

Employee coverage requirements differ between the plans. SIMPLE plans have potentially broader coverage, because every

---

[143] Code Sec. 401(p)(2)(E).

[144] Code Sec. 414(v)(2)(B)(ii).

[145] Code Sec. 401(k)(11)(B)(iii); Reg. § 1.401(k)-4(d)(3).

[146] Reg. § 1.401(k)-4(d)(2)(ii).

employee who earns over $5,000 may make an elective deferral that must be matched (although the actual matching contribution is based entirely on the level of actual participation). If the alternative two percent nonelective contribution is made, an employer contribution is required for all eligible employees. The traditional 401(k) plan requires 70 percent coverage for eligibility, not participation.

The annual limit on elective deferrals under a traditional 401(k) plan is higher than the SIMPLE 401(k) plan ($14,000 v. $10,000 in 2005). However, level of deferral for highly compensated employees under a traditional plan is directly limited by the ADP for the nonhighly compensated employees. No such limit applies to SIMPLE plans.

All employer-matching or nonelective contributions under a SIMPLE plan are immediately vested. Employer contributions under a traditional plan are subject to the normal vesting rules, unless the employer contributions are made in accordance with the fail-safe provisions (QNCs). In either case, employee elective deferrals are nonforfeitable at all times.

Finally, as is usually the case when simpler provisions are introduced, funding flexibility is lost. Employers who adopt a SIMPLE 401(k) plan cannot make contributions other than those allowed under the SIMPLE provisions. Moreover, the employer cannot maintain any other qualified plan under which additional contributions or benefit accruals may be made. In addition, an employer who adopts a SIMPLE 401(k) plan must determine in advance of each calendar year whether it will match employee contributions or make the nonelective contribution (due to the 60-day notice requirement).

.11   Roth 401(k) Plans

Beginning in 2006, 401(k) plans can incorporate a qualified Roth contribution program. Under such a plan, participants can elect to have all or a portion of their elective deferrals treated as Roth contributions. Unlike regular 401(k) elective deferrals, Roth contributions are included in the participant's current income; however, qualified distributions from a designated Roth account are not included in income.[147]

Plan Requirements. Under a qualified Roth contribution program, participants are allowed to make designated Roth contributions in lieu of all or part of elective deferrals that they are

---

[147] Code Sec. 402A.

otherwise allowed to make under the 401(k) plan. These designated Roth contributions are defined in recently issued proposed regulations as elective contributions under a qualified 401(k) arrangement that are: (1) designated irrevocably by the employee at the time of the cash or deferred election as designated Roth contributions; (2) treated by the employer as includible in the employee's income at the time the employee would have received the contribution amounts in cash if the employee had not made the cash or deferred election (i.e., by treating the contributions as wages subject to withholding); and (3) maintained by the plan in a separate account.[148]

These Roth elective deferrals are subject to the same immediate vesting requirements and distribution restrictions normally imposed on regular 401(k) elective deferrals discussed earlier in ¶ 704.04 and ¶ 704.05.[149]

Because qualified distributions are not included in an employee's income, the plan must establish and maintain a separate "designated Roth account" for designated Roth contributions and attributed earnings for each employee. Failure to maintain this separate account and recordkeeping will disqualify the program.[150]

Annual Contribution Limits. Since designated Roth contributions are a part of a participant's eligible 401(k) elective deferrals, they are subject to the same contribution limits. Accordingly, Roth contributions are subject to the annual limit on elective deferrals, reduced by the amount of other elective deferrals under the 401(k) plan, as well as the ADP limits.[151]

If designated Roth contributions exceed these limits, the excess (and attributable earnings) must be distributed by April 15 of the following year. Excess deferrals distributed by this date are not included in the participant's income; however, the earnings attributable to the excess deferral are included in the participant's income upon distribution. Any excess contributions and earnings that are not distributed by the April 15 deadline are included in the participant's income for the year actually distributed.[152] (Note, then, that the excess is double-taxed—first, in the year of deferral (as it does not reduce the participant's income), and second, in the year of the corrective distribution.) Under proposed regulations, a highly-compensated employee who has made elective contributions for a year that includes both pre-tax elective contributions and designated Roth contributions can elect whether excess contributions are

---

[148] Prop. Reg. § 1.401(k)-1(f)(1).

[149] Code Sec. 402A(a)(1); Prop. Reg. § 1.401(k)-1(f)(3).

[150] Code Sec. 402A(b)(2); Prop. Reg. § 1.401(k)-1(f)(2).

[151] Code Sec. 402A(c)(2).

[152] Code Sec. 402A(d)(3).

¶704.11

to be attributed to pre-tax elective contributions or designated Roth contributions.[153]

Distributions. Qualified distributions from a designated Roth account are not included in a participant's income. A qualified distribution from a designated Roth account is basically the same as one from a Roth IRA account. Thus, the distribution must be made after a five-year "nonexclusion" period and:

(1) made on or after the date on which the participant attains age 59½;

(2) made to a beneficiary (or to the participant's estate) on or after the death of the participant; or

(3) attributable to the participant's being disabled.[154]

The five-year nonexclusion period is the five-year period beginning with the earlier of (1) the first tax year in which the participant makes a designated Roth contribution to any designated Roth account under the employer plan, or (2) if the participant has made a rollover contribution to the designated Roth account from another plan, the first year in which the participant made a designated Roth contribution to that previous plan.[155]

Qualified distributions from a designated Roth account may be rolled over to either (1) another designated Roth account for the participant (if the new plan allows for rollovers), or (2) the participant's Roth IRA. Such rollovers are not taken into account for purposes of the annual limits on elective deferrals.[156]

---

[153] Prop. Reg. § 1.401(k)-2(b)(2)(vi)(C).
[154] Code Secs. 402A(d)(1) and (2).

[155] Code Sec. 402A(d)(2)(B).
[156] Code Sec. 402A(c)(3).

Chapter 8

Employer Deduction and Funding Rules

¶801 Introduction

This chapter addresses two distinct aspects concerning employer contributions to qualified plans. First, Code Sec. 404 establishes upper limits with respect to the amount that an employer may deduct for contributions paid to the trust during any taxable year. These ceilings prevent an employer from overfunding a qualified plan in high tax years to obtain a more favorable tax savings. (However, excess contributions may be carried forward to subsequent years.) Second, Code Sec. 412 sets minimum limits on employer contributions to pension plans through its minimum funding standards. These funding requirements were established by ERISA to ensure that benefits promised to employees would be properly funded.

¶802 General Rules for Deductions

Employer contributions to any plan that defers compensation, qualified or nonqualified, are deductible only under the Code Sec. 404 rules.[1] However, in order to be deductible under Code Sec. 404, the contributions must first meet all of the rules regarding business deductions (e.g., the rules under Code Secs. 162 and 212 regarding ordinary and necessary business expenses) before being subjected to the deduction limitations described in Code Sec. 404. Under the uniform capitalization rules, all pension costs, including past service costs, associated with inventory items or capital construction projects must be capitalized instead of currently deducted under the rules which follow.

---

[1] Code Sec. 404(a).

Employer payments to a defined contribution plan that are restorative in nature (e.g., made to restore losses to the plan due to an action that creates a reasonable risk of liability for breach of fiduciary duty) are not considered to be employer contributions. Therefore, any such restorative payments are not subject to the provisions and limitations affecting employer contributions.[2]

.01   Reasonableness of Compensation

In no case is a deduction allowable under Code Sec. 404(a) for any contribution for the benefit of an employee in excess of reasonable compensation. In determining reasonableness, all deductions allowed for compensation for the employee's services (e.g., current pay, deferred compensation, fringe benefits) are considered.[3] Of course, what constitutes "reasonable compensation" depends on the facts in the particular case. Among the elements to be considered in determining this are the personal services actually rendered in prior years as well as the current year, and all compensation and contributions paid to or for the employee in prior years as well as in the current year.

Therefore, a contribution that is in the nature of additional compensation for services performed in earlier years may be deductible, even if the total of the contributions and other compensation for the current year would be in excess of reasonable compensation for services performed in the current year, provided that the total plus all compensation and contributions paid to or for the employee in earlier years represents a reasonable allowance for all services rendered by the employee by the end of the current year.[4] As a result, many (if not most) pension plans, upon adoption, grant credit to employees for prior service.

Because any compensation disallowed as unreasonable would not be considered an ordinary or necessary business expense (under Code Sec. 162 or 212), any unreasonable contribution paid to a plan would also be disallowed. Since the disallowed contribution would not constitute an ordinary and necessary business expense in the year paid or any subsequent year, no carryover of the excess contribution for deduction in future years would be allowed. (See the discussion on limitations in this chapter.)

In the event that an employee's compensation is deemed unreasonable, the deduction for the contribution to the plan must be adjusted accordingly. Unless some adjustment is made, such as reallocation of the unreasonable amount to the other participants, the plan could become discriminatory, due to the possibility that contributions or

---

[2] Rev. Rul. 2002-45, IRB 2002-29 116.
[3] Reg. § 1.404(a)-1(b).

[4] Reg. § 1.404(a)-1(b).

benefits in relation to compensation would be greater for the highly compensated employees than for the rank and file employees. Rev. Rul. 67-341[5] demonstrates two methods under which the unreasonable amounts may be reallocated.

.02 Forms of Contributions

Property. Contributions to a plan on behalf of an employee may be paid in cash or other forms of property. If a contribution is made to a plan in property other than cash, the employer is entitled to a deduction based on the fair market value of the property, determined as of the date of the contribution (rather than the date on which the liability was accrued by the employer).[6] If the contribution is made with appreciated property (i.e., the employer's basis in the property is less than the fair market value), gain is recognized by the employer on the excess.[7] On the other hand, if the employer's basis is greater than the fair market value of the property, no loss is recognized by the employer, because Code Sec. 267 prohibits the deduction for losses on sales or exchanges between related taxpayers.[8]

Generally, the sale or exchange of property between a plan and the sponsoring employer is a prohibited transaction and is subject to an excise tax (see Chapter 12). Any transfer of encumbered property is considered to be a sale, and is thus prohibited.[9] The Supreme Court ruled that even a contribution of unencumbered property would constitute a sale or exchange if it was made to satisfy the minimum funding obligation of a defined benefit plan.[10] Thus, to avoid the prohibited transaction penalties, a contribution of property should be made only if it is unencumbered and only to a plan with a discretionary contribution formula, such as a profit-sharing plan.

Employer Stock. If a corporate employer contributes its own stock to the plan, for example under a stock bonus plan, the above rules regarding the amount of the deduction also apply. That is, the employer is entitled to a deduction for the fair market value of the stock as of the date of the contribution. However, because of Code Sec. 1032, no gain or loss is recognized by the corporation on sales or exchanges with respect to its own stock.

Promissory Notes. A promissory note from the employer is not considered a "payment" under Code Sec. 404(a). Furthermore, it is considered to be a prohibited transaction under Code Sec. 4975, subject to the penalties thereunder.[11]

---

[5] 1967-2 CB 156.
[6] Rev. Rul. 73-583, 1973-2 CB 146.
[7] Rev. Rul. 69-181, 1969-1 CB 196.
[8] Rev. Rul. 61-163, 1961-2 CB 58.

[9] Code Sec. 4975(f)(3).
[10] *Keystone Consolidated Industries, Inc.*, SCt, 93-1 USTC ¶ 50,298, 508 US 152; 113 SCt 2006.
[11] Rev. Rul. 80-140, 1980-1 CB 89.

.03 Timing of Deductions

A contribution to a qualified plan is generally deductible in the employer taxable year when paid. However, Code Secs. 404(a)(6) (qualified plans), 404(h)(1)(B) (SEPs), and 404(m)(2)(B) (SIMPLE retirement accounts) provide that an employer is deemed to have made a contribution to the plan as of its year-end, if the contribution is made on account of that preceding year and is made by the due date of its tax return including extensions. (An employer must actually obtain an extension for filing its tax return to deduct a contribution paid within the extension period.) In effect, a contribution made within this grace period is deductible for the prior year, if the contribution would have been deductible if it had been made by the last day of that year. Thus, for example, employer matching contributions made within the grace period would not be deductible by the employer for the prior tax year, if they are attributable to compensation earned by plan participants after the end of that preceding tax year.[12]

In order to be made on account of the preceding year, the payment must be treated by the plan in the same manner that the plan would have treated a payment actually received on the last day of the preceding employer tax year and either:

(1) the employer must designate the payment in writing to the plan administrator or trustee as a payment on account of the employer's preceding taxable year; or

(2) the employer must claim the payment as a deduction on its tax return for the preceding taxable year.

The above rules apply to both cash or accrual method taxpayers.[13]

.04 Deductions for Contributions to Nonqualified Plans

If a deferred compensation plan does not meet the rules of Code Sec. 401(a) (i.e., it is a nonqualified plan), the deduction for employer contributions is governed by Code Sec. 404(a)(5). Under this provision, an employer is entitled to a deduction for contributions only in the year such contributions are includible in the income of the employee, and *only if* separate accounts are maintained for participants under the plan. Thus, Code Sec. 404(a)(5) provides identical treatment with regard to employer contributions as that under Code Sec. 83(h), which concerns property transferred in connection with performance of services. That is, the employee recognizes income in the year in which the amounts become transferable or no longer subject to a substantial risk of forfeiture (i.e., he vests), and the employer deducts the contribution in the same year. Chapters 14 and 15 discuss these

---

[12] Rev. Rul. 90-105, 1990-2 CB 69; Rev. Rul. 2002-46, IRB 2002-29 117.

[13] Rev. Rul. 76-28, 1976-1 CB 106.

nonqualified deferred compensation plans in detail, including the provisions for employer deductions.

If a qualified plan loses its qualified status for a given year, the deductions for employer contributions must follow the appropriate rules for the year in which the contributions were made. That is, if the status of the trust under the plan changes from qualified to nonqualified (or vice versa) in a succeeding year, the previously made contributions do not change from qualified to nonqualified (or vice versa). Thus, a tracking of each individual's vesting must be made to determine the amount of deductions for the nonexempt years, while a current deduction (subject to the limitations discussed below) is allowed for contributions in exempt years.

¶803   Qualified Plans—Limitations on Deductions

Although Code Sec. 404 determines the rules regarding deductions for contributions to all plans of deferred compensation, it imposes ceilings only on qualified plans. These limits are grouped into four basic categories: (1) pension plans, (2) profit-sharing and stock bonus plans, (3) ESOPs, and (4) SEPs. It should be emphasized that the limitations in Code Sec. 404 apply to the amount of employer *deduction,* and not to the maximum contribution or benefit the plan may provide on behalf of a participant, as described in Code Sec. 415. That is, Code Sec. 415 sets limits on the amounts of contributions and benefits that an employer may provide for an employee, whereas Code Sec. 404 establishes ceilings on the annual deductions for those contributions.

These limits apply to the employer contributions to the plan. Administrative expenses, such as actuarial fees, are not subject to those limits, but rather only to the ordinary and necessary standards. Thus, the total deduction with respect to a qualified plan may exceed the applicable limitations if the employer pays the administrative expenses directly.

.01   Pension Plans

Defined benefit and target benefit plans fall under the ceilings placed on pension plans. The ceiling on the employer deduction for its contribution to the trust under a plan is described in Code Sec. 404(a)(1)(A) as any one (i.e., the one which would provide the greatest deduction for a particular year would be used) of the following:

(1) the amount necessary to satisfy the *minimum funding standard of Code Sec. 412* (discussed later in this chapter) for plan years ending within or with the taxable year (or any prior plan year), if it is greater than the level cost method or the normal cost method (described below);

(2) the amount determined under the *level cost method,* which is the amount that is necessary to provide all employees under the plan with the remaining unfunded cost of their past and current service credits distributed as a level amount, or as a level percentage of compensation, over the remaining future service of each employee. (However, if the remaining unfunded cost for any three individuals exceeds 50 percent of the total unfunded cost, the amount for these individuals must be spread out over at least five years.); or

(3) the amount determined under the *normal cost plus ten-year amortization method,* which is the amount equal to the normal cost of the plan (i.e., that portion of the total cost of the plan which is assigned by the actuarial cost method of the current year), plus an amount that is necessary to amortize any unfunded costs attributable to past service credits or other supplementary pension or annuity credits in equal annual payments (until fully amortized) over ten years.

Notwithstanding the above three limitations, the maximum amount deductible for a year is limited to the full funding limitation of Code Sec. 412, discussed later in ¶ 804.04.

A higher deduction limitation applies to any defined benefit plan that has an unfunded current liability (as determined under Code Sec. 412(1), discussed later in ¶ 804.06). For those plans, the employers may deduct up to 100 percent of the plan's unfunded current liability. This unfunded current liability is determined without regard to any reduction by the credit balance in the funding standard account. However, for plans with 100 or fewer participants for the plan year, the unfunded current liability does not include the liability attributable to benefit increases for "highly compensated employees" that result from plan amendments made (or effective) within the last two years.[14] (For purposes of determining the number of participants in a plan, all defined benefit plans of an employer, or any member of its controlled group, are treated as a single plan, but only employees of such member or employer are taken into account.[15])

In the event a plan is terminated, a special deduction limit applies. For the plan year in which the plan terminates, the deduction limit is up to 100 percent of the amount necessary to make the plan sufficient to meet "benefit liabilities," within the meaning of ERISA sec. 4041(d). (These liabilities relate to plans covered by the PBGC termination insurance program.)[16]

Contributions in Excess of Deduction Limits. If an employer has made contributions to the plan which exceed the appropriate

---

[14] Code Sec. 404(a)(1)(D)(ii).
[15] Code Sec. 404(a)(1)(D)(iii).
[16] Code Sec. 404(a)(1)(D)(iv).

deductible limitation, the excess amount may be carried forward indefinitely, until it can be deducted within the limits.[17] Thus, for example, if an employer contributed $50,000 to a plan in which a $40,000 deduction limit applied, a deduction of $10,000 is allowed for the following year, even if no contributions are made (assuming, of course, that the deduction would be within the appropriate ceiling for the following year).

However, to discourage such excess contributions, Code Sec. 4972 imposes an excise tax on the employer equal to ten percent of the nondeductible contribution. Nondeductible contributions are defined as the sum of (1) the excess of the amount contributed for the taxable year by the employer over the amount allowable as a deduction for that year, and (2) the amount of excess contributions for the preceding year, reduced by the amounts returned to the employer during the year and by the portion of the prior excess contribution that is deductible by the employer for the year.[18]

This penalty does not apply to nondeductible contributions to terminating single-employer defined benefits plans with 100 or fewer participants to the extent that the contributions do not exceed the plan's unfunded current liability (discussed later in this chapter).[19] Employers may elect not to take into account contributions to a defined benefit pension plan, except to the extent that they exceed the accrued liability full funding limit of Code Sec. 412. However, if an employer makes this election, it cannot also benefit from the exception for terminating plans.[20]

If an excess contribution is made for a taxable year, the excise tax will apply for that year and for each succeeding year until the excess is eliminated. Recall from Chapter 6 that an employer can recover such an excess contribution from a continuing plan only if the excess was the result of a mistake of fact. Thus, in many cases, the excess contribution can be corrected only by an undercontribution in the following year. This means that the penalty could not be avoided for the year of overpayment.

Example: XYZ Company maintains a qualified defined benefit pension plan. Its contributions and ceilings on deductions (as determined under the appropriate provision in Code Sec. 404(a)(1)) for 2005-2008 are as follows:

---

[17] Code Sec. 404(a)(1)(E).
[18] Code Sec. 4972(c).

[19] Code Sec. 4972(c)(6).
[20] Code Sec. 4972(c)(7).

Code Sec. 404

Year	Contribution	Applicable Limit	Deduction	Excess Contribution
2005	$100,000	$90,000	$90,000	$10,000
2006	85,000	90,000	90,000	5,000
2007	80,000	90,000	85,000	-0-
2008	80,000	90,000	80,000	-0-

Since XYZ made a contribution of $10,000 in excess of the Section 404 ceiling in 2005, it must pay a penalty tax of 10% on the excess contribution. For 2006, XYZ contributed $85,000, but was able to deduct the ceiling of $90,000 since there was a $10,000 excess contribution carryover from 2005. However, since the entire carryover was not used up, the 10% penalty tax of Code Sec. 4972 will apply again in 2005 on the $5,000 remaining excess contribution carryover. For 2006, a deduction of $85,000 is allowed, which consists of the $80,000 contribution plus the $5,000 contribution carryover. Since this uses up the balance of the excess contribution, no penalty tax applies to 2006. Finally, in 2007, XYZ contributes and deducts its $80,000 contribution.

If the pension plan terminates or loses its qualified status, any excess contribution carry forward deduction in future years is limited to an amount that is computed in a manner similar to the normal cost plus ten-year amortization method.[21]

Penalty for Overstatement of Deduction for Pension Liabilities. In addition to the penalty tax on nondeductible (excess) contributions, a penalty for the "substantial" overstatement of pension liabilities is imposed under Code Sec. 6662(f). A substantial overstatement of pension liabilities exists if the actuarial determination of the liabilities considered in computing the deduction for contributions to a pension trust or to employees' annuities is 200 percent or more of the amount that is determined to be the correct amount of the liability.[22] This may occur, for example, when the valuation of liabilities is based on unreasonable actuarial assumptions or methods.

Code Sec. 6662 imposes a flat 20-percent penalty tax only if an underpayment of income tax is caused by a substantial (200 percent or more) overstatement of pension liabilities.

Example: Suppose A Company's actuary determined the pension liabilities to be $100,000, but the correct amount is later determined by the IRS to be $45,000. As a result of this overstatement, A Company's income taxes are increased from

---

[21] Reg. § 1.404(a)-7(b).   [22] Code Sec. 6662(f)(1).

$30,000 to $40,000. Since the liability claimed ($100,000) is 222% of the correct amount ($45,000), a penalty is assessed at 20% of the $10,000 income tax underpayment, or $2,000.

The penalty is doubled to 40 percent to the extent that a portion of the underpayment is attributable to a gross valuation misstatement. A gross misstatement exists if the actuarial determination is 400 percent or more of the correct amount.[23]

The penalty does not apply if the income tax underpayment is less than $1,000.[24] Additionally, no penalty will be imposed with respect to any portion of an underpayment if it is shown that there was a reasonable cause for such underpayment and that the employer acted in good faith.[25] However, an employer's reliance on an enrolled actuary or other professional as to the proper amount of the deduction will not constitute a reasonable basis or good faith claim by the employer.[26]

Target Benefit Plans. Target benefit plans are treated the same as defined benefit pension plans, i.e., the same ceilings apply. For a target benefit plan, the level cost ceiling basically defines the manner in which contributions are made, i.e., it is the level amount which would provide the targeted benefit.

.02 Profit-Sharing, Money Purchase, and Stock Bonus Plans

An employer may deduct contributions paid into a profit-sharing, money purchase or stock bonus trust up to 25 percent of the compensation paid to employees who are covered under the plan.[27] Note that this limit is less than the limitation under Code Sec. 415(c), under which 100 percent of compensation is the maximum contribution which may be made on behalf of an employee during a year.

The 25-percent limitation is based on the compensation paid or accrued during the employer's taxable year to all employees who are covered under the plan. Compensation is generally defined as the amount paid by an employer for services performed,[28] but also includes: certain imputed disability pay; elective deferrals under a 401(k) plan, SIMPLE, SEP, or 403(b) annuity; and elective contributions or deferrals under a cafeteria plan, qualified transportation fringe benefit plan, or Sec. 457 deferred compensation plan.[29] In addition, Code Sec. 404(l) places a limitation of $210,000 (in 2005) in compensation which may be considered for qualified plans.

In determining the amount of an employer's deduction for contributions to a qualified plan, employee elective deferrals are not

---

[23] Code Sec. 6662(h).
[24] Code Sec. 6662(f)(2).
[25] Code Sec. 6664(c).
[26] Notice 89-47, 1989-1 CB 687.

[27] Code Sec. 404(a)(3)(A).
[28] Code Sec. 414(s)(1).
[29] Code Sec. 404(a)(12).

treated as employer contributions, and are, therefore, not subject to the 25-percent-of-compensation deduction limit. These employee elective deferrals include employee salary reduction contributions to 401(k) plans, SARSEPs, 403(b) annuities, and SIMPLE plans. (Prior to 2002, employee elective deferrals were treated as employer contributions for purposes of the deduction limit. Thus, this change, along with redefining compensation to include elective deferrals, considerably loosened the restrictions on employee and employer contributions caused by the deduction limitations.)[30]

In the case of a self-employed individual, compensation is defined in Code Sec. 404(a)(8) as his "earned income," as defined in Code Sec. 401(c). This definition is the same as that discussed in Chapter 7 under the special rules for Keogh plans. In general, earned income of a self-employed individual includes the net earnings derived from a trade or business and a partner's distributive share of partnership income but is reduced by the deduction under Code Sec. 164(f) for one-half of self-employment taxes. In either case, the personal services of the individual must be a material income-producing factor. Earned income does not include the amount excludable from gross income as the result of a contribution and deduction to a qualified plan. That is, the earned income is reduced by the amount of the deduction allowed under Code Sec. 404. Thus, the limitation for contributions to a profit-sharing plan or money purchase plan on behalf of a self-employed individual is 25 percent of earned income *minus* the deduction. This reduction results in a limitation of 20 percent of earned income before the deduction.

Contributions in Excess of Deduction Limits. Similar to the provisions under pension and annuity plans, any amounts contributed in excess of the 25-percent limitation (referred to as the "primary limitation") may be carried forward and deducted in future years in which contributions are less than 25 percent of compensation.[31]

Example: C Company maintains a qualified profit-sharing plan. For the years 2006 through 2008, the information regarding the compensation of C's employees in the plan and C's contributions to the plan are as follows:

Year	Compensation	Contribution	Deduction	Contribution Carryover
2006	$100,000	$30,000	$25,000	$5,000
2007	120,000	32,000	30,000	7,000
2008	140,000	20,000	27,000	-0-

In 2006, the ceiling on C's deduction is $25,000 (25% × $100,000). Thus, the $5,000 excess contribution is carried

---

[30] Code Sec. 404(n).

[31] Code Sec. 404(a)(3)(A)(ii).

over to 2007. In 2007, C again contributed an amount in excess of the 25-percent limitation of $30,000 (25% × $120,000). This increases C's excess contribution carryover to $7,000. In 2008, when C contributed $20,000, it was able to deduct the entire contribution plus the $7,000 carryover, since the total amount available for deduction, $27,000, was less than the 2008 deduction limitation of $35,000 (25% × $140,000).

As with pension plans, however, any excess contributions (including carryovers) which are not returned to or deducted by the employer as of the end of the year are subject to the ten-percent excise tax under Code Sec. 4972. In the above example, C Company would incur penalty taxes of $500 in 2006 and $700 in 2007, based on the year-end balance of its excess (nondeductible) contribution carryovers of $5,000 and $7,000, respectively. Since the excess contributions were deducted in 2008, no further excise tax would be imposed.

In the event that the profit-sharing or stock bonus plan becomes disqualified or is terminated, any excess contribution carry forward may still be deducted in subsequent years. However, the deduction for any such year is limited to 25 percent of the compensation paid to participants during the one-year period ending on the last day of the last month that the plan was qualified.[32]

.03 401(k) Plans

The 25 percent of compensation deduction limit applies to the employer's contribution to a 401(k) plan. Employee elective deferrals are not treated as employer contributions and are, therefore, not subject to the employer deduction limits. (Prior to 2002, these employee elective deferrals were treated as employer contributions for purposes of determining the employer's deduction limit.)[33] Any nondeductible excess contributions are subject to the ten percent excise tax of Code Sec. 4972.

.04 SIMPLE 401(k) Plans

Employers may deduct contributions to a SIMPLE 401(k) plan that are required under Section 401(k)(11)(B). Thus, the employer's deduction is limited to the greater of: (1) 25 percent of participants' compensation during the year, or (2) the amount that the employer is required to contribute to the SIMPLE 401(k) plan for the year.[34]

---

[32] Reg. 1.404-9(b)(2), adapted to reflect the new 25 percent limit applicable after 2001.

[33] Code Sec. 404(n).

[34] Code Sec. 404(a)(3)(A).

.05 ESOPs

ESOPs are discussed in detail in Chapter 11. However, a general overview of the deduction limitations is provided in this chapter as well.

An ESOP must be a part of a stock bonus (or combined stock bonus-money purchase plan); therefore, it is subject to the normal deduction ceilings for the underlying plan, i.e., 25 percent of compensation. *In addition* to this regular deduction limitation, C corporations are also allowed to deduct (1) contributions to pay an exempt ESOP loan (both interest and principal) and (2) dividends paid on stock held by the ESOP. These additional deductions are not available to S corporations, however.

A C corporation can deduct contributions to a leveraged ESOP, subject to the following special limits:[35]

(1) contributions to an ESOP to pay interest on an exempt loan are fully deductible, without regard to any percentage limitation; and

(2) contributions to an ESOP to pay principal on an exempt loan are subject to a separate limitation of 25 percent of the total compensation of all participants in the plan, with an unlimited carryover of excess contributions. Again, this nondeductible excess contribution is subject to the ten-percent excise tax under Code Sec. 4972. (Note that these higher limitations are not available to S corporations.)

A C corporation can also deduct certain dividends paid on stock held by an ESOP. This deduction is allowed only if the dividend is either:

(1) paid in cash directly to participants (or beneficiaries);

(2) paid to the ESOP and then distributed to participants (or beneficiaries) within 90 days after the plan year-end;

(3) at the election of the participants, either paid in cash to the participants or paid to the plan and reinvested in employer securities; or

(4) used to make payments on an exempt ESOP loan, the proceeds of which are used to acquire employer securities on which the dividend is paid.[36]

.06 Simplified Employee Pension Plans (SEPs)

Code Sec. 404(h) determines the deduction ceiling for SEPs. An employer is entitled to a deduction of up to 25 percent of the

---

[35] Code Sec. 404(a)(9). [36] Code Sec. 404(k).

compensation paid to the employees under the plan. Any excess contributions may be carried forward indefinitely in accordance with the normal Code Sec. 404 rules. Again, any nondeductible excess contribution is subject to the ten-percent excise tax under Code Sec. 4972.

.07   SIMPLE IRA Plans

Code Sec. 404(m) treats employer contributions to SIMPLE IRA plans as if they were made to a qualified plan. No special limitations apply to the employer deduction. The deduction is generally allowed in the tax year with or within which the calendar year for which the contributions were made ends. However, employer contributions made after year-end must be made by the due date for the employer's tax return, including extensions.[37] (Note, however, that employee elective deferrals must be deposited within 30 days after the end of the month to which the contributions relate.)[38]

.08   Deduction Limitations on Combined Plans

Pension or Annuity Plans. Where two or more pension or annuity plans are maintained by an employer, the deductions limitations are applied to each separate plan. However, if any employee is covered by two or more such plans, the total deductions for all such plans are also subject to the limitations that would be applicable as if they constituted a single plan.[39]

Profit-Sharing or Stock Bonus Plans. The deduction limitations for contributions to two or more profit-sharing or stock bonus plans maintained by the same employer are applied on a combined basis. That is, the trusts under all profit-sharing and stock bonus plans are treated as if they were a single trust.[40] Thus, the total deduction cannot exceed 25 percent of the compensation paid to all employees covered under all such plans.

SEPs and Profit-Sharing or Stock Bonus Plans. For any taxable year in which an employer has a deduction for contributions to a SEP, the 25-percent limitation for the deduction to the profit-sharing or stock bonus plan is reduced by the amount paid to the SEP on behalf of any employee who is also a participant in a stock bonus or profit-sharing plan.[41]

Pension Plans and Profit-Sharing or Stock Bonus Plans. In addition to the deduction limitations in Code Secs. 404(a)(1) or (2)

---

[37] Code Sec. 404(m)(2).
[38] Code Sec. 408(p)(5)(A)(i).
[39] Reg. § 1.404(a)-4(c).

[40] Code Sec. 404(a)(3)(A)(iv).
[41] Code Sec. 404(h)(2).

(for pension and annuity plans) and 404(a)(3) (for profit-sharing and stock bonus plans), Code Sec. 404(a)(7) imposes an overall limitation for deductions. If at least one employee is covered in both a pension plan and a profit-sharing (or stock bonus) plan and the employer contributes to both plans, the overall limitation applies. The limit is the greater of:

(1) 25 percent of the compensation paid or accrued during the taxable year to employees who are beneficiaries under any of the plans; or

(2) the amount(s) necessary to meet the minimum funding standard of Code Sec. 412 for the pension plan(s).[42]

For purposes of this combined plan limit, "compensation" and "employer contributions" are defined in the same manner as for profit-sharing and stock bonus plans. Thus, employee elective deferrals are included in the level of compensation and are not treated as employer contributions (and, thus, not subject to the deduction limits.)

If the employer makes contributions to the plans that exceed the overall limitation, the excess may be carried forward to succeeding years, subject to the 25 percent (but not the minimum funding standard) limitation for any such year. This carryover is classified as a Code Sec. 404(a)(7) carryover and not a carryover of any individual plan. That is, all plans must first meet the separate limitations of Code Sec. 404(a)(1), (2), and (3), and then meet the overall limitation of Code Sec. 404(a)(7).

The 10-percent excise tax on nondeductible contributions applies to each set of plans, as well as to the combined plans. However, the penalty does not apply to contributions to one or more defined contribution plans that are not deductible when contributed *solely* because of the Code Sec. 404(a)(7) combined plan limitation, to the extent that they do not exceed the greater of: (1) six percent of compensation paid or accrued during the tax year for which the contributions were made to beneficiaries under the plans; or (2) the sum of the employee's elective deferrals plus the employer's matching contribution. For purposes of this penalty, the combined plan limits are first applied to amounts contributed to the defined benefit plan.[43]

> **Example:** F Corporation maintains both a qualified profit-sharing plan and a defined benefit pension plan which cover the same employees. Below are the facts with regard to the years 2006 through 2008. For simplicity, assume that the pension plan

---

[42] Code Sec. 404(a)(7)(A).

[43] Code Sec. 4972(c)(6)(A).

contribution is equal to the minimum funding requirement under Code Sec. 412. (Thus, there are no excess contribution carryovers for the pension plan.)

Year	Compensation	Profit-Sharing Contribution	Pension Plan Contribution
2006	$150,000	$40,000	$20,000
2007	160,000	25,000	20,000
2008	140,000	5,000	20,000

The deductions and carryover amounts are computed below.

Excess Contribution Carryovers

Year	Deduction	Profit-Sharing	Pension	Code Sec. 404(a)(7)
2006	$37,500	$2,500	$-0-	$20,000
2007	40,000	-0-	-0-	27,500
2008	35,000	-0-	-0-	17,500

Explanation: First, the two plans must meet the individual limitations of their respective Code sections, i.e., the profit-sharing plan deductions cannot exceed 25% of compensation for each year, and the pension plan cannot exceed whichever of the three limitations under Code Sec. 404(a)(1) is applicable. Since the pension plan contributions were assumed to be equal to the minimum funding requirement of Code Sec. 412, there are no excess contribution carryovers for that plan. Once the individual plan limitations are met, the overall limitation of Code Sec. 404(a)(7) applies, i.e., it is in addition to, and not instead of, the individual plan limitations.

2006:

Pension Plan—The $20,000 contribution is fully deductible, since it is the amount required to meet the minimum funding requirement.

Profit-Sharing Plan—The $40,000 contribution exceeds the 25% of the $150,000 compensation by $2,500 (i.e., 25% × $150,000 = $37,500). Thus, the maximum deduction is $37,500, leaving a $2,500 excess contribution carryover with respect to the profit-sharing plan, which is subject to the 10 percent nondeductible contributions penalty tax.

Overall Limitation—The potential deduction for both plans, after meeting their respective limitations, is $57,500 ($20,000 from the pension plan and $37,500 from the profit-sharing plan). Since the maximum deduction allowed is 25% of the $150,000 compensation, or $37,500, there is a $20,000 overall excess contribution carryover under Code Sec. 404(a)(7).

2007:

Pension Plan—The allowable deduction is the same as for 2004, since the contribution was equal to the minimum funding requirement. Thus, a $20,000 deduction is available, with no excess contribution carryover.

Profit-Sharing Plan—The limitation on the deduction for the contribution to the profit-sharing plan is $40,000 (25%×$160,000). The potential deduction for the profit-sharing plan is $27,500, which is the $25,000 contribution plus the $2,500 in excess contribution carryover from 2006. Thus, $27,500 would be allowed as a deduction. This deduction eliminates the excess contribution carryover from the profit-sharing plan.

Overall Limitation—The potential deduction from both plans is $67,500 ($20,000 from the pension plan and $27,500 from the profit-sharing plan in current contributions, plus the $20,000 overall excess contribution carryover). The overall deduction limitation under Code Sec. 404(a)(7) is $40,000 (25%×$160,000). Thus, the total Code Sec. 404(a)(7) carryover is now $27,500, an increase of $7,500 from 2006. This increase ($7,500) may also be calculated as the excess of the 2007 separate plan deductible amounts ($47,500) over the 2007 deduction limitation ($40,000).

2008:

Pension Plan—The deduction for the pension plan is the same as for the prior two years.

Profit-Sharing Plan—The deduction limitation for the profit-sharing plan is $35,000 (25%×$140,000). Thus, the $5,000 contribution would be allowed as a deduction.

Overall Limitation—The potential deduction for all plans is $52,500, which is made up of: the $20,000 from the pension plan; the $5,000 from the profit-sharing plan; and $27,500 from the 2007 overall excess contribution limitation. Since this exceeds the 25% of compensation limitation for 2008 (25%×$140,000 = $35,000), a $17,500 overall excess contribution carryover remains. Stated another way, the potential deduction from the individual plans is $25,000. Since the overall deduction limitation is $35,000, $10,000 of the $27,500 Code Sec. 404(a)(7) carryover may be deducted in 2008, leaving a balance of $17,500.

¶ 804 Minimum Funding Standards

Code Sec. 412 establishes minimum funding requirements for employers who sponsor pension plans. The purpose of these standards is to ensure that the employer will have provided sufficient funding to pay benefits to participants. In general, Code Sec. 412 requires that a "funding standard account" be maintained by the plan to determine the amount of annual contributions required from the sponsoring employer. Thus, the funding standard account is somewhat analogous to an account receivable from the employer. If the employer fails to fund the minimum amount required by the funding standard account, two possibilities exist. First, the employer may be able to obtain a waiver of the deficiency from the IRS, if it can prove that a temporary financial hardship exists. If, however, no waiver is granted, the employer is subject to an excise tax of ten percent of the deficiency per year. If the deficiency is not corrected, a 100-percent penalty is assessed.[44]

The minimum funding standards of Code Sec. 412 apply to qualified pension plans, which include defined benefit, money purchase, and target benefit plans. Specifically excluded from these requirements are:

(1) profit-sharing and stock bonus plans;

(2) plans that are funded exclusively by the purchase of individual annuity contracts, as long as the employer premiums are paid annually when due and no policy loans are allowed;

(3) federal, state, and local government plans;

(4) church plans that have not made the special election under Code Sec. 410(d) have the participation, vesting, and funding provisions apply;

(5) plans under which the employer does not contribute; and

(6) plans of fraternal organizations and tax-exempt employee beneficiary associations, as long as contributions are not made by employers of the plan participants.[45]

SEPs and SIMPLE plans are also exempt from the minimum funding standards.

.01 Definitions

Because the minimum funding provisions of Code Sec. 412 involve several technical terms, some definitions are provided below as a prelude to the discussion of the actual requirements.

Actuarial Methods. ERISA does not allow an employer to fund a pension plan on a "pay as you go" method (where pension payments are funded only as they become due), nor does it allow a terminal funding method (where the entire value of a retirement annuity is funded immediately at retirement).[46] Instead, actuarial cost methods are required. In general, an actuarial cost method is a recognized

---

[44] Code Sec. 4971.
[45] Code Sec. 412(h) and (i).

[46] ERISA Sec. 3(31).

actuarial technique whereby the cost of the projected benefits is funded over the service period of the employee.

The specific cost allocated to a particular year of service of an employee is referred to as the "normal cost" for the year. This normal cost is determined under one of six actuarial techniques allowed under ERISA. In general, all actuarial methods fall within one of two basic approaches of determining normal cost: the "benefit" approach or the "cost" approach. Benefit approaches determine the normal cost of a pension plan for a year as the present value of the pension benefits earned by participants during the year. Cost approaches, on the other hand, determine the normal cost for a year as the level cost that will be sufficient (together with interest accumulations) to provide the estimated total benefit of participants at retirement.

ERISA Sec. 3(31) specifies six acceptable actuarial methods. These acceptable methods are referred to in the Code as "reasonable funding methods."[47] These methods may be categorized into the benefit and cost approaches as follows:

Benefit Approach: Accrued benefit cost method (also known as the unit credit method)

Cost Approach: Entry age normal cost method
Individual level premium cost method
Aggregate cost method
Attained age normal cost method
Frozen initial liability cost method

Example: The basic difference between the two approaches may be demonstrated as follows. Suppose pension plan P provides an annual benefit upon retirement at age 65 equal to 1% of compensation per year of participation. Employee A, who is 35 years old, earns an annual salary of $40,000. It is assumed that employee A's life expectancy at age 65 is 15 years, and that 5% will be the investment return for all years. Under the benefit approach, employee A is assumed to have earned a $400 benefit (which begins at age 65 and lasts for an estimated 15 years) during the current year. The present value of this $400 annuity, beginning 30 years from now (since A is age 35) and computed at 5%, is $960. Stated another way, if A's employer contributed $960 today, it would accumulate, at 5%, to a balance which would provide the $400 annuity that he earned this year. Thus, $960 would be the normal cost.

---

[47] Code Sec. 412(c)(3).

¶804.01

Under the cost approach, employee A's total projected annual benefit at retirement age is $12,000 (1% × $40,000 × 30 years of employment remaining). The normal cost is determined as the level amount required to pay this $12,000 annuity at age 65 for a 15-year life expectancy. This amount is $1,875. That is, if the employer contributes $1,875 each year until A's retirement, the accumulated balance (including interest) would provide A's total projected annual benefit.

The above example demonstrates the significant differences in funding patterns between the two basic actuarial approaches. In general, the normal cost pattern under the benefit approach, expressed as a percentage of salary, increases throughout an employee's career. Under cost approaches, however, normal cost as a percentage of salary tends to be more level. Thus, the specific financial situation and desires of the employer can determine the most appropriate actuarial method to follow.

As mentioned above, Code Sec. 412(c)(3) requires that all costs and liabilities of a pension plan be determined on the basis of assumptions and methods that are reasonable. Regulations further explain that a funding method is considered reasonable only if it produces no experience gains and losses (defined in **Actuarial Assumptions**, below) when each actuarial assumption is exactly realized.[48] In a recent ruling, the IRS identified two specific versions of the aggregate entry age normal funding method that are not reasonable and should not be used.[49]

Plan sponsors may change funding methods only with IRS approval. Revenue Procedure 2000-41 provides the procedures by which a plan sponsor may obtain approval for a change in funding methods.[50]

Actuarial Assumptions. The above example was intentionally oversimplified in order to show the basic differences between actuarial approaches. In the real world, the actuary must make many assumptions when computing the normal cost for the employee group as a whole. Among these assumptions are employee turnover, mortality rates, compensation levels, and investment returns. According to Code Sec. 412(c)(3), these individual actuarial assumptions must be reasonable (taking into account the experience of the plan and reasonable expectations) or result, in the aggregate, in a total plan contribution equivalent to the contribution that would be obtained if each assumption were reasonable. These costs must be the actuary's best estimate of anticipated experience under the plan.

---

[48] Reg. § 1.412(c)(3)-1(c)(2).
[49] Rev. Rul. 2003-83, 2003-30 IRB 128.
[50] 2000-2 CB 371.

Normally, the same actuarial assumptions and cost method must be used for determining both the minimum annual contribution to the plan under Code Sec. 412 and the maximum amount that can be currently deducted under Code Sec. 404.[51]

Obviously, however, an actuary cannot have complete accuracy. Thus, actual results will vary from those which were estimated. These differences are referred to as "experience gains and losses." For example, suppose the actuary estimated the investment return at five percent when it was actually seven percent. In this case, an experience gain would have occurred. For minimum funding purposes, experience gains and losses must be amortized (spread) over a period of five years (15 years for multiemployer plans). A determination of experience gains and losses, as well as a valuation of the plan's liability, must be made at least once every year.[52]

Another type of gain or loss occurs when the actuarial assumptions are changed. These gains and losses are required to be amortized over a period of 10 years (30 years for multiemployer plans). Certain large plans must obtain IRS approval before changing actuarial assumptions in a way that results in large decreases in unfunded current liabilities.[53]

Actuarial assumptions used in small defined benefit plans have come under increased IRS scrutiny in recent years. The IRS appears to be particularly concerned with conservative interest rates assumptions and relatively early normal retirement age assumptions, both of which accelerate the required contributions and allowed deductions.[54] (In the event of an overstatement of 200 percent or more of pension liabilities caused by unreasonable actuarial assumptions, a 20-percent accuracy-related penalty under Code Sec. 6662 is imposed.) However, several courts have upheld some conservative actuarial assumptions, provided they are not substantially unreasonable.[55]

Waived Funding Deficiency. If an employer is unable to satisfy the minimum funding standard for a plan year without substantial business hardship, and if enforcement of the standard would be adverse to the interest of plan participants in the aggregate, the IRS may waive any or all of the funding requirement. In order to obtain a funding waiver for a plan year, an employer must file a waiver application with the IRS no later than two-and-one-half

[51] Code Sec. 404(a)(1)(A).
[52] Code Sec. 412(c)(9).
[53] Code Sec. 412(c)(5)(B).
[54] *See* e.g., *J. Mirza & Associates, Ltd.,* CA-7, 89-2 USTC ¶ 9492; 882 F2d 229.

[55] *See* e.g., *Vinson & Elkins,* 99 TC 9, Dec. 48,340. Aff'd, CA-5, 93-2 USTC ¶ 50,632, 7 F3d 1235; and *Citrus Valley Estates, Inc.* 99 TC 379. Dec. 48,548. Aff'd, CA-9, 95-1 USTC ¶ 50,132, 49 F3d 1410.

¶ 804.01

months following the end of the plan year. This application must establish that the employer cannot satisfy the minimum funding standard without suffering from a *temporary* financial hardship. (This prevents the granting of waivers to employers that will not recover sufficiently to make their waived contributions.) In addition, certain procedural requirements contained in Revenue Procedure 2004-15 must be satisfied.[56] (Terminating defined benefit plans must meet additional conditions contained in Revenue Procedure 2000-17 to obtain a waiver of the penalty tax.[57]) No more than three waivers may be granted for any 15 consecutive plan years.[58] Any amount waived must be amortized (i.e., paid), plus interest, over a period of five years.

.02   Valuation of Plan Assets

Plans subject to the minimum funding requirements must be valued at least once a year, unless regulations require valuations more frequently. Normally, the valuation date must be within the plan year or within one month prior to the start of the plan year. However, in an effort to ease some administrative burden on plan sponsors, plan assets may be valued on any date within the prior plan year, but only if the value of the plan assets is not less than 100 percent of the plan's current liability on that date.[59]

.03   Funding Standard Account

Every qualified pension and annuity plan which is subject to the minimum funding standards must establish and maintain a funding standard account. In general, this account calculates the amount of the contribution that is required from the employer for each year. At the end of the year, if there is no balance, no funding is required. However, if there is a balance, an "accumulated funding deficiency" exists, which if not paid, results in penalty taxes to the employer on this deficiency.

Charges to the Account. Each year the funding standard account is charged with:[60]

(1) the normal cost for the plan year;

(2) the amounts necessary to amortize in equal annual installments, until fully amortized:

    (a) any unfunded past service liability of the plan over 30 years (for plans in existence on January 1, 1974, the amortization period for unfunded past service costs is 40 years);

---

[56] IRB 2004-7, 490.
[57] 2000-1 CB 766.
[58] Code Sec. 412(d)(1).

[59] Code Secs. 412(c)(9)(A) and (B).

[60] Code Sec. 412(b)(2).

(b) separately, with respect to each plan year, the net increase in the past service liability arising from plan amendments, over 30 years;

(c) separately, with respect to each plan year, the net experience loss under the plan, over five years (15 years for multiemployer plans); and

(d) separately, with respect to each plan year, the net loss resulting from changes in actuarial assumptions, over ten years (30 years for multiemployer plans and for changes occuring in a single employer plan before 1988); and

(3) the amount necessary to amortize each waived funding deficiency for each prior plan year in equal annual installments, until fully amortized, over five years (15 years for multiemployer plans);

(4) the amount necessary to amortize in equal annual installments, until fully amortized, any amount credited to the funding standard account because of the use of the alternative minimum funding account (described later) over five years;

(5) the amount necessary to amortize in equal annual installments, until fully amortized, any amount that cannot be contributed to the plan due to the full funding limitations (discussed later in this chapter) over 20 years (a special shorter amortization period applies to any unamortized balance as of the end of the 1998 plan year);[61] and

(6) for plans that are determined to be underfunded, additional funding requirements are imposed (discussed later in this chapter.)

The funding standard account is also charged or credited with interest at the rate used under the plan to determine costs. This interest must be within a "permissible range," of 90 to 110 percent of the weighted average on 30-year Treasury securities during the preceding four-year period.[62] (For plan years beginning in 2004 and 2005, this interest rate is changed to a permissible range of 90-110 percent of the weighted average of the rates of interest on amounts invested in long-term corporate investment-grade bonds.[63]) The funding standard account is also charged with interest on any underpayment of the required quarterly installments of Code Sec. 412(m). The interest rate on any such underpayments is the greater of (1) 175 percent of the applicable federal mid-term rate, or (2) the rate of interest used under the plan to determine costs, including

---

[61] Code Sec. 412(b)(2)(E); Rev. Rul. 2000-20 (2000-1 CB 880) provides guidance for establishing special amortization bases for these 12/31/98 balances.

[62] Code Sec. 412(b)(5).

[63] Code Sec. 412(b)(5)(B)(ii)(II) and 412(l)(7)(C)(i)(IV), as added by the Pension Funding Equity Act of 2004, P.L. 108-218, Sec. 101(b) (April 10, 2004).

¶ 804.03

any adjustments required for plans subject to the minimum funding rules.[64]

Additional charges to the funding standard account are made for certain plans that are determined to be underfunded. These charges are discussed in ¶ 804.06.

Under certain conditions, the DOL may grant an extension of up to ten additional years for the amortization of past service costs, experience losses, and losses resulting from changes in actuarial assumptions.[65] Revenue Procedure 2004-44 describes the method for requesting such an extension of the amortization period.[66]

Credits to the Account. Each year, the funding standard account is credited with:[67]

(1) employer contributions for the plan year;

(2) the amount necessary to amortize in equal annual installments, until fully amortized:

    (a) separately, with respect to each plan year, the net decrease (if any) in unfunded past service liability under the plan arising from plan amendments, over 30 years;

    (b) separately, with respect to each plan year, any net experience gain, over five years (15 years for multiemployer plans); and

    (c) separately, with respect to each plan year, the net gain resulting from changes in actuarial assumptions, over ten years (30 years for multiemployer plans and for changes occurring in single employer plans before 1988);

(3) the amount of the waived funding deficiency for the plan year; and

(4) in a year in which a plan changes back to the funding standard from the alternative funding standard, the excess of any debit balance in the funding standard account over the debit balance in the alternative minimum funding standard account.

.04 Full Funding Limitation

Notwithstanding the minimum funding standard above, an employer is not required to fund a plan if the plan is fully funded. Code Sec. 412(c)(6) provides a special credit to the funding standard

---

[64] Code Sec. 412(m)(1).
[65] Code Sec. 412(e).

[66] IRB 2004-31,134.
[67] Code Sec. 412(b)(3).

account for the amount of the full funding limitation. This limitation is defined in Code Sec. 412(c)(7)(A) as the excess of:

(1) the "accrued liability" (including normal cost) under the plan (determined under the entry age normal method if the plan's funding method does not permit accrued liability to be directly calculated); over

(2) the lesser of the fair market value of the plan's assets or the actuarial value of the assets, as determined under Code Sec. 412(c)(2).

In any event, the full funding limitation may not be less than 90 percent of the plan's current liability of the plan (including the expected increase in current liability due to benefits accruing during the plan year), over the value of the plan's assets. In determining the 90 percent limit, plan assets are not reduced by any credit balances in the funding standard account.[68] "Current liability," for this purpose, is defined as all liabilities to employees and beneficiaries under the plan, i.e., the amount that the plan would have to pay in benefits on termination.[69] It is based on IRS-prescribed mortality tables, using an interest rate within a permissible range that is based on 30-year Treasury securities. (For plan years beginning in 2004 and 2005, this interest rate is changed to a permissible range of 90-110 percent of the weighted average of the rates of interest on amounts invested in long-term corporate investment-grade bonds.)[70] The IRS publishes a monthly announcement updating the rate and resulting permissible ranges. "Accrued liability" is the excess of (1) the present value of the future benefits costs and administrative expenses for all plan participants and beneficiaries, over (2) the present value of future contributions for the normal cost of all applicable plan participants and beneficiaries.[71]

Recall from earlier in this chapter that the deduction for a contribution to a pension plan cannot exceed the full funding limitation. Thus, for example, assume a plan's funding standard account has a year-end debit balance of $100,000 and a full funding limitation of $80,000. The employer needs to make a contribution of only $80,000 to avoid the underfunding penalty, despite the funding standard account's debit balance. Furthermore, the maximum deduction is $80,000; any excess contribution would be carried forward to the following year and is subject to the Code Sec. 4972 excise tax.

---

[68] Code Sec. 412(c)(7)(E).
[69] Code Sec. 412(c)(7)(B).
[70] Code Sec. 412(b)(5)(B)(ii)(II) and 412(l)(7)(C)(i)(IV), as added by the Pension

Funding Equity Act of 2004, P.L. 108-218, Sec. 101(b) (April 10, 2004).
[71] ERISA Sec. 3(29).

.05 Alternative Minimum Funding Standard

Some plans will use the alternative minimum funding standard account instead of the funding standard account, if it results in a smaller amount due from the employer for the year. The use of this alternative account is restricted to plans that use a funding method which requires contributions in all years that are not less than those required under the entry age normal funding method.[72] (Proposed regulations indicate that only a plan that actually uses a method that results in contributions at least as large as those that would be required under the entry age normal funding method may use the alternative minimum funding standard.)[73] In general, the alternative minimum funding standard provides for the immediate recognition of gains and losses by incorporating the excess of accrued liabilities over the fair market value of plan assets.

Each plan year, the alternative minimum funding standard account is charged with:

(1) the lesser of normal cost under the funding method used under the plan or normal cost determined under the unit credit method;

(2) the excess, if any, of the present value of accrued benefits under the plan over the fair market value of the assets; and

(3) an amount equal to the excess of credits to the alternative minimum standard account for all prior plan years over charges to the account for all such years.[74]

Each year the alternative minimum funding standard account is credited with the employer contributions to the plan.[75]

If plan assets decline in value, the alternative minimum funding standard may require a larger contribution from the employer. Thus, the employer will want to switch back to the funding standard account. In order to change, the plan must also maintain the funding standard account records in addition to the alternative account records, so that it may determine the proper contribution. For any year, a plan may use either the standard or the alternative account, whichever requires the smaller funding.[76]

When a plan changes from the alternative account to the standard account, it ceases to maintain the alternative account. If the plan later resumes using the alternative account, a new alternative account with a zero balance is then established.[77]

---

[72] Code Sec. 412(g)(1).
[73] Prop. Reg. § 1.412(g)-1(a).
[74] Code Sec. 412(g)(2)(A).

[75] Code Sec. 412(g)(2)(B).
[76] Prop. Reg. § 1.412(g)-1(b).
[77] Prop. Regs. § 1.412(g)-1(b)(4).

.06 Additional Minimum Funding Requirements for Underfunded Plans

Accelerated funding requirements apply to certain single-employer defined benefit plans. These rules apply to plans with more than 100 participants that are "underfunded." In general, a plan is considered underfunded if it has a funded current liability percentage of less than 90 percent for a plan year. However, a plan that has a funded liability percentage of at least 80 percent is not subject to the special funding rules if it met the 90-percent level in each of the two immediately preceding plan years, or in each of the second and third immediately preceding plan years.[78]

> **Example:** Plan A's funded current liability percentage (defined below) for each of the plan years beginning on January 1, 2004, 2005, 2006, and 2007 is as follows: 95%, 95%, 75%, and 80%. For plan years 2004 and 2005, the plan is not subject to the additional funding rules for underfunded plans because the funded current liability percentage is at least 90%. The plan is subject to the additional funding rules for plan year 2006 because the funded current liability percentage is below 80%. The plan is not subject to the additional funding rules for plan year 2007, because it satisfies the volatility rule.

Definitions. Each of these terms is defined below:

Current liability is all liabilities to employees and beneficiaries under the plan, determined as if the plan terminated;

Unfunded current liability is the excess (if any) of: (1) the current liability of the plan, over (2) the value of the plan's assets; and

Funded current liability percentage is the percentage that the value of the plan assets is of the current liability.[79]

Additional Changes. Any plan that is determined to be underfunded has an added amount charged to its minimum funding standard account equal to the sum of:[80]

(1) the excess (if any) of:

    (a) the "deficit reduction contribution" for the plan year, over

    (b) the sum of the charges for the plan year reduced by the sum of the credits for the plan year; plus

---

[78] Code Sec. 412(l)(1).
[79] Code Sec. 412(l)(8)(B).
[80] Code Sec. 412(l)(1)(A).

(2) the "unpredictable contingent event amount" (if any) for the plan year.

Thus, in general, the minimum required contribution for underfunded plans is the greater of (1) the amount determined under the normal funding rules, or (2) the deficit reduction contribution plus the amount required with respect to benefits that are contingent on unpredictable events.

A *deficit reduction contribution* is defined as the sum of: (1) the "unfunded old liability amount," (2) the "unfunded new liability amount, (3) a 10-year amortization of the unfunded mortality increase; and (4) the expected increase in new current liability due to benefits accruing during the year."[81]

The *unfunded old liability amount* is the amount necessary to amortize any unfunded old liability under the plan in equal annual installments over 18 plan years, for plan years beginning after 1987 and before 1995. The GATT-required changes in interest and mortality assumptions in the unfunded old liability starting with the 1995 plan year are amortized over a 12-year period. As an alternative, employers may elect to amortize the entire amount of the plan's unfunded old liability over the 12-year period beginning with the 1995 plan year.[82]

The *unfunded new liability amount* is defined as the "applicable percentage" times the plan's unfunded new liability. The unfunded new liability is the plan's unfunded current liability for the plan year, reduced by: (1) the unamortized portion of any unfunded old liability and the unamortized portion of the unfunded existing benefit increase liability, (2) the unamortized portion of each unfunded mortality increase; and (3) the liability with respect to any unpredictable contingent event benefits. The applicable percentage is equal to 30 percent, reduced by the product of: (1) .40, times (2) the number of percentage points by which the funded current liability percentage exceeds 60 percent.[83]

> **Example:** A plan's funded current liability percentage is 70%. Thus, its applicable percentage is 26% [30%−(.40×10%)]. If the plan had an unfunded current liability of $5,000,000, of which $800,000 was attributable to unamortized old liability, the plan's new liability amount would be $1,092,000 [26%×($5,000,000−$800,000)].

---

[81] Code Sec. 412(1)(2).
[82] Code Sec. 412(1)(3)(A).
[83] Code Sec. 412(1)(4)(C).

The *unfunded mortality increase* is the increase in the current liability of the plan that results from changing to a new mortality table. The increase is computed as the excess of the current liability of the plan for the first plan year for which the plan uses the new mortality table over the current liability of the plan for the plan year that would have been determined if the mortality table in effect for the preceding plan year had been used.[84]

An unpredictable contingent event benefit means any benefit contingent on an event other than: (1) age, service, compensation, death, or disability, or (2) an event which is reasonably and reliably predictable. Thus, an unpredictable contingent event benefit is one that depends on contingencies such as facility shutdown or contraction in the work force that are not reasonably predictable. The *unpredictable contingent event amount* for a plan year is equal to the greatest of:[85]

(1) the product of:

    (a) 100 percent, reduced (but not below zero percent) by the funded current liability percentage for the plan year, multiplied by

    (b) the amount of unpredictable contingent event benefits paid during the plan year, including (except as provided by regulation) any payment for the purchase of an annuity contract for a participant or beneficiary with respect to such benefits;

(2) the amount which would be determined for the plan year if the unpredictable contingent event benefit liabilities were amortized in equal annual installments over seven plan years, beginning with the plan year in which the event occurs; or

(3) the additional contribution that would be required if the unpredictable contingent event benefit liabilities were included in the determination of unfunded new liability.

Temporary Relief for Certain Industries. In an effort to provide immediate temporary relief to some employers experiencing significant hardships in funding pension plans, Congress passed the Pension Funding Equity Act of 2004 (PFEA '04) effective for the 2004 and 2005 plan years.

PFEA '04 replaces the interest rate used for computing benefits (based on 30-year Treasury securities) with an interest rate based on long-term investment-grade corporate bonds. Since this new rate is significantly higher than the 30-year Treasury securities, the effect

---

[84] Code Sec. 412(l)(10).   [85] Code Sec. 412(l)(5).

is to reduce the calculated current liability and thus reduce the deficit reduction contribution for an underfunded plan.

A second temporary PFEA '04 provision allows employers in the airline and steel industries to elect to reduce the deficit reduction contribution by 80 percent. Employers seeking this deficit reduction contribution election follow the guidance set forth in Announcement 2004-38.[86] Additional guidance is provided in Notice 2004-59.[87]

.07   Quarterly Contribution Requirement

Employers who contribute to single employer defined benefit plans generally must make quarterly installment payments equal to 25 percent of the required annual payment to satisfy the minimum funding requirements.[88] However if the plan's funded current liability percentage in the preceding plan year was at least 100 percent (i.e., the plan was fully funded), quarterly estimated contributions are not required during the current plan year.[89]

The required annual payment is the lesser of:

(1) 90 percent of the amount the employer is required to contribute for the plan year under the minimum funding requirements (without regard to any funding waivers); or

(2) 100 percent of the amount that the employer was required to contribute for the preceding plan year under the minimum funding requirements (but only if the preceding plan was a 12-month period).

Due dates for the quarterly installments for a calendar-year plan are April 15, July 15, and October 15 of the plan year, and January 15 of the following year. For non-calendar year plan years, the due dates are the 15th day of the fourth, seventh, and tenth months of the plan year, and the 15th day of the first month of the following year.[90]

If a required installment is not made by the due date, the funding standard account is charged with interest on the amount of the underpayment from the due date until the date of contribution. The rate of interest is the greater of 175 percent of the midterm applicable federal rate (in effect for the first month of the plan year under Code Sec. 1274) or the rate of interest used under the plan in

---

[86] 2004-18 IRB 878, as modified by Announcement 2004-43, 2004-21 IRB 955.

[87] 2004-36 IRB 447.

[88] Code Sec. 412(m)(3): Rev. Rul. 95-31, Q&A-1, 1995-1 CB 76.

[89] Code Sec. 412(m)(1).

[90] Code Sec. 412(m)(3)(B).

determining costs (including any adjustments required for plans subject to the minimum funding rules).[91]

Any unpredictable contingent event liabilities are not taken into account in computing the required annual payment for purposes of charging interest to the funding standard account. Nevertheless, the quarterly installments are increased by the largest of: the unfunded percentage of the amount of unpredictable event benefits paid during the three-month period preceding the month in which the installment is due; 25 percent of the amount required to be contributed for the plan year if the unpredictable event benefit liabilities were amortized over seven years; or 25 percent of the additional amount contribution would be required if the unpredictable contingent event benefit liabilities were included in the unfunded new liability.[92]

Plan Liquidity Requirements. Defined benefit plans with more than 100 participants have an additional liquidity requirement with respect to their quarterly installments. In general, such plans are required to maintain liquid plan assets at an amount approximately equal to three times the total disbursements from the trust during the 12-month period ending on the last day of each quarter for which the plan has a required quarterly installment. If any such plan has a "liquidity shortfall" at the end of any quarter for which there is a required quarterly contribution, the employer must make a contribution of liquid assets to cover the entire amount of the shortfall by the due date of the quarterly installment. If the employer fails to satisfy the liquidity requirement, the employer is treated as having failed to make a required quarterly installment.[93]

A plan has a liquidity shortfall if its liquid assets are less than the base amount for the quarter. Liquid assets include cash, marketable securities (including stock, notes, and derivatives for which there is a liquid financial market), and certain insurance and annuity contracts. The base amount for a quarter is equal to three times the adjusted disbursements from the plan for the 12 months ending on the last day of the quarter. Disbursements from the plan are all disbursements from the trust, including purchase of annuities, payments of single sums and other benefits, and administrative expenses. Adjusted disbursements means disbursements (as defined above) reduced by the product of: (1) the plan's funded current liability percentage, times (2) the sum of the purchases of annuities, payments of single sums, and other disbursements as provided in regulations.[94]

---

[91] Code Sec. 412(m)(1).
[92] Code Sec. 412(m)(4)(D).

[93] Code Sec. 412(m)(5).
[94] Code Sec. 412(m)(5)(E).

A special rule applies where the liquidity shortfall exceeds an amount equal to 2 times the sum of the adjusted disbursements from the plan for the 36-month period ending on the last day of the quarter. If an enrolled actuary certifies that such excess is the result of nonrecurring circumstances, the base amount for that quarter will be determined without regard to related amounts.[95]

.08 Lien for Unpaid Contributions

If an employer fails to make a required contribution (including a required installment payment) when due to a defined benefit plan with a funded current liability percentage of less than 100 percent, a lien is established in favor of the plan against the employer (and each member of a controlled group). The lien provision applies only to plans covered by the Pension Benefit Guaranty Corporation (PBGC) program.[96] In order for the lien to apply, the unpaid balance of the installment or other payment (including interest), when added to the aggregate unpaid balance of all previous installments or other payments for which payment was not made before the due date (including interest), must exceed $1 million.[97]

The amount of the lien is the aggregate unpaid balance of required installments and other payments (plus interest) not made before the due date.[98] The lien arises on the due date of an unpaid contribution, and continues until the last day of the first plan year in which the plan no longer has total unpaid contributions in excess of $1 million.[99]

.09 Penalties for Underfunding

If a plan has an accumulated funding deficiency for any year in which a waiver from the IRS is not obtained, Code Sec. 4971 imposes severe penalties on the employer. A first-tier tax of ten percent (five percent for multiemployer plans) of the accumulated funding deficiency is imposed on the employer for each year in which the deficiency has not been corrected.[100] (However, the excise tax may be avoided if the employer makes the required contribution within eight-and-a-half months after plan year-end.[101]) If the funding deficiency is not corrected (i.e., paid by the employer) within the 90-day period after the IRS mails the notice of deficiency for the initial tax, a penalty tax of 100 percent of the accumulated funding deficiency is imposed on the employer.[102]

---

[95] Code Sec. 412(m)(5)(E)(ii)(II).
[96] Code Sec. 412(n)(2).
[97] Code Sec. 412(n)(1).
[98] Code Sec. 412(n)(3).
[99] Code Sec. 412(n)(4).
[100] Code Sec. 4971(a).
[101] Code Sec. 412(c)(10).
[102] Code Sec. 4971(b).

In addition, the employer is required to notify participants and beneficiaries that the plan did not meet the minimum funding standards.[103] If an employer fails to make such notification, the employer may be liable for a penalty of up to $100 per day from the date of the failure as well as any other relief the court may order.[104]

---

[103] Code Sec. 417(a)(3)(B)(ii); ERISA Sec. 205(c)(B)(ii).

[104] ERISA Sec. 502(c).

¶ 804.09

Chapter 9

Taxation of Distributions from Qualified Plans

¶ 901 Introduction and General Tax Rules for Distributions

Distributions received by employees and self-employed individuals from qualified retirement plans (as described in Chapters 6-8) are ordinarily taxed when received, usually at or after retirement. Generally, distributions are received in annuity form for a period of years or over the remaining lifetime of the employee and the employee's spouse, if any. Distributions received in annuity form are taxed under the annuity taxation rules of Code Sec. 72. Under Code Sec. 72, if the employee made contributions to the plan (other than voluntary deductible contributions that were allowed prior to 1987 and elective deferrals), a portion of each annuity receipt is nontaxable determined using an exclusion ratio. A simplified method of determining the taxable amount of annuities from qualified plans must generally be used, however, for annuities with starting dates beginning after November 18, 1996 from qualified plans. In addition, Code Sec. 72(e)(2) requires that an exclusion ratio be used in the case of certain amounts not received as an annuity, such as distributions of employer securities and in-service withdrawals.

In some cases, an employee or self-employed individual may receive his retirement benefits in a lump sum. Ordinarily, all of the lump sum is taxed as ordinary income in the year received. However, under special tax rules, a portion of the lump-sum distribution may be taxed as a capital gain and the remaining portion of the distribution may be eligible for special taxation using the ten-year averaging rules. Participants in qualified plans can avoid being taxed on a distribution that is an eligible rollover distribution from a qualified plan by making a direct rollover (a trustee-to-trustee transfer) of the distribution into another eligible qualified plan or into an IRA or IR Annuity. In general, an eligible rollover distribution is a partial or total distribution from a qualified plan that is otherwise taxable to the employee. This chapter covers the taxation of annuity distributions, the taxation of lump-sum distributions, and rollovers of eligible rollover distributions. Finally, the Economic Growth and Tax Relief Reconciliation Act of 2001 (EGTRRA) made some important changes concerning rollovers and certain other aspects of qualified plan distributions. These changes are covered in this chapter.

.01   When Distributions Can and Must Be Made

In the case of pension plans, payments of benefits can generally begin at the time of the employee's death, disability, termination of employment, or at retirement.[1]

The payment of benefits from profit sharing and stock bonus plans can begin at any of the times specified for pension plans, and, in addition, for reasons of hardship or after a "fixed number of years" (under Rev. Rul. 71-295, the fixed period may be as few as two years).[2]

Required Distributions. Under Code Sec. 401(a)(14), benefit payments must begin within 60 days of the latest of:

(1) age 65 or normal retirement age under the plan, if earlier;

(2) the tenth anniversary of participation;

(3) termination of service; or

(4) some later date elected by the participant.

Required Distributions Under Code Sec. 401(a)(9). In addition to the requirements of Code Sec. 401(a)(14), Code Sec. 401(a)(9) provides rules under which employees who are qualified plan participants must begin receiving minimum distribution amounts by April 1 of the calendar year following the later of (1) the calendar year in which the employee reaches age 70½ or (2) the calendar year in which the employee retires. However, participants who own five percent or more of their employer and holders of IRA accounts must begin

---

[1] *See* Reg. § 1.401-1(b)(1)(i); Rev. Rul. 56-693, 1956-2 CB 282, and Rev. Rul. 69-277, 1969-1 CB 116.

[2] *See* Reg. § 1.401-1(b)(1)(ii), (iii); Rev. Rul. 71-295, 1971-2 CB 184, and Rev. Rul. 73-553, 1973-2 CB 130.

receiving minimum distributions by April 1 of the year following the calendar year in which the participant reaches age 70½, regardless of retirement. Prior to 1997, all qualified plan participants had to follow the rule now applicable to five percent owners and IRA account holders. See Chapter 6 for coverage of these rules.

.02 Taxation of Distributions Under Code Sec. 402

As a general rule, amounts that are actually distributed by a qualified plan fund holder to a participant are taxable in the year distributed using the Code Sec. 72 annuity taxation rules.

However, certain lump-sum distributions are not taxed as ordinary income under Code Sec. 72 and, instead, may be partly taxed as long term capital gain income (amount attributable to pre-1974 participation), and the balance may be taxed using the special ten-year forward averaging rules if the participant qualifies as discussed later in the chapter. In addition, the participant can avoid paying tax on a distribution that qualifies as an eligible rollover distribution by making a timely rollover of the distribution into an IRA or another qualified retirement plan.

.03 Special Rules Concerning Qualified Plan Distributions

Special rules apply in the case of life insurance provided by a qualified plan, health and accident payments included in pension and profit-sharing plan benefit payments, distributions of employer securities, distributions of annuity contracts, and loans made to participants.

Life Insurance Provided by the Plan. If a life insurance contract, under which the proceeds of the contract are payable to a plan participant or beneficiary of such participant, is purchased by a qualified plan and paid for with employer contributions to the plan or plan earnings, the cost of the life insurance protection provided is currently taxable to the employee participant.[3] For this purpose, the cost of life insurance protection for a year equals the excess of (1) the death benefit payable under the policy over (2) the cash surrender value of the policy at the end of the year.[4] That cost is based on a premium that is determined by the IRS.

> **Example:** An annual premium policy purchased by a qualified plan for an employee participant provides an annuity of $100 per month upon retirement at age 65, with a death benefit of $10,000. The cash value at the end of the current year is

---

[3] Code Sec. 72(m)(3)(B).   [4] Reg. § 1.72-16(b)(3).

$1,000. Thus, the life insurance protection is $9,000 ($10,000 − $1,000). Assuming that the IRS has determined that a reasonable net premium cost for the employee's age is $6.00 per $1,000, the premium for $10,000 of insurance is therefore $60.00. The cost of life insurance which is includible in the employee's gross income is $54.00 (9,000 ÷ 10,000 × $60.00).

If the trustee has a right under any circumstances to retain any of the proceeds of the life insurance contract, the employee is not taxed on the premiums paid by the qualified plan.[5]

When proceeds are received under a life insurance policy provided by a qualified plan, only the amount of the proceeds in excess of the cash surrender value is excludable under Code Sec. 101(a) as a life insurance benefit payment.[6] The cash surrender value and the amounts of the premiums paid that were taxable to the employee under Code Sec. 72(m)(3) are taxable to the recipient.[7]

Health and Accident Insurance Benefits Included in Pension and Profit-Sharing Plan Distributions. The annuity taxation rules of Code Sec. 72 generally apply to determine the taxability of distributions from qualified pension and profit-sharing plans. However, amounts that are received as accident and health benefits and are not attributable to contributions of the employee (amounts treated as employee contributions for health benefits cannot be treated as employee plan contributions under Code Sec. 72) are includible in gross income except to the extent such amounts are excludable from gross income under Code Sec. 105(b) and (c).[8] This Code section covers amounts which reimburse the individual for medical expenses of the individual, his/her spouse, and his/her dependents and payments for the permanent loss or loss of the use of a member or function of the body or for permanent disfigurement of the individual, his/her spouse, and his/her dependents (see the discussion in Chapter 3 for further coverage). Benefits that are excluded because they are received under accident and health insurance include amounts that are received through an arrangement that has the effect of accident and health insurance for years after 1996.[9]

Distribution of Employer Securities. If securities of the employer are distributed as part of a lump-sum distribution, the net unrealized appreciation in value of the securities is not taxable to the recipient.[10] For this purpose, the net unrealized appreciation

---

[5] Reg. § 1.72-16(b)(6).
[6] Reg. § 1.72-16(c)(2).
[7] Reg. § 1.72-16(c)(2).
[8] Reg. § 1.72-15(c) and (d).

[9] Code Sec. 104(a)(3) as modified by P.L. 104-191, 104th Cong, 2d Sess. (Aug. 21, 1996).

[10] Code Sec. 402(e)(4)(B).

is the fair market value of the securities at the date of distribution minus the qualified plan's basis. The participant is taxed on the appreciation when he actually sells the securities. The rollover of a portion of a lump-sum distribution from a qualified plan to a traditional IRA does not affect the status of the distribution of employer stock for purposes of the tax treatment of the net unrealized appreciation on the stock.[11] Thus, the appreciation in value on the portion rolled over is not recognized at the time of the rollover, and recognition is postponed until the taxpayer actually receives the stock from the IRA and sells the stock. Further, the net unrealized appreciation in value on the portion of the stock that was not rolled over into the traditional IRA is also deferred until the stock is sold.

Alternatively, Code Sec. 402(e)(4)(B) permits the recipient of employer securities as part of a lump-sum distribution to elect to recognize the unrealized appreciation at the time of the distribution. This election may be beneficial if the participant can use the special capital gains treatment and/or the ten-year averaging method (covered later in the chapter) to determine his or her tax on the distribution. That election must be made on the tax return for the year in which the distribution is received.

Under Code Sec. 402(e)(4)(E), securities for purposes of the special distribution rules are shares of stock and bonds or debentures that are issued by the employer corporation (its parent, or subsidiary as defined under the provisions concerning the taxation of incentive stock options, as discussed in Chapter 15) with interest coupons or in registered form.

If employer securities are distributed as part of a nonlump-sum distribution, the net unrealized appreciation that can be excluded is only the amount that is attributable to the amount that the employee contributed toward the cost of the securities when they were purchased by the qualified plan.[12] Employee contributions are treated as being attributable to employer securities if the securities have been specifically earmarked as purchased with employee contributions. If employer securities cannot be so identified, a ratable allocation method may be used.[13] The exclusion is not available for voluntary deductible employee contributions (not allowed after 1986).

The remainder of the distribution (after taking into account the amount excludable as net unrealized appreciation) is taxed according to the rules of Code Sec. 72. Code Sec. 72(e)(8) provides for a pro

---

[11] *See*, e.g., IRS Letter Rulings 200202078 and 200315041.

[12] Code Sec. 402(e)(4)(A).
[13] *See* Reg. § 1.402(a)-1(b)(3).

rata recovery of the employee's investment into the contract (i.e., after-tax contributions made by the employee to the plan). Under this approach, the amount of the distribution (i.e., the cash, if any, and the fair market value of the securities received) minus the excludable net unrealized appreciation is multiplied by an exclusion ratio, the numerator of which is the employee's investment in the plan, and the denominator of which is the employee's account balance in the plan. For this purpose, the account balance must be reduced by the entire net unrealized appreciation on employer securities attributable to employee contributions, whether or not all such securities are distributed.[14]

> **Example (1):** In 2006, Wilson received a distribution of ten shares of his employer's stock from a profit-sharing plan. The stock was worth $100 per share at the time of the distribution. In 1995, the trust had purchased 40 shares of such stock on behalf of Wilson for $50 per share, and Wilson contributed $20 per share of the purchase price.
>
> First, it is useful to determine the net unrealized appreciation in value that is excludable. Since Wilson contributed 40 percent of the purchase price of each share ($20 divided by $50), 40 percent of the unrealized appreciation in value of each share or $20 [($100 − $50)×.40 is excludable. Thus, $200 ($20×10) is excludable as net unrealized appreciation on the ten shares distributed.
>
> Next, the amount of income that Wilson must recognize on the distribution can be determined. To accomplish this, first determine the amount of the distribution which is excludable from gross income. The excludable amount is equal to (1) the amount of the distribution, which is $800 ($1,000 value minus the $200 of excludable net unrealized appreciation) multiplied by (2) the ratio of (a) $800 (Wilson's investment into the plan) divided by (b) $3,200 (Wilson's account balance of $4,000, which is $100 times 40 shares) minus $800 (the net unrealized appreciation on all 40 shares—$20 times 40).
>
> Thus, $200 ($800×$800/$3,200) is excludable. The amount of the distribution which is taxable to Wilson can then be determined, and it is $600 (the $800 amount of the distribution, as determined above, minus the $200 excludable amount).

For purposes of determining gain or loss to the employee on a subsequent sale of the employer securities received in the

---

[14] Notice 89-25, 1989-1 CB 662.

distribution, the basis of the shares will equal the sum of (1) the amount the employee invested in the shares plus (2) the taxable amount of the distribution in which the shares were received that was attributable to the shares.[15]

> **Example (2):** Assume the same facts as in the previous example and that Wilson sells the ten shares of employer stock for $120 per share in 2008. Wilson's basis in the ten shares is $800 (the $200 he was treated as paying for them plus the $600 income that was recognized on the distribution of the shares). Thus, Wilson has a taxable capital gain of $400 on the sale ($1,200 – $800).

Annuity Contracts. The value of an annuity contract that is distributed to a participant from a qualified plan is not taxable in the year in which it is received. Instead, the value of the contract is taxable when the participant receives annuity payments under the contract or when the participant sells the contract.[16] Note that the receipt of annuity contracts can affect the amount of tax payable on a lump-sum distribution using the ten-year averaging rules as discussed later in this chapter.

Tax Treatment of Loans to Participants. Under Code Sec. 72(p)(1)(A), outstanding loans from qualified retirement plans above specified limits to participants are generally treated as deemed distributions from the plan. In mid-2000, the IRS issued final regulations under Code Sec. 72(p). Subsequent modifications were made to the final regulations in 2002 to address additional issues such as refinancing, multiple loans, and repayment during military leaves of absence.[17] These final regulations, subject to specified transition rules, are effective for plan loans, assignments, and pledges made on or after January 1, 2002.[18] The modifications made in 2002 apply with respect to plan loans, assignments, and pledges made on or after January 1, 2004.[19] Important aspects of the final regulations are covered in this and succeeding paragraphs. The deemed distribution treatment applies to both direct and indirect loans made to a plan participant from a qualified plan.[20] Where a qualified plan participant or beneficiary assigns or pledges or agrees to assign or pledge any part of his/her interest in a qualified employer plan as security for a loan, the part of that person's interest in the qualified plan, which is subject to the assignment or pledge is treated

---

[15] Reg. § 1.402(a)-1(b)(3)(vi).
[16] Reg. § 1.402(a)-1(a)(2).
[17] T.D. 9021, 12/3/03, 67 FR 71821.

[18] T.D. 8894, 7/31/00, 65 FR 46588.
[19] T.D. 9021, 12/3/02, 67 FR 71821.
[20] Reg. § 1.72(p)-1, Q&A 1(a).

as a loan from the plan to that person.[21] However, if all or a portion of a participant's or beneficiary's interest in a qualified plan is pledged or assigned as security for a loan from that plan to the participant or beneficiary, only the amount of the loan from the plan actually received by the participant or the beneficiary is treated as a plan loan.[22] The deemed distribution treatment does not apply if there is an express or tacit understanding that the loan will not be repaid, or, for any reason, the transaction does not create a debtor-creditor relationship.[23] In such a case, the purported loan is treated as an actual distribution, subject to all of the rules applicable to actual plan distributions. The deemed distribution treatment also does not apply to residential mortgage loans made by a plan in the ordinary course of an investment program, if the property acquired with the loans is the primary security for the loans, and the amount loaned does not exceed the fair market value of the property.[24] In addition, a distribution of a plan loan offset amount is not treated as a deemed distribution, but rather, it is treated as an actual distribution. A plan loan offset occurs when, under the terms governing a plan loan, the accrued benefit of a plan participant or beneficiary is reduced (offset) to repay the loan. A distribution of a plan loan offset amount can occur in a variety of circumstances, such as where plan terms require that, in the event of the participant's request for a distributor, a loan be repaid immediately or treated as in default. In the event of a plan loan offset, the amount of reduction in the accrued benefit is treated as an actual distribution. Thus, a plan may be prohibited from making such an offset under the provisions of Code Secs. 401(a), 401(k)(2)(B), or 403(b)(11) prohibiting or limiting distributions to an active employee.[25] Code Sec. 72(p) does not prohibit a participant from borrowing from a qualified plan more than once per year. Thus, there is no barrier to credit card loans that otherwise meet the requirements of that section. The regulations indicate that a participant who has an outstanding loan balance that satisfies the requirements of Code Sec. 72(p) may refinance those loans or borrow additional amounts if, under the facts and circumstances, the loans collectively satisfy the amount limitations of Code Sec. 72(p)(1)(A) and the prior loan and the additional loans each satisfy the requirements of Code Secs. 72(p)(1)(B) and (C).[26] Finally, the deemed distribution treatment does not apply to loans falling under the de minimis exception covered below.

---

[21] Reg. § 1.72(p)-1, Q&A 1(b).
[22] *Id.*
[23] Reg. § 1.72(p)-1, Q&A 17.

[24] Reg. § 1.72(p)-1, Q&A 18.
[25] Reg. § 1.72(p)-1. Q&A 13.
[26] Reg. § 1.72-1(p). Q&A 20(a).

¶901.03

A plan loan that is deemed to be a distribution is not treated as an actual distribution for some purposes, but is so treated for other purposes. A deemed distribution under Code Sec. 72(p) is not treated as an actual distribution for purposes of the plan qualification requirements of Code Sec. 401(a) (discussed in chapter 6), certain distribution rules under Code Sec. 402, including the ability to use the special five year averaging rules and the ability to roll over the distribution (plan loans cannot be rolled over under Reg. § 1.402(c)-2 Q&A4), and the distribution restrictions applicable to Code Sec. 401(k) plans (discussed in Chapter 7) and Code Sec. 403(b) plans.[27] However, a plan loan that is a deemed distribution is treated as an actual distribution for purposes of the 10 percent premature distributions tax of Code Sec. 72(t). In addition, if the participant has made after-tax plan contributions, those are taken into account under the annuity taxation rules of Code Sec. 72 in determining the taxable amount of the deemed distribution.[28]

Under a de minimis exception, the full amount of loans outstanding from qualified plans are not taxable to the participants. A loan from a qualified plan that is repayable within five years is treated as a taxable distribution only to the extent that the loan (when added to the outstanding balance of all other loans from all qualified plans of the employer) exceeds the lesser of:

(1) $50,000, reduced by the excess of:

    (a)   the highest outstanding balance of loans from the plans during the one-year period ending on the day before the date on which such loan was made, over

    (b)   the outstanding balance of loans from the plan on the date on which the loan was made, or

(2) the greater of:

    (a)   one-half of the present value of the nonforfeitable accrued benefit of the employee under the plan, or

    (b) $10,000.[29]

Note that the above de minimis amounts apply to loans made or renegotiated after 1986. For loans made or renegotiated prior to 1987, the $50,000 amount was not reduced as indicated above.

---

[27] Reg. § 1.72(p)-1, Q&A 12.
[28] Reg. § 1.72(p)-1, Q&A 11.

[29] Code Sec. 72(p)(2)(A).

Example: An employee borrowed $8,000 from a qualified plan in 2005 at a time when his nonforfeitable accrued benefit was $13,000. In 2006, after repaying $4,000 of principal on the first loan, he borrowed another $8,000. As a result, the employee has received a deemed distribution under Code Sec. 72(p) of $2,000 ($12,000 minus the $10,000 limit which applies in this case.)

The de minimis exceptions to the treatment of outstanding loans as distributions generally do not apply to loans that are payable over more than five years or that are extended by renegotiation or otherwise beyond the five years.[30] Thus, loans made for more than five years or renegotiated beyond five years are fully taxable. Further, the de minimis exception does not apply unless the loan is amortized on substantially a level basis with payments made at least quarterly. Note that the level amortization rule did not apply to loans made before 1987. However, the de minimis exclusion amounts apply even if the loan is not repayable within five years if the loan is used to acquire a dwelling that is to be used within a reasonable time as the principal residence of the plan participant.[31]

Generally, the interest paid by participants on qualified plan loans is deductible, partially deductible, or not deductible depending on the purpose and use of the loan.[32] For example, interest on a plan loan used to purchase the taxpayer's principal residence is deductible as qualified residence interest under Code Sec. 163(h). However, interest on qualified plan loans paid by key employees (as defined in Code Sec. 416) or by any employee if the loan is secured by elective deferral amounts in a Code Sec. 401(k) plan or a Code Sec. 403(b) plan is not deductible and is to be treated as a nondeductible contribution by the employee to the plan.[33] The rule applies to the period beginning on the first day the participant becomes a key employee or that the loan is secured by such elective deferrals.

.04 Effect of Qualification Status

Under Reg § 1.402(b)-1(b)(1), if an employer's qualified retirement plan loses its qualified status during a year and the participant's account balance in the plan is already partly or totally vested, the employee is taxed on that vested balance (on the portion which is attributable to employer contributions) even if it is subject to a substantial risk of forfeiture within the meaning of Code Sec. 83

---

[30] IRS Pub. 575, Pension and Annuity Income, at 16.
[31] Code Sec. 72(p)(2)(B)(ii).

[32] See Code Secs. 163 and 265.
[33] Code Sec. 72(p)(3).

(see the coverage of Code Sec. 83 in Chapter 14). This rule applies only to the portion of the vested balance that is attributable to contributions made during a tax year of the employer that ended with or within a tax-qualified year of the trust.

.05   The Ten-Percent Premature Distribution Tax

Under Code Sec. 72(t), a ten-percent penalty tax applies to any premature taxable distributions including taxable qualified plan loans received from any employer tax-qualified plan. A premature distribution is any taxable distribution from a qualified plan other than the following:

(1) a distribution received by the participant after he or she has reached age 59½;

(2) a distribution after the death of the participant;

(3) a distribution received after the participant has become disabled (as defined in Code Sec. 72(m)(7);

(4) a series of substantially equal periodic distributions at least annually over the life or life expectancy of the participant or the participant and a beneficiary;

(5) a distribution to a participant who has attained age 55 and has separated from service;

(6) a distribution which is used to pay medical expenses to the extent that the expenses are deductible under Code Sec. 213, determined without regard to whether the taxpayer takes itemized deductions;

(7) certain distributions of excess contributions to and excess deferrals under a qualified cash or deferred arrangement;

(8) a distribution of pass-through dividends from an ESOP under Code Sec. 404(k);

(9) certain distributions from an ESOP, if received before 1990;

(10) a distribution made on account of a levy under Code Sec. 6331 on the qualified retirement plan (for distributions after 1999); and

(11) payments to an alternate payee under a QDRO.[34]

EGTRRA has amended Code Sec. 72(t) to also provide that premature distributions from Code Sec. 457 governmental deferred compensation plans (covered in Chapter 14) will generally be subject to the ten percent premature distribution tax to the extent that the distributions consist of amounts that are attributable to rollover distributions previously received from another type of plan.[35]

---

[34] Code Sec. 72(t)(2), as amended by P.L. 105-206, 105th Cong., 2d Sess., Sec. 3436(a) July 22, 1998).

[35] Code Sec. 72(t)(9), as added by P.L. 107-16, 107th Cong., 1st Sess., Sec. 641(a)(2)(C) (June 7, 2001).

In 1989, the IRS issued Notice 89-25[36] in which it set forth three methods for determining whether payments from a retirement plan or an IRA constitute a series of substantially equal periodic payments for purposes of meeting the fourth exception noted above. After the IRS issued the final required minimum distribution regulations under Code Sec. 401(a)(9) in 2002, the IRS issued Rev. Rul. 2002-62[37] in which it modifies the three methods to reflect the provisions of the final minimum distribution regulations and the new life expectancy tables contained in those regulations. The three acceptable methods are:

(1) the required minimum distribution method;

(2) the fixed amortization method; and

(3) the fixed annuitization method.

It should be noted that the IRS, in a posting of FAQs on its web site about Rev. Rul. 2002-62, indicates that the methods contained in that revenue ruling are intended to be safe harbor methods and are not the only acceptable methods of meeting the substantially equal periodic payments exception. The IRS indicates that another method may be used in a private letter ruling request, but would be subject to individual analysis.[38] The IRS has issued a number of private letter rulings concerning the substantially equal periodic payments exception (e.g., concerning situations where the IRA participants proposed to use the fixed amortization method or the fixed annuitization method on an annually recalculated basis).[39]

The provisions of the revenue ruling are effective for any series of payments that commence on or after January 1, 2003 and may be applied to distributions that commenced during 2002.

If the ten-percent penalty tax does not apply because payments are to be made in installments over the life expectancy of the employee participant, the payments must continue in a qualified form for at least five years or until after the participant reaches age 59½, whichever is later. If the payments are changed before the end of the required time such that they no longer qualify for exemption, the ten percent tax is retroactively applied to all distributions actually received before the participant reached age 59½.[40] The tax bears interest for the year in which the distribution is included in gross income through the year in which the payments were modified according to Code Sec. 72(t)(4)(B).

---

[36] 1989-1 CB 662.

[37] 2002-2 CB 710.

[38] *See* e.g., IRS Letter Ruling 299437038.

[39] *See* IRS Letter Rulings 200432021, 200432023, 200432024 and 200503036.

[40] Code Sec. 72(t)(4). (The ten-percent premature distribution tax rules generally apply to qualified plan and IRA distributions made after December 31, 1986.)

¶ **901.05**

Example: Norton started a life expectancy payout from a qualified plan at age 50, then took a lump sum payment at age 58. The 10-percent tax would apply to the lump sum and to each installment payment that had been made before the lump sum was paid. Each increment of tax would bear interest from the first day of the year in which the employee received the installment that generated the tax until the last day of the year in which the lump sum was paid out. Had Norton waited to receive the lump sum payment until after age 59½, the 10-percent tax would have been avoided.

.06 In-Service Withdrawals

Under pre-1986 law, benefits paid by a qualified plan before the participant's annuity starting date (defined later in the chapter) were first treated as a return of capital to the extent of after-tax employee contributions and were taxable only after those contributions were fully recovered.[41]

A pro rata basis recovery rule applies in determining the taxable amount of in-service withdrawals. Under the "pro rata" rule, a participant is not taxed on the portion of the distribution that is attributable to the employee's after-tax contributions to the plan.[42] Thus, the excludable amount of a distribution can be determined using the following formula (which is determined on the distribution data):

$$\text{Amount Received} \times \frac{\text{Employee's After-Tax Plan Contributions}}{\text{Employee's Account Balance}} = \frac{\text{Excludable}}{\text{Amount}}$$

The remaining amount of the distribution is includible in the employee's gross income. For purpose of this calculation, the employee's account balance includes only amounts to which the employee has a nonforfeitable right.

¶ 902   Taxation of Annuity Distributions

Qualified plan distributions other than those eligible for special lump-sum taxation or those rolled over are subject to tax under Code Sec. 72. The determination of the tax depends upon whether the participant made any after-tax contributions to the plan and whether payments are to be made to an alternate payee under a QDRO.

---

[41] Former Code Sec. 72(e)(5)(A) and (f).   [42] Code Sec. 72(e)(8)(B).

Distributions received in annuity form from qualified plans are generally using the rules of Code Sec. 72 and the regulations thereunder.

Under Code Sec. 72(d), as revised by the Small Business Job Protection Act of 1996, most qualified plan annuities with a starting date after November 18, 1996 will be taxed using a statutory simplified method. Annuity distributions with starting dates before November 19, 1996 and those that are not eligible for the statutory simplified method will be taxed using the general annuity taxation rules of Code Sec. 72. Finally, most qualified plan participants receiving annuities from qualified plans with a starting date after July 1, 1986 and before November 19, 1996 could have elected to use the simplified safe-harbor method provided by the IRS in Notice 88-118[43] and IRS Publication 575 to determine the tax on their distributions. In addition, certain individuals with annuity starting dates after July 1, 1986 and before November 19, 1996 and who are using the general exclusion ratio method can switch to the IRS safe harbor method.[44] This safe-harbor approach will be discussed following the discussion of the general annuity exclusion rules and the taxation rules of revised Code Sec. 72(d).

.01 Definition of an Annuity

Under Code Sec. 72, amounts received as annuities may not be fully taxable in the year received. In general, amounts received as an annuity are (1) payable at regular intervals over a period of more than one year after the year in which payments commence and (2) are definitely determinable as of the annuity starting date.[45] Both annuities payable over a term certain (a definite period of time longer than one year) or a period measured by the life (or lives) of the annuitant (the person or persons who are to receive the annuity payments) are considered paid over a period of more than one year.[46] Other payments under annuity contracts are generally considered to be "amounts not received as an annuity," and are taxed under the special rules of Code Sec. 72(e).[47] Such payments are generally taxable when received except to the extent the payments are attributable to the employee's after-tax contributions to the plan.

Insurance, Endowment, and Annuity Contracts. Payments under life insurance, endowment (as well as face amount

---

[43] 1988-2 CB 450, obsoleted by Notice 98-2, 1998-1 CB 266.
[44] IRS Publication 575 at 12 and 13.

[45] Reg. §§ 1.72-1(b) and 1.72-2(b)(3).
[46] Reg. § 1.72-1(e).
[47] Reg. § 1.72-1(d).

¶ 902.01

certificates), and annuity contracts are taxable using the Code Sec. 72 annuity rules. Further, amounts distributed to participants and beneficiaries under qualified employer retirement plans are taxable under Code Sec. 72.[48]

Deferred Annuities Available to Non-natural Persons. Under Code Sec. 72(u), a deferred annuity contract held by a non-individual owner (e.g., a corporation or trust) is not considered to be an annuity contract taxable under the Code Sec. 72 rules. Nonindividual owners of annuity contracts must pay tax each year on any increase in the cash surrender value of the deferred annuity over the basis of the contract during the tax year.[49] However, a deferred annuity contract that is nominally owned by a nonindividual, but is beneficially owned by a natural person, is treated as being owned by the natural person. Consequently, if a corporation purchases a group annuity contract as an agent for a group of persons who are the beneficial owners of the contract, the normal annuity taxation rules of Code Sec. 72 will apply to the contract. However, a deferred annuity contract which is used to fund nonqualified deferred compensation payable by an employer is considered to be owned by the employer and is subject to Code Sec. 72(u), even though the employer only nominally owns the contract for the benefit of the employees.[50]

.02 Taxation of Annuities Under the General Code Sec. 72 Rules

Annuity distributions from qualified plans with (1) an annuity starting date before November 19, 1996 for which the plan participant could not, or did not elect, or has not elected (in a case where the participant can still switch from the general method to the IRS simplified rules) to use the IRS safe-harbor rules described in IRS Pub. 575 and (2) a starting date after November 18, 1996 for which the new simplified Code Sec. 72(d) rules do not apply, are taxable using the general annuity taxation rules (making use of the exclusion ratio) under Code Sec. 72. Under Code Sec. 72, the taxation of amounts received by annuitants and beneficiaries as annuities from employer-maintained qualified plans depends upon whether the qualified plan was noncontributory or contributory. Under a noncontributory plan, the employee participant does not make any after-tax contributions to the plan. Thus, the participant has a zero basis in the plan, and all annuity payments received are fully taxable as ordinary income.

---

[48] Reg. § 1.72-2(a)(3).
[49] Code Sec. 72(u)(2).
[50] TRA '86 Conference Committee Report.

Treatment of Voluntary Deduction Employee Contributions (VDECs). Prior to 1987, in certain cases, employees were permitted to make VDECs to qualified plans. Since VDECs were deductible by the contributing employees, they are not treated as employee contributions for purposes of the Code Sec. 72 annuity rules and any other rules governing the taxation of qualified plan benefits. Instead, VDECs are treated as employer contributions and are taxable to the employee when received.[51] Note that TRA '86 repealed VDECs, effective for tax years beginning after December 31, 1986.[52]

Annuity Exclusion Ratio. If the qualified plan is contributory, the employee will have made after-tax contributions to the plan and thus will have a basis in the plan. In such cases, a proportionate part of each payment will be excludable by the annuitant under Code Sec. 72(b) until the employee's after-tax contributions are fully recovered. The amount excludable is determined by multiplying each annuity payment by the exclusion ratio. The exclusion ratio is the ratio of the taxpayer's "investment in the contract" (generally the sum of his or her after-tax contributions; see the discussion of the term later in the chapter) to the "expected return under the contract" (the total amount receivable under the contract based on the length of time or expected length of time the distributions will be received; see the discussion of the term later in the chapter). Consequently, the exclusion ratio is:

$$\frac{\text{Taxpayer's Investment in the Contract}}{\text{Expectd Return Under the Contract}}$$

The investment in the contract and the expected return under the contract are calculated as of the annuity starting date (defined below).

Example: Assume that Blake is to receive a life annuity paying $200 per month from his employer's qualified plan. As of the annuity starting date, his investment in the contract was $8,000 and his life expectancy was 10 years. The expected return from the contract is $24,000, and the exclusion ratio is $8,000/$24,000 or ⅓. Thus, ⅓ of each $200 payment, or $66.67, is excludable, and the remainder is includible each year until Blake's basis is fully recovered.

Computation and Application of the Exclusion Ratio. The exclusion ratio is computed by taking into account the total expected

---

[51] Code Sec. 72(0)(1).   [52] TRA 86 Sec. 1101.

¶ 902.02

return under the contract on the annuity starting date. Under Code Sec. 72(b)(2), an employee's total exclusion using the exclusion ratio rules is limited to his investment in the annuity contract. If the annuity recipient dies before his investment in the contract is fully recovered, the nonrecoverable amount may be claimed as a deduction in the annuitant's final taxable year.[53] If an annuitant lives long enough to fully recover his investment in the contract through use of the exclusion ratio rules, all payments received after the investment is fully recovered are fully taxable under Code Sec. 72(b)(2).

> **Example:** Assume the same facts as given in the example above. Further assume that Blake actually lives 15 years beyond the annuity starting date. Since the exclusion ratio was based on a life expectancy of 10 years, all amounts received after the tenth year are fully taxable. The exclusion ratio will not apply after the tenth year.

In the case of annuities with a starting date before January 1, 1987, a different rule applies in using the exclusion ratio. Although the exclusion ratio is calculated in the same way as shown above, the annuity recipient is permitted to continue using the exclusion ratio to exclude a portion of each annuity payment as a return of investment, even after his or her investment in the contract is fully recovered. Thus, in the case of a life annuity, if the annuitant lives longer than his life expectancy which is used to determine his expected return under the contract, the annuitant will more than fully recover his investment.[54] However, if the annuitant dies before the investment in the contract is fully recovered, no deduction is permitted for the remaining unrecovered investment.

Three-Year Investment Recovery Rule. Under the three-year recovery rule (applicable to annuities with a starting date before July 1, 1986), the exclusion ratio approach did not apply to any employee annuity under which the employee's investment in the contract (i.e., the sum of his or her after-tax contributions) was recoverable within three years after the annuity starting date.[55]

Special Rule for Qualified Domestic Relations Order (QDRO) Distributions. Under Code Sec. 72(m)(10), the employee's after-tax plan contributions (and other amounts treated as the employee's investment in the contract) must be apportioned between the employee participant and the taxpayer's spouse or former spouse, if that spouse is an alternate payee under a QDRO.

---

[53] Code Sec. 72(b)(3).
[54] *See* former Code Sec. 72(b).

[55] Former Code Sec. 72(c)(4), TRA '86 Sec. 1122(c).

In such a case, the participant's investment in the contract is allocated on a pro rata basis between the present value of the distribution or payment and the present value of all benefits payable to the participant. An exclusion ratio is then separately determined for the participant and the spouse (or former spouse). This rule applies because the spouse or former spouse is treated as the recipient of any payment or distribution made pursuant to a QDRO.[56] A QDRO is an order made pursuant to a state domestic relations law pertaining to the payment of child support, alimony, or marital property rights and satisfies the requirements of Code Sec. 414(p)(1), (2), and (3).

The apportionment rule described above does not apply if the alternate payee is someone other than the participant's spouse or former spouse (e.g., the participant's child). Payments made under a QDRO to alternate payees other than the participant's spouse or former spouse are fully taxable to the alternate payees.[57] In such a case, none of the participant's investment in the contract is allocated to the alternate payee.

Investment in the Contract. Under Code Sec. 72(c)(1), the participant's investment in the contract is the sum of all after-tax contributions made by the participant to the qualified plan plus any premiums and other consideration paid by the participant under the plan minus (1) any nontaxable amount received by the participant before the annuity starting date and (2) any premiums returned or dividends received prior to the date on which the investment in the contract is determined. An adjustment to the investment amount must be made if the contract has a refund feature (see below). The employee participant's investment in the contract is determined as of the later of the annuity starting date or the date on which an amount is first received under the contract.[58]

Adjustment for Refund Feature. The investment in the contract must be adjusted if the annuity contract contains a refund feature. A contract contains a refund feature if (1) the total amount receivable as an annuity under the contract depends, at least partly, on the continuing life of one or more persons, (2) the contract provides for payments to be made to a beneficiary or the estate of an annuitant on or after his or her death if a specified amount or number of payments has not been paid as of that time, and (3) the payments are a refund of the consideration paid.[59] A refund feature basically guarantees payment of a specified amount under the con-

---

[56] Code Sec. 402(a)(9).
[57] Code Sec. 72(m)(10).

[58] Reg. § 1.72-6(a)(1).
[59] Reg. § 1.72-7.

tract even if the annuitant dies before that sum has been paid. Therefore, the investment in the contract amount must be reduced by the value of the refund feature.

The value of the refund feature is determined as of the annuity starting date using Table III or VII of Reg. § 1.72-9. Table VII is gender neutral and is to used for distributions for which the gender neutral tables apply (generally for distributions beginning after June 30, 1986; see the discussion below).

The factors in Tables III and VII (which are based upon the participant's age and the duration of the guaranteed amount) provide a "percentage value" to the refund feature. The appropriate factor is multiplied by the taxpayer's investment in the contract or the total guaranteed return under the annuity contract, whichever is smaller, to determine the dollar value of the refund feature. That dollar value is to be subtracted from the investment in the contract to determine an adjusted investment in the contract to be used in computing the annuity exclusion ratio.

Qualified Plan Contributions on Behalf of Self-Employed Individuals. Amounts paid into a qualified plan annuity contract on behalf of a self-employed individual that are deducted under Code Sec. 404 are treated as consideration furnished by the employer, rather than as employee contributions.[60] Thus, amounts paid by owner-employees into Keogh plans are not treated as an investment in the contract.

Annuity Starting Date. Code Sec. 72(c)(4) provides that the annuity starting date is the later of: (1) the first day of the first period for which an annuity is receivable under a qualified plan or annuity contract, or (2) the date upon which the payment obligation under the contract becomes fixed. Special rules apply if an annuity is assigned or otherwise transferred for consideration. In such a case, the annuity starting date is the first day of the first period for which the transferee received an annuity payment.[61]

The Expected Return from the Plan. The expected return, for purposes of the Code Sec. 72 exclusion ratio calculation, is the expected total amount that will be received under the annuity contract, computed in accordance with IRS actuarial tables, if benefits will be paid over the remaining life of one or more individuals (in which case it is the amount payable per period times the expected return multiple from the applicable IRS table).[62] Otherwise, the

---

[60] Code Sec. 72(m)(2).
[61] Reg. § 1.72-4(b)(2)(ii).

[62] Code Sec. 72(c)(3)(A).

expected return is the total of the amounts receivable under the contract as an annuity.[63] The calculation of the expected return under the general rule of Code Sec. 72 for the more common types of qualified plan annuity benefits is covered below.

Annuities for Term or Amount Certain. The expected return for an annuity for a term certain (i.e., an annuity payable for a specified number of periods) is the amount of each payment multiplied by the number of payments.[64] In the case of an annuity for an amount certain, the expected return is the amount guaranteed.[65]

Use of IRS Actuarial Tables in the Case of Annuities Based on Life Expectancy. If the annuity payments are to be made over the remaining lifetime of one or more individuals, the expected return is computed in accordance with IRS actuarial tables provided in Reg. § 1.72-9. Reg. § 1.72-9 contains two sets of actuarial tables: (1) Tables I-IV in which the expected return multiple(s) depends upon both the age and sex of the qualified plan recipients and (2) Tables V-VII in which the expected return multiples only depend on the age of the qualified plan recipients. In general, Tables I-IV must be used if all of the participant's investment in the contract has been made before July 1, 1986 or if the annuity starting date is before July 1, 1986. Correspondingly, Tables V-VII must be used if at least some of the participant's investment in the contract had been made after June 30, 1986.[66] However, if annuity payments are received after June 30, 1986, a taxpayer may elect to treat all of the investment in the contract as having been made after June 30, 1986, and thus to make use of the gender-neutral Tables V-VII. This election can be made for any taxable year, but once made, it is binding for all future years.[67] As an alternative, if the participant has made both pre-July 1986 and post-June 1986 contributions to the plan, that participant can elect to use the old tables with respect to the employee-participant's contributions prior to July 1, 1986 and the newer gender-neutral tables for the employee contributions made after June 30, 1986.[68] Where there is a choice, the taxpayer should make computations of the exclusion ratio under the choices available to him/her and choose the alternative that produces the larger/largest exclusion ratio. In most cases, the "old" tables should be chosen, where there is a choice, because the expected return multiples are larger in almost all cases under the "new" tables, thus producing a larger expected return and a smaller exclusion ratio. The difference in the age-multiple figures in the

---

[63] Code Sec. 72(c)(3)(B).
[64] Reg. § 1.72-5(c).
[65] Reg. § 1.72-5(d).

[66] Reg. § 1.72-9.
[67] Reg. § 1.72-9.
[68] Reg. § 1.72-6(d)(6).

gender-dependent and the gender-neutral tables is illustrated below for a single life annuity.

Single Life Annuity. If the annuity payments under a qualified plan will be made monthly to the participant for the rest of his or her life, the total annuity payments for one year are multiplied by the multiple listed in Table I or Table V of Reg. § 1.72-9, depending upon whether the last investment into the plan was made before July 1, 1986 or after June 30, 1986, as discussed above.

> **Example:** Assume that Bilko retired on June 15, 1986 and started receiving payments under a qualified plan of $100 per month for life beginning on July 1, 1986. He made contributions of $8,000 in total to the plan prior to July 1, 1986. He is age 66 on July 1, 1986. Because all of Bilko's contributions to the plan were made prior to July 1, 1986, he can use Table I of Reg. § 1.72-9 to calculate his expected return. His expected return is $100 times 12 times the multiple of 14.4, or $17,280. His exclusion ratio would be .46296 ($8,000/$17,280). If Bilko, instead, elected to use the gender-neutral Table V, his expected return would be $100 times 12 times the multiple of 19.2, or $23,040. In that case, his exclusion ratio would be .3472 ($8,000/$23,040). Thus, Bilko would be better off not having elected to use Table V.

If payments are made less frequently than monthly (such as quarterly or annually), an adjustment to the Table I and V multiples may be required. Depending on how many months the first payment is to be made after the annuity starting date, the adjustment to the multiple can be as much as 0.5 in either direction. The adjustment is determined in accordance with the table found in Reg. § 1.72-5(a)(2)(i). For example, if the annuity in the example above were to be paid yearly beginning on July 1, 1986, the multiple would be increased by 0.5.

Joint and Survivor Annuities. A joint and survivor annuity is an annuity contract under which the qualified plan participant will receive periodic payments for life and after his or her death, a designated beneficiary will receive periodic payments in the same or different amounts for life. As discussed in Chapter 6, Code Sec. 417 ordinarily requires certain qualified plans to make distributions in the form of a joint and survivor annuity for the participant and his or her spouse if the participant is married as of the annuity starting date.

If the payments under a joint and survivor annuity are to remain the same, the combined life expectancy of the two individuals based on the ages and sex of the two persons in Table II or the ages of the two persons in Table VI from Reg. § 1.72-9, whichever is applicable, is used to determine the expected return.

Example (1): Kramden retired on June 15, 1996 and will receive benefits under his employer's qualified retirement plan as a joint and survivor annuity. Payments will begin on July 1, 1996, at which time Kramden will be age 65 and his wife, the second annuitant, will be age 64. The payment will be $400 per month. Using Table VI, the expected return will be $400 times 12 times 25.5, or $122,400.

If the amount payable to the designated beneficiary will be different than that payable to the participant, the calculation is more complicated. First, the joint multiple from Table II or VI, whichever is applicable is determined for both parties. Then, the single life multiple for the participant is determined using Table I or V, whichever is applicable. Then, the multiple of the participant is subtracted from the joint multiple which gives the single life multiple for the beneficiary. The total expected return is computed by adding: (1) the yearly payment to the participant multiplied by his or her single life multiple, and (2) the yearly payment to the beneficiary multiplied by his or her single life multiple as determined above.[69]

Example (2): Assume the same facts as in the above example, except that Mr. Kramden is to receive $500 per month for life and, after he dies, Mrs. Kramden will receive $300 per month for life.

Assume that Table VI from Reg. § 1.72-9 is used. The expected return is determined as follows:

Multiple from Table VI	25.5
Subtract: Multiple from Table V (Mr. Kramden)	20.00
Multiple applicable to Mrs. Kramden	5.5
Portion of expected return (Mr. Kramden)	
20 × $6,000	$120,000
Portion of expected return (Mrs. Kramden)	
5.5 × $3,600	$19,800
Expected return under the contract	$139,800

.03 Simplified Annuity Taxation Method Under Revised Code Sec. 72(d)

Under revised Code Sec. 72(d), qualified plan annuity distributions with an annuity starting date after November 18, 1996, must be taxed using the new simplified annuity taxation method unless (1) the participant is age 75 or more on the starting date and (2) there

---

[69] Reg. § 1.72-5(b)(2).

are five years or more of guaranteed payments under the plan (in this case, the general rules covered above must be used).[70]

The amount that is excludable each month under the statutory simplified method is equal to (1) the participant's investment in the contract (generally the total of the participant's after-tax plan contributions) divided by (2) the expected number of annuity payments (based on the appropriate table from Code Sec. 72(d), as discussed below).[71] Note that the statutory method is similar to the IRS simplified alternative method that was effective under prior law.

Expected Number of Annuity Payments. Under the statutory simplified method, the total number of monthly annuity payments expected to be received with respect to annuity starting dates beginning after 1997 is based on the age of the participant at the annuity starting date in the case of single life annuities and on the combined age of the annuitants in the case of annuities payable over the life of more than one individual.[72] For annuity starting dates after November 18, 1996 and before January 1, 1998, the total number of payments expected to be received only depended on the age of the primary annuitant and was the same whether the annuity was a single life annuity or was payable over the life of more than one individual. The expected number of payments for (1) single life annuities and (2) all types of annuities for annuity starting dates after November 18, 1996 and before 1998—based on the age of the primary annuitant is based on the following table found in Code Sec. 72(d)(1)(B)(iii):

Age of Distributee at Annuity Starting Date	Number of Payments
55 and under	360
56-60	310
61-65	260
66-70	210
More than 70	160

For example, a participant in a qualified plan began receiving annuity payments under the plan on November 30, 1997, when he was age 62. The expected number of payments is 260.

The expected number of payments for annuity starting dates after 1997 where the annuity is payable over the life of more than one individual is based on the following table under Code Sec. 72(d)(1)(B)(iv):

---

[70] Code Sec. 72(d)(1)(E), Notice 98-2, 1998-1 CB 266, I and III.
[71] Code Sec. 72(d)(1)(B)(i), Notice 98-2, 1998-1 CB 266, III B and C.

[72] Code Sec. 72(d)(1)(B), as amended by P.L. 105-34, 105th Cong. 1st Sess., Sec. 1075(a) (Aug. 5, 1997), and Notice 98-2, 1998-1 CB 266, III C.

Combined Ages of the Annuitants	Number of Payments
Not more than 110	410
More than 110 but not more than 120	360
More than 120 but not more than 130	310
More than 130 but not more than 140	260
More than 140	210

For example, suppose that Charles, age 67, will start receiving annuity payments monthly from his employer's qualified plan beginning on February 1, 2006 and that payments will be made to his wife, Mildred, age 60 at the annuity starting date, if she should be living after Charles' death. In that case, the expected number of payments is 310 because the couple's combined ages at the annuity starting date are 127.

Investment in the Contract. The participant's investment in the contract is determined in the same manner as described above for the Code Sec. 72 general rules, except that under Code Sec. 72(d)(1)(C), no adjustment is made for a refund feature in the plan. If in connection with the commencement of annuity payments, the participant receives a lump-sum payment, the payment will be taxable under the rules of Code Sec. 72(e), as if received before the annuity starting date, and the investment in the contract will be determined as if the payment had been received. Under Code Sec. 72(d)(2), employee contributions under defined contribution plans may be treated as a separate contract.

Excludable Amount. The participant's investment in the contract is recovered on a level basis over the expected number of months determined from the applicable table above. The excludable portion of each payment is equal to:

$$\frac{\text{Investment in the Contract}}{\text{Number of Monthly Payments}} = \text{Tax Free Portion of Monthly Annuity}$$

The dollar amount excludable each month will remain the same even if the monthly annuity changes (such as will happen in a joint and survivor annuity where the monthly payments for the survivor are typically less than for the participant). If the excludable amount is greater than the monthly payment, each monthly annuity will be completely excludable until the investment in the contract has been recovered. Once the investment in the contract has been recovered, all annuity amounts received are fully taxable. If annuity payments end before the participant's investment in the contract has been fully recovered, a deduction for the unrecovered investment can be taken on the participant's or applicable beneficiary's final income tax return. Where annuity payments are not made on a monthly

¶ 902.03

basis, Code Sec. 72(d)(1)(F) requires that appropriate adjustments must be made to take into account the period on the basis of which the payments are made.

Example (1): Ted Downey, retired at age 67 on March 18, 2006, and will begin receiving annuity payments of $1,200 for the remainder of his life from his employer's pension plan. Ted made $12,000 of after-tax plan contributions. Each month, Ted will exclude $57.14 of the $1,200 monthly payment ($12,000/210—the expected number of payments from the table in Code Sec. 72(d)(1)(B)(iii) which is used because the annuity is a single life annuity) and include $1,142.86. If Ted lives to receive more than the 210 monthly payments, each payment after that will be fully includible in gross income. If he were to die after only receiving 45 payments, the unrecovered investment would be deductible on his final return.

Example (2): David Doran retired at age 63 in 2006, and will receive retirement benefits in the form of a joint and survivor annuity with monthly payments of $2,000 per month for the remainder of his life, and, then, $1,000 per month to his wife, Natalie, age 58 at the annuity starting date, (if she should survive him) for her life. David made $20,000 of after-tax contributions to the plan. The amount excludable each month is $64.52 ($20,000/310—the expected number of payments from the table in Code Sec. 72(d)(1)(B)(iv) which is used because this annuity is payable over the life of more than one individual and the annuity starts after 1997). If David lives to receive 180 payments, each month he will exclude $64.52 and include $1,935.48. Natalie would then, for up to 130 more payments, exclude $64.52 and include $935.48 per month. After the 130 months, the full $1,000 per month received would be includible by Natalie. If Natalie were to die after only receiving 18 payments, the remaining portion of David's investment in the contract would be deductible on Natalie's final return.

A special transition rule is provided in Notice 98-2[73] for qualified plan participants with annuity starting dates after November 18, 1996, and before January 1, 1997. The special rule applies to payor and participants that continued to use the methods for taxing distributions in the law in effect before the effective date of the statutory simplified rules of Code Sec. 72(d) to determine the taxable

---

[73] 1998-1 CB 266, V.

amount of annuities with starting dates from November 19, 1996, through December 31, 1996. Under the transition rule, such payors and participants are permitted to use the former rules to determine the taxable amounts of such annuities for the years 1996 and 1997 and do not have to file amended returns for those years. However, for 1998 and later years, the payors and participants must use the transition rule specified in Notice 98-2, rather than continue to use the former rules. Under the transition rule, the tax-free portion of each annuity payment received on or after January 1, 1998, is to be determined by dividing the remaining investment in the contract by the remaining number of expected payments (the number from the table in Code Sec. 72(d)(1)(B)(iii) minus the number of months between the annuity starting date and the first payment date on or after January 1, 1998).

.04 Simplified IRS Safe-Harbor Method for Determining Tax on Qualified Plan Annuity Distributions (Pre-11/19/96 Annuities)

IRS Notice 88-118[74] and IRS Publication 575 provide a simplified safe-harbor method for determining the tax-free and taxable portions of certain annuity payments made from a qualified plan. The IRS safe-harbor method is applicable to determine the taxation of qualified plan annuity distributions with annuity starting dates prior to November 19, 1996 if the participant elected to use the safe harbor method and the following requirements are met:

(1) the annuity payments commence after July 1, 1986;

(2) the annuity payments are made from a qualified employee retirement plan;

(3) the annuity payments are to be made over the remaining life of the distributee or the joint lives of the distributee and beneficiary; and

(4) the distributee is younger than age 75 when annuity payments commence or, if the distributee is age 75 or older, there are less than five years of guaranteed payments.

If one or more of the above conditions are not met, the annuity distributions must be taxed using the general annuity exclusion rules of Code Sec. 72 (covered above).

Determination of the Taxable Amount Under the IRS Safe-Harbor Rules. The method of determining the excludable

---

[74] 1988-2 CB 450, obsoleted by Notice 98-2, 1998-1 CB 266.

amount and taxable amount of each monthly distribution under the IRS simplified method is the same as under the Code Sec. 72(d) statutory simplified method for annuity starting dates after November 18, 1996, except that the expected number of payments for each age group in the IRS method table is different. The expected number of payments in the IRS simplified method is shown in the following table:

Age of Distributee	Number of Payments
55 and under	300
56-60	260
61-65	240
66-70	170
71 and over	120

The amount excludable each month, then, is equal to the taxpayer's investment in the contract (defined essentially the same way as under the Code Sec. 72(d) method) divided by the expected number of months from the IRS table.

The dollar amount excludable will not change even when the monthly payments will change (e.g., in the case of a joint and survivor annuity where the survivor will receive smaller monthly benefits than the employee participant). If the excludable amount is greater than the amount of the monthly annuity (e.g., in case of reduced survivor benefits), then each monthly annuity will be completely excluded until the entire investment in the contract is recovered. For those participants with annuity starting dates after December 31, 1986, annuity payments received after the investment has been recovered (usually after the set number of payments has been received) are fully taxable. If annuity payments end before the participant's investment has been recovered, a deduction for the unrecovered investment can be taken on the participant's or applicable beneficiary's last tax return. But, for participants with annuity starting dates after July 1, 1986, and before January 1, 1987, the tax-free portion can be excluded from all annuity payments received by the participant and his or her beneficiary, and no deduction is allowed if the annuity payments cease before the participant's investment in the contract has been fully recovered.

Election of the IRS Safe-Harbor Rules. Participants with annuity starting dates before November 19, 1996 can make the election to use the IRS safe-harbor method on his/her income tax return. The change can even be made if the general rule is already being used, according to IRS Pub. No. 575, by filing amended returns for all tax years beginning with the year in which the participant's annuity starting date occurred. Generally, this change is only permitted to be made within three years from the due date of the participant's return for the year in which the first annuity payment was received.

>   **Comment:** Use of the IRS safe-harbor method (applicable for annuity starting dates before November 19, 1996) is generally advisable when it can be used (instead of using the regular Reg. § 1.72-9 rules). That is because the number of payments under the fixed table of Notice 88-118 for a given age is generally less than the expected number of payments under Reg. § 1.72-9 for the same age. That smaller number of payments produces a larger exclusion ratio (because the denominator is smaller while the investment in the contract numerator amount is the same). For example, an individual who is age 60, has a multiple of 260 months under the safe-harbor method and a multiple of 290 months under Reg. § 1.72-9 (Table V for a single life annuity). The results favor the use of the IRS safe-harbor method even more so in the case of a joint and survivor annuity, since the fixed rates are based on single life annuities under the safe-harbor method.

¶ 903   Taxation of Taxable Lump-Sum Distributions

If an employee-participant receives a lump-sum distribution (as defined later in the chapter) from a qualified plan, the entire amount of the distribution minus the amount of after-tax contributions (remember VDECs are treated as employer contributions) made by the participant is subject to taxation in the year in which the distribution is actually received under Code Sec. 402. The taxable amount of the lump-sum distribution (LSD) is generally treated as fully taxable ordinary income. For very large distributions, this can mean that most or all of the distribution will be taxed at the top marginal tax rate for individuals (35 percent after 2002). Prior to 1987, taxpayers meeting specified conditions could elect to determine the tax on all or part of an LSD using the ten-year forward averaging method. The ten-year forward averaging method was generally repealed by TRA '86 with respect to distributions received after 1986. But, under a special transition rule contained in TRA '86, taxpayers who were age 50 on January 1, 1986, can elect to treat the pre-1974 portion of their lump-sum as a long-term capital gain taxed at a rate of 20 percent and use ten-year averaging (on the post-1973 portion of the taxable distribution or, alternatively on the entire taxable distribution, in lieu of treating the pre-1974 portion as a LTCG). An eligible LSD recipient can tax the pre-1974 portion of the taxable LSD as a LTCG and not use ten-year averaging on the post-1973 portion. In that case, the post-1973 portion would be taxed as part of the recipient's taxable income for the year and would be taxable at the recipient's regular income tax rates. For LSDs received prior to 2000, taxpayers, in general (not limited to those who were at least age 50 in 1986), had the choice of using the five-year forward averaging method of former Code Sec. 402(d). However, five-year forward averaging was repealed with respect to distributions received after 1999, and no special transition rules were provided such as those described for the use of ten-year forward averaging.[75] As a result, the five-year forward averaging provisions are not covered in detail in this book.

If the taxpayer desires to avoid taxation on a lump sum altogether, the lump sum must be rolled over into an IRA or another qualified plan as covered later in the chapter. This section of the chapter describes the special taxation of lump-sum distributions. Critical to this coverage is a description of important terms and qualification rules. These are covered immediately below.

.01   Major Definition and Qualifying Rules

Only certain distributions made from qualifying plans under certain circumstances qualify for special tax treatment as indicated below.

Lump-Sum Distributions (LSD). Under Code Sec. 402(e)(4)(D), an LSD is a distribution or payment from a qualified plan "within one taxable year" of the "balance to the credit of an employee," payable:

(1) on account of the death of the employee participant;

(2) after the employee reaches age 59½;

(3) on account of an employee's separation from service (in the case of an employee, but not a self-employed individual); or

(4) after the participant becomes disabled (in the case of self-employed individuals only).

Note, however, that the IRS has stated that an "in-service" distribution from a pension plan does not meet the requirements for an LSD unless the participant has attained the plan's normal retirement age.[76]

A profit-sharing plan distribution made in one taxable year and a pension plan distribution made in a different year are treated as separate LSDs. Consequently, a profit-sharing plan LSD received in

---

[75] Code Sec. 402(d), as repealed by P.L. 104-188, 104th Cong., 2d Sess., Sec. 1401(a) (Aug. 20, 1996).

[76] TIR 1403 (Sept. 1975); TR 8507042.

2006 could be taxed using the ten-year forward averaging provisions, and a pension plan distribution received in 2007 could be rolled over into an IRA. But, in determining the amount of an LSD for purposes of the special averaging tax method, all of an employer's pension plans including both defined benefit and defined contribution plans are treated as a single plan; all of an employer's profit-sharing plans are treated as single plans, and all of an employer's stock bonus plans are considered to be a single plan.[77] However, profit-sharing plan balances need not be aggregated with pension plan balances for this purpose.

Separation from Service. A distribution made to an employee as a result of that employee's separation from service can be treated as an LSD under Code Sec. 402(e)(4)(D). Note that an individual is not considered to have separated from service if he or she continues to perform substantial similar services for the employer in the capacity of an independent contractor or if an individual continues in the same job for a new employer in a merger or consolidation, in which the old employer disappears as a legal entity.[78]

Distribution Within One Taxable Year. A distribution of the balance to the credit of the employee must be made within one taxable year of the recipient to qualify as an LSD.[79] However, this does not have to be the same calendar year in which separation from service (or one of the other qualifying events) occurs.

Balance to the Credit of the Employee. Only a distribution of the "balance to the credit of the employee' at the time of the distribution is eligible for LSD treatment.[80] For this purpose, the date on which the distribution commences is the date on which one of the qualifying events for LSD status (described above) occurs.

The term "balance to the credit of an employee" includes any amount to the credit of the employee under any plans which must be aggregated pursuant to the plan aggregation rules of Code Sec. 402(e)(4)(D)(ii) (described above).[81] Further, the balance to the credit of an employee generally includes any amount which is not forfeited under the plan as of the close of the taxable year of the recipient within which the distribution is made.[82]

However, the balance to the credit of the employee does not include:

(1) Voluntary deductible employee contributions (VDECs).[83] Thus, distributions of VDECs are not eligible for special tax treatment.

---

[77] Code Sec. 402(e)(4)(D)(ii).

[78] *See. e.g. Reinhardt,* 85 TC 511, Dec. 42,413 (1985) and Rev. Rul. 72-440, 1972-2 CB 225.

[79] Prop. Reg. § 1.402(e)-2(d)(1).

[80] Prop. Reg. § 1.402(e)-2(d)(1)(ii).
[81] Prop. Reg. § 1.402(e)-2(d)(1)(v).
[82] Prop. Reg. § 1.402(e)-2(d)(1)(vii).
[83] *See* IRS Form 4972 for ten-year averaging purposes.

¶ 903.01

(2) Amounts payable to an alternate payee under a qualified domestic relations order (QDRO).[84]

Required Minimum Period Service. Code Sec. 402(d)(4)(F) (applicable to taxable years beginning before 2000) indicates that a qualified plan distribution cannot be treated as an LSD unless the employee has participated in the plan for at least five years before the taxable year in which the distribution is made. Note that the five-year participation requirement is not a prerequisite to the use of long-term capital gain treatment for a portion of an LSD.[85] However, a recipient cannot use ten-year averaging if the participant did not satisfy the minimum service requirement.

.02 Capital Gains Treatment for LSDs

The tax treatment of LSDs was significantly altered by TRA '86, effective generally for distributions made after December 31, 1986. In general, LTCG treatment is no longer available on LSDs. However, under a special grandfather rule specified in sec. 1122(h)(3) of TRA '86, individuals who were at least age 50 on January 1, 1986 can elect to treat the pre-1974 participation portion of one taxable LSD as an LTCG taxable at a rate of 20 percent (the age 59½ requirement does not apply in this case). The election can also be made by any individual, trust, or estate with respect to an employee who was age 50 on January 1, 1986. The making of this election precludes the use of special tax treatment (e.g., ten-year forward averaging) on another LSD. However, ten-year averaging can be used to determine the tax on the post-1973 (ordinary income) portion of the same distribution.

Example: Assume that Wyatt received a $500,000 LSD from a qualified pension plan to which only his employer made contributions. Assume that Wyatt's pre-1974 participation in the plan amounted to 27 percent of his total participation time in the plan. In this case, the pre-1974 portion of his taxable LSD is $135,000 ($500,000 × 27%). The tax under the special grandfather rule on this amount is $27,000 ($135,000 × 20%).

Amount Eligible for LTCG Treatment Only the pre-1974 participation portion of an LSD is eligible for the special grandfathered 20 percent LTCG tax treatment described above.[86] The pre-1974 participation portion is determined by dividing the number of calendar months that the employee actually participated in the plan before 1974 by the total number of months that the employee

---

[84] Code Sec. 402(e)(4)(D)(v).
[85] *See* Prop. Reg. § 1.402(e)-2(d)(3).

[86] IRS Pub. No. 575, at 19.

actually participated in the plan.[87] For this purpose, the proposed regulations state that the number of months of active participation is the number of calendar months during that period beginning with the first month in which the employee became a participant under the plan and ending with the earliest of:

(1) the month in which the employee received an LSD from the plan;

(2) the month in which the employee dies;

(3) the month in which an employee who receives an LSD on account of disability became disabled; or

(4) in the case of a self-employed individual, the month in which he or she separates from service.

Any portion of a pre-1974 calendar year of participation is counted as a full year; any portion of a post-1973 month is counted as a full month.[88]

> **Example:** Martin, age 69, began participation in his employer's pension plan on October 24, 1964 and continued active participation in the plan until November 3, 2006, when he retired and separated from service. His total months of participation before 1974 is 120 (1964 is counted as a whole year—1964-1973 is 10 years or 120 months). His total months of participation is 515 (120 before 1974 and 395 after 1973—32 years plus 11 months in 2006, counting November as a whole month). Thus, 120/515 or 23.30 percent of the taxable portion of one LSD he receives could be taxed as an LTCG at a rate of 20 percent. The post-1973 (ordinary income) portion of the same distribution could be taxed by using ten-year averaging since Martin was over age 50 on January 1, 1986.

.03 Taxation of an LSD Using the Ten-Year Averaging and Five-Year Averaging Methods

Prior to 2000, qualified plan participants were permitted to use five-year forward averaging (or ten-year averaging if the participant was age 50 on January 1, 1986) to determine the tax on one LSD (or the post-1973 portion of one LSD if the participant was eligible and elected to use the special LTCG treatment on the pre-1974 portion). If a participant used five-year averaging on one LSD prior to 2000, ten-year averaging (discussed below) cannot be used on another LSD. The five-year forward averaging method was repealed for dis-

---

[87] *Id.*

[88] Prop. Reg. § 1.402(e)-2(d)(3)(ii).

tributions in taxable years beginning after 1999.[89] Thus, after 1999, only ten-year averaging will be available.

Under former Code Sec. 402(d), if a taxpayer elected five-year averaging, he/she determined the tax on the LSD separately from the rest of his/her taxable income. The tax using five-year averaging was determined by (1) dividing the taxable LSD (or the post-1973 portion if LTCG treatment was elected on the pre-1974 portion) by five, (2) determining the tax on that amount using the rates for single filers for the taxable year in which the distribution was received, and (3) multiplying that tax amount by five.

Taxation of LSDs Using Ten-Year Forward Averaging. Under former Code Sec. 402(e)(1), taxpayers prior to 1987 could use ten-year forward averaging to determine the tax on one or more qualifying LSDs prior to reaching age 59½ and on one LSD after becoming age 59½ or older. As noted above, ten-year forward averaging is generally not available after 1986. However, under sec. 1122(h)(5) of TRA '86, a special grandfather rule permits plan participants who were at least age 50 on January 1, 1986 and other recipients such as estates and trusts with respect to a plan participant who was age 50 or more on January 1, 1986, to elect to use ten-year forward averaging (using 1986 tax rates), for one LSD received after 1986. Use of the ten-year forward averaging in such circumstances precludes the use of the method on a subsequent distribution.

Determination of Tax Using Ten-Year Forward Averaging. The tax on a LSD using ten-year forward averaging is determined by (1) dividing the taxable amount of the LSD by ten (the post-1973 participation (ordinary income) portion of the taxable LSD if LTCG treatment is elected for the pre-1974 participation portion) and adding the zero bracket amount applicable to a single-filing taxpayer in 1986; (2) then, determining the tax on that sum using the 1986 tax rates applicable to a single-filing taxpayer for the year 1986; and (3) multiplying that tax amount by ten to determine the tax.[90] This process is undertaken by separating the taxable amount of the LSD from the rest of the taxpayer's taxable income for the year of the distribution.

> **Example:** Charlie Smith, who was age 71 on January 1, 2006, retired in 2006 and received a lump-sum taxable distribution amounting to $400,000 (75% of which was attributable to

---

[89] Code Sec. 402(d), repealed for taxable years beginning after 1999 by P.L. 104-188, 104th Cong., 2d Secs., (Aug. 20, 1996), Sec. 1401(a).

[90] TRA '86, Sec. 1122(h)(5).

post-1973 participation in the plan). First, assume that Smith elects to use 10-year averaging on the post-1973 portion and the special LTCG treatment on the pre-1974 portion. In that case, Smith's tax on the LSD received in 2006 would be $86,330 (the $20,000 determined as follows):

(1) Determine the pre-1974 portion of the taxable LSD
$400,000×.25 .... $100,000

(2) Determine the tax on the pre-1974 portion
$100,000×.20 .... $20,000

(3) Determine post-1973 participation portion of the distribution $400,000×.75.................... $300,000

(4) Divide ordinary income portion by 10
$300,000/10.................................. $30,000

(5) Tax at single rates (1986 rates) on $30,000 plus $2,480
$6,157 + .34($32,480 − $31,080) $6,633

(6) Multiply the tax on 1/10 of the distribution by 10
$6,633 × 10................................. $66,330

(7) Add the tax amounts on the pre-1974 and post-1973 portions to determine the total amount of tax on the distribution
$20,000 + $66,330........................... $86,330

   If Smith had elected to tax the entire taxable LSD using ten-year averaging, the tax on distribution would be $102,602, determined as follows:

(1) Divide the taxable distribution by 10
$400,000/10.................................. $40,000

(2) Tax at single rates (1986 rates) on $40,000 plus $2,480
$8,101.80 + .38 ($42,480 − $36,800) $10,260.20

(3) Multiply the tax on 1/10 of the distribution by 10
$10,260.20 × 10 .... $102,602

   Obviously, Smith would be better off treating the pre-1974 portion of the taxable LSD as a LTCG taxable at 20 percent since that election would save nearly $16,000 in taxes.

   Minimum Distribution Allowance. The total taxable amount of an LSD must be reduced by the minimum distribution allowance (MDA) when the taxpayer uses five-year or ten-year averaging. The MDA is an amount equal to (1) the lesser of: (a) $10,000, or (b) 50 percent of the total taxable amount, reduced (but not below zero) by (2) 20 percent of the total taxable amount in excess of $20,000.[91]

---

[91] *See* IRS Form 4972 and Form 4972 Instructions.

Note that the minimum distribution allowance is zero if the ordinary income portion of the distribution is at least $70,000 because 20 percent of ($70,000 − $20,000), or $10,000, must be subtracted from the maximum MDA of $10,000.

> **Example:** Suppose that Jackson received a $60,000 LSD from a qualified plan in 2006 and that he had made $10,000 of after-tax contributions to the plan. Jackson began participating in the plan in 1976, so that none of the taxable portion of the LSD can be taxed as an LTCG. If Jackson elects to use ten-year forward averaging, his tax on the distribution is computed as follows:

(1) Taxable amount of the distribution $50,000

(2) Minus minimum distribution allowance
$10,000 minus .2 ($50,000 − $20,000) $4,000

(3) Total taxable amount $46,000

(4) Divide $46,000 by 10 . . . . $4,600

(5) Tax on $4,600 using 10-year averaging $587.40

(6) Multiply $587.40 by 10 . . . . $5,874.00

(7) Tax on ordinary income portion. $5,874.00

Note that when an LSD includes an annuity contract, adjustments must be made, if the taxable amount of the LSD is less than $70,000. In effect, a portion of the MDA equal to the portion of the distribution consisting of the actuarial value of the annuity must be allocated to the annuity.[92]

Special Treatment of Annuity Contracts. The current actuarial value of an annuity contract included as part of an LSD is used to figure the tax on the part of the distribution that is taxed using ten-year averaging (recall that such part is the entire taxable LSD or the post-1973 participation (ordinary income) portion if LTCG treatment is properly elected for the pre-1974 participation portion).[93] If an annuity contract is distributed as part of an LSD, the value of the contract is added to the part of the taxable LSD that is taxed using five-year averaging (or ten-year averaging if the taxpayer qualifies for and elects such treatment). The tax using ten-year averaging is then computed on the combined amount. That amount of tax is then reduced by the product of (1) the tax amount multiplied by (2) a fraction, the numerator of which is the value of

---

[92] Prop. Reg. § 1.402(e)-2(c)(1)(B)(2).

[93] *See* IRS Form 4972 and Form 4972 Instructions.

the annuity contract and the denominator of which is the sum of the value of the annuity contract and the part of the taxable LSD taxed using ten-year averaging.[94]

> **Example:** Assume that Raymond, age 71, began participating in a qualified pension plan of his employer on January 1, 1974 and retired on December 31, 2006, receiving a $200,000 LSD and an annuity contract valued at $100,000 on that date. He had made no after-tax contributions to the plan. Since he did not participate in the plan before 1974, none of the distribution is eligible for LTCG treatment. He elected the ten-year forward averaging method to determine the tax on the distribution. That tax is first determined on the combined total of $300,000 ($200,000 + $100,000) and amounts to $66,330, determined as follows:

(1) Divide the taxable portion by ten:
$300,000/10 = ... $30,000

(2) Determine the tax on $30,000 + $2,480
$6,157 + .34 ($32,480 − $31,080) = ... $6,633

(3) Multiply the tax on one-tenth of the distribution by
ten: $6,633 × 10 = ... $66,330

> Next, the tax of $66,330 is multiplied by the fraction of $100,000/$300,000 to yield $22,110. Finally, the combined amount of tax, $66,330, is reduced by the $22,110 to yield, $44,220, which is the tax on the non-annuity portion of the distribution. Another way to calculate the $44,220 of tax payable on the non-annuity portion of the distribution is to multiply the tax on the total amount of the distribution, $66,330 by $200,000 / $300,000, which is the ratio of the non-annuity portion of the distribution to the total distribution.

Taxation of LSDs Under a Qualified Domestic Relations Order (QDRO). For purposes of the LSD rules, when a portion of an LSD is payable to an alternative payee who is a participant's spouse or former spouse pursuant to a QDRO, the balance to the credit of the employee is to be divided under Code Sec. 402(a)(9) between the participant and the alternative payee. Thus, a ratable portion of the after-tax employee contributions will be allocated to that spouse or former spouse. The spouse or former spouse can elect

---

[94] *See* IRS Form 4972 and Form 4972 Instructions.

to tax his or her portion of the LSD using the special rules or roll over the distribution without affecting the taxation of the employee-participant's portion. The employee-participant can use any special methods (as described in this chapter) that are available to him or her.

Deciding Whether to Elect Ten-Year Forward Averaging. The decision of whether to elect ten-year averaging for the ordinary income portion of an LSD or the entire distribution should be based on a consideration of (1) the average (effective) tax rate that would be incurred if ten-year averaging were used, (2) the marginal income tax rate of the taxpayer on the LSD for the year of the distribution, (3) the 20 percent rate that can apply to the portion of the LSD which is eligible for the special LTCG treatment, and (4) whether and in what expected amount future LSDs may be received (this is an important factor because ten-year averaging can be used on only one LSD). If the taxpayer is subject to the top marginal income tax rate of 35 percent in 2003 and later years and (1) receives an LSD with a taxable ordinary income amount of $750,000 or less, and (2) does not expect to receive any larger LSDs in the future, that taxpayer should use ten-year averaging (if possible). The reason is that the effective rate under ten-year averaging will be 34.6 percent or less, compared to the top marginal tax rate of 35 percent that would otherwise apply to the distribution.[95] In addition, the LTCG option should be chosen when it is available except in cases where the entire taxable amount of the LSD is about $250,000 or less (in those cases the effective rate using ten-year averaging is 20 percent or less).

Example: Fredericks, age 70, retired in 2006 and received an LSD from a qualified pension plan amounting to $500,000. Assume the entire distribution is taxable, that the pre-1974 portion (eligible for LTCG treatment) is $100,000, that the taxpayer is a single filer and has other taxable income of $92,000 (thus, the taxpayer is already in the 28 percent bracket), and that he does not expect to receive any future LSDs. In that case, ten-year averaging should be elected for the ordinary income portion of the distribution since the average applicable rate under that method would be 25.7 percent. LTCG treatment using the special 20 percent rate should be chosen on the pre-1974 portion.

If the recipient of an LSD (who was at least age 50 in 1986) expects to receive a larger LSD in the future, careful consideration

---

[95] For a listing of the average (effective) rates applicable to LSDs using ten-year averaging, see Lassila, Dennis R. and Kilpatrick, Bob G., "Tax Planning for Optimum Benefits in Choosing the Form of Pension Income," *The Journal of Taxation,* Vol. 80, No. 4, April 1994, pp. 220-225.

(taking into account present value concepts) should be undertaken to determine whether the special ten-year averaging and, if available, LTCG treatment should be used on the current LSD or should be saved to use on the future distribution. In addition, the taxpayer should make a calculation to determine whether less tax would be paid taxing the pre-1974 portion of the taxable LSD as an LTCG (as described above) or using ten-year forward averaging to tax the entire distribution.

Filled-In Form 4972. The following example and sample form illustrate the ten-year averaging method, and the completion of Form 4972.

Example (1): Assume that Gerald Brown, age 68, received a $200,000 lump-sum distribution in 2004 (80% of which is attributable to post-1973 plan participation) and that he made no after-tax contributions to the plan. If Brown elects to use ten-year forward averaging to determine the tax on the post-1973 participation portion of the distribution, the tax of $26,870 would be determined as follows:

(1) Determine post-1973 participation portion of the distribution ($200,000 × .8). $160,000.00

(2) Divide $160,000 by 10 . . . . $16,000.00

(3) Tax on $16,000 + $2,480 using 1986 single person tax rates $2,160.30 + .23 ($18,480 − $16,190) $2,687.00

(4) Multiply the tax by 10 . . . . $26,870.00

The LTCG portion of the distribution is $40,000 (20% of the distribution). Assuming that Brown elects to treat the pre-1974 participation portion of the distribution as LTCG income under the grandfather rule, the tax on the $40,000 pre-1974 portion is $8,000 ($40,000 X .20). Note that the employer or other payor indicates to the employee the amount of the taxable LSD that is eligible for LTCG treatment and the remaining post-1973 participation (ordinary income) portion on Form 1099-R that is sent to the employee and filed with the IRS for the taxable year of the distribution.

The filled-in Form 4972 is reproduced on the next page.

¶903.03

Form **4972**	**Tax on Lump-Sum Distributions**	OMB No. 1545-0193
Department of the Treasury Internal Revenue Service (99)	(From Qualified Plans of Participants Born Before January 2, 1936) ▶ Attach to Form 1040 or Form 1041.	20**04** Attachment Sequence No. **28**

Name of recipient of distribution	Identifying number

Part I   Complete this part to see if you can use Form 4972

			Yes	No
1	Was this a distribution of a plan participant's entire balance (excluding deductible voluntary employee contributions and certain forfeited amounts) from all of an employer's qualified plans of one kind (pension, profit-sharing, or stock bonus)? If "No," **do not** use this form	1	✔	
2	Did you roll over any part of the distribution? If "Yes," **do not** use this form	2		✔
3	Was this distribution paid to you as a beneficiary of a plan participant who was born before January 2, 1936?	3		✔
4	Were you **(a)** a plan participant who received this distribution, **(b)** born before January 2, 1936, **and (c)** a participant in the plan for at least 5 years before the year of the distribution?	4	✔	
	If you answered "No" to both questions 3 **and** 4, **do not** use this form.			
5a	Did you use Form 4972 after 1986 for a previous distribution from your own plan? If "Yes," **do not** use this form for a 2004 distribution from your own plan	5a		✔
b	If you are receiving this distribution as a beneficiary of a plan participant who died, did you use Form 4972 for a previous distribution received for that participant after 1986? If "Yes," **do not** use the form for this distribution	5b		✔

Part II   Complete this part to choose the 20% capital gain election (see instructions)

6	Capital gain part from Form 1099-R, box 3	6	40,000	00
7	Multiply line 6 by 20% (.20) . . . . ▶	7	8,000	00
	If you also choose to use Part III, go to line 8. Otherwise, include the amount from line 7 in the total on Form 1040, line 43, or Form 1041, Schedule G, line 1b, whichever applies.			

Part III   Complete this part to choose the 10-year tax option (see instructions)

8	Ordinary income from Form 1099-R, box 2a minus box 3. If you did not complete Part II, enter the taxable amount from Form 1099-R, box 2a.	8	160,000	00
9	Death benefit exclusion for a beneficiary of a plan participant who died before August 21, 1996	9		
10	Total taxable amount. Subtract line 9 from line 8	10	160,000	00
11	Current actuarial value of annuity from Form 1099-R, box 8. If none, enter -0-	11		
12	Adjusted total taxable amount. Add lines 10 and 11. If this amount is $70,000 or more, **skip** lines 13 through 16, enter this amount on line 17, and go to line 18	12		
13	Multiply line 12 by 50% (.50), but **do not** enter more than $10,000 . [13]			
14	Subtract $20,000 from line 12. If line 12 is $20,000 or less, enter -0- . . . . . . [14]			
15	Multiply line 14 by 20% (.20) . . . . [15]			
16	Minimum distribution allowance. Subtract line 15 from line 13	16		
17	Subtract line 16 from line 12	17	160,000	00
18	Federal estate tax attributable to lump-sum distribution	18		
19	Subtract line 18 from line 17. If line 11 is zero, **skip** lines 20 through 22 and go to line 23 . .	19	160,000	00
20	Divide line 11 by line 12 and enter the result as a decimal (rounded to at least three places). . . . . [20]			
21	Multiply line 16 by the decimal on line 20 . . . . [21]			
22	Subtract line 21 from line 11 . . . . [22]			
23	Multiply line 19 by 10% (.10)	23	16,000	00
24	Tax on amount on line 23. Use the Tax Rate Schedule in the instructions	24	2,687	00
25	Multiply line 24 by ten (10). If line 11 is zero, **skip** lines 26 through 28, enter this amount on line 29, and go to line 30	25	26,870	00
26	Multiply line 22 by 10% (.10) . . . . [26]			
27	Tax on amount on line 26. Use the Tax Rate Schedule in the instructions . . . . [27]			
28	Multiply line 27 by ten (10)	28		
29	Subtract line 28 from line 25. Multiple recipients, see instructions . . . . . . ▶	29	26,870	00
30	**Tax on lump-sum distribution.** Add lines 7 and 29. Also include this amount in the total on Form 1040, line 43, or Form 1041, Schedule G, line 1b, whichever applies . . . . ▶	30	34,870	00

For Paperwork Reduction Act Notice, see instructions.   Cat. No. 13187U   Form **4972** (2004)

¶903.03

¶904   Rollover of Qualified Plan Distributions Into a Traditional IRA or Other Qualified Plan

An employee may be able to postpone or avoid taxation on a taxable distribution from a qualified plan in the current year by making a timely rollover of all or some of the distribution into a traditional IRA or another qualified plan (the term "traditional IRA" means an IRA that is not a Roth IRA, an Educational IRA or a SIMPLE IRA—see chapter 10 for coverage of those kinds of IRAs). But, in the case of a partial rollover, tax-free treatment applies only to the amount that is rolled over. Further, the special ten-year forward averaging and capital gain treatment are forfeited for the portion of the distribution that is not rolled over. Distributions are subject to 20 percent mandatory income tax withholding unless they are the subject of a direct trustee-to-trustee transfer.

Rollover treatment is permitted only if the rollover is made within 60 days following the day on which the distribution was received. Further, rollovers from qualified plans into traditional IRAs cannot be revoked.[96]

The Economic Growth and Tax Relief Reconciliation Act of 2001 (EGTRRA) has substantially broadened the availability of rollovers in the case of eligible distributions made from qualified plans and traditional IRAs after December 31, 2001. This section describes the types of distributions that can be rolled over taking into account the changes made by EGTRRA, the operational aspects of rollovers and other pertinent rules.

.01   Eligible Rollover Distributions

All eligible rollover distributions can be rolled over. Eligible rollover distributions are distributions received from qualified plans except for:

(1) Distributions that are a part of a series of substantially equal payments that are made at least annually (a) for the life (or life expectancy) or the joint lives (or joint life expectancies) of the employee and the employee's designated beneficiary or (b) for a specified period of ten years or more (e.g., distributions received as a single life annuity or joint and survivor annuity cannot be rolled over);[97]

(2) Required distributions under the minimum distribution rules of Code Sec. 401(a)(9) (as discussed in Chapter 6);[98]

(3) Returns of Code Sec. 401(k) elective deferrals that are returned as a result of the Code Sec. 415 limitations (see Chapter 7);

---

[96] Reg. § 1.402(c)-2 Q&A 13.
[97] Code Sec. 402(c)(4)(A).
[98] Code Sec. 402(c)(4)(B).

(4) Corrective distributions of excess contributions and excess deferrals under Code Sec. 401(k) plans and of excess aggregate contributions under Code Sec. 401(m) plans, together with income allocable to such corrective distributions (see Chapters 6 and 7 for a discussion of these issues);

(5) Plan loans that are treated as distributions under Code Sec. 72(p) and are not excepted by Code Sec. 72(p)(2) (as discussed earlier in this chapter);

(6) Certain qualified plan loans that are in default;

(7) Dividends paid on employer securities as described in Code Sec. 404(k);

(8) The cost of life insurance coverage;

(9) Any distribution that is made upon the hardship of the employee (prior to 2001, the exception was for hardship distributions only coming out of Code Sec. 401(k) and 403(b) plans);[99] and

(10) Other items designated by the IRS in revenue rulings or similar authoritative pronouncements.[100]

For purposes of the rollover rules, a single sum that is not substantially equal to payments being made periodically (e.g., in annuity form) and that is made before, with, or after the commencement of the periodic payments, is not treated as one of the series of payments, and therefore, may be rolled over.[101]

> **Example:** Ben received 35 percent of the balance to his credit from his employer's money purchase pension plan, and the remainder will be paid to him in the form of a single life annuity. The 35 percent amount can be rolled over into another qualified plan or a traditional IRA.

If the amount (or, if applicable, the method of calculating the amount) of the payments under a plan changes such that the subsequent payments are not substantially equal to payments that have already been made, a new determination must be made about whether the remaining payments are a series of substantially equal payments for which rollover treatment is not permitted. This determination is made without taking into account the payments made before the change.[102]

In the case of a defined contribution plan, a series of payments will be considered a series of substantially equal periodic payments over a period, if, for each year of the period, the amount of the

---

[99] Code Sec. 402(c)(4)(C), as added by P.L. 105-206, 105th Cong., 2d Sess., Sec. 6005(c)(2) (July 22, 1998), and amended by P.L. 107-16, 107th Cong., 1st Sess., Sec. 636(b)(1) (June 7, 2001). See Notice 99-5, 1999-1 CB 10 and Notice 2000-32, 2000-1 CB 1274 for an explanation of this pro-

vision prior to its 2001 amendment along with a description of applicable transition rules.

[100] Reg. § 1.402(c)-2, Q&A 4.

[101] Reg. § 1.402(c)-2, Q&A 6.

[102] Reg. § 1.402(c)-2Q&A5(c).

distribution is determined by dividing the account balance by the remaining number of years in the period. Or, if a participant's account balance in a defined contribution plan is to be distributed in annual installments until the account balance has been reduced to zero, the period of years over which the installments are treated as distributed in order to determine whether there is a series of substantially equal periodic payments must be determined using reasonable actuarial assumptions.[103]

.02 Tax Consequences of Making a Rollover in the Year of the Rollover and in Future Years

The amount of an eligible rollover distribution that is rolled over on a timely basis is not includible in the gross income of the recipient of the distribution and is not subject to FICA and FUTA taxes.[104] Further, the amount rolled over is not subject to the 10 percent premature distribution penalty tax of Code Sec. 72(t). However, the amount of an eligible rollover distribution is subject to income tax withholding at a rate of 20 percent (as discussed below) except to the extent that the distribution is the subject of a direct trustee-to-trustee rollover transfer.[105] Amounts distributed that are not rolled over are fully includible in the recipient's gross income (except for the portion that is equal to nondeductible employee plan contributions) in the year of the distribution. Further, ten-year averaging and LTCG treatment (that are applicable to one LSD received by an individual who was at least age 50 on January 1, 1986—discussed in ¶903.03) are not available with respect to any distribution from a plan (or other plans deemed aggregated with the plan from which the distribution is made) after a rollover is made with respect to a distribution from the same plan.[106] Thus, except for amounts rolled over in future years from the plan, future distributions are fully taxable except for nondeductible employee plan contribution amounts.

If the rollover was made into another qualified plan, a later distribution of the rollover amount and other amounts from the second plan will be taxed like any other qualified plan distributions unless such distributions are rolled over into yet a third qualified plan. Thus, if a distribution from the second plan is a qualifying lump-sum distribution, the distributed amount may be subject to the ten-year averaging and long-term capital gains treatment under sec. 1122(h) of TRA '86 for individuals who were age 50 or older on January 1, 1986. Otherwise, the distribution will be taxed as ordinary income and may be subject to the ten percent premature distributions tax.[107] However,

---

[103] Reg. § 1.402(c)-2, Q&A 5(d).
[104] Code Secs. 402(c)(1), 3121(a)(5), and 3306(b)(5).
[105] Code Secs. 402(c)(1) and 3405(b).
[106] IRS Pub. 575 at 18.
[107] *Id.*

with respect to Code Sec. 403(b) plans and Code Sec. 457 governmental deferred compensation plans which, after 2001, can accept eligible rollover distributions from other types of retirement plans (as noted in ¶ 904.05 below), ten-year averaging and long-term capital gains treatment will not be available for any distributions made from such plans that have accepted eligible rollover distributions.[108] In order to preserve such special treatment, the initial distribution from the other type of plan should first be made into a conduit IRA (as discussed in ¶ 904.06 below) and then, later, distributed into the Code Sec. 403(b) plan or Code Sec. 457 governmental deferred compensation plan.

If the rollover was made into a traditional IRA or IR annuity, any amounts later distributed on account of that rollover are taxable in the same manner as other distributions from traditional IRAs and IR annuities (see ¶ 1002.06), unless the later distribution is rolled over into yet another traditional IRA or IR annuity (see ¶ 1002.10) or another qualified plan (if the traditional IRA was a conduit IRA as discussed later in this chapter). The penalty taxes noted above may also apply. No special tax rules such as ten-year averaging can be used unless amounts are rolled over from conduit IRA to qualified plans.[109]

.03 Rollover of Property

If a taxpayer receives a distribution of property other than cash from a qualified plan, he or she may roll over the property into an eligible retirement plan (as defined in ¶ 904.05 below). Further, the taxpayer can sell part or all of the property and roll over the proceeds into an eligible retirement plan. No gain or loss on the sale of such property is recognized if all of the proceeds are rolled over.[110]

> **Example:** On June 3, 2006, Joe received a distribution of $80,000 cash and property worth $70,000 as an LSD from his employer's qualified plan. In early July he sold the property for $85,000. On July 25, 2006, he rolled over the cash received from his employer's plan plus the cash received from the sale into a traditional IRA. The $15,000 gain on the sale is not recognized.

If the taxpayer does not roll over all of the proceeds from the sale of property received from a qualified plan, the gain attributable to the portion of the proceeds not rolled over must be recognized.[111] Further, the portion of the distribution attributable to the value of the property (on the date of the distribution) which is not rolled over is taxable to the recipient and possibly subject to the ten percent premature distribution tax of Code Sec. 72(t). For example, if the taxpayer in the above

---

[108] P.L. 107-16, 107th Cong., 1st Sess., Sec. 641(f) (June 7, 2001).
[109] See IRS Pub. 590

[110] Code Sec. 402(c)(6)(D).
[111] Code Sec. 402(c)(6)(C).

example rolls over only half of the proceeds from the sale of the property, half of the $15,000 gain or $7,500 would have to be recognized. In addition, since only half of the proceeds are rolled over, one-half of the value of the property (as of the date of the distribution) is taxable to Joe and could be subject to the ten percent premature distribution tax of Code Sec. 72(t).

.04 Rollovers and Qualified Domestic Relations Orders (QDROs) and Rollovers Made by Surviving Spouses of Plan Participants

The Retirement Equity Act of 1984 created an additional class of payees for qualified plans—alternate payees under QDROs. As noted earlier in the chapter, nondeductible employee contributions to qualified plans are apportioned between the participant and any alternate payees who are spouses or former spouses, and the participant and the alternate payees are separately taxed on distributions received.

Alternate payees who are spouses or former spouses can also roll over eligible rollover distributions they receive. If the alternate payee receives a distribution from a qualified plan and rolls over any portion of the distribution into an eligible retirement plan, the portion rolled over is not taxable to the alternate payee.[112]

If a surviving spouse of a plan participant receives a distribution from a plan from which eligible rollover distributions may generally be made, that surviving spouse (for distributions received prior to 2002) could only roll over the amount into a traditional IRA or IR annuity.[113] However, as a result of EGTRRA, surviving spouses that receive eligible rollover distributions after the death of the plan participant spouse can roll over such distributions to any eligible retirement plan (as defined in ¶ 904.05 below).[114] That is because, pursuant to EGTRRA, all of the provisions concerning rollovers apply just the same to surviving spouses of plan participants as they do to plan participants for distributions received after 2001.

> **Example:** Jill's husband died, and Jill was the designated beneficiary under his qualified plan. Jill received a lump-sum distribution and elected to roll over that distribution. If the distribution were received in 2001, it could only be rolled over into a traditional IRA or IR annuity. If the distribution were received in 2002 or later, it can be rolled over into any eligible retirement plan.

---

[112] Code Sec. 402(e)(1)(B).
[113] Code Sec. 402(c)(9), as amended by P.L. 107-16, 107th Cong., 1st Sess., Sec. 641(d) (June 7, 2001).

[114] Former Code Sec. 402(c)(9).

.05 Basic Taxation Rules Concerning Rollovers

To qualify for tax-free treatment, rollovers of eligible rollover distributions must be made within 60 days after the day on which the employee receives the distribution.[115] However, in the case of distributions made after December 31, 2001, the IRS is permitted to waive the 60-day requirement in situations where the requirement was not met because of casualty, disaster, or other events beyond the reasonable control of the individual subject to the requirement.[116] The IRS has recently provided guidance concerning obtaining such waivers of the 60-day requirement.[117] According to the guidance, a taxpayer must generally apply for the hardship exception waiver to the 60-day roll-over requirement by using the same procedure as outlined in Rev. Proc. 2005-4 (and successor procedures in coming years)[118] for obtaining letter rulings accompanied by the user fee that is set forth in Rev. Proc. 2005-8 (and successor procedures in coming years).[119] The IRS has indicated that it will issue a favorable ruling in cases where the failure to waive such requirement would be against equity or good conscience, including casualty, disaster, or other events beyond the reasonable control of the taxpayer. In determining whether to grant a waiver, the IRS will consider all relevant factors and circumstances, including (1) errors committed by a financial institution, (2) inability to complete a roll-over due to death, disability, hospitalization, incarceration, restrictions imposed by a foreign country or postal error; (3) the use of the amount distributed; and (4) the time elapsed since the distribution occurred. The IRS has issued a number of letter rulings in response to taxpayer requests on the basis of its published guidance. The IRS has granted waivers in a number of varying situations (e.g., where due to a recent stroke, a taxpayer failed to make a tax-free rollover within the 60 days, but did so soon after the omission was discovered).[120] In a number of other instances, the IRS has denied such waivers (e.g., an unemployed individual withdrew funds from his IRA for living expenses and, on becoming employed again, requested the waiver from the IRS).[121] The IRS also noted that no application is required for a waiver if (1) a financial institution receives funds on behalf of taxpayer prior to the expiration of the 60-day rollover period, (2) the taxpayer follows all procedures required by the financial institution for depositing the funds into an eligible retirement plan within the

---

[115] Code Sec. 402(c)(3).
[116] Code Sec 402(c)(3)(B), as added by P.L. 107-16, 107th Cong., 1st Sess., Sec 644(a) (June 7, 2001).
[117] Rev. Proc. 2003-16, 2003-1 CB, 305.
[118] IRB 2005-1, 128.

[119] IRB 2005-1, 243.
[120] *See* e.g., IRS Letter Rulings 200507019, 200507020, 200402028, and 200332026.
[121] *See* e.g., IRS Letter Rulings 200428034 and 200415011.

60-day period, and (3) solely due to an error on the part of the financial institution, the funds are not deposited into the eligible retirement plan within the 60-day period.

The 60-day period is also extended in the case of frozen deposits. The period during which the amount is a frozen deposit is not counted in the 60-day period allowed for a tax-free rollover to a traditional IRA or other qualified plan. After the release of the funds, the 60-day period continues, but will not end for at least ten days after the release.[122]

A frozen deposit is any deposit that may not be withdrawn because of:

(1) the bankruptcy or insolvency of any financial institution, or

(2) any requirement imposed by the state in which the institution is located due to the bankruptcy or insolvency (or threat of bankruptcy or insolvency) of one or more financial institutions in the state.[123]

Finally, Rev. Proc. 2005-27[124] also indicates that the time for making a rollover may be postponed in the event of service in a combat zone or in the case of a Presidentially declared disaster or a terroristic or military action.

Amounts rolled over will not be taxed until distributed later to the participant from the traditional IRA or eligible qualified plan as noted above.

Limit on the Amount that Can Be Rolled Over. EGTRRA has expanded the limit on the amount that can be rolled over. For distributions received from plans other than traditional IRAs and IR annuities after December 31, 2001, the nontaxable portion of the distribution (that amount which is attributable to after-tax plan contributions made by the participant) can be rolled over in addition to the taxable portion of the distribution (the amount which would be taxable if the rollover were not made) if:[125]

(1) the nontaxable portion is transferred in a direct trustee-to-trustee transfer (direct rollover) to a qualified trust which is part of a plan which is a defined contribution plan, and that trust agrees to separately account for the nontaxable portion (and the earnings, thereon) and the taxable portion, if any, of the rollover; or

(2) the nontaxable portion is rolled over into a traditional IRA or IR annuity.

---

[122] Code Sec. 402(c)(7)(A).
[123] Code Sec. 402(c)(7)(B).
[124] Rev. Proc. 2005-27, IRB 2005-20, 1050, superseding Rev. Proc. 2004-13, IRB 2004-4,

335, superseding Rev. Proc. 2002-71, 2002-2 CB 850.
[125] Code Sec. 402(c)(2), as amended by P.L. 107-16, 107th Cong., 1st Sess., Sec. 643(a) (June 7, 2001).

The new rules did not mandate separate accounting for the taxable and nontaxable portions of the distribution when the direct rollover is made to a traditional IRA or IR annuity because there are already provisions in place that require that such amounts be kept separate under the IRA rules as covered in ¶ 1002.05 and ¶ 1002.06. In the case of distributions from traditional IRAs and IR annuities after 2001 (as noted in the following section), only the taxable portion of the distribution can be rolled over into some other type of plan.[126]

For distributions received prior to 2002 and rollovers of distributions received after 2001 which did not meet the guidelines noted in the above paragraph, the maximum amount that could have been rolled over is the taxable portion of the distribution (the amount that would be subject to tax if no rollover were made).[127] The amount that would be taxable if the distribution were not rolled over is the amount of cash plus the fair market value of the property received in the distribution minus any nondeductible contributions relating thereto.

Eligible Retirement Plans. EGTRRA has expanded the types of qualified plans from which eligible rollover distributions may be made after December 31, 2001. Under the expanded rules, rollovers can be made of eligible rollover distributions from qualified pension, profit-sharing, stock bonus plans, Code Sec. 403(a) annuity plans, Code Sec. 403(b) tax sheltered annuity plans, governmental Code Sec. 457 plans (covered in Chapter 14) and traditional IRAs (only the taxable portion of an IRA distribution can be rolled over into other types of plans—for further discussion see the coverage on IRA rollovers in ¶ 1002.10) into an eligible retirement plan as defined in Code Sec. 402(c)(8)(B).[128] For purposes of the preceding sentence, distributions that are made from SIMPLE IRAs are treated like distributions from traditional IRAs once the employee has participated in the SIMPLE IRA for at least two years, and thus can be rolled over into eligible retirement plans.[129] Prior to 2002, tax-free rollovers from Code Sec. 457 plans could not be made; rollovers from traditional IRAs (except for conduit IRAs covered below) could only be made to other traditional IRAs; and rollovers from Code Sec. 403(b) plans could only be made to other Code Sec. 403(b) plans or traditional IRAs. Under Code Sec. 402(c)(8)(B), as amended by

---

[126] Code Sec. 408(d)(3)(A), as amended by P.L. 107-16, 107th Cong., 1st Sess., Sec. 642 (June 7, 2001).

[127] Code Sec. 402(c)(2) and Former Code Sec. 402(c)(2).

[128] Code Sec. 457(e)(16)(A), as added by P.L. 107-16, 107th Cong., 1st Sess., Sec. 641(a)(1)(A)

(June 7, 2001); and Code Sec. 408(d)(3)(A), as amended by P.L. 107-16, 107th Cong., 1st Sess., Sec. 642 (June 7, 2001).

[129] Code Sec. 408(d)(3)(G), as amended by P.L. 107-16, 107th Cong., 1st Sess., Sec. 642 (June 7, 2001).

EGTRRA, the following can be considered eligible retirement plans after 2001 (prior to 2002, only the first four were considered to be eligible retirement plans):[130]

(1) qualified pension, profit-sharing and stock bonus plans under Code Sec. 401;

(2) Code Sec. 403(a) annuities;

(3) traditional IRAs;

(4) IR annuities;

(5) Code Sec. 403(b) tax sheltered annuities; and

(6) Code Sec. 457 governmental employer (as described in Code Sec. 457(e)(1)(A)) deferred compensation plans (Code Sec. 457 plans are covered in Chapter 14).

It should be noted that in order for a Code Sec. 457 governmental deferred compensation plan to accept rollovers from a qualified plan, a Code Sec. 403(a) annuity, a traditional IRA, IR annuity, or a Code Sec. 403(b) plan, the recipient Code Sec. 457 plan must agree to account for such rollovers separately.[131] The reason for this separate accounting rule is that premature distributions from Code Sec. 457 plans will generally be subject to the ten-percent premature distribution tax (discussed in ¶901.05) to the extent that the distributions consist of amounts that are attributable to rollovers from another type of plan.[132]

Although eligible retirement plans can accept rollovers of eligible retirement distributions, there is no requirement that they have to do so.[133] Thus a participant, who had worked for one employer maintaining a plan from which eligible rollover distributions can be made, will only be able to roll over an eligible rollover distribution into a traditional IRA if the plan of that participant's new employer does not accept rollover contributions.

Revocations of Rollovers Not Permitted. Taxpayers cannot revoke rollovers of eligible rollover distributions that are made into a traditional IRA.[134] Consequently, the taxpayer may not change his mind and try to use ten-year forward averaging or LTCG treatment with respect to the distribution.

> **Comment:** The rule preventing revocation of rollovers puts a higher premium on careful planning as to whether a distribu-

---

[130] Code Sec. 402(c)(8)(B), as amended by P.L. 107-16, 107th Cong., 1st Sess., Sec. 641 (June 7, 2001).

[131] Code Sec. 402(c)(10), as added by P.L. 107-16, 107th Cong., 1st Sess., Sec. 641(a)(2)(B) (June 7, 2001).

[132] See Code Sec. 72(t)(9), as added by P.L. 107-16, 107th Cong., 1st Sess., Sec. 641(a)(2)(C) (June 7, 2001).

[133] See, e.g., HR Rep. No. 107-51, 107th Cong., 1st Sess. (2001).

[134] Reg. § 1.402(c)-2, Q&A 13.

¶**904.05**

tion should be rolled over. Making the rollover into a traditional IRA precludes current and future use of five-year and ten-year forward averaging and capital gains treatment with respect to the distribution and any future distributions from that plan or other employer plans of the same type. Because the rollover must be made within 60 days of receiving the distribution, planning should begin before the distribution is actually received.

Although a taxpayer cannot revoke a rollover election (to a traditional IRA) to secure ten-year averaging treatment, the IRS, in a Field Service Advice, has indicated that there is another way in which the result could be achieved.[135] The taxpayer could reclassify the rollover contribution as being a nondeductible traditional IRA contribution (see ¶1002.05 for a discussion of nondeductible traditional IRA contributions). That reclassification could require payment of the 6 percent excise tax on excess contributions to a traditional IRA (see the discussion of that tax in ¶1002.05).

There is no prohibition against revocation of rollovers of eligible rollover distributions to other qualified plans.

Distribution of Amounts Rolled Over To an Eligible Retirement Plan. Under Rev. Rul. 2004-12,[136] if an eligible retirement plan (as defined above) separately accounts for amounts attributable to rollover contributions to the plan, that plan may permit the distribution of amounts attributable to the amounts rolled over at any time, at the participant's request. Such distributions are not subject to the distribution limitations that apply with respect to employer contributions to most qualified plans as covered in Chapters 5, 6, and 7. Thus, a Code Sec. 401(k) plan can distribute amounts attributable to rollover contributions under such circumstances without regard to the restrictions on distributions from 401(k) plans, in general, as covered under the final Code Sec. 401(k) regulations. However, rollover amounts are still subject to the following recipient plan requirements: (1) the Code Sec. 401(a)(9) required minimum distribution rules as covered in Chapter 6, (2) the joint and survivor annuity requirements of Code Secs. 401(a)(11) and 417 as covered in Chapter 6, and (3) the ten percent premature distributions tax under Code Sec. 72(t), as discussed in ¶901.05.

.06 Conduit IRAs

If a qualifying distribution is rolled over into a traditional IRA or IR annuity, such amount is ordinarily not eligible to be taxed using the special ten-year averaging rules and/or long-term capital

---

[135] IRS Field Service Advice 1999-775.   [136] IRB 2004-7, 478.

gain treatment at a later time. However, one method can preserve the possibility of using ten-year forward averaging and/or long-term capital gain treatment at a later date to determine tax on the amount rolled over. That method is to use a traditional IRA as a conduit; that is, to roll over the eligible rollover distribution into a traditional IRA and later roll over the balance in that IRA into another employer's qualified plan.[137] Such an IRA is called a conduit IRA. Use of the conduit IRA enables the taxpayer to roll over an eligible rollover distribution into another employer's qualified plan after the end of the statutory 60-day rollover period if the eligible rollover distribution is rolled over into the conduit IRA within the required 60 days.

In order to use a traditional IRA as a conduit, only the assets received in the eligible rollover distribution (plus any earnings thereon) can be invested in the IRA.[138] No additional contributions can be made to that IRA. (However, contributions can be made to some other IRA of the taxpayer in accordance with the rules described in Chapter 10.) Once part or all of the funds in the conduit IRA are withdrawn, they must be reinvested into the second qualified plan within 60 days.[139]

Amounts that are withdrawn from conduit IRAs and that are timely re-rolled over into other traditional IRAs, IR annuities, or eligible qualified plans are not includible in the recipient's gross income. There is no limit on the amount of time that a rollover distribution can remain in a conduit IRA before it is rolled over into another qualified plan.

.07 Income Tax Withholding Rules Applicable to Eligible Rollover Distributions

Eligible rollover distributions (as defined above) are subject to income tax withholding at a rate of 20 percent regardless of whether the distributions are rolled over, except for amounts rolled over in the form of direct trustee-to-trustee transfers.[140] The 20 percent withholding rule is mandatory, even if the distribution is made on account of hardship.[141] However, distributees may elect to have more than 20 percent withheld from eligible rollover distributions.[142]

> **Example:** Charles, an employee of Wixon Corporation, received a $300,000 taxable distribution from the corporation's

---

[137] *See* e.g., IRS Pub. 590 at 24, P.L. 107-16, 107th Cong., 1st Sess., Sec. 642(c), and HR Rep. No. 107-85 (107th Cong., 1st Sess., 2001).

[138] *Id.*

[139] Code Sec. 408(d)(3)(D).

[140] Code Sec. 3405(c).

[141] As to what constitutes hardship, see Reg. § 1.401(k)-1(d)(3).

[142] Reg. § 31.3405(c)-1, Q&A 3.

qualified profit-sharing plan. Charles will receive only $240,000, since the remaining $60,000 ($300,000 × 20 percent) will be withheld for income tax purposes.

The income tax withheld is treated as a refundable credit on the taxpayer's return for that year. Thus, the taxpayer will not be able to get back the withheld tax until after the end of the year, even if the distribution was rolled over, and therefore, not includible in gross income.

Under a de minimis rule, a payor or plan administrator does not have to withhold income tax from an eligible rollover distribution which is not the subject of a direct trustee-to-trustee transfer if the amount of the distribution is less than $200. But, for this purpose, all eligible rollover distributions received by the taxpayer within one year must be aggregated.[143]

Impact of the Income Tax Withholding Rule on Rollovers. An amount equal to the income tax that is withheld from a distribution is not considered to be rolled over and is includible in the taxpayer's gross income and could be subject to penalty taxes, such as the premature distributions penalty tax under Code Sec. 72(t) unless:

(1) the income tax withheld is refunded to the taxpayer within the normal 60 day rollover time limit period and is rolled over within that time; or

(2) the employee replaces the income tax withheld amount with other funds which are rolled over.[144]

Thus, where more than 80 percent of an eligible rollover distribution is rolled over and is subject to income tax withholding, the taxpayer will generally have to replace withheld amounts from a separate source to avoid further tax consequences.

Direct Trustee-to-Trustee Transfer (Direct Rollover) Exception to the Income Tax Withholding Rules If an eligible rollover distribution is transferred directly by the trustee of the plan making the distribution directly to the trustee of an eligible retirement plan for direct transfer purposes (as defined below), no part of the distribution is taxable and subject to income tax withholding.[145] EGTRRA has expanded the amount of distributions which may be part of a direct rollover.

In the case of distributions made after December 31, 2001, a direct rollover may be made of the nontaxable portion (an amount

---

[143] Reg. § 31.3405(c)-1, Q&A 14.
[144] Reg. § 1.402(c)-2, Q&A 11.

[145] Code Secs. 3405(c)(2), 402(e)(6), and 401(a)(31).

attributable to after-tax employee contributions) in addition to the taxable portion (the amount that would be taxable if no rollover were made) from employer qualified plans (rollovers of the nontaxable portion of traditional IRAs and IR annuities are not permitted) into an eligible retirement plan if:[146]

(1) the eligible retirement plan agrees to separately account for the nontaxable portion (and any earnings, thereon) and the taxable portion; or

(2) the recipient plan is a traditional IRA or IR annuity.

For distributions made prior to December 31, 2001, a direct rollover could only be made of the taxable portion of a distribution.[147]

EGTRRA has also made the direct rollover the default option for involuntary cash-outs amounting to $1,000 or more of a qualified plan participant's vested account balance from an eligible plan.[148] An eligible plan is a plan that provides that any nonforfeitable accrued benefit for which the present value (as determined under Code Sec. 411(a)(1)—note that involuntary cash-outs are discussed in Chapter 6) does not exceed $5,000 must be immediately distributed to the participant.[149] Under the provision, the distribution must be rolled over immediately into a designated IRA, unless the participant elects to have that distribution (1) transferred to a different IRA or qualified plan or (2) distributed directly to the participant. This provision was scheduled to take effect as of the effective date of regulations to be issued by the Department of Labor (DOL) concerning ERISA-related issues with respect to rollovers of cash-out distributions.[150] Such regulations were issued by the DOL and are effective for distributions occurring after March 28, 2005.[151] Thus, the default option provisions are also effective for distributions occurring after that date. The IRS has issued Notice 2005-5,[152] in which it provides guidance on the automatic rollover requirements of Code Sec. 401(a)(31)(B).

A direct rollover may be accomplished by any reasonable means of direct payment, including, for example, a wire transfer or the mailing of a check to the eligible retirement plan. The payee has to

---

[146] Code Sec. 401(a)(31)(B), as amended by P.L. 107-16, 107th Cong., 1st Sess., Secs. 641(e)(3) and 643(b) (June 7, 2001) effective for distributions received after December 31, 2001, and prior to the effective date of safe harbor IRS regulations mandated by Act Sec. 657(c)(2)(A). Code Sec. 401(a)(31)(C), as amended by P.L. 107-16, 107th Cong., 1st Sess., Secs. 641(e)(3) and 643(b) (June 7, 2001) effective when the IRS issues the safe harbor regulations.

[147] Former Code. Sec. 401(a)(31)(B).

[148] Code Sec. 401(a)(31)(B), as amended by P.L. 107-16. 107th Cong., 1st Sess., Secs. 641(e)(3) and 641(b) (June 7, 2001), effective when the Department of Labour issues safe harbor regulations mandated by Act Sec. 657(c)(2)(A). The DOL has issued such regulations that apply to distributions after March 28, 2005.

[149] *Id.*

[150] *Id.*

[151] *See* 29 CFR 2550.404a-2, 69 FR 58017.

[152] IRB 2005-3, 337.

be the trustee of the eligible retirement plan. It is acceptable to permit the taxpayer to deliver the check to the eligible retirement plan as long as the check is made payable to the trustee of that plan.[153]

Eligible Retirement Plans for Direct Rollover Purposes. The types of eligible retirement plans under the direct rollover rules have been expanded as a result of EGTRRA. For distributions after December 31, 2001, eligible retirement plans for this purpose are eligible retirement plans as defined in revised Code Sec. 402(a)(8)(B) (covered in ¶ 904.05 above), except that a qualified plan under Code Sec. 401 must be a defined contribution plan.[154] Thus, for distributions after 2001, eligible retirement plans are:

(1) Qualified plans that are defined contribution plans that accept rollovers;

(2) Code Sec. 403(a) annuity plans;

(3) Traditional IRAs and IR annuities;

(4) Code Sec. 403(b) plans; and

(5) Code Sec. 457 governmental deferred compensation plans.

For distributions received prior to January 1, 2002, only the first three were eligible retirement plans for the direct rollover provisions.[155]

Although defined benefit plans are not specifically listed in the Code as being eligible retirement plans for direct rollover purposes, the regulations indicate that if direct rollover of an eligible rollover distribution is made into a defined benefit plan, the rollover will not be subject to the mandatory 20 percent withholding.[156]

Requirement that a Qualified Plan Provide for Direct Rollovers. In order to maintain qualified plan status, a plan must provide for optional direct rollovers of eligible rollover distributions at the request of, and in the form requested by, the taxpayer distributee.[157] However, a qualified plan does not have to accept direct rollovers.[158] Thus, if an employee terminates his/her employment with one employer and, as a result, receives a qualified plan distribution that he/she will roll over, the 20 percent income tax withholding rules will apply if his/her new employer's plan has no provision for accepting direct transfers and he/she does not or cannot find an IRA or IR annuity to which such a direct transfer can be made.

---

[153] Reg. § 1.401(a)(31)-1 Q&A's 3 and 4.
[154] Code Sec. 401(a)(31)(D), as amended by P.L. 107-16, 107th Cong., 1st Sess., Secs. 641(e)(3) and 643(b) (June 7, 2001), effective for distributions received after December 31, 2001. Once the IRS issues safe harbor regulations mandated by Act Sec. 657(c)(2)(A), this Code Sec will be redesignated Code Sec. 401(a)(31)(E).
[155] Former Code Sec.401(a)(31)(D).
[156] Reg. § 31. 3405(c)-1 Q&A 8.
[157] Code Sec. 401(a)(31)(A).
[158] Reg. § 1.401(a)(31)-1, Q&A 13.

The direct rollover option is considered to be a distribution option, such that the spousal-consent rule and other participant and beneficiary protection rules (as discussed in Chapter 6) apply. Similarly, because a direct rollover is generally considered to be a distribution from a transferor plan, rights and options that were available under the transferor plan need not be preserved in the transferee plan.[159]

In order to enhance the portability of amounts in qualified plans, the final regulations under Code Sec. 401(a)(31) were amended in April, 2000, to allow eligible retirement plans that accept invalid rollover contributions to retain their tax qualified status if certain conditions are met.[160] An eligible retirement plan accepting an invalid rollover will be permitted to treat the rollover as a valid rollover for purposes of determining the plan's qualified plan status, if the following two conditions are met:

(1) when accepting the amount from the participant as a rollover contribution, the plan administrator reasonably concludes that the contribution is a valid rollover contribution; and

(2) if the plan administrator of the eligible retirement plan later determines that the contribution is not a valid rollover contribution, the amount of that contribution, plus any earnings attributable to it, is distributed to the participant within a reasonable period of time after the distribution.

For this purpose, an invalid rollover contribution is one that does not meet the requirements of an eligible rollover distribution under Code Sec. 402(c)(2) or 408(d)(3) or does not satisfy other requirements of Code Secs. 402(c), 408(d), and 401(a)(31).[161]

Notice Requirement. The administrator of a qualified plan must, within a reasonable period of time before making an eligible rollover distribution, provide a written explanation to the taxpayer recipient of the following:

(1) the plan provisions pursuant to which the recipient may have the distribution directly transferred to another eligible retirement plan and that the automatic distribution by direct transfer applies to certain distributions in accordance with Code Sec. 401(a)(31)(B);

(2) the plan provisions requiring the withholding of income tax on the distribution to the extent it is not directly transferred to another eligible retirement plan;

---

[159] Reg. § 1.401(a)(31)-1, Q&A 15.
[160] Reg. § 1.401(a)(31)-1, Q&A 14(a), as modified by T.D. 8880, 4/21/00.

[161] Reg. § 1.401(a)(31)-1, Q&A 14(b) as added by T.D. 8880, 4/21/00.

¶ 904.07

(3) whether the distribution will be subject to tax if transferred to an eligible retirement plan within 60 days after the day on which the recipient receives the distribution;

(4) if applicable, the rules concerning lump-sum and annuity contract distributions to alternate payees or nonresident aliens;

(5) With respect to distributions received after December 31, 2001, a discussion of the potential restrictions and tax consequences that may apply to distributions from the eligible retirement plan receiving the rollover that are different from those applicable to the plan which made the distribution (e.g., penalties that may apply for early withdrawals, availability of hardship withdrawals, availability of ten-year averaging and/or long-term capital gain treatment for amounts that were rolled over, and other important considerations).[162]

The IRS has provided a model notice that employers can use to satisfy the notice requirement. The latest notice reflects the changes made by EGTRRA and is required to be used for distributions made after December 31, 2001. The notice became enforceable by the IRS 90 days after its release date (December 26, 2001).[163] A plan administrator is deemed to have complied with the notice requirement if the administrator provides the model notice as issued, or with modifications that are appropriate to the plan.[164]

The required notice must be provided by the plan administrator to the distributee no more than 90 days before and no later than 30 days before distribution is made. However, if a participant, after having received the notice, affirmatively elects to not make a direct rollover, the reasonable time period requirement will not be violated just because the election is implemented in less than 30 days after notice was given if two requirements are met:

(1) the participant must be given the opportunity to consider the decision whether to elect a direct rollover for at least 30 days after the notice has been provided, and

(2) the plan administrator must provide information to the participant clearly indicating that the participant has a right to this period for making the decision.[165]

---

[162] Code Sec. 402(f)(1), as amended by P.L. 107-16, 107th Cong., 1st Sess., Secs. 641 and 657(b) (June 7, 2001), effective generally with respect to distributions received after December 31, 2001. The second part of the first notice requirement noted above is effective for distributions after March 28, 2005, as discussed above under the coverage of involuntary cash-outs. *See* Notice 2005-5, IRB 2005-3, 337, for IRS guidance concerning involuntary cash-outs and the default direct rollover provision. For distributions received before 2002, only the first four requirements above applied (and only the first part of the first requirement).

[163] H.R. Conf. Rep. No. 107-84, 107th Cong, 1st Sess. (June 7, 2001).

[164] Notice 2002-3, 2002-1 CB 289.

[165] Reg. § 1.402(f)-1 Q&A 2.

¶905 Choosing the Appropriate Form of Distribution from a Qualified Plan

In cases where a participant in a qualified plan has a choice to receive a distribution from the plan in lump-sum form or in the form of annuity for life or for a term certain, careful planning can lead to a maximization of that participant's (and/or his beneficiary's) after-tax monthly income on account of the distribution from the qualified plan. In such a case, the participant would have to evaluate the following alternative courses of action:

(1) The participant could decide to leave the balance to his credit in the qualified plan and receive an annuity for life (or a joint and survivor annuity) or for a term certain. The amounts received would be taxed as ordinary income in accordance with the Code Sec. 72 annuity taxation rules described in this chapter. The key factors in determining his monthly after-tax income from this alternative would be the rate of return earned on his account balance and his expected applicable marginal income tax rates in the years the monthly payments are received.

(2) The participant could decide to receive the balance to his credit in the year of the distribution and roll over the amount into a traditional IRA (or, if possible, another qualified plan) and then receive monthly payments from the IRA for life or some other period. Again, the key decision points would be the rate of return that could be earned on the funds in the IRA and his expected applicable marginal income tax rates in the years the monthly payments are received. A variation of this second alternative where the balance in the plan is rolled over into a traditional IRA would be to afterwards convert some or all of the traditional IRA into a Roth IRA—see the discussion of Roth IRAs and conversions of traditional IRAs into Roth IRAs in chapter 10. In some cases, that strategy could lead to a higher rate of return as compared to leaving the amount in the traditional IRA and receiving monthly payments from that IRA.

(3) The participant could decide to receive the balance to his credit in the year of the distribution and pay tax on the distribution. Then, the after-tax proceeds could be invested to produce monthly income. The key factors here would be the amount of tax that would be paid in the year of the distribution in addition to the factors described in numbers (1) and (2) above. The difference with this alternative is that no tax would be paid as monthly payments are received on the amount of the distribution that is already taxed in the year of the distribution. In addition, to evaluate this alternative versus the first two, the taxpayer would have to determine the lowest possible amount of tax on the distribution. For most qualified plan distribution recipients, the only choice is to treat the taxable portion of the

distribution as ordinary income and part of their taxable income for the year of the distribution. In that case, the distribution would be subject to the marginal income tax rate(s) of the taxpayer applicable in that year. However, for recipients who were at least age 50 on January 1, 1986, and have not chosen to determine the tax on an LSD under any special method after 1986, ten-year averaging treatment and long-term capital gain (LTCG) treatment may be available as an alternative on one LSD. To determine the lowest amount of tax in such cases, the recipient should compare:

(a) the additional amount of tax payable if the entire taxable distribution is taxed as part of recipient's taxable income (i.e., taxed as ordinary income);

(b) the amount of tax payable on the entire taxable distribution using ten-year averaging;

(c) the amount of tax payable on the LSD if the pre-1974 participation portion of the taxable distribution, if any, is taxed as a LTCG at the special 20-percent rate, and the remainder is taxed using ten-year averaging; or

(d) the amount of tax payable on the LSD if the pre-1974 participation portion of the taxable distribution, if any, is taxed as a LTCG at the special 20 percent rate, and the remainder is taxed as part of the recipient's taxable income (i.e., taxed as ordinary income).

In making the retirement income choice, it is obvious that the only difference between the first two alternatives above (leaving the money in the plan versus taking the rollover) is the rate of return that can be obtained. The alternative with the higher rate of return will produce the higher amount of after-tax monthly income over the same period of time. Thus, the better of the first two alternatives would be compared against the after-tax income that could be obtained by receiving the lump-sum, paying tax on it, and investing the proceeds to produce a monthly income over a comparable period. In some cases, using a combination of the first two alternatives may be better than taking one or the other (because, e.g., a higher rate of return could be obtained). In that case, the combined alternative of rolling over part of the balance to the credit of the employee and leaving the remaining balance in the plan would be compared with the third alternative.

Example: Charlie Clark, age 72, expects to retire in December 2006 and expects to have a marginal income tax rate of 28% during his retirement years. He has a choice of receiving the balance to his credit in the retirement plan in the form of a life annuity or in a lump sum. Charlie has a 20-year life expectancy.

Further assume that he began participating in the plan in January 1992 such that he will have 15 years of participation in the plan at the time of the distribution. His account balance in his noncontributory was $200,000. Assume that nine percent interest can be earned on that balance if he leaves it in the plan, eight percent on amounts he rolls over into an IRA, and 10 percent if he takes the lump sum, pays the tax on it, and invests the rest to produce equal monthly income for life.

Step 1: Charlie would choose to leave his money in the plan rather than roll over any amounts into an IRA, since he can get a higher rate of return (9% versus 8%). His monthly after-tax income from leaving the money in the plan and taking a life annuity is determined as follows:

(1) Account balance $200,000

(2) Divided by present value of an annuity factor, 20 years at 9% annual rate 111.45

(3) Monthly pre-tax income. $1,799

(4) Monthly after-tax income $1,295.28

Step 2: Charlie would next calculate the after-tax monthly income that would be generated from taking the lump sum, paying tax on it, and investing the proceeds to produce a monthly annuity for life at 10% interest. To do this, he must first determine the amount he has left after tax to invest. He would use ten-year forward averaging since he was at least 50 on January 1, 1986, and the average tax rate on the taxable distribution using that method is less than the marginal rate that would be applicable if the taxable distribution were just taxed as part of his taxable income. Capital gains treatment is not available since he did not participate in the plan before 1974. The amount of tax will be $36,922 using ten-year forward averaging. This leaves $173,088 to invest ($200,000 minus the tax of $36,922). The after-tax monthly income for life on that investment would be computed as follows:

(1) Investment in annuity contract $173,088

(2) Monthly present value factor, 20 years at 10% annual rate 103.6246

(3) Monthly amount receivable ($173,088/103.6246) $1,670

(4) Total amount receivable under the annuity contract ($1,670 × 240). $400,800

(5) Exclusion ratio under Code Sec. 72 ($173,088/$400,800). 0.43186

(6) Amount of each payment excludable in gross income
($1,670 × .43186) $721.21

(7) Amount of each payment includible.............. $948.79

(8) After-tax monthly income
($1,670 − .28 ($948.79)) $1,404.34

Since this alternative produces a higher monthly income than the alternative of leaving the money in the plan and receiving a life annuity ($1,295.28), Charlie should take the lump sum, pay tax on it, and invest the proceeds to receive a life annuity at 10%.

The above example produces an economic approach to determining which form of retirement benefit should be chosen. Of course, other factors might impact such a decision, such as the flexibility associated with the retirement alternative. Taking a lump sum and paying tax on it affords the greatest flexibility, virtually giving the taxpayer an unlimited number of choices of what to do with the money. The danger of taking the lump sum up front, of course, is that the taxpayer may squander the money quickly. The least flexibility may result by leaving the money in the plan to pay a life (or other period) annuity. Here, the taxpayer may not be able to control what can be done with the undistributed balance in his account. The health of the taxpayer may also be a factor. If he has a short time to live, he may want to take the lump sum and enjoy the time he has left. In addition, other tax factors such as estate tax consequences associated with the alternatives may be important.

Chapter 10

Traditional IRAs/SEPs/SIMPLE IRAs/Roth IRAs/Deemed IRAs

¶1001   Introduction

Traditional individual retirement accounts (IRAs) are tax-favored arrangements tailored to help meet the retirement planning needs of individuals who either are not covered by a qualified plan (such as a pension plan) or who desire to provide for additional retirement income. In this chapter and book, the term "traditional IRA" is used to refer to the original type of IRA and to distinguish this type of IRA from the more recently enacted SIMPLE IRAs and Roth IRAs that are also discussed in this chapter.

Currently, traditional IRA contributions can be made by individuals into individual retirement accounts and individual retirement annuities (IR annuities). The term "IRA" is generally used to refer to both types of plans. In addition, employers can make IRA contributions on behalf of executives and other employees into employer trust accounts or under simplified employee pension plans (SEPs), or (beginning in 1997) under the Savings Incentive Match Plan for Employees (SIMPLE). Finally, for plan years beginning after December 31, 2002, as a result of the Economic Growth and Tax Relief Reconciliation Act of 2001 (EGTRRA), voluntary employee contributions under a qualified plan made to a separate account or annuity that meets the traditional IRA or Roth IRA requirements will be treated as contributions to a traditional IRA or Roth IRA, as the case may be. Such accounts or annuities are called "Deemed IRAs."

The basic features of and tax rules covering traditional IRAs are similar to those applicable to qualified plans, in general, with some specifically applicable rules. Individuals can contribute and deduct (subject to specified limitations) up to the lesser of (1) $4,000 per year for 2005 through 2007 (up from $3,000 per year for 2002 through 2004 and $2,000 per year before 2002) and $5,000 per year in 2008 (after 2008, the yearly maximum will be adjusted for inflation), or (2) the amount of taxable compensation they receive per year. Further, IRA participants who are at least or become age 50 during the calendar year can make additional dollar contributions beginning in 2002 above the dollar limit stated in the last sentence. The additional contribution limit is $500 per year in 2002 through 2005 and $1,000 per year after 2005. Many permissible IRA account holders have made contributing to traditional IRAs and Roth IRAs (discussed below) much easier for investors in recent years and have expanded the types of available investments for the money contributed. The amounts contributed to traditional IRAs earn a tax-free rate of return since earnings on IRA invested funds are not subject to income taxes. Thus, the value of a traditional IRA account will ordinarily grow to a much higher value than a comparable account with taxable earnings. Traditional IRA account holders are generally not taxed until they actually withdraw amounts from their IRAs. Amounts withdrawn from traditional IRAs are taxable as ordinary income to the recipient except to the extent the withdrawals are attributable to nondeductible contributions made to the IRA. Amounts withdrawn can also be subject to a 10-percent premature distribution tax if the distribution takes place prior to the time the IRA account holder reaches age 59½. Finally, traditional IRAs are subject to the qualified plan minimum distribution rules under which IRA distributions must commence at a minimum rate once the account holder reaches age 70½. A 50-percent penalty tax will apply to an amount that should have been, but was not, distributed.

Employers can set up a simplified employee pension plan (SEP) as an alternative or companion to qualified retirement plans discussed in Chapters 5 through 9. Under a SEP, EGTRRA has increased (for tax years beginning after 2001) the maximum amount that employers can contribute and deduct up to the lesser of 25 percent (up from 15 percent in 2001 and earlier years) of the employee's compensation or the Code Sec. 415(c)(1)(A) defined contribution plan limit ($40,000 in 2002—adjusted for inflation after 2002 (in 2005, the limit is $42,000) and up from $35,000 in 2001) to a participating employee's SEP IRA account. SEPs are generally less costly to maintain than other qualified retirement plans and are subject to less reporting and disclosure requirements.

¶ **1001**

Beginning in 1997, employers can set up a Savings Match Incentive Plan for Employees (SIMPLE). Under one type of SIMPLE plan, the contributions are made directly into designated IRAs of participating employees (known as SIMPLE IRA). An employer with 100 or fewer employees that have received compensation of at least $5,000 in the previous two years may adopt a SIMPLE plan as long as that employer does not currently maintain another qualified plan. Under a SIMPLE plan, employees can make elective pre-tax (elective deferral) contributions, expressed as a percentage of compensation, of up to $10,000 in 2005 (after 2005, the maximum dollar amount will be increased on account of inflation—prior to 2005, the maximum dollar amounts had been increased by $500 per year from the $6,500 maximum in 2001 as a result of EGTRRA). Further, SIMPLE IRA plan participants that are at least or become age 50 during the applicable calendar year can make additional contributions of $1,500 (in 2004 (in 2003, the amount was $1,000)—the maximum additional contribution is increasing by $500 each year through 2006, and the maximum will be adjusted for inflation after that, as a result of EGTRRA). Employers must generally match employee contributions on a dollar-for-dollar basis up to three percent of each participating employee's compensation, or make a nonelective contribution equal to two percent of employees' compensation. SIMPLE IRA plans are in many ways less expensive to maintain than other qualified plans because contributions are made directly into the IRA accounts of the participants, no nondiscrimination rules apply, and the top heavy plan rules do not apply.

Since the beginning of 1998, an additional type of IRA called the Roth IRA has been available to taxpayers as a result of the Taxpayer Relief Act of 1997. Unlike most contributions made to traditional IRAs, contributions made to Roth IRAs are totally nondeductible. In essence, the tax advantages of a Roth IRA will be "backloaded." Just as with traditional IRAs, the earnings on amounts contributed to a Roth IRA will not be taxed while amounts are left in the plan. And, if the taxpayer satisfies a five-year holding period requirement and one of four specified requirements, all amounts (including plan earnings) withdrawn from the Roth IRA will be totally excludable. To be treated as a Roth IRA, the taxpayer's account must be designated as such. The same annual contribution limit that applies to traditional IRAs (discussed above) applies to Roth IRAs. However, it should be noted that this limit is a combined limit (e.g., if a 30-year-old individual contributed $2,500 to a traditional IRA in 2005, that individual could only contribute $1,500 to a Roth IRA). However, unlike traditional IRAs, contributions can be made to Roth IRAs even after the taxpayer reaches age 70½. Further, the maximum dollar amount of Roth IRA contributions is phased out ratably for taxpayers with more than $150,000 but not more than $160,000 of modified adjusted gross income. The maximum amount that can be contributed to a Roth IRA is subject to income limits and will be phased out for taxpayers with adjusted gross income in excess of specific amounts. Finally, amounts in one Roth IRA can be rolled over into another Roth IRA subject to the rollover time period rules that apply to IRAs generally, and taxpayers with AGI of $100,000 or less can roll over amounts from traditional IRAs to Roth IRAs (such amounts will be taxed as ordinary income).

Finally, as noted above, EGTRRA enacted a provision, effective after 2002, permitting "Deemed IRAs" under employer qualified plans. If an eligible retirement plan permits employees to make voluntary employee contributions to a separate account or annuity that (1) is established under the plan and (2) meets the requirements applicable to either traditional IRAs or Roth IRAs, the separate account or annuity shall be deemed a traditional IRA or a Roth IRA and will be treated as such for all purposes of the Internal Revenue Code.

The tax rules and considerations of establishing, making contributions to, making withdrawals from and other aspects of traditional IRAs, SEPs, SIMPLE IRA plans, and Roth IRAs are covered in the following paragraphs. Education IRAs, which were enacted by the Taxpayer Relief Act of 1997 to provide taxpayers with a savings vehicle to pay higher education expenses of dependents, are not covered in this book because they are not compensation-related and do not have any relationship to traditional IRAs or Roth IRAs. As noted above, the Economic Growth and Tax Relief Reconciliation Act of 2001 (EGTRRA) made substantial changes to the amounts that can be contributed to traditional IRAs, Roth IRAs, SEP plans, and SIMPLE IRAs as well as other important changes such as the enactment of "Deemed IRAs." These changes will be discussed in detail below.

¶ 1002   Traditional Individual Retirement Accounts (IRAs)

Any individual who has received or earned taxable compensation during the taxable year can establish and make contributions to a traditional IRA.[1] Individuals can establish a traditional IRA whether or not they are covered under any other qualified plan. In addition, an individual can set up a spousal IRA for his or her spouse

---

[1] Code Sec. 219(b) and (f)(1).

whether or not that spouse has any compensation.[2] Spousal IRAs are specifically covered below.

Under Code Sec. 219(f)(1), compensation is generally considered to be earned income as defined in Code Sec. 401(c)(2). Thus, wages, salaries, tips, professional fees, bonuses, commissions on sales and other amounts received for personal services performed are compensation. In addition, net income from the operation of a sole proprietorship and a partner's share of partnership net income (in cases where the partner actively participates in and performs services for the partnership) is considered to be compensation. However, a net loss from a sole proprietorship or partnership does not have to be subtracted from other compensation in determining the amount that can be contributed to a traditional IRA. Compensation does not include any amount received as a pension or annuity payment as deferred compensation, or as unemployment compensation.[3] Further, earnings and profits from property, such as rental income, interest income, and dividend income and nontaxable income such as foreign earned income eligible for the foreign earned income exclusion are not compensation.[4] However, taxable alimony and separate maintenance payments received by an individual under a decree of divorce or separate maintenance are treated as compensation. Finally, in determining the compensation of married persons in community property states, the usual community property rules do not apply.[5] Thus, compensation earned by one spouse is treated as compensation earned by that spouse alone and is not split between the spouses.

.01 Limits on Contributions and Deductions

Except in the case of spousal IRAs and rollovers (covered later), individuals under age 70½ who are not active participants in another qualified plan, can contribute and deduct in arriving at adjusted gross income (AGI) the lesser of: (1) their taxable compensation, or (2) as a result of increases made by EGTRRA, $4,000 (per year in years 2005 through 2007 and $5,000 in 2008, adjusted for inflation after 2008—the maximum per year was $3,000 per year in 2002 through 2004 and $2,000 per year before 2002) to a traditional IRA.[6] Also, as a result of EGTRRA, traditional IRA participants who are at least or become age 50 during the applicable calendar

---

[2] Code Sec. 219(c)(1).

[3] Code Sec. 219(f)(1); Prop. Reg. § 1.219(a)-1(b)(3).

[4] IRS Pub. No. 590, Individual Retirement Arrangements (IRAs), at 9 (hereafter referred to as IRS Pub. 590).

[5] Code Sec. 219(f)(2).

[6] Code Secs. 219(b)(1) and (b)(5), as amended by P.L. 107-16, 107th Cong., 1st Sess., Secs. 601(a)(1) and (a)(2) (June 7, 2001).

year are entitled to make additional dollar contributions (assuming their compensation is that high or higher). The maximum additional contribution is $500 per year in 2002 through 2005 and $1,000 per year after 2005.[7] Thus, the dollar limits on traditional IRA contributions in the years 2001 through 2008 are as follows:

Year	Maximum Dollar Limit for IRA Participants, In General	Maximum Additional Dollar Limit for Participants Age 50 or More	Maximum Dollar Limit for Participants Age 50 or More
2001	$2,000	$ 0	$2,000
2002	$3,000	$ 500	$3,500
2003	$3,000	$ 500	$3,500
2004	$3,000	$ 500	$3,500
2005	$4,000	$ 500	$4,500
2006	$4,000	$1,000	$5,000
2007	$4,000	$1,000	$5,000
2008	$5,000	$1,000	$6,000

Example: David, age 35, is an unmarried participant in a traditional IRA. Assuming that his compensation is $45,000, he could contribute $4,000 to his IRA for 2005. If he were, instead, at least age 50, he could contribute $4,500. If the year were 2006, the respective limits would be $4,000 and $5,000.

If an individual maintains more than one traditional IRA, the limit applies to the total of the contributions made to all of the IRAs during the year.[8] In addition, any amounts contributed by the individual to his or her traditional IRA reduces the amount that can be contributed by that individual to a Roth IRA (subject to the same dollar maximums as discussed in ¶ 1005.01). In general, the contribution must be made by cash, check, or money order.[9] Property contributions cannot be made except in the case of certain roll-overs from qualified deferred compensation plans, as discussed in Chapter 9 and later in this chapter under "Traditional IRA to IRA Rollovers."

For purposes of the traditional IRA contribution and deduction limits and Roth IRA contribution limits (see the discussion of Roth IRAs in ¶ 1005), contributions to pay broker's commissions on brokerage accounts used for the IRA are considered to be IRA contributions.[10] However, a financial institution's wrap fees are not treated as IRA contributions if the account holders pay such fees separately to the institution.[11]

[7] *Id.*
[8] IRS Pub. No. 590, at 10.
[9] Code Sec. 219(e).

[10] Rev. Rul. 86-142, 1986-2 CB 61.

[11] IRS Letter Ruling 200507021.

In the case of married taxpayers where both spouses have compensation, each spouse can set up a traditional IRA. The contribution for each spouse is determined separately and depends on how much the spouse earns. Spouses cannot establish a joint IRA.[12] However, see the discussion of spousal IRAs later in this chapter for coverage of circumstances where the spouse that has less than $4,000 (in 2005 through 2007—$4,500 (in 2005 and $5,000 in 2006 through 2008), if the spouse is at least or becomes age 50 during the calendar year) of compensation can still have up to that much contributed to his or her IRA if the spouses file a joint return.

Example: George and Gracie (both under age 50) are married and both work but are not covered by any qualified plans. In 2006, George received $1,900 of compensation and Gracie, $21,000. If the spouses were to file separate income tax returns, George would be able to contribute and deduct $1,900 to his IRA (limited to the amount of his compensation, since that amount is less than $4,000) and Gracie, $4,000. If the spouses file a joint return, they can contribute and deduct $4,000 to George's IRA account under the Spousal IRA rules discussed later in this chapter and $4,000 to Gracie's account or a total of $8,000.

.02 When Contributions Can Be Made

To be deductible, contributions to a traditional IRA must be made during the applicable tax year or by the due date for filing the individual's tax return for that year not including extensions.[13] The last day for most people will be April 15.

Caution: If an individual contributes an amount to his or her IRA account between January 1 and April 15, that individual must tell the IRA account holder which year the contribution is for (the current year or immediately preceding year). In absence of information to the contrary, the sponsor must assume that the contribution is made for the current year.

An individual can actually claim that a traditional IRA contribution has been made on his or her tax return before the contribution is actually made. In such a case, the individual must actually make the contribution before the due date of the return, not including extensions.[14] A taxpayer can make use of this rule, for

---

[12] IRS Pub. No. 590, at 10.
[13] Code Sec. 219(f)(3).

[14] Rev. Rul. 84-18, 1984-1 CB 88.

example, to finance his/her IRA contribution, in part, with a tax refund that is partially attributable to the IRA contribution.

.03   Limit on Deductible Contributions for Active Qualified Plan Participants

Under Code Sec. 219(g), if the taxpayer is an active participant in a qualified employer retirement plan, the individual will be entitled to a full (i.e., up to the lesser of $4,000 (in 2005 through 2007—$4,500 (in 2005 and $5,000 in 2006 and 2007) if the participant is at least or becomes age 50 during the calendar year as discussed in ¶1002.01 above) or amount of compensation received limit), a partial, or no IRA deduction depending on how much modified AGI the individual has (and his or her spouse has, if applicable) and the individual's tax return filing status. For purposes of the IRA deduction limitation rules, modified AGI is the taxpayer's AGI (and that of his or her spouse, if applicable) figured without taking into account the IRA deduction amount, the foreign earned income exclusion, the foreign housing exclusion, Series EE bond interest that is excludable because the bonds are used to pay the costs of higher education, and, for tax years beginning after December 31, 2004, the manufacturing deduction allowed the taxpayer under Code Sec. 199.[15]

Full Deduction. An individual will be permitted a full deduction if: (a) the individual and his/her spouse do not actively participate in any qualified employer-sponsored retirement plan, or (b) the individual's modified AGI (and the modified AGI of his or her spouse, if applicable) is equal to or less than the beginning amount of the deduction phaseout range based on the individual's filing status under Code Sec. 219(g)(3). The beginning amount of the phaseout range in 2005 is zero for married persons filing separate returns, $50,000 for unmarried individuals, and $70,000 for married persons filing a joint return. In 2006 and 2007, respectively, the beginning amount will increase to $75,000 and $80,000, respectively, for married taxpayers filing joint returns but will not change from the 2005 amount for single individuals.[16]

Partial Deduction. Under Code Sec. 219(g)(2), the full IRA deduction for individuals actively participating in any qualified employer-sponsored retirement plan is reduced proportionally over a specified $10,000 ($20,000 for married taxpayers filing joint returns

---

[15] IRS Pub. No. 590, at 10; Code Sec. 219(g)(3)(A)(ii), as amended by P.L. 108-357, 108th Cong., 2d Sess., Sec. 102(d)(1) (Oct. 22, 2004).

[16] Code Sec. 219(g)(3)(B) as amended by P.L. 105-34, 105th Cong., 1st Sess., Sec. 301(a) (Aug. 5, 1997).

beginning in 2007) phaseout range. That phaseout range in 2006 is between $0 and $10,000 for married persons filing separate returns, $50,000 and $60,000 for unmarried individuals, and $75,000 and $85,000 for married persons filing a joint return.

The phase-out ranges applicable in 1998 and later years are the dollar amounts indicated in the following tables:[17]

Tax Years Beginning in	Single Taxpayers
1998	$30,000—$40,000
1999	$31,000—$41,000
2000	$32,000—$42,000
2001	$33,000—$43,000
2002	$34,000—$44,000
2003	$40,000—$50,000
2004	$45,000—$55,000
2005 and Later Years	$50,000—$60,000

Tax Years Beginning in	Married Taxpayers Filing Joint Returns
1998	$50,000—$60,000
1999	$51,000—$61,000
2000	$52,000—$62,000
2001	$53,000—$63,000
2002	$54,000—$64,000
2003	$60,000—$70,000
2004	$65,000—$75,000
2005	$70,000—$80,000
2006	$75,000—$85,000
2007 and Later Years	$80,000—$100,000

The amount deductible on account of IRA contributions made by individuals whose modified AGI falls within the applicable phase-out range can be determined by use of the following formula (beginning in 2007, the married filing jointly phase-out range will become $20,000 wide and, therefore, $20,000 will be substituted in the formula in both the numerator and denominator for those taxpayers then):

$$\frac{\$10,000 - \text{Excess AGI}}{\$10,000} \times \frac{\text{Full IRA}}{\text{Deduction Limit}} = \text{Deduction Limit}$$

In the formula, "excess AGI" is the individual's modified AGI (and that of his or her spouse, if applicable) above the beginning

---

[17] Code Sec. 219(g)(3)(g)(1) and (7), as amended by P.L. 105-34, 105th Cong., 1st Sess., Sec. 301(b) (Aug. 5, 1997).

amount of the applicable phaseout range. In using the formula, the taxpayer must round up to the next highest $10 level.[18] For example, if the formula calculation resulted in a deduction limit of $1,523, the taxpayer would have to round up to $1,530. If the formula calculation results in a deduction amount of more than $0, but less than $200, then the deduction limit is set at $200 under Code Sec. 219(g)(2)(B). Of course, if the deduction limit exceeds the individual's compensation amount or his or her actual IRA contribution, the lower amount is deductible.

Example: Sara Mills (age 35), who in 2006 has modified AGI of $57,202, is unmarried and an active participant in a qualified plan. Her excess AGI is $7,202 ($57,202 – $50,000). Her IRA deduction limit is $839.40 which must be rounded to $840, computed as follows:

$$\frac{\$10,000 - \$7,202}{\$10,000} \times \$3,000 = \$839.40$$

Special Rule for Married Couples Where Only One Spouse Is an Active Participant in a Qualified Plan. In a case where a married couple files a joint return and one of the spouses is an active participant in a qualified plan, the deduction for IRA contributions of the spouse that actively participates in a qualified plan is phased out using the phase-out rules and ranges described above. However, the spouse that does not actively participate in a qualified plan will be able to deduct his/her IRA contributions subject to a different phase-out range than applies (as discussed above) for individuals who are active qualified plan participants. The phase-out range is from $150,000 to $160,000 of modified AGI for the married couple. The phase-out formula presented above can be used to determine the deduction limit, which will be at least $200 if the actual calculation results in a dollar amount of from $10 to $190 (rounded up to the nearest $10).[19]

Example: David (age 55) is employed and is covered by his employer's Section 401(k) plan. His wife, Sandra (age 52), is employed, but is not an active participant in a qualified plan. Assume that the couple's modified AGI is $127,000 in 2006. In that case, David would not be able to deduct any amount contributed to a traditional IRA, but Sandra would be able to contribute and deduct up to $5,000 to her IRA (she can contribute and

---

[18] IRS Pub. No. 590, at 19.
[19] Code Secs. 219(g)(1) and (7), as amended by P.L. 105-35, 105th Cong., 1st Sess., Sec. 301(b) (Aug. 5, 1997) and by P.L. 105-206, 105th Cong., 2d Sess., Sec 6005(a) (July 22, 1998).

deduct an additional $1,000 above the $4,000 year 2006 limit because she is age 50 or more). If the couple's modified AGI were $156,000, Sandra would be able to deduct only $2,000, computed as follows:

$$\frac{\$10,000 - \$6,000}{\$10,000} \times \$5,000 = \$2,000$$

If the couple's modified AGI were $160,000 or more, none of Sandra's contributions would be deductible.

No Deduction. No deduction is permitted for traditional IRA contributions made by an individual: (1) whose modified AGI (and that of his/her spouse, in the case of a joint return) is at least $10,000 for married persons filing separate returns, or in the case of unmarried individuals and married persons filing joint returns is at least as much as the top dollar figure of the phase out range (listed earlier in this chapter) applicable to the taxable year for which the contribution is made and (2) who actively participates in a qualified plan. For example, in 2006, no deduction is permitted with respect to an individual who is an active participant where that individual's modified AGI is at least $60,000 (if the individual is not married) or, if the individual is married and a joint return is filed, the modified AGI of that individual and his/her spouse is at least $85,000. However, as covered above, where a married couple files a joint return and only one of the spouses is an active participant in a qualified plan, the non-participating spouse's deduction will be phased out ratably over the range of $150,000 to $160,000 of modified AGI (but will be at least $200 for modified AGI amounts over that range) and becomes $0 if the modified AGI of the couple is $160,000 or more.[20]

Special Rule for Separated Married Persons Who File Separate Returns. If an individual is married, files a separate return, does not actively participate in a qualified plan, and lives apart from his or her spouse the entire year, that individual can make a full deductible contribution to his or her IRA account regardless of the amount of modified AGI that each spouse has.[21] This rule applies even if the individual's spouse actively participates in a qualified plan.

Example: John and Joy Benson (both under age 50), a two-earner married couple, lived apart during 2006 and filed separate returns. John, who participates in a qualified plan, received

---

[20] *See* Code Secs. 219(g)(1)-(3) and (7), as amended by P.L. 105-34, 105th Cong., 1st Sess., Secs. 301(a)-(c) (Aug. 5, 1997) and by P.L. 105- 206, 105th Cong., 2d Sess., Sec. 6005(a) (July 22, 1998).
[21] Code Sec. 219(g)(4).

$58,000 of compensation and Joy received $11,000 of compensation. John cannot deduct any IRA contributions because his modified AGI is $10,000 or more. However, Joy can contribute and deduct up to $4,000 to her IRA, since her deduction is not affected by John's active qualified plan participation.

IRA Deduction Rule Tables. The tables on the following page, adapted from IRS Pub. No. 590 which pertains to the year 2004, summarize the circumstances under which individuals are permitted a full deduction, partial deduction, or no deduction for their IRA contributions based on the deduction phase out ranges applicable in the year 2002. These tables can be used for later years by substituting in the phase out range amounts applicable in those later years (see those figures as listed earlier in this chapter).

Table 1-2. Effect of Modified AGI[1] on Deduction If You Are Covered by a Retirement Plan at Work

If you are covered by a retirement plan at work, use this table to determine if your modified AGI affects the amount of your deduction.

IF your filing status is ...	AND your modified adjusted gross income (modified AGI) is ...	THEN you can take ...
single or head of household	$45,000 or less	a full deduction.
	more than $45,000 but less than $55,000	a partial deduction.
	$55,000 or more	no deduction.
married filing jointly or qualifying widow(er)	$65,000 or less	a full deduction.
	more than $65,000 but less than $75,000	a partial deduction.
	$75,000 or more	no deduction.
married filing separately [2]	less than $10,000	a partial deduction.
	$10,000 or more	no deduction.

[1] Modified AGI (adjusted gross income). See *Modified adjusted gross income (AGI)*, later.
[2] If you did not live with your spouse at any time during the year, your filing status is considered Single for this purpose (therefore, your IRA deduction is determined under the "Single" filing status).

Table 1-3. Effect of Modified AGI[1] on Deduction If You Are NOT Covered by a Retirement Plan at Work

If you are not covered by a retirement plan at work, use this table to determine if your modified AGI affects the amount of your deduction.

IF your filing status is ...	AND your modified adjusted gross income (modified AGI) is ...	THEN you can take ...
single, head of household, or qualifying widow(er)	any amount	a full deduction.
married filing jointly or separately with a spouse who is not covered by a plan at work	any amount	a full deduction.
married filing jointly with a spouse who is covered by a plan at work	$150,000 or less	a full deduction.
	more than $150,000 but less than $160,000	a partial deduction.
	$160,000 or more	no deduction.
married filing separately with a spouse who is covered by a plan at work [2]	less than $10,000	a partial deduction.
	$10,000 or more	no deduction.

[1] Modified AGI (adjusted gross income). See *Modified adjusted gross income (AGI)*, later.
[2] You are entitled to the full deduction if you did not live with your spouse at any time during the year.

Active Participation in a Qualified Plan. Under Code Sec. 219(g)(5), an active participant in a qualified plan is an individual who actively participates in one or more of the following:

(1) a qualified pension, profit-sharing, stock bonus, money purchase pension, or other qualified plan described in Code Sec. 401;

(2) a qualified annuity plan;

(3) a plan established for its employees by a federal, state, or local government, or any political subdivisions, agencies, or instrumentalities (other than an eligible state deferred compensation plan covered by Code Sec. 457);

(4) a tax-sheltered annuity plan covered by Code Sec. 403(b);

(5) a simplified employee pension plan (SEP);

(6) a Code Sec. 501(c)(18) trust (a certain tax-exempt trust created before June 25, 1959 that is funded by employee deductible contributions pursuant to Code Sec. 219(b)(3));

(7) a union plan (a qualified pension or profit-sharing plan, created by a collective bargaining agreement between employee representatives and one or more employers);

(8) a cash-or-deferred plan under Code Sec. 401(k); or

(9) a SIMPLE plan.

Specific rules are used to determine whether an individual actively participates in a qualified plan. The rules differ depending on whether the plan is a defined contribution or a defined benefit plan (see Chapter 5 for a definition of these terms).

Defined Benefit Plan. A taxpayer is considered to be actively participating in a defined benefit plan if the taxpayer is not specifically excluded from the eligibility provisions of an employer's plan for the plan year that ends with or within the individual's taxable year.[22] Thus, a taxpayer may be an active participant in a defined benefit plan even if no benefits accrue to the taxpayer's benefit during the year. Further, it is not necessary that the taxpayer be an active participant in the defined benefit plan until the end of the year. The Tax Court has held that an individual was an active participant in a defined benefit plan for the year 1988 even though the individual participated in the plan only for the first half of that year and withdrew her plan contributions upon termination of her employment just after that time.[23] More recently, the Tax Court held that a part-time employee was an active participant in a defined benefit plan despite the employee's "nominal" amount of plan

---

[22] IRS Pub. No. 590, at 11-12.
[23] *S.E. Wanes,* 65 TCM 2058, Dec. 48,895(M),

TC Memo. 1993-84. *See also R. Freese,* 71 TCM 3004, Dec. 51,342(M), TC Memo. 1996-224.

participation.[24] The employee argued that she was not an active participant because she had earned only .083 years of service credit during 1996 (the year in concern) and, at that rate, it would take over 120 years to accumulate the minimum 10 years of credited service to receive a retirement benefit. The court noted that it had previously held that a person can be an active participant even though that person had only forfeitable rights to plan benefits and those rights were, in fact, forfeited prior to becoming vested. Thus, it rejected the taxpayer's argument under current law.

Defined Contribution Plan. An individual is considered covered by a defined contribution plan if any employer or employee contributions, or forfeitures, are allocated to that individual's account for the plan year that ends with or within the individual's taxable year.[25] For example, an individual was considered to be an active participant in a situation where forfeitures were allocated to his account under his employer's profit-sharing plan.[26]

Certain Individuals Not Treated as Active Participants. Under Code Sec. 219(g)(6), members of reserve units of the armed forces who have served 90 days or less on active duty (other than active duty for training) and volunteer firefighters whose accrued benefit as of the beginning of the taxable year is no more than an annual benefit of $1,800 (when expressed as a single life annuity commencing at age 65) are not treated as active participants in a qualified plan.

In addition, coverage under Social Security or a railroad retirement plan does not count as active participation in an employee retirement plan. Finally, if an individual is receiving benefits from a previous employer's plan, he or she is not considered to be actively participating in the plan.[27]

.04 Spousal IRAs

A spousal IRA is a special arrangement under which an individual can make a traditional IRA contribution into an IRA account on behalf of a nonworking spouse or a spouse that has less taxable compensation. Code Sec. 219(c)(1) provides that, under a Spousal IRA, up to $4,000 (in 2005 through 2007—$4,500 (in 2005—$5,000 in 2006 and 2007) for participants that are at least or become age 50 during the calendar year as discussed in ¶1002.01 above (the amount was $2,000 in 2001 and earlier years)) can be contributed

---

[24] *J. Wade*, 81 TCM 1613. Dec. ¶54,337(M), TC Memo. 2001-114.

[25] IRS Pub. No. 590 at 13-14.

[26] *O.H. Tolley, Jr.*, 73 TCM 2877, Dec. 52,063(M), TC Memo. 1997-244.

[27] *Id.*

to IRA accounts of each spouse, even if one spouse has little or no compensation income.[28] Specifically, the limit on the deductible contributions that can be made to the IRA of the spouse with the smaller amount of compensation is the lesser of:

(1) 4,000 (in 2005 through 2007—$4,500 (in 2005—$5,000 in 2006 and 2007)) for participants who are at least or become age 50 during the calendar year, as phased out for active qualified plan participants, or

(2) the sum of:

  (a) the taxable compensation of the lower-paid spouse, and

  (b) the taxable compensation of the higher-paid spouse, reduced by: (I) the deduction permitted to the higher-paid spouse for traditional IRA contributions, (II) the amount of any designated nondeductible contribution on behalf of the higher-paid spouse, and (III) the amount of any contribution on behalf of the higher-paid spouse to a Roth IRA.[29]

See the discussion of Roth IRAs later in this chapter.

Example: During 2006, Mack (age 35) had taxable compensation of $2,800. His wife, Maria (age 32) had $1,700 of compensation. Mack contributed $2,800 to his traditional IRA which he designated to be treated as a nondeductible contribution. The couple's $4,500 of taxable compensation must be reduced by Mack's $2,800 nondeductible contribution in determining the maximum that Maria could have contributed. Thus, Maria could only contribute $1,700, as the sum of the couple's IRA contributions can be no higher than their taxable compensation.

In general, the Spousal IRA rules apply to any individual if (1) he or she files a joint income tax return with his or her spouse for the year and (2) the total amount of compensation of that individual includible in gross income is less than that of his or her spouse.[30] Note that the spouses may not maintain a "joint IRA." Separate IRA accounts must be maintained. While an individual may not make deductible contributions to his or her own IRA beginning with the taxable year in which he or she reaches age 70½, that individual may make contributions for a nonworking spouse until the spouse reaches age 70½. The individual's age is not relevant for purposes of this rule.[31]

---

[28] Code Sec. 219(c)(1), as amended by P.L. 104-188, 104th Cong., 2d Sess., Sec. 1427(a) (Aug. 20, 1996), and by P.L. 106-554. 106th Cong., 2d Sess., Sec. 316(d) (Dec. 21, 2000).

[29] Code Sec. 219(c)(1)(B)(ii). as amended.
[30] Code Sec. 219(c)(2), as amended by P.L. 104-188, 104th Cong., 2d Sess., Sec. 1427(a) (Aug. 20, 1996).
[31] IRS Pub. 590, at 9-10.

¶ 1002.04

Amount Deductible Under Spousal IRAs After 1997. The rules governing the deductibility of contributions to spousal IRAs are the same as those described for traditional IRAs above. That is, if neither spouse is an active participant in a qualified plan, a full deduction may be taken by each spouse (i.e., up to $4,000 in 2005 through 2007—$4,500 (in 2005—$5,000 in 2006 and 2007) for participants who are at least or become age 50 during the calendar year of contributions made to the account of each spouse).[32] If either spouse does actively participate in a qualified plan, a full deduction can be taken by the actively participating spouse only if the couple's modified AGI is at or below the bottom of the phase out range (see the phase out range list for years after 1997 earlier in this chapter) applicable for the year for which the contribution is made. For example, in 2006, the bottom of the phase out range is $75,000. If the couple's modified AGI is more than the dollar figure at the bottom of the phase out range but less than the top of that range applicable for that year, a partial deduction is computed through the use of the following formula (beginning in 2008, the range in the bracket will be $20,000; thus, in the following formula, $20,000 will replace $10,000 in both the numerator and denominator):

$$\frac{\$10,000 - \text{Excess AGI}}{\$10,000} \times \frac{\text{Applicable}}{\text{Dollar Limit}} = \text{Deduction Limit}$$

Note that the $200 minimum deduction rule also applies in the case of spousal IRAs. Finally, where the modified AGI of the couple is equal to or more than the top dollar amount of the phase out range applicable for the year for which the contribution is made, no deduction is permitted with respect to the contributions of the actively participating spouse.

If only one spouse is an active participant in a qualified plan, the other spouse can deduct his or her own IRA contribution (up to the applicable annual contribution limit) provided that the couple's modified AGI is below $150,000. The deduction is phased out ratably (but not below $200) over the $10,000 range from $150,000 to $160,000, using the above formula. If the couple's modified AGI is $160,000 or more, no deduction is allowed for IRA contributions of either spouse.[33]

Example: Charles and Elizabeth (both under age 50) are married and file a joint return. Their 2006 modified AGI was

---

[32] Code Sec. 219(b), (c) and (g).

[33] Code Secs. 219(g)(1)-(3) and (7), as amended by P.L. 105-34, 105th Cong., 1st Sess., Secs. 301(a)-(c), (Aug. 5, 1997).

$81,000, and Charles participated in his employer's pension plan. Assume that Charles earned $37,000, and Elizabeth earned $700 and that they will establish Spousal IRAs. Both can contribute up to $4,000 to their respective IRAs. The amount contributed to Elizabeth's IRA is fully deductible because Elizabeth does not actively participate in a qualified plan and the couple's modified AGI is less than $150,000. However, of the amount contributed to Charles' IRA, only $1,600 is deductible (because the regular phase out range for 2006 applies in determining Charles' deduction) computed as follows:

$$\frac{\$10,000 - \$6,000}{\$10,000} \times \$4,000 = \$1,600$$

.05 Nondeductible Contributions

Under Code Sec. 408(o), the excess of the maximum allowable contribution to a traditional IRA or Spousal IRA over the amount of the contribution that is deductible under Code Sec. 219(g) (if that amount if less) can be treated as a nondeductible contribution to the IRA.

> **Example:** Assume that each spouse of a working couple (both under age 50) can make IRA contributions of up to $4,000 for 2006, but only $1,600 of each such contribution can be deducted under the rules of Code Sec. 219(g). Under Code Sec. 408(o), each spouse could contribute $4,000 and treat $2,400 of such contribution as a nondeductible contribution.

Alternatively, nondeductible amounts contributed during a given year can be withdrawn tax free (except for any earnings on them) by April 15 of the next calendar year (or a later date, if the taxpayer has an extension to file his return) as long as the taxpayer (1) did not take a deduction for such amount and (2) withdraws any earnings on the contributions (taxable as ordinary income and subject to the penalty tax on premature distributions, see the discussion on premature distributions later).[34]

Reporting Requirements. If an individual decides to treat the excess of amounts contributed to a traditional IRA over the deduction limit as a nondeductible contribution, that designation must be reported to the IRS with the individual's tax return for the applicable year. Code Sec. 408(o)(4)(B) specifically requires

---

[34] Code Sec. 408(d)(4).

individuals who decide to designate traditional IRA contributions as nondeductible to supply the following information:

(1) the amount of the designated nondeductible contributions for the taxable year;

(2) the aggregate amount of designated nondeductible contributions for all preceding taxable years that have not been withdrawn by the taxpayer;

(3) the aggregate balance of all IRAs of the individual as of the close of the taxable year; and

(4) the amount of withdrawals made from IRAs during the taxable year.

Form 8606, Nondeductible IRAs, is to be used by taxpayers to supply this required information.[35] It is obvious that the making of nondeductible contributions results in considerable recordkeeping responsibilities for the affected taxpayers.

In addition to the required recordkeeping, it is wise for taxpayers maintaining IRAs to keep more specific records concerning contributions to and withdrawals from each IRA maintained, including the specific date of each IRA transaction. For more information, see CCH, *Keeping Track of Your IRAs.*

Tax Rules Governing Nondeductible Contributions. If a taxpayer designates some IRA contributions as nondeductible, that taxpayer acquires a basis in such contribution and will be able to recover such contributions tax-free; see the discussion under, "Distributions from IRAs When Nondeductible Contributions Have Been Made," later in this chapter. Otherwise, Code Sec. 408(o) specifies that the usual traditional IRA rules apply in the case of nondeductible contributions. Thus, the rules covered earlier concerning the maximum allowable yearly contributions, when the contributions have to be made, who can make traditional IRA contributions, and the tax treatment of earnings on such IRA contributions and other applicable IRA rules apply to nondeductible contributions.

Election to Treat Deductible Contributions as Nondeductible. Code Sec. 408(o)(2)(B) permits taxpayers to elect to treat otherwise deductible traditional IRA contributions as being nondeductible. While such an election would create a tax basis in such contributions and allow their tax-free withdrawal when the withdrawal is made, this election is ordinarily not economically beneficial. Unless tax rates are expected to dramatically increase in the future, it is better to have a current tax deduction for contributions rather

---

[35] IRS Pub. No. 590, at 15.

than tax-free withdrawals in some future year. Further, in such a case, if the taxpayer qualifies, it would be better to make the contributions into a Roth IRA (discussed in ¶1005 below) because withdrawals made from a Roth IRA as qualified distributions are totally tax-free (including the earnings withdrawn).

Excess Contributions and Applicable Penalty Tax. Code Sec. 4973(a) imposes a six percent penalty tax each year on excess contributions made to a traditional IRA. The penalty tax applies to each year in which the excess is left in the account unless eliminated or reduced as discussed below. An excess contribution to an IRA is the excess of the amounts actually contributed to the IRA (excluding rollover contributions) over the maximum amount that can be contributed to an IRA under Code Sec. 219, including both deductible and nondeductible contributions (recall that such maximum is the lesser of (1) the applicable dollar limit, or (2) 100 percent of the taxpayer's compensation).[36]

> **Example:** Ray Berndt (age 40), a single individual with compensation of $21,000, contributed $4,800 to his traditional IRA in 2006. He has made an excess contribution of $800 ($4,800 – $4,000) that will be subject to the six percent penalty tax each year unless and until the excess is eliminated or reduced.

The six percent penalty tax can be avoided by eliminating the excess contribution. The rules concerning elimination of the excess depend upon whether the elimination takes place by the tax return due date for the year in which the excess amount is contributed.

Elimination of Excess Contribution on or Before Due Date of Tax Return. Under Code Sec. 408(d)(4), a taxpayer can withdraw an excess contribution amount free of tax before the due date (including any extended due date) if (1) no deduction was taken for the excess amount, and (2) the net income attributable to the excess amount is also withdrawn. While the excess contribution withdrawn is not taxable, the attributable net income is subject to tax and possibly the 10 percent premature distribution penalty discussed later in this chapter.

The IRS has recently issued final regulations that indicate the method to be used for calculating the net income attributable to excess contributions.[37] The final regulations adopt the new method which was originally set forth in Notice 2000-39,[38] as modified by

---

[36] Code Sec. 4973(b).
[37] Reg. § 1.408-11, TD 9056,68 FR 23586.

[38] 2000-2 CB 132.

¶1002.05

proposed regulations,[39] issued in 2002. The final regulations are applicable for calculating income allocable to IRA contributions made on or after January 1, 2004.[40] For purposes of determining net income applicable to IRA contributions made during 2002 and 2003, taxpayers may continue to apply the rules set forth in Notice 2000-39 or the proposed regulations.[41]

Under the "new method" as applied under the final regulations (and, also, the proposed regulations), the net income attributable to an excess IRA contribution is determined by allocating to the contribution a pro-rata portion of the earnings accrued by the IRA during the period the IRA held the contribution.[42] The new method is represented by the following formula:

$$\text{Net Income} = \text{Contribution} \times \frac{(\text{Adjusted Closing Balance} - \text{Adjusted Opening Balance})}{\text{Adjusted Opening Balance}}$$

The adjusted opening balance is the fair market value of the IRA at the beginning of the computation period plus the amount of any contributions, distributions or transfers (including the contribution that is distributed as a returned contribution pursuant to Code Sec. 408(d)(4) and recharacterizations of contributions made pursuant to Code Sec. 408A(d)(6)—as discussed later in ¶1005.05 under Roth IRAs) made to the IRA during the computation period.[43] A special rule is provided for an IRA asset that is not normally valued on a daily basis. In this case, the fair market value of the asset at the beginning of the computation period is deemed to be the most recent, regularly determined, fair market value of the asset, determined as of a date that concides with or precedes the first day of the computation period.[44] The adjusted closing balance is the fair market value of the IRA at the end of the computation period plus the amount of any distributions or transfers (including recharacterizations of contributions pursuant to Code Sec. 408A(d)(6)—see the discussion of recharacterizations under Roth IRAs at ¶1005.04 later in this chapter) made from the IRA during the computation period.[45] The computation period is the period beginning immediately prior to the time the excess contribution is made to the IRA and ending immediately prior to the removal of the contribution being returned. If more than one contribution was made as a regular contribution and is being returned from the IRA, the computation period begins immediately prior to the time the first contribution being returned

---

[39] Prop. Reg. § 1.408-11, REG-124256-02, 67 FR 48067.

[40] T.D. 9056, 68 FR 23586.

[41] Id.

[42] Reg. § 1.408-11(a).

[43] Reg. § 1.408-11(b)(1).

[44] Reg. § 1.408-11(c).

[45] Reg. § 1.408-11(b)(2).

was contributed.[46] The final regulations retain the rule (from the proposed regulations), without modification, that net income calculations and allocations must be based on the overall value of an IRA and the dollar amounts contributed, distributed, or recharacterized to or from the IRA. Even in a recharacterization of an amount contributed to a Roth IRA where the Roth IRA contains both regular contributions and conversion contributions, the final regulations do not permit net income, including any losses, to be allocated other than pro rata.[47]

> **Example (1):** Morris, who is single, age 40, and not an active participant in a qualified plan contributed $5,000 to his traditional IRA on June 1, 2006 when the IRA had a fair market value of $8,500. Morris does not maintain a Roth IRA and had no other transactions related to the Traditional IRA during the computation period. Assume that Morris withdraws the contribution and allocable net income on March 1, 2007, and that the balance in the account immediately after the withdrawal is $13,000. The net income for the computation period which begins June 1, 2006 and ends March 1, 2007 is $37, determined as follows:

> $1,000 × ($14,000 − $13,500) / $13,500

> Where $14,000 is the adjusted closing balance ($13,000 plus the $1,000 returned excess contribution, and $13,500 is the adjusted opening balance ($8,500 plus the $5,000 contribution).

A second way of avoiding the excess contributions penalty by taking action on or before the due date of the applicable tax return is to make use of the rules governing the deadline for making traditional IRA contributions. The deadline for making an IRA contribution for a particular year is the due date (not including extensions) of the tax return for that year.[48] Thus, contributions made during the period of January 1 through April 15 of a given year can be treated as contributions for the previous year or the current given year. In some cases the judicious use of this rule could avoid the excess contribution penalty tax.

> **Example (2):** During 2005, Mark contributed $800 to his traditional IRA. On March 14, 2006, he contributed another $5,000 to his IRA. Assuming that Mark makes no other 2005 and 2006 contributions, the penalty tax can be avoided if at

---

[46] Reg. § 1.408-11(b)(3).
[47] T.D. 9056. 68 FR 23,586.

[48] Code Sec. 219(f)(3).

¶ 1002.05

least $1,000 of the March 2005 contribution is treated as a contribution for 2005.

A third way of avoiding the penalty tax by taking action by the applicable tax return due date is to transfer the excess contributions (and any earnings allocable thereto) into a Roth IRA (see the discussion of Roth IRAs later in this chapter). No gross income is recognized in that case, provided that no deduction was taken with respect to any of the amount transferred.[49]

Elimination of Excess Contribution After the Due Date of Tax Return. After the due date of the applicable tax return, excess contributions can be eliminated or corrected by (1) taking a taxable distribution from the traditional IRA (see the discussion concerning taxable distributions following this section),[50] (2) by taking a nontaxable distribution that satisfies the provisions of Code Sec. 408(d)(5),[51] (3) by filing an amended return within the required time limits and taking a distribution of the excess,[52] or (4) by making contributions to a traditional IRA in future years of less than the maximum allowable amount.[53] The latter three approaches are explained immediately below.

Nontaxable Distributions Under Code Sec. 408(d)(5). Code Sec. 4973(b)(2)(B) states that excess contributions can be eliminated or reduced by means of a nontaxable distribution within the rules of Code Sec. 408(d)(5). Under that section, a nontaxable distribution of an excess contribution can be made after the due date of the applicable return if:

(1) the aggregate IRA contributions for the particular taxable year were the applicable dollar amount ($4,000 in 2005 through 2007—$4,500 (in 2005—$5,000 in 2006 and 2007)) for participants who are at least or become age 50 during the calendar year or less but do exceed the amount deductible for that year, and

(2) no deduction has been allowed for the excess amount.

In such a case, the net income attributable to the excess amount need not be withdrawn. Note that the limit is increased by the amount of any employer's contribution during the year to the IRA under a Simplified Employee Pension Plan (SEP) or SIMPLE plan; see the discussion on SEPs and SIMPLE plans later in this chapter.

---

[49] Code Sec. 408A(d)(3)(D), as added by P.L. 105-34. 105th Cong., 1st Sess. Sec. 302(a) (Aug. 5. 1997).

[50] Code Sec. 4973(b)(2)(A).

[51] Code Sec. 4973(b)(2)(B).

[52] IRS Pub. No. 590, at 46.

[53] Code Sec. 4973(b)(2)(C).

If the total traditional IRA contributions for the year are more than the applicable dollar amount, the taxpayer must include in gross income any excess over the applicable dollar amount that is withdrawn unless it is an excess rollover contribution attributable to erroneous information (see the discussion on IRA rollover below).[54] The excess over the applicable dollar amount may also be subject to the 10 percent penalty tax on premature distributions discussed below.

Filing an Amended Return for the Year of the Excess Contribution. If a taxpayer deducted an excess contribution in an earlier taxable year for which the total contributions were the applicable dollar amount or less, the excess may still be withdrawn tax free. The tax-free withdrawal can be accomplished if the taxpayer files Form 1040X, Amended U.S. Individual Income Tax Return, for that year, does not deduct the excess contribution on the amended return, and withdraws the excess amount from his or her traditional IRA.[55] An amended return may generally be filed within three years after the taxpayer filed his return.

Making Less Than the Maximum Allowable Traditional IRA Contribution in Future Years. Excess traditional IRA contributions can be reduced or eliminated in a future taxable year by: (1) contributing less than the maximum allowable IRA amount, and (2) treating the difference between the maximum allowable amount and the actual contribution for the year as coming from the excess contribution amounts.[56] In that way, the excess can be "worked off" in future years. Note that the additional contribution can be considered made even if a deduction was taken for the excess amount.[57] However, no deduction may be taken for the excess contribution being "worked off" if that amount was incorrectly deducted for a year which is considered a closed tax year (one for which the period to assess a deficiency has expired).[58]

> **Example:** Roy Moore (age 30) contributed $4,900 to his traditional IRA in 2005 and thus has a $900 excess contribution ($4,900 – $4,000). The $900 excess can be eliminated in 2006 if Moore contributes $3,100 or less to his IRA in 2006 and treats the $900 excess contribution of 2005 as an IRA contribution in 2006. Such treatment will eliminate the 2005 excess.

---

[54] IRS Pub. No. 590, at 46.
[55] *Id.*
[56] Code Sec. 219(f)(6).

[57] Prop. Reg. § 1.219(a)-2(d).

[58] IRS Pub. No. 590, at 46.

.06 Traditional IRA Distributions, General Rules

Unless amounts distributed or withdrawn from a traditional IRA are rolled over to another IRA within 60 days (see the discussion on rollovers later in the chapter), the distributions are taxed to the recipient using the annuity rules of Code Sec. 72.[59] However, traditional IRA distributions are not subject to the mandatory 20 percent withholding rules that apply to eligible rollover distributions from qualified plans (as covered in Chapter 9). For this purpose: (1) all traditional IRAs are to be treated as one contract, (2) all distributions are to be treated as one distribution, and (3) the value of the contract, investment in the contract, and income in the contract is to be determined as of the end of the taxable year.[60] Under these rules, all amounts withdrawn from a traditional IRA are taxable if the taxpayer has made no nondeductible IRA contributions and the withdrawal is not of an excess contribution under the special rules of Code Sec. 408(d)(5) (described above). If the taxpayer has made nondeductible contributions to his or her traditional IRAs, a portion of the withdrawal will be tax-free as determined below.

Distributions from Traditional IRAs Where Nondeductible IRA Contributions Have Been Made. If nondeductible contributions have been made to a traditional IRA by a taxpayer, a portion of an amount withdrawn from an IRA by that taxpayer will be treated as a tax-free return of capital. The taxable portion of the distribution is the amount of the distribution minus the return of capital amount.[61] The following formula can be used to calculate the return of capital amount:

$$\frac{\text{Total Nondeductible Contributions (Minus Tax-free Withdrawals Made in Previous Years)}}{\text{Total Balance of All Traditional IRAs} + \text{Distribution Amount} + \text{Outstanding Rollover}} \times \text{Distribution Amount}$$

For purposes of the above formula, an outstanding rollover is any amount withdrawn from a traditional IRA within 60 days before the end of the tax year, not rolled over into another traditional IRA before the end of that year, but rolled over in the following year within the 60-day requirement; see the discussion on rollovers below.[62] The total IRA account balances, the total nondeductible contributions, and the distribution amount for an individual participant for a taxable year are each to be adjusted to reflect

---

[59] Code Sec. 408(d)(1) and (3).
[60] Code Sec. 408(d)(2).

[61] *See* Notice 87-16, 1987-1 CB 446.
[62] Notice 87-16, 1987-1 CB 446.

recharacterized amounts contributed to, or distributed from, the traditional IRAs. For purposes of making this adjustment, the contribution that is being recharacterized as a contribution to the second IRA is treated as having been originally contributed to the second IRA on the same date and (in the case of a regular contribution) for the same taxable year that the contribution was made to the first IRA. If the recharacterization transaction occurs after the close of the taxable year and if the recharacterization transaction involves a regular contribution from the prior taxable year, the recharacterization is disregarded for the prior taxable year in determining the total IRA account balances.[63]

Example: George made the following investments to his traditional IRAs:

Year	Deductible	Nondeductible
2000	$2,000	0
2001	$2,000	0
2002	$2,000	0
2003	$1,000	$1,000
2004	$1,000	$1,000
2005	0	$2,000
2006	0	$2,000

In 2006, George withdraws $5,000. At the end of 2006, the total balance in his IRA accounts, including accumulated earnings, total $17,500. He did not have any tax-free withdrawals in previous years. The tax-free amount of the $5,000 distribution is $1,333, determined as follows:

$$\frac{\$6,000}{\$17,500 + \$5,000} \times \$5,000 = \$1,333$$

Thus, $3,667 ($5,000 – $1,333) of the distribution is taxable as ordinary income to George in 2006.

Losses on Traditional IRA Investments. A loss on traditional IRA investments by a taxpayer can be recognized only when all the amounts in all of the taxpayer's traditional IRA accounts have been withdrawn and the total withdrawals are less than the taxpayer's unrecovered basis (i.e., total nondeductible contributions minus any tax-free withdrawals made).[64]

---

[63] Notice 2000-30, 2000-1 CB 1266, modifying Notice 98-49, 1998-2 CB 365, and Notice 87-16, 1987-1 CB 446.

[64] *Id.*

¶ 1002.06

Example: During 2006, Martin's traditional IRA had a loss of $7,500. At the end of the year, the balance in the IRA was $3,100. He withdrew that amount on December 31, 2006. He had made total contributions of $8,000 to the IRA (this IRA was his only one), of which $4,000 were nondeductible contributions. He had made no withdrawals in previous years. Martin can deduct a loss of $900, the $4,000 basis he has in the IRA minus the $3,100 withdrawn.

.07 Required Distributions

In general, traditional IRAs are subject to the required distribution rules of Code Sec. 401(a)(9).[65] Reg. § 1.408-8 specifies the required distribution rules of Reg. § 1.401(a)(9) (covered in Chapter 6) are to apply except to the extent modified by Reg. § 1.408-8. The final regulations were issued by the IRS in April of 2002 and apply for determining required minimum distributions (RMD's) for calendar years beginning on or after January 1,2003.[66] Taxpayers are permitted to use the final regulations, the proposed regulations issued in 2001 or the proposed regulations issued in 1987 to determine RMD's for calendar years beginning on or after January 1, 2002 and before January 1, 2003.[67] The rules in the final regulations are described, as applicable, in the following paragraphs. For a description of the RMD rules under the 2001 proposed regulations, see IRS Publication 590 (issued in early 2002) and Prop. Reg. §§ 1.401(a)(9)-l through -8 issued in 2001. For a description of the RMD rules under the earlier proposed regulations, see IRS Publication 590 (issued in early 2001) and Prop. Reg. §§ 1.401(a)(9)-1 and 1.408-8 issued in 1987. A 50-percent penalty tax is imposed on amounts that should have been distributed but have not been in accordance with the required distribution rules.[68]

In the case of distributions from traditional IRAs, the required "beginning date" is April 1 of the calendar year following the calendar year in which the individual reaches age 70½.[69] Thus, a lump-sum distribution from each traditional IRA of the individual must be made by that date or annuity or installment distributions must commence by that time. Note that the change in the law applicable to qualified deferred compensation plans (see the discussion in Chapter 6) allowing minimum distributions to commence in the year following the later of (1) the year in which the participant

---

[65] Code Sec. 408(a)(6) and (b)(3).
[66] *See* T.D. 8987.4/16/ 02, 67 FR 36676.
[67] *Id.*

[68] Code Sec. 4974.

[69] Prop. Reg. § 1.408-8, A-3.

reaches age 70½. or (2) the calendar year in which the participant retires does not apply to traditional IRAs and IR Annuities.[70]

Reg. § 1.408-8, Q&A 10 requires IRA trustees to report to the IRS and IRA owners information about RMDs, which an IRA owner must begin to receive by April 1 of the year following the year in which the owner reaches age 70½. In that regard, Notice 2002-27[71] provides that if a minimum distribution must be made from an IRA for a calendar year after 2002 and the IRA owner is alive at the beginning of the year, the trustee that held the IRA as of the end of the prior year has to provide a statement to the IRA owner by January 31 of the calendar year concerning the RMD. This require-ment may be met through the provision of (1) a statement indicating the RMD amount and the date by which it must be distributed or (2) a statement that informs the IRA owner that an RMD is required for the calendar year and the date by which it must be distributed together with an offer to furnish, on request, a calculation of the RMD amount. Under Notice 2003-3,[72] an IRA trustee need not use the same alternative for all IRA owners and, thus, can provide statements satisfying the first alternative to some IRA owners and statements satisfying the second alternative to others. The required statements may be transmitted electronically to IRA owners if specified requirements are met. Beginning with 2004, IRA trustees will have to report to the IRS annually on Form 5498 whether the IRA account holder is required to take an RMD from his or her account.[73]

Periodic Distributions. If a taxpayer does not withdraw the entire balance by April 1 of the year following when he or she reaches age 70½, payments must be made to him or her over one of the following periods (or any combination thereof, in accordance with IRS regulations):

(1) the taxpayer's life;

(2) the lives of the taxpayer and his designated beneficiary;

(3) a period that does not extend beyond the taxpayer's life expec-tancy; or

(4) a period that does not extend beyond the joint life and last sur-vivor expectancy of the taxpayer and his or her designated beneficiary.[74]

---

[70] Code Sec. 401(a)(9)(C)(ii), as amended by P.L. 104-188, 104th Cong., 2d Sess., Sec. 1404(a) (Aug. 20, 1996).

[71] 2002-1 CB 814.

[72] 2003-1 CB 258.

[73] Notice 2002-27, 2002-1 CB 814.

[74] Code Sec. 401(a)(9)(A).

¶ 1002.07

The minimum amount required to be distributed (as determined under one of the above methods) may be distributed in a series of installments (e.g., monthly or quarterly), provided that the total payments made by the required date aggregate to the minimum required for the year. Of course, the taxpayer may withdraw more than the minimum amount in any year. However, if in any given year, the participant receives more than the RMD, that taxpayer will not receive credit for that extra amount in determining the amount of the RMD in a future year. This does not mean that the participant does not reduce his or her IRA account balance by the amount of the distribution taken. It means that the participant cannot count the amount distributed in one year that is more than the RMD for that year as a distribution of an amount required to be distributed in another year.[75] However, any amount that is actually distributed in the taxpayer's 70½ year will be credited toward the amount that must be distributed by April 1 of the following year.[76]

If the taxpayer has more than one traditional IRA, the RMD must be calculated separately for each of the IRAs. However, such amounts may then be totaled and the total distribution may be taken from any one or more of the individual IRAs. For this purpose, only the IRAs which the taxpayer holds as the owner can be taken into account.[77]

Distributions Beginning Before Traditional IRA Owner's Death. If periodic distributions are to be received, a minimum amount must be distributed to the taxpayer each year beginning April 1 of the year following the year in which the taxpayer reaches age 70½. Under Reg. § 1.401(a)(9)-2, Q&A 3, a participant attains age 70½ as of the date six calendar months following the participant's 70th birthday. The required minimum distribution for any year after the taxpayer's 70½ year must be made by December 31 of that later year. Thus, for taxpayers who reach age 70½ in 2005, the first required minimum distribution must be made by April 1, 2006, the second by December 31, 2006, the third by December 31, 2007, and so on.[78]

> **Example:** Wyatt became 70 on May 18, 2005. Thus, he reaches age 70 ½ on November 18, 2005. Wyatt must receive RMDs starting April 1, 2006. His first distribution would have to be received on or before April 1, 2006. The second distribution would have to be received on or before December 31, 2006.

---

[75] Reg. § 1.401(a)(9)-5, Q&A 2 and IRS Pub. 590, at 30.
[76] IRS Pub. 590, at 30 and 31.

[77] Reg. § 1.408-8, Q&A 10.
[78] Reg. § 1.401(a)(9)-5, Q&A 5(c).

Minimum Amount of Periodic Distributions. In general, the RMD for a distribution calendar year equals the account balance (as determined in Reg. § 1.401(a)(9)-5 Q&A 3) divided by the applicable distribution period (as determined under Q&A 4 or Q&A 5 of that regulation, whichever is applicable). The first distribution calendar year is the year in which the participant reaches age 70½. In the example above, the first distribution year is 2005.

The account balance is the balance in the participant's account as of the last valuation date in the calendar year immediately preceding the particular distribution calendar year. This balance is (1) increased by the amount of any contributions or forfeitures allocated to the account after the valuation date and (2) decreased by distributions made in the particular distribution calendar year after the valuation date. For example, the account balance in the example above which would be used to determine his RMD on April 1, 2006 would be the account balance on December 31, 2004 adjusted for items (1) and (2), if any.[79]

The applicable distribution period is, in general, based on the participant's age as of his/her birthday in the distribution calendar year and is determined using the Uniform Lifetime Table in Q&A 2 of Reg. § 1.401(a)(9)-9. This is generally the case regardless of the number of and the age of the participant's designated plan beneficiaries, if any (for an exception, see the discussion after the example below concerning the case where the surviving spouse of the participant is the sole beneficiary).[80] In addition, the making of distributions based on the methods found in Reg. § 1.401(a)(9)-5 satisfies the minimum distribution incidental benefit rule.[81]

> **Example:** Assume that Baker was born on October 12, 1934. He became age 70½ on April 12, 2005. His first distribution calendar year is 2005, and he must receive his first RMD by April 1, 2006. His designated beneficiary is his son, Walt, age 49. Baker's account balance in his Traditional IRA was $125,000 on December 31, 2004. No contributions, forfeitures, or distributions occurred during 2005. Baker's RMD on April 1, 2006 is $4,717 ($125,000 divided by 26.5—which is the distribution period from the table in Q&A2 of Reg. § 1.401(a)(9)-9 based on Baker's attained age of 71 as of his birthday in 2005, the distribution calendar year.
>
> Next, assume that Baker's account balance on December 31, 2005 was $132,000, and that there were no contributions or

---

[79] Reg. § 1.401(a)(9)-5. Q&A 3.
[80] Reg. § 1.401(a)(9)-5, Q&A 4.

[81] Reg. § 1.401(a)(9)-5, Q&A 1(d).

forfeitures during 2006. Baker did take the $4,717 RMD on April 1, 2006 (for 2005 distribution calendar year). Baker's RMD for the 2006 distribution calendar year would have to be distributed by December 31, 2006. That RMD would equal $4,971 ($132,000 minus the $4,717 distribution divided by 25.6 from the table in Q&A 2 of Reg. § 1.401(a)(9)-9 based on his attained age of 72 in 2006).

The applicable distribution period when the participant's spouse is the *sole* designated beneficiary is the greater of (1) the distribution period based on the participant's age as of his/her birthday in the distribution calendar year from the table in Q&A 2 of Reg. § 1.401(a)(9)-9 or (2) the joint life expectancy of the participant and his/her spouse based on their attained ages in the distribution calendar year and using the table in Q&A 3 of Reg. § 1.401(a)(9)-9.

> **Comment:** Based on an observation of the life expectancy tables, it is apparent that when the participant's spouse is the sole beneficiary and is not more than 10 years younger than the participant, the figures in the Q&A 2 table can be used in all situations.

The table in Q&A 2 of that regulation cannot be used if the sole beneficiary spouse is more than 10 years younger than the participant.[82] In such a case, the table in Q&A 3 of that regulation is to be used.

> **Planning Opportunity:** Assume a participant in a Traditional IRA has a designated beneficiary to whom the participant was not married at the time RMDs had to begin. In that case, the RMD, according to the rules above, has to be determined based on the participant's age using the table in Q&A 1 of Reg. § 1.401(a)(9)-9. Further assume that the beneficiary is, say, 16 years younger than the participant. If the participant later marries the beneficiary and rolls over that IRA in a trustee-to-trustee transfer to another Traditional IRA, an IRS letter ruling indicates that under the final regulations, the RMDs in the new Traditional IRA can be determined using the longer joint life expectancy of the participant and his new spouse using the joint life expectancy table under Q&A 3 of Reg. § 1.401(a)(9)-9.[83]

---

[82] Reg. § 1.401(a)(9)-9, Q&A 2.

[83] IRS Letter Ruling 200250037, 9-19-02, CCH IRS LETTER RULINGS REPORTS.

Undistributed Amount at IRA Owner's Death. If distributions began by April 1 following the IRA owner's 70½ year, and began in accordance with the prescribed minimum distribution method (under the new final regulations) before the owner's death the RMD for the calendar year in which the participant dies is determined as if the participant lived the entire year. For example, if Baker in the example above died on November 14, 2006, the RMD for 2006 would be determined the same way as it was in the example. The applicable distribution period for distribution calendar years after the distribution calendar year in which the taxpayer-owner died depends on whether that taxpayer had a beneficiary and, if so, whether that beneficiary was the taxpayer's surviving spouse as follows:[84]

(1) If the taxpayer had no designated beneficiary, the applicable distribution period measured by the taxpayer's remaining life expectancy is the remaining life expectancy of the taxpayer as of the taxpayer's birthday in the calendar year of the taxpayer's death. In subsequent years, the applicable distribution period is reduced by one for each calendar year elapsed since the calendar year of death. The participant's remaining life expectancy is based on the age as of the participant's birthday in the year following the year of the participant's death. For each year following the year after the participant's death, subtract one for determining the age to use. Use the table in Q&A 1 of Reg. § 1.401(a)(9)-9.

(2) If the taxpayer had a designated beneficiary who is not the taxpayer's surviving spouse, the applicable distribution period is the longer of (1) the remaining life expectancy of the designated beneficiary or (2) the remaining life expectancy of the employee. The remaining life expectancy of a nonspouse designated beneficiary is determined using the beneficiary's age as of his/her birthday in the calendar year following the year in which the participant died. Use the table in Q&A 1 of Reg. § 1.401(a)(9)-9, as a general rule to determine the applicable period based on that age. For each succeeding year, reduce that age by one year.

(3) If the taxpayer's sole designated beneficiary is the surviving spouse, the applicable distribution period is measured by the surviving spouse's life expectancy using the attained age of that surviving spouse in each such year and using the table in Q&A 1 of Reg. § 1.401(a)(9)-9. This is done through the year of the surviving spouse's death. After that surviving spouse dies, additional rules apply. For calendar years after the calendar year of the spouse's death, the spouse's remaining life expectancy is the life expectancy of the spouse using the age of the spouse as

---

[84] Reg. § 1.401(a)(9)-5, Q&A 5 and 6.

¶ 1002.07

of the spouse's birthday in the calendar year of the spouse's death. In subsequent calendar years, the applicable distribution period is reduced by one for each successive calendar year.

Example: Assume the same facts as in the immediately preceding example and that Baker dies on November 14, 2006. As noted above, the RMD for 2006 will not change. Further assume that on December 31, 2006, Baker's account balance was $130,000 and that Walt, his sole beneficiary, inherited the account. Walt attained age 49 in 2006 and 50 in 2007. Walt will have to receive an RMD by December 31, 2005 of at least $3,801 ($130,000 divided by 34.2—Walt's age multiple from the table in Q&A 1 of Reg. § 1.401(a)(9)-9 based on his attained age of 50 in 2007, the year following the participant's death. In each succeeding year, Walt would reduce the 34.2 by one year to determine his RMD.

If there is more than one designated beneficiary and/or one or more contingent beneficiaries, the rules of Reg. § 1.401(a)(9)-5, Q&A 7 should be consulted for determining the applicable distribution period. In general, the beneficiary with the shortest life expectancy (i.e., the oldest individual) is treated as the designated beneficiary in such a case for purposes of determining the RMDs. Where a trust is a beneficiary, the rules provided under Q&A 5 of Reg. § 1.401(a)(9)-4 apply. If an IRA is divided into separate accounts, the RMD rules are to apply separately to each account, effective for years after the year in which the separate accounts were created, or, if later, the date of death of the IRA owner. Reg. § 1.401(a)(9)-8 provides specific rules concerning separate accounts.[85]

Required Distributions if IRA Owner Dies Before April 1 After His or Her 70½ year. If the IRA owner dies before April 1 after his or her 70½ year, the determination of the RMDs once again depends upon whether the participant has a designated beneficiary and, if so, whether the participant's surviving spouse is the sole designated beneficiary as follows:[86]

(1) RMDs where the participant has no designated beneficiary— Use the 5-year rule of Code Sec. 401(a)(9)(B)(ii), under which the account balance of the participant must be distributed by the end of the calendar year containing the 5th anniversary of the

---

[85] *See* IRS Letter Ruling 20044033 for a situation in which the IRS permitted a decedent's IRA to be subdivided into separate IRAs for the beneficiaries of a trust. *See also* IRS Letter Ruling 200349009.

[86] Reg. § 1.401(a)(9)-3 and Reg. § 1.401(a)(9)-5, Q&A 5.

participant's death. For example, if a participant died on February 22, 2006, under the 5-year rule, his or her entire interest would have to be distributed by the end of 2011.

(2) RMDs where the participant has a designated beneficiary who is not the participant's surviving spouse—Distributions must commence by the end of the year following the year of the participant's death and are based on the remaining life expectancy of the beneficiary according to his or her attained age in that following year. That life expectancy is based on the table in Q&A 1 of Reg. § 1.401(a)(9)-9, and is reduced by one in each succeeding year. Note that a Traditional IRA or other qualified plan can provide that the 5-year rule (described in 1 above) will apply to some or all instances where an employee has a designated beneficiary or that a participant or a beneficiary can make an election to use the 5-year rule in lieu of the life expectancy rule in such a case under Q&A 4 (c) of Reg. § 1.401(a)(9)-3.

(3) RMDs where the participant's sole designated beneficiary is the participant's surviving spouse—Distributions must commence by the later of (1) the end of the calendar year immediately following the calendar year in which the participant died or (2) the end of the calendar year in which the participant would have attained age 70½. The RMDs are to be based on the surviving spouse's attained age for the year in which distributions must commence and for each year after that. The table in Q&A 1 of Reg. § 1.401(a)(9)-9 is used to obtain the life expectancies. Note that a surviving spouse can roll over the account into his or her own IRA and circumvent this rule.

If there is more than one designated beneficiary, see Reg. § 1.401(a)(9)-8 Q&A's 2 and 3 and Reg. § 1.401(a)(9)-5 Q&A 7 for the applicable rules. Reg. § 1.401(a)(9)-6, which was issued in June of 2004, provides guidelines for determining RMDs with respect to annuity contracts that are purchased with a participant's account balance under a traditional IRA or an employee's account balance under a defined contribution retirement plan.

Penalty for Insufficient Distributions. A 50-percent excise tax must be paid on insufficient distributions from an IRA.[87] The 50-percent tax applies to the difference between the required distribution amount and the amount actually distributed. It is important to note that since IRA account administrators must report that an IRA account holder has an RMD requirement for years after 2003 (as discussed above), there is now a greater likelihood that the 50 percent penalty could be assessed. This is just simply too great a penalty

---

[87] Code Sec. 4974(a).

to ignore. It is generally advisable to take the RMD, even though it is taxable, to avoid the 50 percent penalty.

> **Example:** Assume the same facts as in the example above concerning required distributions except that Baker received a distribution of only $2,000 by April 1, 2004 (he should have received $4,717). Baker will have to pay a penalty tax of $1,358.50 (50% of ($4,717 minus $2,000)) due to the insufficient distribution.

Minimum Distribution Incidental Benefit (MDIB) Requirement. Distributions from a traditional IRA must satisfy the MDIB requirement.[88] This is to ensure that the IRA is used primarily to provide retirement benefits to the IRA owner. After the owner's death, only "incidental" benefits are expected to remain for distribution to the owner's beneficiary or beneficiaries. Under the final regulations, the MDIB rules will be satisfied if distributions are made in accordance with the rules contained in Reg. § 1.401(a)(9)-5.[89] The same rule applied under the 2001 proposed regulations. The MDIB rules under the 1987 proposed regulations are described in IRS Publication 590 (the version published in early 2001).

.08 Penalty for Premature Distributions

Under Code Sec. 72(t), distributions from traditional IRAs (including deemed distributions covered later in the chapter, such as investing IRA funds in "collectibles") received by the IRA owner before he or she reaches age 59½ are subject to a ten-percent penalty tax in addition to the regular income tax. The ten-percent penalty tax applies to the portion of the distribution includible in the taxpayer's gross income. Form 5329 is to be used to figure the penalty tax. Finally, a penalty of 25 percent (rather than 10 percent) is applicable in taxable years beginning after 1996 to premature distributions from a SIMPLE plan IRA account (SIMPLE IRA plans are covered later in this chapter) during the two-year period beginning on the date the participant first participated in the employer's SIMPLE IRA plan.[90]

> **Example:** Ted, who is 40 years old, withdrew $3,000 from his traditional IRA. Ted must include the $3,000 in gross income and pay an additional penalty tax of $300 (10 percent of $3,000) with respect to the withdrawal.

---

[88] Code Sec. 408(a)(6), IRS Pub. No. 590 at 30.

[89] Reg. § 1.401(a)(9)-5, Q&A 1(d).

[90] Code Sec. 72(t)(6), as added by P.L. 104-188, 104th Cong. 2d Sess., Sec. 1421(b)(4)(A) (Aug. 20. 1996).

Exceptions to the Imposition of the Ten-Percent Penalty Tax. Under Code Sec. 72(t)(2) and (3), the ten-percent penalty tax does not apply to the following distributions:

(1) portions of any distributions that are treated as return of capital nondeductible distributions;

(2) distributions made after the death of the IRA owner;

(3) distributions made because of the disability (as defined in Code Sec. 72(m)(7)) of the IRA owner;

(4) distributions that are a part of a series of substantially equal payments over the life of the IRA owner or the lives of the IRA owner and his beneficiary (see Rev. Rul. 2002-62, 2002-2 CB 710, and Letter Ruling 200313016 for a description of approved methods for using this exception to avoid the ten-percent penalty tax—the IRS has issued a number of other letter rulings applying the provisions of Rev. Rul. 2002-62 (see the discussion in ¶ 901.05);

(5) for taxable years beginning after 1996, distributions that are made from an IRA to the participant to pay medical expenses of the participant to the extent the distributions do not exceed the amount allowable to the participant as a medical expense deduction (determined without regard to whether the participant takes itemized deductions on his or her tax return);

(6) for taxable years beginning after 1996, distributions that are made from an IRA to the participant to pay for medical insurance for the participant, his or her spouse, and his or her dependents (as defined in Code Sec. 152, determined without regard to subsections (b)(1), (b)(2), and (d)(1)(B) thereof for tax years beginning after December 31, 2004, and as defined under Code Sec. 152 for tax years beginning before January 1, 2005) where all four of the following conditions apply: (a) the participant has lost his or her job; (b) the participant has received unemployment compensation under any Federal or State law for at least 12 consecutive weeks; (c) the distributions are made during either the year in which the participant received unemployment benefits or the succeeding year, and (d) where the participant has become employed again, the distributions are made no later than 60 days after the reemployment began;[91]

(7) for taxable years beginning after 1997, distributions that are made from an IRA to a participant to the extent the distributions are used to pay qualified higher education expenses of the participant, the participant's spouse, or any child (as defined

---

[91] Code Sec. 72(t)(2), as amended by P.L. 104-191, 104th Cong. 2d Sess., Secs. 361(a) and (b) (Aug. 21, 1996), and by P.L. 108-311, 108th Cong., 2d Sess., Sec. 207(6) (Oct. 4, 2004).

under Code Sec. 152(f)(1) for tax years beginning after December 31, 2004 and under Code Sec. 151(c)(3) for tax years beginning before January 1, 2005) or grandchild of the participant or participant's spouse. Qualified higher education expenses include tuition, fees, books, supplies and equipment required for enrollment or attendance at a post-secondary educational institution, including graduate level education. For this purpose, qualified educational expenses must be reduced by the sum of (a) qualified scholarships received by the individual and which are excludable under Code Sec. 117, (b) educational assistance allowances received by the individual, and (c) any other payments which are excludable from gross income (other than gifts, bequests, devices, or inheritances) for the individual's educational expenses;[92] and

(8) for taxable years beginning after 1997, distributions from an IRA which are considered to be qualified first-time homebuyer distributions. Qualified first-time homebuyer distributions are distributions from the participant's IRA of no more than $10,000 during the participant's lifetime and that are used within 120 days after the distribution to pay qualified acquisitions costs related to the purchase, building, or rebuilding of a "first" home which is the principal residence of the participant, the participant's spouse, or any child grandchild or ancestor of the participant or participant's spouse. Qualified acquisition costs include any usual or reasonable settlement, financing, or other closing costs. In general, a first-time homebuyer is an individual (and, if married the individual's spouse) who had no present ownership interest in a principal residence during the 2-year period ending on the date of acquisition of the principal residence to which the IRA distribution relates. Thus, the term "qualified first-time homebuyer" is not necessarily someone buying a home for the first time. A "first" home is considered to be acquired on the date on which a binding contract is entered into or when the building or rebuilding begins. In the case of a delay or cancellation of the purchase or building of the "first" home, the amount of the IRA distribution may be put back into the IRA within 120 days of receipt.[93]

Planning Pointer: While the ten-percent penalty tax is meant to discourage the use of IRAs as short-term investments, it does not fully eliminate their usefulness as short-term investments. A taxpayer can still achieve a greater return by investing in an IRA than investing in a taxable return investment if he leaves his money in

---

[92] Code Secs. 72(t)(2)(E) and (t)(7), as added by P.L. 105-34, 105th Cong., 1st Sess., Secs. 203(a) and (b) (Aug. 5, 1997) and by P.L. 108-311, 108th Cong., 2d Sess., Sec. 207(7) (Oct. 4, 2004).

[93] Code Secs. 72(t)(2)(F) and (t)(8), as added by P.L. 105-34, 105th Cong., 1st Sess., Secs. 303(a) and (b) (Aug. 5. 1997) and amended by P.L. 105-206, 105th Cong., 2d Sess., Sec. 6005(c)(1)(July 22, 1998).

the IRA long enough such that the after-tax rate of return from the IRA exceeds that from the taxable investment.

.09   IRA Rollovers

Under Code Sec. 408(d)(3) rollovers that are made from one traditional IRA or on account of eligible rollover distributions from qualified plans into a traditional IRA within 60 days are: (1) not subject to: (a) income tax, (b) any penalty taxes on excess contributions, excess distributions, and premature distributions; and (2) not subject to the limitations on contribution amounts for IRAs (discussed above) and simplified employee pension plans (discussed later). In addition, rollovers from traditional IRAs are not subject to 20 percent income tax withholding. Amounts rolled over into an IRA will grow at a tax-free rate of return since the net income on such amounts is not taxable until distributed. For distributions after December 31, 2001, under EGTRRA, the taxable portion of eligible rollover distributions from traditional IRAs may also be rolled over into qualified employee plans, Code Sec. 403(a) annuity plans, Code Sec. 403(b) tax-sheltered annuity plans, and Code Sec. 457 governmental deferred compensation plans.[94] Through the use of a conduit IRA, amounts that originated as an eligible rollover distribution can be re-rolled over into another employer's qualified plan. When such amounts are finally distributed to the taxpayer, the amounts may still be eligible for special ten-year averaging and long-term capital gains treatment as covered in Chapter 9.

Rollovers from qualified plans to traditional IRAs and conduit IRAs were discussed in Chapter 9. Rollovers from one traditional IRA to another, trustee to trustee, IRA transfers (direct rollovers), and rollovers from traditional IRAs to qualified employee plans, Code Sec. 403(a) plans, Code Sec. 403(b) plans, and Code Sec. 457 governmental deferred compensation plans (for distributions after December 31, 2001) are covered in the following paragraphs.

Traditional IRA to IRA Rollovers. Under Code Sec. 408(d)(3), a taxpayer may withdraw, tax-free, part or all of the assets from one traditional IRA and reinvest them in another traditional IRA. But, no rollover is permitted for amounts required to be distributed because the taxpayer has reached age 70½ (see required distributions as covered earlier in the chapter). Rollovers from SIMPLE IRAs (discussed in ¶1004 below) can be made into traditional IRAs when such rollovers are made no sooner than the time at which

---

[94] Code Sec. 402(c)(8)(B), as amended by P.L. 107-16, 107th Cong., 1st Sess., Sec. 641 (June 7. 2001).

¶1002.09

the participating employee has participated in the SIMPLE IRA for at least two years.[95] The reinvestment must generally be completed within 60 days. Otherwise, the distribution will be taxable except in the case of trustee to trustee transfers discussed below. However, a special rule permits traditional IRA deposits in financially distressed institutions to be rolled over into another IRA, even though the rollover does not take place within the requisite 60-day period.[96] The 60-day period does not include any period during which the amount transferred qualifies as a "frozen deposit." A "frozen deposit" is any deposit that may not be withdrawn because of: (1) the bankruptcy or insolvency of any financial institution, or (2) any requirement imposed by the state in which the institution is located due to the bankruptcy or insolvency (or threat of bankruptcy or insolvency) of one or more financial institutions in that state. In addition, for distributions after 2001, the IRS may waive the 60-day requirement where the failure to waive the requirement would be against equity or good conscience, including casualty, disaster, or other events beyond the control of the taxpayer.[97] Rev. Proc. 2003-16[98] provides IRS requirements concerning the circumstances under which and how taxpayers can obtain a waiver from the IRS under the post-2001 rules (see a discussion of this Rev. Proc. at ¶ 904.05). Finally, Rev. Proc. 2005-27[99] indicates that the time for making a rollover may be postponed in the event of service in a combat zone or in the case of a presidentially declared disaster or a terroristic or military action.

Limit of One Rollover Per Year. Code Sec. 408(d)(3)(B) permits only one rollover distribution from each of the taxpayer's traditional IRAs per year. The one-year period begins on the date the taxpayer receives an IRA distribution, not the date that the distribution is rolled over. However, the rule applies separately to each traditional IRA owned by the taxpayer. Thus, a tax-free rollover from the taxpayer's first traditional IRA account to another during 2006 does not prevent a tax-free rollover from being made from another one of his or her traditional IRAs that same year.

Example: At the start of 2006, Charlie Smith had three traditional IRAs: IRA_1, IRA_2, and IRA_3. On April 3, 2006, he

---

[95] Code Sec. 408(d)(3)(G) before and after amendment by P.L. 107-16, 107th Cong., 1st Sess., Sec. 642(b)(3) (June 7, 2001).

[96] Code Secs. 408(d)(3)(F) and 402(a)(6)(H).

[97] Code Sec. 408(d)(3)(I), as added by P.L. 107-16, 107th Cong. 1st Sess., Sec. 644(b)(June 7, 2001).

[98] 2003-1 CB 305. As discussed in ¶ 904.05, the IRS has issued a number of letter rulings applying Rev. Proc. 2003-16, some of which waive the requirement and some of which do not, depending on the facts and circumstances. See that discussion for citations to some of the pertinent letter rulings.

[99] IRB 2005-20, 1050, superseding Rev. Proc. 2004-13, IRB 2004-4, 335, superseding Rev. Proc. 2002-71, 2002-2 CB 850.

withdrew $5,000 from IRA$_1$ and reinvested that amount into a new IRA, IRA$_4$, on May 22, 2006. Under the IRA rollover limitation rules, Charlie cannot roll over another amount from IRA$_1$ tax-free until April 3, 2007. However, during that period he may make a tax-free rollover from any of his other IRAs.

Rollover of Property. If the taxpayer withdraws property such as stock from an IRA, the same property must be invested in a new IRA to receive tax-free rollover treatment.[100] The taxpayer is taxed on the withdrawal to the extent that the property is not reinvested in a new IRA within the requisite 60-day period. Similarly, cash that is received from one traditional IRA must be rolled over into another traditional IRA to receive tax-free rollover treatment. Thus, a taxpayer, who used cash withdrawn from one traditional IRA to buy stock which was then invested into a second traditional IRA, was held to be taxable on the withdrawal.[101] The rollover rules did not apply since the cash must have been invested into the second traditional IRA.

Planning Pointer: The traditional IRA rollover rules provide the taxpayer with flexibility in choosing whether to leave funds in a particular IRA or transfer some or all of the funds to another IRA free of tax consequences. However, the taxpayer should take account of any penalty charges that might be imposed by the bank or other agency holding the IRA account with respect to withdrawals (e.g., early withdrawal penalties). Care must be taken to reinvest any withdrawn funds within 60 days. Otherwise, withdrawn funds will be subject to income taxes and possibly the ten-percent premature withdrawal penalty.

Direct Rollovers. A transfer of funds in the taxpayer's traditional IRA from one trustee directly to another, either at the taxpayer's request or at the trustee's request, is not a rollover. It is a transfer that is not affected by the one-year waiting period. Such a transfer is not includible in the taxpayer's gross income, and more than one trustee-to-trustee transfer from one of the taxpayer's IRAs can be made in a given year.[102]

Rollovers from IRAs to Employer Plans. After 2001, eligible rollover distributions from traditional IRAs can be made into qualified employer plans (e.g., pension plans and profit-sharing plans), Code Sec. 403(a) annuity plans, Code Sec. 403(b) tax-shel-

---

[100] Code Sec. 408(d)(3)(A)(i).
[101] *A. Lemishow,* 110 TC 110, Dec. 52,274(1998).

[102] IRS Pub. No. 590, at 23.

tered annuity plans, and Code Sec. 457 governmental deferred compensation plans that agree to accept such distributions (there is no requirement that they do so).[103] For this purpose, rollovers from SIMPLE IRA plans are treated as rollovers from traditional IRAs when such rollovers are made at least two years after the time the employee began participating in the SIMPLE IRA.[104] Under the new rules, an eligible rollover distribution from an IRA is the amount of a distribution that is includible in gross income. Thus, distributions of nontaxable amounts (amounts attributable to nondeductible IRA contributions) may be rolled over to another IRA, but not to qualified employee plans and other plans eligible to receive rollover distributions from traditional IRAs under the new rules.[105] In addition, required minimum distributions and distributions to beneficiaries from inherited IRAs may not be rolled over unless the beneficiary is the participant's surviving spouse who is permitted to treat the IRA as his or her own.[106]

A special formula applies to determine the portion of an IRA distribution that is includible in gross income and therefore eligible to be rolled over into an eligible retirement plan (employer qualified plans and other plans noted in the above paragraph). Under new Code Sec. 408(d)(3)(H), an amount that is rolled over from a traditional IRA to an eligible retirement plan (and not another traditional IRA) is first considered to come from amounts that are includible in gross income. Amounts attributable to nondeductible IRA contributions are considered distributed last. In a case where a rollover distribution is made under these rules, appropriate adjustments are to be made to determine the amount taxable in the case of a future distribution from the IRA that is not a rollover distribution.[107]

> **Example:** Wes, an unmarried individual, has three traditional IRA accounts. From 1996 through 2005, he was unable to deduct his contributions, but contributed $2,000 per year in the form of nondeductible contributions. Assume that his account balances were $21,000, $25,000, and $28,000, in the three accounts, respectively, on the date he rolled over $15,000 into his employer's Code Sec. 403(b) tax-sheltered annuity plan

---

[103] Code Sec. 408(d)(3)(ii) as amended by P.L. 107-16, 107th Cong., 1st Sess., Sec. 642(a) (June 7, 2001).

[104] Code Sec. 408(d)(3)(G), as amended by P.L. 107-16, 107th Cong., 1st Sess., Sec. 642(b)(3) (June 7, 2001).

[105] Code Sec. 408(d)(3)(ii).

[106] Code Secs. 408(d)(3)(C) and (E).

[107] Code Sec. 408(d)(3)(H), as added by P.L. 107-16, 107th Cong., 1st Sess., Sec. 643(c) (June 7, 2001).

in 2006. That rollover could be made from any of the three IRAs since the amount remaining overall in the IRAs would not be less than the $20,000 of after-tax contributions made from 1996 through 2005.

The one rollover per year limit and the 60-day limit covered above apply to rollovers made from traditional IRAs to other types of plans discussed above.[108] However, a direct rollover (trustee-to-trustee transfer) is not considered a rollover for these purposes. Thus, several direct rollovers could be made from one IRA in one year.[109]

Finally, it should be noted that the special ten-year averaging rules and LTCG treatment that may apply to a lump-sum distribution taken by a participant who was at least age 50 in on January 1, 1986, do not apply to distributions from a qualified plan to which an IRA rollover contribution has been previously made.[110] To preserve that special treatment, a rollover from a qualified plan should be first made into a conduit IRA (covered in ¶ 1002.10) and then into another employer qualified plan.

.10 Types of Traditional IRAs

As noted at the beginning of this chapter, the term "traditional IRA" is being used to denote all the types of arrangements covered by the traditional IRA rules. The specific types of traditional IRAs and their basic requirements are covered below.

Individual Retirement Account. Perhaps the most common type of traditional IRA is the individual retirement account. Under Code Sec. 408(a) and (n), a taxpayer can set up an individual retirement account (either by investing in a trust account or a custodial account) with a bank, a federally insured credit union, a savings and loan association, or any other person who has specific approval to act as a trustee or custodian. The account must be established in the United States and must be for the exclusive benefit of the taxpayer and/or the taxpayer's beneficiaries. For this purpose, beneficiaries include the taxpayer's spouse, dependents, estate, or any other persons designated to receive benefits from the taxpayer's account after his or her death.[111]

---

[108] Code Secs. 408(d)(3)(A)(1) and (F).
[109] IRS Pub. 590 at 22.
[110] P.L. 107-16, 107th Cong., 1st Sess., Sec. 642(c)(2) (June 7, 2001).

[111] Reg. § 1.408-2(b)(2).

The individual retirement account must be created by a written document and satisfy all of the following requirements:[112]

(1) the trustee or custodian must be a bank, federally insured credit union, savings and loan association, or a person approved by the IRS to act as a trustee or custodian. The taxpayer cannot be his own trustee;

(2) the IRA trustee custodian cannot accept contributions of more than $4,000 (in 2005 through 2007—$4,500 in 2005 and $5,000 in 2006 and 2007) for participants who are age 50 or more per year, and contributions other than rollover contributions from qualified employer plans must be in cash. However, rollover contributions and contributions to simplified employee pension plans (covered later in this chapter) can be more than the applicable dollar limit. Rollover contributions can be in the form of property (such as stock);

(3) the amount in the taxpayer's account must be fully vested at all times;

(4) no part of the taxpayer's account can be used to purchase life insurance;

(5) the assets in the taxpayer's account cannot be combined with other property, except in a common trust fund or common investment fund;

(6) the taxpayer must begin receiving distributions from his or her account by April 1 of the year after the year in which he or she becomes age 70½ as discussed under Required Distributions earlier in this chapter;

(7) the account must be set up in the United States; and

(8) the account must be for the exclusive benefit of the taxpayer and his beneficiaries.

Model Trust or Model Custodial Account. The IRS has created a model trust account and a model custodial account that meet the requirements for an individual retirement account. A taxpayer can establish a model trust account by using Form 5305, Individual Retirement Trust Account and a model custodial account by using Form 5305-A, Individual Retirement Custodial Account.[113]

Individual Retirement Annuity. The benefits of a traditional IRA can be obtained through the purchase of an individual retirement annuity (IR annuity) from an insurance company. An IR annuity must be issued in the taxpayer's name as the owner, and

---

[112] Code Sec. 408(a), as amended by P.L. 107-16, 107th Cong., 1st Sess., Secs. 601(b)(1) and 641(e)(8) (June 7, 2001); and IRS Pub. 590 at 7-8.

[113] Rev. Proc. 87-50, 1987-2 CB 647, modified by Rev. Proc. 92-38, 1992-1 CB 859, and Rev. Proc. 97-29, 1997-1 CB 698.

either the taxpayer or the taxpayer's beneficiaries can be the only ones to receive the benefits or the payments.[114]

An IR annuity contract must be nontransferable and the owner's interest must be fully vested at all times. The contribution limit is the same as that for individual retirement accounts described above, and the contract must provide for flexible premiums such that if the compensation of the taxpayer-owner changes, the premium can also change. The taxpayer must use any refunded annuity premiums to pay for future premiums or to purchase additional benefits. Finally, the rules for required distributions in the case of IR annuities are the same as those given above for individual retirement accounts.[115]

Endowment Contracts. With respect to contracts issued before November 7, 1978, endowment contracts that provide life insurance protection are treated as an IR annuity contract if the requirements of Code Sec. 408(b) (noted above) are satisfied. In addition, Reg. § 1.408-3(e) states that the contract must:

(1) mature no later than the contract-owner's 70½ year,

(2) provide a cash value at maturity that is at least equal to the death benefit payable at any other time (assuming required premium payments have been timely made);

(3) preclude any increase in premiums;

(4) prior to maturity provide a death benefit greater than the cash value or sum of premiums paid;

(5) prevent an increase in the life insurance element over the term of the contract (other than through the purchase of additional benefits); and

(6) not provide insurance coverage other than incidental life insurance and waiver of premiums upon disability.

Tax Treatment of Death Benefit. If an endowment contract owner dies before the contract matures, the portion of the payment that represents life insurance is excludable under Code Sec. 101(a). The rest of the payment is taxable.

Tax Treatment of Contributions. Under Code Sec. 219(d)(3), the portion of the net premium that is attributable to life insurance protection cannot be deducted. The insurance portion is the net premium cost multiplied by the excess of the death benefit over the cash value.[116]

---

[114] Code Sec. 408(b).
[115] *Id.*

[116] Reg. § 1.219-1(b)(3).

Individual Retirement Bonds. Individual retirement bonds (IR bonds) are retirement bonds that were issued by the federal government prior to May 1, 1982. The bonds that were issued have the following features and requirements:

(1) the taxpayer-owner is paid interest on the bonds when they are cashed in;

(2) the owner is not paid any further interest once he or she reaches age 70½. If the owner dies, interest will be paid until five years after his or her death, or the date he or she would have reached age 70½, whichever is earlier;

(3) the taxpayer is not permitted to transfer the bonds; and

(4) The bonds cannot be sold, discounted, or used as collateral or security.[117]

Amounts received upon redemption of IR bonds are taxable and subject to the ten percent premature distribution penalty if received before age 59½.[118]

Employer and Employee Association Trust Accounts. The taxpayer's employer, labor union, or other employee association can establish a trust to provide IRAs for its employees or members. Under such arrangements, contributions can be made directly from the employer or association into the respective participating employee's accounts.

Under Code Sec. 408(c), employer and employee association plans must meet the same exclusive benefit rules that govern qualified pension plans and trusts. The principal and income of the trust must be used to benefit only the plan participants and their beneficiaries. The trust document must prohibit the use of the trust principal or income for any other purpose.

Code Sec. 408(c)(1) states that these plans must satisfy the same requirements that apply to individual retirement accounts (covered above). In addition, Code Sec. 408(c)(2) states that the trustee must keep separate records for each participant, and the assets of each trust may not be commingled with other property. The trustee may invest the assets of the plan in a common trust fund, common investment fund, or common fund for all the persons covered under the plan program.[119]

The employer or employee association may use Form 5305 (which is considered to meet the statutory requirements) to set up the plan. The IRS will issue an opinion letter to an employer or

---

[117] IRS Pub. No. 590. at 8.
[118] Id.

[119] IRS Pub. No. 590, at 8.

¶ **1002.10**

employee association that establishes an IRA for the benefit of its employees or members as to whether the IRA meets the specified requirements. Requests for such opinions are to be made on Form 5306, which should be submitted to the IRS, Attention Employer Plans Letter Rulings, P.O. Box 27063, McPherson Station, Washington, D.C. 20038.[120] Each such request must be accompanied by the payment of a $480 user fee. For opinion letters requested under the mass submitter program, the fee is $1,300.[121]

Taxability of Employer Contributions. Employer contributions under employer traditional IRA trust plans or into individual employee accounts (e.g., through payroll deduction) must be reported as income to the employee on Form W-2.[122] Such contributions are deductible by the employee within the specified limits of Code Sec. 219(b), (c), and (f). Income tax withholding on such employer contributions is not required if the employer believes the employee can deduct them.[123] However, employer contributions to IRAs of employees are subject to FICA and FUTA taxes.

Inherited IRAs. The successor (by beneficiary designation, will or inheritance) to the deceased owner of a traditional IRA is not permitted to treat that IRA as his or her own account.[124] Thus, the successor may not deduct amounts contributed to inherited IRAs and may not roll over the amount in an inherited IRA to another traditional IRA.[125] These rules do not apply, however, to a successor who is the surviving spouse of the deceased owner.[126] Thus, a surviving spouse can make deductible contributions to and rollover distributions from an inherited account in accordance with the general rules covered earlier. Distributions from an inherited IRA are taxable to the recipient to the extent such distributions are attributable to deductible contributions made to the plan by the deceased participant.[127] In a case where a trust was designated as the beneficiary of a traditional IRA of a deceased participant, the IRS has privately held that that trust may divide the inherited IRA into four equal IRAs corresponding with the separate beneficial trust interests without creating a taxable event.[128] In fact, it is a good idea to split up inherited IRAs jointly held with others, since the required minimum distributions (RMDs) from the split IRA may be less for a particular heir if that heir holds his or her portion as a separate account than if the heir holds a proportional interest of one account where the RMD will be based on the age of the oldest

---

[120] Rev. Proc. 2005-8, IRB 2005-1, 243.
[121] *Id.*
[122] Code Sec. 219(f)(5).
[123] Code Sec. 3401(a)(12)(C).
[124] Code Secs. 219(d)(4) and 408(d)(3)(C).

[125] *See* e.g., IRS Letter Ruling 200513033.
[126] Code Sec. 408(d)(3)(C)(ii)(II).
[127] Code Sec. 408(d)(1).
[128] IRS Letter Ruling 200008040, 11-29-99, CCH IRS Letter Rulings Reports.

co-owner. For the application of the required minimum distribution rules to inherited IRAs, see the discussion on required minimum distributions in ¶ 1002.07 above.

IRA of Divorced Spouses. Under Code Sec. 408(d)(6), the transfer of an individual's interest in a traditional IRA to his or her former spouse under a divorce decree or under a written instrument incident to that divorce is not a taxable transfer. After the transfer, the IRA is considered to belong to the former spouse. Thus, the former spouse as the new owner of the IRA can make deductible contributions to the IRA and rollover distributions from the IRA.

Under Code Sec. 219(f)(1) amounts paid to former spouses that are taxable alimony payments are treated as compensation to the former spouse for IRA purposes and, therefore, can be the basis of IRA contributions by the former spouse.

.11 Prohibited IRA Investments and Prohibited Transactions

Certain types of traditional IRA investments and certain types of transactions are treated as taxable distributions under Code Sec. 408. The rules concerning such events are covered in the following paragraphs.

Investing in Collectibles. A taxpayer who invests in traditional IRAs can make use of many types of investments including certificates of deposit, money market accounts, stocks and bonds, mutual funds, etc. However, Code Sec. 408(m) states that any amounts invested from an IRA in "collectibles" are treated as a taxable distribution that may be subject to the ten-percent premature distribution penalty. Collectibles include art works, rugs, antiques, metals, gems, stamps, coins, alcoholic beverages, and certain other tangible personal property considered to be collectibles by the IRS. In effect the tax advantages associated with IRAs do not apply to investments in collectibles. However, a taxpayer's IRA may invest in one, one-half, one-quarter, or one-tenth ounce U.S. gold coins, or one-ounce silver coins minted by the Treasury Department and coins issued under the laws of any state.[129] In addition, in taxable years beginning after 1997, a taxpayer's IRA may invest in any gold, silver, platinum, or palladium bullion of a fineness that equals or exceeds the minimum fineness that a contract market requires for metals which may be delivered in satisfaction of a regulated futures contract.[130]

---

[129] Code Sec. 408(m)(3).

[130] Code Sec. 408(m)(3)(B), as added by P.L. 105-34, 105th Cong., 1st Sess., Sec. 304(a)(Aug. 5, 1997).

Prohibited Transactions and Their Impact on a Taxpayer's Traditional IRA Account. If a taxpayer engages in a prohibited transaction in connection with his or her traditional IRA at any time during the year, it will not be treated as an IRA account as of the first day of the year.[131] Thus, the fair market value of the portion of the assets of the IRA with respect to which the prohibited transaction occurred must be included in the taxpayer's gross income, and that amount may be subject to the ten-percent premature distribution tax. For this purpose, the value of the IRA assets is measured as of the first day of the applicable year.

Some examples of prohibited transactions with a traditional IRA are:

(1) borrowing money from the IRA;

(2) selling property to the IRA;

(3) receiving unreasonable compensation for managing the IRA; and

(4) using the IRA as security for a loan.[132]

In addition, Code Sec. 408(e) specifies certain events that are treated as traditional IRA distributions. They are described in the following paragraphs.

Pledging an Account as Security. Code Sec. 408(e)(4) states that any part of a traditional IRA that is used as security for a loan is treated as a distribution that is includible in the account owner's gross income. The amount that is considered a distribution may be subject to the ten-percent premature distribution penalty tax.

Borrowing Against an IR Annuity Contract. Under Code Sec. 408(e)(3), if the taxpayer borrows money against his or her IR annuity contract, he or she must include the fair market value of the annuity contract as of the first day of the applicable year in gross income. The taxpayer may also have to pay the ten percent premature distribution tax on that amount.

Prohibited Transaction with Respect to Trust Account Set Up by an Employer or Employee Association. The taxpayer's traditional IRA will not lose its IRA tax treatment if the taxpayer's employer or employee association, with whom he or she has his or her account engages in a prohibited transaction as specified in Code Sec. 4975.[133] However, if the taxpayer participates with the employer or employee association in the prohibited transaction, his or her account will lose its IRA tax treatment.

---

[131] Code Sec. 408(e)(2).
[132] Code Sec. 4975(c).

[133] Code Sec. 408(e)(6).

¶ 1003   Simplified Employee Pension Plans (SEPs)

The simplified employee pension plan (SEP) rules were enacted to provide retirement benefits under an arrangement that is less complex and costly to maintain than qualified retirement plans covered earlier. An SEP is a plan program under which the employer makes contributions directly to an IRA of each participating employee.[134] The general IRA contribution limits do not apply in the case of employer contributions to SEPs. Instead, employers can generally contribute and deduct the lesser of: (1) 25 percent of the participating employee's compensation, or (2) the Code Sec. 415 defined contribution limit ($42,000 in 2005) to the participating employee's IRA account under an SEP. Such contributions are excludable to the employee up to an amount equal to the lesser of (1) 25 percent of the employee's compensation or (2) $42,000 (see the discussion concerning the tax treatment of the employee as to why the exclusion percentage limit is less than the employer's contribution and deduction percentage limit). Note that only the first $210,000 of compensation for plan years beginning in 2005 may be taken into account for purposes of determining SEP contributions.[135] Certain small employers may maintain salary reduction SEP plans for employees if certain conditions are fulfilled (no SEP salary reduction arrangements may be set up in years beginning after 1996).[136]

In any event, the participating employees can make their own contributions to their traditional IRAs up to the maximum limit the lesser of (1) $4,000 (in 2005 through 2007—$4,500 in 2005 and $5,000 in 2006 and 2007 for individuals who are at least or become age 50 during the calendar year (the dollar maximum was $2,000 in 2001 and earlier years)) or (2) 100 percent of the taxable compensation of the taxpayer) and deduct them (where possible) in addition to the SEP contributions made by their employer. Once the employer contributions have been made to the employee IRA accounts, the traditional IRA rules described earlier concerning distributions, etc. apply to the contributed salary reduction amounts.

If certain conditions are satisfied, employees may have elective deferral contributions made to an SEP. Under an elective deferral (salary reduction) SEP, the amount contributed reduces the employee's taxable compensation amount from the sponsoring

---

[134] Code Sec. 408(k).
[135] Code Secs. 402(h), 404(h)(1)(C), and 408(k)(3)(C), as amended by P.L. 107-16, 107th Cong., 1st., Sess., Secs. 616(a) and 611(c)(1) (June 7, 2001).

[136] Code Sec. 408(k)(6)(H), as added by P.L 104-188, 104th Cong. 2d Sess., Sec. 1421(c) (Aug. 20, 1996), as amended by P.L. 105-34, 105th Cong., 1st., Sess., Sec. 1601(d)(1)(B)(Aug. 5. 1997).

employer. No elective deferral SEP arrangements may be set up in years beginning after 1996. Nevertheless, salary reduction SEPs established before 1997 may continue to operate and new employees hired after 1996 can participate in those salary reduction SEPs.[137]

A number of nondiscrimination rules must be satisfied, and amounts contributed to employee IRA accounts must be immediately 100 percent vested under Code Sec. 408(k).

The following paragraphs cover the basic tax rules concerning SEPs.

.01 Taxation of SEP Contributions, in General

An employer can generally contribute to a covered employee's IRA under an SEP and deduct the lesser of: (1) 25 percent of the covered employee's compensation, or (2) $42,000 (the deduction limit on contributions to a defined contribution plan in 2005—adjusted for inflation after 2005).[138] The maximum deductible percentage was adjusted upward by EGTRRA from the former limit of 15 percent that applied in 2001 and earlier years, and the dollar limit was raised up from $35,000 in 2001 to $40,000 in 2002, and has been adjusted upward for inflation since then). For purposes of the contribution limit, an employee's compensation, as defined below, does not include the amount of the employer's SEP contribution or other qualified plan contributions.[139] The employer's deduction for a year cannot exceed 25 percent (15 percent in 2001 and earlier years) of total compensation paid to employees who are plan participants during the year. If the employer makes contributions during a particular year in excess of the maximum limit, such excess may be carried over and deducted in the succeeding tax years, subject to the 25 percent limit for these years.[140] Only the first $210,000 of compensation for plan years beginning in 2005 (adjusted for inflation after 2005—the dollar maximum of $170,000 in 2001 was increased to $200,000 in 2002 and has been adjusted for inflation since then as a result of the enactment of EGTRRA) can be taken into account in determining the amount of SEP contributions.[141]

Example: Mary's employer maintains an SEP for its employees. During 2006, Mary (age 35) had compensation of $80,000

---

[137] *Id.*

[138] Code Secs. 404(h)(1)(C) and 408(j), as amended by P.L. 107-16, 107th Cong., 1st Sess., Secs. 601(b)(4) and 616(a) (June 7, 2001). IR-2004-127 (October 20, 2004).

[139] Prop. Reg. § 1.404(h)-1(a)(1).

[140] Code Sec. 404(h)(3).

[141] Code Secs. 408(k)(3)(C) and (8), as amended by P.L. 107-16, 107th Cong., 1st Sess., Sec. 611(c)(1) (June 7, 2001). IR-2002-111 (October 18, 2002).

from her employer. Mary's employer can contribute up to $20,000 (25% × $80,000) to Mary's SEP-IRA. In addition, Mary could make a contribution of up to $4,000 on her own to her personal (traditional or Roth) IRA. She would not be able to deduct any of that IRA contribution because she is covered by the SEP (a qualified plan) and her adjusted gross income exceeds the maximum level below which some or all of the IRA contribution is deductible.

Deduction Limitation for Employers Maintaining Other Qualified Plans. If the employer who maintains an SEP also maintains a profit-sharing or stock bonus plan, the limitation on deductions applicable to such a plan (see Chapter 6) must be reduced by the deductible amount of SEP contributions for the same taxable year.[142] The same rule applies to the overall deduction limitations for employers that maintain qualified plans of different types (see Chapter 6 for a coverage of these limits).[143]

Reduction of Employer Contributions in Integrated Plans. The annual limitation for SEP contributions ($42,000 in 2005, $205,000 in 2004) must be reduced for highly compensated employees (as defined in Code Sec. 414(q)) to the extent the employer treats FICA or self-employment tax payments as SEP contributions.[144]

Minimum Contribution for Top-Heavy SEPs. If an SEP arrangement is top heavy (see Chapter 7 for a definition of top heavy and coverage of the top-heavy rules), the employer must contribute at least three percent of the compensation of each non-key employee (as defined under Code Sec. 416; see Chapter 7).[145] Further, all SEPs must contain contingency provisions to take effect in the event the SEP becomes top heavy.[146]

Compensation Defined. Compensation, for purposes of determining the SEP contribution limit and for other SEP purposes (except for purposes of the Code Sec. 408(k)(2)(C) rule that permits employers to disregard employees earning less than $450 in 2003 through 2005 for participation requirement purposes, as noted below), has the same meaning as given the term under Code Sec. 414(s) (covered in Chapter 6).[147]

Timing of Employer Contributions. For calendar-year employers, SEP contributions made on or before the due date of

---

[142] Code Sec. 404(h)(2).
[143] Code Sec. 404(h)(3).
[144] Code Sec. 402(h)(2)(B).
[145] Code Sec. 416(k)(1)(B).

[146] Reg. § 1.416-IT-36 and-37.

[147] Code Sec. 408(k)(7)(B). IR 2004-127 (October 20, 2004).

the employer's tax return of that calendar year (including extensions) are considered made for that year and are deductible for that year.[148]

> **Example:** The Mason Company is a calendar-year taxpayer that maintains an SEP. Mason filed for an automatic 3-month extension to file its 2004 income tax return until June 15, 2005. Mason made its 2004 SEP contribution on May 12, 2005. That SEP contribution is deductible for the year 2004.

An employer with a fiscal tax year may choose to use its own tax year rather than the calendar year for purposes of determining contributions to an SEP.[149] In such a case the employer may make an SEP contribution by the due date of its fiscal year tax return (including extensions). Thus, a company with a fiscal year ending July 31 would normally have until the following October 15 to actually make its SEP contribution for that fiscal year.

Tax Treatment of the Employee. Employer contributions to SEPs are excludable from the employee's gross income and are not subject to FICA and FUTA taxes to the extent that the contributions do not exceed the Code Sec. 402(h) limit. That limit is the lesser of (1) 25 percent of the employee's compensation or (2) $42,000 in 2005.[150]

Treatment of Excess Employer Contributions. If the employer contributes more to the employee's SEP-IRA than the lesser of 25 percent of the employee's compensation or the Code Sec. 415(c) defined contribution plan dollar contribution limit ($44,000 in 2005, $41,000 in 2004), the employee must withdraw the excess employer contributions before the due date of the employee's tax return, to avoid the Code Sec. 4979 six percent penalty tax.[151] See the discussion concerning excess contributions in the traditional IRA section of this chapter.

If the excess employer contributions are withdrawn after the due date of the employee's return and the employer's total contributions for the year are $42,000 or less (in 2005), the employee can withdraw the excess without having to pay the ten percent premature distribution tax. However, the excess contribution is subject to the annual six-percent excise tax until withdrawn.[152]

---

[148] Code Sec. 404(h)(1)(B).
[149] *Id.*
[150] Code Secs. 402(b)(2), 3121(a)(5)(C) and 3306(b)(5)(C).

[151] IRS Pub. No. 590. at 44.

[152] *Id.*

¶ 1003.01

.02   Requirements for SEPs

SEPs must satisfy specific participation, coverage, vesting, and nondiscrimination requirements. In addition, there are specific rules concerning the integration of SEPs with Social Security (FICA) contributions of the employer. These provisions are discussed in the following paragraphs followed by a discussion of salary reduction SEP plans.

Participation Requirements. An SEP will receive qualified treatment only if the employer contributes to the SEP-IRA of each employee who (1) has attained at least the age of 21, (2) has performed services for the employer during at least three of the immediately preceding five years, and (3) has received at least $450 in 2003 through 2005 of compensation (as defined above) from the employer for the year.[153] Note that the minimum compensation amount is adjusted for inflation in the same manner as the limit on qualified plan contributions and benefits under Code Sec. 415(d). Employees who are eligible to have employer contributions made on their behalf under a salary reduction plan (see the discussion below) are treated as if the contribution was made.

Code Sec. 408(k)(2) also specifies that employees that can be excluded from participation under Code Sec. 410(b)(3)(A) and (C) can be excluded from participation in the employer's SEP. These employees are: (1) employees covered by a collective bargaining agreement in which there has been good faith bargaining concerning retirement benefits, and (2) employees who are nonresident aliens and have no earned income from U.S. sources.

> **Comment:** There is no provision in the Code which covers whether an employee can refuse to participate in an SEP. Thus, it seems that an SEP will not qualify unless all eligible employees have IRAs and participate in the SEP.

Leased Employees. Pursuant to Code Sec. 414(n)(3)(B), leased employees may have to be included in an SEP maintained by the person or company for whom these employees are performing services. An individual is a leased employee and is treated as an employee of the recipient of the services if:

(1) the individual's services are provided under an agreement between the recipient and the leasing organization;

---

[153] Code Sec. 408(k)(2). IR-2004-127 (October 20, 2004).

(2) the individual's services are performed for the recipient, or for the recipient and related persons, on a substantially full-time basis, for a period of at least one year; and

(3) the services are of a type historically performed by employees in the recipient's field of business.

Vesting Rules. Since SEPs involve the use of the participating employees' IRA accounts, all contributions made to SEPs by the employer are immediately 100 percent vested with the employee. Employee withdrawals of amounts contributed to SEPs cannot be prohibited.[154]

Nondiscrimination Rules. Under Code Sec. 408(k)(3), an SEP arrangement will not qualify unless the employer's contributions do not discriminate in favor of highly compensated employees as defined in Code Sec. 414(q) (see the discussion concerning highly compensated employees in Chapter 6). For purposes of this rule, employees that can be excluded from participation (see above) do not have to be taken into account.[155]

Employer contributions must also bear a uniform relationship to the total compensation of each participating employee.[156] Thus, the same percentage of compensation (determined under a written formula; see below) will have to be contributed on behalf of each participant. However, a contribution rate that decreases as compensation increases will not be considered to be discriminatory.[157] For this purpose only the first $210,000 for plan years beginning in 2005 (adjusted for inflation after 2005—the limit in 2004 was $205,000) of employee compensation can be taken into account.[158]

Integration with Social Security. Code Sec. 408(k)(3)(D) provides that the permitted disparity rules of Code Sec. 401(1)(2) will apply in testing the nondiscrimination of employer SEP contributions integrated with the employer's Social Security benefit contributions. Under this rule, a limited disparity is permitted between the contribution percentages applicable to compensation below and compensation above the OASDI tax wage base ($90,000 in 2005). Thus, an SEP contribution on compensation in excess of the integration level (the FICA wage base), expressed as a percentage of compensation, cannot exceed the percentage contribution for compensation below the integration level by more than the percentage contribution for compensation below that level, or the old-age portion of the OASDI rate (5.7 percent), if less.[159]

---

[154] Code Sec. 408(k)(4).
[155] Code Sec. 408(k)(3)(B).
[156] Code Sec. 408(k)(3)(C).
[157] Prop. Reg. § 1.408-8(c)(1).

[158] Code Secs. 408(k)(3)(C) and (8), as amended by P.L. 107-16, 107th Cong., 1st Sess., Sec. 611(a)(1) (June 7, 2001). IR 2004-127 (October 20, 2004).
[159] *See* Code Sec. 401(1).

Example: Walker Company contributes five percent of compensation below the FICA tax wage base (the integration level). Walker's contribution with respect to compensation above that level cannot exceed ten percent.

Written Allocation Formula. Under Code Sec. 408(k)(5), employer contributions to an SEP must be determined under a definite written allocation formula that specifies (1) the requirements an employee must satisfy to share in allocation, and (2) the manner in which the amount allocated is computed. Of course, the allocation (that is, the percentage of compensation contributed on behalf of covered employees) cannot be discriminatory as covered above.

Withdrawals Must Be Permitted. An SEP will not be qualified unless the employees have the right to withdraw any or all employer contributions immediately.[160] This requirement goes hand in hand with the immediate vesting rule covered above.

.03 Salary Reduction SEPs

A SEP may include a salary reduction (elective deferral) arrangement which provides participating employees with benefits similar to those available under a Code Sec. 401(k) plan. Thus, participating employees can elect to defer salary tax-free to the accounts in the plan. The maximum amount that is excludable per year on account of SEP elective deferrals has been increased as a result of EGTRRA. In 2005 and 2006, respectively, the limit amounts are $14,000 and $15,000 (the amounts have been increased by $1,000 each year from $12,000 in 2002 until the $15,000 2006 limit has been reached).[161] Thereafter, the limit will be adjusted upward for inflation.[162] In addition, in 2005 and 2006, respectively, salary reduction SEP participants that are at least or become age 50 during the calendar year will be permitted to make additional elective deferral contributions of $4,000 and $5,000. That additional elective deferral limit has been increased by $1,000 per year from the 2002 amount of $1,000 until it reaches $5,000 in 2006.[163] Thereafter, that limit will be adjusted for inflation.[164] The elective deferral limits applying to salary reduction SEPs for 2001 through 2006 are as follows:

---

[160] Code Sec. 408(k)(4).
[161] Code Secs. 402(g)(1) as amended by P.L. 107-16, 107th Cong., 1st Sess., Sec. 611(d)(1) (June 7, 2001).
[162] Code Sec. 402(g)(4), as amended by P.L. 107-16, 107th Cong., 1st Sess., Sec. 611(d)(2) (June 7, 2001).

[163] Code Sec. 414(v)(1)(B)(i), as added by P.L. 107-16, 107th Cong., 1st Sess., Sec. 631(a) (June 7, 2001). *See also* Reg. § 1.414(v)-1.
[164] Code Sec. 414(v)(1)(C), as added by P.L. 107-16, 107th Cong., 1st Sess., Sec. 631(a) (June 7, 2001).

Year	Elective Deferral Limit	Additional Contribution Limit for Participants Age 50 or More	Total Elective Deferral Limit for Participants Age 50 or More
2001	$10,500	$ 0	$10,500
2002	11,000	1,000	12,000
2003	12,000	2,000	14,000
2004	13,000	3,000	16,000
2005	14,000	4,000	18,000
2006	15,000	5,000	20,000

Example: A 30-year-old participant in a salary reduction SEP plan could make elective deferral contributions of up to $15,000 to the SEP plan in 2006. If that participant were at least age 50 in 2006, the maximum allowable elective deferral would be $20,000. In 2005, the respective limits are $14,000 and $18,000.

Note that the elective deferral (and additional catch-up elective deferral) limits apply to the combined amount of elective deferral contributions made by a taxpayer to any Code Sec. 401(k) plans and Code Sec. 403(b) plans, as. well as the salary reduction SEP plans. In addition, elective deferrals made to a SIMPLE plan count toward that overall limit.

Under Code Sec. 408(k)(6)(H), no new salary reduction SEP arrangements may be set up in years beginning after 1996. Salary reduction SEP plans already in existence at that date may continue to operate under the rules of Code Sec. 408(k)(6), and new employees hired after 1996 can participate in those plans.[165]

Under Code Sec. 408(k)(6)(A), (B), and (D), the following conditions must be satisfied with respect to an elective deferral SEP:

(1) at least 50 percent of the employees of the employer maintaining the plan must elect to have amounts contributed to the SEP;

(2) the employer must have no more than 25 employees who were eligible to participate (or would have been required to be eligible to participate if a pension plan were maintained) at any time during the preceding year. Thus, elective deferral SEPs can only be maintained by small businesses; and

---

[165] Code Sec. 408(k)(6)(H) as added by P.L. 104-188, 104th Cong. 2d Sess., Sec. 1421(c) (Aug. 20, 1996) and as amended by P.L. 105-34. 105th Cong., 1st Sess., Sec. 1601(d)(1)(B) (Aug. 5, 1997).

¶1003.03

(3) the amount deferred each year by each highly compensated employee of the employer during the year (as defined under Code Sec. 414(q); see the discussion of the term in Chapter 6) can be no more than 125 percent of the average deferral percentage of all other employees (the ADP test). This test is determined in the same way as it is for Code Sec. 401(k) plans (see Chapter 7).

Tax Treatment of Excess Salary Reduction Contributions. Code Sec. 408(k)(6)(C) states that if an employer makes an excess contribution (i.e., a contribution on behalf of a highly compensated employee that exceeds the maximum amount of contributions that is permitted under the ADP test noted above), the excess is subject to the ten percent excise tax provided by Code Sec. 4979. However, the ten percent excise tax is inapplicable if any excess deferral plus the earnings attributable to that excess deferral are distributed by the SEP within two-and-one-half months after the plan year in which the excess deferral occurred.[166]

Exception for State, Local and Tax-Exempt Pensions. Under Code Sec. 408(k)(6)(E), an elective deferral arrangement cannot be part of an SEP that is maintained by a state or local government, or any of their political subdivisions, agencies, or instrumentalities, or by an exempt organization.

FICA and FUTA Taxation of SEP Contributions. Employer contributions to SEPs are not subject to FICA and FUTA taxes if the employer has reason to believe that those contributions are excludable by the participating employees.[167] However, amounts contributed by employers that constitute elective deferrals of the participants are subject to FICA and FUTA taxes.[168]

.04   Tax Treatment of SEP Distributions

Since employer contributions on behalf of participating employees to SEPs are made into nonforfeitable IRA accounts of the participants, the rules concerning IRA distributions apply to any distributions under SEP plans. Thus, such distributions are ordinary income when received and are subject to the ten percent premature distribution penalty discussed earlier in this chapter. Further, the required distribution rules under which participants must receive minimum distribution amounts starting April 1 after their 70½ year apply in the case of SEPs.

Establishing an SEP. Any employer can establish an SEP by executing a written document including the employer's name, the

---

[166] Code Sec. 4979(f).
[167] Code Secs. 3121(a)(5)(D) and 3306(b)(5)(D).

[168] Code Secs. 3121(v) and 3306(r).

signature of a responsible officer, a description of the participation requirements, and a definite allocation formula.[169] The allocation formula must specify the requirements an employee must fulfill to share in an allocation and the method by which the amount allocated to the account of each participant is determined.[170] Each participant must be directed to establish an IRA account to which the employer's contributions can be made. The employer must establish the SEP, communicate it to the employees and make contributions to it by April 15 following the calendar year for which the contributions are made.[171]

Model SEPs. An employer can establish either a model SEP or a nonmodel SEP. A model SEP is established by filing Form 5305-SEP or 5305A-SEP (for elective deferral plans, prior to 1997). The appropriate form is not filed with the IRS but is distributed to each participant. The advantage of using a model SEP is that it is easy to complete (the employer's name, two blanks, two check options and a date constitute the form), and it satisfies the SEP requirements covered earlier. However, not all employers can establish a model SEP. Contributions to a model SEP cannot be integrated with Social Security. In addition, an employer cannot establish a model SEP if the employer:

(1) currently maintains another qualified plan;

(2) has maintained a qualified defined benefit plan at any time;

(3) has one or more eligible employees who have not set up their own IRAs;

(4) uses the services of leased employees (see the discussion concerning leased employees above);

(5) is a member of an affiliated service group (as defined in Code Sec. 414(m) or controlled group (Code Sec. 414(b) or (c)), unless all employees of the group participate in the SEP; or

(6) integrates SEP contributions with Social Security.[172]

Nonmodel SEPs. A nonmodel SEP can be established through the filing of Form 5306A with the IRS or by adopting a prototype SEP that the IRS has previously approved. Form 5306A is used to seek IRS approval of a prototype SEP and for any subsequent amendments (a copy of the amendment and an explanation of its effect on the SEP agreement must be included with the form).

---

[169] Prop. Reg. § 1.408-7(b).
[170] Prop. Reg. § 1.408-7(e).

[171] Prop. Reg. § 1.408-7(b).
[172] Instructions, Form 5305-SEP.

¶ **1003.04**

.05 Reporting and Disclosure Requirements

The nature and extent of the SEP reporting and disclosure requirements depend upon whether the employer's SEP is a model or nonmodel SEP.

Model SEPs. The IRS and Department of Labor (DOL) reporting and disclosure requirements for model SEPs are satisfied if the employer furnishes to each participant:

(1) A copy of the completed and unaltered Form 5305-SEP or 5305A-SEP including the questions and answers printed on the form, and

(2) A written statement each year showing any contribution made to the participant's SEP account (such information can be indicated on the participant's Form W-2).[173]

In addition, the DOL requires any employer who influences an employee to choose a particular IRA which restricts the withdrawal of invested funds by a participant to provide each participant with (1) a written explanation of these restrictions, and (2) a statement that other IRAs may not have such restrictions.

Nonmodel SEPs. The reporting and disclosure rules for nonmodel SEPs are somewhat more extensive than for model SEPs. However, the IRS requirements for general information can be met by furnishing each participant with a copy of Notice 81-1.[174] The SEP specific information requirement can be met by providing a copy of an understandable SEP agreement to each participant.

The employer must also disclose the contribution made on behalf of each participant by filing a statement with each participant (the amount can be placed on Form W-2).

For DOL purposes, the reporting and disclosure requirements are usually considered fulfilled when the IRS requirements (stated above) are satisfied.[175] However, an employer who has a nonmodel SEP plan is subject to the full DOL reporting and disclosure requirements if the employer selects, recommends, or substantially influences the participants to choose IRAs that will restrict withdrawal of plan contributions made into them.

¶ 1004 Savings Incentive Match Plans for Employees (SIMPLEs)

Savings Incentive Match Plans for Employees (SIMPLE plans) were enacted in order to provide small businesses with a less costly

---

[173] DOL Reg. § 2520.104-48; Notice 81-1, 1981-1 CB 610.

[174] Notice 81-1, 1981-1 CB 610.
[175] DOL Reg. § 2520. 104-49.

means of providing a qualified deferred compensation plan for their employees and thus, resulted in more employees in small businesses being covered by a qualified plan. A SIMPLE IRA plan (SIMPLE Code Sec. 401(k) plans are covered in Chapter 7) is a plan under which the employer makes contributions (consisting of employee elective deferral and employer matching or nonelective plan contributions) directly into a SIMPLE IRA account of participating employees (an IRA account into which only SIMPLE plan contributions and rollovers can be made).[176] The general IRA contribution limits covered earlier in this chapter do not apply to SIMPLE IRA plans. Instead, employee participants may elect to make contributions on a pre-tax basis, expressed as a percentage of compensation, or as a specific dollar amount, which has been increased by EGTRRA by $1,000 per year from the $7,000 maximum in 2002 to the $10,000 maximum in 2005 (the 2005 limit will be adjusted for inflation in years after 2005).[177] In addition, participants who are at least or become age 50 during the calendar year can make additional "catch-up" elective deferral contributions to SIMPLE plans beginning in 2002. The additional contribution limit has been increased by $500 per year from the $500 additional limit in 2002 to $2,000 in 2005 and $2,500 in 2006. After 2006, the then $2,500 limit will be adjusted upward for inflation.[178] In addition, employers must match employee elective deferral contributions at a rate of up to three percent of a participant's compensation (under certain circumstances, the matching contribution can be a rate lower than three percent) or make nonelective contributions at a rate of two percent of compensation on behalf of each employee who is eligible to participate in the plan.[179] The elective deferral employee contributions and the employer contributions are exempt from income tax. However, the elective deferral contributions are subject to FICA and FUTA taxes.[180] Only employers that had 100 or fewer employees who received at least $5,000 of compensation in the preceding year may establish SIMPLE IRA plans, provided that the employer (or a predecessor) does not maintain another qualified plan that covers the same employees.[181] While no nondiscrimination rules apply, and the top-heavy rules (covered in Chapter 7) do not apply to SIMPLE IRA plans, contributions made immediately vest with the participants,

---

[176] Code Sec. 408(p), as enacted by P.L. 104-188, 104th Cong. 2d Sess. (Aug. 20, 1996), Sec. 1421(a), Notice 98-4, 1998-1 CB 269, Q&As A-1 and A-2.

[177] Code Sec. 408(p)(2)(E), as amended by P.L. 107-16, 107th Cong., 1st Sess., Secs. 611(f)(1) and (2) (June 7, 2001).

[178] Code Secs. 414(v)(2)(B)(ii) and (C), as added by P.L. 107-16, 107th Cong., 1st Sess., Sec. 631(a) (June 7, 2001).

[179] Notice 98-4, 1998-1 CB 269, Q&As D-4 and D-5; Code Secs. 408(p)(2)(A) and (B).

[180] *Id.*, Q&As I-1 and I-2.

[181] *Id.*, Q&As B-1-B-3, Code Secs. 408(P)(1) and (2).

and a number of administrative requirements apply.[182] SIMPLE IRA plans are covered in the following paragraphs.

.01 SIMPLE IRA Plan Requirements

SIMPLE IRA plans must meet a number of requirements including participation, employer notification, employee election, and vesting requirements covered in the following paragraphs. SIMPLE IRA plans, however, are not subject to the general qualified plan nondiscrimination rules (covered in Chapter 6) and the top heavy plan rules (covered in Chapter 7).[183]

Participation Requirements. If an employer establishes a SIMPLE IRA plan, all employees of the employer who received at least $5,000 in compensation from the employer during any two preceding calendar years (whether consecutive or not) and who are reasonably expected to receive $5,000 in compensation during the current year must be eligible to participate. The term employees includes employees and self-employed individuals. However, an employer may elect to exclude from eligibility employees described in Code Sec. 410(b)(3) (e.g., employees who are covered by a collective bargaining agreement and certain nonresident aliens). Employers may impose less restrictive eligibility requirements by reducing or eliminating prior year and/or current year compensation requirements (e.g., minimum compensation can be reduced from $5,000 to, say, $3,000).[184]

Under Notice 98-4 (Q&A C-4), compensation for purposes of these requirements means wages subject to income tax withholding pursuant to Code Sec. 3401(a) and elective deferrals under SIMPLE plans and other elective deferral plans. Compensation for self-employed individuals means net earnings from self employment, determined under Code Sec. 1402(a) prior to subtracting any SIMPLE plan contributions.

Employer Notification Requirements. Under Notice 98-4 (Q&As G-1 through G-3), an employer must notify each employee immediately before the employee's 60-day election period (described below) of the employee's opportunity to enter into a salary reduction agreement or to modify any existing agreement under the SIMPLE plan. An employer may also inform an employee at the same time if the employer is making reduced matching or nonelective contributions to the plan. The notification must contain a copy of the

[182] *See, e.g., id.,* Q&As F and G.
[183] H.R. Rep No 737, 104th Cong. 2d Sess. (Aug. 20, 1996); Code Sec. 416(g)(4).
[184] Notice 98-4. 1998-1 CB 269, Q&As C-1 and C-2; Code Sec. 408(p)(4).

summary plan description that must be provided to employees on an annual basis. If applicable, the notification must inform the employee of his or her right to select the financial institution that will serve as the trustee of the employee's SIMPLE IRA (ordinarily, the employee must have the right to select that institution). In that case, completed pages of Form 5304-SIMPLE can be supplied to employees to meet the notification requirement. If the employer designates the financial institution for all employees (by meeting the requirements of Q&A J of Notice 98-4), completed pages one and two of Form 5305-SIMPLE can be supplied to employees to meet the notification requirement. A penalty of $50 per day applies if an employer fails to provide one or more of the required notices (but not if the employer can show the failure was due to reasonable cause and not willful neglect).

Employee Elections. During the 60-day period immediately preceding January 1 of a calendar year, an eligible employee must be given the right to enter into a salary reduction agreement for the year or to modify or terminate a prior agreement. However, for the year in which the employee becomes eligible to participate, the period during which the employee may enter into a salary reduction agreement or modify a prior agreement is a 60-day period that includes either the date the employee becomes eligible or the previous day.

> **Example:** An employer establishes a SIMPLE plan effective as of July 1, 2004. Each eligible employee must be permitted to make salary reduction contributions on that date, and the 60-day period must begin no later than July 1 and must not end before June 30, 2004.

A SIMPLE plan can provide additional or longer periods (e.g., 80 days) for permitting employees to enter into salary reduction agreements or to modify an existing one.[185] An employee must be given the right to terminate plan participation at any time during the calendar year. If that is done, the employee cannot resume participation until the next year.[186]

Finally, under Notice 98-4 (Q&A E-4), an employee must generally be permitted to choose the financial institution to which the SIMPLE plan contributions will be made. However, if the requirements of Notice 98-4 (Q&A J-1 through J-5) are met, the employer

---

[185] *Id.*, Q&As E-1 and E-2.   [186] *Id.*, Q&A E-3.

may designate the financial institution to which contributions on behalf of all participating employees are to be made.

Timing of Contributions. Employers must contribute employees' salary reduction contributions under a SIMPLE plan within 30 days after the end of the month to which the contributions relate. The matching or non elective employer contributions must be made by the due date of the employer's tax return for that tax year, including extensions.[187]

Vesting and Withdrawal Requirements. All contributions made to SIMPLE IRAs vest 100 percent immediately with the participants and must be immediately available for withdrawal pursuant to Code Sec. 408(p)(3). Note that early withdrawal penalty taxes (as discussed earlier in the chapter) may apply to premature distributions.

.02 Amount of Employee and Employer Contributions

Amounts that can be contributed to SIMPLE IRA plans are generally more limited than contributions that can be made to qualified plans.

Employee Salary Reduction Contributions. Employees can elect (in lieu of receiving cash compensation) to have pre-tax contributions made to a SIMPLE IRA, expressed as a percentage of compensation or as a specific dollar amount. The maximum specific dollar amount of pre-tax contributions that can be made to a SIMPLE plan by an employee has been increased by EGTRRA by $1,000 per year from the $7,000 maximum in 2002 to the $10,000 maximum in 2005 (the 2005 limit will be adjusted for inflation in years after 2005).[188] In addition, participants who are at least or become age 50 during the calendar year can make additional "catch-up" elective deferral contributions to SIMPLE plans beginning in 2002. The additional contribution limit has been increased by $500 per year from the $500 additional limit in 2002 to $2,000 in 2005 and $2,500 in 2006. After 2006, the then $2,500 limit will be adjusted upward for inflation.[189] Thus, the elective deferral limits for SIMPLE plans for the years 2001 through 2005 are as follows:

---

[187] *Id.,* Q&As G-5 and G-6, Code Sec. 408(p)(5)(A).

[188] Code Sec. 408(p)(2)(E), as amended by P.L. 107-16, 107th Cong., 1st Sess., Secs., 611(f)(1) and (2) (June 7, 2001).

[189] Code Secs. 414(v)(2)(B)(ii) and (C), as added by P.L. 107-16, 107th Cong., 1st Sess., Sec. 631(a) (June 7, 2001). *See also* Reg. § 1.414(v)-1.

Year	Elective Deferral Limit	Additional Elective Deferral for Participants Age 50 or More	Total Elective Deferral Limit for Participants Age 50 or More
2001	$ 6,500	$0	$ 6,500
2002	7,000	500	7,500
2003	8,000	1,000	9,000
2004	9,000	1,500	10,500
2005	10,000	2,000	12,000

Example: John, a 30-year-old participant in a SIMPLE plan, had $130,000 of compensation in 2005 and elects to have five percent of that compensation, $6,500, contributed on a pre-tax basis, to the plan. That amount is below the $10,000 maximum that he could have contributed ($12,000 if he were age 50 or more).

The pre-tax contributions that are made to a SIMPLE plan count toward the overall elective deferral limit that applies to Code Sec. 401(k) and other elective deferral plans as discussed in ¶ 1003.03 (concerning salary reduction SEP plans) and in Chapters 5 and 7. That limit in 2005 is $14,000 ($18,000 for individuals who are at least or become age 50 during the calendar year). Thus, for example, assume that an individual participates in a SIMPLE plan maintained by one employer and a Code Sec. 401(k) plan maintained by a second employer for whom the individual works. If that individual contributed $4,000 in 2006 on a pre-tax basis to the SIMPLE plan, the most he/she could contribute on an elective deferral basis to the Code Sec. 401(k) plan of the second employer is $10,000 ($14,000 minus the $4,000 SIMPLE plan contribution—the maximum amount would be $14,000 if the individual were age 50 or more ($18,000 minus $4,000)). Compensation for this purpose has the same meaning as for employee eligibility purposes (covered above).[190]

Matching contributions to SIMPLE IRAs that are made on behalf of self-employed individuals are not treated as salary reduction contributions and thus, are not subject to subject to the $10,000 annual limitation (in 2006—$2,000 for participants who are at least or become age 50 during the calendar year) that applies to SIMPLE IRA elective deferrals.[191]

Employer Matching Contributions. Under Notice 98-4 (Q&As D-4 and D-5), an employer generally is required to make a

---

[190] Notice 98-4, 1998-1 CB 269, Q&As D-1-D-3; Code Secs. 408(p)(2)(A) and 402(g)(3)(D).

[191] Code Sec. 408(p)(9), as added by P.L. 105-34, 105th Cong., 1st Sess., Sec. 1501(b) (Aug. 5, 1997).

¶ 1004.02

dollar-for-dollar matching contribution on behalf of each eligible employee equal to the employee's salary reduction contributions, up to the limit of three percent of the employee's compensation for the entire year. An employer's matching contribution is not subject to the employee compensation limitation under Code Sec. 401(a)(17) which is $210,000 in 2005 (adjusted for inflation after 2005 and up from $205,000 in 2004).[192] However, an employer's nonelective contribution (discussed below) is subject to this limitation.[193]

> **Example:** Consider the same facts as in the above example. The participant's employer would ordinarily have to contribute $1,200 to the employee's SIMPLE IRA account (three percent of the employee's $40,000 compensation). If the employee's compensation had been $180,000 and the employee's pre-tax contribution had been $6,000, then the employer's matching contribution would be $5,400 (3% × $180,000).

The three percent limit on matching contributions can be reduced to as low as one percent if (1) the limit is not reduced for more than two years out of the five-year period that ends with (and includes) the year for which the election is effective and (2) employees are notified of the reduced limit within a reasonable period of time before the 60-day election period during which employees can enter into a salary reduction agreement.

Employer Nonelective Contributions. As an alternative to making matching contributions under a SIMPLE IRA plan, an employer may make nonelective contributions equal to two percent of each eligible employee's compensation for the entire year. An employer that chooses to make a nonelective contribution must make it for each eligible employee regardless of whether the employee elects to make salary reduction contributions for that year. The employer may, but is not required to, limit nonelective contributions to eligible employees who have at least $5,000 (or some lower amount selected by the employer) of compensation for that year.[194]

As noted above, the amount of compensation that can be taken into account in determining the employer nonelective contributions is limited to $210,000 in 2005 (adjusted for inflation after 2005). An employer may substitute the two percent nonelective contributions in place of the matching contributions for a year only if: (1) eligible

---

[192] Code Sec. 401(a)(17), as amended by P.L. 107-16. 107th Cong., 1st Sess., Sec. 611(c) (June 7, 2001). IR-2004-127 (October 20, 2004).
[193] Code Sec. 408(p)(2)(B)(ii).

[194] Notice 98-4, 1998-1 CB 269, Q&A D-6; Code Sec. 408(p)(2)(B).

employees are notified that the nonelective contributions will be made instead of the matching contributions and (2) that notice is provided within a reasonable time before the 60-day election period during which employees can enter into a salary reduction agreement.[195]

.03 Tax Treatment of SIMPLE IRA Plan Contributions

The tax treatment of SIMPLE plan contributions with respect to the participating employees and the contributing employer are covered in the following paragraphs.

Employee's Tax Treatment. Contributions made on behalf of employees to SIMPLE IRA plans are excludable for income tax purposes. For FICA and FUTA tax purposes, employee salary reduction contributions are taxable, whereas employer matching and nonelective contributions are not subject to tax.[196]

Employer's Tax Treatment. Under Notice 98-4 (Q&A I-7), pursuant to Code Sec. 404(m), employer matching or nonelective contributions to a SIMPLE IRA plan are deductible in the tax year of the employer with or within which the calendar year for which the contributions are made ends. Contributions will be treated as made for a particular taxable year if they are made on account of that taxable year and are made by the due date (including extensions) of the employer's income tax return.

Tax Treatment for Self-Employed Individuals with No Employees. One portion of a self-employed individual's contribution to a SIMPLE IRA is similar to employee contributions to SIMPLE IRAs discussed above. This portion is referred to below as the "deemed employee contribution." The deemed employee contribution can be any fixed percentage or fixed amount of compensation, not to exceed the applicable dollar amount ($10,000 in 2005— $12,000 for individuals who are at least or become age 50 during the calendar year) as discussed in ¶1004.02 above. "Compensation" as applied to self-employed individuals means net earnings from self-employment without regard to any contribution, reduced by the self-employment tax deduction.[197] The deemed employee contribution is reported by a self-employed individual as a deduction for AGI on Form 1040, page 1. Although the deemed employee contribution is deferred for federal income tax purposes, it is nevertheless subject to the self-employment tax. (The manner of reporting this contribution

---

[195] Code Sec. 401(a)(17), as amended by P.L. 107-16, 107th Cong., 1st Sess., Sec. 611(c) (June 7, 2001); Notice 98-4, 1998-1 CB 269. IR-2002-111 (October 18, 2002).

[196] Notice 98-4, 1998-1 CB 269, Q&A I-1.

[197] Code Sec. 408(p)(6)(A)(ii).

on Form 1040, Page 1, rather than on Schedule C, facilitates this tax treatment because Schedule C net earnings, which are subject to employment tax, are not reduced by the amount of the deemed employee contribution.)

The other portion of a self-employed individual's contribution to a SIMPLE IRA is similar to employer contributions previously discussed. This portion is referred to below as the "deemed employer contribution." The deemed employer contribution is equal to the lesser of: (a) the amount of the deemed employee contribution, or (b) three percent of "compensation" as defined above, without regard to the $210,000 (in 2005) compensation limitation under Code Sec. 401(a)(17). This amount is reported as a deduction on Schedule C. This manner of reporting the deemed employer contribution facilitates its deferral from federal income tax and its exemption from self-employment tax.

> **Example:** John-Paul (age 42) is self-employed and has earned income of $10,000 in 2005. If his "deemed employee contribution" is fixed at $7,000, he may contribute an additional $300 as a "deemed employer contribution" (i.e., $7,000, not to exceed three percent of $10,000). On his tax return, he would report a $7,000 deduction on Form 1040, page 1, and a $300 deduction on Schedule C. The amount of net self-employment earnings subject to federal income tax would be $2,700 (i.e., $10,000 – $7,300). The amount subject to self-employment tax would be $9,700 (i.e., $10,000 – $300).
>
> If John-Paul's earned income were $300,000 instead of $10,000, his "deemed employer contribution" would be $7,000 (i.e., the lesser of $7,000 or $9,000 = 3% X $300,000). On his tax return, he would report the $7,000 deemed employee contribution as before, i.e., as a deduction on Form 1040, page 1. The deemed employer contribution would be $7,000 instead of $300, and would be reported as a deduction on Schedule C. The amount of net self-employment earnings subject to federal income tax would be $286,000 (i.e., $300,000 – $14,000). The amount subject to self-employment tax would be $293,000 (i.e., $300,000 – $7,000).

.04   Tax Treatment of Distributions from SIMPLE IRAs

Under Notice 98-4 (Q&A 1-2), amounts distributed from SIMPLE IRAs are generally taxed as ordinary income like other IRA distributions and can be subject to the 10 percent premature distributions tax under Code Sec. 72(t). However, as noted earlier, the 10 percent premature distributions tax, when applicable, is increased to 25 percent for distributions from a SIMPLE IRA made during the two-year period beginning on the date the participant first participated in any SIMPLE plan maintained by his or her employer.

In general, distributions from SIMPLE IRAs can be rolled over tax-free into other IRAs or, beginning in 2002, qualified employer plans in which the taxpayer participates, subject to the limitations on IRA rollovers discussed earlier in the chapter. In addition, amounts transferred in a direct trustee-to-trustee transfer from a SIMPLE IRA are not subject to income tax. However, a premature distribution made during the two-year period described in the above paragraph will be taxable unless the distribution is rolled over or transferred directly in a trustee-to-trustee transfer into another SIMPLE IRA.

.05 Employers That Can Establish SIMPLE IRA Plans

SIMPLE IRA plans may be established only by employers that had no more than 100 employees who earned $5,000 or more in compensation during the preceding calendar year. For this purpose, all employees employed at any time during the calendar year are counted, regardless of whether they are eligible to participate in the plan. This includes all self-employed individuals working for the employer. Under a grace period rule, an employer that ceases to meet the 100-employee limitation is treated as satisfying the 100-employee limitation for the two calendar years immediately following the calendar year for which it last met the 100-employee limitation.[198] However, if an employer fails to satisfy the 100-employee requirement, the exclusive plan requirement, or the participation rules due to an acquisition, disposition, or similar transaction, the SIMPLE IRA plan may be maintained as a qualified salary reduction arrangement during a transition period that begins on the date of the transaction and ends on the last day of the second calendar year following the calendar year in which the transaction occurs. To make use of the transition period, the employer must satisfy requirements similar to those stated in Code Sec. 410(b)(6)(C)(i)(II). In addition, it is necessary that the qualified salary reduction arrangement maintained by the employer would have satisfied the requirements for qualified salary reduction arrangements after the transaction if the employer which maintained the plan before the transaction had remained a separate employer.[199] Certain related employers (trades or businesses under

---

[198] *Id.*, Q&As B-1 and B-2.

[199] Code Sec. 408(p)(10), as added by P.L. 105-206, 105th Cong., 2d Sess., Sec. 6016(a)(1)(B) (July 22, 1998).

¶ 1004.05

common control) are treated as a single employer for purposes of the 100-employee limitation. These related employers include controlled groups of corporations, under Code Sec. 414(b), partnerships or sole proprietorships under common control under Code Sec. 414(c), and affiliated service groups under Code Sec. 414(m). In addition, leased employees as defined in Code Sec. 414(n) are treated as employed by the employer.[200]

Under Notice 98-4 (Q&A B-3), an employer cannot make contributions under a SIMPLE plan for a calendar year if the employer, or a predecessor employer, maintains another qualified plan under which any of its employees received an allocation of contributions (in the case of a defined contribution plan) or has an increase in a benefit accrued or treated as an accrued benefit (in the case of a defined benefit plan) for any plan year beginning or ending within the current calendar year. However, the fact that an employer maintains another qualified plan that only covers collectively bargained employees, who are excluded from participation under the employer's SIMPLE IRA plan under Code Sec. 408(p)(4)(B), will not prevent the employer from maintaining the SIMPLE IRA plan for its noncollectively bargained employees. Tax-exempt employers and governmental entities can establish SIMPLE IRA plans just like any other employers.[201]

.06 SIMPLE Plan Establishment

An employer may establish a SIMPLE Plan, effective on any date between January 1 and October 1 of a year beginning after December 31, 1996, provided that the employer (or any predecessor employer) did not previously maintain a SIMPLE plan. An employer beginning business on or after October 1 of a year can establish a SIMPLE plan for that year if it does so as soon as administratively feasible after the employer comes into existence. If an employer (or predecessor employer) previously maintained a SIMPLE plan, the employer may establish the SIMPLE plan effective only on January 1 of the year. A SIMPLE IRA must be established for an employee prior to the first date by which a contribution is required to be deposited into the employee's SIMPLE IRA.[202]

The IRS has issued model plan forms that can be used by employers to establish SIMPLE IRA plans and make required notifications to employees. Form 5305-SIMPLE is to be used as the

---

[200] Notice 98-4, 1998-1 CB 269, Q&A B-5.
[201] *Id.*, Q&A B-4, Code Sec. 408(p)(2)(D)(i), as amended by P.L. 105-34. 105th Cong., 1st Sess., Sec. 1601(d)(1)(E) (Aug. 5, 1997).

[202] *Id.*, Q&As K-1 and K-2.

model plan form for establishing a SIMPLE IRA where the employer designates the financial institution to be used by all employees participating in the plan. Form 5304-SIMPLE is to be used where the employer will permit the plan participants to select the financial institution where the participants' SIMPLE IRAs are to be established.[203]

.07 Reporting and Disclosure Requirements

SIMPLE IRA plans are subject to simplified reporting and disclosure requirements. A SIMPLE IRA trustee or the issuer of an annuity for a SIMPLE IRA must provide the employer sponsoring the plan each year with a summary description containing the following information: (1) the name and address of the employer and the trustee or annuity issuer, (2) the requirements for eligibility for participation, (3) the benefits provided with respect to the arrangement, (4) the time and method of making elections with respect to the arrangement, and (5) the procedures for, and effects, withdrawals (including rollovers) from the arrangement. Generally, a trustee or annuity issuer must provide the summary description to the employer early enough to allow the employer to meet its notification requirements (discussed earlier).

In the case of a SIMPLE PLAN established using Form 5305-SIMPLE or Form 5304-SIMPLE, a trustee or annuity issuer may satisfy this obligation by providing the employer with a current copy of the form, with instructions, the information necessary to complete Article VI, and the name and address of the financial institution. The trustee or annuity issuer should supply guidance to the employer concerning the need to complete the first two pages of the form in accordance with its plan's terms and to distribute completed copies to eligible employees. The trustee or annuity issuer of a transfer SIMPLE IRA does not have to provide this summary description. A transfer SIMPLE IRA is not one to which the employer has made contributions under its SIMPLE plan.[204]

Under Notice 98-4 (Q&A H-2), within 31 days after the close of each calendar year, a SIMPLE IRA trustee or annuity issuer must provide each participant on whose behalf an account is maintained with a statement of his or her account balance as of the close of that calendar year and the account activity during that calendar year. The trustee or annuity issuer must also provide any other information required to be furnished to IRA account holders (e.g., disclosure statements for IRAs referred to in Reg § 1.408-6).

---

[203] *Id.,* Q&A K-3.

[204] Notice 98-4, 1998-1 CB 269, Q&A H-1.

Notice 98-4 (Q&A H-3) indicates that a trustee of an IRA or issuer of an IRA annuity must also make reports regarding these accounts to the IRS, pursuant to Code Sec. 408(i). The IRS will be modifying Form 5498, Individual Retirement Arrangement Information, to require that the amount of contributions to a SIMPLE IRA, rollover contributions, and the fair market value of the account be reported, and that contributions to a SIMPLE IRA be identified as such.

These are the only reports that must be made by the trustee, annuity issuer, or employer to the IRS concerning the employer's SIMPLE plan.[205] The general reporting requirements for qualified plans do not apply. Under Notice 98-4 (Q&A's H-1 through H-3), a trustee or annuity issuer that fails to file any of the reports described above incurs a $50 penalty (generally for each day the failure continues, except that it is $50 for each failure in the case of failure to file Form 5498), unless it is shown the failure is due to reasonable cause. A trustee or annuity issuer will not be assessed a penalty for failing to provide the summary plan description to the employer, if the employer, trustee, or annuity issuer has provided the required information to eligible employees within the required time period. Also, the penalty for failure to provide participants with an account statement will not be imposed if the statement is provided by January 31 following the calendar year to which the statement relates.

Planning Pointer: The annual contribution limit and the requirement that SIMPLE plan contributions be made annually should carefully be considered by an employer in deciding whether to establish a SIMPLE plan or some other type(s) of qualified plans. The annual contribution limit may be significantly less for a SIMPLE plan (e.g., $10,000 in 2005—$12,000 for individuals who are at least or become age 50 during the calendar year for employee salary reduction contributions plus three percent of compensation for employer contributions) than applies generally in the case of other defined contribution plans (e.g., under Code Sec. 401(k) plans, up to $14,000 (in 2005—$18,000 for participants who are at least or become age 50 during the calendar year) of salary reduction contributions can be made, and employer matching contributions or nonelective contributions can be made above this amount). Further, SIMPLE plan contributions must be made yearly even when the employer is having loss years. Under a profit-sharing plan, contributions need not be made yearly as discussed in Chapter 5.

---

[205] Code Sec. 408(1)(2)(A).

¶ 1005   Roth IRAs

Beginning in 1998, taxpayers were able to make contributions into a new type of plan called a Roth IRA.[206] A Roth IRA is an individual retirement plan that is designated at the time of establishment of the plan as a Roth IRA.[207] In general, the tax rules concerning Roth IRAs are the same as for traditional IRAs covered in the first section of this chapter.[208] Accordingly, this section of the chapter will focus on the rules concerning Roth IRAs that are different than the rules covering traditional IRAs. See the first section of this chapter for a discussion of IRA tax rules, in general. Roth IRAs are different than traditional IRAs in that the tax advantages of Roth IRAs are "backloaded." That is, contributions made to Roth IRAs are totally nondeductible.[209] In addition, unlike the case of IRAs, contributions can be made into Roth IRAs even after the taxpayer reaches age 70½.[210] But, the total amount of contributions that a taxpayer can make to all IRA plans (other than employer contributions to SEP IRAs and SIMPLE IRAs) including the taxpayer's Roth IRAs in one taxable year cannot exceed the maximum dollar limit for contributions to IRAs which has been increased by EGTRRA to $4,000 per year in 2005 through 2007 ($4,500 per year in 2005 and $5,000 per year in 2006 and 2007 for individuals age 50 or more (the maximum was $2,000 in 2001 and earlier years)) (see the discussion of those dollar limits in ¶ 1002.01).[211] The maximum amount that a taxpayer can contribute to a Roth IRA is phased out ratably over a $15,000 range ($10,000 for married persons filing joint returns) for single taxpayers and married taxpayers filing joint returns with modified AGI amounts above $95,000 and $150,000 respectively.[212]

If the taxpayer meets a five-year holding period and one of four other specified requirements, distributions from a Roth IRA (called qualified distributions) are totally tax free (including any amount of earnings on the taxpayer's Roth IRA plan contributions.[213] Amounts contributed to a Roth IRA can be rolled over tax-free into another Roth IRA subject to the rollover time limit rules that apply to IRAs generally, and taxpayers with AGI of $100,000 or less can roll over amounts from traditional IRAs to Roth IRAs (such amounts will be taxed as ordinary income—special recognition rules applied to such rollovers made before 1999) or convert an IRA into a Roth IRA.[214] In February of 1999, the IRS issued final regulations concerning Roth

---

[206] Code Sec. 408A, as added by P.L. 105-34, 105th Cong., 1st Secs., Sec. 302(c)(Aug.5, 1997).

[207] Code Sec. 408A(b).

[208] Code Sec. 408A(a).

[209] Code Sec. 408A(c)(1).

[210] Code Sec. 408A(c)(4).

[211] Code Sec. 408A(c)(2).

[212] Code Secs. 408A(c)(2)(A) and (C)(ii).

[213] Code Secs. 408A(d)(1) and (2).

[214] Code Secs. 408(c)(3)(B), (d)(3), and (e).

IRAs.[215] These regulations provide extensive coverage and details concerning Roth IRAs. The following paragraphs cover the more important aspects of Roth IRAs.

> **Comment:** Effective for tax years beginning after 2005, participants in Code Sec. 401(k) and 403(b) plans will be permitted to make after-tax contributions in lieu of some or all of the elective deferral contributions they would have otherwise made to a qualified Roth contribution program, if the employer's plan then adds such a program.[216] Such contributions will be made to a separate designated Roth IRA account for each participating employee (subject to the maximum elective deferral limitations covered in Chapters 5 and 7). The limitations that normally apply to Roth IRA contributions under Code Sec. 408A will not apply to those designated Roth IRA accounts. However, the rules concerning the taxability of distributions from Roth IRAs (discussed below) will apply, and rollovers will be able to be made from the designated Roth IRA accounts to other Roth IRAs of the taxpayer. For further discussion of this issue, see Chapter 7.

.01   Roth IRA Contribution Rules

Taxpayers, including those who cannot make contributions to traditional IRAs because they are over age 70½ may be able to make contributions to a Roth IRA. Under Code Secs. 408A(c)(1) and (2), taxpayer contributions to Roth IRAs are not deductible and cannot exceed the excess of (1) the maximum amount allowable as a deduction to a traditional IRA, computed without regard to the rule not allowing contributions on behalf of a beneficiary who is at least age 70½ and the limitation on deductions for active participants in qualified plans over (2) the aggregate amount of contributions made to traditional IRAs for the benefit of that taxpayer. That effectively means that no more than $3,000 in 2002 through 2004 ($3,500 for individuals who are at least or become age 50 during the calendar year—the limit for 2001 was $2,000—see the discussion on the dollar limits for IRA contributions in ¶ 1002.01 for limits in other years) can be contributed per year to all of the traditional and Roth IRAs, owned by a particular taxpayer. The maximum amount that can be contributed to a Roth IRA for a given year is phased out ratably over a $15,000 range ($10,000 for married persons filing jointly) for single taxpayers and married taxpayers filing joint

---

[215] T.D. 8816, 2/4/99, 64 FR 5597.
[216] See Code Sec. 402A, as added by P.L. 107-16, 107th Cong., 1st Secs., Sec. 617(a), effective in tax years beginning after December 31, 2005 (June 7, 2001).

returns with modified AGI in excess of $95,000 and $150,000 respectively.[217] The phase out range for married persons filing separate returns (where the spouses lived together during any part of the taxable year) is from $0 to $10,000. For the purpose of determining the maximum allowable Roth IRA contribution, modified AGI is defined in the same way as it is for IRA purposes (discussed earlier in this chapter) except that any income that must be recognized on a rollover from (or the conversion of) an IRA into a Roth IRA (as discussed under Rollovers below) is not taken into account, and any deduction for contributions to IRAs under Code Sec. 219 is to be taken into account.[218] For taxable years beginning after December 31, 2004, amounts received as RMDs (as discussed earlier in this chapter) under Code Sec. 401(a)(9) from a traditional IRA and any amount distributed from a traditional IRA under the minimum distribution incidental benefit rules will not be taken into account in determining modified AGI (such amounts were included in determining modified AGI for taxable years beginning before January 1, 2005).[219] Under a special rule, Code Sec. 408A(c)(2)(D) with a cross reference to Code Sec. 219(g)(4) indicates that married persons filing separate returns and that live apart the entire year are not to be treated as married persons. This rule allows such individuals to use the more favorable phase-out range beginning at $95,000 instead of the $0 to $10,000 range that applies to married persons filing separate returns, in general. Specifically, the amount that can be contributed to the Roth IRA taking into account the phase-out rule is (1) the maximum contribution amount multiplied by (2) a fraction, the numerator of which is $15,000 ($10,000 for married persons) minus the amount of taxpayer's modified AGI in excess of $95,000 ($150,000 in the case of married persons filing jointly and $0 generally for married persons filing separate returns) and the denominator of which is $15,000 ($10,000 for married persons filing jointly). If the amount after the phase out is more than $0 but less than $200, it is raised to $200 under Code Sec. 408A(c)(2)(A). In addition, this Code Sec. provides that an amount is rounded down to the nearest $10 (however, note that IRS Pub 590 indicates that the Roth IRA plan contribution after phase-out is to be rounded up to the nearest $10).

Example: Ken and Diane (both under age 50) are married and file a joint return and have modified AGI of $154,411 in 2006. Ken does not contribute any amount to a traditional IRA. The

---

[217] Code Secs. 408A(C)(3)(A) and (C).
[218] Code Secs. 408A(c)(3)(C)(i).

[219] Code Sec. 403(c)(3)(C)(i), as modified by P.L. 105-206, 105th Cong., 2d Sess., Sec.7004(b) (July 22, 1998).

maximum amount Ken can contribute to his Roth IRAs, in total, for 2006 is $2,240, computed as follows:

$$\frac{\$10,000-\$4,411}{\$10,000} \times \$4,000 = \$2,235.60$$

This amount is to be rounded up to $2,240, according to IRS Publication 590.

Note that the taxpayers, whose contribution to a Roth IRA is partially or totally phased out, may contribute the difference between the applicable dollar limit and the Roth IRA contribution limit (after phase-out) to a traditional IRA on a nondeductible basis.

A taxpayer can make a contribution to a Roth IRA by converting an excess contribution made to an IRA (see the first section of this chapter for the definition of excess IRA contributions) into a contribution to the Roth IRA. This can be done to correct excess contributions made to an IRA.

Under Code Sec. 408A(c)(7), a taxpayer is considered to have made an Roth IRA contribution on the last day of the preceding taxable year if the contribution is made by the due date of that taxpayer's return, not including extensions.

.02 Excess Contributions

Excess contributions to Roth IRAs are subject to the Code Sec. 4973 six percent penalty tax.[220] Under Code Sec. 4973(f)(1), an excess contribution to a Roth IRA is defined as the amount contributed for the tax year to the taxpayer's Roth IRAs (other than amounts properly and timely rolled over from a Roth IRA or converted from a traditional IRA as described later) minus the allowable contribution limit. In addition, an excess contribution includes an excess contribution from the preceding taxable year minus the sum of (1) distributions out of the Roth IRA accounts during the year plus (2) the excess, if any, of the taxpayer's maximum contribution limit for the year over amounts contributed to all of the taxpayer's IRAs (other than Education IRAs) for the year.[221] Therefore, any excess contributions from prior years remain subject to the six percent excise tax until the excess is corrected by making less than the maximum allowable contribution in the current or future year. Code Sec. 4973(f) indicates that the rule of Code Sec. 408(d)(4) applies such that in computing the amount of the excess contribution,

---

[220] Code Sec. 4973(f), as added by P.L. 105-34, 105th Cong., 1st Sess., Sec 302(b) (Aug., 5, 1997).

[221] Code Sec. 4973(f)(2).

any contribution distributed from a Roth IRA under the rule permitting correction of an excess contribution by making a distribution before the due date of the taxpayer's return is treated as an amount not contributed to the account. This treatment only applies if any earnings on the contributions are also withdrawn and reported as income earned and receivable in the year the contribution was made.[222] There is another way to accomplish that result as well. If the account holder timely filed his or her tax return without withdrawing the excess contributions, he or she can still make the withdrawal no later than six months after the due date of the applicable tax return, excluding extensions. In that case, the taxpayer should file an amended return with "Filed Pursuant to Section 301.9100-2" written at the top. Any related plan earnings for the year should also be reported on the amended return.[223] For further coverage of the rules under Code Sec. 408(d)(4), see ¶ 1002.05 covering traditional IRAs in this chapter.

.03 Spousal IRAs

Contributions can be made to a Roth IRA for the taxpayer's spouse even if the spouse has attained age 70½.[224] However, the amount contributed on behalf of the spouse into a Roth IRA reduces the amount that can be. contributed into other IRAs under a Spousal IRA arrangement on behalf of the spouse for that year.[225] Thus, the maximum contribution an individual and his or her spouse can make during a taxable year to all of their traditional and Roth IRAs is the lesser of 100 percent of their combined compensation or $8,000 in 2005 through 2007 ($8,500 in 2005 and $9,000 in 2006 and 2007 if one spouse is at least or becomes age 50 during the calendar year and $9,000 in 2005 and $10,000 in 2006 and 2007 if both spouses meet that age requirement—in 2001, the maximum limit was $4,000). For further coverage on Spousal IRAs, see ¶ 1002.04.

.04 Conversions, Recharacterizations, and Reconversions

Taxpayers may be able to move (convert) amounts from either a traditional, SEP, SIMPLE, or other Roth IRA into a Roth IRA.[226] Taxpayers also may be able move (transfer) contributions made to one IRA to a different IRA and recharacterize them as having been made directly to the different IRA.[227]

---

[222] IRS Pub. No. 590 at 57.

[223] Instructions for Form 5329, p. 4.

[224] Code Sec. 408A(c)(4).

[225] Code Sec. 219(c)(1)(B)(ii), as amended by P.L. 105-34, 105th Cong., 1st Sess., Sec. 302(c) (Aug. 5, 1997).

[226] Reg. § 1.408A-4, Q&A 4(a) and (b).

[227] IRS pub. No. 590 at 56.

Conversions. Taxpayers can convert a traditional IRA to a Roth IRA if two requirements are met. First the IRA owner must satisfy the $100,000 modified AGI and tax return limitations described below. Second, the amount contributed to the Roth IRA must meet the definition of a qualified rollover contribution under Code Sec. 408A(e) (i.e., it must satisfy the requirements for a contribution as defined in Code Sec. 408(d)(3)—applicable to traditional IRAs as discussed earlier—except that the one-rollover-per-year limitation does not apply).[228] There are three ways to convert amounts from a traditional IRA to a Roth IRA:[229]

(1) *Rollover*—The taxpayer can receive a distribution from a traditional IRA and roll it over to a Roth IRA within 60 days after the distribution.

(2) *Trustee-to-trustee transfer*—The taxpayer can direct the trustee of a traditional IRA to transfer an amount from the traditional IRA to the trustee of the Roth IRA.

(3) *Same trustee transfer*—If the trustee of the traditional IRA also maintains the Roth IRA, the taxpayer can direct the trustee to transfer an amount from the traditional IRA to the Roth IRA.

A conversion from a traditional IRA to a Roth IRA by one of the above methods will be treated as a qualified rollover, and the 10 percent early distributions tax will not apply. If property is withdrawn from the traditional IRA, the same property must be rolled over into the Roth IRA to qualify as a conversion. If only a portion of an amount withdrawn from a traditional IRA is rolled over into the Roth IRA, the amount that the taxpayer keeps will be taxable (except to the extent it is attributable to nondeductible contributions made to the traditional IRA) and will be subject to the 10 percent premature distributions tax, unless it is excepted from that tax. Amounts that must be distributed from a traditional IRA for a particular year under the minimum required distribution rules (discussed earlier) cannot be converted into a Roth IRA. In addition, traditional IRAs that have been inherited by the taxpayer from someone other than the taxpayer's spouse cannot be converted into Roth IRAs.[230]

A taxpayer can convert amounts from a traditional IRA into a Roth IRA only if both of the following requirements are met:[231]

(1) The taxpayer's modified AGI (together with that of his or her spouse in the case of married persons filing joint returns) is not more than $100,000.

---

[228] Reg. § 1.408A-4, Q&A 1(a).
[229] IRS Pub. No 590 at 57.

[230] *Id.*, at 57.
[231] Reg. § 1.408A-4, Q&A 2.

(2) If the taxpayer is married, that taxpayer and his or her spouse must file joint returns. However, if a married couple lives apart the entire year, each spouse can make a conversion even though a separate return is filed as long as his or her modified AGI is not more than $100,000.

If a taxpayer, who does not meet both of these requirements, makes a conversion from a traditional IRA to a Roth IRA, that conversion is treated as a failed conversion. In that case, the taxpayer can recharacterize the contribution (see the discussion below on recharacterizations) as having been made to the traditional IRA. If the taxpayer does not recharacterize the distribution, it will be treated as a regular contribution to a Roth IRA and will be considered to be an excess contribution to the extent it exceeds the regular contribution limit.[232]

Under Code Sec. 408A(d)(3)(A), amounts converted from a traditional IRA to a Roth IRA are includible in the taxpayer's gross income to the extent the amounts would have been taxable if retained by the taxpayer. Thus converted amounts attributable to nondeductible traditional IRA contributions would not be taxable. Further, the 10 percent premature distributions tax will not apply to a conversion, as noted above.

Recently, the IRS issued new temporary and proposed regulations which explain how to value annuity contracts that are held in a traditional IRA or IR Annuity which is converted to a Roth IRA. These temporary and proposed regulations clarify that the fair market value of the annuity rather than the cash surrender value is to be used in determining the amount of gross income the taxpayer has from the conversion. The temporary regulations apply to conversion transfers made after August 18, 2005.[232.1]

> **Comment:** Note that amounts that are taxable under the conversion rules are included in income for all purposes. Thus, for example, the amount is counted for purposes of determining the taxable portion of social security benefits under Code Sec. 86 and in determining the phase-out of the $25,000 exemption under Code Sec. 469(i) relating to the disallowance of real estate rental losses under the passive activity rules.[233] Thus, a converted amount can, in some cases, increase a taxpayer's adjusted gross income by more than the amount that is converted. In such a case, the taxpayer may want to consider recharacterization of the contribution, as discussed below. An actual example of the impact of conversions on a taxpayer's adjusted gross income is in

---

[232] *Id.*, Q&As 2 and 3.
[232.1] T.D. 9220, 70 FR 48868 (August 22, 2005) and REG-122857-05, 70 FR 48924 (August 22, 2005).

[233] *Id.*, Q&A 9.

¶ 1005.04

the case of *Robert and Sara Helm.*[234] In that case, the Tax Court in a Summary Opinion held that it was proper to take into account the amount of income that resulted from the taxpayers' conversion of a Traditional IRA into a Roth IRA for purposes of determining the amount of taxable social security benefits that the couple received. The conversion triggered the taxation of some of the social security benefits they received.

Under an exception to the income inclusion rule, gross income attributable to amounts converted from a traditional IRA to a Roth IRA prior to January 1, 1999 were includible in gross income over a four-year period beginning with 1998. However, a taxpayer could have elected to include such gross income entirely in 1998, if the election were made by the due date (including extensions) for that taxpayer's 1998 tax return.[235]

> **Example:** Charles rolled over a $16,000 distribution received from an IRA in 1998 to a Roth IRA. Assume that Charles had made no nondeductible contributions to the IRA. As a result, the $16,000 is includible in gross income. But, since the rollover took place before 1999, the $16,000 is includible at a rate of $4,000 per year beginning with 1998. The 10 percent premature distributions tax does not apply, even if Charles were under age 59½. A Charles, however, could have elected to recognize the entire $16,000 as gross income for 1998.

If the taxpayer included the taxable portion of a pre-1999 conversion ratably over the four-year period and in 1998, 1999, or 2000 withdraws from the Roth IRA any amount allocable to the taxable part of the conversion, that taxpayer would generally have to have been included in income both the ratable (one-quarter) portion for the year and the part of the withdrawal made during the year that was allocable to the taxable part of the conversion.[236] Special rules apply to taxpayers using the four-year spread that died, changed from married filing jointly to married filing separately, or divorced during that four-year period. See Reg. § 1.408A-4, Q&A 11 for details.

Conversion from a SIMPLE IRA. Under Reg. § 1.408A-4, Q&A 4, amounts in a taxpayer's SIMPLE IRA can be converted to a Roth IRA using the same rules that pertain to converting traditional IRAs to Roth IRAs. However, a taxpayer cannot convert an amount distributed from a SIMPLE IRA during the two-year period beginning on the date the taxpayer first participated in any SIMPLE IRA maintained by the taxpayer's employer.

---

[234] TC Summary Opinion 2002-138.
[235] Reg. § 1.408A-4, Q&A 8.
[236] IRS Pub. No. 590, at 39.

Conversions from Other Retirement Plans. Amounts in other retirement plans in which the taxpayer participates cannot be converted directly into a Roth IRA. However, such amounts can be rolled over into a traditional IRA under the rules discussed in Chapter 9 and then can be converted into a Roth IRA.[237]

Rollover from One Roth IRA into Another Roth IRA. Taxpayers can withdraw, tax-free, all or part of the assets from one Roth IRA if those assets are contributed within 60 days to another Roth IRA. In addition, trustee-to-trustee transfers from one Roth IRA to another are considered rollovers. In general, rollovers from one Roth IRA to another must meet the general requirements that apply to IRA rollovers, in general, as discussed earlier in connection with traditional IRAs. However, the one-rollover-per account-per-year limitation does not apply.[238]

Recharacterizations. Taxpayers who have made a failed conversion from a traditional IRA to a Roth IRA (because, e.g., their modified AGI is more than $100,000) can undo the conversion by recharacterizing the contribution. In that case, the converted amount will be treated as having been moved to the traditional IRA. More generally, taxpayers may be able to treat a contribution made to one type of IRA as having been made to a different type of IRA. This process is called recharacterizing the contribution. To recharacterize a contribution, the taxpayer must generally have the contribution transferred from the first IRA (the one to which the contribution was made) to the second IRA in a trustee-to-trustee transfer. If the transfer is made by the due date (including extensions) for that taxpayer's tax return for the year during which the contribution was made, the taxpayer can elect to treat the contribution as having been originally made to the second IRA instead of the first IRA. It will be treated as having been made to the second IRA on the same date that it was actually made to the first IRA. The IRS has granted extensions to taxpayers in individual instances where the taxpayers' failure to do the recharacterization by the required time was due to circumstances beyond their control.[239] For recharacterization purposes, a distribution from a traditional IRA that is received in one tax year and rolled over into a Roth IRA in the next year, but still within 60 days of the distribution from the traditional IRA, is treated as a contribution to the Roth IRA in the year of the distribution from the traditional IRA.[240] A recharacterization is not

---

[237] Reg. § 1.408A-4, Q&A 5.

[238] IRS Pub. No. 590, at 57.

[239] See, e.g., IRS Letter Ruling 200219040.2-14-02, CCH IRS Letter Rulings Reports, IRS Letter Ruling 200234073. 5-28-02, CCH IRS Letter Rulings Reports, IRS Letter Ruling 200235033,

6-12-02, CCH IRS Letter Rulings Reports. IRS Letter Ruling 200431016, and IRS Letter Ruling 200428035.

[240] Reg. § 1.408A-5. Q&A 5. IRS Pub. No. 590 at 57-58.

treated as a rollover for purposes of the one-rollover-per-account-per-year limitation that applies to traditional IRAs according to Reg. § 1.408A-5, Q&A 8.

Under the Reg. § 1.408A-5, Q&A 2, the contribution will not be treated as having been made to the second IRA unless the transfer includes all of the net earnings attributable to the contribution. See Reg. § 1.408A-5, Q&A 2(c) and Reg. § 1.408-11 for the process of determining the net earnings attributable to the contribution (the methods are similar to those described in ¶ 1002.05 concerning net earnings attributable to excess contributions made to traditional IRAs). No deduction is allowed for the contribution to the first IRA, and any net earnings transferred with the recharacterized contribution are treated as earned in the second IRA. The contribution will not be treated as having been made to the second IRA to the extent any deduction was allowed with respect to the contribution to the first IRA.[241]

Effect of Previous Tax-Free Transfers. If a contribution has been moved from one IRA to another in a tax-free transfer, such as a rollover, the contribution to the second IRA cannot be recharacterized. However, if an amount is erroneously rolled over or transferred from a traditional IRA to a SIMPLE IRA, the contribution can subsequently be recharacterized as a contribution to another traditional IRA.[242]

A contribution to one IRA that has been moved between IRAs in tax-free transfers can be treated as if it remained in the first IRA, the IRA that received the original contribution. This means that the taxpayer can elect to recharacterize the contribution to the first IRA by having a trustee-to-trustee transfer of the contribution made from the IRA in which it now resides to a second IRA and treat the contribution as having been made to the second IRA on the same date it was actually made to the first IRA. If both IRAs involved in the trustee-to-trustee transfer are maintained by the same trustee, the taxpayer need only direct the trustee to transfer the contribution.[243]

Employer Contributions. Under Reg. § 1.408A-5, Q&A 5, a taxpayer cannot recharacterize employer contributions (including elective deferrals) under a SEP or a SIMPLE IRA plan (discussed earlier in this chapter) as contributions to another IRA.

Recharacterization Procedures. To recharacterize a contribution, the taxpayer must notify both the trustee of the first IRA (the one to which the contribution was actually made) and the trustee of the second IRA that the taxpayer has elected to treat, for federal tax purposes, as having been made to the second IRA rather than the

---

[241] IRS Pub. No. 590 at 57-58
[242] Reg. § 1.408A-5. Q&A 4.

[243] *Id.*, Q&A 7.

first. The taxpayer must make the notifications by the date of the transfer. Only one notification is required if both IRAs are maintained by the same trustee. The notification(s) must include all of the following information:

(1) The type and amount of the contribution to the first IRA that is to be recharacterized.

(2) The date on which the contribution was made to the first IRA and the year for which it was made.

(3) A direction to the trustee of the first IRA to transfer in a trustee-to-trustee transfer the amount of the contribution and any net income allocable to the contribution to the second IRA.

(4) The name of the trustees of the first and second IRAs.

(5) Any additional information needed to make the transfer.

The recharacterization election and the transfer must take place on or before the due date (including extensions) for filing the taxpayer's return for the year for which the contribution was made to the first IRA. After the transfer has taken place, the taxpayer cannot change the election to recharacterize.[244]

> **Example:** In June of 2005, Wyatt, who is single, converted his traditional IRA to a Roth IRA. Later in 2005, he discovered that his modified AGI would be more than $100,000 due to an unexpected bonus he received. In January of 2006, to make the necessary adjustment to remove the failed conversion, Wyatt set up a traditional IRA with the same trustee and instructed that trustee to make a trustee-to-trustee transfer of the conversion contribution made to the Roth IRA (along with earnings on that contribution) to the new traditional IRA. The trustee was informed that Wyatt was recharacterizing the contribution to the Roth IRA such that it would be treated as having been contributed to the new traditional IRA. As a result of the recharacterization, Wyatt has no gross income to report from the 2005 conversion, and the resulting rollover to the traditional IRA is not treated as a rollover for purposes of the one-rollover-per-year rule.

Reconversions. If an IRA owner converts an amount from a traditional IRA to a Roth IRA and then recharacterizes the amount back to a traditional IRA in a recharacterization, may the IRA owner subsequently reconvert that amount from the traditional IRA to a Roth IRA? In general, that IRA owner may not reconvert that amount from the traditional IRA to a Roth IRA before the beginning

---

[244] IRS Pub. No. 590 at 57-58.

¶ 1005.04

of the taxable year following the taxable year in which the amount was originally converted to a Roth IRA, or, if later, the end of the 30-day period beginning on the day on which the IRA owner transfers the amount from the Roth IRA back to a traditional IRA by means of a recharacterization. Any attempted conversion before that time will be treated as a failed conversion.[245]

.05 Distributions from Roth IRAs

Any qualified distribution from a Roth IRA is not includible in the gross income of the recipient under Code Sec. 408A(d)(1). In addition, (1) amounts rolled over from one Roth IRA to another Roth IRA on a tax-free basis under Code Sees. 408(d)(3) and 408A(e) and (2) contributions (other than the earnings thereon) that are returned to the Roth IRA owner in accordance with Code Sec. 408(d)(4) (corrective distributions) are not includible in the taxpayer's gross income.[246] On the other hand, nonqualified distributions may be at least partially taxable and subject to the 10 percent premature distributions tax, unless that tax is not applicable. The mandatory distribution rules that apply to IRAs held by persons who are at least age 70½ do not apply to Roth IRAs. Thus, Roth IRAs are not subject to the minimum distributions rules of Code Sec. 401(a)(9) or the incidental death benefit rules.[247] These rules are covered in the first section of this chapter concerning traditional IRAs.

In determining the tax consequences of distributions (using the rules of Code Sec. 408(d)(2)) from Roth IRAs, those distributions are accounted for separately from distributions from traditional IRAs.[248] Thus, all Roth IRAs are to be treated as one contract; all distributions from Roth IRAs are to be treated as one distributions; and the value of the contract, income on the contract, and investment in the contract are to be computed as of the close of the calendar year in which the taxable year ends.

Qualified Distributions. Under Code Sec. 408A(d)(2)(A), a qualified distribution means any payment or distribution from a Roth IRA:

(1) made on or after the date on which the distributee attains age 59½;

(2) made to a beneficiary (or to the estate of the distributee) on or after his or her death;

(3) attributable to the distributee's being disabled; or

---

[245] Reg. § 1.408A-5, Q&A 9.
[246] Reg. § 1.408A-6, Q&A 1(b).

[247] Code Sec. 408A(c)(5).
[248] Code Sec. 408A(d)(4).

(4) made to a distributee that is a qualified first-time homebuyer as defined in Code Secs. 72(t)(2)(F) and (8) (discussed in the first section of this chapter).

In addition, Code Sec. 408A(d)(2)(B) specifies that a five-year holding period must be met. Thus, any distribution received prior to the end of the five-year period will not be a qualified distribution. The five-year period begins on the.first day of the taxpayer's taxable year for which the first regular contribution is made to any Roth IRA of the taxpayer or, if earlier, the first day of the taxpayer's taxable year in which the first conversion contribution is made to any Roth IRA of the taxpayer. The five-year period ends on the last day of the individual's fifth consecutive taxable year beginning with the taxable year described in the previous sentence. For example, if an individual using the calendar tax year made a first-time regular Roth IRA contribution any time between January 1, 1998 and April 15, 1999, for 1998, the five-taxable-year period began on January 1, 1998. Thus, each Roth IRA owner has only one five-taxable-year period for all Roth IRAs he or she owns or will own. Further, no qualified distributions could have been made from any Roth IRAs before the year 2003 under this rule, since contributions could not be made to Roth IRAs prior to 1998. For purposes of these rules, the amount of any contribution that is distributed as a corrective distribution is treated as if it was never contributed.[249] Special rules apply in determining the five-year period with respect to the beneficiaries of a deceased Roth IRA owner. See Reg. § 1.408A-6, Q&A 7.

Nonqualified Distributions. A distribution that does not meet one of the four requirements specified above and/or fails the five-tax-year holding period requirement is treated as a nonqualified distribution. A distribution that is not a qualified distribution, and is neither contributed to another Roth IRA in a qualified rollover contribution nor constitutes a corrective distribution, may be partly or totally taxable and subject to the 10 percent premature distributions tax unless excepted from that tax under Code Sec. 72(t). In general, the amount of a nonqualified distribution is includible in gross income to the extent that (1) the amount of the distribution, when added to the amount of all previous distributions from the owner's Roth IRAs (including any qualified distributions) and reduced by previous distributions that were includible in gross income exceeds (2) the owner's contributions to all his or her Roth IRAs.[250] The 10 percent premature distributions tax will apply (unless an exception under Code Sec. 72(t) applies) to any Roth IRA distribution that is includible in the taxpayer's gross income.

---

[249] Reg. § 1.408A-6, Q&A 2.　　　　[250] *Id.*, Q&A 4.

A separate five-year period applies with respect to the 10 percent premature distributions tax and conversion contributions. If within the five-year period starting with the year of a conversion contribution, any part of a distribution from a Roth IRA is from the taxable part of the amount converted, the 10 percent tax will apply, unless one of the Code Sec. 72(t) exceptions applies. The tax applies only to the portion of a conversion contribution that is includible in gross income because of the conversion. And, it applies as though the amount is includible in gross income in the year of the distribution. Note that this five-year period is not necessarily the same as the five-year period that applies in deciding whether distributions are qualified distributions as discussed above.[251]

The final regulations detail how it is determined whether amounts distributed from Roth IRAs are allocated to regular contributions, conversion contributions, and Roth IRA earnings for the purpose of determining the taxable amount of nonqualified distributions. Any amount distributed from a Roth IRA is treated as made in the following order (determined as of the end of the taxable year and exhausting each category before moving to the following category):[252]

(1) From regular contributions.

(2) From conversion contributions, on a first-in, first-out basis (generally, total conversions from the earlier year first). These conversion contributions are taken into account as follows: (a) the taxable portion (the amount required to be included in gross income because of the conversion) first, and then the (b) nontaxable portion.

(3) Earnings on the Roth IRA contributions.

To determine the taxable amounts withdrawn (distributed), distributions are grouped and added together as follows:[253]

(1) All distributions from all of the taxpayer's Roth IRAs during the year are added together.

(2) All regular contributions made during and for the year (contributions made after the close of the year, but before the due date of the taxpayer's return) are added together. This total is added to the total undistributed regular contributions made in prior years.

(3) All conversion contributions made during the year are added together. For purposes of the ordering rules, in the case of

---

[251] *Id.*, Q&A 5.
[252] Reg. § 1.408A-6, Q&A 8, IRS Pub. No. 590 at 59.
[253] Reg. § 1.408A-6, Q&A 9, IRS Pub. No. 590 at 60-61.

any conversion in which the conversion distribution is made in 2005 and the conversion contribution is made in 2006, the conversion contribution is treated as contributed prior to other conversion contributions made in 2006.

Any recharacterized contributions that end up in a Roth IRA are added to the appropriate contribution group for the year that the original contribution would have been taken into account if it had been made directly to the Roth IRA. Any recharacterized contribution that ends up in an IRA other than a Roth IRA is disregarded for the purpose of aggregating both contributions and distributions. Any amount withdrawn to correct an excess contribution (including the earnings withdrawn) is also disregarded for this purpose.[254]

Example: On October 15, 2001, Justin converted all $80,000 in his traditional IRA to his Roth IRA. His forms 8606 from prior years show that $20,000 of the amount converted is his basis (due to nondeductible contributions). Justin included $60,000 ($80,000 − $20,000) in his gross income for 2001. Further, Justin made a $3,000 regular contribution to his Roth IRA in each year of 2001 through 2005 and did not take any distributions through the end of 2004. On September 27, 2005, Justin took an $85,000 distribution from his Roth IRA. That $85,000 withdrawal is a nonqualified distribution because it is made prior to the expiration of the required five-year holding period. Nevertheless, the amount included in gross income is $0,—the $85,000 distribution minus the $85,000 nontaxable amounts determined as follows:

(1) The first $15,000 of the distribution equal to the regular contributions made during 2001 through 2005 is nontaxable.

(2) The next $60,000 is a return of taxable conversion contributions made in 2001 that were taxable in 2001.

(3) The remaining $10,000 of the distribution is equal to the 2001 conversion contributions that were not taxable.

Even though none of the distribution is includible in gross income, $60,000 of the distribution will be subject to the 10 percent premature distributions tax (unless excepted from that tax) because the conversion contribution that was includible in gross income is distributed within the five-year period beginning with the year of the conversion contribution (2001).

If the owner of a Roth IRA dies prior to the end of the five-taxable-year period for qualified distributions, each type of

---

[254] *Id.*

¶ 1005.05

contribution made by the owner is allocated on pro-rata basis to his or her beneficiaries, for purposes of determining their tax consequences on a distribution.[255]

Minimum Distribution Rules. No minimum distributions are required to be made from a Roth IRA while the owner is alive. However, the post-death minimum distribution rules under Code Sec. 401(a)(9)(B) that apply to traditional IRAs, with the exception of the at-least-as-rapidly rule described in Code Sec. 401(a)(9)(B)(i), also apply to Roth IRAs. The minimum distribution rules apply to the Roth IRA as though the Roth IRA owner died before his or her required beginning date. See ¶ 1002.07 for the specific rules concerning required minimum distributions after the death of the account owner. If the sole beneficiary is the decedent's spouse, such spouse may delay distributions until the decedent would have attained age 70½ or may treat the Roth IRA as his or her own. If he or she elects to treat the Roth IRA as his or her own, that individual's five-year period would be used to determine whether a distribution is qualified and no minimum distributions would have to be taken.[256]

.06 Reporting Requirements

Reg. § 1.408A-7, indicates that, in general, the reporting requirements applicable to IRAs other than Roth IRAs also apply to Roth IRAs, except that, pursuant to Code Sec. 408A(d)(3)(D), the trustee of a Roth IRA must include on Forms 1099-R and 5498 additional information that is described on the instructions to those forms. Any conversion of amounts from an IRA other than a Roth IRA to a Roth IRA is treated as a distribution for which a Form 1099-R must be filed by the trustee maintaining the non-Roth IRA. In addition, the owner of such IRAs must report the conversion by completing Form 8606. In the case of a recharacterization, owners must report such transactions in the manner prescribed in the instructions to the applicable federal tax forms. A trustee may rely on representations of a Roth IRA contributor or distributee in fulfilling reporting obligations.

¶ 1006 Deemed IRAs Under Employer Plans

As a result of the enactment of EGTRRA, for plan years beginning after December 31, 2002, employees participating in employer qualified plans will, if certain requirements are met, be permitted to make contributions to "Deemed IRAs." Deemed IRAs have been referred to as "Sidecar IRAs" by some practitioners because they are an added element to an employee retirement plan such as a

---

[255] Reg. § 1.408A-6, Q&A 11.   [256] *Id.,* Q&A 14

profit-sharing plan or Code Sec. 401(k) plan but are not subject to most of the rules that apply to the regular qualified plan, as indicated in this section.[257] Under the new rules, if an eligible retirement plan permits employees to make voluntary employee contributions to a separate account or annuity that (1) is established under the plan and (2) meets the requirements applicable to either traditional IRAs or Roth IRAs, the separate account or annuity will be deemed a traditional IRA or a Roth IRA and will be treated as such for all purposes of the Internal Revenue Code.[258] Thus, all of the rules relating to traditional IRAs and Roth IRAs as covered in this chapter apply to the Deemed IRAs. For example, the annual contribution limitations and rules concerning deductibility of the contributions (in the case of Traditional IRAs) apply with respect to the Deemed IRA. To illustrate this, assume that an employer maintains a qualified profit-sharing plan with a Deemed IRA. One of the plan participants, who is single and age 41 with AGI of $55,000 in 2006, maintained one other traditional IRA to which he contributed $3,000 for 2006. That participant could only contribute an additional $1,000 to the Deemed IRA ($4,000 annual limit minus the $3,000 already contributed to the other traditional IRA). In addition, only one-half of the contributions would be deductible, since the employee's $55,000 AGI is half way through the phase-out range covered in ¶1002.03. In July of 2004, the IRS issued final regulations that explain and interpret the Deemed IRA rules.[259] The final regulations apply to accounts or annuities established under Code Sec. 408(q) on or after August 1, 2003.[260] Under the final regulations, where an employer desires to have an effective Deemed IRA plan, that employer's qualified plan documents must contain the Deemed IRA provisions, and a Deemed IRA has to be in effect at the time the Deemed IRA contributions are accepted. However, employers that desired to provide for Deemed IRAs for plan years beginning before January 1, 2004 (but, after December 31, 2002), were not required to have such provisions in their plan documents before the end of such plan years.[261]

The Deemed IRA, and the voluntary contributions made to it are not subject to the Internal Revenue Code rules that pertain to the eligible retirement plan and are not taken into account in applying the rules of the Code to any other contributions under the employer's plan.[262] For example, the Deemed IRA or "Sidecar

---

[257] *See* eg., Miller. Girard, "Coming in January 2003: Sidecar IRAs in Your DC Plan," *Employee Benefit Plan Review,* (November, 2002): 22-25.

[258] Code Sec. 408(q)(1), as amended by P.L. 107-16. 107th Cong., 1st Sess., Sec. 602(a) (June 7, 2001). Prop. Reg. § 1.408(q)-1(b) and (c).

[259] Reg. § 1.408(q)-1, T.D. 9142, 69 FR 43735 (July 22, 2004).

[260] Reg. § 1.408(q)-1(i).

[261] Reg. § 1.408(q)-1(d)(1).

[262] Code Sec. 408(q)(1). Reg. § 1.408(q)-1(a).

¶1006

IRA" is not (1) subject to the spousal consent/benefits requirements under Code Secs. 401(a)(11) and 417, (2) taken into account in applying the $5,000 cashout provisions under Code Sec. 401(a)(11), (3) subject to the coverage and nondiscrimination rules of Code Secs. 410(b) and 401(a)(4) (but, it should be noted that to the extent nonhighly compensated employees elect to contribute amounts into the Deemed IRA rather than elective deferral contributions under a Code Sec. 401(k) plan, the nondiscrimination testing with respect to highly compensated participants under the plan could be negatively affected), or (4) subject to the annual addition limits under Code Sec. 415(c) and the elective deferral limits under Code Sec. 402(g) (thus, for example, in 2006, a 55-year-old participant in a Code Sec. 401(k) plan could make a regular contribution of $15,000 and a catch-up contribution of $5,000 to the 401(k) plan and could make an additional contribution to the Deemed IRA). The Deemed IRA and contributions to it are subject to the exclusive benefit and fiduciary rules of ERISA to the extent they are otherwise applicable to the eligible retirement plan. However, they are not subject to the ERISA reporting and disclosure, participation, vesting, funding, and enforcement requirements that apply to the eligible retirement plan.[263]

An eligible retirement is a qualified employer pension or profit-sharing plan or other qualified plan under Code Sec. 401(a), a Code Sec. 403(b) tax-sheltered annuity plan, or a governmental Code Sec. 457 deferred compensation plan.[264]

> **Comment:** The use of Deemed IRAs should be beneficial for both employers (and plan sponsors) and employee participants. For employers and plan sponsors, Deemed IRAs should have a number of benefits including (1) the ability to offer an additional benefit to employees, (2) the ability to commingle IRA and qualified plan funds for investment purposes within a single plan, and (3) the probable increase in plan assets through employee contributions (and, presumably) rollovers into the Deemed IRA as well as the ability to use the Deemed IRA as the default IRA for automatic cashouts. For employees, Deemed IRAs should be beneficial because, among other considerations, the Deemed IRAs could provide one convenient place for all of the employee's retirement contributions and rollovers providing coordination of the employee's retirement investments and possibly lower investment costs.

---

[263] Conf. Rep. No. 107-84, 107th Cong., 1st Sess. (June 7, 2001).

[264] Code Sec. 408(q)(3)(A). Reg. § 1.408(q)-1(h)(1).

Chapter 11

Employee Stock Ownership Plans

¶1101 Introduction

An employee stock ownership plan (ESOP) is a qualified plan under Code Sec. 401(a) which is designed to invest primarily in the employer's securities. First created as a distinct type of employee benefit plan with the passage of ERISA in 1974, ESOPs have shown a tremendous growth in popularity among publicly and privately held firms. This growth has been largely due to continued legislative encouragement.

The goals of this ESOP legislation have focused on improving the U.S. economy by (1) broadening ownership of new wealth in the form of corporate stock; (2) providing a source of funds for capital formation through tax-favored leveraging techniques; and (3) improving the economic performance of sponsoring corporations.

Legislation enacted over the past ten years includes several provisions that encourage the use of ESOPs by S corporations. SBA '96 allowed qualified retirement plan trusts to be shareholders in S corporations, thus opening the door for S corporations to establish ESOPs. (Prior to 1998, only C corporations could establish ESOPs because of the restrictions on ownership of S corporation shares.) TRA '97 further provided that the flow-through income and loss items from the S corporation are *not* treated as unrelated business taxable income (UBTI), and thus, not subject to tax until it is distributed to the ESOP participants as a plan distribution. Subsequent to TRA '97, however,

Congress became aware that these rules allowed S corporation owners to obtain "inappropriate" tax deferral or avoidance. Consequently, EGTRRA '01 effectively eliminated the deferral feature for certain "disqualified" owners.

¶1102   Unique Features of ESOPs

ESOPs provide three basic tax advantages to both the employer and its employees. Because the ESOP is a qualified plan under Code Sec. 401(a), employees defer recognition of income until the stock is actually distributed to them, at which time favorable distribution treatments (such as rollovers) are available. Second, the employer is able to fund the plan with contributions of stock, thereby avoiding any drain on cash flows. Finally, the company may be able to deduct amounts above the normal qualified limits if the special leveraging techniques are used. While all of these features will be discussed at length later on in the chapter, some of the unique features of ESOPs are briefly introduced below.

Leveraging. Probably the most unique feature is the "leveraged ESOP," so-called because of the tax-favored borrowing techniques available to ESOPs. For qualified plans, the lending and borrowing of money, including the guaranteeing of loans, is a prohibited transaction. However, ESOPs are allowed a special exemption under Code Sec. 4975 which actually encourages this type of transaction.

A leveraged ESOP involves three basic steps. First, the trust of the ESOP secures a loan from a lending institution, and the employer guarantees that it will make contributions to the ESOP which will be adequate to repay the loan. Second, the ESOP then uses the loan proceeds to purchase employer securities, and the company is free to use the money for whatever purpose it desires. Third, as the employer makes contributions, to the ESOP to repay the loan, the amounts representing interest are fully deductible, and only the amounts representing principal are subject to the 25 percent of compensation limitation. Thus, the company is able to *deduct both principal and interest on the repayment of the loan.*

Some of the more common usages of this money by the ESOP include purchasing newly issued employer stock (in which case the company could use the funds for working capital, expansions, etc.), acquisitions and divestitures of subsidiaries, leveraged buyouts, and buying out existing owners.

Closely Held Buyouts. Probably the most common usage of ESOPs is the purchase of stock by the employees from a retiring owner in a privately held firm. In fact, the majority of all active

ESOPs are sponsored by privately held firms. Code Sec. 1042 allows certain owners to defer recognition of any gain realized from the sale of company stock to the ESOP. In general, if the ESOP owns more than 30 percent of the company's stock after the buyout, the owner is allowed to roll over the gain by purchasing any domestic corporate security, including stocks and bonds of both publicly and privately held companies. The owner's basis and holding period are carried over to the new securities, and, thus, the gain is deferred until the disposition of the new stock.

Deductible Dividends. Another unique feature of ESOPs is the ability to deduct any dividends paid to ESOP participants. As long as the dividends are paid directly to the participants or distributed through the ESOP to them within 90 days or used to make payments on an ESOP loan (the proceeds of which were used to acquire employer securities), the company is allowed to deduct the amount paid, without affecting the contribution limitations. This deduction is also available to employers for dividends paid to an ESOP that an employee may elect to reinvest back into the ESOP for more of the employer's stock.[1]

¶1103   Types of ESOPs

Although it is not designed to be a "retirement plan," an ESOP must meet all of the qualification requirements under Code Sec. 401(a). An ESOP is a type of defined contribution plan which must contain a stock bonus plan element.[2] ESOPs take the form of either a nonleveraged ESOP or a leveraged ESOP. Although these forms share many common features of defined contribution plans, each one possesses some unique characteristics.

.01   Nonleveraged ESOPs

A nonleveraged ESOP is a stock bonus plan or a combination stock bonus and money purchase pension plan which is not designed to borrow money. Thus, a nonleveraged ESOP has the traditional characteristics of a stock bonus plan and is eligible for the ESOP tax incentives which were introduced in 1984. (Stock bonus plans are similar to profit-sharing plans, except that benefits are distributable in employer stock.) In addition, an ESOP may invest primarily, or even exclusively, in employer securities, exempting it from the "prudent man," or fair return, investment requirements.

---

[1] Code Sec. 404(k)(2)(A).   [2] Code Sec. 4975(e)(7).

The normal deduction limitations of stock bonus plans apply to nonleveraged ESOPs, namely, that contributions are limited to 25 percent of the compensation of participating employees.

.02 Leveraged ESOPs

A leveraged ESOP is a stock bonus or combination stock bonus and money purchase pension which is specially designed to borrow money (hence the term leveraged) under the tax-favored provisions of Reg. § 54.4975-7. The leveraged ESOP thus allows the company to not only provide employee benefits, but to also obtain favorable debt financing. ESOP leveraging results in favorable debt financing because the company is allowed to deduct both the principal and the interest for its contributions to the ESOP to repay the loan.

¶ 1104 Statutory Requirements for ESOPs

An ESOP is formally defined under Code Sec. 4975(e)(7) as a stock bonus plan or combined stock bonus and money purchase pension plan which is qualified under Code Sec. 401(a), and which is designed to invest primarily in qualified employer securities.[3] In addition to complying with the general requirements imposed on defined contribution plans, ESOPs must also comply with requirements concerning voting rights, diversification requirements, and account allocation restrictions.

The requirements for a qualified plan under Code Sec. 401(a) were discussed at length in Chapter 6. Therefore, only those requirements which are unique to ESOPs are discussed below.

.01 General Requirements

First, the ESOP must meet all the requirements relating to qualified stock bonus plans and, if applicable, money purchase pension plans. These include the participation, vesting, and non-discrimination rules. If the ESOP is a part of a plan, the remainder of which is a qualified plan that is not an ESOP, the ESOP portion is generally treated separately in applying these rules. In addition, the plan document must formally designate the plan as an ESOP and must specifically state that it is designed to invest primarily (or exclusively, if desired) in qualifying employer securities.[4]

---

[3] Code Sec. 4975(e)(7).

No Social Security Integration. An ESOP created after November 1, 1977, is not allowed to integrate with Social Security. However, ESOPs which were in existence and already integrated before this date may remain integrated.[5]

"Qualifying Employer Securities" Defined. Employer securities are defined under Code Sec. 409(1) as common stock issued by the employer (or by a corporation which is a member of the same controlled group) which is readily tradable on an established securities market. If there is no common stock which meets this definition, then "employer securities" means employer (or a member of the same controlled group) common stock which has a combination of voting power and dividend rights at least equal to those classes of common stock which have the greatest voting power and the greatest dividend rights. Employer securities also include noncallable preferred stock which is convertible at any time into qualifying common stock.

.02 Voting Rights

Under the requirements of Code Sec. 401(a)(22), certain voting rights apply to all qualified stock bonus plans, which, therefore, includes all ESOPs. If a company is not publicly traded, voting rights must pass through to participants if more than ten percent of the total assets of the plan consists of employer securities. However, this pass-through does not apply to employers whose business consists of publishing a newspaper for general circulation on a regular basis.

In addition to the general rule for the pass-through of voting rights, Code Sec. 409(e) contains requirements which are applicable to both publicly and privately held employers. If an employer has registration-type securities (this would include businesses with more than $1 million in assets and more than 500 shareholders required to be registered under section 12 of the Securities Exchange Act of 1934), the ESOP must permit each participant to direct the manner in which the securities allocated to his account are voted. If a company does not have registration-type securities, voting rights must be passed through only: (1) for corporate matters which must be decided by a more than majority vote of outstanding shares, (2) if the employer stock is not publicly traded, and (3) if the plan has invested more than ten percent of its assets in employer securities. Those

---

[4] Reg. §§ 54.4975-11(a)(2) and (b).

[5] Reg. § 54.4975-11(a)(7)(ii).

majority-required corporate matters include mergers and consolidations, acquisitions, reclassifications, sales of substantially all of the corporate assets, liquidations, dissolutions, or similar transactions which may be designated by the Secretary of the Treasury under regulations.[6]

To the extent that shares have not been released from loan covenants under a leveraged transaction, the fiduciary may use his own discretion in voting those shares. An ESOP may provide each participant with one vote as long as the trustee votes all shares held by the ESOP in proportion to the votes of all participants.[7] Thus, under this provision, the trustee must relinquish control over those unallocated shares.

.03 Diversification Requirements

Ordinarily, the fiduciary is charged with the responsibility of selecting proper investments and properly diversifying the assets of the trust to ensure a reasonable return. (Fiduciary standards are discussed in detail in Chapter 12.) Because ESOPs are designed to invest primarily in employer securities, they are exempt from these requirements to the extent of their investment in qualifying employer securities.[8] Thus, qualifying employer securities held by an ESOP are not required to produce the return which would normally be expected from similar types of plans. Nevertheless, the Third Circuit held that when fiduciaries are aware that the employer's financial condition is rapidly deteriorating, they could be liable for failure to diversify the trust investments in a plan that invests *exclusively* in employer stock, if the terms of the plan require a *primary*, but not *exclusive*, investment in employer stock.[9]

An ESOP must allow employees who are near retirement age to diversify the investments in their own accounts. An ESOP must give a "qualified participant" an election to have a portion of his account balance invested in something other than employer securities each year during his "qualified election period." The election applies to all employer stock acquired after 1986.[10]

A qualified participant is an employee who is at least age 55 and who has completed ten years of participation in the ESOP.[11] The qualified election period is the six-plan-year period beginning with

---

[6] Code Sec. 409(e)(3).
[7] Code Sec. 409(e)(5).
[8] ERISA Sec. 404(a)(2).

[9] *Moench v. Robertson.* 62 F.3d 553 (3d Cir., 1995).
[10] Code Sec. 401(a)(28)(B).
[11] Code Sec. 401(a)(28)(B)(iii).

the plan year in which the individual first becomes a qualified participant.[12] During the first 90 days of each of these plan years, a qualified participant must be allowed to elect to diversify up to 25 percent of his post-1986 stock, reduced by any amounts previously subject to diversification. In the final plan year, 50 percent of such employer securities are subject to the diversification election. Because of the reduction for previous elections, the only amounts which are subject to the election in the second through the sixth years are the increments in the participant's account from additional contributions and earnings if the maximum 25 percent was elected in all prior years. However, the election is cumulative, so that if an election is made to diversify only 15 percent in one year, an election could be made to catch up the shortage in a subsequent year.[13]

> **Example:** Joe first became eligible to make a diversification election in his employer's calendar-year ESOP in 2006. As of December 31, 2005, Joe's account was credited with 200 shares of employer stock that had been contributed to the plan after 1986. The value of the employer stock on December 31, 2005 was $30 per share. The ESOP must allow Joe to diversify the value of up to 50 shares (25% × 200) of employer stock. This election must be permitted through March 31, 2006. Joe makes the election to diversify the maximum value of 50 shares.
>
> During 2006, Joe's account is credited with an additional 40 shares from the 2006 employer contribution. Thus, as of December 31, 2006, Joe's account contains 190 shares of post-1986 employer stock. Joe must be permitted to diversify 10 additional shares through March 31, 2007, computed as follows: 25% of 240 shares (i.e., 60 shares), less the 50 shares previously diversified.

The diversification requirements may be met in one of three ways under Code Sec. 401(a)(28)(B)(ii). First, the ESOP may offer at least three different investment options. Any investment option selected must be implemented within 90 days after the end of the election period. Second, the ESOP may distribute the amount so elected to the participant within 90 days after the close of the diversification election period. The amount may be distributed in cash or in stock (in which case the usual put option rules will apply). This amount is eligible for a rollover into an IRA or for a transfer to another qualified defined contribution plan that offers at least three investment options.[14] Finally, the plan may permit

---

[12] Code Sec. 401(a)(28)(B)(iv).
[13] Notice 88-56, 1988-1 CB 540.
[14] Code Sec. 402(a)(5)(D)(i).

the participant to direct a transfer of the diversification amount into another qualified plan that provides for employee-directed investment and in which the required diversification options are available.

.04   Individual Account Allocations

The general rules of Code Sec. 415(c) for allocating contributions among plan participants apply to ESOPs. Thus, the amount of "annual additions" to a participant's account is limited to the lesser of $42,000 (in 2005) or 100 percent of the participant's compensation. As in other qualified plans, "annual additions" include employer contributions (to all defined contribution plans in which the employee is a participant), forfeitures allocated to the participant's account, and employee contributions. Dividends paid on employer stock to an ESOP that are used to repay an exempt loan are not considered annual additions.

Two special provisions apply to ESOPs, both of which can substantially increase the amount of annual additions available to participants. Recall that "annual additions" include employer contributions, forfeitures allocated to an account, and employee contributions. Under Code Sec. 415(c)(6), if no more than one-third of the employer contributions for a year are allocated to highly compensated employees, then the following items will not be included in "annual additions" for purposes of applying the general limitations for defined contribution plans under Code Sec. 415(c)(1) (which limits annual additions to the lesser of $42,000 or 100 percent compensation):

(1) forfeitures of stock which was acquired by the ESOP with an exempt loan; and

(2) employer contributions to the ESOP used to pay interest on an exempt loan.

.05   Distribution Rules

An ESOP may make distributions either in cash or in stock, but must provide participants with the right to demand payment in the form of qualifying employer securities.[15] If the employer securities are not readily tradable on an established market, Code Sec. 409(h)(1)(B) requires that the participant be given the right to a "put" option, requiring the employer (not the ESOP) to repurchase the securities under a fair valuation formula. However, under Code Sec. 409(h)(2), if the employer's corporate charter or bylaws

---

[15] Code Sec. 409(h)(1)(A).

restrict ownership of substantially all employer securities to employees or to a trust under a qualified plan, the ESOP may distribute all benefits in cash. Such a plan may distribute employer securities subject to a requirement that they be resold to the employer under the put option of Code Sec. 409(h)(1)(B). Similarly, an ESOP that is maintained by an S corporation may distribute all benefits in cash.[16]

Required Distributions. All qualified plans are required to begin benefit payments to a participant under Code Sec. 401(a)(14) no later than 60 days after the end of the plan year in which the latest of the following occurs: the participant (1) attains age 65 or an earlier normal retirement age under the plan; (2) reaches the tenth anniversary of his participation in the plan; or (3) terminates employment.

However, Code Sec. 409(o) requires additional rules which allow for early distributions for separation from service before normal retirement age. Unless the participant otherwise elects in writing, the ESOP must begin benefit payments of the participant's account balance no later than one year after the close of the plan year: (1) in which the participant terminates employment due to retirement, disability, or death, or (2) which is the fifth plan year following the plan year in which the employee separated from service for any other reason, provided that he was not reemployed within the five-year period. For these purposes, the participant's account balance does not include employer securities which were acquired with a loan in a leveraged ESOP until the close of the plan year in which the loan is repaid in full.[17]

If the general rules were to provide a starting date sooner than the ESOP rules, those general rules, of course, must be followed in order to maintain the qualified status of the plan. Thus, the required starting date for distributions is the earlier of the rules in Code Sec. 401(a)(14) or 409(o).

Code Sec. 409(o)(1)(C) also provides rules which limit the length of time over which a distribution may be made. Unless the participant otherwise elects, the ESOP must distribute his account balance in substantially equal periodic payments over a period of no longer than five years in at least annual payments. If the account balance exceeds $850,000, however, the payment term may be lengthened by one year for each $170,000, or fraction thereof, over $850,000, with a maximum payout period not to exceed ten years. (These amounts apply to 2005 and are subject to cost-of-living adjustments in the same manner as the dollar limits of defined

---

[16] Code Sec. 409(h)(2)(B).

[17] Code Sec. 409(o)(1)(B).

benefit pension plans.)[18] The chart below demonstrates the payout rules for 2005:

Account Balance	Maximum Payout Period
$1—$850,000	5 years
$850,001—$1,020,000	6 years
$1,020,001—$1,190,000	7 years
$1,190,001—$1,360,000	8 years
$1,360,001—$1,530,000	9 years
$1,530,001 and over	10 years

Put Option Requirement. An ESOP maintained by a privately held employer (i.e., one whose securities are not readily traded on an established securities market) is required by Code Sec. 409(h)(1)(B) to give participants the right to require the employer to repurchase any distributed securities under a fair valuation formula. (The ESOP may, but cannot be required to, purchase the securities instead.)

This right, referred to as a "put option," applies to all distributions from a leveraged ESOP which are attributable to shares acquired after September 30, 1976.[19] Banks that maintain a plan are allowed a special rule under Code Sec. 409(h)(3), whereby the put option rule is waived if the bank is prohibited by law from redeeming or purchasing its own securities.

This put option must be open for at least 60 days following the distribution, and if not exercised within the 60-day period, must be open for another 60 days in the following plan year.[20] This additional option period allows the holder to wait until a new valuation has been established in the event the earlier valuation was low. Payment requirements attributable to stock acquired after 1986 differ depending upon whether a complete distribution of the participant's account balance is made within one taxable year, termed a "total distribution," or over an installment period.

For total distributions, the employer may elect to pay the put option price over a period not to exceed five years. The price must: (1) be paid in substantially equal installments at least annually, (2) include a reasonable rate of interest, (3) be adequately secured, and (4) commence within 30 days after the distributee exercises the option.[21] If the former participant exercises options for stock which was distributed on an installment basis, the employer is required to pay the entire purchase price within 30 days after the exercise of the put option.[22]

---

[18] IRS News Release. IR-2004-127. October 20, 2004.

[19] Reg. § 54.4975-7(b)(10).

[20] Code Sec. 409(h)(4).

[21] Code Sec. 409(h)(5).

[22] Code Sec. 409(h)(6).

Right of First Refusal. Under Reg. § 54.4975-7(b)(9), privately held employers are allowed to attach a right of first refusal on stock held by a former participant. This right allows the employer or the ESOP (but no other person) to purchase securities before they are sold to a third party. The only securities which may be subject to such a right are stock, other equity securities, and debt securities which are convertible into stock or other equity securities. The purchase price is required to be at least equal to the greater of the fair market value or the purchase price and other terms offered by a third-party buyer making a good-faith offer to buy the stock. Under Reg. § 54.4975-11(d)(5), appraisal of fair market value must be made in good faith, based on all relevant factors and must be made at least annually by an independent person who customarily makes such appraisals. This right must lapse no later than 14 days after the holder of the stock gives written notice that a third-party offer has been received.

.06 Loan Exemption

Qualified plans are prohibited by Code Sec. 4975(c)(1)(B) from engaging in any direct or indirect lending of money or other credit extension with a disqualified person, which of course includes the employer. This rule would generally prohibit not only direct loans (in any direction), but also the guarantee of an ESOP loan by the employer. As was discussed earlier, however, one of the most unique features of a leveraged ESOP is the ability to engage in such transactions.

In order to accomplish this, the leveraged ESOP must use an "exempt loan" which meets the requirements set forth in Reg. §§ 54.4975-7 and 54.4975-11. An exempt loan is one which is made to an ESOP by a disqualified person or a loan made to an ESOP which is guaranteed by a disqualified person.[23] Such a loan must meet the following requirements.

Primary Benefit Requirement. The loan must be primarily for the benefit of the ESOP participants and their beneficiaries. At the time the loan is made, the interest rate for the loan and the price of the securities to be acquired with the loan proceeds should not be such that the plan assets might be drained off. The terms of the loan must be at least as favorable to the ESOP as the terms of a comparable loan resulting from an arm's-length transaction between independent parties.[24]

---

[23] Reg. § 54.4975-7(b)(1).

[24] Reg. § 54.4975-7(b)(3).

Loan Terms. The following conditions must be met with respect to the loan itself.

(1) The interest rate and loan terms must be reasonable. In determining whether all of these terms are reasonable, factors such as the amount and duration of the loan, the security and guarantee involved, the credit standing of the ESOP and the guarantor, and the prevailing interest rate, including variable rates (if reasonable), for comparable loans should be considered.[25]

(2) The loan must be for a specific term. It may not be payable upon demand, except in the case of default.[26]

(3) An exempt loan must be without recourse against the ESOP. In addition, the only assets of the ESOP that may be pledged as collateral on an exempt loan are qualifying employer securities which were either acquired with the proceeds of the loan or which were used as collateral on a prior exempt loan repaid with the proceeds of the current exempt loan.[27]

(4) The ESOP liability for repayment of the loan must be limited to the securities pledged as collateral on the loan, contributions made to the ESOP for loan repayment purposes (other than contributions of employer securities), and the earnings attributable to such contributions and collateral.[28]

(5) In the event of a default on an exempt loan, the value of plan assets transferred in satisfaction of the loan cannot exceed the amount of default. If the lender is a disqualified person, the loan must provide for a transfer of plan assets upon default only to the extent of the failure of the plan to meet the payment schedule of the loan.[29]

(6) Any securities pledged by the ESOP as collateral to secure an exempt loan must be released on a proportionate basis as the loan is repaid. The release may be in proportion to the principal and interest payments or it may be in relation to principal payments only, as long as the principal is reduced at a rate which is at least as rapid as level annual payments over ten years.[30]

Use of Loan Proceeds. After an ESOP receives the proceeds of an exempt loan, it must, within a reasonable time, use the proceeds only for the following purposes: (1) to acquire qualifying employer securities; (2) to repay such loan; and/or (3) to repay a prior exempt loan. Except for a right of first refusal and a put option in favor of the participant, no security acquired with the proceeds of an exempt loan may be subject to a put, call, or other option, or buy-sell or similar arrangement.[31]

---

[25] Reg. § 54.4975-7(b)(7).
[26] Reg. § 54.4975-7(b)(13).
[27] Reg. § 54.4975-7(b)(5).
[28] Reg. § 54.4975-7(b)(5).

[29] Reg. § 54.4975-7(b)(6).
[30] Reg. § 54.4975-7(b)(8).
[31] Reg. § 54.4975-7(b)(4).

Suspense Accounts and Allocation to Participants' Accounts. Under Reg. § 54.4975-11(c), assets acquired by an ESOP with the proceeds of an exempt loan must be held in a suspense account. They are withdrawn from the suspense account in accordance with the rules regarding the release of such collateral, discussed above. As of the end of each plan year, the ESOP must allocate to the participants' accounts nonmonetary units representing interests in assets withdrawn from the suspense account. In addition, income with respect to such securities must be allocated as income of the plan except to the extent that the ESOP provides for the use of income from the securities to repay the loan.[32] AJCA '04 added a similar provision that allows an S corporation ESOP to use dividends paid with respect to the S stock held by the ESOP to repay an ESOP loan acquired to purchase the S stock.[33]

Interest Exclusion. SBA '96 repealed the Code Sec. 133 exclusion for interest on ESOP loans made after August 20, 1996, with the exception of certain refinancing loans and loans made pursuant to a binding contract in effect since June 9, 1996.[34] For ESOP loans made prior to that date (and the loan exceptions described above), however, banks, insurance companies, corporations actively engaged in the business of lending money, and regulated investment companies (mutual funds) may exclude 50 percent of the interest earned on a securities acquisition loan. Thus, the following discussion relates to the interest exclusion for ESOP loans made prior to August 20, 1996 and loans qualifying for the exception described above. Note that a loan made to refinance an ESOP loan that was originally made before August 21, 1996 (including one made pursuant to a binding contract in effect before June 10, 1996) qualifies for the interest exclusion if: (1) the refinancing loan meets the requirements described below; (2) immediately after the refinancing, the outstanding principal amount of the loan is not increased; and (3) the term of the refinancing does not extend beyond the term of the original ESOP loan.[35]

The loan may be made to either the ESOP or to the sponsoring employer to the extent that the proceeds are used to acquire qualifying employer securities (or those of a member of the same controlled group) for the ESOP or to refinance an exempt loan. Where the loan is to the employer and the employer loans the proceeds to the ESOP, the loan from the employer to the ESOP

---

[32] Reg. § 54.4975-11(d)(2) and (3).
[33] Code Sec. 4975(f)(7), added by AJCA Sec. 240(a).
[34] Section 1602(a) of the Small Business Job Protection Act of 1996 (P.L. 104-188), repealing Code Sec. 133.
[35] Section 1602(a) of the Small Business Job Protection Act of 1996, P.L. 109-188.

must be on substantially similar repayment terms.[36] However, if the term of the loan exceeds seven years, the interest exclusion applies only to interest which accrues during the first seven years.[37]

Loans to the employer which are not reloaned to the ESOP may also qualify for the exclusion. In order to qualify, however, employer securities must be transferred within 30 days to the plan in an amount equal to the loan proceeds. These securities must be allocable to the participants' accounts within one year of the loan. In addition, the loan period must not exceed seven years.[38]

Additional requirements for loans generally made after July 10, 1989 apply. The partial interest exclusion will apply to a securities acquisition loan only if:

(1) immediately after the acquisition of the securities acquired with the loan, the ESOP must own more than 50 percent of each class of outstanding stock of the employer-corporation, or 50 percent of the total value of all its outstanding stock;[39]

(2) the term of the loan must not exceed 15 years;[40] and

(3) each participant must be entitled to direct the plan as to the manner in which shares allocated to the participant's account that were acquired with a securities acquisition loan are to be voted.[41]

The exclusion will not apply to any interest received that is allocable to any period during which the stock ownership requirement is not met, unless the ESOP acquires stock to meet the requirement within 90 days of the first date on which the failure occurred, or within a longer period (not to exceed 180 days) which may be provided by the IRS in future regulations.[42]

A ten-percent excise tax on the amount realized from the disposition of Code Sec. 133 stock may be imposed on an employer maintaining an ESOP under Code Sec. 4978B. The tax is imposed if, within three years after the employer securities are acquired by the ESOP, a disposition of Code Sec. 133 stock held by the ESOP occurs in which:

(1) the total number of employer securities held by the ESOP after the disposition is less than the total number of employer securities held after the acquisition; or

(2) the value of the employer securities held by the ESOP after the disposition is 50 percent or less of the total value of all employer

---

[36] Code Sec. 133(b)(3).
[37] TRA '86 Sec. 1173(c)(2)(B)(11).
[38] Code Sec. 133(b)(1)(B).
[39] Code Sec. 133(b)(6).

[40] Code Sec. 133(b)(1).
[41] Code Sec. 133(b)(7).
[42] Code Sec. 133(b)(6)(B).

securities as of the time of the disposition (unless provided otherwise in future regulations).[43]

The tax is also imposed if employer securities are disposed of before being allocated to the accounts of participants or beneficiaries and the proceeds of such disposition are not so allocated.[44] Certain distributions, however, do not result in the excise tax. These allowable distributions include certain distributions to employees (e.g., by reason of death, retirement, disability, or separation from service), exchanges of employer securities in various reorganizations, dispositions required to meet the diversification requirements of Code Sec. 401(a)(28), and certain forced dispositions occurring by operation of state law.[45]

.07 Employer Deductions

The normal limits under Code Sec. 404(a)(3) and (7) allow a maximum deduction for contributions of 25 percent of total compensation paid or accrued to all participants under the plan, with an unlimited carryover period for excess contributions.

Deduction for Payments of Interest and Principal on ESOP Loans. C corporations have additional deductions available, above and beyond the normal deduction limitations described above. A C corporation can deduct its contributions to a *leveraged* ESOP for payments that apply to both the interest and principal on an exempt ESOP loan.

Payments that apply to interest are fully deductible, while payments that apply to the loan principal are deductible up to 25 percent of total compensation of all participants for the plan year.[46] For many years, a misconception among a large number of practitioners was that the deduction limit that applied to principal repayments on a leveraged ESOP loan was integrated with the normal limit of Code Sec. 404(a)(3), i.e., that the sum of regular contributions plus loan principal repayments could not exceed 25 percent of the total compensation for all plan participants. However, in a recent letter ruling,[47] the IRS clarifies that the leveraged ESOP principal repayment is, in fact, a separate deduction limit from regular contributions. Thus, an employer could contribute (and deduct) up to 25 percent of total participant compensation as a normal contribution, and then contribute (and deduct) an additional ESOP principal loan repayment of up to 25 percent of total participant compensation, along with any interest payment on the loan.

---

[43] Code Sec. 4978B(c)(1).
[44] Code Sec. 4978B(c)(2).
[45] Code Sec. 4978B(d).

[46] Code Sec. 404(a)(9)(A) and (B).

[47] IRS Letter Ruling 200436015 (June 9, 2004).

However, the normal contribution limits of Code Sec. 415(c) still apply, i.e., the maximum annual contribution cannot exceed the lesser of $42,000 (in 2005) or 100 percent of compensation.

Note, however, that the additional deductions for ESOP loan principal and interest are not available for S corporations.[48]

Deduction for Payment of Dividends. Code Sec. 404(k) provides a deduction to a sponsoring C corporation (but *not* to an S corporation) for certain "applicable" dividends paid on stock held by a tax-credit ESOP or an ESOP that meets the requirements of Code Sec. 4975(e)(7). The deduction applies only to cash dividends paid on employer stock or stock of another member of the employer's controlled group under the following conditions:

(1) the dividend is paid in cash directly to the participants in the plan or to their beneficiaries;

(2) the dividend is paid to the ESOP and then distributed by the ESOP in cash to the participants in the plan or to their beneficiaries within 90 days after the end of the plan year in which the corporation paid the dividend;

(3) the dividend is, at the election of the participants or their beneficiaries, payable as provided in either of the two methods above, or paid to the plan and reinvested in qualified employer securities; or

(4) the dividend is used to make payments on an exempt ESOP loan (for principal or interest), the proceeds of which were used to acquire the securities with respect to which the dividends were paid.[49]

The deduction is allowed for the corporation's year in which the dividend is distributed to the participants or used to repay the loan, rather than for the year in which the corporation paid the dividend. The employer is allowed a deduction even if participants can elect to receive or not receive the dividends.[50] This deduction is in addition to the regular deduction limits allowed for contributions to an ESOP under Code Sec. 404 and is not considered to be an annual addition to participants' accounts for purposes of the Code Sec. 415 limits. For AMT purposes, however, Code Sec. 404(k) dividends are not taken into account in computing earnings and profits. Thus, an employer cannot deduct them in computing its ACE adjustment.[51]

In an effort to thwart abuse of this deduction, EGTRRA expanded the IRS's authority to disallow deductions for payments of dividends paid with respect to ESOP stock if the dividends

---

[48] Code Sec. 404(a)(9)(C).
[49] Code Sec. 404(k)(2).
[50] Temp. Reg. § 1.404(k)-1T. Q&A-2.
[51] Reg. § 1.56(9)-1(d)(3)(iii)(E).

constitute, in substance, an avoidance or evasion of tax. The committee reports suggest that this provision was added to disallow a deduction for dividends deemed to be unreasonable.[52] This provision followed a 2001 ruling in which the IRS determined that a corporation's payments in redemption of stock held by an ESOP that were used to make cash distributions to terminating ESOP participants were not "applicable dividends" within the meaning of Code Sec. 404(k), and, accordingly were not deductible, because treating such payments as dividends would have, in substance, constituted an evasion of tax.[53] Despite this ruling, the Ninth Circuit, on facts substantially identical to those of Rev. Rul. 2001-06, reached the opposite result in *Boise Cascade,* holding that such payments did not qualify as a stock redemption (as there was no meaningful reduction in the ESOP's proportionate interest in the company), but were instead to be treated as dividend payments and deductible under Code Sec. 404(k).[54] The IRS has since issued Chief Council Notice 2004-38 reiterating its position and instructing IRS agents to continue disallowing claims for deduction of such amounts in cases outside the Ninth Circuit,[55] and has subsequently issued proposed regulations in 2005 confirming that such dividend payments are not deductible.[56]

Note, again, that S corporations cannot deduct cash dividends with respect to stock held by an ESOP.[57]

Payments which are distributed to participants are not considered a return of any nondeductible employee contributions.[58] Rather, such payments are considered to be ordinary income to the recipient,[59] and are not eligible to be rolled over into an IRA.[60] These dividends are not eligible for the reduced tax rates on qualified dividends.[61] These payments are not subject to employer withholding under Code Sec. 3405(d)(1)(B). Finally, the payments are not subject to the ten-percent premature distribution tax of Code Sec. 72(t).[62]

.08 Valuation of Securities Contributed to an ESOP

The value assigned to qualifying securities of a nonpublicly traded employer is extremely important. This value must be determined for several purposes, including:

(1) determining the amount of a deduction for contributions of securities to the ESOP by the employer;

---

[52] Code Sec. 404(k)(5)(A), as amended by EGTRRA Sec. 662(b).
[53] Rev. Rul. 2001-6, 2001-6 IRB 491.
[54] *Boise Cascade Corp.,* CA-9, 2003-1 USTC ¶ 50,472.
[55] Chief Council Notice 2004-38 (Oct. 1, 2004).
[56] Prop. Reg. § 1.404(k)-3.

[57] Code Sec. 404(k)(1).
[58] Temp. Reg. § 1.404(k)-1T, Q&A-3.
[59] Code Sec. 72(e)(5)(D).
[60] Reg. § 1.402(c)-2, Q&A-4.
[61] Code Sec. 1(h)(11)(B)(ii).
[62] Code Sec. 72(t)(2)(A)(vi).

(2) establishing the sales price for a sale of employer securities to an ESOP (otherwise, if the trustee paid an amount in excess of the fair market value, it would be deemed a prohibited transaction);

(3) determining the amount of securities which may be allocated to participants' accounts for purposes of the Code Sec. 415 contribution limits; and

(4) establishing values for put options and rights of first refusal.

In establishing a fair market value, Reg. § 54.4975-11(d)(5) requires a good-faith estimation based on all relevant factors. Presumably, this includes the factors set out in Rev. Rul. 59-60,[63] which relates to the valuation of property for estate tax purposes. These factors were successfully employed in *Las Vegas Dodge, Inc.,*[64] and included the following:

(1) the nature and history of the company;

(2) the general economic conditions;

(3) the dividend-paying capacity of the company;

(4) the leadership of the company;

(5) other sales of the company's stock;

(6) the market for stocks of similar companies;

(7) the book value of the company stock; and

(8) the location of the business.

Reg. § 54.4975-11(d)(5) requires that a determination of fair market value be made at least annually and be performed by an independent person who customarily makes such appraisals. Under Code Sec. 401(a)(28)(C), this independent appraiser must meet requirements similar to those imposed under Code Sec. 170(a)(1), relating to charitable contributions. If no disqualified person (defined in Code Sec. 4975(e)(2)) is involved in a transaction, the most recent such valuation will suffice. However, if a disqualified person is involved in a transaction, the regulation requires that the value be set as of the transaction date.

¶ 1105   S Corporation ESOPs

As mentioned in the Introduction section of this chapter, S corporations have only recently been allowed to establish ESOPs. The most important aspect of this legislation is that the flow-through income from the S corporation to shares held by the ESOP is tax-deferred (e.g., if the ESOP owns 25 percent of an S corporation, then 25 percent of the corporation's profits are not currently taxed).

---

[63] 1959-1 CB 237.   [64] DC Nev., 85-2 USTC ¶ 9546.

However, as discussed in ¶ 1105.02, the ability to defer income on behalf of certain owners is limited.

S Corporation ESOPs, often referred to as SESOPs, do not enjoy all the benefits that are available to C corporation ESOPs. As noted throughout the discussion in ¶ 1104, C corporations have expanded deduction limits for ESOP contributions relating to interest payments on loans and for certain dividend payments, neither of which are available to SESOPs. In addition, the gain rollover provisions of Code Sec. 1042 (discussed in ¶ 1106) are not available to S corporation owners.

The special rules applicable to SESOPs follow.

.01 Limit on Number of S Corporation Shareholders

Pursuant to AJCA '04, the number of shareholders allowed in an S corporation was expanded to 100.[65] For purposes of determining the numbers of shareholders in an S corporation, a SESOP counts as only one shareholder.[66]

.02 Prohibited Allocations.

As mentioned in the ¶ 1101, TRA '97 provisions allowed SESOPs to avoid unrelated business income tax on the sponsoring S corporation's flow-through income. Thus, income tax is deferred on the S corporation income until the SESOP actually distributes the stock to participants covered under the plan. (Note that this income could be deferred even further if the participant rolls the distributed S corporation stock over into an eligible retirement plan in accordance with the rules of Code Sec. 402(c), discussed in chapter 9.) Because Congress was concerned about techniques that SESOPs could use to avoid income recognition by owners without providing broad-based employee coverage that benefits rank and file employees, complex new rules under EGTRRA '01 effectively limit the ability to defer income on shares held by a SESOP on behalf of individuals who own 10 percent of the company, or who are part of a family which owns 20 percent of the company.

Specifically, these rules require a SESOP to provide that no portion of the assets of the plan attributable to (or allocable in lieu of) the S corporation stock may, during a nonallocation year, accrue directly or indirectly to a disqualified person. Any violation of this

---

[65] Code Sec. 1361(b)(1)(A), as amended by the American Jobs Creation Act of 2004, P.L. 108- 357, Sec. 232(a) (Oct. 22, 2004).
[66] IRS Letter Ruling 199906044.

provision is referred to as a "prohibited allocation." These rules are generally effective for plan years beginning after December 31, 2004.

Consequences of a Prohibited Allocation. The plan itself is not disqualified because a prohibited allocation occurs. However, if a prohibited allocation occurs:

(1) the amount allocated in a prohibited allocation to a disqualified person is treated as distributed to that individual (that is, the value of the prohibited allocation is includible in the gross income of the individual receiving the prohibited allocation);[67] and

(2) an excise tax is imposed on the S corporation equal to 50 percent of the amount allocated to the account of a disqualified person or any synthetic equity interest owned by a disqualified person.[68]

> **Example:** John and Marsha each own 40 percent of the shares in Mack Corporation, an S corporation. The remaining shares of Mack are held in its ESOP for the benefit of Mack employees. The flow-through income from Mack to the shares held by the ESOP is allocated to John's and Marsha's accounts. John and Marsha are disqualified persons because they own more than 20 percent of Mack's shares. Therefore, the allocation is a prohibited allocation. John and Marsha must treat the allocations to their accounts as distributions and include the amounts in income for the year. In addition, Mack Corporation is subject to the excise tax equal to 50 percent of the amount allocated to John's and Marsha's accounts.

The value on which the 50 percent excise tax is based in a prohibited allocation is the fair market value of the stock. A special rule applies to the first nonallocation year, regardless of whether there is a prohibited allocation. In that year, the excise tax also applies to the fair market value of the deemed-owned shares of any disqualified person held by the ESOP, even though those shares are not actually allocated to that disqualified person in that year. For synthetic equity interests, the excise tax is based on the value of the shares on which the synthetic equity is based.

Definitions. Several terms included in the new rules require defining:

---

[67] Code Sec. 409(p).

[68] Code Sec. 4979A.

Nonallocation year. A nonallocation year generally means any plan year of an S corporation's ESOP if, at any time during the plan year, disqualified persons own at least 50 percent of the total outstanding shares of the S corporation.[69]

For purposes of determining whether there is a nonallocation year, ownership of stock generally is attributed under the rules of Code Sec. 318, except that (1) the family attribution rules are modified to include certain other family members, (2) option attribution does not apply (but instead special rules relating to synthetic equity apply), and (3) deemed-owned shares held by the ESOP are treated as held by the individual with respect to whom they are deemed owned. For this purpose, the family members of an individual are (1) the individual's spouse, (2) the individual's and his or her spouse's ancestor or lineal descendant, (3) the individual's and his or her spouse's siblings and any lineal descendant of the sibling, and (4) the spouse of any person described in (2) or (3).[70]

Disqualified person. An individual is a disqualified person if he or she is either (1) a member of a "deemed 20 percent shareholder group" or (2) a "deemed 10 percent shareholder." An individual is a member of a deemed 20 percent shareholder group if the aggregate number of deemed-owned shares of the person and his or her family members is at least 20 percent of the deemed-owned shares of stock in the S corporation. (An individual is also treated as a disqualified person if he or she has deemed owned shares and is a family member of a member of this "deemed 20 percent shareholder group.") An individual is a deemed 10 percent shareholder if he or she is not a member of a deemed 20 percent shareholder group and his or her deemed-owned shares are at least 10 percent of the number of deemed-owned shares of stock of the corporation.[71]

Deemed-owned shares. Deemed-owned shares include (1) S corporation-employer stock allocated to the account of an individual under the ESOP, and (2) a share of unallocated stock held by the ESOP that is attributable to an individual. Unallocated stock held by an ESOP is attributed to an individual if it would be allocated to him/her in the same proportion as shares were allocated in the most recent allocation of stock under the terms of the plan.[72]

---

[69] Code Sec. 409(p)(3); Temp. Reg. § 1.409(p)-1T(c)(1).

[70] Temp. Reg. § 1.409(p)-1T(c)(3).

[71] Code Sec. 409(p)(4)(A) and (B); Temp. Reg. § 1.409(p)-1T(d)(1).

[72] Code Sec. 409(p)(4)(C); Temp. Reg. § 1.409(p)-1T(e)(1).

Example: ABC Corporation is a calendar year S corporation that maintains an ESOP for the benefit of its employees. During 2006, ABC's 1,000 outstanding shares of common stock are owned by the following unrelated individuals: A (not an employee), 100 shares; employee B, 100 shares; and the ESOP, 800 shares. The ESOP's 800 shares are allocated to the accounts of the following employees:

Employee	Deemed-Owned ESOP Shares (800 total)	Percentage Deemed-Owned ESOP Shares
B	200	25%
C	100	12.5%
D	50	6.25%
E	50	6.25%
Other employees	400 (none exceeding 10 shares)	1% or less

Employees B and C are disqualified persons because each owns at least 10% of ABC's deemed-owned ESOP shares. (Note that A is not a disqualified person because he is not a participant in the ESOP.) However, 2006 is not a nonallocation year because the disqualified persons, B and C, do not own at least 50% of ABC's outstanding shares. (B owns 100 shares directly and has 200 deemed-owned shares, and C has 100 deemed-owned shares, for a total of 400 shares, or 40%.)

Synthetic equity interest. Synthetic equity generally includes any stock option, warrant, restricted stock, deferred issuance stock right, or similar interest that gives the holder the right to acquire or receive the S corporation stock in the future. Synthetic equity also includes a stock appreciation right, phantom stock unit, or similar right to a future cash payment based on the value of the stock or appreciation in the value.[73] Temporary regulations also include nonqualified deferred compensation (even if it is not payable in, or calculated with respect to, stock in the S corporation) and rights to acquire interests in a related entity.[74]

The stock on which a synthetic equity interest is based is treated as outstanding stock of the S corporation and as deemed-owned shares of the individual holding the synthetic equity interest if such treatment would result in (1) the treatment of any individual as a disqualified person or (2) the treatment of any year as a nonallocation year. Thus, for example, disqualified persons for a year

---

[73] Code Sec. 409(p)(6).   [74] Temp. Reg. § 1.409(p)-1T(f)(2).

include those individuals who are disqualified persons under the general rule (i.e., treating only those shares held by the ESOP as deemed-owned shares) and those individuals who are disqualified individuals if synthetic equity interests are treated as deemed-owned shares. Ownership of a synthetic equity interest is attributed under the rules of Code Secs. 318(a)(2) and (3) (relating to attribution to and from partnerships, estates, trusts, and corporations), but is not attributed under the family attribution rules.[75]

> **Example:** Refer to the preceding example. The facts are the same, except that employee C also has an option to acquire 250 shares of the common stock of ABC from the company. C's option constitutes 250 shares of synthetic equity. Employees B and C are now deemed to own 650 shares (100 shares of direct ownership + 200 deemed-owned shares for employee B; 100 deemed-owned shares + 250 synthetic equity shares for employee C). These 650 shares equal 52% of the 1,250 outstanding and synthetic equity shares of ABC. Thus, 2006 is a nonallocation year for ABC because disqualified persons own at least 50% of its total outstanding and synthetic equity shares.

.03   Distributions of S Corporation Stock.

As discussed in Chapter 9, any net unrealized appreciation on employer stock distributed as part of a qualified lump-sum distribution is excluded from the participant's gross income. This net unrealized appreciation is measured as the excess of the stock's fair market value at the time of distribution, over the cost or other basis of the stock to the SESOP. Thus, only the SESOP's basis is included in the participant's gross income. In a recent revenue ruling, the IRS clarified that employer stock held by a SESOP is subject to the same basis adjustments under Code Sec. 1367(a) as stock held by any other S corporation shareholder. That is, despite the fact that the sponsoring S corporation's flow-through income is not currently taxable to the SESOP trust, the basis in the employer stock is nevertheless adjusted for those items. Thus, the total flow-through income would be taxable to the participant upon distribution, unless the participant rolls the distribution over into an eligible retirement plan.[76]

---

[75] Code Sec. 409(p)(5).

[76] Rev. Rul. 2003-27. IRB 2003-11, 597.

Example: Blue Corporation, an S corporation, maintains Plan B, a SESOP. Plan B purchases several shares of Blue stock for $100 per share with employer contributions. Plan B's pro rata share of Blue's income over the period the shares were held is $20 per share. As part of a qualified lump-sum distribution, Plan B distributes shares of Blue to Jill, a participant in the plan, when the fair market value is $130 per share. Under the IRS ruling, the amount of net unrealized appreciation in the stock is $10 per share, the excess of the fair market value of the stock ($130) over Plan B's adjusted basis in the stock ($120, which is the $100 purchase price of the stock plus the $20 of flow-through income). Thus, Jill has $120 of ordinary income per share as a result of the distribution (unless, of course, she rolls the stock over into an eligible retirement plan.)

As discussed at the beginning of this section, ESOPS are generally required to provide for distributions in the form of employer stock. If a ESOP permits distributions of employer securities, Code Sec. 401(a)(31) requires the ESOP to also permit participants to elect to have any such stock that is part of an eligible rollover distribution be paid in a direct rollover to an eligible retirement plan, including an IRA. An IRA trustee or custodian, however, is not a permissible S corporation shareholder under Code Sec. 1361, therefore, possibly causing loss of the S corporation's election due to such a rollover. Thus, SESOPs are permitted to provide for distributions only in cash. SESOPs are also permitted to provide that any employer stock distributed is subject to an immediate repurchase by the S corporation on a direct rollover of the stock from the SESOP to an IRA. The IRS has recently accepted the position that the S corporation's election is not affected as a result of a SESOP's distribution of S corporation stock where the participant directs that the stock be distributed to an IRA in a direct rollover, provided that: (1) the terms of the SESOP require that the S corporation repurchase its stock immediately upon the rollover to an IRA; (2) either, pursuant to the terms of the SESOP, the S corporation or the SESOP actually repurchases its stock contemporaneously with, and effective on the same day as, the distribution; and (3) no income, loss, deduction, or credit flow-through items attributable to the S corporation stock is allocated to the participant's IRA.[77]

---

[77] Rev. Proc. 2004-14, 2004-7 IRB 489, modifying and superseding Rev. Proc. 2003-23, 2003-1 CB 599.

¶ 1106   Nonrecognition of Gain on Employer Securities Sold to ESOPs

Code Sec. 1042 allows shareholders (other than C corporation shareholders) of privately held C corporations a method of liquidating their ownership without recognizing gain. Code Sec. 1042 provides a rollover treatment on the sale of qualified employer securities to an ESOP if qualified replacement property is acquired within the specified time period. Assuming all the provisions are met, the shareholder's basis and holding period are carried over, and gain is recognized only upon the disposition of the replacement property. Note, however, that the nonrecognition of gain provision does not apply to shareholders who are C corporations.[78] In addition, sales of S corporation stock to an ESOP are not eligible for the nonrecognition provision.[79]

As an overview, the shareholder must first sell the qualifying securities of the employer to the ESOP, purchase qualified replacement property within a 15-month period, and elect to apply Code Sec. 1042 treatment to the transaction within the filing period of the taxable year in which the sale occurs. The ESOP must own at least 30 percent of the employer stock after the sale and not benefit the shareholder or other related parties with the acquired stock. Finally, the employer must consent to the application of a potential excise tax in the event of an early disposition of the acquired stock.

In order for the nonrecognition of gain to apply, however, several rules apply to the employer, the shareholder, the replacement property, and the ESOP. Each of these are discussed below.

.01   Employer Requirements

Qualifying securities are employer securities as defined in Code Sec. 409(1), and include common stock issued by the employer or a member of the same controlled group. The employer must be a domestic C corporation (S corporation stock is ineligible) which has no outstanding stock that is readily tradable on an established securities market. Thus, the employer may have publicly traded debt instruments and still qualify.[80]

The employer corporation must also give written consent to have the rules of Code Sec. 4978 apply. Under Code Sec. 4978, if the ESOP disposes of the shares acquired in the Code Sec. 1042 transaction within three years of acquisition, the employer corporation will be assessed with a ten percent excise tax on the

---

[78] Code Sec. 1042(c)(7).
[79] Code Sec. 1042(c)(1)(A).

[80] Code Sec. 1042(c)(1)(A).

amount realized (fair market value) on the disposition. The specific shares are not tracked; instead, a disposition would be deemed to occur if either: (1) the percentage of the total outstanding shares of employer securities held by the ESOP after any disposition is less than the percentage of the total outstanding shares held immediately after the Sec. 1042 purchase; or (2) the value of the employer securities held by the ESOP after the disposition is less than 30 percent of the total value of all employer securities outstanding at that time.[81] However, routine dispositions by the ESOP, defined as those made to a participant on account of death, disability, retirement after age 59½, and separation from service which would constitute a one-year break in service, will not cause the penalty to be imposed.[82]

.02 Shareholder Requirements

The shareholder must not have acquired the qualifying employer securities from a qualified plan, through the exercise of statutory or nonqualified stock options, or from any other plan to which Code Sec. 83 (property transferred in connection with the performance of services) applies.[83] The shareholder must have held the qualifying employer securities for at least three years before selling it to the ESOP.[84]

In order to have the nonrecognition rules apply, the shareholder must purchase qualified replacement property (defined below) within a 15- month replacement period, which begins three months prior to the sale. Thus, the replacement period runs from three months before the sale to 12 months after the sale.[85] To the extent that the proceeds from the sale are used to purchase qualified replacement property, no gain will be recognized. The taxpayer's basis in the new property is reduced by the gain not recognized in the sale, and the holding period of the old stock is carried over to the replacement property. If more than one item of replacement property is purchased, the old basis is divided proportionately among the items, based on their cost. In the event that the total proceeds are not used to buy qualified replacement property within the requisite period, gain will be recognized.[86] If the taxpayer disposes of any qualified replacement property, he will recognize any gain that was not previously recognized in the Code Sec. 1042 transaction.

> **Example:** On May 1, 2006, Ed sells 1,000 shares of X Company stock with a basis of $15,000 to the X Company ESOP for $35,000. Ed elects under Code Sec. 1042 to not recognize the

---

[81] Temp. Reg. § 54.4978-1T, Q&A 1.
[82] Code Sec. 4978(d).
[83] Code Sec. 1042(c)(1)(B).

[84] Code Sec. 1042(b)(4).
[85] Code Sec. 1042(c)(3).
[86] Code Sec. 1042(d).

$20,000 gain ($35,000 – $15,000). On January 15, 2007, Ed purchases 600 shares of Y Company stock for $40,000. His basis in the Y stock is $20,000 ($40,000 cost, minus the $20,000 gain not recognized under Code Sec. 1042). The holding period of the X stock is tacked on to the Y stock. Upon the sale of the Y stock for $50,000, Ed will recognize a $30,000 gain ($50,000 – $20,000 basis).

If the Y stock had cost $30,000 instead of $40,000, Ed must recognize a $5,000 gain ($35,000 sale of X stock, minus the $30,000 cost of Y stock) on the sale of the X stock to the ESOP. His basis in the Y stock would be $15,000 ($30,000 cost, minus the $15,000 gain not recognized).

For these purposes, certain dispositions by the corporation that issued the qualified replacement property will trigger recognition of gain by the taxpayer. If the corporation that issued the securities (but not another member of the same controlled group) disposes of a substantial portion of its assets other than in the ordinary course of business at a time when it was controlled by the taxpayer, the taxpayer is treated as if he had disposed of the qualified replacement property at that time. Gain recognition will not apply: (1) to Code Sec. 368 reorganizations, unless the shareholder owns stocks representing control of the acquiring or acquired corporation; (2) because of the shareholder's death; (3) to gifts; or (4) to any transaction subject to Code Sec. 1042.[87]

Shareholder Reporting. The taxpayer or executor must make an election to have Code Sec. 1042 apply to the sale of the securities to the ESOP. The election must be attached to the taxpayer's return, along with the employer's consent to have Code Sec. 4978 apply (see above), by the due date of the taxpayer's return (including extensions, if applicable) for the year in which the sale occurred.[88] (The election may not be made subsequently in an amended return.)[89]

In addition, the shareholder must file a notarized statement of purchase describing the replacement property, the date of purchase, and the cost of the property, and declaring the property to be qualified replacement property with respect to the sale of qualified securities. The original temporary regulations required this statement to be notarized within 30 days after the purchase. However, the IRS has subsequently relaxed this 30-day requirement and allows the statement to be notarized no later than the time the taxpayer filed his or her tax return for the tax year in which the

---

[87] Code Sec. 1042(e).
[88] Code Sec. 1042(b)(3) and (c)(6).

[89] *J.W. Clause Est.*, 122 TC 1155 (2004).

sale occurred. If the taxpayer has not purchased qualified replacement property at the time of the filing of the statement of election, the election will be invalid unless taxpayer attaches the notarized statement of purchase to his income tax return filed for the tax year following the year for which the Code Sec. 1042 election was made.[90]

.03 Qualified Replacement Property Requirement.

Qualified replacement property is defined as any security (including stock, bonds, etc.) issued by a domestic operating corporation where the corporation does not have passive investment income in excess of 25 percent of its gross receipts. In addition, the corporation may not be a member of the same controlled group as the one which issued the securities that were sold to the ESOP.[91] The corporation may be privately or publicly held. Government securities are specifically excluded from the definition.[92]

An operating corporation is one in which more than 50 percent of the corporation's assets are used in the active conduct of a trade or business. Financial institutions and insurance companies are deemed to be operating corporations.[93] For purposes of the passive income test, gross receipts of the year prior to acquisition are to be used.[94] In applying the test, controlling and controlled groups are treated as a single entity.[95]

ESOP Notes. Because the deferred gain on a Code Sec. 1042 stock sale is recognized upon the sale of the replacement securities, "ESOP notes" (also known as floating rate notes) are an increasingly popular alternate form of replacement property. ESOP notes are regulated securities issued by highly-rated public companies (e.g., Ford Motor Credit, ITT Financial) that have a 40-60 year maturity and bear a floating rate coupon indexed to 30-day commercial paper or some other market index. Typically, these ESOP notes can be margined up to 75-90 percent of their fair market value, allowing the taxpayer to access a substantial portion of the stock sale proceeds without triggering any tax liability.

> **Example:** Mr. X invests $1 million in ESOP notes as qualified replacement property, in which he has $800,000 of deferred Code Sec. 1042 gain (i.e., a basis of $200,000). He then borrows $900,000 against the ESOP notes. The interest earned on the $1 million could produce approximately enough income to pay the interest charged by the lender on the $900,000 borrowed. Thus, Mr. X has approximately $900,000 of cash to create an actively-

---

[90] Temp. Reg. § 1.1042-1T, Q&A-3; Prop. Reg. § 1.1042-1T, Q&A 3.
[91] Code Sec. 1042(c)(4).

[92] Code Sec. 1042(c)(4)(D).
[93] Code Sec. 1042(c)(4)(B).
[94] Code Sec. 1042(c)(4)(A)(i).

managed portfolio without triggering any tax liability on the deferred Code Sec. 1042 gain.

.04 ESOP Requirements.

Immediately after the Code Sec. 1042 transaction, the ESOP must own at least 30 percent of the outstanding stock of the employer corporation. This test is met by owning 30 percent of either (1) each class of outstanding stock of the corporation, or (2) the total value of all outstanding stock. Both tests exclude any nonconvertible preferred stock. In applying the ownership test, the attribution rules of Code Sec. 318(a)(4) are to apply, i.e., if options to buy stock are owned, the stock is deemed owned by the holder.[96]

An excise tax of 50 percent under Code Sec. 4979A will be assessed to the employer if the assets acquired by the ESOP in the Code Sec. 1042 transaction accrue to either the shareholder or individuals related to the shareholder (within the meaning of Code Sec. 267(c)) within a certain nonallocation period, or at anytime to another person who owns more than 25 percent of any class of employer securities. For the shareholder seeking nonrecognition, this nonallocation period is the ten-year period beginning on the later of: (1) the date of the sale of the qualified securities, or (2) the date of the plan allocation attributable to the final payment of acquisition indebtedness incurred in connection with the sale.[97] Thus, the ESOP must contain express provisions to prohibit these individuals from accruing any benefits from the securities in the transaction during this period. However, individuals who are lineal descendants of the shareholder may receive an allocation during the nonallocation period as long as the total amount allocated to all such lineal descendants does not exceed five percent of all securities held by the ESOP.[98]

The penalty is based on the amount of any prohibited allocation.[99] Note, however, that this provision only penalizes the employer. That is, Code Sec. 1042 provisions still apply to the transaction and provide the same results to the taxpayer.

¶ 1107   The Uses of Leveraged ESOPs

One of the chief goals of ESOP legislation has been to provide a source of funds for capital formation through tax-favored leveraging techniques. Not surprisingly, then, the ESOP is the only form of qualified employee benefit plan which is permitted to borrow funds to acquire employer stock. As discussed earlier in this chapter, when

---

[95] Code Sec. 1042(c)(4)(C).
[96] Code Sec. 1042(b)(2).

[97] Code Sec. 409(n)(3)(C).
[98] Code Sec. 409(n)(3)(A).

the employer corporation repays this loan through contributions to the ESOP, it is allowed to deduct amounts which represent both principal and interest. In addition, the limitations for allocations to participants' accounts and deductions for such contributions by the employer are increased if the special rules are met. Two of the most common uses of leveraged ESOP transactions are outlined below.

.01   Financing Corporate Growth

The basic steps in using an ESOP to finance corporate growth are as follows:

(1) the employer corporation creates an ESOP;

(2) the ESOP borrows money from a bank to buy stock in the employer corporation, and the employer guarantees the loan;

(3) the ESOP uses the money to purchase employer stock and pledges the stock as collateral on the note;

(4) the employer uses the proceeds for working capital, for plant expansion, or to acquire another corporation;

(5) each year, the employer corporation contributes enough cash to the ESOP to enable the ESOP to make the payments on the loan. All amounts so contributed, both principal and interest, are generally deductible up to the limits imposed under Code Sec. 404(a)(9);

(6) as the loan is paid off, the bank releases the pledged stock, which is then allocated to the individual accounts of the participants.

The result of the above transaction is that the employer corporation has expanded, the employees have acquired an equity interest in their employer, and the lender has earned a higher rate of return than normal, since 50 percent of the interest earned on the ESOP loan may be excludable from taxable income (for loans made prior to August 20, 1996).

.02   Leveraged Buyouts

Perhaps the most classical use of ESOPs, however, is in leveraged buyouts, or "going private." Instead of purchasing new shares (or treasury shares) from the employer corporation, the ESOP purchases the stock from the existing shareholders. This is usually accomplished in one of two ways.

The first method involves setting up a new company, commonly referred to as the "Newco" approach. The basic steps involved under this approach are:

(1) key management of the employer corporation forms a new corporation, the "Newco";

(2) the Newco forms an ESOP;

(3) the ESOP secures a loan from a lending institution, with the Newco providing the guarantee for its repayments;

(4) the ESOP purchases stock from the Newco at the same time as the employer corporation merges into the Newco;

(5) pursuant to the statutory merger, the shareholders of the employer corporation receive cash from the Newco;

(6) Newco annually contributes enough cash to the ESOP to service the ESOP loan.

The second method of leveraged buyout is the use of a public tender offer. The steps involved in this case are not very complicated, and are similar to the steps in financing corporate growth:

(1) the corporation forms an ESOP;

(2) the ESOP obtains a loan from a financial institution, with the corporation as the guarantor;

(3) the ESOP makes a public tender offer to buy the stock of the corporation;

(4) the corporation annually contributes enough cash to the ESOP to service the ESOP debt.

Each of the two methods has advantages and disadvantages. The chief advantage of the tender offer is that it takes much less time to accomplish, which would make outside competition more difficult. Thus, financing should be easier to obtain. The main advantages of the Newco approach are that there is less public notice, which would reduce the chances of a hostile takeover, and the costs of SEC registration for a tender offer are avoided.

Chapter 12

Fiduciary Responsibilities and Prohibited Transactions

¶1201 Introduction

One of the chief purposes of the Employee Retirement Income Security Act of 1974 (ERISA) was to ensure that employees receive the benefits promised them from employee welfare and pension plans. To achieve this purpose, ERISA's Title I, Part 4 provides standards of fiduciary responsibility and prohibitions against specific transactions by persons dealing with those plans. While the Department of Labor (DOL) has primary responsibility for enforcing these standards of conduct, the IRS shares some responsibility in ensuring that certain prohibited transactions do not occur.

The ERISA Sec. 401 standards apply to employee welfare benefit plans and employee pension benefit plans (including nonqualified plans as well as qualified plans), other than:

(1) government plans,

(2) church plans not electing coverage under Code Sec. 410(d),

(3) workers' compensation, unemployment compensation, or disability plans,

(4) plans maintained outside the United States for the benefit of nonresident aliens,

(5) unfunded deferred compensation plans maintained for the benefit of executives,

(6) unfunded excess benefit plans,

(7) deferred compensation plans for retiring partners described in Code Sec. 736,

(8) funds held by an insurance company, unless the funds are held in a separate account,

(9) funds held by regulated investment companies, and

(10) plans without employees, e.g., a Keogh plan which covers only the self-employed individuals (owners, partners, and their spouses).

The ERISA fiduciary responsibilities are grouped in two categories: (1) a set of general standards to which the fiduciary must adhere, and (2) a set of specific transactions in which the fiduciary and other parties in interest are prohibited from engaging. The general standards are contained in ERISA only and are enforced by the DOL. A breach of these duties by the fiduciary generally results in personal liability for losses which are incurred. The specific prohibited transactions are contained in ERISA and in the Internal Revenue Code. These prohibited transactions also require correction and, in addition, can result in excise penalty taxes to the person involved in the transaction.

¶ 1202   Fiduciary Defined

Before discussing the duties of the fiduciary, one must first identify who is considered to be a fiduciary under the ERISA provisions. Every employee benefit plan covered by ERISA must provide for one or more named fiduciaries who jointly or severally have authority to control and manage the operation and administration of the plan.[1] ERISA Sec. 3(21) defines the term fiduciary as any person (including a corporation):

(1) who exercises any discretionary authority or discretionary control respecting management of the plan or exercises any authority or control respecting management or disposition of its assets;

(2) who renders investment advice for a fee or other compensation, direct or indirect, with respect to any monies or other property of the plan, or has any authority or responsibility to do so; or

(3) who has any discretionary authority or discretionary responsibility in the administration of the plan.

Trustees, plan administrators, and investment managers would obviously be classified as fiduciaries. In addition, the authority to administer a plan and select investments normally rests with the sponsoring company or the plan committee. Thus, the company and/or the plan committee are also considered fiduciaries under ERISA. Even if the company hires a third party to administer the plan, the company or plan committee is still classified as a fiduciary, since these third party administrators generally limit their

---

[1] ERISA Sec. 402(a).

activities to carrying out the directions of the company or plan committee.

Persons other than those named in the plan can also be considered as fiduciaries, particularly because some actions can fall within the investment advice provision. However, IRS regulations indicate that a person would be deemed to be rendering "investment advice" only if: (1) the person renders advice to the plan as to the value of securities or other property or makes recommendations as to the advisability of investing in, purchasing, or selling securities or other property; and (2) the person either directly or indirectly (a) has discretionary authority or control with respect to purchasing or selling securities or other property for the plan, or (b) renders any advice on a regular basis to the plan with the understanding that the advice will serve as a primary basis for investment decisions and that the person will render individualized investment advice to the plan based on the particular needs of the plan regarding such matters as investment policies or strategy, overall portfolio composition, or diversification of plan investments.[2] Thus, ordinarily an accountant, attorney, or actuary acting in such capacity would not be considered a fiduciary unless he or she renders investment advice to the plan on a regular basis.

¶ 1203 Fiduciary Responsibilities

.01 Duties of the Fiduciary

Any person who is classified as a fiduciary must follow the general standards under ERISA Sec. 404. These require that the fiduciary discharge his duties to the plan solely in the interest of the participants and beneficiaries:

(1) for the exclusive purpose of providing benefits to participants and beneficiaries;

(2) with the care, skill, prudence, and diligence under the circumstances prevailing that a prudent person, acting in a like capacity and familiar with such matters, would use in the conduct of an enterprise of a like character and with like aims (referred to as the "prudent expert" standard);

(3) by diversifying the investments of the plan so as to minimize the risk of large losses, unless under the circumstances it is clearly prudent not to do so; and

(4) in accordance with the documents and instruments governing the plan insofar as such documents and instruments are consistent with ERISA.

ERISA Sec. 404(c) contains a special provision in the case of a plan which provides for individual accounts and permits a

---

[2] Reg. § 54.4975-9(c)(1).

participant or beneficiary to exercise control over the assets in his account (i.e., he can direct his investments). If the participant or beneficiary actually directs the investment of the assets in his account, the participant or beneficiary is not deemed to be a fiduciary by reason of such exercise of control. In addition, any other person who is a fiduciary is not liable for any loss which results from the participant's or beneficiary's exercise of control over the investment of the assets in his own account. However, for purposes of the excise tax on prohibited transactions (discussed in ¶ 1204), Code Sec. 4975 does not contain a similar exception from the definition of fiduciary for plan participants who direct their own account investments.

.02 Liability for Breach of Fiduciary Duties

A fiduciary who breaches any of the responsibilities or duties imposed under ERISA is personally liable to make good to the plan any losses resulting from the breach, and to restore to the plan any profits earned through the use of the plan assets by the fiduciary. In addition, the fiduciary may be subject to other remedial relief as a court may deem appropriate, such as the removal of the fiduciary.[3] This civil action may be brought by the Secretary of Labor, participants, beneficiaries, or another fiduciary.[4]

A plan may expressly provide for procedures for allocating fiduciary responsibilities (other than trustee responsibilities of managing or controlling the assets of the plan) among named fiduciaries and procedures for named fiduciaries to designate persons other than named fiduciaries to carry out fiduciary responsibilities under the plan.[5] Thus, a fiduciary would not ordinarily be liable for a breach of another fiduciary who has responsibility for the specific act. However, a fiduciary may be liable for breaches of fiduciary responsibility by another fiduciary of the same plan in the following situations:

(1) if he knowingly participates in, or knowingly undertakes to conceal, an act or omission of another fiduciary, knowing that the act or omission is a breach;

(2) if, by breaching his own fiduciary responsibilities, he enables another fiduciary to commit a breach; or

(3) if he has knowledge of a breach by another fiduciary and does not make a reasonable effort to remedy the breach.[6]

¶ 1204 Prohibited Transactions

Both ERISA and the Internal Revenue Code contain a list of transactions in which fiduciaries and other parties may not engage.

---

[3] ERISA Sec. 409(a).
[4] ERISA Sec. 502(a)(2).

[5] ERISA Sec. 405(c)(1).
[6] ERISA sec 405(a).

As will become evident in the discussion below, the scope of these prohibited transactions is broadly defined; consequently, both ERISA and the Code contain several narrowly-defined exceptions for certain transactions.

The prohibited transactions listed in ERISA Sec. 406 apply to all plans which are subject to the ERISA reporting requirements, whereas the prohibited transactions under Code Sec. 4975(c) apply only to plans qualified under Code Sec. 401(a), employee annuities under Code Sec. 403(a), IRAs, Archer medical savings accounts (MSAs), health savings accounts (HSAs), and SEPs. Another significant difference between the two sets of prohibited transactions is that the penalties under ERISA are the same as those for breach of fiduciary responsibilities, i.e., that the fiduciary must restore any losses to the plan and face possible removal from his position. The penalties under the Internal Revenue Code carry a 15 percent excise tax, which increases to a 100 percent excise tax if not corrected within the requisite time period.

The specific prohibited transactions contained in ERISA and the Code are, for the most part, identical. These requirements provide that, with respect to a plan, a fiduciary is not to engage in the following direct or indirect transactions:

(1) The sale or exchange, or leasing, of any property between a plan and a party in interest or disqualified person.[7] Both the Code and ERISA provide that a transfer of real or personal property by a party in interest or a disqualified person to a plan will be treated as a sale or exchange if the property is subject to a mortgage or similar lien which the plan assumes, or if it is subject to a mortgage or similar lien which a party in interest or disqualified person placed on the property within the ten-year period ending on the date of the transfer.[8] Moreover, the Supreme Court has ruled that even a contribution of unencumbered property would constitute a sale or exchange if it was made to satisfy the minimum funding obligation of a defined benefit plan.[9] Thus, a contribution of property should be made only if it is unencumbered and only to a plan with a discretionary contribution formula, such as a profit-sharing plan.

An exception to this provision applies to ESOPs maintained by S corporations. The sale of employer securities to the ESOP by a shareholder-employee, family member (as defined in Section 267) of the shareholder-employee, or corporation in which the shareholder-employee owns at least 50 percent of the stock will not be considered a prohibited transaction.[10]

---

[7] ERISA Sec. 406(a)(1)(A) and Code Sec. 4975(c)(1)(A).

[8] ERISA Sec. 406(c) and Code Sec. 4975(f)(3).

[9] *Keystone Consolidated Industries, Inc.* SCt. 93-1 USTC ¶ 50,298. 508 US 152. 113 SCt 2006.

See also *N.M. Baizer,* 75 TCM 1671, Dec. 52,540(M), TC Memo. 1998-36. Aff'd, CA-9, 2000-1 USTC ¶ 50,249, 204 F3d 1231.

[10] Code Sec. 4975(f)(6).

(2) The lending of money or other extension of credit between a plan and a party in interest or disqualified person.[11] Thus, the contribution of a promissory note or other form of debt instrument to the plan by the employer would constitute a prohibited transaction. In addition, the guarantee of a plan loan by a disqualified person would fall within this category of prohibited transactions.

There are, however, two exceptions to this provision. Guarantees by an employer of plan loans to an ESOP which meets the requirements of Code Sec. 4975(e)(7) will not be considered a prohibited transaction (as discussed in Chapter 11).[12] In addition, loans to plan participants will not be considered a prohibited transaction if certain requirements are met.[13] These specific requirements will be discussed in detail later in this chapter.

There are also recent instances in which courts have deemed prohibited loans to have been made. For example, in *J.R. Rollins,* the taxpayer's wholly owned company's 401(k) plan made loans to three entities partially owned by the taxpayer. The court ruled that the taxpayer was a disqualified person and a fiduciary and that he directly benefited from the loans, even though none of the assets were actually transferred to the disqualified person. The fact that the plan may have benefited from a favorable rate of interest had no impact on the decision against self-dealing.[14]

(3) The furnishing of goods, services, or facilities between a plan and a party in interest or disqualified person.[15] However, there are three exceptions to this provision:

(a) Any contract or reasonable arrangement made with a disqualified person for office space, or legal, accounting, or other services necessary for the establishment or operation of the plan will not be a prohibited transaction if no more than reasonable compensation is paid for the services.[16]

(b) A U.S. or state bank or financial institution which is a fiduciary of the plan may provide ancillary services if it meets both of the following conditions: (i) it has adopted adequate internal safeguards which assure that the ancillary service is consistent with sound banking and financial practice, as determined by federal or state supervisory authority; and (ii) the extent to which the ancillary service provided is subject to specific guidelines issued by the bank or financial institution, and the service cannot be provided in an excessive or unreasonable manner or in a manner that would be

---

[11] ERISA Sec. 406(a)(1)(B) and Code Sec 4975(c)(1)(B).

[12] ERISA Sec. 408(b)(3) and Code Sec. 4975(d)(3).

[13] ERISA Sec. 408(b)(1) and Code Sec. 4975(d)(1).

[14] 88 TCM 447, TC Memo. 2004-260.

[15] ERISA Sec. 406(a)(1)(C) and Code Sec. 4975(c)(1)(C).

[16] ERISA Sec. 408(b)(2) and Code Sec. 4975(d)(2).

inconsistent with the best interests of participants and beneficiaries of the plan.[17]

(c) A plan can pay a fiduciary any reasonable compensation for services rendered, or for the reimbursement of expenses properly and actually incurred in the performance of his duties with the plan. However, no "double-dipping" is allowed in the case of a fiduciary who also received full-time pay as an employee of the employer or employee organization, except that the plan may reimburse properly incurred expenses.[18]

(4) The transfer to, or use by or for the benefit of, a party in interest or disqualified person of any asset or income of the plan.[19] According to Conference Committee Reports, the purchase or sale of securities by a plan to manipulate the price of the securities to the advantage of a disqualified person constitutes a use of assets of the plan for the benefit of a disqualified person.[20]

(5) The act by a fiduciary whereby he deals with the income or assets of the plan in his own interest or for his own account.[21]

(6) The receipt of any consideration for his own personal account by a fiduciary from any party dealing with the plan in connection with a transaction involving the income or assets of the plan.[22]

(7) The acquisition, on behalf of the plan, of certain employer securities or employer real property.[23] (The Internal Revenue Code has no similar provision.) Note that this provision includes not only purchases or exchanges by the plan, but also acquisitions by employer contributions of securities or real property to the plan. However, under ERISA Sec. 407, a plan may hold "qualifying employer securities" or "qualified employer real property" if the aggregate value of these securities and properties do not exceed ten percent of the value of the assets of the plan. This exception will be explored in detail later in this chapter.

.01 Parties in Interest/Disqualified Persons

These prohibited transactions prevent the fiduciary from engaging the plan in transactions with certain persons. ERISA refers to these persons as "parties in interest," while the Code refers to them as "disqualified persons." Although the two terms are basically identical, there are some minor differences. Under ERISA Sec. 3(14)

---

[17] ERISA Sec. 408(b)(6).
[18] ERISA Sec. 408(c)(2).
[19] ERISA Sec. 406(a)(1)(D) and Code Sec. 4975(c)(1)(D).
[20] Conference Committee Report to P.L. 93-406 (1974), H.R. Conference Report No. 93-1280.

[21] ERISA Sec. 406(b)(1) and Code Sec. 4975(c)(1)(E).
[22] ERISA Sec. 406(b)(3) and Code Sec. 4975(c)(1)(F).
[23] ERISA Sec. 406(a)(1)(E).

and Code Sec. 4975(e)(2), a "party in interest" and a "disqualified person" include the following:

(1) any fiduciary (including, but not limited to, any administrator, officer, trustee, or custodian), counsel, or employee of the employee benefit plan;

(2) a person providing services to the plan;

(3) an employer whose employees are covered by the plan;

(4) an employee organization whose members are covered by the plan;

(5) an owner, direct or indirect, of 50 percent or more (as determined under Code Sec. 267(c)) of: (a) the combined voting power of all classes of stock entitled to vote or the total value of all classes of stock of a corporation, (b) the capital interest or the profits interest of a partnership, or (c) the beneficial interest of a trust or unincorporated enterprise which is an employer or an employee organization whose employees are covered by the plan;

(6) a relative (which includes a spouse, ancestor, lineal descendant, or spouse of a lineal descendant) of any individual listed in (1) through (5), above;

(7) a corporation, partnership, or trust or estate of which (or in which) 50 percent or more is owned directly or indirectly (as determined under Code Sec. 267(c)) by persons described in (1) through (5), above;

(8) a highly compensated employee, officer, director, or a ten-percent-or-more shareholder (directly or indirectly) of a person described in (2) through (5), above (Note, however, that the Internal Revenue Code's definition requires a highly "compensated employee" to earn more than ten percent of the total annual wages of the employer, while ERISA's definition includes all employees.); and

(9) a ten-percent-or-more (directly or indirectly in capital or profits, as determined under Code Sec. 267(c)) partner or joint venturer of a person described in (2) through (5), above.

As discussed earlier in ¶ 1203, ERISA specifically excepts from the definition of fiduciary, any participant who directs the investment of his or her own account. However, for purposes of the excise tax on prohibited transactions, Code Sec. 4975 contains no such exception. As a result, a profit-sharing plan participant's majority-owned corporation was determined to be a disqualified person and subject to the excise tax when the participant directed the plan to lend money to the corporation from his plan account.[24]

---

[24] *Flahertys Arden Bowl, Inc.*, 115 TC 269, Dec.   ¶ 50,770, 271 F3d 763.
54,052. Aff'd, *per curiam*, CA-8, 2001-2 USTC

¶ 1204.01

.02   Consequences of a Prohibited Transaction

Both ERISA and the Internal Revenue Code impose sanctions for engaging in a prohibited transaction. The sanction under ERISA for a prohibited transaction is the same as that imposed for a breach of fiduciary responsibility, i.e., the restoration of any lost profits by the fiduciary or party in interest to the plan and the possible removal of the fiduciary and/or some other remedial relief determined by a court. Under the Internal Revenue Code, however, an excise tax is imposed on the disqualified person or persons participating in the prohibited transaction. (All participating disqualified persons are jointly and severally liable for the tax.) Any disqualified person who participates in a prohibited transaction must report the transaction on Form 5330, Return of Initial Excise Taxes Related to Pension & Profit-Sharing Plans. The due date for filing Form 5330 and paying the initial tax is the last day of the seventh month after the end of the disqualified person's tax year.

The Excise Tax. Code Sec. 4975 imposes an excise tax on the disqualified person for each prohibited transaction in which he or she engages. The initial tax is 15 percent of the "amount involved" with respect to the prohibited transaction for each year, or part thereof, of the "taxable period." If the transaction is not corrected within the taxable period (see below), an additional tax is imposed, which is equal to 100 percent of the amount involved in the transaction.

"Amount Involved." The term "amount involved" is defined in Code Sec. 4975(f)(4) as the greater of the amount of money and the fair market value of the other property either given or those amounts received. For services, the amount involved means only the excess compensation received.

For the initial 15 percent tax, the fair market value is determined as of the date on which the prohibited transaction occurs. However, for the 100-percent tax, fair market value is the highest fair market value during the period which begins on the date of the prohibited transaction and ends 90 days after the mailing of the notice of deficiency for the initial tax.

IRS regulations under Code Sec. 4941 (Taxes on Self-Dealing with Private Foundation) define several of the same terms which are found in Code Sec. 4975. Included in these regulations are some guidelines for determining the measurement of the amount involved in certain prohibited transactions. Where the use of money (e.g., a prohibited loan) or other property (e.g., a lease) is involved, the amount involved is the greater of the amount paid for such use or the fair market value of such use for the period for which the money or other property is used. Thus, for example, in the case of a loan which constitutes a prohibited transaction, the amount involved is the greater of the actual amount of interest paid by the disqualified person or the fair market value for the use of money (i.e., the going rate) as of the loan date.[25]

"Taxable Period." The term "taxable period" means, with respect to any prohibited transaction, the period beginning with the date on which the prohibited transaction occurs and ending on the earliest of:

(1) the date of mailing a notice of deficiency for the 15 percent tax;

(2) the date on which the 15 percent tax is assessed; or

(3) the date on which correction of the prohibited transaction is completed.[26]

"Correcting" the Prohibited Transaction. Basically, to correct a prohibited transaction means to undo the transaction to the extent possible. In any case, the plan must be placed in a financial position not worse than that in which it would be if the disqualified person were acting under the highest fiduciary standards.[27]

ERISA Provisions. The Employee Benefit Security Administration (EBSA) division of the Department of Labor has created a Voluntary Fiduciary Correction (VFC) program to encourage voluntary self-correction of certain violations of fiduciary duty under ERISA and thus avoid civil penalties. Under the VCF program, an applicant is not required to consult with the DOL, but instead follows the procedures below:[28]

(1) Identify any violations and determine whether they fall within the transactions covered by the VFC program;

(2) Follow the process for correcting specific violations (e.g., improper loans or incorrect valuation of plan assets);

(3) Calculate and restore any losses or profits, with interest, if applicable, and distribute any supplemental benefits to participants; and

(4) File an application with the appropriate EBSA regional office that includes documentation showing evidence of corrective action taken.

Transactions covered by the VFC program are:

(1) Delinquent participant contributions and participant loan repayments to pension plans;

(2) Fair market interest rate loans with parties in interest;

(3) Below market interest rate loans with parties in interest;

---

[25] Reg. § 53.4941(e)-1(b)(2).
[26] Code Sec. 4975(f)(2).
[27] Code Sec. 4975(f)(5).

[28] EBSA, Adoption of Amended and Restated Voluntary Fiduciary Correction Program, 70 FR 17515-17547 (April 6, 2005).

(4) Below market interest rate loans with non-parties in interest;

(5) Below market interest rate loans due to a delay in perfecting the security interest;

(6) Participant loan amounts in excess of plan limitations;

(7) Participant loan durations in excess of plan limitations;

(8) The purchase of assets by plans from parties in interest;

(9) The sale of assets by plans to parties in interest;

(10) The sale and leaseback of property to sponsoring employers;

(11) The purchase of assets from non-parties in interest at other than fair market value;

(12) The sale of assets to non-parties in interest at other than fair market value;

(13) The holding of an illiquid asset previously purchased by a plan;

(14) Benefit payments based on improper valuation of plan assets;

(15) The payment of duplicate, excessive, or unnecessary compensation; and

(16) The payment of dual compensation to plan fiduciaries.

VFC program applicants must restore the plan and its participants to the condition they would have been in had the prohibited transaction or breach not occurred. While specific rules are provided for corrections involving the transactions listed above, applicants generally must:

(1) Conduct valuations of plan assets using generally recognized markets for the assets or obtain written appraisal reports from qualified professionals that are based on generally accepted appraisal standards;

(2) Restore to the plan the principal amount involved, plus the greater of (a) lost earnings, starting on the date of the loss and extending to the recovery date; or (b) profits resulting from the use of the principal amount, starting on the date of the loss and extending to the date the profit is realized;

(3) Pay the expenses associated with correcting transactions, such as appraisal costs or fees associated with recalculating participant account balances; and

(4) Make supplemental distributions to former employees, beneficiaries, or alternate payees when appropriate, and provide proof of the payments.

Code provisions. Again, the regulations under Code Sec. 4941 provide further explanation (with examples) of how a correction is to be effected.

To correct a prohibited sale by a plan to a disqualified person, Reg. § 53.4941(e)-1(c)(2) requires the disqualified person to sell the property back to the plan. In order to protect the plan's financial position, the repurchase price paid by the plan to the disqualified person must be equal to the *lesser* of: (1) the original sales price paid by the disqualified person, (2) the fair market value of the property as of the original prohibited sale date, or (3) the fair market value of the property as of the correction date. If, however, the disqualified person has sold the property in an arm's-length transaction to a bona fide purchaser (who is not a disqualified person), obviously no resale can occur. In such case, the disqualified person must pay over to the plan the excess (if any) of the greater of (1) the fair market value of the property on the date on which the correction occurs or (2) the amount realized by the disqualified person from the arm's-length resale over the amount which would have been paid by the plan to the disqualified person if the arm's-length resale had not occurred. In either case, the disqualified person must also pay to the plan any income earned on the property in excess of the income which the plan earned on the cash received from the original sale.

To correct a prohibited sale by a disqualified person to the plan, Reg. § 53.4941(e)-1(c)(3) again requires the rescission of the sale where possible. Again, to protect the financial position of the plan, the repurchase price to be paid by the disqualified person must equal the *greater* of (1) the original sales price paid by the plan, (2) the fair market value of the property at the time of the original sale, or (3) the fair market value of the property as of the correction date. If the plan has sold the property to a bona fide purchaser, no rescission can be made. Instead, the disqualified person must pay the plan the excess (if any) of the amount which the disqualified person would have paid to the plan if the property were resold over the amount realized by the plan from the arm's-length sale. The disqualified person must also pay the plan any income he realized from the cash received from the original sale which exceeds the income derived by the plan from the property during the correction period.

Finally, to correct a prohibited use of plan property by a disqualified person, Reg. § 53.4941(e)-1(c)(4) first requires the termination of the use of the property. In addition, the disqualified person must pay the plan: (1) the excess (if any) of the fair market value of the use of the property over the amount paid by the disqualified person, and (2) the excess (if any) of the amount which would have been paid by the disqualified person for the use of the property on or after the date of the termination if termination had not occurred, over the fair market value of use for that period.

¶1204.02

.03 Exemption for ESOP Loans

A loan or guarantee of a loan to an ESOP by a disqualified person will not be a prohibited transaction if the loan meets the criteria of Code Sec. 4975(d)(3). Basically, these provisions require that the loan must be primarily for the benefit of the participants and beneficiaries of the plan, that it be made at a reasonable rate of interest, and that if any collateral is given by the plan to a disqualified person, it must consist only of "qualifying employer securities." In addition, the ESOP must meet several requirements specified in Reg. § 54.4975-11. These requirements are discussed at length in Chapter 11.

.04 Exemption for Participant Loans

Although loans from a plan to a participant would normally constitute a prohibited transaction, ERISA Sec. 408(b)(1) and Code Sec. 4975(d)(1) provide an exemption for certain loans to plan participants. This exemption for loans to participants is available to an owner-employee in a Keogh plan and to an S corporation shareholder-employee.[29]

In order for a loan to be exempt from the prohibited transaction rules, the following requirements must be met:

(1) Loans must be made available to all participants and beneficiaries on a reasonably equal basis. A plan must, of course, take into consideration the creditworthiness of plan participants in providing or rejecting loan applications because of the responsibilities imposed on the plan fiduciaries. Thus, a written loan policy must be adopted to enforce such actions.

(2) The plan must not make loans available to highly compensated employees (within the meaning of Code Sec. 414(q)) in an amount greater than the amount made available to other employees. The "amount" of the loan may be either an absolute or a relative number. That is, a plan can impose a maximum dollar limit of the amount of a participant's loans under the plan (e.g., $20,000), or it may impose a maximum loan expressed as a percentage of the participant's vested accrued balance (e.g., 50 percent of each participant's vested balance).

(3) Loans must be made in accordance with specific loan provisions set out in the plan. Again, in order to prevent any potential discrimination in loans, specific provisions must be adopted in the plan. In addition, this would require that a policy for determining repayment, interest, and collateral terms be specifically incorporated into the loan provisions.

---

[29] Code Sec. 4975(f)(6)(B)(iii) and ERISA Sec. 408(d)(2)(C), effective for loans after 2001.

(4) Loans must bear a reasonable rate of interest. The loan should be approximately equal to that which a bank or other financial institution would charge for a similar loan. In past years when all consumer interest was deductible, plan loans provided a tax advantage if the participant was allowed to direct the investments of his own account. That is, a participant was allowed to borrow from the plan and pay deductible interest to his own account, which was tax-exempt. While this is still possible for home loans, caution must be exercised to not abuse the reasonableness requirement. Otherwise, the IRS could attempt to reclassify the excess interest payments to the plan as employee contributions, which could possibly have an impact on the plan's qualified status. See Chapter 6.

(5) Loans must be adequately secured. A participant is allowed to pledge his vested accrued benefit as security, as long as the loan does not exceed his balance. If a loan is secured by a vested accrued benefit that is subject to the joint survivor annuity rule, consent of the participant's spouse is required. If the loan is for an amount in excess of his vested balance, other adequate security must be pledged as collateral. One problem with allowing the participant's vested benefit to be pledged as security concerns defined benefit and money purchase pension plans. As discussed in Chapter 5, one of the requirements of these plans is that there must be definitely determinable benefits. If the participant defaults on his loan and the plan forecloses on his vested accrued benefit, a distribution is deemed to occur. Thus, a pension plan would not qualify if it allowed such a deemed distribution prior to the employee's termination of employment. Therefore, in the case of a defined benefit or money purchase pension plan, property other than the participant's vested accrued benefit must be pledged as collateral. Another possibility which has been proposed by some experts in the area is to make a loan default by a participant grounds for dismissal. Thus, the defaulting participant would immediately have terminated employment, allowing a qualifying distribution to be made from his vested accrued benefit to repay the loan. However, there is no certainty that such a provision would withstand IRS scrutiny.

Taxation of Participant Loans. A loan from a qualified plan is generally treated as a distribution to the participant (and subject to the 10 percent early distribution tax of Code Sec. 72(t)). However, Code Sec. 72(p) provides an exception for certain plan loans. In order for the exception of Code Sec. 72(p) to apply to a loan, certain requirements must be met. In general, these provisions:

(1) require the loan to be evidenced by a legally enforceable agreement which specifies the amount and term of the loan and the repayment schedule (This agreement must be set forth either in a

written document or in an electronic medium that satisfies certain requirements contained in regulations.[30]);

(2) limit the amount of the loan;

(3) limit the repayment term of the loan; and

(4) require the loan to be amortized in level installments.

In addition, spousal consent to use a participant's accrued benefit as security for a plan loan is required.

A distribution is *deemed* to occur at the first time that a loan does not satisfy any of the above requirements. This may occur at the time the loan is made or at a later date. If the terms of the loan do not meet the repayment term requirement or the level amortization requirement, or if the loan is not evidenced by an enforceable agreement, the entire outstanding balance of the loan is a deemed distribution made at the time the loan is made. If the loan satisfies those requirements, but the amount of the loan exceeds the limitations of Code Sec. 72(p)(2)(A), discussed below, only the excess amount is deemed distributed at the date the loan is made. If the loan initially satisfies all of the above requirements, but payments are not made in accordance to the loan terms, the entire outstanding balance is deemed distributed at the time of the failure (although a grace period may be allowed under the loan terms).[31] Any amount included in income as a result of a deemed distribution must be reported on Form 1099-R.[32] Note that, despite part or all of a loan being deemed distributed, repayments on the loan by the employee may still occur. Any such repayments are considered to be nondeductible employee contributions and are not taxed a second time when actually distributed from the employee's account.[33]

Such deemed distributions are not treated as actual distributions for some purposes, but are for others. A deemed distribution does not violate the in-service distribution qualification requirements (and, thus, would not cause disqualification of the plan), nor is it eligible for rollover or averaging. However, a deemed distribution is subject to the 10 percent tax on early distributions and the 10 percent tax on distributions to 5-percent owners. In addition, the normal rules for taxing distributions apply. Thus, if an employee's account includes after-tax contributions, a portion of the deemed distribution may not be taxable.[34]

Loan Limits. Code Sec. 72(p)(2)(A) places a cap on the amount of loans which a participant may borrow from a qualified plan. Only that portion of a loan which is in excess of the limit is treated as a taxable

---

[30] Reg. § 1.72-1(p), Q&A 3(b).
[31] Reg. § 1.72(p)-1, Q&As 4, 10.
[32] Reg. § 1.72(p)-1, Q&A 14.

[33] Notice 82-22. 1982-2 CB 751.

[34] Reg. § 1.72(p)-1, Q&As 11, 12.

distribution. This limit, which applies to the total outstanding loan balance, is defined as the lesser of:

(1) $50,000, or

(2) the greater of: (a) one-half of the present value of the participant's vested accrued benefit at the loan date, or (b) $10,000.

However, the $50,000 limit is reduced by the excess of:

(1) the highest outstanding balance of loans from the plan during the preceding one-year period ending on the day before the date on which the new loan was made, over

(2) the outstanding balance of loans from the plan on the date on which the new loan was made.

Example (1): Ms. B, a participant in Plan X, has a vested accrued benefit of $18,000. The maximum amount Ms. B may borrow is $10,000, computed as the lesser of: (1) $50,000; or (2) the greater of $10,000 or $9,000 (half of her vested accrued benefit). Thus, if Ms. B receives a $12,000 loan (which meets the repayment requirements), she would have a deemed distribution of $2,000, which is the excess of the $12,000 loan over her $10,000 limit.

Example (2): Mr. A is a participant in Plan X and wishes to borrow the maximum amount possible from Plan X on January 1, 2006. As of that date, he has a vested accrued benefit of $90,000. During 2005 (the one-year period ending the day before the loan date), Mr. A's maximum loan balance was $40,000. On January 1, 2006, his current loan balance is $25,000. The maximum amount that Mr. A can borrow on January 1, 2006 is $10,000, computed as follows. His maximum loan balance cannot exceed the lesser of:

(1) $35,000, which is $50,000 less $15,000 (the excess of $40,000, his highest aggregate loan balance during 2005, over $25,000, his current loan balance), or

(2) $45,000, which is the greater of $45,000 (one-half of his vested accrued benefit) or $10,000.

Since the maximum loan balance cannot exceed $35,000, Mr. A has only $10,000 available in additional loans.

Note from the above example that whenever a participant's loan balance reaches the $50,000 maximum, he would be precluded from any additional borrowings for the next one-year period, regardless of his current loan balance. For example, suppose Mr. A's maximum loan balance during 2005 had been $50,000, instead of $40,000. The $50,000 limit would be reduced by $50,000 minus $25,000, or $25,000. Thus, his maximum loan balance is $25,000, which is his current loan balance. Therefore, Mr. A could not borrow any additional funds until one year after his maximum balance was reduced below $50,000. Thus, this provision essentially eliminates the possibility of extending a loan by rolling over an old loan into a new one.

Repayment Terms. Code Sec. 72(p)(2)(B) requires that plan loans must be repaid within five years. If the term of a loan is five years or more, the entire amount of the loan is treated as a distribution.

Any loan used to acquire a principal residence is exempt from the five-year repayment requirement. However, a loan to improve an existing principal residence, refinance a principal residence loan (in general), or buy a second home is subject to the normal five-year repayment rule.

The loan payments must be substantially equal, and payable at least quarterly, over the term of the loan.[35] Thus, disallowed loans include those which provide for interest-only payments with a balloon payment at the end of the loan or demand loans. However, this level amortization requirement does not prevent repayment of loans prior to the end of the loan period (e.g., a plan could require full repayment upon termination of employment), nor does it prohibit the use of a variable interest rate.

Refinanced Loans. A participant may refinance a loan if (1) the original and new loans collectively satisfy the amount limitations, and (2) the original loan and the new loan each satisfy the repayment requirements. However, if an original loan is replaced by a new loan and the term of the new loan ends after the latest permissible term of the original loan, then the new loan and the original are both treated as outstanding on the date of the transaction. Thus, if the sum of the original loan and the new loan exceed the loan limit, part or all of the new loan results in a deemed distribution.[36]

> **Example (1):** Chris, a participant in Plan Y with a vested account balance of $150,000, borrows $40,000 from the Y plan on January 1, 2005, to be repaid in 20 quarterly installments (i.e., ending on December 31, 2009) of $2,491 each. On January 1, 2006, when the outstanding balance on the loan is $33,322, the loan is refinanced and is replaced by a new $40,000 loan from the plan to be repaid in 20 quarterly installments (i.e., ending on December 31, 2010) of $2,491 each.
>
> The maximum loan balance on January 1, 2006 cannot exceed $43,322, which is $50,000 reduced by $6,678 (the excess of

---

[35] Code Sec. 72(p)(2)(C).

[36] Reg. § 1.72(p)-1, Q&A 20.

the $40,000 maximum outstanding loan balance during 2005 over the $33,322 outstanding balance on January 1, 2006). However, because the term of the new loan ends later than the term of the original loan, both the new loan and the original loan balance must be taken into account for purposes of applying the $43,322 loan amount limitation. Accordingly, the sum of the new loan ($40,000) and the outstanding balance on January 1, 2006 of the original loan ($33,322) is $73,322. Since $73,322 exceeds the $43,322 limit by $30,000, Chris has a deemed distribution of $30,000 on January 1, 2006.

However, the regulations allow the new loan to be treated as consisting of two separate loans, i.e., the original loan that continues to be amortized in substantially level payments over its original term, and a new loan (to the extent the amount of the new loan exceeds the balance of the original loan) that is also amortized in substantially level payments over the new loan's term, thus avoiding the requirement to treat both loans as outstanding on the date of the transaction.

> **Example (2):** Refer to the preceding example. Under the terms of the new loan, the amount of the first 16 installments is $2,907, which is the sum of the $2,491 scheduled quarterly installment payment amount under the original loan, plus $416 (the amount required to repay, in level quarterly installments over five years beginning on January 1, 2006, the excess of the refinanced loan over the January 1, 2006 balance of the first loan ($40,000 − $33,322 = $6,678)), and the amount of the four remaining installments was equal to $416.
>
> The new loan may be treated as consisting of two qualifying loans, one of which is in the amount of the first loan ($33,322), amortized in substantially level payments over a period ending December 31, 2009 (the last day of the term of the first loan), and the other of which is in the additional amount ($6,678) borrowed under the new loan. Since the total of the two loans is $40,000 (which is less than the maximum balance of $43,322), no distribution is deemed made to Chris.

Of course, many loans are refinanced to take advantage of reduced interest rates, as well as extending the loan life or increasing the loan balance. Thus, despite the fact that the new loan payments may be below the original payments, the new loan can still be treated as two separate loans, resulting in the same conclusions as that reached in Example (2), i.e., no deemed distribution.

Other Provisions. Code Sec. 72(p)(3) imposes substantial limitations on the deductibility of interest payments (above the general limitations applicable to consumer interest deductions) on these loans by certain individuals. Any interest deduction, including interest on a loan which is used to acquire a principal residence of the participant, will be denied if the loan is either:

(1) made to a key employee (as defined in the top-heavy rules under Code Sec. 416(i)); or

(2) secured by amounts attributable to elective Code Sec. 401(k) or 403(b) deferrals.

The effect of this provision is to severely limit the attractiveness of loans from qualified plans, since the interest is not deductible.

.05 Exemption for Holding Qualifying Employer Securities and Real Property

One of the transactions prohibited under ERISA Sec. 406 is the acquisition of any employer security or employer real property which is not "qualified." The term "qualified employer security" refers to stock or marketable obligations (bonds, debentures, notes, certificates, or other evidence of indebtedness) issued by the employer whose employees are covered by the plan, or by an affiliate of the employer. The term "qualifying employer real property" means real property (and related personal property) which is leased to an employer (or an affiliate). The parcels of real property must be dispersed geographically and adaptable for more than one use.[37]

In the case of a plan other than an "eligible individual account plan," stock is considered a qualifying employer security only if (1) not more than 25 percent of the aggregate stock of the same class outstanding at the time of acquisition by the plan is held by the plan, (2) at least 50 percent of the aggregate amount of the stock is held by persons independent of the issuer; and (3) not more than 25 percent of the assets of the plan may be invested in obligations of the employer.[38]

In addition to this prohibition, ERISA Sec. 407 prohibits the acquisition of any qualifying employer security or qualifying employer real property, if immediately after the acquisition the aggregate fair market value of all employer securities and employer real property held by the plan exceeds 10 percent of the fair market value of the assets of the plan.[39] However, this percentage limitation does not apply to an "eligible individual account plan."

An eligible individual account plan includes a profit-sharing, stock bonus, thrift or savings plan, an ESOP, or a money purchase pension plan which was invested primarily in qualifying employer

---

[37] ERISA Sec. 407(d).
[38] ERISA Sec. 407(d)(5) and (f).

[39] ERISA Sec. 407(a)(2).

securities on the date of the enactment of ERISA (September 2, 1974). However, ERISA requires that the portion of a 401(k) plan consisting of employee elective deferrals must be treated as a separate plan, subject to the 10 percent limitation, if more than 1 percent of deferrable compensation is required to be invested in employer securities or employer real property.[40] (Note, however, that this provision was added in 1997. Any elective deferrals that were invested in qualified employer securities and/or qualified employer real property before January 1, 1999 were grandfathered and not subject to the 10 percent restrictions.[41])

Thus, the restriction applies to defined benefit pension plans, money purchase pension plans (other than those which did not meet the above requirements), IRAs, and post-1998 elective deferrals in a 401(k) plan. However, if a plan that would otherwise be an eligible individual account plan has its benefits taken into account in determining the benefits payable to a participant under any defined benefit plan, the plan will not be considered an eligible individual account plan.[42]

In order for a plan to be treated as an eligible individual account plan (i.e., the plan is allowed to hold more than ten percent of its assets in the form of qualifying employer real property or qualifying employer securities), it must explicitly provide for acquisition and holding of such assets in excess of the limit.[43] Any arrangement established after December 17, 1987, consisting of a defined benefit plan and a plan that would otherwise be an individual account plan, but for the fact that the individual account plan is taken into account in determining the benefits payable to a participant under the defined benefit plan (i.e., a floor-offset arrangement), will be treated as a single plan for purposes of the ten percent limit.[44]

To qualify an acquisition or sale by a plan of qualifying employer securities or the acquisition, sale or lease by a plan of qualifying employer real property as an exemption, the following requirements must be met:

(1) the acquisition, sale, or lease must be for adequate consideration;

(2) no commission can be charged; and

(3) the plan must either be an eligible individual account plan or the acquisition or lease must not violate the ten percent limit imposed under ERISA Sec. 407.[45]

---

[40] ERISA Sec. 407(b).
[41] EGTRRA Sec. 655(a), amending Sec. 1524 of the Taxpayer Relief Act of 1997.
[42] ERISA Sec. 407(d).

[43] ERISA Sec. 407(d)(3)(B).
[44] ERISA Sec. 407(d).
[45] ERISA Sec. 408(e).

Despite this exception for eligible individual account plans to hold employer stock, fiduciaries may still have a responsibility to limit investment in company stock if the fiduciary knows (or should know) the investment is unsuitable. For example, in *Moench v. Robertson*,[46] a fiduciary was held liable for failure to diversify the trust investments in an ESOP when the company's financial condition was rapidly deteriorating, despite the fact that the terms of the plan required a primary investment in company stock.

---

[46] CA-3, 62 F3d 553 (1995).

Chapter 13

Reporting and Disclosure

¶1301 Introduction

In seeking to protect the rights of participants and their beneficiaries under employee benefit plans, ERISA imposes several reporting and disclosure requirements on the plan administrators. Since ERISA divided the jurisdiction over employee benefit plans among the IRS, the Department of Labor (DOL), and the Pension Benefit Guaranty Corporation (PBGC), certain reporting requirements are required by all three entities. In addition, ERISA requires that certain disclosures concerning benefits be provided or made available to plan participants and beneficiaries. The purpose of this chapter is to provide a review of these reporting and disclosure requirements.

Employee pension benefit plans, welfare benefit plans, and fringe benefit plans all fall within these ERISA reporting requirements. Under the definitions provided in ERISA Sec. 3, the following types of plans are affected by the requirements:

Pension Benefit Plans:	Defined benefit pension plans
	Money purchase pension plans
	Profit-sharing plans
	Stock bonus plans
	ESOPs
	Thrift and savings plans
Welfare Benefit Plans:	Life insurance plans
	Medical/hospital/surgical plans
	Dental plans
	Disability insurance plans
	Accident insurance plans
	Supplemental unemployment payment plans
	Funded scholarship plans
	Prepaid legal services plans
	Dependent care plans
Fringe Benefit Plans:	Cafeteria plans (Code Sec. 125)
	Education assistance programs (Code Sec. 127)
	Adoption assistance programs (Code Sec. 137)

Certain plans are statutorily excluded from ERISA coverage. These include government plans, church plans not electing coverage under Code Sec. 410(d), plans maintained to comply with workers' compensation, unemployment compensation or disability laws, qualified foreign plans, and unfunded excess benefit plans.[1] In addition, several other plans are exempt under Department of Labor Regulations, including certain employer practices and arrangements which do not meet the definition of a welfare plan, unfunded pension benefit plans, unfunded or fully insured welfare benefit plans, IRAs, SEPs, health plans that participate in a group insurance arrangement, SIMPLE IRAs, and tax-sheltered annuities.

As mentioned above, ERISA requires reporting to the IRS, the DOL, and the PBGC, as well as disclosure to plan participants and beneficiaries. To reduce duplication of reporting, the IRS, DOL, and PBGC have designed consolidated annual return/report forms. These annual report forms, which are filed with DOL's Employee Benefit Security Administration (EBSA), satisfy the annual reporting requirements of all three government agencies. However, these agencies may require special reports if certain events occur. Accordingly, the reporting requirements of each of these agencies is discussed below. In addition, the ERISA requirements for disclosure to plan participants and beneficiaries is discussed.

---

[1] ERISA Sec. 4(b).

More detailed reporting information is available in the EBSA's *Reporting and Disclosure Guide for Employee Benefit Plans.* The guide provides information and overview charts on basic ERISA disclosures; PBGC reporting and disclosure requirements for single-employer defined benefit pension plans; and annual reporting requirements for Form 5500 and Form M-1. The guide also contains a list of EBSA and PBGC resources, including agency web sites that contain laws, regulations and other guidance relating to ERISA's reporting and disclosure requirements.

¶1302 Reporting to the IRS

The plan administrator must file certain information with the IRS with respect to the financial condition of the plan and, if a determination letter is sought, regarding the qualification and operations of the plan.

.01 Setting Up the Plan—Determination Letters

An advance determination letter is not required to secure the qualification of a plan. However, it is generally advisable to obtain an advance ruling from the IRS prior to the establishment of the plan, as receiving a favorable determination letter provides the employer with assurance that the plan is qualified under Code Sec. 401(a) and the trust is exempt under Code Sec. 501(a). The 5300 series of forms are used to obtain an IRS determination letter regarding the status of a newly adopted plan. These include:

Form Number	Type of Plan
5300	Individually designed defined benefit or defined contribution plan.
5307	Short-form application for an employer who has a previously qualified master or prototype plan.
5309	ESOP

The IRS issues an annual revenue procedure that provides detailed guidelines for filing for determination letters on the qualified status of the plan and the status for exemption of any related trusts or custodial accounts.[2] Over the past few years, the IRS has simplified the application procedures for determination letters for qualified plans. Employers can now elect to have a plan reviewed for compliance with the form requirements only or both the form requirements and the coverage and nondiscrimination requirements.

---

[2] *See,* e.g., Rev. Proc. 2005-6, IRB 2005-1, 200.

Certain information is required for all determination letter applications. A complete copy of the plan and the trust instrument must be filed if the plan is not an IRS-approved prototype plan. Schedule Q, Nondiscrimination Requirements, must be attached to Forms 5300 or 5307 only if the employer wants a determination letter that relates to certain coverage and nondiscrimination requirements.

Form 8717, User Fees for Employer Plan Determination Letter Request, accompanies any application form. Because the IRS allows applicants to modify the scope of a determination letter request and the type of review for the plan, a graduated user fee schedule is provided on Form 8717. Depending on the nature of the request, fees can cost hundreds or thousands of dollars. (The IRS provides an annual schedule of user fees for various types of determination letter requests.[3]) However, certain small employer pension benefit plans are not required to pay a user fee for certain determination letter requests. In general terms, these plans are sponsored by employers with no more than 100 employees who received at least $5,000 in compensation from the employer in the preceding year and have at least one employee participating in the plan who is not a highly compensated employee (as defined in Chapter 6).[4]

Note that standardized prototype plans typically need not be filed with the IRS for approval since, by their terms, they cannot violate the qualification requirements.

.02 Annual Reports

No annual reports are required to be filed directly with the IRS. Instead, information from the Form 5500 series (which is technically an IRS-produced form) which are filed with the DOL's Employee Benefit Security Administration is forwarded to the IRS. (In prior years, Form 5500 was filed with the IRS.)

.03 Distributions and Withholding

Withholding is required on any distribution from a qualified retirement plan that is not transferred directly to another qualified retirement plan or IRA. Periodic payments (annuities) are subject to withholding as if the payments were wages paid by an employer to an employee for the appropriate payroll period.[5] Nonperiodic distributions are subject to a flat withholding rate of 10 percent, except that "eligible rollover distributions" (see Chapter 9) are subject to a 20 percent withholding rate.[6]

---

[3] *See* e.g., Rev. Proc. 2005-8, IRB 2005-1, 243.
[4] Notice 2002-1, 2002-1 CB 283.

[5] Code Sec. 3405(a).
[6] Code Sec. 3405(b) and (c).

Information concerning distributions from qualified retirement plans, both periodic and nonperiodic, is reported on Form 1099-R. Form 1099-R must be filed with the IRS no later than February 28 of the year following the calendar year in which the payments were made. Information concerning employee contributions and the capital gain and ordinary income portions of distributions is also required.

.04 Plan Amendments

A determination letter may be requested from the IRS for minor amendments to a plan (including some corrections of plan document or operational failures) on which a favorable determination letter has been issued. This request is filed on Form 6406, Short Form Application for Determination for Amendment of Employment Benefit Plan. The entire plan need not be submitted with the request. Instead, the plan amendments and an explanation of the effects of the amendments must be submitted, as well as a copy of the latest determination letter.

Determination letter requests for plan amendments that involve a significant change to plan benefits or coverage, or that may affect other portions of the plan so as to cause disqualification, should be filed on the appropriate Form 5300 series.

.05 Other Reports

Form 5310 (Application for Determination For Terminating Plan). A Form 5310 is filed in connection with a termination of a qualified retirement plan to receive an IRS determination letter with respect to the plan's qualified status upon its termination. The Schedule Q (Form 5300), Nondiscrimination Requirements, must accompany Form 5310. Form 6088, Distributable Benefits from Employee Pension Benefit Plans, is also required to report accrued benefits payable to participants in the terminating plan.

Form 5310-A (Notice of Plan Merger or Consolidation, Spin-off, or Transfer of Plan Assets or Liabilities; Notice of Qualified Separate Lines of Business). Form 5310-A is filed at least 30 days before assets are transferred from one qualified plan to another in connection with a merger or consolidation, or a transfer of plan assets or liabilities. Filing is imposed on plan administrators of the transferor plan *and* the recipient plan. Filing is not required if the transfer is in compliance with Reg. § 1.414(1)-1(d), (h), (m), or (n)(2). Form 5310-A is also used to provide notice to the IRS that the employer is applying the separate line of business (SLOB) rules. The filing date for SLOB notification is the later of ten-and-a-half months after the close of the testing year or October 15 of the year after the close of the testing year.

Form 5330 (Return of Excise Taxes Related to Employee Benefit Plans). Form 5330 is used to report and pay excise taxes resulting from various penalty provisions, such as a minimum funding deficiency (Code Sec. 4971), nondeductible contribution to a qualified plan (Code Sec. 4972), prohibited transaction (Code Sec. 4975), reversion of plan assets to employers (Code Sec. 4980), as well as several other penalty taxes.

¶ 1303 Reporting to the Department of Labor

The U.S. Department of Labor's Employee Benefits Security Administration (EBSA) is the agency charged with reporting and disclosure of plan information under Title I of ERISA. While TRA '97 eliminated the requirement that plan administrators automatically file certain documents, such as summary plan descriptions and summaries of material modifications with the DOL, these documents (and others, such as the trust agreement) must be furnished to the DOL upon request.[7] If any documents are not provided within 30 days of the request, the plan administrator may be subject to a civil penalty of up to $110 per day (up to $1,100 per request). However, no penalty will be imposed if a failure to provide a requested document results from matters reasonably beyond the plan administrator's control.[8]

.01 Setting Up the Plan

Upon establishing a plan, the plan administrator must prepare a Summary Plan Description (SPD). The SPD, which is a booklet given to plan participants and beneficiaries, informs them of their benefits under the plan. The specific contents of the SPD are discussed under the disclosures to participants section later in this chapter.

.02 Annual Reports

The 5500 series of forms must be filed annually with the Employeee Benefits Security Administration (EBSA) division of the DOL by all nonexempt pension benefit, welfare benefit, and fringe benefit plans. As mentioned earlier, this set of forms satisfies the annual reporting requirements of the IRS, DOL, and PBGC. The EBSA processes the reports and provides information from the reports to the IRS and PBGC for use in enforcement and other

---

[7] ERISA Sec. 104(a)(6).   [8] ERISA Sec. 502(c)(6).

program activities. (In prior years, the annual Form 5500 was filed with the IRS.

The Form 5500 annual report consists of the main Form 5500 and, depending on the type of filer, one or more of 13 schedules. These forms contain information concerning the plan's qualification, operations, and financial condition.

Each of the 5500 series is due by the end of the seventh month after the plan year-end (July 31 for calendar-year plans). An automatic extension of two-and-a-half months may be obtained by filing Form 5558 with the IRS by the normal due date. The DOL can assess a civil penalty of up to $1,100 per day against the plan administrator for his failure or refusal to file an annual report. An annual report that has been rejected by the DOL is treated as not having been filed for purposes of this penalty.[9]

The specific forms are:

Form Number	Description
5500	*Annual Return/Report of Employee Benefit Plan.* This form is filed by an employee benefit plan with more than 100 participants. It is required to be filed annually.
5500-C/R	*Return/Report of Employee Benefit Plan.* This combined form is filed by an employee benefit plan with fewer than 100 participants. The Form 5500-C part must be filed for the first and final plan years. Additionally, it is filed once every three years. The Form 5500-R part is basically a condensed version of Form 5500-C that is filed in the two years between the normal Form 5500-C filings. An exception exists for plans with 80 to 120 participants. Generally, under the filing requirements explained above, if the number of plan participants increases from under 100 to 100 or more, or decreases from 100 or more to under 100, from one year to the next, the plan administrator would file Form 5500 instead of a 5500-C. However, the same form which was filed in the previous year may be filed in the current year, provided that at the beginning of the plan year, the plan had at least 80 participants, but not more than 120.[10]

---

[9] ERISA Sec. 502(c).   [10] DOL Reg. § 2520.103-1(d).

5500-EZ	*Annual Return of One-Participant Retirement Plan.* This form is filed annually by a one-participant pension benefit plan. A one-participant pension benefit plan is a pension benefit plan that covers only an individual (or an individual and his/her spouse) who owns a trade or business, whether incorporated or not. In the case of a partnership, a one-participant plan is one which covers only the partners (or the partners and their spouses). A pension benefit plan includes defined benefit, money purchase, profit-sharing, stock bonus, ESOP, and 401(k) plans. In order to file this simplified version of Form 5500, the one-participant plan must also meet the minimum coverage requirements of Code Section 410(b) without being combined with another plan maintained by the employer. Form 5500-EZ cannot be used if the plan covers a business that is a member of an affiliated group, a member of a controlled group of corporations, or a member of a group of corporations under common control. Note, however, that no Form 5500-EZ (or any other form) is required if a one-participant plan has *never* had more than $100,000 in plan assets at plan year-end. This $100,000 limit applies to aggregate assets, if an employer maintains two or more one-participant plans.[11]

Schedules. In addition to the appropriate 5500 form, certain schedules must accompany the annual report. The contents of the more commonly used schedules are outlined below.

Schedule	Description
A	*Insurance Information.* If some or all of the benefits under the plan are purchased from and guaranteed by an insurance company or similar organization (such as Blue Cross/Blue Shield or an HMO), this schedule must be filed with the appropriate 5500 form. In general, this schedule summarizes premium rate and claim payments for each carrier. Schedule A is not required for a one-participant plan (as defined earlier), filed on Form 5500EZ.

---

[11] Form 5500-EZ, Instructions.

¶ 1303.02

B	*Actuarial Information.* This schedule is required to accompany the appropriate 5500 form for a defined benefit plan which is subject to the minimum funding standards of Code Sec. 412. An enrolled actuary must prepare and certify the detailed actuarial information contained in the report. Included in the report is such information as the value of assets at the beginning of the plan year, the present value of vested and nonvested benefits, contributions made during the year, the funding standard account, the actuarial cost method, and the assumptions used.
E	*ESOP Annual Information.* This schedule is required for all ESOPs.
H or I	*Financial Information.* Schedule H is required for large plans (those with 100 or more participants), while Schedule I is required for small plans (those with fewer than 100 participants).
P	*Annual Return of Fiduciary of Employee Benefit Trust.* A fiduciary (trustee or custodian) may file this schedule as an attachment to the 5500 form. This form starts the running of the statute of limitations on the collection of taxes which may be due from the plan.[12]
R	*Retirement Plan Information.* This schedule is required for defined benefit plans or plans otherwise subject to Code Sec. 412.
SSA	*Annual Registration Statement Identifying Separated Participants with Deferred Vested Benefits.* This schedule lists any plan participants who have separated from service with a deferred vested benefit that was neither paid nor forfeited.
T	*Qualified Pension Plan Coverage Information.* This schedule is required unless the plan is permitted to rely on coverage testing information for the prior year.
Audited Financial Statements	ERISA Sec. 103(a) requires separate financial statements to be filed with the Form 5500 (i.e., for plans with 100 or more participants) which must be audited by an independent qualified public accountant. These plans must file the statements and the accountant's audit report. Audited financial statements are not required for small plans.

---

[12] Code Sec. 6501(a).

.03 Amendments

If requested by the DOL, the plan administrator must file a summary of material modifications (SMM) for any changes that are not contained in the summary plan description. Automatic filing with the DOL is not required.

¶ 1304 Reporting to the PBGC

As discussed in Chapter 6, the PBGC provides termination insurance for most defined benefit pension plans. The filing requirements for these defined benefit pension plans fall into three categories: the filing for the payment of premiums to the PBGC, the reporting of certain events required by the PBGC, and the notification of the intent to terminate a plan.

.01 Premium Payments

An annual return for the payment of termination insurance premiums is required for all defined benefit plans subject to PBGC insurance. The premium for PBGC coverage for single-employer pension plans consists of a flat-rate premium of $19 per participant, plus a variable-rate premium of $9 for each $1,000 of unfunded vested benefits as of the end of the preceding plan year.

> **Example:** Plan A covers 20 participants and has unfunded vested benefits totaling $200,000 on the last day of its preceding plan year. Plan A's premium would total $2,180, consisting of a flat-rate premium of $380 (20 participants × $19) and a variable-rate premium of $1,800 ([$200,000/$1,000] × $9).

The premium is filed and paid with PBGC Form 1, Annual Premium Payment. Certain single employer plans are exempt from the variable rate premium and file Form 1-EZ instead of Form 1. A single employer plan is exempt from the variable rate premium only if it is one of the following:

- a plan with no vested participants;
- a Code Sec 412(i) plan;
- a fully-funded plan that has fewer than 500 participants;
- a plan terminating in a standard termination; or
- a plan at the full funding limit for the preceding plan year.

The due date for filing and payment depends upon the size of the plan.

Large Plans. For single-employer plans with 500 or more participants as of the end of the prior year, the plan administrator must file PBGC Form 1-ES with an estimated or final participant count and pay the flat-rate premium by the last day of the second month following the close of the previous plan year. (This date is referred to by the PBGC as the first filing due date.) The plan administrator must then file PBGC Form 1 or Form 1-EZ and pay the variable-rate premium and any unpaid flat-rate premium within nine-and-a-half months after the plan year-end. (This date is referred to by the PBGC as the "final filing due date.")

Small Plans. Defined benefit pension plans with fewer than 500 participants are not required to make the flat rate premium filing and payment by the first filing due date. Instead, small plans file PBGC Form 1-EZ or Form 1 and pay the entire premium by the final filing due date (nine-and-a-half months after plan year-end).

New Plans. Regardless of the number of participants, a new plan must file PBGC Form 1 or Form 1-EZ and pay the premium by the latest of the following dates:

(1) the 15th day of the 10th calendar month following (a) the *beginning* of the plan year, or (b) the date the plan became effective for benefit accruals from future service; or

(2) 90 days after (a) the date of the plan adoption or (b) the date the plan became covered under ERISA Sec. 4021.

Penalties for Underpayment of Premiums. If the premium amount due for a plan year is paid after its due date, or, in the case of large plans, is underpaid on the first filing due date, the plan may be assessed late payment interest and penalty charges. Interest charges accrue at the rate imposed under Code Sec. 6601(a) and cannot be waived. The penalty rate is equal to five percent of the unpaid premium per month, up to 100 percent of the unpaid premium. (This penalty rate drops to only one percent per month if the late payment is made on or before the date when the PBGC issues a premium invoice, a past-due filing notice, or a letter indicating an audit.) However, a large plan will not incur a late payment penalty charge (but will still incur a late payment interest charge) if the premium paid by the first filing due date is at least 90 percent of the full premium ultimately due for the plan year or is at least based on the participant count reported on its previous PBGC Form 1 filing.

.02 Reportable Events

In addition to the normal annual report filed with the IRS on the IRS/DOL/PBGC 5500 series of forms, defined benefit pension plan administrators are required to file with the PBGC a notice of certain reportable events. Generally, these events signal potential problems with the plan or sponsoring employer. The notice must contain information about the plan, the plan administrator, contributing employers and any affiliated companies, and a description of the event.[13]

Post-Event Notice. The plan administrator and each contributing sponsor of a plan for which a reportable event has occurred must file a post-event reportable event notice with PBGC. PBGC Form 10 (*Post-Event Notice of Reportable Event*) is used to provide this notice, which must be filed within 30 days after the plan administrator or contributing sponsor knows, or has reason to know, that a reportable event has occurred. For the following cases, notice must be given to the PBGC within the 30-day period after the occurence of any of the following events:

- a 20 percent reduction in active participants;
- the failure to make minimum funding payments;
- the inability to pay benefits when due;
- excess distributions to a substantial owner within a 12-month period;
- a transfer of 3 percent or more of benefit liabilities outside the controlled group;
- an application for minimum funding waiver;
- a transaction involving a change in the contributing sponsor or controlled group;
- the liquidation or dissolution of a contributing sponsor or a controlled group member;
- the declaration of an extraordinary dividend or stock redemption;
- a loan default of $10 million or more; and
- bankruptcy, insolvency, or similar settlements with creditors.

Advance Notice. ERISA also requires that certain contributing sponsors notify PBGC at least 30 days in advance of certain reportable events. This advance notice requirement applies *only* to

---

[13] PBGC Reg. §§ 2615.3 through 2615.23

¶ 1304.02

non-public companies that (1) are members of a controlled group whose plans have aggregate unfunded vested benefits of more than $50 million and an aggregate funded vested benefit percentage of less than 90 percent; and (2) are reporting about events relating to themselves or other companies in the group. PBGC Form 10-Advance (*Advance Notice of Reportable Event*) is used for this purpose. For the following cases, notice must be given to the PBGC within the 30-day period before any of the following events:

- a change in contributing sponsor or controlled group;
- liquidation of contributing sponsor or controlled group member;
- extraordinary dividend or stock redemption;
- transfer of benefit liabilities;
- application for minimum funding waiver;
- loan default; or
- bankruptcy or similar settlement.

Notice of Failure to Make Required Contributions. In the event that a plan's funded current liability percentage (see ¶ 804 for discussion) is less than 100 percent, the plan has a lien on the contributing sponsor's assets. ERISA Sec. 302(f)(4)(A) and Code Sec. 412(n)(4)(A) require that the PBGC be notified whenever there is a failure to make a required payment and the total of unpaid balances (including interest) exceeds $1 million. Form 200 (*Notice of Failure to Make Required Contributions Over $1 Million*) is used to provide such notice to the PBGC. The Form 200 notice must be provided within 10 days of the due date for the required payment.

.03 Notice of Intent to Terminate

Under ERISA, only two types of voluntary terminations are allowed for single employer plans covered by the PBGC: standard terminations and distress terminations.

A standard termination occurs when a plan has sufficient assets to pay all "benefit liabilities" under the plan (these generally include all nonforfeitable benefits, including early retirement supplements or subsidies and plant closing benefits). A plan's benefit liability includes all benefit obligations to employees, both fixed and contingent (as defined in Code Sec. 401(a)(2)). This includes those liabilities that vest solely due to plan termination and other contingent benefits for which a participant has not satisfied all of the conditions for entitlement prior to termination (e.g., early retirement benefits).[14]

---

[14] ERISA Sec. 4041(b)(1)(D).

In the case of a standard termination, the plan administrator must issue a Notice of Intent to Terminate (NOIT) to affected parties other than PBGC (e.g., participants, beneficiaries) at least 60 days and not more than 90 days before the proposed termination date. (PBGC has developed a model NOIT that may be used or adapted by a plan administrator.) The NOIT is followed by a Notice of Plan Benefits, which describes the amounts and forms of participants' benefits payable at the proposed termination date. The plan administrator must file Form 500, Standard Termination Notice/Single-Employer Plan Termination, within 180 days after the proposed termination date. Form 500 contains an enrolled actuary's certification (Schedule EA-S) that the plan is projected to be sufficient for all benefit commitments as of the proposed date of final distribution of plan assets. However, this certification by the enrolled actuary is not required in the case of a standard or distress termination of plans funded exclusively by individual insurance contracts. PBGC Form 501, Post-Distribution Certification for Standard Terminations, must be filed within 30 days of the final distribution of plan assets. If the plan administrator fails to comply with the filing and notice requirements or to meet the deadlines, it may cause the proposed termination to be nullified, which could require the entire process to be restarted.

A distress termination occurs if the plan does not have sufficient assets to pay all benefit commitments under the plan and certain distress criteria are met. These criteria require the sponsor employer and each substantial member of the same controlled group (a five-percent owner of the entire controlled group) to meet one of the following: (1) it is involved in liquidation under bankruptcy, or insolvency proceedings; (2) it is involved in reorganization under bankruptcy or insolvency proceedings; (3) it is unable to pay debts and continue operating; or (4) the pension costs are unreasonably burdensome. The distress criteria must be satisfied as of the proposed date of plan termination. The PBGC determines whether any of these criteria are met. If a distress.termination is requested because of bankruptcy or insolvency proceedings, the bankruptcy or other appropriate court must determine that the employer will be unable to pay its debts when due or will be unable to continue in business if the plan is not terminated. In addition, the bankruptcy judge must approve the termination.[15]

In the case of a distress termination, the plan administrator must give written notice of intent to termination (NOIT) to affected

---

[15] ERISA Sec. 4041(c)(2).

¶ 1304.03

parties and to PBGC on PBGC Form 600, Distress Termination/Notice of Intent to Terminate, which includes the proposed termination date, to the PBGC at least 60 days and not more than 90 days before the proposed termination date. If the PBGC determines that the termination may proceed, the plan administrator must submit a second notice to the PBGC on PBGC Form 601, Distress Termination Notice/Single-Employer Plan Termination, within 120 days after the proposed termination date. Form 601 contains information sufficient to enable the PBGC to determine that the criteria for a distress termination are met as of the proposed termination date and, if applicable, the proposed distribution date. In addition, it must contain an enrolled actuary's certification concerning the degree to which the plan is funded, i.e., whether, as of the proposed termination date, the plan is sufficient for benefit commitments, guaranteed benefits, or neither. However, this certification is not required to be furnished if the PBGC determines that it is not necessary for purposes of its determination relating to plan sufficiency for guaranteed benefits and benefit liabilities, or for purposes of plan sponsor liability. After the plan administrator receives PBGC approval, benefits may be distributed. A post-distribution certificate must be filed on PBGC Form 602 within 30 days of the final distribution of plan assets.

¶ 1305   Disclosure Requirements to Participants and Beneficiaries

Plan administrators have a duty to disclose certain information to participants and beneficiaries. Some disclosures must be automatically furnished, while other disclosures are required only upon a participant's request. In addition, administrators must make certain materials available to participants for inspection.

.01   Setting Up the Plan

Prior to filing a request with the IRS for a determination letter for the adoption of a qualified pension, profit-sharing, or stock bonus plan, a "notice to interested parties" must be made. Interested parties generally include all employees who are eligible to participate in the plan and all other present employees who have the same place of business as any employee who is eligible to participate.[16] (For a determination letter which involves an amendment to the plan, "interested parties" also includes beneficiaries receiving benefits.)[17] The notice may be

---

[16] Reg. § 1.7476-1.   [17] Reg. § 1.7476-2.

given by posting or in person within 7 to 21 days prior to the filing for a determination, or by mailing within 10 to 24 days prior to the filing. It may be provided separately or by printing in an employer publication that is distributed in such a manner as to be reasonably available to employees. Proposed regulations permit greater flexibility in the manner in which this notice must be given, by allowing that the notice may be provided by any method (e.g., e-mail) that reasonably ensures that all interested parties will receive it.[18]

Information required in the notice to interested parties includes a description identifying the class(es) of eligible employees, the name of the plan, the name and identification of the plan administrator, the name and identification of the sponsor, a statement as to the type of determination letter requested (e.g., initial, amendment, termination), and the procedure under which any interested party may submit comments concerning the determination letter request. The annual IRS procedure[19] discusses the information which is required in the notice and provides a model notice of interested parties which may be used.

.02 Summary Plan Description

ERISA Sec. 102(a) requires that a summary plan description (SPD) of any employee benefit plan must be furnished to participants and beneficiaries. Each participant and each beneficiary receiving benefits under the plan must be furnished with a copy of the SPD within 90 days after he becomes a participant (or starts receiving benefits) or if later, within 120 days after the plan is established.[20]

Basically, the SPD is the employee booklet which describes the major features of each plan. It must be written in a manner calculated to be understood by the average plan participant and must be sufficiently comprehensive to apprise the plan's participants and beneficiaries of their rights and obligations under the plan. Thus, the administrator must consider such factors as the level of comprehension and education of typical participants in the plan and the complexity of the terms of the plan. If enough participants do not speak English, the SPD must include a prominent notice in the familiar language offering assistance in understanding the plan.[21]

The Labor Regulations specifically identify the required contents of the SPD. This information must accurately reflect the contents of the plan as of a date not earlier than 120 days prior to the date that the SPD is disclosed. The following information must

---

[18] Prop. Reg. § 1.7476-2(c).
[19] *See.* e.g., Rev. Proc. 2005-6, IRB 2005-1, 200.
[20] ERISA Sec. 104(b)(1).
[21] DOL Reg. § 2520.102-2.

be included:[22]

(1) the name and type (e.g., profit-sharing, defined benefit) of the plan, including the type of administration of the plan (e.g., insurer administration);

(2) the name, address, and employer identification number of the plan sponsor;

(3) the names and addresses of the plan administrator, trustees, and legal agent;

(4) the plan's requirements with respect to eligibility for participation and benefits;

(5) a statement describing any joint or survivor benefits provided under the plan;

(6) a statement clearly identifying circumstances which may result in disqualification, ineligibility, and forfeiture of benefits;

(7) a description of plan provisions for determining vesting of benefits;

(8) a statement as to whether benefits under a pension plan are guaranteed by the PBGC;

(9) how the plan will be funded (e.g., by employer contributions only or partly by employee contributions), and the identity of the funding medium used to accumulate the assets through which benefits are provided (e.g., trust fund, insurance company); and

(10) the procedures for claiming benefits under the plan and the remedies available if claims are denied in part or in whole.

An updated SPD that integrates all plan amendments must be furnished to each plan participant and to each beneficiary receiving benefits every five years.

.03 Summary Annual Report

A Summary Annual Report (SAR) must be provided annually to all participants and beneficiaries receiving benefits under the plan. The SAR summarizes the plan's financial information which is reported on the appropriate Form 5500 Annual Report. It must be furnished to participants within nine months after the close of the plan year. In practice, the SAR is typically attached to each participant's most recent benefit statement. The SAR must contain the same information prescribed on a model form at DOL Reg. sec. 2520.104b-10(d). (Any portion of the model form which is not applicable to the plan may be omitted.) For years in which a Form 5500-R was filed (by firms with fewer than 100 participants), either a copy of

---

[22] DOL Reg. § 2520.102-3.

the Form 5500-R filed on behalf of the plan or a written notice stating that a copy will be furnished free of charge upon receipt of a written request must be furnished to plan participants and beneficiaries. Employers whose plans are funded below 70 percent of the current liability must include a statement in the annual reports of the extent to which the plan is funded.[23]

.04 Plan Amendments

Any significant plan amendments which have occurred since the last summary plan description must be furnished to participants and beneficiaries in the form of a summary of material modifications (SMM). As with the SPD, the SMM must be written in a manner which is understandable to the average plan participant. It must be furnished within seven months after the close of the plan year in which the modification was adopted, unless the modification is already incorporated in a new SPD.[24]

Although the regulations do not specify what changes are considered to be material, some guidance was provided in Form EBS-1 (was now-discontinued form which was used to file the plan description with the DOL). According to the EBS-1, a material modification included changes in the name and address of the plan sponsor, administrator, and fiduciaries; the name or type of the plan; eligibility requirements and vesting provisions; benefit accrual; break-in-service rules; circumstances that cause a loss of benefits; and the procedure for presenting claims.

In the event that a plan is amended to significantly reduce the rate of future benefit accruals, a special notification is required. This notice, typically referred to as the "204(h) notice," is required for any amendment to a defined benefit plan or money purchase plan which provides for a significant reduction in the rate of future benefit accruals, including amendments which reduce any early retirement benefit or retirement-type subsidy. The plan administrator must provide written notice to each participant, beneficiary, and employee organization representing affected participants and beneficiaries whose rate of future benefit accrual is reasonably expected to be significantly reduced by the amendment. The content of the notice must be sufficient to allow the recipient to determine the approximate magnitude of the reduction that applies to him or her (e.g., by including illustrative examples satisfying certain conditions contained in the regulations or by providing individualized statements).[25] This statement must generally be provided at least 45 days

---

[23] ERISA Sec. 103(d)(10).
[24] DOL Reg. § 2520.104b-3(a).

[25] Reg. § 54.4980F-1. Q&A 11.

before the effective date of the amendment; however, a 15-day period is permitted for small plans and multiemployer plans, as well as for amendments in connection with an acquisition or disposition.[26]

If the notice requirements are not met, the employer may be liable for an excise tax of $100 per day of noncompliance, per participant or beneficiary affected, up to a maximum of $500,000. (The plan is liable for the excise tax in the case of a multiemployer plan.[27]) In addition, if any failure to provide the notice is determined to be "egregious," affected participants and beneficiaries will be entitled to the greater of (1) the benefits to which they would have been entitled without the amendment; or (2) the benefits under the plan to which they would have been entitled under the amendments. An egregious failure occurs if the failure is within the control of the plan sponsor and either: (1) the failure is intentional, including failures to promptly provide the notice after an unintentional failure is discovered; or (2) the failure is one in which most of the affected individuals were not provided with most of the information they were entitled to receive.[28]

.05   Other Required Disclosures for Participants

Distribution Forms. As discussed above, the plan administrator must file returns with the IRS or Social Security Administration to disclose any distributions made for a calendar year. Form 1099-R is used to report annuity distributions and lump-sum distributions from retirement plans. In addition to actual distributions, amounts includible as deemed distributions from plan loans are reported on Form 1099-R.[29] A Form 1099-R must be provided to recipients by January 31 of the year following the calendar year in which the distributions were made.

In addition to the above forms, Code Sec. 402(f) requires plan administrators to give recipients of lump-sum distributions a written explanation of the rules relating to the taxation of the amounts, including the availability of the direct rollover option, the provision requiring 20 percent withholding if a direct rollover is not elected, the rules permitting employees to rollover a distribution within 60 days of receipt, and the availability of capital gains treatment and averaging. This notice must generally be provided to distributees no less than 30 days and no more than 90 days before the date of the distribution. These notices may also be provided through an electronic medium, such as e-mail. EGTRRA requires that the notice

---

[26] Reg. § 54.4980F-1, Q&A 9.

[27] Code Sec. 4980F(b)-(d).

[28] ERISA Sec. 204(h)(6); Reg. § 54.4980F-1, Q&A 14.

[29] Prop. Reg. § 1.72(p)-1, Q&A 14.

include an explanation of the potential restrictions and tax consequences that may apply to distributions from a new plan to which a
distribution is rolled over from the plan making the distribution. It
is anticipated that the IRS will update its model 402(f) notice (Notice
92–48[30]) to reflect this new explanation.

Survivor Annuities. As discussed in Chapter 6, any qualified
retirement plan that provides a benefit in the form of an annuity
must provide that annuity in the form of a qualified joint and survivor annuity (QJSA) and a qualified pre-retirement survivor
annuity (QPSA). A qualified plan must furnish a notice to participants indicating their right to waive the QJSA and QPSA (which
must also have spousal consent). The notices must be made: in the
case of the QJSA, within a reasonable period of time before the
annuity starting date; and in the case of the QPSA, within the period
beginning on the first day of the plan year in which the participant
attains age 32 and ending with the close of the plan year preceding
the plan year in which the participant attains age 35.[31]

Blackout Period Notice. A blackout period generally includes any period during which the ability of participants or
beneficiaries to direct or diversify assets credited to their accounts,
to obtain loans from the plan or to obtain distributions from the plan
will be temporarily suspended, limited or restricted. Typically,
blackout periods occur when plans change recordkeepers or investment options, or when plans add participants due to a corporate
merger or acquisition.

The *Blackout Period Notice*, a recent addition to the notice
requirements for individual account plans (e.g., a 401(k) plan), requires at least 30 days' (but not more than 60 days') advance notice
before a plan is closed to participant transactions. A blackout notice
should contain information on the expected beginning and end
date of the blackout. The notice should also provide the reason for
the blackout and what rights will be restricted as a result. The notice
must specify a plan contact for answering any questions about the
blackout period. The DOL regulations provide a model notice that
may be used for this purpose.[32]

Termination of Employment. Upon the termination of employment by a participant, a statement of his or her deferred vested
benefit or must be provided. This must be furnished to the participant no later than the date the Schedule SSA of Form 5500 must be
reported to the IRS.[33]

---

[30] 1992–2 CB 377.
[31] Code Sec. 417(a)(3) and ERISA Sec. 205(c)(3).
[32] DOL Reg. § 2520.101-3.
[33] Reg. § 301.6057-1(e).

Notice of Waiver Requests. An employer is required to notify plan participants, beneficiaries, and alternate payees that a waiver of funding has been requested. The notice must describe the extent to which the plan is funded with respect to guaranteed benefits and benefit liabilities.[34]

Notice of Failure to Fund. An employer must notify all plan participants, beneficiaries, and alternate payees of any failure to make an installment or other payment required to meet the minimum funding standard to a plan within 60 days following the due date of the payment. If the employer has filed a waiver request with respect to the plan year that includes the required installment, no notice is required. However, if the waiver request is denied, the employer must provide notice within 60 days after the date of the denial.[35]

A sanction is imposed on employers who fail to notify participants and beneficiaries of the failure to make required contributions. A court may require an employer who fails to make the notification to pay the affected participants and beneficiaries up to $100 per day from the date of the failure.[36]

Funding Status. Plan administrators of defined benefit plans subject to PBGC coverage are required to provide participants with a statement indicating the percentage of funded benefits as of the beginning of the plan year. This statement is not required of plans that are at least 90 percent funded. The notice is due within two months after the due date of the prior year's Form 5500.[37]

Defined Benefit Plan Terminations. As discussed earlier, the plan administrator must give a *Notice of Intent to Terminate* to plan participants, beneficiaries of deceased participants, alternate payees, and any employee organization representing participants between 60 and 90 days before the proposed termination date. For a standard termination, a second *Notice of Plan Benefits* concerning information about his/her benefit commitments must be given to each plan participant or beneficiary by the required submission date for the PBGC notice (see earlier discussion). In the case of a distress termination, a *Notice of Benefit Distribution* must be given to each participant and beneficiary receiving benefits within 60 days of the PBGC's determination that the plan is sufficient to pay guaranteed benefits.

Qualified Domestic Relations Order. ERISA Sec. 206(d)(3)(G) requires. the plan administrator to promptly notify a

---

[34] Code Sec. 412(f)(4)(A).

[35] ERISA Sec. 101(d).

[36] ERISA Sec. 502(c).

[37] ERISA Sec. 4011. *See* PBGC Technical Update 96-5 for a model notice.

participant and any other alternate payee of the receipt of a domestic relations order affecting the participant's account. In addition, the notice must describe the plan's procedures for determining the qualified status of the order, followed by a notice of the determination of the qualified status of the order.

.06 Information Provided Upon Request

ERISA Sec. 104(b)(4) requires the plan administrator to provide, upon the written request by a participant or beneficiary, the latest updated SPD, the plan description, the latest annual report (Form 5500 series), and any terminal report, as well as the bargaining agreement, trust agreement, contract, or other instruments under which the plan is established or operated. After receiving a request, the plan administrator has 30 days to supply the information. The administrator may make a reasonable charge to cover the cost of furnishing such complete copies.

Accrued Benefits Statement. ERISA Sec. 105(a) requires the plan administrator to provide a statement of a participant's accrued benefits upon the participant's written request. The statement must include the total benefits accrued and the amount which is nonforfeitable (vested), or the earliest date on which benefits will become vested. However, no participant or beneficiary is entitled to receive more than one report during any 12-month period.[38]

.07 Documents Available for Inspection

Certain information must be available for review by participants and beneficiaries. This information includes: copies of the plan description, latest annual report, and copies of the documents under which the plan is established and operated. All these documents must be current, readily accessible, and clearly identified. They must be available at all times in the plan administrator's principal office, the employer's principal office, and each employer establishment in which at least 50 participants covered under the plan are customarily working.[39]

---

[38] ERISA Sec. 105(b).   [39] ERISA Sec. 104(b).

¶ 1305.06

Chapter 14

Nonqualified Deferred Compensation, in General

¶1401 Introduction

Employers have become increasingly interested in nonqualified deferred compensation arrangements in recent years to supplement and/or replace their qualified deferred compensation plans for executives and other key employees. This added interest is due to the relatively severe requirements for qualified plans and the maximum contributions that can be made to and benefits that can be paid from qualified plans. Although the Economic Growth and Tax Relief Reconciliation Act of 2001 (EGTRRA) increased (1) the maximum dollar contribution (annual addition) defined contribution plan percentage and amount to the lesser of (a) 100 percent (up from 25 percent in 2001 and earlier years) of compensation or (b) $40,000 (adjusted for inflation after 2002 (the 2005 limit is $42,000) and up from $35,000 in 2001); and (2) the maximum dollar benefit under defined benefit plans to $160,000 (adjusted for inflation after 2002 (the 2005 limit is $170,000) and up from $140,000 in 2001), such maximums are still rather small compared to the total amount of compensation paid to some executives and owner-employees. Further, the $210,000 maximum amount of employee compensation (in 2005, up from $170,000 in 2001 and $200,000 in 2002 and 2003) that can be taken into account in determining contributions that can be made to qualified plans has made nonqualified plans more attractive to highly compensated employees desiring more retirement income than would be provided them under a qualified plan. Nonqualified plans are attractive because (1) they can be established to primarily or exclusively cover certain key employees such as executives, and (2) there is no statutory limit on the amount of benefits they can provide and less limitation on the benefits that can be provided.

The enactment of Code Sec. 409A by Section 885 of the American Jobs Creation Act of 2004 (AJCA) is the most profound tax development concerning nonqualified deferred compensation in the last 50 years. Code Sec. 409A provides that all amounts deferred under a nonqualified deferred compensation plan for all taxable years are currently includible in gross income to the extent not subject to a substantial risk of forfeiture and not previously included in gross income, unless certain requirements under the section are met. The new Code section also includes rules applicable to certain trusts or similar arrangements associated with nonqualified deferred compensation, where such arrangements are located outside of the United States or are restricted to the provision of benefits in connection with a decline in the financial health of the sponsor. The new Code section, which is generally applicable to amounts deferred in taxable years beginning on or after January 1, 2005, will have a significant impact on nonqualified deferred compensation planning and compliance. While the new section does not end the capability of employers and employees to enter into elective nonqualified deferred compensation arrangements after 2004 and use vehicles such as rabbi trusts (under Rev. Proc. 92-64) to secure the employer's promise to pay the deferred compensation, the new requirements will have to be carefully analyzed and taken into account in the design of deferred compensation arrangements to assure deferral of income recognition and avoidance of the rather Draconian consequences under the section for failing to meet the requirements.

The decrease of individual marginal income tax rates by the Jobs Growth and Tax Relief Reconciliation Act of 2003 (JGTRRA) effective for 2003 and later years (with the greatest decreases in the highest rates—e.g., the top rate that was slated to be 38.6 percent for 2003 was reduced to 35 percent) should continue to have a positive impact on both employer and employee interest in nonqualified plans. In addition, the top marginal individual tax rate of 35 percent is no higher than the top corporate rate of 35 percent and is higher than the 34 percent marginal rate that applies to corporations with less than $10 million of taxable income. As a result, the value to the employee of having income recognition deferred is frequently not less and is sometimes greater than the cost to the employer of postponing the deduction of compensation paid to a future year due to the provision of deferred rather than current compensation.

The decrease in the top rate applicable to long-term capital gain income for individuals from 20 percent to 15 percent under JGTRRA (from 10 percent to 5 percent for taxpayers with marginal tax rates of 15 percent or less) effective for sales after May 5, 2003 of capital assets held for more than one year has made certain nonqualified deferred compensation plans that give rise to capital gains income more desirable forms of deferred compensation. For example, the desirability of restricted stock and property plans (discussed later in this chapter) and nonqualified and incentive stock options (discussed in Chapter 15) that can produce capital gain income to the recipient no doubt has increased in some cases compared to forms of nonqualified deferred compensation that only produce ordinary income for the recipient. However, the recent requirement that public companies must expense the value of granted stock options on their financial statements may cool the enthusiasm for such nonqualified deferred compensation in some cases in the coming years.

The Sarbanes-Oxley Act of 2002 (P.L. 107–204, 116 Stat. 745 (2002)) could also have an impact on certain nonqualified arrangements. For example, since the Act prohibits public companies from making certain loans to executives, arrangements such as split-dollar life insurance plans which are treated as loans may be prohibited for such executives.

This chapter covers nonqualified deferred compensation, in general. The chapter begins with an introduction to nonqualified plans that includes a comparison of nonqualified plans and qualified plans, the major forms of nonqualified plans, factors that should be taken into account in setting up nonqualified plans, and the advantages and disadvantages of nonqualified plans. The chapter next analyzes new Code Sec. 409A and other important tax rules and doctrines that impact nonqualified deferred compensation. The chapter then discusses and evaluates nonqualified deferred compensation arrangements in light of these rules. After that, Code Sec. 83 restricted property and stock plans are covered. Finally, the chapter concludes with a coverage of Code Sec. 457 deferred compensation plans that can be offered by state governments and tax-exempt organizations.

¶1402 General Considerations

Nonqualified deferred compensation is deferred compensation that does not satisfy the qualification requirements of qualified plans such as the vesting and minimum coverage rules. Thus, there are a number of differences between qualified and nonqualified plans. These differences, as well as the typical types of nonqualified plans and the factors that should be taken into account in considering nonqualified plans, are covered below.

.01 Nonqualified v. Qualified Plans

Nonqualified deferred compensation plans differ from qualified plans in terms of the tax benefits available under the two types of plans, the rules for qualification of the plans, the flexibility associated with the plans, and the applicable reporting and disclosure rules.

Tax Benefits. As noted in Chapter 5, qualified deferred compensation plans provide five major tax benefits:

(1) deferral of income recognition for the employee until amounts are actually received under the plan;

(2) exemption of contributions into (except for elective deferral employee contributions) and distributions from qualified plans from FICA and FUTA taxes;

(3) tax free accumulation of earnings on employer and employee contributions to the qualified plan;

(4) favorable tax treatment of distributions from qualified plans in certain cases; and

(5) within limits, a current deduction for employer contributions to qualified deferred compensation plans.

On the other hand, most nonqualified plans provide only one of the major tax advantages of a qualified plan. If a nonqualified plan is properly structured, such that the requirements of new Code Sec. 409A are met, where applicable, and/or other relevant tax rules and doctrines are met, it can provide a deferral of income to the recipient-employee, i.e., the employee will not be taxed until he or she receives or has a nonforfeitable right to receive the income. The employer is entitled to a deduction when the employee includes the ordinary income.[1]

Qualification Rules. The tax benefits of qualified plans are not available unless such plans satisfy an array of nondiscrimination requirements that were made more stringent by TRA '86 and other later tax laws. These include the following:

(1) Qualified plans must generally cover a large percentage of the rank and file employees (i.e., those who are not highly compensated) under Code Secs. 401 and 410.

---

[1] Code Secs. 83(h), 404(a), and 409A.

¶1402.01

(2) Qualified plans are subject to rules which not only limit the deferral of income, but also require minimum funding of benefits (in defined benefit plans) and put a ceiling on employer contributions (in the case of defined contribution plans) under Code Secs. 401, 412, and 415.

(3) Qualified plans must provide for the vesting of employer contributions and earnings on contributions to qualified plans over specified minimum time periods under Code Sec. 411.

(4) Qualified plans must make distributions to participants in accordance with restrictions that limit the timing and the amount of the distributions under Code Secs. 401 through 403.

On the other hand, none of these requirements have to be satisfied in the case of nonqualified plans.

Flexibility. The qualification requirements for qualified plans limit the flexibility of such plans to provide for deferred compensation and retirement benefits of executives, shareholder-employees and other key employees. Because nonqualified plans do not have to satisfy any of the qualification requirements, they can be designed in a more flexible manner so as to provide the particular benefits that are desirable in specific circumstances. The following elements of flexibility are inherent in nonqualified plans:

(1) Nonqualified plans do not have to cover a minimum number of employees or employees of a specific class. Nonqualified plans usually cover only key employees such as executives and shareholder-employees.

(2) Nonqualified plans can be designed to provide flexibility in the amounts that can be deferred and, to the extent permitted under the requirements of Code Sec. 409A where that section is applicable, in the timing of the payments of the deferred amounts.

(3) Nonqualified plans do not have to provide vested benefits. Thus, employees' rights to benefits under nonqualified plans do not have to vest in accordance with any statutory schedule. Instead, nonqualified plans can provide that benefits are fully vested immediately or can postpone vesting for a number of years as a means of retaining certain key employees. Of course, the requirements of new Code Sec. 409A, where applicable, must be taken into account with respect to the decision of whether and when benefits from nonqualified plans should be vested.

(4) Nonqualified plans are not limited as to the form, timing, and amounts of distributions thus providing maximum flexibility in planning for distributions.

.02 Reporting and Disclosure Rules and Exceptions for Top Hat and Excess Benefit Plans

Qualified deferred compensation plans are subject to the fiduciary, reporting, disclosure, and other requirements of Title I of the Employee Retirement Income Security Act of 1974 (ERISA). The requirements of ERISA can significantly increase the cost of maintaining qualified plans for rank-and-file employees.

Exception for Top Hat Plans. An unfunded, nonqualified deferred compensation plan that is "maintained by an employer primarily for the purpose of compensation for a select group of management or highly compensated employees," known as a "top hat" plan, is eligible for an alternative method of compliance with the reporting and disclosure requirements of Title I. Under the alternative method, only a statement that the employer maintains a top hat plan or plans, the number of such plans, and the number of participants in such plan is required of the employer.[2] Further, such a plan is not subject to the participation and vesting, funding, fiduciary responsibility, and termination insurance requirements.[3] Although the DOL has not defined what is considered to be a "select group" of management or highly compensated employees for purposes of this rule, it has stated that in order to qualify for the exemption, the plan cannot cover employees beyond the select group.[4] The phrase "select group of management or highly compensated employees" will likely be interpreted narrowly by the DOL and will include a very limited number of employees of the employer. In that respect, the DOL has taken narrow views constituting the definition of the terms "management" and "highly compensated" in determining whether a top-hat plan exists. The DOL has stated that, under a top hat plan, the participants must have, by virtue of their position or compensation level, the ability to affect or substantially influence the design and operation of their deferred compensation plan, taking into consideration the risks attendant thereto, and therefore would not need the substantive rights and protections of Title I of ERISA.[5]

On the other hand, the courts have taken a less conservative path toward evaluating the phrases "select group of management" or "highly compensated employees" and have examined the facts and circumstances of the various cases. In determining what constitutes a "select group" the courts, like the DOL, have in many

---

[2] DOL Reg. § 2520.104–23.
[3] ERISA Secs. 201(2), 301(a)(3), 401(a)(1), and 4021(b)(6).

[4] DOL Op. Ltr. 90–14A (May 8, 1990)
[5] *Id.*

¶ 1402.02

instances focused on the size of the group relative to the employer's total workforce. For example, one court held that a plan benefited a "select group" because the number of participants was relatively small compared to the employer's work force and rejected the DOL's position that the plan may not be considered a top hat plan if it includes employees who are neither management nor highly compensated.[6] The District Court in *Belka v. Rowe Furniture Corp.*[7] held that a deferred compensation plan covering only 4.6 percent of the employees of the employer was a "select group" of employees. But, the District Court, in *Darden v. Nationwide Mutual Insurance Co.*,[8] held (a holding that was not contested on appeal) that a group of employees that constituted almost 20 percent of the employer's employees was too large to be considered a "select" group of employees. However, the Second Circuit Court of Appeals in *Demery v. Extebank Deferred Compensation Plan B*[9] held that an unfunded deferred compensation plan which was offered to 15.34 percent of a bank's employees was a top hat plan. The court noted that the circumstances in this case were different than those in *Darden* because the deferred compensation plan in *Demery* was offered only to bank officers, most of whom were employed in managerial positions, and found that the plan participant's average compensation was more than twice the average of the bank's employees, in general. The court also noted that there is no existing authority that establishes when a plan is too large to be deemed "select." Finally, the court stated that while the percentage of employees offered the plan is at or near the upper limit of the acceptable size for a "select group," this fact alone did not make the deferred compensation plan too broad to be a top hat plan without considering the positions held in the bank by the plan participants. Thus, it may be possible to cover a fairly large percentage of employees with a top hat plan if the eligible participants are mostly or entirely managerial employees who earn compensation substantially in excess of the rest of the employer's employees. As noted above, the ability of the participants to affect or substantially influence the design and operation of the plan is also an important factor in deciding whether a plan is a top hat plan. For example, in *Duggan v. Hobbs*[10] the Ninth Circuit Court of Appeals found that a severance pay arrangement provided to one executive employee of the employer constituted a top hat plan because the employee was the only individual ever successful in entering into such a deferred

---

[6] *Loffland Brothers Co, v. C.A. Overstreet*, 758 P2d 813 (Okla., 1988).

[7] 571 FSupp. 1249 (D., MI, 1983).

[8] 117 FSupp. 388 (E.D., NC, 1989). aff'd 922 F2d 203 (CA-4, 1991), rev'd 503 US 318 (USSC, 1992).

[9] 216 F3d 283 (CA-2, 2000), aff'g summary judgment, ED, NY (1998).

[10] 99 F3d 307 (CA-9, 1996).

compensation arrangement. As such, the employee was able to influence the nature of the plan and thus, constituted a select group of management or highly paid employees. In *Carrabba v. Randall Food Markets,*[11] the District Court found that the Management Security Plan maintained by the employer to provide deferred compensation to certain management employees was not a top hat plan because the plan participants were not able to exert influence over the plan and the level of benefits. The court stated that the exception granted to top hat plans from ERISA general requirements was based on the notion that top hat plan participants are in a position to exert influence over their plan and plan benefits.

Because of the favorable treatment of top hat plans under ERISA, unfunded nonqualified plans (other than excess benefit plans covered in the next paragraph), including the various types of unfunded nonqualified plans (such as rabbi trusts) covered below, will generally be set up to qualify as top hat plans.

Exception for Unfunded Excess Benefit Plans. Unfunded excess benefit plans are exempt from all of the requirements of Title I of ERISA.[12] An excess benefit plan is a nonqualified employee pension benefit plan of an employer that is maintained by the employer solely for the purpose of providing contributions (benefits in the case of a defined benefit plan) for certain employees in excess of the limits on contributions and benefits imposed by Code Sec. 415 on plans to which that Section applies.[13] Apparently, this definition means that other compensation limits such as the Code Sec. 401(a)(17) limitation on the amount of compensation that can be taken into account in determining qualified plan contributions ($210,000 in 2005, adjusted for inflation after 2005) cannot be incorporated into determining employer contributions under excess benefit plans. The DOL has not yet provided any guidance on this matter. However, courts have held that the term "solely" does mean benefits in excess of the Code Sec. 415 limitations, and does not include benefits in excess of the Code Sec. 401(a)(17) compensation limits.[14] Therefore, excess benefit plans (to escape meeting the requirements of Title I of ERISA) should be structured only to provide contributions (benefits) in excess of those permitted by Code Sec. 415. Employers desiring to set up plans to provide contributions (benefits) in excess of those permitted by other Code Sections (such

---

[11] 38 FSupp 2d 468 (ND, TX, 1999), aff'd 252 F3d 721 (CA-5, 2001).

[12] ERISA Sec. 4(b)(5).

[13] ERISA Sec. 3(36).

[14] *See e.g., Irving D. Isko vs. Engelhard Corporation,* Civ. No. 05-333 (DC NJ April 29, 2005).

Garratt vs. Knowles, 245 F3d 941 (CA-7, 2001), *Olander v. Bucyrus-Erie Co.,* 187 F3d 599 (CA-7, 1999); *Petkus v. Chicago Rawhide Manufacturing Co.,* 763 FSupp 357 (ND, IL, 1991).

as Code Sec. 401(a)(17)) should set up the plan as a top hat plan (described above). It should be noted that excess benefit plans need not be restricted to managerial or highly compensated individuals such as top hat plans must be. In cases where an employer wishes to cover a fairly large group of employees (such as all computer technicians, some of whom may not be managerial employees or highly compensated), it may be desirable to set up an excess benefits plan, rather than a top hat plan. Finally, note that the IRS has privately ruled in Letter Ruling 9747033 that the adoption of an excess benefit plan by an employer to provide benefits that could not be provided due to the Code Sec. 415 limitations would not affect the qualified status of the qualified plan.[15]

.03 Considerations in Designing Nonqualified Plans

Nonqualified plans present advantages for both employees and employers. In addition there are a number of factors and potential drawbacks that employees and employers should take into account with respect to nonqualified plans.

Employee Considerations. Perhaps the most important advantage to employees under nonqualified plans is the deferral of income recognition. This advantage is predicated on the assumption that the employees will pay less income tax by having the amounts paid to them at some future time when they expect to be subject to a lower marginal income tax rate and for plans subject to Code Sec. 409A, that the requirements for deferral under that section are met. In some cases over time, the employee's marginal income tax rate has not turned out to be lower in the future because (1) inflation has increased the employee's income to a point that the applicable marginal tax rate is not lower, and/or (2) marginal income tax rates increased from the time of deferral until the time of payout. However, the reduction of individual marginal tax rates through at least 2010 by EGTRRA and JFTRRA tends to mitigate this concern, at least in the near term, because those reductions make it more likely that in many situations marginal tax rates applicable to deferred compensation receipts in the future will be smaller than rates applicable today on current compensation.

Another factor that should be taken into account by employees is their current and projected future cash flow needs. If the employee expects to have higher cash flow needs in the future or needs that will not be met after retirement by Social Security and other retirement income, it may be wise to defer certain amounts of compensation.

---

[15] *See also* IRS Letter Ruling 9950044, 9–20–99, CCH IRS LETTER RULINGS REPORTS, IRS Letter Ruling 200148081, 9–5–01, CCH IRS LETTER RULINGS REPORTS, and IRS Letter Ruling 200410024.

The rate of return on amounts deferred could be very important. If the employee will be paid only the absolute amount that is deferred, the value of the deferred compensation could be seriously eroded by inflation. For that reason, employees would ordinarily prefer to have deferred amounts increased by a specified interest rate or invested in some manner so that the deferred amount will be increased by some rate of return. Where the deferred amounts are increased by a rate of return, the result to the employee can be similar to that which can be achieved through a qualified retirement plan. Of course, if the employer invests amounts to produce a rate of return on the deferred compensation, the employer is taxed on the income earned unless the amounts are invested in tax-exempt securities.

> **Example:** Assume that an employee elects to defer $10,000 of 2006 compensation such that the compensation will be paid on January 1, 2011 (to meet the requirements of Code Sec. 409A as to when the deferred compensation is permitted to be paid). In addition, assume that the deferred $10,000 earns six-percent interest per year. If the deferred compensation is distributed on January 1, 2011, the employee will receive $10,497.05 (i.e., $10,000 \times 1.06^5 \times 0.74$) after taxes, assuming that the applicable marginal rate will still be 26 percent in that year. On the other hand, if the employee received the $10,000 in 2006, taxes of $2,600 would be payable, leaving only $7,400 to invest. Even if the employee were to receive seven percent interest on that amount, the interest may be taxable yearly (unless, for example, the investment was in tax-exempt bonds). Far less would be accumulated by 2011 than if the compensation were deferred.

Nonqualified deferred compensation may be attractive to employees as a retirement supplement in cases where their maximum qualified plan benefits are limited because of the $170,000 (in 2005) annual benefit limit under a defined benefit plan or the maximum $42,000 (in 2005) annual contribution that can be made into a defined contribution plan (adjusted for inflation after 2005).

Finally, employees will naturally be concerned with the ultimate ability of the employer to pay the deferred amounts in the future. Unfortunately, many arrangements that either provide for funding of the payment of the deferred amounts or provide the employee with security on the deferred amounts may make it impossible for the employee to defer recognition of the compensation altogether. Thus, the deferral of compensation and employee security may be competing considerations, and care must be taken to achieve both, as will be discussed below.

Employer Considerations. Nonqualified deferred compensation plans can serve many important purposes for employers. A prime consideration for employers is the attraction and retention of key employees. A nonqualified deferred compensation plan can be used to:

(1) substitute for qualified plan benefits lost to the employee as a result of a job change;

(2) allow certain employees to share in profits to reward superior performance;

(3) permit companies with temporary cash flow problems to offer a larger compensation package for recruiting purposes; and

(4) retain key employees for years into the future by making deferred compensation payable to them forfeitable unless they remain employed with the employee for a special period of time.

The use of nonqualified deferred compensation plans, such as phantom stock plans, can avoid the potential dilution of earnings or minority shareholder problems associated with stock options and restricted stock compensation. Equity plans are discussed in the next chapter.

Employers can use nonqualified plans to induce certain employees to take early retirement. Because the maximum benefit that can be paid to early retirees from qualified plans must be reduced in the same fashion as social security benefits are reduced for persons who retire before reaching age 65, some employees may face a serious reduction in income as a result of early retirement. Amounts deferred under a nonqualified plan could make up for this shortfall.

One other important concern of employers is to secure deductions with respect to nonqualified deferred compensation plan contributions. Ordinarily, a deduction is permitted to employers in the same year an employee includes nonqualified deferred compensation in gross income. Care must be taken to satisfy any requirements that must be met for deductions such as maintaining separate employee accounts which apply in some cases. Corresponding employer deductions under nonqualified plans are covered later in this chapter.

Finally, employers need to take account of Code Sec. 409A and its applicability to their nonqualified deferred compensation plans. Existing plans should be amended or terminated and new ones developed to comply with the provisions of that section to avoid the rather Draconian tax consequences to employees or other service providers for failure to meet the section's requirements.

Tax Considerations. As indicated earlier, a major goal of most nonqualified plans is to defer the recognition of income to the employee until a future year when the income is received by or made available to the employee. Achieving that goal requires a close consideration of the tax factors related to nonqualified plans, such as new Code Sec. 409A and other applicable tax considerations, including the constructive receipt doctrine, the economic benefit doctrine, and the Code Sec. 83 restricted property rules. These are covered in detail below.

.04 Common Forms of Nonqualified Plans

Common forms of nonqualified plans used to compensate executives and other key employees include excess benefit plans, supplemental executive retirement plans, salary continuation plans, deferred compensation arrangements, restricted stock plans, incentive bonus plans (performance unit plans and phantom stock), stock appreciation rights, and nonqualified stock options. The first four are summarized below. Restricted stock plans are covered in detail later in this chapter and other equity-based plans are covered in Chapter 15.

Excess Benefit Plans. Excess benefit plans are designed exclusively to provide retirement benefits that exceed the maximum benefit (or contribution) permitted under Code Sec. 415 for qualified retirement plans. Note that the maximum benefit under a defined benefit plan is $170,000 per year in 2005 and that this amount must be actuarially reduced if the employee takes early retirement.

Supplemental Executive Retirement Plans (SERPs). SERPs usually provide benefits in a form similar to defined benefit pension plans (i.e., an annuity for the remainder of the employee's life, commencing at retirement). For example, the employer could promise to pay an executive a benefit equal to a specified dollar amount or a percentage of the final year's compensation. The benefits payable under SERPs can be based upon an employee's qualified retirement benefits from the employer and Social Security benefits and can be reduced if retirement benefits are received from another employer. In some cases, an SERP is designed as an excess benefit plan to achieve exemption from the requirements of Title I of ERISA, as covered earlier in this chapter.

Because of the higher defined benefit plan limitation enacted as part of **EGTRRA** (increased to $160,000 for limitation years ending after December 31, 2001—adjusted for inflation in later years (the 2005 plan year limit is $170,000) and up from $140,000 in 2001), some employers may want to consider doing a "SERP Shift." That is, an employer can use some amounts deferred under a SERP to fund the increased benefits that can be paid to the higher-paid participants in defined benefit plans.

Salary Continuation Plans. Under a salary continuation plan, the employer agrees to continue to pay all or a percentage of the employee's salary in the event of the employee's death or disability for a specified period of years or upon separation from service.

Deferred Compensation Arrangements. Deferred compensation arrangements are agreements under which the employee elects to forgo the receipt of some of his or her current compensation. The deferred amounts are to be paid at some later time, typically increased by some rate of interest. This is the most common form of nonqualified deferred compensation. This type of plan is also referred to as a salary reduction plan.

Shadow or Nonqualified Code Sec. 401(k) Plans. A shadow or nonqualified Code Sec. 401(k) plan is an unfunded nonqualified plan of an employer designed to allow employees to defer a portion of their current compensation in excess of the elective deferral limit under Code Sec. 401(k) ($15,000 in 2006—20,000 for participants who are at least or become age 50 during the applicable calendar year) and the Code Sec. 401(a)(17) limit on compensation ($20,000 in 2005—adjusted for inflation after 2005) that can be taken into account in determining plan contributions. This plan will ordinarily coordinate with a Code Sec. 401(k) plan where, under the 401(k) plan, a shadow plan participant will contribute the maximum allowable on a pre-tax basis, and then, an additional amount will be contributed to the shadow plan. The IRS has issued a number of favorable private letter rulings concerning shadow Code Sec. 401(k) plans stating that in those arrangements, the Code Sec. 401(k) requirements were not violated and deferral of income recognition under the companion shadow plan was permitted. See, e.g., IRS Letter Rulings 9424032, 9807027, and 200031060. In those rulings, the plans were found not to violate the contingent benefit rule that applies to Code Sec. 401(k) plans under Code Sec. 401(k)(4)(A). That analysis is based on an IRS statement found in Reg. § 1.401(k)-1(e)(6)(iii) (in the recently issued final Code Sec. 401(k) regulations—Reg §. 1.401(k)-1(e)(6)(iv) in the old, previously issued final regulations) to the effect that if deferred compensation under a nonqualified plan is dependent on an employee having made the maximum deferral elective deferrals under Code Sec. 402(g) (which applies to Sec. 401(k) plans) or the maximum elective contributions permitted under the terms of the plan, that deferred compensation is not treated as contingent.

Impact of Code Sec. 409A. The provisions of Code Sec. 409A apply to all of the common nonqualified deferred compensation plans generally discussed above for amounts deferred in calendar years beginning after January 1, 2005. Thus, many such plans will have to be redesigned to take into account the requirements of new Code Sec. 409A. This will be particularly true for SERPs and shadow (nonqualified) Code Sec. 401(k) plans which historically have had provisions such as allowing participants to elect early distributions subject to a reduction or "haircut" and to further defer a scheduled distribution. Some employers may consider breaking the tie between their nonqualified and qualified plans in order to comply with Code Sec. 409A. Certainly all of the nonqualified plans summarized above, and, especially, SERP and shadow 401(k) plans, will have to become more prescriptive concerning the timing and manner of deferrals and benefit payments.

¶ 1403 Code Sec. 409A Nonqualified Deferred Compensation Rules

Code Sec. 409A, the most important development in the taxation of nonqualified deferred compensation in at least the last 50 years, was enacted into law as part of the American Jobs Creation Act of 2004 (ACJA).[16] The provisions of the new section are generally effective for amounts deferred in taxable years beginning after December 31, 2004 (subject to some transition rules under Notice 2005-1, covered below). Amounts deferred in taxable years beginning before January 1, 2005, are subject to the new provision only if the plan under which the deferral is made is materially modified after October 3, 2004 (e.g., the addition of any benefit, right, or feature is a material modification, subject to IRS transition rules). Earnings on amounts deferred before the effective date are subject to the provision to the extent that such amounts deferred are subject to the provision.[17]

Under Code Sec. 409A(a), a nonqualified deferred compensation plan is required to satisfy specific requirements concerning (1) the permissible timing of distributions from the nonqualified deferred compensation plan (e.g., compensation deferred under the plan may not be distributed earlier than specified times including a specified time (or pursuant to a fixed schedule) indicated under the plan at the date the compensation is deferred or the date of the participant's death); (2) the prohibition of the acceleration of the time or schedule

---

[16] Code Sec. 409A, as enacted by P.L. 108-357, 108th Cong., 2d Sess., Sec. 885 (Oct. 22, 2004), 118 Stat. 1418.

[17] P.L. 108-357, 108th Cong., 2d Sess., Sec. 885(d) (Oct. 22, 2004).

of any compensation payments under the plan with certain exceptions as provided by the IRS (e.g., an early payment with a reduction in the amount—a haircut—is not permitted); and (3) the permissible timing of employee or other service provider deferral elections with certain exceptions to be provided by the IRS (e.g., in general, the deferral election must be made no later than the close of the preceding taxable year).

If at any time during a taxable year a nonqualified deferred compensation plan fails to meet the Code Sec. 409A requirements, or is not operated in accordance with those requirements, all amounts deferred under the plan for the taxable year and all previous taxable years by any participant to whom the failure relates are includible in that participant's gross income to the extent the amounts are not subject to a substantial risk of forfeiture. The amount required to be included is also subject to an additional income tax equal to 20 percent of the compensation required to be included and interest.[18] The employer or other service recipient is entitled to a deduction for the amount required to be included in gross income.

Code Sec. 409A applies to any plan or arrangement (not limited to arrangements between employer and employee) that provides for the deferral of compensation. For purposes of applying the Code Sec. 409A rules and consequences for failure to meet them, the IRS considers (1) all account balance plans (generally, defined contribution nonqualified plans) to be one plan, (2) all nonaccount balance plans (generally, defined benefit nonqualified plans) to be one plan, and (3) all plans which are neither account balance or nonaccount balance plans (generally, equity plans such as stock appreciation rights covered in Chapter 15) to be one plan.[19] A number of plans are not considered to be nonqualified plans subject to the requirements of Code Sec. 409A, including (1) qualified retirement plans (e.g., pension plans and Code Sec. 457(b) plans); (2) incentive stock option plans; (3) employee stock purchase plans; (4) most restricted stock and property plans covered under Code Sec. 83; (5) annual bonus plans with amounts to be paid within two-and-one-half months after the end of the taxable year in which the services are performed; (6) nonqualified stock options where the option price equals the value of the stock when the option is granted and where there is no other deferral feature; (7) any bona fide vacation leave, sick leave, compensatory time, disability pay, or death benefit plan; and (8) certain stock appreciation rights and other plans specified in

---

[18] Code Sec. 409A(c)(4).

[19] Notice 2005-1, IRB 2005-2, 274, Q&A 9.

guidance from the IRS.[20] Therefore, the types of nonqualified plans subject to the provisions of Code Sec. 409A include unfunded, unsecured plans, top hat plans, SERPs, and others described earlier in this chapter as well as Code Sec. 457(f) plans (plans of governmental and tax-exempt entities that are not eligible for the general Code Sec. 457 provisions described later in this chapter). In addition, phantom stock plans, certain stock appreciation rights, discounted nonqualified stock options and certain other equity-based nonqualified plans covered in Chapter 15 are subject to Code Sec. 409A.

Code Sec. 409A also contains rules under which its income recognition provisions will apply to instances where (1) assets are set aside in offshore rabbi trusts (rabbi trusts are covered later in this chapter) unless substantially all of the employee's services are performed in the same jurisdiction as the trust, and (2) a plan or rabbi trust would become funded if there is an adverse change in the financial health of the employer or other service provider.[21] Finally, it should be noted that the provisions of Code Sec. 409A do not alter or affect the application of any other provision of the Internal Revenue Code or common law tax doctrine, such as the constructive receipt doctrine. Thus, nonqualified deferred compensation not required to be included in gross income under Code Sec. 409A may nevertheless be included under some other applicable doctrine.[22] The following paragraphs cover the requirements and related planning considerations concerning new Code Sec. 409A in more detail.

.01 Code Sec. 409A Nonqualified Plan Requirements

There are three general requirements specified under Code Sec. 409A which concern (1) the permissible timing of distributions from the nonqualified deferred compensation plan, (2) the general prohibition of acceleration of benefit payments (distributions) under the plan, and (3) the permissible timing of elections to defer the payment of compensation under the plan.[23]

Permissible Distributions. Under Code Sec. 409A(a)(2), distributions from a nonqualified deferred compensation plan may be permitted only (1) upon the employee's or other service provider's separation from service (as specified in IRS guidance); (2) upon the employee's or other service provider's death; (3) at a specified time (or pursuant to a fixed schedule); (4) upon a change in ownership or control of the employer corporation (to the extent provided in IRS

---

[20] H.R. Conf. Rep. No. 108-755, 108th Cong., 2d Sess. (Oct. 22, 2004).
[21] Code Sec. 409A(b).
[22] Code Sec. 409A(c).

[23] Code Secs. 409A(a)(2), (3), and (4).

regulations); (5) upon the occurrence of an unforeseeable emergency, or (6) if the employee or other service provider becomes disabled. A nonqualified deferred compensation plan may not allow distributions other than for the permissible distribution events and, except as provided in IRS regulations, may not permit acceleration of a distribution.

Special rules apply concerning deferrals of payments to a specified person upon separation from service. Distributions may not be made to specified persons earlier than six months following such person's separation from service or the death of the specified person. For purposes of these rules, specified persons are key employees (as defined under Code Sec. 416(i)—see the discussion of key employees under the top heavy plan rules in Chapter 7) of publicly-traded corporations.[24]

Amounts payable at a specified time (e.g., December 31, 2011) or pursuant to a fixed schedule (a ratable payment to be made yearly on December 31 for five years beginning on December 31, 2011) must be specified under the plan at the time of the initial deferral under the plan. Deferred amounts payable upon the occurrence of an event are not treated as amounts payable at a specified time. For example, amounts payable when an individual attains age 65 are payable at a specified time, while amounts payable when an individual's child begins college are payable upon the occurrence of an event. In the latter case, the deferral would not satisfy the Code Sec. 409A distributions requirements.[25]

The Conference Committee Report indicates that distributions upon a change in the ownership or effective control of a corporation, or in the ownership of a substantial portion of the assets of a corporation, may be made to the extent provided by the IRS in regulations or other guidance. The IRS is to use a similar, but more restrictive, definition of change in control as is used for purposes of the golden parachute provisions of Code Sec. 280G and the regulations thereunder (see coverage of Code Sec. 280G at the end of Chapter 3), consistent with the purposes of the provision.[26] In response, the IRS has published detailed initial guidance in Question and Answers 11 through 14 of Notice 2005-1.[27] Under the Notice, a plan may permit a payment upon the occurrence of a change in the ownership of the corporation, a change in effective control of the corporation, or a change in the ownership of a substantial portion of the assets of the

---

[24] Code Sec. 409A(a)(2)(B) and H.R. Rep. No. 108-755, 108th Cong., 2d Sess. (Oct. 22, 2004).
[25] H.R. Rep. No. 108-755, 108th Cong., 2d Sess. (Oct. 22, 2004).

[26] *Id.*
[27] IRB 2005-2, 274.

corporation. The Notice collectively refers to these events as change in control events. To qualify as a change in control event, the occurrence of the event must be objectively determinable and any requirement that any other person, such as a plan administrator or board of directors compensation committee, certify the occurrence of a change in control event must be strictly ministerial and not involve any discretionary authority. For purposes of these rules, a payment also will be treated as occurring upon a change in control event if the right to the payment arises due to the corporation's exercise of discretion under the terms of the plan to terminate the plan and distribute the compensation deferred thereunder within 12 months of the change in control event. The plan may provide for a payment on any change in control event, and need not provide for a payment on all such events, provided that each event upon which a payment is provided qualifies as a change in control event.[28] To constitute a change in control event as to the plan participant (the employee or other service provider), the change in control event must relate to (1) the corporation for whom the participant is performing services at the time of the change in control event; (2) the corporation that is liable for the payment of the deferred compensation (or all corporations liable for the payment if more than one corporation is liable); or (3) a corporation that is a majority shareholder of a corporation identified in (1) or (2), or any corporation in a chain of corporations in which each corporation is a majority shareholder of another corporation in the chain, ending in a corporation identified in (1) or (2). For these purposes, a majority shareholder is a shareholder owning more than 50 percent of the total fair market value and total voting power of the indicated corporation.[29] The Notice specifies that the stock attribution rules of Code Sec. 318(a) apply for determining stock ownership. Also, stock underlying a vested option is considered owned by the individual that holds the vested option.[30]

A change in ownership occurs when any one person, or more than one person acting as a group, acquires ownership of stock of the corporation that, together with stock held by such person or group, constitutes more than 50 percent of the total fair market value or total voting power of the stock of such corporation. However, increases in ownership by one person or a group that already owns at least 50 percent of the corporation is not considered a change in ownership.[31]

---

[28] Notice 2005-1, IRB 2005-2, 274, Q&A 11(a).
[29] Notice 2005-1, IRB 2005-2, 274, Q&A 11(b).
[30] Notice 2005-1, IRB 2005-2, 274, Q&A 11(c).
[31] Notice 2005-1, IRB 2005-2, 274, Q&A 12(a).

¶1403.01

A change in effective control occurs if (1) any one person, or more than one person acting as a group, acquires (or has acquired during the 12-month period ending on the date of the most recent acquisition by such person or persons) ownership of stock of the corporation possessing 35 percent or more of the total voting power of the stock of such corporation; or (2) a majority of members of the corporation's board of directors is replaced during any 12-month period by directors whose appointment or election is not endorsed by a majority of the members of the corporation's board of directors before the date of the appointment or election. A change in the board of directors is only relevant for purposes of Code Sec. 409A if such change occurs in the parent corporation.[32]

A change in the ownership of a substantial portion of a corporation's assets occurs if one person, or more than one person acting as a group, acquires (or has acquired during the 12-month period ending on the date of the most recent acquisition by such person or persons) assets from the corporation that have a total gross fair market value equal to or more than 40 percent of the total gross fair market value of all of the assets of the corporation immediately before that acquisition or acquisitions. For this purpose, gross fair market value means the value of the assets of the corporation, or the value of the assets being disposed of, determined without regard to any liabilities associated with such assets. However, no change in control occurs for purposes of Code Sec. 409A if the assets are transferred to specified entities that are controlled by the shareholders of the transferring corporation.[33]

As noted above, a nonqualified deferred compensation plan may make distributions to a plan participant upon the occurrence of an unforeseeable emergency. Under the Conference Report, an unforeseeable emergency is defined as a severe financial hardship to the participant: (1) resulting from an illness or accident of the participant, the participant's spouse, or a dependent (as defined in Code Sec. 152(a)); (2) loss of the participant's property due to casualty; or (3) other similar extraordinary and unforeseeable circumstances arising as a result of events beyond the control of the participant. The amount of the distribution must be limited to the amount needed to satisfy the emergency plus taxes reasonably anticipated as a result of the distribution. Distributions may not be allowed to the extent that the hardship may be relieved through reimbursement or compensation by insurance or otherwise, or by liquidation

---

[32] Notice 2005-1, IRB 2005-2, 274, Q&A 13(a).   [33] Notice 2005-1, IRB 2005-2, 274, Q&A 14(a).

of the participant's assets (to the extent such liquidation would not itself cause a severe financial hardship).[34]

Finally, a distribution may be made if the plan participant becomes disabled. Under the Conference Report, a participant is considered disabled if he or she is (1) unable to engage in any substantial gainful activity by reason of any medically determinable physical or mental impairment which can be expected to result in death or can be expected to last for a continuous period of not less than 12 months; or (2) due to any medically determinable physical or mental impairment which can be expected to result in death or can be expected to last for a continuous period of not less than 12 months, receiving income replacement benefits for a period of not less than three months under an accident and health plan covering employees of the participant's employer.[35]

Acceleration of the Timing or Schedule of Plan Payments. Under Code Sec. 409A(a)(3), a nonqualified deferred compensation plan may not permit the acceleration of the time or schedule of any payment under the plan, except as provided in IRS regulations. The new provision prevents certain common provisions that have been included in nonqualified deferred compensation plans such as "haircut" provisions. Under a haircut provision, a plan participant could receive a benefit payment in an earlier year than permitted under the plan if that participant agreed to receive a smaller amount than he or she would have received in the scheduled year of payment. However, the Conference Report notes that the accelerations provision is not violated merely because a plan provides a choice between cash and taxable property if the timing and amount of income inclusion is the same regardless of the medium of distribution. For example, the choice between a fully taxable annuity contract and a lump-sum payment may be permitted. The Conference Report also notes that the IRS should provide rules (1) under which the choice between different forms of actuarially equivalent life annuity payments is permitted, and (2) which provide other, limited, exceptions to the prohibition on accelerated distributions, such as when the accelerated distribution is required for reasons beyond the control of the participant and the distribution is not elective.[36]

Question and Answer 15 of Notice 2005-1 provides a number of exceptions to the general rule prohibiting an acceleration of benefits. A payment of benefits under any of the listed circumstances is not

---

[34] H.R. Conf. Rep. No. 108-755, 108th Cong., 2d Sess. (Oct. 22, 2004).

[35] *Id.*
[36] *Id.*

considered a prohibited acceleration of payment. In addition, the IRS has requested comments as to other circumstances under which a plan should be allowed to accelerate plan payments.

The following exceptions are provided in the Notice:

(1) Waiving or accelerating a condition constituting a substantial risk of forfeiture. It is not an acceleration of the time or schedule of payment of a deferral of compensation if an employer or other service recipient waives or accelerates the satisfaction of a condition which is a substantial risk of forfeiture applicable to such deferral of compensation, if the requirements of Code Sec. 409A are otherwise met with respect to that deferral of compensation. For example, if a nonqualified deferred compensation plan provides for a lump sum payment of the vested benefit upon separation from service, and the benefit vests under the plan only after 10 years of service, it is not a violation of the requirements of the Code section if the service recipient reduces the vesting requirement to five years of service, even if an employee or other service provider becomes vested as a result and qualifies for a payment in connection with a separation from service.

(2) De minimis and specified amounts. A nonqualified deferred compensation plan may be amended to be allowed to make a payment of not more than $10,000 to a participant under the plan before that individual is scheduled to receive deferred compensation payments under the plan if the payment is made (1) in termination of the participant's interest in the plan; and (2) on or before the later of (a) December 31 of the calendar year in which the participant separates from service with the employer or other service recipient, or (b) the date two-and-one-half months after the participant's separation from service with the service recipient. Such an amendment may be made with respect to previously deferred amounts under the plan as well as amounts to be deferred in the future. In addition, a nonqualified deferred compensation plan that otherwise complies with Code Sec. 409A may be amended with regard to future deferrals to provide that, if a participant's interest under the plan has a value below an amount specified by the plan at the time that amounts are payable under the plan, then the participant's entire interest under the plan can be distributed as a lump sum payment.

(3) Domestic relations order. A plan may permit an acceleration of the time or schedule of a payment under the plan to an individual other than the plan participant which may be necessary to fulfill a domestic relations order (as defined in Code Sec. 414(p)(1)(B)—see the discussion of domestic relations orders in Chapter 6).

(4) Conflicts of interest. A plan may permit an acceleration of the time or schedule of a payment under the plan that may be necessary to comply with a certificate of divestiture (as defined in Code Sec. 1043(b)(2)).

(5) Section 457 plans. A plan subject to Code Sec. 457(f) (a plan that does not meet the general Code Sec. 457 requirements, covered in ¶ 1407.06) may permit an acceleration of the time or schedule of a payment to a participant to pay income taxes due upon a vesting event, as long as the amount of the payment is not more than the income tax withholding that would have been remitted by the employer if there had been a payment of wages equal to the income includible by the participant under Code Sec. 457(f) at the time of the vesting.

(6) Payment of employment taxes. A plan may permit early payments of amounts deferred under the plan to allow a participant to pay FICA taxes imposed by Code Sec. 3121(v)(2), and with respect to any amount of income tax withholding under Code Sec. 3401 that relates to that early payment. The total amount paid under this exception may not exceed the amount of such FICA taxes and the related income tax withholding amount.

For purposes of the rules permitting certain acceleration of deferred compensation payments, the term "plan" has the same general meaning as it does for purposes of Code Sec. 409A, in general (as covered in ¶ 1403.03 below), except that the plan aggregation rules do not apply. Thus, an employer could incorporate certain permitted acceleration provisions in one account balance plan and not in others.

Timing of Deferral of Income Elections. The third Code Sec. 409A requirement concerns the permissible timing of elections to defer the payment of compensation under a nonqualified deferred compensation plan. Under Code Sec. 409A(a)(4)(B), the initial election by the employee or other service provider to defer the payment of compensation must generally be made no later than the close of the taxable year preceding the year in which the related services are to be performed or at another time as provided by IRS regulations. For example, the initial election to defer payment of compensation with respect to services to be performed by an employee during 2006 must be made by December 31, 2005. Further, in the first year that an employee or other service provider becomes eligible for participation in a nonqualified deferred compensation plan, the election may be made within 30 days after the date that the employee is first eligible to participate in the plan. It should be noted that these initial deferral provisions are similar to those permitted under the IRS ruling policy that prevailed with respect to amounts deferred prior to December 31, 2004 under plans that are subject to Code Sec. 409A.[37]

The permissible timing of initial deferrals of performance-based compensation is subject to special rules. Code Sec. 409A(a)(4)(B)(iii) provides that a deferral election related to performance-based compensation based on services performed over a period of at least 12 months may be made no later than six months before the end of the period. The Conference Committee Report notes that the IRS is to determine the definition of performance-based compensation and that such compensation must meet certain requirements similar to those under Code Sec. 162(m) (see the discussion of that section in Chapter 2), but would not be required to meet all of the requirements under that section.[38] In January, 2005, the IRS supplied initial guidance in Question and Answer 22 of Notice 2005-1 concerning under what conditions deferral elections may be made with respect to bonus (performance-based) compensation. Along with the initial guidance, which the IRS refers to as transition relief, the IRS notes that additional guidance is expected to be issued which will be more restrictive than the initial guidance. Thus, taxpayers may have to review and perhaps alter the structure of performance-based plans once further guidance is issued.

Under the IRS initial guidance, a deferral election with respect to bonus compensation based on services performed over a period of at least 12 months will be treated as meeting the statutory requirements if the election is made at least six months before the end of the service period. For purposes of the initial guidance, bonus compensation is compensation deferred under an arrangement where (1) the payment of or the amount of the compensation is contingent on the satisfaction of organizational or individual performance criteria, and (2) the performance criteria are not substantially certain to be met at the time a deferral election is permitted. Bonus compensation may include payments based upon subjective performance criteria. However, (1) any subjective performance criteria must relate to the performance of the participant service provider, a group of service providers that includes the participant service provider, or a business unit for which the participant service provider provides services (which may include the entire organization); and (2) the determination that any subjective performance criteria have been met must not be made by the participant service provider or a family member of the participant service provider (as defined in Code Sec. 267(c)(4), applied as if the family of an individual includes the spouse of any

---

[37] *See* e.g., Rev. Proc. 71-19, 1971-1 CB 698 and Rev. Proc. 92-65, 1992-2 CB 428.

[38] H.R. Conf. Rep. No. 108-755, 108th Cong., 2d Sess. (Oct. 22, 2004).

member of the family). Bonus compensation may also include payments based on performance criteria that are not approved by a compensation committee of the board of directors (or similar entity in the case of a non-corporate service recipient) or by the stockholders or members of the service recipient. In any event, bonus compensation does not include any amount or portion of any amount that will be paid either (1) regardless of performance, or based upon a level of performance that is substantially certain to be met at the time the criteria is established; or (2) that is based solely on the value of, or appreciation in value of, the service recipient or the stock of the service recipient.

As noted earlier, the time and form of distributions must be specified at the time of initial deferral. A plan could specify the time and form of payments that are to be made as a result of a distribution event (e.g., a plan could specify that payments upon separation of service will be paid in a lump sum within 30 days of separation from service) or could allow participants to elect the time and form of payment at the time of the initial deferral election. If a plan allows participants to elect the time and form of payment, that election is subject to the rules regarding initial deferral elections under Section 409A. Multiple payout events are permissible. For example, a participant could elect to receive 25 percent of his or her account balance at age 50 and the remaining 75 percent at age 60. A plan could also allow participants to elect different forms of payment for different permissible distribution events. For example, a participant could elect to receive a lump-sum distribution upon disability, but an annuity beginning when the participant attains age 65.[39]

Additional Deferrals After the Initial Deferral. Code Sec. 409A(4)(C) permits employees or other service providers to change the time and/or form of the deferred compensation distribution by means of an election made subsequent to the time of the initial deferral election under specified circumstances. A nonqualified deferred compensation plan may allow a subsequent election to delay the timing or form of distributions only if: (1) the plan requires that such election cannot be effective for at least 12 months after the date on which the election is made; (2) except for elections relating to distributions on account of death, disability or unforeseeable emergency, the plan requires that the additional deferral for which such election is made is for a period of not less than five years from the date such payment would otherwise have been made; and (3) the plan requires that an election related to a distribution to be made

---

[39] *Id.*

upon a specified time may not be made less than 12 months before the date of the first scheduled payment. The Conference Report indicates that in limited cases, the IRS can issue guidance, consistent with the purposes of Section 409A, concerning (1) the extent to which elections to change a stream of payments are permissible, and (2) elections with respect to payments under nonelective, supplemental retirement plans.[40]

.02 Failure of a Plan to Meet the Requirements of Code Sec. 409A

Under Code Sec. 409A(a)(1), if a nonqualified deferred compensation plan at any time fails to meet the requirements of Code Sec. 409A(a)(2), (3), and/or (4) or is not operated in accordance with those requirements (discussed in ¶ 1403.01 above), all amounts deferred under that plan for all taxable years are currently includible in gross income to the extent the amounts (1) are not subject to a substantial risk of forfeiture; and (2) have not previously been included in gross income. Further, the income tax payable with respect to the current income inclusion is to be increased by the sum of (1) the interest at the IRS underpayment rate plus one percentage point on the underpayments of tax that would have occurred had the compensation been includible in income when first deferred, or if later, when not subject to a substantial risk forfeiture; and (2) an additional tax equal to 20 percent of the compensation which is required to be included in gross income. The tax consequences associated with a failure to meet or comply with the Code Sec. 409A requirements only apply with respect to the plan participants for whom the requirements are not met. For example, suppose a plan covering all executives of an employer (including those subject to Section 16(a) of the Securities and Exchange Act of 1934) allows distributions to individuals subject to Section 16(a) upon a distribution event that is not permitted under Code Sec. 409A (e.g., when their annual bonus falls below a specified amount). The individuals subject to Section 16(a), rather than all participants of the plan, would be required to include amounts deferred in gross income and would be subject to interest and the 20 percent additional tax.[41]

> **Example:** Wesley is a participant in an unfunded nonqualified deferred compensation plan that took effect on June 1, 2005. Under the plan, Wesley elected to defer $20,000 of his 2005 compensation and $30,000 of his 2006 compensation with a payment date set for July 1, 2012. During 2006, the plan was amended

---

[40] Id.   [41] Id.

with respect to Wesley, allowing him to receive 70 percent of the amounts deferred in 2005 and 2006 on December 31, 2008, if he so elected (in lieu of waiting until July 1, 2012). The amendment violates the acceleration of payment rules described in ¶ 1403.01 above. Therefore, all $50,000 of the amounts deferred in 2005 and 2006 is includible in Wesley's gross income in 2006. In addition, interest as described in Code Sec. 409A is payable, and Wesley must pay an additional $10,000 tax ($50,000 × 20 percent) on the includible amount. Wesley's employer can deduct the $50,000 included by Wesley in 2006.

Substantial Risk of Forfeiture. As noted above, amounts are includible for violations of one or more of the Code Sec. 409A requirements to the extent the amounts are not subject to a substantial risk of forfeiture.[42] Similar to the definition provided under Code Sec. 83 and Reg. § 1.83-3 (as discussed in ¶ 1406.02), compensation is subject to a substantial risk of forfeiture if entitlement to the amount is conditioned on the performance of substantial future services by any person or the occurrence of a condition related to a purpose of the compensation, and the possibility of forfeiture is substantial.[43]

For purposes of Code Sec. 409A, a condition related to a purpose of the compensation must relate to the employee's or other service provider's performance for the service recipient or the service recipient's business activities or organizational goals (for example, the attainment of a prescribed level of earnings, equity value or a liquidity event). Any addition of a substantial risk of forfeiture after the beginning of the service period to which the compensation relates, or any extension of a period during which the compensation is subject to a substantial risk of forfeiture, whether elected by the service provider, service recipient or other person (or by agreement of two or more of such persons), is disregarded for purposes of determining whether such compensation is subject to a substantial risk of forfeiture. Further, an amount is not subject to a substantial risk of forfeiture merely because the right to the amount is conditioned, directly or indirectly, upon the refraining from performance of services. Finally, for purposes of Code Sec. 409A, an amount will not be considered subject to a substantial risk of forfeiture beyond the date or time at which the recipient otherwise could have elected to receive the amount of compensation, unless the amount subject to a substantial risk of forfeiture (not taking into account earnings) is materially greater than the amount the recipient otherwise could

---

[42] *Id.*

[43] Notice 2005-1, IRB 2005-2, 274, Q&A 10(a).

have elected to receive. For example, a deferral of a straight salary amount generally may not be made subject to a substantial risk of forfeiture. However, where an election is granted to receive a materially greater bonus amount in a future year rather than a materially lesser bonus amount in an earlier year, the materially greater bonus may be made subject to a substantial risk of forfeiture.[44]

Similar to the requirements under Reg. § 1.83-3(c)(3) for purposes of restricted stock and property plans (as discussed in ¶ 1406.02), a risk of forfeiture is not considered substantial unless the employer or other service provider can and will enforce the condition. This is particularly questionable in cases where the employee or other service provider owns a significant amount of the total combined voting power or value of all classes of stock of the service recipient corporation or of its parent corporation. In such a case, the IRS will take into account the same factors enumerated under Reg. § 1.83-3(c)(3): (1) the service provider's relationship to other stockholders and the extent of his or her control, potential control and possible loss of control of the corporation; (2) the position of the service provider in the corporation and the extent to which the service provider is subordinate to other service providers; (3) the service provider's relationship to the officers and directors of the corporation; (4) the person or persons who must approve the service provider's discharge; and (5) past actions of the service recipient in enforcing the restrictions.

> **Example:** If the service provider owns 20 percent of the single class of stock in the transferor corporation, and if the remaining 80 percent of the class of stock is owned by an unrelated individual (or members of such an individual's family) so that the possibility of the corporation enforcing a restriction on such rights is substantial, then such rights are subject to a substantial risk of forfeiture. On the other hand, if 4 percent of the voting power of all the stock of a corporation is owned by the president of such corporation and the remaining stock is so diversely held by the public that the president, in effect, controls the corporation, then the possibility of the corporation enforcing a restriction on the right to deferred compensation of the president is not substantial, and those rights are not subject to a substantial risk of forfeiture.[45]

Finally, it should be noted that Code Sec. 409A does not alter or affect the application of any other provisions of the Code or common

---

[44] *Id.*

[45] Notice 2005-1, IRB 2005-2, 274, Q&A 10(b).

law tax doctrine to nonqualified deferred compensation plans. Accordingly, deferred compensation not required to be included in income under Code Sec. 409A may nevertheless be required to be included in income under Code Sec. 451, the constructive receipt doctrine, the cash equivalency doctrine, Code Sec. 83, the economic benefit doctrine, the assignment of income doctrine or any other applicable provision of the Code or common law tax doctrine.[46]

.03 Nonqualified Deferred Compensation Plans and Terminology Under Code Sec. 409A

For purposes of Code Sec. 409A, the term "nonqualified deferred compensation plan" is any plan that provides for the deferral of compensation with the exception of certain plans specified in the Code and/or IRS guidance.[47] The application of Code Sec. 409A is not limited to arrangements between an employer and employee. Section 409A may apply to arrangements between a service recipient and an independent contractor or between a partner and a partnership.[48] A nonqualified deferred compensation plan can contain an agreement or arrangement that includes only one person.

Plans Not Considered Nonqualified Deferred Compensation Plans Under Code Sec. 409A. The following types of plans are not considered to be nonqualified deferred compensation plans or are considered not to provide for the deferral of compensation subject to Code Sec. 409A:[49]

(1) Qualified employer retirement plans including Code Sec. 401(a) pension and profit-sharing plans, Code Sec. 401(k) plans, Code Sec. 403(b) tax sheltered annuity plans, SIMPLE plans, Simplified Employee Pension Plans, IRAs, and Code Sec. 457(b) deferred compensation plans of governmental and tax-exempt entities (discussed in ¶ 1407), and qualified government excess benefit arrangements as described in Code Sec. 415(m);

(2) Any bona fide vacation leave, sick leave, compensation time, disability pay or death benefit plan;

(3) Archer MSAs covered under Code Sec. 220, Health Savings Accounts under Code Sec. 223, and any other health reimbursement arrangement that satisfies the requirements of Code Secs. 105 and 106 (e.g., health FSAs covered in Chapter 4);

(4) Incentive stock option plans (ISOs) (covered in Chapter 15) and employee stock purchase plans;

---

[46] Notice 2005-1, IRB 2005-2, 274, Preamble.
[47] Code Sec. 409A(d)(1).
[48] Notice 2005-1, IRB 2005-2, 274, Q&A 3(a).
[49] Code Secs. 409A(d)(1) and (2), H.R. Conf. Rep. No. 108-755, 108th Cong., 2d Sess. (Oct. 22, 2004), and Notice 2005-1, IRB 2005-2, 274, Q&As 3 and 4.

(5) Nonqualified stock options (covered in Chapter 15) where the option price is equal to the value of the stock when the option is granted, and there is no feature for the deferral of compensation other than the deferral of recognition of income until the later of exercise or disposition of the option under Reg. § 1.83-7;

(6) Restricted property and stock plans covered by Code Sec. 83, even in cases where the employee or service provider makes the Code Sec. 83(b) election to recognize income in the year of the grant (see the discussion of restricted stock and property plans in ¶ 1406);

(7) Annual bonuses or other annual compensation amounts paid within two-and-one-half months after the close of the taxable year in which the relevant services required for payment have been performed (see further discussion of this exception below under the short-term deferral exception to what constitutes a deferral of compensation); and

(8) Certain stock appreciation rights (see the discussion below and in Chapter 15 for further details of the application of Code Sec. 409A to stock appreciation rights).

Therefore, the types of nonqualified plans which are likely to be affected by the Code Sec. 409A requirements include unfunded, secured deferred compensation plans, top hat plans, excess benefit plans, supplemental executive retirement plans, and Code Sec. 457(f) plans—plans of governmental and tax-exempt entities that do not meet the Code Sec. 457 requirements. In addition, the following plans based on stock or stock values (covered in chapter 15) may be covered: phantom stock plans; certain stock appreciation rights; discounted nonqualified stock options (option price is less than the fair market value at the date of grant); and non-qualified stock options with deferral features other than the right to exercise the option.

Deferral of Compensation. A nonqualified deferred compensation plan only includes arrangements that provide for the deferral of compensation. Notice 2005-1 first provides a fairly broad definition of what constitutes a deferral of compensation, and then provides some specific important exceptions. Under the broad definition, a plan provides for the deferral of compensation only if, under the plan and the relevant facts and circumstances, the employee or other service provider has a legally binding right during a taxable year to compensation that has not been actually or constructively received and included in gross income and is payable to (or on behalf of) the service provider in a later year. A service provider does not have a legally binding right to compensation if that compensation may be unilaterally reduced or eliminated by the employer or other service recipient or another person after the services creating the right to the compensation have been performed. However, if the facts and circumstances indicate that the discretion to reduce or eliminate the compensation is available or exercisable only upon a condition that is unlikely to occur, or the discretion to reduce or eliminate the compensation is unlikely to be exercised, a service provider will be considered to have a legally binding right to the compensation. For this purpose, compensation is not considered subject to unilateral reduction or elimination merely because it may be reduced or eliminated by operation of the objective terms of the plan, such as the application of an objective provision creating a substantial risk of forfeiture (defined above). Similarly, a service provider does not fail to have a legally binding right to compensation merely because the amount of compensation is determined under a formula that provides for benefits which can be offset by benefits provided under a qualified employer retirement plan or because benefits are reduced, for example, because of actual or notional investment losses.[50]

The first exception to what constitutes a deferral of compensation is compensation that is payable under the employer's or other service recipient's customary payment timing arrangement. Under this exception, a deferral of compensation does not occur just because the service recipient pays compensation after the end of the service provider's taxable year under a timing arrangement under which the service recipient normally compensates service providers for services performed during a payroll period. For example, where an employer typically pays employees on the following January 20 for services rendered during the previous December, there is no deferral of compensation under Code Sec. 409A.[51]

The second exception is for what the Notice refers to as short-term deferrals. Until the IRS issues further guidance, if amounts are payable under the terms of a plan and not pursuant to a deferral election of the employee or other service provider within a short time period after the amounts are fully vested and earned, the plan does not provide for the deferral of compensation. The amounts must be actually or constructively received by the employee or other service provider within the later of (1) two-and-one-half months following the end of the service provider's first taxable year in which the amounts have become fully vested or (2) two-and-one-half months following the end of the service recipient's first taxable year in which the amounts have become fully vested to the service provider.[52] It should be noted that this exception applies not only to short-term bonus plans but, by its terms, applies to long-term bonus or incentive plans where the plans require payment within the applicable

---

[50] Notice 2005-1, IRB 2005-2, 274, Q&A 4(a).
[51] Notice 2005-1, IRB 2005-2, 274, Q&A 4(b).
[52] Notice 2005-1, IRB 2005-2, 274, Q&A 4(c).

two-and-one-half month period following the year in which the plan benefits vest with the employee or other service provider (that is, the year in which such benefits are no longer subject to a substantial risk of forfeiture as defined above). Thus, various long-term deferred compensation arrangements can be exempt from the provisions of Code Sec. 409A under this exception.

The other exceptions for plans or arrangements that do not provide for deferral of compensation were discussed above under plans not considered to be nonqualified deferred compensation plans subject to Code Sec. 409A. These plans are nonqualified stock options not issued at a discount, incentive stock options, employee stock purchase plans, and restricted property and stock plans.

Service Recipients and Service Providers. For purposes of Code Sec. 409A, the service recipient is the person (generally an employer company) for whom the services are performed, all persons with whom such person would be considered a single employer under Code Sec. 414(b) (employees of controlled group of corporations), and all persons with whom such person would be considered a single employer under Code Sec. 414(c) (employees of partnerships, proprietorships, etc., which are under common control).[53]

Until the IRS issues additional guidance, a service provider under Code Sec. 409A includes (1) individuals who are employees or independent contractors, (2) personal service corporations or entities that would be so classified if they were incorporated, and (3) qualified personal service corporations or entities that would be so classified if they were incorporated. However, Code Sec. 409A does not apply to arrangements between (1) taxpayers, all of whom use the accrual method of accounting, and (2) a service provider and a service recipient if (a) the service provider is actively engaged in the trade or business of providing substantial services, other than as an employee or as a director of a corporation; and (b) the service provider provides such services to two or more service recipients to which the service provider is not related and that are not related to one another.[54]

"Plan" for Purposes of Code Sec. 409A. The term "plan" is defined broadly by the IRS for purposes of Code Sec. 409A. This broad definition can have significant consequences as noted below. A plan includes any agreement, method or arrangement, including an agreement, method or arrangement that applies to one person or individual. A plan may be adopted unilaterally by the service recipient or may be negotiated among or agreed to by the service recipient and one or more service providers or service provider representatives. An agreement, method or arrangement may

---

[53] Notice 2005-1, IRB 2005-2, 274, Q&A 5.   [54] Notice 2005-1, IRB 2005-2, 274, Q&A 8.

constitute a plan regardless of whether it is an employee benefit plan under Sec. 3(3) of the Employee Retirement Income Security Act of 1974 (ERISA). Further, for most purposes, similar types of nonqualified deferred compensation plans subject to Code Sec. 409A are combined. The following types of plans are combined for determining whether the requirements of Code Sec. 409A are met and the consequences of not meeting such requirements:[55]

(1) All compensation deferred with respect to a service provider under account balance plans (as defined under Reg. § 31.3121(v)(2)-1(c)(1)(ii)(A)—generally, defined contribution nonqualified plans);

(2) All compensation deferred with respect to a service provider under a nonaccount balance plan (as defined in Reg. § 31.3121(v)(2)-1(c)(2)(i)—generally, defined benefit nonqualified plans such as SERPs); and

(3) All compensation deferred under plans that are neither account or nonaccount balance plans (such as discounted nonqualified stock options, certain stock appreciation rights or other equity-based compensation described in Reg. § 31.3121(v)(2)-1(b)(4)(ii).

Under the foregoing rules, a severance pay plan is either an account balance plan or nonaccount balance plan depending on the nature of the plan.

The plan aggregation rules can have significant adverse consequences for taxpayers in some circumstances under Code Sec. 409A. For example, suppose that an executive is covered by three separate nonaccount balance plans under which compensation is deferred after December 31, 2004. Assume that all three plans are covered by the Code Sec. 409A rules and that in 2007, one or more of the Code Sec. 409A requirements are violated under one of the three plans. Because all three plans are combined and considered to be one plan for the general purposes of Code Sec. 409A, all of the compensation deferred after 2004 under all three plans is recognized as gross income in 2007 (and subject to interest and the additional 20 percent tax) to the extent not previously recognized as income and not subject to a substantial risk of forfeiture.

.04 Foreign Trusts and Triggers Upon Financial Health

One of the common means of securing the payment of nonqualified deferred compensation is through the use of rabbi trusts (as discussed in ¶ 1405.02) and similar arrangements. In brief, a rabbi trust is a trust or other fund established by the employer to hold assets from which nonqualified deferred compensation payments

---

[55] Notice 2005-1, IRB 2005-2, 274, Q&A 9.

¶ 1403.04

will be made. The trust or fund is generally irrevocable and does not permit the employer to use the assets for purposes other than to provide nonqualified deferred compensation, except that the terms of the trust or fund provide that the assets are subject to the claims of the employer's creditors in the case of insolvency or bankruptcy. In an attempt to place assets set aside in such trusts beyond the reach of creditors, some employers have established rabbi trusts and similar arrangements in foreign jurisdictions. Because Congress felt that such arrangements violate the intent of the provisions allowing for deferral of compensation set aside in such trusts, Congress enacted Code Sec. 409A(b)(1). Under that Code section, where assets are set aside (directly or indirectly) in a trust (or other arrangements as specified in forthcoming IRS guidance) for purposes of paying non-qualified deferred compensation, such assets are treated as property transferred in connection with the performance of services under Code Sec. 83 (this results in the inclusion of the value of such property in gross income—see the discussion of Code Sec. 83 in ¶ 1406) at the time the assets are set aside if (1) those assets (or the applicable trust or other arrangement) are then located outside of the United States; or (2) those assets (or the applicable trust or other arrangement) are subsequently transferred outside of the United States. Any subsequent increases in the value of, or any earnings on such assets are treated as additional transfers of property subject to tax. However, this rule does not apply if substantially all of the services to which the nonqualified deferred compensation relates are performed in the same jurisdiction as the assets set aside.[56]

Some employers have also tried to keep assets intended to be used to pay nonqualified deferred compensation beyond the reach of creditors by restricting the availability of such assets to pay the deferred compensation if the financial condition of the employer deteriorates to a specified point. Congress enacted Code Sec. 409A(b)(2) to attack such situations. Under that Code section, a transfer of property in connection with the performance of services under Code Sec. 83 (and, thus, current inclusion in gross income) occurs with respect to compensation deferred under a nonqualified deferred compensation plan if the plan provides that upon a change in the employer's financial health, assets will be restricted to the payment of nonqualified deferred compensation. An amount is treated as restricted even if the assets are available to satisfy the claims of general creditors. For example, the provision applies in the case of a plan that provides that upon a change in financial health, assets will be transferred to a rabbi trust.

---

[56] H.R. Conf. Rep. No. 108-755, 108th Cong., 2d Sess. (Oct. 22, 2004).

The transfer of property occurs as of the earlier of when the assets are so restricted or when the plan provides that assets will be restricted. It is intended that the transfer of property occurs to the extent that assets are restricted or will be restricted with respect to such compensation. For example, in the case of a plan that provides that upon a change in the employer's financial health, a trust will become funded to the extent of all deferrals, all amounts deferred under the plan are treated as property transferred under Code Sec. 83. If a plan provides that deferrals of certain individuals will be funded upon a change in financial health, the transfer of property would occur with respect to compensation deferred by such individuals. The new rule is not intended to apply when assets are restricted for a reason other than change in financial health (e.g., upon a change in control) or if assets are periodically restricted under a structured schedule and scheduled restrictions happen to coincide with a change in financial status. Any subsequent increases in the value of, or any earnings with respect to, restricted assets are treated as additional transfers of property. [57]

Of course, amounts includible under each of the above provisions are also subject to the interest and the 20 percent additional tax of Code Sec. 409A. [58]

.05 Effective Date and Transition Rules

Except as provided under transition guidance (generally applicable only for calendar year 2005) specified in Notice 2005-1, Code Sec. 409A is effective for (1) amounts deferred in taxable years beginning after December 31, 2004, and (2) amounts deferred in taxable years beginning before January 1, 2005, if the plan under which the deferral is made is materially modified after October 3, 2004. Section 409A applies to earnings on amounts deferred only to the extent that the section applies to the amounts deferred. Thus, Code Sec. 409A does not apply to earnings on amounts deferred in taxable years beginning before January 1, 2005, unless that section applies to the amounts that are deferred. [59]

For purposes of determining whether Code Sec. 409A is effective with respect to an amount of compensation, the amount is considered deferred before January 1, 2005, if (1) the service provider has a legally binding right to be paid the amount, and (2) the right to the amount is earned and vested. For this purpose, a right to an amount is earned and vested only if the amount is not subject to either a substantial risk of forfeiture (as defined in Reg. § 1.83-3(c)) or a requirement to perform further services. Thus, amounts to which the service provider

---

[57] *Id.*
[58] *Id.*

[59] Notice 2005-1, IRB 2005-2, 274, Q&A 16(a).

does not have a legally binding right before January 1, 2005 (for example, because the service recipient retains discretion to reduce the amount) will not be considered deferred before January 1, 2005. In addition, amounts to which the service provider has a legally binding right before January 1, 2005, but which are subject to a substantial risk of forfeiture or a requirement that the service provider must perform further services after December 31, 2004, are not considered deferred before January 1, 2005. Nevertheless, an amount to which the service provider has a legally binding right before January 1, 2005, but for which the service provider must continue performing services to retain the right only through the completion of the payroll period which included December 31, 2004, will not be treated as subject to a requirement to perform further services (or a substantial risk of forfeiture) for purposes of the effective date rules.[60]

Determination of Amounts Deferred Before January 1, 2005. Detailed rules are provided in Question and Answer 17 concerning how the amount of compensation deferred under a nonqualified deferred compensation plan before January 1, 2005 is determined. The amount deferred under a plan which is a nonaccount balance plan (e.g., a defined benefit nonqualified plan) equals the present value as of December 31, 2004 of the amount to which the participant would be entitled under the plan if the participant voluntarily terminated services without cause on that date and received a full payment of benefits from the plan on the earliest possible date permitted to the extent the right to the benefit is earned and vested. Reasonable actuarial assumptions must be used in the determination. For account balance plans (defined contribution nonqualified plans), the amount deferred before January 1, 2005 equals the vested and earned portion of the participant's account balance as of December 31, 2004. For equity-based nonqualified plans, the amount deferred prior to January 1, 2005 is deemed to be the amount of the payment available to the participant on December 31, 2004, the right to which is earned and vested and excludes the exercise price or other amount that the participant must pay. Earnings on amounts deferred under a plan before January 1, 2005 include only income (notional or actual) attributable to the amounts deferred under a plan as of December 31, 2004. For example, notional interest earned on amounts deferred in an account balance plan as of December 31, 2004 will be treated as earnings on amounts deferred under the plan before January 1, 2005. For purposes of determining the amount deferred prior to January 1, 2005, nonqualified plans of similar types are not aggregated like they must be for purposes of the general rules of Code Sec. 409A.

---

[60] Notice 2005-1, IRB 2005-2, 274, Q&A 16(b).

When A Plan Is Considered to Be Materially Modified.
With the exception of certain transition rules applicable to the year
2005, a plan is considered to be materially modified if a benefit or right
existing in that plan on October 3, 2004 is enhanced or a new benefit or
right is added. A benefit enhancement or addition is a material modification whether it occurs via an amendment to the plans or the exercise
of the discretion of the service provider under the plan (even if the
enhanced or added benefit would be permitted under Code Sec. 409A).
For example, a material modification would occur if a service recipient
exercised discretion to accelerate the vesting of a benefit under the plan
to a date on or before December 31, 2004. However, the following are
not considered to be material plan modifications: (1) a service recipient
exercises discretion over the time and manner of payment of a benefit
to the extent the discretion is allowed under the plan as of October 3,
2004; (2) a change in a notional investment measure to, or to add, an
investment measure that qualifies as a predetermined actual investment within the meaning of Reg. § 31.3121(v)(2)-1(d)(2); (3) to amend a
plan to bring the plan into compliance with the provisions of Code Sec.
409A; and (4) the reduction of an existing benefit under a plan, such as
the removal of a "haircut" provision.[61]

In general, the adoption of a new arrangement or the grant of an
additional benefit under an existing arrangement after October 3,
2004 is presumed to constitute a material modification of a plan.
However, the presumption may be rebutted by demonstrating that
the adoption of the arrangement or grant of the additional benefit
is consistent with the service recipient's historical compensation
practices. For example, the presumption that the grant of a stock
appreciation right on November 1, 2004 is a material modification of
a plan may be rebutted by demonstrating that the grant was consistent
with the historic practice of granting substantially similar stock appreciation rights (both as to terms and amounts) each November for a
significant number of years. Further, the grant of an additional benefit
under an existing arrangement that consists solely of a deferral of
additional compensation not otherwise provided under the plan as of
October 3, 2004, will be treated as a material modification of the plan
only as to the additional deferral of compensation, if the plan explicitly
identifies the additional deferral of compensation and provides that
the additional deferral of compensation is subject to Code Sec. 409A.[62]

The amendment of a plan or arrangement to stop future deferrals under it is not a material modification of the arrangement or
plan. Further, the amendment of a plan or arrangement on or before
December 31, 2005 to terminate that arrangement and distribute

---

[61] Notice 2005-1, IRB 2005-2, 274, Q&A 18(a).   [62] Notice 2005-1, IRB 2005-2, 274, Q&A 18(b).

¶ **1403.05**

the amounts of deferred compensation under it will not be treated as a material modification if all amounts deferred under the plan are included in gross income in the year the termination occurs.[63]

Special rules apply concerning the cancellation and reissuance of equity-based deferred compensation plans if that cancellation and reissuance occurs before the end of 2005 in order to bring the plan to the state that its provisions do not constitute a deferral of compensation under Code Sec. 409A.[64] See further discussion of this point in Chapter 15.

For purposes of the rules described above concerning whether a material plan modification occurs, the general rules of Code Sec. 409A requiring aggregation of similar types of plans do not apply. Any changes to particular plans are evaluated separately.[65]

Transition Rules for Calendar Year 2005. Question and Answers 19 through 21 and 23 of Notice 2005-1 provide detailed transition rules that apply specifically to calendar year 2005. Highlights of these rules are covered in the following discussion.

Probably the most important of the transition rules is that a plan adopted before December 31, 2005 will not be treated as violating the general Code Sec. 409A requirements (those of Code Sec. 409A(a)(2) through (4)) if (1) the plan is operated in good faith compliance (as defined in the Notice) with the provisions of Code Sec. 409A and Notice 2005-1; and (2) the plan is amended on or before December 31, 2005 to conform to such rules for amounts that are subject to Code Sec. 409A.[66]

For amounts subject to Code Sec. 409A, a plan may be amended to provide for new payment elections with respect to amounts deferred prior to the election without violating the rules of Code Sec. 409A(a)(3) and (4) if that plan is so amended and the participant makes the election on or before December 31, 2005. Similar rules apply to stock options and stock appreciation rights.[67] A plan providing severance pay benefits that is amended on or before December 31, 2005 to comply with Code Sec. 409A and that is either (1) a collectively bargained plan, or (2) covers no key employees (as defined in Code Sec. 416(i)) does not have to meet the requirements of Code Sec. 409A during calendar year 2005 with respect to such severance pay benefits.[68] Of course, this transition rule is relevant only to severance pay plans that would otherwise be subject to Code Sec. 409A. Severance pay plans could be set up to meet the

---

[63] Notice 2005-1, IRB 2005-2, 274, Q&A 18(c).
[64] Notice 2005-1, IRB 2005-2, 274, Q&A 18(d).
[65] Notice 2005-1, IRB 2005-2, 274, Q&A 18(e).

[66] Notice 2005-1, IRB 2005-2, 274, Q&A 19(a) and (b).
[67] Notice 2005-1, IRB 2005-2, 274, Q&A 19(c).
[68] Notice 2005-1, IRB 2005-2, 274, Q&A 19(d).

short-term deferral exception of Question and Answer 4(c) of Notice 2005-1 and escape treatment under Code Sec. 409A.

A plan adopted before December 31, 2005 may be amended to allow a participant all or part of 2005 to terminate his or her participation in the plan or cancel a deferral election without causing the plan to fail the three Code Sec. 409A requirements (the requirements in Code Sec. 409A(2) through (4)) if (1) the amendment is enacted and effective before the end of 2005, and (2) the amounts subject to that termination are includible in gross income by the participant in 2005, or, if later, in the taxable year in which the amounts are earned or vested. Neither the availability of nor the making of such election will cause the participant to be subject to Code Sec. 409A with respect to the applicable amount, and the constructive receipt doctrine will not apply. A partial termination or cancellation in accordance with these provisions is also permitted. For purposes of the transition rule described in this paragraph, plans are not aggregated such as they are for purposes of the general Code Sec. 409A requirements.[69]

Taxpayers had an opportunity to make an election on or before March 15, 2005 under which the requirements of Code Sec. 409A(4)(B) concerning the timing of deferral elections would not be applicable to deferrals relating totally or in part to services performed on or before December 31, 2005. For the election to apply, the following requirements had to be met: (1) the amounts to which the deferral election related could not have been paid or become payable at the time of election; (2) the plan under which the deferral election was made had to be in existence on or before December 31, 2004; (3) the elections to defer compensation were made in accordance with the terms of the plan in effect on or before December 31, 2005 (other than a requirement to make a deferral election after March 15, 2005); (4) the plan was otherwise operated in accordance with Code Sec. 409A with respect to deferrals subject to Code Sec. 409A; and (5) the plan is amended to comply with the requirements of Code Sec. 409A during 2005. Neither the making nor availability of this election caused the constructive receipt doctrine to apply to the subject amounts.[70]

Finally, for periods ending on or before December 31, 2005, an election concerning the timing and form of a payment under a nonqualified deferred compensation plan that is controlled by a payment election made by the participant under a Code Sec. 401(a) qualified retirement plan (such as an election under a shadow Code Sec. 401(k) plan as described in ¶ 1402.04 above) will not violate Code Sec. 409A if made in accordance with the terms of the plan as of October 31, 2004. However, such deferrals continue to be subject to other provisions of

---

[69] Notice 2005-1, IRB 2005-2, 274, Q&A 20.   [70] Notice 2005-1, IRB 2005-2, 274, Q&A 21.

¶ 1403.05

the Code and common law doctrines, such as the constructive receipt doctrine.[71] This transition provision suggests that the IRS will carefully review shadow 401(k) plans after 2005, so, as discussed as the end of ¶ 1402, taxpayers will need to pay close attention to the structure of shadow Code Sec. 401(k) plans and other nonqualified plans that have been traditionally tied to qualified retirement plans.

.06 Wage Withholding and Information Reporting Requirements

Section 885 of the ACJA also includes specific wage withholding and information reporting requirements connected with nonqualified deferred compensation that is subject to the provisions of Code Sec. 409A. The additions to the Code include modifications to Code Sec. 3401(a) and added Code Secs. 6041(g) and 6051(a)(13). Question and Answers 24 through 36 of Notice 2005-1 provide detailed guidance as to the withholding and reporting requirements and should be consulted for specific rules. Although it is beyond the scope of this work to cover these requirements, it should be noted that Code Sec. 3401(a) requires income tax withholding on any amounts includible in gross income under the Code Sec. 409A provisions. Further, annual reporting of amounts deferred under a nonqualified plan is required, regardless of whether such amounts are includible in gross income. Reporting of includible amounts and amounts deferred with respect to independent contractors is also required. However, reporting of deferrals is not required with respect to persons for whom a Form 1099 or a Form W-2 is not required to be filed.

.07 Applicability of Code Sec. 409A for FICA and FUTA Tax Purposes

Section 885 of the ACJA and the provisions of Code Sec. 409A do not affect the imposition of employee tax and employer tax under FICA on wages paid and received for employment under a nonqualified deferred compensation plan as defined in Code Sec. 409A(d). Thus, the applicability of FICA taxes to nonqualified deferred compensation continues to be governed by the rules under Code Sec. 3121(v)(2) and the regulations thereunder as described in ¶ 1405.02.[72] Without a doubt, the same conclusion applies for FUTA taxes which are still governed by Code Sec. 3306(r) and the regulations thereunder.

¶ 1404 Other Tax Factors Affecting Nonqualified Deferred Compensation

As noted in ¶ 1403 above, new Code Sec. 409A does not alter or affect the application of any other provision of the Code or common

---

[71] Notice 2005-1, IRB 2005-2, 274, Q&A 23.

[72] Notice 2005-1, IRB 2005-2, 274, Q&A 37.

law tax doctrine to nonqualified plans to which the new section applies. Thus, deferred compensation not required to be included under Code Sec. 409A may nonetheless be required to included under the constructive receipt doctrine, the cash equivalency doctrine, the economic benefit doctrine, Code Sec. 83, or any other applicable provision of the Code or common law doctrine. Further, these other provisions continue to apply to amounts deferred that are not subject to the provisions of Code Sec. 409A because they are excepted under that section's effective date provisions (i.e., amounts deferred in taxable years beginning before January 1, 2005 where no material modifications to the subject plan have been made after October 3, 2004) and to certain nonqualified plans not covered under Code Sec. 409A or not covered because of the 2005 transition rules under Notice 2005-1. Thus, in order to ensure the deferral of income recognition overall, not only must taxpayers concern themselves with Code Sec. 409A but also must take into account the other tax factors as well. The more important of these other factors, the constructive receipt doctrine, the cash equivalency doctrine, the economic benefit doctrine, and the Code Sec 83 restricted property rules, are covered below.

.01 Constructive Receipt

The doctrine of constructive receipt is of extreme importance in planning for nonqualified deferred compensation. If the deferred compensation amounts are considered to be constructively received during the year in which the employee performs the related services, the employee will have to pay tax on a current basis on amounts to be received in the future. Under Reg. § 1.451–2, income is considered constructively received by the taxpayer "in the taxable year during which it is credited to his account, set apart for him, or otherwise made available so that he may draw upon it at any time or so that he could have drawn upon it during the taxable year if notice of intention to withdraw had been given." However, income is not constructively received if the taxpayer's control of its receipt is subject to substantial limitations or restrictions. Thus, if a corporation credits its employees with a bonus, but the bonus is not available to such employees until some future date, the mere crediting on the books of the corporation does not constitute receipt. Amounts which are subject to the unfettered control of the taxpayer will be constructively received, regardless of whether the taxpayer elects to exercise that control. However, if the taxpayer's control of the amount is subject to substantial limitations or restrictions imposed by someone else (such as the taxpayer's employer), there will be no constructive receipt.

Although the question of whether income is constructively received will be decided on the facts of each case, the courts have indicated that the doctrine is to be applied sparingly, gathering only the more flagrant cases within its sweep.[73] Thus, in general, a deferred compensation arrangement will be honored unless the arrangement is a sham transaction that is designed to provide the employee with the benefits of deferring income recognition while also permitting access to the deferred amounts. The following paragraphs describe the position of the IRS and the prevailing position of the courts concerning deferred compensation arrangements.

The IRS Position. Rev. Rul. 60–31[74] sets out the principles under which the IRS will permit the deferral of income recognition under deferred compensation arrangements. This ruling distinguished between (1) a mere contractual right to receive income at a future date, not evidenced by a note or security, and (2) cases in which the employee had the right to receive the compensation income, but instead had it put into trust or escrow for him or held on demand by the employer until a future tax year. Under the ruling, a "mere promise to pay, not represented by notes or secured in any way, is not regarded as a receipt of income within the intendment of the cash receipts and disbursements method. . ." Thus, the recognition of compensation can be deferred if the employer and employee enter into a contract to defer a certain amount or percentage of compensation before the income is earned (that is, before the services are performed) and the employer does no more than make a basic bookkeeping entry of the liability to pay the deferred amount in the future. The employee's future right to the compensation does not have to be subject to a substantial risk of forfeiture and the employer can credit the deferred amount with interest.

The deferral of compensation was also permitted in Rev. Rul. 69–650,[75] where certain compensation was deferred until termination of employment, and in Rev. Rul. 71–419,[76] where director's fees were deferred pursuant to an unfunded deferred compensation plan. In these rulings, the IRS also stated that if the right to defer compensation prior to the rendition of services is pursuant to a periodic election, that election must be irrevocable.

The IRS Ruling Policy. The IRS will issue an advance ruling on nonqualified deferred compensation plans in accordance with the provisions of Rev. Proc. 71–19, as modified by Rev. Proc. 92–65.[77]

---

[73] *JA. Brander*, 3 BTA 231, Dec. 1095 (1925).
[74] 1960 –1 CB 174.
[75] 1969 –2 CB 106.

[76] 1971 –2 CB 220.
[77] 1971 –1 CB 698 and 1992–2 CB 428.

This ruling policy will not apply to situations where Code Sec. 409A (discussed in ¶ 1403) applies to include amounts deferred under nonqualified plans. Beginning in 2005, the ruling policy (unless or until it is revised) will likely apply with respect to the applicability of the doctrine of constructive receipt to nonqualified plans that pass muster under Section 409A.

Under Rev. Proc. 71–19, the IRS will issue a letter ruling concerning whether an employee's election to defer recognition of compensation can actually defer the recognition under the following circumstances:

(1) When an employee initially makes an election to defer compensation, the election must be made before the beginning of the period of service for which compensation is payable, regardless of forfeiture provisions in the plan.

(2) In the case of elections other than an initial election, an election may be made by an employee after the beginning of the service period if the plan contains substantial forfeiture provisions that must remain in effect throughout the entire period of deferral.

Rev. Proc. 71–19 does not specifically define the terms "substantial forfeiture provisions" and "period of service." The revenue procedure does state, however, "that a substantial forfeiture provision will not be considered to exist unless its conditions impose on the employee a significant limitation on duty which will require a meaningful effort on the part of the employee to fulfill and there is a definite possibility that the event which will cause the forfeiture could occur." Rev. Proc. 92–65 indicates that the period of service for purposes of the first requirement is ordinarily the employee's tax year for cash-basis, calendar-year taxpayers. Rev. Proc. 92–65 also provides two exceptions to the first requirement above, as follows:

(1) In the year in which the plan is first implemented, the employee participant may make an election to defer compensation for services to be performed subsequent to the election within 30 days after the effective date of the plan.

(2) In the first year in which an employee becomes eligible to participate in the plan, the newly eligible employee-participant may make an election to defer compensation for services to be performed subsequent to the election within 30 days after the date the employee becomes eligible.

¶ 1404.01

In addition, Rev. Proc. 92–65 has established additional requirements that must be met with respect to elective deferral ruling requests, as follows:

(1) The plan must define the time and method for payment of deferred compensation for each event that entitles an employee participant to receive benefits (e.g., separation from service). The plan must specify the date of payment or provide that payment will begin within 30 days after the occurrence of a stated event.

(2) The plan must permit an employee participant to receive benefits in the case of an unforeseeable emergency. The term "unforeseeable emergency" must be defined in the plan as an unanticipated emergency that is caused by an event beyond the control of the employee participant or beneficiary and that would result in severe financial hardship to the individual if early withdrawal were not permitted. The amount allowed to be withdrawn, however, must be limited to the actual expenses of the emergency. Language similar to that contained in Reg. § 1.457–6(c)(2) may be used.

(3) The plan must provide that the participants have the status of general unsecured creditors and the plan must be unfunded (i.e., the employer has only made a promise to pay future amounts). If the plan contains or refers to a trust, it must conform to the requirements of the model trust described in Rev. Proc. 92–64 (see the discussion of this revenue procedure under the heading Rabbi Trusts later in this chapter). Finally, the plan must state that the parties intend that the arrangements be unfunded for tax purposes and under Title I of ERISA.

(4) The plan must provide that a participant's rights to benefits under the plan are not subject to anticipation, alienation, sale, transfer, assignments, pledge, encumbrance, attachment, or garnishments by the creditors of the participant or the participant's beneficiary.

For an example of letter rulings in which the taxpayer received a favorable response allowing the deferral of compensation at least in part on the basis of meeting the requirements of Rev. Proc. 92–65, see Letter Rulings 9807004 and 9817015.

As an exception to its general ruling policy concerning unfunded deferred compensation plans, the IRS will not rule on the tax consequences of nonqualified deferred compensation arrangements with respect to controlling shareholder-employees and unidentified independent contractors who participate in the plan.[78]

---

[78] Rev. Proc. 2005–3, IRB 2005–1, 118.

The Courts' Position. The courts have adopted a more liberal stance than the IRS ruling requirements concerning elective deferrals. In general, unless the deferred compensation arrangement is clearly a sham or the employee already controls the amounts sought to be deferred, deferred compensation arrangements have been approved where the agreement was executed before or, even in some cases, after the services were performed. Beginning in 2005, these court rulings will not apply to amounts deferred under non-qualified plans to which Code Sec. 409A applies. However, the rulings still could have application to amounts deferred under the few non-qualified plans that are not subject to the requirements of that section and to amounts deferred prior to the effective date of Code Sec. 409A.

In cases where compensation deferral arrangements are executed before the services are rendered, the courts have generally ruled that the deferred amounts have not been constructively received. Deferral has even been permitted where the amount deferred constitutes a portion of the employee's original regular annual compensation, rather than an additional payment, such as a bonus.

For example, in *Robinson*,[79] the Tax Court permitted "Sugar Ray" Robinson to defer a portion of his earnings from a championship bout, where the agreement was entered into before the fight even though the employer might have been willing to make payments immediately after the fight. The court also indicated that the fact that the deferral agreement was instituted solely at the taxpayer's request was immaterial as long as the contracting parties viewed the agreement as binding. Further, in *Goldsmith*,[80] the Court of Claims (now the U.S. Court of Federal Claims) indicated that amounts could be deferred even though the deferral agreement was made after the original salary payments were fixed by an earlier employment agreement. Finally, the courts have not required that the receipt of the deferred compensation be subject to a substantial risk of forfeiture. The courts simply require that the employee not exercise control over the deferred compensation during or before the period of the deferral.

The courts have permitted the deferral of compensation in some cases under arrangements entered into after the services have been performed. Unless the arrangement is considered a sham, amounts will not be held to be constructively received where a deferral agreement is entered into after services are performed, but the likelihood or the amount of the payment is not determinable on the date of the deferral. Thus, an election to defer a bonus will not cause the bonus

---

[79] 44 TC 20, Dec. 27,321 (1965), acq. 1976–2 CB 2.   [80] CtCls, 78–2 USTC ¶ 9804, 586 F2d 810 (1978).

to be constructively received where the amount of the bonus cannot be determined as of the date of the deferral. For example, in *Veit*,[81] the employee was entitled to a bonus in 1941 based on the employer's 1940 net profits. The bonus was to become due and payable when the 1940 net profits were calculated sometime in 1941. In November 1940, the employer and employee entered into an agreement to defer payment of the bonus until 1942. The Tax Court held that the bonus was not constructively received in 1941 because the agreement was an arm's-length business transaction, and the agreement was entered into prior to the date that the bonus was definitely determinable. A similar ruling was handed down in *Oates*.[82] In that case, following their retirement, the taxpayers were entitled to receive certain commissions on renewal premiums. At the time of their retirement on April 27, 1944, the taxpayers had the right to receive the renewal commissions or elect to receive them in monthly installments of $1,000 per month over a period not to exceed 180 months. The taxpayers elected to receive the monthly installments. The IRS argued that the amounts were constructively received at retirement. The Tax Court did not agree (and the decision was upheld by the Seventh Circuit Court of Appeals) and instead held that the amounts were only taxable when received. This ruling was partly based on the fact that the amount of the previously earned commissions was not exactly known and was not payable at the time of the deferral. The IRS acquiesced in the Tax Court's decision.[83]

The courts have even permitted additional deferrals of compensation that have already been deferred by prior agreement if the subsequent deferral arrangement was entered into prior to the payment date specified in the original agreement. For example, in the second *Veit* case,[84] a revised deferral agreement was executed in late 1941 providing that the deferred amounts subject to the original deferral agreement which was the subject of the first *Veit* case (described above) would be further deferred over a five-year period. In the second *Veit* case, the Tax Court ruled that the further deferral of the amounts did not result in constructive receipt of the amounts because under the initial deferral contracts, "there was never a time when the [compensation] was unqualifiedly subject to the taxpayer's demand or withdrawal." The taxpayer did not voluntarily refrain from collecting the money available to him, nor did he agree to deferral of money that was available to him. Thus, under the second *Veit* case, further deferrals of income will be permitted even if the amounts are ascertainable as long as the employee cannot withdraw

---

[81] 8 TC 809, Dec. 15,718 (1947). Acq. 1947–2 CB 4.
[82] 18 TC 570, Dec. 19,049 (1952). Acq. 1960-1 CB 5, aff'd, CA-7, 53–2 USTC ¶ 9596, 207 F2d 711 (1953).
[83] Acq. 1960.1 CB 5.
[84] 8 TCM 919, Dec. 17,240(M).

the money or otherwise exercise control over it. The IRS did not acquiesce in this decision.

Section 132 of the Revenue Act of 1978. Section 132(a) of the Revenue Act of 1978 required the IRS to abide by the principles set forth in regulations, rulings and judicial decisions which were in effect on February 1, 1978, in dealing with the application of the constructive receipt doctrine to unfunded nonqualified deferred compensation arrangements. Thus, even though its ruling policy in Rev Procs. 71-19 and 92-65 was stronger, it was likely bound by its acquiescences to the first *Veit* case and the *Oates* case and by its revenue rulings (such as Rev. Rul. 60-31) issued prior to that date in applying the doctrine of constructive receipt to unfunded nonqualified plans. Beginning in 2005, Section 132(a) of the 1978 Act is no longer is applicable to amounts deferred under plans to which the requirements of Code Sec. 409A apply and which take precedence over the earlier cases and rulings. However, Section 132(a) likely still applies with respect to the application of the doctrine of constructive receipt to plans that meet the requirements of Code Sec. 409A, to amounts deferred under plans not subject to the requirements of Code Sec. 409A, and to amounts deferred that are exempt from Code Sec. 409A because of its effective date provisions.

.02 The Economic Benefit and Cash Equivalency Doctrines

The economic benefit doctrine is frequently confused with the constructive receipt doctrine, but is logically different. The constructive receipt doctrine indicates when income is taxable. By contrast, the economic benefit doctrine defines what income is.

The economic benefit doctrine is a principal of taxation developed in court decisions and IRS rulings and applies where an economic benefit is presently conferred on the taxpayer even though there may be no right and no opportunity on the part of the taxpayer to receive the money currently. Beginning in 2005, the economic benefit doctrine will still apply to nonqualified deferred compensation plans where its requirements are not contrary to the provisions of Code Sec. 409A, and to amounts deferred under nonqualified plans not covered under Code Sec. 409A or which are not subject to that section under its effective date provisions.

In general, the economic benefit doctrine will apply to a nonqualified deferred compensation plan that: (1) provides to the employee rights to the employer's property that are in some way superior to those of the employer's general creditors, (2) permits the employee to assign or otherwise anticipate the income before it is due, or (3) conveys some other immediate economic benefit on the employee. In *Sproul*,[85] the Tax Court held that economic benefit was conferred where an amount of compensation for past services was irrevocably placed in trust for future distribution to an employee. Similarly, the employee was immediately taxable on amounts irrevocably placed in escrow. However, the economic benefit doctrine did not apply to a case in which insurance policies that were to be used to pay deferred compensation in the future were subject to claims of the employer's creditors.[86] Similarly, in *Minor*, the Ninth Circuit Court of Appeals held that the economic benefit doctrine did not apply to a trust created to provide for the payment of deferred compensation to the company's physician beneficiaries. The economic benefit doctrine did not apply because the trust was not required by the deferred compensation plan, the employer was the beneficiary of the trust, and the trust assets were subject to the claims of the employer's general creditors.[87]

It is not clear how narrowly the nonqualified plan can define the class of creditors that may have access to the assets of the plan and still avoid application of the economic benefit doctrine. The IRS has approved arrangements in which the class of creditors was limited to judgment creditors of the employer.[88] But if the class of creditors is defined too narrowly, the IRS might assert that the assets of the plan are effectively insulated from the creditors of the firm and that, as a result, the economic benefit doctrine applies to the plan.

In summary, if funds placed into a nonqualified plan remain subject to the rights of the employer's creditors or the employee does not have a vested right to those funds, the economic benefit doctrine should not apply.

Under the cash equivalency doctrine, if an employer issues an employee a promissory note equal to the amount of compensation that is deferred and payable in a subsequent taxable year, the amount of the note may be recognized as compensation income by the employee when received. In *Cowden*,[89] the Fifth Circuit Court of Appeals held that "if a promise to pay of a solvent obligor is unconditional and assignable, not subject to set-offs, and is of a kind that is frequently transferred to lenders or investors at a discount not substantially greater than the generally prevailing premium for

---

[85] 16 TC 244, Dec. 18,080. Aff'd *per curiam*, CA-6, 52–1 USTC ¶ 9223, 194 F2d 541 (1952).

[86] *See* Rev. Rul. 68–99, 1968–1 CB 193 and Rev. Rul. 72–25, 1972–1 CB 127.

[87] *R.H. Minor*, CA-9, 85–2 USTC ¶ 9717, 722 F2d 1472. *See also R.A Childs*. 103 TC 634, Dec. 50,239. Aff'd, CA-11, 96–2 USTC ¶ 50,504,89 F3d 856.

[88] See IRS Letter Ruling 8325100. 3–23–83, CCH IRS Letter Ruling Reports and IRS Letter Ruling 8439012, 6–22–84, CCH IRS LETTER RULINGS REPORTS.

[89] *Cowden*, CA-5, 7 AFTR2d 1160 (1961).

the use of money, such promise is the equivalent of cash and taxable in like manner as cash would have been taxable had it been received by the taxpayer rather than the obligation." Thus, unless the instrument evidencing the promise to pay the deferred compensation is issued by an employer-maker of doubtful solvency or for other reasons under which the instrument may not be negotiable in the marketplace, an employee that receives such a note evidencing the promise will be taxable in the year the note is received. Beginning in 2005, the cash equivalency doctrine will still apply to nonqualified deferred compensation plans where its requirements are not contrary to the provisions of Code Sec. 409A, and to amounts deferred under nonqualified plans not covered under Code Sec. 409A or which are not subject to that section under its effective date provisions.

.03   Code Sec. 83 Restricted Property Rules

To a large extent, the Code Sec. 83 restricted property rules have replaced the economic benefit doctrine in applying to nonqualified plans. Under Code Sec. 83, an employee is taxed on the fair market value of property (including the employer's stock) minus any amount paid for the property by the employee when that property is transferred to him (or to a trust on his behalf) in connection with the performance of services for the employer. However, the employee will not be taxed until the year in which his rights in the property are either transferable or are not subject to a substantial risk of forfeiture. Since nonqualified deferred compensation which is subject to the provisions of Code Sec. 83 is generally not subject to the provisions of Code Sec. 409A, as discussed in ¶ 1403 above, Section 83 remains an important authority governing the provision of certain forms of nonqualified deferred compensation.[90] Code Sec. 83 is covered extensively in the discussion of restricted property plans later in this chapter.

.04   Employer Deductibility of Deferred Amounts

Under Code Sec. 404(a)(5), amounts deferred pursuant to a nonqualified deferred compensation plan are deductible in the year in which the deferred amounts are included in the income of the deferring employee. Thus, the timing of the employer's deduction is matched with the timing of the employee's income recognition. This rule also applies to nonqualified deferred compensation which is included in gross income under new Code Sec. 409A in a year earlier than the year in which it is actually payable to an employee. In the

---

[90] *See* Notice 2005-1, IRB 2005-2, 274, Q&As 3 and 4.

case of a funded arrangement, an employer is entitled to a deduction for a contribution to such a plan in the tax year during which the last day of the employee's tax year in which the income was recognized falls.[91] However, if the funded plan has more than one participant, a deduction will be permitted only if separate accounts are maintained for each participant. In addition, Code Sec. 404(a)(5) also applies to deferred bonus arrangements of accrual basis employers if such bonuses are not paid within two and one-half months after the year in which the services were performed.[92] For this purpose, no amount of compensation is treated as having been paid to an employee until the employee actually receives payment of the amount.[93] Thus, payments under vacation plans and severance pay plans must be received by employees within the applicable 2½ month period to avoid being treated as deferred compensation. Payments made within the 2½ month period are deductible in the year in which they are accrued, rather than the year in which they are paid.

The timing of the deductibility of accrued interest on nonqualified deferred compensation has been the subject of heated debate. The Ninth Circuit Court of Appeals ruled in 1993 in *Albertsons Inc.* that accrued interest on unpaid nonqualified deferred compensation accounts is deductible in the year it is accrued, rather than in the year the compensation is paid.[94] Needless to say, the ruling sparked vigorous protests from the IRS, fearing the loss of revenue, and subsequently generated numerous articles by commentators. Eventually, at the request of the IRS, the Ninth Circuit reheard the decision. In the rehearing, the Court reversed the earlier ruling and held that interest on nonqualified deferred compensation is deductible in the year in which the compensation is paid.[95] The Court, instead of citing technical reasons for its decision cited the basic differences between qualified and nonqualified plans (discussed earlier in this chapter) as forming the reason for the decision. According to the Court, the interest on the deferred amounts in a nonqualified plan should not be deductible until paid, so as not to provide an undue advantage with respect to nonqualified plans that do not have to meet the qualification rules that must be met by qualified plans. Of course, if, under Code Sec. 409A, amounts deferred under a nonqualified plan and the earnings thereon are

---

[91] Reg. § 1.404(a)-12(b).

[92] Code Sec 404(a)(6).

[93] Code Sec. 404(a)(11) as added by P.L. 105–206, 105th Cong. 2d Sess., Sec. 7001(a) (July 22, 1998).

[94] *Albertsons Inc.*, CA-9, 94–1 USTC ¶50,016,38 F3d 1046. Rev'g 95 TC 415. Dec. 46,915.

[95] *Albertsons Inc.*, CA-9, 94–2 USTC ¶50,619,42 F3d 537. Rev'd on rehearing CA-9, 94–1 USTC ¶50,016,38 F3d 1046. Rev'g 95 TC 415. Dec. 46,915(1990), cert. denied, U.S. Sup. Ct. No. 941796(1994).

taxable to an employee in a year earlier than the year in which they are payable under the plan, the employer may then deduct both the deferred amounts and related earnings in the same year they are includible by the employee.

Nonqualified deferred compensation is not deductible unless the requirements of Code Sec. 162 are met. Thus, such payments must be reasonable in amount. As noted in Chapter 2, whether nonqualified deferred compensation is reasonable is based on a consideration of the year in which the services are performed.[96]

.05   Applicability of FICA and FUTA Taxes

Nonqualified deferred compensation is part of the taxable wage base for both FICA and FUTA tax purposes. Under Code Secs. 3121(v) and 3306(r), amounts deferred under a "nonqualified deferred compensation plan" are included as wages for FICA and FUTA tax purposes in the later of:

(1) the year in which the services are performed; or

(2) the year in which there is no substantial risk of forfeiture of the amounts.

Since new Code Sec. 409A does not apply with respect to the applicability of FICA and FUTA taxes to nonqualified deferred compensation plans, Code Secs. 3121(v) and 3306(r) continue to provide the authority for that applicability.[97]

In early 1999, the IRS issued final Regulations § 31.3121(v)(2)-1 that provide guidance on the determination of FICA and FUTA taxes under Code Secs. 3121(v) and 3306(r). In general, the final regulations apply to amounts deferred on or after January 1, 2000; to amounts deferred before January 1, 2000, which cease to be subject to a substantial risk of forfeiture on or after January 1, 2000, or for which a resolution date occurs on or after January 1, 2000; and to benefits actually or constructively paid on or after January 1, 2000. For periods before January 1, 2000, (including amounts deferred before then and any benefits actually or constructively paid before then that are attributable to those amounts deferred), an employer may rely on a reasonable, good faith interpretation of Code Sec. 3121(v)(2) taking into account pre-existing guidance.[98] Under Reg. § 31.3121(v)(2)-1(b), the rules apply to plans that provide for the deferral of compensation. A plan provides for the deferral of compensation only if an employee has a legally binding

---

[96] *Lucas v. Ox Fibre Co.*, SCt, 2 USTC ¶ 522, 281 US 115 (1930).

[97] *See* Notice 2005-1, IRB 2005-2, 274, Q&A 37.
[98] Reg. § 31.3121(v)(2)-1(g).

right to compensation that has not been actually or constructively received and that is payable in a subsequent year. However, the following types of plans are not covered by the rules of the regulations (that means that for these plans, FICA and FUTA taxes will apply in the same year income taxes apply): (1) stock appreciation rights, (2) non-qualified stock options, (3) restricted stock and property plans under Code Sec. 83, and (4) certain welfare benefit plans, such as vacation benefits, severance pay, and disability pay.

Only the amount deferred under a non-qualified plan is subject to FICA and FUTA taxes. Under Reg. § 31.3121(v)(2)-1(c), the determination of the amount deferred depends upon whether the plan is an account balance or a non-account balance plan. If amounts are credited under an account balance plan (a plan that credits an absolute dollar amount such as an elective deferral plan), the amount deferred equals the principal amount credited to the employee for the period plus any income attributable to that amount through the date the amount is taken into account for FICA and FUTA tax purposes. If the plan is a non-account balance plan (meaning that an amount other than a fixed amount is credited to the employee's account—e.g., an excess benefit plan designed to provide benefits over those allowed for defined benefit pension plans), the amount deferred equals the present value of the future payments to which the employee has obtained a legally binding right during the period. In determining this present value amount, employers can use any reasonable actuarial method.

Under Reg. § 31.3121(v)(2)-1(d), an amount deferred is generally considered taken into account when the amount is included in computing the amount of FICA and FUTA taxes. Under a non-duplication rule, once an amount deferred is taken into account for employment tax purposes, neither the amount deferred nor the income related to the amount will again be taken into account for these purposes.[99]

In accordance with the statutory rules indicated above, Reg. § 31.3121(v)(2)-1(e) indicates that deferred compensation amounts must ordinarily be taken into account for the year in which the related services are performed unless there is a substantial risk of forfeiture as defined in Reg. § 1.83–3(c). The services that create the right to an amount deferred are considered performed when, under the terms of the plan and all relevant facts and circumstances, the employee has performed all the services necessary to obtain a legally binding right to the amount deferred, disregarding any substantial

---

[99] Reg. § 31.3121(v)(2)-1(a)(2)(iii).

risk of forfeiture. If an amount deferred under a non-account balance plan is not reasonably ascertainable, the amount need not be taken into account until the earliest date the amount is reasonably ascertainable. Finally, an amount that is required to be taken into account at some point during a calendar year may be taken into account as late as December 31 of that year.

> **Comment:** The provisions of Code Secs. 3121(v) and 3306(r) affect nonqualified deferred compensation plans (covered under the proposed regulations) entered into after 1993 because the 1.45 percent Medicare portion of the FICA tax applies to all wages (without limit) paid or taxable during a given year. Therefore, unless the deferred compensation is subject to a substantial risk of forfeiture, the Medicare tax will apply to deferred amounts for the year in which the related services are performed, causing the executive or other employee participant to be taxed on amounts not yet received. To a lesser degree, this rule will have an impact with respect to the OASDI portion of FICA taxes (applicable to the first $84,900 of compensation in 2002).

¶ 1405   Types of Nonqualified Plans

Taking into account the general tax consequences associated with nonqualified deferred compensation arrangements, the following classifications can be made of nonqualified plans:

(1) unfunded, unsecured plans;

(2) unfunded, secured plans;

(3) funded, unsecured plans; and

(4) funded, secured plans.

.01   Unfunded, Unsecured Plans

Under Rev. Rul. 60–31,[100] an unfunded, unsecured nonqualified deferred compensation agreement will result in the deferral of income recognition until the compensation is actually paid to the employee. The constructive receipt doctrine will not apply because the employee does not have control over or a right to receive the compensation until the time specified in the contract. The economic benefit doctrine and Code Sec. 83 do not apply because the employer has only made a bookkeeping entry, a mere promise to pay the amount in the future. And, beginning in 2005, no amount under an

---

[100] 1960–1 CB 174.

unfunded, unsecured plan that is subject to the requirements of Code Sec. 409A will be taxable earlier than in the year payable, if the plan meets the requirements of Code Sec. 409A, as covered in ¶ 1403.01. Under this rule, a deferred compensation arrangement may credit investment earnings (such as interest) to the base amount of compensation deferred. This crediting may be done as a bookkeeping entry, or the employer may actually "segregate" and invest the amount of deferred compensation. In the latter case, as long as the assets remain subject to the claims of the employer's creditors, the employee will not be taxed on the deferred amounts until they are received. The IRS has issued a number of private letter rulings indicating that the crediting of investment earnings to unfunded deferred compensation arrangements does not result in current taxation to the employee.[101]

Because of their basic characteristics, unfunded and unsecured plans have three fundamental disadvantages. First, if the employer credits the employee's deferred amount with interest, the right of the employee to receive the deferred compensation is an employer liability which increases yearly. Second, the employer's obligation may have to be paid when the employee is no longer performing services for the company and thereby not helping to produce the funds needed to pay the deferred compensation. Finally, the employee runs the risk that the employer will become financially unable to meet the contractual obligation to pay the deferred compensation at the scheduled future dates of payment. For example, consider the plights of star athletes who entered into unfunded deferred compensation contracts with teams in the defunct U.S. Football League. Employees who have deferred compensation under unfunded, unsecured plans are only general creditors, and if the employer becomes bankrupt, the employee may collect nothing or, at best, a small percentage of the amount promised to be paid.

.02 Unfunded, Secured Plans

To overcome the major disadvantages of unfunded, unsecured plans, employers arrange to provide funding to meet their contractual obligations arising from nonqualified plans. The trick is to "secure" a plan in a way such that some form of security can be provided to the employee without bringing the constructive receipt or economic benefit doctrine into play. The following methods can

---

[101] *See.* e.g., IRS Letter Ruling 7941001, 11-22-98, CCH IRS Letter Rulings Reports, IRS Letter Ruling 7914047, 1-4-79, CCH IRS Letter Rulings Reports, IRS Letter Ruling 7914076, 1-8-79, CCH IRS Letter Rulings Reports, IRS Letter Ruling 9403008, 10–19–93, CCH IRS Letter Rulings Reports, IRS Letter Ruling 9825007, 3-16-98, CCH IRS Letter Rulings Reports, and IRS Letter Ruling 200110005, 11-14-00, CCH IRS Letter Rulings Reports.

be used to "secure" the payments to be made under nonqualified plans:

(1) life insurance;

(2) reserve funds;

(3) revocable trusts;

(4) vesting trusts;

(5) rabbi trusts;

(6) third-party guarantees; and

(7) surety bonds and deferred compensation insurance.

Each of the methods is covered in order below. Beginning in 2005, care will have to be taken to meet the requirements of Code Sec. 409A, discussed in ¶ 1403.01, where amounts deferred under the underlying plans are subject to that new section.

Life Insurance. Employer-owned life insurance on the life of the compensated employee is a method of securing the payment of deferred compensation to the employee. By retaining ownership in the policy and making the proceeds payable to itself, the employer transfers no property interest beyond its control for the benefit of the employee. Thus, the employee does not have to recognize income under the either the constructive receipt or economic benefit doctrine. The employee is not taxable until he actually receives the compensation[102] or some right constituting an incidence of ownership.[103] One of the downsides of using employer-owned life insurance is that Code Sec. 264 generally prohibits employers from deducting (1) premiums for the contracts funding the nonqualified plan where the employer remains owner and beneficiary, and (2) most interest expense costs associated with such policies.

The life insurance method of "funding" covered above works well (from the employee's perspective) except if the employer becomes insolvent before all benefits have been paid to the employee. Since the policy is held by the employee as one of its unsecured assets, it can be attached by the creditors or the trustee in the case of bankruptcy.

---

[102] Rev. Rul. 72–75, 1972–1 CB 401.

[103] In *Brodie*, 1 TC 275. Dec. 12,907 (1942), the Tax Court held that a nonassignable, nonliquidating, single premium annuity purchased by an employer on behalf of an employee was taxable compensation to the employee under the economic benefit doctrine because the employee could designate a beneficiary. The Court did not find any evidence of the constructive receipt doctrine, given that the employee (1) had no advance knowledge of the bonus, (2) had no option to receive cash in lieu of the policy, and (3) could not begin receiving payments until after his 70th birthday. However, the Court viewed the employee's right to designate a beneficiary to be an incidence of ownership, a right that was superior to the employer's, and therefore an economic benefit, taxable as compensation.One of the downsides of using employer-owned life insurance is that Code Sec. 264 generally prohibits employers from deducting (1) premiums for the contracts funding the nonqualified plan where the employer remains owner and beneficiary and (2) most interest expense costs associated with such policies.

However, attempts to further "secure" an employee's rights while retaining deferral of taxation may face severe obstacles. For example, if the insurance policy is placed in trust or escrow for unconditional payment to the employee, the economic benefit doctrine will apply and make the employee immediately taxable on the cash value of the policy and additional premiums as they are paid.[104] Also, under Code Sec. 402(b), the employee would be immediately taxable unless his rights under the trust are subject to a substantial risk of forfeiture according to Code Sec. 83.

Split-dollar life insurance is another type of insurance-related arrangement which may be used to "fund" or fulfill an employer's obligation under a nonqualified deferred compensation plan. It is not a particular type of life insurance but rather a method by which the employee can share the costs and/or benefits of a life insurance policy with the employer. Care must be taken to structure arrangements taking into account the rules under Reg. §§ 1.61-22 and 1.7872-15. In addition, Section 402(k)(1) of the Sarbanes-Oxley Act of 2002[105] may prohibit split-dollar arrangements that are treated as loans with respect to executives of public corporations. See Chapter 3 for further coverage of split-dollar life insurance.

Reserve Fund. Another method of "securing" the employer's promise to pay is for the employer to establish a reserve fund which is invested in a portfolio of securities or other assets. Since the fund is part of the employer's general assets, it is subject to the claims of the firm's general creditors. Thus, the economic benefit doctrine does not apply.

The employer could provide the employees with the right to direct the investment of their portion of the reserve fund as long as they have no formal secured right to that fund. That is, the fund could not be formally assigned as collateral for the deferred compensation obligations.

Revocable Trust. The employer could establish a revocable trust for the benefit of the employees participating in the nonqualified plan. The plan should be regarded as unfunded for tax purposes since the trust assets essentially belong to the employer.[106] In addition, the transfer of assets to the trust should not be considered a transfer of property subject to the provisions of Code Sec. 83 (see the discussion on Code Sec. 83 later in this chapter) since the trust assets remain subject to the claims of the firm's general creditors.

---

[104] *See, e.g., P.L. Frost,* 52 TC 89, Dec. 29, 535(1969).

[105] P.L. 107-204, 107th Cong., 2nd Sess. (July 30, 2002). 116 Stat. 745 (2002).

[106] *See* Rev. Rul. 67-289, 1967-2 CB 163.

The trust may also be considered unfunded for purposes of ERISA since the employer can revoke the trust.

Since the trust is revocable, the employer is taxable on the earnings of the trust under the grantor trust rules of Code Sec. 676. The employer should thus receive a deduction under Code Sec. 404(a)(5) for the amount transferred to the employee when the deferred compensation is paid rather than when contributions are made to the trust.

Vesting Trusts. Under a vesting trust arrangement, the employer makes contributions to a trust to "secure" the compensation payable under a nonqualified plan. However, an employee's right to the amounts accumulated in the trust will not vest until the occurrence of specified events. An employee's rights will typically vest when he or she terminates employment, attains a specific age, retires from the company, or when there is a change in control of the employing company. The deferred compensation is generally paid to the employee when his rights to the compensation vest. Thus, it is not necessary that the assets of the trust be subject to the claims of the general creditors of the employer.

The employee-participants will not be taxed on their interest in a vesting trust until those interests become transferable or are no longer subject to a substantial risk of forfeiture.[107] The economic benefit doctrine should not apply because the employee's have not been provided any current cash equivalent right. Finally, the constructive receipt doctrine should not apply since the employees are not entitled to any of the deferred amounts until they vest.

If the vesting trust is revocable, or the assets of the trust can be used to satisfy the employer's legal liabilities, the employer will be taxable on the income of the trust under the grantor trust rules of Code Sees. 671 to 678. The use of assets of the trust to pay the deferred compensation due to participating employees would likely be a discharge of the employer's legal liability to pay the deferred compensation. Consequently, most vesting trusts are grantor trusts.

Under Code Sec. 404(a)(5), the employer can deduct its contributions to the extent that the amounts are taxable to the employees in the year of receipt as long as a separate account is maintained for each participant. Ordinarily, Reg. § 1.404(a)-12(b)(1) provides that the employer's deduction will be limited to the value of the assets (which may be greater) at the time the employee becomes vested,

---

[107] *See* Code Secs. 83 and 402(a).

¶ 1405.02

which is the amount includible in the employee's income under Reg. § 1.402(b)-1(b)(1). However, if the vesting trust is a grantor trust under which the employer is taxable on the income, the employer should get a deduction for the value of the assets in the trust at the time of the employee's vesting, rather than the amount contributed to the trust.

Rabbi Trusts. A rabbi trust is an arrangement under which the employer places assets into an irrevocable trust to "secure" the payment of promised deferred compensation to selected employees. The trust agreement will generally provide that the assets placed in the trust will remain subject to the claims of the employer's general creditors in the event the employer becomes insolvent or files for bankruptcy. If the trust agreement does not provide the employees with vested ownership rights in the trust assets before they receive the deferred compensation payments, the employee will be taxed only when the payments are received. This type of deferred compensation arrangement is called a rabbi trust because the first letter ruling that approved deferral of compensation under such an arrangement involved a rabbi.[108] The IRS has established a model rabbi trust agreement and ruling procedures (discussed below) under which, if the employer's trust meets the model trust provisions, the IRS will issue a favorable ruling which will allow the deferral of the compensation. As a practical matter, therefore, employers desiring to secure deferred compensation payments through the use of a rabbi trust should set up their trust in accordance with the model trust provisions.

Under a rabbi trust arrangement, no income will be recognized by the employee participants until they actually receive the promised deferred compensation payments since the assets of the trust remain subject to the claims of the general creditors of the employer.[109] For the same reason, the economic benefit doctrine should not apply. The constructive receipt doctrine should not apply because the employee cannot receive the deferred compensation until some future time such as the termination of employment or retirement. Finally, beginning in 2005, as long as the requirements of Code Sec. 409A, as stated in ¶ 1403.01, are met for plans subject to that section and employing rabbi trusts and the rabbi trust assets are not located abroad and are not payable as result of a change in the employer's financial health, as discussed in ¶ 1403.04, the use of a rabbi trust will not cause deferred amounts to be taxed in a year earlier than when paid to the participants under Section 409A.

---

[108] *See* IRS Letter Ruling 8113107, 12-31-80, CCH IRS LETTER RULINGS REPORTS.

[109] Code Secs. 83 and 402(b).

Since the assets of the trust may be used to satisfy the liabilities of the employer, the employer will be taxable on the income of the trust under the grantor trust rules. The employer will be able to deduct the deferred compensation payments to the employees from a rabbi trust by virtue of Code Sec. 404(a)(5) and Reg. § 1.404(a)-12(b)(2). In addition, it is not necessary to maintain separate accounts in a rabbi trust for each employee as a condition for getting the deduction.[110]

The IRS has provided a model rabbi trust agreement in Rev. Proc. 92-64[111] that is intended to serve as a safe harbor for taxpayers that adopt and maintain rabbi trusts and other grantor trusts in connection with unfunded deferred compensation plans (only funds that actually defer the receipt of compensation will be approved). If the model language is used, the constructive receipt doctrine will not apply solely on account of adoption or maintenance of the trust. Rev. Proc. 92-64 also provides guidance for requesting IRS letter rulings on plans that use rabbi trusts. Rulings will only be issued in rare and unusual circumstances if the model language is not used. One example of a ruling issued where there was a rare and unusual circumstance was IRS Letter Ruling 9332038 (May 18, 1993). In that instance, the deferred compensation agreement did not adopt the model trust format because the participant was employed by a Canadian sports franchise necessitating that the agreement had to comply with both U.S. and Canadian tax law.

The model trust language includes all the provisions necessary for operation of the trust except for provisions concerning the trustee's investment powers. However, the revenue procedure indicates that the trustee must be an independent third party and must be given reasonable investment discretion within broad guidelines described in the trust. In general, the model trust language must be used except that the taxpayer may substitute his/her language for any optional provision, but the substituted language must be consistent with the model trust language. The trust can be revocable or irrevocable, but it must be intended to be a grantor trust with the employer as the grantor. The principal and earnings of the trust must be held apart from other employer funds and used exclusively for the purposes of plan participants and employer creditors. Assets of the trust must remain subject to the claims of the employer's creditors, and the Board of Directors and Chief Executive Officer of the employer have the obligation to

---

[110] IRS Letter Ruling 8936072, 6-15-89, CCH   [111] 1992-2 CB 422.
IRS Letter Rulings Reports.

inform the trustee in writing of the employer's insolvency. Finally, any provision of the model trust agreement that is prohibited by state law will be ineffective.

Taxpayers who adopt the model trust and desire to obtain a ruling concerning the plan must include a representation that the plan is not inconsistent with the terms of the trust and must follow the guidelines of Rev. Procs. 92-64 and 92-65 (covered earlier in this chapter). Rulings issued by the IRS will continue to express no opinion concerning whether the trust is funded for purposes of Title I of ERISA. However, the DOL has indicated that rabbi trusts are not considered funded for purposes of ERISA where rabbi trusts are used in connection with top hat or excess benefit plans.[112] The request for a ruling must be accompanied by a representation that the trust conforms to the model trust language, including the order in which sections of the model trust language appear and that the trust adopted does not contain any inconsistent language, in substituted portions or elsewhere, that conflicts with the model trust language. A copy of the trust language must be provided with all substituted language underlined or highlighted.

The provisions of Rev. Proc. 92-64 apply with respect to rulings requested on or after July 28, 1992 and do not affect any letter rulings issued before that date. Since the issuance of Rev. Proc. 92-64, the IRS has issued favorable rulings in a number of instances where the trust language conformed to that in the revenue procedure.[113]

Because the assets of the trust remain subject to the claim of the employer's creditors, there is a chance (as discussed in the case of life insurance "secured" plans above) that the employee will not be paid the deferred compensation if the employer becomes bankrupt. Provisions could be put in the trust instrument that call for the acceleration of payment of the deferred compensation in such an event. However, such provisions may cause the employee to be taxed at the time the employer makes contributions to the trust under the economic benefit doctrine or Code Sec. 83 since such provisions could determine the rights of the firm's creditors to the trust assets.

---

[112] DOL Advisory Opinion 91-16A (April 5, 1991).

[113] *See*, e.g., IRS Letter Ruling 9301017. 10-9-92, CCH IRS LETTER RULINGS REPORTS. IRS Letter Ruling 9324040, 2-25-93. CCH IRS LETTER RULINGS REPORTS, IRS Letter Ruling 9530007, 4-20-95, CCH IRS LETTER RULINGS REPORTS, IRS Letter Ruling 9701024, 9-30-96, CCH IRS LETTER RULINGS REPORTS, IRS Letter Ruling 199901013, 9-30-98, CCH IRS LETTER RULINGS REPORTS, IRS Letter Ruling 200046012, 8-8-99, CCH IRS LETTER RULINGS REPORTS, IRS Letter Ruling 200128006, 3-27-01, CCH IRS LETTER RULINGS REPORTS, IRS Letter Ruling 200308032, 11-8-02, CCH IRS LETTER RULINGS REPORTS and IRS Letter Ruling 200434008.

In Notice 2000–56,[114] the IRS held that when (1) a parent corporation contributes parent stock to a rabbi trust to assist a subsidiary in meeting the subsidiary's deferred compensation obligation to the subsidiary's employees or service providers, and (2) the parent stock is both subject to the claims of the creditors of the parent corporation and subject to the requirement that any parent stock not transferred to the subsidiary's employees will revert to the parent on termination of the trust, then the parent corporation will be considered the grantor and owner of the parent stock held in the trust. This holding applies even if the parent stock is also subject to the claims of the general creditors of the subsidiary. If these conditions are met, the parent stock (or other assets) will not be considered transferred to the subsidiary until when they are used to satisfy the subsidiary's deferred compensation obligation to its employees or service providers or when a claim is made against the trust by a creditor of the subsidiary in the case of the subsidiary's insolvency. Under these circumstances, the provisions of Rev. Proc. 92-64 will not fail to be satisfied.

Third-Party Guarantees. Under this arrangement, the employer promises to pay deferred compensation and a third party guarantees to pay the deferred compensation in the event that the employer is unable to pay. The guarantee could be from a shareholder of the employer, a related corporation, or possibly in the form of an irrevocable letter of credit from a bank issued in the favor of the employee. As long as the employer's promise to pay and the guarantor's obligation is not evidenced by notes or secured in any manner, the existence of the guarantee should not trigger recognition of income to the employee before the employee actually receives the compensation.

The IRS has approved third-party guarantee arrangements in some private letter rulings. For example, in Letter Ruling 8509023, the IRS approved a third-party guarantee as a method of providing "security" for the employer's payment. In that situation, the guarantor was the employer's parent corporation. The IRS has also issued favorable rulings for third-party guarantees in Letter Rulings 8741078, 8752037, 875037, and 9241030.

Surety Bonds and Deferred Compensation Insurance. The IRS, in Letter Ruling 8406012, permitted the deferral of compensation in an arrangement under which an executive purchased a financial surety bond from an independent insurance company

---

[114] 2000-2 CB 393.

¶ 1405.02

to "secure" payment of the employer's promise to pay deferred compensation to the executive. The surety bond insured payments under the nonqualified plan if, for any reason, the employer was unable to make the payments. The executive paid the premiums for the bond without being reimbursed by the employer. The IRS reasoned that the purchase of the surety bond was similar to the purchase of a life insurance policy and did not create a current property right or change the employee's rights to the deferred compensation. Thus, it seems that if the employer plays no part in obtaining the insurance and does no business with the insurance company that issues the surety bond, deferral of compensation should be permitted where the employee pays for the policy.

More recently, however, the IRS has informally indicated that where surety bonds are used to secure an unfunded, unsecured promise to pay, the surety bonds may be treated as property under Code Sec. 83, thereby causing income to be recognized currently. For example, in Tech. Adv. Memo 9443006, the IRS held that an irrevocable standby letter of credit purchased by an employer to secure the employer's obligation to pay unpaid vacation benefits accrued during the taxable year constituted property for purposes of Code Sec. 83. If the employer failed to pay the vacation benefits, the issuer of the letter of credit would be requested to pay the benefits. Since the general creditors of the employer had no rights with respect to the payments made or to be made under the letter of credit, the IRS concluded that the employer's secured promise to pay constituted property for purposes of Code Sec. 83, making the employees taxable currently on the accrued benefits.

> **Comment:** There is an important distinction between the two rulings above. In the first, the employee obtained the insurance on his own, whereas the vacation payments in the second ruling were secured by "insurance" (the letter of credit) purchased by the employer. If the employee independently (and without getting an increase in compensation to fund the payment) purchases insurance which will pay the deferred compensation in the event the employer fails to do so, the recognition of compensation should be deferred. In that case, the employer still only has an unfunded, unsecured obligation.

The degree of employer involvement with respect to the insurance will be a significant concern of the IRS in deciding whether the recognition of income can be deferred. See IRS Letter Ruling 9344038.

.03 Funded, Unsecured Plans

An employer may actually provide funding as a part of a nonqualified deferred compensation plan in order to ensure that it will be able to make the promised deferred compensation payments. Funding the deferred compensation payments will, of course, reduce the risk to the employee that the promised amounts won't be paid and will more easily enable the employer to make them. The problem with funded plans is that the employee is currently taxable on the funded amounts under the economic benefit doctrine and Code Sec. 83. However, this problem can be overcome if (1) the corporation retains ownership of the assets, (2) the assets used for the funding remain subject to the claim of the creditors of the employer, or (3) the rights of the employee to the deferred compensation are subject to a substantial risk of forfeiture. Arrangements under which the employer can provide some type of "funding" and still preserve deferral, such as the use of the vesting trusts and rabbi trusts, are covered in the section describing unfunded, secured plans. Beginning in 2005, plans employing such funding arrangements must further meet the requirements of Code Sec. 409A, as covered in ¶ 1403.01, where amounts deferred under the plans are subject to Section 409A and must not run afoul of the foreign trust and employer health change provisions, as covered in ¶ 1403.04. Obviously, there is considerable overlap in the overall classification of plans.

.04 Funded, Secured Plans

The ultimate means of making certain that the deferred compensation amounts will actually be paid is to provide funding of the deferred amounts and to provide the participating employees with security that the amounts will be paid. Thus, a nonqualified plan could be funded by contributions to a trust, by contributions to an escrow account, or by the purchase of annuity for the benefit of the employee. However, such strategy will ordinarily trigger the recognition of income in the current year under Code Sec. 83, which provides that amounts contributed to such plans will be immediately taxable to the employee unless the employee's rights to the deferred compensation are subject to a substantial risk of forfeiture.

Secular Trusts. One important type of funded and secured plan is the secular trust. A secular trust is a funded, irrevocable trust which is used to provide nonqualified deferred compensation to executives and other employees. Because such trusts are funded and the funds are beyond the reach of the employer's creditors, the employees enjoy more security than is available under rabbi trusts and other similar vehicles discussed above, and as a result, there is no deferral of income recognition.

Secular trusts came into favor after 1986 because under TRA '86, the top corporate marginal income tax rate of 34 percent was higher than the top individual income tax rate of 28 percent (31 percent in 1991 and 1992). For the period of 1987 through 1992, this relationship of the top corporate and individual marginal tax rates made the employer's tax deduction for compensation more valuable than the tax cost to the employee of not having the benefit of deferral of income recognition. However, for the period of 1993 through 2002, as a result of RRA '93 and EGTRRA, the top individual marginal tax rate (39.6 percent for 1993 through 2000, 39.1 percent in 2001, and 38.6 percent in 2002) was higher than the top corporate rate of 35 percent. Even with the reduction in individual marginal tax rates for 2003 and later years under JGTRRA (the top rate has been reduced to 35 percent), the top individual rate will still not be less than the top 35 percent corporate rate. As a result, secular trusts have become less favored because the corporate tax deduction is generally less valuable than the tax cost to the employee of not having deferral of income recognition.

The desirability of secular trusts has been further diminished as a result of a series of letter rulings issued by the IRS in late 1991. Under Letter Rulings 9206009 and 9207010, the IRS held that where an employer made contributions to a trust to be allocated to the accounts of participants to secure deferred compensation payments, the trusts could not be treated as employer grantor trusts. As a result, the trust has to be treated as a taxable entity in such a situation, and the earnings on employer contributions are taxed to the trust (using the most progressive tax rate schedule in revised Code Sec. 1(e)). In addition, the IRS held that Code Sec. 402(b)(4), which provides a special income inclusion rule for highly compensated employees (as defined in Code Sec. 414(q), discussed in Chapter 6) if the trust fails to meet the minimum coverage rules of Code Sec. 410(b) and/or Code Sec. 401(a)(26) (these sections require that a certain minimum number of nonhighly compensated employees be covered under the plan in order for the plan to be qualified; see the discussion in Chapter 6), applies to determine the taxability of highly compensated plan participants. Since most secular trusts violate one or both of these sections because secular trusts generally cover only executives and other highly compensated employees, the highly compensated participants are taxed on their vested accrued benefit in the trust at the end of each year minus their investment in the arrangement (amounts taxed in previous years are not taxed again). For years in which the employer retains the right to allocate trust income among the participants, the taxable amount to the highly compensated participants will be the lesser of the present value of their trust account balance payable when provided under the plan or the present value of the participant's benefit under the plan. The nonhighly compensated participants are taxable on an amount equal to the portions of the participant's trust account attributable to employer contributions (other than contributions for amounts that have already been included in gross income) to the trust account which are substantially vested to the participants.

> **Comment:** Two observations can be made from the above discussion. First, since the trust is taxable on the earnings on the plan contributions and the highly compensated participants are also taxable on such earnings, there is double taxation of this kind of secular trust. Second, the IRS is applying the Code Sec. 402(b)(4) taxation of highly compensated employee rules to trusts that never were qualified plan trusts. Some practitioners feel that such rules were intended only to apply to cases where qualified plans become disqualified as a result of failing to meet the Code Sec. 410(b) and/or Code Sec. 401(a)(26) requirements. Their view is that Code Sec. 402(b)(4) should not apply to secular trusts that have never been qualified plan trusts. However, the IRS has indicated that Code Sec. 402(b)(4) does apply to non-qualified plans, and, in particular, to secular trusts.

Finally, in Letter Rulings 9206009 and 9207010, the employer was not permitted to deduct its plan contributions because the IRS found that the employer's power to reallocate trust income from the accounts of those not yet in benefit status violated the separate account requirement of Code Sec. 404(a)(5). The employer could only deduct contributions as the participants received their benefits. As a result, there is no matching of employer deductions and trust and employee income recognition in such arrangements. Also see IRS Letter Ruling 9302017.

In two other Letter Rulings 9212019 and 9212024 with similar facts, the tax consequences for the trust participants and the trusts were the same as described above. However, since the employer did not have the power to reallocate trust income, the employer was allowed a current deduction for its trust contributions.

In all of the rulings concerning secular trusts described above, the employer was not permitted to take a full deduction for the amounts includible by the employees from the trusts. Instead, the employer was only able to deduct its trust contributions at some point. The IRS has formalized its position on the amount deductible by an employer under secular trusts in Prop. Reg. § 1.671-1(g)(1). Under that proposed regulation, an employer is not treated as an owner of any portion of a nonqualified deferred compensation trust, regardless of the powers the employer holds over the trust. Thus, the employer cannot deduct more than the amounts it contributes to those trusts.

To avoid the double taxation of trust income described above, secular trusts will have to be set up as employee grantor trusts or as simple trusts. In order to be classified as an employee grantor trust, the employees would have to make contributions to the trust that are more than incidental as compared to those of the employer (i.e., they would have to exceed those made by the employer).[115] Such a trust arrangement could be made similar to the ones described in Letter Rulings 8841023 and 8843021 which allowed the participants to receive cash compensation or have their employers contribute a like amount to an irrevocable trust set up for their exclusive benefit. See Letter Ruling 9316018 for a more recent illustration where double taxation was avoided through use of an employee secular trust. In that instance, as in the earlier rulings, the employees were treated as the owners of the trust and were taxable on the trust income.

As an alternative, the trust could be made a simple trust by requiring that trust income be distributed yearly to the participants. This would eliminate taxation on the trust because of the distribution deduction allowed to such trusts under Code Sec. 661. An example of a simple trust used for secular trust purposes can be found in Letter Ruling 9502030 where the IRS held that the trust was entitled to a deduction under Code Sec. 661 for the amounts paid or credited and were taxable to the participants. To mitigate the employee's taxation, the employer could indemnify the participants for the taxes that result from the funding of the arrangement.

Finally, it should be noted that the provisions of Code Sec. 409A, described in ¶ 1403, should not apply to secular trusts since employer contributions to such trusts are taxable to the employee participants under Code Sec. 83 in the year the contributions are made and there is no deferral or attempt to defer the recognition of compensation.

---

[115] *See* Reg. § 1.402(b)-1(b)(6) and IRS Letter Ruling 9212024, 12-20-91, CCH IRS LETTER RULINGS REPORTS.

¶1406   Code Sec. 83 Restricted Property and Stock Plans

Code Sec. 83 has been mentioned many times in this chapter due to its potential application to various types of deferred compensation plans. In fact, Code Sec. 83 directly provides the rules governing a major form of nonqualified deferred compensation called restricted property or restricted stock plans. Under this type of arrangement, the employee receives property, but his rights to keep or dispose of the property are subject to a substantial risk of forfeiture. The property is typically stock of the employer, and the forfeiture provision typically requires the employee to perform substantial services for the employer for a specified minimum amount of time. Otherwise, the employee will forfeit the stock or other property. Such an arrangement provides a substantial disincentive for leaving the employing company. Ordinarily, the employee is taxable in the year in which the receipt of the property is no longer subject to a substantial risk of forfeiture, or, if earlier, when the property can be transferred by the employee free of risk of forfeiture. However, under Code Sec. 83(b), the employee can elect to be taxed on the property in the year in which the property is initially transferred or granted to the employee. The following sections describe the operating rules of Code Sec. 83 and relevant planning considerations. Finally, as noted in ¶1403.03, restricted property and stock plans under Code Sec. 83 are not subject to the requirements of Code Sec. 409A, and thus, the rules of Code Sec. 83 and the regulations thereunder continue to apply to such plans.

It should be noted that restricted stock plans have increased in popularity beginning in 2003 relative to non-qualified stock option plans (covered in Chapter 15) as a means of rewarding executives and other employees.[116] Microsoft Corporation indicated in July of 2003 that it plans to stop issuing stock options to its employees, and instead will provide them with restricted stock.[117] In addition, General Mills in the same month indicated that it is leaning toward putting more emphasis on restricted stock as opposed to stock options.[118] Two of the reasons for this change in emphasis overall may be (1) the relatively poor stock market performance of many stocks beginning in 2000 which has decreased (or eliminated) the value of stock options (restricted stock is a less risky form of compensation under which employees will receive some compensation even if the stock price

---

[116] McGeehan. Patrick, "Executives Still Gobble Up Stock Options," *Houston Chronicle*, May 7, 2003.

[117] *See*, e.g., Guth, Rob, "Cultural Evolution–At Maturing Microsoft Corp., Entrepreneurial Ethos Goes the Way of Stock Options," *Wall Street Journal*, July 10, 2003, p. B1.

[118] Forster. Julie, "General Mills Leaning to an Options Change–Other Firms Assess Compensation Programs," *Minneapolis StarTribune*, July 21, 2003, p. D1.

falls and does not recover) and (2) the fact that the FASB has formally adopted a requirement that stock options must be expensed on the financial statements of issuing publicly traded companies.[119]

.01 Code Sec. 83, in General

Under Code Sec. 83(a), if, in connection with the performance of services, property (including stock of the employer) is transferred to the employee that performed the services or someone other than the employer, the person who performed the services must include in gross income the excess of:

(1) the fair market value of the property (determined without regard to any lapse restriction, i.e., a restriction other than one by its terms will never lapse) at the first time that the rights of the person having a beneficial interest in that property are (a) transferable or (b) not subject to a substantial risk of forfeiture, whichever occurs earlier, over

(2) the amount (if any) paid for the property, by the person who performed the services.

The amount is includible by the employee in the first taxable year in which the rights of the person having the beneficial interest in the property are transferable or are not subject to a substantial risk of forfeiture, whichever is applicable. If the property is sold after that time, the excess of the selling price over the fair market value of the property at the time the Code Sec. 83 income is recognized is treated as a capital gain. If less than that fair market value is obtained upon the sale of the property, the employee recognizes a capital loss. If the employee (or other person holding a beneficial interest in the property) receives income from that property, such as dividends received on restricted stock shares, while it is nonvested (that is, while there is a substantial risk of forfeiture) the amount received is treated as additional compensation to the employee.[120]

> **Example (1):** In 2006, the Dayton Company granted one of its employees, Bates, the right to purchase 25 shares of the Dayton Company stock for $2,000. Bates's rights to the shares are subject to a substantial risk of forfeiture which will end in 2010. In 2006, the 25 shares were worth $3,000, and they are worth $8,000 in 2010 at the time the risk of forfeiture ends. Under Code Sec. 83(a), Bates will include $6,000 ($8,000–$2,000) as ordinary income in 2008. If Bates sold the stock, for $9,000 in 2012, he would recognize a long-term capital gain of $1,000 ($9,000–$8,000).

---

[119] Financial Accounting Standards Board, Statement No. 123(R), Share-Based Payment, December 2004.

[120] Reg. § 1.83-1(a)(1).

However, if the restricted property is sold before the property becomes transferable or before it is no longer subject to a substantial risk of forfeiture, the amount includible in the employee's gross income is the excess of the selling price over the amount paid for the property, if any.[121]

> **Comment:** Note that under Code Sec. 83(a), an employee may have to include an amount in gross income and pay the tax before he/she has funds from the deferred compensation to use to pay the tax. That is, the rules of Code Sec. 83 may force the employee to sell the property in the same year the income is recognized to obtain funds to use in paying the tax. Of course, the employee may be able to borrow money using the stock as collateral. This might be a useful strategy if the stock (or other property) is expected to increase in value in a future year. But, if the property is listed stock, SEC restrictions may prevent the use of the stock as collateral to secure a loan with which to pay the tax. Note that the courts have held income must be includible under Code Sec. 83 even if the employee is barred from making a public sale by SEC rules and cannot obtain the market price in a private sale.[122]

In lieu of recognizing income under the general rules of Code Sec. 83(a), the employee can elect to be taxed under the provisions of Code Sec. 83(b). Under Code Sec. 83(b), the employee can elect to recognize as income in the year in which the restricted property is granted, the excess of the fair market value of the property at the time of the grant minus the amount, if any, that must be paid for the property. If the election is made and the property is later transferred by the employee, any increase in value of the property after the time the right to the property is granted to the employee will be treated as a capital gain. This capital gain treatment can be particularly advantageous since the maximum rate on long-term capital gains is 15 percent (5 percent for taxpayers with regular marginal income tax rates of 15 percent or less) for sales and exchanges after May 5, 2003 of capital assets held longer than one year (the maximum rate was generally 20 percent for sales of such assets prior to that date and after May 6, 1997).[123] However, if the property is forfeited, the employee is not permitted any deduction on account of the amount previously included in income.[124] However, a capital loss would be permitted for the amount paid for the property, if any, minus the

---

[121] Reg. § 1.83-1(b)(1).
[122] *See*, e.g., *P.N. Cassetta*, 39 TCM 188, Dec.36, 330(M), TCMemo. 1979-384.

[123] Code Sec. 1(h)(1), as modified by P.L. 108-27, 108th Cong., 1st Sess., Sec. 301(a) (May 28, 2003).
[124] Reg. § 1.83-2(a).

amount which the individual receives from the employer as a result of the forfeiture.[125]

> **Example (2):** Assume the same facts as in the example above. If Bates made the Code Sec. 83(b) election, he would have to recognize $1,000 of income ($3,000−$2,000) in 2006. He would have a long-term capital gain of $6,000 ($9,000−$3,000) when the stock is sold in 2011. However, if he forfeited the stock prior to 2010, no deduction would be permitted on account of the $1,000 previously included in gross income. He would only be permitted a $2,000 long-term capital loss on his initial stock purchase (i.e., if the employer provided no reimbursement). The holding period would begin with the grant date.

A good understanding of restricted property and stock plans requires an understanding of the operational rules and terminology of Code Sec. 83. These rules and a detailed analysis of the Code Sec. 83(b) election are presented in the following paragraphs. The meaning of these terms is discussed in the following paragraphs.

.02 Code Sec. 83 Operating Provisions

The operating provisions of Code Sec. 83 are largely made up of rules concerning the following specific terms: (1) property, (2) property transferred in connection with the performance of services, (3) a transfer of property, (4) a substantial risk of forfeiture, (5) transferability of property, (6) substantially vested and nonvested property, (7) nonlapse and lapse restrictions, (8) fair market value of the property, and (9) amount paid for the property. These terms are discussed in the following paragraphs.

Property. Code Sec. 83 applies only to transfers of property in return for services performed. Thus, property is one of the key terms under Code Sec. 83. Reg. § 1.83-3(e) states that "property" includes real property and personal property other than money or an unfunded and unsecured promise to pay money in the future. Thus, as noted earlier, unfunded, unsecured deferred compensation plans are not subject to Code Sec. 83. Further, the term "property" includes a beneficial interest in assets (including money) which are transferred or set aside from claims of creditors of the employer, for example, in a trust or escrow account. The term "property" also has been extended to include intangible assets. For example, the IRS has held that an overriding oil and gas royalty interest transferred to a promoter in connection with the acquisition and development of oil

---

[125] *Id.*

and gas leases was a property interest.[126] Similarly, the IRS has held that a letter of credit purchased by an employer to secure its obligations to pay accrued vacation pay to its employees constituted property for purposes of Code Sec. 83.[127] In what could be viewed as a departure from the general understanding of the term "property" under Section 83, the Ninth Circuit Court of Appeals in *Theophilos*[128] recently held that an executory contract requiring an employee to purchase stock of an employer was considered to be property. The Court held that a contractual right to acquire stock is not unfunded and unsecured where it is a binding obligation (as opposed to being an option) secured by a valuable consideration. Finally, nonqualified stock options (covered in Chapter 15) are subject to the provisions of Code Sec. 83.

Under recently issued Reg. § 1.83-3(e), the term property also includes the cash surrender value and all other rights (including any supplemental agreements thereto and whether or not guaranteed), other than current life insurance protection, with respect to a contract, or any undivided interest therein, providing death benefit protection (including a life insurance contract, retirement contract, or endowment contract). This addition to the term "property" became effective when final regulations were issued under split dollar life insurance arrangements as covered in Chapter 3.

Property Transferred in Connection with the Performance of Services. Under Reg. § 1.83-3(f), property transferred to an employee or beneficiary of an employee in recognition of the performance of, or refraining from performance of, services is considered transferred in connection with services under Code Sec. 83. Such a transfer is subject to Code Sec. 83 whether the related services were performed in a past year or the current year or are to be performed in the future. However, if other persons can buy stock on the same terms and conditions as an employee, whether pursuant to a public or private offering, a transfer of stock to the employee is not in recognition of the performance of services. Thus, Code Sec. 83 should not apply to stock obtained by employees under their employer's dividend reinvestment plan which permits shareholders (whether or not they are employees) to buy corporate stock at a certain percentage of market value such as 90 or 95 percent. Similarly, a shareholder who receives an option to purchase the corporation's stock in return for guaranteeing a loan to the corporation is not considered to have received the option in connection

---

[126] Rev. Rul. 83-46, 1983-1 CB 16.
[127] Technical Advice Memorandum 9443006, 4-29-94, CCH IRS LETTER RULINGS REPORTS.

[128] CA-9, 96-1 USTC ¶ 50,293, 85 F3d 440 (1996). Rev'g and rem'g 67 TCM 2106, Dec. 49,653(M), TC Memo. 1994-45.

with the performance of services.[129] In summary, the courts have noted that in evaluating the phrase "property transferred in connection with the performance of services," Code Sec. 83 does not require the property to be transferred as compensation for the performance of services. Rather the Code envisions some sort of relationship between the services performed and the property transferred. The courts have considered four factors in deciding whether this relationship is found under the facts of a case:[130]

(1) whether the property right is granted at the time the employee or independent contractor signs his/her employment contract;

(2) whether the property restrictions are linked explicitly to the employee's or independent contractor's tenure with the employing company;

(3) whether the consideration furnished by the employee or independent contractor in exchange for the transferred property is services; and

(4) the employer's intent in transferring the property.

Transfer of Property. Under Reg. § 1.83-3(a), a transfer of property occurs when a person acquires a beneficial ownership interest in the property, disregarding any lapse restriction (other than one which by its terms will never lapse). For example, assume that a company sells 100 shares of its own stock to an employee for $900 (at a time when the stock is worth $2,900) on January 19, 2006, subject to the stipulation that the stock must be returned if the employee does not reach targeted sales goals by December 31, 2006. Since the lapse restriction is not one that by its terms will never lapse, the employee is considered to be the beneficial owner, and, therefore, a transfer of property occurs on January 19, 2006.

The grant of an option to purchase property does not constitute a transfer of that property under Reg. § 1.83-3(a)(2). Further, if the property is paid for with borrowed money, the repayment of which is secured by the transferred property, and the employee is not personally liable on the debt, the transaction is substantively an option to purchase.

No transfer of property may occur if the property is transferred under conditions that require its return upon the happening of an event that is certain to occur, such as the termination of

---

[129] *Centel Communications Co., Inc.*, CA-7. 90-2 USTC ¶50,603, 920 F2d 1335. Aff'g, 92 TC 612, Dec. 45, 548 (1989).
[130] *See, e.g., Montelepre Systems, Inc.*, 61 TCM 1782, Dec. 47,154(M), TC Memo. 1991-46. Aff'd on other issue, CA-5, 92-1 USTC ¶50,196, 956 F2d 496. *See also* Technical Advice Memorandum 200043013, 6-30-00, CCH IRS LETTER RULINGS REPORTS.

employment. In such a case, whether there is, in fact, a transfer depends upon a consideration of all of the relevant facts and circumstances. Factors indicating that no transfer may have occurred are as follows:

(1) the extent to which the conditions relating to the transfer are similar to an option;

(2) the extent to which the consideration to be paid the transferee upon surrendering the property does not approach the fair market value of the property at the time of surrender; and

(3) the extent to which the transferee does not incur the risk of a beneficial owner that the value of the property at the time of the transfer will decline substantially.[131]

> **Example:** On January 4, 2006, the Wilbur Corporation purports to transfer to Jack, an employee, 100 shares of Wilbur stock. The Wilbur stock is subject to the sole restriction that Jack must sell the stock to Wilbur if he terminates his employment for any reason for an amount equal to the excess (if any) of the book value of the Wilbur stock when he terminates employment over the book value on January 4, 2006. The stock is not transferable to Jack, and the restrictions concerning transfer are stamped on the certificate. In this case, there is no transfer of stock under Code Sec. 83.[132]

Substantial Risk of Forfeiture. The key to deferring the recognition of compensation under restricted property plans is to make certain that the employee's right to the property is subject to a substantial risk of forfeiture. Under Code Sec. 83(c)(1), the rights of a person in the property are subject to a substantial risk of forfeiture if that person's rights to the full enjoyment of the property are conditioned upon the future performance of substantial services by any individual (most often the employee). The regulations give a somewhat more encompassing interpretation of the term in stating that a substantial risk of forfeiture exists where rights in the transferred property are conditioned, directly or indirectly, upon (1) the future performance (or refraining from performance) of substantial services by any person, or (2) the occurrence of a condition related to a purpose of the transfer, and the possibility of forfeiture is substantial if the condition is not satisfied.[133]

The courts have shed further light on its meaning by taking the position that a substantial risk of forfeiture is based not on the

---

[131] Reg. § 1.83-3(a).
[132] Reg. § 1.83-3(a)(7), Ex. 3.

[133] Reg. § 1.83-3(c)(1).

likelihood of a forfeiture-triggering event, but on the likelihood of forfeiture once a triggering event occurs. For example, in *Robinson*,[134] an employee received a restricted stock option that carried a risk of forfeiture beyond the exercise date. The triggering event that would cause forfeiture, a sale by the employee of the stock within one year of the exercise date, was unlikely to occur. Thus, the IRS argued that recognition should occur at the exercise date, not one year later when the restricted period lapsed. Its argument centered on the remote probability of the employee selling the stock within the one-year restricted period, since such a sale would most probably be avoided by the employer. The court rejected the IRS argument and allowed deferral until one year later, when the restriction was lifted. It applied the following reasoning in its decision:

> Whether a condition creates a substantial risk or [sic] forfeiture is not a function of time, nor, as the Commissioner urges in this appeal, is it a function of the likelihood of triggering the event that will require the forfeiture to take place. To the extent that the substantiality of the risk depends on probability, the probability should be measured by the likelihood of the forfeiture taking place once the triggering event occurs.

Property is not transferred subject to a substantial risk of forfeiture to the extent that the employer is required to pay the fair market value of a portion of that property to the employee upon the return of the property. The risk that the value of property will decline during a certain period of time does not constitute a substantial risk of forfeiture. Finally, the IRS indicates that a nonlapse restriction, standing by itself, is not considered a substantial risk of forfeiture.[135] The District Court has held that no substantial risk of forfeiture existed where a taxpayer used borrowed money to purchase employer stock under a stock option plan and, after the stock was purchased, the employer had no right to get the stock back. The fact that the lender held the stock as collateral for the loan and could keep the stock in foreclosure was not equivalent to a substantial risk of forfeiture as the term is described under Reg § 1.83-3(c).[136]

The most common type of condition to be satisfied in the case of restricted property plans is that the employee remain employed and perform significant services for the employer for a specified minimum period of time. For example, the IRS has privately held that a substantial risk of forfeiture existed when the employee's rights to

---

[134] CA-1, 86-2 USTC ¶ 9790.805 F2d 38.
[135] Reg. § 1.83-3(c)(1).

[136] *Kent Miller*, DC CA, 2005-1 USTC 50101 (2004).

the deferred benefits became nonforfeitable only if the participant remained employed with the employer until the earliest of the participant's retirement with immediate benefit, death, separation from service due to disability or attainment of age 70½.[137] Reg. § 1.83-3(c)(2) states that the regularity of the performance of services and the time spent performing the services will tend to indicate whether services required by a condition are substantial. For example, regular services of full-time managers should be considered substantial. However, if the person performing services has the right to decline to perform such services, the services may not be substantial. Thus, where employees were not required to return certain bonuses even if they failed to fulfill the requirements of their one-year employment or consulting contract, the transfer of annuity contracts which were the bonuses was not subject to a substantial risk of forfeiture. This finding resulted in the bonuses being taxable when they were received.[138] Further, requirements that the property be returned if the employee is discharged for cause or for committing a crime will not be considered a substantial risk of forfeiture. Finally, an enforceable requirement that the property be returned to the employer if the employee accepts a job with a competing company will not ordinarily be considered a substantial risk of forfeiture unless the particular facts and circumstances indicate otherwise.

> **Example (1):** Black Corporation transferred 100 shares of its stock to Meyer, an executive, in connection with the performance of service in May 2006 for $90 per share. Under the terms of the transfer, Meyer is subject to a binding commitment to resell the stock to the corporation at $90 per share if he leaves the employment of Black Corporation for any reason prior to the expiration of a three-year period from the date of the transfer. Since Meyer must perform substantial services for Black Corporation and will not be paid more than $90 for the stock, regardless of its value, if he fails to perform such services during that three-year period, Meyer's rights in the stock are subject to a substantial risk of forfeiture during that period.[139]

In some instances, a covenant not to compete is the condition that has to be fulfilled by the employee. The factors which may be taken into account in determining whether a covenant not to

---

[137] See IRS Letter Ruling 9628011, 4-11-96, CCH IRS LETTER RULINGS REPORTS and IRS Letter Ruling 9642046, 7-19-96, CCH IRS LETTER RULINGS REPORTS.

[138] IRS Letter Ruling 199928013, 4-12-99, CCH IRS LETTER RULINGS REPORTS.

[139] See Reg. § 1.83-3(c)(4), Ex. 1.

compete constitutes a substantial risk of forfeiture include (1) the age of the employee, (2) the availability of alternative employment opportunities, (3) the likelihood that the employee can obtain alternative employment, (4) the employee's background and skills, (5) the employee's health, and (6) the practice of the employer to enforce such covenants.[140] Similarly, the rights in property transferred to a retiring employee subject to the sole requirement that it be returned unless he or she renders consulting services upon the request of his former employee will not be considered subject to a substantial risk of forfeiture unless he or she is expected to perform substantial services.

Under Code Sec. 83(c)(3), the rights of a person, in stock or other property, are subject to a substantial risk of forfeiture and are not transferable if the sale of the stock or other property would subject the person to suit under sec. 16(b) of the Securities Exchange Act of 1934. Under sec. 16(b) of the Act, a taxpayer who is an officer or owns at least ten percent of the stock of a company subject to Securities and Exchange Commission (SEC) registration requirements is subject to suit if he or she realizes a profit from a sale of his or her company's stock within a period of less than six months of its acquisition.[141] Under the current rules of the Securities and Exchange Commission, the time between the grant of a stock option and its exercise is counted toward the six-month period.[142] These profits can be recovered as damages by the company or by a shareholder on behalf of the company. Consequently, the employee in such cases is effectively prevented from selling the stock. The stock is considered forfeitable and nontransferable until the earlier of (1) the expiration of the six-month period after the purchase of the stock, or (2) the first day on which the sale of that stock at a profit will not subject the person to suit under Sec. 16(b).[143] Code Sec. 83(b) does not apply after the initial six-month period provided under Sec. 16(b). An example of this rule can be found in the Tax Court case of *Paul A. Tanner, Sr.*[144] In that case, the provisions of Code Sec. 83(c) did not apply after six months after the grant of an option even though the taxpayer had agreed with the grantor of the option that a sale of the option stock within two years would be subject to Sec. 16(b). The Tax Court's ruling has been affirmed by the Fifth Circuit Court of Appeals.[145]

---

[140] Reg. § 1.83-3(c)(2).

[141] Securities Exchange Act of 1934, 48 Stat. 881, sec. 16(b)(June 6, 1934).

[142] Sec. Rel. Nos. 34-28869 and 35-25254, 56 Fed. Reg. 7242 (Feb. 21, 1991).

[143] Reg. § 1.83-3(j).

[144] 117 TC 237, Dec. 54,559.

[145] *Tanner*, CA-5, 2003-1 USTC ¶ 50,385. Aff'g 117 TC 237 (2001).

Other examples of substantial risk of forfeiture provisions given in the regulations include: (1) stock transferred to an underwriter prior to a public offering in a case in which the full enjoyment of the stock is expressly or impliedly conditioned upon the successful completion of the underwriting, and (2) property received by an employee from an employer subject to a requirement that it be returned if the total earnings of the employer do not increase.[146] Finally, example four of Reg. § 1.83-3(c)(4) indicates that if stock is transferred subject to a substantial risk of forfeiture but the forfeiture restriction for a specific portion of the stock is removed periodically, that portion of the stock ceases to be subject to a substantial risk of forfeiture, and the employee has to recognize income with respect to that portion.

Example (2): Martin Corporation agrees to transfer 200 shares of its common stock to Davis which he is obligated to return if he terminates his employment for any reason. However, for each year following the year of the transfer that Davis remains employed performing substantial services for Martin Corporation, he ceases to be obligated to return 20 shares of the stock. Under Reg. § 1.83-3(c)(4) (Examples 3 and 4), Davis will be taxed on the value of 20 shares of Martin stock for each of the 10 years following the year of the transfer.

Enforcement of the Forfeiture Conditions. A condition of forfeiture will not be substantial unless the corporation can and will enforce the condition.[147] The regulations indicate that the following factors will be taken into account in determining whether a condition of forfeiture is substantial where the employee-transferee owns a significant amount of the total combined voting power or value of all classes of stock of the employer corporation or its parent:

(1) the employee's relationship to other shareholders and the extent of their control, potential control, or loss of control of the corporation;

(2) the position of the employee in the corporation and the extent to which he is subordinate to other employees in the corporation;

(3) the employee's relationship to the officers and directors of the corporation;

(4) the person or persons who must approve the employee's discharge; and

---

[146] Reg. § 1.83-3(c)(2).   [147] Reg. § 1.83-3(c)(3).

(5) past actions of the employer in enforcing the provisions of the restrictions. (See IRS Letter Ruling 9615023 for an example of a case where no substantial risk of forfeiture existed because there was no consistent past enforcement of forfeiture conditions by the employer.)

Example: If the employee-transferee owns 20 percent of the single class of stock of the employing corporation and the other 80 percent is held by an unrelated individual and his family so that the possibility of the corporation enforcing a forfeiture condition is substantial, then a transfer to the employee can be subject to a substantial risk of forfeiture. On the other hand, if four percent of the stock of a corporation is owned by the CEO of the corporation and the remaining stock is so diversely held by the public that the CEO, in effect, controls the corporation, then the possibility of the corporation enforcing a restriction on rights in property transferred to the CEO is not substantial. Thus, the CEO's rights in such property are not subject to a substantial risk of forfeiture.

Transferability of Property. As indicated earlier, the recipient of restricted property is ordinarily taxable on the value of the property at the time at which his rights are no longer subject to a substantial risk of forfeiture, or if earlier, when his beneficial interest in the property is transferable.[148] Code Sec. 83(c)(2) indicates that the rights of a person in property are transferable only if the rights in that property of any transferee are not subject to a substantial risk of forfeiture. Thus, property is considered transfereble unless it is subject to a substantial risk of forfeiture. As a practical matter, therefore, the application of Code Sec. 83 hings on the existence of the substantial risk of fortfieture.

Property is transferable if the transferee can sell, assign, or pledge (as collateral for a loan or otherwise) his or her interest in the property to any person other than the employer-transferor and if the transferee is not required to give up the property in the event that the substantial risk of forfeiture materializes.[149] For example, the Tax Court has held that stock was transferable even in a case where that stock could be transferred only to one specific transferee who was someone other than the transferor of the stock.[150] Note that to be nontransferable, restricted property or its value must be recoverable. For example, if an employer transfers restricted stock or other property to an employee, the restrictions should be stamped on the ownership instrument (i.e., the certificate, deed, etc.) if the property is to be nontransferable and

---

[148] Code Sec. 83(a).
[149] Reg. § 1.83-3(d).

[150] S. *Schulman*, 93 TC 623, Dec. 46,181.

not subject to current taxation. However, property is not transferable merely because the person performing the services or receiving the property can designate a beneficiary to receive the property in the event of the person's death.[151]

Substantially Vested and Substantially Nonvested Property. Property is substantially nonvested if it is subject to a substantial risk of forfeiture and is nontransferable. Property is substantially vested if it is either transferable or not subject to a substantial risk of forfeiture.[152] Thus, the employee must recognize income in the first year in which his rights to the property become substantially vested.

Nonlapse and Lapse Restrictions. Code Sec. 83(a) provides that the amount of compensation realized in restricted property plans is the fair market value of the property, determined without regard to any lapse restriction, minus the amount paid for the property, if any. Under Reg. § 1.83-3(i), a lapse restriction is any restriction other than a nonlapse restriction and includes (but is not limited to) a restriction that carries a substantial risk of forfeiture. In that regard, restrictions on stock that is granted to employees that require employees to sell the stock back to the employing company with the exception that the stock need not be sold back in the event of a corporate reorganization of the employing company or some other major event are considered to be lapse restrictions.[153]

Under Reg. § 1.83-3(h), a nonlapse restriction or a restriction which by its terms will never lapse is a permanent limitation on the transfer of property that: (1) will require the transferee of the property to sell, or offer to sell, the property at a price determined under a formula, and (2) will continue to apply to and be enforced against the transferee or any later holder (other than the employer-transferor).

In the case of property subject to a nonlapse restriction, Reg. § 1.83-5(a) indicates that the price determined under the formula will be considered to be the fair market value of the property (and, thus, the amount taxable to the employee minus the amount paid by the employee) unless established to the contrary by the IRS. The burden of proof is on the IRS with respect to that value.

Example: On September 4, 2006, the Ratton Corporation, whose shares are closely held and not regularly traded, transfers

---

[151] Reg. § 1.83-3(d).
[152] Reg. § 1.83-3(b).

[153] See *Riverton Investment Corporations*, DC Va., 2001-1 USTC ¶ 50,318 (2000).

to Bill, an employee, 100 shares of Ratton stock subject to the condition that if Bill desires to dispose of the stock while he is employed with Ratton, he must resell it to Ratton at its then existing book value. In addition, Bill or his estate is obligated to sell the stock at his retirement or death to Ratton at its then existing book value. The shares of stock are subject to a nonlapse restriction. Therefore, the fair market value of the stock is includible in Bill's gross income as compensation for the tax year 2006. However, in determining the fair market value of the Ratton stock, the book value formula price is treated as the stock's fair market value.[154]

A limitation subjecting the property to a permanent right of first refusal in a particular person at a price determined under a formula is a permanent nonlapse restriction. Such a limitation is not a condition that would result in a substantial risk of forfeiture. If the right of first refusal is at the fair market value of the property (determined without regard to a formula), however, that would not be a nonlapse restriction.[155]

If stock in a corporation is subject to a nonlapse restriction that requires the transferee to sell that stock only at a formula price based on book value, a reasonable multiple of earnings, or a reasonable combination thereof, the price so determined will ordinarily be regarded as the market value of the stock for purposes of Code Sec. 83.[156]

If a nonlapse restriction is canceled, Code Sec. 83(d) provides that the fair market value of the property (computed without regard to the restriction) at the time of the cancellation minus the sum of (1) the fair market value of the property (taking into account the restriction) immediately before the cancellation and (2) the amount paid for the cancellation, will be recognized as compensation income in the year of the cancellation. This rule applies unless the taxpayer establishes that:

(1) the cancellation was not compensatory, and (2) the person who would be allowed a deduction if the cancellation were treated as compensatory will in fact treat the transaction as not compensatory.

Fair Market Value of the Property. Ordinarily, the employee or other transferee must recognize as income the fair market value of the restricted property when the property becomes substantially vested.[157] However, as noted above, if the receipt of the property is

---

[154] Reg. § 1.83-5(c), Ex. 1.
[155] Reg. § 1.83-3(h).

[156] Reg. § 1.83-5(a).
[157] Code Sec. 83(a).

subject to a nonlapse restriction wherein a price is to be determined on the basis of a formula, the formula price will be the property's market value.[158]

Amount Paid for the Property. Under Code Sec. 83(a), the amount paid for the property reduces the amount included in gross income by the employee. Reg. § 1.83-3(g) provides that the "amount paid" is the amount of any money or property paid for the transfer of property to which Code Sec. 83 applies, and does not refer to any amount paid for the right to use that property or to receive the income from that property.

> **Example:** Blue Corporation transferred a home to its employee Wilson (as compensation) for $40,000 subject to the restriction that the home would be forfeited if Wilson did not remain employed with Blue Corporation for at least 5 years thereafter and charged Wilson $400 per month rent for the 5 years. The $40,000 would be considered to be an amount paid but the rent would not.

The amount paid does not include any interest paid by the employee or unstated interest determined under Reg. § 1.483-1. Further, if an indebtedness treated as an amount paid is forgiven, canceled in whole or in part, that amount would be included in the employee's gross income.[159] Thus, the IRS ruled that an employee recognized compensation income when that employee and his employer agreed to reduce the principal amount of a recourse note that was issued by the employee to the exercise price of an option to purchase stock of the employer. The compensation was recognized in the year the agreement was made and was equal to the agreed reduction in the principal required to be repaid.[160]

.03 The Code Sec. 83(b) Election

Under Code Sec. 83(b), the person providing the services can elect to recognize income from the restricted property in the year in which the services are performed instead of waiting until the time the person's (or other transferee's) rights to the property become substantially vested. If the election is made, the service performer must recognize, as income, the fair market value of the property at the time of the transfer (determined without regard to lapse restrictions) minus the amount paid for the property. The election can be made even if the amount paid equals the fair market value of the

---

[158] Reg. § 1.83-5(a).
[159] Reg. § 1.83-4(c).

[160] Rev. Rul. 2004-37, 2004-1 CB 583.

property at the time of the transfer.[161] The amount included in income is added to the taxpayer's basis in the property.[162] Thus, any appreciation in value of the property after that time is treated as capital gain income. This capital gain treatment can be advantageous for the employee because the top tax rate applicable to long-term capital gains is only 15 percent (5 percent for taxpayers with marginal income tax rates of 15 percent or less) for sales and exchanges after May 5, 2003 of stock and other capital assets held longer than one year whereas the top marginal tax rate on ordinary income is 35 percent for 2003 and later years.[163] Even though the top individual marginal rate has been reduced from 38.6 percent to 35 percent for 2003 and later years under JGTRRA, that rate is still significantly higher than the top 15 percent rate on long-term capital gains.[164] Further, if the transferee should receive dividends or other income from the property, that income is not treated as compensation income. This can be an advantage connected with making the Code Sec. 83(b) election after 2002 in circumstances where the income received is dividends from restricted stock, since qualifying dividends received beginning in 2003 are taxed at a top rate of 15 percent (5 percent for taxpayers with a marginal tax rate of 15 percent or less).[165] If the Code Sec. 83(b) election were not made, dividends received on the restricted stock would be treated as compensation received which would be fully taxable at regular rates and also would be subject to payroll taxes.

The main drawback of making the Code Sec. 83(b) election is the rather detrimental tax treatment associated with a forfeiture of the restricted property. If the rights to the restricted property are forfeited, no deduction is permitted to the employee under Code Sec. 83(b) for the amount that was previously included in gross income as a result of making the election. A capital loss, however, will be permitted if the transferee received less than the amount paid for the property. If more is received, the excess is treated as a capital gain.

> **Example:** Benson Corporation gives its employee, Blake, the right to buy 100 shares of its stock at $40 per share at a time when the stock is worth $140 per share. However, Blake must return the stock to the corporation for $40 per share if

---

[161] Reg. § 1.83-2(a).
[162] Id.
[163] Code Sec. 1(h)(1). as modified by P.L. 108-27, 108th Cong., 1st Sess., Sec. 301(a) (May 28.2003).
[164] Code Sec 1(i), as added by P.L. 107-16, 107th Cong., 1st Sess., Sec. 101(a) (June 7. 2001). as modified by P.L. 108-27, 108th Cong., 1st Sess., Sec. 104(c)(2) (May 28,2003).
[165] Code Sec. 1(h)(11), as added by P.L. 108-27, 108th Cong., 1st Sess., Sec. 302(a) (May 28, 2003).

he should leave the employ of Benson Corporation for any reason within three years after the transfer. If Blake makes the Code Sec. 83(b) election, he will include $10,000 (100 shares × ($140−$40)) in the year of the transfer. His basis in the stock becomes $14,000. But if he forfeits the right to the stock; no deduction is permitted for the $10,000 previously included in income.

Mechanics of the Election. The Code Sec. 83(b) election must be made within 30 days after the transfer of the property.[166] If the 30-day deadline for filing is not met, the taxpayer forfeits his/her right to make the election.[167] However, the election can be made before the date of the transfer.[168] The 30-day period may be extended under the provisions of Code Sec. 7508 for taxpayers serving in the armed forces or in support of the armed forces in a combat zone.[169] Under Reg. § 1.83–2(c), the election is made by filing one copy of a written statement of the election (signed by the person filing the election) with the IRS officer with whom the person who performed the services files his return. In addition, one copy of the statement must be submitted with that person's tax return covering the year of the election. The statement must include several pieces of information including (1) the taxpayer's name and address, (2) a description of the restricted property, (3) the date of transfer, (4) the nature of the restrictions to which the property is subject, (5) the fair market value of the property at the time of the transfer, (6) the amount paid for the property, and (7) a statement to the effect that copies of the election statement have been supplied to the other persons as required in Reg. § 1.83-3(d). The requirement that the Code Sec. 83(b) election statement be signed by the person making the election may be met if the person's employer files the election statement and has been properly authorized by the person to do so.[170]

Under Reg. § 1.83-2(f), the Code Sec. 83(b) election may not be revoked except with the consent of the IRS. That regulation indicates (1) that the consent will be granted only in a case where the transferee is under a mistake of fact concerning the underlying transaction and (2) that the consent must be requested within 60 days of the date on which the mistake first becomes known. However, a mistake concerning the value, or decline in the value, of the property or a failure to perform an act contemplated at the time of the transfer of the property does not constitute a mistake of

---

[166] Code Sec. 83(b)(2).
[167] *L.T. Welsh*, 83-1 USTC ¶ 9369, ClsCt.
[168] Reg. § 1.83-2(b).

[169] See e.g., Rev. Proc. 2005-27, IRB 2005-20, 1050.
[170] Service Center Advice 200203018.

fact. Thus, the service performer must be very careful in deciding whether to make the Code Sec. 83(b) election.

Deciding to Make the Code Sec. 83(b) Election. There are two general advantages of making the Code Sec. 83(b) election:

(1) Any increase in value of the property after the making of the election is taxed as a capital gain. This can be an important advantage because the top capital gains rate is 15 percent (5 percent for taxpayers with a marginal rate of 15 percent or less) on stock and other capital assets that are sold after May 5, 2003 and that have been held more than one year; thus, the capital gains rate is much lower than the top marginal rate of 35 percent in 2003 and later years.

(2) The employee or other transferee will not have to pay tax on that further appreciation until he or she disposes of the property and has the wherewithal to pay the tax. If the election is not made, tax will have to be paid in the year the property becomes vested whether or not it is sold or otherwise disposed of.

The disadvantage of the election is that if the service performer forfeits his or her rights to the property, no deduction is permitted for the amount of income that is recognized in the year the property is transferred.[171] Therefore, the choice of when to recognize compensation from restricted property plans is between: (1) no income recognition in the year in which the property is transferred and the recognition of ordinary compensation income in the year in which the property becomes substantially vested, minus the amount paid for the property, and (2) recognition of ordinary income equal to the value of the property at the time of the transfer minus the amount paid for the property and the possibility of capital gain income in the future.

The service performer should make the choice which maximizes the expected present value of the after-tax income to him from the plan. The choice which minimizes the expected present value of the employee's tax liability with respect to the income from the plan will be the one that maximizes the present value of his after-tax income.

In general, the decision hinges on the following factors:

(1) the market value of the property at the time of the transfer;

(2) the amount paid for the property, if any;

(3) the expected market value of the property when the property becomes substantially vested;

---

[171] Code Sec. 83(b)(1).

(4) the marginal income tax rate of the service performer in the year of the transfer;

(5) the expected marginal income tax rate of the service performer applicable to ordinary compensation income in the year the property becomes substantially vested;

(6) the expected marginal income tax rate of the service performer applicable to capital gains in the year the property is sold or otherwise disposed of;

(7) the expected after-tax rate of return of the service performer on investments;

(8) the probability that the property will become substantially vested (that is, the probability that the service performer will satisfy the restriction(s) constituting the substantial risk of forfeiture); and

(9) the length of time the employee expects to retain the property.

A mathematical present value analysis process can be used to assist an employee or other service performer in deciding whether to make the Code Sec. 83(b) election. Under this analysis, the present value of the tax liability, assuming that the Code Sec. 83(b) election is made, can be compared with the present value of the tax liability assuming that the election is not made. The present value of the tax liability if the election is not made is calculated as follows:

Compute the present value (using the expected after-tax rate of return of the service performer) of:

(1) the service performer's expected marginal income tax rate in the year in which the property becomes substantially vested; multiplied by

(2) the expected market value of the property at the time the property becomes substantially vested (minus the amount that has to be paid for the property); multiplied by

(3) the probability that the property will become substantially vested.

The present value of the tax liability if the Code Sec. 83(b) election is made can be expressed as:

Compute the present value (using the service performer's expected after-tax rate of return) of the sum of:

(1) the service performer's marginal income tax rate in the year the property is transferred multiplied by the fair market value of the property on the date of the transfer (minus the amount paid for the property); plus

¶ 1406.03

(2) the service performer's expected tax rate applicable to capital gains in the year in which the property becomes substantially vested multiplied by (a) the difference between the fair market value of the property at the date the property becomes substantially vested and its value at the date of the transfer and (b) the probability that the property will become substantially vested.

In this calculation process, it is assumed that the property will be sold at the date it becomes substantially vested. This permits a constant base of comparison. This assumption also takes account of the fact that retention of the restricted property beyond the year in which the substantial risk of forfeiture ends is only one of many investment choices available to the employee. That is, once the employee can sell the property, he or she is free to consider investment possibilities other than retaining the property.

Example: Assume that the Walton Corporation transfers 100 shares of its stock worth $10,000 in 2006 to an employee named Simpson at no charge. However, Simpson must return the stock to the employer unless he remains employed with Walton Corporation for at least four years after the date of the transfer. Simpson expects that the stock will be worth $15,000 at that time. Simpson has a marginal income tax rate of 35% in the current year and expects to be subject to a 33% marginal rate in 2010 when the stock would become substantially vested. He expects that his capital gains tax rate at that time will be 15%. His expected aftertax rate of return is 6%. Finally, he estimates that there is a 90% chance that he will remain employed by the corporation for another four years.

The expected present value of the taxes payable if the Code Sec. 83(b) election is not made is $3,849.50 or (33% × $15,000 × 90% or $4,455/1.2625 to get the present value).

The expected present value of the taxes payable if the Code Sec. 83(b) election is made is $4,035 or (35% × $10,000 or $3,500) plus ($15,000 minus $10,000 or $5,000 multiplied by 15% and multiplied by 90% which equals $675 divided by 1.2625 to obtain a present value of $535).

Simpson should not make the Code Sec. 83(b) election in this case because, by not making the election, he minimizes the expected present value of his tax liability, which in turn, maximizes the present value of his after-tax income.

While the Code Sec. 83(b) election is not advisable in the above illustration, it is advisable in some cases and may be desirable in other cases. The Code Sec. 83(b) election should be made if the taxpayer has to pay an amount equal to the fair market value of the property at the date of the grant. In that case, there would be no tax due upon making the election and no risk associated with it. In that case, the election is only beneficial because under the election, no tax would be paid until the stock or other property is sold. In cases where the employee must pay near market value of the stock or other property and/or the stock or other property is expected to sharply increase in value, the election may be advisable. Finally, the substantial reduction in the top rate on long-term capital gain income from 20 percent to 15 percent (from 10 percent to 5 percent for taxpayers with a marginal income tax rate of 15 percent or less) for sales and exchanges after May 5, 2003, as a result of JGTRRA compared to the relatively more modest decrease in regular marginal tax rates effective for 2003 and later years (e.g., a reduction of the top rate from 38.6 percent to 35 percent) has made the election more worthwhile after 2002 as compared to before 2003.

.04 Tax Consequences to the Employer

Under Code Sec. 83(h), the employer is generally entitled to a deduction equal to the amount of compensation income that the service performer includes in income as compensation in the year in which the income is recognized. Thus, there is supposed to be a parallel between compensation income recognition and deductions under Code Sec. 83. The IRS position is that the amount included as compensation by the employee or other service provider for this purpose is (1) the amount that was actually reported by the employee on an original or amended return or (2) the amount that is included by the employee in gross income as a result of the determination of the IRS in an audit of the taxpayer. According to the IRS, the employer should not be permitted a deduction where no amount has actually been included in the tax return of the employee or other service provider. Recently, however, the Court of Appeals for the Federal Circuit in reversing the Court of Federal Claims and disagreeing with an earlier decision of the Sixth Circuit Court of Appeals,[172] held that an employer may deduct the amount with respect to restricted compensation that the employee should have included in gross income even though the amount was not actually reported as gross income by the employee.[173]

Ordinarily, the employer gets a deduction in the year in which the property becomes substantially vested for the fair market value

---

[172] *Venture Funding Ltd.*, 110 TC 236, Dec. 52,637 (1998). Aff'd CA-6 (unpublished *per curium* opinion), 99-2 USTC ¶50. 972, Cert. denied, 2000.

[173] *J.G. Robinson*, CA Fed Circ, 7/15/2003, rev'g 2002-2 USTC ¶50,524,52 FedC1 725.The Supreme Court has declined to review the Federal Circuit Court's ruling in this case.

of the property at the time it becomes substantially vested. However, if the Code Sec. 83(b) election is made by the service performer, the employer can deduct in the year in which the transfer is made the fair market value of the property (minus the amount paid by the employee for the property) at the time of the transfer. Note that the timing of the employer's deduction may also be a factor in considering whether the Code Sec. 83(b) election should be made (as discussed above). If the employer's marginal tax rate is higher than that of the employee, the value of the current deduction the employer receives as a result of making the Code Sec. 83(b) election could be greater than the tax cost to the employee of current income recognition. In such a case, if the employer would share some of the benefit of the current deduction with the employee, the Code Sec. 83(b) election could become more worth-while. Note, however, that if the employer is a corporation, its marginal income tax rate will be no more than that of many typical restricted property compensation recipients because the top individual marginal rate has been reduced to 35 percent for 2003 and later years, which is the same as the top rate incurred by corporations. Of course, if the top corporate rate were reduced (reductions are being proposed as part of at least one tax bill being considered in Congress as this book went to press), the deduction would become less valuable to corporations.

Under Reg. § 1.83–6(a)(2), the employee (or other service provider) is considered to have included an amount as compensation income (thus allowing the employer or other service recipient to take a deduction even if the employee or other service provider fails to actually include the amount as income on his/her tax return) in tax years after 1994 if the employer (or other person for whom the services are performed) complies with all the tax reporting requirements of Code Sec. 6041 or 6041A (that is, reports the compensation to the IRS on a Form W2). Prior to 1995, the employer had to withhold income tax on the amount of the employee's compensation as a condition for obtaining the deduction. The U.S. Tax Court has, in a divided opinion, upheld the pre-1995 requirements by not allowing a deduction for an amount of compensation under Section 83 where the employer failed to issue the employees Forms W2.[174] Further, Reg. § 1.83–6(a)(4) indicates that no deduction is allowed with respect to restricted property transfers to the extent the transfer constitutes a capital expenditure, an item of deferred expense, or an amount includible in the inventory items. Finally, if property with respect to which a Code Sec. 83(b) election was made is

---

[174] *Venture Funding Ltd.*, 110 TC 236, Dec. 52,637 (1998). Aff'd, CA-6 (unpublished *per curiam* opinion), 99-2 USTC ¶ 50,972. Cert. denied, 2000.

forfeited, Reg. § 1.83–6(c) requires the employer to include in gross income any deduction it took with respect to the making of the election by the employee.

Recognition of Gain or Loss. If the property transferred under a restricted property plan is the employer's stock, no gain or loss is recognized by the employer on the transfer under Code Sec. 1032. Under proposed regulations, a similar nonrecognition rule applies with respect to the transfer of an interest in partnership capital in return for services performed by an existing or prospective partner.[175] However, if the transfer involves property other than the employer's stock, Reg. § 1.83-6(b) indicates if the employer receives more than its adjusted basis upon the transfer of the property, gain is recognized to the extent of that excess. In addition, at the time the employer is entitled to a deduction with respect to a transfer of restricted property, the employer will recognize gain or loss to the extent of the difference between (1) the sum of the amount paid for the property plus the amount allowed to the employer as a deduction under Code Sec. 83(h) and (2) the sum of the employer's basis in the property plus any gain recognized at the time of the initial transfer of the property.

.05 Basis and Holding Period

Reg. § 1.83-4(b) states that the service performer's (or other transferee's) basis in the restricted property is generally equal to the amount paid for the property plus the amount of compensation income that the service performer must recognize under Code Sec. 83(a), (b), or (d)(2). Thus, once the service performer recognizes compensation income on the restricted property, any subsequent appreciation in value of the property is recognized as capital gain income rather than ordinary compensation income.

The holding period of restricted property generally begins at the time the property becomes substantially vested. Therefore, if the property is sold at that date or very shortly thereafter, any gain or loss on its sale will be short-term.[176] However, if the Code Sec. 83(b) election is made, the holding period of the property begins at the time the property is transferred.[177] Thus, any gain upon the sale of the property at or after (or even before) the time the property becomes substantially vested will be treated as a long-term capital gain if the period of time between transfer date and sales date exceeds one year.

---

[175] Prop. Reg. § 1.83-6(b).
[176] Reg. § 1.83-4(a).

[177] *Id.*

.06 Special Rules for Property Transfers By Shareholders

Special rules apply to transfers of property made to a service provider by a shareholder of the employer corporation under Reg. § 1.83-6(d). Under those rules, if a shareholder of a corporation transfers property to an employee of that corporation or other service provider (or beneficiary thereof), in consideration of services performed for the corporation, the transaction will be considered (1) a contribution of that property to the capital of the corporation and (2) immediately afterward, a transfer of that property to the employee or other service provider under the Code Sec. 83 rules. For purposes of these rules, such a transfer will be treated as being in consideration for services performed for the corporation if either the property is substantially nonvested at the time of transfer or an amount is includible in the gross income of the employee or other service provider at the time of.transfer. In the case of such a transfer, any money or other property paid to the shareholder for such stock or property will be considered paid to the corporation and transferred immediately by the corporation to the shareholder as a distribution to which Code Sec. 302 applies (i.e., such amount may be considered a dividend distribution).

If following a transaction described in the above paragraph, the transferred property is forfeited to the shareholder, the provisions of Reg. § 1.83-6(c) shall apply both with respect to the shareholder and to the corporation. In addition, the corporation shall, in the taxable year of the forfeiture, be allowed a loss (or realize a gain) to offset any gain (or loss) realized under Reg. § 1.83-6(b) (covered at the end of ¶ 1405.04 above).

> **Example** If a shareholder transfers property to an employee of the corporation as compensation for services, and, as a result, the shareholder's basis of $20,000 in such property is allocated to his stock in that corporation and the corporation recognizes a short-term capital gain of $80,000, and is allowed a deduction of $100,000 on the transfer, upon a subsequent forfeiture of the property to the shareholder, the shareholder will recognize $20,000 of gross income, and the corporation will recognize $100,000 of gross income and a short-term capital loss of $80,000.

¶ 1407 Code Sec. 457 Deferred Compensation Plans

Under Code Sec. 457, state governments and tax-exempt organizations may establish deferred compensation plans under which the doctrine of constructive receipt (covered earlier in this chapter) can be avoided, and the compensation deferred under the plan will not be recognized as income until it is paid or otherwise made available (until the amounts are paid with respect to governmental Code Sec. 457 plans for distributions made after December 31, 2001) to the participant or other beneficiary. Participation in a state government or tax-exempt organization plan is restricted to employees and independent contractors who perform services for the sponsoring employer, and only a limited amount of each participant's compensation can be deferred each year. The Economic Growth and Tax Relief Reconciliation Act of 2001 (EGTRRA) has made some substantial changes to the rules concerning Code Sec. 457 plans. In July of 2003, the IRS issued comprehensive new final regulations under Code Sec. 457 to replace the existing final regulations and that take into account the provisions of EGTRRA and other revisions to Code Sec. 457 that have occurred since the publication of the old final regulations. The final regulations are, in general, effective for taxable years beginning after December 31, 2001.[178] This effective date is subject to a number of specified transition rules including one applicable for taxable years beginning after December 31, 2001, and before January 1, 2004 under which a plan did not fail to be an eligible plan if it was operated in accordance with a reasonable, good faith interpretation of Code Sec. 457(b).[179] In May of 2005, the IRS issued proposed regulations which, among other considerations, deal with deferrals after severance from employment, including sick, vacation, and back pay under an eligible Code Sec. 457 plan.[180] Finally, it should be noted that new Code Sec. 409A discussed in ¶1403 (see ¶1403.03 for coverage of plans not subject to Code Sec. 409A) does not apply to Code Sec. 457 deferred compensation plans of state governments and tax-exempt organizations, except for plans that are not eligible for general Code Sec. 457 treatment under Code Sec. 457(f) (see the discussion in ¶1407.06). The following paragraphs cover the plan requirements, the maximum deferral rules, distribution requirements, and other pertinent considerations regarding Code Sec. 457 deferred compensation plans and reflect the provisions of EGTRRA, the 2003 final regulations, the 2005 proposed regulations (where applicable) and the applicability of Code Sec. 409A to Code Sec. 457 plans that are not eligible under Code Sec. 457(f).

.01 Plan and Eligibility Requirements

The Code Sec. 457 deferred compensation rules apply only to plans that are maintained by eligible employers and that meet

---

[178] TD 9075, 68 FR 41230 (July 11, 2003).
[179] *Id.*

[180] REG-130241-04, 70 FR 31213 (May 31, 2005).

specified requirements concerning administration of the plan, who can participate, limits on how much can be deferred, and timing of distributions.

Eligible Plans. An eligible Code Sec. 457 deferred compensation plan is a plan maintained by an eligible employer (as defined in Code Sec. 457(e) and covered below) that satisfies the requirements of Code Sec. 457(b) in both form and operation (i.e., the plan must be an eligible deferred compensation plan as defined in that section) and provides benefits to eligible participants (as defined in Code Sec. 457(b)(1) and Reg. § 1.457-2(j) and covered below).[181] Eligible employers may, alternatively, maintain ineligible plans (plans which do not meet all of the Code Sec. 457 requirements). Eligible plans may be eligible governmental plans or eligible plans of tax-exempt employers. The Code Sec. 457(b) requirements specify the limits on how much may be deferred under Code Sec. 457 plans (including additional deferrals that may be made by persons who are at least age 50—see Code Sec. 457(e)) and catch-up deferrals as covered in ¶ 1407.02 below. An eligible plan must be established in writing, must include all of the material terms for benefits under the plan, and must be operated in compliance with the requirements reflected in the proposed regulations. An eligible plan may contain certain optional features not required for plan eligibility under Code Sec. 457(b), such as distributions for unforeseeable emergencies, loans, plan-to-plan transfers, additional deferral elections, acceptances of rollovers to the plan, and distributions of smaller amounts to eligible participants. However, except as otherwise provided in the proposed regulations, if an eligible plan contains any optional provisions, the optional provisions must meet, in both form and operation, the relevant requirements under Code Sec. 457 and the proposed regulations.[182]

An eligible plan must provide that, in general, compensation can be deferred for any calendar month only if the agreement providing for the deferral of that compensation is entered into before the first day of the month in which the compensation is paid or made available. A new employee may defer compensation payable in the calendar month during which the participant first becomes an employee if an agreement providing for the deferral is entered into on or before the first day on which the participant performs services for the eligible employer. An eligible plan may provide that if a participant enters into an agreement providing for the deferral of compensation will remain in effect until the participant revokes or

---

[181] *Id.*

[182] Reg. § 1.457-3(a).

alters the terms of the agreement. Nonelective employer contributions are treated as being made under an agreement entered into before the first day of the calendar month.[183] The agreement which provides for deferral of compensation into a Code Sec. 457 plan before the beginning of a month may be in the form of an automatic election under which a fixed percentage of an employee's compensation is automatically deferred under the plan unless the employee affirmatively elects to actually receive the amount.[184]

Benefits under eligible governmental plans are excludable from the gross income of plan participants until paid, in the case of an eligible plan of a tax-exempt employer, until paid or made available to the plan participant.[185] Benefits under ineligible plans are, under Code Sec. 457(f) includible in income when deferred or, if later, when the rights to the benefits are not subject to a substantial risk of forfeiture (see the discussion of what constitutes a substantial risk of forfeiture under the Code Sec. 83 provisions in ¶ 1406.02. Further, ineligible plans covered by Code Sec. 457(f) are subject to the provisions of Code Sec. 409A (see the coverage of Code Sec. 409A in ¶ 1403), as discussed in ¶ 1407.06.)

An eligible governmental plan must provide for the timely distributions of excess deferrals (deferrals in excess of the limitations covered in ¶ 1407.02 below) along with any net income attributable to such benefits.[186] An eligible plan of a tax-exempt employer that fails to comply with the deferral limitations will be an ineligible plan under which the benefits from the plan will be taxable under the provisions of Reg. § 1.457-11. Further, such plan will be subject to the requirements of Code Sec. 409A (see the coverage of that new section in ¶ 1403), as discussed in ¶ 1407.06. However, a such a plan may distribute to a participant any excess deferrals (and any income allocable to such amount) not later than the first April 15 following the close of the taxable year of the excess deferrals. In such a case, the plan will continue to be treated as an eligible plan.[187]

In order to be an eligible governmental plan, all amounts deferred under the plan, all property and property rights purchased with such amounts, and all income attributable to such amounts, property, or rights, must be held in trust for the exclusive benefit of participants and their beneficiaries.[188] In order to be an eligible plan of a taxexempt entity, the plan must be unfunded and plan assets must not be set aside for participants or their beneficiaries. An eligible plan of a tax-exempt entity must provide that (1) all amounts

---

[183] Reg. § 1.457-4(b).
[184] Rev. Rul. 2000-33, 2000-2 CB 142.
[185] Reg. § 1.457-7 (b) and (c).
[186] Reg. § 1.457-4(e)(2).
[187] Reg. § 1.457-4(e)(3).
[188] Reg. § 1.457-8(a).

deferred under the plan, (2) all property and rights to property purchased with such amounts, and (3) all income attributable to such amounts, property, or rights, remain (until paid or made available to the participant or beneficiary) solely the property and rights of the eligible employer (without being restricted to the provision of benefits under the plan), subject only to the claims of the eligible employer's general creditors.[189]

An eligible plan may provide that a participant who has not had a severance from employment may elect to defer accumulated sick pay, accumulated vacation pay, and back pay under such a plan if the Code Sec. 457(b) requirements for eligibility are met. For example, the plan must provide that these amounts may be deferred for any calendar month only if an agreement providing for the deferral is entered into before the beginning of the month in which the amounts would otherwise be paid or made available and the participant is an employee on the date the amounts would otherwise be paid or made available. For purposes of Section 457, compensation that would otherwise be paid for a payroll period that begins before severance from employment is treated as an amount that would otherwise be paid or made available before an employee has a severance from employment. In addition, deferrals may be made for former employees with respect to (1) compensation described in Prop. Reg. § 1.415(c)-2(e)(3)(ii) (relating to certain compensation paid within two-and-one-half months following severance from employment), (2) compensation described in Prop. Reg. § 1.415(c)-2(g)(4) (relating to compensation paid to participants who are permanently and totally disabled), and (3) compensation relating to qualified military service under Code Sec. 414(u).[190]

Avoidance of the Constructive Receipt Doctrine. Amounts deferred under Code Sec. 457 tax-exempt employer plans are not considered to be constructively received by the participants merely because the participants have the right to elect to defer specific amounts. In addition, Code Sec. 457 plans may contain the following features that do not cause amounts deferred to be constructively received:

(1) the plan may permit participants to choose among various investment modes in determining how deferred amounts should be invested;[191]

(2) the plan may permit a participant to transfer deferred amounts to another eligible Code Sec. 457 plan;[192]

---

[189] Reg. § 1.457-8(b).
[190] Prop. Reg. § 1.457-4(d)(1).

[191] Reg. § 1.457-7(c)(1).
[192] Code Sec. 457(e)(10).

(3) the plan may permit a participant to elect to receive a lump-sum payment (or the plan may distribute the amount to the participant without his/her consent) of $5,000 or less only if (a) no amount has been deferred under the plan during the two-year period ending on the date of the distribution and (b) there has been no prior distribution to the individual by the plan.[193] For distributions received after December 31, 2001, the distributed amount must be determined without regard to any rollover contributions made to the plan for the participating employee receiving the lump-sum distribution;[194] and

(4) the plan may permit (in taxable years beginning after 1996) participants to defer commencement of distributions under the plan if (a) the election is made after amounts may be available under the plan but before commencement of distributions and (b) the participant may make only one such election per year.[195]

Plans Not Covered by Code Sec. 457 Compensation Deferral Rules. A Code Sec. 457 plan does not include a qualified pension, profit-sharing, or stock bonus plan, a Code Sec. 403(b) tax-sheltered annuity plan, a Code Sec. 83 restricted stock or property plan, or a nonexempt trust.[196] Further, a Code Sec. 457 plan does not include bona fide vacation leave, sick leave, compensatory time, severance pay, disability pay, or death benefit plans and for taxable years beginning after 1996, any plan paying solely length of service awards to bona-fide volunteers (or their beneficiaries) on account of qualified services performed by such volunteers.[197] Code Sec. 457 also does not apply to nonelective deferred compensation that is attributable to services that are performed by the participant in a capacity other than as an employee and to plans maintained by a church or a qualified church organization.[198] Under Code Sec. 457(e)(12)(B), deferred compensation is to be treated as nonelective only if all individuals (other than those who have not met any applicable initial service requirement) with the same relationship to the payor are covered under the same plan with no individual variations or plan options. However, certain nonelective plans in existence on December 31, 1987, and maintained pursuant to a collective bargaining agreement remain eligible for Code Sec. 457 treatment.[199] In addition, nonelective plans described in Code Sec.

---

[193] Code Sec. 457(e)(9).

[194] Code Sec. 457(e)(9), as amended by P.L. 107-16, 107th Cong., 1st Sess., Secs. 648(b) and 649(b)(2) (June 7, 2001).

[195] Code Sec. 457(e)(9)(B), as added by P.L. 104-188,104thCong.,2dSess.,Sec.1447(a)(Aug.20,1996).

[196] Code Sec. 457(f)(2).

[197] Code Sec. 457(e)(11), as amended by P.L. 104–188, 104th Cong., 2d Sess., Sec. 1458(a) (Aug. 20, 1996).

[198] Code Sec. 457(e)(12)(A) and (13).

[199] *See* P.L. 100-647, Sec. 6064(d) (Nov. 10, 1988) and Reg. § 1.457-2(k).

457(e)(12) generally are subject to the provisions of Code Sec. 409A (see the coverage of that Code section in ¶ 1403).[200] Thus, administrators of such plans must take care to meet the applicable requirements of Code Sec. 409A. Finally, the Code Sec. 457 rules do not apply to qualified state judicial plans (i.e., retirement plans of states for the exclusive benefit of judges or their beneficiaries and that have been in continuous existence since December 31, 1978).[201]

Eligible Employers and Plan Participants. Under Code Sec. 457(e)(1), the term "eligible employer" means (1) a state (including political subdivisions, agencies, and instrumentalities of the state, e.g., a state university) and (2) any tax-exempt organization. Tax-exempt rural cooperatives such as rural electric cooperatives can also maintain Code Sec. 457 plans. In order to be eligible, governmental Code Sec. 457 plans must invest the elective deferral amounts into a trust under which the amounts are held for the exclusive benefit of the participants and their beneficiaries.[202] That requirement does not apply to Code Sec. 457 plans maintained by other tax-exempt entities. For distributions after December 31, 2001, governmental Code Sec. 457 plans will not lose their eligibility solely because they make cash-out distributions pursuant to Code Sec. 457(e)(9)(A) (see the discussion under item (3) of "Avoidance of the Constructive Receipt Doctrine" above).[203] Finally, the IRS has publicly held that a plan offered and administered by a union can be an eligible governmental Code Sec. 457 plan for employers of governmental employees that adopt the plan and meet the Code Sec. 457 rules for governmental employers.[204]

A participant in an eligible plan is an individual who is deferring compensation, or who has previously deferred compensation under the plan by salary reduction or by nonelective employer contribution and who has not received a distribution of his/her entire benefit under the eligible plan. Only individuals who perform services for an eligible employer as employees or independent contractors can participate in a Code Sec. 457 plan.[205]

.02 Maximum Deferral Limitation

EGTRRA substantially increased the amount of compensation that can be deferred under a Code Sec. 457 plan for years beginning after December 31, 2001. After 2001, the maximum amount that can

---

[200] Notice 2005-1, IRB 2005-2, 274, Q&A 6.
[201] P.L. 95–600, sec. 131(c), as amended by P.L. 97–248, sec. 252. Reg. § 1.457-2(k).
[202] Code Sec. 457(g).

[203] Code Sec 457(d)(3), as added by P.L. 107-16, 107th Cong., 1st Sess., Sec. 649(b)(2)(B) (June 7, 2001).
[204] Rev. Rul. 2004-57, IRB 2004-24, 1048.
[205] Reg. § 1.457-2(j).

be deferred (except for the special catch-up deferral of Code Sec. 457(b)(3) covered below and not counting rollover contributions) is the lesser of (a) 100 percent of compensation or (b) the applicable dollar amount (in 2001, the maximum deferral was the lesser of (a) 33⅓ percent of compensation or (b) $7,500, as adjusted for inflation—the applicable amount in 2001 was $8,500).[206] In 2006, the applicable amount is $15,000 (the amount was $11,000 in 2002 and had been adjusted upward by $1,000 each succeeding year). After 2006, the $15,000 applicable amount will be adjusted upward on account of inflation.[207] Further, Code Sec. 457 plan participants who are at least or become age 50 during the calendar year are permitted to make additional catch-up contributions beginning in 2002. The maximum dollar amount of the additional catch-up contributions for 2006 is $5,000 (the additional amount started at $1,000 in 2002 and was adjusted upward by $1,000 each succeeding year). The $5,000 maximum will be adjusted upward for inflation after 2006.[208] Thus, the applicable dollar limits on Code Sec. 457 deferrals in the years 2001 through 2006 will be as follows:

Year	Applicable Dollar Limit	Maximum Additional Dollar Limit for Participants Age 50 or More	Maximum Dollar Limit for Participants Age 50 or More
2001	$ 8,500	$ 0	$ 8,500
2002	$11,000	$1,000	$12,000
2003	$12,000	$2,000	$14,000
2004	$13,000	$3,000	$16,000
2005	$14,000	$4,000	$18,000
2006	$15,000	$5,000	$20,000

Example: Jack is a participant in a Code Sec. 457 plan. In 2006, he had includible compensation of $90,000. Thus, if he were age 40 he could contribute, on an elective deferral basis, $15,000 to the plan. If he were at least age 50, the maximum contribution would be $20,000. In 2005, the respective maximums are $14,000 and $18,000.

For this purpose, includible compensation means compensation as defined in Code Sec. 415(c) for services performed for the eligible employer. Thus, elective deferrals under Code Sec. 457 and other sections are not subtracted in determining the amount of includible

---

[206] Code Secs. 457(b)(2) and (e)(15), as amended by P.L. 107-16, 107th Cong., 1st Sess., Secs. 611(e)(1)(A), 611(e)(2), and 632(c)(1) (June 7, 2001).

[207] Code Sec. 457(e)(15)(B), as amended by P.L. 107-16, 107th Cong., 1st Sess., Sec. 611(e)(2) (June 7, 2001).

[208] Code Secs. 414(v)(1)(B) and (C), as added by P.L. 107-16, 107th Cong., 1st Sess., Sec. 631(a) (June 7, 2001), *See also* Reg. § 1.414(v)-1.

compensation in taxable years beginning after December 31, 2001. Community property laws do not apply in determining the amount of includible compensation.[209] For taxable years beginning prior to 2002, includible compensation for Code Sec. 457 limitation purposes was reduced by Code Sec. 457 elective deferrals. Thus, the former 33⅓ percent of includible compensation limit for elective deferrals that applied to taxable years beginning before 2002 was actually 25 percent, without subtraction of the Code Sec. 457 deferral amount according to Reg. § 1.457-2(m), example 1.

Under Code Sec. 457(c), the applicable dollar limit ($15,000 in 2006—$20,000 for participants who are at least or become age 50 during the calendar year) must be reduced dollar for dollar by amounts deferred under other Code Sec. 457 plans. However, for years beginning after December 31, 2001, for purposes of determining how much can be electively deferred under a Code Sec. 457 plan, no reduction is required on account of elective deferrals made by the employee under another elective deferral plan such as a Code Sec. 403(b) plan.[210] Thus, a participant in a Code Sec. 403(b) plan can make elective deferrals to that plan up to the maximum and to a Code Sec. 457 plan up to the maximum. Prior to 2002, elective deferrals made to other plans had to be taken into account in determining the maximum that could be deferred under a Code Sec. 457 plan. Also note that a Code Sec. 457 plan of an employer is not disqualified merely because that employer does not reduce the maximum deferral limit with respect to a particular employee for Code Sec. 457 deferrals that the employee has with another employer. However, such deferrals with other employers do reduce the amount excludable by the employee on account of the Code Sec. 457 plan.

> **Example:** Chester, age 40, an employee of Texas A&M University, received a salary of $50,000 in 2006. Texas A&M maintains a Code Sec. 457 plan for its employees. The maximum amount of compensation that Chester can defer under the plan is $15,000 (the lesser of (1) 100 percent of compensation (assuming that the definition of compensation includes any elective deferrals) or (2) $15,000, the applicable dollar limit for 2006). If Chester also participates in a Code Sec. 403(b) plan, he can also defer up to $15,000 under that plan.

---

[209] Code Sec. 457(e)(5), as amended by P.L. 107-47, 107th Cong., 2d Sess., Sec. 411(0)(9) (March 9, 2002), Reg. § 1.457-2(g).
[210] Code Sec. 457(c), as amended by P.L. 107-16, 107th Cong., 1st Sess., Sec. 615(a) (June 7, 2001).

See also Reg. § 1.457-5(a) and Prop. Reg. § 1.457-5(d), Example 2.

Catch-Up Deferral. Under Code Sec. 457(b)(3), as amended by EGTRRA, a participant during one or more of his/her last three taxable years ending before he/she attains normal retirement age under the plan may make an elective deferral taking into account the maximum limit under the Code Sec. 457(b)(3) catch-up rules, rather than the general limits under Code Sec. 457(b)(2) (as covered above). Under the catch-up rules, the maximum amount that can be deferred is the lesser of:[211]

(1) twice the applicable dollar amount under Code Sec. 457(b)(2)(A) ($30,000 for 2006—$28,000 in 2005), or

(2) the normal Code Sec. 457(b)(2) deferral limit plus so much of the Code Sec. 457(b)(2) deferral limit that has not been used in prior years.

Note that the additional dollar amount for participants over age 50 (e.g., $5,000 in 2006) does not apply in a year in which the participant uses the catch-up rules of Code Sec. 457(b)(3). So, in effect, if for a particular year a participant is eligible for both catch-up provisions, the provision that produces the larger deferral limit will be the one that applies.[212]

Example: In 2006, Roy Moore, a 63-year-old participant in a Code Sec. 457 plan with a normal retirement age of 65, received a salary of $62,000 from the state of Texas. He has underutilized his allowable deferrals by $14,000 in earlier years. He can elect to defer $27,000 in 2006, i.e., the lesser of (1) $30,000 or (2) the normal Code Sec. 457(b)(2) limit, which would be $13,000 plus the $14,000 underutilized deferral amounts from prior years or a total of $27,000. Moore would use the Code Sec. 457(b)(3) catch-up provision to defer $27,000 rather than the $20,000 maximum that would be permitted normally as discussed above (the $15,000 applicable dollar limit for 2006 plus the $5,000 additional dollar limit for participants age 50 or more).

.03 Distribution Requirements

A Code Sec. 457 deferred compensation plan must provide that distributions of deferred amounts cannot be made available to participants earlier than the year in which the participant:[213]

---

[211] Code Sec. 457(b)(3), as amended by P.L. 107-16, 107th Cong., 1st Sess., Sec. 611(e)(1)(B) (June 7, 2001).

[212] Reg. § 1.457-4(c)(2)(ii).

[213] Code Sec. 457(d)(1), as amended by P.L. 107-16, 107th Cong., 1st Sess., Sec. 641(a)(1)(C) (June 7, 2001).

(1) has a severance from employment (prior to 2002, the wording "separates from service" applied) with the employer,

(2) is faced with an unforeseeable emergency, or

(3) reaches age 70½.

Under the new final regulations, an employee is considered to have a severance from employment with the eligible employer if the employee dies, retires, or otherwise has a severance from employment.[214] An independent contractor is considered to have a severance from employment upon the expiration of his or her contract (or contracts, if there is more than one) under which services are performed for the eligible employer if the expiration constitutes a good-faith and complete termination of the contractual relationship.[215]

Amounts deferred under a tax-exempt employer eligible Code Sec. 457 plan will not be considered made available to the participant or beneficiary if under the plan the participant or beneficiary may irrevocably elect, prior to the time any such amounts become payable, to defer payment of some or all of such amounts to a fixed or determinable future time.[216] For this purpose, the time at which amounts become payable (the first permissible payout date) is the earliest date on which a plan permits payments to begin after separation from service (i.e., disregarding payments to a participant who has an unforeseeable emergency or attains age 70½, or under the in-service distribution provision of Code Sec. 457(e)(9)(A) if the amount payable is $5,000 or less).[217] In addition, amounts deferred (including amounts previously deferred) under an eligible plan will not be considered made available to the participant solely because the participant is permitted to choose among various investment modes under the plan for the investment of such amounts whether before or after payments have commenced under the plan.[218]

An unforeseeable emergency is an event which causes severe financial hardship to the participant due to a sudden and unexpected illness or accident of the participant or beneficiary, the participant's or beneficiary's spouse, or the participant's or beneficiary's dependent (as defined in Code Sec. 152, and for taxable years beginning on or after January 1, 2005, without regard to Code Sec. 152(b)(1), (b)(2), and (d)(1)(B)), a casualty loss involving property of the participant, or a similar extraordinary and unforeseeable circumstance arising from events beyond the participant's control. For example, the imminent foreclosure of or eviction notice from the participant's or primary beneficiary's primary residence may constitute an

---

[214] Reg. § 1.457-6(b)(1).
[215] Reg. § I.457-6(b)(2).
[216] Reg. $ 1.457-7(c)(1).

[217] Reg. § 1.457-7(c).
[218] Reg. § 1.457-7(c)(1).

unforeseeable emergency. However, the purchase of a home or payment for the college education of a dependent is not considered to be an unforeseeable emergency. Whether a participant or beneficiary is faced with an unforeseeable emergency permitting a distribution from the Code Sec. 457 plan is to be determined based on the relevant facts and circumstances of each case, but, in any case, may not be made to the extent that such emergency is or may be relieved through reimbursement or compensation from insurance or otherwise—e.g., through liquidation of the participant's assets, to the extent that such liquidation would not cause severe financial hardship. Distributions because of an unforeseeable emergency must be limited to the amount reasonably necessary to satisfy the emergency need.[219]

Minimum Distribution Rules. Pursuant to EGTRRA, a Code Sec. 457 plan meets the minimum distribution requirements if its participants are subject to the required beginning date and minimum distributions requirements of Code Sec. 401(a)(9) that apply to qualified deferred compensation plans (see Chapter 6).[220] EGTRRA thus conforms the minimum distribution requirements under Code Sec. 457 plans with those that apply to qualified plans, in general, for distributions made after December 31, 2001. See the discussion of those minimum distribution requirements for qualified plans in Chapter 6 and for traditional IRAs in Chapter 10.

For distributions made prior to 2002, the minimum distribution rules under Code Sec. 401(a)(9) also generally applied to Code Sec. 457 plan participants.[221] However, additional distribution requirements applied under former Code Sec. 457(b)(2)(B) to deal with required distributions after the death of the Code Sec. 457 plan participant. Under those rules, distributions that began before the death of the participant, the distributions must be made in a form under which the amounts payable with respect to the participant will be paid at times specified by the IRS and not later than the time determined under Code Sec. 401(a)(9)(G) (relating to incidental death benefits).

If a participant died before receiving his entire plan balance, any amounts not distributed had to be distributed at least as rapidly as under the method of distributions used during the participant's life. In the case of a distribution that began after the participant's death,

---

[219] Reg. § 1.457-6(c)(2). *See also* Prop. Reg. § 1.457-6(c)(2)(i).

[220] Code Sec. 457(d)(2), as amended by P.L. 107-16, 107th Cong., 1st Sess., Sec. 649(a) (June 7, 2001).

[221] Former Code Sec. 457(d)(2)(B)(i).

the entire amount payable with respect to the participant had to be paid over a period of no more than 15 years (or the life expectancy of the surviving spouse if he or she is the beneficiary).[222] Any distributions payable over a period of more than one year could only be made in substantially nonincreasing amounts (paid at least annually).[223]

.04 Rollovers from and into Code Sec. 457 Governmental Plans

As a result of EGTRRA for distributions after December 31, 2001, tax-free rollovers of eligible rollover distributions as defined in Code Sec. 402(c)(4) of money and property (e.g., lump-sum distributions and other non-annuity distributions that are not excepted by that section such as required minimum distributions—see the discussion of eligible rollover distributions in ¶ 904.01) can be made from Code Sec. 457 plans maintained by state and local governments and political subdivisions thereof into eligible retirement plans as defined in Code Sec. 402(c)(8) (e.g., other Code Sec. 457 governmental plans, employer qualified plans under Code Sec. 401, and traditional IRAs—see the discussion concerning eligible retirement plans in ¶ 904.05).[224] The rules that pertain to rollovers under Code Sees. 402(c)(2) through (c)(7) and (c)(9) and Code Sec. 402(f) all apply with respect to rollovers from Code Sec. 457 governmental deferred compensation plans (see the discussion of these rules under ¶ 904). These rules include, for example, requirements that eligible rollover distributions that are not directly rolled over in a direct trustee-to-trustee transfer must be rolled over within 60 days (unless the frozen deposit or hardship exception applies). Presumably, the 20 percent withholding rules under Code Sec. 3405 that apply to eligible rollover distributions that are not the subject of a direct trustee-to-trustee transfer (direct rollover) also apply.

Example: Norton, age 67, retired in 2006 from a position with Montana State University which maintains a Code Sec. 457 governmental deferred compensation plan. In 2006, he received a lump-sum distribution of $240,000. Of that amount, he rolled over $180,000 into a traditional IRA within 60 days and kept the rest. As a result, he is taxable in 2006 on $60,000, and the $180,000 rolled over into his IRA is not taxable in 2006.

After December 31, 2001, Code Sec. 457 governmental deferred compensation plans will also be permitted to accept eligible rollover distributions from employer qualified plans under Code Sec. 401

---

[222] Former Code Sec. 457(d)(2)(B)(ii).

[223] Former Code Sec. 457(d)(2)(C).

[224] Code Sec. 457(e)(16). as added by P.L. 107-16, 107th Cong., 1st Sess., Sec. 641(a)(1)(A) (June 7, 2001). *See also* Reg. § 1.457-10(e).

plans, Code Sec. 403(a) annuity plans, Code Sec. 403(b) tax-sheltered annuity plans, other Code Sec. 457 governmental deferred compensation plans, and traditional IRAs.[225] Only the taxable portion of rollovers from traditional IRAs can be made into Code Sec. 457 governmental plans. In order to accept rollovers from plans other than other Code Sec. 457 governmental deferred compensation plans, the recipient Code Sec. 457 governmental plan must agree to account for such rollovers separate from other amounts participants have in the plan.[226] The reason for the separate accounting requirement is that amounts that are distributed later from the recipient Code Sec. 457 plan will generally be subject to the ten percent premature distributions tax under Code Sec. 72(t) (see the discussion of that tax in ¶ 901.05) to the extent the distributions consist of rollovers received from other types of plans.[227] Finally, the special ten-year averaging rules and long-term capital gain treatment applicable to lump-sum distributions that may be available with respect to plan participants who were at least age 50 on January 1, 1986 will not be available for any distributions from a governmental Code Sec. 457 plan which has received a rollover contribution from another type of plan.[228]

Tax-free rollovers cannot be made from or into Code Sec. 457 plans that are maintained by tax-exempt organizations other than state and local governments and political subdivisions, thereof.[229] The same was true with respect to governmental Code Sec. 457 plans for distributions prior to January 1, 2002.[230]

.05 Applicability of Withholding Tax and FICA and FUTA Taxes

Notice 2003–20,[231] which was issued by the IRS in mid-2003, indicates the applicability of federal income tax withholding and FICA and FUTA taxes to Code Sec. 457 plan contributions and distributions. The provisions of the notice are generally applicable for periods after December 31, 2001. However, for deferrals or distributions made after December 31, 2001, and before January 1, 2004, the IRS will not assert that there has been a failure to comply with applicable reporting and withholding requirements if the applicable reporting and withholding requirements set forth in Notice

---

[225] Code Sec. 402(c)(8), as amended by P.L. 107-16, 107th Cong., 1st Sess., Sec. 641(a)(2)(A) (June 7, 2001).

[226] Code Sec. 402(c)(10), as amended by P.L. 107-16, 107th Cong., 1st Sess., Sec. 641(a)(2)(B) (June 7, 2001).

[227] Code Secs. 72(t)(9) and 457(a)(2), as added by P.L. 107-16, 107th Cong., 1st Sess., Secs. 641(a)(2)(C) and 649(b)(1) (June 7, 2001).

[228] P.L. 107-16, 107th Cong., 1st Sess., Sec. 641(f)(3)(June 7,2001).

[229] Code Sec. 457(e)(16), as added by P.L. 107-16, 107th Cong., 1st Sess., Sec. 641(a)(1)(A) (June 7, 2001) and Rev. RuL 86-103, 1986-2 CB 62. *See also* Reg. § 1.457-10(e).

[230] *Id.*

[231] IRB 2003-19,894.

2000–38[232] (which was superceded by Notice 2003–20) have been satisfied.

Federal income tax withholding does not apply to elective deferral contributions that are made into Code Sec. 457 plans by participants. Rather, withholding is required when amounts are paid or made available under Code Sec. 457 plans maintained by tax-exempt organizations and when paid under governmental Code Sec. 457 plans.

Distributions that are paid or made available from Code Sec. 457 plans maintained by nongovernmental tax-exempt organizations are subject to income tax withholding the same way as normal wages in accordance with Code Sec. 3402(a). Thus, the withholding is determined in the same manner as withholding on other types of taxable wage payments. Such distributions are generally reported on Form W-2.

With respect to governmental plans, income tax withholding is determined using the rules of Code Sec. 3405. Thus, governmental Code Sec. 457 plan distributions that qualify as eligible rollover distributions as defined under Code Sec. 402(c)(4) (see the discussion of the eligible rollover distributions in ¶ 904.01) are subject to mandatory 20 percent income tax withholding unless the distribution qualifies as a direct rollover. Periodic distributions that are not qualified rollover distributions from such plans are subject to income tax withholding under Code Sec. 3405(a) just like normal compensation, and nonperiodic distributions that are not eligible rollover distributions from such plans are subject to withholding at a rate of 10 percent under Code Sec. 3405(b). For both periodic and nonperiodic distributions that are not qualified rollover distributions, the recipient can elect not to have withholding apply. Distributions from governmental Code Sec. 457 plans are to be reported on Form 1099-R.

The applicability of FICA taxes to Code Sec. 457 plan contributions and distributions depends upon whether the employer is a nongovernmental tax-exempt organization or a state or local government or political subdivision thereof. In the case of nongovernmental taxexempt organizations, FICA taxes are applied using the rules of Code Sec. 3121(v) and Reg. § 31.3121(v)(2)-1 (see a discussion of those rules in ¶ 1404.05). In general, that means that amounts deferred under Code Sec. 457 plans of nongovernmental tax-exempt organizations are subject to FICA taxes at the later of

---

[232] 2000 –2 CB 174.

(1) the year in which the related services are performed or (2) when the amounts are no longer subject to a substantial risk of forfeiture (within the meaning of Code Sec. 83 as discussed in ¶ 1406.02). The same rules apply with respect to governmental Code Sec. 457 plans under which the employees (1) are subject to Medicare tax under Code Sec. 3121(u), (2) are subject to FICA taxes under Code Sec. 3121(b)(7)(E) because the governmental unit has entered into a Section 218 agreement with the Social Security Administration to cover its employees under FICA, or (3) are subject to FICA taxes under Code Sec. 3121(b)(7)(F) because they are not members of a state or local government retirement system.

FUTA taxes do not apply to compensation deferred under governmental Code Sec. 457 plans, since employees of state and local governments or political subdivisions thereof are not subject to FUTA taxes under Code Sec. 3306(c)(7). However, FUTA taxes do apply to compensation deferred under nongovernmental tax-exempt employer maintained Code Sec. 457 plans using the same timing rules as discussed in the above paragraph concerning when FICA taxes apply to that compensation.

.06 Tax Treatment of Participants Under an Ineligible Plan

If a state government or tax-exempt organization deferred compensation plan does not meet the requirements of Code Sec. 457 or ceases to meet those requirements, any compensation that has been deferred will be taxable to the participants in the first year in which the receipt of the compensation is not subject to a substantial risk of forfeiture.[233] If amounts under an ineligible Code Sec. 457 plan are subject to a substantial risk of forfeiture, the amount that is includible in gross income for the first year in which there is no substantial risk of forfeiture includes earnings thereon up to the date on which there is no substantial risk of forfeiture.[234] Earnings credited on the compensation deferred under the agreement or arrangement that are not includible in gross income currently because there is a substantial risk of forfeiture are includible in the gross income of the participant or beneficiary only when paid or made available to the participant or beneficiary, as long as the interest of the participant or beneficiary in any assets (including amounts deferred under the plan) of the entity sponsoring the agreement or arrangement is not senior to the entity's general creditors.[235] For purposes of these rules, the rights of a person to compensation are subject to a substantial risk of forfeiture if that person's rights to the compensation

---

[233] Code Sec 457(f)(1).
[234] Reg. § 1.457-11(a)(2).

[235] Reg. § 1.457-11(a)(3).

are conditioned upon the future performance of substantial services for the employer by any individual.[236]

The discussion and authorities concerning the substantial risk of forfeiture under Code Sec. 83 (discussed earlier in this chapter) are also relevant for determining whether stated conditions under an ineligible Code Sec. 457 plan constitute a substantial risk of forfeiture.

Amounts paid or made available to a participant or beneficiary under an ineligible Code Sec. 457 plan are includible in the gross income of the participant or beneficiary under Code Sec. 72, relating to annuities.[237] For that purpose, the participant or beneficiary is treated as having an investment in the contract equal to the amount included, including any earnings thereon, under the Code Sec. 457(f) rules when the amounts are no longer subject to a substantial risk of forfeiture.[238]

The provisions of Code Sec. 409A discussed in ¶ 1403 (subject to the effective date and transition rules applicable under Code Sec. 409A) apply to ineligible Code Sec. 457(f) plans in addition to the requirements already applicable to such plans under Code Sec. 457(f). Pending additional guidance, state and local government and tax-exempt entities may rely on the definitions of bona fide vacation leave, sick leave, compensatory time, disability pay, and death benefit plans for purposes of Code Sec. 457(f) as being applicable for purposes of applying the Code Sec. 409A rules to nonqualified deferred compensation plans under Code Sec. 457(f). However, state and local government and tax-exempt entities may not rely upon the definition of a deferral of compensation that applies under Code Sec. 409A as being applicable for purposes of the Code Sec. 457(f) definition of a deferral of compensation. For example, for purposes of Code Sec. 457(f), a deferral of compensation includes stock options and arrangements in which an employee or independent contractor of a state or local government or tax-exempt entity earns the right to future payments for services, even if those amounts are paid immediately upon vesting. However, under Code Sec. 409A, a deferral of compensation occurs when an employee or other service provider has a legally binding right during a taxable year to compensation that has not been actually or constructively received and included in gross income and that is payable to the service provider in a later taxable year.[239]

---

[236] Code Sec. 457(f)(3).
[237] Reg. § 1.457-11(a)(4).
[238] Reg. § 1.457-11(c).

[239] Notice 2005-1, IRB 2005-2, 274, Q&As 4 and 6.

Chapter 15

Equity-Oriented Arrangements

¶ 1501 Introduction

The compensation package for an executive is usually made up of a mixture of elements. Typically, this mixture includes: a base salary; some type of annual incentive, such as a bonus; fringe benefits, such as medical insurance; deferred compensation such as retirement benefits; and long-term equity-oriented incentives, which involve some form of a stock arrangement. These stock arrangements can average more than 30 percent of the typical executive's compensation package in large companies. In fact, every one of the top 100 U.S. industrial companies employs some form of stock arrangement in order to attract and retain key executives.

The prevalence of these incentives indicate companies' involvement in aligning management's interests with that of the stockholders. In addition to benefiting the company, many of these stock arrangements provide tax advantages to the executive by deferring what would otherwise be currently taxable compensation, and converting ordinary income into capital gains. This chapter will focus on the most prevalent forms of equity-oriented arrangements, as well as some recent developments in the stock acquisition area. In addition to examining the tax consequences of each type of plan, some innovative financing techniques used in these plans are presented.

¶ 1502 New Deferred Compensation Rules and Equity-Oriented Plans

While there are many forms of equity-based compensation plans, the most common forms are discussed in this chapter. These include: nonqualified stock options (NQSOs); incentive (or qualified) stock options (ISOs); stock appreciation rights (SARs); performance shares or units; restricted stock; and phantom stock.

As discussed in detail in Chapter 14, Code Sec. 409A provides major changes in the rules for nonqualified deferred compensation plans. In general, Code Sec. 409A provides that unless specified requirements are met, all amounts deferred in taxable years after 2004 are currently includible in gross income (to the extent not subject to a substantial risk of forfeiture and not previously included in gross income) and subject to a 20 percent tax penalty. (This rule also applies to amounts deferred before 2005 if the plan was materially modified after the enactment of AJCA '04.) As it relates to equity-based compensation plans, the following provisions must be met to avoid current taxation under Code Sec. 409A (see Chapter 14 for detailed discussion):

(1) Elections to defer compensation for services performed during a taxable year must be made before the beginning of that year (with exceptions for the first year of eligibility and performance-based compensation);

(2) Distributions can be made only at a time specified under the plan, separation from service, death, disability, or a change in control of the employer; and

(3) The time or schedule of any payment under the plan cannot be accelerated (with limited exceptions, including *de minimis* amounts, domestic relations orders, and divestiture requirements).

Code Sec. 409A casts a broad net by defining a nonqualified deferred compensation plan as any arrangement that provides an employee (or other service provider) with a legally binding right, during a taxable year, to compensation that (1) has not been actually or constructively received and included in gross income, (2) is payable to the employee in a later year, and (3) is not subject to a substantial risk of forfeiture. As discussed in Chapter 14, however, some arrangements are specifically excluded from the new rules (e.g., qualified retirement plans and annuities, SEPs, SIMPLEs).[1]

Thus, this general definition could include virtually any form of equity-based incentive award. (For example, the ability to exercise a stock appreciation right or option is considered an acceleration clause, thereby violating the distribution restrictions and triggering current income recognition.) However, the related legislative history indicates that the new rules are not intended for arrangements taxable under

---

[1] Notice 2005-1, Q&As 3 & 4, IRB 2005-2, 274.

Code Sec. 83 (certain options and restricted stock), nor are the new rules intended to change the tax treatment of incentive stock options or options granted under an employee stock purchase plan. Shortly after the passage of AJCA '04, the IRS issued Notice 2005-1 to serve as initial transitional guidance in implementing the requirements of Section 409A to new and existing arrangements. Notice 2005-1 clarifies which types of equity-based deferred compensation arrangements are covered and which are exempt from the Code Sec. 409A rules, shown in the table below. The impact on specific arrangements is explained in the appropriate sections of ¶ 1503.

Equity-Based Plans Subject to Code Sec. 409A	Equity-Based Plans Not Subject to Code Sec. 409A
• Discounted stock options • Stock appreciation rights • Phantom stock & restricted stock units	• Nondiscounted stock options • Statutory stock options • Restricted stock

Grandfathering Provisions. Amounts deferred before 2005 under equity-based compensation plans may be grandfathered and thus avoid the Code Sec. 409A rules. For purposes of the grandfathering provision, the "amount deferred" is the amount earned and vested (including earnings thereon) and for which payment is available to the employee on December 31, 2004 (or that would be available if the right were immediately exercisable). However, this grandfather provision is allowed only if no material modifications to the grandfathered benefit were made after the enactment of AJCA '04.[2] (See ¶ 1403 for discussion.)

¶ 1503 Specific Equity-Based Compensation Plans

The tax treatment concerning the specific equity-based compensation plans discussed in this section applies to pre-2005 deferrals that qualify under the AJCA grandfather provisions and post-2004 deferrals that are either exempt from, or meet the requirements specified under, Code Sec. 409A. The tax treatment of noncompliant equity-based compensation plans follows the tax treatment under Code Sec. 409A (discussed in Chapter 14), i.e., all amounts deferred under the arrangement become immediately taxable (to the extent not already included) and subject to the 20-percent penalty tax.

---

[2] Notice 2005-1, Q&As 16 & 17(c), IRB 2005-2, 274.

.01   Nonqualified Stock Options (NQSOs)

Nonqualified stock options (NQSOs) are one of the most popular method of stock-based plans. A NQSO is a right granted by an employer corporation that allows an employee to purchase the employer's stock at a fixed price for a stated period of time. The employee thus benefits from the potential appreciation in the value of the underlying stock from the date of grant to the date of exercise of the option. These options are sometimes referred to as nonstatutory options, because they are not described anywhere in the Code. As their names indicate, NQSOs are not "qualified" within the meaning of Code Secs. 421-424. Thus, NQSOs are not afforded any favorable tax treatment; rather, they are taxed under Code Sec. 83, which was discussed in Chapter 14.

The most advantageous feature of NQSOs is their flexibility. There are no statutory restrictions concerning transferability, exercise periods, or holding periods, all of which are common in qualified stock options. They need not be nontransferable, although most NQSOs are generally not transferable in order to avoid current taxation under Code Sec. 83(a)(1). The exercise period may extend well beyond ten years, a feature which is not available to qualified options. There are no minimum holding requirements, although most plans require a period of continued service before the option can be exercised.

Applicability of Code Sec. 409A. Nonqualified stock options (NQSOs) are subject to Code Sec. 409A. However, NQSOs are exempt from the Code Sec. 409A provisions if: (1) the exercise price is at least equal to the fair market value of stock on the date of grant (i.e., a nondiscounted option); (2) the receipt, transfer or exercise is taxable under Code Sec. 83; and (3) there is no deferral feature (other than the deferral of recognition of income until the later of exercise or disposition of the option).

If the exercise price is or could become less than the fair market value of the stock on the date of grant (i.e., a discount stock option), the grant of a NQSO would become subject to the new Code Sec. 409A rules. Thus, the value of the deferral, less amounts previously included in income, is currently taxed and subject to the 20-percent penalty tax. For purposes of determining the fair market value of the stock at the date of grant, any reasonable valuation method may be used. Such methods include, for example, the valuation method described in § 20.2031-2 of the Estate Tax Regulations.[3]

---

[3] Notice 2005-1, Q&A 4(d)(ii), IRB 2005-2, 274.

Tax Consequences to the Employee. Assuming the requirements under Notice 2005-1 are met, NQSOs are taxed under Code Sec. 83, which provides that property transferred in connection with the performance of services will be taxed in the year in which the property either becomes transferable or is no longer subject to a substantial risk of forfeiture. The amount of the income taxable to the executive is the excess of the fair market value of the stock, measured on the date at which it becomes transferable or free of the substantial risk of forfeiture, over the amount paid for the stock, which is the exercise price of the option.[4]

The employee will not have taxable income on the date of grant, unless: (1) the exercise price is or could become less than the fair market value of the stock on the date of grant (in which case Code Sec. 409A applies); or (2) the option has a readily ascertainable fair market value at the time of the grant. While a readily ascertainable fair market value generally requires that the option be actively traded on an established market, it may also be established if:

(1) the option is immediately exercisable;

(2) it is transferable and free of restrictions which would constitute a substantial risk of forfeiture; and

(3) the fair market value can be determined by considering any difference between the option price and the value of the stock at the grant date, as well as the value of the option privilege for the remainder of the option period. Thus, it is necessary to consider whether the value of the property subject to the option can be ascertained, the probability of an increase or decrease in such property's value, and the length of the option's exercise period.[5]

NQSOs will not normally satisfy all of these conditions, because either an established market does not exist (NQSOs often have exercise periods extending over five to 10 years), the options are not transferable, or the right to exercise the options is conditioned upon the future performance of services by the executive. Ordinarily, then, the employee will be taxed at the date of exercise on the difference, or spread, between the market value of the stock on the exercise date and the exercise price of the option. This income is treated as ordinary income (and is subject to withholding). The holding period for the stock (for purposes of determining long-term capital gains) begins with the exercise date.[6] The employee's basis in the stock is equal to the amount paid for the NQSOs (if any) plus the

---

[4] Code Sec. 83(a).
[5] Reg. § 1.83-7(b).

[6] Code Sec. 83(f).

exercise price plus the amount of income recognized upon the exercise of the option.[7]

If the options have a readily ascertainable market value, as defined in Reg. § 1.83-7(b), the excess of the value of the options over the cost, if any, is taxed as ordinary income at the date of grant. Upon the exercise of the option, the employee would realize no income.[8] The holding period starts on the grant date, not the exercise date; basis includes the exercise price plus the amount paid for the NQSOs (if any) plus the income recognized at the grant date.

Tax Consequences to the Corporation. Code Sec. 83(h) provides a "matching" of employee inclusion of income and employer deduction. Thus, the employer deducts an amount equal to that which the employee includes for the employer period in which the taxable year of the employee ends.[9]

It should be noted that in order to deduct this compensation expense, the company must comply with the reporting requirements applicable to the payment (i.e., report the payment on the employee's Form W-2 identified as Code "V").[10] This reporting requirement applies to all of the stock compensation plans discussed in this chapter, where the company is allowed a deduction for the compensation element. It should also be noted that, although withholding is not required to deduct the compensation expense, the compensation element is still subject to income tax withholding, FICA taxes, and FUTA taxes under the normal rules.[11]

> **Example:** On May 25, 2005, when its stock was selling at $15 per share, X Co. granted nonqualified stock options to Mr. Watkins to purchase 1,000 shares of X Co. stock at $15. On the grant date, the NQSOs had no readily ascertainable market value. (Note that the option price may not be below the market value of the stock on the grant date, if the plan is to be exempt from Code Sec. 409A.) The options were exercisable anytime after May 25, 2006 and before May 25, 2015. (Note that a specified distribution date is not required under this plan, as it is exempt from Code Sec. 409A.) Mr. Watkins exercised his options on October 16, 2006, when the X stock was selling for $22. He sold the shares on June 12, 2007 for $25 per share.
>
> *Results*: Mr. Watkins recognizes no taxable income on the date of the grant of the options. He recognizes $7,000 of ordinary

---

[7] Reg. § 1.83-4(b).
[8] Code Sec. 83(e)(3) and (4).
[9] Reg. § 1.83-6(a)(1).

[10] Reg. § 1.83-6(a)(2).
[11] Reg. § 1.83-6(a)(2).

compensation income on October 16, 2006, when he exercises the options [($22−$15) × 1,000]. X Co. will be allowed a deduction of the same $7,000 for its taxable year which contains December 31, 2006, Mr. Watkins's year-end. Mr. Watkins will also recognize a $3,000 short-term capital gain upon the sale of the stock on June 12, 2005, since his holding period was less than twelve months (October 16, 2006 - June 12, 2007).

.02 Incentive Stock Options (ISOs)

Incentive stock options (ISOs) have become very popular in recent years because of their favorable tax treatment for the employee. ISOs are referred to as qualified, or statutory, stock options because they are defined in Code Sec. 422. ISOs were created by the Economic Recovery Tax Act of 1981 (ERTA) to provide a tax-advantaged form of stock option. Unlike the NQSO, the ISO does not trigger any ordinary income recognition at the grant date or the exercise date. Instead, all of the potential income is treated as capital gain and is not recognized until the ultimate disposition of the stock by the employee.

In order to qualify for ISO tax treatment, a number of specific requirements are set forth in Code Sec. 422:

(1) ISOs must be issued pursuant to a written plan approved by shareholders within twelve months of board adoption that specifies the maximum number of shares to be issued under the plan through ISOs and the employees, or class of employees, eligible to receive the options;[12]

(2) ISOs must be granted within ten years from the date of adoption of the plan (or shareholder approval, if earlier);[13]

(3) ISOs may be granted only to employees and must be exercised by the employee either during employment or within three months of termination of employment;[14]

(4) ISOs cannot be transferable by the employee, except by will or the laws of descent and distribution, and must be exercisable only by the employee during his lifetime;[15]

(5) the option price must be equal to, or exceed, the fair market value of the stock on the date of the grant;[16]

(6) the maximum term of an ISO cannot be longer than ten years from the date of the grant;[17]

---

[12] Code Sec. 422(b)(1); Reg. § 1.422-2(b).
[13] Code Sec. 422(b)(2); Reg. § 1.422-2(c).
[14] Code Sec. 422(a)(2); Reg. § 1.421-1(h).

[15] Code Sec. 422(b)(5); Reg. § 1.421-1(b)(2).
[16] Code Sec. 422(b)(4); Reg. § 1.422-2(e).
[17] Code Sec. 422(b)(3); Reg. § 1.422-2(d).

(7) all shares acquired from the exercise of ISOs must be held for two years from the date of the grant and one year from exercise date (this holding period does not apply to an estate or a beneficiary following the death of the ISO holder, nor does it apply for ISO holders who are insolvent);[18]

(8) ISOs may not be granted to an individual who owns more than ten percent of the total combined voting power of all classes of stock of the employer corporation, or its parent or subsidiary corporation.[19] However, this rule will not apply if, at the time the option is granted, (a) the option price is at least 110 percent of the fair market value of the stock subject to the option, and (b) the option is not exercisable after five years from the date the option was granted;[20] and

(9) the maximum aggregate value of the stock (determined as of the grant date) which is first *exercisable* during any one calendar year may not exceed $100,000 for any employee.[21] Thus, for example, an ISO award could permit acquisition of up to $500,000 worth of stock if it provided that the options were exercisable in five installments, each of which becomes exercisable in a different year and does not exceed $100,000.

Applicability of Code Sec. 409A. Code Sec. 409A does not apply to incentive stock options (ISOs) or to options granted under employee stock purchase plans under Code Sec. 423.[22]

Tax Consequences to the Employee. Under Code Sec. 422(a), the employee does not recognize any taxable income at the date of grant or date of exercise. When the employee disposes of the stock acquired, the difference between the selling price and the exercise price is treated as long-term capital gain, since the required holding period of the stock is at least one year from the exercise date.

However, for alternative minimum tax (AMT) purposes, an ISO is essentially treated as a NQSO. The spread between the ISO exercise price and the market value of the stock on the date the rights become freely transferable or no longer subject to a substantial risk of forfeiture (normally the exercise date) is treated as a positive adjustment item (i.e., recognized as income for AMT). (Thus, if the employee is subject to AMT in the year he or she exercises an ISO, the deferral benefit is lost.) The stock's AMT basis is increased by the income recognized. The disposition of the stock triggers a

---

[18] Code Sec. 422(a)(1); Reg. § 1.422-1(a).
[19] Code Sec. 422(b)(6).
[20] Code Sec. 422(c)(6); Reg. § 1.422-2(f).

[21] Code Sec. 422(d); Reg. § 1.424-4.
[22] Notice 2005-1, Q&A 4(d)(iii), IRB 2005-2, 274.

negative adjustment for AMT, since the AMT basis includes the income recognized. However, Code Sec. 55(b)(3) spares taxpayers from paying the higher AMT rates. If the capital gain is taxed at a 5 percent or 15 percent rate for regular tax purposes, it is also taxed at the same rate for AMT purposes.

Tax Consequences to the Corporation. Under the same matching concept as NQSOs, the corporation has no tax deduction, because the employee recognizes no ordinary income at the grant date or the exercise date. (Even if the employee is subject to the AMT for the year in which the ISOs are exercised, the corporation is not entitled to a deduction for regular income tax or AMT purposes.) However, in the event a disqualifying disposition is made by the employee, the corporation would be allowed a deduction for the amount and in the year in which the employee recognizes income.[23]

For the past few years, a controversy existed over whether the employer is required to withhold and remit FICA and FUTA taxes upon the exercise of an ISO. (The IRS had proposed regulations in 2001 that would have required such withholding, but then suspended them one year later.) AJCA '04 eliminated all uncertainty concerning this issue, by changing the definition of wages for FICA tax purposes to *exclude* any compensation element (i.e., the spread between the exercise price and market value at the exercise date) pursuant to an exercise of an ISO or on account of a disposition of stock acquired through such an exercise. Thus, no withholding is required.[24]

> **Example:** On May 25, 2005, when its stock was selling at $15 per share, X Co. granted incentive stock options to Mr. Watkins to purchase 1,000 shares of X Co. stock at $15 after one year of employment. The options were exercisable anytime between May 25, 2006, and May 24, 2015. (Note that the option price must equal the market value of the stock on the grant date, and the option period may not exceed 10 years.) Mr. Watkins exercised his options on October 16, 2006, when the stock was selling for $22. He sold the shares on June 12, 2008, for $25 per share.
>
> *Results:* Mr. Watkins recognizes no taxable income on the grant date, nor does he recognize any on the exercise date. Because Mr. Watkins has met the required holding period for the stock (two years from May 25, 2005, and one year from October 16, 2006), he recognizes a long-term capital gain in 2008 from the sale of the stock totaling $10,000 [$25 − $15 × 1,000]. X Co. is not

---

[23] Code Sec. 421(a) and (b).

[24] Code Secs. 3121(a) and 3306(b), as amended by AJCA '04, Sec. 251(a).

allowed any deduction in connection with the ISOs, since no ordinary income was recognized by Mr. Watkins.

For AMT purposes, however, the $7,000 spread between the exercise price and the market value of the stock on the date his right to purchase the stock becomes freely transferable or is no longer subject to a substantial risk of forfeiture (October 16, 2006, the exercise date) is treated as a positive adjustment. This positive adjustment is taxed at the special AMT rate provided under Code Sec. 55(b)(3) (usually 15 percent). His AMT basis in the stock is thus increased by this $7,000. Upon the sale of the stock in year 2008, a negative $7,000 adjustment is made for AMT. In essence, his year 2008 AMT gain from the sale is only $3,000, since his AMT basis is $22,000 ($15,000 exercise price + $7,000 AMT income).

Comparison of ISOs and NQSOs. The table below compares the above example with the NQSO example presented earlier with a $15 option price:

Income Recognized

Date	*Market Price*	*NQSO*	*ISO*
Grant date	$15	None	None
Exercise date	$22	$7,000 ordinary income	None (However, the $7,000 is an AMT positive adjustment)
Sale of stock	$25	$3,000 capital gain	$10,000 capital gain ($3,000 for AMT purposes, i.e., a $7,000 negative adjustment)

As the above table illustrates, the ISO allows the employee to postpone the recognition of any income (except for AMT purposes) until the ultimate disposition of the stock. In addition, all of the income is treated as long-term capital gain. If the employee intends to hold the stock for a considerable length of time, postponement of the tax payment under an ISO would be an attractive element. Perhaps more significantly, however, all income recognized with an ISO for regular tax purposes is long-term capital gain, currently taxed at a maximum rate of 15 percent. Since part of the income recognized with a NQSO is ordinary income, that portion could conceivably be taxed at the maximum 35 percent rate. Thus, the favorable character and timing of income recognized under an ISO probably outweigh their inherent restrictions.

Disqualifying Dispositions. If the employee does not hold the stock acquired from the exercise of an ISO for the requisite holding period (two years from the date of grant and one year from the date of exercise), the gain, up to the spread at the exercise date, will be treated as compensation income. Any excess will be treated as capital gain.[25] Thus, an early disposition disqualifies the ISO and treats the transaction as if it were a NQSO, with the exception of the date of income recognition. The example below illustrates the effects of a disqualifying disposition.

> **Example:** Suppose that Mr. Watkins sold his shares on January 12, 2007, at $25 per share. Because the stock was not held for two years from the date of grant, May 25, 2005 (nor was it held for one year from the exercise date, October 16, 2006), Mr. Watkins made a disqualifying disposition of the stock. As before, Mr. Watkins will recognize no income on the grant date or on the exercise date. On January 12, 2007, however, Mr. Watkins will recognize ordinary income to the extent that he would have recognized such income on the exercise of a NQSO. That is, he will recognize $7,000 in ordinary income [($22 − 15) × 1,000] and $3,000 in short-term capital gain [($25 − $22 basis) × 1,000]. The holding period of a disqualified ISO begins on the exercise date; thus, Mr. Watkins' holding period is short-term (from the October 16, 2006, exercise date to the January 12, 2007, sale date). X Co. is allowed a corresponding deduction of $7,000 for its year which includes December 31, 2007, Mr. Watkins's year-end. (Mr. Watkins cannot file an amended return for 2006 to eliminate the AMT positive adjustment.)[26]
>
> For AMT purposes, the results are the same as the previous ISO example, i.e., Mr. Watkins has a $7,000 positive AMT adjustment in 2006, giving him a $22,000 basis for AMT purposes. Thus, upon the disqualifying disposition of the stock in 2007, his gain for AMT purposes is only $3,000 (i.e., he has a $7,000 negative AMT adjustment in 2007).

If the sales price of the stock sold in a disqualifying disposition is less than its fair market value on the exercise date, but more than its exercise price, the amount of ordinary income is limited to the amount of gain. The employer is allowed a deduction for the same amount. (Similar to the requirements for NQSOs, the employer must comply with the reporting requirements in order to deduct the compensation element resulting from a disqualifying disposition,

---

[25] Reg. § 1.421-2(b)(1).
[26] IRS Letter Ruling 8809061, 12–8–87, CCH IRS Letter Rulings Reports.

i.e., it must report the compensation element on the employee's Form W-2.) If the sales price of the stock sold in a disqualifying disposition is less than the exercise price, the employee recognizes a capital loss and the employer is not entitled to any deduction.[27]

.03 Stock Appreciation Rights (SARs)

In prior years (i.e., before Code Sec. 409A was enacted), SARs played a vital role in executive compensation. Traditionally, a SAR allowed an employee the flexibility to receive a payment in cash or stock based on the difference between a specified amount per share of stock (usually the market value at the grant date) and the market price per share at any time after it vested. SARs are similar to NQSOs in that the employee enjoys the economic benefits of stock ownership from the potential appreciation in the value of the stock without risk of loss. SARs differ from NQSOs in that NQSOs require a cash payment *from* the employee in acquiring the stock, whereas SARs can provide a cash payment to the employee, with no transfer of stock to the employee.

Applicability of Code Sec. 409A. SARs are subject to Code Sec. 409A. The new rules effectively eliminate the traditional SAR by prohibiting the ability to control the timing of deferred compensation payable in cash. However, Code Sec. 409A does provide a very narrow exception to its tax treatment for SAR arrangements. A SAR is exempt from Code Sec. 409A *only if* (1) the exercise price is at least equal to the fair market value of stock on the date of grant; (2) the underlying stock is traded on an established securities market; (3) the exercise may *only* be settled in stock; and (4) there is no deferral feature (other than the deferral of income until the exercise of the right).

Thus, cash-payable SARs, discounted SARs, SARs that have some post-exercise deferral feature, and all private company SARs are subject to Section 409A, meaning that these types of awards must have a fixed payment date to be compliant with Code Sec. 409A.

SARs granted under a plan in effect prior to October 4, 2004 (a pre-AJCA SAR) may be exempt from Code Sec. 409A, subject to two requirements: (1) the SAR exercise price may never be less than the fair market value of the underlying stock on the date the right is granted; and (2) the right does not include any feature for the deferral of compensation other than the deferral of recognition of income until the exercise of the right. (Note, however, that the IRS warns that this exception may be changed or eliminated in future

---

[27] Code Sec. 422(c)(2).

guidance.) Thus, absent modification to this rule, an employee can still control the timing of a pre-AJCA SAR arrangement payable in cash and not fall under the Code Sec. 409A treatment.[28]

Notice 2005-1 provides several options for bringing into compliance with Code Sec. 409A existing SAR arrangements that are otherwise noncompliant. Plans must be amended to adopt these correction methods on or before December 31, 2005.

Tax Consequences to the Employee. Pre-AJCA SARS and 409A-compliant SARs are taxed identically to NQSOs. The employee has no taxable income at the date of grant. Upon the exercise of the SARs, the employee must recognize ordinary income to the extent of the spread between the preestablished value (exercise price) and the market value of the stock at the exercise date.[29] Thus, the amount of ordinary income recognized is equal to the value of stock (or cash, in the case of a qualifying pre-AJCA SAR or a 409A-compliant SAR) received upon the exercise.

Tax Consequences to the Corporation. Similar to NQSOs, the corporation is allowed a deduction for the same amount that was included by the employee. The deduction is allowed for the employer year which includes the employee's year-end.[30]

Example: Refer to the example under the NQSO discussion in ¶ 1502.01. Assume that SARs were issued instead of NQSOs. The results, and a comparison with NQSOs, are presented in the figure below.

	NQSOs	Pre-AJCA SARs (cash received)	409A-Compliant SARs (stock received)
Income Recognized:			
Grant date	None	None	None
Exercise date	$7,000 ordinary income	$7,000 ordinary income	$7,000 ordinary income
Cash Flow:			
Received (Paid) at exercise	$(15,000)	$7,000	None
Tax (35% rate)	$(2,450)	$(2,450)	$(2,450)
Net Cash In (Out)	$(17,450)	$4,550	$(2,450)
Shares Held	1,000 (basis of $22,000)	None	318 (basis of $7,000)

---

[28] Notice 2005-1, Q&A 4(d)(iv), IRB 2005-2, 274.
[29] Code Sec. 61(a)(1)(cash); Code Sec. 83(a)(stock).

[30] Code Sec. 83(h).

Before the enactment of Code Sec. 409A, one of the most popular uses of SARs was their issuance in conjunction with options, both NQSOs and ISOs. The employee had the election to exercise either SARs or options, or any combination of the two. Thus, the specific cash flow situation of the employee can determine the most advantageous exercise path. However, as discussed earlier, Code Sec. 409A has effectively eliminated this type of arrangement, except for qualifying pre-AJCA SARs.

.04   Performance Plans

Performance plans represent awards which are contingent upon the attainment of some predetermined goal measured over a period of time, typically three to five years. The most common goals are stated in terms of growth in earnings-per-share (EPS), although some goals are tied to divisional sales or similar measures, depending upon the particular employee's position. Performance plans exist most often in the form of a performance unit program, although some firms use a performance share approach. The difference between the two forms is the unit of measurement. Performance units are assigned some arbitrary dollar amount, whereas performance shares are measured by the company's stock. Generally, the payment of the award is made in the same measure as the unit valuation, i.e., performance units are typically paid in cash and performance shares are usually paid in stock.

The typical plan establishes some performance target and period. For example, the following target and award may be made for a five-year performance period:

Growth in EPS	Unit Value
6.0%	$200
2.5%	0

Intermediate values between the growth rates may be computed on a pro rata basis. The awards are normally paid in cash at the close of the performance period.

Applicability of Code Sec. 409A. Whether Code Sec. 409A applies to a performance plan depends on the specific form of the arrangement. For example, if vesting and payment occur at the same time under the plan, the plan itself is not a deferred compensation plan; however, if deferral of a vested amount is allowed under the plan, the plan is subject to the Code Sec. 409A provisions. Additionally, if the plan qualifies as performance-based (and subject to Code Sec. 409A), deferral elections are allowed up to six months before the end of the performance period.

¶ 1503.04

Recall that the Code Sec. 409A rules encompass any arrangement that provides an employee with a legally binding right to compensation that (1) has not been actually or constructively received and included in gross income, (2) is payable to the employee in a later year, and (3) is not subject to a substantial risk of forfeiture. Notice 2005-1 defines compensation as being subject to a substantial risk of forfeiture if entitlement to the amount is conditioned on the occurrence of a condition related to a purpose of the compensation, and the possibility of forfeiture is substantial. Specifically included in this "condition related to a purpose of the compensation" description are the employer's organizational goals (e.g., the attainment of a prescribed level of earnings, equity value, or a liquidity event).[31] Presumably, the substantial risk of forfeiture would be deemed to exist during the performance period even if the performance measure currently exceeds the performance goal, because the possibility exists that the measure could decrease and thus eliminate the attainment of the goal and payment of the award.[32]

Thus, until the end of the performance period over which the plan encompasses, at which time vesting and payment both generally occur simultaneously (although a two-and-one-half-month deferral is allowed), the plan is technically not a deferred compensation plan, as defined in Code Sec. 409A.[33] However, if the plan allows for deferrals of a vested amount (longer than two-and-one-half months), such deferrals are subject to Code Sec. 409A, although the plan would probably qualify as "performance-based compensation," allowing deferral elections to be made up to six months before the end of the performance period. (These deferral elections are discussed in detail in Chapter 14.)

Tax Consequences to the Employee. The employee will recognize no income until the completion of the performance period, because: (1) the rights are normally nonassignable, and (2) during the performance period, the goal would be considered to be subject to a substantial risk of forfeiture.

Tax Consequences to the Corporation. The corporation will deduct the performance unit award in the year in which it is properly includible by the employee.[34]

.05 Restricted Stock

Under a restricted stock program, an employee is awarded stock that is subject to certain restrictions of transferability and to a substantial risk of forfeiture for a specific period of time. The stock

---

[31] Notice 2005-1, Q&A 10(a), IRB 2005-2, 274.
[32] Reg. § 1.83-3(c)(2).

[33] Notice 2005-1, Q&A 4(c), IRB 2005-2, 274.
[34] Code Sec. 83(h).

may be provided under outright grants at no cost to the employee or through some nominal purchase arrangement. The employee's ownership rights are typically made contingent on his continued employment with the company for a certain period. These restrictions generally expire over a period of time (either ratably or nonratably) or at retirement. In the event the shares are forfeited (for example, because the employee terminates employment before the specified period of time has expired), employers normally will provide a repurchase price equal to the original cost paid by the employee.

Applicability of Code Sec. 409A. Restricted stock plans are a form of restricted property plan. Thus, as discussed in Chapter 14, they are generally excepted from the provisions of Code Sec. 409A. However, Code Sec. 409A would apply if an employee obtains a legally binding right to receive stock in a future year, whether or not it is restricted.

Tax Consequences to the Employee. Under Code Sec. 83(a), when property is transferred to an employee in connection with the performance of services, the excess of the fair market value of the property over the price paid (if any) by the employee is included in his income when the property is transferable or no longer subject to a substantial risk of forfeiture. Thus, under the normal rules, an employee would recognize ordinary income upon the expiration of the restrictions. The employee's basis in the stock is equal to the amount paid for the property, plus any amount included in gross income.[35] Holding period for the stock would begin on the date the restrictions expire.[36]

Until the property becomes substantially vested, the employer is treated as the owner of the stock. Thus, any dividends received on the stock by the employee during the restriction period are considered additional compensation income and included in gross income in the year received.[37]

A timely election may be made by the employee under Code Sec. 83(b) to recognize ordinary income on the date of the transfer, rather than deferring tax recognition until the expiration of the restrictions. Under this election (which was discussed in detail in Chapter 14), the employee is taxed on the difference between the amount paid (if any) for the stock and the market value on the grant date (computed without regard to any restrictions other than those which will never lapse; see Reg. § 1.83-5 for examples of restrictions which will never lapse). Thus, any appreciation subsequent to the grant date will be treated as capital gain. Additionally, the holding

---

[35] Reg. § 1.83-4(b).
[36] Reg. § 1.83-4(a).

[37] Reg. § 1.83-1(a)(1).

period would begin as of the transfer date.[38] Even though the stock remains subject to restrictions, the employee is now considered the owner of the stock. Thus, any dividends received on the stock by the employee during the restriction period are not considered compensation, from the employer, but as dividends.[39]

Tax Consequences to the Corporation. Under the matching concept of Code Sec. 83(h), the company would be allowed a deduction for the amount which the employee recognizes as ordinary income. The deduction is allowed for the company year which includes the employee's year-end in which income was recognized.

If no Code Sec. 83(b) election was made by the employee, the company would deduct the difference between the price paid by the employee and the market value of the stock as of the date on which the restrictions expire. Recall that until the restrictions lapse, the employer is treated as the owner of the stock. Thus, any dividends paid on the stock to the employee are deductible as compensation.

If, however, the employee makes the Code Sec. 83(b) election, the company also accelerates its deduction to the grant date and deducts the spread on the grant date. Even though the property remains subject to restriction, the employee is considered the owner of the stock because of the Code Sec. 83(b) election. Thus, any dividends paid during the restriction period are not deductible as compensation.[40]

Example: On January 1, 2005, M Corporation transferred 100 shares of its common stock to Mr. Watkins, an executive of M, as a bonus for his work for the year. The stock was issued with the restriction that if Mr. Watkins leaves M's employment within the next two years, he must return the shares to the corporation. On the date of the transfer, the stock had a market value of $35 per share. On January 1, 2007, when the restrictions expired, the stock was selling at $60 per share.

Results	No Code Sec. 83(b) Election	Code Sec. 83(b) Election
2005:		
Income Recognized (and Deduction by M)	None	$3,500
2007:		
Income Recognized (and Deduction by M)	$6,000	None
Holding Period Begins	1/1/07	1/1/05

---

[38] Reg. § 1.83-4(a).
[39] Reg. § 1.83-2(a).

[40] Reg. § 1.83-2(a).

In this example, Mr. Watkins will have taxable income of $3,500 in 2005 under the special election of Code Sec. 83(b), or he may postpone recognizing any taxable income until the expiration of the restrictions in 2007. However, his recognized income would be $2,500 more. One of the principal advantages of the Code Sec. 83(b) election is the conversion of what would be ordinary income into a more-favorable capital gain. For example, if Mr. Watkins were to sell the stock at its market value on the date of the lapse of the restrictions, January 1, 2007, the entire gain of $6,000 would have been taxed as ordinary income without the election. With the election, he would have converted $2,500 of the income into long-term capital gain. Since the tax rate on long-term capital gains is 15 percent (versus up to 35 percent for ordinary income), the Code Sec. 83(b) election may be advantageous, despite accelerating the recognition of a portion of the income.

A potential hazard of the Code Sec. 83(b) election occurs when the stock is forfeited by the employee. For example, suppose Mr. Watkins left the employment of M Corp. in 2006 and was required to return the stock. If no election was made, there would never have been any taxable events. However, if the Code Sec. 83(b) election was made to include $3,500 in his 2005 income, the forfeiture does not trigger a taxable event for Mr. Watkins. In other words, he has chosen to include $3,500 in his 2005 income, but receives no deduction for his surrender of his stock.[41] M Corp. would have to include $3,500 of income on its 2006 return to recapture the previously deducted amount.[42]

It may appear that because of the disallowance of a deduction in the event of forfeiture, the Code Sec. 83(b) election is too risky. However, this may not be true in all situations. If the employee intends to hold the stock for a substantial period of time, the election to recognize income at the grant date would prove advantageous if the stock is expected to increase significantly in value by the date on which the restrictions expire. For example, paying a tax on $3,500 today may be more economical than paying a tax on $10,000 in five years, depending on the employee's opportunity cost of money. Thus, a careful analysis comparing the employee's intentions concerning length of ownership, the spread at the grant date (i.e., the amount that is included in income under the Section 83(b) election), and the expected growth rate of the stock with an assessment of the probability of a forfeiture should be performed to determine the most economical election.

---

[41] Code Sec. 83(b)(1).

[42] Reg. § 1.83–6(c).

.06   Phantom Stock and Restricted Stock Units

Phantom stock and restricted stock unit (RSU) arrangements are based on hypothetical investments in company stock. These arrangements involve the crediting of shares of stock to an employee's account without ever issuing the actual shares to the employee (i.e., a bookkeeping entry only). These plans use "units," which are analogous to actual shares of stock, whereby the employee receives either an amount equal to the value of the stock at some future date specified under the plan (e.g., at termination of employment) (or the increase in the value in the stock between the grant date and the payment date), and (typically) an amount equal to the dividends paid over the period of time specified in the arrangement. Measurement may be in terms of either the market value or the book value of the stock. Phantom stock arrangements are normally settled in cash. When settlement is payable in employer stock, the arrangement is often referred to as a restricted stock unit arrangement.

Phantom stock plans appear to be popular in smaller closely-held firms, because issuing real shares of stock may not be desirable or feasible. S corporations may grant phantom stock units to employees without jeopardizing their S corporation status. The IRS has privately ruled that as long as any phantom stock units issued to an employee are not excessive relative to the services performed by the employee, the phantom stock units would not be treated as a second class of stock.[43]

Applicability of Code Sec. 409A. Phantom stock plans are treated as deferred compensation subject to the requirements of Code Sec. 409A. Thus, unless a predetermined payout is specified at the grant date, the value of the phantom stock would be subject to tax (plus the 20-percent penalty tax) at the time of vesting.

Tax Consequences to the Employee. Assuming a phantom stock arrangement complies with the requirements of Code Sec. 409A, the employee recognizes ordinary income only upon the receipt of cash or stock at the settlement date specified under the plan. However, if the plan allows for settlement at the employee's discretion, the incremental value of the phantom stock vested during each year would be included in that year's income (plus the 20-percent penalty tax).

Tax Consequences to the Corporation. The corporation is allowed a deduction under Code Sec. 83(h) for compensation expense when the employee recognizes the income. Thus, the corporation

---

[43] IRS Letter Ruling 9840035, 7-2-98, CCH IRS LETTER RULINGS REPORTS.

deducts the amount of cash or market value of stock paid to the employee on the settlement date specified under the plan.

.07   Effect of Insider Trading Rules

Section 16(b) of the Securities Exchange Act of 1934 requires that any short swing profits made by a corporate "insider" must be returned to the corporation. Corporate insiders include officers, directors, and more-than-ten-percent shareholders of publicly traded companies. Under sec. 16(b), a profit made on any purchase and sale by insiders of their corporation's stock which can be matched within a six-month period must be paid to the corporation. Under sec. 16(b) the time between the grant of an option and its exercise is counted toward the six-month period. This rule applies to all of the corporation's stock held by the insider, and not just to specific shares. Thus, a purchase of one block of stock may be matched with the sale of another block of stock if they occur within a six-month period. The order of the transactions (purchase-sell or sell-purchase), of course, has no bearing on the application of sec. 16(b).

Shares received by a corporate insider under an incentive stock plan are considered to be a purchase of stock subject to the above rules. Because of the potential loss of any profit from a sale within the six-month period, these shares are deemed to be subject to a substantial risk of forfeiture and nontransferable under Code Sec. 83(c)(3) and do not constitute a feature for the deferral of compensation under Code Sec. 409A.[44] Thus, ordinary income is imposed at the later of the expiration of these restrictions or the acquisition date.[44.1] Of course, a Code Sec. 83(b) election may be made with respect to this "restricted stock," which would accelerate the taxable event.

> **Example:** Mr. Watkins, the president of M Corporation, is considered to be a corporate insider subject to the sec. 16(b) rules. On October 16, 2006, M granted to Mr. Watkins nonqualified stock options for 1,000 shares of M stock at $15 per share. Mr. Watkins exercised the options on November 30, 2006, when the M stock had a market value of $22. Since the restricted period includes the time between the grant date and the exercise date, if Mr. Watkins sells M stock within six months of October 16, 2006, any profit (the excess of the selling price over his $15 purchase price) must be returned to M Corporation. Suppose on April 16, 2007, when the sec. 16(b) restrictions lapse with respect to this purchase, the M stock had a market value of $25 per share.

---

[44] Notice 2005-1, Q&A 4(b)(ii), IRB 2005-2, 274.

[44.1] See, e.g., Rev. Rul. 2005-48, IRB 2005-32, 259.

Results: Under the normal rules of Code Sec. 83(a), Mr. Watkins would recognize no income on the grant date or on the exercise date. He would recognize $10,000 of ordinary income on April 16, 2007, when the restrictions expire. If, however, Mr. Watkins made a Code Sec. 83(b) election, he would recognize $7,000 on November 30, 2006. Of course, if he sells the stock within the six-month restriction period and forfeits the profits to M Corporation, he would not be allowed any deduction for the amount previously included under his Code Sec. 83(b) election.

Certain aspects of stock acquisition plans may qualify for an exemption from the application of the sec. 16(b) rules under SEC Rule 16(b)(3). For example, the grant of options to purchase stock is not deemed a purchase of stock. Likewise, the cancellation or surrender of stock options is not deemed a sale of stock. In addition, an exchange of shares to exercise a stock option is not deemed a sale, to the extent of the shares traded in. Any additional shares received in the exchange are deemed to be a purchase. (The exercise of options with an exchange of stock will be discussed in the next section of this chapter.)

¶ 1504 Cashless Exercises

Stock acquisition plans may occasionally require a substantial cash outflow for the executive. For example, consider Mr. Watkins's cash flow with regard to the nonqualified stock option example presented earlier in the chapter. X Company had granted Mr. Watkins 1,000 options at $15. When he exercised the options, the stock had a market value of $22. Thus, Mr. Watkins recognized $7,000 of ordinary income. Assuming Mr. Watkins is in the 35 percent marginal tax bracket, his total cash outflow resulting from the exercise of his options is $17,450 ($15,000 exercise price plus $2,450 in taxes).

Because of potential financing problems for the executive, many companies provide alternative methods for their employees to acquire stock. Three of the most popular financing methods are discussed below.

.01 Stock Swaps

A popular technique for cashless exercise of options is the stock swap. By using a stock swap, an employee is able to exercise his options with no cash outflow except for the payment of any related income taxes. Instead of using cash, the employee pays the company in previously acquired stock with a market value equivalent to the exercise price of the options. Since the market value of the stock will exceed the exercise price of the options, the employee receives more shares than he surrenders. For example, if the exercise price of the options is $10 per share, and the market value of the stock is $20 on the date of the exercise, the surrender of one share (with a value of $20) will exercise two options (an exercise price of $20). Thus, the employee has given up one share to acquire two. (Recall that, under the insider trading rules, the one share traded in is not normally considered to be a "sale" or a "purchase." However, the additional share received in the swap is considered to be a purchase of employer stock subject to the six-month restriction period.)

Stock swaps may be used with NQSOs and ISOs. However, because the rules for ISOs are more technical than NQSOs, the two forms of options are discussed separately.

Nonqualified Stock Option Swaps. Revenue Ruling 80-244[45] lays out the working rules for the exercise of NQSOs with previously acquired stock. These rules provide the following results:

(1) The exchange of the previously acquired stock for the same number of new shares in the exercise is a tax-free exchange under Code Sec. 1036(a). In addition, Code Sec. 1031(d) provides that the basis and holding period of the old stock are carried over (i.e., "tack") to the same number of shares acquired in the exchange.

(2) Additional shares acquired in the exchange are considered to be property transferred in connection with the performance of services, and, accordingly, trigger ordinary compensation recognition under Code Sec. 83(a) by the recipient. The amount of income to be recognized is the difference between the market value of the stock on the exercise date and the cost of the stock. In this case, the cost of these excess shares is zero. Thus, the employee will recognize as ordinary income the total market value of these excess shares. His basis in these shares is equal to the income recognized on the transaction (their fair market value), and his holding period begins with the date of exercise.

> **Example:** On April 1, 2005, X Corporation granted NQSOs to Mr. Watkins for 5,000 shares of X stock with an exercise price of $10 per share (its fair market value). On September 1, 2006, when the X stock had a market value of $25 per share, Mr. Watkins exercised the options with 2,000 shares of X stock which he had acquired on July 5, 2003, on the open market. (2,000 shares @ $25 = $50,000 total value, which equals the total exercise price of 5,000 shares @ $10.) Assume that his basis in the 2,000 shares was $5 per share.
>
> *Results:* (1) The exchange of 2,000 shares with a total value of $50,000 for 2,000 shares, also with a value of $50,000, qualifies

---

[45] 1980-2 CB 234.

¶1504.01

for a tax-free exchange under Code Sec. 1036. Mr. Watkins's basis and holding period for the 2,000 shares tack onto these 2,000 shares he received in the exchange, i.e., a basis of $5 per share and a holding period which began on July 5, 2003. (2) The additional 3,000 shares received by Mr. Watkins are considered compensation for services under Code Sec. 83(a). Mr. Watkins will recognize $75,000 in ordinary income, which is the fair market value of the stock. The basis of these shares is the same as the amount included in gross income ($75,000); his holding period for these shares begins on the exercise date. It should be noted that Mr. Watkins recognizes the same amount of taxable income as if he had exercised all of the options with cash, i.e., [($25 − $10) × 5,000 = $75,000]. However, his overall cash outlay is reduced by $50,000 since he is able to exercise the NQSOs using stock instead of cash.

Incentive Stock Option Swaps. The rules discussed above also apply to the exercise of an ISO with either: (1) stock acquired from a means other than a previous ISO; or (2) stock acquired from a previous ISO which was held for the required period of time. Thus, the exercise of an ISO with such stock will not trigger taxable income to the employee. As before, the basis and holding period for the shares surrendered tack to the same number of shares acquired in the swap. However, the holding period of the old shares does not tack for purposes of the special holding requirements of ISO stock. The basis in the stock not acquired pursuant to the Code Sec. 1036 exchange is zero, and the holding period of that stock begins with the date of the transfer.[46]

Example (1): Assume the options in the previous example were ISOs. Upon the exchange of his previously acquired 2,000 shares (basis of $5 and holding period starting July 5, 2003), Mr. Watkins will now recognize no income on the exchange. He owns 2,000 shares with a basis of $5 each and a holding period which began on July 5, 2003, and 3,000 shares with a basis of zero and a holding period which began on September 1, 2006. For purposes of the special ISO holding requirements, however, the holding period for all 5,000 shares began on September 1, 2006.

There are two major differences with respect to an ISO swap, both of which are caused by a disqualifying disposition of ISO stock. The tax-free exchange protection of Code Sec. 1036 will not apply to an exchange of stock which was previously acquired under another ISO plan if the required holding period has not been satisfied as of

---

[46] Reg. § 1.422-5(b)(3).

the date of the exchange.[47] Thus, the exercise of an ISO with stock acquired from a previous ISO will trigger ordinary income recognition with respect to the surrendered stock. However, it will not affect the tax treatment for the stock received under the ISO.

Special rules apply under the regulations if a disqualifying disposition is made of ISO stock which was acquired under a stock swap. The employee is deemed to have disposed of the stock having the lowest basis of all the stock acquired in the ISO exercise. For purposes of income character recognition upon a disqualifying disposition, the regulations assume that the amount paid for the stock acquired under the Code Sec. 1036 exchange was its fair market value on the exchange date and that the amount paid for the excess stock was zero.[48]

> **Example (2):** Assuming the same facts as the previous example, suppose Mr. Watkins sells 4,000 shares of the ISO stock on February 1, 2007, for $30 per share. Mr. Watkins has made a disqualifying disposition of the 4,000 shares because he did not hold them for one year from the exercise date and two years from the grant date. Therefore, Mr. Watkins has sold all 3,000 of the non-Code Sec. 1036 shares and 1,000 of the Code Sec. 1036 shares. The total amount of income which Mr. Watkins must recognize from the disqualifying disposition on February 1, 2007, is $115,000, which is the total sales price (4,000 shares @ $30) minus his total basis of $5,000 (3,000 shares with a zero basis and 1,000 shares with a $5 basis). The character of the income to be recognized is as follows:

> (1) $75,000 of ordinary compensation income;

> (2) $25,000 of long-term capital gain; and

> (3) $15,000 of short-term capital gain.

> *Explanation*: (1) The amount of compensation attributable to his disqualifying disposition on February 1, 2007, of the 4,000 shares is $75,000, which is the difference between the fair market value on the date of exercise, $100,000 (4,000 shares x $25, the market value of the stock on the September 1, 2006 exercise date), and the amount deemed paid for the stock, $25,000 (3,000 shares @ $0 plus 1,000 shares @ $25). (2) The long-term capital gain represents the difference between the sales price ($30) and the basis of the 1,000 shares from the Code Sec. 1036 exchange ($5), which had a carryover holding period which began July 5, 2003. (3) The short-term capital gain

---

[47] Code Sec. 424(c)(3); Reg. § 1.424-1(c)(3).   [48] Reg. § 1.422-5(b)(2).

represents the difference between the sales price ($30) and the basis of the extra 3,000 shares which were not involved in the Code Sec. 1036 exchange ($25). This basis of $25 was the result of including the $75,000 as compensation in the disqualifying disposition, i.e., ($75,000/3,000 shares = $25 per share). The holding period of these 3,000 shares began on September 1, 2006, which was the exercise date.

.02 Stock Pyramiding

Stock pyramiding allows the employee to benefit from the gain inherent in a stock option with a nominal investment. Pyramiding involves a series of ever-increasing stock swaps. For example, the employee exercises one or more options with cash, and then swaps those shares to exercise more options. The process is repeated until all the options have been exercised.

The tax treatment for pyramiding NQSOs follows the general rules of Code Sec. 83(a). That is, the employee will recognize ordinary income upon the exercise of the options. Thus, the total recognizable income in a pyramid is exactly the same as if the options had been exercised with cash, through a stock swap, or with tandem SARs.

Pyramiding is not allowed for ISO grants. Under Code Sec. 424(c)(3), pyramiding is treated as a series of sales and purchases of stock acquired under an ISO. Thus, the ISO holding periods would not be met. Accordingly, these disqualifying dispositions would trigger ordinary income recognition for the employee.

Example: On April 1, 2006, X Corporation granted NQSOs to Mr. Watkins to purchase 1,000 shares of X stock at $5 per share (the fair market value on April 1). On September 1, 2006, when the X stock had a market value of $25 per share, Mr. Watkins exercised all of the options via a stock pyramid. The results are presented in the figure below:

Step	Option Price Paid	Shares Received	Total Options Exercised	Shares Retained	Income Recognized
1	$ 5	1 sh.	1	–0–	$20
2	1 sh.	5 sh.	6	–0–	$100
3	5 sh.	25 sh.	31	–0–	$500
4	25 sh.	125 sh	156	–0–	$2,500
5	125 sh.	625 sh.	781	581.2 sh.	$12,500
6	43.8 sh.	219 sh.	1,000	219 sh.	$4,380
	Totals	800.2 sh.			$20,000

In order to start the process, Mr. Watkins had to exercise the first option with a cash outlay of $5, the exercise price of one option. The share obtained from this exercise was worth $25. This share was then used to exercise (swapped) five more options, which had a total cost of $25 (5 options at $5). These five shares, worth $125, were then used to exercise twenty-five more options. This process continued until all of the options were exercised. The end result is that Mr. Watkins used $5 cash and wound up with 800.2 shares of X stock. Of course, he must also pay the tax on the $20,000 recognized as ordinary income.

.03 Pre-AJCA SARs in Tandem with Options

Prior to AJCA '04, a very popular method of providing flexibility of financing for the employee was to issue stock appreciation rights (SARs) in tandem with options. Under this type of arrangement, the employee may choose to exercise only the options, only the SARs, or some combination of the two, depending on his desires and specific cash flow situation. Usually, under these types of plans, there is a fixed number of SARs/options which may be exercised, so that the exercise of SARs will reduce the number of shares which may be acquired through the options.

However, under Notice 2005-1, if a plan provides for a tandem arrangement involving options and stock appreciation rights, the entire arrangement is considered a deferral of compensation.[49] Thus, the entire plan would be subject to the rules under Code Sec. 409A. As discussed in ¶1503.03, the loss of an employee's ability to control the timing of a SAR redemption effectively eliminates cash-payable SARs as a viable method of compensation. Thus, such tandem arrangements are not likely in the future.

Pre-AJCA Tandem SARs. As discussed in ¶1503.03, qualifying pre-AJCA SARs were grandfathered. Thus, the tax treatment of tandem NQSO-SARs that were granted prior to the enactment of Code Sec. 409A (absent any material modifications to the plan) is relatively straight-forward.

The employee recognizes taxable income on the date of exercise in the amount of the spread between the market price of the stock (as of the exercise date) and the exercise price of the NQSO or SAR. Thus, regardless of the combination of NQSOs and SARs exercised, the taxable income is the same. The treatment of pre-AJCA tandem ISO-SARs is equally simple, because each is taxed individually, as if the other were not attached. That is, the employee would recognize income on the

---

[49] Notice 2005-1, Q&A 4(d)(ii), IRB 2005-2, 274.

¶**1504.03**

exercise date only to the extent of SARs exercised, and would have a positive adjustment item for alternative minimum tax purposes amounting to the spread at exercise on the ISOs actually exercised.

> **Example (1):** Prior to October 3, 2004, X Corporation granted tandem NQSO-SARs for 1,000 shares of its stock to Mr. Watkins with an option price of $15. On the grant date, the X stock had a market value of $15. Mr. Watkins exercised the 300 SARs and 700 NQSOs, when the X stock had a market value of $25.
>
> *Results*: Mr. Watkins will recognize $10,000 of ordinary income on the exercise date. This amount includes $3,000 from the SARs [($25 − $15) × 3001 and $7,000 from the NQSOs. His net cash outflow is $11,000 ($3,000 inflow from the SARs; $10,500 outflow from the NQSOs; and $3,500 outflow in taxes, assuming a 35% tax bracket).
>
> Had Mr. Watkins exercised 750 SARs and 250 NQSOs, he would still recognize $10,000 in ordinary income. His cash flow, however, is now a $250 inflow ($7,500 inflow from the SARs; $3,750 outflow from the NQSOs; and $3,500 outflow in taxes). Of course, he now owns 250 shares, as opposed to the 700 shares in the original example.

Pre-AJCA SARs were also issued in tandem with incentive stock options. Tandem arrangements with ISOs are considered an "alternative right" under the final regulations (issued in 2004). Such alternative rights (e.g., a taxable payment of cash in exchange for the cancellation of an ISO) do not disqualify an ISO, as long as it is not inconsistent with the ISO requirements. Thus, if the SARs were issued in connection with ISOs, they had to meet the following requirements:[50]

(1) the SAR must expire no later than the expiration of the underlying ISO;

(2) the SAR cannot be for more than the difference between the exercise price of the ISO and the market price of the stock at the exercise date;

(3) the SAR can be transferable only when the underlying ISO is transferable, and under the same conditions;

(4) the SAR can be exercised only when the underlying ISO is eligible to be exercised; and

---

[50] Reg. § 1.422-5(d)(3).

(5) the SAR can be exercised only when there is a positive spread between the market price of the stock and the exercise price of the option.

Example (2): Refer to the previous example in which Mr. Watkins exercised 300 SARs and 700 NQSOs. If the grant had been tandem ISO-SARs, Mr. Watkins would recognize only $3,000 in ordinary income, all from the exercise of the 300 SARs. He would also have a $7,000 positive adjustment item for alternative minimum tax purposes from the exercise of the ISOs.

¶ 1505 Summary

In choosing the optimal equity-based incentive program, a company must consider factors which will meet the objectives of both the employee and the company. Of course, a major issue relates to the tax consequences to the executive compared with the total cost to the company. Because of the Internal Revenue Code's matching of the deduction by the company with the inclusion of income by the executive, the costs to the executive and to the company are inversely related. That is, a tax-free transfer of stock to the employee results in no deduction by the company. Thus, these programs (such as ISO plans) result in a higher cost to the company. Additional consideration must be given to other factors such as the motivational value of various stock plans, as well as their financial reporting consequences. Only after consideration of all of these factors can a company determine whether a particular plan or group of plans is compatible with the company's overall compensation package.

This chapter has provided an analysis of the tax consequences of the most popular equity-based programs used by large U.S. firms, as well as some financing techniques provided by firms to assist their employees in taking advantage of these plans. Many recent developments in equity-based incentive plans, such as the enactment of Code Sec. 409A and FASB Statement No. 123R, are likely to cause a realignment of the popularity of certain plans versus others. Thus, the area of stock compensation plans will most likely see some major new trends as companies strive to develop programs to meet their objectives.

Index

References are to paragraph (¶) numbers

CODE

CODE

QUA